Theories of Race and Racism

A Reader

Theories of Race and Racism: A Reader is an important and innovative collection that brings together extracts from the work of scholars, both established and up and coming, who have helped to shape the study of race and racism as a historical and contemporary phenomenon.

This second edition incorporates new contributions and editorial material and allows readers to explore the changing terms of debates about the nature of race and racism in contemporary societies. All six parts are organised around the contributions made by theorists whose work has been influential in shaping theoretical debates. The various contributions have been chosen to reflect different theoretical perspectives and to help readers gain a feel for the changing terms of theoretical debate over time. As well as covering the main concerns of past and recent theoretical debates it provides a glimpse of relatively new areas of interest that are likely to attract more attention in years to come.

Les Back is Professor of Sociology at Goldsmiths College, University of London. His primary research interests focus on the culture of racism with particular reference to social identity and popular culture.

John Solomos is Professor of Sociology at City University, London. He has researched and written widely on aspects of race and ethnic relations, the politics of race, equal opportunity policies, race and football, and racist movements and ideas.

Routledge Student Readers

Series Editor: Chris Jenks, Professor of Sociology,
at Brunel University West London.

Theories of Race

and Racism

A Reader
Second edition

Edited by

Les Back and John Solomos

Routledge
Taylor & Francis Group

LONDON AND NEW YORK

First published 2000
Second edition published 2009
by Routledge
2 Park Square, Milton Park, Abingdon, Oxon, OX14 4RN

Simultaneously published in the USA and Canada
by Routledge
711 Third Avenue, New York, NY 10017

Routledge is an imprint of the Taylor & Francis Group, an informa business

© 2009 Les Back and John Solomos, editorial material;
individual contributors, their chapters

Typeset in Perpetua and Bell Gothic by
Florence Production Ltd, Stoodleigh, Devon

British Library Cataloguing in Publication Data
A catalogue record for this book is available from the British Library

Library of Congress Cataloging in Publication Data
A catalog record for this book has been requested

ISBN 10: 0–415–41253–6 (hbk)
ISBN 10: 0–415–41254–4 (pbk)
ISBN 10: 0–203–88191–5 (ebk)

ISBN 13: 978–0–415–41253–7 (hbk)
ISBN 13: 978–0–415–41254–4 (pbk)
ISBN 13: 978–0–203–88191–0 (ebk)

For Nikolas Solomos, Daniel Solomos,
Stephanie Back, Sophie Back and Charlie Back,
in the hope of a better future

Contents

PART TWO
Sociology, race and social theory

PART THREE
Racism and Anti-Semitism

PART FOUR
Colonialism, race and the other

Notes on Contributors

The editors

Les Back is Professor of Sociology at Goldsmiths, University of London, where he has been working since 1993. Before that he taught at the Department of Cultural Studies, University of Birmingham. His main focus over the years has been on race and racism, multiculturalism, urban life, popular culture and music and youth. In addition to the co-authored work with John Solomos his books include *The Art of Listening* (2007), *The Auditory Cultures Reader* (co-editor with Michael Bull) (2003), *Out of Whiteness: Color, Politics and Culture* (co-author with Vron Ware) (2002) and *New Ethnicities and Urban Culture: Racisms and Multiculture in Young Lives* (1996).

John Solomos is Professor of Sociology in the Department of Sociology, City University London. He is Director of the Centre on Race, Ethnicity and Migration. Before that he was Professor of Sociology in the Faculty of Humanities and Social Science at South Bank University, London, and he has previously worked at the Centre for Research in Ethnic Relations, University of Warwick and Birkbeck College, University of London and the University of Southampton. He has published on various aspects of race and ethnic studies, including *The Changing Face of Football: Racism, Identity and Multiculture and the English Game* (co-author with Les Back and Tim Crabbe) (2001), and *Race and Racism in Britain*, third edition (2003). He has also edited *A Companion to Racial and Ethnic Studies* (co-editor with David Theo Goldberg) (2002), *Researching Race and Racism* (co-editor with Martin Bulmer) (2004) and *Racialization: Studies in Theory and Practice* (co-editor with Karim Murji) (2005) among other edited books. He is Editor of the international journal *Ethnic and Racial Studies*, published nine times a year by Routledge.

Contributors

Theodor W. Adorno (1903–69) was one of the leading figures in the Frankfurt Institute for Social Research from the 1920s onwards, including a period as an émigré in the United States. He published a number of books on various aspects of critical theory, including *Prisms* (1967), *Negative Dialectics* (1973) and *The Culture Industry: Selected Essays on Mass Culture* (1990).

Claire Alexander is Reader in Sociology at the London School of Economics. Her research interests are in the area of race, ethnicity, masculinity and youth identities, particularly in relation to ethnography. Her main publications include *The Art of Being Black* (1996) and *The Asian Gang* (2000). She is co-editor of *Beyond Difference* (Special Issue of *Ethnic and Racial Studies*, July 2002), and *Making Race Matter: Bodies, Space and Identity* (2005) and editor of *Writing Race: Ethnography and Difference* (Special Issue of *Ethnic and Racial Studies*, May 2006).

K. Anthony Appiah is Laurence S. Rockefeller University Professor of Philosophy at the Center for Human Values, Princeton University. He has researched and written on the history of ideas about race and on philosophical thought and race. His books include *In My Father's House: Africa in the Philosophy of Culture* (1992), *The Dictionary of Global Culture* (with Henry Louis Gates Jr) (1997) and *Cosmopolitanism: Ethics in a World of Strangers* (2006).

Michael Banton is Professor Emeritus of Sociology at the University of Bristol. He is a former President of the Royal Anthropological Institute of Great Britain. He has written widely on race and ethnicity, and his previous books include *Racial and Ethnic Competition* (1983), *Promoting Racial Harmony* (1985), *Racial Theories* (1987 and 1998), *International Action against Racial Discrimination* (1996) and *The International Politics of Race* (2002).

Zygmunt Bauman is Professor Emeritus in Sociology at the University of Leeds. He is the author of a wide range of studies in social theory, including *Liquid Modernity* (2000), *Society Under Siege* (2002), *Wasted Lives: Modernity and Its Outcasts* (2004) and *Liquid Fear* (2006).

Robert Bernasconi is (from Fall 2009) Edwin Erle Sparks Professor of Philosophy at Penn State. He was previously Moss Professor of Philosophy at Memphis State University. His primary research and teaching interests lie in critical philosophy of race, particularly in continental philosophy, especially figures such as Sartre, Levinas and Heidegger. He is the author of *How to Read Sartre* (2007) and editor of *Race and Racism in Continental Philosophy* (with Sybol Cook) (2003).

Homi K. Bhabha is Anne F. Rothenberg Professor of the Humanities, Department of English, and Director of the Humanities Center, Harvard University. He is one of the most influential theorists in the field of postcolonialism and he has written widely on key issues related to colonialism and postcolonialism. He is the author of *The Location of Culture* (1994) and editor of *Nation and Narration* (1990).

Eduardo Bonilla-Silva is Professor of Sociology at Duke University. He is the author of *White Supremacy and Racism in the Post-Civil Rights Era* (2001), *Racism Without Racists: Color-Blind Racism and the Persistence of Racial Inequality in the United States* (2003), *White Out: The Continuing Significance of Racism* (with Ashley Doane) (2003) and *White Logic, White Methods: Racism and Social Science* (with Tukufu Zuberi) (2008). His recent research has been on the connections between the discourses of citizenship, democracy and human rights, the Latin Americanization of racial stratification in the USA, and on the meaning and significance of the political ascendancy of Barack Obama.

Avtar Brah is Professor of Sociology, School of Continuing Education, Birkbeck College, University of London. She is the author of *Cartographies of Diaspora* (1996) and of numerous articles and reports on aspects of race, gender and identity. She is a member of the editorial collective of *Feminist Review*.

Hazel V. Carby is Charles C. and Dorothea S. Dilley Professor of African American Studies, Yale University. She is the author of *Reconstructing Womanhood: The Emergence of the Afro-American Woman Novelist* (1987) and *Race Men* (1998).

Patricia Hill Collins is Distinguished University Professor, Department of Sociology, University of Maryland. She was previously Charles Phelps Taft Professor of Sociology in the Department of African-American Studies at the University of Cincinnati. She has written widely on issues of gender, race and social class, especially in relation to African-American women. She has written *Black Feminist Thought: Knowledge, Consciousness, and the Politics of Empowerment* (1990), *Fighting Words: Black Women and the Search for Justice* (1998) and *From Black Power to Hip Hop: Racism, Nationalism, and Feminism* (2006).

Oliver C. Cox (1901–74) was born in Trinidad and spent most of his life in the United States. He taught at Lincoln University and Wayne State University. He researched various aspects of the history of capitalism and its evolution, including the history of race and racism. He published a number of studies of the history of capitalism, including *The Foundations of Capitalism* (1959) and *Capitalism as a System* (1964).

Kimberlé Williams Crenshaw is Professor of Law at UCLA and the Columbia School of Law in New York. She is one of the leading scholars in the area of race and law and in developing what is called a Critical Race Theory in legal studies. She is a co-editor, along with N. Gotanda, G. Peller and K. Thomas, of *Critical Race Theory* (1995).

W. E. B. Du Bois (1868–1963) was a student at Fisk, Harvard and Berlin and became a leading black sociologist and activist. He was a staff member of the National Association for the Advancement of Colored People (NAACP) and the editor of its journal *The Crisis* from 1910 to 1934. He published a wide range of books during his lifetime, including *The Philadelphia Negro* (1899), *Dusk of Dawn* (1940) and *Black Reconstruction* (1956).

Frantz Fanon (1925–61) was born in the French Caribbean island of Martinique. He studied medicine and psychiatry in France and worked in a hospital in Algeria between 1953 and 1956. He identified with Algeria's struggle for independence. He was the author of a number of books, including *The Wretched of the Earth* (1961) and *A Dying Colonialism* (1967).

Ruth Frankenberg (1957–2007) was Associate Professor of American Studies at the University of California, Davis. She researched and wrote widely on racism, antiracism and whiteness. She was the author of *Living Spirit, Living Practice* (2004) and editor of *Displacing Whiteness* (1997).

Sander L. Gilman is a distinguished Professor of the Liberal Arts and Sciences at Emory University. He has researched and written on the history of medicine, sexuality and race. Among his books are *Difference and Pathology* (1985), *Jewish Self-Hatred* (1986) and *Smart Jews* (1996).

Paul Gilroy is Anthony Giddens Professor of Sociology at the London School of Economics. He was previously Professor of African American Studies and Sociology at Yale University and Professor of Sociology and Cultural Studies at Goldsmiths, University of London. He is one of the leading theorists on questions of race and culture in relation to the African diaspora and his major books include *There Ain't No Black in the Union Jack* (1987), *The Black Atlantic* (1993), *Small Acts* (1993), *Between Camps: Nations, Cultures and the Allure of Race* (2004) and *After Empire: Melancholia or Convivial Culture?* (2004).

David Theo Goldberg is Director of the University of California Humanities Research Institute. He has researched and written on the history and contemporary expression of racism and was one of the founding editors of the journal *Social Identities*. He is the author of *Racist Culture* (1993) and *The Racial State* (2002) and he has edited a number of influential collections, including *Anatomy of Racism* (1990), *Multiculturalism* (1994) and *Race Critical Theories: Text and Context* (with Philomena Essed) (2002).

Stuart Hall is Professor Emeritus in Sociology at the Open University. He is the co-author of the influential text *Policing the Crisis: Mugging, the State, and Law and Order* (1978), the author of *The Hard Road to Renewal: Thatcherism and the Crisis of the Left* (1988) and the editor of numerous volumes, including *New Times: The Changing Face of Politics* (1988) and *Formations of Modernity* (1992).

Jennifer L. Hochschild is the Henry LaBarre Jayne Professor of Government and Professor of African and African American Studies at Harvard University. She studies the intersection of American politics and political philosophy – particularly in the areas of race, ethnicity and immigration – and educational policy. She also works on issues in public opinion and political culture. She is the co-author of *The American Dream and the Public Schools* (2003), and author of *Facing Up to the American Dream: Race, Class, and the Soul of the Nation* (1995), *The New American Dilemma: Liberal Democracy and School Desegregation* (Press, 1984) and *What's Fair: American Beliefs about Distributive Justice* (1981).

Max Horkheimer (1895–1973) was the Director of the Frankfurt Institute for Social Research from 1930 to 1958, including a period as an émigré in the United States. He was the author of a number of books, including *Eclipse of Reason* (1947) and *Critical Theory: Selected Essays* (1972).

Matthew F. Jacobson is Professor of American Studies and History, Yale University. He is the author of *Special Sorrows: The Diasporic Imagination of Irish, Polish and Jewish Immigrants in the United States (1995)* and *Roots Too: White Ethnic Revival in Post-Civil Rights America* (2006).

Winthrop D. Jordan (1931–2007) was William F. Winter Professor of History at the University of Mississippi. He published a number of books on the history of race relations in the United States, including *White Over Black: American Attitudes Toward the Negro 1550–1812* (1968), *The White Man's Burden* (1974) and *Tumult and Silence at Second Creek* (1993).

Anne McClintock is Simone de Beauvoir Professor, Department of English, University of Wisconsin, Madison. She has written on gender, race and sexuality in a number of journals, including *Social Text, Transition* and *Critical Inquiry*. Her books include *Dangerous Liaisons: Gender, Nations, and Postcolonial Perspectives* (edited with Aamir Mufti and Ella Shohat) (1997).

Albert Memmi is a writer and critic and Professor Emeritus of Sociology at the University of Paris, Nanterre. He was born and raised in Tunis and lives in Paris. He has written *The Colonizer and the Colonized* (1957), *Dominated Man* (1968) and a number of works of fiction.

Kobena Mercer is a writer and critic and Senior Lecturer in the School of Arts and Education at Middlesex University. He was formerly Visiting Professor at New York University and a Fellow at Cornell University, is the author of landmark texts in visual culture and has an international research profile in cultural studies. Among his recent books is *Exiles, Diasporas and Strangers* (2008).

Robert Miles is Director of the Study Abroad Programme at the University of North Carolina, Chapel Hill. He has written widely on various aspects of racism and has carried out extensive research on the history of racism in Britain. Among his books are *Racism and Migrant Labour* (1982), *Racism* (1989) and *Racism after 'Race Relations'* (1993).

Chandra Talpade Mohanty is Professor of Women's Studies at Syracuse University. She has worked extensively on questions of feminist theory, pedagogy and democratic culture. Her books include *Feminism without Borders: Decolonizing Theory, Practicing Solidarity* (2006) and she is the co-editor of *Feminist Genealogies, Colonial Legacies, Democratic Futures* (edited with M. Jacqui Alexander) (1997) and *Third World Women and the Politics of Feminism* (edited with Ann Russo and Lourdes Torres) (1991).

George L. Mosse (1918–1999) was Professor Emeritus of History at the University of Wisconsin, Madison. He previously held academic positions in the UK, South Africa, Holland and Israel. He was involved in the Wiener Library and was a co-editor of the prestigious *Journal of Contemporary History*. He has written and researched on a wide range of issues, including studies of modern German and European history. His books include *The Crisis of German Ideology* (1966), *The Nationalization of the Masses* (1975) and *Nationalism and Sexuality* (1985).

Gunnar Myrdal (1898–1987) was a leading Swedish economist and sociologist who carried out research on a wide range of social and economic issues. He was commissioned by the Carnegie Corporation to conduct one of the first systematic studies of the position of black Americans. The study was eventually published as *An American Dilemma* (1944) and he also published a number of other influential books, including *Value in Social Theory* (1958) and *Asian Drama* (1968).

Robert E. Park (1864–1944) was one of the leading figures in the Chicago School of Sociology. He, along with his students, made major contributions to the development of urban sociology, and the study of race relations, collective behaviour and social control. He published *An Introduction to the Science of Sociology* (1924) and numerous papers that were published in edited collections after his death, including *Race and Culture* (1950).

John Rex is Professor Emeritus of Sociology at the University of Warwick. He has researched and written widely on theories of race relations and on race relations in Britain. Among his books are *Race, Colonialism and the City* (1973), *Race and Ethnicity* (1986) and *Ethnic Minorities in the Modern Nation State* (1996).

David R. Roediger teaches history and African American Studies at the University of Illinois. He born in southern Illinois and educated in public schools in that state, with a B.S. in Ed. from Northern Illinois University. He completed a doctorate in History at Northwestern in 1979. Roediger has taught labour and Southern history at Northwestern, the University of Missouri and the University of Minnesota. He has also worked as an editor of the Frederick Douglass Papers at Yale University. He has written on US movements for a shorter working day, on labour and poetry, on the history of radicalism, and on the racial identities of white workers and of immigrants. His books include *The Wages of Whiteness* (1991), *Towards the Abolition of Whiteness* (1994), *Colored White* (2002) and *Working Towards Whiteness* (2005). He has edited *Black on White: Black Writers on What It Means to Be White* (1998). He has been active in labour support and anti-racist organising.

Kimberly Springer is Senior Lecturer, American Studies, King's College, London. Her work engages questions of race, gender and representation as defined by the sociological imagination and feminist theory. She is the author of *Still Lifting, Still Climbing: African American Women's Contemporary Activism* (1999) and *Living for the Revolution: Black Feminist Organizations, 1968–1980* (2005) and her work has appeared in journals and edited collections.

Sarita Srivastava is Assistant Professor, Department of Sociology, Queen's University. Her research has focused on social movements, the sociology of gender and race and the sociology of emotions. Her primary interest is the interdisciplinary, historical and organisational study of race and gender. She has published a number of articles on these topics in journals, including *Signs* and *Critical Sociology*.

Stephen Steinberg is a Professor in the Department of Urban Studies at Queen's College and the Ph.D. Program in Sociology at the Graduate Center, City University of New York. His books include *The Ethnic Myth* (1981), *Turning Back: The Retreat from Racial Justice in American Thought and Policy* (1995) and *Race Relations: A Critique* (2007).

Ann L. Stoler is Willy Brandt Distinguished Professor of Anthropology and Historical Studies at the New School for Social Research. She has written widely on race and sexuality in colonial societies, including *Race and the Education of Desire* (1995) and *Carnal Knowledge and Imperial Power: Race and the Intimate in Colonial Rule* (2002), and co-edited *Tensions of Empire: Colonial Cultures in a Bourgeois World* (with Frederick Cooper) (1997).

Pierre-André Taguieff is a research director at CNRS in Paris and teaches at the Political Studies Institute. He works in the areas of philosophy, political science and the history of ideas. Among his books are *The Force of Prejudice: On Racism and its Doubles* (2001) and *Rising from the Muck: The New Anti-Racism in Europe* (2004).

Tzvetan Todorov works at the Centre Nationale de la Recherche Scientifique in Paris. He has written a wide range of books, including *Mikhail Bakhtin* (1977), *The Conquest of America* (1984), *The Morals of History* (1995), *Imperfect Garden: The Legacy of Humanism* (2002) and *Hope and Memory: Reflections on the Twentieth Century* (2005).

Patricia J. Williams is a Professor of Law at Columbia University. She also writes a column for *The Nation*, and her books include *The Rooster's Egg* (1995) and *Seeing a Color-Blind Future* (1997).

Howard Winant is a Professor of Sociology at the University of California, Santa Barbara. He is the author, with Michael Omi, of *Racial Formation in the United States* (1994), *Racial Conditions* (1994) and *The World Is a Ghetto: Race and Democracy since World War II* (2001).

Lola Young is a member of the House of Lords and a freelance consultant. She is a former professional actress and was Professor of Media and Cultural Studies at Middlesex University. She has published widely on questions about race and the cinema, including her book on *Fear of the Dark* (1996).

Preface to Second edition

IT IS PERHAPS A SIGN OF THE TIMES that the study of race and racism has been transformed even in the short period since the production of the first edition of this Reader. We have seen a proliferation of monographs, edited collections, journals and related publications on aspects of race, ethnicity and racism in a wide range of disciplines and fields of research. Indeed if one looks at diverse parts of the world there can be little doubt that the study of race and racism is now at a significantly different level from the situation that existed even a decade ago. This marks out the current period as a high point in the scholarly study of race and racism, both in terms of theory and empirically focused research. We are aware that even an extensive Reader such as this one cannot hope to cover all aspects of this fast changing field of research. We have, however, sought to produce a Reader that provides a systematic overview of the field as a whole, that will speak directly to the students taking courses in this field at a variety of levels.

In producing this second edition we have tried to remain true to the ambition and breadth of issues that underpinned the original while introducing some new extracts to reflect currents and debates that we feel were perhaps insufficiently explored first time round. This explains the fact that we have chosen to drop some of the original content and to add some new elements in the form of new extracts and a revision of our own introductory material. In doing so we have sought to enhance the coverage of some issues and to further develop the key preoccupations that helped to give shape and meaning to the first edition. In addition we have thoroughly revised the editorial material to take account of advances and changes in the research agendas of the issues we cover and to guide readers through the core arguments of the six component parts.

John Solomos would like to acknowledge the help of a number of colleagues during the period when this Reader was being produced: Claire Alexander, Alice

Bloch, Martin Bulmer, Michael Keith, Caroline Knowles, Eugene McLaughlin, Karim Murji, Steve Pile, Liza Schuster, Fran Tonkiss and Tony Woodiwiss. Students in the Department of Sociology at City University provided useful comments on various aspects of the first edition, and these were helpful in helping us put together the second edition. Chris, Nikolas and Daniel reminded me to get out of my office and study occasionally, and that there is a life beyond. The Baggies' rise to the Premier League and their 'yo-yo' existence these past few years have been heartening experiences. The memorable 'great escape' experience that saved the Baggies from relegation emphasised the need to think the impossible, which in many ways is the very definition of being a Baggie. Les Back would also like to acknowledge friends and colleagues who have similarly helped shape his thinking on issues of race and racism during the period in which this second edition was compiled, in particular: Stephen Dobson, Michael Keith, Claire Alexander, Vikki Bell, Paul Gilroy, Vron Ware, Chetan Bhatt, Stuart Hall, Max Farrar, Yasmeen Narayan, Emma Jackson, Kimberly Keith, Thomas Zacharias, Alex Reese Taylor, Hiroki Ogasawara, Pete Merchant, Ron Warshow and Earl Green. He'd also like to thank Debbie and his children Steph, Sophie and Charlie for their patience and love.

We have received support throughout the production of this second edition from our publisher at Routledge, Gerhard Boomgaarden. We are grateful for his patience and encouragement, even when we had to delay the project for what must have seemed unfathomable reasons. We are also indebted to him for the enthusiasm which first encouraged us to think of a second edition.

Les Back
Goldsmiths College, University of London
John Solomos
City University London
July 2008

Preface to First edition

THE PRODUCTION OF A READER of this kind is a long and arduous process, and is in many ways more demanding than writing a book on the same topic. As usual we have accumulated a range of debts on the way that need to be acknowledged. In particular we are grateful to the encouragement and advice in one way or another of Martin Bulmer, Chetan Bhatt, David Theo Goldberg, Clive Harris, Michael Keith, Tony Kushner, Marco Martiniello and Liza Schuster at various stages of the project. The comments of the anonymous academic referees used by Routledge to look at a draft of the whole Reader (a thankless task) were also extremely helpful in influencing us to revise it somewhat in ways that have hopefully made it more useful. Even if we did not listen to all the suggestions, we thought about them. Jeffrey Weeks, Dean of the Faculty of Humanities and Social Science at South Bank University, was helpful in facilitating the final stages of work on the project. The help of our publisher, Mari Shullaw, who first suggested to us that we put this Reader together, has been important at a number of stages. Even after all the delays she believed in the project and we hope that the final product justifies her faith. We are also grateful for the hard work of Geraldine Williams in tracking down copyright holders and ensuring that we gained permission to use the extracts that we wanted to use. Liza Schuster diligently searched for some of the less accessible books and articles and made our job easier; she also kindly read a draft of all the introductory material and provided useful suggestions.

Finally, but not least, we are both aware that projects such as this one would not be feasible without the help and indulgence of our families. They put up with the time taken by yet another book with a sense of humour and patience, and provided us with the love and care we needed as well as encouragement. Though this may be a lost cause, we do hope to make up for time lost in the future. For John Solomos numerous trips to watch the Baggies play the beautiful game and struggle to return to their place in the sun have as usual provided a source of inspiration and a distraction from the pettiness of academic life, helping to put things in perspective. Various London-based Baggies provided good company, a sense of humour and a fair degree of cynicism on our often wasted trips. Our memorable 'retro' trip to Norwich stands out. The struggle continues.

John Solomos, *South Bank University*
Les Back, *Goldsmiths College*
May 1999

Acknowledgements

The publishers would like to thank the following for their permission to reproduce material under copyright:

Beacon Press for permission to reprint Stephen Steinberg, 'America Again at the Crossroads', from *Turning Back: The Retreat from Racial Justice in American Thought and Policy*, 1995, pp. 205–13, 214–20. Copyright © 1995, 2001 by Stephen Steinberg. Reprinted by permission of Beacon Press, Boston.

Berg for permission to reprint Avtar Brah, 'Difference, Diversity, Differentiation', from John Wrench and John Solomos (eds), *Racism and Migration in Western Europe*, 1993, pp. 166–78.

Cambridge University Press for permission to reprint Ann Laura Stoler, 'Sexual Affronts and Racial Frontiers', *Comparative Studies in Society and History*, Volume 34, Number 3, 1992, pp. 514–17, 521–2, 523–33, 537–47, 548–51.

Duke University Press for permission to reprint Chandra Talpade Mohanty, 'Under Western Eyes: Feminist Scholarship and Colonial Discourse', from *boundary* 2, Volume 12, Number 3, pp. 333–58. Copyright, 1984, Duke University Press. All rights reserved. Used by permission of the publisher.

Emerald Publishing Group for permission to reprint Michael Banton, 'The Idiom of Race: A Critique of Presentism' from *Research in Race and Ethnic Relations*, Volume 2, 1980, pp. 21–2, 24–30, 32–8, 39–40.

Georges Borchardt and Grove Atlantic Press for permission to reprint Frantz Fanon, 'The Fact of Blackness', from *Black Skin, White Masks*, 1986, pp. 109–22, 130–5 (Pluto Press edn). Translated by Charles Lam Markham. English Translation © 1967 by Grove Press, Inc. Originally published in French as *Peau Noire, Masques Blancs* by Editions du Seuil. Copyright 1952 by Editions du Seuil. Reprinted by permission of Georges Borchardt, Inc., for Editions du Seuil. Copyright © 1967 by Grove Press, Inc. Used by permission of Grove/Atlantic, Inc.

Harvard University Press for permission to reprint Tzvetan Todorov, 'Race and Racism', from *On Human Diversity: Nationalism, Racism and Exoticism in French Thought*, 1993, pp. 90–5, 153–7. Matthew F. Jacobson, 'Looking Jewish, Seeing Jews', from *Whiteness of a Different Color: European Immigrants and the Alchemy of Race*, 1998, pp. 171–6, 176–82, 183–7,188. Patricia J. Williams, 'Race and Rights', from *The Alchemy of Race and Rights*, 1991, pp. 166–78.

Kimberlé Williams Crenshaw for permission to reprint 'Race, Reform and Retrenchment', from Kimberlé Crenshaw, Neil Gotanda, Garry Peller and Kendall Thomas (eds), *Critical Race Theory: The Key Writings that Formed the Movement*, 1995, pp. 103, 112–16, 117–18, 119.

MIT Press Journals for permission to reprint Jennifer L. Hochschild, 'Looking Ahead: Racial Trends in the United States', from *Daedalus*, Volume 134, Number 1, 2005, pp. 70–81. © 2005 by the American Academy of Arts and Sciences.

Monthly Review Foundation for permission to reprint Oliver C. Cox, 'Race Relations', from *Caste, Class and Race*, 1948, pp. 321–2, 331–4, 345–8.

Polity Press for permission to reprint Zygmunt Bauman, 'Modernity, Racism, Extermination', from *Modernity and the Holocaust*, 1989, pp. 61–70, 72–82.

Princeton University Press for permission to reprint K. Anthony Appiah, 'Racial Identity and Racial Identification', in K. Anthony Appiah and Amy Gutmann, *Color Conscious: The Political Morality of Race*, 1996, pp. 76–83, 89–90, 92–3, 97–9.

Profile Books for permission to reprint Paul Gilroy, 'The Dialectics of Diasporic Identification', from *Small Acts: Thoughts on the Politics of Black Cultures*, 1993, pp. 120–7, 131–42.

Routledge/Taylor and Francis Books for permission to reprint John Rex, 'Race Relations in Sociological Theory', from *Race and Culture: Essays in the Sociology of Contemporary Man*, 1970, pp. 81–4, 100–4, 114–16; Robert Miles, 'Apropos the Idea of 'Race'', from *Racism After Race Relations*,1993, pp. 28–34, 35–43, 44–50; Sander L. Gilman, 'Are Jews White?', from *The Jew's Body*, 1991, pp. 169–80; Lola Young, 'Imperial Culture', from *Fear of the Dark: Race, Gender and Sexuality in the Cinema*, 1996, pp. 55–6, 57–62, 63–8, 70–4, 79–83; Anne McClintock, 'The White Family of Man', from *Imperial Leather: Race, Gender and Sexuality in the Colonial Context*, 1995, pp. 232–3, 238–44, 248–57; Homi Bhabha, 'Race, Time and the Revision of Modernity', from *The Location of Culture*, 1994, pp. 236–51; Hazel V. Carby, 'White Woman Listen!', from *The Empire Strikes Back: Race and Racism in '70s Britain*, 1982, pp. 212, 224, 228–33; Patricia Hill Collins, 'Black Feminist Thought', from *Black Feminist Thought: Knowledge, Consciousness and the Politics of Empowerment*, 1990, pp. 19–28, 33–6, 37–9; Kobena Mercer, 'Identity and Diversity in Postmodern Politics', from *Welcome to the Jungle: New Positions in Black Cultural Studies*, 1994, pp. 259–63, 265–71, 274–85.

Simon and Schuster for permission to reprint Robert Park, 'The Nature of Race Relations', from *Race and Culture: Essays in the Sociology of Contemporary Man*, 1950, pp. 81–4, 100–4, 114–16.

Taylor and Francis for permission to reprint Claire Alexander, 'Beyond Black', from *Ethnic and Racial Studies*, Volume 25, Number 4, 2002; Eduardo Bonilla-Silva, 'From Bi-Racial to Tri-Racial USA', from *Ethnic and Racial Studies*, Volume 27, Number 6, 2004, pp. 931–950; Howard Winant, 'Race and Racism', from *Ethnic and Racial Studies*, Volume 29, Number 5, 2006.

Transaction Publishers for permission to reprint Gunnar Myrdal, 'Racial Beliefs in America', from *An American Dilemma*, 1962, pp. 84–8, 88–9, 90–3, 97–9.

University of California Press for permission to reprint David R. Roediger, 'All About Eve, Critical White Studies, and Getting Over Whiteness', from *Colored White: Transcending the Racial Past*, 2002, pp. 3–26. © 2002 Regents of the University of California. Published by the University of California Press.

University of Chicago Press for permission to reprint Sarita Srivastava, 'You're Calling Me a Racist?', from *Signs*, Volume 31, Number 1, 2005, pp. 29–62; Kimberly Springer, 'Third Wave Black Feminism?', *Signs*, Volume 27, Number 4, 2002, pp. 1059–81.

University of Minnesota Press for permission to reprint Ruth Frankenberg, 'White Women, Race Matters', from *White Women, Race Matters: The Social Construction of Racism*, 1993, pp. 1–10, 236–8, 239–40, 242–3; Albert Memmi, 'Racism and Difference', from *Racism*, 2000, pp. 39–43, 45–6, 47–52, 55–67. First published in French as *La Racisme*. Copyright 1982, 1994 by Éditions Gallimard. English translation copyright 2000 by the Regents of the University of Minnesota; Pierre-André Taguieff, 'On Antiracism' from *The Force of Prejudice: On Racism and Its Doubles*, 2001, pp. 230–59. First published in French as *La force du préjugé: Essai sur la racisme et ses doubles*. Copyright 1987 Éditions la Decouverte. English translation copyright 2001 by the Regents of the University of Minnesota; Stuart Hall, 'Old and New Identities, Old and New Ethnicities', from Anthony D. King (ed.), *Culture, Globalisation and the World System: Contemporary Conditions for the Representation of Identity*, 1997, pp. 42–5, 47–9, 51–7, 59–61.

University of North Carolina Press for permission to reprint Winthrop D. Jordan, 'First Impressions', from *White Over Black: American Attitudes to the Negro, 1550–1812*, University of North Carolina Press, 1968, pp. 3–8, 11–15, 20–36, 43.

Verso for permission to reprint Theodor Adorno and Max Horkheimer, 'Elements of Anti-Semitism', from *Dialectic of Enlightenment*, 1976, pp. 168–70, 173–6, 183–6

Wiley Blackwell for permission to reprint Robert Bernasconi, 'Who Invented the Concept of Race', from Robert Bernasconi (ed.), *Race*, 2001, pp. 11, 12–13, 14–18, 19–21, 23–30; David Theo Goldberg 'Racial Knowledge' from *Racist Culture: Philosophy and the Politics of Meaning*, 1993, pp. 149–55. 163–6, 168–77.

The publishers have made every effort to contact authors and copyright holders of works reprinted in *Theories of Race and Racism: A Reader* (Second edition). This has not been possible in every case, however, and we would welcome correspondence from individuals or companies we have been unable to trace.

Introduction:
Theories of race and racism:
genesis, development and
contemporary trends

■   Les Back and John Solomos

O UR MAJOR OBJECTIVE IN PUTTING the second edition of this
Reader together has been to bring together in one single volume a rounded
overview of the emergence and development of race and racism as a field of
scholarship and research. We have decided to organise it around a mixture of both
classical and more contemporary texts that have helped to set the agenda for this
field, and to include our own introductory material in order to guide readers through
the complexities of the debates and the contributions of the specific authors that
we have selected for inclusion in this volume. In choosing the various extracts that
make up this volume we have had to make choices, and no doubt other contributions
could have been included in place of the ones that we have chosen. We believe,
however, that the selections we have been able to include are important contributions
to this scholarly field, and will help readers gain a critical understanding of the
six thematic areas we have sought to cover.

Given the feedback we have had on the first edition we are also aware that
this is a field of scholarly research that is rapidly changing all the time, and a
Reader such as this one cannot ignore these changes. Indeed, in the relatively short
period since the Reader was published we have seen important developments in
both research and teaching agendas in this field. We have seen a seemingly ever-
expanding range of books and journals that address questions about race, racism
and related topics from a variety of disciplinary and conceptual perspectives (for
an overview of some of these developments see Bulmer and Solomos 1999 and
2004; Essed and Goldberg 2002; Goldberg and Solomos 2002; Steinberg 2007).
It is also clear that there is growing academic and public recognition of the
importance of studying these phenomena and developing conceptual tools for
analysing the role and impact of racial inequality, racist movements and parties
and forms of racial and ethnic violence (Feagin 2006).

It is as a result of this growing recognition of the need for greater theoretical clarity and conceptual analysis that we have put together this second edition of *Theories of Race and Racism*. In doing so we had two related sets of objectives.

- First, to provide for students and the general reader a collection that introduces them to the key arenas around which theoretical debates have been conducted, and the range of perspectives that have emerged over the years in this field. We have consciously tried to reflect different perspectives and avoid the obvious danger of putting together extracts from texts close to our own theoretical starting point. This is not to say that we have not been selective in terms of the authors and the particular extracts we have chosen to include. Given the breadth of material we had to cover in one volume we have inevitably been selective and in places the choice of extracts may seem arbitrary. But we hope that whether readers agree with our choice of texts or not they find them of interest and reflective of the range of positions and attitudes that have shaped the study of race and racism in the contemporary period.
- Second, we have used texts that cover a range of disciplines, historical situations and geographical contexts. This arises partly out of our concern to show the diversity of theoretical and empirical work that has been evident in this field. In addition, however, we wanted to provide in one single volume a range of original sources that could be critically evaluated and analysed in some detail in relation to the conceptual issues they seek to explore or the situations they are attempting to understand. Part of the problem with the current proliferation of textbooks and monographs in this field is that there has been a noticeable neglect of some important texts, along with a lack of historical perspective about the origin of current theoretical debates. It is partly in order to balance this neglect that we have included extracts from works published at various stages of the twentieth century as well as more contemporary texts.

Bearing these twin objectives in mind we have also sought, as far as is possible in a single volume, to make the main ideas more accessible by organising them into six inter-related parts and providing introductory material that outlines the main themes. Although all the component parts of the Reader link up, we have divided the main debates around key themes and illustrated them by including extracts from some of the main contributors to each sub-field.

- **Part One** explores the question of the origins of race and racism, and includes extracts from the work of some of the main scholars in this field. This is an issue that has in fact attracted much attention in the past two decades and the various extracts included in this part address questions that are still the subject of intense scholarly debate.

- From this starting point, **Part Two** moves on to explore some important facets of social theorising about race and what is often called race relations. Bringing together both classical and more contemporary theorising in this field, the main objective of this part is to provide an overview of the place of race and racism within social theory.

- **Part Three** shifts the focus somewhat by looking at one specific manifestation of racism, but one which has had murderous consequences, namely anti-semitism. Anti-semitism is an issue that tends to be treated somewhat separately from other expressions of racism, and relatively few attempts have been made to include it within the core of contemporary debates about race and racism. But, as we attempt to illustrate in this part, any comprehensive analysis of racism has to include anti-semitism as a key component.

- **Part Four** focuses on the complex linkages between colonialism and constructions of race, which are explored in some detail. This is an issue that has been at the heart of much contemporary scholarship, both in the social sciences and in the humanities and cultural studies, and the extracts included here highlight the shifting boundaries of race in colonial and postcolonial situations.

- **Part Five** includes a number of influential contributions to the development of a feminist, or more specifically a black feminist, perspective on racism. The main concern that holds the somewhat divergent extracts included in this part together is the argument that theories of race and racism need to be re-imagined in such a way that a gendered perspective comes more to the fore. As a number of the contributors to this part emphasise, the interplay between race, class and gender can take complex forms in specific situations.

- **Part Six** takes as its guiding theme the changing boundaries and spaces within which contemporary debates about race and racism are being carried out. One of the shared concerns to be found in a number of the contributions to this part is the need to place questions about race and racism within an analytic framework that allows for change and diverse experiences. Another underlying theme in this part is the question of what issues are likely to shape academic and public discourses in this field in the coming period.

In addition to these substantive overviews we have included an annotated **Guide to Further Reading** at the end of each part in order to provide a basis for exploring important themes and debates in an organised manner. We have listed a series of key texts and background reading for each part, focusing particularly on contributions that have played an important part in debates within their particular sub-fields.

We are aware that many of the linkages in theoretical debates are by no means self-evident or easy to place within the parameters of wider theoretical debates. This is partly because a number of the issues that have been the focus of much current debate in this field are conceptually difficult. But it is also the case that many of the core texts in this field are written with little concern about their accessibility to students and even less so for the wider public. The fixation with theoretical abstraction has produced a plethora of texts that may in some fashion have something valuable to say, but that in practice are addressed to other scholars in very narrow specialised fields. Some of the difficulties this has given rise to are evident in the readings we have included in this Reader, though we have made an effort to avoid this. In order to provide a starting point for using this Reader in the most productive manner we have therefore felt it important to include substantive introductory overviews of the main themes covered in this volume as a whole, written by us as editors. We have done this in the form of this **Introduction** and in brief introductions at the beginning of each part. In doing so we are not intending to simplify what are often complex scholarly debates, but to provide a map of key themes and terminology that is suggestive and contemplative rather than exhaustive. Our concern here is more basic, in the sense that we have sought to use the introductory overviews as a way of engaging with the main arguments of the authors that we have chosen to include. It is to this mapping that we now turn before moving on to the substantive parts that make up *Theories of Race and Racism*.

Race and racism in perspective

One of the more reliable, if depressing, predictions about the twentieth century was made by the black American scholar W. E. B. Du Bois back in 1903 when he asserted that 'the problem of the twentieth century is the problem of the colour line – the relation of the darker to the lighter races of men in Asia and Africa, in America and in the islands of the sea' (1903: xx). It is perhaps with Du Bois's words in mind that the black British scholar Stuart Hall asserted a few years ago that 'the capacity to *live with difference* is, in my view, the coming question of the twenty-first century' (Hall 1993: 361). This is because, argues Hall, in contemporary societies we are seeing an increasing diversity of subject positions, social experiences and cultural identities that cannot be grounded in a set of fixed trans-cultural or transcendental racial categories and which therefore are constantly evolving and changing (see contribution by Hall in Part Two).

At the beginning of the twenty-first century these contrasting statements provide an important point of reference for those of us thinking about both the past and the future of race and racism. It is of course not possible to make any sensible comment on the relevance of Du Bois or Hall's predictions for the current century. But one reason to counterpose the two statements here is that one of the vital questions we have to reflect on is the meanings that are attached to ideas about race and ethnicity in the contemporary social context. One way to see the different language used by Du Bois and Hall is to remember that while for scholars of Du Bois's generation the 'colour line' was an everyday reality based on institutional patterns of racial domination in the current period questions about race and racism have been refashioned in ways that emphasise cultural difference. This is not to say of course that for writers such as Hall questions about race and racism are in practice less important. It is clear that whatever the changing terms of language that are used to talk about race and ethnicity in the present day environment, we have in practice seen growing evidence of forms of racial and ethnic conflict in many parts of the globe. The shifts in conceptual language that have become evident in the past two decades are symptomatic of wider debates about the analytical status of race and racism, as well as related shifts in political and policy agendas.

The study of race and 'race relations' as important social issues can be traced back to the early part of the twentieth century, at least in relation to the United States of America. It has to be said, however, that the expansion of research and scholarship in this field is far more recent. It is really in the period since the 1960s, in the aftermath of the social transformations around questions of race that took place during that decade, that we have witnessed a noticeable growth of interest in the theorisation of race and racism and more generally what is called the 'sociology of race relations' (Anderson and Massey 2001; Holloway and Keppel 2007). The publication in 1967 of Michael Banton's book on *Race Relations* and in 1970 of John Rex's *Race Relations in Sociological Theory* can be seen as symptomatic of wider social trends and of their impact on the course of scholarly research and debate.

Banton's study looked at race relations from a global and historical perspective, concentrating particularly on situations of cultural contact, beliefs about the nature of race, and the social relations constructed on the basis of racial categories. By looking at the experience of changing patterns of interaction between racial and ethnic groups from a historical perspective Banton argued that six basic orders of race relations could be delineated: namely institutionalised contact, acculturation, domination, paternalism, integration and pluralism (Banton 1967).

It was during the period of the 1960s that what Banton and others have called the 'race relations problematic' became the dominant approach in this field (Banton 1991). While often utilising racial classifications this literature also incorporated anthropological perspectives on ethnicity and social boundaries. Richard Jenkins among others has shown that there are continuities between the methodological and theoretical approach applied to tribal societies and their 'modern' equivalent – *ethnic groups* (Jenkins 1986 and 1997).

John Rex's *Race Relations in Sociological Theory*, along with his subsequent output, represents another important attempt to construct a theoretical framework for the analysis of race relations and racism. Rex's work has exercised a major influence over this field and his contribution remains one of the most ambitious attempts to provide a theoretical grounding for research in this field. According to Rex's analytic model the definition of social relations between persons as race relations is encouraged by the existence of certain structural conditions, e.g. frontier situations of conflict over scarce resources, the existence of unfree, indentured, or slave labour, unusually harsh class exploitation, strict legal inter-group distinctions and occupational segregation, differential access to power and prestige, cultural diversity and limited group interaction, and migrant labour as an underclass fulfilling stigmatised roles in a metropolitan setting (Rex 1983). From this perspective the study of race relations is concerned with situations in which such structured conditions interacted with actors' definitions in such a way as to produce a racially structured social reality.

What is also interesting about Rex's work is that he has attempted to utilise his conceptual framework in two seminal studies of race relations in Birmingham during the 1960s and the 1970s. In the study conducted by Rex and his associates in the Handsworth area of Birmingham during the mid 1970s (Rex and Tomlinson 1979) the basic research problem was to explore the degree to which immigrant populations shared the class position of their white neighbours and white workers in general. The substance of the analysis goes on to outline a class structure in which white workers have been granted certain rights that have been won through the working class movement through the trade unions and the Labour Party. For Rex an important feature of the position of migrant workers and their children is that they are located outside the process of negotiation that has historically shaped the position of white workers. They experience discrimination in all the areas where the white workers had made significant gains, such as employment, education, housing. It follows from this that the position of migrant workers placed them outside of the working class in the position of an 'underclass':

> The concept of underclass was intended to suggest . . . that the minorities were systematically at a disadvantage compared with their white peers and that, instead of identifying with working class culture, community and politics, they formed their own organisations and became effectively a separate underprivileged class. (Rex and Tomlinson 1979: 275)

From this point Rex and Tomlinson develop a model for analysing the changing position of minority communities within the context of class and political relations is societies such as Britain. In the process of this analysis they also explore the differential positioning of minorities, through a comparison between Asian and West Indian communities. Within Asian communities they highlight the concentration on capital accumulation and social mobility. In the West Indian community they point to a pattern of withdrawal from competition altogether with an emphasis on the construction of a black identity. This all leads to what Rex refers to elsewhere as the 'politics of defensive confrontation' (Rex 1979).

As can be seen from the extracts included in Parts One and Two, the approach adopted by scholars such as Banton and Rex has much in common with the arguments to be found in the work of American sociologists of the time. Quite apart from the classical work of Robert Park, whose early studies of American race relations continue to influence key aspects of contemporary debates, there are important links with the arguments to be found in the work of contemporary scholars. A case in point is the work of William Julius Wilson, whose early theoretical work in this field attempted to outline a historical and comparative framework for the analysis of race relations, focusing particularly on the situation in the USA and South Africa (Wilson 1973). A recurrent theme in the work of Wilson, which was produced in the aftermath of the riots and turmoil that characterised American race relations in the 1960s, was the relationship of the concepts of racism and power and their role in explaining processes of change in the context of race relations. This is indeed a theme that is a recurring point of reference in much of the scholarship in this field in the United States in the period since the civil rights movement (Patterson 1998; Spickard and Daniel 2004).

Rethinking the boundaries of race and racism

The arguments articulated by writers as diverse as Banton, Rex and Wilson were in many ways shaped by the discussion of race relations that was developing during the 1960s and the 1970s in both the USA and Britain. This was a time when social reforms implemented in the aftermath of the Civil Rights Movement, urban violence and unrest, and the development of black power ideas and forms of cultural nationalism helped to reshape the politics of race in America, as well as in other parts of the world.

It became clear, however, by the early 1980s that a number of fundamental criticisms of the whole field of race relations research were emerging. These critiques were influenced to some extent by theoretical arguments that emanated from neo-Marxist, feminist, postcolonial and related theoretical perspectives. Such criticisms were influenced both by theoretical and political considerations, and they helped to stimulate new areas of debate. As a result there has been a rapid expansion of scholarship on race and racism within the social sciences and the humanities, particularly in sociology, political science, philosophy, anthropology, psychology, cultural studies and geography (Rex and Mason 1986; Goldberg 1990). A number of questions have come to the fore in the current period: What kinds of meanings can be given to the category race? How should racism be identified as a political force within European societies, the USA and other parts of the globe? Have we seen a growth of new forms of racist expression in contemporary societies?

While it is clear what questions are being asked, what remains in dispute is exactly how to respond to them. A number of distinct paradigms have emerged in response to these key questions, influenced in particular by changing research agendas as well as by political transformations. In the context of the concerns of this volume we want to focus particularly on the influence of (i) the neo-Marxist approach articulated by Robert Miles, and (ii) the approach associated with the collectively produced volume *The Empire Strikes Back* that emanated from the Race and Politics Group of the Centre for Contemporary Cultural Studies at the University of Birmingham.

The starting point of Miles's critique was his opposition to the existence of a sociology of race, and his view that the object of analysis should be racism, which he viewed as integral to the process of capital accumulation and class relations in capitalist societies (Miles 1982; 1986, 1993). His analysis was first articulated in *Racism and Migrant Labour*, and it is perhaps the most sustained attempt to include the study of racism within the mainstream of Marxist social theory. His empirical research has focused specifically on the situation in Britain and the rest of Europe, and has looked at the role of political, class and ideological relationships in shaping our understandings of racial conflict and change in these societies. As can be seen from a number of extracts in Parts Two, Four and Five in particular, Miles was not alone in making these criticisms of the conceptual focus on 'race'. His influence on contemporary debates can be seen in the way that the status of race as a social and analytical concept has been an important and recurring area of concern.

For Miles the idea of race refers to a human construct, an ideology with regulatory power within society. Analytically race constitutes a paper tiger (Miles 1988) that may be a common term of reference within everyday discourse, but which presents a serious theoretical problem. It is here that Miles diverges from what he sees as the race relations problematic. While Rex is concerned with models of social action (i.e. for Rex it is enough that race is utilised in everyday discourse as a basis for social action), Miles is concerned with the analytical and objective status of race as a basis of action (Miles 1982: 42). Race is thus an ideological effect, a mask that hides real economic relationships (Miles 1984). Thus the forms of class consciousness that are legitimate for Miles must ultimately be seen as shaped by economic relations that are hidden within the process of racialisation (for rather different accounts of processes of racialisation see Martinot 2003 and Memmi 2000).

For Miles the process of racialisation is inter-related with the conditions of migrant communities. Its effects are the result of the contradiction between 'on the one hand the need of the capitalist world economy for the mobility of human beings, and on the other, the drawing of territorial boundaries and the construction of citizenship as a legal category which sets boundaries for human mobility' (Miles 1988: 438). Within the British setting this ideological work, conducted primarily by the state, acts as a means of crisis management and results in racialising fragments of the working class. Race politics are thus confined to the forces of regulation. For Miles the construction of political identities that utilise racial consciousness plays no part in the development of a progressive politics.

Miles's work raises some fundamental questions about the nature of racism and migration in contemporary societies. The most important of these is the degree to which black and minority politics are really distillations of class conflict. If this is true any movements away from class-based political action (i. e. movements towards any notions of black community politics) are doomed to failure (Miles 1988; Miles and Brown 2003). If one takes this argument further, class-based political action is ultimately in opposition to any sort of sustained political organisation around a notion of race. For Miles the politics of race is narrowly confined to the struggle against racism. This is neatly captured in the way he uses Hall's (1980: 341) statement on the relationship between class and race. He concludes that it is not race but racism that can be the modality in which class is lived and fought through (Miles 1988).

Miles's insistence that racial differentiations are always created in the context of class differentiation (Miles and Brown 2003) is a core feature of his critique of the work of Banton and Rex. One danger of his position, however, is that it can result in a kind of class reductionism that ultimately limits the scope of theoretical work on conceptualising racism and racialised social relations. For example, in some contexts class exploitation may be incidental to the construction of situations of racial dominance (Goldberg 1992). However, the greatest contribution that Miles makes is his insistence that 'races' are created within the context of political and social regulation. Thus 'race' is above all a political construct. It is within this context that the concepts of *racial categorisation* and *racialisation* have been used to refer to what Miles defines as those instances where social relations between people have been structured by the signification of human biological characteristics in such a way as to define and construct differentiated social collectivities (Miles and Brown 2003). His work constitutes an attempt to reclaim the study of racism from an apoliticised sociological framework and locate it squarely in a Marxist theorisation of social conflict.

In contrast to Miles's approach, the arguments articulated in *The Empire Strikes Back* were less concerned with the development of a neo-Marxist analysis of racism than with the analysis of the changing nature of the politics of race and the development of new forms of racial ideology. The theoretical approach of this volume was influenced by the work of Stuart Hall in particular (Hall 1980). This volume attracted widespread attention at the time and it still remains a point of reference in current debates (Bulmer and Solomos 1999). The approach articulated in this volume has also been extended in the work of key authors associated with it, including Hazel Carby, Paul Gilroy and John Solomos.

A major concern of the CCCS Group was the need to analyse the complex processes by which race is constructed as a social and political relation. They emphasised that the race concept is not simply confined as a process of regulation operated by the state but that the meaning of race as a social construction is contested and fought over. In this sense they viewed race as an open political construction where the political meaning of terms like black are struggled over. Collective identities spoken through race, community and locality are for all their spontaneity also a powerful means to co-ordinate action and create solidarity (Gilroy 1987). In some ways *The Empire Strikes Back* shared Rex's concern with social action but it rejected his overall framework as being at best ill-founded and at worst politically spurious.

Within this model of political action a multiplicity of political identities can be held. An inclusive notion of black identity can prevail and at the same time allow heterogeneity of national and cultural origins within this constituency. In his subsequent work, for example, Gilroy argues that the crucial question here is the extent to which notions of race can be re-forged into a political colour of opposition (Gilroy 1987: 236; see also Gilroy 1990). He holds little hope that this process can be developed within the arena of representative democracy. Instead he views pressure group strategies that have evolved out of community struggles that utilise a specifically black political vernacular as the way forward. Gilroy argues for a radical revision of class analysis in metropolitan contexts. He suggests that political identities that are spoken through race can be characterised as social movements that are relatively autonomous from class relations.

It should also be noted that *The Empire Strikes Back* was one of the first books on race relations in Britain to look in any depth at the question of gender and the role of sexism in the context of racialised relations. The contributions of Hazel Carby and Pratibha Parmar to this volume provided a point of reference and debate in the debates about the interplay between race, class and gender during the 1980s. Along with the interventions of bell hooks and Angela Y. Davis in the USA they were among the first authors to argue for a specifically black feminist voice. They also highlighted the relevance of looking at this dimension of racial relations in a context where the bulk of research remained gender blind.

In exploring these issues *The Empire Strikes Back* acted as a catalyst to a politicisation of debates about the role of research in relation to race relations. In a sense the political struggles that were occurring around the question of race during the 1980s were being echoed in the context of the production of knowledge about racism. The sociology of race relations stood accused of being implicitly conservative and unable to articulate the theorisation of racism with an analysis of class divisions and structural inequalities in power. Sociologists of race and ethnic relations were also criticised for letting their theoretical imaginations be coloured by an implicit Eurocentrism. The result was that the sociological literature demonstrated an inability to record the experiences of minority communities in a sympathetic way.

The arguments to be found in the work of Miles and *The Empire Strikes Back* marked an attempt to articulate a theoretical debate about how to understand racism within the political environment of the 1980s, including the ideological challenge of the Conservative New Right. It is quite clear that the preoccupation with prioritising the analysis of racism was linked to a concern to fix the theoretical debate on questions of power and inequality. In this sense the radical critiques of race relations that became a recurrent refrain in the literature on race and racism from the 1990s onwards were produced in an environment where the main question that interested many researchers was the role of racism in structuring the social and political marginalisation of minority communities. However, in making the conceptualisation of racism a priority, these critiques failed to develop a theo-retical framework for an elaborated analysis of the complex ways in which questions about race tie up to wider social and cultural processes. As we shall see later on in this Introduction, this is an issue that has come more to the fore in the current period.

Racism, anti-semitism and 'the Jew'

One of the most noticeable gaps in many contemporary texts on race and racism is a failure to examine the question of anti-semitism in a substantive fashion. Yet it should be clear from the whole history of racism over the past two centuries that anti-semitism has been a central theme in racial discourses and in political mobilisations around questions of race. This relative absence is all the more surprising since it seems to be an inescapable fact of our recent history that the experience of the Holocaust and the genocidal policies of the Nazi state are an integral part of any contemporary discussion about race and racism. Although there is by now a very substantial literature on the racial theories and practice of the Nazis and on the Holocaust (Proctor 1988; Weindling 1989; Burleigh and Wippermann 1991), little of this has been fed into broader discussions about race and racism.

This gap is beginning to be filled, particularly through the growing body of work that explores the interrelationship between anti-semitism and racism from both a conceptual and a political perspective. It is partly for this reason that we have chosen to focus in Part Four of this Reader on *Racism and Anti-Semitism,* with the inclusion of a set of extracts that explore this dimension in some detail. This concern to link the analysis of racism to discussions about anti-semitism is embedded in our awareness of the important role that the rise of Nazism had on scholarship and research in this field. The actual term anti-semitism came into popular usage at the end of the nineteenth century. But it is widely accepted that as a term it captures the long history of resentment and hatred of Jews. Anti-semitism can be seen therefore as a term that refers to the conception of Jews as an alien, hostile and undesirable group, and the practices that derive from, and support, such a conception. The history of anti-semitism is of course much more complex and of longer historical origin than the racial theories of the Nazis (Poliakov 1974; Gilman and Katz 1991). It has existed in a variety of historical contexts and it has been legitimised by a wide range of beliefs and folklore about Jews. Indeed it seems quite clear that if one looks at all the major European countries they all have quite specific histories of anti-semitism, influenced both by sets of beliefs about Jews and by broader socio-political processes. In the British context, for example, there is evidence of anti-semitism at different historical conjunctures. But it is perhaps in the period of the late nineteenth century that the arrival of sizeable number of Jewish migrants from Eastern Europe became a focus of political debate, leading to the development of a political anti-semitism in particular localities. The political influence of anti-semitism in France towards the end of the nineteenth century can also be seen as related to the changing political and social relations in French society at the time.

Not surprisingly in the aftermath of the Holocaust, one of the main concerns of research on political anti-semitism has been in relation to Germany. Although the history of anti-semitism in Germany was by no means unique, it is certainly the case that in the aftermath of the Holocaust the German experience has been at the heart of most research. Whatever the limitations of this focus on the German experience the wealth of research on the social and political context within which various kinds of anti-semitism developed in Germany has provided some important insights into the ways in which racial ideologies and practices are constructed by and through specific political movements. A case in point is Theodor Adorno's and Max Horkheimer's *Dialectic of Enlightenment,* an extract from which is included in Part Three. Adorno and Horkheimer sought on the one hand to situate anti-semitism in the broader context of class and political struggles in German society and on the other to underline its specific and unique characteristics. Although they sought to locate anti-semitism in the broader framework of capitalist society they also highlighted the murderous consequences of the fascist construction of the Jews as a 'degenerate race':

> The fascists do not view the Jews as a minority but as an opposing race, the embodiment of the negative principle. They must be exterminated to secure the happiness of the world. (Adorno and Horkheimer 1986: 168)

The usages of racial theories by the Nazis thus provided not only a basis for the articulation of anti-semitism but a means of justifying the 'final solution to the Jewish question' and the inevitability of a 'race war'. From this perspective the political consequences of Nazi racial theories, with their emphasis on race as a total criterion, provided the basis for the extermination of Jews. The Holocaust itself needs to be analysed in the context of what actually happened during the period of Nazi rule from 1933 to 1945. As a number of studies have shown, a key feature of the Nazi state was precisely its 'racial' nature.

A fascinating discussion of the role that anti-semitism played in German society during the nineteenth and early twentieth centuries is provided by George Mosse's magisterial study on *The Crisis of German Ideology*. Mosse provides perhaps the best insight into the variety of factors that helped to shape the articulation between anti-semitism and racism in the period from the second half of the nineteenth century to the rise of Adolf Hitler. He also illustrates the complex variety of processes that went into the transformation of latent anti-semitism, including the role of educational institutions, youth organisations and political parties. Mosse's rich account of Volkish thought during the nineteenth century provides perhaps the best and most powerful account of the social and political roots of German anti-semitism, highlighting the contrast in images of 'the uprootedness of the Jew' with those of the 'rootedness of the Volk' (Mosse 1966: 27–8). He also provides a detailed analysis of the linkages between the growth of anti-semitism and the rise of national socialism as a mass political movement:

> That the Volkish ideology, wedded as it was to anti-modernity, could be absorbed by the modern mass movement techniques of National Socialism led to its final realisation. To be sure, if it had not been for very real grievances and frustrations, both on a personal level and on the national level, Germany's development in modern times might have taken a different turn. But the most important question is: Why did millions of people respond to the Volkish call? (Mosse 1966: 317)

In some ways of course Mosse's question has not been fully answered, even when one takes into account the wealth of research on this question. What is clear is that the fact that the Nazis used racial anti-semitism as an important plank of their platform has cast a long shadow over subsequent debates about racism.

This has been highlighted by one of the most challenging attempts to rethink the whole experience of the Holocaust, namely Zygmunt Bauman's *Modernity and the Holocaust.* Bauman seeks to reinterpret the meaning of the Holocaust and its role in contemporary history from the perspective of contemporary sociological theory. One of the ironies that he points to is that anti-semitism in Germany at the beginning of this century was weaker than in many other European countries. He points to the ways in which there were many more Jewish professionals and academics than in Britain, France and America. He also cites evidence that popular anti-semitism was not that widespread in Germany, although it grew rapidly in the aftermath of the First World War. Perhaps most controversially, Bauman contends that the Holocaust was not an aberration but an integral feature of modernity:

> The Holocaust was born and executed in our modern society, at the high stage of our civilisation and at the peak of human cultural achievement, and for this reason it is a problem of that society, civilisation and culture. (Bauman 1989: 13)

From this perspective Bauman argues that a core feature of Nazism was its view of the need for 'social engineering' through its racial policies. The use of genocide by the Nazis was a means to an end, an element in the construction of the 'perfect society' (Bauman 1989: 91). In this sense Bauman is agreeing with the arguments articulated by historians such as Mosse. But he also wants to go beyond such historical accounts and explore more deeply the implications of the Holocaust for how we think about our societies today.

The Nazi attempt to construct a 'racially pure' society and to use state power to help bring this about has exerted a major influence in discussions about race and racism in the post-1945 period. In particular it helped to emphasise and warn against the destructive and genocidal consequences of racist theorising and political mobilisation. It also helped to highlight the complex forms which racist ideologies can, and do, take in particular historical conjunctures. It also highlighted the genocidal impact of the use of state power as a tool of racial policy, an issue that has attracted greater attention from scholars working in this field in relation to both historical and contemporary situations (Wolf 1999; Goldberg 2002; Lentin 2004).

Colonialism, race and the other

While much of the literature on racism and of race relations tends to leave the question of anti-semitism to one side there has been a noticeable growth of interest in the issue of the role of racial ideologies and practices during the colonial period. This has been reflected in important and valuable accounts of the impact of colonialism on our understandings of race and culture. A key point of reference in this discussion has been the work of the psychiatrist Frantz Fanon (1967), along with the work of Edward Said on orientalism. Among other things this work has helped to highlight, for example, the complex processes of racial and gender identification experienced by the colonised during the colonial and postcolonial periods. Other studies have sought to show that the oppressed themselves have produced their own discourses about race and identity in the context of their own experiences of domination and exclusion.

In much of the literature on the development of racist ideologies and practices an important role is assigned to the ways in which colonialism and imperialism helped to construct images of the 'other' (Mannoni 1964). In particular there have been numerous studies of the development of images of colonised peoples and the ways these were popularised and reproduced in British society. There have also been a number of attempts to analyse the ways in which ideas about race were in one way or another the product of attempts to analyse the 'differences' between coloniser and colonised. Such studies have certainly done very much to shed light on an issue that has by and large been marginal to the study of race and racism. Part of the problem in discussing the interplay between imperialism and colonialism with racism is the tendency to over-generalise without exploring in any detail the connections between the institutionalisation of imperial domination and colonisation and the emergence of racist ideas and practices. Mosse is surely right when he argues that: 'Imperialism and racism . . . were never identical; their interrelationship was dependent upon time and place' (Mosse 1985: x). It is precisely the nature of this relationship that remains to be fully analysed, particularly if we are to understand how and why commonsense images about race were influenced by the role that countries such as Britain played as colonial and imperial powers.

A variety of critical research on the politics of colonialism has shown that images of the 'other' played a central role in colonial discourses (Ross 1982; Pratt 1992; Parry 1998). Such images were closely tied to racial stereotypes, but it was also clear that they related to all aspects of the relationship between the colonised and colonisers. Sander Gilman has made this linkage clear when he argues:

> In the nineteenth century, in the age of expanding European colonies, the black became the primitive per se, a primitivism mirrored in the stultifying quality of his or her dominant sense, touch, as well as the absence of any aesthetic sensibility. (Gilman 1991: 20)

From this perspective the linkage of colonised peoples with images of the 'primitive' was the product of complex historical processes and it took different forms in specific colonial situations. A case in point is the impact of the 'scramble for Africa' on images of the peoples of the 'dark continent', and the circulation of these images in the metropolitan societies. While, as we have shown above, European images of Africa had taken shape over some centuries it is also the case that the expansion of colonial power during the nineteenth century helped to invent new images and to institutionalise specific forms of class, gender and racial relations (Mudimbe 1988 and 1994; Appiah 1992; Coombes 1994).

What of the impact of these images on racial ideas and values in the colonial powers themselves? In the British context it seems clear that in the Victorian era the experience of colonialism and imperial expansion played an important role in shaping ideas about race, both in relation to Africa and India. It was also during this period that the question of the Empire became an integral part of British politics and society. Images of colonial peoples were not the outcome of any singular process. In the context of both Africa and Asia, for example, a number of interlinked processes were at work in the construction of images of both the 'natives' and the 'colonisers' (Dirks 1992; Spurr 1993; Sharpe 1993). We need to remember that most Victorians had no personal contact with the exotic peoples and places that they were assuming responsibility for. Their opinions were formed according to the sources of their information, and these sources were for the most part the popular press and literature. The linkages between colonialism and racism became evident throughout the late nineteenth and early twentieth centuries in the form of the articulation between nationalism and patriotism in the construction of the very definition of 'Englishness' and 'Britishness'.

It would be a mistake, however, to see such racial images in isolation from wider sets of social relations. As a number of commentators have forcefully argued, an important aspect of racial thinking during the nineteenth century was the similarity between discourses about race and those about class. This was evident in both Britain and the rest of the Empire. Douglas Lorimer's study of racial attitudes in Victorian society brings out the parallels between the colour and the class prejudice of middle-class Victorians in the most clear manner. He notes the similarities between the attitudes of those middle class travellers whose tourism took them to India, to Egypt, and to the East End of London, in order to view the strange, the primitive and the exotic creatures of the world (Lorimer 1978).

It is also clear that during the high point of imperialism in the late nineteenth and early twentieth centuries racialised notions of national identity were pertinent outside the colonial context. By the late nineteenth and early twentieth centuries imperialist ideologies had developed a racial notion of national identity to refer to other European nations as well as colonial people. It was during this period that nationalist movements and ideals began to gain a degree of influence in many European countries.

What this process made clear is the variety of ways in which the idea of race could be used to refer to the putative 'racial' differences between competing nations and states. Interestingly enough, in the period before the First World War it was precisely such ideas about 'race' that gained an important role in political discourses of the time. This is not to say that colonialism and imperialism did not also have an important impact on political ideologies, literature and popular culture. Certainly if one looks at literary and cultural output from the period at the end of the nineteenth century, and well into the twentieth, it is redolent with images of the role of Britain as an imperial power and as a source of civilised culture for the colonies. Some of the most interesting research in this field has been about the role that colonialism and imperialism played in influencing political discourses and values through popular culture at this time. In the British context a number of valuable studies have helped to show the depth of the impact that imperialism had on popular cultural expressions throughout the late nineteenth and early twentieth centuries. John MacKenzie has shown in his interesting studies of imperialism and

popular culture both the complexity and the depth of the impact of imperial propaganda on popular culture, education, literature and other cultural forms (MacKenzie
1984; MacKenzie 1986). Other studies of colonial societies have also highlighted
the depth of the cultural and political imagery of colonialism and its impact on
Western societies (Miller 1990; Pieterse 1992). The important role of sexuality
in constructions of the 'native' has also been highlighted by on-going research
about imperial culture (Hyam 1990; Parker *et al.* 1992; Young 1995).

Yet it has to be said that one of the major lacunae in the existing literature
is that while much has been written about the impact of colonial expansion and
imperial domination on racial attitudes, there has been surprisingly little comment
on the role and impact of anti-colonial ideas and movements. Given the extent of
its influence on political and social discourses during this period it is indeed
surprising that we have little knowledge of both the nature of the anti-colonialist
movements and the role that they had on the changing ideas about race in Britain
and elsewhere. It is perhaps this absence that has helped to produce a rather
monolithic view of the impact of the Empire on domestic British political culture.

It has to be noted here that in practice current research has tended, if anything,
to question the idea of a uniform and unchanging colonial view of 'race' that was
prevalent at all stages of colonial history and European expansion. Rather a number
of scholars have shown that in practice colonial societies were by no means static
and unchanging in their articulation of racial ideologies and social relations. In
summary, while it is important in analysing the history of racism to include the
role played by processes of domination and colonisation it would be misleading to
construct a simplistic one-to-one relationship between the two. It is perhaps
understandable in the immediate aftermath of the decline of colonialism that much
of the attention of researchers has focused on its role in fostering and spreading
racial stereotypes and myths in metropolitan societies. The danger, however, is
that in so doing we may lose sight of the complexity and diversity of colonial
social relations and blame many of our contemporary mores on the 'experience'
of colonial domination.

Feminism, race and gender

Alongside the increased attention given to colonialism and postcolonialism we
have seen a proliferation of feminist writings on race and racism from a variety
of angles. Indeed, it can be said that during the past decade some of the most
important contributions to the analysis of racism have come from writers whose
work can be seen as deriving from feminism, though often also influenced by some
of the perspectives we have touched upon already. From the early 1980s a growing
number of studies, chiefly from the USA and Britain, have sought in one way or
another to place questions about sexism, gender and sexuality on the agenda of
the study of racial relations. This has led to some valuable insights into the everyday
social processes that helped to shape the interrelationship between race and gender
in particular historical contexts (Hall 1992; Ware 1992). It has also produced a

wealth of theoretical interventions by black and minority feminist writers into debates about contemporary racisms and their socio-political contexts (Carby 1987 and 1998; Williams 1991).

As we noted earlier in discussing the British context, for example, *The Empire Strikes Back* was one of the first books on race relations in Britain to look in any depth at the question of gender and the role of sexism in the context of racialised relations. The contributions of Hazel Carby and Pratibha Parmar to this volume provided a point of reference and debate in the literature about the interplay between race, class and gender during the 1980s (CCCS 1982). They also highlighted the relevance of looking at this dimension of racial relations in a context where the bulk of research remained gender blind. Carby's contribution in particular is a point of reference in discussions within feminism about racism, and is included in the readings we have selected for this part of the Reader.

At the same time a vibrant and critical discussion about the position of black and other minority women in relation to feminism was emerging in the USA. This took a number of forms. The work of writers such as bell hooks addressed the limits of feminist theory in dealing with questions of race and class. The work of other writers questioned the limitations of black nationalist politics when dealing with questions of gender. A particularly controversial example of this trend was the book by Michele Wallace *Black Macho & The Myth of the Superwoman*, that was originally published in 1979, and which sought to explore important aspects of the relationship between black men and women (Wallace 1990). Another influential text was *Ain't I A Woman: Black Women and Feminism* by bell hooks, originally published in 1981, which was concerned with both establishing the possibility of a dialogue between black women and feminism and with a critical analysis of the limits of feminism in relation to the question of race (hooks 1981). The work of theorists such as Gyatri Spivak and Chandra Talpade Mohanty also helped to bring questions about non-western versions of feminist thought into academic discussion about this issue (see Part Five).

In the aftermath of these debates a growing number of studies have begun to explore the interrelationship between racism and sexism, racial inequality and gender inequality and the position of African-Caribbean, Asian and other migrant women in British society. This has helped to overcome the gender blind approach of many studies of racial relations, though there are still many aspects of the position of black and ethnic minority women that have received little attention. Most attention has focused on: (a) the role of women in the migration process; (b) the employment and social position of black women; (c) family relations; and (d) the links between racial and gender equality. All these studies have contributed to a growing awareness of the complex sets of interrelationships that take place between racial, class and gender relations in specific socio-economic contexts (Anthias and Yuval-Davis 1992; Winddance Twine and Blee 2001). They have also helped to shed light on often neglected but nevertheless crucial aspects of racialisation (Murji and Solomos 2005).

Debates between feminists about the boundaries of identity and the different positionings of black and white women have been an important undercurrent in the past two decades and this is one of the central themes that is explored in a number of the extracts in Part Five. Perhaps one of the most controversial areas of debate has been the issue of whether feminists have over concentrated on patriarchy, and neglected race and ethnicity as sources of women's oppression (Collins 2006). This is certainly a theme that pervades many of the early black feminist critiques of the mainstream of feminist politics, and it has continued to be a key area of debate. It is certainly the case that many feminist texts from the 1960s and 1970s showed little or no awareness of the historical background and contemporary context of racial inequalities. Whatever the merits of the specific debates that have taken place over this issue it is worth emphasising that contemporary feminism has had to take on board questions about race and ethnicity in a systematic manner. The mainstream of contemporary feminism has been forced in one way or another to come to terms with questions about race and racism. There is now a wealth of literature that has arisen out of the on-going debates between white and black feminists over the past decade. What is more important, however, is that this dialogue has encouraged the development of grounded research on the position of black and minority women (Mohanty *et al.* 1991; Alexander and Mohanty 1997; Mohanty 2003).

One interesting example of this is the growth of research on the position of migrant women in various societies. Studies of migration have tended in the past to make assumptions about migration that have either excluded or underplayed the position of women in the migration process. More recently an increasing amount of research has focused either directly or indirectly on the position of migrant women. A number of important studies have explored the impact of immigration and nationality legislation on black and ethnic minority women, their employment patterns, the impact of racism on their lives, and their struggles to improve their social and economic position.

Quite apart from the academic research that has taken up the question of race and gender, over the past decade we have seen a massive growth of writings by and about black and minority women. The works of novelists such as Toni Morrison have explored key aspects of the experience of black women in America through the form of the novel and have become another important contribution to current debates. A good example of the impact of Morrison's work is her novel *Beloved* whose narrative provides a powerful and chilling account of the experience of black Americans through and after slavery. As Morrison herself comments about the contemporary situation in America:

> For both black and white American writers, in a wholly racialised society,
> there is no escape from racially inflected language, and the work writers
> do to unhobble the imagination from the demands of that language is
> complicated, interesting, and definitive. (Morrison 1992: 12–13)

In this context it is perhaps not surprising that literary texts such as those of Morrison and Alice Walker among others have come to occupy an important and vibrant role in contemporary debates about the historical interface between race and gender. This is perhaps because more than traditional sociological studies they have done much to give voice to the experience of black women and to highlight the lived realities of racial ideologies and practices.

Another important area in current research has been the issue of the construction of black female sexuality in racial ideologies. There is a wealth of research that has shown that at various historical conjunctures sexuality has played an important role in the fantasies that make up the world of racism. This research has tended to have a historical focus, and to be concerned specifically with slavery and colonialism. It is also clear that aspects of contemporary popular culture and advertising involve the reproduction of images of black female sexuality and sensuality. The role that such images play in the articulation of racialised culture in the context of contemporary societies remains to be fully investigated (see extract from Stoler in Part Four and Stoler 1995).

Perhaps the main achievement of the debates outlined above has been that they have helped to establish the complex historical linkages between racism and sexism and encouraged theoretical debate about the interrelationship between the two (Collins 1990; James and Busia 1993). Despite important contributions, however, questions about gender and sexism have remained a neglected aspect of the mainstream of studies of racial and ethnic relations. The main research centres in this field have been largely unaffected by the debates discussed above and they have done little or no substantive research with a clear gender dimension. Even where issues of race have been looked at there has been an implicit assumption that 'the three worlds of inequality' (race, class and gender) are somehow separate from each other. There is a long way to go before the gender dimension is fully integrated into the study of race and racism, but as we shall see in Part Five and other parts of this Reader it would be impossible to analyse important aspects of contemporary racism without serious consideration of the changing social relations which shape the position of minority women.

Race, culture and identity

A major dilemma we faced in putting together *Theories of Race and Racism* derives from the fact that we were attempting to provide an overview of a field that was constantly changing. Whilst it may have been possible two decades ago to provide a reliable guide to the sociology of race relations and see that as a relatively complete survey of key theoretical debates, this is no longer the case. In the current period it has become increasingly difficult to provide a reliable map of this field, particularly as it has become increasingly multidisciplinary and as it has spread out to include arenas that were largely neglected by previous generations of scholars. Thus whilst the debates of the 1970s and 1980s continue to influence research agendas, a number of current developments have led to a questioning of many of the certainties that dominated theorising in this field even a decade ago. Perhaps the most important influence in this new situation has been the decline of both mainstream and neo-Marxist approaches. In this context some have called for a radical revision of class analysis in order to incorporate political movements that mobilise around forms of identity other than class. Others have suggested a need for a move away from both narrow sociological and neo-Marxist theoretical models as a framework of analysis and have (i) sought to develop a self-consciously multi-disciplinary approach to the study of race and racism and (ii) have taken on board some of the concerns of post-structuralism and postmodernism in relation to the analysis of changing forms of social and cultural identity.

One of the results of this shift is the growing concern with the status of cultural forms and a return to an analysis of the nature of ethnicity in metropolitan settings. The political naivety of the early work on ethnicity meant that for much of the 1980s the analysis of cultural processes and forms was rejected in favour of a focus on the politics of racism. The rejection of culture was tied up with the notion that one of the inherent dangers of focusing research on the culture of minority communities was the tendency to shift attention from racism to the characteristics of racialised minorities. However, the question of cultural production and the politics of identity are fast becoming an important area of contemporary debate. New perspectives are being developed which examine the ways in which cultural forms are being made and re-made producing complex social phenomena. These new syncretic cultures are being plotted within the global networks which have been formed by diasporic and transnational communities.

The process of reclaiming culture in critical debate has simultaneously involved a re-examination of how racism is conceptualised. As a number of the extracts that are included in Part Six make clear, a major influence in current theoretical debates has been an engagement of theories about race and racism with wider controversies in the social sciences surrounding questions of culture and identity. One of the constant refrains in this discussion has been the need to avoid uniform and homogeneous conceptualisations of racism. Although not yet part of the agenda of mainstream research on race relations, a range of studies of racialised discourses in the mass media, literature, art and other cultural forms have begun to be produced. Reacting against what they see as the lack of an account of cultural forms of racial discourse a growing number of scholars have sought to develop a more rounded picture of contemporary racial imagery by looking at the role of literature, the popular media and other cultural forms in representing changing images of race and ethnicity.

David Goldberg has pointed out that 'the presumption of a single monolithic racism is being displaced by a mapping of the multifarious historical formulations of *racisms'* (Goldberg 1993). In this context it is perhaps not surprising that a core concern of many current texts in this field is to explore the interconnections between race and nationhood, patriotism and nationalism rather than analyse ideas about biological inferiority (Juan Jr 2002; Taguieff 2001; Winant 2001). One of the core ideas that is explored in a number of the extracts in Part Six is precisely this issue of the complex and varied nature of contemporary forms of racist discourses and political symbols.

Let us take the example of the changing terms of debate about race in Britain during the 1980s and 1990s. The ascendancy of the political right in Britain during the 1980s prompted commentators to identify a 'new racism', or what Fanon (1967) referred to as 'cultural racism', within the political culture and in everyday life. This 'new racism' has been conceptualised as having its origins in the social and political crisis afflicting Britain. Its focus is the defense of the mythic 'British/English way of life' in the face of challenges posed by the incursion of 'foreign influences'. In this environment it has become all too easy for new forms of racial discourse to achieve common currency in everyday debates about the role and position of minorities in British society. Similar trends towards the articulation of forms of cultural racism have been noted by commentators on the situation in a number of other societies in the current period, including France, Germany and the USA. We make this point because it seems to us that it points to the need to situate racism and ideas about race as changing and historically situated. From this perspective the question of whether race is an ontologically valid concept or otherwise is in many ways not the most relevant question to ask, since it is perhaps more important to understand why certain racialised subjectivities become a feature of social relations at particular points in time and in particular geographical spaces.

One of the most important features of the contemporary situation is that manifestations of race are coded in a language that aims to circumvent accusations of racism (see contributions by Stuart Hall and David Goldberg in Part Two). In the case of contemporary racist discourses, for example, race is often coded in terms of 'difference' and 'culture'. However, the central feature of these processes is that the qualities of social groups are fixed, made natural, confined within a pseudo-biologically defined culturalism. What is clear from these writings is that a range of discourses on social differentiation may have a metonymic relationship to racism. As Goldberg shows clearly in his work on racist culture, the semantics of race are produced by a complex set of inter-discursive processes where the language of culture and nation invokes a hidden racial narrative. The defining feature of this process is the way in which it naturalises social formations in terms of a racial/cultural logic of belonging (Smith 2006; Spickard and Daniel 2004; Steinberg 2007).

Another focus within the emerging literature on the cultural politics of racism has been the social construction of race and difference in literature and the cinema. This has been a neglected area of research but in the past two decades this has been remedied by the publication of a number of important studies of race, culture and identity. Originating largely from the United States such studies have looked at a number of areas, including literature, the cinema and other popular cultural forms. They have sought to show that within contemporary societies our understandings of race, and the articulation of racist ideologies, cannot be reduced to economic, political or class relations. This type of approach is in fact more evident outside of sociology. The work of literary and cultural theorists in the United States and Britain has begun to explore seriously the question of race and racism, and has led to a flowering of studies which use the debates around post-structuralism and postmodernism as a way of approaching the complex forms of racialised identities in colonial and postcolonial societies.

Equally, it has also become clear that there is a need to shed the narrow confines of the race relations problematic and develop a more sophisticated analysis of the impact of various racisms on the white majority. A growing literature now exists on the politics of whiteness that is attempting to develop such a focus of inquiry. However, there are immediate difficulties with this endeavour, as David Roediger shows in his analysis of critical white studies in Part Six. From a different perspective bell hooks has graphically discussed the terrorising effect that whiteness has on the black imagination (Roediger 2002 and 2005). Writing on her experience of growing up as a black woman in the American South she comments: 'whiteness in the black imagination is often a representation of terror' (hooks 1992: 342). Clearly there is a need for a research agenda which looks at the way white subjectivities are racialised, and how whiteness is manifested in discourse, communication and culture (Hartigan 1999; Jacobson 2006; Ware and Back 2002).

This turn within critical writing has important implications. One of the fundamental criticisms of the sociology of race and ethnic relations is that it has too often focused on the victims rather than the perpetrators of racism. Prioritising whiteness as an area of critical endeavour has the potential to disrupt the sociological common sense that equates the discussion of racism with the empirical scrutiny of black communities. Toni Morrison in her analysis of whiteness in American novels comments:

> My project is an effort to avert the critical gaze from the racial object
> to the racial subject; from the described and imagined to the describers
> and imaginers; the serving to the served. (Morrison 1992: 90)

In the context of Britain, Stuart Hall, among others, has pointed out the urgency of deconstructing the meanings of whiteness, not just in order to counter racism but also in order to understand the complex realities faced by the African and Asian diaspora living in Britain (Hall 1993). There is already an emerging literature that is trying to provide a critical analysis of the complex meanings that are attached to ideas about whiteness in everyday cultural processes (Frankenberg 1993; Back 1996).

The analysis of whiteness is certainly an important theme in many current debates, though it is not always clear how far it has helped to develop a better analysis of contemporary expressions of racism. There are a number of possible shortcomings in the turn towards whiteness. In the hurry to shift the critical gaze there is always a danger of suspending reflection on the analytical terms of this project. Like many of the debates on the ontological status of culture, there is a danger of reifying whiteness and reinforcing a unitary idea of race. In order to avoid this it is crucial to locate any discussion of whiteness in specific empirical and historical contexts. Equally, it is important to understand that whiteness is a political definition that has gained historical meaning in the context of white supremacy. Any discussion of whiteness must, therefore, incorporate an appreciation of how gendered processes are inextricably articulated within the semantics of race. In this sense interrogating whiteness as a form of identity and a political discourse must (i) focus on de-colonising the definition of 'normal', and (ii) avoid the reification of whiteness as a social identity.

Whatever the merits of the turn towards an emphasis on culture and identity in the literature on race and racism, it is evident that questions of cultural production and change are an integral component of any contemporary conceptualisation of racism. Nevertheless, these theoretical debates need to be contextualised within a shifting political context. The certainties of the debates that dominated much of the discussion on racism in the 1980s and 1990s have all but disappeared. What seems to characterise the contemporary period is, on the one hand, a complex spectrum of racisms, and, on the other, the fragmentation of the definition of blackness as a political identity in favour of a resurgence of ethnicism and cultural differentiation. At the same time, and perhaps paradoxically, new cultures and ethnicities are emerging in the context of dialogue and producing a kaleidoscope of cultural syncretisms (Bhatt 1997), ethnic nationalism (Wimmer 2002 and 2004) and ideologies that emphasise the search for ethnic and racial purities (Mann 2005).

Shifting research and teaching agendas

As we have tried to show in this Introduction, the study of race and racism has been rapidly transformed over the past three decades and this has in turn led to a reformulation of research agendas and the boundaries of scholarship in this field. In this period of change our main hope in putting together *Theories of Race and Racism* is that it can help to provide an overview of important debates about the status of race and racism and explore important theoretical and political dilemmas that are faced at the present time. We are aware that this process is not simply an academic process, since researchers in this field are almost inevitably forced to confront questions about politics. While some authors writing in the tradition of race and ethnic relations studies have been careful to separate the research process from political action, such a separation is in some ways impossible and even undesirable.

Perhaps the main lessons that we can learn from the rapid expansion of studies of race and racism in the past three decades are the following:

- first, that there is a need for greater theoretical clarity on key concepts;
- second, that there is a need to broaden the research agenda to cover issues that have been neglected, such as culture and identity;
- third, that there is a need for research agendas to address political and policy dilemmas in order to understand racism and how to counter it;
- fourth, that there is a need to integrate the analysis of racism with a conceptualisation of related issues, such as gender and sexuality (Zack, Shrage and Sartwell 1998).

Precisely because the question of how to conceptualise racism is not purely an academic matter, it is important to develop analytic frameworks that explain the role of ideas about race in specific historical and political conjunctures. It is from this starting point that we can begin to understand the complex mechanisms through which contemporary racisms have evolved and adapted to new circumstances.

A good example of the unpredictability of these new circumstances can be found in the public debates about security and terrorism that we have seen since 2001. The 9-11 terrorist attacks on the World Trade Center, and subsequent attacks in various parts of the globe, were not in themselves closely linked to questions about race and immigration as such. It is true to say, however, that debates about immigration, racism, belonging and identity have been animated in new ways in the wake of these events and the subsequent prosecution of the 'war on terror.' As Stuart Hall has commented, 'September 11th did make a profound change in explicitly making cultural difference and multiculturalism dangerous' (Hall and Back forthcoming). In America this culminated in a reworking of a 'clash of civilisations' discourse which sought to situate the cultural politics of religious identity in the context of incommensurable struggles between Islam and the West (see Calhoun, Price and Timmer 2002; Appiah 2007). Equally, in the context of Europe the so-called 'death of multiculturalism' has produced a debate about the degree to which social solidarity and cultural diversity are incompatible. The fear of terror and violence from the 'enemy next door,' directed racism's ire against what Paul Gilroy calls 'the half different and the partially familiar' (Gilroy 2004: 137). Here the complexities of ambivalences within contemporary racism play a part in producing a 'politics of misrecognition' in which suspects are detained by the security forces without cause, or even shot and killed (Back 2007). Our larger point is that the current martial climate of ongoing armed conflict and securitization gives the political elsewhere of Afghanistan, Iraq and Middle East an increasingly significant role in the politics of racism and cultural dynamism of cities in the United States or Europe. This challenges analysts of racism to be more attentive of global relations and networks as well as sensitive to the impact of geopolitical events in shaping racism's future.

In this context unitary or simplistic definitions of racism become hard to sustain. However, it seems clear that contemporary racisms share some central features. They attempt to fix human social groups in terms of *natural* properties of belonging within particular political and geographical contexts. The assertion that racialised subjects do not belong within, say, British society is then associated with social and cultural characteristics designated to them within the logic of particular racisms. It follows from the above argument that racist discourses need to be rigorously contextualised. This means that racisms need to be situated within specific moments. The effect of a particular racist discourse needs to be placed in the conditions surrounding the moment of its enunciation.

In this context the meanings of race and racism need to be located within particular fields of discourse and articulated to the social relations found within that context. It is then necessary to see what kinds of racialised identities are being formed within these contexts. Take, for example, the definition of the category 'black'. It is clear that it is a notion used somewhat differently in specific national situations, and that this has been influenced by particular historical and cultural processes. The contrasting usages of the category 'black' in America and Britain is a case in point. With regard to the ontological status of these classifications we view them as political constructions of identity that need to be situated within specific social and discursive contexts. We in no way accept that these identifications relate to 'natural communities' or that one notion is more politically legitimate than others. Rather they constitute moments where community and identity is defined: manifestations of racial and ethnic closure. We are suggesting a position that builds into any analysis a rigorous scrutiny of racialised definitions, whether they are operated by the state or through political mobilisations that are occurring around racial and ethnic identities within minority communities (Dawson 2001). This approach seeks to decipher the meanings of racialised identities without attempting to prioritise one classification as more legitimate than another.

We are suggesting a model for conceptualising racisms that is:

- sensitive to local and contextual manifestations of racist discourse;
- able to connect local manifestations with wider or national public discourses;
- able to develop a sensitivity to the trans-local matrices of racist culture and ethnic absolutist movements.

Here we are particularly thinking of the ways in which racist cultures are being integrated across time and space through technological advances such as the Internet. In this way we are suggesting a model that situates racisms at local, national and global levels. As yet much theoretical work on racism has produced accounts of racism that derive contemporary forms of racism from public political discourse. This evidence is then used to generalise about broader trends within British society. We are suggesting that there is a need to move beyond the limits of this approach by situating racisms within particular settings before moving towards a more general account of their wider significance.

Theories of Race and Racism provides a guide through the complex debates about the ways in which ideas about race and racism need to be conceptualised in the present political environment. We are aware that this whole field of research is going through a rapid period of change and that it is not possible to cover all these transformations in one volume. It is clear that the coming period will pose serious questions with regard to the way racism is conceptualised, particularly in a context where new forms of racial and ethnic conflict have come to the fore in various parts of the globe. But precisely because of these uncertainties there is a need to go beyond the limited perspectives that have dominated academic discourses over the past few decades and develop theoretical and conceptual tools of relevance to the analysis of the present. We hope that in putting this Reader together we have provided some of the tools for moving beyond current preoccupations in order to analyse new trends and developments.

Using the Reader

We want to conclude this Introduction by emphasising how to make it accessible and usable to a range of audiences, including students and researchers. We have therefore included a number of features to help you get the most out of it. We have provided a general overview of the main thematic issues covered by the Reader in the course of this chapter and so it is best to go carefully through the arguments here before moving on to the specific parts. In particular we have signposted some of the key themes that underpin the structure of the six component parts. In addition, at the beginning of each part we have included an introduction that surveys the main arguments to be found in each contribution. The main point of these introductions is to provide a guide to the specific themes covered by the extracts in each part and to clarify important points of debate.

In order to follow up other relevant important texts we have included at the end of each part introduction a Guide to Further Reading that provides suggestions for readings that follow up the key themes in that particular part of the Reader. The suggestions contained there are not meant to be complete, but we have attempted to include texts that reflect a variety of conceptual perspectives and which are important contributions to their fields of study. Finally, at the end of each part introduction we have included lists of Key Questions that can serve as a point of departure for thinking through the main themes that are covered in each part.

References

Adorno, T. W. and Horkheimer, M. (1986) *Dialectic of Enlightenment*, London: Verso.

Alexander, M. J. and Mohanty, C. T. (eds) (1997) *Feminist Genealogies, Colonial Legacies, Democratic Futures*, New York: Routledge.

Anderson, E. and Massey, D. S. (eds) (2001) *Problem of the Century: Racial Stratification in the United States*, New York: Russell Sage Foundation.

Anthias, F. and Yuval-Davis, N. (1992) *Racialized Boundaries*, London: Routledge.

Appiah, K. A. (1992) *In My Father's House: Africa in the Philosophy of Culture*, London: Methuen.

—— (2006) *Cosmopolitanism: Ethics in a World of Strangers*, New York: Basic Books.

Back, L. (1996) *New Ethnicities and Urban Culture*, London: UCL Press.

—— (2007) *The Art of Listening*, Oxford: Berg.

Banton, M. (1967) *Race Relations*, New York: Basic Books.

—— (1991) 'The Race Relations Problematic', *British Journal of Sociology* 42, 1: 115–130.

Bauman, Z. (1989) *Modernity and the Holocaust*, Oxford: Blackwell.

Bhatt, C. (1997) *Liberation and Purity: Race, New Religious Movements and the Ethics of Postmodernity*, London: UCL Press.

Bulmer, M. and Solomos, J. (eds) (1999) *Ethnic and Racial Studies Today*, London: Routledge.

—— (eds) (2004) *Researching Race and Racism*, London: Routledge.

Burleigh, M. and Wippermann, W. (1991) *The Racial State: Germany 1933–1945*, Cambridge: Cambridge University Press.

Calhoun, C., Price, P. and Timmer, A. (eds) (2002) *Understanding September 11*, New York: New Press.

Carby, H. V. (1987) *Reconstructing Womanhood*, New York: Oxford University Press.

—— (1998) *Race Men*, Cambridge, MA: Harvard University Press.

Centre for Contemporary Cultural Studies (1982) *The Empire Strikes Back: Race and Racism in 70s Britain*, London: Hutchinson.

Collins, P. H. (1990) *Black Feminist Thought*, London: Unwin Hyman.

—— (1998) *Fighting Words: Black Women and the Search for Justice*, Minneapolis: University of Minnesota Press.

—— (2006) *From Black Power to Hip Hop: Racism, Nationalism, and Feminism*, Philadelphia: Temple University Press.

Coombes A. (1994) *Reinventing Africa*, New Haven and London: Yale University Press.

Davis, A. Y. (1982) *Women, Race and Class*, London: The Women's Press.

Dawson, M. C. (2001) *Black Visions: The Roots of Contemporary African-American Political Ideologies*, Chicago: University of Chicago Press.

Dirks, N. B. (ed.) (1992) *Colonialism and Culture*, Ann Arbor: University of Michigan Press.

Du Bois, W. E. B. (1996) [1903] *The Souls of Black Folk*, New York: Penguin.

Essed, P. and Goldberg, D. T. (eds) (2002) *Race Critical Theories: Text and Context*, Oxford: Blackwell.

Fanon, F. (1967) *Towards the African Revolution*, New York: Monthly Review Press.

Feagin, J. R. (2006) *Systemic Racism: A Theory of Oppression*, New York: Routledge.

Fredrickson, G. M. (2003) *Racism: A Short History*, Princeton: Princeton University Press.

Gilman, S. L. (1991) *The Jew's Body*, New York: Routledge.

Gilman, S. L. and Katz, S. T. (eds) (1991) *Anti-Semitism in Times of Crisis*, New York: New York University Press.

Gilroy, P. (1987) *There Ain't No Black in the Union Jack*, London: Hutchinson.

—— (1990) 'One Nation Under a Groove: The Cultural Politics of "Race" and Racism in Britain' in D. T. Goldberg (eds) *Anatomy of Racism*, Minneapolis: University of Minnesota Press.

—— (2004) *After Empire: Melancholia or Convivial Culture?*, London: Routledge.

Goldberg, D. T. (1993) *Racist Culture*, Oxford: Blackwell.

—— (2002) *The Racial State*, Oxford: Blackwell.

Goldberg, D. T. (ed.) (1990) *Anatomy of Racism*, Minneapolis: University of Minnesota Press.

Goldberg, D. T. and Solomos, J. (eds) (2002) *A Companion to Racial and Ethnic Studies*, Oxford: Blackwell.

Guillaumin, C. (1995) *Racism, Sexism, Power and Ideology*, London: Routledge.

Hall, C. (1992) *White, Middle Class and Male: Explorations in Feminism and History*, Cambridge: Polity Press.

Hall, S. (1980) 'Race Articulation and Societies Structured in Dominance' in UNESCO *Sociological Theories: Race and Colonialism*, Paris: UNESCO.

—— (1990) 'Cultural Identity and Diaspora' in J. Rutherford (ed.) *Identity: Culture, Community, Difference*, London: Lawrence and Wishart.

—— (1993) 'Culture, Community, nation', *Cultural Studies* 7, 3: 349–63.

Hall, S. and Back L. (Forthcoming) 'At Home and Not at Home', *Cultural Studies*.

Hartigan Jr, J. (1999) *Racial Situations: Class Predicaments of Whiteness in Detroit*, Princeton: Princeton University Press.

Holloway, J. S. and Keppel, B. (eds) (2007) *Black Scholars on the Line: Race, Social Science, and American Thought in the Twentieth Century*, Notre Dame: University of Notre Dame Press.

hooks, b. (1981) *Ain't I A Woman: Black Women and Feminism*, Boston: South End Press.

—— (1992) 'Representing Whiteness in the Black Imagination' in L. Grossberg, C. Nelson and P. Treichler (eds) *Cultural Studies*, London: Routledge.

Hyam, R. (1990) *Empire and Sexuality: The British Experience*, Manchester: Manchester University Press.

Jacobson, M. F. (2006) *Roots Too: White Ethnic Revival in Post Civil-Rights America*, Cambridge, MA: Harvard University Press.

Jenkins, R. (1986) 'Social Anthropological Models of Inter-Ethnic Relations' in J. Rex and D. Mason (eds) *Theories of Race and Ethnic Relations*, Cambridge: Cambridge University Press.

—— (2008) *Rethinking Ethnicity: Arguments and Explorations*, 2nd edition, London: Sage.

Juan Jr, E. S. (2002) *Racism and Cultural Studies: Critiques of Multiculturalist Ideology and the Politics of Difference*, Durham and London: Duke University Press.

Klineberg, E. (2002) *Heat Wave: A Social Autopsy of Disaster in Chicago*, Chicago: University of Chicago Press.

Kohn, M. (1995) *The Race Gallery: The Return of Racial Science*, London: Jonathan Cape.

Lentin, A. (2004) *Racism and Anti-Racism in Europe*, London: Pluto.

Lorimer, D. A. (1978) *Colour, Class and the Victorians*, Leicester: Leicester University Press.

MacKenzie, J. M. (1984) *Propaganda and Empire: The Manipulation of British Public Opinion 1880–1960*, Manchester: Manchester University Press.

MacKenzie, J. M. (ed.) (1986) *Imperialism and Popular Culture*, Manchester: Manchester University Press.

Mann, M. (2005) *The Dark Side of Democracy: Explaining Ethnic Cleansing*, Cambridge: Cambridge University Press.

Mannoni, O. (1964) *Prospero and Caliban: The Psychology of Colonisation*, New York: Fredrick A. Praeger.

Martinot, S. (2003) *The Rule of Racialization: Class, Identity, Governance*, Philadelphia: Temple University Press.

Memmi, A. (2000) *Racism*, Minneapolis: University of Minnesota Press.

Miles, R. (1982) *Racism and Migrant Labour*, London: George Allen and Unwin.

—— (1984) 'Marxism Versus the "Sociology of Race Relations"?', *Ethnic and Racial Studies* 7, 2: 217–37.

—— (1986) 'Labour Migration, Racism and Capital Accumulation in Western Europe', *Capital and Class* 28: 49–86.

—— (1988) 'Racism, Marxism and British Politics', *Economy and Society* 17, 3: 428–60.

—— (1993) *Racism after 'Race Relations'*, London: Routledge.

Miles, R. and Brown, M. (2003) *Racism*, Second edition, London: Routledge.

Miller, C. L. (1990) *Theories of Africans*, Chicago: University of Chicago Press.

Mohanty, C. T. (2003) *Feminism Without Borders: Decolonizing Theory, Practicing Solidarity*, Durham and London: Duke University Press.

Mohanty, C. T., Russo, A. and Torres, L. (eds) (1991) *Third World Women and the Politics of Feminism*, Bloomington: Indiana University Press.

Morrison, T. (1992) *Playing in the Dark: Whiteness and the Literary Imagination*, Cambridge MA: Harvard University Press.

Mosse, G. L. (1966) *The Crisis of German Ideology: Intellectual Origins of the Third Reich*, London: Weidenfeld and Nicolson.

—— (1985) *Toward the Final Solution: A History of European Racism*, Madison: University of Wisconsin Press.

Mudimbe, V. Y. (1988) *The Invention of Africa: Gnosis, Philosophy and the Order of Knowledge*, Bloomington: Indiana University Press.

—— (1994) *The Idea of Africa*, Bloomington: Indiana University Press.

Murji, K. and Solomos, J. (eds) (2005) *Racialization: Studies in Theory and Practice*, Oxford: Oxford University Press.

Parker, A., Russo, M., Sommer, D. and Yaeger, P. (eds) (1992) *Nationalisms and Sexualities*, New York: Routledge.

Parry, B. (1998) *Delusions and Discoveries: Studies on India in the British Imagination 1880–1930*, London: Verso.

Patterson, O. (1998) *Rituals of Blood: Consequences of Slavery in Two American Centuries*, Washington DC: Civitas.

Pieterse, J. N. (1992) *White on Black: Images of Africa and Blacks in Western Popular Culture*, New Haven and London: Yale University Press.

Poliakov, L. (1974) *The Aryan Myth*, Brighton: Chatto, Heinemann for Sussex University Press.

Pratt, M. L. (1992) *Imperial Eyes: Travel Writing and Transculturation*, London: Routledge.

Proctor, R. N. (1988) *Racial Hygiene: Medicine Under the Nazis*, Cambridge, MA: Harvard University Press.

Rattansi, A. (2007) *Racism: A Very Short Introduction*, Oxford: Oxford University Press.

Rex, J. (1983) *Race Relations in Sociological Theory*, Second edition, London: Routledge and Kegan Paul.

—— (1979) 'Black Militancy and Class Conflict' in R. Miles and A. Phizacklea (eds) *Racism and Political Action in Britain*, London: Routledge and Kegan Paul.

Rex, J. and Mason, D. (eds) (1986) *Theories of Race and Ethnic Relations*, Cambridge: Cambridge University Press.

Rex, J. and Tomlinson, S. (1979) *Colonial Immigrants in a British City*, London: Routledge and Kegan Paul.

Roediger, D. R. (2005) *Working Toward Whiteness: How America' Immigrants Became White*, New York: Basic Books.

—— (2002) *Colored White: Transcending the Racial Past*, Berkeley: University of California Press.

Ross R. (ed.) (1982) *Racism and Colonialism*, The Hague: Martinus Nijhoff.

Said, E. (1978) *Orientalism*, Harmondsworth: Penguin.

Sharpe, J. (1993) *Allegories of Empire: The Figure of Woman in the Colonial Text*, Minneapolis: University of Minnesota Press.

Smith, M. M. (2006) *How Race is Made: Slavery, Segregation and the Senses*, Chapel Hill, NC: University of North Carolina Press.

Solomos, J. and Back, L. (1996) *Racism and Society*, Basingstoke: Macmillan.

Spickard, P. and Daniel, G. R. (eds) (2004) *Racial Thinking in the United States: Uncompleted Independence*, Notre Dame: University of Notre Dame Press.

Spivak, G. C. (1988) *In Other Worlds: Essays in Cultural Politics*, London: Routledge.

Spurr, D. (1993) *The Rhetoric of Empire*, Durham and London: Duke University Press.

Steinberg, S. (2007) *Race Relations: A Critique*, Stanford: Stanford University Press.

Stoler, A. L. (1995) *Race and the Education of Desire: Foucault's History of Sexuality and the Colonial Order of Things*, Durham, NC: Duke University Press.

Taguieff, P.-A. (2001) *The Force of Prejudice: On Racism and its Doubles*, Minneapolis: University of Minnesota Press.

Wallace, M. (1990) *Black Macho and the Myth of the Superwoman*, London: Verso.

Ware, V. (1992) *Beyond the Pale: White Women, Racism and History*, London: Verso.

Ware, V. and Back, L. (2002) *Out of Whiteness: Color, Politics, and Culture*, Chicago: University of Chicago Press.

Weindling, P. (1989) *Health, Race and German Politics Between National Unification and Nazism 1870–1945*, Cambridge: Cambridge University Press.

Williams, P. J. (1991) *The Alchemy of Race and Rights*, Cambridge, MA: Harvard University Press.

Wilson, W. J. (1973) *Power, Racism and Privilege*, New York: Macmillan.

Wimmer, A. (2002) *Nationalist Exclusion and Ethnic Conflict: Shadows of Modernity*, Cambridge: Cambridge University Press.

Wimmer, A. *et al.* (eds) (2004) *Facing Ethnic Conflicts: Toward a New Realism*, Lanham: Rowman and Littlefield.

Winant, H. (2001) *The World is a Ghetto: Race and Democracy Since World War II*, New York: Basic Books.

Winddance Twine, F. and Blee, K. M. (eds) (2001) *Feminism and Antiracism: International Struggles for Justice*, New York: New York University Press.

Wolf, E. (1999) *Envisioning Power: Ideologies of Dominance and Crisis*, Berkeley: University of California Press.

Young, R. J. C. (1995) *Colonial Desire: Hybridity in Theory, Culture and Race*, London: Routledge.

Guide to Further Reading

Key texts

Bulmer, M. and Solomos, J. (eds) (2004) *Researching Race and Racism*, London: Routledge (a collection of first-hand accounts of real-life research projects by leading scholars and researchers).

Feagin, J. R. (2006) *Systemic Racism: A Theory of Oppression*, New York: Routledge (a critical analysis of the everyday realities of racism in American society and the possibility of developing anti-racist strategies in the future).

Fredrickson, G. M. (2003) *Racism: A Short History*, Princeton: Princeton University Press (a synoptic overview of the history of racism, written from the perspective of a practising historian but highly relevant for sociologists).

Winant, H. (2001) *The World Is a Ghetto: Race and Democracy since World War II*, New York: Basic Books (a synoptic overview of the key global trends that have shaped racial orders in the period since 1945).

Background reading

Gates Jr, H. L. (ed.) (1986) *'Race', Writing and Difference*, Chicago: University of Chicago Press (an influential collection of papers written largely from a literary perspective).

Malik, K. (2008) *Strange Fruit: Why Both Sides are Wrong in the Race Debate*, Oxford: Oneworld Publications (a critical exploration of current debates about the meaning of race in scientific and social science discourses).

Miles, R. and Brown, M. (2003) *Racism*, Second edition, London: Routledge (an updated edition of a classic Marxist analysis of racism as a social and historical phenomenon).

Montagu, A. (1997) *Man's Most Dangerous Myth: The Fallacy of Race*, Sixth edition, Walnut Creek, CA: AltaMira Press (a new edition of a classic critique of the mythologies of race thinking).

Mosse, G. L. (1985) *Toward the Final Solution: A History of European Racism*, Madison: University of Wisconsin Press (an insightful historical analysis of the processes that shaped European racism, leading to the final solution).

Rex, J. and Mason, D. (eds) (1986) *Theories of Race and Ethnic Relations*, Cambridge: Cambridge University Press (an important collection of papers that provides an insight into key debates about the theories of race and ethnicity).

UNESCO (1980) *Sociological Theories: Race and Colonialism*, Paris: UNESCO (a collection of papers that outline different theories of race and racism, including papers by Rex, Hall and Guillaumin).

Winant, H. (1994) *Racial Conditions: Politics, Theory, Comparisons*, Minneapolis: University of Minnesota Press (an attempt to link theoretical debates with a historical analysis).

Zack, N., Shrage, L. and Sartwell, C. (eds) (1998) *Race, Class, Gender and Sexuality: The Big Questions*, Cambridge, MA: Blackwell (a collection of papers that links the analysis of race to other social phenomena).

PART ONE

Origins and transformations

INTRODUCTION

THE FOCUS OF THE EXTRACTS in this part of the Reader is on the origins of the idea of race and the development of ideologies about this social phenomenon. This is not because we see the issue of origins as simple, since it is now commonly agreed that there is no single point of origin for modern racial ideologies.

While we do not aim to cover all possible aspects of this dimension we have chosen to include contributions that reflect both the growing interest in the genealogy of racial thinking and the concern to place the question of racism within a historical framework. Given the fact that all six parts of the Reader are closely interlinked it is best to see Part One as essentially concerned with outlining the broad contours of ongoing debates about the origins and development of ideas about race. Indeed, a number of the themes that will be touched upon in this part are ones that we shall return to, albeit from rather different angles, in other parts of the Reader. As we have indicated in the *Guide to Further Reading* at the end of this introduction this is now one of the key areas of research and debate, and so if you want to follow up the issues that are touched upon here it may be as well for you to read some of the texts that we list in there.

We begin this part of the Reader with the question of the impact of European expansion and exploration, particularly after 1492, and its impact on the construction of ideas about race and 'other' peoples. This is a subject that is imaginatively explored in Winthrop Jordan's classic reconstruction of the narratives of first contact that rapidly became evident in the case of English ideas about Africans. Jordan's reconstruction of these images, and his attempt to place them in context, helps us to see the ways in which, from the earliest stages of European expansion into Africa and other parts of the globe, corporeal properties such as skin colour, hair and other phenotypical differences constructed an epidermal schema not only for anchoring difference but for placing different groups of types of humankind into distinct types. Jordan's account also usefully shows that the historical backdrop of European expansion and patterns of domination over the past few centuries is an important point of reference for any historically grounded of racial ideas and the development of institutional forms of racism in different societies.

The dilemmas faced in analysing the history of ideas about race while avoiding the dangers of presentism are explored sympathetically by Michael Banton. Banton's research into the history of the idea of race and the variety of ways it has been used to categorise humankind since the eighteenth century has played an important role in the development of the historical and sociological study of racial relations. In this particular piece he seeks to highlight important dilemmas that we face when we seek to analyse the development of ideas such as race, or indeed racism, over a long period of time without adequate recognition of the shifts in meaning that have emerged and taken shape over time. For Banton the most obvious consequence of presentism is that it means scholars have paid insufficient attention to the social, cultural and intellectual context within which ideas about race have emerged and spread. But he is also concerned to highlight the need to avoid the danger of reading directly from the present into the past.

The concern to place the changing meanings attached to race in context is also at the heart of Tzvetan Todorov's account of the development of ideas about race in French political and social thought in the eighteenth and nineteenth centuries. Although Todorov is writing from a perspective that is quite removed theoretically from that of Banton he also shows an acute awareness of the importance of locating the development of ideas about race within the intellectual and social changes that have shaped societies such as France over the past three centuries or so. In particular he is concerned with the question of how the values of the Enlightenment were distorted by racism and nationalism in such a way that led to the development of ideologies of racial superiority and hatred of 'Others'. From this perspective Todorov sees the nineteenth century as the highpoint of racial thinking, a period in which modern ideas which can be defined as racist took the form that we are familiar with today.

The next extract is by Oliver C. Cox, one of the first generation of black scholars to make an impact on academic debates in this field. Cox's contribution reflects one of the earliest attempts to place the question of racism, or racial prejudice, as he prefers to call it, centrally within a Marxist analytic framework. Cox's work was written from the perspective of historical sociology and he was particularly interested in the ways in which the origins of race prejudice could be seen to link up quite closely to European expansion from the end of the fifteenth century onwards. For Cox the development of race prejudice was a social attitude propagated by exploiting classes for the purpose of stigmatising some group as inferior so that the exploitation of either the group itself or its resources or both may be justified. It is from this angle that Cox sought to analyse both the Atlantic slave trade and the plantation slavery that came to characterise the Americas in the aftermath of European expansion. But he also used the same model to analyse other patterns of racial domination and exclusion in other parts of the globe historically and in contemporary times.

The focus of Cox's account is essentially on the economic underpinnings of racism and slavery. In the following extract Robert Bernasconi contends that classical philosophers such as Immanuel Kant played a key role in the diffusion of ideas about race. Bernasconi's account foregrounds the role of Enlightenment philosophy in the development of racial thinking. In doing so he reminds us that the history of race as a concept cannot merely be seen through the lens of economic processes, and he also reminds us that key philosophical thinkers such as Kant were very much a product of the intellectual and cultural transformations of their time.

The extract from the work of W. E. B. Du Bois, which is the oldest of the extracts included in this Reader, is an example of the contribution of black thinkers such as Du Bois to a reconceptualisation of the role of race in shaping the experience of race in the United States of America. Written at end of the nineteenth century the Du Bois piece is particularly concerned with the position of the 'Negro race' in the context of American culture and society. What is interesting about this extract from Du Bois's work is the way it shows him attempting to engage in an evaluation of scientific ideas about race in order to question the way such ideas positioned American blacks, and other Africans, in the hierarchy of 'races'. Although this particular extract represents merely one facet of the rich diversity of Du Bois's scholarship it provides an interesting insight into the development of early black scholarship about race and racism, and the linkages with wider trends in research and debate. We have included a number of more contemporary black scholars in subsequent parts of this Reader and it may be helpful to compare their perspectives to those of Cox and Du Bois.

The extract from Gunnar Myrdal is focused on the development of what he calls racial beliefs in the United States. Myrdal's analysis was originally published in 1942 and he was concerned to explore the history of the 'Negro problem' in the United States. In this particular extract he seeks to look at the development of racial ideas and values about American blacks from the nineteenth century onwards. Myrdal's core concern was to explore the contradictions to be found in American society's treatment of black Americans in the context of the wider vision of a society based on equality of opportunity and justice. He was particularly concerned with how ideas of racial superiority became an established element of American culture and society. Much of Myrdal's study is taken up with detailed accounts of institutional processes of exclusion against American blacks and their role at different historical points. But he also showed an acute awareness of the role of racial ideologies in facilitating institutionalised behaviour. Indeed for Myrdal the 'chief hindrance to improving the Negro is the white man's firm belief in his inferiority'.

It is also worth emphasising, however, that racism as an ideology is not premised on ideas of the inferiority of some races as compared to others. As Albert Memmi reminds us racism as a set of ideas and values has been often preoccupied about ideas of difference. While conceding the argument that racist ideologies are an integral component of racialised forms of domination Memmi also wants us to think about the complex ways in which racist discourses rely on notions of 'differential characteristics' and their attribution to specific groups and communities.

The final extract in this part is by Pierre-André Taguieff focuses on the discourses of antiracism and their role in shaping contemporary discourses about race and racism. Taguieff's analysis traces the origins of antiracism to the attempts in the 1930s to counter the racial ideologies of fascist mass movements, such as the Nazis in Germany. He suggests, however, that the main currents of antiracist thinking offer little in the way of a systematic and rounded analysis of racism. Rather, he argues forcefully that antiracism relies on a 'conspiracist representation of racism' and therefore cannot move beyond rhetoric and propaganda. This is in many ways a critique of antiracism as a set of ideas that will not be recognised by many who are active in countering racism in practice, but Taguieff's analysis highlights the need to ask the following questions: What are defining features of antiracism? What does it mean to be an antiracist today? In doing so he gives voice to a critical perspective that needs to be part of this debate.

Chapter 1

Winthrop D. Jordan

FIRST IMPRESSIONS

[. . .]

ENGLISH VOYAGERS did not touch upon the shores of West Africa until after 1550, nearly a century after Prince Henry the Navigator had mounted the sustained Portuguese thrust southward for a water passage to the Orient. Usually Englishmen came to Africa to trade goods *with* the natives; the principal hazards of these ventures proved to be climate, disease, and the jealous opposition of the "Portingals" who had long since entrenched themselves in forts along the coast. The earliest English descriptions of West Africa were written by adventurous traders, men who had no special interest in converting the natives or, except for the famous Hawkins voyages, in otherwise laying hands on them. Extensive English participation in the slave trade did not develop until well into the seventeenth century. The first permanent English settlement on the African coast was at Kormantin in 1631, and the Royal African Company was not chartered for another forty years.[1] Initially, therefore, English contact with Africans did not take place primarily in a context which prejudged the Negro as a slave, at least not as a slave of Englishmen. Rather, Englishmen met Negroes merely as another sort of men.

Englishmen found the natives of Africa very different from themselves. Negroes looked different; their religion was un-Christian; their manner of living was anything but English; they seemed to be a particularly libidinous sort of people. All these clusters of perceptions were related to each other, though they may be spread apart for inspection, and they were related also to circumstances of contact in Africa, to previously accumulated traditions concerning that strange and distant continent, and to certain special qualities of English society on the eve of its expansion into the New World.

[. . .] The most arresting characteristic of the newly discovered African was his color. Travelers rarely failed to comment upon it; indeed when describing Negroes they frequently began with complexion and then moved on to dress (or rather lack of it) and manners. At Cape Verde, "These people are all blacke, and are called Negros, without any apparell, saving before their privities."[2] Robert Baker's narrative poem recounting his two voyages to the West African coast in 1562 and 1563 first introduced the natives with these engaging lines:

> And entering in [a river], we see
>   a number of blacke soules,
> Whose likelinesse seem'd men to be,
>   but all as blacke as coles.
> Their Captaine comes to me
>   as naked as my naile,
> Not having witte or honestie
>   to cover once his taile.[3]

Even more sympathetic observers seemed to find blackness a most salient quality in Negroes: "although the people were blacke and naked, yet they were civill."[4]

Englishmen actually described Negroes as *black* – an exaggerated term which in itself suggests that the Negros complexion had powerful impact upon their perceptions. Even the peoples of northern Africa seemed so dark that Englishmen tended to call them "black" and let further refinements go by the board. Blackness became so generally associated with Africa that every African seemed a black man. In Shakespeare's day, the Moors, including Othello, were commonly portrayed as pitchy black and the terms *Moor* and *Negro* used almost interchangeably.[5] With curious inconsistency, however, Englishmen recognized that Africans south of the Sahara were not at all the same people as the much more familiar Moors.[6] Sometimes they referred to Negroes as "black Moors" to distinguish them from the peoples of North Africa. During the seventeenth century the distinction became more firmly established and indeed writers came to stress the difference in color, partly because they delighted in correcting their predecessors and partly because Negroes were being taken up as slaves and Moors, increasingly, were not. In the more detailed and accurate reports about West Africa of the seventeenth century, moreover, Negroes in different regions were described as varying considerably in complexion. In England, however, the initial impression of Negroes was not appreciably modified: the firmest fact about the Negro was that he was "black."

The powerful impact which the Negro's color made upon Englishmen must have been partly owing to suddenness of contact. Though the Bible as well as the arts and literature of antiquity and the Middle Ages offered some slight introduction to the "Ethiope," England's immediate acquaintance with black-skinned peoples came with relative rapidity. While the virtual monopoly held by Venetian ships in England's foreign trade prior to the sixteenth century meant that people much darker than Englishmen were not entirely unfamiliar, really black men were virtually unknown except as vaguely referred to in the hazy literature about the sub-Sahara which had filtered down from antiquity. Native West Africans probably first appeared in London in 1554; in that year five "Negroes," as the legitimate trader

William Towerson reported, were taken to England, "kept till they could speake the language," and then brought back again "to be a helpe to Englishmen" who were engaged in trade with Negroes on the coast. Hakluyt's later discussion of these Negroes, who he said "could wel agree with our meates and drinkes" though "the colde and moyst aire doth somewhat offend them," suggests that these "blacke Moores" were a novelty to Englishmen.[7] In this respect the English experience was markedly different from that of the Spanish and Portuguese who for centuries had been in close contact with North Africa and had actually been invaded and subjected by people both darker and more highly civilized than themselves. The impact of the Negro's color was the more powerful upon Englishmen, moreover, because England's principal contact with Africans came in West Africa and the Congo where men were not merely dark but almost literally black: one of the fairest-skinned nations suddenly came face to face with one of the darkest peoples on earth.

Viewed from one standpoint, Englishmen were merely participating in Europe's discovery that the strange men who stood revealed by European expansion overseas came in an astounding variety of colors. A Spanish chronicle translated into English in 1555 was filled with wonder at this diversity: "One of the marveylous thynges that god useth in the composition of man, is coloure: whiche doubtlesse can not bee consydered withowte great admiration in beholding one to be white and an other blacke, beinge coloures utterley contrary. Sum lykewyse to be yelowe whiche is betwene blacke and white: and other of other colours as it were of dyvers liveres"[8] As this passage suggests, the juxtaposition of black and white was the most striking marvel of all. And for Englishmen this juxtaposition was more than a curiosity.

In England perhaps more than in southern Europe, the concept of blackness was loaded with intense meaning. Long before they found that some men were black, Englishmen found in the idea of blackness a way of expressing some of their most ingrained values. No other color except white conveyed so much emotional impact. As described by the *Oxford English Dictionary*, the meaning of *black* before the sixteenth century included, "Deeply stained with dirt; soiled, dirty, foul. . . . Having dark or deadly purposes, malignant; pertaining to or involving death, deadly; baneful, disastrous, sinister. . . . Foul, iniquitous, atrocious, horrible, wicked. . . . Indicating disgrace, censure, liability to punishment, etc." Black was an emotionally partisan color, the handmaid and symbol of baseness and evil, a sign of danger and repulsion.

Embedded in the concept of blackness was its direct opposite – whiteness. No other colors so clearly implied opposition, "beinge coloures utterlye contrary"; no others were so frequently used to denote polarization:

> Everye white will have its blacke,
> And everye sweete its sowre.[9]

White and black connoted purity and filthiness, virginity and sin, virtue and baseness, beauty and ugliness, beneficence and evil, God and the devil.[10]

Whiteness, moreover, carried a special significance for Elizabethan Englishmen: it was, particularly when complemented by red, the color of perfect human beauty, especially *female* beauty. This ideal was already centuries old in Elizabeth's time,[11] and their fair Queen was its very embodiment: her cheeks were "roses in a bed of lillies." (Elizabeth was naturally pale but like many ladies then and since she freshened her "lillies" at the cosmetic table.)[12]

[. . .] Black human beings were not only startling but extremely puzzling. The complexion of Negroes posed problems about its nature, especially its permanence and utility, its cause and origin, and its significance. Although these were rather separate questions, there was a pronounced tendency among Englishmen and other Europeans to formulate the problem in terms of causation alone, for if that nut could be cracked the other answers would be readily forthcoming; if the cause of human blackness could be explained, then its nature and significance would follow.

   Not that the problem was completely novel. The ancient Greeks had touched upon it without ever really coming to grips with it. The story of Phaëton's driving the chariot sun wildly through the heavens apparently served as an explanation for the Ethiopian's blackness even before written records, and traces of this ancient fable were still drifting about during the seventeenth century.

> The Æthiopians then were white and fayre,
> Though by the worlds combustion since made black
> When wanton Phaëton overthrew the Sun.[13]

Less fancifully, Ptolemy had made the important suggestion that the Negro's blackness and woolly hair was caused by exposure to the hot sun and had pointed out that people in northern climates were white and those in temperate areas an intermediate color.[14] Aristotle, Antigonus, Pliny, and Plutarch, an impressive battery of authorities, had passed along the familiar story of a black baby born into a white family (telltale trace of some Ethiopian ancestor), but this was scarcely much help as to original cause. The idea that black babies might result from maternal impressions during conception or pregnancy found credence during the Middle Ages and took centuries to die out, if indeed it ever has entirely.[15] Before the fifteenth century, though, the question of the Negro's color can hardly be said to have drawn the attention of Englishmen or indeed of Europeans generally.

   The opening of West Africa and the development of Negro slavery, which for the first time brought Englishmen frequently into firsthand contact with really black Negroes, made the question far more urgent and provided an irresistible play-ground for awakening scientific curiosity. The range of possible answers was rigidly restricted, however, by the virtually universal assumption, dictated by church and Scripture, that all mankind stemmed from a single source. Giordano Bruno's statement in 1591 that "no sound thinking person will refer the Ethiopians to the same protoplast as the Jewish one" was unorthodox at best. Indeed it is impossible fully to understand the various efforts at explaining the Negro's complexion without bearing in mind the strength of the tradition which in 1614 made the chronicler, the Reverend Samuel Purchas, proclaim vehemently: "the tawney Moore, blacke Negro, duskie Libyan, ash-coloured Indian, olive-coloured American, should with the whiter European become *one sheep-fold*, under *one great Sheepheard*, till *this mortalitie being swallowed up of Life*, wee may all *be one, as he and the father are one*

. . . without any more distinction of Colour, National, Language, Sex, Condition, all may bee *One* in him that is One, *and onely blessed for ever.*"[16]

In general, the most satisfactory answer to the problem was some sort of reference to the action of the sun, whether the sun was assumed to have scorched the skin, drawn the bile, or blackened the blood. People living on the Line had obviously been getting too much of it; after all, even Englishmen were darkened by a little exposure. How much more, then, with the Negroes who were "so scorched and vexed with the heat of the sunne, that in many places they curse it when it riseth."[17] The sun's heat was itself sometimes described as a curse — a not unnatural reaction on the part of those Englishmen who visited the West African coast where the weather was "of such putrifying qualitie, that it rotted the coates of their backs."[18] This association of the Negro's color with the sun became a commonplace in Elizabethan literature; as the Prince of Morocco apologized, "Mislike me not for my complexion,/ The shadow'd livery of the burnish'd sun,/ To whom I am a neighbour and near bred."[19]

Unfortunately this theory ran headlong into a stubborn fact of nature which simply could not be overridden: if the equatorial inhabitants of Africa were blackened by the sun, why not the people living on the same line in America? Logic required them to be the same color. As Ptolemy's formidably authoritative *Geographia* stated this logic, "Reason herself asserts that all animals, and all plants likewise, have a similarity under the same kind of climate or under similar weather conditions, that is, when under the same parallels, or when situated at the same distance from either pole."[20]

Yet by the middle of the sixteenth century it was becoming perfectly apparent that the Indians living in the hottest regions of the New World could by no stretch of the imagination be described as black. They were "olive" or "tawny," and moreover thay had long hair rather than the curious wool of Negroes; clearly they were a different sort of men. Peter Martyr, the official Spanish court chronicler whose accounts Richard Eden translated in 1555, made the point as early as 1516, a trifle over-enthusiastically to be sure: "in all the navigation, he [Columbus] never wente oute of the paralelles of Ethiope. . . . [Yet] the Ethiopians are all blacke, havinge theyr heare curld more lyke wulle then heare. But these people [in America] . . . are whyte, with longe heare, and of yellowe colour." Fortunately it did not take long to calm down this entrancing, overly Nordic presentation of the Indian. Toward the end of the century Richard Hakluyt picked up Eden's own account of a voyage of 1554 which had carefully noted that the Indians were "neither black, nor with curlde and short wooll on their heads, as they of Africke have, but of the colour of an Olive, with long and blacke heare on their heads."[21] Clearly the method of accounting for human complexion by latitude just did not work. The worst of it was that the formula did not seem altogether wrong, since it was apparent that in general men in hot climates tended to be darker than in cold ones. The tenacity of the old logic was manifest in many writers who clung to the latitudinal explanation and maintained stoutly that for one or many reasons the actual climate on the ground was more temperate in America than in Guinea and men accordingly less dark.[22]

Another difficulty with the climatic explanation of skin color arose as lengthening experience augmented knowledge about Negroes. If the heat of the sun caused the

Negro's blackness, then his removal to cold northerly countries ought to result in his losing it; even if he did not himself surrender his peculiar color, surely his descendants must. By mid-seventeenth century it was becoming increasingly apparent that this expectation was ill founded: Negroes in Europe and northern America were simply not whitening up very noticeably. Still, the evidence on this matter was by no means entirely definite, and some observers felt that it was not yet all in hand. Though they conceded that lightening of black skin by mixture with Europeans should be ruled out of the experiment, these writers thought they detected a perceptible whitening of the unmixed African residing in colder climates, and they bolstered their case by emphasizing how long it was going to take to whiten up the African completely.[23]

[. . .] While distinctive appearance set Africans over into a novel category of men, their religious condition set them apart from Englishmen in a more familiar way. Englishmen and Christians everywhere were sufficiently acquainted with the concept of heathenism that they confronted its living representatives without puzzlement. Certainly the rather sudden discovery that the world was teeming with heathen people made for heightened vividness and urgency in a long-standing problem; but it was the fact that this problem was already well formulated long before contact with Africa which proved important in shaping English reaction to the Negro's defective religious condition.

In one sense heathenism was less a "problem" for Christians than an exercise in self-definition: the heathen condition defined by negation the proper Christian life. In another sense, the presence of heathenism in the world constituted an imperative to intensification of religious commitment. From its origin Christianity was a universalist, proselytizing religion, and the sacred and secular histories of Christianity made manifest the necessity of bringing non-Christians into the fold. For Englishmen, then, the heathenism of Negroes was at once a counter-image of their own religion and a summons to eradicate an important distinction between the two peoples.

The interaction of these two facets of the concept of heathenism made for a peculiar difficulty. On the one hand, to act upon the felt necessity of converting Negroes would have been to eradicate the point of distinction which Englishmen found most familiar and most readily comprehensible. Yet if they did not act upon this necessity, continued heathenism among Negroes would remain an unwelcome reminder to Englishmen that they were not meeting their obligations to their own faith – nor to the benighted Negroes. Englishmen resolved this implicit dilemma by doing nothing.

Considering the strength of the Christian tradition, it is almost startling that Englishmen failed to respond to the discovery of heathenism in Africa with at least the rudiments of a campaign for conversion. Although the impulse to spread Christianity seems to have been weaker in Englishmen than, say, in the Catholic Portuguese, it cannot be said that Englishmen were indifferent to the obligation imposed upon them by the overseas discoveries of the sixteenth century. While they were badly out of practice at the business of conversion (again in contrast to the Portuguese) and while they had never before been faced with the practical difficulties involved in Christianizing entire continents, they nonetheless were able to contemplate with equanimity and even eagerness the prospect of converting the heathen. Indeed they went so far as to conclude that converting the natives in America was sufficiently important to demand English settlement there. As it turned out, the well-publicized English program for converting Indians produced very meager results, but the avowed intentions certainly were genuine. It was in marked contrast, therefore, that Englishmen did not avow similiar intentions concerning Africans until the late eighteenth century. Fully as much as with skin color, though less consciously, Englishmen distinguished between the heathenisms of Indians and of Negroes.

The suggestive congruence of these twin distinctions between Negroes and Indians is not easy to account for. On the basis of the travelers' reports there was no reason for Englishmen to suppose Indians inherently superior to Negroes as candidates for conversion. While in the sixteenth and seventeenth centuries the Englishmen who had first-hand contact with Africans were not, unlike many of the Portuguese, engaged in missionary efforts, the same may be said of most English contact with Indians. On the other hand, America was not Africa. Englishmen contemplated settling in America, where voyagers had established the King's claim and where supposedly the climate was temperate; in contrast, Englishmen did not envision settlement in Africa, which had quickly gained notoriety as a graveyard for Europeans and where the Portuguese had been the first on the scene. Certainly these very different circumstances meant that Englishmen confronted Negroes and Indians in radically different social contexts and that Englishmen would find it far easier to contemplate converting Indians than Negroes. Yet it remains difficult to see why Negroes were not included, at least as a secondary target, by extension from the program actually directed at the Indians. The fact that English contact with Africans so frequently occurred in a context of slave dealing does not entirely explain the omission of Negroes, since in that same context the Portuguese and Spanish did sometimes attempt to minister to the souls of Negroes (somewhat perfunctorily, to be sure) and since Englishmen in America enslaved Indians when good occasion arose. Given these circumstances, it is hard to escape the conclusion that the distinction which Englishmen made as to conversion was at least in some small measure modeled after the difference they saw in skin color.

Although Englishmen failed to incorporate Negroes into the proselytizing effort which was enjoined by the Christian heritage, that heritage did much to shape the English reaction to Negroes as a people. Paradoxically, Christianity worked to make Englishmen think of Negroes as being both very much like themselves and very different. The emphasis on similarity derived directly from the emphatic Christian doctrine which affirmed that mankind was one. The Old Testament, most notably the book of Genesis, seemed absolutely firm on this point: all men derived from the same act of creation and had at first shared a common experience. So too the New Testament declared all nations to be of one blood. The strength of this universalist strain in Christianity was evident in the assurances offered by a number of English travelers in Africa that they had discovered rudiments of the Word among the most barbarous heathens. In 1623 Richard Jobson exclaimed that "they have a wonderous reference, to the leviticall law, as it is in our holy Bible related; the principalls whereof they are not ignorant in, for they do report concerning *Adam* and *Eve*, whom they call *Adama* and *Evahaha*, talking of *Noahs* flood, and of

Moses, with many other things our sacred History makes mention of." Another commentator hinted at covert Calvinism in the jungle: "They keep their *Fetissoes* [Fetish] day, one day in seven, and that Tuesday (a Sabbath it seems is natural) more solemnly and strictly than the *Hollanders* do their Sunday."[24] To call the Sabbath "natural" among heathens was an invitation to the missionary to harvest the seed planted everywhere by God. Such a description also serves to demonstrate how powerfully the Christian tradition operated to make Englishmen and other Europeans consider the new peoples of the freshly opened world as being inherently similar to themselves.

At the same time, Christianity militated against the unity of man. Because Englishmen were Christians, heathenism in Negroes was a fundamental defect which set them distinctly apart. However much Englishmen disapproved of Popery and Mehometanism, they were accustomed to these perversions. Yet they were not accustomed to dealing face to face with people who appeared, so far as many travelers could tell, to have no religion at all.[25] Steeped in the legacy and trappings of their own religion, Englishmen were ill prepared to see any legitimacy in African religious practices. Judged by Christian cosmology, Negroes stood in a separate category of men.

[. . .] The condition of savagery – the failure to be civilized – set Negroes apart from Englishmen in an ill-defined but crucial fashion. Africans were *different* from Englishmen in so many ways: in their clothing, huts, farming, warfare, language, government, morals, and (not least important) in their table manners. Englishmen were fully aware that Negroes living at different parts of the coast were not all alike; it was not merely different reactions in the observers which led one to describe a town as "marveilous artificially builded with mudde walles . . . and kept very cleane as well in their streetes as in their houses" and another to relate how "they doe eate" each other "alive" in some places but dead in others "as we wolde befe or mutton."[26] No matter how great the actual and observed differences among Negroes, though, none of these black men seemed to live like Englishmen.

To judge from the comments of voyagers, Englishmen had an unquenchable thirst for the details of savage life. Partly their curiosity was a matter of scientific interest in the "natural productions" of the newly opened world overseas. To the public at large, the details of savage behavior appealed to an interest which was not radically different from the scientist's; an appetite for the "wonderful" seems to have been built into Western culture. It is scarcely surprising that civilized Englishmen should have taken an interest in reports about cosmetic mutilation, polygamy, infanticide, ritual murder and the like – of course *English* men did not really *do* any of these things themselves. Finally, reports about savages began arriving at a time when Englishmen very much needed to be able to translate their apprehensive interest in an uncontrollable world out of medieval, religious terms. The discovery of savages overseas enabled them to make this translation easily, to move from miracles to verifiable monstrosities, from heaven to earth.

As with skin color, English reporting of African customs constituted an exercise in self-inspection by means of comparison. The necessity of continuously measuring African practices with an English yardstick of course tended to emphasize the differences between the two groups, but it also made for heightened sensitivity to instances of similarity. Thus the Englishman's ethnocentrism tended to distort his perception of African culture in two opposite directions. While it led him to emphasize differences and to condemn deviations from the English norm, it led him also to seek out similarities (where perhaps none existed) and to applaud every instance of conformity to the appropriate standard. Though African clothing and personal etiquette were regarded as absurd, equivalents to European practices were at times detected in other aspects of African culture. Particularly, Englishmen were inclined to see the structures of African societies as analogous to their own, complete with kings, counselors, gentlemen, and the baser sort. Here especially they found Africans like themselves, partly because they knew no other way to describe a society and partly because there was actually good basis for such a view in the social organization of West African communities.[27]

Most English commentators seem to have felt that Negroes would behave better under improved circumstances; a minority thought the Africans naturally wicked, but even these observers often used "natural" only to mean "ingrained." (English accounts of West Africa did not emphasize ingrained stupidity in the natives; defect of "Reason" was seen as a function of savagery.)[28] Until well into the eighteenth century there was no debate as to whether the Negro's non-physical characteristics were inborn and unalterable; such a question was never posed with anything like sufficient clarity for men to debate it. There was no precise meaning in such statements about the Africans as, "Another (as it were) innate quality they have [is] to Steal any thing they lay hands of, especially from Foreigners . . . this vicious humor [runs] through the whole race of *Blacks*," or in another comment, that "it would be very surprizing if upon a scrutiny into their Lives we should find any of them whose perverse Nature would not break out sometimes; for they indeed seem to be born and bred Villains: All sorts of Baseness having got such sure-footing in them, that 'tis impossible to lye concealed."[29] These two vague suggestions concerning innate qualities in the Negro were among the most precise in all the English accounts of West Africa. It was sufficient to depict and describe. There might be disagreement as to the exact measure of tenacity with which the African clung to his present savage character, but this problem would yield to time and accurate description.

Despite the fascination and self-instruction Englishmen derived from expatiating upon the savage behavior of Africans, they never felt that savagery was as important a quality in Africans as it was in the American Indians. Two sets of circumstances made for this distinction in the minds of Englishmen. As was the case with heathenism, contrasting social contexts played an important role in shaping the English response to savagery in the two peoples. Inevitably, the savagery of the Indians assumed a special significance in the minds of those actively engaged in a program of bringing civilization into the American wilderness. The case with the African was different: the English errand into Africa was not a new or a perfect community but a business trip. No hope was entertained for civilizing the Negro's steaming continent, and Englishmen lacked compelling reason to develop a program for remodeling the African natives. The most compelling necessity was that of pressing forward the business of buying Negroes from other Negroes. It was not until the slave trade came to require justification, in the eighteenth century, that some Englishmen found special reason to lay emphasis on the Negro's savagery.

[. . .] If Negroes were likened to beasts, there was in Africa a beast which was likened to men. It was a strange and eventually tragic happenstance of nature that the Negro's homeland was the habitat of the animal which in appearance most resembles man. The animal called "oran-outang" by contemporaries (actually the chimpanzee) was native to those parts of western Africa where the early slave trade was heavily concentrated. Though Englishmen were acquainted (for the most part vicariously) with monkeys and baboons, they were unfamiliar with tailless apes who walked about like men.[30] Accordingly, it happened that Englishmen were introduced to the anthropoid apes and to Negroes at the same time and in the same place. The startlingly human appearance and movements of the "ape" – a generic term though often used as a synonym for the "orang-outang" – aroused some curious speculations.

In large measure these speculations derived from traditions which had been accumulating in Western culture since ancient times. Medieval bestiaries contained rosters of strange creatures who in one way or another seemed disturbingly to resemble men. There were the *simia* and the *cynocephali* and the *satyri* and the others, all variously described and related to one another, all jumbled in a characteristic amalgam of ancient reports and medieval morality. The confusion was not easily nor rapidly dispelled, and many of the traditions established by this literature were very much alive during the seventeenth century.

The section on apes in Edward Topsell's *Historie of Foure-Footed Beastes* (1607) serves to illustrate how certain seemingly trivial traditions and associations persisted in such form that they were bound to affect the way in which Englishmen would perceive the natives of Africa.[31] Topsell, who built principally upon the work of the great Swiss naturalist Konrad von Gesner (1516–65), was careful to distinguish tailless apes from monkeys. They were to be found in three regions: south of the Caucasus, India, and "*Lybia* and all that desart Woods betwixt *Egypt, Æthiopia* and *Libia*." When he came to describe the various kinds of "apes," however, Topsell was far less definite as to location than as to their general character: above all else, "apes" were venerous. In India the red apes were "so venerous that they will ravish their Women." Baboons were "as lustful and venerous as goats"; a baboon which had been "brought to the French king . . . above all loved the companie of women, and young maidens; his genitall member was greater than might match the quantity of his other parts." Pictures of two varieties of apes, a "Satyre" and an "Ægopithecus, graphically emphasized the "virile member."

In addition to stressing the "lustful disposition" of the ape kind, Topsell's compilation contained suggestions concerning the character of simian facial features. "Men that have low and flat nostrils," readers were told in the section on apes, "are Libidinous as Apes that attempt women, and having thicke lippes the upper hanging over the neather, they are deemed fooles, like the lips of asses and Apes." This rather explicit association was the persistent connection made between apes and devils. In a not altogether successful attempt to distinguish the "Satyre-apes" from the mythical creatures of that name, Topsell straightened everything out by explaining that it was "probable, that Devils take not any dænomination or shape from Satyres, but rather the Apes themselves from Devils whom they resemble, for there are many things common to the Satyre-apes and devilish Satyres." Association of apes and/or satyrs with devils was common in England: James I linked them in his *Daemonology* (1597).[32] The inner logic of this association derived from uneasiness concerning the ape's "indecent likenesse and imitation of man"; it revolved around evil and sexual sin; and, rather tenuously, it connected apes with blackness.

Given this tradition and the coincidence of contact, it was virtually inevitable that Englishmen should discern similarity between the man-like beasts and the beast-like men of Africa.[33] A few commentators went so far as to suggest that Negroes had sprung from the generation of ape-kind or that apes were themselves' the offspring of Negroes and some unknown African beast.[34] These contentions were squarely in line with the ancient tradition that Africa was a land "bringing dailie foorth newe monsters" because, as Aristotle himself had suggested, many different species came into proximity at the scarce watering places. Jean Bodin, the famous sixteenth-century French political theorist, summarized this wisdom of the ages with the categorical remark that "promiscuous coition of men and animals took place, wherefore the regions of Africa produce for us so many monsters."[35] Despite all these monsters out of Africa, the notion that Negroes stemmed from beasts in a literal sense did not receive wide credence; even the writers who advanced it did not suggest that the Negro himself was now a beast.

Far more common and persistent was the notion that there sometimes occurred "a beastly copulation or conjuncture" between apes and Negroes, and especially that apes were inclined wantonly to attack Negro women.[36] The very explicit idea that apes assaulted female human beings was not new; Negroes were merely being asked to demonstrate what Europeans had known for centuries. Englishmen seemed ready to credit the tales about bestial connections, and even as late as the 1730's a well-traveled, intelligent naval surgeon, John Atkins, was not at all certain that the stories were false: "At some Places the *Negroes* have been suspected of Bestiality with them [apes and monkeys], and by the Boldness and affection they are known under some Circumstances to express to our Females; the Ignorance and Stupidity on the other side, to guide or control Lust; but more from the near resemblances are sometimes met to the Human Species would tempt one to suspect the Fact." Atkins went on to voice the generally received opinion that if offspring were ever produced by such mixtures they would themselves be infertile: "Altho' by the way, this, like other *Hebridous* productions, could never go no farther; and as such a monstrous generation would be more casual and subject to Fatality, the Case must be uncommon and rare."[37]

[. . .] It was no accident that this affinity between Negroes and apes was so frequently regarded as sexual, for undertones of sexuality run throughout many English accounts of West Africa. To liken Africans — any human being — to beasts was to stress the animal within the man. Indeed the sexual connotations embodied in the terms *bestial* and *beastly* were considerably stronger in Elizabethan English than they are today, and when the Elizabethan traveler pinned these epithets upon the behavior of Negroes he was frequently as much registering a sense of sexual shock as describing swinish manners: "They are beastly in their living," young Andrew Battell wrote, "for they have men in women's apparel, whom they keep among their wives."[38]

Lecherousness among the Negroes was at times merely another attribute which one would expect to find among heathen, savage, beast-like men. A passage in

Samuel Purchas's collection makes evident how closely interrelated all these attributes were in the minds of Englishmen: "They have no knowledge of God; those that traffique and are conversant among strange Countrey people are civiller then the common sort of people, they are very greedie eaters, and no lesse drinkers, and very lecherous, and theevish, and much addicted to uncleanenesse: one man hath as many wives as hee is able to keepe and maintaine."[39] Sexuality was what one expected of savages.

Clearly, however, the association of Africans with potent sexuality represented more than an incidental appendage to the concept of savagery. Long before first English contact with West Africa, the inhabitants of virtually the entire continent stood confirmed in European literature as lustful and venerous. About 1526 Leo Africanus (a Spanish Moroccan Moor converted to Christianity) supplied the most authoritative and influential description of the little-known lands of "Barbary," "Libya," "Numedia," and "Land of Negroes"; and Leo was as explicit as he was imaginative. In the English translation (*ca.* 1600) readers were informed concerning the "Negroes" that "there is no Nation under heaven more prone to Venery." Having reduced the "Numedians" to being "principally addicted unto treason, Treacherie, Murther, Theft and Robberie" and the inhabitants of Libya to living a "brutish kind of life" destitute of "any Religion, any Lawes, or any good form of living," Leo went on to disclose that "the Negroes likewise leade a beastly kind of life, being utterly destitute of the use of reason, of dexteritie of wit, and of all arts. Yea, they so behave themselves, as if they had continually lived in a Forrest among wild beasts. They have great swarmes of harlots among them; whereupon a man may easily conjecture their manner of living."[40] Nor was Leo Africanus the only scholar to elaborate upon the classical sources concerning Africa. In a highly eclectic work first published in 1566, Jean Bodin sifted the writings of ancient authorities and concluded that heat and lust went hand in hand and that "in Ethiopia . . . the race of men is very keen and lustful." Bodin announced in a thoroughly characteristic sentence, "Ptolemy reported that on account of southern sensuality Venus chiefly is worshiped in Africa and that the constellation of Scorpion, which pertains to the pudenda, dominates that continent."[41]

Depiction of the Negro as a lustful creature was not radically new, therefore, when Englishmen first met Negroes face to face. Seizing upon and reconfirming these long-standing and apparently common notions about Africa, Elizabethan travelers and literati spoke very explicitly of Negroes as being especially sexual. Othello's embraces were "the gross clasps of a lascivious Moor." Francis Bacon's *New Atlantis* (*ca.* 1624) referred to "an holy hermit" who "desired to see the Spirit of Fornication; and there appeared to him a little foul ugly Æthiop." Negro men, reported a seventeenth-century traveler, sported "large Propagators."[42] In 1623 Richard Jobson, a sympathetic observer, reported that mandingo men were "furnisht with such members as are after a sort burthensome unto them"; it was the custom in that tribe not to have intercourse during pregnancy so as not to "destroy what is conceived." During this abstinence, Jobson explained, the man "hath allowance of other women, for necessities sake," though this was not to be considered "overstrange" since in the twenty-third chapter of Ezekiel two incontinent sisters were "said to dote upon those people whose members were as the members of asses." Jobson's explanation for the unusual size of these men was incorporated neatly into the context of scriptural anthropology. "Undoubtedly," he wrote, "these people originally sprung from the race of *Canaan*, the sonne of *Ham*, who discovered his father *Noahs* secrets, for which *Noah* awakening cursed *Canaan* as our holy Scripture testifieth[;] the curse as by Scholemen hath been disputed, extended to his ensuing race, in laying hold upon the same place, where the originall cause began, whereof these people are witnesse."[43]

The neatness of Jobson's exegesis was unusual, but his initial observation was not. Another commentator, the anonymous author of *The Golden Coast* (1665), thought Negroes "very lustful and impudent, especially, when they come to hide their nakedness, (for a *Negroes* hiding his Members, their extraordinary greatness) is a token of their Lust, and therefore much troubled with the Pox."[44] By the eighteenth century a report on the sexual aggressiveness of Negro women was virtually *de rigueur* for the African commentator. By then, of course, with many Englishmen actively participating in the slave trade, there were pressures making for descriptions of "hot constitution'd ladies" possessed of a "temper hot and lascivious, making no scruple to prostitute themselves to the *Europeans* for a very slender profit, so great is their inclination to white men."[45] And surely it was the Negro women who were responsible for lapses from propriety: "If they can come to the Place the Man sleeps in, they lay themselves softly down by him, soon wake him, and use all their little Arts to move the darling Passion."[46]

While the animus underlying these and similar remarks becomes sufficiently obvious once Englishmen began active participation in the slave trade, it is less easy to see why Englishmen should have fastened upon Negroes a pronounced sexuality virtually upon first sight. Certainly the ancient notions distilled in the alembics of Bodin and Leo Africanus must have helped pattern initial English perceptions. Yet it is scarcely possible that these notions were fully responsible for the picture of Negro sexuality which developed so rapidly and in such explicit terms in the sixteenth and early seventeenth centuries.

Another tradition was of possible relevance – the curse upon Ham's son Canaan. According to the Scriptural account Ham's offense was that he had "looked upon the nakedness of his father." To the post-Freudian ear this suggests castration. To early Jewish commentators it suggested not merely castration but other sexual offenses as well. The Hebraic literature of *ca*. 200–600 A.D. which saw the posterity of Ham and Canaan as smitten in the skin speculated as to whether Ham's offense was (variously) castrating his father Noah (described in the Midrash Rabbah as Noah's saying "You have prevented me from doing something in the dark"), and (in the same source) as copulating "in the Ark," and (again) copulating "with a dog . . . therefore Ham came forth black-skinned while the dog publicly exposes its copulation." The depth and diffuse pervasiveness of these explosive associations are dramatized in the mystic Zohar of the thirteenth century, where Ham, it was said, "represents the refuse and dross of the gold, the stirring and rousing of the unclean spirit of the ancient serpent."

What is especially striking in these commentaries is that for centuries they remained peculiar though not secret to Jewish scholars. Although some Christian writers in the early centuries of the church seem to have been aware of sexual connotations in Ham's offense, they appear never to have dilated upon them. With the onset of European expansion in the sixteenth century, some Christian commentators, or rather some commentators who were Christians, suddenly began speaking in the same mode which Jews had employed a thousand years and more before. Though the genealogy of Noah's descendants was always somewhat tangled, Ham always represented for the ancient Jews the southward peoples *including* the Canaanites, whom the Jews drove from the promised land and upon whom they fastened the millstone of sexual offenses which are repeatedly and so adamantly condemned and guarded against in the Pentateuch. More than two thousand years later a similar disquietude seems to have come over Europeans and Englishmen as they embarked upon a program of outward migration and displacement and exploitation of other peoples. The curse upon Ham's posterity took on for Christian Englishmen a potential immediacy and relevance which it could never have had if Englishmen had not as a people been undergoing an experience which they half sense was in some measure analogous to that of the ancient special people of God's word.[47]

[. . .] It was the case with English confrontation with Negroes, then, that a society in a state of rapid flux, undergoing important changes in religious values, and comprised of men who were energetically on the make and acutely and often uncomfortably self-conscious of being so, came upon a people less technologically advanced, markedly different in appearance and culture. From the first, Englishmen tended to set Negroes over against themselves, to stress what they conceived to be radically contrasting qualities of color, religion, and style of life, as well as animality and a peculiarly potent sexuality. What Englishmen did not at first fully realize was that Negroes were potentially subjects for a special kind of obedience and subordination which was to arise as adventurous Englishmen sought to possess for themselves and their children one of the most bountiful dominions of the earth. When they came to plant themselves in the new World, they were to find that they had not entirely left behind the spirit of avarice and insubordination. Nor does it appear, in light of attitudes which developed during their first two centuries in America, that they left behind all the impressions initially gathered of the *Negro* before he became pre-eminently the *slave*.

Notes and references

1   Kenneth G. Davies, *The Royal African Company* (London, 1957), 38–46; John W. Blake, trans. and ed., *Europeans in West Africa, 1450–1560; Documents to Illustrate the Nature and Scope of Portuguese Enterprise in West Africa, the Abortive Attempt of Castilians to Create an Empire There, and the Early English Voyages to Barbary and Guinea* (Works Issued by the Hakluyt Society, 2d Ser., 87 [1942]), II, 254–60.

2   "The voyage made by M. John Hawkins . . . to the coast of Guinea and the Indeas of Nova Hispania . . . 1564," in Richard Hakluyt, *The Principal Navigations, Voyages, Traffiques and Discoveries of the English Nation* . . . 12 vols., 1598 ed. (Glasgow, 1903–05), X, 15. See Katherine Beverly Oakes, "Social Theory in the Early Literature of Voyage and Exploration in Africa" (unpubl. Ph.D. diss., University of California, Berkeley, 1944), 120–23.

3   "The First Voyage of Robert Baker to Guinie . . . 1562," in Richard Hakluyt, *The Principall Navigations, Voiages and Discoveries of the English Nation* . . . (London, 1589), 132. The entire poem was omitted in the 1598 edition.

4   "The Voyage of M. George Fenner . . . Written by Walter Wren" (1566), Hakluyt, *Principal Navigations*, VI, 270. All ensuing references are to this reprinted 1598 edition unless otherwise indicated.

5   Warner Grenelle Rice, "Turk, Moor and Persian in English Literature from 1550–1660, with Particular Reference to the drama" (unpubl. Ph.D. diss., Harvard University, 1926), 401–2n; Robert R. Cawley, *The Voyagers and Elizabethan Drama* (Boston, 1938), 31; Samuel C. Chew, *The Crescent and the Rose: Islam and England during the Renaissance* (N. Y., 1937), 521–24; Wylie Sypher, *Guinea's Captive Kings: British Anti-Slavery Literature of the XVIIIth Century* (Chapel Hill, 1942), 26.

6   An early instance is in "The Second Voyage to Guinea . . ." (1554), in Hakluyt, *Principal Navigations*, VI, 167–68. See the associations made by Leo Africanus, *The History and Description of Africa and of the Notable Things Therein Contained* . . ., trans. John Pory [*ca.* 1600], ed. Robert Brown, 3 vols. (London, 1896), I, 130.

7   Hakluyt, *Principal Navigations*, VI, 176, 200, 217–18. Just how little Europeans knew about Africa prior to the Portuguese explorations is evident in T. Simar, "La géographie de l'Afrique central dans l'antiquité et au moyen âge," *La Revue Congolaise*, 3 (1912), 1–23, 81–102, 145–69, 225–52, 288–310, 440–41.

8   Francisco López de Gómara, in Peter Martyr (D'Anghera), *The Decades of the Newe Worlde* . . . trans. Richard Eden (London, 1555), in Edward Arber, ed., *The First Three English Books on America* . . . (Birmingham, Eng., 1885), 338.

9   Thomas Percy, *Reliques of Ancient English Poetry* . . . , ed. Robert A. Willmott (London, 1857), 27 (Sir Cauline, pt. 2, stanza 1).

10 Numerous examples in Middle English, Shakespeare, the Bible, and Milton are given by P. J. Heather, "Colour Symbolism," *Folk Lore*, 59 (1948), 169–70, 175–78, 182–83; 60 (1949), 208–16, 266–76. See also Harold R. Isaacs, "Blackness and Whiteness," *Encounter*, 21 (1963), 8–21; Caroline F. E. Spurgeon, *Shakespeare's Imagery and What It Tells Us* (Boston, 1958), 64, 66–69, 158; Arrah B. Evarts, "Color Symbolism," *Psychoanalytic Review*, 6 (1919), 129–34; Don Cameron Allen, "Symbolic Color in the Literature of the English Renaissance," *Philological Quarterly*, 15 (1936), 81–92; and for a different perspective, Francis B. Gummere, "On the Symbolic use of the Colors Black and White in Germanic Tradition," *Haverford College Studies*, 1 (1889), 112–62.

11 Walter Clyde Curry, *The Middle English Ideal of Personal Beauty; As Found in the Metrical Romances, Chronicles, and Legends of the XIII, XIV, and XV Centuries* (Baltimore, 1916), 3, 80–98.

12 Elkin Calhoun Wilson, *England's Eliza* (Cambridge, Mass., 1939), 337; Charles Carroll Camden, *The Elizabethan Woman* (Houston, N. Y., and London, 1952), chap. 7; Cawley, *Voyagers and Elizabethan Drama*, 85; Elizabeth Jenkins, *Elizabeth the Great* (London, 1958), 62, 100, 159, 296; Gamaliel Bradford, *Elizabethan Women*, ed. Harold O. White (Boston, 1936), 82, 212; Violet A. Wilson *Queen Elizabeth's Maids of Honour and Ladies of the Privy Chamber* (N. Y., n.d.), 4–5. Hugh Plat *Delightes for Ladies, Written Originally by Sir Hugh Plat, First Printed in 1602, London, England* ed. Violet and Hal W. Trovillion (Herrin, Ill., 1939), 87–94, 99, 102–3, contains advice on cosmetics.

13   R. Warwick Bond, ed., *The Poetical Works of William Basse (1602–1653)* (London, 1893), 279; Conway Zirkle, "The Early History of the Idea of the Inheritance of Acquired Characters and of Pangenesis," American Philosophical Society, *Transactions*, New Ser., 35 (1945–46), Pt. ii, 145. The original story of Phaëton is in Thomas Bulfinch, *Bulfinch's Mythology* (N. Y.: Modern Library, n.d.), 36–42; Edith Hamilton, *Mythology* (N. Y.: Mentor, 1953), 131–34.

14   [Claudius] Ptolemy, *Tetrabiblos*, trans. and ed. F. E. Robbins (Cambridge, Mass., and London, 1940), 121–25, 439.

15   Conway Zirkle, "The Knowledge of Heredity before 1900," L. C. Dunn, ed., *Genetics in the 20th Century: Essays on the Progress of Genetics during Its First 50 Years* (N. Y.: 1951), 42; Thorndike, "De Comlexionibus," *Isis*, 49 (1958), 400; Don Cameron Allen, *The Legend of Noah: Renaissance Rationalism in Art, Science and Letters* (Urbana, 1949), 119. For an interesting modification, Browne, "Of the Blackness of Negroes," Sayle, ed., *Works of Browne*, II, 375–76.

16   T[homas] Bendyshe, "The History of Anthroplogy," Anthropological Society of London, *memoirs*, 1 (1863–64), 355; Samuel Purchas, *Purchas his Pilgrimage. Or Relations of the World and the Religions Observed in All Ages and Places Discovered, from the Creation unto This Present*, 2d ed. (London, 1614), 656.

17   "Second Voyage to Guinea," Hakluyt, *Principal Navigations*, VI, 167; Cawley, *Voyagers and Elizabethan Drama*, 88–89, 159–60. A remarkably early suggestion that sun-blackened skin afforded protection against the sun "as if naturaliz'd" was made by John Ogilby, *Africa: Being an Accurate description of the Regions of Ægypt, Barbary, Lybia and Billedulgerid, the Land of Negroes, Guinee, Æthiopia, and the Abyssines . . . Collected and Translated from Most Authentick Authors, and Augmented with Later Observations* (London, 1670).

18   "The First Voyage to Guinea and Benin" (1553), Hakluyt, *Principal Navigations*, VI, 148.

19   *The Merchant of Venice*, II, i, 1–3; also Ben Jonson, "Masque of Blackness," Gifford, ed., *Works of Jonson*, VII, 12.

20   Edward L. Stevenson, trans. and ed., *Geography of Claudius Ptolemy* (N. Y., 1932), 31–32.

21   Martyr, *Decades of Newe Worlde*, trans. Eden, 88, 387–88; "Second Voyage to Guinea," Hakluyt, *Principal Navigations*, VI, 176.

22   Both Martyr and Hakluyt did so in the preceding passages; James Spedding, Robert L. Ellis, Douglas D. Heath, eds., *The Works of Francis Bacon . . . 14 vols.* (London, 1857–74), II, 473; John Selden's notes in *Works of Michael Drayton*, II, 675; John Ovington, *A Voyage to Suratt, in the Year 1869*, ed. H. G. Rawlinson (London, 1929), 285. For a more general statement of the influence of climate on complexion, Matthew Hale, *The Primitive Origination of Mankind, Considered and examined According to the Light of Nature* (London, 1677), 200–201.

23   A widely popular work, [Thomas Burnet], *The Theory of the Earth . . . the First Two Books . . .* , 2d ed. (London, 1691), 191, bk. II, chap. 2, announced that "after some generations they become altogether like the people of the Country where they are." Ovington, *Voyage to Suratt*, ed. Rawlinson, 285, was at pains to deny this "current Opinion."

24   Jobson, *Golden trade*, ed. Kingsley, 78 (probably there was good basis for Jobson's contention since the Negroes he referred to were Muslims); *The Golden Coast*, 80.

25   For example, Hakluyt, *Principal Navigations*, VI, 144.

26   Both seem to be eyewitness reports. "Voyage of Thomas Candish," Hakluyt, *Principal Navigations*, XI, 293; anonymous author on Hawkins' third voyage quoted in James A. Williamson, *Sir John Hawkins: The Time and the Man* (Oxford, 1927), 509. There is an interesting description of (almost certainly) the now well-known symbiotic relationship between Negroes and Pygmies in *The Golden Coast*, 66–67, "I have not found so much faith, nor faithfulness, no not in Israel."

27   An early instance is in Clements R. Markham, ed., *The Hawkins' Voyages during the Reigns of Henry VIII, Queen Elizabeth, and James I (Works Issued by the Hakluyt Soc., 1st Ser., 57 [1878]),* 19.

28   For example, H[eylyn], *Microcosmus*, 379. But compare a later and precursively environmentalist argument that culturally dictated lack of mental and moral exercise had literally weakened the African brain: John Atkins, *The Navy Surgeon . . . and Physical Observations on the Coast of Guiney*, 2d ed. (London, 1742), 366–67; also his *Voyage to Guinea*, 80–88.

29   Ogilby, *Africa*, 452; William Bosman, *A New and Accurate Description of the Coast of Guinea, Divided into the Gold, the Slave, and the Ivory Coasts . . .*, trans. from the Dutch (London, 1705), 117.

30   H. W. Janson, *Apes and Ape Lore in the Middle Ages and the Renaissance* (London, 1952), chap. 11; also Robert M. and Ada W. Yerkes, *The Great Apes: A Study of Anthropoid Life* (New Haven, 1929), 1–26; John C. Greene, *The Death of Adam: Evolution and Its Impact on Western Thought* (Ames, Iowa, 1959), chap. 6. I have oversimplified the confused state of terminology concerning simians; see M. F. Ashley Montague, *Edward Tyson, M.D., F.R.S., 1605–1708, and the Rise of Human and Comparative Anatomy in England; A Study in the History of Science* (Phila., 1943), 228, 244–49. By 1600 "baboons," "marmosets," "monkies," "apes" were common in literature; several (probably baboons) were on show in London. Yet a foreign visitor in 1598 did not list any sort of "apes" in the Tower menagerie, though there were lions there. W. Strunk, Jr., "The Elizabethan Showman's Ape," *Modern Language Notes*, 32 (1917), 215–21; Emma Phipson, *The Animal-Lore of Shakespeare's Time . . .* (London, 1883), 5.

31   Edward Topsell, *The Historie of Foure-Footed Beastes . . . Collected out of All the Volumes of Conradus Gesner, and All Other Writers to This Present Day* (London, 1607), 2–20.

32   G. B. Harrison, ed., *King James the First Daemonologie (1597) . . .* (London, 1924), 19.

33   Jobson, *Golden Trade*, ed. Kingsley, 186; Thomas Herbert, *A Relation of Some Yeares Travaile, Begunne Anno 1626. Into Afrique and the Greater Asia, Especially the Territories of the Persian Monarchie . . .* (London, 1634), 16–17; Herbert, *Some Years Travels* (1677), 16–17.

34   Herbert, *Some Years Travels*, 18; Zirkle, "Knowledge of Heredity," Dunn, ed., *Genetics in the 20th Century*, 39–40.

35   Quotation from Alexander B. Grosart, ed., *The Complete Works of Thomas Nashe*, 6 vols. (London and Aylesbury, 1883–85), I, 160: Aristotle, *Historia Animalium*, trans. D'Archy W. Thompson, in J. A. Smith and W. D. Ross, eds., *The Works of Aristotle*, IV (Oxford, 1910), 606b; Bodin, *Method of Easy Comprehension of History*, 105.

36   Quotation from Herbert, *Some Years Travels*, 18. Montague, *Edward Tyson*, 250–52; John Locke, *An Essay Concerning Human Understanding*, 2 vols. in 1 (London, 1721), II, 53 (Bk. III, chap. 6, sec. 23); Phillips, *Journal*, Churchill, comps., *Voyages*, VI, 211; William Smith, *A New Voyage to Guinea . . .* (London, 1744), 52; Zirkle,

"Knowledge of Heredity," Dunn, ed., *Genetics in the 20th Century*, 39–40; Janson, *Apes and Ape Lore*, 267–76.

37 Atkins, *Voyage to Guinea*, 108; also his *Navy Surgeon*, 369.

38 Ernest George Ravenstine, ed., *The Strange Adventures of Andrew Battell of Leigh, in Angola and the Adjoining Regions. Reprinted from "Purchas His Pilgrimes"* (*ca.* 1607) (*Works Issued by the Hakluyt Soc.*, 2d Ser., 6 [London, 1901]), 18. The term *bestiality* was first used to denote sexual relations with animals early in the 17th century; it was thus used frequently only for about 150 years!

39 "A Description . . . of Guinea . . ." in Samuel Purchas, *Hakluytus Posthumus or Purchas His Pilgrimes, Contayning a History of the World in Sea Voyages and Lande Travells by Englishmen and Others*, 20 vols. (Glasgow, 1905–07), VI, 251.

40 Leo Africanus, *History and Description of Africa*, trans. Pory, ed. Brown, I, 180, 187. Leo continues concerning the Negroes, "except their conversation perhaps bee somewhat more tolerable, who dwell in the principall Townes and Cities: for it is like that they are somewhat more addicted to Civilitie." Leo's work was available to Englishmen in Latin from 1556.

41 Bodin, *Method for Easy Comprehension of History*, 103–6, 143.

42 Rice, Turk, Moor, and Persian, 401; *Othello*, I, i, 127; Spedding, Ellis, and Heath, eds., *Works of Francis Bacon*, III, 152; Ogilby, *Africa*, 451.

43 Jobson, *Golden Trade*, ed. Kingsley, 65–67.

44 *The Golden Coast*, 75–76.

45 Smith, *New Voyage to Guinea*, 146; Barbot, *Description of the Coasts*, Churchill, comps., *Voyages*, V, 34.

46 Smith, *New Voyage to Guinea*, 221–22, clearly based on Bosman, *New and Accurate Description*, 206–7.

47 I hope to discuss this complex matter more fully on another occasion and in the meantime cite only the sources directly quoted. Freedman and Simon, trans., *Midrash Rabbah*, I, 293; Sperling and Simon, trans., *Zohar*, I, 246.

Chapter 2

Michael Banton

THE IDIOM OF RACE
A critique of presentism

[. . .]

T**HE HISTORICAL STUDY** of racial thought and attitudes has often been flawed by an unreflecting presentism. Earlier writers are held up to scorn without any adequate attempt to locate their understandings within the context of the knowledge available to their generation. Modern writers all too easily neglect the shifts in the meaning attributed to the word "race" (for a recent example of serious study vulnerable to this criticism, see Horsman, 1976). This essay will contend that as new modes of explanation of human variation have arisen, so the word "race" has been used in new ways, but the old uses have often continued side by side with the new ones. "Race" and associated words suggesting commonality of descent or character were developed into popular modes of thought and expression in many European languages in the eighteenth century so that they constituted an idiom in which people related themselves to others and developed conceptions of their own attributes. In the nineteenth century this idiom was extended through the identification of race with nation (and *Volk*), and the rise of potent beliefs about national character. Where previously there had been an emphasis upon supposed innate differences between persons distant in social rank, the stress was shifted to differences between people of distinct nations. Political circumstances helped mold these changes but they cannot be fully appreciated without taking account of changes in scientific understanding.

Possibly the most notable feature of race as a concept is the way it has inveigled observers into assuming that the main issue is that of the nature of differences between populations, and that they should concentrate upon what "race" *is*, as if this would determine the one scientifically valid use for the word. Physical differences catch people's attention so readily that they are less quick to appreciate that the validity of "race" as a concept depends upon its value as an aid in explanation. From this standpoint, the main issue is the use of the word "race," both in rational argument and in more popular connections, for people use beliefs about race, nationality, ethnicity and class as resources when they cultivate beliefs about group identities.

The failure to allow for changes in the sense in which the word race has been used has important consequences, for those who misunderstand the past of their society are likely to misunderstand the present, because people judge the present in the light of what they believe the past to have been. The past cannot be properly understood if changes in the significance of words are not allowed for. Historians and sociologists judge their predecessors, but will themselves be judged by a later generation because they are not standing outside history. Since the limitations of their knowledge will bemuse their successors, they should be charitable in assessing the limitations of their predecessors.

Race as descent

[. . .] Up to the eighteenth century at least, the dominant paradigm in Europe for explaining the differences between groups of people was provided by the Old Testament. It was the story of God's creating the world and, on the sixth day, of his making "Adam" (alternatively translated as "the man") in his own image. The Old Testament provided a series of genealogies by which it seemed possible to trace the peopling of the world and the relations which different groups bore to one another. Thus Augustine derided the idea that there might be men in unknown lands on the other side of the world because the suggestion that some of Adam's descendants might have sailed there was "excessively absurd." Many writers attempted to ascertain the date when the world was created by working back through these genealogies. Others attempted to explain the assumed inferiority of black people by reference to a curse supposedly placed by Noah on the descendants of Ham, decreeing that they should be servants of his sons Shem and Japheth; or by relating it to the despersal of peoples after the fall of the tower of Babel. Implicit in such arguments is the assumption that differences are to be explained by tracing them back to particular events the consequences of which are then transmitted genealogically. This is also a view of the world in which God is likely to intervene to punish or reward particular individuals and in which men are therefore less motivated to develop and improve classificatory concepts like that of species. A species was seen simply as the product of an arbitrary action by the Creator.

Within a paradigm of explanation in terms of descent there were several possible ways of accounting for physical variation. First, it could be held that differences of color and such like were all part of God's design for the universe; perhaps, as in the hypothesis about the curse on Ham's descendants, they were the result of divine judgment; perhaps, though, they were a part of God's plan that had not yet been revealed or that man could not properly understand, and this led to a line of reasoning which may be called racial romanticism. Secondly, it could be held that physical differences were related in some way to climate and environment and were irrelevant to the important questions of man's obligations to do God's will. Thirdly, it was sometimes argued that since the differences between Europeans, Africans and Asians were repeated in successive generations they must have had separate ancestors. It was hazardous and perhaps unnecessary to challenge the story of Adam directly, so the doubters suggested that the Old Testament account was incomplete: Adam was the ancestor of the Europeans alone. The debate about whether mankind consisted of one or many stocks had to be cast in terms of the dominant paradigm and therefore it was phrased as a choice between monogenesis and polygenesis.

The use of "race" as a term in explanations of its kind is reflected in the first major definition of the word given in the *Oxford English Dictionary* (1910), viz. "I. A group of persons, animals, or plants, connected by common descent or origin." This is the principal sense in which the word is used in English in the sixteenth, seventeenth and eighteenth centuries, and it continues to be used, though rather less frequently, in this sense. But already in the sixteenth century the notion of likeness because of descent was generalized and "race" was used to denote instances of likeness without any claim of common descent, like Dunbar's reference in 1508 to "backbiters of sundry races" and Sidney's of 1580 to "the race of good men." As the Dictionary records, this use continued into the nineteenth century, as with Lamb's reference to "the two races of men", the men who borrow and the men who lend, but thereafter it was less frequent.

If there was a principle explaining the differences in the appearance of peoples, either theistic or atheistic, then it could have operated through either moral or physical causes. Moral causes would today be called cultural: they consisted of the ways in which men responded to their environment. Physical causes were inherited dispositions and capacities. Both monogenists and polygenists used the word "race" to designate the outwardly identifiable populations of their time, but the same word meant different things to them. The monogenists believed that men started off the same and had become different because of climate and their different response to environmental opportunities. The polygenists suspected that men must have been different to begin with and their understanding of race was later systematized as "type."

For an illustration of how people subscribing to these two schools of thought could use the same word in what superficially appears to be the same sense, but draws upon two different modes of explanation, it is appropriate to turn to an essay by the historian Macaulay on the capacities of Negroes. It was written in response to a report by a Major Moody, who contended that though blacks in the West Indies could work hard, their preference for leisure was such that they would not do so unless coerced. According to Macaulay's reading, Moody maintained that there was an instinctive and unconquerable aversion between the white and black races which stemmed from a physical cause. Against this, Macaulay contended that the blacks did not work harder because, unless they emigrated, they could not get an adequate return for their labor. The antagonism, he said, was caused by slavery and for the major to prove his case he needed to provide evidence of the alleged aversion in circumstances unaffected by slavery or the memory of it. Both men used the word "race" to designate blacks and whites: "the two races could not live together," wrote Moody, while his critic referred to the "policy which excludes strangers, of all races, from the interior of China and Japan". Where Moody stressed "the consequences arising from physical differences in form, colour, feature and smell," Macaulay referred to 'the Gypsey race, one of the most beautiful and intelligent on face of the earth . . . persecuted under a thousand pretexts . . . yet the remnant of a race still preserves its peculiar language and manners" (Macaulay, 1827: 137–38, 151–52). It should be noted that Macaulay, who elsewhere displayed his own variety of ethnocentrism, misrepresented his opponent's arguments (Williams, 1978), but yet it is still clear that for the one writer the history of a race was determined by its physical nature; for the other, its history was the story of how more varied circumstances caused it to become or remain distinctive.

Race as type

Classification by descent was more easily manageable so long as the number of species was fairly limited, but with the revival of observation and the exploration of new continents in early modern times, the number of known kinds of plants increased rapidly. It was time for someone to distinguish essential forms from accidental variations, and to define a stable unit on which botanical classification could be based. The problem was most pressing in botany, but in principle it applied to all biology. The man who did most to resolve it was the Swedish naturalist known to later generations as Linnaeus (1707–1778).

In Linnaeus' view, natural history consisted of describing the various productions of the earth, their appearance, their habits, their relations to each other, and their uses. Implicit in this conception of classification as the goal of science was the belief that nature had been constructed on a pattern discoverable, at least in part, by human reason. It was man's duty to study nature diligently so that he could come closer to God, could better understand his purpose, and could glorify Him in his works. At the heart of the conception of nature to which Linnaeus came was the idea of an *oeconomia*, a rationally ordered system of means and ends. The earth, with its delightful variety of climate and topography, was populated with an equally varied assemblage of living beings, each perfectly adapted to the region in which it lived. The economy of nature lay in the balance between its constituent elements. Linnaeus never tired of describing the mechanisms which maintained the adaptation of organism and environment and the equilibrium of species (Greene, 1959: 134–37). God had created not a series of individual species but a self-regulating system. He did not need to intervene in the day-to-day affairs of his creation.

The man who more than anyone else extended the method of Linnaeus to the study of the animal kingdom and – though only in outline – to that of man, was the French comparative anatomist Cuvier (1769–1832). The system which he hoped to discover by relating animal structure to conditions of existence was the "great catalogue in which all created beings have suitable names, may be recognized by distinctive characters, and [are] arranged in divisions and sub-divisions." Cuvier's method of classification rested heavily upon the conception of a type (defined by the *Oxford English Dictionary* as "a person or thing that represents the characteristic qualities of a class; a representative specimen"). If the right representative specimen was chosen, then the essential of the category could be understood. Cuvier divided man into three main subspecies (which he called races): Caucasian, Mongolian, and Ethiopian, which were further subdivided. He stated that they were all one species but they had been separated by some great natural catastrophe. He presented the three races as differing permanently in ability because of the biological differences between them that were as yet little understood. Thus the earlier physical cause interpretation of human variation was given a new foundation.

Cuvier's influence was immense, and during the course of the nineteenth century the notion of type was extended to the analysis of poetry, aesthetics, biography, personality, culture, social movements, and many kinds of differences other than those of interest to biologists. His teaching was one of the principal factors behind the emergence in the middle years of the nineteenth century of an international school of anthropological thought. It is important to note that the conception of type was independent of the Linnaean classificatory system. A zoological type could be a genus, a species, or a subspecies. Critics therefore protested that the notion of type was redundant since the Linnaean classifications would serve. As the usual criterion for a species was that its members could breed with one another, and since the races of man engaged so frequently in interbreeding, *Homo sapiens* must be one species. The typologists criticized the orthodox definition of species. Prominent among them were Charles Hamilton Smith, Samuel George Morton, Joseph Arthur de Gobineau, Robert Knox, Josiah Clark Nott, George Robins Gliddon, James Hunt, and Karl Vogt. They are often identified as proponents of "scientific racism" but their key concept was that of the permanence of types and their theory is better designated as "racial typology." Though there were variations from one writer to another and Vogt at least changed his opinions significantly, they more or less agreed in presenting man as a genus divided into types which in effect were species. They believed that each type was permanent and was suited to a particular zoological province of the earth's surface, but they recognized that the actual races of the contemporary world were all mixed. They accounted for this by arguing that hybrids were ultimately sterile so that though because of human foolishness, races might deviate from their type, nature kept the deviation within bounds. An alternative interpretation was advanced by Gobineau who believed that the mixing had gone much too far and had spoiled the stocks responsible for progress so that humanity was going into decline (see Banton 1977: 32–55).

The typological mode of explanation differed from the previous one in being agnostic about origins. The typologists rejected earlier beliefs that the earth was about six thousand years old. Whatever might have happened in earlier epochs, within the period for which there wasn't anatomical evidence types appeared to have been constant. One of the main attractions of typology was that it offered a theory of history purporting to explain the differential pattern of human progress. The record of history also contributed to the theory by revealing the special cultural attributes of types that went along with the physical differences. Since changes were the outcome of the essential characteristics of types in relation to particular environments, the theory attributed little significance to purely contingent events like the reported curse upon Ham's descendants. Though the typological theory could be reconciled with a belief in polygenesis it was really of a very different kind. For its appeal it relied on the one hand upon science rather than the Bible, and on the other, upon the growing European acceptance of an association between differences in physical appearance and ability to build a progressive civilization.

Some of these writers, like Smith, Nott, Gliddon, and Broca, made a clear distinction between "type" and "race." Gobineau, Knox and Hunt utilized the distinction but were less careful, and Knox indeed usually used "race" where on his own terms "type" would have been preferable. In the subsequent period a few writers did try to keep to the expression "type" but it is noticeable that in the very considerable literature about the nature of racial differences published in the United States after the Civil War there is a strong tendency to use the word "race" in the sense of "type." It is unfortunate that the major study on American writing in this period – apart from its strong inclination to presentism – regards race and type as synonymous. It does indeed quote a passage in which Nott refers to the "permanence of races, types, species, or permanent varieties, call them what you please" (Haller, 1971: 80) but when Nott, in *Types of Mankind* (1854: 95) wrote, "every race, at the present time, is more or less mixed," he was clearly referring to actual physically distinguishable populations and not to permanent types. Many of the passages in Haller's book (e.g., the reference in the American context to "both races," 1971: 208) refer to the latter usage and the interpretation of them is less clear than it would be were the distinction drawn. It would probably be worthwhile engaging in further more detailed research into the usage of the authors of the period in the light of Mayr's analysis (1972) of the multiple nature of the reorientation necessitated by Darwin's discovery of natural selection.

It could also be of interest to trace the ways in which the European idiom was carried to other continents. In South Africa before World War I, any reference to the races was likely to relate to the English-speaking and the Afrikaans-speaking sections of the white population. Equally, it was common to refer to the Zulu race, the Xhosa race, the Tswana race, differentiating groups within the African section of the population. Before World War II it seems to have been unusual to employ "race" to distinguish blacks from whites. Field Marshal Smuts wrote of the European type and the African type, identifying ethnic groups within these types as races (Graaff, 1973: 4). Most writers were less meticulous but it is interesting to note that the memorandum of Association marking the foundation in 1929 of the South African Institute of Race Relations sets out as the main objective the encouragement of "co-operation between the various sections and races of the population of South Africa" as if blacks and whites constituted sections that were divided into races (Horrell, 1976).

[. . .] It was noted in the previous section that the explanation of human differences by reference to descent was associated with a concern about the original creation and God's design for the world. One outcome of this was the conclusion that God had created men of different colors for a purpose, and that each color category had its part to play in his plan. The most striking illustration of this approach to race is found in the early nineteenth-century school of thought rather misleadingly called *natur-philosophie* (see Banton, 1977: 35–40). An echo of it can be heard in the New England writer Ralph Waldo Emerson who in 1844 was insisting that the civility of no race could be perfect so long as another race was degraded, for mankind was one. Yet within a decade Emerson had been attracted to Knox's explanations and was arguing that England's economic prowess was the result of "the rare coincidence of a good race and a good place" (Nicoloff, 1961: 124, 139). It is difficult to be certain but it looks as if here, in less than a decade, Emerson switched from a sense of race as descent to that of race as type. It is also relevant that he did so in a book that tried to analyze the character of the Englishman. In later years there was to be a minor literary industry producing volumes about national character, and it was rooted in the presuppositions of racial typology.

Race as subspecies

Darwin cut the ground from under the feet of the typologists by demonstrating that there were no permanent forms in nature. Each species was adapted to its environment by natural section, so that people of one racial type who migrated to a new habitat would there undergo change. The ups and downs of history could therefore not be explained in terms of the qualities of particular types. In the *Origin of Species* Darwin recognized "geographical races or sub-species" as local forms completely fixed and isolated, but concluded that since they did not differ from each other in important characteristics there was no certain way of deciding whether they should be considered species or varieties. He employed the word race primarily when referring to domestic races as the outcome of human breeding, and presented them as incipient species, for as his subtitle suggested, it was by natural selection that favored races became species (Darwin, 1859: 62–63, 73).

Darwin's revolution was so complex (Mayr, 1972) that it took decades even for the specialists to appreciate its implications. In the 1930s, more than seventy years after the publication of the *Origin of Species*, new lines of reasoning and research in biology led to the establishment of population genetics. Human variation was to be comprehended statistically in terms of the frequencies of given genes within the gene pool of the relevant population. This meant that for biologists, "population" was the successor concept to the discredited notion of racial type, and race could be legitimately used only as a synonym for subspecies, as explained above.

Yet the first adaptations of Darwinian thought to social affairs preserved much of the older mode of explanation, in part because the reorientation demanded of people was so great, and in part because of the particular circumstances of the late nineteenth century. That period saw unparalled technological advances which helped knit together the peoples of Europe in larger, more effective units, and to increase the gap between them and the peoples of most other regions. Social evolution was pictured therefore not as adaptation to changing environments but as the story of man's progress to superior modes of living. Sociologists represented it as a process in which men first lived in small bands, then successively as members of clans, tribes, peoples, states and empires. Groups designated as races were often thought to belong somewhere in such a scale; skin color and similar traits served as signs of membership in groups that had progressed in different measure, and therefore functioned as boundary markers. The conception of race as subspecies is not easily grasped by the man in the street, whereas that of race as type is much simpler and can easily be twisted to deal with conflicting evidence. The idea of race in the popular mind in the twentieth century has therefore usually been that of race as type. This conception was invalidated by Darwin's work, whereas that of race as descent was not. Although confusing, it is therefore still legitimate to use the word "race" in the earlier sense.

Race in current usage

The idea of race was important to Europeans in the late nineteenth century on account of its value in philosophies of history. It was widely believed that the success of the European powers sprang from the qualities inherent in the white race, or races, and that these promised continuing European supremacy. Probably there would be less support for such views in Europe and North America in the 1970s. The bulk of the population is more likely to believe that the ups and downs of nations in history are a reflection of technological skill and material resources, though this is not a question that has been thought worth detailed investigation. Probably more people would agree that the cultural characteristics of racial groups are an outcome of environment and opportunity than would consider them genetically determined. Those who believe that the universe was built by divine design and that everything in it has a place in that design might well echo the racial romanticism of an earlier era. One twentieth-century expression of this, though scarcely contemporary, is to be found in a history of the British and Foreign Bible Society (Canton, 1925), entitled *The Five Colours*. After the title page comes the verse:

> Not for one race nor one colour alone
> Was He flesh of your flesh and bone of your bone!
> Not for you only – for all men He died.
> 'Five were the colours', The Angel said,
> 'Yellow and black, white, brown and red;
> Five were the wounds from which he bled,
> On the Rock of Jerusalem crucified'.
> "The Vision of Peter"

If race remains a word in popular usage, religious groups concerned for international harmony may well stress the complementarity of races and again employ metaphors of this kind.

In England in the years preceding and following World War II, the tendency was for less use to be made of the idiom of race. Sir Julian Huxley and A. C. Haddon, the senior anthropologist at Cambridge, set the tone in *We Europeans*, in which they declared that "the term race as applied to human groups should be dropped from the vocabulary of science" because it had "lost any sharpness of meaning" (1935: 107). Ideal types had to be distinguished from the existing mixed populations which might also be political and cultural units and were best called ethnic groups. The unity of race as a concept in either biological or social science was doubted by the leading authorities in both fields, while the extravagancies of Nazi rhetoric, coupled with the growing threats presented by their regime, helped to descredit it in popular usage. Earlier practices, such as that of identifying the French- and English-speaking sections of the Canadian population as "the two races" began to appear quaint. The same could be said of Sir Winston Churchill's rather archaic usage in his *History*, of which Book I was entitled "The Island Race." In 1957 he could still write about the early twentieth century, "meanwhile in Europe the mighty strength of the Teutonic race, hitherto baffled by division or cramped in lingering mediaeval systems, began to assert itself with volcanic energy" (1958: Preface). This echo of a previous century's parlance was a reminder of the change that had been occurring.

From the scientific standpoint it is unfortunate that just as the word "race" was being less used in any context where it might be thought to claim explanatory value, New Commonwealth immigration into England led to its greatly increased use in the press and in popular speech to designate the different population groups. An examination of the present use of the words "race," "races," and "racial" would probably show that they are employed chiefly to designate outwardly identifiable categories, and that people differ greatly in the degree to which they believe or assume that the labels explain anything. If questioned about why such groups should be called races, or what is the nature of race, many people will say that they are not sure but leave such matters to the experts. Since there are few situations in everyday life which require a precise use of "race" its employment in a diverse and loose fashion causes few problems.

Two situations calling for precise definition of ethnic or racial identification are provided by censuses and legislation. In the United States after World war II social scientists moved away from the use of race to designate social categories, preferring to write about minorities. The Federal government has been more slow to change: until recently they were using five "racial/ethnic categories," viz.:

1   *American Indian or Alaskan Native*: A person having origins in any of the original peoples of North America.
2   *Asian or Pacific Islander*: A person having origins in any of the original peoples of the Far East, Southeast Asia, or the Pacific Islands. This area includes, for example, China, Japan, Korea, the Philippine Islands, and Samoa.
3   *Black/Negro*: A person having origins in any of the black racial groups of Africa.
4   *Caucasian/White*: A person having origins in any of the original peoples of Europe, North Africa, the Middle East, or the Indian subcontinent.
5   *Hispanic*: A person of Mexican, Puerto Rican, Cuban, Central or South American, or other Spanish culture or origin, regardless of race.

[This list is quoted from the Federal Interagency Committee on Education Report, vol. 2(1), May 1975.]

The Association of Indians in America – i.e. of Indians from Asia – protested against their classification as whites. In May 1977 the President's Office issued a revision of Circular A–46. It modified category 1 by adding the qualification "and who maintains cultural identification through tribal affiliation or community recognition." To the first sentence of category 2 it added "the Indian subcontinent."

Category 3 was redesignated "Black." The numbers of categories 4 and 5 were changed round; 5 is now designated simply "White," and the reference to the Indian subcontinent has been deleted. The circular further states that if separate race and ethnic categories are used, the minimum designations are:

(a)   Race:
  - American Indian or Alaskan Native
  - Asian or Pacific Islander
  - Black
  - White
(b)   Ethnicity
  - Hispanic origin
  - Not of Hispanic origin.

Thus "ethnicity" becomes a subdivision of the categories Black and White alone. The circular also lays down that when someone is "of mixed racial and/or ethnic origins" the category to be used is that which "most closely reflects the individual's recognition in his community." The designation "non-white" is no longer acceptable.

In Britain there is [currently] a controversy about categories to be used in the 1981 census. It is said that the procedure almost certain to be recommended by the Office of Population Censuses and Surveys contains the instruction: "*Race or ethnic group* (1) Please tick the appropriate box to show the race or ethnic group to which the person belongs or from which the person is descended. 1. White; 2. West Indian; 3. African; 4. Arab; 5. Turkish; 6. Chinese; 7. Indian; 8. Pakistani; 9. Bangladeshi, 10. Sri Lanka; 11. Other" (Mack, 1978).[1] It will be unfortunate if the word "race" is retained in this context by the American and British governments since this will add legitimacy to the lingering remains of the typological doctrine that were on their way to the lumber room of discarded science. The United States government's use of ethnicity as a subdivision of a racial category has little support in contemporary social science, but their practice of classifying individuals by their having origins in particular peoples seems far preferable to the British assumption that a person can belong to a race. It should also be noted that though the British Race Relations Act of 1976 penalizes discrimination on racial grounds, it does not define race, and that there is at present little case law that bears upon this question. The Act does, in Section 3 (i) define racial groups but only as "a group of persons defined by reference to colour, race, nationality or ethnic or national origins."

Consideration of these issues does, however, suggest that a fourth use of the word "race" is now being established. It is an administrative and political use which does not pretend to any explanatory significance but will doubtless be used to support old-style racial explanations. The political implications of the racial idiom have always been complex. It can be argued, for example, that a salient feature of the use some Englishmen made of it in the middle and later decades of the nineteenth century was to celebrate the positive qualities of their own stock and that the disparagement of the qualities of other stocks was to start with only an incidental consequence of their self-centeredness. (Sir Charles Dilke's *Greater Britain* of 1868 is an illustration of this.) Only as contact and conflict between Europeans and non-Europeans became closer did the political use of racial doctrines become important. In recent times peoples who have been the victims of such doctrines have been inclined to turn the tables by appealing for nonwhite solidarity against whites. In the United States some blacks prefer to identify themselves in racial terms because they believe that their experience of disadvantage has been so much more profound than that of white ethnic minorities. In the United Kingdom it seems as if people who stand to the left in political terms are the more inclined to identify New Commonwealth immigrant minorities in racial terms because they wish to challenge the typological preconceptions which seem still to be widespread in the white population. This appears to have been the major reason why the agency established under the 1976 Act has been called The Commission for Racial Equality whereas its predecessor was the Community Relations Commission. Therefore though it may seem desirable on strictly academic grounds to abandon the use of the word race, there are political pressures, from non-whites as well as whites, from radicals as well as conservatives, which are likely to keep it in current use and to shape the fourth stage in the career of this troublesome concept.

Other perspectives

If the meaning of the word race has changed in the way suggested, reflecting changes in popular understanding of the significance of phenotypical variation, then it is reasonable to expect that the character of the arguments which get classified as "racist" will have changed likewise. When race meant descent, then it may be expected that whites considered alliance with blacks as socially dishonorable. When race meant type, whites would have seen sexual union with blacks as producing stock physicaly inferior to whites but superior to blacks. When race meant subspecies, most members of the public would not have comprehended the workings of inheritance and selection, and since it takes time for scientific advances to reach the wider public it might be expected that the typological doctrine would have retained its appeal.[2] Now that race is coming to be defined by bureaucratic and political concerns it is not surprising that there is no agreement upon a clear definition of racism.

Historical evidence is not lacking to support this thesis at least in respect to the change between the first and second stages. In 1771 the Viceroy of Brazil ordered the degradation of an Amerindian chief who, "disregarding the signal honours which he had received from the Crown, had sunk so low as to marry a Negress, staining his blood with this alliance" (Boxer, 1963: 121). Such a statement recalls a judgment that in eighteenth-century Latin America the "almost pathological interest in genealogy" and honorable descent was characteristic of the age (Mörner, 1967: 59). It suggests that it is the social rather than the physical consequences of marriages between persons of contrasting status which are to be avoided, and can be placed alongside the French memoire du roi of 1777 that declared of the transplanted Africans in Saint Dominque:

> Whatever distance they may be from their origin, they always keep the stain of slavery, and are declared incapable of all public functions. Even gentlemen who descend in any degree from a woman of color cannot

enjoy the prerogatives of nobility. This law is harsh, but wise and necessary. In a country where there are fifteen slaves to one white, one cannot put too much distance between the two species . . .

(Hall, 1972: 183–84).

This is an explicitly political argument which utilizes a doctrine of descent – to which Europeans admitted exceptions when it suited them – in order to exclude a category of people from civil rights. It lacks the biological presupposition which a twentieth-century reader might expect.

Conclusion

[. . .] Physical differences between peoples have been observed throughout human history; all over the world people have developed words for delineating them. "Race" is a concept rooted in a particular culture and a particular period of history which brings with it suggestions about how these differences are to be explained. It lends itself to use in a variety of contexts and gets elaborated into a whole style or idiom of interpretation. In the earliest phase of its career "race" meant descent at a time when people understood little of the biology of descent. In the nineteenth century "race" became identified with a controversial scientific theory that was found to be erroneous and which, had science been a more logical and less human enterprise, should have been discarded after 1859. Instead, the old idea was salvaged and rebuilt on a foundation quite different from that of the pre-Darwinian era, while in the present it is being used for purely political purposes to identify communities without intending to imply that the chief differences between then stem from inheritance.

Some scholars overlook these differences in the meaning that has been given to the word; they interpret the racial attitudes of earlier centuries in terms of their own generation's understanding of biological variation and condemn anything which to a modern reader smacks of racial intolerance. This practice diminishes some of the differences between periods of history; it distracts attention from the forces for change which exist in the present and will extend into the future. Presentism tends to slow down the process whereby erroneous or unhelpful formulations are discarded, and it can be pernicious when analyses of past events are distorted by a desire to support a contemporary political strategy. Since all writers will be influenced in some degree by the circumstances of their own time, and most believe that it is possible to learn lessons from history, the problem is implicit in any account of another period, but it can still be kept under control. Since people's ideas about the special characteristics of their own time are influenced by their beliefs about previous periods they have a particular reason to be on their guard against presentism.

Notes

1   In March 1980 it was announced that the 1981 United Kingdom census would not contain any question on race or ethnic origin. See also White, 1979.

2　　Although overlain by some other lines of thought, sophisticated writers for a time advanced social Darwinist theses that racial prejudice served an evolutionary function, while the slogan 'survival of the fittest' seemed to justify white aggressiveness overseas.

References

Banton, Michael 1977. *The Idea of Race*, London: Tavistock.

Boxer, C. R. 1963. *Race Relations in the Portuguese Colonial Empire, 1415–1825*, Oxford: Clarendon Press.

Canton, William 1925. *The Five Colours*. London: The Bible House.

Churchill, Winston S. 1956–1958. *A History of the English-speaking Peoples*, London: Cassell.

Darwin, Charles 1959. *On the Origin of Species by Means of Selection; or, The Preservation of Favoured Races in the Struggle for Life*, (page references to New York: Mentor Books edition).

Graaff, J. F. de V. 1973. "Kosmos and Chaos: The racial attitudes of Jan Christian Smuts", unpublished MSc. Thesis, University of Bristol.

Greene, John C. 1959. *The Death of Adam*, New York: Mentor Books.

Hall, Gwendolyn Midlo 1972. "Saint Domingue," pp. 172–192 in David N. Cohen and Jack P. Greene (eds), *Neither Slave nor Free: The Freedmen of African Descent in the Slave Societies of the New World*, Baltimore: Johns Hopkins University press.

Haller, John S. 1971. *Outcasts from Evolution: Scientific Attitudes of Racial Inferiority 1859–1900*, Urbana: University of Illinois Press.

Horrell, Muriel 1976. Personal communication.

Horsman, Reginald 1976. Origins of racial Anglo-Saxonism in Great Britain before 1850", *Journal of the History of Ideas* 37: 387–410.

Huxley, Julian S. And Haddon, A. C. 1935. *We Europeans: A Survey of 'Racial' Problems*, London: Cape.

Macaulay, Thomas B. 1827. "The social and industrial capacities of Negroes", reprinted in *Race*, 1971, 13: 133–164.

Mack, Joanna 1978. "A question of race", *New Society* 43, 5 Jan: 8–9.

Mayr, Ernst 1972. "The nature of the Darwinian revolution" *Science*, 176: 981–989.

Mörner, Magnus 1967. *Race Mixture in the History of Latin America*, Boston: Little, Brown.

Nott, J. C. and Gliddon, Geo. R. 1854. *Types of Mankind: or, Ethnological Researches*, Philadelphia: Lippincott.

Nicoloff, Philip L. 1961. *Emerson on Race and History: an examination of "English Traits"*, New York: Columbia University Press.

White, R. M. 1979. "What's in a name? Problems in official and legal usages of 'race'", *New Community*, 7: 333–349.

Williams, David O. 1978. "Macaulay and the commission to Tortola", unpublished MSc. Thesis, University of Bristol.

Chapter 3

Tzvetan Todorov

Translated by Catherine Porter

RACE AND RACISM

[. . .]

THE WORD "RACISM," in its usual sense, actually designates two very different things. On the one hand, it is a matter of *behavior*, usually a manifestation of hatred or contempt for individuals who have well-defined physical characteristics different from our own; on the other hand, it is a matter of *ideology*, a doctrine concerning human races. The two are not necessarily linked. The ordinary racist is not a theoretician; he is incapable of justifying his behavior with "scientific" arguments. Conversely, the ideologue of race is not necessarily a "racist," in the usual sense: his theoretical views may have no influence whatsoever on his acts, or his theory may not imply that certain races are intrinsically evil. In order to keep these two meanings separate, I shall adopt the distinction that sometimes obtains between "racism," a term designating behavior, and "racialism," a term reserved for doctrines. I must add that the form of racism that is rooted in racialism produces particularly catastrophic results: this is precisely the case of Nazism. Racism is an ancient form of behavior that is probably found worldwide; racialism is a movement of ideas born in Western Europe whose period of flowering extends from the mid-eighteenth century to the mid-twentieth.

Racialist doctrine, which will be our chief concern here, can be presented as a coherent set of propositions. They are all found in the "ideal type," or classical version of the doctrine, but some of them may be absent from a given marginal or "revisionist" version. These propositions may be reduced to five.

1 *The existence of races.* The first thesis obviously consists in affirming that there are such things as races, that is, human groupings whose members possess common physical characteristics; or rather (for the differences themselves are self-evident) it consists in affirming the relevance and the significance of that notion.

From this perspective, races are equated with animal species, and it is postulated that there is the same distance between two human races as between horses and donkeys: not enough to prevent reproduction, but enough to establish a boundary readily apparent to all. Racialists are not generally content to observe this state of affairs; they also want to see it maintained: they are thus opposed to racial mixing.

The adversaries of racialist theory have often attacked the doctrine on this point. First, they draw attention to the fact that human groups have intermingled from time immemorial; consequently, their physical characteristics cannot be as different as racialists claim. Next, these theorists add a two-pronged biological observation to their historical argument. In the first place, human beings indeed differ from one another in their physical characteristics; but in order for these variations to give rise to clearly delimited groups, the differences and the groups would have to coincide. However, this is not the case. We can produce a first map of the "races" if we measure genetic characteristics, a second if we analyze blood composition, a third if we use the skeletal system, a fourth if we look at the epidermis. In the second place, within each of the groups thus constituted, we find greater distances between one individual and another than between one group and another. For these reasons, contemporary biology, while it has not stopped studying variations among human beings across the planet, no longer uses the concept of race.

But this scientific argument is not really relevant to the argument against racialist doctrines: it is a way of responding with biological data to what is actually a question of social psychology. Scientists may or may not believe in "races," but their position has no influence on the perception of the man in the street, who can see perfectly well that the differences exist. From this individual's viewpoint, the only properties that count are the immediately visible ones: skin color, body hair, facial configuration. Furthermore, the fact that there are individuals or even whole populations that are the product of racial mixing does not invalidate the notion of race but actually confirms it. The person of mixed race is identified precisely because the observer is capable of recognizing typical representatives of each race.

2   *Continuity between physical type and character*. But races are not simply groups of individuals who look alike (if this had been the case, the stakes would have been trivial). The racialist postulates, in the second place, that physical and moral characteristics are interdependent; in other words, the segmentation of the world along racial lines has as its corollary an equally definitive segmentation along cultural lines. To be sure, a single race may possess more than one culture; but as soon as there is racial variation there is cultural change. The solidarity between race and culture is evoked to explain why the races tend to go to war with one another.

Not only do the two segmentations coexist, it is alleged, but most often a causal relation is posited between them: physical differences *determine* cultural differences. We can all observe these two series of variables, physical and mental, around us; each one can be explained independently, and the two explanations do not have to be related after the fact; or else the two series can be observed without requiring any explanation at all. Yet the racialist acts as if the two series were nothing but the causes and effects of a single series. This first assertion in turn implies the hereditary transmission of mental properties and the impossibility of modifying those properties by education. The quest for unity and order in the variety of lived experience clearly relates the racialist attitude to that of the scholar in general, who tries to introduce order into chaos and whose constructions affirm the kinship of things that remain separate in the phenomenal world. It must be added that up to now, no proof has been provided for the relation of determinism or even for the interdependence of race and culture. This does not mean, of course, that proof might not one day be found, or that the search for proof is in itself harmful. We must simply note that, for the time being, the hypothesis has turned out to be unproductive.

Here I should like to mention a recent proposal to maintain the causal relation while overturning it. This view no longer holds that physical characteristics determine mental ones; rather, it holds that culture acts on nature. If, within a given population, tall people are preferred to short people, or blonds are preferred to brunettes, the population as a whole will evolve toward the desired end: its value system will serve as a genetic filter. We can also imagine a population that would prefer physical strength to intelligence, or vice versa; once again, conditions will be favorable for an extension of the qualities valued. Such an inversion of perspective opens up new possibilities for the study of mind–body interactions.

3   *The action of the group on the individual*. The same determinist principle comes into play in another sense: the behavior of the individual depends, to a very large extent, on the racio-cultural (or "ethnic") group to which he or she belongs. This proposition is not always explicit, since it is self-evident: what is the use of distinguishing races and cultures, if one believes at the same time that individuals are morally nondetermined, that they act in function of their own will freely exercised, and not by virtue of their group membership – over which they have no control? Racialism is thus a doctrine of collective psychology, and it is inherently hostile to the individualist ideology.

4   *Unique hierarchy of values*. The racialist is not content to assert that races differ; he also believes that some are superior to others, which implies that he possesses a unitary hierarchy of values, an evaluative framework with respect to which he can make universal judgments. This is somewhat astonishing, for the racialist who has such a framework at his disposal is the same person who has rejected the unity of the human race. The scale of values in question is generally ethnocentric in origin: it is very rare that the ethnic group to which a racialist author belongs does not appear at the top of his own hierarchy. On the level of physical qualities, the judgment of preference usually takes the form of aesthetic appreciation: my race is beautiful, the others are more or less ugly. On the level of the mind, the judgment concerns both intellectual and moral qualities (people are stupid or intelligent, bestial or noble).

5   *Knowledge-based politics*. The four propositions listed so far take the form of descriptions of the world, factual observations. They lead to a conclusion that constitutes the fifth and last doctrinal proposition – namely, the need to embark upon a political course that brings the world into harmony with the description

provided. Having established the "facts," the racialist draws from them a moral judgment and a political ideal. Thus, the subordination of inferior races or even their elimination can be justified by accumulated knowledge on the subject of race. Here is where racialism rejoins racism: the theory is put into practice.

The refutation of this last inference is a task not for the scientist but rather for the philosopher. Science can refute propositions like the first three listed, but it may also turn out that what appears self-evident to biologists today may be considered an error tomorrow. Even if this were to happen, however, it would not justify behavior that could be properly condemned on other grounds. Geneticists are not particularly well qualified to combat racism. Subjecting politics to science, and thus subjecting what is right to what is, makes for bad philosophy, not bad science; the humanist ideal can be defended against the racist ideal not because it is more true (an ideal cannot be more or less true) but because it is ethically superior, based as it is on the universality of the human race.

The whole set of features described constitutes racialist doctrine; each of them taken alone can also be found independently of racialism. They are all necessary to racialism; the absence of any one of them produces a related but nevertheless distinct doctrine. We shall discover that the first proposition was rejected as early as the nineteenth century, leading to a "culturalism" that is in other respects very similar to racialism. In the twentieth century, the fourth proposition has also been frequently rejected, in situations where relativist neutrality has been favored over the obligation to judge (whereas this proposition was the only common feature of racialism and universalist humanism). There are also racialists who have no interest whatsoever in any possible political implications of their doctrines (this is the case with the most famous racialist of them all, Gobineau). Still, the conjunction of the five features must be considered the classical model of racialism. On the other hand, the supplementary elements of the doctrine mentioned here are optional – for example, the fear of racial mixing, or the belief that mental faculties are inherited, or the explanation of racial warfare.

Several common features indicate that racialism belongs to the spiritual family of scientism. Indeed, we have seen how the latter is characterized by its affirmation of an integral determinism (which includes the relation of the moral realm to the physical as well as the relation of the individual to the group). Scientism is also characterized by its demand that science formulate society's goals and indicate legitimate means for attaining them. One might call racialism the tip of the scientistic iceberg. Racialist theories are no longer in fashion today, but the scientistic doctrine continues to flourish. This is why I am inclined to conduct parallel analyses of racialist ideas as such and their general scientistic context.

[. . .] The most significant change in the notion of race in the late nineteenth century is its transposition from the physical to the cultural plane, under the influence of such authors as Renan, Taine, and Le Bon. [. . .] Let us now consider the notion of "historical" race shared by Taine and Le Bon.

Hippolyte Taine's place in the history of racialism is somewhat difficult to pin down. His influence is quite considerable, although his writings include only a few pages devoted to the issue of race. Moreover, there is a troubling discrep-ancy between his programmatic exposés and his own practice. Like Renan, his contemporary, Taine in fact swings back and forth between physical and cultural interpretations of the word "race," thus authorizing his disciples to find arguments in his writings in support of contradictory theses.

In his statements of principle, as we have seen, Taine aligns himself with an integral determinism (this is not the case with his practice). In his introduction to the *History of English Literature*, Taine's systematic presentation of the factors governing human behavior reduces them to three: race, surroundings, and epoch – that is, what man contributes in himself, what the external environment imposes on him, and finally the results of the interaction of these two factors. The "epoch" (*le moment*) is not actually the result of the era in which one lives, but rather the result of the phase of an internal evolution proper to each human group; in other words, it combines the two preceding factors, yet it becomes a determining factor in turn. "With the forces within and without, there is the work which they have already produced together, and this work itself contributes to produce that which follows". But just what does the contribution from "within" (called "race") consist of? What are its nature and its scope?

In "The Philosophy of Art in the Netherlands" ("Philosophy de l'art dans les Pays-Bas"), Taine attempts to draw a rigorous distinction between race and nation (or people), but he does so with the help of a metaphor that leaves room for a certain interpretive license. "I shall first show you the seed, that is to say the race, with its fundamental and indelible qualities, those that persist through all circumstances and in all climates; and next the plant, that is to say the people itself, with its original qualities expanded or contracted, in any case grafted on and transformed by its surroundings and its history" (*Philosophie de l'art*, in English *The Philosophy of Art*, II. But just what do these vegetable images yield when they are transposed onto the human species?

When he sets out to illustrate the influence of race, in the *History of English Literature*, Taine resorts to an example that seems to confirm the foregoing distinction. "A race, like the old Aryans, scattered from the Ganges as far as the Hebrides, settled in every clime, and every stage of civilization, transformed by thirty centuries of revolutions, nevertheless manifests in its languages, religions, literatures, philosophies, the community of blood and of intellect which to this day finds its offshoots together." Let us note here that while Taine may be talking about "blood" and "intellect," his list includes only intellectual products, languages and literatures, religions and philosophies; the common denominator of activities as numerous and varied as these can hardly be very powerful. In any event, race is presented here as a supranational entity.

However, the same text also includes statements that tend to identify race with nation. Races, according to Taine, "vary with various peoples." Why, then, are two terms needed instead of just one? He goes on to give examples of "regulating instincts and faculties implanted in a race" that involve the Germanic, Hellenic, and Latin races – or rather Spain, England, and France, which is to say nations and not races. In another passage, where he lists "the fundamental causes" that govern human behavior, Taine specifies that he means "nationality, climate, temperament"; here "nationality" appears again as a synonym for "race." At the same time, Taine says he intends to complete the task Montesquieu had set for himself: the description of "the special psychology of each special formation" – that is, the spirit of nations. And it must be said that in practice, physical characteristics play only a small part in Taine's analyses; thus, contrary to what his own distinctions imply, his races are nations, understood as "cultures."

We find the same ambiguity in the description of "race" itself. Race is what is innate; but is what is innate modifiable? Is it radically distinct from what is acquired? On the one hand, Taine implies that race is a stable entity. "There is one [fixed element], a character and spirit proper to the race, transmitted from generation to generation, remaining the same through cultural change, organizational shifts, and variation in products" (*Essais*, preface to the second edition, pp. xviii–xix). These are "the universal and permanent causes, present at every moment and in every case, everywhere and always acting, indestructible, and finally infallibly supreme" (*History of English Literature*). So much for the immutable side.

But at the same time, Taine makes precisely the opposite claim. The brief passages in the *History of English Literature* that describe the entity called "race" are oddly focused on the search for the *origin* of races – which is nothing other than an adaptation to the surroundings. The inside that was supposed to be opposed to the outside is only a slightly older outside. "As soon as an animal begins to exist, it has to reconcile itself with its surroundings; it breathes and renews itself, is differently affected according to the variations in air, food, temperature. Different climate and situation bring it various needs, and consequently a different course of activity; and thus, again, a different set of habits; and still again, a different set of aptitudes and instincts." It is no longer race and surroundings that are in opposition, but long and short time periods. "The race emigrates, like the Aryan, and the change of climate has altered in its case the whole economy, intelligence, and organization of society." Taine then falls back on another comparison in which he has given up the qualitative difference between seed and plant: the race is "a kind of lake, a deep reservoir wherein other springs have, for a multitude of centuries, discharged their several streams." Certain waters flow out of the lake, and others flow into it; but there is no difference in nature between them.

When he turns to the study of the "surroundings," Taine mentions the climate and geographical features, political circumstances, and social conditions as being among the most powerful environmental forces that act on men; taken together, "these prolonged situations, these surrounding circumstances" produce "the regulating instincts and faculties implanted in a race – in short, the mood of intelligence in which it thinks and acts at the present time." Thus, race no longer produces history, but rather history produces race (or the spirit of the nation). Moreover, by modifying the institutions or forms of social life, one can transform race: such actions "are to nations what education, career, condition, abode are to individuals." The possibility of an educational project alluded to here is at the opposite pole from racialist thought, and it allows us to measure the full ambivalence of Taine's position (although properly speaking there is no contradiction, and Taine was probably conscious of the apparent inconsistency).

In his books (*Philosophy de l'art, Essais de critique*), Taine deals at length with "the spirit of nations." He uses the term "race," but he often leaves the impression that the word is only a substitute, sometimes synonymous with "nation," sometimes with "essential element" or "dominant faculty." Whatever the case, starting with Taine the word "race" comes into play with renewed vigor.

In the transformations that Renan and Taine, or even le Bon, bring to racialist doctrine, we can see a prefiguration of its contemporary outlines. The term 'race," having already outlived its usefulness, will be replaced by the much more appropriate term "culture"; declarations of superiority and inferiority, the residue of an attachment to the universalist framework, will be set aside in favor of a glorification of difference (a difference that is not valorized in itself). What will remain unchanged, on the other hand, is the rigidity of determinism (cultural rather than physical, now) and the discontinuity of humanity, compartmentalized into cultures that cannot and must not communicate with one another effectively. The period of classical racialism seems definitely behind us, in the wake of the widespread condemnation of Nazi Germany's policies toward Jews; thus, we can establish its chronological limits with a precision that is unusual in the history of ideas: from 1749 (Buffon) to 1945 (Hitler). Modern racialism, which is better known as "culturalism," originates in the writings of Renan, Taine, and Le Bon; it replaces physical race with linguistic, historical, or psychological race. It shares certain features with its ancestor, but not all; this has allowed it to abandon the compromising term "race" (and thus the first "proposition" of classical racialism). Nevertheless, it can continue to play the role formerly assumed by racialism. In our day, racist behaviors have clearly not disappeared, or even changed; but the discourse that legitimizes them is no longer the same; rather than appealing to racialism, it appeals to nationalist or culturalist doctrine, or to the "right to difference." [. . .]

Chapter 4

Oliver C. Cox

RACE RELATIONS
Its meaning, beginning, and progress

I N   A   D I S C U S S I O N   O F "the origin" of race relations it should be well to
determine at the outset exactly what we are looking for. We shall proceed,
therefore, by first eliminating certain concepts that are commonly confused with
that of race relations. These are: ethnocentrism, intolerance, and "racism."

Ethnocentrism, as the sociologists conceive of it, is a social attitude which
expresses a community of feeling in any group – the "we" feeling as over against
the "others." This attitude seems to be a function of group solidarity, which is not
necessarily a racial phenomenon. Neither is social intolerance [. . .] racial antagonism,
for social intolerance is social despleasure or resentment against that group which
refuses to conform to the established practices and beliefs of the society. Finally,
the term "racism" as it has been recently employed in the literature seems to refer
to a philosophy of racial antipathy. Studies on the origin of racism involve the
study of the development of an ideology, an approach which usually results in
the substitution of the history of a system of rationalization for that of a material
social fact.[1] Indeed, it is likely to be an accumulation of an erratic pattern of
verbalizations cut free from any on-going social system.

What then is the phenomenon, the beginnings of which we seek to determine?
It is the phenomenon of the capitalist exploitation of peoples and its complementary
social attitude. Again, one should miss the point entirely if one were to think of
racial antagonism as having its genesis in some "social instinct" of antipathy between
peoples. Such an approach ordinarily leads to no end of confusion.[2]

The beginning of racial antagonism

Probably a realization of no single fact is of such crucial significance for an
understanding of racial antagonism as that the phenomenon had its rise only in
modern times.[3] In a previous chapter on "the origin of caste" we have attempted

to show that race conflict did not exist among the early Aryans in India, and we do not find it in other ancient civilizations. Our hypothesis is that racial exploitation and race prejudice developed among Europeans with the rise of capitalism and nationalism, and that because of the world-wide ramifications of capitalism, all racial antagonisms can be traced to the policies and attitudes of the leading capitalist people, the white people of Europe and North America.

[. . .] In the study of race relations it is of major importance to realize that their significant manifestations could not possibly have been known among the ancients. If we had to put our finger upon the year which marked the beginning of modern race relations we should select 1493–94. This is the time when total disregard for the human rights and physical power of the non-Christian peoples of the world, the colored peoples, was officially assumed by the first two great colonizing European nations. Pope Alexander VI's bill of demarcation issued under Spanish pressure on May 3, 1493, and its revision by the Treaty of Tordesillas (June 7, 1494), arrived at through diplomatic negotiations between Spain and Portugal, put all the heathen peoples and their resources – that is to say, especially the colored peoples of the world – at the disposal of Spain and Portugal.[4]

Sometimes, probably because of its very obviousness, it is not realized that the slave trade was simply a way of recruiting labor for the purpose of exploiting the great natural resources of America.[5] This trade did not develop because Indians and Negroes were red and black, or because their cranial capacity averaged a certain number of cubic centimeters; but simply because they were the best workers to be found for the heavy labor in the mines and plantations across the Atlantic.[6] If white workers were available in sufficient numbers they would have been substituted. As a matter of fact, part of the early demand for labor in the West Indies and on the mainland was filled by white servants, who were sometimes defined in exactly the same terms as those used to characterize the Africans. Although the recruitment of involuntary labor finally settled down to the African coasts, the earlier kidnapers did a brisk business in some of the most enlightened European cities. Moreover, in the process of exploiting the natural resources of the West Indies, the Spanish conquistadors literally consumed the native Indian population.

This, then, is the beginning of modern race relations. It was not an abstract, natural, immemorial feeling of mutual antipathy between groups, but rather a practical exploitative relationship with its socio-attitudinal facilitation – at that time only nascent race prejudice. Although this peculiar kind of exploitation was then in its incipience, it had already achieved its significant characteristics.[7] As it developed and took definite capitalistic form, we could follow the white man around the world and see him repeat the process among practically every people of color. Earl Grey was directly in point when he described, in 1880, the motives and purpose of the British in one racial situation:

> Throughout this part of the British Dominions the colored people are generally looked upon by the whites as an inferior race, whose interest ought to be systematically disregarded when they came into competition with their own, and who ought to be governed mainly with a view of the advantage of the superior race. And for this advantage two things

are considered to be especially necessary: first, that facilities should be afforded to the white colonists for obtaining possession of land heretofore occupied by the native tribes; and secondly, that the Kaffir population should be made to furnish as large and as cheap a supply of labor as possible.[8]

But the fact of crucial significance is that racial exploitation is merely one aspect of the problem of the proletarianization of labor, regardless of the color of the laborer. Hence racial antagonism is essentially political-class conflict. The capitalist exploiter, being opportunistic and practical, will utilize any convenience to keep his labor and other resources freely exploitable. He will devise and employ race prejudice when that becomes convenient.[9] As a matter of fact, the white proletariat of early capitalism had to endure burdens of exploitation quite similar to those which many colored peoples must bear today.

However, the capitalist spirit, the profit-making motive, among the sixteenth-century Spaniards and Portuguese, was constantly inhibited by the philosophy and purpose of the Roman Catholic Church. A social theory supporting the capitalist drive for the impersonal exploitation of the workers never completely emerged. Conversion to Christianity and slavery among the Indians stood at cross-purposes; therefore, the vital problem presented to the exploiters of labor was that of circumventing the assimilative effects of conversion to Christianity. In the West Indies the celebrated priest, Las Casas, was touched by the destructive consequences of the ruthless enslavement of the Indians, and he opposed it on religious grounds. But work had to be done, and if not voluntarily, then some ideology had to be found to justify involuntary servitude. "The Indians were represented as lazy, filthy pagans, of bestial morals, no better than dogs, and fit only for slavery, in which state alone there might be some hope of instructing and converting them to Christianity."[10]

The capitalist exploitation of the colored workers, it should be observed, consigns them to employments and treatment that is humanly degrading. In order to justify this treatment the exploiters must argue that the workers are inately degraded and degenerate, consequently they naturally merit their condition. It may be mentioned incidentally that the ruling-class conception of degradation will tend to be that of all persons in the society, even that of the exploited person himself; and the work done by degraded persons will tend to degrade superior persons who attempt to do it. [. . .]

The progress of racial antagonism

This, then, is the nature of racial antagonism; developing in Europe, it has been carried to all parts of the world. In almost fateful terms Kipling's celebrated poem written in 1899 describes a desperate conflict, "the white man's burden," a like obligation, incidentally, never assumed by any other race in all the history of the world:

> Take up the White Man's burden –
> Send forth the best ye breed –
> Go bind your sons to exile

> To serve your captives' need;
> To wait in heavy harness,
> On fluttered folk and wild —
> Your new-caught, sullen peoples,
> Half-devil and half-child.[11]

The Europeans have overthrown more or less completely the social system among every colored people with whom they have come into contact. The dynamism and efficiency of capitalistic culture concluded this. The stability of color and inertness of culture, together with effective control over firearms, subsequently made it possible for whites to achieve a more or less separate and dominant position even in the homeland of colored peoples. "The white man's conception of himself as the aristocrat of the earth came gradually through the discovery, as surprising to himself as to anyone else, that he had weapons and organization which made opposition to his ambition futile."[12]

It should be made clear that we do not mean to say that the white race is the only one *capable* of race prejudice. It is probable that without capitalism, a cultural chance occurrence among whites, the world might never have experienced race prejudice. Indeed, we should expect that under another form of economic organization, say socialism, the relationship between whites and peoples of color would be significantly modified.[13]

The depreciation of the white man's color as a social gift goes hand in hand with the westernization of the conquered peoples of color. The Hindus, for example, are the same color today as they were in 1750, but now the white man no longer appears to them to be the cultural magician of other days. His secret of domination has been exposed, and the Hindus are now able to distinguish between his white skin and that secret. Therefore, he is now left with only his nationalism and superior might, for should he pull a cultural rabbit out of his hat, some Hindu would promptly pull another, which might even overmatch the first. Krishnalal Shridharani puts it thus: "[The Saxon] has been accustomed to regarding himself as a supreme being for centuries. Now he faces a world which refuses to recognize him as such. With all his civilized values, he will have to go on the role of military tyrant."[14] There is no assumption, then, that race prejudice is a biological heritage of the white race.

But we should not lose sight of the fact that whites have pre-empted this attitude.[15] Since the belief in white superiority — that is to say, white nationalism — began to move over the world, no people of color has been able to develop race prejudice independent of whites. It may be, however, that the Japanese have now reached that stage of industrial development, nationalistic ambition, and military power sufficient to question their assignment to inferior racial rank; no other colored race has ever dared to do this.[16] Indeed, since 1905 the Japanese have known how it felt to overcome the white man and make him like it.

Furthermore, the Japanese are culturally ripe for a belief of their own in yellow superiority. But the problem now confronting them is not similar to that which lay before the Europeans when they began to take on the burden of exploiting the colored peoples of the world. The white opportunists had then come upon no race able to fathom their cultural superiority and power. Today, however, the

Japanese are not only blocked at every point by powerfully entrenched whites but also relatively limited in their possible area of dominance.

A still more crucial question is whether this world is large enough to accommodate more than one superior race. Barring the apparent illogic of the superlative, we should bear in mind that color prejudice is more than ethnocentrism; race prejudice must be actually backed up by a show of racial excellence, secured finally by military might.[17] No race can develop color prejudice merely by wishing to do so. It would be ridiculous for the Chinese to say that they are prejudiced against whites when Europeans segregate the Chinese even in China.[18] [. . .]

Notes

1   See Hannah Arendt; "Race-Thinking Before Racism," *The Review of Politics*, Vol. 6, January 1944, p. 36–73; and Frederick G. Detweiler, "The Rise of Modern Race Antagonisms," *The American Journal of Sociology*, vol. 37, March 1932, pp. 738–47.

2   Consider, for instance, the following definitive statement by professor Robert E. Park: "This [prejudice against the Japanese] is due to the existence in the human mind of a mechanism by which we inevitably and automatically classify every individual human being we meet. When a race bears an external mark by which every individual member of it can infallibly be identified, that race is by that fact set apart and segregated. Japanese, Chinese, and Negroes cannot move among us with the same freedom as members of other races because they bear marks which identify them as members of their race. This fact isolates them. . . . Isolation is at once a cause and an effect of race prejudice. It is a vicious circle – isolation, prejudice; prejudice, isolation." In Jesse F. Steiner, *The Japanese Invasion*, p. xvi.

Since, however, we may assume that all races "bear marks which identify them as members of their race," it must follow, according to Park, that a certain human capacity for classification makes it impossible for races to come together without racial antagonism and prejudice. We shall attempt to show that this instinct hypothesis is too simple.

3   Cf. Ina Corine Brown, *National Survey of the Higher Education of Negroes*, J. S. Office of Education, Misc. No. 6, Vol. I, pp. 4–8.

4   As early as 1455 Pope Nicholas V had granted the Portuguese exclusive right to their discoveries on the African coast, but the commercial purpose here was still very much involved with the crusading spirit.

5   In a discussion of the arguments over slavery during the Constitutional Convention, Charles A. Beard observes: "South Carolina was particularly determined, and gave northern representatives to understand that if they wished to secure their commercial privileges, they must make concessions to the slave trade. And they were met half way. Ellsworth said: 'As slaves multiply so fast in Virginia and Maryland that it is cheaper to raise than import them, whilst in the sickly rice swamps foreign supplies are necessary, if we go no farther than is urged, we shall be unjust towards South Carolina and Georgia. Let us not intermeddle. As population increases, poor laborers will be so plenty as to render slaves useless.'" *An Economic Interpretation of the Constitution*, p. 177. Quote from Max Farrand, *Records*, Vol. II, p.371.

6   In a discussion of the labor situation among the early Spanish colonists in America, Professor Bailey W. Diffie observes: "One Negro was reckoned as worth two, four, or even more Indians at work production." *Latin American Civilization*, p. 206.

7   Francis Augustus MacNutt describes the relationship in Hispaniola: "Columbus laid tribute upon the entire population of the island which required that each Indian above fourteen years of age who lived in the mining provinces was to pay a little bell filled with gold every three months; the natives of all other provinces were to pay one *arroba* of cotton. These amounts were so excessive that in 1496 it was found necessary to change the nature of the payments, and, instead of the gold and cotton required from the villages, labour was substituted, the Indians being required to lay out and work the plantations of the colonists in their vicinity." *Bartholomew De Las Casas*, p. 25.

8   Quoted by E. D. Morel, *The Black Man's Burden*, p. 30.

9   In our description of the uses of race prejudice in this essay we are likely to give the impression that race prejudice was always "manufactured" in full awareness by individuals or groups of entrepreneurs. This, however, is not quite the case. Race prejudice, from its inception, became part of the social heritage, and as such both exploiters and exploited for the most part are born heirs to it. It is possible that most of those who propagate and defend race prejudice are not conscious of its fundamental motivation. To paraphrase Adam Smith: They who teach and finance race prejudice are by no means such fools as the majority of those who believe and practice it.

10 Francis Augustus MacNutt, *Bartholomew De las Casas*, p. 83.

It should be kept clearly in view that this colonial movement was not a transference of the feudal manorial economy to America. It was the beginning of an entirely different economic enterprise – the dawn of colonial capitalism, the moving out of "white" capital into the lands of colored peoples who had to be exploited unsentimentally and with any degree of ruthlessness in the interest of profits.

11 *Rudyard Kipling's Verse, 1885–1926*, p. 320.

12 Josef W. Hall (Upton Close), *The Revolt of Asia*, p. 4. In this early period there was a more or less conscious development of the exploitative system. In later years, however, the infants that were born into the developed society had, of course, to take it as they found it. The social system determined their behavior *naturally*; that is to say, the racial exploitation and racial antagonisms seemed natural and the *conscious* element frequently did not exist. In other words, the racial fate of the individual was determined before he was born.

13 See a popular discussion relative to this by Hewlett Johnson, *The Soviet Power*, Book V; Bernhard J. Stern, "Soviet Policy on national Minorities," *American Sociological Review*, June 1944, pp. 229–35, and particularly Joseph Stalin, *Marxism and the National Question*.

14 *Warning to the West*, p. 274.

15 Pearl S. Buck likes to repeat the fact that "we differ in one important regard from the peoples of Asia. Race has never been a cause for any division among those people. But race prejudice divides us deeply." "The Spirit Behind the Weapon," *Survey Graphic*, Vol. XXXI, No. 11, November 1942, p. 540.

In a broad historical description of this process Leonard Woolf says: "In no other period of the world's history has there been such a vast revolution as the conquest of Asia and Africa by Europe. . . . Until very nearly the end of the nineteenth century, Europeans themselves regarded it with complacent pride as one of the chief blessings and glories of Western Civilization. The white race of Europe, they held, was physically, mentally, and morally superior to all other races; and God, with infinite wisdom and goodness, had created it and developed it so that it might be ready, during the reign of Queen Victoria in England, to take over and manage the affairs of all other people on earth and teach them to be, in so far as that was possible for natives and heathens, good Europeans and good Christians. Indeed, until the very end of the century, the natives and heathens themselves seemed to acquiesce in this view of the designs of providence and the blessings of being ruled by Europeans. It is true that in almost every case originally a considerable number of Africans and Asiatics had to be killed before the survivors were prepared to accept the domination or, as it was called, protection of the European State; but once the domination was established there were few revolts against European rule which could not be met with a punitive expedition." *Imperialism and Civilisation*, New York, 1928, pp.15–16.

16   And we should expect that all peoples of color will be gratified and inspired by this kind of accomplishment. It tends to restore their self-respect as nothing else can. "When the white man began his series of retreats before the yellow hordes," Krishnalal Shridharani writes, "it was soothing balm to the ancient wounds of Asia. More than any Japanese words the Japanese deeds made propaganda. The white man, the most hated creature in Asia, was put to flight at Hong Kong, in Malaya, in Burma, and above all at Singapore." *Warning to the West*, New York, 1942, p. 196.

Dr. Sun Yat-sen finds inspiration for all the colored peoples in Asia in the exploits of Japan. "Japan," he says, "is a good model for us, if we wish for prosperity of China. . . . Formerly it was thought that of all the people in the world only the whites were intelligent and gifted"; but today Japan has shown all this to be false and hope has returned to the peoples of Asia. *Le Triple Demisme*, French trans. By Pascal M. D'Elia, pp. 20–21.

One fairly widely read East Indian, P. S. Joshi, puts it in this way: "The whiteism steps an insane dance in all the continents of the world. There are in Asia only a handful of whites . . . . Still they have, by reason of their political might, introduced the colour bar in India, China, the Philippines and other countries. Had not Japan been triumphant over Russia, had not white prestige suffered a severe blow, the same colour bar would have spread . . . throughout the continent of Asia." *The Tyranny of Colour*, p. 4.

17   Raymond Kennedy emphasizes the point that in the belief of racial superiority the confidence in superior might is elemental. Thus he writes: "The European peoples were enabled, some four hundred years ago, to extend conquest over the entire 'native' world. The 'natives,' who were just as good, man for man, as the Europeans, lacked the superior material equipment of the latter, and were either slaughtered or subjugated. The possessors of guns came to believe that they were also possessors of superior racial endowments, and attributed their success not to material advantages, but to innate mental and physical superiority. They were white and the beaten peoples mostly black, brown, yellow, and red; consequently inferiority must be linked with color and race." *The Ageless Indies*, pp. 185–86. To the same effect see Leonard Woolf, op. cit, p. 12.

Lin Yutang puts the idea in his own way: "How did nineteenth century imperialism begin, and how did the white man go about conquering the world, and what made him think he was superior to other peoples? Because the white man had guns and the Asiatics had none. The matter was as simple as that." And he brings the argument up to date: "China will never . . . be accorded true equality until she is like Japan, twenty years from now, when she can build her own tanks and guns and battleships. When that time comes, there will be no need to argue about equality, such being the standards of the modern age." *Between Tears and Laughter*, pp. 21, 4.

18 In reporting on social conditions in China, Theodore H. White says: "No one can understand China today . . . who does not understand the hatred and bitterness of the intelligent Chinese for the foreign businessman who treated him like a coolie in his own land. In some cities this foreigner closed the public parks to Chinese; on some boats Chinese were not allowed to ride first-class." See "Life Looks at China," *Life*, May, 1, 1944, p. 100. See also Nathaniel Peffer, *The White Man's Dilemma*, Chap. IX.

Chapter 5

Robert Bernasconi

WHO INVENTED THE CONCEPT
OF RACE?

W HO INVENTED THE scientific concept of race? This question admits
of a variety of answers depending on what one takes to be decisive about
the concept and on whether one believes that what defines the moment in which
a technical term is introduced is the first usage of the word in the required sense
or the definition that secures its status and influence. It will quickly become clear
that by "the inventor of the concept of race" I mean the one who gave the concept
sufficient definition for subsequent users to believe that they were addressing
something whose scientific status could at least be debated. The terms and basis
of the definition might continue to be scrutinized, but, so long as the term was
being used only loosely, it made no sense to contest the concept. The invention
of the concept of race in this sense took place some time after the introduction
of the broad division of peoples on the basis of color, nationality, and other inherited
characteristics that could not be overcome subsequently, as religious differences
could be overcome by conversion.[1] One need only think of the purity of blood
statutes of fifteenth-century Spain that were used against the *conversos*, Jews who
had converted to Christianity but who were still not accepted. Then there were
the debates in sixteenth-century Spain when the opponents of Bartolomé de Las
Casas justified the mistreatment of Native Americans on the grounds that they
were not human. One can also look at the Atlantic trade in African slaves that
began in the sixteenth century and was already a large operation in the seventeenth
century. It was possible for the Spanish or the English to exploit Jews, Native
Americans, and Africans, as Jews, Native Americans, and Africans, without having
the concept of race, let alone being able to appeal to a rigorous system of racial
classification. We have no difficulty identifying these as cases of racism, but they
were not sustained by a scientific concept of race. However, the introduction of
that concept lent an air of apparent legitimacy to these practices. By investing the
concept of race with a scientific status, members of the academy certainly have in

the past contributed to making racism more respectable and have even seemed to provide a basis for it, but the academy of itself is now virtually powerless to undo those effects. However, we can at least try to throw some light on that history.

[. . .]

It is usually agreed that the term "race" was first used in something like its contemporary meaning at the end of the seventeenth century. Europeans had long been aware of the multiplicity of different peoples and had often embellished their sense of it with tales of fabulous monsters. Since the end of the fifteenth century, Europeans had been increasingly exposed to travel reports written by missionaries, traders and explorers that detailed some of the differences between peoples, although that was rarely their main focus of attention. On some occasions "specimens" were brought back by travellers to exhibit to the curious. However, in the sixteenth and seventeenth centuries, the primary issue raised by the diversity of peoples was theological and focused on the question of baptism.[2] It was not until the end of the seventeenth century that European scholars attempted to organize the mass of information now available to them and to sort the different peoples into a few groupings. In 1684 an anonymous essay, now usually attributed to François Bernier, acknowledged four or five different types. He did not give them all names, but they correspond roughly to Europeans, Africans, Orientals and Laplanders, while allowing for the possibility of two additional types, the Native Americans and the Hottentots. Within the first group, that included Europeans, he also placed Moroccans, Egyptians, and Indians. What made Bernier's classification so important retrospectively was not the list itself, but the fact that he employed the term "race" for the purpose. Nevertheless, his title, "A new division of the earth, according to the different species or races of men who inhabit it," with its equation of race and species, also indicates that the terminology was not yet fixed or precise.[3] The absence of any distinction between race and species is reflected in Leibniz's response to Bernier.

> I remember having read somewhere, but I cannot locate the passage again, that a certain traveler had divided humans into certain tribes, races, or classes. He gave one particular race to the Lapps and Samoyedes, another to the Chinese and neighboring peoples, another to Negroes, and still another to the Caffres, or Hottentots. Further, in America, there is a marvelous difference between the Galibs, or Caribs, who are very brave and indeed spirited, and the people of Paraguay, who seem to be children or novices all their lives. That does not prevent all human beings who inhabit the earth from being of the same race, which has been altered by different climates, just as we see that beasts and plants change their nature and improve or degenerate.[4]

The distinction between race and species that would preoccupy subsequent theorists, is here elided for lack of a clear terminology.
[. . .]
The idea of a single author of the concept of race is at best only a useful fiction, but I shall argue that, if any one person should be recognized as the author of the first theory of race worthy of the name, it should be the German philosopher Immanuel Kant. There is no shortage among Kant's writings of remarks that would

today unquestionably be characterized as racist. Although the most notorious comment is his remark in *Observations on the Feeling of the Beautiful and Sublime*, that the fact that someone as completely black from head to toe was clear proof that what he said was stupid,[5] it is, by no means the most problematic. Because I have discussed Kant's racism elsewhere,[6] I shall concentrate here on the philosophical motivation for his definition of race as a "class distinction between animals of one and the same line of descent (*Stamm*), which is unfailingly transmitted by inheritance" (AA VIII 100).

Kant expended more energy on securing the concept of race than one would ever guess from the secondary literature about him. In 1775 Kant published the first version of "Of the Different Human Races" (AA II 429–43) as the preliminary announcement for his lectures on *Physical Geography*.[7] Kant regularly lectured on Anthropology and on Physical Geography at the University of Königsberg. Both courses included discussions of race drawn from his own independent reading of the travelogues, which were still the main source of information for the natural scientists of his day. However, they did not provide the same level of theoretical discussion to be found in "Of the Different Human Races." Kant prefaced the first publication of the essay with a statement that the essay, like the lecture course it was advertising, was more like a game than profound investigation (AA II 429), but this warning was dropped when he expanded the essay for republication in 1777.[8] The two versions of this essay were in fact Kant's only publications between the 1770 inaugural lecture and the first edition of the *Critique of Pure Reason* in 1781. However, an even better guide to Kant's preoccupation with the concept of race is that he came to its defense during the 1780s, when he was completing the critical project. Even though "Of the Different Human Races" was reprinted again in 1783,[9] Kant published "Bestimmung des Begriffs einer Menschenrasse" in November 1785. In this essay Kant largely reiterates his earlier position. It is probable that he felt obliged to do so as a result of Herder's denial of race in the second part of his *Ideen zur Philosophie der Geschichte der Menschheit*, which had appeared in August of the same year. However, in 1786, under the title "Still More About the Human Races," Georg Forster attacked Kant's position. Georg Forster, who favored empirical science, challenged Kant's distinction between natural history and natural description, a distinction Kant had employed to justify giving a role to teleological explanation in science.[10] Georg Forster was better placed than most to marshall the information about the South Pacific which reached Europe in the second half of the eighteenth century through reports of the voyages of George Anson, Samuel Wallis, Phillip Carteret, Louis Antoine de Bougainville, and James Cook.[11] Georg Forster had accompanied his father on Captain Cook's voyage and assisted his father with the task of writing a report on the voyage.[12] It was small wonder therefore that Kant, in his reply early in 1788 in "On the Use of Teleological Principles in Philosophy," retreated from some of his empirical claims and turned to a discussion of method (AA VIII 157–84).[13] This essay, which was predominantly concerned with race, was not in any sense an interruption of the writing of his major philosophical works. Indeed, it appears that it was in the course of this controversy that Kant recognized that he needed to expand his Critique of Taste into what we now know as the *Critique of Judgment* by adding the second part on the Critique of Teleological Judgement.[14] A number of the most important questions posed in the course of the Critique of Teleological Judgment can be understood as suggested by issues Kant raised in his essay on race fifteen years earlier.

My claim about Kant's place in the construction of the scientific concept of race is not new. In the 1920s Walter Scheidt maintained that although Buffon was the first anthropologist, Kant was the originator of "the first theory of race which really merits the name."[15] There is no doubt that Scheidt had arrived at this conclusion after a careful study of the history of the concept, although perhaps because he was Director of the Rassenbiologische Institut of the Hanseatic University at Hamburg, there might have been suspicion that he had been misled by a desire to find support for the concept from such an exalted source. However, Kant's role in establishing the concept of race has been widely acknowledged by historians of the concept of race.[16] It is only philosophers who have ignored it, until Emmanuel Eze restated the argument for them.[17] Even so, a great deal more work needs to be done, both to establish the context of Kant's discussion of race with reference to his sources and to clarify the various aspects of Kant's theory of race that have been treated largely in isolation from each other. Before exploring Kant's theory, I will examine other possible candidates for the dubious honor of being the inventor of the concept of race.

The Swedish researcher, Carolus Linnaeus, certainly contributed to what would subsequently become race thinking in the twelve editions of his *Systema naturae sive regna tria naturae* that were published from 1735 until his death. Linnaeus was the first to include human beings within a formal classification of animals and plants. He included under the heading *homo sapiens* four geographical varieties, corresponding not only to the four regions of the world then recognized by Europeans, but also to the medieval theory of the four humors.[18] Although a great deal is sometimes made of the fact that they were not organized hierarchically, Linnaeus's descriptions included not only physical differences but also differences in character, clearly derived in large part from stereotypes already emerging in the travel literature. So one finds in the tenth edition of 1758, after the feral or wild man, the following classes: *homo americanus*, who was allegedly obstinate, content, free, and governed by habit; *homo Europaeus*, who was allegedly gentle, very acute, inventive and governed by customs or religious observances (*ritus*); *homo Asiaticus*, who was allegedly severe, haughty, covetous, and governed by opinions; and *homo Africanus*, who was allegedly crafty, indolent, negligent and governed by caprice.[19] However, although Linnaeus took great care in making his classifications and subjected them to constant revision, he made little attempt to clarify the status of the varieties thus differentiated. There was a tension in his works between his theoretical commitment to the constancy of species and the clear evidence to the contrary that was available to him.[20] The above list was followed by a record of *homo monstrosus* after whom Linnaeus proceeded to *homo troglodytes*. Linnaeus also appears to have been willing to try to accommodate in his *Systema natura* that for which he did not have clear evidence.[21]

From the outset, Buffon presented his theory as an alternative to that of Linnaeus. He began the publication of his *Histoire naturelle générale et particulière* in 1749 with a discussion of methodology that rejected the classifications of Linnaeus as arbitrary.[22] In spite of the fact that Buffon tended to disdain questions of classification and nomcenclature, it has sometimes been claimed that Buffon was the originator of the concept of race.[23] The importance of Buffon's definition of species and the means by which he secured it is undeniable. To Buffon, a species was "a constant succession of similar individuals that can reproduce together" (HN IV 384–5). The definition, presented in his essay on the ass from 1753, was widely disseminated, so that, for example, it is quoted verbatim in Diderot's *Encyclopédie*.[24] The definition was accompanied by an account of how one separates one species from another: the mark of separation lay where a pair of individuals are unable to reproduce with each other across successive generations. Often known as Buffon's rule, it seems to have been expounded by John Ray in the seventeenth century.[25] According to Buffon, species were fixed and constant, although he did concede that the general prototype that was found in the first individual and that was imprinted in all subsequent individuals left some room for variation (HN IV 215–16). This variation was represented by the various types, breeds, or races, but those terms themselves remained without clear definition.[26]

The argument that Buffon introduced a determinate concept of race is hampered by his failure not only to propose a definition of race as he did of species, but also to use the term with any consistency. The best evidence that he was working toward a precise notion of race is to be found in "On the Degeneration of Animals" where, in 1766, Buffon indicated that quasi-permanent change from an original stock could take place as a result of climate, geography and especially food. In this context Buffon came to acknowledge "constant and general characters by which one recognizes the races and even the different nations which compose the human genus" (HN XIV 316). However, this formulation is not as decisive as it might appear to be. In 1753 in his essay on "The Ass," Buffon had already applied his rule and the notion of degeneration to the variations within the human species. There he had focused on the differences between Blacks and Whites, Laplanders and Patagonians, but the addition of Giants and Dwarfs to the list, as well as mention of the enormous legs of certain people in Ceylon and the occurrence of six fingers and toes in certain families, shows that he did not consider that his framework was sufficient to establish a new category (HN IV 387–9). Indeed, he explicitly warned against doing so. Having identified the difference between two species on the basis that they cannot give rise to a succession of individuals that can mix, he added:

> This is the most fixed point that we have in Natural History; all other resemblances and differences that we can grasp in the comparison of beings, are neither so constant, real, nor certain. These intervals are also the sole lines of separation that one will find in our work. We shall not divide beings otherwise than they are in fact. Each species, each succession of individuals which reproduce and cannot mix will be considered apart and treated separately, and we shall not use families, kinds, orders and classes which are set by Nature. (HN IV 385–6)

Even after 1766 Buffon demonstrated no clear commitment to the terminology of race, still less an interest in clarifying its theoretical status.

A word should also be said about Blumenbach's claim to being the originator of the anthropological concept of race.[27] Although his name is often mentioned in this regard, Kant's credentials over against Blumenbach are easily secured. Kant's first essay on race, "Of the Different Human Races," was published in 1775, some months before Johann Friedrich Blumenbach submitted *De generis humani varietate nativa* as his dissertation for the doctorate in medicine to the University of Göttingen at the age of twenty-three.[28] Furthermore, one needs to attend to the history of the publication of Blumenbach's treatise. It was twice republished, in 1781 and 1795, but the revisions between the first and second editions were extensive and those between the second and third were such that the latter is better thought of as a new book, albeit published under the tame title. All three editions were written in Latin, and it was not until the third edition, which was the first to be translated into German, that the terms *gens* and *gentilitius* began to predominate in a way that suggests that Blumenbach had begun to develop a concept of race. In the first edition he had relied almost exclusively on the same general term that had been used by Linnaeus: *varietas*.[29] Furthermore, while it is true that Blumenbach's system of classification was more complex than Kant's, which was based almost solely on color, in the first edition Blumenbach did not include any theoretical reflection on the status of these varieties, other than to say that the different human varieties run into each other so that no definite limits can be drawn between them (GHV1 40–1; NVM 98–9), a position he repeated in the third edition (GHV3 285 and 322; NV 203–4 and 224; NVM 264 and 275). Indeed in his *Handbuch der Naturgeschichte* Blumeubach excitly acknowledges that Kant was the first to distinguish precisely races and varieties.[30] By setting out clearly the distinction between race and variety, where races are marked by hereditary characteristics that are unavoidable in the offspring, whereat the distinguishing marks of varieties are not always transmitted, Kant introduced a language for articulating permanent differentiations within the notion of species (AA VIII 180n). Buffon had not argued for a clear distinction along these lines because he was not concerned with organizing in a systematic way the raw data provided by travellers.

Another indication of Blumenbach's relation to Kant can be found in the former's defense of color as a way of differentiating the races. From the outset Kant relied almost exclusively on color for his classification of the races, even though this led to severe difficulties. Already in 1775, the year of Kant's first essay on race, it was becoming clear that the appeal to color as a criterion could not be sustained without anomalies. For example, in that year, John Hunter of Edinburgh included under the label "light brown," Southern Europeans, Sicilians, Abyssinians, the Spanish, Turks, and Laplanders, and under the label "brown," Tartars, Persians, Africans on the Mediterranean, and the Chinese.[31] In 1786 Forster directly challenged Kant's appeal to color by presenting him with the case of two people of two different races having a child that was the same color as both the parents.[32] Color was simply not a viable indicator. It is ironic that at the very time that Kant was giving the concept of race intellectual coherence, his criterion for distinguishing the different races was collapsing. And yet it is some measure of the growing proximity of Kant and Blumenbach that, although in 1775 Blumenbach had dismissed color as an indicator of human varieties, on the grounds that so many additional factors contribute to the differences (GHV1 50–7; NVM 107–13), some twenty years later, with specific references to Kant's 1785 and 1788 essays on race, he granted that color is the most constant character of the human varieties (GHV3 114–15; NV 91; NVM 207).

Some commentators have made much of Kant's own acknowledgment of his debt to Blumenbach, but the balance of the debt goes in the other direction, as I shall show later. It is not usually noticed that in his essay on teleology, which is one of the places where Kant praised Blumenbach's notion of a formative drive or *Bildungstrieb* (AA VIII 180n), Kant also argued for a distinction between "race" and "variety" (AA VIII 163–5). Kant again acknowledged the importance of the notion of *Bildungstrieb* in the *Critique of Judgment* but in the context of showing Blumenbach's conformity with Kant's longstanding attempt to unite the teleological and mechanical frameworks (AA V 42).[33] The growing proximity of Kant and Blumenbach is confirmed by Christoph Girtanner's *Über das Kantische Prinzip für die Naturgeschichte* of 1796.[34] Girtanner dedicated his book on race to Blumenbach, with whom he had studied from 1780 to 1782, and in his *Anthropology* Kant endorsed Girtanner's book as "in keeping with my principles" (AA VII 320). Not only is Kant's chronological primacy secured, but so is the importance of his theoretical contribution, even if it was Blumenbach and the Göttingen school who, by undertaking empirical research, such as the measurement of skulls, set the tone for nineteenth-century research in Germany not just for the science of race but the biological sciences generally. Unlike Kant, Blumenbach did not base his account on Buffon's rule of fertile progeny, which he recognized as an entirely impractical criterion for scientists to have to utilize, condemning them to endless attempts to persuade different types from different parts of the world to copulate (GHV3 67–9; NV 59–60; NVM 188–9). Blumenbach relied on morphological considerations and the application of a revised version of Buffon's notion of degeneration. However, it was through Blumenbach that Kant's concept of race came to have an impact on the larger scientific community. Kant's writings on race seem to have disappeared from view until the advent of Darwinism reopened some of the theoretical issues, and interest in them was revived.[35]

[. . .]

Buffon was a particularly important figure in the debate against polygenesis not only because he was an unambiguous supporter of the claim that there was only one human species (HN III 529–30), but especially because his "rule" appeared to provide scientific support for this claim. Buffon had argued that any two animals that can procreate together are of the same species, if their issue can also procreate. Following this rule it was clear that all dogs were of the same species, but that a horse and an ass were not because their issue, a mule, cannot procreate. The fact that all human beings, however different they are, are able to procreate and have fertile offspring, led Buffon to the conclusion that they all belong to the same species. It is a testimony to Buffon's importance that Henry Home, Lord Kames, defended polygenesis largely by attacking Buffon.

Kames introduced his *Sketches of the History of Man* by asking "whether all men be of one lineage, descended from a single pair, or whether there be different races originally distinct."[36] It quickly became clear that Kames favored the second alternative. Kames even had some fun at Buffon's expense with the latter's notion of degeneration. According to Kames, people degenerate in a climate to which they are not suited by nature, except around Charleston where Europeans die so fast from the heat that they do not have time to degenerate (SHM. I 11). However,

Kames's serious point was that people do not adapt to a new climate, but that different races are fitted by nature for different climates (SHM I 10). Hence Kames posed the following question to Buffon:

> But is he seriously of opinion, that any operation of climate, or of other accidental cause, can account for the copper colour and smooch chin universal among the Americans, the prominence of the *pudenda* universal among Hottentot women, or the black nipple no less universal among female Samoides? (SHM 112)

Although Kames seems to have had little doubt as to the conclusion that should be drawn from the evidence, he was reluctant to express it directly, placing it in quotation marks so as to avoid having to take full responsibility for it:

> That God created many pairs of the human race, differing from each other both externally and internally; that he fitted these pairs for different climates, and placed each pair in its proper climate; that the peculiarities of the original pairs were preserved entire in their descendants. (SHM I 38–9)

That the Biblical account of the creation of a single pair is "not a little puzzling" was as much as he was willing to say outright at the outset. Later in the book he returned to the topic that had occupied La Peyrère and argued for the separate origin of the American Nations (SHM II 70–2). However, even here, in an effort to assuage believers in the Biblical account, he proposed a way of reconciling his account with theirs:

> supposing the human race to have been planted in America by the hand of God later than the days of Moses, Adam and Eve might have been the first parents of mankind, i.e. of all who at that time existed, without being the first parents of the Americans. (SHM II 75)

Voltaire, by contrast, not only contested the Biblical account openly. His opposition to the Bible seems to have been one of his main reasons for adopting polygenesis.

In his adherence to polygenesis, Voltaire was more concerned with polemic than with argument. In his *Essai sur les moeurs et de l'esprit des nations* he was satisfied with the claim that "only the blind could doubt that the Whites, the Blacks, the Albinos, the Hottentots, the Laplanders, the Chinese, the Americans, are entirely different races."[37] This was not meant as an exhaustive list. Voltaire was also open to the possibility of further types that had disappeared. Elsewhere, albeit in a text that was first published posthumously in 1784, Voltaire was even more direct in declaring that "bearded Whites, wooly haired Blacks, yellow-skinned peoples with their long manes, and beardless men do not come from the same man."[38] However, Voltaire, who had been a leading advocate of the importance of Indian and especially Chinese civilization, was critical of Africa. He offered a hierarchical model in which Blacks were not only not at the highest level, but adding insult to injury, placed explicitly above "apes and oysters."[39]

Kant's 1775 essay on race included an attack on the theory of "local creations" in the context of which Voltaire was mentioned explicitly (AA II 440; IR 19).[40] Kant's interest in defending monogenesis emerged in other writings also. In January 1786, Kant published "Speculative Beginning of Human History" in which he argued that the speculation of philosophy about the first beginnings coincided with the account to be found in Genesis, including the fact of a single original pair (AA VIII 110).[41] Two years later, Kant returned to the issue when Georg Forster revived the theory of "local creations."[42] Fully aware that polygenesis was deprived of the rhetoric of human brotherhood as a tool to combat racism, Forster simply responded: "Let me ask whether the thought that Blacks are our brothers has ever anywhere even once abated the raised whip of the slave driver was put away."[43] Although polygenesis lent itself to those who wanted to defend the enslavement of Africans, one cannot establish a correlation between these two positions.[44] Although it is significant that the concept of race was given precision in an effort to combat polygenesis, that does not constitute an ethical defence of the concept, any more than La Peyrère's good intentions in introducing Preadamism are relevant to assessing its merits. However, it does alert us to the complexity of the issues being discussed.

The fact that the scientific concept of race was developed initially in Germany rather than in Britain or America suggests that it was not specifically the interests of the slaveowners that led to its introduction, but rather, as Kant's essays themselves confirm, an interest in classification and above all the attempt to provide a theoretical defense of monogenesis.[45] The appeal of monogenesis in large measure lay in its conformity to the Biblical account, but it also lent itself to discussions of "human fraternity," so that within the context of the late eighteenth century the idea of race was a resource for those who opposed slavery, just as polygenesis lent itself to the upholders of slavery, without there being any necessary connection between one's position on the monogenesis-polygenesis dispute and one's position on slavery. Nevertheless, none of this means that there was not a strong connection between the concept of race and racism. What the natural historians and philosophers in Europe knew about the different human varieties or races came from travel reports that were increasingly being written with an eye to the debate over slavery.

[. . .]

Already in "Of the Different Human Races," Kant was concerned with the kind of causality that produced the races. Kant proposed a review of the entire human genus over the whole earth with a view to finding either the natural or the purposive causes of the various deviations, depending simply on whichever kind of cause was most readily discernible (AA II 435; DHR 14). More specifically, Kant attempted to explain differences in skin color, as this was the basis on which he distinguished the four fundamental races: Whites, Blacks, Hindustanic, and Kalmuck. Kant's explanation of the production of these differences was in terms of the effects of air and sun, but he argued that these developments must have been preformed and could not be understood as simply a product either of chance or the application of mechanical laws alone. Kant argued that by the solicitude of nature, human beings were equipped with seeds (*Keime*) and natural predispositions (*Anlagen*) that were developed or held back depending on climate (AA II 434–5; DHR 13–14).

That is to say, the seeds of the races were latent from the start in everyone, and the appropriate seed was actualized to serve a purpose that arose from the circumstances. The thrust of Kant's account, therefore, was to support the use of teleology within biology as opposed to providing merely mechanical explanations, as had become the tendency. Mechanical explanations would allow for the effects of climate to produce further changes in species or parts of the species. This was a possibility Kant rejected, just as he rejected all evolutionary theories. Such changes that had occurred were all preformed. They we also irreversible.

Although Kant had already indicated in 1775 that race is an ex-speciation which cannot return to the original stem, it was only in 1777 that he made absolutely clear that the races, once formed resist further remodeling (AA II 442; DHR 21). This was crucial. He emphasized the same point in the 1785 essay (AA VIII 105) and again 1788 (AA VIII 166). Race cannot be undone by further differences in climate. It is permanent. Whichever germ was actualized by the conditions, the other germs would retire into inactivity.[46] It was also in 1777 that Kant first identified the stem genus as White (AA II 441; DHR 20). Buffon had already argued in 1749 that "White appears to be the primitive color of Nature" (HN III 502).[47] However, Kant was not rehearsing Buffon's argument which relied on the claim that Blacks can have White children but that the reverse cannot happen. Kant did not concede until 1785 that, because it is now impossible to reproduce the original stock, we will never be able to tell for sure what it was like (AA VIII 82). See also (AA V 420; CJ 306).

In appealing to the idea of "pre-existing seeds" Kant was adopting a view that had arisen in the seventeenth century under the influence of Malebranche and that came to be associated with certain works of Charles Bonnet in the early 1760s.[48] Buffon had explicitly rejected the language of germs when he dismissed attempts to refer generation back to God, on the grounds that they placed it beyond the reach of human investigation (HN II 32–3). However, it can be argued that both Bonnet and Buffon were trying to solve the same problem that faced all mechanical theories of generation of how a complex order could be created from an originally chaotic arrangement of particles. Indeed, Buffon's appeal, in his essay on the horse, to the idea of a general prototype of every species that is found in the first of its kind, which in turn acts as an external model and internal mold of all the individuals of the species (HN IV 215–16), was not so distant from Bonnet.[49] Kant's introduction of Bonnet's vocabulary in an essay whose main framework was formed by Buffon was not therefore as extraordinary as it might otherwise appear. Nevertheless, no reader of Kant could underestimate the significance of the fact that he replaced Buffon's simply mechanical explanation of the diversity of human types with an account that appealed to teleological causes.[50]

[. . .]

Early discussions of the various human types were by no means always focused on Africans. A great deal of attention and animosity was reserved for Lapps and often Native Americans were placed below all the other types. However, insofar as color was regarded as the most striking characteristic differentiating the various types and insofar as Whites considered themselves clearly superior to everyone else, then one obvious way of organizing these types hierarchically that occurred to Europeans was from white to black.[51] Even before the last quarter of the eighteenth century, which was when the proslavery faction became directly involved in providing descriptions of Africa that served their cause, European travellers to Africa were only too happy to support this growing prejudice again Africans by exaggerating what they observed in an effort to gain the public's attention.[52] The blackness of Africans was not only a subject of theoretical speculation, it became the characteristic around which all the prejudices against Africans were gathered. Already in 1728 Ephraim Chambers wrote: "The origin of *Negroe's* [sic], and the cause of that remarkable difference in complexion from the rest of mankind, has much perplexed the naturalists; nor has any thing satisfactory been yet offered in that head."[53] That it had been possible at one time to pose the question without any hint of the prejudice with which it subsequently became infused can be illustrated by turning to Sir Thomas Browne. When he explored the question "Of the Blackness of Negroes," it was a strictly theoretical inquiry, and even if he did not go so far as to ask why Whites were white, in the course of dismissing the account of the "curse of Ham," he did not neglect to ask why observers would consider it a curse to be that color.[54] For Browne it was quite clear that beauty could not "reasonably" be associated with one color over another, as beauty is determined by what custom leads one to regard as natural: "And by this consideration of Beauty, the Moors also are not excluded, but hold a common share with all mankind."[55] The praise that is sometimes lavished on Kant for having come to a similar insight is for that reason not fully deserved (AA V 234; CJ 82).[56] He was repeating a standard observation of the time, but it is noteworthy that the emphasis is no longer, as in Bernier, that there are beautiful women everywhere, but that each culture has its own idea of what constituted human beauty.

The problem, of why Blacks were black, obsessed scientists throughout the eighteenth century. Some anatomists sought and sometimes claimed to find a physiological explanation, such as black bile.[57] Although most natural scientists were inclined to include some environmental explanation in terms of air, food, or climate, not least because it could easily be reconciled with a belief in Adam as the source of all mankind,[58] on its own this ran counter to the evidence that skin color was transmitted largely unchanged across generations. Buffon favored the environmental explanation of color but he was unusual in being prepared to draw the consequences. He insisted in 1749 that if Africans were brought North their skin color would lighten, albeit slowly and that possibly they would end up as white as northerners (HN III 523–4). In his essay "On the Degeneration of Animals" Buffon even described a possible experiment to establish this. He proposed transporting some Blacks from Senegal to Denmark, the country of white skin, blonde hair and blue eyes. If the Blacks were enclosed "with their women" and all possibility of crossbreeding excluded, he suggested that we would learn how long it would take to "reintegrate (*réintégrer*) in this respect the nature of man" (HN XIV 314). The term "reintegrate," of course, had its source in Buffon's belief that white was the original color. A similar question arose in the course of Kant's debate with Forster. Kant held that one showed one's "true" color only in a mild climate: "one can more correctly judge in France the color of a Negro, who has lived there a long time, or better still was born there, insofar as that determines his or her class distinction from other men, than one can judge it in the fatherland of the Blacks" (AA VIII 92). Indeed, Kant claimed that the true color of the South Sea Islanders was not yet known for certain and would not be until one of them was born in Europe (AA VIII 92), a proposition to which Georg Forster, who had taken the trouble to travel to the South Pacific, objected strongly.[59] However, one important characteristic of Kant's theory is that he excluded the possibility of any such reintegration as described by Buffon. This was a decisive difference because it established the distinction between, on the one hand, race as a permanent characteristic that is unfailingly inherited and, on the other hand, characteristics, such as hair color, sickness or deformity, for which there was only a tendency to hereditary transmission (AA VIII 93–4). It was this distinction that in "On the Use of Teleological Principles in Philosophy" was redrawn as a distinction between race and variety, thereby challenging Blumenbach to introduce a similar distinction, as noted earlier (AA VIII 180n).

Kant speculated about the physical basis for blackness, appealing to iron particles in 1777 (AA II 440) and to phlogiston in 1785 (AA VIII 103). But the most important consequence of Kant's interest in the question of the color of Africans was that it seems to have kept him focused on the question of the adequacy of mechanistic explanations offered in isolation from teleology. In Kant's first essay on race the purposive nature of racial (which meant for him color) differences was assumed but not argued on the basis that because neither chance nor mechanical laws could have brought about the developments that enabled organic bodies to adapt to the climates into which they first moved, those developments must be construed as preformed (AA II 435; DHR 14). He was more direct in the 1785 essay when he wrote that the purposive nature of color was visible in the Negro race (AA VIII 103).[60] However, for the other races, Kant was obliged simply to assume that color was purposive. And yet it was from the presence of purposiveness that Kant inferred the existence of seeds (AA VIII 102). The blackness of Blacks provided Kant with one of his most powerful illustrations of purposiveness within the biological sphere. But perhaps it worked as a powerful example among his White audience because it addressed their fascination with the fact of Blackness.

However, the issue in "On the Use of Teleological Principles in Philosophy," as in the second part of the Critique of Judgment, is a much larger one and it arises in relation to a new point of contact between Kant and Blumenbach. What brought Kant and Blumenbach together was Kant's recognition that in his notion of Bildungatrieb or formative drive, Blumenbach had gone beyond natural description and an account of mechanical forces to posit a teleology in nature. Like his book on human varieties, Blumenbach's essay on the Bildungstrieb appeared in three very different versions. The first, published in 1780, was barely twenty pages.[61] The following year it was expanded into a treatise of some 87 pages.[62] In 1789, Blumenbach published a text of 116 pages on the Bildungstrieb that was reprinted two years later.[63] Blumenbach had discovered the Bildungstrieb while conducting some experiments on polyps while on holiday. He found that if their arms or tentacles were cut off, they would grow again within a few days, albeit they would be smaller (B3 28–9). On this basis he came to posit in the unformed generative matter of organized bodies a lifelong drive that initially takes on a determinate form, maintains it lifelong, and reproduces itself where possible, if it is in any way mutilated (B3 31).

Because Blumenbach's essay was an attack on Haller's conception of preformed seeds, it appears to be in stark contrast with Kant's theory of race, which also appeals to seeds. However, the appearance is somewhat deceptive.[64] Blumenbach's argument against preformed seeds was based on the existence of hybrids. Indeed, in the 1781 edition, Blumenbach even appealed to the fact that the mixing of pure varieties, such as Blacks and Whites, produces mulattoes and blendings (B2 60), an example which lay at the heart of Kant's reflections on race. The theory of seeds that Blumenbach is attacking is the same as that found in the theory of evolution that Kant rejects in section 81 of the Third Critique. Indeed, if Kant ends that section by applauding Blumenbach's account of the *Bildungstrieb*, he has done much more than take over this notion from Blumenbach (AAV 424; CJ 311). The whole way Kant frames the issue as a question of the advantages of the theory of epigenesis over that of evolution was taken from Blumenbach (B3 13–14)1.[65] I judge Kant to have been quite genuine in his praise for Blumenbach when in 1790 he wrote to thank Blumenbach for sending him *Über den Bildungstrieb* (B3) in which Blumenbach's combination of the physico-mechanical principle of explicating organic nature was in line with his own recent work (AA XI 185).[66] It is worth noting that although Blumenbach had only recently arrived at the theory of epigenesis, Kant had long maintained it, as is reflected in the *Critique of Pure Reason*.[67] The transformation of Blumenbach's philosophy of science in the ten years after 1788 was largely toward a form of Kantianism.[68] However, Kant preferred to emphasize the conformity of his views with those of Blumenbach, because Blumenbach brought to Kant a scientific legitimacy that Kant was unable to provide on his own account. The advantage to Kant is nowhere clearer than in Blumenbach's adoption of the Kantian language of race. Even though it is far from clear that Blumenbach fully recognized the status Kant gave to the concept of race, which is one of the subjects of the next section, he came to frame his discussion of human varieties, like Kant, in terms of the conjunction of the physico-mechanical and teleological principles (GHV3 82–3; NV 69; NVM 194).

[. . .]

That Kant's three essays on race are important sources for understanding the genesis of the *Critique of Judgment* has been recognized by a number of Kant scholars.[69] Indeed, Girtanner, Kant's contemporary, already saw the relevance of the *Critique of Judgment* for Kant's discussions of race.[70] Kant seems to have decided to address the vexed problem of the grouping of species by taking the model he had developed in his investigation of race and extending it to cover broader groupings of species.[71] In drawing on this model Kant not only described how creatures of a less purposive form gave birth to others "better adapted to their place of origin" (AA V 419; CJ 305), thereby recalling the way climate served to develop the races, he also returned to the language of "predisposition": "nothing is to be taken up into the generative force that does not already belong to one of the being's undeveloped original predispositions" (AA5 420; CJ 306). For Kant, when certain individuals undergo accidental change leading to the altered character being taken up into the generative force (*Erzeugungskraft*) and thereby becoming hereditary, this has to be judged as the development of a purposive predisposition already in the species for the sake of its preservation:

> If we find that the altered character of these individuals becomes
> hereditary and is taken up into their generative force, then the only
> proper way to judge it is as the development, on [a given] occasion,
> of a purposive predisposition that was originally present in the species
> and that serves the preservation of the kind (*Art*). (AA V 420; CJ
> 305–6)[72]

This sentence so clearly evokes what Kant had said about racial differences that it is no surprise to find one English translator introducing "race" as a translation of *Art* in the last sentence.[73] If Kant did not mention "race" explicitly in the second half of the *Critique of Judgment*, it is perhaps because he knew from his debate with Herder how controversial it still was and that it might interfere with the general acceptance of his theory.

Herder's polemic against Kant in his *Ideas on the Philosophy of the History of Humankind* and Kant's response in his reviews of the first two parts of Herder's book came to a head around the notion of race. Although an opponent of polygenesis,[74] Herder, who had attended Kant's lectures on *Physical Geography* in which the concept of race had been championed, explicitly denied the reality of race: "there are neither four nor five races, nor are there exclusive varieties on earth."[75] Herder's questioning of race did not stop him, for example, from citing Camper's studies on the angle of the head which places the head of Africans and Kalmucks closer to apes than Europeans, and which allegedly was Nature's means of discriminating the varieties of creation as they approximate to the most perfect form of beauty in human beings (IGM 134–35). But Herder believed that the language of race was divisive. He opened his criticism of the concept of race in these terms:

> Nature has provided for each kind and given each one its own inheritance.
> She has distributed the apes in as many species and varieties and spread
> them out as far as she could spread them; you human, however, should
> honour yourself. Neither the pongo nor the gibbon is your brother,
> whereas the American and the Negro certainly are. You should not
> oppress him, nor murder him, nor steal from him; for he is a human
> being just as you are: you may not enter into fraternity with the apes.
> (IGM 255; PH 25–6)

Herder understood peoples as the fundamental units of history and, although he primarily conceived of them in cultural terms, their biological basis was retained in his works, as when he wrote of "the original root-character of a nation" (*die ursprungliche Stammgebilde der Nation*) (IGM 255–6; PH 26). Whereas Kant was among those who advocated a division into only four or five kinds, Herder advocated recognition of the diversity of human peoples; whereas Kant focused on color divisions, Herder saw continuity: "the colors run into one another" (IGM 256; PH 26). Like Blumenbach, Herder believed that if we only knew more about the different peoples, we could perhaps complete the shadings of the portraits of these peoples without finding a single break (IGM 231).[76] Whereas Kant regarded the division of races as permanent, according to Herder, "the characters of peoples are gradually extinguished in the general run of things" (IGM 685).

Herder disagreed with Kant on the role the latter gave to seeds. Herder in the first part of the *Ideas* complained: "No eye has ever seen these preformed seeds, lying ready ever since the creation; what we observe from the first moment of a creature's genesis are effective *organic powers*" (IGM 171). In his anonymous review of the first part of Herder's *Ideas* Kant merely noted this difference and attacked Herder as the one who was explaining the obscure by the more obscure (AA VIII 48 and 53–4; OH 31 and 37). In his review of the second part of the *Ideas*, in which Herder had denied race explicitly, Kant took up the argument more directly. Herder had acknowledged that the inner vital principle modifies itself according to variations in external conditions, most notably climate. Kant proposed that if these adaptations were limited to a certain number of variations and were such that, once established, they could no longer revert to the original form or change into another type, then it would be legitimate to reintroduce the contested language of seeds and original dispositions (AA VIII 62; OH 48). In this way Kant attempted to persuade Herder that his objections to the notion of seeds applied to an account of seeds that was not Kant's own and that Herder could readily accommodate Kant's conception, properly understood. However, it might seem Kant did not have a good response for Herder's accusation that the seeds were somewhat mysterious. Kant described them as limitations that cannot be rendered comprehensible (AA VIII 62–3; OH 68).

That is why, when Kant referred Herder's hostility to classification based on hereditary colorization to Herder's not yet having "clearly determined the concept of a race" (AA VIII 62; OH 47), something more was at stake than the conception of seeds. At issue was the conception of scientific investigation that afforded them a status. In the *Critique of Pure Reason* Kant distinguished those people who assume that there are certain hereditary characteristics in each nation and race and those who insist that in all such cases nature made the same provision for all and that such differences that one does find are due to external and accidental conditions (KrV A667, B695). Kant negotiated the two positions by granting that we cannot speak from insight into the nature of the objects concerned. He made clear, however, that looking for order in nature, such as Leibniz and Bonnet did in proposing what came to be known as the chain of being, is a legitimate and excellent regulative principle of reason (KrV A668; B696). This same insight governed all Kant's writings on race and is most clearly expressed in his observation that the word *variety*, but not the word *race*, belongs to the description of nature and that nevertheless an observer of nature finds the word *race* necessary from the viewpoint of natural history (AAVIII 163). This is what underlies Kant's crucial explanation of the status of the concept of race, whereby it corresponds to nothing in the world, but nevertheless is "necessary from the viewpoint of natural history":

> What is a *race?* The word certainly does not belong in a systematic description of nature, so presumably the thing itself is nowhere to be found in nature. However, the *concept* which this expression designates is nevertheless well established in the reason of every observer of nature who supposes a conjunction of causes placed originally in the line of descent of the genus itself in order to account for a self-transmitted

peculiarity that appears in different interbreeding animals but which does not lie in the concept of their genus. (AA VIII 163)[77]

A similar insight at a more general level can be found in the *Critique of Judgment*. If one applies what Kant says about regulative concepts in the *Critique of Judgment* to his discussions of race, then Kant is saying that in the present state of our knowledge the idea of race imposes itself. It is also what underlies his observations in notes written when preparing his response to Forster, which read: "to accept that any part of a creature which adheres constantly to the species is without purpose is just like accepting that an event in the world has arisen without a cause" (AA XXIII 75). As Kant understood it, racial differences called for a purposive account.[78] To this extent, Kant was right to say that Herder had not yet clearly understood what he meant by the concept of race. Nevertheless, Herder's debate with Kant about race for all of its misunderstandings was a philosophical debate that shows that the concept had finally reached sufficient precision in Kant to allow one to say he brought it to fruition.

The scientific concept of race underwent many changes after Kant introduced it. At times the reality of race was not in question. Race was a given. However, now that the reality of race is being questioned by Appiah on the grounds that it is no longer in conformity with our best scientific knowledge, one must still ask whether we call do without it. In response to Appiah, Lucius Outlaw has argued, "As we struggle to realize social justice with harmony in America, given this nation's history of race relations, we are unable to do away with the notion of 'race.'"[79] When he writes that we cannot do away with the notion of race, Outlaw seems to be proposing an argument about strategy within a particular context, rather than a Kantian style argument about whether or not race still imposes itself on us according to some regulative principle of reason. But if we acknowledge, as Appiah does, that our current ways of talking about race are the residue of earlier views, then it is prudent to develop a deeper understanding of the history of race thinking as well as of racial practices.[80]

Notes

1   See Richard Popkin, "The Philosophical Bases for Modern Racism," *The High Road to Pyrrhonism*, San Diego, Austin Hill Press, 1980, pp. 79–102.

2   For example, Lewis Hanke, *Aristotle and the American Indians*, Bloomington, Indiana University Press, 1959, esp. pp. 44–73. John Locke, *An Essay concerning Human Understanding*, Oxford, Oxford University Press, 1975, pp. 454–5. See Robert Bernasconi, "Locke's Almost Random Talk of Man: The Double Use of Words in the Natural Law Justification of Slavery," *Perspektiven der Philosophie*, 18, 1992, pp. 293–318.

3   Anon. "Nouvelle division de la Terre, par les differentes Especes on Races d'hommes qui l'habitent, envoyée par on fameux Voyageur à Monsieur *****[sic] à peu prés en ces termes," *Journal des scavans*, Monday 24 April, 1684, pp. 148–55; trans. "A new division of the earth, according to the different species or races of men who inhabit it, sent by a famous traveller to Mons. , [sic] nearly in these terms," in T. Bendyshe, "The History of Anthropology," Appendix 1, in *Memoirs Read before the Anthropological Society of London*, vol. 1, 1863–64, pp. 360–4. Bendyshe's translation has now been reprinted

in *The Idea of Race*, eds. Robert Bernasconi and Tommy Lott, Indianapolis, Hackett, 2000, pp. 1–4.

4   G. W. Leibniz, *Otium Hanoverium sive Miscellanea*, 2nd ed., Leipzig, Christian Martin, 1737, pp. 37–8. That the essay attributed to Bernier is meant is confirmed at *Miscellanea*, pp. 158–9.

5   Kant, *Beobachtungen über das Gefühl des Schönen und Erhabenen, Gesammelte Schriften*, Berlin, de Gruyter, 1902, vol. II, p. 255; trans. John T. Goldthwait, *Observations on the Feeling of the Beautiful and Sublime*, Berkeley, University of California Press, 1973, p. 113. Whenever possible German reference will be to the Akademie Ausgabe, abbreviated as AA followed by the volume number. On Kant's "witticism" see Ronald A. T. Judy, *(Dis)forming the American Canon*, Minneapolis, University of Minnesota Press, 1993, esp. pp. 108–17.

6   Robert Bernasconi, "Kant as an Unfamiliar Source of Racism," in *Philosophers on Race*, eds. T. Lott and J. Ward, Oxford, Blackwell, forthcoming.

7   Two very different editions of the *Physische Geographie* were published in Kant's lifetime: the authorized version in two volumes edited by Friedrich Theodor Rink and published by Gobbels and Unzer in Königsberg in 1802 has formed the basis of all subsequent editions, but the unauthorized edition in four volumes published by Gottfried Bollmer of Mainz and Hamburg between 1801 and 1805 remains a largely neglected source of information about Kant's extensive knowledge of the travel literature of his day.

8   This version can now be found in a new translation by Jon Mark Mikkelsen in *The Idea of Race*, pp. 8–22. Henceforth DHR.

9   I. Kant, "Von der verschiedenen Racen der Menschen," *Der Philosoph für die Welt*, ed. J. J. Engel, Reuttlingen, Joh. Georg Fleischhauer, 1783, Part 2, pp. 100–31. The Akadamie Ausgabe does not list this edition, which my cursory examination suggests is an unchanged version of the 1777 text.

10   Georg Forster, "Noch etwas über die Menschenrassen," Werke 8, ed. Siegfried Scheibe, Berlin, Akademie Verlag, 1991, pp. 142–3.

11   See P. J. Marshall and G. Williams, *The Great Map of Mankind*, Cambridge, Harvard University Press, 1982, pp. 258–98.

12   Johann Reinhold Forster, *Observations made during a Voyage round the World*, eds. Nicholas Thomas et al., Honolulu, University of Hawaii Press, 1996. On Georg Forster's role in the book, see Thomas P. Saine, Georg Forster, New York, Twayne Publishers, 1972, p. 24.

13   An English translation by Jon Mark Mikkelsen is given in chapter 2. Because references to the Academy edition are given in parentheses within the main body of the translation, I have not included references to the translation in this paper.

14   See F. C. Beiser, *The Fate of Reason. German Philosophy from Kant to Fichte*, Cambridge, Harvard University Press, 1987, p. 155.

15   Walter Scheidt, "Beiträge zur Geschichte der Anthropologie. Der Begriff der Rasse in der Anthropologie und die Einteilung der Menschenrassen von Linné bis Deniker," *Archiv für Rassen- und Gesellschaftsbiologie* 15, 1924, p. 383; trans. "The Concept of Race in Anthropology and the Divisions into Human Races from Linneus to Deniker," *This is Race*, ed. Earl W. Count, New York, Henry Schuman, 1950, p. 372. It is worth noting that Count also provides an English translation of "Von der verschiedenen Racen der Menschen," but it is incomplete and follows more closely the 1777 edition than the 1775 edition in spite of giving the earlier date. "On the Distinctiveness of the Races in General," *This is Race*, pp. 16–24.

16   For example, Wilhelm A. Mühlmann, *Geschichte der Anthropohogie*, Bonn, Universitäts-Verlag, 1948, p. 60 and Earl W. Count, *This is Race*, p. 704.

17   Enmanuel Eze, "The Color of Reason: The Idea of 'Race' in Kant's Anthropology," *Anthropology and the German Enlightenment: Perspectives on Humanity*, ed. Katherine M. Faull, Lewisburg, Bucknell University Press, 1995, pp. 219–20.

18   Carolus Linnaeus. *Systema naturae*, Facsimile of the First Edition, eds. M. S. J. Engel-Ledeboer and H. Engel, Nieuwkoop, B. de Graaf, 1964. See Gunnar Broberg, "Homo Sapiens. Linnaeus's Classification of Man," *Linnaeus. The Man and His Work*, ed. Tore Frängsmyr, Canton, Science History Publications 1994, pp. 156–94.

19   The Latin text of the 1758 edition is quoted by T. Bendyshe, "The History of Anthropology," *Memoirs Read before the Anthropological Society of London*, vol. 1, 1863–64, pp. 424–6. A partial English translation can be found in Winthrop D. Jordan, *White over Black*, Baltimore, Penguin, 1969, pp. 220–1. However, I have modified Jordan's translation to reflect the ambiguity of *ritus*.

20   James L. Larson, Reason and Experience. *The Representation of Natural Order in the Work of Carl von Linné*, Berkeley, University of California Press, 1971, pp. 98–9.

21   Londa Schiebinger, *Nature's Body. Gender in the Making of Modern Science*, Boston, Beacon Press, 1993, pp. 80–1.

22   George Louis le Clerc, Comte de Buffon, "Premier Discours. De la manière d'étudier et de traiter l'Histoire Naturelle," *Histoire Naturelle, Générale et Particulière, avec la description du cabinet du Roi*, Paris, De l'imprimerie royale, 1749, vol. 1, pp. 1–62, esp. 37–40. All further references to this edition are designated HN followed by the volume number.

23   See, for example, Michèle Duchet, *Anthropologie et Histoire au siècle des lumières*, Paris, François Maspero, 1971, pp. 270–3 and Philip Sloan, "The Gaze of Natural History," *Inventing Human Science*, eds. Christopher Fox, Roy Porter and Robert Wokler, Berkeley, University of California Press, 1995, p. 135.

24   Eds. D. Diderot and d'Alembert, *Encyclopédie on Dictionnaire Raisonné des Sciences, des Arts et des Métiers*, Elmsford, NY, Pergamon Press Reprint of 1777 edition, vol. 5, p. 957.

25   Frank W. P. Dougherty, "Buffons Bedeutung für die Entwicklung des anthropologischen Denkens im Deutschland der zweiten Hälfte des 18. Jahrhunderts," *Die Natur des Menschen*, eds. Gunter Mann and Franz Dumont, Soemmerning Forschungen VI, Stuttgart, Gustav Fischer, 1990, p. 255.

26   Paul L. Farber, "Buffon and the Concept of Species," *Journal of the History of Biology*, 5 (2), 1972, p. 278.

27   For example, M. F. Ashley Montagu, *Man's Most Dangerous Myth: The Fallacy of Race*, New York, Columbia University Press, 1945, p. 28.

28   Ivan Hannaford presents Kant's "On the Different Races of Man" as an answer to Blumenbach, but he focuses on the *Anthropology* and seems largely unconcerned with Kant's essays on race. See *Race. The History of an Idea in the West*, Baltimore, Johns Hopkins University Press, 1996, pp. 218–19. It is not clear to me why the chronology is so often ignored so as to make Kant's essay a response to Blumenbach. More than one commentator, while stating correctly that Blumenbach was born in 1752, even moved the date of the first edition of *De generis humani varietate nativa* forward from 1775 to 1770. Kenneth A. R. Kennedy, "Race and Culture," *Main Currents in Cultural Anthropology*, eds. Raoul and Frada Naroll, Englewood Cliffs, Prentice Hall, 1973, pp. 142 and 151. See also Michael Banton, "The Classification of Races in Europe and North America: 1700–1850," *International Social Science Journal*, 39 (1), 1987, p. 47.

29   Io. Frid. Blumenbach, *De generis humani varietate nativa*, Göttingen, Vandenhoeck, 1776. Henceforth GHV1. See also the second edition: Io. Frid. Blumenbach, *De generis humani varietate nativa*. Göttingen, Vandenhoek, 1781. Henceforth GHV2. The third edition was the only one translated into German. *De generis humani varietate nativa*, Göttingen,

Vandenhoeck et Ruprecht, 1795; trans. Johann Goetfried Gruber, *Über die naturlichen Verschiedenheiten im Menschengeschlechte*, Leipzig, Breitkopf und Hartel, 1798. Henceforth GHV3 and NV respectively. The first and the third edition are translated by Thomas Blendyshe in Johann Friedrich Blumenbach, *On the Natural Varieties of Mankind*, London: Longman, Green, Longman, Roberts, & Green, 1865. Henceforth NVM. Blumenbach's linguistic usage is discussed by Eric Voeghin, "The Growth of the Race Idea," *Review of Politics*, 2, 1940, p. 297.

30 J. F. Blumenbach, *Handbuch der Naturgeschichte*, fifth ed. Göttingen, Heinrich Dieterich, 1797, p. 23n. Blumenbach also praised the precision of the distinctions by which Kant authorized the concept of race and other related terms in his conversations with Gruber. See NV 259–61.

31 John Hunter, "An Inaugural Disputation of the Varieties of Man," appended to Blumenbach, *On the Natural Varieties of Mankind*, p. 367.

32 Forster, "Noch etwas über die Menschenrassen," p. 148.

33 See the translation by Werner S. Pluhar, *Critique of Judgment*, Indianapolis, Hackett, 1987, p. 311. Henceforth CJ.

34 Christoph Girtanner, *Über das Kantische Prinzip für die Naturgeschichte*, Göttingen, Vanderoek und Ruprecht, 1796. On Girtanner, see Phillip R. Sloan, "Buffon, German Biology and the Historical Interpretation of Biological Species," *British Journal for the History of Science*, vol. 12, no. 41, 1979, pp. 137–141.

35 Kant's essays on race were reprinted with other related works and some commentary by Fritz Schultze in *Kant und Darwin*, Jena, Hermann Dufft, 1875.

36 This formulation of the question is found first in the second edition. Henry Home, Lord Kames, *Sketches of the History of Man*, Edinburgh, William Creech, 1778, vol. 1, p. 2. All subsequent references will be to the first edition: *Sketches of the History of Man*, Edinburgh, W. Creech, 1774. Henceforth SHM (followed by the volume number).

37 Voltaire, *Essai sur les moeurs et l'esprit des nations*, Oeuvres complètes, vol. 11, ed. Louis Moland, Paris, Garnier Frères, 1878, p. 12.

38 Voltaire, *Trasté de métaphysique*, ed. W. H. Barber, *The Complete Works of Voltaire*, vol. 14, Oxford, The Voltaire Foundation, 1989, p. 423.

39 Ibid., p. 452. Voltaire also advocated the idea of a hierarchy of "degrees descending from man to the animal" when he placed albinos beneath Blacks (*négres*) and Hottentots but above apes. *Essai sur les moeurs*, vol. 2, Oeuvres complètes, vol. 12, pp. 367–8.

40 Blumenbach also specified his opposition to polygenesis. GHV1 40–1; NVM 98. GHV3 65–6; NV 58; NYM 188.

41 I. Kant, "Conjectural Beginning of Human History," *On History*, ed. Lewis White Beck, Indianapolis, Bobbs-Merrill, 1963, p. 54. Henceforth OH.

42 Ludwig Uhlig, *Georg Forster*, Tübingen, Max Niemeyer, 1965, pp. 57–62.

43 Georg Forster, "Noch etwas über die Menschenrassen," p. 154.

44 Hans-Konrad Schmutz, "Friedrich Tiedemann (1781–1861) und Johann Friedrich Blumenbach (1752–1840) – Anthropologie und Sklavenfrage," *Die Natur des Menschen*, eds. C. Mann and F. Dumont, pp. 353–63, esp. 354.

45 Nevertheless the advocates of slavery came to see that the science of racial differences could be used to support their case. This is never more clear than in the transmission of the European science of race to the USA. See, for example, the presentation of Julien Joseph Virey's *Histoire naturelle du genre humain* in J. H. Guenebault, *Natural History of the Negro Race*, Charleston, D. J. Dowling, 1837.

46 See Arthur O. Lovejoy, "Kant and Evolution," *Forerunners of Darwin: 1745–1859*, eds. Bentley Glass, Owsei Temkin, and William L. Straus, Baltimore: Johns Hopkins Press, 1959, p. 188.

47   Later, in 1775, in the second volume of the *Suppléments* Buffon explored the possibility that the Black race might be older than the White race. This led him to speculate in 1778 that Whites were an improved race, the first truly civilized culture, and indeed the only variety of mankind worthy of being called people. See also J. H. Eddy. "Buffon, Organic Alterations, and Man," *Studies in History of Biology*, vol. 7, eds. William Coleman and Camille Limoges, Baltimore, Johns Hopkins University Press, 1984, p. 35.

48   See Peter J. Bowler, "Preformation and Pre-existence in the Seventeenth Century," *Journal of the History of Biology*, 4 (2) 1971, pp. 221–44; and Elizabeth B. Gasking, *Investigations into Generation*, London, Hutchinson, 1967.

49   This is the argument of Peter J. Bowler, "Bonnet and Buffon: Theories of Generation and the Problem of Species," *Journal of the History of Biology*, 6 (2), 1973, pp. 259–81.

50   Jean Ferrari, "Kant, lecteur de Buffon," *Buffon 88*, ed. Jean Gayon, Paris, Vrin, 1992, p. 159.

51   Philip D. Curtin, *The Image of Africa. British Ideas and Action, 1780–1850*, Madison, University of Wisconsin Press, 1964, p. 39.

52   "Travellers have exaggerated the mental varieties far beyond the truth, who have denied good qualities to the inhabitants of other countries, because their mode of life, manners and customs have been excessively different from their own." John Hunter, "An Inaugural Disputation on the Varieties of Man," p. 352.

53   *Cyclopaedia: Or an Universal Dictionary of Arts and Sciences* (1728), s. v. "Negro's [sic]." Cited by J. H. Eddy, "Buffon, Organic Alterations and Man," *Studies in the History of Biology*, eds. William Coleman and Camille Limoges, vol. 7, 1984, p. 25.

54   Sir Thomas Browne, *Pseudoxia*, Works, vol. 2, ed. Charles Sayle, Edinburgh, John Grant, 1927, pp. 383–4.

55   Ibid., p. 385.

56   Sandor Gilman gives Kant too much credit for what appears to be a common trope. See *On Blackness without Blacks*, Boston, G. K. Hall, 1982, pp. 33–4. Compare also Adam Smith, *The Theory of Moral Sentiments*, eds. D. D. Raphael and A. L. Maclie, Oxford, Oxford University Press, 1976, p. 199.

57   J. H. Eddy, "Buffon Organic Alterations and Man," pp. 25–7.

58   A. Owen Aldridge, "Feijoo and the Problem of Ethiopian Color," *Racism in the Eighteenth Century*, ed. Harold A. Pagliaro, Cleveland, The Press of Case Western University, 1973, pp. 265 and 275.

59   Georg Forster, "Noch etwas über die Menschenrassen," pp. 134–7.

60   It seems to me that it is to this passage that Kant must be referring when he wrote in 1788 that in a short essay on human races he had tried to show the necessity of resorting to teleological principles where theory proves inadequate (AA VIII 159). For an alternative, see J. D. McFarland, *Kant's Concept of Teleology*, Edinburgh University Press, 1970, p. 61n.

61   J. Blumenbach, "Über den Bildungstrieb und seinen Einfluss auf die Generation und Reproduktion," *Göttingsches Magazin der Wissenschaft und Literatur* 1, no. 5, 1790, pp. 247–66.

62   Johann Friedrich Blumenbach, *Über den Bildungstrieb und das Zeugungsgechäfte*, Göttingen, Johann Christian Dieterich, 1781. Henceforth B2.

63   Johann Friedrich Blumenbach, *Über den Bildungstrieb*, Göttingen, Johann Christian Dieterich, 1791. Henceforth B3.

64   Kant went out of his way to show that the language of preformation could still be used to describe the theory of epigenesis Blumenbach embraced (AAV 423; CJ 311). Furthermore, Girtanner persisted with the language of seeds. *Über das Kantische Prinzip*, p. 11

65 It is worth noting that section 80 of the *Critique of Judgment* with its praise of comparative anatomy, especially bone structure, was already clearly about Blumenbach.

66 I thus disagree with James Larson's understanding of the letter in "Vital Forces: Regulative Principles or Constitutive Agents," *Isis* 70, 1979, p. 237.

67 See J. Wubnig, "The Epigenesis of Pure Reason," *Kane Studien* 60, 1968–69, pp. 147–57.

68 See Timothy Lenoir, "Kant, Blumenbach, and Vital Materialism in German Biology," *Isis*, 71, 1980, p. 77. Unfortunately, in this essay Lenoir ignores Kant's 1775 essay, so that Kant's originality is not fully appreciated.

69 In addition to the works by Lovejoy, Beiser, Lenoir, McFarland, and Zammito listed elsewhere in these notes, see Paul Bommersheim, "Der Begriff der organischen Selbstreguitation in Kants *Kritik der Urteilskraft*," *Kant Studien* 23, 1919, pp. 209–20; Manfred Riedel, "Historizismus und Kritizismus. Kants Streit mit G. Forster und J. G. Herder," *Kant Studien*, 72, 1981, pp. 41–57; and John H. Zammito, *The Genesis of Kant's Critique of Judgment*, Chicago, University of Chicago Press, 1992, pp. 213–18.

70 Christoph Girtanner, *Über das Kantische Prinzip für die Naturgeschichte*, pp. 17–30. See also Theodor Elsenhans, *Kants Rassentheorie und ihre bleibende Bedeutung*, Leipzig, Wilhelm Engelman, 1904, pp. 40–52.

71 Timothy Lenoir, "Teleology Without Regrets. The Transformation of Physiology in Gernsaisy: 1790–1847," *Studies in the History of Philosophy and Science*, 12, 1981, pp. 307–8.

72 This passage was important to Girtanner. He quoted it at *Über das Kantische Prinzip für die Naturgeschichte*, p. 20.

73 J. H. Bernard in *Critique of Judgment*, New York, Hafner, 1951 at p. 269.

74 J. G. Herder, *Auch eine Philosophie der Geschichte zur Bildung des Menschheit*, eds. J. Brummack and M. Bollacher, Frankfurt, Deutscher Klassiker, 1994, p. 11.

75 J. G. Herder, *Ideen zur Philosophie des Geschichte der Menschheit*, ed. M. Bollacher, Frankfurt, Deutscher Klassiker, 1989, p. 256. Henceforth IGM. A translation by Tom Nenon of the crucial chapter can be found in *The Idea of Race*, pp. 23–6. Henceforth PH.

76 Blumenbach insisted on the same point particularly in the first two editions of his treatise. GHV1 40–1 and 50; NV 98–9 and 107. See also GHV2 48–9 and 64.

77 Few commentators have recognized the importance of these sentences. Exceptions include Philip R. Sloan, "Buffon, German Biology and the Historical Interpretation of Biological Species," pp. 133–4 and Andrea Figl, "Immanuel Kant und die wissenschaftliche Werke des Rassismus," *Zeitschrift für Afrika Studien* 13/14, 1992, pp. 10–11. Unfortunately, this second essay came to my notice too late to take full advantage of it.

78 Herder and Kant shared the idea that the history of mankind should be written with reference to a conception of nature according to which nothing arises aimlessly. However, they approached the task very differently. For example, Herder had a greater respect for the distinctness of different peoples than Kant and believed that every people contributed to the idea of humanity by virtue of the realization of their own dispositions. See R. Bernasconi, "'Ich mag in keinen Himmel wo Weisse sind'," *Acta Institutionis Philosophiae et Aestheticae* (Tokyo), vol. 13, pp. 69–81. I intend to explore elsewhere the question of Kant's difficulties rewriting his cosmopolitanism with his view of races. Some indication of the problems can be found in Mark Larrimore, "Sublime Waste: Kant on the Destiny of the 'Races'," in *Civilization and Oppression* ed. Catherine Wilson, *Canadian Journal of Philosophy*, Supplementary volume 25. pp. 99–125.

79 Lucius Outlaw, *On Race and Philosophy*, New York, Routledge, 1996, p. 157.

80 K. Anthony Appiah, "Race, Culture, Identity," in *Color Conscious*, New Jersey, Princeton University Press, 1996, p. 38.

Chapter 6

W. E. B. Du Bois

THE CONSERVATION OF RACES

T HE AMERICAN NEGRO HAS ALWAYS felt an intense personal interest in discussions as to the origins and destinies of races: primarily because back of most discussion of race with which he is familiar, have lurked certain assumptions as to his natural abilities, as to his political, intellectual and moral status, which he felt were wrong. He has, consequently, been led to deprecate and minimize race distinctions, to believe intensely that out of one blood God created all nations, and to speak of human brotherhood as though it were the possibility of an already dawning to-morrow.

Nevertheless, in our calmer moments we must acknowledge that human beings are divided into races; that in this country the two most extreme types of the world's races have met, and the resulting problem as to the future relations of these types is not only of intense and living interest to us, but forms an epoch in the history of mankind.

It is necessary, therefore, in planning our movements, in guiding our future development, that at times we rise above the pressing, but smaller questions of separate schools and cars, wage discrimination and lynch law, to survey the whole question of race in human philosophy and to lay, on a basis of broad knowledge and careful insight, those large lines of policy and higher ideals which may form our guiding lines and boundaries in the practical difficulties of every day. For it is certain that all human striving must recognize the hard limits of natural law, and that any striving, no matter how intense and earnest, which is against the constitution of the world, is vain. The question, then, which we must seriously consider is this: What is the real meaning of Race; what has, in the past, been the law of race development, and what lessons has the past history of race development to teach the rising Negro people?

When we thus come to inquire into the essential difference of races we find it hard to come at once to any definite conclusion. Many criteria of race differences have in the past been proposed, as color, hair, cranial measurements and language. And manifestly, in each of these respects, human beings differ widely. They vary in color, for instance, from the marble-like pallor of the Scandinavian to the rich, dark brown of the Zulu, passing by the creamy Slav, the yellow Chinese, the light brown Sicilian and the brown Egyptian. Men vary, too, in the texture of hair from the obstinately straight hair of the Chinese to the obstinately tufted and frizzled hair of the Bushman. In measurement of heads, again, men vary; from the broad-headed Tartar to the medium-headed European and the narrow-headed Hottentot; or, again in language, from the highly-inflected roman tongue to the monosyllabic Chinese. All these physical characteristics are patent enough, and if they agreed with each other it would be very easy to classify mankind. Unfortunately for scientists, however, these criteria of race are most exasperatingly intermingled. Color does not agree with texture of hair, for many of the dark races have straight hair; nor does color agree with the breadth of the head, for the yellow Tartar has a broader head than the German; nor, again, has the science of language as yet succeeded in clearing up the relative authority of these various and contradictory criteria. The final word of science, so far, is that we have at least two, perhaps three, great families of human beings – the whites and Negroes, possibly the yellow race. That other races have arisen from the intermingling of the blood of these two. This broad division of the world's races which men like Huxley and Raetzel have introduced as more nearly true than the old five-race scheme of Blumenbach, is nothing more than an acknowledgement that, so far as purely physical characteristics are concerned, the differences between men do not explain all the differences of their history. It declares, as Darwin himself said, that great as is the physical unlikeness of the various races of men their likenesses are greater, and upon this rests the whole scientific doctrine of Human Brotherhood.

Although the wonderful developments of human history teach that the grosser physical differences of color, hair and bone go but a short way toward explaining the different roles which groups of men have played in Human Progress, yet there are differences – subtle, delicate and elusive, though they may be – which have silently but definitely separated men into groups. While these subtle forces have generally followed the natural cleavage of common blood, descent and physical peculiarities, they have at other times swept across and ignored these. At all times, however, they have divided human beings into races, which, while they perhaps transcend scientific definition, nevertheless, are clearly defined to the eye of the Historian and Sociologist.

If this be true, then the history of the world is the history, not of individuals, but of groups, not of nations, but of races, and he who ignores or seeks to override the race idea in human history ignores and overrides the central thought of all history. What, then, is a race? It is a vast family of human beings, generally of common blood and language, always of common history, traditions and impulses, who are both voluntarily and involuntarily striving together for the accomplishment of certain more or less vividly conceived ideals of life.

Turning to real history, there can be no doubt, first, as to the widespread, nay, universal, prevalence of the race idea, the race spirit, the race ideal, and as to its efficiency as the vastest and most ingenious invention for human progress. We, who have been reared and trained under the individualistic philosophy of the

Declaration of Independence and the laisser-faire [sic] philosophy of Adam Smith, are loath to see and loath to acknowledge this patent fact of human history. We see the Pharaohs, Caesars, Toussaints and Napoleons of history and forget the vast races of which they were but epitomized expressions. We are apt to think in our American impatience, that while it may have been true in the past that closed race groups made history, that here in conglomerate America *nous avons changer tout cela* – we have changed all that, and have no need of this ancient instrument of progress. This assumption of which the Negro people are especially fond, cannot be established by a careful consideration of history.

We find upon the world's stage today eight distinctly differentiated races, in the sense in which History tells us the word must be used. They are, the Slavs of eastern Europe, the Teutons of middle Europe, the English of Great Britain and America, the Romance nations of Southern and Western Europe, the Negroes of Africa and America, the Semitic people of Western Asia and Northern Africa, the Hindoos of Central Asia and the Mongolians of Eastern Asia. There are, of course, other minor race groups, as the American Indians, the Esquimaux and the South Sea Islanders; these larger races, too, are far from homogeneous; the Slav includes the Czech, the Magyar, the Pole and the Russian; the Teuton includes the German, the Scandinavian and the Dutch; the English include the Scotch, the Irish and the conglomerate American. Under Romance nations the widely-differing Frenchman, Italian, Sicilian and Spaniard are comprehended. The term Negro is, perhaps, the most indefinite of all, combining the Mulattoes and Zamboes of America and the Egyptians, Bantus and Bushmen of Africa. Among the Hindoos are traces of widely differing nations, while the great Chinese, Tartar, Corean and Japanese families fall under the one designation – Mongolian.

The question now is: What is the real distinction between these nations? Is it the physical differences of blood, color and cranial measurements? Certainly we must all acknowledge that physical differences play a great part, and that, with wide exceptions and qualifications, these eight great races of to-day follow the cleavage of physical race distinctions; the English and Teuton represent the white variety of mankind; the Mongolian, the yellow; the Negroes, the black. Between these are many crosses and mixtures, where Mongolian and Teuton have blended into the Slav, and other mixtures have produced the Romance nations and the Semites. But while race differences have followed mainly physical race lines, yet no mere physical distinctions would really define or explain the deeper differences – the cohesiveness and continuity of these groups. The deeper differences are spiritual, psychical, differences – undoubtedly based on the physical, but infinitely transcending them. The forces that bind together the Teuton nations are, then, first, their race identity and common blood; secondly, and more important, a common history, common laws and religion, similar habits of thought and a conscious striving together for certain ideals of life. The whole process which has brought about these race differentiations has been a growth, and the great characteristic of this growth has been the differentiation of spiritual and mental differences between great races of mankind and the integration of physical differences.

The age of nomadic tribes of closely related individuals represents the maximum of physical differences. They were practically vast families, and there were as many groups as families. As the families came together to form cities the physical differences lessened, purity of blood was replaced by the requirement of comicile, and all who lived within the city bound became gradually to be regarded as members of the group; *i.e.*, there was a slight and slow breaking down of physical barriers. This, however, was accompanied by an increase of the spiritual and social differences between cities. This city became husbandmen, this, merchant, another warriors, and so on. The *ideals of life* for which the different cities struggled were different. When at last cities began to coalesce into nations there was another breaking down of barriers which separated groups of men. The larger and broader differences of color, hair and physical proportions were not by any means ignored, but myriads of minor differences disappeared, and the sociological and historical races of men began to approximate the present division of races as indicated by physical researches. At the same time the spiritual and physical differences of race groups which constituted the nations became deep and decisive. The English nation stood for constitutional liberty and commercial freedom; the German nation for science and philosophy; the Romance nations stood for literature and art, and the other race groups are striving, each in its own way, to develop for civilization its particular message, its particular ideal, which shall help to guide the world nearer and nearer that perfection of human life for which we all long, that

"one far off Divine event."

This has been the function of race differences up to the present time. What shall be its function in the future? Manifestly some of the great races of today – particularly the Negro race – have not as yet given to civilization the full spiritual message which they are capable of giving. I will not say that the Negro race has yet given no message to the world, for it is still a mooted question among scientists as to just how far Egyptian civilization was Negro in its origin; if it was not wholly Negro, it was certainly very closely allied. Be that as it may, however, the fact still remains that the full, complete Negro message of the whole Negro race has not as yet been given to the world: that the messages and ideal of the yellow race have not been completed, and that the striving of the mighty Slavs has but begun. The question is, then: How shall this message be delivered; how shall these various ideals be realized? The answer is plain: By the development of these race groups, not as individuals, but as races. For the development of Japanese genius, Japanese literature and art, Japanese spirit, only Japanese, bound and welded together, Japanese inspired by one vast ideal, can work out in its fullness the wonderful message which Japan has for the nations of the earth. For the development of Negro genius, of Negro literature and art, of Negro spirit, only Negroes bound and welded together, Negroes inspired by one vast ideal, can work out in its fullness the great message we have for humanity. We cannot reverse history; we are subject to the same natural laws as other races and if the Negro is ever to be a factor in the world's history – if among the gaily-colored banners that deck the broad ramparts of civilization is to hang one uncompromising black, then it must be placed there by black hands, fashioned by black heads and hallowed by the travail of 200,000,000 black hearts beating in one glad song of jubilee.

For this reason, the advance guard of the Negro people – the 8,000,000 people of Negro blood in the United States of America – must soon come to realize that if they are to take their just place in the van of Pan-Negroism, then their destiny is *not* absorption by the white Americans. That if in America it is to be proven for the first time in the modern world that not only Negroes are capable of evolving individual men like Toussaint, the Saviour, but are a nation stored with wonderful possibilities of culture, then their destiny is not a servile imitation of Anglo-Saxon culture, but a stalwart originality which shall unswervingly follow Negro ideals.

It may, however, be objected here that the situation of our race in America renders this attitude impossible; that our sole hope of salvation lies in our being able to lose our race identity in the commingled blood of the nation; and that any other course would merely increase the friction of races which we call race prejudice, and against which we have so long and so earnestly fought.

Here, then, is the dilemma, and it is puzzling one, I admit. No Negro who has given earnest thought to the situation of his people in America has failed, at some time in life, to find himself at these cross-roads; has failed to ask himself at some time: What, after all, am I? Am I an American or am I a Negro? Can I be both? Or is it my duty to cease to be a Negro as soon as possible and be an American? If I strive as a Negro, am I not perpetuating the very cleft that threatens and separates Black and White America? Is not my only possible practical aim the subduction of all that is Negro in me to the American? Does my black blood place upon me any more obligation to assert my nationality than German, or Irish or Italian blood would?

It is such incessant self-questioning and the hesitation that arises from it, that is making the present period a time of vacillation and contradiction for the American Negro; combined race action is stifled, race responsibility is shirked, race enterprises languish, and the best blood, the best talent, the best energy of the Negro people cannot be marshalled to do the bidding of the race. They stand back to make room for every rascal and demagogue who chooses to cloak his selfish deviltry under the veil of race pride.

Is this right? Is it rational? Is it good policy? Have we in America a distinct mission as a race – a distinct sphere of action and an opportunity for race development, or is self-obliteration the highest end to which Negro blood dare aspire?

If we carefully consider what race prejudice really is, we find it, historically, to be nothing but the friction between different groups of people; it is the difference in aim, in feeling, in ideals of two different races; if, now, this difference exists touching territory, laws, language, or even religion, it is manifest that these people cannot live in the same territory without fatal collision; but if, on the other hand, there is substantial agreement in laws, language and religion; if there is a satisfactory adjustment of economic life, then there is no reason why, in the same country and on the same street, two or three great national ideals might not thrive and develop, that men of different races might not strive together for their race ideals as well, perhaps even better, than in isolation. Here, it seems to me, is the reading of the riddle that puzzles so many of us. We are Americans, not only by birth and by citizenship, but by our political ideals, our language, our religion. Farther than that, our Americanism does not go. At that point, we are Negroes, members of a vast historic race that from the very dawn of creation has slept, but half awakening in the dark forests of its African fatherland. We are the first fruits of this new nation, the harbinger of that black to-morrow which is yet destined to soften the whiteness of the Tuetonic to-day. We are that people whose subtle sense of song has given America its only American music, its only American fairy tales, its only touch of pathos and humor amid its mad money-getting plutocracy. As such, it is our duty to conserve our physical powers, our intellectual endowments, our spiritual ideals; as a race we must strive by race organization, by race solidarity, by race unity to the realization of that broader humanity which freely recognizes differences in men, but sternly deprecates inequality in their opportunities of development.

For the accomplishment of these ends we need race oganizations: Negro colleges, Negro newspapers, Negro business organizations, a Negro school of literature and art, and an intellectual clearing house, for all these products of the Negro mind, which we may call a Negro Academy. Not only is all this necessary for positive advance, it is absolutely imperative for negative defense. Let us not deceive ourselves at our situation in this country. Weighted with a heritage of moral iniquity from our past history, hard pressed in the economic world by foreign immigrants and native prejudice, hated here, despised there and pitied everywhere; our one haven of refuge is ourselves, and but one means of advance, our own belief in our great destiny, our own implicit trust in our ability and worth. There is no power under God's high heaven that can stop the advance of eight thousand thousand honest, earnest, inspired and united people. But – and here is the rub – they *must* be honest, fearlessly criticising their own faults, zealously correcting them; they must be *earnest*. No people that laughs at itself, and ridicules itself, and wishes to God it was anything but itself ever wrote its name in history; it *must* be inspired with the Divine faith of our black mothers, that out of the blood and dust of battle will march a victorious host, a mighty nation, a peculiar people, to speak to the nations of earth a Divine truth that shall make them free. And such a people must be united; not merely united for the organized theft of political spoils, not united to disgrace religion with whoremongers and ward-heelers; not united merely to protest and pass resolutions, but united to stop the ravages of consumption among the Negro people, united to keep black boys from loafing, gambling and crime; united to guard the purity of black women and to reduce that vast army of black prostitutes that is today marching to hell; and united in serious organizations, to determine by careful conference and thoughtful interchange of opinion the broad lines of policy and action for the American Negro.

This, is the reason for being which the American Negro Academy has. It aims at once to be the epitome and expression of the intellect of the black-blooded people of America, the exponent of the race ideals of one of the world's great races. As such, the Academy must, if successful, be

(a)   Representative in character.
(b)   Impartial in conduct.
(c)   Firm in leadership.

It must be representative in character; not in that it represents all interests or all factions, but in that it seeks to comprise something of the *best* thought, the most unselfish striving and the highest ideals. There are scattered in forgotten nooks and corners throughout the land, Negroes of some considerable training, of high minds, and high motives, who are unknown to their fellows, who exert far too little influence. These the Negro Academy should strive to bring into touch with each other and to give them a common mouthpiece.

The Academy should be impartial in conduct; while it aims to exalt the people it should aim to do so by truth – not by lies, by honesty – not by flattery. It should continually impress the fact upon the Negro people that they must not expect to have things done for them – they MUST DO FOR THEMSELVES; that they have on their hands a vast work of self-reformation to do, and that a little less complaint and whining, and a little more dogged work and manly striving would do us more credit and benefit than a thousand Force or Civil Rights bills.

Finally, the American Negro Academy must point out a practical path of advance to the Negro people; there lie before every Negro today hundreds of questions of policy and right which must be settled and which each one settles now, not in accordance with any rule, but by impulse or individual preference; for instance: What should be the attitude of Negroes toward the educational qualification for voters? What should be our attitude toward separate schools? How should we meet discriminations on railways and in hotels? Such questions need not so much specific answers for each part as a general expression of policy, and nobody should be better fitted to announce such a policy than a representative honest Negro Academy.

All this, however, must come in time after careful organization and long conference. The immediate work before us should be practical and have direct bearing upon the situation of the Negro. The historical work of collecting the laws of the United States and of the various States of the Union with regard to the Negro is a work of such magnitude and importance that no body but one like this could think of undertaking it. If we could accomplish that one task we would justify our existence.

In the field of Sociology an appalling work lies before us. First, we must unflinchingly and bravely face the truth, not with apologies, but with solemn earnestness. The Negro Academy ought to sound a note of warning that would echo in every black cabin in the land: *Unless we conquer our present vices they will conquer us*; we are diseased, we are developing criminal tendencies, and an alarmingly large percentage of our men and women are sexually impure. The Negro Academy should stand and proclaim this over the housetops, crying with Garrison: *I will not equivocate, I will not retreat a single inch, and I will be heard*. The Academy should seek to gather about it the talented, unselfish men, the pure and noble-minded women, to fight an army of devils that disgraces our manhood and our womanhood. There does not stand today upon God's earth a race more capable in muscle, in intellect, in morals, than the American Negro, if he will bend his energies in the right direction; if he will

> Burst his birth's invidious bar
> And grasp the skirts of happy chance,
> And breast the blows of circumstance,
> And grapple with his evil star.

In science and morals, I have indicated two fields of work for the Academy. Finally, in practical policy, I wish to suggest the following *Academy Creed*:

1   We believe that the Negro people, as a race, have a contribution to make to civilization and humanity, which no other race can make.
2   We believe it the duty of the Americans of Negro descent, as a body, to maintain their race identity until this mission of the Negro people is accomplished, and the ideal of human brotherhood has become a practical possibility.
3   We believe that, unless modern civilization is a failure, it is entirely feasible and practicable for two races in such essential political, economic and religious harmony as the white and colored people of America, to develop side by side in peace and mutual happiness, the peculiar contribution which each has to make to the culture of their common country.
4   As a means to this end we advocate, not such social equality between these races as would disregard human likes and dislikes, but such a social equilibrium as would, throughout all the complicated relations of life, give due and just consideration to culture, ability, and moral worth whether they be found under white or black skins
5   We believe that the first and greatest step toward the settlement of the present friction between the races – commonly called the Negro problem – lies in the correction of the immorality, crime and laziness among the Negroes themselves, which still remains as a heritage from slavery. We believe that only earnest and long continued efforts on our own part can cure these social ills.
6   We believe that the second great step toward a better adjustment of the relations between the races, should be a more impartial selection of ability in the economic and intellectual world, and a greater respect for personal liberty and worth, regardless of race. We believe that only earnest efforts on the part of the white people of this country will bring much needed reform in these matters.
7   On the basis of the foregoing declaration, and firmly believing in our high destiny, we, as American Negroes, are resolved to strive in every honorable way for the realization of the best and highest aims, for the development of strong manhood and pure womanhood, and for the rearing of a race ideal in America and Africa, to the glory of God and the uplifting of the Negro people.

Chapter 7

Gunnar Myrdal

RACIAL BELIEFS IN AMERICA

[. . .]

WHEN THE NEGRO WAS FIRST ENSLAVED, his subjugation was not justified in terms of his biological inferiority. Prior to the influences of the Enlightenment, human servitude was taken as a much more unquestioned element in the existing order of economic classes and social estates, since this way of thinking was taken over from feudal and post-feudal Europe. The historical literature on this early period also records that the imported Negroes – and the captured Indians – originally were kept in much the same status as the white indentured servants.[1] When later the Negroes gradually were pushed down into chattel slavery while the white servants were allowed to work off their bond, the need was felt, in this Christian country, for some kind of justification above mere economic expediency and the might of the strong. The arguments called forth by this need were, however, for a time not biological in character, although they later easily merged into the dogma of natural inequality. The arguments were broadly these; that the Negro was a heathen and a barbarian, an outcast among the peoples of the earth, a descendant of Noah's son Ham, cursed by God himself and doomed to be a servant forever on account of an ancient sin.[2]

The ideas of the American Revolution added their influence to those of some early Christian thinkers and preachers, particularly among the Quakers, in deprecating these arguments. And they gave an entirely new vision of society as it is and as it ought to be. This vision was dominated by a radically equalitarian political morality and could not possibly include slavery as a social institution. The philosophical ideas of man's natural rights merged with the Golden Rule of Christianity, "Do unto others as you would have them do unto you."

How it actually looked in the minds of the enlightened slaveholders who played a prominent role in the Revolution is well known, since they were under the urge to intellectual clarity of their age, and in pamphlets, speeches, and letters frequently discussed the troubles of their conscience. Most of them saw clearly the inconsistency between American democracy and Negro slavery. To these men slavery was an "abominable crime," a "wicked cause," a "supreme misfortune," an "inherited evil," an "cancer in the body politic." Jefferson himself made several attacks on the institution of slavery, and some of them were politically nearly successful. Later in his life (1821) he wrote in his autobiography:

> it was found that the public mind would not bear the proposition [of gradual emancipation], nor will it bear it even at this day. Yet the day is not far distant when it must bear it, or worse will follow. Nothing is more certainly written in the book of fate than that these people are to be free.[3]

It was among Washington's first wishes ". . . to see a plan adopted for the abolition of it [slavery]; but there is only one proper and effectual mode by which it can be accomplished and that is by legislative authority. . . ."[4]

Even in terms of economic usefulness slavery seemed for a time to be a decaying institution. Slave prices were falling. Public opinion also was definitely in motion. In the North where it was most unprofitable, slavery was abolished in state after state during this revolutionary era. Also Southern states took certain legislative steps against slave trade and relaxed their slave codes and their laws on manumission. It is probable that the majority of Americans considered Negro slavery to be doomed. But in the South the slaves represented an enormous investment to the slave owners, and the agricultural economy was largely founded on slave labor. When the Constitution was written, slavery had to be taken as an economic and political fact. It is, however, indicative of the moral situation in America at that time that the words "slave" and "slavery" were avoided. "Somehow," reflects Kelly Miller, "the fathers and fashioners of this basic document of liberty hoped that the reprobated institution would in time pass away when there should be no verbal survival as a memorial of its previous existence."[5]

In the first two decades of the nineteenth century, the Abolitionist movement was as strong in the South as in the North, if not stronger. A most fateful economic factor had, however, entered into the historical development, and it profoundly changed the complexion of the issue. Several inventions in the process of cotton manufacture, and principally Eli Whitney's invention of the cotton gin in 1794, transformed Southern agriculture. Increased cotton production and its profitability gave impetus to a southward and westward migration from the old liberal Upper South, and raised the prices of slaves which had previously been declining.[6]

In explaining the ensuing ideological reaction in the South we must not forget, however, that the revolutionary movement, typified by the Declaration of Independence, represented a considerable over-exertion of American liberalism generally, and that by the time of the writing of the Constitution a reaction was on its way. In Europe after the Napoleonic Wars a reaction set in, visible in all countries and in all fields of culture. The North released itself rather completely from the influences of the European reaction. The South, on the contrary, imbibed it and continued on an accentuated political and cultural reaction even when the

European movement had turned again toward liberalism. Around the 1830's, the pro-slavery sentiment in the South began to stiffen. During the three decades leading up to the Civil War, an elaborate ideology developed in defense of slavery. This Southern ideology was contrary to the democratic creed of the Old Virginia statesmen of the American Revolution.

The pro-slavery theory of the *ante-bellum* South is basic to certain ideas, attitudes, and policies prevalent in all fields of human relations even at the present time. The central theme in the Southern theory is the moral and political dictum that slavery did not violate the "higher law," that it was condoned by the Bible and by the "laws of nature," and that "free society," in contrast, was a violation of those laws.

More and more boldly as the conflict drew nearer, churchmen, writers, and statesmen of the South came out against the principle of equality as formulated in the Declaration of Independence. This principle came to be ridiculed as a set of empty generalities and meaningless abstractions. Common experience and everyday observation showed that it was wrong. Indeed, it was "exuberantly false, and arborescently fallacious":

> Is it not palpably nearer the truth to say that no man was ever born free and no two men were ever born equal, than to say that all men are born free and equal? . . . Man is born to subjection. . . . The proclivity of the natural man is to domineer or to be subservient.[7]

Here we should recall that Jefferson and his contemporaries, when they said that men were equal, had meant it primarily in the moral sense that they should have equal rights, the weaker not less than the stronger.[8] This was fundamentally what the South denied. So far as the Negroes were concerned, the South departed radically from the American Creed. Lincoln later made the matter plain when he observed that one section of the country thought slavery was *right* while the other held it to be *wrong*.

The militant Northern Abolitionists strongly pressed the view that human slavery was an offense against the fundamental moral law. Their spiritual ground was puritan Christianity and the revolutionary philosophy of human rights. They campaigned widely, but most Northerners – sensing the dynamite in the issue and not liking too well the few Negroes they had with them in the North – kept aloof. In the South the break from the unmodified American Creed continued and widened. Free discussion was effectively cut off at least after 1840. Around this central moral conflict a whole complex of economic and political conflicts between the North and the South grew up. The most bloody contest in history before the First World War became inevitable. De Tocqueville's forecast that the abolition of slavery would not mean the end of the Negro problem came true. It is with the American nation today, and it is not likely to be settled tomorrow.

It should be observed that in the pro-slavery thinking of the *ante-bellum* South, the Southerners stuck to the American Creed *as far as whites were concerned*; in fact, they argued that slavery was necessary in order to establish equality and liberty for the whites. In the precarious ideological situation – where the South wanted to defend a political and civic institution of inequality which showed increasingly great prospects for new land exploitation and commercial profit, but where they also wanted to retain the democratic creed of the nation – *the race doctrine of biological inequality between whites and Negroes offered the most convenient solution.*[9] The logic forcing the static and conservative ideology of the South to base itself partly on a belief in natural inequality is parallel but opposite to the tendency of the original philosophy of Enlightenment in Europe and the American Revolution to evolve a doctrine of natural equality in order to make room for progress and liberalism.[10]

[. . .] After the War and Emancipation, the race dogma was retained in the South as necessary to justify the caste system which succeeded slavery as the social organization of Negro–white relations. In fact, it is probable that racial prejudice increased in the South at least up to the end of reconstruction and probably until the beginning of the twentieth century.[11]

The North never had cleansed its own record in its dealing with the Negro even if it freed him and gave him permanent civil rights and the vote. In the North, however, race prejudice was never so deep and so widespread as in the South. During and after the Civil War it is probable that the North relaxed its prejudices even further. But Reconstruction was followed by the national compromise of the 1870s when the North allowed the South to have its own way with the Negroes in obvious contradiction to what a decade earlier had been declared to be the ideals of the victorious North and the polity of the nation. The North now also needed the race dogma to justify its course. As the North itself did not retreat from most of the Reconstruction legislation, and as the whole matter did not concern the average Northerner so much, the pressure on him was not hard, and the belief in racial inequality never became intense. But this period was, in this field, one of reaction in the North, too.

The fact that the same rationalizations are used to defend slavery and caste is one of the connecting links between the two social institutions. In the South the connection is psychologically direct. Even today the average white Southerner really uses the race dogma to defend not only the present caste situation but also *ante-bellum* slavery and, consequently, the righteousness of the Southern cause in the Civil War. This psychological unity of defense is one strong reason, among others, why the generally advanced assertion is correct that the slavery tradition is a tremendous impediment in the way of improvement of the Negro's lot. The caste system has inherited the defense ideology of slavery.

The partial exclusion of the Negro from American democracy, however, has in no way dethroned the American Creed. This faith actually became strengthened by the victorious War which saved the Union and stopped the Southerners from publicly denouncing the cherished national principles that all men are born equal and have inalienable civil rights. The question can be asked: What do the millions of white people in the South and in the North actually think when, year after year, on the national holidays dedicated to the service of the democratic ideals, they read, recite, and listen to the Declaration of Independence and the Constitution? Do they or do they not include Negroes among "all men"? The same question is raised when we observe how, in newspaper editorials and public speeches, unqualified and general statements are made asserting the principles and the fact of American democracy. Our tentative answer is this: In solemn moments, Americans try to forget about the Negroes as about other worries. If this is not possible they think in vague and irrational terms; in these terms the idea of the Negroes' biological inferiority is a nearly necessary rationalization.

The dogma of racial inequality may, in a sense, be regarded as a strange fruit of the Enlightenment. The fateful word *race* itself is actually not yet two hundred years old. The biological ideology had to be utilized as an intellectual explanation of, and a moral apology for, slavery in a society which went out emphatically to invoke as its highest principles the ideals of the inalienable rights of all men to freedom and equality of opportunity. It was born out of the conflict between an old harshly nonequalitarian institution – which was not, or perhaps in a short time could not be, erased – and the new shining faith in human liberty and democracy. Another accomplishment of early rationalistic Enlightenment had laid the theoretical basis for the racial defense of slavery; the recognition of *Homo sapiens* as only a species of the animal world and the emerging study of the human body and mind as biological phenomena. Until this philosophical basis was laid, racialism was not an intellectual possibility.

The influences from the American Creed thus had, and still have, a double-direction. On the one hand, the equalitarian Creed operates directly to suppress the dogma of the Negro's racial inferiority and to make people's thoughts more and more "independent of race, creed or color," as the American slogan runs. On the other hand, it indirectly calls forth the same dogma to justify a blatant exception to the Creed. The race dogma is nearly the only way out for a people so moralistically equalitarian, if it is not prepared to live up to its faith. A nation less fervently committed to democracy could, probably, live happily in a caste system with a somewhat less intensive belief in the biological inferiority of the subordinate group. *The need for race prejudice is, from this point of view, a need for defense on the part of the Americans against their own national creed, against their own most cherished ideals.* And race prejudice is, in this sense a function of equalitarianism. The former is a perversion of the latter.[12]

[. . .] This split in the American soul has been, and still is, reflected in scientific thought and in the literature on the Negro race and its characteristics. Thomas Jefferson, the author of the Declaration of Independence and the supreme exponent of early American liberalism, in his famous *Notes on Virginia* (1781–1782) deals with the Negro problem in a chapter on "The Administration of Justice and the Description of the Laws." He posits his ideas about race as an argument for emancipating the slaves, educating them, assisting them to settle in Africa:

> Deep-rooted prejudices entertained by the whites; ten thousand recollections, by the blacks, of the injuries they have sustained; new provocations; the real distinctions which nature has made; and many other circumstances, will divide us into parties, and produce convulsions, which will probably never end but in the extermination of the one or the other race.[13]

He goes on to enumerate the "real distinctions" between Negroes and whites and gives a fairly complete list of them as they were seen by liberal people of his time:

color, hair form, secretion, less physiological need of sleep but sleepiness in work, lack of reasoning power, lack of depth in emotion, poverty of imagination and so on. In all these respects he is inclined to believe that "it is not their condition, then, but nature, which has produced the distinction." But he is cautious in tone, has his attention upon the fact that popular opinions are prejudiced, and points to the possibility that further scientific studies may, or may not, verify his conjectures.[14]

This guarded treatment of the subject marks a high point in the early history of the literature on Negro racial characteristics. In critical sense and in the reservation for the results of further research, it was not surpassed by white writers until recent decades. As the Civil War drew nearer, intellectuals were increasingly mobilized to serve the Southern cause and to satisfy the Southern needs for rationalization. After Reconstruction their theories were taken over by the whole nation. Biology and ethnology were increasingly supplanting theology and history in providing justification for slavery and, later, caste. Even the friends of the Negroes assumed great racial differences, even if, out of charity, they avoided elaborating on them. The numerous enemies of the Negro left a whole crop of pseudo-scientific writings in the libraries, emphasizing racial differences. Robert W. Shufeldt's book, *America's Greatest Problem: the Negro*[15] which had considerable influence for a time – illustrating the inferiority argument by a picture of a Negro lad between two monkeys and filled with an imposing mass of presumed evidences for Negro inferiority – is a late example of this literature at its worst.[16]

Without much change this situation continued into the twentieth century. At this time the heavily prejudiced position of science on the race problem was, however, beginning to be undermined. Professor Franz Boas and a whole school of anthropologists had already come out against these arguments for racial differences based on the primitive people's lack of culture.[17] The outlines of a radically environmentalistic sociology were being drawn by W. G. Sumner, W. I. Thomas and C. H. Cooley. The early research on intelligence pronounced that there were considerable racial differences but it had already encountered some doubts as to validity.[18] Improved techniques in the fields of anatomy and anthropometry had begun to disprove earlier statements on Negro physical traits.[19]

The last two or three decades have seen a veritable revolution in scientific thought on the racial characteristics of the Negro. This revolution has actually a much wider scope: it embraces not only the whole race issue even outside the Negro problem, but the fundamental assumptions on the nature–nurture question. The social sciences in America, and particularly sociology, anthropology, and psychology,[20] have gone through a conspicuous development, increasingly giving the preponderance to environment instead of to heredity.

In order to retain a proper perspective on this scientific revolution, we have to recall that American social science is not many decades old. The biological sciences and medicine, firmly entrenched much earlier in American universities, had not, and have not yet, the same close ideological ties to the American Creed. They have been associated in America, as in the rest of the world, with conservative and even reactionary ideologies.[21] Under their long hegemony, there has been a tendency to assume biological causation without question, and to accept social explanations only under the duress of a siege of irresistible evidence. In political questions, this tendency favored a do-nothing policy. This tendency also, in the main, for a century and more, determined people's attitudes toward the racial traits of the Negro. In the years around the First World War, it exploded in a cascade of scientific and popular writings[22] with a strong racialistic bias, rationalizing the growing feeling in America against the "new" immigrants pouring into the country whose last frontier was now occupied and congregating in the big cities where they competed with American labor. In addition to the social friction they created, the idea that these newcomers represented an inferior stock provided much of the popular theory for the restrictive immigration legislation.[23]

The wave of racialism for a time swayed not only public opinion but also some psychologists who were measuring psychic traits, especially intelligence, and perhaps also some few representatives of related social sciences.[24] But the social sciences had now developed strength and were well on the way toward freeing themselves entirely from the old biologistic tendency. The social sciences received an impetus to their modern development by reacting against this biologistic onslaught. They fought for the theory of environmental causation. Their primary object of suspicion became more and more the old static entity, "human nature," and the belief that fundamental differences between economic, social, or racial groups were due to "nature."

From the vantage point of their present research front, the situation looks somewhat like this: a handful of social and biological scientists over the last fifty years have gradually forced informed people to give up some of the more blatant of our biological errors. But there must be still other countless errors of the same sort that no living man can yet detect, because of the fog within which our type of Western culture envelops us. Cultural influences have set up the assumptions about the mind, the body, and the universe with which we begin; pose the questions we ask; influence the facts we seek; determine the interpretation we give these facts; and direct our reaction to these interpretations and conclusions.

Social research has thus become militantly critical. It goes from discovery to discovery by challenging this basic assumption in various areas of life. It is constantly disproving inherent differences and explaining apparent ones in cultural and social terms. By inventing and applying ingenious specialized research methods, the popular race dogma is being victoriously pursued into every corner and effectively exposed as fallacious or at least unsubstantiated. So this research becomes truly revolutionary in the spirit of the cherished American tradition. A contrast is apparent not only in comparison with earlier strands of American social science but also with contemporary scientific trends in other countries. The democratic ones have, on the whole, followed a similar course, but America has been leading. It is interesting to observe how on this point the radical tendency in American social research of today dominates even the work and writings of scientists who feel and pronounce their own political inclination to be conservative.

What has happened is in line with the great traditions of the American Creed, the principles of which are themselves, actually, piecemeal becoming substantiated by research and elaborated into scientific theory. American social scientists might – in a natural effort to defend their objectivity – dislike this characterization, but to the outsider it is a simple and obvious fact that the social sciences in America at present have definitely a spirit in many respects reminiscent of eighteenth century Enlightenment. The ordinary man's ideas have not, however, kept up to those of the scientist. Hardly anywhere else or in any other issue is there – in spite of intensive and laudable efforts to popularize the new results of research – such a wide gap between scientific thought and popular belief. At least potentially these ideas have, however, a much greater importance in America than could be assumed upon casual observation and for the reason that the ordinary American has a most honored place in his heart for equalitarianism.

This trend in social sciences to discount earlier notions of great differences in "nature" between the advantaged and the disadvantaged groups (rich–poor, men–women, whites–Negroes) runs parallel to another equally conspicuous trend in American political ideology since the First World War: an increased interest and belief in social reforms. The latter trend broke through in the course of the Great Depression following the crisis of 1920; and it materialized in the New Deal, whose principles, even if not methods, are now widely accepted. We have already stressed the strategic importance for political liberalism and radicalism of the modern social science point of view on the basic problem of nurture *versus* nature. The scientific trend in non-democratic countries during the same period – and specifically the sway of racialism over German universities and research centers under the Nazi regime – provides a contrast which vividly illustrates our thesis.

As always, we can, of course, assume that basically both the scientific trend and the political development in a civilization are functions of a larger synchronized development of social ideology. A suspicion is, then, natural that fundamentally the scientific trend in America is a rationalization of changed political valuations. This trend has, however, had its course during a remarkable improvement of observation and measurement techniques and has been determined by real efforts to criticize research methods and the manner in which scientific inferences are made from research data. It has, to a large extent, been running against expectation and, we may assume, wishes. This is the general reason why, in spite of the natural suspicion, we can feel confident that the scientific trend is, on the whole, a definite approach toward objective truth.

[. . .] Our characterization of the race dogma as a reaction against the equalitarian Creed of revolutionary America is a schematization too simple to be exact unless reservations are added. Undoubtedly the low regard for the Negro people before the eighteenth century contained intellectual elements which later could have been recognized as a racial theory in disguise. The division of mankind into whites, blacks, and yellows stretches back to ancient civilization. A loose idea that barbarism is something inherent in certain peoples is equally old. On the other hand, the masses of white Americans even today do not always, when they refer to the inferiority of the Negro race, think clearly in straight biological terms.

The race dogma developed gradually. The older Biblical and socio-political arguments in defense of slavery retained in the South much of their force long beyond the Civil War. Under the duress of the ideological need of justification for Negro slavery, they were even for a time becoming increasingly elaborated. Their decline during recent decades is probably a result of the secularization and urbanization of the American people, which in these respects, as in so many others, represents a continuation of the main trend begun by the revolutionary ideological impulses of the eighteenth century. In this development, the biological inferiority dogma threatens to become the lone surviving ideological support of color caste in America.

In trying to understand how ordinary white people came to believe in the Negro's biological inferiority, we must observe that there was a shift from theological to biological thinking after the eighteenth century. As soon as the idea was spread that man belongs to the biological universe, the conclusion that the Negro was *biologically* inferior was natural to the unsophisticated white man. It is obvious to the ordinary unsophisticated white man, from his everyday experience, that the Negro is inferior. *And inferior the Negro really is*; so he shows up even under scientific study. He is, on the average, poorer; his body is more often deformed; his health is more precarious and his mortality rate higher; his intelligence performance, manners, and morals are lower. The *correct* observation that the Negro is inferior was tied up to the *correct* belief that man belongs to the biological universe, and, by twisting logic, the *incorrect* deduction was made that the inferiority is biological in nature.

Race is a comparatively simple idea which easily becomes applied to certain outward signs of "social visibility," such as physiognomy. Explanations in terms of environment, on the contrary, tax knowledge and imagination heavily. It is difficult for the ordinary man to envisage clearly how such factors as malnutrition, bad housing, and lack of schooling actually deform the body and the soul of people. The ordinary white man cannot be expected to be aware of such subtle influences as the denial of certain outlets for ambitions, social disparagement, cultural isolation, and the early conditioning of the Negro child's mind by the caste situation, as factors molding the Negro's personality and behavior. The white man is, therefore, speaking in good faith when he says that he sincerely believes that the Negro is racially inferior, not merely because he has an interest in this belief, but simply because he has seen it. He "knows" it.

Tradition strengthens this honest faith. The factors of environment were, to the ordinary white man, still less of a concrete reality one hundred years ago when the racial dogma began to crystallize. Originally the imported Negro slaves had hardly a trace of Western culture. The tremendous cultural difference between whites and Negroes was maintained[25] and, perhaps, relatively increased by the Negroes being kept, first, in slavery and, later, in a subordinate caste, while American white culture changed apace. By both institutions the Negroes' acculturation was hampered and steered in certain directions. The Negroes, moreover, showed obvious differences in physical appearance.

From the beginning these two concomitant differences – the physical and the cultural – must have been associated in the minds of white people. "When color differences coincide with differences in cultural levels, then color becomes symbolic and each individual is automatically classified by the racial uniform he wears."[26] Darker color, woolly hair, and other conspicuous physical Negro characteristics became steadily associated with servile status, backward culture, low intelligence performance and lack of morals. All unfavorable reactions to Negroes – which for social if not for biological reasons, are relatively much more numerous than favorable reactions – became thus easily attributed to *every* Negro as a Negro, that is, to the *race* and to the individual only secondarily as a member of the race.

Whites categorize Negroes. As has been observed also in other racial contacts, visible characteristics have a power to overshadow all other characteristics and to create an illusion of a greater similarity between the individuals of the out-race and greater difference from the in-race than is actually warranted.[27]

This last factor is the more important as the unsophisticated mind is much more "theoretical" – in the popular meaning of being bent upon simple, abstract, clear-cut generalizations – than the scientifically trained mind.[28] This works in favor of the race dogma. To conceive that apparent differences in capacities and aptitudes could be cultural in origin means a deferment of judgment that is foreign to popular thinking. It requires difficult and complicated thinking about a multitude of mutually dependent variables, thinking which does not easily break into the lazy formalism of unintellectual people.

We should not be understood, however, to assume that the simpler concept of race is clear in the popular mind. From the beginning, as is apparent from the literature through the decades, environmental factors to some extent, have been taken into account. But they are discounted, and they are applied in a loose way – partly under the influence of vulgarized pre-Darwinian and Darwinian evolutionism – to the race rather than to the individual. The Negro race is said to be several hundreds of thousands of years behind the white man in "development." Culture is then assumed to be an accumulated mass of memories *in the race*, transmitted through the genes. A definite biological ceiling is usually provided: the mind of the Negro race cannot be improved beyond a given level. This odd theory is repeated through more than a century of literature: it is phrased as an excuse by the Negro's friends and as an accusation by his enemies. The present writer has met it everywhere in contemporary white America.

Closely related to this popular theory is the historical and cultural demonstration of Negro inferiority already referred to. It is constantly pointed out as a proof of his racial backwardness that in Africa the Negro was never able to achieve a culture of his own. Descriptions of hideous conditions in Africa have belonged to this popular theory from the beginning. Civilization is alleged to be the accomplishment of the white race; the Negro, particularly, is without a share in it.

Notes and references

1   See, for example: John H. Russell, *The Free Negro in Virginia, 1619–1865* (1913); J. C. Ballagh, *A History of Slavery in Virginia* (1902); John C. Hurd, *The Law of Freedom and Bondage in the United States* (1858–1862).

2   A weak variation of this popular theory – weak because it looked forward only to temporary subordination of backward peoples – was that in making the Negroes slaves, white men were educating and Christianizing them. This variation is known as the "white men's burden" doctrine and played an especially important role in nineteenth century exploitation. For some statements of this doctrine, see W. O. Brown, "Rationalization of Race Prejudice," *The International Journal of Ethics* (April, 1933), pp. 299–301.

3   H. A. Washington (editor), *The Writings of Thomas Jefferson* (1859), Vol. 1, p. 49.

4   Letter to Robert Morris, dated April 12, 1786. Jones Viles (editor), *Letters and Addresses of George Washington* (1908), p. 285.

5   "Government and the Negro," *Annals of the Academy of Political and Social Science* (November, 1928), p. 99.

6   This materialistic explanation is not a new idea. It was already seen clearly by some in the *ante-bellum* South. George Fitzhugh, for example, writes:

> "Our Southern patriots, at the time of the Revolution, finding Negroes expensive and useless, became warm anti-slavery men. We, their wiser sons, having learned to make cotton and sugar, find slavery very useful and profitable, and think it a most excellent institution. We of the South advocate slavery, no doubt, from just as selfish notices as induce the Yankees and English to deprecate it."
>
> "We have, however, almost all human and divine authority on our side of the argument. The Bible nowhere condemns, and throughout recognises slavery."
>
> (*Sociology for the South* [1854], p. 269)

7   Chancellor William Harper, "Memoir on Slavery," paper read before the Society for the Advancement of Learning of South Carolina, annual meeting at Columbia, South Carolina, 1837 (1838), pp. 6–8.

8   This stress on moral equality has not been lost throughout the ages. T. J. Woofter, Jr., a representative of modern Southern liberalism, writes:

> "It is desirable frankly to recognize the differences as they actually exist, but there is absolutely no ethical justification for the assumption that an advantaged group has an inherent right to exploit and oppress, and the prejudice based upon the assumptions is the most vicious enemy to human peace and cooperation."
>
> (*Basis of Racial Adjustment* [1925], p. 11)

Vance, another Southern liberal, writes:

> "In a field where doubts abound, let us make one sweeping statement. If biological inferiority of the whole Negro group were a proved fact, it would, nevertheless, be to the benefit of both white and black to behave as though it did not exist. Only in this way can the Section be sure of securing, in the economic sphere, the best of which both races are capable." (Rupert B. Vance,
>
> *Human Geography of the South* [1932], p. 463)

9   "Prejudice of any sort, racial or otherwise, is regarded as derogatory to intellectual integrity, incompatible with good taste, and perhaps morally reprehensible. Hence the prejudiced in order to be secure in their illusions of rationality, impeccable taste, and moral correctness find rationalizations essential. The rationlization inoculates against insights as to the real nature of one's reactions. It secures the individual in his moral universe. It satisfies his impulse to rationality. The mind thus becomes an instrument, a hand-maiden, of the emotions, supplying good reasons for prejudiced reaction in the realm of racial, class, or sectarian contacts." (Brown, *op. cit.*, p. 294).

10   In this connection it is interesting to note, as an example of how political reaction fosters racialism, that in the *ante-bellum* South racial thinking also turned toward beliefs in biological differences between whites. The legend was spread that the white Southerners were a "master race" of Norman blood while New England was settled by descendants of the ancient British and Saxon serfs. The Northerners and Southerners, it was said, "are the same men who cut each other's throats in

England, under the name of Roundheads and Cavaliers." The Southerners were a Nordic race with greater capacity to rule. (See James Truslow Adams, *America's Tragedy* [1934], pp. 95 ff, 121, and 128 ff.) A late example of this ideology will be found in a chapter entitled "The Tropic Nordics," of H. J. Eckenrode, *Jefferson Davis, President of the South* (1923). The present writer has on several occasions in conversation with Southerners met vague reminiscences of this popular theory, usually related to the myth that the South, unlike the North, was settled mainly by English aristocrats. The more common theory of Southern racial superiority nowadays is, however, simply the assertion that the white Southerners belong predominantly to "the pure Anglo-Saxon race," as the South has received so few immigrants in recent decades when these were recruited from other European countries. In addition, one often meets the idea that "the poor whites" and generally the lower classes of whites are racially inferior, as they descend from indentured servants.

11   Guion G. Johnson, "History of Racial Ideologies,' unpublished manuscript written for this study (1940). Vol. 1, pp. 149, *passim*; Vol. 2, pp. 331, *passim*.

12   The same principle operates also outside the Negro problem. The American Creed, in its demand for equality, has strong support from the very composition of the new nation. As immigrants, or the descendants of immigrants with diverse national origins, Americans have an interest – outside of the Negro problem – in emphasizing the importance of environment and in discounting inheritance. In order to give a human and not only political meaning to the legend *e pluribus unum*, they feel the need to believe in the possibility of shaping a new homogeneous nation out of the disparate elements thrown into the melting pot. This interest plays on a high level of valuations where the individual identifies himself with the destiny of the nation. In daily life, however, the actual and obvious heterogeneity in origin, appearance, and culture of the American people acts as a constant stimulus toward prejudiced racial beliefs.

Thus – even outside the Negro problem – there is in America a considerable ambivalence in people's thoughts on race. On a lower valuation level, there appears to be in America an extreme belief in and preoccupation with all sorts of racial differences, while on a higher level a contrary ideology rules, equally extreme when compared with more homogeneous nations. The former side of the American personality is responsible for much friction and racial snobbishness in social life. The latter side finds its expression not only in empty speeches – what the Americans call "lip-service" – but also in national legislation and in actual social trends.

13   H. A. Washington (editor), *The Writings of Thomas Jefferson* (1854), Vol. 8, pp. 380–381.

14   *ibid*, pp. 380 ff.

15   1915.

16   Concerning this literature, see G. G. Johnson, *op. cit.*, Vol. 1, pp. 149, *passim*, Vol. 2, pp. 250–258 and 311–338.

17   Much of the earliest literature of this sort is summarized in W. I. Thomas (editor), *Sourcebook for Social Origins* (1909).

18   Cooley challenged Galton's hereditary explanation of racial genius in 1897. (Charles H. Cooley, "Genius, Fame and the Comparison of Races," *Annals of the American Academy of Political and Social Science* [May, 1897], pp. 317–358); see Chapter 6, Section 3.

19   Several scientists, for example, had criticized much of the early research on brain and skull differences. One of the most notorious of the exposés was that of Robert B. Bean by Franklin P. Mall. Bean was a Southern student of Mall's in the latter's laboratory at Johns Hopkins. In an elaborate study of Negro skulls and brains, he attempted to show that the skulls were smaller than the skulls of white men, and that the brains were less convoluted and otherwise deficient. After Bean published his findings (Robert B. Bean, "Some Racial Peculiarities of the Negro Brain," *American Journal of Anatomy* [September, 1906], pp. 27–432), Mall repeated the measurements on many of the same specimens and found that Bean had completely distorted his measurements and conclusions. (Franklin P. Mall, "On Several Anatomical Characters of the Human brain, Said to Vary According to Race and Sex, With Especial Reference to the Weight of the Frontal Lobe," *American Journal of Anatomy* [February, 1909], pp. 1–32). Bean's sample, too, was grossly inadequate; it consisted of 103 Negroes and 49 whites in the Baltimore morgue who had been unclaimed at death.

20   The change toward environmentalism in American psychology has been most radical in child psychology, psychiatry and educational psychology, applied psychology, "social psychology," and other branches which are in close relation to social practice and social science. Undoubtedly the biologistic approach has still a stronghold in academic psychology proper. But even there a change is under way which can be registered by comparing the present situation with the one prevalent two or three decades ago. An indication is the almost complete abandonment of the "instinct" psychology.

21   This connection between biology and conservatism will have to be remembered when explaining why, with some outstanding exceptions, the medical profession has, on the whole, in all countries, taken a rather reactionary stand on questions of social and health reforms.

22   Perhaps the most influential of the popular racialistic writers were: Madison Grant, *The Passing of the Great Race* (1916); Lothrop Stoddard, *The Rising Tide of Color* (1920); Charles W. Gould, *America, A Family Matter* (1920).

23   The acts restricting immigration not only cut down the total number of immigrants admitted to the country, but also provided that those allowed entrance should be predominantly from Western and Northern Europe. The 1921 act permitted an immigration from each country equal to 3 per cent of the number of foreign-born from that country resident in the United States in 1910. The 1924 act reduced the quota to 2 per cent and set the determining date back to 1890. Immigration from the orient was completely prohibited, but that from independent countries in the Americas and from Canada was not restricted at all.

24   As examples we may cite the following: Carl C. Brigham, an outstanding psychologist who has since repudiated his book (*A Study of American Intelligence* [1923]); William McDougall, the father of many trends in psychology (*The Group Mind* [1920], and *Is America Safe for Democracy?* [1921]); Albert Bushnell Hart and H. H. Bancroft, the eminent historians (*The Southern South* [1920], and *Retrospection, Political and Personal* [1912]).

25   When we say that cultural differences were maintained, we do not refer one way or the other to the retention of African culture.

26   Reuter, *The Mulatto in the United States*, pp. 99–100.

27   Edward K. Strong, *The Second-Generation Japanese Problem* (1934), p. 100. The classic statement on the difference between categoric and sympathetic contacts is that of Nathaniel S. Shaler, *The Neighbor* (1904), pp. 207–227.

28   The tendencies of unsophisticated thinking to be "theoretical" are worthy of much more study than they have been given hitherto. They can be illustrated from all spheres of human life. To give an example outside our problem: The most human concept, *bona fide*, in jurisprudence is a late juristical development in all civilizations; originally legal systems are formalistic and behavioristic (they do not consider people's intentions); *bona fide* is even today only the trained lawyer's way of thinking and has, as yet, never and nowhere really been understood by the mass of laymen whose thinking of legal matters always seems formalistic to the lawyer. Similarly the simple "economic laws" are thought-forms adhered to by business people when they speculate in this strange field, while the economic theorists, instead, devote their labor to criticising, demolishing, and complicating economic theory. It is the common man, *and not the statistician who* "thinks in averages," or, rather, in pairs of *contrasting types*: good–bad, healthy–sick, man–woman, white–black. And the common man is likely to handle averages and types as if they applied to the individuals. He will confidently tell you something about "all Negroes," in the same breath as he observes an exception.

He is, further, likely to construct his types without a thought as to sampling difficulties. He has a tendency to forget about range and spread. He has, of course, a pragmatic understanding that things and happenings have their causes. Otherwise he would not be able to get on with his several pursuits in a rational way. But particularly when it comes to social questions, causation becomes to the untrained mind divested of complications. Social causation is to him mostly monistic, direct, apparent and simple. The very idea of causal interrelations within a mutually dependent system of a great many factors is usually entirely absent. In his thoughts on social causation he mingles his ideas about what is right and wrong. The unsophisticated mind is not questioning; it answers questions before they are stated.

Generally speaking, it is a fact that "to think in concrete terms" when reaching for generalizations is the endeavor of theoretical training and a mark of the highest intelligence, while "theoretical," abstract and formalistic thinking is the common man's philosophy.

Chapter 8

Albert Memmi

RACISM AND DIFFERENCE

[. . .]

THE FACT REMAINS THAT *difference is the principal notion around which the racist enterprise revolves.*[1] The idea of difference has become quite fashionable today; the banner of the "right to difference" has been raised by many revindicating social struggles. But this has not simplified things; within the swelling ranks of its proponents, there are those who sometimes go to foolish extremes. Similarly, in advertising campaigns, one finds such slogans as "taste the difference," or a product that offers "more than difference." Difference is made to be a quality in and of itself, the essential property of a mineral water or a car, the meaning of its carbonation or of some accessory gadget. This becomes a serious matter when, and with all due respect, certain retrograde practices become glorified as "ethnic" under the guise of the "right to difference," though they are actually quite harmful: female genital mutilation, for instance, or certain unhealthy practices of magic.

But do we really have to choose between a "differentialism" that extols all within a cultural tradition as good and worthy of protection on the one hand, and a condemnation of all particularism on the other?[2] Having been one of those responsible for promoting the question of difference (see my *Portrait of a Jew*), I would like to address a certain misunderstanding that has become attached to it. In reviewing the issue, I recall that it is not so much difference itself that is important as the significance given to it.

Not to keep this in mind would be, by an irony of history, to join forces with the other side, the most hardened traditionalists as well as those of the radical right. Any historical approach of the notion of difference shows that its importance varies, even within one and the same group. Often, blown by the winds of destiny, it shifts, like a pendulum, from a vague background notion to an overglorified affirmation. Its importance is always clearly linked to the meaning that people need to give it at any particular moment. This process can be seen at work in many individuals who at times feel closely allied with their group but at other times may keep their distance and insist on what divides them from it.

When I first began to reflect on these questions, the notion of "difference" did not have a good reputation among those of us involved in anti-colonialist and anti-racist movements. On the contrary, the conservatives and the partisans of colonialism upheld the concept of difference. The arguments advanced by both sides seemed quite clear (and how the wheel of history has turned!). For us, any insistence on difference was suspect, and rightly so; it constituted the very foundation of racist discourse and prepared all its criminal actions. The conservatives, who defend their colonialist social order by basing it on a supposed natural order, accomplished two things at once. They affirmed difference and, by always doing so in their own favor, reduced the colonized to a subhuman level; in treating the colonized as inferior, the colonialists simultaneously constructed themselves as superior. Difference thus signified inequality. Since biological and cultural inequality implied economic and political inequality (i.e., domination), the conservatives gave themselves the right to do as they liked, to do whatever was to their advantage. The same mechanism works against Black people, or against women, to the benefit of Whites, or men. The argument goes that it would be wrong to entrust Black people with the functions of government (and would even be a disservice to them) because it would be contrary to their biological and cultural nature; these responsibilities must be reserved for Whites, who can perform them properly and thus protect everyone's interests. The same holds for women: they must be protected, even from themselves. The authority of men and Whites is thus founded on the delegitimization of women and Blacks. With certain subtle differences, the same mechanism operates with respect to the Jews: "The economic or political success of the Jews would be a disaster for everyone, including the Jews. It is better to prevent it, in the general interest."

In the other camp, namely ours, the commonality and confraternity of all peoples were a matter of principle, based on a very simple metaphysics: only one human nature exists, which is uniform across all time and space. A natural confraternity of people logically implied a natural equality: "all men are born free and equal." The small phrase "in rights" had been added by the revolution, but this minor correction, though important, was given scant attention. The main point was that natural equality necessarily implied social equality. Domination, "the exploitation of man by man," was nothing but an abuse, a crime that had to be firmly combated.

While our enemy's position enraged me, there was also something troubling about that of my friends. They affirmed that differences did not exist, from which point everything else followed coherently. If all "men" were "cut from the same cloth," then nothing provided any ground for social inequality except violence and injustice. This generous *Jacobin myopia* derives from the history of the French nation itself, which, in order to constitute itself, fought hard against the particularism or desire for autonomy of certain provinces, at times with terrible excesses.[3] Yet it accepted that leap, even if it were a denial of the real. But what if it were mistaken in its fundamental premises? Suppose difference existed – what would become of the Jacobin position, and in its wake, of *our* entire social philosophy? Would we be obliged to accept the thinking of our adversaries, to resign ourselves to their iniquitous social order, to their colonialism, racism, and masculinism? Such a con-clusion was unthinkable to us, though it had a certain logic. If we were to avoid it, there was only one thing to do: submit our own premises to serious review. After all, such things do not depend on opinion but on knowledge. For science, do biological or other differences exist or not, yes or no? The a priori assumption that humans were either the same or different was in either case something that arose from a partisan interest, as a tactic, or from passion. Only the facts could prove one right and the other wrong – or what would be most embarrassing, that differences existed in some cases but not in all.

Let me emphasize this. What I've argued is that differential characteristics can be wholly conceptual, or over-estimated, or simply invented and then imposed on designated groups like a veneer, with no obligation to point out (though not without risk of misunderstanding) what might also be real and objective. This is so for Black people (who have themselves remarked on it), for women, for young people with respect to adults, and again for immigrants, arriving in Europe in greater and greater numbers, who are culturally different and whose real cultural differences sometimes pose certain problems by their proximity. In all these cases, the denial of differential characteristics would obviously not be without serious psychological and sociological significance.

[. . .]

My own thinking soon led me to the unexpected conclusion that both sides, ourselves and our adversaries, had been wrong. Both had fundamentally supposed that *it was bad to be different*. That is, both presupposed, implicitly or explicitly, that a model existed, a good model incarnated in the dominant group.[4] For both, to be different signified to be different from the dominant. In Tunisia, even a liberal and nondenominational schoolteacher, devoted to his "indigenous" Tunisian students, believed himself invested with a mission: to produce little French people in his own image, the image of France's civilization, its good customs, its refined taste and articulateness. Later, when I went to France (the "Metropole"), I found that the corresponding schoolteacher, the pride of Jacobin democracy, had a similar attitude toward the peasants of his own country, or toward the Bretons or the Alsatians. It was the same old story. For our part, we had to be docile and accede to everything in order to resemble our masters, and we generally did that, even though it meant killing a certain part of our souls.

[. . .]

In sum, like all apparently irresolvable problems, the question of difference had been badly posed – both by the colonialists, who affirmed differences in order to crush the colonized, and by the anti-colonialists, who denied differences in order to protect the colonized. By establishing some distance from the generous but blind republican (anti-colonialist) stance, in order to look directly at what was real, I saw clearly that *differences existed*. What a revelation! How could I have believed for such a long time that they didn't exist! In the street, on the bus, in the markets, the crowd had always been visibly cosmopolitan and diverse! But furthermore, this discovery conceded nothing to racist reasoning, because the diversity was to be found at the interior of each group, including that of any racist, and the boundaries between communities were neither fixed nor clear. We were undeniably different, one from the other.

Later, when I enrolled in the Sorbonne, it made me laugh to hear my companions seriously proclaim that differences between people didn't exist. I let it go, because they had the best intentions in the world. But then, they had only to look at things with their eyes, and not with their minds. In their own country, France, which I traveled through with delight, the population changed from region to region and climate to climate. Everywhere there was this same generosity in all native-born French, this same Jacobin myopia mixed with republican pride – it was an unforeseen outcome of the centralism of the pre-revolutionary aristocratic state [*ancien régime*]. That famous parable of the "forty kings who made France," thanks to "a law, a king, a faith" [*une loi, un roi, une foi*], reappeared after the revolution in secularized form as the "republic one and indivisible."[5]

During the same period, there were also many seminars and conferences on the reawakening of colonized peoples and the future of colonialism, which began to bring intellectuals together. I attended a number of these meetings. At the first "Congress of Black Intellectuals," I argued that, despite certain notable achievements, the policy of assimilation had been, up to that time, more or less of a failure. Not always, certainly, and not at the hands of the colonized themselves, who had wanted it most of all. But no one else had wanted them. The right refused even to envision such a horror, whose dreaded result would be the mixing of blood and racial impurity [*métissage*]. They feared, of course, that they would thereby lose their privileges. And the left could not imagine working for anything other than what had effectively brought them together themselves. They truly sought a kind of freemasonry of the colonized that would be both socialist and universalist, but not Moslem, fetishist, or Jewish – that is, it would not express the character of each formerly colonized people in its singularity and its own particular differences.

What remained for the colonized (and in general, for all oppressed people, I would later argue) was simply to accept themselves, since no one else would accept them. Where good faith and solicitude had led only to humiliation, only self-vindication remained. There was no other way out. To refuse oneself, to denounce one's defeated ancestors out of shame, to abjure one's language because it was said to be clumsy or one's traditions because they were considered ineffective, was unconscionable. From the moment the oppressed began to speak, they testified to painful and vain acrobatic performances, trying to fulfill the perspective of the dominant, to see themselves through his eyes in order to adopt his perspective, and in the end, they only found themselves living his injurious contempt. To live, one must, in one way or another, affirm oneself.[6] If one cannot affirm oneself through identification with something, one must affirm oneself through difference. To take this one step further: "To be is to be different" (see *Portrait of a Jew*). To affirm one's difference becomes the condition for self-affirmation, the banner for the individual or collective reappropriation of one's self. Where, in the first instance, the dominant affirmed their differences over and against those they oppressed, in the last, the oppressed reclaim their differences against the dominant. I called this second symmetrical movement "the return of the pendulum."

Since then, many experiences have confirmed what has now become the common understanding. But it has not been without pain, occasioned by wrenching and impassioned discussions, by discord and breaks in relations, and by many mistakes. For instance, in several Arab countries, the Jewish citizens, many of whom had contributed to the struggle for national independence, were afterward told to leave. The same happened to the Spanish of the Maghreb. It is rare that the "return of the pendulum" is content merely to correct an unjust situation. Carried away by its own momentum [*élan*], the pendulum swings far over to the other side, at times perpetrating injustices of its own; thus, there were the expropriations of small colonists and the harassment of minorities who were innocently caught in the situation.[7] Self-affirmation sometimes takes on mythic proportions; to the injurious myths of the past, one counterposes substitute myths that are just as deluded. The least important ancestor becomes a legendary hero, and a folk dance the pinnacle of art. Having struggled for the recognition of differences, I have dissented as well against these new excesses – and do so still. None of them were inscribed in what we had originally sought to reclaim. When, during the first Congress of Black Intellectuals, a participant, recalling Molière, wrote superbly, "I am in rags, perhaps, but these rags are mine," by his intentional use of the word "rags," he refused to hyperbolize his blackness, while at the same time refusing to disown it. As with the slogan "Black is Beautiful" [in English, in the original], one's being a woman, or a Jew, or a Breton can be glorified. Or the Arab Moslem can be proposed as the paragon of civilization. This fierce faith seems to me as debatable as the self-devaluations of the past. No one needs to be ashamed of their past or their heart; to accept oneself is also to accept one's personal and collective history. But is it necessary to pass from self-refusal all the way to hypervaluation? To valorize oneself in excess because one has been devalorized in excess? Does one not risk committing the same errors as the racist partisans of difference? Does one not soon risk affirming oneself against others?

The same holds for other associated notions that have become popular, such as identity, roots, and so on. If they are difficult to define, they are of doubtful utility as well. All this is explainable as probably necessary after having been downtrodden for so long, but one must watch out for what new delusions one may then confront. It is an irony of history that, whether coming upon or returning to an exaltation of roots and collective identities, the first to preach that exaltation were those of the right. It is no wonder we are witnessing a rebirth of right-wing movements in Europe. At base, it is a movement to recapture the past, and as is often the case, that is an ambiguous project. A common past is generally fictional because it is usually an invention by certain partisan interests, and thus neither common nor a past. One must ask, common to whom? Whose past? The responses to such questions will be full of surprises. Who can really be sure of their supposed ancestors? Some serious research would have to be done . . . if it were possible. And if one really wanted to; I am not sure that many people really wish to disturb their comfortable sense of their own history. In any case, to be is to be different, yes, but to be different is to be other. Therefore, everyone is different and everyone is other. In short, all self-affirmation must be by definition relative. Whatever its importance in one's voyage of recovery, difference cannot be considered an end in and of itself. No one can take the prize in this.

In effect, the real stakes against racism, which must also inform anti-racism, do not concern difference itself but the use of difference as a weapon against its victim, to the advantage of the victimizer.

Therein lies the real depravity of racism. This can all be summed up in three points. Differences can exist or not exist. Differences are not in themselves good or bad. One is not racist or anti-racist in pointing out or in denying differences, but one is racist in using them against someone to one's own advantage.

[. . .]

Whatever its little detours may be, ultimately, *the goal of racism is dominance*. This is the last point I will elicit from its relation to colonialism. It is a point of correlation, however, that provides an essential insight into the structure of racism. As in billiards, where one aims at one ball in order to hit another, though racism levies its accusatory derogations under many different pretexts, it does so always in order to reject, to injure, and to oppress. In looking first at the colonial relation, I was led to elucidate and then systematize that same relation in other forms of racism, those enmeshed in other, yet similar, conditions of oppression. Of course, the case of the Jews, with which I preoccupied myself next, was one I knew from the inside, without having to reflect on it. But the elaboration of my general reflections in *The Colonizer and the Colonized* also came naturally. Then, by passing from the colonial situation to other forms of oppression, I was able to extend the formula given above: *racism illustrates and symbolizes oppression*.

That said, if we now reexamine the importance of myth in the racist discourse, we can see its limits. It is necessary, but it is relative; it is crucial, but it is not the whole of racism. *Racism is an opinion, but it is an opinion that declares an intention and signals a mode of conduct*.

One opinion does not suffice to make a racist, assuming he could stop there. Racism is both the ideology and the active manifestation of domination. Each time one explores a relation of oppression, one discovers within it a racism, like a ghost or a shadow, as its inevitable extension. An aspect of all forms of dominance, it is a laborious and self-concerned form of bad faith. If I dominate you, it is *because* you are an inferior being; the responsibility is yours, and the differences that exist between us prove it. Whites can exploit [*asservir*] Blacks because Blacks are not White – that is, they are afflicted with the insufficiency of being Black, and thus deprived of the virtue of being White. Men have the right to use women because women are different and because femininity is a deficiency. Whatever the seductions of those deficiencies, a certain distorted conduct is authorized: one can be a "ladies' man" and still have contempt for women; one can be infatuated with Black women or Jewish women, or Arab boys, without ceasing to despise the world each comes from.

Thus, the general effect of the dominance-subjection relation is to destroy both parties, each by the other, and each in a specific manner. Though the corrosive suffering of the victim is wholly incommensurate with and overshadows the psychic deformation of the victimizer, one nevertheless does not transform oneself into an executioner without great cost. There is a double erosion of personhood in all racism, because its only purpose is to torment other people through an attempt to reduce them to nothing, and to harass people to the point of destroying them. I do not mean this symbolically, or as a moment of the racist's imagination, but as a concrete process of constant humiliation, of gratuitous constraint imposed on the other's life; at its worst, the other finally engages in forms of self-destruction.

That is, the *interiorization* of racist denigration is not the least criminal aspect of it; it is the ingestion of a poison that eats away from the inside, and whose end is the victim's wholehearted adoption of the imposed image. How is one to defend oneself if one is driven into agreement with one's persecutor? Before the French Revolution, a person named Moreau de Saint-Mery developed a classification of the people of the Antilles that included "negroes," "mulattoes," "quadroons," *métis, mamelouques, sang-mêlés, marabouts, griffés,* and *sacatros,*[8] along with various other designations. When I went to the Antilles myself, I was shocked to find that Saint-Mery's schema was not only still in effect, but enriched! The people of the Antilles had adopted and preserved this infernal scale of diminished dignity, measured by a person's distance from the "White Father" (their own expression), with all the implicit social and psychological damage one might imagine. The scars of past oppression are not easily healed. It reminded me of a Tunisian concierge who became very angry at me one day but could only express it through a reflection on herself: "You are nothing but a Tunisian, like us!"

Yet one's racism is not a road to paradise, either. Because it is bad faith, it demands constant defense, argument, and hostility. It is a bottomless pit, an endless debate in which no one is ever completely convinced – neither those victimized, despite their harassment and torment, nor those who think in racist terms and who sense their lack of being, their obsessive need for an endless campaign that never brings them peace of mind. During my trip to the Antilles, I spent time with many *Békés* (French people born on the islands), and they never stopped talking about "all that."

Let it be said in passing (I will return to this later) that the necessity for endless defensiveness and self-explanation is not a totally bad sign. At the risk of sounding confused, I would say that, in a manner of speaking, the racist deserves some credit. A hardened criminal does not talk, he kills. But behind racism's evil aspect, there is something that could be called *the ethical paradox of the racist stance*, and it offers a glimmer of hope. Animals devour their prey without due process when they are hungry. More vigorous plants tend to crowd out the weaker. Humans, like all living things, seize, crush, or kill, both their own kind and others. But they find it necessary to talk about it as well, to explain and to justify themselves to others, to obtain approbation. Do I dominate? Do I have privileges? Certainly, but it is because I have rights! On this land, my father, after all . . . my ancestors . . . and so on. It is a pitiful legitimacy, of course, fallacious, fictional, and out of joint. But it is proclaimed, insisted on, and even theorized. There are philosophies and moralities founded on race, psychology, sex, culture, and metaphysics. One does for oneself what one can for the sake of a slightly easier conscience. How much of the behavior of "grand" families or of "national" politics is nothing more than rapaciousness at the level of the group? Yet still, the necessity to rationalize it as preserving a sacred familial patrimony or the "national interest" remains inescapable. In one way or another, the need to justify one's gains is ineluctable.

[. . .]

There is always some benefit or advantage to be gained. That is the very thing that commands attention: *the racist undertaking is never disinterested*, even if what it seeks to gain is not immediately evident.

What would the advantage be? Of what could it consist? On the surface, it could be anything: psychological, economic, political, cultural . . . whatever one seeks, more or less consciously, to the detriment of the other. At the risk of redundancy, we can define the benefits of racism as *all that produces an advantage or privilege through the devaluation of the other.*

An objection that Marxism might raise should perhaps be addressed. For most Marxists, the diversity of racism's social advantages is a deception, in the strong sense of the term. "Man" is, essentially, an economic animal, driven principally by economic needs. The rest is diversion, ruse, and ideology. In these terms, racism is fundamentally an economic weapon. Racist discourse becomes an alibi disguising an interminable appropriation of natural resources and, more to the point, the "exploitation of man by man." According to the familiar formula, "economics is the ultimate motor of history."

I am in partial agreement with the Marxists here. They are right to suspect that racism seeks another end, behind all its disparagements and attacks. I am quite convinced that there are usually two levels to a discourse – an explicit content and a hidden meaning. Often, the hidden meaning is much more important and more revelatory than the literal. For racism, the real meaning must be mystified in order not to reveal its basic injustice. Its primary need is to fool its prey, to forestall their reactions, which would be counteractive. But also, oppression needs disguises for itself as well; it is not always possible to assent to privilege with an easy conscience. At times, an iron-fisted regime becomes necessary, which is not particularly pleasant to live in and, moreover, is costly. A good disguise or an adroit defense is worth the effort, at least as an economy of means. One virtue of the ideology of domination is that it is pragmatic – which contributes to its stability and power.

The Marxists are not wrong, either, in suspecting contemporary racism of economic motivation. Frequently, that is the case, though it may not always be evident. Examples are not hard to find in history, sociology, or even literature. The small anti-Semitic businessman enmeshed in his problems, or a victim of his own greed, will hope to gain immediate benefit from the destruction of his Jewish competitors. It is not an accident that economic recession always seems to call up the lurking monster of anti-Semitism.

My agreement with the Marxists ends there. I think they are wrong to think that privilege always reduces itself to economic advantage – even as "ultimate determinant," according to their customary expression. Which is, of course, an ambiguous formula; if one rejects consideration of intermediary forms, it becomes false, while if one admits the importance of these forms, then the formula has only theoretical interest. A similar argument would apply to explanations based on the Oedipus complex, for instance. I am well aware that it is no longer possible to lump all Marxists together. Having aged, the doctrine has become diversified, as with old religions, and the faithful wisely counsel tolerance toward dissident sects and heretics. Marxists, however, even those who no longer support the necessity of one exclusive interpretation, still accept the primacy of economics "in the final analysis" (as they say). Yet it suggests, more or less directly, an economic determinism. Human reality is more complex; one could not know for certain what unique factor governs all the rest, nor could one know even if such a thing exists. Human needs are multiple, even if they are not endlessly multiplied. Priorities are variable and fluid. The need for security, or the need for love, is often as important as the need for nourishment. In short, one might adopt a racist stance for many different reasons, and not simply for calculable economic return – even though, for all, the mechanism whereby those gains are achieved may be the same.

[. . .]

The phenomenon of the scapegoat illustrates this point. The Ancients had an extraordinary intuition. To exorcise misfortune, they sacrificed an expiatory animal to the gods; by loading the poor beast with all the sins of the community, they thus unburdened it of its collective guilt. The notion of a tragic hero works in a similar way, and it is no accident that this was so successful as theater. Accused of being the source of whatever calamities have struck, the hero must perish in order to bring them to an end. In some cases, he is not responsible, being instead a pawn of fatal destinies (like Oedipus) or of occult divine machinations. Whatever the case, the collective conscience does not recoil from choosing an innocent person to pay for the crimes and comforts of others. The myth of Jesus Christ is of this genre: a man of good repute and purity of being who, as a saint and son of a virgin, is designated to redeem the sufferings and sins of humanity. Agamemnon sacrificed his daughter as virginal martyr in order to appease the wrath of the gods, as if her purity, like clean linen, was needed to wipe away the stains of former corruption. It is as if the purity of the victim becomes the coin wjh which to pay the costs charged by destiny or divinity.[9] Naturally, such an interpretation does not exhaust these myths. But what it signifies is that to load one's mistakes and misfortunes upon another makes an adverse situation more tolerable, whether the sacrificial victim is a competitor or a neighbor, a member of a minority or of another nation, an institution or nature itself. To attribute our private or public failures, our sports or professional defeats, to the treachery of an adversary excuses our own deficiencies. In the film *The Little Soldier*, Charlie Chaplin's hero shoots at a stone, which he holds responsible for his misfortunes. Isn't this what the bigot does? Or as a humorist once said, "Why the Jews, and not bicyclists?" To which the anti-Semite would reply: "Because the Jews fill the bill."

The derogatory stance, the act of denigrating another, permits people to close ranks with each other; the identification of an external threat, whether real or imagined, restores fraternity. Our modern leaders have only revived a very old recipe; one has only to designate a responsible party, however innocent she or he may be, to vindicate the rest. Name the misfortune, give it a face, and thereby create the illusion of having mastered it! The effect is to assuage the collective self as much as the individual self.

For these purposes, the marginalized are "well placed," as they say in horse racing. Foreigners are less protected by the law; minorities, or those who are different, are already suspect. They make excellent hooks on which to hang collective anxiety. It is not an accident that the inquisitions of Europe killed so many female witches and so few male ones. Women are different and less adept at defending themselves. General fear and resentment are more easily incorporated in them. In more recent times, Black people in the United States have been burned by lynch mobs, as women were burned during the Inquisition. The genocidal campaign against the Jews, in which fully a third of the world's Jews were exterminated, was the latest avatar of this ongoing butchery. To exteriorize evil by incarnating it in another separates it from society and renders it less threatening. It can be manipulated, managed, destroyed by fire. The common denominator must be understood: fire purifies all, including ourselves . . . but only by burning the other. That is where it is most economical.

These are extreme cases, in which the inner meanings are more clearly seen, but the same meanings can then be discovered in other places and other events. At the individual level, one destroys in the other what one would like to destroy in oneself, by imputing to that other one's own faults. Indeed, it is the vehemence of the apologies, the excessive protestations about our own virginal innocence against the baseness of the other, that betrays as much as it affirms. The protestations are too shrill. The outcome of the trial is never in question; the victim is convicted in advance, with the public in solidarity with the prosecution. And the executioners, whether they work with hot coals or words, whether they roast their enemies or only designate them as such, always proclaim for themselves a great love for the collective soul. Through them, we are no longer the guilty, because the other is. Of course, we are never wholly convinced, since we must continue to argue and debate. But even these efforts, though a furtive avowal of our deficiencies, become a part of our self-purification. Like ritual baths, they are more effective when all take them together. We evoke our faults in common; we account for and cleanse ourselves collectively. Henceforth, we are pure, because we all participate in the same purity. What transcends and envelops us we have drawn out of ourselves, and we now find the evil outside, beyond us. Thus, we give ourselves mutual self-absolution.

One could go on about the necessity for purity. Having already found biological purity to be inconceivable, we have dispensed with its pretenses. *Psychological purity is no more intelligible* (see *A Contre-courants*). But why is there such an obsessive preoccupation with it? The answer is easy: since purity cannot be documented, it can only appear as a promise, made at the behest of a nostalgia or a hope. The racist mind aspires to the image of a perfect nation, though one it is nevertheless unable to really describe. One finds it difficult to say if the ideal is a return to a former state or the establishment of a new order, a lost paradise, or a messianic golden age. The Italian fascists combined the two: ancient Rome and the avant-garde of European modernity. The PanGerman movement conjured up. a past splendor as legitimation for imposing its rule on the world. In general, a future seen as a projection of the past is amalgamated with a past reconstructed as a function of the future. It is both a regret for not living in that past state of grace and a desire to recapture it. And against all intruders, all those strangers who threaten to tarnish or obstruct the enactment of promised communion, however illusory it might be, there is recourse to a familiar violence. In that moment, one comes face to face with the scapegoat.

The trauma and drama of this process have seduced philosophers and inspired poets. Even psychoanalytic interpretations suggest themselves: "Ah, how good it was to be all *together*, myself between Papa and Mama, in the warmth of the home, sheltered from the cold external world!" "Ah, how good it was *before* that new baby arrived, that shitting, pissing stranger who has polluted everything, disturbed the family harmony, absorbed all the milk, monopolized all parental love and the attentions of visitors." But while the poets dream, and philosophers and psychologists interpret; the racist acts. Since a return to the carefree world of infancy is impossible, he says, let us make a future in its image; let us constitute our homogeneity in solidarity *against* all who disturb or defile it; let us rid ourselves of the intruders, the immigrants, the invaders, the polluters, by means of their destruction if necessary. And I wonder if the desecraters of Jewish tombs, the ragged slanderers and occasional assassins of poor immigrant workers, do not get some real sensual pleasure from committing their crimes, though they have probably convinced themselves that they act for the public good. Indeed, many participants in white lynch mobs have acknowledged a kind of deranged ecstasy in defending the mythic integrity of the white race. This miserable plague, this scandal, which I have already shown is delusory, must be brought to an end if a life-affirming social order is to be established. There are children who would kill that unacceptable little brother if they could, and sometimes they can. The obsession with purity arises from a fear of pollution and a vow to obviate it.

Notes

1   By *difference*, it goes without saying, I am referring to a trait differential and not to its concrete being or actual substantiality; in any ease, it is wiser to employ the plural: *differences*.

2   Albert Memmi, *A Contre-courants*, illustrations by Michel Ciardi (Paris: Nouvel Objet, 1993).

3   [The Jacobins were the radicals of the French Revolution, who sought the most complete dismantling of the old feudal aristocratic structure in the name of the equality of "man." They introduced the Declaration of the Rights of Man into the revolutionary process. In attempting to unify France under the republic, the revolution ended up fighting not only the aristocracy, many of whom had fled to England as a base of counterrevolutionary operations, but local armies of peasants and former serfs who resisted the revolution in the name of loyalty to that same nobility. This conflict reached its most critical level in the province of Vendfe, in western France. Victor Hugo's novel *Ninety-Three* is a brilliant portrait of the human issues involved in that struggle. – Trans.]

4   [This type of realization initiated the contemporary critique of humanism, now associated with poststructuralist thought. In the process of anti-colonial struggle, many people came to realize that the human being that Western humanism spoke about was the White European human being, and that humanism had imposed it as an ideological concept, derived from a European cultural background, on other cultures that were different. The purpose of the critique of humanism was not to "throw humanism out," as some of its detractors have claimed, but to reveal its limits and biases, and thus to open the notion of the humane, which humanism had sought to place in the center of human activity, to a multiplicity of nonimpositional contexts. – Trans.]

5   On the importance of ideology for racism, see the works of Colette Guillaumin, in particular *L'idéologie raciste: Genèse et langage actuel* (La Haye: Mouton, 1972).

6   [This is a question that Frantz Fanon addresses in *The Wretched of the Earth* – that is, the dislocating and unbalancing psychological effects of colonialism and its

brutality, and what the process of national liberation, in its many forms, offered as practical therapy – and perhaps, he theorized, the only practical therapy – for the psychological ills suffered by the colonized. Frantz Panon, *The Wretched of the Earth*, preface by Jean-Paul Sartre, trans. Constance Farrington (New York: Grove Press, 1965); originally published as *Les damnés de la terre*, preface by Jean-Paul Sartre (Paris: Maspero, 1961). – Trans.]

7   On "the return of the pendulum," see my essay by that name in Albert Memmi, *Dominated Man: Notes toward a Portrait* (Boston: Beacon Press, 1969); originally published as *L'Homme dominé* (Paris: Gallimard, 1968).

8   [I leave these terms for degrees of "racial mixture" in French, since the English equivalents have become archaic and do not need to be resurrected here. – Trans.]

9   I have developed this notion of "costs to be paid" for all such "services rendered" in my article "Dependence," in "Le Prix de la Santé," *Perspective et santé publique* (December 1982).

Chapter 9

Pierre-André Taguieff

ON ANTIRACISM

[. . .]

U NDERSTANDING THE CONTEMPORARY forms of racism involves submitting ordinary antiracism to critical reason Avoiding any analogical or metaphorical reduction of the present to the past (and to a certain past, one that nourishes an ever-effective political imaginary: the Dreyfus Affair, the Nazi genocide of the Jews. . .), engaging in an analysis without pity of the antiracist discourses on "racism" that seem to play the role of collective screen-memories: such are the conditions of an active departure from the circle of exorcising practices, pious ceremonies, and lazy repetitions of the same formulas of defensive magic.

Classical antiracism, a system engendered by the ideologization[1] of the humanist tradition, hardened into a rhetoric that is today on the way to being totally instrumentalized by the political struggles for power (as well as for cultural hegemony), may be briefly characterized by a set of traits that sketch an ideal type.[2]

1. Antiracism represents the *functional survival* of an ideological apparatus brought into focus in the 1930s to fight against the National Socialist regime, its diffuse influence, and the growing power of its allies, beginning with Italian fascism. The latter underwent the misadventure, through the unfathomable paths of propaganda, of quite involuntarily giving its name to the *demonized/demonizing entity*, *fascism*, a term that lumps together all the contemporary motifs and objects of political hatred but that above all has few traits in common with Italian fascism as a historical reality.[3] A discourse of propaganda destined to fight against a state racism that represented a real danger for the European democracies no less than for the communist system, antiracist antifascism constituted the least common ideological denominator between pluralist democracies and Stalinist totalitarianism, a shared polemical position strictly tied to conjuncture. When the latter disappeared, antiracism had to find new negative objects, outside the communist field of influence,

as by definition. As South Africa alone precisely corresponded to this model, anti-racism after 1945 was slowly displaced from the preferential denunciation of "neo-Nazism" (from 1945 to the early 1960s) to that of the apartheid regime practiced by South Africa,[4] not without integrating, in its left wing (Third-Worldist and/or Christian-communist), the stigmatization of "Zionism," which was progressively demonized to the point of being likened to "racism" and to an apartheid regime, in the extension of Soviet and Arab propaganda.[5] The antiracist left allowed itself to be instrumentalized bit by bit by a complex of propagandas, while the antiracist right tended to reduce, as if by reaction, its field of investigation to a general struggle (but an expressly political one: anticommunism continued by humanitarianist means) against "anti-Semitism".[6] Now, the tendency to typify antiracism in general as "the struggle against anti-Semitism" may appear especially anachronistic and at the very least paradoxical. For, on the one hand, the new forms of anti-Jewish discourse no longer carry a racist legitimation (so no longer an "anti-Semitic" ideology in the strict sense) except as a remnant, and, on the other hand, the regime designated as the principal enemy (and sometimes, significantly, the only enemy) is incarnated by the Soviet Union,[7] whose victims one risks reducing to the sole category of unassimilated Jews – that is, in essence, religious or "Zionist" Jews, in the broad sense.[8]

Let us summarize: the antiracist ideologization of humanism, an apparatus that remained unitary until the defeat of the Axis powers, has since evolved in the direction of a differentiation into two opposing camps, which may be schematized by the "anti-imperialist" and the anticommunist poles of antiracism. That is why it is perhaps not excessive to deem that today, in spite of the ideological homogeneity suggested by the term *antiracism*, the latter masks the reality of political scission and covers with a single and thereby equivocal name two rhetorical systems that are fundamentally heterogeneous and hence antinomic. Antiracism must be stated in at least two senses: antiracism is a homonymic term.

2. Antiracism puts into play a received idea, a first piece of evidence that it posits as a univocal and sufficient definition: racism is in its essence *the rejection of difference*, the refusal or impossibility of accepting another as different – that is, as not identical to nor resembling oneself. Antiracism limits racism a priori, by a primal definition, to *heterophobia*. It thereby even prohibits merely considering the racializations that proceed from the praise of difference, that build on anthropological pluralism in order to hold up factual cultural differences as supreme values and to prescribe their unconditional defense as a categorical imperative. So doing, antiracism first commits a grave error concerning the rhetorical functioning of ordinary language, in the order of what Aristotle called the epideictic genre:[9] for if praise and blame are continually converted to each other, then racism may indiscriminately be constituted by blame (of difference/differences) or praise (of difference/differences). But racism has a demerit whose practical consequences are graver: it dissimulates the functional ambiguity of the racism that proceeds in wavering between blame and praise; it prohibits its access to knowledge in the very name of the conviction of knowing its nature. The *illusion of knowing* is worse than ignorance. Thus the antiracist risks dreaming with his eyes open, sure of himself and accusing, laughing, or lamenting, never belied by the facts nor disappointed by his radical inefficacy.

3. Antiracism continually modulates a basic statement, which one will note is common to the left (communist or not) and to the liberal-democratic right: "Crisis breeds racism, which breeds fascism."[10] If crisis breeds racism, it is because it leads to the designation of scapegoated victims.[11] Explanation by "crisis" is willingly stated as a law "any crisis. . ."), and a causal law. Let us give two examples of statements of the *crisological formula*, the first restricted, the second developed. The editorial board of a socialist monthly posited, in November 1984, the following axiom: "Any economic crisis, by the disarray and anguish it incites, is accompanied by a rise in intolerance and xenophobia."[12] Thus is satisfied the mesological desire, the reduction of xenophobia to an effect of specific social conditions that are themselves achieved in being assigned to an economic determinism. In the framework of the ideology of the supposedly omnipotent middle, explanation by crisis tends to be presented as an explanation by *economic* crisis, which responds to the dominant, fundamentally economophile objectivist need. Hence the entry into circulation of ideological evidence: the phenomena of society considered aberrant may be only, in the last analysis, effects produced by economic dysfunctionings. The "roots" of xenophobia and racism are of an economic order, first and essentially by reason of the axiom that the economy is the real.

[. . .]

Referring to "crisis" achieves the most common incantatory naming of Evil (or of its favorable conditions: "in favor of crisis") in contemporary ideological space. An indistinct name, *crisis* signifies and designates without distinction the cause and the effect, the essence and the accident, the "seed" and the manifestation. A well-advised political scientist has accurately characterized the ideological advantage of such a great confusion: "Political vocabulary offers the term *crisis*, the most confused word in contemporary social thought. Because it has no content, because its use is not governed by any discipline, it may designate any situation at all."[13] But we might note here a general trait of political discourse, if it is true that the latter is constituted around a systematic avoidance of any precise definition of the terms it employs.[14]

The universalist antiracists stigmatize as "racist" the reactions that the supposed racists, who proudly designate themselves as "national" or "nationalist," describe as natural and legitimate: reactions of legitimate defense before the threat of an invasion or of a destruction of community identity, of a theft of work, or of a rape of the national body. Hence the same imperative, "We must defend against the foreign invasion" (certain foreigners constituting an invasion more than others), is interpreted in two rigorously opposite ways: as typically "racist" by the dominant group of antiracists and as a prescription for self-defense against "anti-French racism" (and the invasion that supposedly accompanies it) by the "racists" (those so named by the former). But the two opposing collective subjects, "antiracists" and "racists," agree on the broad diagnosis of "crisis," linking economic crisis (unemployment), social and moral crisis (values in crisis), and the identity crisis affecting France and the French.

What we have called the "crisological formula" applies perfectly to monocausal explanation by "economic crisis." At issue here is a sloganized form (thus calling for struggle against the so-called crisis) of the economic conception of the world, which must be conceived as a system of illusory explanation appeasing a specific *dogmatic need*. Now, economistic monomania long ago left the limited ideologicopolitical territory of the "materialist conception of history," in which Max Weber situated it exclusively at the beginning of the twentieth century. The liberal-socialist consensus on the primacy of the economy has instead been put forth as absolute ideological evidence: modernity is achieved as economolatry. In 1904, Weber perfectly identified this new axiom of the historico-social sciences, this economistic principle of sufficient reason that certain circles insisted on as governing the methodology of these sciences. Indeed, he stigmatized

> the peculiar condition that their need for a causal explanation of an historical event is never satisfied until somewhere or somehow economic causes are shown (or seem) to be operative. Where this however is the case, they content themselves with the most threadbare hypotheses and the most general phrases since they have then satisfied their dogmatic need to believe that the economic "factor" is the "real" one, the only "true" one, and the one which "in the last instance is everywhere decisive."[15]

But we must carry the critique of economistic monocausalism to its very spiritual-cultural roots: we must in this sense conceive it as one of the ideologico-scientific figures of "the inevitable monistic tendency"[16] that, on the basis of some science or other (biology, physics, economics, and so on), claims to construct a conception of the world endowed with an explanatory omnipotence. This monistic presumption, thus postulated as an a priori of the human mind, characterizes "every type of thought which is not self-critical."[17] Incarnated by its "eager dilettantes,"[18] economistic dogmatism claims to reduce historical becoming in its totality, "in the last instance," to the rivalry of economic interests. Hegemonic antiracism does nothing but apply to its specific domain the scheme of economorphic gnosis.

4. Antiracism assumes a manipulatory, even *conspiracist, representation*[19] of racism. The rhetorical schema that subtends the antiracist representation of racism is the following: there exists a social power, anonymous or personalized, whose activity consists of dissimulating (in its objectives and tactics), of both inventing and diffusing erroneous models of interpretation of social and economic questions, of proposing illusory solutions based on the designation of those responsible (the racists) for "the crisis," in order to channel the dissatisfactions and hatreds in the direction of a scapegoated minority victim, foreign to the average (or ideal) type of the "homegrown" population. In short, racism would be an ideological and discursive device destined to get people to believe so as to get them to do, thus fulfilling a supplementary function: to camouflage the true problems, to turn attention away from the real causes of social discontent. (These causes waver between the class struggle and the welfare state, between left antiracism and right antiracism.) The placement in discourse of these interpretive schemes, which also play the role of arguments in ideological warfare, is most commonly effected by the metaphor of "orchestration" or according to the model of the "campaign," whether political or journalistic (or the conjunction of the two). The manipulatory representation of racism involves focusing on the power to deceive, on the mystifying agency

that would be its true subject, the latter all the more dangerous since it would not itself believe in the racist propositions that it would banalize in opinion. This mystifying and overpowerful subject is formally distinguished from the "racist" who practices in the open. The latter is only the "maneuver" of the former.[20] The "racist" of journalistic discourse is hence reduced, in the elaborate representation that antiracist "theory" gives of him, to the subaltern role of manipulated collaborator in a cause that he cannot know in its truth. Stated otherwise, the dominant antiracist view of racism assumes a distinction between the real and the apparent subject of racism, deceptive and deceived, abusive and abused, cynical and naive. But, even here, racism is no longer defined as an ideology (in spite of the usage of ideologistic vocabulary); rather, it is in turn reduced to the functional status of an instrumental myth, to a fiction of propaganda. Racism no longer stems so much from the spontaneous collective imaginary, from ideological production, as it does from an intention of and will to indocrination, in the service of an occult poitics. [. . .]

5. Antiracism tends to serve as a *means of diversion*, insofar as the denunciation of racism[21] is susceptible of turning public attention away from real social, economic, or military problems. This ideologization and politicization of antiracism confer on it an instrumental function in an ideological war of which one objective is to paralyze the adversary through disinformation. That is why the tactical function of antiracism is willingly brought into evidence by conservative ideologues and anticommunists, whether "nationalists" (the National Front) or "liberals" (who express themselves in *Le Figaro* or *Le Quotidien de Paris*). Antiracism may in certain cases be denounced as a method of intellectual terrorism, an enterprise of obfuscation and blinding. On the side of xenophobic nationalism, the affair has long been understood, inasmuch as some trait of antiracism remains one of the rare ideological means of confronting it. In the following, François Brigneau devotes himself to disqualifying antiracism for the reason that the latter would target only a "straw man": "Today, the straw man is racism. Even if the word cannot be applied to reality, it sounds out the sweeties and rounds up the cuties."[22] Its function of rallying the lefts would enable an understanding of racism as the last means of "blackmail" and of "intellectual terrorism of the left." The first "straw man" was clericalism, which, under the Third Republic, was denounced only to serve to rejoin the bloc of lefts. The second "straw man" was fascism, whose proclaimed threatening return, brandished like a flag, allowed one "to forget the Soviet Union." The third "straw man," finally, is racism, which is stirred up in order to effect; "a particularly repugnant operation against French nationalism."[23] It will be noted in the passage that the defensive argument for nationalism is able to integrate one of the real characteristics of antiracism. But if the argument does not reproach the latter for a fictional property, it nonetheless integrates the motif of the instrumentality of antiracism in a conspiracist grand narrative in which the enemy is, as if in a mirror, demonized: "We are in the presence of a vast incantation against the French France and its natural defenders."[24] The reaction to the anti-Magheebian and anti-Jewish murders and incidents of late March 1985, instigated by SOS-Racisme, is interpreted in the framework of this paranoid vision of the world:

> Menton. Miramas. Paris. The bomb at the Jewish festival (eighteen
> slightly wounded) whose sound drowns out the small echo from

Guadaloupe (a bomb at a National Front café owner's): the campaign of feigned indignation and real intimidation unleashed by the anti-French racists touches on delirium. By their clamors, their denunciations, their displays, their acts of lumping together, they want to provoke the worst. We leave them with the responsibility for their undertaking. We see perfectly its mainsprings and tricks.[25]

Among ex-communists who have become conservatives and anticommunists, who are particularly sensitive to the techniques of ideological instrumentalization (they know them from the inside), the critique of antiracism is also based on the grievance of obfuscation] diversion: "By continuing to struggle 'against racism,' we are in the process of falsifying, distorting, occulting the diversity of motives that command individual and collective decisions."[26] But what is essential is elsewhere for "systemic" anticommunism: antiracism is only understood in the framework of the communist strategy in western Europe that, "based on a union with a possibly radicalizing social democracy," would strive to "revive the 'progressive' tradition of the 1930s."[27] Antiracism is reduced to a single element in the discourse of communist propaganda. After analyzing the linked acts of lumping together implied by communist antiracism/antifascism, Annie Kriegel moves on to decoding the "struggle against anti-Semitism":

The "struggle against anti-Semitism" was drowned and diluted [by the MRAP and similar organizations] in a struggle against racism or rather "against all racisms," one of which was Zionism. It is in this way that, by an apparent broadening of a single theme – from the struggle against anti-Semitism to the struggle against all racisms – the communists were successful with the tour de force, for example after the incident on the Rue Copernic, of lining up the leaders of the Jewish community behind a banner that, implicitly, for the ones who read it from the communist point of view, included the state of Israel among the purveyors of hatred against the Jews.[28]

The critical argument is quite simple: generalized and generic antiracism (which subsumes all humanitarianist "struggles") is advantageous to international communism, its true initiator and sponsor. Unfortunately for our desire for objectivity, the mythical slant of such a demystifying critique is quickly revealed, as much through the neglect of empirical "details" (we are content with a few striking illustrations of "theory") as through a singular speed of elevation to the great anticommunist view of the world, a new paranoid picture that has no cause to envy the old communist view. The simplism of conspiracist pseudoexplanation (to whom is this advantageous?) in fact blocks scientific investigation. The renewed communist imaginary remains within the limits of diabolical causality. Good analyses are not done with disappointment, resentment, and vindictive recycling.

6. Antiracism is founded on a *postulate of exteriority* of the antiracist spectator-actor with respect to the racist, that is, of the one who designates "racist" in the face of the one who is designated as such. The antiracist, having the power of qualification, therefore presupposes himself, by the fact of spotting a "racist" and

qualifying her as such, as a subject situated on the exterior of the racist world, or at least the world of racists. This is the *postulate of radical separability* of the antiracist and the racist, to which is surreptitiously added a *postulate of inequality*: for the antiracist does not doubt for an instant that his antiracist position is superior to the racist position he stigmatizes. Here is a paradox of egalitarian ideology in general, which necessarily arises in the particular field of antiracist egalitarianism: one may not affirm the value of equality to be superior to that of inequality without postulating a hierarchical scale of values; in the same way, one may not affirm antitacist values without assuming them to be superior to racist values, therefore without putting into play an inegalitarian relation (between the antiracist and the racist types) that one otherwise impugns absolutely, precisely as an index of racism.[29] But the antiracist representation of the racist goes beyond the relation of inequality: the racist tends to be treated, by an only slightly elaborated rhetorical reversal, in the very same way the racist treats the racized. The racist – as the Other rejected from the world of properly human values, excluded from dialogue, likened to a delinquent – tends to become the representative of that demonized entity who bore the names, in the racist tradition, of the "inferior race" or the "antirace."[30] We see an inversion of the process of racism: the racist is *demonized*, after being thrown off into inhumanity.[31] The operation of designating the racist enemy, implied by the "fight against racism," thus enables the antiracist to exclude himself from what he blames and, absolutely innocent, to hold himself up as a tribunal for a set of behaviors that he judges to be infrahuman, indeed satanic.

A typology of antiracist attitudes may be sketched according to the types of "racists" disiguished or blamed.

a. The ignorant racist:[32] if racism is measured and produced by ignorance, the antiracist struggle will merge with the task of education and upbringing. This is an optimistic postulate: no one is a racist voluntarily. The antiracist is an educator. His mission is twofold: on the one hand, to teach differences, to make them "known" and "liked"; on the other hand, to teach that differences are negligible and that what alone is worthy of absolute respect in each human being is shared by all human beings. This is a pedagogical hesitation inherent in contemporary antiracism, revealing the antinomy that it cannot surmount by its own means (see trait 8 below).

b. The wicked racist: it is no longer ignorance, a mere lack, but rather hatred, negative power, that is designated as the source of racism. To fight against racism is to disqualify and isolate it, to keep it from doing harm – to the point of excluding it: "I judge it unacceptable," declares Bernard-Henri Levy, "that Le Pen is considered a politician like the others. . . . I am a partisan of the exclusion of the bearers of xenophobic thoughts and racist ideology."[33] The antiracist realm is populated with rituals of counterexclusion, according to the simple logic of give-and-take: "The only just attitude, in the face of Le Pen: exclude him by all possible means from the family circle of established politics. The only imperative: draw around him the ideological and ethical line that, alone, will keep him out of action,"[34] As Leszek Kolakowski has duly noted, at issue here is one of those arguments most often invoked against tolerance, which presupposes the uniqueness of the supreme value of each domain of value in question: there is only one truth, only one good, only one type of beauty. Besides an unwavering axiological dogmatism, such a position illustrates almost as a caricature the relationship of mimetic rivalry (everyone excludes everyone), practiced as unsurpassable (or normal) while offering a good example of a phobic attitude: one must avoid contact with the group of plague victims or lepers; one must mark off the distance, separate, even differentiate – in a word, discriminate. In pseudoethnographic terms adorned with vague psychoanalysis, the antiracist will demand that taboo be restored, that there be respect for the border that absolutely separates the legitimate-respectable ones from the untouchables. That which is feared is displayed as a submersion in the "mud," the rising mire. Levy explained and prescribed, in November 1985:

> I insist on the case of Le Pen. The base of the affair, of course, is the taboo that has leaped out of the way. It is the lock that has come undone. It is that old mud, held back for years, that rises all at once, oozes into consciousness. And in the face of this oozing, in the face of this flood. . ., I believe we must no longer be afraid to call things by name – nor to call, literally, for *a restoration of Prohibition*.[35]

The wicked one is hence rejected, under the blow of metaphors, into the muck, the mire, the muddy element from which he should never emerge. This is an unconditional norm: the antiracist must protect herself from that which soils, covers with stains; she must be sufficiently vigilant not to fall into the (racist) mud, where there is risk of getting bogged down and dirtied, indeed of getting sucked in. Not only does the antiracist attribute to herself the monopoly on good intentions, but she also captures the superior position (she may fall into the mud if she is not careful) and the possession of purity, far above the muddy swamp in which the subhumans wallow, vile and corrupt. We should therefore be done, according to the distinguished antiracist, with a certain laxity toward the presumed bearers of racism: they are dangerous because they are endowed with a power of contamination, which is deployed every time they are allowed to come up from the bottom of this muddy marsh that is their natural element. We should in some way lock back up the sites of access to terra firma and clean air. The program is clear, simple. But is it not a transparent *petitio principii*? Just what is the prohibition that must be restored? Is the law of July 1972 insufficient? By which new and firmer means must we exclude the presumed racists? And how do we identify them without too much risk of being deceived? For the clandestine racists are legion. . . . This is precisely the question: for antiracist legislation to be effective, it should be applicable to all forms of racism, especially including those which in no way resemble the recognized and therefore recognizable forms. That is hardly possible: ineffectiveness seems to be guaranteed. Thus, to demand the restoration of prohibitions, and all the more so of Prohibition, is to speak and say nothing – at least nothing other than a barely shameful dream of the authoritarian organization of society. This is a wholly literary activism, a flagging antiracism.

[. . .]

c. The mad racist: in a certain way a mentally ill person (moving between neurosis and psychosis), the racist must be vigorously cared for. Racism, without referring to a type of mental illness, designates the set of symptoms distributed in the nosographic field. The antiracist is a polymorphous therapist. Let us take an exemplary text by Roger Ikor, whose intransigent democratic individualism draws on a militant rationalism whose polemical tendency is to pathologize any attitude perceived as irrational. By defining racism as "a flight, a fear, a hatred that attempts to find a justification and an excuse," Ikor believes he can explain that "this madness, specific to modern man, can be only furious."[36] Hence the hardly amenable description of the racist, at once bestialized and pathologized: "Yes, at the start, the racist is simply a beast who is afraid of his emerging soul and whom fear makes mad."[37] And the illness of this mad beast becomes a threatening epidemic: "Virus, terrain: there remains the opportunity that may unleash the illness."[38] In the racist are condensed the ordinary figures of threat, from the "dangerous madman" to "the proliferation of the racist cancer."[39] Antiracism has its own version of the catastrophist myth, with its obsessional and phobic anxieties.

d. *The stupid racist*: the grievance of stupidity ("he's a moron"; "he's a simpleton") has the advantage of unconditionally disqualifying the racist, but the disadvantage of being unable to be specific or to justify except by recourse to an inegalitarian theory of intelligence that, in antiracist milieus, is in general likened to racism and eugenicism (there are many slogans based on this chain of equivalence: elitism = eugenicism = racism = fascism). To fight against stupidity is first to ridicule it, thereby to exclude it from legitimate dialogue, to render it shameful and speechless. The antiracist is part of the intellectual elite that detests the racist, that weak and narrow mind.[40]

e. *The ill-bred racist*: racism may be the effect, no longer of a lack of education, but of a poor upbringing. The racist is the one who says things that should not be said, who makes inappropriate remarks. And also the one whose thoughts are supposedly dominated by "prejudices," "stereotypes," "clichés." The antiracist henceforth makes an effort to teach her methodical mistrust before received ideas; he will apply himself to reeducate her to speak correctly, for words are bearers and vectors of "racist prejudice." At issue is inculcating her with good habits, which begin with the right choice of denominations: the most virtuist will advise that one not say "Negroes" but "blacks," no longer say "Jews" but "Israelites" ("French people of the Israelite faith"), or Israelis, when that is the case; no longer to speak of "races" but rather of "cultures" or "ethnic groups"; to term "different" the peoples one tends, spontaneously and very inadvertently, to declare "inferior," "primitive," or "savage" (these qualifiers must always be preceded by the cautious adjective *so-called*), and so on. The racist must reeducate one to speak, to think, to behave appropriately, by way of the standardized euphemisms in the use of which may be socially recognized the distinguished antiracist. The height of antiracist euphemization is the suspension of judgment: it is necessary to teach human beings not to judge and above all to *abstain from judging* what differs from "Us" – and to abstain all the more as the intended individuals belong to "otherized" or "excluded" categories, as they incarnate victimizable types. The reeducated antiracist must be able to content herself with affirming that there is difference, while adding that one must respect, indeed love, differences – in such a way that the antiracist offers himself as a reeducator without borders, part teacher, part police officer, part master of ceremonies.[41]

The disadvantage of such an antiracist attitude is that one may too easily come under the grievance of conformism: the antiracist becomes the right-thinking person who is shocked by racist behavior, thus held up as a member of an oppressed minority, inventive and on the fringe, a martyr to the contestation of the last taboos of postmodern society.

f. The racist as social symptom: the status of "symptom" makes the racist radically innocent, reduced to a mere effect of structure. The presupposition in question is that society as a whole is in a state of dysfunction, that there is discontent in civilization, and so on, the causes of which once recognized. may be modified in order to act on the effects. As the racist is reproached as *nouveau pauvre*, unemployed person, and delinquent by social fate, his disappearance will of itself be effected, with all those effects of a bad society, once the latter is improved. The most common schema is the masterpiece of socialist-communist utopia: to be a consequential antiracist is to bring on revolution in order to destroy the class bases of racism. A revolutionary dream: in a classless society, racism will disappear for lack of function, like an organ that has become useless. "The cure for anti-Semitism will only be found in the complete transformation of the societies in which we live," declared Daniel Cohn-Bendit in 1978.[42]

7. Antiracism effects *a placement in evidence and in relief of the "racial," "ethnic," or "cultural" identity* of individuals, which it likens to an unsurpassable origin. This operation comes down to legitimating, of course involuntarily, the racist reduction, which one claims to combat, of the individual to a fixed class of affiliation, which is confused with his "origins" (racial, ethnic, cultural). Racist fatalism is hence renewed, comforted, confirmed. This perverse effect of antiracism turns up again in the reclaiming of identity, from the moment it absolutizes the differences and identities of origin.[43] In short, whether one calls oneself "racist" (rarely) or "antiracist" (commonly), one legitimates the racial criterion of differentiation among humans; one tends to present it as the principal and determining criterion of the classification of individuals. It is such a "cementing" of collective differences, flowing into the exclusive vocabulary of race, that constitutes the dominant perverse effect of antiracism. To the antiracists' "Live together with our differences"[44] responds the racists' "Live separately with our differences." It is clear that the reference to racial differentiation represents a presupposition common to the declared ideological enemies, which envelopes a second and implicit postulate: differences are treated as unsurpassable or as uncrossable boundaries. In brief, everything happens as if it were within the same circle of prejudices that the fraternal enemies confront each other, agreed on a "differentialist" reductionism and fatalism.

On this point, one may only be in agreement with these remarks formulated by Annie Kriegel:

> The "fight against racism" is currently led in such a manner as ineluctably to end up in a "panracialization" of the social bonds: unduly privileged and even held up as the only significant factor is the dimension of personal identity that stems from the affiliation with one or another ethnic community. This is an extraordinarily questionable and dangerous trend: ethnic identity – a prudish qualifier to designate race – is not and should not be the constitutive criterion of the intermediary groups that a complex society such as French society is made up of.[45]

8. The ideological hesitations manifested by the store of slogans produced for a number of years now throw a certain light on the *major theoretical contradiction* of the contemporary antiracist vulgate. The analysis of slogans and watchwords in the sphere of influence of what is conveniently called spectacle antiracism, originating in the recruitment of the confirmed stars of "humanitarian" causes and the selection of a new generation of media personalities, indeed enables a placing in evidence of a contradiction between the two principal demands formulated by the antiracist actors endowed with a spokesperson's legitimacy.

a. On the one hand, *to call for the respect and safeguard of difference*, to practice the praise of difference against the supposedly heterophobic "racists." The partisans of "multiracial," "pluriethnic," or "multicultural" society develop the logic of good multiplicity and presuppose an absolutely positive valorization of interracial/ethnic/cultural difference. The slogan launched in the spring of 1985 by the MRAP, "Live together with our differences,"[46] illustrates it as much as that of the marchers in "Convergence 84": "For a rainbow France that recognizes the diversity of rights and cultures."[47] The basic axiological postulate here is that difference is good in itself and of itself.

b. On the other hand, *to call for mixing, hold up* métissage *as a method of salvation*, as at once the hybridization of ethnically diverse populations and "intercultural exchanges" that must result in a new culture. Numerous statements illustrate such a praise of *métissage*, presented as the new royal road to the ideal of assimilation through the radical abolition of the distinctive traits of ethnocultural groups, these characteristics being implicitly evaluated as so many stigmata destined to be erased. Two slogans in the form of definitions of France, launched on the occasion of the second March for Equality (1984), bear witness: "France is like a moped: to move forward, it needs a mixture";[48] "Great! France moves toward mixture."[49] The axiological postulate is here that difference is not as good as exchange and mixture, which rend toward a lack of differentiation. The latter seems desirable insofar as difference is evaluated as a source of nonequality: the primacy accorded to the requirement for equality implies the position of the final abolition of differences, holds up the state of the lack of differentiation as the horizon of antiracist desirability. The normative and prescriptive statement that "*It needs* a mixture" is itself propped up on a constative statement: "France is like a moped: to move forward, it has always needed a mixture."[50] The basic argument is that mixture has already taken place, that there is a precedent of mixture, that France has always "moved forward" toward mixture. The constative legitimates the normative and the prescriptive: mixture is needed because mixture has already taken place. "To 'each in his own home,' we respond with the mixture that already exists."[51]

The inegalitarian interpretation of difference functions as the founding ideological evidence of the production of such slogans as this one: "Different, that is, unequal."[52] It follows that difference may not be claimed as a positive value and norm. From this moment on it is understood that "resemblance" tends to be substituted for "difference" in antiracist statements: "Let us live in equality with our similarities, whatever our differences."[53] But the ideological indeterminacy remains, marked by the hesitation renewed by the spontaneous remarks of one marcher or another: "'Convergence' means a crossroads. A crossroads of men and women who fight for the ideal of Equality. . . . Equality with our similarities,

Equality with our differences."[54] We see a wavering between the primacy of the mixed and the primacy of difference, a norm of interethnic mixture and a prescription of respect for ethnocultural diversity, an ideal of assimilation through the similarity of all to all (pure egalitarian reciprocity: a state of absolute lack of differentiaton) and a celebration of the "multiracial" or the "pluricultural":[55] these figures of hesitant ideological steps reproduce and renew the fundamental antinomy that has structured ideological debates in France since the French Revolution; these two series of demands, contradictory to each other, are two contemporary variants of the antinomy formed by the *logic of assimilation* and the *logic of differentiation*.

The logic of assimilation is not linked to one or another instrument of sociopolitical realization; rather, it may resort, simultaneously or successively, to the operators of uniformization of language, the legal system, mores, or *métissage*. In all cases, assimilationist antiracist action has as its final cause the ideal of a lack of differentiation through similarity, through the sharing of bloods and cultures,[56] through equal distribution/allotment of all traits of all to all: it is the case that similarity is the relationship in which the ideal of egalitarian reciprocity is best incarnated. From such a valorization of the homogeneity of the population, one will easily find formulations on the left and the right. We must insist on the fact that the positive valorization of *métissage* is currently received as one of the surest criteria of the absence of racism: the criterion of decisive identification of the antiracist attitude is the praise of *métissage* pronounced by the subject in question. That *mixophilia* is hence held up as a major index and in the essence of antiracism constitutes an absolute piece of evidence belonging to the *individuo-universalist* view. "All the same not racist because Élie Faure believes in the virtue of *métissage*," notes for example Pierre Guiral after a quotation from the philosopher-doctor that may be rather disturbing to a convinced antiracist.[57] The positive value of *métissage* is sufficient to remove the diagnosis of "racism" concerning the subject who offers proof of it (that is, who *declares* his mixophilia, whatever his other judgments may be). The mixophile affirmation plays the role of absolute proof of antiracism.

As for the logic of differentiation, let us say that it is expressly opposed to what is generally perceived as the "Jacobin" model of centralizing and authoritarian integration: differentialist antiracism is elaborated on the basis of the federalist countermodel of regionalisms or ethnicisms – whose right and left versions interfere with each other and are sometimes confused.

Two distinct types of evaluation may therefore be gauged in the corpus of contemporary antiracist statements.

a. Difference is better than nondifference (leveling of cultures, destruction of collective identities, lack of respect for what is "other," and so on): *differentialist antiracism*.

b. Mixture, as exchange and sharing of ethnic as well as cultural traits, is better than the refusal of contact (communication, communion, fusion); *métissage* is infinitely better than "each in his own home": *assimilationist antiracism*. Two political versions of this type of antiracism must be distinguished: either one extols the mixture of all with all as the surest means of realizing the "Jacobin" ideal of the assimilation of individuals in a national body; or one expects that generalized *métissage* will shake up the basic consensus on which the republican ideal of assimilation rests. Moreover, it will be noted that this mixophilic formulation of assimilation appears, in the discourses, to be concurrent with a mimetic formulation: the similarity of all to all is the normative state that gives its meaning to antiracist action.

[. . .]

9. Antiracism presents a ninth trait, borrowed from *pacifist ideology*: it defines its final objective by the idea of an achievement of peace in the world. Antiracist discourse is regularly accompanied by a denunciation of conflict in general, by a condemnation of the principle of war, by a violent reproof of the passions that are supposed to lead to fighting among human beings. Hatred and contempt are the two passions most often stigmatized – to the point of a symptomological practice that seems characteristic of antiracism: the latter believes it can recognize the presence of racism in the manifestations, verbal or not, of hatred or contempt. This belief implies a certain ability to decipher ambiguous indices. This violent denial of conflict, which is reduced to an antivalue, identified with radical evil, this *polemophobia* may not be expressed without paradoxes: hatred of hatred (in the objective genitive), contempt for contempt, an intellectual fight against the idea of fighting, war against war. The specter of the polemical element is willingly presented under the positive appearance of an absolute love of peace and of a position taken in favor of "friendship among peoples."[58] The self-representation of antiracism integrates the will to concord, the desire for pacific exchanges, the wish for an amicable planetary dialogue. Several dominant figures of the ideal of universal sympathy may be inventoried, according to empirical models transposed analogically. The model of the couple: the difference of the sexes at the origin of a union of complementaries. The model of familial relations: a primacy of sentiment, a centering on love as a gift. The model of intracommunity relations: the mutual aid and solidarity of the members of the same grouping, friendship. The model of commercial relations: exchange in order mutually to enrich, a presumed factor of peace. The more general model of the complementarity of parts or agencies in interaction: differences are good for the sole reason that they are the occasion to make ties, to form new series, to institute networks of groupings, among those who are different and complementary. Such is the horizon of empathy or sympathy that antiracism must hold up as a regulatory ideal of its action. If racism is violence, its legitimation, and its cult, antiracism is nonviolence.

The nightmare of the war of all against all is hence reversed into the dream of universal and perpetual peace. The ideal of the total and definitive pacification of humanity is imposed as the last finality of antiracist action. Now, the achievement of peace on earth involves the abolition of differences that are not reducible to the various types of treatment reserved by antiracism. The bad differences, those that cannot cash themselves out as fertile complementarity or enriching cooperation – these negative differences must be eliminated. For they would be able only to impose oppositions that would lead to war, which must be avoided absolutely. What governs the imaginary and axiological universe of antiracism is therefore not the mere consideration that war is not desirable; it is rather the idea that war is what should be *unconditionally avoided*. The total abolition of conflict in all its forms furnishes the content of the categorical imperative that antiracism presupposes.

It follows from such an ideal of absolute pacification that one must declare war on war and that it is necessary to dedifferentiate the part of humanity that presents differences irreducible to the criterion of nonpolemical complementarity. Antiracist pacifism hence unveils its normative dream of a unified, homogenized human universe or of a humanity absolutely reconciled with itself. But there must be a preliminary surgical operation: to amputate from the body of humanity the members suspected of provoking and maintaining the gangrene of conflict. To trim, to clean, to scrub up by the destruction of germs of opposition: the pacifist ideal reveals its hidden thanatological motor, its fundamental distrust with regard to the world of life, populated with impure contradictions, made up of troublesome oppositions Thus antiracism founders in the inconsequence of engaging in total war against its enemy ("racism," "the racists") while legitimating its action of an absolute condemnation of war. Total pacificism henceforth appears to be the most effective means of self-legitimation of a warlike action, insofar as it absolutely delegitimates its enemy. . . .

Notes

1   The ideologization of humanist philosophy is a process homologous to "the ideologization of tradition" studied by Darius Shayegan in the case of the Iranian "Islamic revolution," in his fundamental book *Qu'est-ce qu'une révolution religieuse?* (Paris: Les Presses d'Aujourd'hui, 1982), 179–238.

2   By ideal type (*Idealtypus*) I understand a theoretical construction that plays the role of an interpretive schema of a determined social reality (here of the ideological order), very exactly in the Weberian sense of the term: "An ideal type is formed by the one-sided accentuation of one or more points of view and by the synthesis of a great many diffuse, discrete, more or less present and occasionally absent *concrete individual* phenomena, which are arranged according to those one-sidedly emphasized viewpoints and into a unified analytical construct (*Gedankenbild*). In its conceptual purity, this mental construct (*Gedankenbild*) cannot be found empirically anywhere in reality. It is a *utopia*" (Max Weber, "'Objectivity' in Social Science and Social Policy," in *Max Weber on the Methodology of the Social Sciences*, trans. Edward A. Shils and Henry A. Finch [Glencoe, Ill.: Free Press, 1949, 90).

3   For a critical analysis of the contemporary functioning of the fascism/antifascism pair, in large part transposable to that of the racism/antiracism pair, see Edgar Morin, *Pour sortir du vingtième siècle* (Paris: Nathan, 1981), 65–64. The projection outside history of "fascism" or "Nazism," which have become exemplary foils and objects of ritual moral condemnation, can only nourish a new obscurantism: legitimate horror is then placed in the service of the refusal to understand. Hence the rush to imprecation and conjuration, in spite of their ineffectiveness.

4   This is a shift that does not involve a substitution, but rather the production of transitional forms, such as the following slogan, illustrative of a current condensation: "Apartheid, the new face of Nazism" (communiqué from the MRAP, March 26, 1985). Antiracist rhetoric grafts itself onto this shift, extending the metaphor, the motif of "liberation": "The South African and Namibian peoples will be able to win their freedom; apartheid, the other face of Nazism, will be eliminated from South Africa" (ibid.).

5   The paradoxical "antiracist" racialization of the State of Israel and Zionism in general found its international outcome in the United Nations General Assembly, on November 10, 1975, when a resolution was voted stating that "Zionism is a form of racism and racial discrimination." See Pierre-André Taguieff, *Les Fins de l'antiracisme* (Paris: Michalon, 1995), 435–36.

6   In a book filled with subtle analyses and questionable theses, *Cry of Cassandra: The Resurgence of European Anti-Semitism*, trans. Norman S. Posel (Bethesda, Md.: Zenith, 2985), Simon Epstein has notably shown, with force, how certain propagandistic acts of lumping together (anti-Semitism racism = fascism, and so on) have paired up with mythical confusions used within the Jewish community in order to engender a system of assuring illusions. Hence the necessity to distinguish clearly three categories of acts, ordinarily confused under and by the polemical etiquette of "anti-Semitism" (and/or "racism"), whose main effect is that of blindness to strategic realities: (1) that which is an international phenomenon and stems from destabilizing terrorism aimed at the Western states (attacks termed "blind"); (2) that which stems from the Israeli-Arab war, waged in France (symbolic attacks with bombs, at symbolic sites); and (3) that which is properly a manifestation of French "anti-Semitism": the small anti-Jewish acts and incidents, the acts of intimidation, and so on, which become massive once they are inventoried. A fourth category is illustrated by the murder of persons "of Jewish origin" committed by isolated, psychopathic, or fanatical "neo-Nazi" individuals.

7   (Let us again remember that Taguieff is writing in 2986. – Trans.]

8   By way of example, we will refer to the *Cahiers de la LICRA* 3 (November 1981) ("If you are different from me, far from doing me wrong, you enrich me"), which presents the general action of the International League against Racism and Anti-Semitism (Ligue Internationale Contre le Racisme et l'Antisémitisme – LICRA). The analysis in chapter 4, on the subject of "the international action of LICRA," illustrates in striking fashion the centering of anticommunist antiracism on the various manifestations of anti-Semitism, symbolic holdovers (Nazism), or sociopolitical realities (the USSR, Arab countries, Argentina). The chapter in fact encompasses the following: "The Hunt for Nazi Criminals" (33–37); "The USSR: Lands of Scorned Freedom" (37–43); "The Right to Life of the State of Israel" (43–46); "Apartheid in South Africa" (47–49); "A Few Other Hot Spots in the World" (49–37: A] Racial Segregation in the United States / B] The Fate of Jews in the Arab Countries / C] The Genocide of the Kurdish People / D] The Cambodian Drama / E] Anti-Semitism in Argentina / F] The Extinction of the Indians of the Amazon"). The important corpus of French anoracist texts that have appeared since the early 1930s still awaits its analyst, who will have to be a historian as much as a semanticist, a political scientist and sociologist as much as a psychologist.

9   See Aristotle, *Rhetoric* 1.3, 1358b (2–7; 10–19). We know that the Stagirite distinguished three genres of discourse, involving as many values and different aims to be realized: the deliberative, advising the useful, that is, the best; the forensic, pleading for the just; the epideictic, which treats of praise and blame, and only has to be concerned with what is beautiful or ugly. The argument of epideictic discourse is meant to "increase the intensity of adherence to certain values"; "the speaker tries to establish a sense of communion centered around

particular values recognized by the audience, and to this end he uses the whole range of means available to the rhetorician for purposes of amplification and enhancement" (Chaïm Perelman and L. Olbrechts-Tyteca, *The New Rhetoric: A Treatise on Argumentation*, trans. John Wilkinson and Purcell Weaver [Notre Dame, Ind.: Notre Dame University Press, 1969], 51). Epideictic discourse is essentially a stimulant for a disposition to action. But, as Gabriel Tarde noted (in *La Logique sociale* [Paris: Alcan, 1895], 43–44), it recalls a procession more than a struggle; hence it is made to be "practiced by those who, in a society, defend the traditional and accepted values, those which are the object of education, not the new and revolutionary values which stir up controversy and polemics" (Perelman and Olbrechets-Tyteca, *New Rhetoric*, 51). If it is true that "there is an optimistic, lenient tendency in epideictic discourse" (ibid.), it is found with no trouble in commemorative antiracism, whose real political aims are masked by the appeal to values of unanimity, even universality, and declamatory spectacle. In short, its (ideological) strength and its (analytic) weakness stem from the fact that the epideictir tends to be reduced to the exclusive use of techniques favoring a *communion* with the listener.

10   A recurring formula in the press releases of the MRAP that follow racist attacks and incidents. It has various placements in discourse: "For as long as crisis, unemployment, and the latter's corollary, racism, continue to exist, the Le Pen movement has fine days ahead of it" (André Chambraud [Jean-François Kahn], in *L'Evénement du Jeudi*, quoted in Olivier Malentraide, "L'Effet Le Pen, c'est le fait Le Pen," *Écrits de Paris* (March 1985): 16–17).

11   Let us recall in passing that René Girard attempted to construct a theory of such s process in his bunk *The Scapegoat*, trans. Yvonne Freccero (Baltimore: Johns Hopkins University Press, 1986).

12   *Latitudes* 1 (November 1984): 1 (editorial). Editor: Philippe Farine [socialist leader].

13   Françoise Jouer, *Le Bon Usage du mot crise* (Grenoble: Institute of Political Science, 1984), quoted in Frédéric Bon, "Langage et politique," in *Traité de science politique*, ed. Madeleine Grawitz and Jean Leca (Paris: Presses Universitaires de France, 1985), 3:564. See the remarks by Maurice Tournier, in *Mots* 10 (March 1983): 2.31–35.

14   Jean-Claude Milner, *Les Noms indistincts* (Paris: Seuil, 1983), 80–93. The common core of the arguments of the left and the right is the economistic evidence of "crisis."

15   Weber, *Max Weber on the Methodology of the Social Sciences*, 68–69.

16   Ibid., 69.

17   Ibid.

18   Ibid.

19   I understand by a conspiracy theory of society, following Karl R. Popper, "The view that whatever happens in society – including things which people as a rule dislike, such as war, unemployment, poverty, shortages – are the results of direct design by some powerful individuals or groups" ("Prediction and Prophecy in the Social Sciences," in *Conjectures and Refutations: The Growth of Scientific Knowledge* [New York: Basic Books, 1962], 341). On the specter of plots as "causes" of historical events, see Léon Poliakov, *La Causalité diabolique: Essai sur l'origine des*

persécutions (Paris: Calmann-Levy, 1980), which departs notably from the Popperian analysis (53–27, 241). See also Pierre-André Taguieff, *Les Protocoles des Sages de Sion: Faux et usages d'un faux* (Paris; Berg International 1992.), vol. 1.

20   We will note the following paradox: only the apparent "racists," the "noble" or "poor" manipulated people, are legally pursued, whereas the manipulators, the "bigwigs," so to speak, those truly responsible, may not be pursued or condemned. Whence the headlong flight into mythical denunciation, called for by juridical impotence, stimulated and justified by the sense of scandal.

21   Let us specify: of "racism" in the singular, in general, as ideological evidence. In short, of "racism" as an operator of lumping together. Here is an example of the diversionary use of antiracism, enabling an effacement of the true nature of the Soviet Union in a unanimist anti-Nazism: "Tuesday, May 7, 1985: all of France against racism. Rallies for memory, solidarity, and hope. Forty years after the victory of *the free peoples* over Nazism, France is confronted with a rise in the ideology of racist violence" (leaflet from the MRAP, April 1985; I underscore the designation that lumps together the victors over Nazism, Stalinist totalitarianism, and pluralist democracies).

22   François Brigneau, *Minute* (April 5–12, 1985): 7.

23   Ibid.

24   Ibid., 6.

25   François Brigneau, "La France aux Français," *Présent* 807 (April 1–2, 1985): 1.

26   Annie Kriegel, "Le Slogan nouveau est arrivé," *Information Juive* (April 1985): 5.

27   Annie Kriegel, *Israël eat-il coupable?* (Paris: R. Laffont, 1982), 36–37.

28   Ibid., 37–38.

29   The paradox of egalitarianism was formulated by Juliers Freund in his talk at the eighteenth national colloquium of the GRECE (Versailles, November 11, 1984): egalitarianism "has, paradoxically, a hierarchy as its basis, from the fact that it accords the rank of supreme or at least superior value to equality. Stated otherwise, equality itself has value only by the place it is assigned in a hierarchical system of values."

30   On the distinction between "inferior race" and "antirace" in Nazi ideology, see Pierre-André Taguieff, "Let Présuppositions définitionnelles d'un indéfinissable: 'Le Racisme,'" *Mots* 8 (March 1984): 101–2.

31   Ibid., 71ff., 104–5. Every racialization is the inscription of a category of otherized/excluded ones in a dubious humanity or (inferior) subhumanity. But another type of racialization must be noted, which may be either added to or substituted for the first one: the inscription of the Other in a (rival) antihumanity. The ambivalence of the maximally racized one, half-inferior and half-rival, at once beastly (the underman) and dangerous (the mortal enemy), characterized the Jew in Nazi anti-Judaism and today tends to be invested in the demonized type of the Maghrebian, in the nationalist imaginary (the Algerian, especially, rapes, kills, is parasitic, but also prepares the destruction of France). See chapter 4 in this book.

32   In an intellectualist perspective, assuming that no one is wicked voluntarily but only out of ignorance (a mere lack of knowledge), the first two types identified are but one, the second folded over the first. Cf., for example, these remarks by Spinoza: "Finally, Hate comes also from mere report — as we see in the Hate

the Turks have against the Jews and the Christians, the Jews against the Turks and the Christians, and the Christians against the Jews and the Turks, etc. For how ignorant most of these are of one another's religion and customs" (Spinoza, *Short Treatise on God, Man, and His Well-Being*, in *The Collected Works of Spinoza*, trans. Edwin Curley [Princeton, N.J.: Princeton University Press, 19851, part 2, chapter 3, 101). Intercommunity hatred would hence derive from the first kind, through sign and hearsay – the realm of rumor.

33   Bernard-Henri Lévy, quoted in *Présent* (February 22, 1985).

34   Bernard-Henri Lévy, in *Globe* 1 (November 1985): 13 (Bloc-notes). The whole argument, which expressly develops an intolerance passed off as antiracist, rests on the norm of the defense of "the democratic order." The democratic system, for humanitarians of atheist or agnostic stripe (those religious spirits unfit for the religious), represents a level of accessible substitutive holiness. Thus is it held up as a supreme transcendent value: the unconditional defenders of democracy in their own way make up a cult on a supraempirical order. They transmute the party of order into the Order of democratic mysticism. It is therefore necessary, in order for Le Pen to be an authentic enemy, one worthy of the name, that he be a guaranteed "real" danger to democracy. This is precisely what Le Pen is in Lévy's rhetoric, because he must be: a "phenomenon" that risks bringing on the "disintegration of the democratic order" (ibid.).

36   Roger Ikor, "La grande question," *La Nef* 19–20 (September–December 1964): Ikor's argument presupposes the basic evidence of the individuo-universalist universe. On the one hand, it offers the affirmation of an immoderate universalism, enveloping a proclaimed intolerance toward any particularism, an attitude representing itself as progressive: "All that is particular finds me hostile, or at least on my guard . . . . I do not dream of breaching the boundaries that separate them (human beings), the artificial and even the natural ones . . . . Everything that separates seems to me reactionary" (Roger Ikor, *Leure ouverte aux Juifs* (Paris: Michel, 1970), 16). On the other hand, Ikor's argument interprets the opposition between individualism and racism as that between good and evil: "It is racism that threatens us: it is therefore toward individualism that we must deliberately lean" (La grande question," 39).

37   Ikor, "La grande question," 34.

38   Ibid.

39   Ibid., 39.

40   There is an antiracist pathos of distance: at issue is keeping away the racist. Contempt may nonetheless not declare itself as such but rather must have reasons: the racist is defined by ignorance coupled with pretentious vulgarity, stupidity mixed with crudeness or brutality. Hence the current usage – for example, in the intellectual class partially followed by the (established) political class – of antipopulist motifs recast in the antifascist-antiracist vulgate. One detests the topics of the "Small Business Café" and "Poujadist" [after Pierre Poujade, the founder, in 1953, of the Union for the Defense of the Tradesman and Artisans of France – Trans.] attitudes, contemporary avatars of contempt for the vulgarity of the "little corporal" of base extraction, a contempt that, detracting from analysis (one is not going to "waste time getting one's hands dirty"), engenders a lack of knowledge of the real danger. Blindness in the face of National Socialism

was long nourished by such a contempt. Certainly, sometimes Hitler becomes a Poujade, but sometimes he becomes a Hitler.

41   The racist must be reeducated insofar as she is assumed to be afflicted by a deep evil, endowed with roots, that is, her racist "prejudice." At issue is not only teaching her; at issue is transforming her, uprooting her prejudice, by acting on the structures outside the consciousness of the subject. Reeducation involves a twofold and simultaneous movement: uneeaching while teaching. An interview that brought together, on December 17, 1967, at *France-Inter*, four representatives of various trends in antiracist militancy, illustrates the type-argument of the antiracist reeducator: "Les Mécanismes du préjugé," interview with S. Agblemagnon, Albert Memmi, Pierre Paraf, and R. P. Aubert, in *Droit et Liberté* 259 (February 1967): 24. The view of the social therapist is grafted onto the juridico-policing conception of social behaviors and ideological attitudes. But who is going to reeducate the reeducators? And how does one avoid policing minds? How does one limit the development of the seeds of authoritarianism contained in the will to submit opinions and beliefs to a system of values posited as an absolute?

42   Daniel Cohn-Bendit, interview in *L'Arche* (June 1978), quoted in Epstein, *Cry of Cassandra*, 150.

43   Cf. the remarks by Erika Apfelbaum and Ana Vasquez on the reduction of identity: "In the sociopolitical context in which a person finds himself reduced to being no more, for example, than 'the Portuguese,' a label of negative connotation, devalorized and devalorizing, 'cultural identity' is none other than a stigma assigned in order to pin him in a determinate place, to exclude him, and to paralyze him in his attempts to be, as a whole, a man, a father, and a worker, who likes to love, who knows how to dance, and so on" ("Les réalités changeantes de l'identité,' *Peuples Méditerranéens* 24 [July–September 1983]: 98).

44   On this slogan, characteristic of left differentialist and dialogic antiracism, see Pierre-André Taguieff, "Le Néo-racisme différentialiste," *Langage et Société* 34 (December 1985): 69–98.

45   Kriegel, "Le Slogan nouveau est arrivé," 1.

46   "Vivre ensemble avec nos differences," *Appel pour la tenue des assises nationales contre le racisme* (leaflet), March 17–58, 1984, 69–98.

47   See *La Ruée vers l'égalité (Mélanges)* (Paris, 1985), 42. Let us recall that the first march took place at the end of 1983 and that the second (in November 1984) was christened "Convergence 84 for Equality." In November 1985, a third march took place, the "March for Civil Rights."

48   Cf. *La Ruée vers l'égalité*, 8, 28: the origin of the slogan was a handwritten sign carried by a demonstrator in the march of 1983. See Jean-Michel Ollé, "Deux marches, c'est beaucoup," *Différences* 51 (December 1985): 7.

49   See Dominique Garcette, "Super, la France marche au mélange!" reprinted in *La Ruée vers l'égalité*, 29.

50   *La Ruée vers l'égalité*, 8; cf. also 68: "For many the idea of 'mixture' has had the function of a new idea. But, as F. B. [Farida Belghoul] said, '*mixture is never claimed, but observed*,' And then it is already at work. But we want new conditions of mixture. The inevitable argument of 'mixture' goes in this direction. But we cannot be content with it. It will run dry if we do not feed it with external or

internal sources. The '*internal source*' is the recognition of the diversity of supplies, the stabilization in France of cultural and linguistic homes other than French" (Albano Cordeiro, "Grandeurs et miseres de Convergence," in *La Ruée vers l'égalité*, 68). From such a rhapsody of militant clichés, three dominant values stand out: "mixture" is valuable in itself, it must be wanted (or desired) for itself; the "new" also represents a value in itself – mixture must be of a new type in order to be fully desirable; finally, "diversity" is good, but insofar as it feeds mixture – there must be difference for there to be mixture. The value of values here remains mixture, a sort of final cause of antiracist action.

51 *La Ruée vers l'égalité*, 11.

52 Ibid. "This is the slogan that summarizes our seeps," comments the "call" for "Convergence 84 for Equality."

54 Ibid., 17. Mixture, metaphorized by individuals' placement at a "crossroads," is here finalized by "equality": mixture is to equality as the means are to the end.

55 We will not insist on the usual confusion between the strictly bioanthropological motif of "multi*racial*" and the call for the "pluri*cultural*." But the interchangeability of the lexical usages sufficiently indicates that "culturalist" vocabulary intervenes in order to *euphemize* the vocabulary of race. In the ordinary social imaginary, beneath the levels of distinct language in which they are distributed, the field of "race" and that of "culture" have the same connotative effects.

56 "We would like a reciprocal multicultural exchange," declares Jérôme, a marcher in Convergence 84 (quoted in Garrerte, "Super, la France marche au mélange!" 29). We see a paradoxical coupling of similarity, reciprocity, and equality with such a "multicultural" ideal: "Sure, differences exist, but the similarities are much greater than the differences," adds Tarek for his part (ibid.). Similarity seems to measure lived proximity: "I feel closer to JerOme than to a young person living in the Maghrebe [*sic*]," Tarek goes on to declare (ibid.). See Pierre-André Taguieff, *Les Fins de l'antiracisme* (Paris: Michalon, 1995), 517–62.

57 See Pierre Guiral, "Vue d'ensemble sur l'idée de race et la gauche française," in *L'Idée de race dana la pensée politique française contemporaine*, ed. Pierre Guiral and Émile Temime (Paris: Editions du CNRS, 1977), 44; the text quoted is excerpted from Élie Faure, *Les Trois Gouttes de sang* (Paris: E. Malfère, 1929), 105 (not 36, as Guiral wrongly indicates).

58 Until 1978, the acronym MRAP designated the Mouvement contre le racisme, l'antisémitisme, et pour la paix (Movement against Racism and Anti-Semitism and for Peace). It was then modified to Mouvement contre le Racisme et pour l'Amitié entre les Peuples (Movement against Racism and for Friendship among Peoples). The transformation of the semantic content of the acronym took place according to two objectives: to erase the specificity of "anti-Semitism" by presupposing it as one form among others of "racism" (that is, racism targeting Jews), to recenter the self-designating formula on the naming of a single enemy to which the prescription for peace, itself defined by "friendship among peoples," is opposed. The antiracist is identified with the party of pacificism and universal brotherhood while attributing to himself the ethical quality par excellence (the respect for the human person), in the face of the racist, identified with the party of warmongering accompanied (indeed founded) by nonrespect for the human person. The absolute evidence, at the basis of commemorative antiracism, is that

racism is violence, can be nothing but violence, is essentially violence. But the violence at issue is most often reduced to "the 'sad everyday reality' of the numerous [racist] attacks." Ritualized antiracism cannot move beyond a legal-policing view of violence. Hence it only projects on its Other, the racist, the dominant characteristic of its conceptions and practices: trailing, driving out, denouncing, and condemning the outlaws. It is a legal-policing view of the social world.

Guide to Further Reading

Key texts

Abufalia, D. (2008) *The Discovery of Mankind: Atlantic Encounters in the Age of Columbus*, New Haven and London: Yale University Press (an innovative analysis of the impact of exploration on ideas about mankind).

Abu-Lughod, J. L. (1989) *Before European Hegemony: The World System A.D. 1250–1350*, New York: Oxford University Press (a survey of the origins of the modern world system which questions Eurocentric interpretations).

Banton, M. (1998) *Racial Theories*, Second Edition, Cambridge: Cambridge University Press (a masterful analysis of the origins and development of ideas about race).

Gossett, T. F. (1997) *Race: The History of an Idea in America, New edition*, New York: Oxford University Press (a classic account of the development of racial thinking in America).

Gould, S. J. (1984) *The Mismeasure of Man*, London: Penguin (a study of the history and usages of scientific attempts to measure human intelligence, including a discussion of race and IQ).

Livingstone, D. N. (2008) *Adam's Ancestors: Race, Religion & the Politics of Human Origins*, Baltimore: Johns Hopkins University Press (a study of the evolution of ideas about human origins and their impact on social and political values).

Wolf, E. R. (1997) *Europe and the People Without History* Berkeley: University of California Press (an exploration of European expansion after 1400 and its impact on the relationship between Europe and the rest of the world).

Background reading

Baker, L. D. (1998) *From Savage to Negro: Anthropology and the Construction of Race, 1896–1954*, Berkeley: University of California Press (an exploration of changing ideas about race in American anthropology).

Banton, M. (1977) *The Idea of Race*, London: Tavistock (an account of the origins of ideas about race in European and American thought).

Barkan, E. (1992) *The Retreat of Scientific Racism*, Cambridge: Cambridge University Press (an insightful investigation of the retreat from discourses based on scientific racism).

Barzun, J. (1938) *Race: A Study in Modern Superstition*, London: Methuen (a classic attempt to undermine myths about race).

Benedict, R. (1943) *Race and Racism*, London: Routledge and Kegan Paul (an early attempt to provide arguments against racism, influenced by debates in American anthropology and the Nazi experience).

Cox, O. C. (1970) *Caste, Class and Race*, New York: Monthly Review Press (a classic attempt to write a history of racial domination from a Marxist perspective).

Gilman, S. L. (1985) *Difference and Pathology: Stereotypes of Sexuality, Race and Madness*, Ithaca: Cornell University Press (an innovative analysis of the use of race in the construction of stereotypes).

Hannaford, I. (1996) *Race: The History of an Idea in the West,* Baltimore: The Johns Hopkins University Press (an attempt to trace the history of thinking about race in Western thought).

Hobson, J. M. (2004) *The Eastern Origins of Western Civilisation,* Cambridge: Cambridge University Press (a trenchant reworking of the history of modernity which questions Eurocentric accounts of the rise of the West).

Jahoda, G. (1999) *Images of Savages: Ancient Roots of Modern Prejudice in Western Culture,* London: Routledge (a historical analysis of how ideas and images about 'savages' developed in Western thought and influenced ideas about race).

Jordan, W. D. (1968) *White Over Black: American Attitudes Towards the Negro 1550–1812,* New York: W. W. Norton (a historical analysis of changing ideas about Africans from the early stages of European exploration to the eighteenth century).

Kohn, M. (1995) *The Race Gallery: The Return of Racial Science,* London: Jonathan Cape (an influential analysis of contemporary debates about race in scientific thought).

Lal, B. B. (1990) *The Romance of Culture in an Urban Civilization: Robert E. Park on Race and Ethnic Relations in Cities,* London: Routledge (an analysis of the theories of Robert Park about race and ethnicity in urban environments).

Montagu, A. (ed.) (1964) *The Concept of Race,* New York: Free Press (a classic collection of essays on the idea of race).

Pieterse, J. N. (1992) *White on Black: Images of Africa and Blacks in Western Popular Culture,* New Haven: Yale University Press (an account of the usages of images of Africa and blacks in popular cultural forms).

Rediker, M. (2007) *The Slave Ship: A Human History,* London: John Murray (a book that seeks to capture the everyday realities of life on slave ships in the classic age of Atlantic slavery).

Roediger, D. R. (1991) *The Wages of Whiteness: Race and the Making of the American Working Class,* London: Verso (a historical account of the emergence and impact of white working class racism in America).

Snowden, F. M. Jr (1983) *Before Color Prejudice: The Ancient View of Blacks,* Cambridge, MA: Harvard University Press (a reconstruction of ancient ideas about blacks).

Stanfield II, J. H. (ed.) (1993) *A History of Race Relations Research: First Generation Recollections,* London: Sage (a collection of interesting biographical recollections of early American researchers on various aspects of race relations).

Stepan, N. (1982) *The Idea of Race in Science,* Basingstoke: Macmillan (an important analysis of the development of ideas about race in scientific discourses).

Thornton, J. (1998) *Africa and Africans in the Making of the Atlantic World, 1400–1800,* Cambridge: Cambridge University Press (a critical account of the history of the formation of the Atlantic World after 1400).

Todorov, T. (1993) *On Human Diversity: Nationalism, Racism and Exoticism in French Thought,* Cambridge, MA: Harvard University Press (an account of ideas about race in French political and social thought).

Walvin, J. (2007) *The Trader, The Owner, The Slave: Parallel Lives in the Age of Slavery,* London: Jonathan Cape (an exploration of slavery through the stories of three individuals who lived through the Atlantic slave system).

Wey Gómez, N. (2008) *The Tropics of Empire: Why Columbus Sailed South to the Indies*, Cambridge, MA: MIT Press (an imaginative re-telling of the discovery of the new world and its impact on subsequent historical developments).

Key Questions

- What role did the process of European expansion and exploration play in shaping images of Africans and of 'races'?
- Michael Banton argues that 'the historical study of racial thought and attitudes has often been flawed by an unreflecting presentism'. What are the implications of this argument for how we analyse the history of racial ideas?
- Robert Bernasconi argues that Kant played a key role in the invention of the race concept. Critically evaluate this argument and its implications for the analysis of racism.
- Examine Cox's argument that the origins of racism can be directly linked to the development of capitalism?
- In what ways does the work of Du Bois contribute to the analysis of the race question in the Unites States?
- How relevant is Gunnar Myrdal's account of 'The American Dilemma' for an understanding of racial relations in the United States.
- 'Difference is the principal notion around which the racist enterprise revolves' (Albert Memmi). Critically evaluate this argument in relation to both historical and contemporary trends.
- Critically assess Taguieff's argument that 'antiracism assumes a manipulatory, even conspiracist, representation of racism'.

PART TWO

Sociology, race and social theory

INTRODUCTION

THE MATERIAL INCLUDED IN PART ONE has hopefully helped to provide some of the background to contemporary theoretical debates about race and racism. We move on in this part to an exploration of attempts to locate the issue of race within the bounds of social theory. As we saw in the previous part from the extracts by Du Bois and Myrdal this is not completely a recent phenomenon as such, and attempts to theorise about racial relations have been made throughout the twentieth century. Indeed the first extract that we have chosen to include in here is from Robert Park, one of the founding figures of the Chicago School of sociology, whose writings from the 1920s and 1930s continue to exercise the interest of contemporary scholars. Park's work was centrally concerned with the development of race relations in the United States, and particularly in the context of the complex social and cultural relations that developed in the major urban conurbations. In the extract included in this volume he reflects on the meaning of the notion of 'race relations', and in doing so he attempts to provide an overview of the key elements of his theoretical perspective. Park's writings on race are difficult to summarise but a recurrent concern in his writings is with the subjective dimensions of racial consciousness that help to produce the conditions for the emergence of racial conflict.

The next extract by John Rex is taken from one of his early works and reflects his first sustained attempt to outline the broad theoretical contours of his analysis of race relations. Rex's work over the years has been concerned with the need to locate the study of race relations on a firm theoretical footing and in this piece he sets out the main elements of his conceptual model. Drawing to some extent on the work of Max Weber as well as Robert Park, among others, he attempts to develop a theoretical model for the analysis of different patterns of race relations that could potentially be applied to a variety of national situations. An important concern in Rex's work, and certainly the one that has exercised the most influence on subsequent generations of students and scholars, is the need to link the analysis of race relations to class as well as other social processes. Although Rex has been a vociferous critic of the more reductionist elements of neo-Marxist theories of race and racism he has also consistently argued for the need to examine the interrelationships between race and class based forms of social consciousness.

In contrast to Rex the extract from Robert Miles can be seen as a rejection of the whole idea of developing a sociology of race or race relations. In its place he seeks to develop an analytical model that is based on a broadly neo-Marxist theoretical framework, although one that is quite distinct from that of earlier Marxist such as Oliver Cox (see Part One). Miles is particularly concerned to expose what he sees as the limitations of the whole 'race relations problematic' and to highlight the need to move beyond the category of race in social analysis. Over the past two decades Miles has been one of the most productive scholars in this field and has attempted to outline key elements of his theory both in more conceptual as well as more empirical work. But a recurrent theme in his work, which is reflected in this extract, is the attempt to reject the language and analytical models of 'race relations' in favour of an analytical model that seeks to analyse the processes that produce 'racialised groups' in specific social and historical conditions. Perhaps the most important theme in his work is the need to analyse racism as an ideology which is produced by specific economic and social processes, such as the defence of domination, subordination and privilege.

The following extract from Stuart Hall is an example of the shifting terms of theoretical debates in this field in the past two decades. Hall's piece is a particularly fine example of a growing body of work that seeks to explore the changing dimensions of how identities are formed and reformed in multicultural societies. An important point of departure for Hall, and other writers who have followed in his footsteps, is a recognition that an analysis of race and ethnic relations in contemporary societies needs to recognise the diversity of subject positions that have been formed over time. From this there follows an emphasis on the need to see racial identities as constantly crossed and recrossed by the categories of gender, class and ethnicity. In this regard Hall's argument has much in common with important undercurrents in recent feminist theorising about race and gender (see in particular the contributions in Part Five).

Some of the themes touched upon by Hall are explored further by Claire Alexander in her discussion of the ways in which the languages of colour and culture are utilised by researchers. Alexander's account draws in places on her own experiences of carrying out ethnographic research in the British context and she provides a forceful and critically informed account of how the move from colour to culture has inflected much scholarly debate in this field. Mindful of the dangers of current fascinations with cultural diversity she explores the possibilities for developing a sharper and more grounded understanding of cultural difference in contemporary societies.

The final piece in this section of the Reader is by David Goldberg, and it is concerned particularly with the question of how racial knowledge is produced and reproduced, both historically and in the present. Goldberg's work is inspired by the need to understand the historical, social and cultural conditions that produce racial knowledge and lead to the articulations of racist ideas and practices. An important aspect of Goldberg's innovative account of these issues is the argument that we need to locate the role of specific kinds of racism within particular time periods as well as geographical spaces. In this respect his arguments can be seen as tied up with a concern to understand how ideas about race, and the role of specific racial identities, help to structure political institutions, social relationships and cultural processes.

Chapter 10

Robert E. Park

THE NATURE OF RACE RELATIONS

R ACE RELATIONS, AS THAT TERM is defined in use and wont
in the United States, are the relations existing between peoples distinguished
by marks of racial descent, particularly when these racial differences enter into
the consciousness of the individuals and groups so distinguished, and by so doing
determine in each case the individual's conception of himself as well as his status
in the community. Thus anything that intensifies race consciousness; anything,
particularly if it is a permanent physical trait, that increases an individual's visibility
and by so doing makes more obvious his identity with a particular ethnic unit or
genetic group, tends to create and maintain the conditions under which race relations, as here defined, may be said to exist. Race consciousness, therefore, is to
be regarded as a phenomenon, like class or caste consciousness, that enforces social
distances. Race relations, in this sense, are not so much the relations that exist
between individuals of different races as between individuals conscious of these
differences.

Thus one may say, without doing injustice to the sense in which the term is
ordinarily used, that there are, to be sure, races in Brazil – there are, for example,
Europeans and Africans – but not race relations because there is in that country
no race consciousness, or almost none. One speaks of race relations when there
is a race problem, and there is no race problem in Brazil, or if there is, it is very
little if at all concerned with the peoples of African and European origin.[1]

On the other hand, when one speaks of race relations and the race problem
in South Africa one does not think of the African and the European. The African
does, to be sure, constitute a problem, but in South Africa, it is described as the
"native problem." South Africa has, also, the problem of the Cape Coloured, a
hybrid people of mixed Hottentot and European origin. The native, as the term
is there used, is a Bantu, and of a quite different racial origin than the "native."
South Africa has, likewise, the problem of the East Indian. Hindus were first

imported into Natal about 1860 in the interest of the sugar industry in that province. However, when one speaks or writes in common parlance of the race problem in South Africa, it is to the relations existing between the English and the native Dutch or Africanders that this expression refers.

In this context and in this sense the expression race relations seems to describe merely the sentiments and attitudes which racial contacts invariably provoke and for which there is, apparently, no more substantial basis than an existing state of the public mind. For the purpose of this chapter, however, the term has been employed in a somewhat wider universe of discourse, in which it includes all the relations that ordinarily exist between members of different ethnic and genetic groups which are capable of provoking race conflict and race consciousness or of determining the relative status of the racial groups of which a community is composed.

Race relations, in this more inclusive sense, might comprise, therefore, all those situations in which some relatively stable equilibrium between competing races has been achieved and in which the resulting social order has become fixed in custom and tradition.

Under such circumstances the intensity of the race consciousness which a struggle for status inevitably arouses, where it did not altogether disappear, would be greatly diminished. The biracial organizations of certain social institutions that have come into existence in Southern states since emancipation exhibit the form which such racial accommodations sometimes take. Some of these, as in the case of the churches and the labor organizations, seem to have grown up quite spontaneously and have been accepted by both races as offering a satisfactory *modus vivendi*. In other instances, as in the case of the public school, the segregation which such dual or biracial organizations necessitate, in spite of certain advantages they offer, has been bitterly opposed even when they have later been reluctantly accepted by the colored people. They were opposed (1) because of the discrimination they inevitable involve and (2) because the separation of the races in the schools as elsewhere has seemed to imply the acceptance of an inferior civic and social status.

All this suggests that the term *race relations*, as here conceived, includes relations which are not now conscious or personal, though they have been; relations which are fixed in and enforced by the custom, convention, and the routine of an expected social order of which there may be at the moment no very lively consciousness.

Historically, the races of mankind at different times and places have lived together in a wide variety of ways. They have lived over long periods of time in a relationship not unlike that existing between the plant and animal species occupying the same territory, that is to say, a relationship of biotic interdependence, without interbreeding. Under these conditions the different races, like the different species, have been able to maintain their integrity as distinct races while living in a form of association that might be described as symbiotic rather than social. Examples of this sort of symbiosis among human creatures are the gypsies of Western Europe or the Wild Tribes of India, particularly the so-called "Criminal Tribes."

On the other hand, other racial stocks, notably those that have fused to create the existing peoples of Europe, have lived together in an intimacy so complete that the original racial differences that once distinguished them have almost wholly disappeared, or at best can now only be clearly determined by the formal investigations of anthropologists. This is the case, for example, of the Germanic and Slavic tribes which, politically united by the conquests of the Markgraf of Brandenburg and the Teutonic Knights, in the thirteenth century, eventually fused to produce the Prussian people.[2]

Evidence of this modern instance of racial amalgamation are the occasional "racial islands," particularly in East Prussia, where, because the process of fusion has not been completed, some remnants of the Slavic peoples and their cultures still persist. Perhaps the most notable example of this incomplete amalgamation and assimilation is the existence, a short distance from Berlin, of an ancient Wendish folk, which still preserves it language and culture, and still cherishes a kind of tribal identity. They are called the *Spree-wälder*, i.e., the people of the Spree Forest, where they exist in the midst of a German population, as a kind of racial and cultural enclave.

There are, however, numerous examples of such isolated racial islands nearer home. There are, for example, the interesting little communities of Negro, Indian, and white mixed bloods, of which there are a great number scattered about in out-of-the-way corners of the Southern and Eastern estates. Perhaps the most notable of these is the community of white and Negro half-castes, living near Natchitoches, Louisiana, described by Lyle Saxon in his recently published novel, *Children of Strangers.*[3]

All these various and divergent types of isolated, and more or less outcast racial and cultural groups, have recently been classed, for the purposes of comparison and study, as minority groups, although the term as originally used acquired its meaning in a European rather than American context. Among these such sectarian and religious groups as the Amish of Eastern Pennsylvania, or the Mormons of Utah, have sometimes been included.

The classic examples of such racial minorities, however, are the Jewish communities in Europe and the Near East, where Jews have maintained, in spite of their very intimate association with other peoples, their racial identity and their ancient tribal religion.

All these relations of cultural or racial minorities with a dominant people may be described, for our purposes, as types of race relationship, even though no evidences exist either of active race conflict, on the one hand, or of obvious racial diversity on the other.

[. . .] In the modern world, and particularly outside of Europe, wherever race relations – or what, in view of the steadily increasing race mixture, we have called race relations – have assumed a character that could be described as problematic, such problems have invariably arisen in response to the expansion of European peoples and European civilization.

In the period of four hundred years and more since Vasco da Gama rounded the Cape of Good Hope and Columbus landed at San Salvador, European discoveries and European enterprise have penetrated to the most remote regions of the earth. There is nowhere now, it seems – either in the jungles of the Malayan peninsula or the remote islands of New Guinea – a primitive people that has not, directly or indirectly, come under the influence of European peoples and European culture.[4]

The growth of European population is, among other evidences of European expansion, the one that is perhaps least obvious. However, the growth and decline of populations are basic to every other form of social or cultural change.

Between 1800 and 1930 the population of Europe increased from 180,000,000 to 480,000,000, and the number of individuals of European origin overseas amounts at the present to 160,000,000. During this period, and indirectly as a result of this emigration of European peoples, a corresponding movement of African and Asiatic peoples has been in progress. The number of people of African origin in the New World, that is, in North America, the West Indies, and South America, is at the present time, as near as can be estimated 37,000,000. Of this number something over 12,000,000 are in the United States and Canada; 8,148,000 are in Bermuda, Central America, and the West Indies; 14,200,000, including, according to the best estimates, 8,800,999 mulattoes, are in Brazil. The remainder, 2,400,000, are in South America.

Meanwhile oriental peoples, mainly Chinese and East Indians, in response to the demands for crude labor to do the rough work on Europe's advancing frontier, have been imported into almost every part of the world outside of Europe. There are settlements of both Hindus and Chinese in the West Indies, in Australia, South and East Africa, and the islands of the Pacific, particularly the Dutch East Indies, the Philippines, and the Hawaiian Islands. They are employed mainly, but not wholly, in plantation agriculture. They are imported to work in the gold mines. There are Chinese in Cuba, in Jamaica, and British Guiana. They were imported in the first instance to replace Negroes on the sugar plantations after emancipation. There are Japanese in Brazil as in the United States. They were brought to Brazil to work in the coffee plantations in São Paulo and to the United States to work in the fruit and vegetable gardens of the Pacific coast.

The number of Chinese, Indians, and Japanese who have gone abroad and are now living outside of their native states has been estimated at 16,084,371. There is in South Africa a Chinese community in the Transvaal and an Indian community in Natal. The Chinese were imported as laborers to work in the Rand gold mines; the Indians, to work on sugar plantations in Natal. In the West Indies, Indians and Chinese took the places, after emancipation in 1834, of Negroes on the plantations. Japanese, who are more recent emigrants, have gone mainly to Hawaii and Brazil.

There are, at the present time, between 16,000,000 and 17,000,000 people of Asiatic origin living in the diaspora, if I may use that term to designate not merely the condition but the place of dispersion of peoples.[5]

Of the Orientals in this diaspora, 10,000,000, it is estimated, are Chinese 2,125,000 are Indians, and 1,973,960 are Japanese. There are 1,900,000 Chinese in Siam; 1,800,000 in Malaya; 1,240,000 in the Dutch East Indies; 700,000 in Indo-China; 150,000 in Burma; 74,954 in the United States; 45,000 in Canada; and 4,090,046 in other parts of the world.

Of the 4,125,000 Indians abroad, 1,300,000 are in Burma; 628,000 in Malaya; 1,133,000 in Ceylon; 281,000 in the island of Mauritius; 278,000 are in South and East Africa; 133,277 are in the British island of Trinidad; 181,600 in British and Dutch Guiana; 76,000 are in the Fiji Islands; 6,101 in the United States and Canada, and 100,225 in other countries.

Of the 1,969,371 Japanese living outside Insular Japan, 1,351,383 are in Korea, the Island of Sakhalin, Manchuria, Formosa, or other parts of the world including China, which have become, or are in a process of incorporation in, the Japanese Empire. Of the remaining 617,988 Japanese abroad, 162,537 are in Brazil, and 297,651 are in the Unites States and Canada. Of the number of Japanese in the United States, 139,634 are in Hawaii.[6]

The Hawaiian Islands are occupied by what, from the point of race and cultural differences, is probably the most thoroughly scrambled community in the world. The census for the Hawaiian Islands, where, different from continental America, the population is classified by racial origin, recognizes twelve different racial categories, two of them hyphenated. They are: Hawaiian, Caucasian–Hawaiian, Asiatic–Hawaiian, Other Caucasian, Portuguese, Chinese, Japanese, Korean, Porto Rican, and Filipino. Among the laborers that have a various times been imported to perform the work on the plantations a considerable number were from Europe, among the Scandinavians, Germans, Galicians, Russians, Poles, Portuguese, and Spaniards.

Of the total population of 347,799 in Hawaii in 1930, 236,673 were Orientals, 562 were Negroes, and 46,311 were hybrids. Of this 46,311, or 47,560 according to another and different calculation, 5,404 were person who counted their ancestry in more than two races.[7] Commenting on the situation, one of these products of miscegenation, a very charming young lady, incidentally, remarked: "Mixed? Yes; I am a kind of league of nations in myself."

I have conceived the emigration of European peoples and the emigration of extra-European peoples – since most, if not all, of these movements have taken place in direct and indirect response to conditions in Europe – as integral parts of a single mass migration. So considered, this is, undoubtedly, the most extensive and momentous movement of populations in history. Its consequences, likewise, have been in proportion to its numbers. Everywhere that European peoples – including their commerce and culture – have penetrated they have invariably disturbed the existing population balance; undermined the local economic organization; imposed upon native societies, sometimes a direct form of control, more often political and judicial processes which were strange to them, but processes which have, at any rate, more or less completely superseded those of the native and local authorities. The invaders have frequently, but not always, inoculated the native peoples with new and devastating diseases. They have invariably infected them with the contagious ferment of new and subversive ideas.

All this disorganization and demoralization seems to have come about, however, in the modern world as it did in the ancient, as an incident of ineluctable historical and cultural processes; the processes by which the integration of peoples and cultures have always and everywhere taken place, though not always and everywhere at a pace so rapid or on so grand a scale.

It is obvious that race relations and all that they imply are generally, and on the whole, the products of migration and conquest. This was true of the ancient world and it is equally true of the modern. The interracial adjustments that follow such migration and conquest are more complex than is ordinarily understood. They involve racial competition, conflict, accommodation, and eventually assimilation, but all of these diverse processes are to be regarded as merely the efforts of a new social and cultural organism to achieve a new biotic and social equilibrium.

[. . .] What then, finally, is the precise nature of race relations that distinguish them, in all the variety of conditions in which they arise, from other fundamental forms of human relations? It is the essence of race relations that they are the relations of strangers; of peoples who are associated primarily for secular and practical purposes; for the exchange of goods and services. They are otherwise the relations of people of diverse races and cultures who have been thrown together by the fortunes of war, and who, for any reason, have not been sufficiently knit together by intermarriage and interbreeding to constitute a single ethnic community, with all that it implies.

Obviously that does not imply as much in the modern world as it did in the ancient; it does not imply as much in the Occident as it does in the orient, where society is still organized on the familial pattern. It possibly implies less in America, or parts of America where divorce is easy and people are not generally interested in genealogies, than it does in Europe.

Although people in America and the modern world are no longer bound and united as people once were by familial and tribal ties, we are, nevertheless, profoundly affected by sentiments of nationality, particularly where they have an ethnic and a cultural basis. Furthermore, national and cultural differences are often re-enforced by divergence of physical and racial traits. But racial differences would not maintain social distances to the extent they actually do if they were not symptoms of differences in custom, tradition, and religion, and of sentiments appropriate to them. Differences of race and custom mutually re-enforce one another, particularly when they are not broken up by intermarriage.[8]

Traditions and customs are ordinarily transmitted through the family and can be most effectively maintained by intermarrying, i.e., endogamous groups. Evidence of this is the fact that every religious society tends to assume the character of a caste or endogamous group in so far at least as it prohibits or discourages marriage outside of the church or the sect. The Catholic clergy are profoundly opposed to marriage outside of the church, and the Jews who are, perhaps, the most mixed of peoples, have only been able to preserve their tribal religion for three thousand years and more because by endogamy they converted a religious society into a racial minority.

It has become commonplace among students of anthropology that most of the traits which we attribute to the different historic races are, like language and a high-school education, acquired by each succeeding generation for itself, sometimes by painful experience and always by a more or less extended formal education. Nevertheless, it is likewise becoming more obvious to students of human nature and society that the things that one learns in the intimate association of the family are likely to be the more permanent and more profound in their effects upon one's character in determining the individual's conception of himself, his outlook on life, his relations to other people.

It is obvious that society, so far as it is founded on a familial or genetic basis is concerned – as a secular society based on commercial and political interest is not – with maintaining not merely a definite life program, but a manner, moral order, and style of life consistent with that conception.

All this implies that the family and religion, the home and the church, in spite of public schools and social welfare institutions of every sort, still have the major responsibility for directing the career of youth and transmitting that intimate personal and moral order in accordance with which individuals freely govern themselves. Where custom breaks down, order may still be maintained, not by custom but by the police.

The consequence of this is that where there are racial and cultural minorities, whether Jews, Negroes, Catholics or religious sects that do not intermarry, the conflicts ordinarily described as racial but which are mainly cultural, do everywhere tend to arise. They arise even in an equalitarian society, like our own where "all men are," in principle if not in fact, "born equal," and they arise perhaps more readily here than they do in a society based on caste, because in theory they should not arise.

The obvious source and origin of most, if not all of the cultural and racial conflicts which constitute our race problems, are, therefore, conflicts of the "we groups" and the "other groups," as Sumner calls them, groups which are, however, integral parts of a great cosmopolitan and a free society. They are the ineluctable conflicts between the "little world" of the family in its struggle to preserve its sacred heritage against the disintegrating consequences of contact with an impersonal "great world" of business and politics.

They are, in fact, individual instances of an irrepressible conflict between a society founded on kinship and a society founded on the market place; the conflict between the folk culture of the provinces and the civilization of the metropolis.

Looking at race relations in the long historical perspective, this modern world which seems destined to bring presently all the diverse and distant peoples of the earth together within the limits of a common culture and a common social order, strikes one as something not merely unique but milennial! Nevertheless, this new civilization is the product of essentially the same historical processes as those that preceded it. The same forces which brought about the diversity of races will inevitably bring about, in the long run, a diversity in the peoples in the modern world corresponding to that which we have seen in the old. It is likely, however, that these diversities will be based in the future less on inheritance and race and rather more on culture and occupation. That means that race conflicts in the modern world, which is already or presently will be a single great society, will be more and more in the future confused with, and eventually superseded by, the conflicts of classes.

Notes and references

1   See unpublished MS by Donald Pierson, *The Black Man in Brazil*.
2   "In 1226 the Polish Duke Conrad of Masovia invited the Teutonic Knights into his territory to combat the heathen Prussians. After a difficult struggle, the Order conquered the territory of the heathen Prussians, exterminated most of the native population, and invited German peasants and townspeople into the country as settlers. In the fourteenth century the State ruled by the Knights was a power in northeastern Germany. It acquired Pommerellia and for a time the Neumark also, and through its connection with the Order of the Sword, of Livonia, extended its influence as far as Estonia. A string of flourishing cities sprang up along its coast" (*Encyclopaedia Britannica*, 14th ed., XVIII, 654).

3   Boston, 1937.

4   The situation seems to have brought about something approaching an anthropo-logical crisis. Since there are now, or soon will be, no living examples of primitive peoples to investigate, anthropologists seem to have arrived at a crossroads with the following result: One school of thought is directing its attention more exclusively to antiquarian and prehistorical investigation, seeking to extend the limits of our knowledge of historical facts; another school is more particularly interested in the historical processes they observe going on about them in contemporary life – the processes of history in the making. But the processes of history, so far as they reveal the manner in which new societies and new civilizations have arisen on the ruins of their predecessors, are the processes by which new and more sophisticated types of personality have succeeded earlier and simpler types. Anthropology thus merges into sociology.

5   Diaspora is a Greek term for a nation or part of a nation separated from its own state or territory and dispersed among other nations but preserving its national culture. In a sense Magna Graecia constituted a Greek diaspora in the ancient Roman Empire, and a typical case of diaspora is presented by the Armenians, many of whom have voluntarily lived outside their small national territory for centuries. Generally, however, the term is used with reference to those parts of the Jewish people residing outside Palestine. It was used at first to describe the sections of Jewry scattered in the ancient Greco-Roman world and later to designate Jewish dispersion throughout the world in the twenty-five hundred years since the Babylonian captivity. Diaspora has its equivalents in the Hebrew words *galuth* (exile) and *golah* (the exiled), which, since the Babylonian captivity, have been used to describe the dispersion of Jewry. *Encyclopaedia of the Social Sciences*, V, 120–127.

6   Radhakamal Mukerjee, *Migrant Asia* (Rome, 1936), Appendix A. The figures for the Japanese in the United States and Brazil have been corrected in accordance with more recent figures.

7   Romanzo Adams, *Interracial marriage in Hawaii* (New York, 1937), pp. 12–20. See also Appendix C. pp. 334–345, for data relating to interracial marriages.

8   *Ibid.*

Chapter 11

John Rex

RACE RELATIONS IN SOCIOLOGICAL THEORY

THE PROBLEM OF RACE AND RACISM challenges the conscience of the sociologist in the same way as the problem of nuclear weapons challenges that of the nuclear physicist. This is not to say that sociology can dictate to men and nations how they should behave toward one another any more than the nuclear physicist had some special competence to advise the American President whether or not he should drop the atom bomb on the Japanese. But it is to say that, in so far as whole populations have been systematically discriminated against, exploited and even exterminated, the sociologist might legitimately be asked to lay the causes of these events bare. The aim of this book is to provide a conceptual basis for doing this.

Conceptual discussion might well appear to some to involve fiddling while the gas ovens burn. Yet it is important to realise that sociology as a discipline has had some difficulty in coming to grips with this problem. The claim of the racists in the Europe of the nineteen-thirties was that race was a biological category, and that appeared to exclude sociological discussion. And, when the falseness of racist biology was systematically exposed, some sociologists were inclined to argue that the problem simply did not exist. Race was a category based upon some sort of false consciousness, and it was the duty of sociologists to reduce all statements about racial difference to statements about some other kind of socially differentiated structure, such as class. Only recently has the question been raised as to whether class really does have some kind of superior ontological status to race, and whether there is not a sense in which the 'race war' is not a more important central structural and dynamic principle in sociology than the class war.[1] A time has therefore arrived at which there is an urgent necessity for a reassessment of the rôle of the race concept in sociological theory.

It might perhaps be said that the fact that the concept of race and the problem of racism is primarily a problem for social science rather than for biology has been established in a quite uniquely authoritative way by a consensus of world experts. For, after the Second World War, UNESCO called together first a group of biologists and social scientists (in 1947) and then on two occasions groups of biologists (in 1951 and 1964), in order to give an authoritative opinion on the race question.[2] The biologists' final statement, made in 1964 and issued as the 'Moscow Declaration', represents the most up-to-date biological opinion on the subject. The full significance of this declaration can be assessed in the light of papers prepared for the Moscow conference and particularly from the introduction to these papers prepared by the Belgian biologist Jean Hiernaux, who has summarised the areas of agreement and disagreement among the experts.[3]

The biologists' conclusions are complex and technical and it would be quite beyond the scope of the present book to set them out in detail. Nonetheless it is important that we should indicate that they do not support certain popular conceptions as to the nature of race, which are systematically propagated by racist theorists, and which even today are widely accepted, even though they may not be so systematically rationalised as they were.

The popular conceptions to which we refer are as follows: first, that the differences in rights which exist between groups of men, within a nation, between nations and between groups which are internationally dispersed, rest upon differences of behaviour and of moral qualities which are genetically determined. Thus the maintenance of a particular political order in the world is represented as being 'scientifically' determined, rather than being based upon force, violence and usurpation. Many subsidiary propositions flow from these basic ones, but they are the essential intellectual core of the racist position.

The general position adopted by the biological experts in Moscow is that the concept of race, and more generally of genetic inheritance, which they feel justified in using, gives no support whatever to these popular conceptions. But this is best understood if we look briefly at what it was that the experts actually said under the headings of the use of the concepts of race and population, the rôle of heredity and environment in determining human characteristics, the actual nature of inter-group differences, the single or multiple origin of the human species, the degree of independence or association between different traits, the rôle of biological and cultural factors in evolution, the consequences of intergroup marriage, the survival value of proved differences between populations, and the possible inheritance of psychic characteristics.

The principal conclusions reached on these points appear to be as follows:[4]

1   Race is a taxonomic concept of limited usefulness as a means of classifying human beings, but probably less useful than the more general concept of populations. The former term is used to refer to 'groups of mankind showing well developed and primarily heritable physical differences from other groups'. The latter refers to a 'group whose members marry other members of the group more frequently than people outside the group' and hence have a relatively limited and distinctive range of genetic characteristics. In any case, however, whether we use the concept of race or population, the experts agree that human population groups constitute a continuum, and that the genetic diversity within groups is probably as great as that between groups.

2   It is agreed that observable human characteristics are, in nearly all cases, the result of biological and environmental factors. The sole difference which could be attributed to biological heredity alone was that relating to blood-groups and the populations which shared the same blood-group by no means coincided with 'races' in the popular usage of the term.

3   The various characteristics commonly grouped together as racial, and said to be transmitted en bloc, are, in fact, transmitted either independently or in varying degrees of association.

4   'All men living today belong to a single species and are derived from a common stock' even though opinions may differ as to how and when groups diverged from this common stock. Interbreeding between members of different groups is possible and productive and in 1964 as distinct from 1951 the experts saw a 'positive biological aspect of this process' (i.e. saw interbreeding as possibly beneficial from an adaptive point of view) 'while at the same time repeating the denial, at all events in the light of present scientific knowledge, of any negative aspect for mankind in general'.

5   Taking into account the possibility of a looser usage of the term 'race' to refer to a national inbreeding population, it may not be desirable from a standpoint of combatting racism to deny that a particular national group may be referred to as a race, but rather to affirm that it is not justifiable to attribute cultural characteristics to the effect of genetic inheritance.

6   Human evolution has been affected to a unique degree as compared with the evolution of other species by migration and cultural evolution. The capacity to advance culturally is one shared by all members of *homo sapiens* and, once it exists, is of far greater significance for the evolution of the species than biological or genetic evolution.

Taken together these findings point clearly to one single conclusion. The concept of race as used by the biologists has no relevance to the political differences among men, and since the whole notion of race and racism as it appears in popular discussion is concerned with these political differences, the question which we have to face is what the characteristics are of those situations which men call racial.

If the possibility of racial differences being biologically based is excluded, two other possible bases, neither of them necessarily sociological, might in principle be considered. One is that there are psychological differences between members of different racial groups, the other that the term merely refers to culturally distinct groups. Neither of these possibilities, however, provides an adequate explanation of how it is that men come to be classified as racially different.

Many problems arise in the attempt to assess psychological differences between races. There are few tests if any which are so free of cultural content as to permit comparisons between subjects drawn from different cultural backgrounds, and it would certainly seem to be the case here, as it is more generally with biological characteristics, that differences between individuals within the same population are at least as great as those between groups. In any case, however, it is somewhat difficult to see what could be meant by a purely psychological determination of intergroup differences divorced from the notion of differences of genetic inheritance. If psychic character is thought of as the consequence of the socialisation process then we should have to say (a) that a variety of types emerges from the socialisation process amongst all groups and (b) that insofar as socialisation processes do vary between cultures and produce differing distributions of the various personality types, the psychological determination of intergroup differences would appear to be dependent upon cultural differences.

So far as the cultural causation of intergroup differences in appearance, behavioural characteristics, institutions, psychic character and so on is concerned, no one would deny it. There certainly are different nations and cultural minorities within nations to be observed in the world. The question is whether the problem of the differences between these groups is coincident with the differences between groups which are said to be racial. Our answer to this question is that, although these cultural differences, or as it is sometimes said, differences between ethnic groups, may sometimes become the basis of a race relations structure and of a race relations problem, this need by no means always be the case. Our task then would appear to lie in discovering which of these culturally differentiated groups come to be thought of as races, and also what other types of groups are so classified.

It would appear to be the case that there are two observable features of any situation in which a problem of race is said to exist. One is the obvious one that the groups are called races, with whatever deterministic overtones that term might appear to have. The other is that there seem to be a definite and restricted number of social structures in relation to which in popular conceptions the term racial is used and in which there would appear to be a need for some distinctive sociological term. At this point we have to look at the problem of race sociologically.

Clearly the problem of a sociology of race relations is a peculiar one as compared with most other special sociologies. It starts with the task of unmasking false biological or related theories. Having done this, the question is what it has to do next. A few writers have taken the view that beyond this all the sociologist has to do is to show the consequences of such theories being held, so that phenomena like those connected with anti-semitism in twentieth-century Europe would be seen or studied simply as the consequence of the preaching of racist ideas. This, however, would appear to involve cutting off the investigation of a causal chain more arbitrarily than is common in sociology. We should surely look not merely at the consequences of racist theory, but also at its causes and at its functions.

[. . .] The first American attempt at a theory of race relations and one which remains prominent even to the present day was W. Lloyd Warner's theory of colour-caste.[5] According to this theory American society includes both class and caste divisions. The white population may be classified as belonging to one of a number of strata (or, as Warner would prefer to say, classes), which are arrived at by placing individuals in terms of two methods, which Warner elaborated in his studies of Yankee City. One of these classified the individuals according to their score on an index of objective and quantifiable status characteristics. The other was based upon the subjective assessments which individuals made of one another's status. Having elaborated this picture of the American stratification system Warner then went on to consider its relationship to the absorption of ethnic minorities. The Yankee City studies showed that most European minority groups moved up the stratification hierarchy over two or three generations, but that, so far as the negro population were concerned, however much they might achieve an improved position in terms of such objective status characteristics as income, they still found that there were barriers preventing their free association with whites at an equivalent level.

Warner suggested that the best way to conceptualise the relationship of the negroes to the stratification system was to begin by imagining that at the bottom of the stratification system there was a barrier far more impenetrable than those which divided the various strata or classes. When some of those beneath this barrier began to acquire characteristics which *prima facie* should have placed them higher up in the stratification system, the effect was not to breach the barrier but to tip it diagonally, so that there was the possibility of an individual negro becoming an upper-class negro, just as there was a possibility of a white becoming a poor white. There would, however, be less association between these two groups than there would between poor whites and middle-class whites or between upper class, middle-class and lower-class negroes.

Warner suggested that the barrier which thus split the stratification system into two was a caste barrier, at least in an incipient form, and he drew attention to similarities with the Hindu caste system, such as the taboos on intermarriage, eating together, and any other intimate form of association. Whether this fairly loose usage of the term caste is justified has been disputed, and probably the weight of opinion is against the introduction of the term caste to explain white–black relations in the United States. Nonetheless Warner's view that these relations cannot be explained in terms of normal stratification models survives, even if his notion of caste is rejected. Any adequate race relations theory must necessarily deal with this point.

O. C. Cox,[6] approaching the problem of the American negro from a sophisticated Marxist point of view, has sought to show that there are several crucial dissimilarities between intercaste and interracial relations as they occur in the United States, which make the use of the term caste in the latter case impermissible. He believes that a better theoretical construct for explaining race relations is that which may be derived from the Marxist theory of class conflict. Cox notes that the Hindu caste system is one in which there is a large measure of assent to the social inequalities and taboos on association amongst higher and lower castes, and that the central and characteristic feature of the system is the occupational specialisation of the castes. Neither of these two conditions prevails in the United States. The position of the negro worker in that society is that of the most exploited worker within a capitalist system of social relations of production. The absence of a race relations problem of the North American kind in Portuguese and Spanish Latin America is thus seen as explicable in terms of their being less advanced capitalist countries. So far from Catholic religion being a determining variable, its presence, like the absence of a race relations problem, is held to be dependent on the kind of economic system which exists.

Clearly the difficulty in sustaining Cox's theory is to show why it is that white workers are not in the same position as negro workers. The simplest Marxist way out of this is simply to attribute the subjectively felt divisions within the working class to a state of 'false consciousness' fostered in its own interest by the bour-geoisie. A non-Marxist alternative would involve the introduction of a secondary hypothesis at this point. Thus it could be said that the position of the negro was explicable in terms of his relation to the means of production, but that a prior distinction had been made as to who should fill inferior working class rôles, and that this distinction was based upon non-economic criteria. As we shall argue later, this modified Marxist position does have considerable value in understanding the race relations situation not merely of the United States, but, even more, that of the Union of South Africa.

[. . .] From this review of some of the basic sociological theories about the kinds of societies in which race relations situations and problems occur, we may now define our own approach to the problem of defining the sociological field of race relations. It includes the following three elements:

1   a situation of differentiation, inequality and pluralism as between groups;
2   the possibility of clearly distinguishing between such groups by their physical appearance, their culture or occasionally merely by their ancestry;
3   the justification and explanation of this discrimination in terms of some kind of implicit or explicit theory, frequently but not always of a biological kind.
     [. . .]

Notes and references

1   See, for instance, R. Segal, *The Race War*, Cape, London, 1966; R. Debray, *Revolution in the Revolution*, Pelican, London, 1968; F. Fanon, *The Wretched of the Earth*, Macgibbon and Kee, London, 1965.
2   UNESCO, Paris, *Statements on Race and Race Prejudice*, 1950, 1951, 1964 and 1967.
3   Hiernaux, Introduction: 'The Moscow Expert Meeting', *International Social Science Journal*, Vol. XVII, No. 1, 1965, UNESCO, Paris.
4   *Ibid.*
5   W. Lloyd Warner, 'American Class and Caste', *American Journal of Sociology*, Vol. XLII, Sept. 1936, pp. 234–7.
6   O. C. Cox, *Caste, Class and Race*, Monthly Review Press, New York, 1959.

Chapter 12

Robert Miles

APROPOS THE IDEA OF
'RACE' . . . AGAIN

[. . .]

The idea of 'race' and the concept of racism

THE HISTORY OF THE CONSTRUCTION and reproduction of the idea of 'race' has been analysed exhaustively (e.g. Barzun 1938, Montagu 1964, Jordan 1968, 1974, Guillaumin 1972, Stepan 1982, Banton 1987). As a result, it is well understood that the idea of 'race' first appeared in the English language in the early seventeenth century and began to be used in European and North American scientific writing in the late eighteenth century in order to name and explain certain phenotypical differences between human beings. By the mid-nineteenth century, the dominant theory of 'race' asserted that the world's population is constituted by a number of distinct 'races', each of which has a biologically determined capacity for cultural development. Although the accumulation of scientific evidence during the early twentieth century (e.g. Barkan 1992) challenged this theory, it was the use of 'race' theory by the National Socialists in Germany that stimulated a more thorough critical appraisal of the idea of 'race' in Europe and North America and the creation of the concept of racism in the 1930s.

The concept of racism is therefore a recent creation in the English language (Miles 1989a: 42–3). It was first used as a title for a book written in the German language by Magnus Hirschfeld in 1933/4 which was translated and published in English in 1938. In *Racism*, Hirschfeld refuted nineteenth-century arguments which claimed the mantle of science to sustain the notion of the existence of a hierarchy of biologically distinct 'races'. But he did so without offering any formal definition of racism and without clarifying how racism is to be distinguished from the concept of xenophobia (1938: 227). During the same decade, a number of other books were published which sought to demonstrate that the idea of 'race' employed in Nazi ideology lacked any scientific foundation, some of which also used the concept of racism to label these ideologies (Huxley and Haddon 1935, Barzun 1938, Montagu 1974, Benedict 1983).

But on one matter, these writers were divided, that of whether or not 'races' nevertheless existed. On the one hand, Benedict (1983) legitimated nineteenth-century biological and anthropological classifications of the human population into three 'races'. On the other hand, Montagu (1974) argued that, in so far as there were biological differences between human beings, they did not correspond to these earlier classifications and he therefore recommended that the term 'race' be excised completely from scientific discourse.

Hence, the scientific and political critique of fascist ideologies that resulted in the creation of the concept of racism was not accompanied by a consistent rejection of either the idea of 'race' or the belief that the human population was divided into biologically distinct 'races'. Indeed, the dispute about whether or not the term 'race' should be used within science to refer to populations characterised by particular genetic profiles continues to this day (Miles 1982: 15–19). Thereby, the basis for the continued confusion of the two terms was created and has been maintained. All the while that it is thought that 'races' exist then there is the possibility, indeed even the necessity, to constitute a theory of how different 'races' interact with one another. In so far as the ideology of racism is identified as one determinant of these 'race relations', a theory of racism becomes entangled in a theory of 'race relations'. And in so far as Marxist writers have incorporated an idea of 'race' as an analytical, or even a descriptive, concept into their theorising about racism, they too have become similarly entangled.

A Marxist theory of 'race relations'?

One of the earliest Marxist texts to analyse 'race relations' was O.C. Cox's *Caste, Class and Race* (1970). It was first published in the United States in 1948. Despite the existence of another tradition of Marxist writing in the USA which claimed to theorise 'race', Cox's book was cited for a long time by Marxists and non-Marxists alike (e.g. Castles and Kosack 1972: 16, Rex 1983: 15–16), as *the* seminal Marxist statement, and the work of the Frankfurt school (which was produced during its exile from Germany: see Outlaw 1990: 69–72) was largely ignored.

Now, it is referred to rarely in the British and North American literature (see, for example, the passing reference in Omi and Winant 1986: 31), although recently one of the original British architects of the 'race relations' problematic has shown a renewed interest in it (Banton 1991). This silence results partly from the fact that there is no longer any widespread interest in Cox's central theme, namely a comparison between caste and 'race' relations. It is also because Cox denied Afro-Americans any autonomous political role, a view that is contrary to more recent political philosophies of 'black' resistance which advocate autonomous political organisation on the part of 'black' people. Finally, as we shall see, Cox rejected the use of racism as an analytical concept, a concept that has in the past three decades become central to Marxist analysis and to critical analysis more generally.

Nevertheless, at the time of its publication, *Caste, Class and Race* was a work of some originality and it remains a work of considerable scholarship. Cox set out to construct a Marxist theory of 'race relations' (1970: ix). He attempted this largely by means of an extended critique of extant writing on 'race relations' in the USA, most of which defined its object of analysis as 'race relations' in the southern States. His central argument was that 'race relations' were not similar, or equivalent, to 'caste relations', as most writers claimed at the time. As a result, a large part of *Caste, Class and Race* sought to establish the nature of caste in Indian society and then to demonstrate that 'race relations' in the USA did not exhibit the defining features of 'caste relations'. The decline in the significance of the caste thesis means that much of this argument has little relevance to contemporary concerns.

But Cox's alternative theorisation is of interest because of the way in which it incorporated the ideas of 'race' and 'race relations' and attributed them with analytical status within the framework of Marxism. As a result, Marxists could claim, *contra* 'bourgeois' theorists, that they too had a theory of 'race relations', a theory that was (at least as far as they were concerned) superior. But the ideas of 'race' and 'race relations' had no specifically Marxist content. Cox, in the manner of mainstream sociological thinking, noted and then passed by the uncertainties about the biological meaning of 'race', and defined 'race' as 'any group of people that is generally believed to be, and generally accepted as, a race in any given area of ethnic competition' (1970: 319). What distinguished a group as a 'race' was their real or imputed physical characteristics (1970: 402), and hence he defined 'race relations' as 'behaviour which develops among peoples who are aware of each other's actual or imputed physical differences' (1970: 320).

The process by which these significations were established and reproduced did not capture Cox's interest and, consequently, he accepted the existence of 'races' as distinctive, immutable collectivities. This verged on reification when he argued that it was impossible for human beings to establish 'new races' and that an individual becomes a member of a 'race' by birth in the course of inheriting certain inalienable physical characteristics (1970: 423). Thus, although he claimed that 'races' were social, and therefore human, constructions, once created they were attributed with the character of permanence: they became 'things in themselves', discrete social collectivities whose presence had to be related to other social collectivities. The problem then became one of locating 'races' within Marxist analysis, which attributes primacy to class and class relations.

In order to assess Cox's attempt to do this, another conceptual matter requires attention. In the light of the centrality of the concept of racism to much contemporary Marxist writing, it is intriguing that Cox explicitly rejected its use. He noted that the concept had been used, by Ruth Benedict, to refer to a 'philosophy of racial antipathy' (1970: 321, 480), and he repudiated this on the grounds that it tended to lead to the study of the origin and development of specific ideas. Although Cox did not use this terminology, he was in fact rejecting idealism. Cox sought alternatively to develop a materialist analysis that identified the class interests and exploitative practices which gave rise to what he preferred to describe as 'race prejudice', a notion that predated the creation of the concept of racism.

In the manner of the mechanistic and economistic Marxism that had not been challenged from within the Marxist tradition in the late 1940s, a now familiar argument resulted from this materialism. Cox proposed that, historically, 'race prejudice' was a recent phenomenon, and that its origin lay in the development of capitalism. He claimed that 'race relations' arose from the proletarianisation of labour power in the Caribbean, 'race prejudice' being the rationalisation developed by the bourgeoisie for its inhuman and degrading treatment of the work force. Thus, 'race prejudice' was defined as 'a social attitude propagated . . . by an exploiting class for the purpose of stigmatising some group as inferior so that the exploitation of either the group itself of its resources or both may be justified' (1970: 393). It therefore facilitated a process of labour exploitation, and hence arose after that system of exploitation had been established (1970: 532).

But exploitation and proletarianisation are, within the framework of Marxist theory, universal capitalist processes. Because 'race relations' are not deemed to have arisen from the process of proletarianisation within, for example, Europe, it follows that it is necessary to identify what distinguishes the exploitation and proletarianisation that give rise to 'race relations' in the Caribbean. 'Race relations', Cox argued, arose when the bourgeoisie successfully proletarianised 'a whole people' (i.e. a 'race'). This happened in the Caribbean and the USA but not in Europe, where only a section of 'white people' (i.e. part of the 'white race') were proletarianised (1970: 344). For Cox, this did not alter the *essential* identity of the two processes: in both instances, a group of people was subordinated to a bourgeoisie whose primary interest was the exploitation of the former's labour power. Hence, for Cox, 'racial antagonism' was in essence class conflict (or political-class conflict as he conceptualised class struggle) because the latter arose from the exploitation of labour power (1970: 333, 453, 536). It follows that 'race relations' and 'race prejudice' arose from the historically specific processes of colonialism and imperialism that accompanied the development of capitalism as a world economic system (1970: 483).

Cox theorised 'race relations' as, simultaneously, a specific form of group relations and a variant of class relations. Their specific character arose from the imputed existence of 'races' as collectives distinguished by real or alleged physical differences. Much of Cox's attention was focused upon 'races' distinguished by skin colour, and he referred to 'whites' and 'Negroes' as distinct 'races'. In this respect, his theoretical approach remained wholly within an emergent academic tradition which had incorporated common-sense understandings and definitions about 'race' into scientific analysis in the course of breaking with nineteenth-century biological and anthropological analysis. The work of Park, Warner, Dollard and Myrdal, about which Cox was so critical, was characterised by what was at the time a radical view that 'race relations' were social relations between collectivities which defined themselves as 'races', rather than biologically determined relations between biologically distinct and discrete 'races' (Banton 1987: 86–93, 99–110). These writers established 'race relations' as a particular sociological specialisation or field of study and Cox sustained and reinforced this paradigm by seeking and claiming to offer a Marxist theory of 'race relations'.

It is easy to criticise Cox's analysis for being functionalist and economistic (Miles 1980, 1982: 81–7, George 1984: 139–47). Here I identify an additional difficulty with Cox's analysis, the significance of which will be discussed further later in this chapter. We have seen that Cox argued that 'race prejudice' was a rationalisation of proletarianisation in the Caribbean. Cox did not elaborate on this interpretation, but it is not consistent with the Marxist conception of capitalism as a mode of production (although it is consistent with Wallerstein's (1979) 'world systems' analysis of capitalism).

If capitalism is understood as a mode of generalised commodity production in which the ownership and control of the means of production are held in the hands of the bourgeoisie, to which the working class is thereby forced to sell its labour power in return for a wage with which it can then purchase the means of subsistence in the form of commodities, the concept of proletarianisation refers to the social process by which a section of the population is transformed into sellers of labour power. Historically, this has entailed the divorce of a section of the population from the means of production in order that it should have no choice but to transform its labour power into a commodity which is exchanged within a labour market.

But this is not what happened during the colonisation of the Caribbean in the seventeenth century (Miles 1987: 73–93). In order to establish commodity production, those who gained control over much of the land (by a combination of force and the establishment of private property rights) brought first European and then African migrants to the region and created indentured and, subsequently, slave relations of production. Under these relations, the labourer did not commodify labour power but was forced to provide labour power to the person who either purchased by contract the right to utilise that labour power or purchased the individual as a chattel. There was no labour market where the buyers and sellers of labour power met to realise their material interests. Rather, labour power was exploited and a surplus realised by means of unfree relations of production. What distinguished the establishment of agricultural commodity production in the Caribbean, and in several other parts of the world, was the *absence* of proletarianisation.

It has been noted many times that Marx's theoretical and historical analysis of the development of the capitalist mode of production, by virtue of being confined to the example of England and more generally to Europe, is of little value to an analysis of the historical development of the forces and relations of production outside Europe (e.g. Robinson 1983). With certain exceptions, much of the theoretical and historical work intended to 'rescue' Marxist analysis from this lacuna was undertaken only after the 1960s. Consequently, when Cox was formulating his Marxist theory of 'race relations', he was doing so in a Eurocentric vacuum. Few attempts had been made within the Marxist tradition at that time to analyse systematically the activities of merchant and finance capital outside Europe.

Hence, we may regard his creation of a Marxist theory of 'race relations' as a refraction of the then contemporary silence within Marxist theory about the formation of unfree relations of production in the colonial context. In an attempt to comprehend and explain that context, Cox identified 'race relations' as the unique characteristic of the process of colonisation, a process which in all other respects had a universal, capitalistic character. Hence, Cox focused on the signification of phenotypical difference which was used subsequently by the colonising class to frame the expropriation of labour power, and so elevated the ideological notion of 'race' to the status of a theoretical concept within Marxist theory. [. . .]

The challenge of migration theory

The post-1945 migrations from the Caribbean and the Indian subcontinent brought to Britain men and women in search of a wage who were understood by state officials and large sections of the British population to be members of distinct 'races'. Rather than signify them as British subjects, which they were, they were designated as 'coloured' and 'colonial' people whose presence would change the 'racial character' of the British population (e.g. Carter *et al.* 1987: 335, also Joshi and Carter 1984). In the light of the fact that sections of the British ruling class commonly justified colonialism as an attempt to 'civilise inferior races' and sought special methods of administration and economic compulsion to achieve this (e.g. Lugard 1929), this is unsurprising. However, there was little political or academic interest in this migration until the hostile, and largely racist, reaction to the migration found a place on the domestic political agenda (Miles 1984b).

Up until 1958, 'race relations' were, in common-sense terms, a colonial 'problem': the racist attacks on British subjects of Caribbean origin in that year in England were interpreted by the state as evidence that the problem of 'race relations' had been transferred to the 'Mother Country'. When British academics began to take an interest in these domestic developments, they drew upon concepts, theories and political strategies derived from the United States and South Africa (Rich 1986a: 191–200), all of which had 'race relations' as the object of analysis. Most of these academics were anthropologists by training and liberal in political perspective (e.g. Banton 1967).

The first major challenge from within the Marxist tradition to this 'race relations' paradigm came with the work of Castles and Kosack published in the early 1970s (1972, 1973, cf. Bolaria and Li 1985). They demonstrated the parallels between determinants and consequences of migration to other nation states in north-west Europe. Thereby, they deflected the institutionalised comparison between British and the United States and South Africa (evident, for example, in the early writing of Banton (1967) and Rex (1970)), arguing that it was more useful to analyse comparatively the British experience of post-1945 migration in the context of the reconstruction of capitalism throughout Europe.

Castles and Kosack opened their seminal work by rejecting the dominant sociological paradigm of 'race relations'. They argued that all contemporary capitalist societies contain a distinct stratum of people who occupy the worst jobs and live in inferior housing, and that in many of these societies this stratum is composed of immigrants or the descendants of immigrants. This immigration was explained as a consequence of uneven capitalist development on a world scale and immigrant workers were identified as having a specific socio-economic function found in all capitalist societies, namely to fill undesirable jobs vacated by the indigenous working class in the course of the periodic reorganisation of production. This stratum of immigrant workers thereby came to constitute a 'lower stratum' of the working class, which was thereby fragmented. Hence, for Castles and Kosack, the analytical focus was not 'race' or 'race relations', but the interconnections between capital accumulation, migration and class formation (1973: 1–13).

But in proposing this paradigm shift, Castles and Kosack did not reject 'race' as an analytical concept. Rather, they subordinated it to a political economy of labour migration and class relations: that is, they retained the category of 'race' in order to deny its explanatory significance. When referring to the total number of eight million immigrants in western Europe, Castles and Kosack claimed that 'At the most two million of them can be considered as being racially distinct from the indigenous population' (1973: 2). In other words, because only a minority of the immigrants occupying this subordinate proletarian position were members of a 'race' distinct from that of the majority, neither 'race' nor racism could be the factor which determined occupation of this structural site in class relations (1973: 2). Rather, their social position was determined by the 'normal' working of the capitalist mode of production. The fact that Castles and Kosack used the idea of 'race' as a classificatory concept in this way without explanation or definition testifies to its unproblematic status amongst Marxist writers during the 1970s.

This political economy of migration paradigm has been embraced by Sivanandan (1982, 1990), who also criticised academic 'race relations' analysis and sought an alternative perspective on the British situation. Sivanandan reproduced several of the central themes in the work of Castles and Kosack (1973), and of Nikolinakos (1975). He referred specifically to the importance of a reserve army of labour (or an underclass) to sustain capitalist expansion and to divide the working class, and to the 'cheapness' of a migrant labour system wherein the costs of the production and reproduction of labour power are met within the social formation from which the migrant originates and to which he or she is returned (Sivanandan 1982: 105–6, 1990: 153–60, 189–91).

Sivanandan's initial focus was not so much upon western European capitalism in general as on British capitalism in particular. For example, he devoted considerable attention to the state immigration controls of the 1960s which transformed British subjects from the Commonwealth into aliens who could enter Britain only on a temporary basis with a work permit (Sivanandan, 1982: 108–11; 1983: 2–3). But his analysis of the British situation was effected by a set of general Marxist categories and via an analysis of capitalism as a world system, categories and a perspective which equally structure his more recent interest in Europe (1990: 153–60). Formally, there is little that is new in this aspect of Sivanandan's work. This is confirmed by his critique of the recent neo-Marxist analysis of Thatcherism which is signalled by the notion of 'New Times', a critique which reaffirms the importance of the fundamental struggle between capital and labour (1990: 19–59). What does distinguish Sivanandan's work, making his voice and contribution distinctive, is the central place that the idea of 'race' occupies in his analysis: for example, the journal that he edits is called Race and Class, a title that places the idea of 'race' on an analytical level equivalent to class.

Sivanandan's use of the idea of 'race' is usually subordinated to the concept of racism. Put another way, his focus on 'black struggle' highlights the resistance of some British citizens of Asian and Caribbean origin to the racism, particularly institutionalised racism, that structures their lives: in the course of analysing the nature and effects of racism, Sivanandan employs the idea of 'race'. For example, Sivanandan claims that the migrant labour system 'prevents . . . the horizontal conflict of classes through the vertical integration of race – and, in the process, exploits both race and class at once' (1982: 104). Elsewhere, he refers to hierarchies of 'race' within the working class (1982: 113) and to the significance of learning about 'other races, about other people's cultures' (1983: 5). In these formulations 'race' is attributed with an independent reality, equivalent to class as well as to sex, as in the argument that 'racism is not . . . a white problem, but a problem of an exploitative white power structure; power is not something white people are born into, but that which they derive from their position in a complex race/sex/class hierarchy' (1985: 27). More recently, in an interview, he has commented concerning the journal that he edits: 'Yet *Race and Class* never subsumes race under class. It looks at race in terms of class, while at the same time bringing to an understanding of the class struggle the racial dimension' (1990: 14).

What Sivanandan means by his use of the idea of 'race' is rarely clearly stated: it usually functions to mark a symbolic site for the organisation of autonomous political resistance to capitalism, imperialism and racism, and, for this very reason, clarification of its meaning is unnecessary for him. But, in one of his less commonly cited papers in which he analyses South Africa as an exceptional capitalist formation, he does address (and reject) the argument that the use of the idea of 'race' implies a legitimation of racist classifications of the human species (1982: 161–71). He defends the common-sense definition of 'race' as a reference to a group of persons who share the same descent or origin, adding that group differences (presumably phenotypical differences) are 'an observable fact' (1982: 163). Thus, Sivanandan uses the idea of 'race' to refer to distinct, biologically defined groups of people. As a result, 'race' is as much a reality as class, both concepts referring to some quality that all people possess. Sivanandan observes, for example that 'Each man was locked into his class and his race, with the whites on top and the blacks below' (1982: 166), and that 'The settlers . . . were (and are) a slender minority, distinguished by race and colour' (1982: 168).

For Sivanandan, 'racial groups' therefore have a reality *sui generis*, a reality which parallels but also mediates class: hence, South Africa is exceptional only because 'race is class and class race – and the race struggle is the class struggle' (1982: 170). Yet, it is not the supposed reality of racial difference that matters theoretically or politically, but rather the use made of that difference by the 'race' (as mediated by class) that possesses the greatest amount of power. In other words, what matters most is the 'racist ideology that grades these differences in a hierarchy of power – in order to rationalise and justify exploitation' (1982: 163). For Sivanandan, the primary object of political struggle is the racism that legitimates capitalist exploitation and, hence, he observes that racism cannot be abolished by rejecting the idea of 'race' (1982: 162). However, it does not follow from this that the critique of the idea of 'race' is not an important moment in the struggle against racism.

The shift in Marxist theory away from the construction of a Marxist theory of 'race relations' towards an analysis of the expression and consequences of racism within the framework of a political economy of migration represented a major theoretical break. It permits an analysis of the expression and consequences of racism within the framework of the dynamic process of capital accumulation, and situates the analysis of racism at the centre of Marxist theory (e.g. Miles 1982, 1986). But, for the Marxist writers mentioned to this point (see also Wolpe 1980, 1986, Wallerstein 1988), this was accomplished in the absence of any critical evaluation of 'race' and 'race relations' as analytical concepts. Rather than sweep the theoretical shelf clean, these writers retained certain core ideas of the 'race relations' paradigm and repackaged them with the central Marxist concepts of class, capital accumulation, reserve army of labour, etc. For Castles and Kosack, and for Sivanandan, the idea of 'race' has been retained in a form which suggests that the human population is composed of a number of biological 'races'.

Marxist theories of political and ideological crisis

The development of a political economy of migration has been largely ignored by another strand of Marxist theory which has been concerned almost exclusively with the political and ideological crisis of British capitalism. This concern results from a preoccupation with the rejection of economism and an adoption of a field of analysis usually described as cultural studies. Given its concern with the social construction of meaning, one might expect that a cultural studies perspective, especially one that is allied with Marxism, would regard the critical evaluation of the idea of 'race' as a central and urgent task. Surprisingly, this has not been so.

The important work of Stuart Hall is central to this strand of Marxist theory. Hall's focus has been upon the role of the British state in reconstructing British society in the face of a series of political and ideological conflicts which have occurred in a conjuncture dominated by the declining profitability of British capital. Hall has devoted some attention to the role of the expression of racism in the resulting organic crisis of British capitalism and the rise of the authoritarian state (e.g. Hall *et al.* 1978, Hall 1978, 1980). While his observations have been theoretically grounded and influential, they are fragmented and have not been accompanied by a rigorous theoretical examination of the concepts employed.

Elsewhere, I have suggested that, in the absence of such theoretical work, Hall represents 'race' as an independent force in itself (Miles, 1982: 176–7). Here, I cite another example: in a much celebrated paper, Hall argues that 'At the economic level, it is clear that race must be given its distinctive and "relatively autonomous" effectivity, as a distinctive feature' (1980: 339). This reification of 'race' is reproduced in the equally well-known work of the 'Race and Politics Group' of the Centre for Contemporary Cultural Studies (CCCS), of which Hall was previously the Director. Hall's previously cited assertion was subsequently echoed approvingly in the work of the CCCS group (1982: 11, my emphasis):

> Although . . . we see race as a means through which other relations are secured or experienced, this does not mean that we view it as operating merely as a mechanism to express essentially non-racial contradictions and struggles in racial terms. These expressive aspects must be recognised, but *race must also be approached in its autonomous effectivity*.

In both these formulations, 'race' is represented as a determinant force, something which has real effects and consequences (although for the 'Race and Politics Group' these effects are absolutely rather than relatively autonomous). But what 'race' is, what the character of this 'feature' is, is never defined. We are left to search for the clues which identify the meaning that lies behind the silence.

Hall refers to 'different racial and ethnic groups' (1980: 339), suggesting that he employs 'race' to identify groups differentiated by biological characteristics (see also 1980: 342). If this is his meaning, it parallels Sivanandan's usage. But this does not help us comprehend the claim that 'race' is a reality which has relatively autonomous effects within social relations. Without additional clarification, the claim remains vacuous and each new, approving citation only reinforces its unintelligibility.

Similarly, the meaning attributed to the idea of 'race' in the work of the CCCS 'Race and Politics Group' (1982) is unclear and problematic (see Miles 1984a). One of the members of this group, Paul Gilroy, has subsequently responded to this critique, and to the broader argument upon which the critique was based (Miles 1982), as a prelude to an important analysis of the historical and contemporary expression of racisms, and their articulation with nationalism in Britain. Given that Gilroy states his agreement with my critique of 'race relations sociology' (1987: 40n), one expects him to reject the use of 'race' as an analytical concept in his more recent work. But this is not so. Moreover, the manner in which the idea of 'race' is theorised and celebrated in this recent text is characterised by a number of contradictions (Miles 1988).

Gilroy begins by claiming that the idea of 'race' has a descriptive value (1987: 149) *and* that it is an analytical concept (1987: 247): '"Race" must be retained as an analytical category not because it corresponds to any biological or epistemological absolutes, but because it refers investigation to the power that collective identities acquire by means of their roots in tradition.' But if there is a reason to attribute the idea of 'race' with analytical status, *that is if one represents it as a concept which can be employed to explain social processes*, it must refer to a real, identifiable phenomenon which can have (autonomous) effects on those processes. Yet, if this is so, it is not clear why ambiguity should be expressed about the concept by the (inconsistent) use of inverted commas around it. Is Gilroy wishing to signal that there is something essentially problematic about the use of the term (which is the justification for my consistent use of inverted commas)? Or is the occasional absence of inverted commas an indication of some real (but unexplained) difference in the usage and meaning of the term?

If 'race' is an analytical category that identifies a material object, what are its features? Gilroy offers several definitions. 'Race' is variously described as an effect of discourse (1987: 14), a political category that can accommodate different meanings (1987: 38, 39), and a relational concept (1987: 229). These descriptions are confusing. If 'race' is an effect of discourse, or a political category, or a relational concept, how is it distinguished from the other effects of discourse or other political categories or other relational concepts? These descriptions by themselves do not refer to any specifically identifiable phenomenon: they do not provide identifying criteria.

Elsewhere, 'race' is represented both as a thing in itself when Gilroy refers to the 'transformation of phenotypical variation into concrete systems of differentiation based on "race" and colour', as well as a social collectivity when he refers to 'racial groups' (1987: 18), when he defines 'race formation' as the 'manner in which "races" become organised in politics' (1987: 38), and when he claims that 'Races are political collectivities not ahistorical essences' (1987: 149). The former implicitly refers to what he subsequently identifies as an ahistorical essence because it has a biological character (although the distinction between 'race' and skin colour adds to the confusion), while the latter identifies a specific form of social collectivity – but we are not told how this differs from any other social collectivity (for example, classes). Hence, within Gilroy's text, 'races' are represented as really existing collectivities, although there is an ambiguity over whether these collectivities are biologically constituted or are the product of the articulation of racism and the expression of resistance by those thereby excluded and exploited. Ironically, his complaint that the Scarman Report fails to define what is meant by the reference to the Brixton riots as 'racial' (1987: 106) refracts precisely the same ambiguity in his own text.

This ambiguity is further expressed in the contradiction between the representation of 'race' as a particular type of social group and the argument that 'race' has never been anything other than an idea, a social representation of the Other as a distinct sort of human being. The latter is expressed in the claims that '"Race" has to be socially and politically constructed' (1987: 38) and that 'race' is only a device for the categorisation of human beings (1987: 218). These assertions parallel my own arguments (Miles 1982, 1984a) and hence I can agree with his claim that 'the attempt to make "race" always already a meaningful factor, in other words to racialise social and political phenomena, may be itself identified as part of the "race" problem' (Gilroy 1987: 116).

But Gilroy resists accepting the logical conclusion of this observation. The definition of a 'race' problem is synonymous with the racialisation of social relations, and this process of attributing meaning to real or invented somatic (and cultural) variation can only be analysed and deconstructed consistently by eliminating all conceptions of 'race' as a thing in itself, with the power to have effects. This does not require denying that the idea of 'race' is a constituent element of everyday common sense: the issue is whether or not such usage is transferred into the conceptual language that it used to comprehend and explain that common sense. I see no reason to do this. There are no 'races' and therefore no 'race relations'. There is only a belief that there are such things, a belief which is used by some social groups to construct an Other (and therefore the Self) in thought as a prelude to exclusion and domination, and by other social groups to define Self (and so to construct an Other) as a means of resisting that exclusion. Hence, if it is used at all, the idea of 'race' should be used only to refer descriptively to such uses of the idea of 'race'.

A comment is also required on Gilroy's apparent rejection of Marxism. Throughout '*There Ain't No Black in the Union Jack*' (1987), he allies himself with those who argue that a Marxist analysis of capitalism based on the historical instance of nineteenth-century Europe is inappropriate in the late twentieth century. This argument takes a number of (not always consistent) forms, but usually includes the assertion that the number of people involved directly in industrial production in advanced 'capitalist' social formations is declining and that, as a result, the industrial proletariat can no longer be the leading and progressive political force that it was in the past.

Echoing writers such as Gorz and Touraine, Gilroy claims that the leading forces of resistance in the contemporary western world are social movements

based around 'race', gender, demands for nuclear disarmament, etc., all of which
are conceived as being disconnected from production relations. Consequently, 'if
these struggles . . . are to be called class struggles, then class analysis must itself
be thoroughly overhauled. I am not sure whether the labour involved in doing this
makes it either a possible or a desirable task' (Gilroy 1987: 245). Class struggle,
for Gilroy, has been transcended by 'the forms of white racism and black resistance' which he describes as 'the most volatile political forces in Britain today'
(1987: 247).

If, in Gilroy's view, class theory cannot be overhauled, he has dispensed with
a theory of class struggle in favour of what is sometimes called 'race' struggle.
Here, Gilroy seems to identify with the 'Black radical tradition' as Robinson (1983)
describes it, a tradition which rejects Marxism as an adequate theory of revolution
for 'black people' (1983: 1–6) and which is terminating the 'experimentation with
Western political inventories of change, specifically nationalism and class struggle'
(1983: 451). This is confirmed by Gilroy's approval (1987: 38) of the work of
Omi and Winant, which rejects class analysis on the grounds that it neglects 'the
specificity of race as an autonomous field of social conflict' (Omi and Winant 1986:
52). [. . .]

'Race' as an ideological construction

Certain currents in the French materialist tradition offer a more reflexive and
critical approach to the use of the idea of 'race' as an analytical concept, reaching
conclusions which parallel my own (Miles 1982, 1984a, Miles and Phizacklea 1984:
1–19) and which are emergent within some critical, if not Marxist, writing in the
USA (e.g. Fields 1982, 1990, Goldberg 1990b). The work of Colette Guillaumin
is the most important in this context (e.g. 1972, 1980, 1988).

She has argued that use of the idea of 'race' necessarily suggests that certain
social relationships are natural and therefore inevitable. Social relations described as
'racial' are represented as somatically determined and therefore outside historical,
social determination. Consequently, the idea of 'race' is transformed into an active
subject, a biological reality which determines historical processes. This amounts to
a process of reification, as a result of which that which should be explained becomes
an explanation of social relations. Guillaumin writes (1980: 39):

> Whatever the theoretical foundations underlying the various
> interpretations of 'racial' relations, the very use of such a distinction
> tends to imply the acceptance of some essential difference between type
> of social relation, some, somewhere, being specifically racial. Merely
> to adopt the expression implies the belief that races are 'real' or
> concretely apprehensible, or at the best that the idea of race is uncritically
> accepted; moreover, it implies that races play a role in the social process
> not merely as an ideological form, but as an immediate factor acting
> as both determining cause and concrete means.

Guillaumin concludes (1980: 39, see also 1988: 26):

the fact that such relationships are thought of as racial by those concerned
(and sometimes this is as true of the oppressed as of the oppressors) is
a social fact, and it ought to be examined as carefully and sceptically
as any other explanation offered by a society of its own mechanisms.
Such explanations can only refer to a particular time and place.

The analytical task is therefore to explain why certain relationships are interpreted
as determined by or expressive of 'race', rather than to accept without criticism and
comment that they are and to freeze and legitimate that representation in the idea
of 'race relations' as social relations between 'races'. Hence, any analytical use of
the idea of 'race' disguises the fact that it is an idea created by human beings in certain
historical and material conditions, and used to represent and structure the world in
certain ways, under certain historical conditions and for certain political interests.
The idea of 'race' is therefore *essentially* ideological (Guillaumin 1980: 59).

These arguments do not deny that there is considerable somatic variation
between individual human beings. But the signification of phenotypical features in
order to classify human beings into groups simultaneously designated as *natural* is
not a universal feature of social relations. In Europe, it began in the eighteenth
century: for the idea of naturalness is even more 'modern' than the idea of 'race'
(Guillaumin 1988). Certain somatic features (some real and some imagined) were
socially signified as natural marks of difference (e.g. skin colour), a difference that
became known as a difference of 'race'. Moreover, these marks, conceived as
natural, were then thought to explain the already existing social position of the
collectivity thereby designated by the mark (cf. Fields 1990: 106). This social
process of signification was (and remains) an important ideological moment in a
process of domination. The idea of 'race' thereby came to express *nature*, something
given and immutable, with the result that what was in fact the consequence of
social relations became understood as *natural*: and so 'race' was thought of as a
determinate force, requiring social relations of domination to be organised in a
specific form, thereby obscuring their human construction. By utilising the idea of
'race' as an analytical concept, social scientists deny the historicity of this social
process, freezing it with the idea that the naturalness of somatic difference ineluctably
constitutes eternal human collectivities.

These arguments have been rarely addressed directly by Marxist writers, many
of whom continue to defend the retention of 'race' as an analytical concept. Anthias
(1990), for example, argues not only that 'race' should be retained as an analytical
concept but also that its relationship to class should be specified. Anthias advocates
retention of the idea of 'race' as an analytical concept to denote 'a particular way in
which communal or collective differences come to be constructed and understood',
one that refers to 'immutable fixed biologically or physiognomically based difference'
(1990: 22). If this is all the meaning that the idea of 'race' embodies in being
transformed into a concept, then this is precisely the meaning that is denoted by
the concept of racialisation (Miles 1982: 120, 150, 1989: 74–7). In other words,
the *social process* that Anthias refers to with the idea of 'race' is better denoted by the
concept of racialisation.

But why does she ignore this concept in order to retain the idea of 'race' as
an analytical concept? It is because she has chosen arbitrarily the class/'race'

articulation as the starting point for her analysis (1990: 19): having made such a choice, she is required to theorise the idea of 'race' into an analytical concept in order to sustain the paradigm which constitutes her point of departure. Thus, rather than *first* reflect critically on the historical evolution of the idea of 'race', and on the implications of its attributed meaning through time, in order to *second* reach a conclusion about the validity of transforming it into an analytical concept, Anthias precludes the very possibility of such an epistemological evaluation by electing without any critical reflection to employ the idea of 'race' as a concept positioned relative to class. As a result, while acknowledging the 'mythological representations that surround it' (1990: 23) and while agreeing with me that the concept of racism should be separated from the idea of 'race' (1990: 22–4), she invests those very same mythological representations with an analytical status by treating the idea of 'race' as a scientific concept with an object in the real world. This is expressed in her various references to 'race formation', 'race processes', to the distinct ontological status of 'race', to 'race phenomena' and to 'racially organised communities' (Anthias 1990: 20, 21, 35).

So, the case against the incorporation of the idea of 'race' into Marxist theory (and indeed into sociological theory) as an analytical concept can be summarised as follows (see also Miles 1982, cf. Goldberg 1990b). First, all theoretical work is an integral part of the social world. We live in a world in which the nineteenth-century biological conception of 'race', although discredited scientifically, remains an important presence in 'common sense': large numbers of people continue to believe, and to act as if they believe, that the world's population is divided into a number of discrete, biologically distinguishable groups, i.e. 'races' (cf. Fields 1990: 95–101). Although this conception (especially in its explicitly racist incarnation) is rejected by most sociologists and Marxists, their conceptions and theories of 'race' and 'race relations', where they resonate in the wider structure of social relations, fail to challenge common sense. Indeed, by failing to explain consistently and explicitly their sociological conception of 'race' as a social construction, they implicitly (and often explicitly) endorse common sense (Rozat and Bartra 1980: 302, Smith 1989: 3, 11), and hence sustain an ideology which Barzun called a 'Modern Superstition' (1938) and which Montagu described as 'Man's [sic] Most Dangerous Myth' (1974).

A recent example of such an endorsement of the commonsense idea of 'race' is found in an argument which is intended to explicate 'the salience of race as a *social construct*': Smith (whose work, while not falling formally within the Marxist tradition, is nevertheless influenced by writing that is) suggests that the analysis of the salience of 'race' (1989: 3) 'should centre not on what race explains about society, but rather on the questions of who, why and with what effect social significance is attached to racial attributes that are constructed in particular political and socio-economic contexts'. Here, the reference to 'racial attributes' resonates with all those 'mythological representations' of the nineteenth-century idea of 'race' as a biological type of human being characterised by certain somatic attributes. While there are all the usual sociological qualifiers (in the form of references to social processes of signification and construction), Smith's reference to 'racial attributes' as the *object* of the ascription of meaning implies that there is some biological 'reality' underlying the somatic features thereby signified: an attribute denotes the existence of some other thing which, given the description 'racial', can only mean that that thing is a 'race'. This is an example of the way in which the idea of 'race' as a natural division lives on, is reconstituted and renewed, by a critical sociological analysis which seeks to deny such a 'reality' by reprocessing the idea of 'race' as an analytical concept.

This is also illustrated by a paper in a collection of essays intended to demonstrate recent advances in the critical analysis of racism (Goldberg 1990a). Christian (1990) offers a radical analysis of Afro-American women's literature which prioritises as the conceptual framework 'the intersection of . . . race, class, and gender' (1990: 135). The novel that is the central focus of her analysis is described as 'an exploration of the ways in which race affects the relations among women', and its author is considered to have demonstrated 'not only that race, class, and gender intersect but that they are never pure, exclusive categories. None of these categories exist on their own. Rather there are men or women of one class or another, of one race or another' (1990: 136, 143).

Thus, second, the reification of 'race' as an active subject, and 'race relations' as a distinct variety of social relations, represents somatic differentiation as an active determinant of social processes and structures. It follows that 'the ideological notion of "race" does not have the rigour of an objective scientific definition, despite all later attempts to rationalise it' (Lecourt 1980: 282). Its use obscures the active construction of the social world by those people who articulate racism and by those who engage in exclusionary practices consistent with racism. Our object of analysis, the active determinant of exclusion and disadvantage, is therefore not physical difference in itself, but the attribution of significance to certain patterns of, or the imagined assertion of, difference and the use of that process of signification to structure social relationships. The use of 'race' (and 'race relations') as analytical concepts disguises the social construction of difference, presenting it as somehow inherent in the empirical reality of observable or imagined biological difference.

Third, the incorporation of ideological conceptions into Marxist and sociological theory has structured historical and empirical investigation in a manner which leads to comparative analyses of limited theoretical and political (including policy) relevance. By defining 'race' and 'race relations' as the subject of study, comparative attention is directed to those other social formations where identical social definitions prevail, usually South Africa and the USA. In other words, comparative analysis is determined by certain common ideological features (i.e. by phenomenal forms), rather than by a historical materialist analysis of the reproduction of the capitalist mode of production (i.e. by essential relations). Yet, considered in terms of the historical dynamic of capitalist development, these two social formations (by virtue of their colonial origin and historical dependence on unfree labour) have little in common with post-1945 economic and political developments in Britain, despite sharing a common ideological definition of 'race' as a social problem (but see Small (1991) for an important alternative analysis).

Attention has thereby been distracted from the other social formations of north-west Europe where the interdependence of capital accumulation and labour migration has resulted, since 1945, in the permanent settlement of populations which are often culturally distinct from the indigenous populations. It is only in Britain that the political definition of this settlement as problematic has been defined as a matter of 'race': elsewhere it has been defined as a 'minority problem' or 'immigrant problem', for example. But these ideological variations are grounded in a common economic and political process, leaving one to pose the question 'Why?'. This question can only be investigated by first deconstructing 'race' as an analytical concept, for only then does investigation come to focus upon the political and ideological processes by which the idea of 'race' has been utilised to comprehend this process of migration and settlement.

Conclusion

In so far as Marxism asserts that all social relationships are socially constructed and reproduced in specific historical circumstances, and that those relationships are therefore in principle alterable by human agency, then it should not have space for an ideological notion that implies, and often explicitly asserts, the opposite. The task is therefore not to create a Marxist theory of 'race' which is more valid than conservative or liberal theories, but to deconstruct 'race', and to detach it from the concept of racism. By deconstructing the idea of 'race', the effects of the process of racialisation and of the expression of racism within the development of the capitalist world economic system are more clearly exposed (Miles 1982, 1987, 1989, Miles and Phizacklea 1984: 4–19) because the role of human signification and exclusionary practices is prioritised. And where racialisation and racism structure aspects of the reproduction of the capitalist mode of production or any other mode of production, then that mode appears in another of its historically specific forms.

This can be illustrated by returning to consider the argument that 'race relations' arose from the proletarianisation of labour in the Caribbean. I have already argued that there was no proletarianisation of labour in this region during the seventeenth and eighteenth centuries because slave rather than wage relations of production predominated after an initial period during which indentured labour was prevalent. In a context where unfree relations of production were widespread, the initial enslavement of Africans was not in itself remarkable. It was only after Africans were enslaved that African people were represented in negative terms as an Other and that certain of their phenotypical characteristics were signified as expressive of their being a different (and inferior) type of human being. This racialisation of a population that was confined to the provision of labour power under slave relations of production was intensified with the emergence of the idea of 'race' and its utilisation to dichotomise the owners of the means of production and the suppliers of labour power as being naturally different 'types' of human being.

Similar processes of racialisation and a similar expression of racism occurred elsewhere in the world (and not only outside Europe) in the eighteenth and nineteenth centuries as colonial settlement was followed by the expansion of commodity production. As in the case of the Caribbean, these instances were usually accompanied by the forced migration of a group of people who were destined to provide labour power under relations of direct politico-legal compulsion. I have argued elsewhere (1987: 186–95) that in all these instances of unfree relations of production, through a process of racialisation, racism became an ideological relation of production: that is to say, the ideology of racism constructed the Other as a specific and inferior category of being particularly suited to providing labour power within unfree relations of production. Racialisation and racism were thereby ideological forces which, in conjunction with economic and political relations of domination, located certain populations in specific class positions and therefore structured the exploitation of labour power in a particular ideological manner. [. . .]

References

Anthias, F. (1990) 'Race and class revisited – conceptualising race and racisms', *Sociological Review*, 38(1): 19–42.

Banton, M. (1967) *Race Relations*, London: Tavistock.

——(1987) *Racial Theories*, Cambridge: Cambridge University Press.

——(1991) 'The race relations problematic', *British Journal of Sociology*, 42(1): 115–30.

Barkan, E. (1992) *The Retreat of Scientific Racism: Changing Concepts of Race in Britain and the United States Between the World Wars*, Cambridge: Cambridge University Press.

Barzun, J. (1938) *Race: A Study in Modern Superstition*, London: Methuen.

Benedict, R. (1983) *Race and Racism*, London: Routledge and Kegan Paul.

Bolaria, B.S. and Li, P. (1985) *Racial Oppression in Canada*, Toronto: Garamond Press.

Carter, B., Harris, C. and Joshi, S. (1987) 'The 1951–55 Conservative government and the racialisation of black immigration', *Immigrants and Minorities*, 6: 335–47.

Castles, S. and Kosack, G. (1972) 'The function of labour immigration in western European capitalism', *New Left Review*, 73: 3–21.

——and Kosack, G. (1973) *Immigrant Workers and Class Structure in Western Europe*, London: Oxford University Press.

CCCS (Centre for Contemporary Cultural Studies) (1982) *The Empire Strikes Back: Race and Racism in 70s Britain*, London: Hutchinson.

Christian, B. (1990) 'What Celie knows that you should know', in D.T. Goldberg (ed.) *Anatomy of Racism*, Minneapolis: University of Minnesota Press.

Cox, O.C. (1970) *Caste, Class and Race*, New York: Monthly Review Press.

Fields, B.J. (1982) 'Ideology and race in American history', in J.M. Kousser and J.M. McPherson (eds) *Region, Race and Reconstruction: Essays in Honour of C. Vann Woodward*, New York: Oxford University Press.

——(1990) 'Slavery, race and ideology in the United States of America', *New Left Review*, 181: 95–118.

George, H. (1984) *American Race Relations Theory: A Review of Four Models*, Lanham: University Press of America.

Gilroy, P. (1987) *'There Ain't No Black in the Union Jack': The Cultural Politics of Race and Nation*, London: Hutchinson.

Goldberg, D.T. (ed.) (1990a) *Anatomy of Racism*, Minneapolis: University of Minnesota Press.

——(1990b) 'The social formation of racist discourse', in D.T. Goldberg (ed.) *Anatomy of Racism*, Minneapolis: University of Minnesota Press.

Guillaumin, C. (1972) *L'idéologie Raciste: Genèse et Langage Actuel*, Paris: Mouton.

——(1980) 'The idea of race and its elevation to autonomous scientific and legal status', in UNESCO, *Sociological Theories: Race and Colonialism*, Paris: UNESCO.

——(1988) 'Race and nature: the system of marks', *Feminist Issues*, 1988: 25–43.

Hall, S. (1978) 'Racism and reaction', in Commission for Racial Equality, *Five Views of Multi-Racial Britain*, London: Commission for Racial Equality.

——(1980) 'Race, articulation and societies structured in dominance', in UNESCO, *Sociological Theories: Race and Colonialism*, Paris: UNESCO.

——, Critcher, C., Jefferson, T., Clarke, J., and Roberts, B. (1978) *Policing the Crisis: Mugging, the State and Law and Order*, London: Macmillan.

Hirschfeld, M. (1938) *Racism*, London: Gollancz.

Jordan, W.D. (1968) *White Over Black: American Attitudes Toward the Negro, 1550–1812*, Chapel Hill: University of North Carolina Press.

——(1974) *The White Man's Burden: Historical Origins of Racism in the United States*, London: Oxford University Press.

Joshi, S. and Carter, B. (1984) 'The role of Labour in creating a racist Britain', *Race and Class*, 25: 53–70.

Lecourt, D. (1980) 'Marxism as a critique of sociological theories', in UNESCO, *Sociological Theories: Race and Colonialism*, Paris: UNESCO.

Lugard, F.D. (1929) *The Dual Mandate in British Tropical Africa*, Edinburgh: William Blackwood & Sons Ltd.

Miles, R. (1980) 'Class, race and ethnicity: a critique of Cox's theory', *Ethnic and Racial Studies*, 3(2): 169–87.

——(1982) *Racism and Migrant Labour: A Critical Text*, London: Routledge and Kegan Paul.

——(1984a) 'Marxism versus the "sociology of race relations"?', *Ethnic and Racial Studies*, 7(2): 217–37.

——(1984b) 'The riots of 1958: the ideological construction of "race relations" as a political issue in Britain', *Immigrants and Minorities*, 3(3): 252–75.

——(1986) 'Labour migration, racism and capital accumulation in western Europe', *Capital and Class*, 28: 49–86.

——(1987) *Capitalism and Unfree Labour: Anomaly or Necessity?*, London: Tavistock.

——(1988) 'Racism, Marxism and British politics', *Economy and Society*, 17(3): 428–60.

——(1989) *Racism*, London: Routledge.

——and Phizacklea, A. (1984) *White Man's Country: Racism in British Politics*, London: Pluto Press.

Montagu, A. (ed.) (1964) *The Concept of Race*, New York: Free Press.

——(1974) *Man's Most Dangerous Myth: The Fallacy of Race*, New York: Oxford University Press.

Nikolinakos, M. (1975) 'Notes towards a general theory of migration in late capitalism', *Race and Class*, 17(1): 5–18.

Omi, M. and Winant, H. (1986) *Racial Formation in the United States: From the 1960s to the 1980s*, New York: Routledge and Kegan Paul.

Outlaw, L. (1990) 'Toward a critical theory of "race"', in D.T. Goldberg (ed.) *Anatomy of Racism*, Minneapolis: University of Minnesota Press.

Rex, J. (1970) *Race Relations in Sociological Theory*, London: Weidenfeld and Nicolson.

——(1983) *Race Relations in Sociological Theory*, 2nd edition, London: Routledge and Kegan Paul.

Rich, P.B. (1986a) *Race and Empire in British Politics*, Cambridge: Cambridge University Press.

Robinson, C.J. (1983) *Black Marxism*, London: Zed Press.

Rozat, G. and Bartra, R. (1980) 'Racism and capitalism', in UNESCO, *Sociological Theories: Race and Colonialism*, Paris: UNESCO.

Sivanandan, A. (1982) *A Different Hunger: Writings on Black Resistance*, London: Pluto Press.

——(1983) 'Challenging racism: strategies for the '80s', *Race and Class*, 25(2): 1–12.

——(1985) 'RAT and the degradation of the black struggle', *Race and Class*, 26(4): 1–34.

——(1990) *Communities of Resistance: Writings on Black Struggles for Socialism*, London: Verso.

Small, S. (1991) 'Racialised relations in Liverpool: a contemporary anomaly', *New Community*, 17(4): 511–37.

Smith, S.J. (1989) *The Politics of 'Race' and Residence*, Cambridge: Polity Press.

Stepan, N. (1982) *The Idea of Race in Science: Great Britain, 1800–1945*, London: Macmillan.

Wallerstein, I. (1979) *The Capitalist World-Economy*, Cambridge: Cambridge University Press.

——(1988) 'Universalisme, racisme, sexisme: les tensions idéologiques du capitalisme', in E. Balibar and I. Wallerstein, *Race, Nation, Classe: Les Identités Ambiguës*, Paris: Editions La Découverte.

Wolpe, H. (1980) 'Capitalism and cheap labour-power in South Africa: from segregation to apartheid', in H. Wolpe (ed.), *The Articulation of Modes of Production: Essays from Economy and Society*, London: Routledge and Kegan Paul.

——(1986) 'Class concepts, class struggle and racism', in J. Rex and D. Mason (eds) *Theories of Race and Ethnic Relations*, Cambridge: Cambridge University Press.

Chapter 13

Stuart Hall

OLD AND NEW IDENTITIES, OLD AND NEW ETHNICITIES

[. . .]

WHAT I AM GOING TO DO first is to return to the question of identity and try to look at some of the ways in which we are beginning to reconceptualize that within contemporary theoretical discourses. I shall then go back from that theoretical consideration to the ground of a cultural politics. Theory is always a detour on the way to something more important.

I return to the question of identity because the question of identity has returned to us; at any rate, it has returned to us in British politics and British cultural politics today. It has not returned in the same old place; it is not the traditional conception of identity. It is not going back to the old identity politics of the 1960s social movements. But it is, nevertheless, a kind of return to some of the ground which we used to think in that way. I will make a comment at the very end about what is the nature of this theoretical–political work which seems to lose things on the one side and then recover them in a different way from another side, and then have to think them out all over again just as soon as they get rid of them. What is this never-ending theoretical work which is constantly losing and regaining concepts? I talk about identity here as a point at which, on the one hand, a whole set of new theoretical discourses intersect and where, on the other, a whole new set of cultural practices emerge. I want to begin by trying, very briefly, to map some of those points of intersection theoretically, and then to look at some of their political consequences.

The old logics of identity are ones with which we are extremely familiar, either philosophically, or psychologically. Philosophically, the old logic of identity which many people have critiqued in the form of the old Cartesian subject was often thought in terms of the origin of being itself, the ground of action. Identity is the ground of action. And we have in more recent times a psychological discourse of the self which is very similar: a notion of the continuous, self-sufficient, developmental, unfolding, inner dialectic of selfhood. We are never quite there, but always on our way to it, and when we get there, we will at last know exactly who it is we are.

Now this logic of identity is very important in a whole range of political, theoretical and conceptual discourses. I am interested in it also as a kind of existential reality because I think the logic of the language of identity is extremely important to our own self-conceptions. It contains the notion of the true self, some real self inside there, hiding inside the husks of all the false selves that we present to the rest of the world. It is a kind of guarantee of authenticity. Not until we get really inside and hear what the true self has to say do we know what we are "really saying."

There is something guaranteed about that logic or discourse of identity. It gives us a sense of depth, out there, and in here. It is spatially organized. Much of our discourse of the inside and the outside, of the self and other, of the individual and society, of the subject and the object, is grounded in that particular logic of identity. And it helps us, I would say, to sleep well at night.

Increasingly, I think one of the main functions of concepts is that they give us a good night's rest. Because what they tell us is that there is a kind of stable, only very slowly-changing ground inside the hectic upsets, discontinuities and ruptures of history. Around us history is constantly breaking in unpredictable ways but we, somehow, go on being the same.

That logic of identity is, for good or ill, finished. It's at an end for a whole range of reasons. It's at an end in the first instance because of some of the great de-centerings of modern thought. One could discuss this very elaborately – I could spend the rest of the time talking about it but I just wanted to slot the ideas into place very quickly by using some names as reference points.

It is not possible to hold to that logic of identity after Marx because although Marx does talk about man (he doesn't talk about women making history but perhaps they were slotted in, as the nineteenth century so often slotted women in under some other masculine title), about men and women making history but under conditions which are not of their own choosing. And having lodged either the individual or collective subject always within historical practices, we as individuals or as groups cannot be, and can never have been, the sole origin or authors of those practices. That is a profound historical decentering in terms of social practice.

If that was not strong enough, knocking us sideways as it were, Freud came knocking from underneath, like Hamlet's ghost, and said, "While you're being decentered from left to right like that, let me decenter you from below a bit, and remind you that this stable language of identity is also set from the psychic life about which you don't know very much, and can't know very much. And which you can't know very much by simply taking thought about it: the great continent of the unconscious which speaks most clearly when it's slipping rather than when it's saying what it means." This makes the self begin to seem a pretty fragile thing.

Now, buffeted on one side by Marx and upset from below by Freud, just as it opens its mouth to say, "Well, at least I speak so therefore I must *be* something," Saussure and linguistics comes along and says "That's not true either, you know. Language was there before you. You can only say something by positioning yourself in the discourse. The tale tells the teller, the myth tells the myth-maker, etc. The enunciation is always from some subject who is positioned by and in discourse." That upsets that. Philosophically, one comes to the end of any kind of notion of a perfect transparent continuity between our language and something out there which can be called the real, or the truth, without any quotation marks.

These various upsets, these disturbances in the continuity of the notion of the subject, and the stability of identity, are indeed, what modernity is like. It is not, incidentally, modernity itself. That has an older, and longer history. But this is the beginning of modernity as trouble. Not modernity as enlightenment and progress, but modernity as a problem.

It is also upset by other enormous historical transformations which do not have, and cannot be given, a single name, but without which the story could not be told. In addition to the three or four that I have quoted, we could mention the relativisation of the Western narrative itself, the Western episteme, by the rise of other cultures to prominence, and fifthly, the displacement of the masculine gaze.

Now, the question of trying to come to terms with the notion of identity in the wake of those theoretical decenterings is an extremely problematic enterprise. But that is not all that has been disturbing the settled logic of identity. Because as I was saying earlier when I was talking about the relative decline, or erosion, the instability of the nation-state, of the self-sufficiency of national economies and consequently, of national identities as points of reference, there has simultaneously been a fragmentation and erosion of collective social identity.

I mean here the great collective social identities which we thought of as large-scale, all-encompassing, homogeneous, as unified collective identities, which could be spoken about almost as if they were singular actors in their own right but which, indeed, placed, positioned, stabilized, and allowed us to understand and read, almost as a code, the imperatives of the individual self: the great collective social identities of class, of race, of nation, of gender, and of the West.

These collective social identities were formed in, and stabilized by, the huge, long-range historical processes which have produced the modern world, just as the theories and conceptualizations that I just referred to very briefly are what constituted modernity as a form of self-reflection. They were staged and stabilized by industrialization, by capitalism, by urbanization, by the formation of the world market, by the social and the sexual division of labor, by the great punctuation of civil and social life into the public and the private; by the dominance of the nation- state, and by the identification between Westernization and the notion of modernity itself.

I spoke in my previous talk about the importance, to any sense of where we are placed in the world, of the national economy, the nation-state and of national cultural identities. Let me say a word here about the great class identities which have stabilized so much of our understanding of the immediate and not-so-immediate past.

[. . .] Identity means, or connotes, the process of identification, of saying that this here is the same as that, or we are the same together, in this respect. But something we have learnt from the whole discussion of identification, in feminism and psychoanalysis, is the degree to which that structure of identification is always constructed through ambivalence. Always constructed through splitting. Splitting between that which one is, and that which is the other. The attempt to expel the other to the other side of the universe is always compounded by the relationships of love and desire. This is a different language from the language of, as it were, the Others who are completely different from oneself.

This is the Other that belongs inside one. This is the Other that one can only know from the place from which one stands. This is the self as it is inscribed in the gaze of the Other. And this notion which breaks down the boundaries, between outside and inside, between those who belong and those who do not, between those whose histories have been written and those whose histories they have depended on but whose histories cannot be spoken. That the unspoken silence in between that which can be spoken is the only way to reach for the whole history. There is no other history except to take the absences and the silences along with what can be spoken. Everything that can be spoken is on the ground of the enormous voices that have not, or cannot yet be heard.

This doubleness of discourse, this necessity of the Other to the self, this inscription of identity in the look of the other finds its articulation profoundly in the ranges of a given text. And I want to cite one which I am sure you know but won't remember necessarily, though it is a wonderful, majestic moment in Fanon's *Black Skin, White Masks*, when he describes himself as a young Antillean, face to face with the white Parisian child and her mother. And the child pulls the hand of the mother and says, "Look, Mama, a black man." And he said, "For the first time, I knew who I was. For the first time, I felt as if I had been simultaneously exploded in the gaze, in the violent gaze of the other, and at the same time, recomposed as another."

The notion that identity in that sense could be told as two histories, one over here, one over there, never having spoken to one another, never having anything to do with one another, when translated from the psychoanalytic to the historical terrain, is simply not tenable any longer in an increasingly globalized world. It is just not tenable any longer.

People like me who came to England in the 1950s have been there for centuries; symbolically, we have been there for centuries. I was coming home. I am the sugar at the bottom of the English cup of tea. I am the sweet tooth, the sugar plantations that rotted generations of English children's teeth. There are thousands of others beside me that are, you know, the cup of tea itself. Because they don't grow it in Lancashire, you know. Not a single tea plantation exists within the United Kingdom. This is the symbolization of English identity – I mean, what does anybody in the world know about an English person except that they can't get through the day without a cup of tea?

Where does it come from? Ceylon – Sri Lanka, India. That is the outside history that is inside the history of the English. There is no English history without that other history. The notion that identity has to do with people that look the same, feel the same, call themselves the same, is nonsense. As a process, as a narrative, as a discourse, it is always told from the position of the Other.

What is more is that identity is always in part a narrative, always in part a kind of representation. It is always within representation. Identity is not something which is formed outside and then we tell stories about it. It is that which is narrated in one's own self. I will say something about that in terms of my own narration of identity in a moment – you know, that wonderful moment where Richard II says, "Come let us sit down and tell stories about the death of kings." Well, I am going to tell you a story and ask you to tell one about yourself.

We have the notion of identity as contradictory, as composed of more than one discourse, as composed always across the silences of the other, as written in and through ambivalence and desire. These are extremely important ways of trying to think an identity which is not a sealed or closed totality.

[. . .] Now I can turn to questions of politics. In this conception of an identity which has to be thought through difference, is there a general politics of the local to bring to bear against the great, over-riding, powerful, technologically-based, massively-invested unrolling of global processes which I was trying to describe in my previous talk which tend to mop up all differences, and occlude those differences? Which means, as it were, they are different – but it doesn't make any difference that they are different, they're just different.

No, there is no general politics. I have nothing in the kitbag. There is nothing I can pull out. But I have a little local politics to tell you about. It may be that all we have, in bringing the politics of the local to bear against the global, is a lot of little local politics. I do not know if that is true or not. But I would like to spend some time later talking about the cultural politics of the local, and of this new notion of identity. For it is in this new frame that identity has come back into cultural politics in Britain. The formation of the Black diasporas in the period of post-war migration in the fifties and sixties has transformed English social, economic and political life.

In the first generations, the majority of people had the same illusion that I did: that I was about to go back home. That may have been because everybody always asked me: when was I going back home? We did think that we were just going to get back on the boat; we were here for a temporary sojourn. By the seventies, it was perfectly clear that we were not there for a temporary sojourn. Some people were going to stay and then the politics of racism really emerged.

Now one of the main reactions against the politics of racism in Britain was what I would call "Identity Politics One," the first form of identity politics. It had to do with the constitution of some defensive collective identity against the practices of racist society. It had to do with the fact that people were being blocked out of and refused an identity and identification within the majority nation, having to find some other roots on which to stand. Because people have to find some ground, some place, some position on which to stand. Blocked out of any access to an English or British identity, people had to try to discover who they were. [. . .] It is the crucial moment of the rediscovery or the search for roots.

In the course of the search for roots, one discovered not only where one came from, one began to speak the language of that which is home in the genuine sense, that other crucial moment which is the recovery of lost histories. The histories that have never been told about ourselves that we could not learn in schools, that were not in any books, and that we had to recover.

This is an enormous act of what I want to call imaginary political re-identification, re-territorialization and re-identification, without which a counter-politics could not have been constructed. I do not know an example of any group or category of the people of the margins, of the locals, who have been able to mobilize themselves, socially, culturally, economically, politically in the last twenty or twenty-five years who have not gone through some such series of moments in order to resist their exclusion, their marginalization. That is how and where the margins begin to speak. The margins begin to contest, the locals begin to come to representation.

The identity which that whole, enormous political space produced in Britain, as it did elsewhere, was the category Black. I want to say something about this category which we all now so take for granted. I will tell you some stories about it.

I was brought up in a lower middle class family in Jamaica. I left there in the early fifties to go and study in England. Until I left, though I suppose 98 per cent of the Jamaican population is either Black or coloured in one way or another, I had never ever heard anybody either call themselves, or refer to anybody else as "Black." Never. I heard a thousand other words. My grandmother could differentiate about fifteen different shades between light brown and dark brown. When I left Jamaica, there was a beauty contest in which the different shades of women were graded according to different trees, so that there was a Miss Mahogany, Miss Walnut, etc.

People think of Jamaica as a simple society. In fact, it had the most complicated colour stratification system in the world. Talk about practical semioticians; anybody in my family could compute and calculate anybody's social status by grading the particular quality of their hair versus the particular quality of the family they came from and which street they lived in, including physiognomy, shading, etc. You could trade off one characteristic against another. Compared with that, the normal class stratification system is absolute child's play.

But the word "Black" was never uttered. Why? No Black people around? Lots of them, thousands and thousands of them. Black is not a question of pigmentation. The Black I'm talking about is a historical category, a political category, a cultural category. In our language, at certain historical moments, we have to use the signifier. We have to create an equivalence between how people look and what their histories are. Their histories are in the past, inscribed in their skins. But it is not because of their skins that they are Black in their heads.

I heard Black for the first time in the wake of the Civil Rights movement, in the wake of the de-colonization and nationalistic struggles. Black was created as a political category in a certain historical moment. It was created as a consequence of certain symbolic and ideological struggles. We said, "You have spent five, six, seven hundred years elaborating the symbolism through which Black is a negative factor. Now I don't want another term. I want that term, that negative one, that's the one I want. I want a piece of that action. I want to take it out of the way in which it has been articulated in religious discourse, in ethnographic discourse, in literary discourse, in visual discourse. I want to pluck it out of its articulation and rearticulate it in a new way."

In that very struggle is a change of consciousness, a change of self-recognition, a new process of identification, the emergence into visibility of a new subject. A subject that was always there, but emerging, historically.

You know that story, but I do not know if you know the degree to which that story is true of other parts of the Americas. It happened in Jamaica in the 1970s. In the 1970s, for the first time, Black people recognized themselves as Black. It was the most profound cultural revolution in the Caribbean, much greater than any political revolution they have ever had. That cultural revolution in Jamaica has never been matched by anything as far-reaching as the politics. The politics has never caught up with it.

You probably know the moment when the leaders of both major political parties in Jamaica tried to grab hold of Bob Marley's hand. They were trying to put their hands on Black; Marley stood for Black, and they were trying to get a piece of the action. If only he would look in their direction he would have legitimated them. It was not politics legitimating culture, it was culture legitimating politics.

Indeed, the truth is I call myself all kinds of other things. When I went to England, I wouldn't have called myself an immigrant either, which is what we were all known as. It was not until I went back home in the early 1960s that my mother who, as a good middle-class colored Jamaican woman, hated all Black people, (you know, that is the truth) said to me, "I hope they don't think you're an immigrant over there."

And I said, "Well, I just migrated. I've just emigrated." At that very moment, I thought, that's exactly what I am. I've just left home – for good.

I went back to England and I became what I'd been named. I had been hailed as an immigrant. I had discovered who I was. I started to tell myself the story of my migration.

Then Black erupted and people said, "Well, you're from the Caribbean, in the midst of this, identifying with what's going on, the Black population in England. You're Black."

At that very moment, my son, who was two and a half, was learning the colors. I said to him, transmitting the message at last, "You're Black." And he said, "No. I'm brown." And I said, "Wrong referent. Mistaken concreteness, philosophical mistake. I'm not talking about your paintbox, I'm talking about your head." That is something different. The question of learning, learning to be Black. Learning to come into an identification.

What that moment allows to happen are things which were not there before. It is not that what one then does was hiding away inside as my true self. There wasn't any bit of that true self in there before that identity was learnt. Is that, then, the stable one, is that where we are? Is that where people are?

I will tell you something now about what has happened to that Black identity as a matter of cultural politics in Britain. That notion was extremely important in the anti-racist struggles of the 1970s: the notion that people of diverse societies and cultures would all come to Britain in the fifties and sixties as part of that huge wave of migration from the Caribbean, East Africa, the Asian subcontinent, Pakistan, Bangladesh, from different parts of India, and all identified themselves politically as Black.

What they said was, "We may be different actual color skins but vis-a-vis the social system, vis-a-vis the political system of racism, there is more that unites us than what divides us." People begin to ask "Are you from Jamaica, are you from Trinidad, are you from Barbados?" You can just see the process of divide and rule. "No. Just address me as I am. I know you can't tell the difference so just call me Black. Try using that. We all look the same, you know. Certainly can't tell the difference. Just call me Black. Black identity." Anti-racism in the seventies was only fought and only resisted in the community, in the localities, behind the slogan of a Black politics and the Black experience.

In that moment, the enemy was ethnicity. The enemy had to be what we called "multi-culturalism." Because multi-culturalism was precisely what I called previously "the exotic." The exotica of difference. Nobody would talk about racism but they were perfectly prepared to have "International Evenings," when we would all come and cook our native dishes, sing our own native songs and appear in our own native costume. It is true that some people, some ethnic minorities in Britain, do have indigenous, very beautiful indigenous forms of dress. I didn't. I had to rummage in the dressing-up box to find mine. I have been de-racinated for four hundred years. The last thing I am going to do is to dress up in some native Jamaican costume and appear in the spectacle of multi-culturalism.

Has the moment of the struggle organized around this constructed Black identity gone away? It certainly has not. So long as that society remains in its economic, political, cultural, and social relations in a racist way to the variety of Black and Third World peoples in its midst, and it continues to do so, that struggle remains.

Why then don't I just talk about a collective Black identity replacing the other identities? I can't do that either and I'll tell you why.

The truth is that in relation to certain things, the question of Black, in Britain, also has its silences. It had a certain way of silencing the very specific experiences of Asian people. Because though Asian people could identify, politically, in the struggle against racism, when they came to using their own culture as the resources of resistance, when they wanted to write out of their own experience and reflect on their own position, when they wanted to create, they naturally created within the histories of the languages, the cultural tradition, the positions of people who came from a variety of different historical backgrounds. And just as Black was the cutting edge of politics vis-a-vis one kind of enemy, it could also, if not understood properly, provide a kind of silencing in relation to another. These are the costs, as well as the strengths, of trying to think of the notion of Black as an essentialism.

What is more, there were not only Asian people of color, but also Black people who did not identify with that collective identity. So that one was aware of the fact that always, as one advanced to meet the enemy, with a solid front, the differences were raging behind. Just shut the doors, and conduct a raging argument to get the troops together, to actually hit the other side.

A third way in which Black was silencing was to silence some of the other dimensions that were positioning individuals and groups in exactly the same way. To operate exclusively through an unreconstructed conception of Black was to reconstitute the authority of Black masculinity over Black women, about which, as I am sure you know, there was also, for a long time, an unbreakable silence about which the most militant Black men would not speak.

To organize across the discourses of Blackness and masculinity, of race and gender, and forget the way in which, at the same moment, Blacks in the under class were being positioned in class terms, in similar work situations, exposed to the same deprivations of poor jobs and lack of promotion that certain members of the white working class suffered, was to leave out the critical dimension of positioning.

What then does one do with the powerful mobilizing identity of the Black experience and of the Black community? Blackness as a political identity in the light of the understanding of any identity is always complexly composed, always historically constructed. It is never in the same place but always positional. One always has to think about the negative consequences of the positionality. You cannot, as it were, reverse the discourses of any identity simply by turning them upside down. What is it like to live, by attempting to valorise and defeat the marginalization of the variety of Black subjects and to really begin to recover the lost histories of a variety of Black experiences, while at the same time recognizing the end of any essential Black subject?

[. . .] Third generation young Black men and women know they come from the Caribbean, know that they are Black, know that they are British. They want to speak from all three identities. They are not prepared to give up any one of them. They will contest the Thatcherite notion of Englishness, because they say this Englishness is Black. They will contest the notion of Blackness because they want to make a differentiation between people who are Black from one kind of society and people who are Black from another. Because they need to know that difference, that difference that makes a difference in how they write their poetry, make their films, how they paint. It makes a difference. It is inscribed in their creative work. They need it as a resource. They are all those identities together. They are making astonishing cultural work, the most important work in the visual arts. Some of the most important work in film and photography and nearly all the most important work in popular music is coming from this new recognition of identity that I am speaking about.

Very little of that work is visible elsewhere but some of you have seen, though you may not have recognized, the outer edge of it. Some of you, for example, may have seen a film made by Stephen Frears and Hanif Kureishi, called *My Beautiful Laundrette*. This was originally made as a television film for local distribution only, and shown once at the Edinburgh Festival where it received an enormous reception. If you have seen *My Beautiful Laundrette* you will know that it is the most transgressive text there is. Anybody who is Black, who tries to identify it, runs across the fact that the central characters of this narrative are two gay men. What is more, anyone who wants to separate the identities into their two clearly separate points will discover that one of these Black gay men is white and one of these Black gay men is brown. Both of them are struggling in Thatcher's Britain. One of them has an uncle who is a Pakistani landlord who is throwing Black people out of the window.

This is a text that nobody likes. Everybody hates it. You go to it looking for what are called "positive images" and there are none. There aren't any positive images like that with whom one can, in a simple way, identify. Because as well as the politics – and there is certainly a politics in that and in Kureishi's other film, but it is not a politics which invites easy identification – it has a politics which is grounded on the complexity of identification – it has a politics which is grounded on the complexity of identifications which are at work.

I will read you something which Hanif Kureishi said about the question of responding to his critics who said, "Why don't you tell us good stories about ourselves, as well as good/bad stories? Why are your stories mixed about ourselves?" He spoke about the difficult moral position of the writer from an oppressed or persecuted community and the relation of that writing to the rest of the society. He said it is a relatively new one in England but it will arise more and more as

British writers with a colonial heritage and from a colonial or marginal past start to declare themselves.

"There is sometimes," he said, "too simple a demand for positive images. Positive images sometimes require cheering fictions – the writer as Public Relations Officer. And I'm glad to say that the more I looked at *My Beautiful Laundrette*, the less positive images I could see. If there is to be a serious attempt to understand present-day Britain with its mix of races and colours, its hysteria and despair, then writing about it has to be complex. It can't apologize, or idealize. It can't sentimentalize. It can't attempt to represent any one group as having the total, exclusive, essential monopoly on virtue.

A jejune protest or parochial literature, be it black, gay or feminist, is in the long run no more politically effective than works which are merely public relations. What we need now, in this position, at this time, is imaginative writing that gives us a sense of the shifts and the difficulties within our society as a whole.

If contemporary writing which emerges from oppressed groups ignores the central concerns and major conflicts of the larger society, and if these are willing simply to accept themselves as marginal or enclave literatures, they will automatically designate themselves as permanently minor, as a sub-genre. They must not allow themselves now to be rendered invisible and marginalized in this way by stepping outside of the maelstrom of contemporary history." [. . .]

Chapter 14

Claire Alexander

BEYOND BLACK

[. . .]

ABOUT EIGHT YEARS AGO, while still finishing my PhD on black young men, I was invited to present a paper to the African-American studies programme seminar at Princeton University. Knowing that my research interests seemed ill-fitting in the American context, and deciding that an upfront defence would be my best shot at forestalling any attack, I prefaced my talk with the explanation that in the British context, 'black' included peoples of African *and* Asian descent. What I had imagined as a minor contextualizing, tactical step actually turned out to be a major diversionary manoeuvre – after this statement, no-one seemed to hear the rest of the paper and the questions returned again and again to this seemingly bizarre British anomaly.

Eight years on, what strikes me is that this British peculiarity (to paraphrase Gilroy 1993), would now seem anomalous even within Britain. Where, at the time of my doctoral research, concerns were aimed less at the race/ethnicity disjunction than gender difference – it was the fact that I was a woman talking about men rather than an Asian talking about African-Caribbeans which people found most odd – less than a decade later it is almost inconceivable, even to me, that I should attempt such a project. It has become something of a truism to recount the splintering of the 'black' consensus in Britain through the 1980s, the fragmentation of political action in the multiculturalist scramble for resources and failure of collective identities in the fallout of *The Satanic Verses* affair. With the benefit of 1990s' hindsight, that inclusive version of black Britain seems a distant mirage of unfulfilled and unfulfillable idealism and optimism, inevitably lost in the grim reality of real lives, incompatible needs and the competition for too-limited opportunities. As we enter the new millennium, the emphasis is firmly on 'difference' – at its most optimistic, within a common national framework, Parekh's 'community of communities' (2000), at its least, of 'cultural enclaves and feuding nationalisms' (Sivanandan 2000) in a hostile homogenized landscape.

While the older spectre of 'black' lingers on, recalcitrant and unrepentant, in some political circles and campaigns, the same cannot be said of the academy. Indeed, the alacrity with which academics – white, black and Asian – have abandoned 'black' as a unifying category in the (neo-anthropological) search for new, emergent, previously undiscovered and preferably unimaginable identities is matched only by the haste to discard the empirical analysis of racism in the rush to gain the more fashionable (and morally pure) high ground of theoretical marginality. As Ash Sharma, John Hutnyk and Sanjay Sharma note: 'Ethnicity is in. Cultural difference is in. Marginality is in' (1996, p.1). This is as much true of the intellectual marketplace as the all-consuming appetite for 'the Other' which continues to define the global market in goods, and products and people. 'Black' in Britain today has re-defined the landscape of similarity and difference, locally and globally, rendering its older contours obsolete and unthinkable. While almost all would accept these changes, and perhaps few would wish things otherwise, these shifts have implications for the theorization of race and ethnicity in Britain, which have been largely unexplored. The too easy valorization of an increasingly inward-looking and (apparently) self-defining 'difference' has led not only to the erection of seemingly insurmountable boundaries between Britain's African, Caribbean and Asian communities, which are empirically unsustainable, but has denied its more subtle ramifications for the way in which we think about these communities. Difference may be in, it may be all there is, but it is applied differentially to communities and often obscures as much as it reveals.

The present article is a preliminary working through of some concerns about the idea of 'difference'. It originates in, and draws implicitly on, my research work, first on African-Caribbean young men and more recently on Asian young men. As perhaps the only British academic to have done ethnographic work on both (certainly in recent years) (1996; 2000a), I have been struck firstly by the similarities of process, negotiation and constraint that mark all of these young men and secondly by the very different ways in which these identities have been defined in current academic debates. It is this latter aspect which concerns me here. The article argues that there are two theoretical versions of 'difference' which have marked out African-Caribbean and Asian communities in distinct and opposing ways, and explores some of the implications of these 'differences' for the under-standing of racial and ethnic identities. At the risk of being unfashionably parochial, this is a local, British story.

Black: a peculiarly British history

In 'Old and new identities, old and new ethnicities', Stuart Hall asserts, 'Black is not a question of pigmentation. The Black I am talking about is a historical category, a political category, a cultural category' (2000a, p.149). In Britain, the story of 'black' as a historical, political and cultural category has a common, generally accepted narrative – at least in its beginnings. Its endings, while avowedly not 'happily ever after', are more contested. Unlike the United States, in whose borrowed costume the dominant current plotline is arrayed, in Britain 'black' related less specifically to an identifiable 'racial' group, though it has come increasingly to refer, similarly, only to (selected) peoples of African descent. Throughout the 1970s and the early years of the 1980s, Asian, African and Caribbean groups organized, mobilized and resisted racial disadvantage and discrimination under the banner of 'black', a movement which Hall argues was crucial in contesting the pathologies of cultural and ethnic difference which underpinned 'race relations' thinking:

> In that moment, the enemy was ethnicity. The enemy had to be what we called "multiculturalism". Because multiculturalism was precisely what I called previously "the exotic". The exotica of difference. (2000a, p.151)

Interestingly, and perhaps ironically in the light of later developments, strands from an emergent black academia avowedly denied the emphasis on 'culturalist' overdetermination as a basis for sociological explanation (CCCS 1982) and insisted on a unified and inclusive use of 'black' to reflect a shared experience of historical distortion and exploitation, and contemporary structural disadvantage and discrimination. More than this, this identification marked the move away from the idea of black communities as passive objects of study and sympathy towards a recognition of an active political subjectivity and resistance (Mercer 2000a). Hall comments, 'So long as that society remains in its economic, political, cultural and social relations in a racist way . . . that struggle remains' (2000a, p.151).

Although few would dispute that the conditions for struggle remain, the discourse on how to wage that struggle has changed almost beyond recognition. 'Black' as a symbolic unity now seems naïve and anachronistic, at once idealistic and reductively undesirable. Hall, for example, argues in 'Frontlines and Backyards' (2000b):

> A decade ago . . . African-Caribbeans and Asians were treated by the dominant society as so much alike that they could be subsumed and mobilised under a single political category. But today that is no longer the case. Today we have to recognise the complex internal cultural segmentation, the internal frontlines which cut through so-called Black British identity. (2000b, p.127)

Three important transitions are discernible in the above quote: firstly, the move away from the equation of 'black' with *structural* positioning and disadvantage, due to an apparent splintering of socio-economic experiences between 'black' (most especially between African-Caribbean and 'Asian' groups); secondly, the emphasis on '*cultural* segmentation' as a revitalized form of salient difference; and thirdly, the implication of boundaries and oppositions *between* Britain's 'black' communities, emotively symbolized as 'frontlines'. This latter, tensely loaded image suggests particularly a move not only towards fragmentation but also towards mutual competition and antagonism.

The re-emergence of culture as a defining feature of Britain's black communities throughout the 1980s, with the dominant ethos of liberal 'multiculturalism' (and its incumbent scattershot resourcing in the aftermath of the disturbances of 1980/1 and 1985) can perhaps be read as a partial return to the race relations paradigm of earlier decades. The solution to structural issues of discrimination was to re-define them as cultural incompatibilities and inadequacies, and to seek new forms of integration and support – what nowadays appears under the guise of 'social inclusion'. However, where black politics in the 1970s eschewed the 'saris, steelbands and samosas' version of cultural pathologization (Rattansi 1992), the mid-eighties and nineties saw the seizing of cultural difference as a source of community pride and a convenient funding (or promotion) opportunity. Within the academy, the return to culture saw increasingly vocal concerns about the silencing of Asian experience and agendas (Hall 2000b), concerns which seemed fully justified in the confused response, or absence of response, to *The Satanic Verses* affair (Modood 1992b; Gilroy 1993).

The re-definition and reclamation of the new, improved, States-style, additive-free version of 'black' has been accompanied by the rise of 'Asian' as a political category and object of study (Rattansi 2000). At the same time, a focus on 'race' and racism has been superseded by a resurgent interest in 'ethnicity' and culture as the locus for identity politics or, increasingly, simply identity. The triumph of ethnicity, particularly when suffused with notions of religious exclusivity, has led to the further splintering of 'Asian' as a collective label/identification, privileging and reifying aspects of identity as axiomatic markers of difference (Rattansi 2000). As I shall argue below, the category 'Asian' carries with it notions of fixity and bounded certainty (Housee & Sharma 1999) which mark it out from, and in opposition to, the more fluid, and more theoretically fashionable, accounts of identity formation which define contemporary slimline 'black' identities; what one might call 'cultural difference' versus 'the politics of difference', or 'old' versus 'new' ethnicities (Alexander 2000a).

The aim of this article is not to revisit the place of 'black' within the arena of political activism, or to argue for its reclamation or rejection as a valid label: my concern is rather to recognize the split and explore its implications for the conception of African-Caribbean and Asian communities within British academe. In particular, it is to examine the way in which the resurgence of notions of ethnicity have impacted in the formation of black and Asian identities and the theorization of cultural difference. It is to this issue that I now turn.

Of difference and difference

While the British history of 'black' can be traced in an almost circular movement from notions of naturalized racial/cultural difference through social, historical and political construction and contestation back to cultural difference (whether natural or constructed), it is also true that some strands of thought within the academy have simply never moved at all. This is particularly true of accounts of Asian communities in Britain, where the dominant paradigm has remained that of 'race relations', though perhaps with a minor makeover of the red-flocked discursive scenery (Parekh 1997).

Although some have argued that the use of 'black' rendered silent and invisible the Asian experience (Modood 1992a; Hall 2000b), it is also true that Asian communities have retained a separate and acute visibility within the field of race and ethnicity, or, more accurately, within the study of ethnicity. Sue Benson (1996) has argued that research in Britain from the 1950s heralded an academic division of labour between sociologists and anthropologists, with the former seizing on issues of race and racism in relation to primarily black/African-Caribbean communities, abandoning Asians to the culturalist microscopes of the anthropologists. Studies of 'black' communities then focused on structural issues of inequality, disadvantage and discrimination (Alexander 1996), whereas studies of Asian communities pored endlessly over the fascinating cultural features of arranged marriages, kinship systems and religious rituals. This division was legitimated and reinforced by a twofold approach to race and culture; i.e. that African-Caribbean communities have no distinct culture, whereas Asian communities have too much (CCCS 1982); that African-Caribbeans have 'race' and Asians have 'ethnicity'; or, as Benson succinctly encapsulates, 'Asians have culture, West Indians have problems' (1996).

The notion of weak black cultures and pathologized identities continues to underpin popular debates on crime, underachievement and 'nihilism' in black communities and to define black cultural events.[1] In the academy, however, in the wake of the cultural studies revolution, black identity and culture have received a postmodern makeover and moved, reclaimed and feted, centre-stage in the debates on difference. Hall, for example, notes that while black people remain at 'the receiving end of systematic structures of deprivation and victimization' they are also the 'dominant defining force in street-oriented British youth culture' (Hall 2000b, p.128). It is, I think, significant that while the former attribute hearkens back, at least potentially, to a more inclusive, political version of peculiarly British blackness, the second looks explicitly towards a trans-Atlantic, African-American cultural trajectory, which demands a more exclusive, racially homogeneous notion of 'black' (particularly centred on hip-hop).

It can be argued that, at least in relation to African-Caribbean communities, the cultural turn in sociology has precipitated a partial inversion of the 'Asians have culture; West Indians have problems' dichotomy. Asians still have culture, though as I shall argue below, this has increasingly become a problem in itself, while African-Caribbeans have become the incumbents of a global, creative, cutting-edge and infinitely marketable culture-of-desire (Gilroy 2000a). While there are problems with the commodification of blackness (Gilroy 1993; 2000a) and its erasure of continued structures of disadvantage and discrimination, it is nevertheless true that current theories on representation, identity and the 'politics of difference' have tended to focus primarily on African-Caribbean cultural production. Notions of hybridity, diaspora, syncretism – of new ethnicities and urban cultures (Back 1996) -have tended to talk across the black (African-Caribbean)/white divide as the primary lines of communication and transgression, leaving Asian cultures,[2] untouched and undesired, on the theoretical sidelines.

If African-Caribbean cultures have become the epitome of dangerous and desirable marginality, theoretical high fashion, Asian cultures have remained largely transfixed and 'invisible' (West 1993) behind reinvented cultural barricades, made visible and translated by the (largely white) anthropological gaze (Shaw 1988; Werbner 1999). Where black/African-Caribbean identities have become defined as fluid, fragmented, negotiated and creative, Asian identities have been defined –

in opposition – as static, bounded, internally homogeneous and externally impenetrable (Housee & Sharma 1999). 'Difference' in this case, then, is imagined in
cultural absolutes and oppositions, less an engagement with the other than the
reification of irreducible and antipathetic 'Others'. The dilemmas of these two
versions of 'difference' are most clearly apparent in relation to youth: where
African-Caribbean youth cultures are seen as moving outwards, into mainstream
cultures, transforming and transgressing ideas of integral British cultural identity,
Asian youth cultures, if acknowledged any existence outside the black hole of
'community' identity, are seen as mysterious, incomprehensible to 'outsiders' and
exclusive (Baumann 1996). In addition, against the backdrop of cultural uniformity
and stasis, change is automatically cast as loss and as conflict – in relation to Asian
youth, at least, the 'between two cultures' thesis is alive and kicking (Anwar,
1994, 1998; Parekh 2000, p. 31).

The initial dichotomy identified by Benson has undergone transformation in
the wake of current theoretical divisions about what 'cultural identity' means.
Where African-Caribbeans once had 'race', they now have 'difference'; Asians *still*
have (too much) culture, but with the additional weight of a stifling demand for
authenticity. It has also precipitated a number of additional dualisms around an
increasingly naturalized black/Asian divide. Where notions of 'the black community'
have been largely deconstructed and demonized within the academy as 'ethnic
absolutism', 'community' remains the privileged location of Asian identity; where
African-Caribbean identities are envisaged as dynamic, fractured and continuously
invented, Asian identities remain possessions of birth and blood, the repository of
'tradition' and 'being'; where African-Caribbean identities call for a dismantling
of notions of culture and nation and belonging (Rattansi 2000), Asian identities
resurrect the barricades and call for a benign and untrammelled multiculture (Parekh
2000). Increasingly, millennial 'black' identities are conceptualized around the
'politics of difference', which can increasingly be read as a bid for inclusion in the
(re)imagination of the national culture, whereas Asian identities are constructed
through 'cultural difference' and placed outside the boundaries of this imagined
culture indeed, providing the 'Other' against which this inclusive 'cool Britannia'
multiracial (and barely multicultural, unless commercially viable) society defines
itself.

The *Windrush* trajectory

It is ironic, given that one of the main stated reasons for abandoning 'black' as an
inclusive term was the erasure of Asian experience, that the version of 'black
British' as an exclusively African-Caribbean experience (with grudging African add-
ons) has enabled not a plurality of black histories, or even black and Asian histories,
but a flat, monochrome narrative, substituting selected and extremely partial
highlights for an altogether more nuanced story. This takes the history of post-
war race and racism in Britain from the arrival of the Empire *Windrush* in 1948,[3]
and traces it through Nottingham and Notting Hill Gate riots, Enoch Powell's
'river of blood' speech, campaigns about e.s.n and sinbins, Notting Hill Carnival
1976, the murder of Blair Peach, the New Cross fire, the disturbances of 1980/81

and 1985 (minus Southall), to the murder of Stephen Lawrence. In earlier versions, this story paid at least token gestures towards the existence of Asian communities and their role in the struggles (Sivanandan 1981/2; CCCS 1982); since the partition of 'black', however, this history has been reinvented and claimed as exclusively African-Caribbean, with exclusively African-Caribbean events and signposts.[4] This narrative is, most of all, a story of 'becoming'; of becoming *British*, which begins with the arrival of strangers and ends with the 'irresistible rise' of the black English – black MPs, Trevor MacDonald, Linford Christie (Phillips & Phillips 1999). Within this version, Asians remain largely invisible and silenced, on the margins of struggle and outside the structures of discrimination and disadvantage. Toted as 'The Irresistible Rise of Multi-Racial Britain' (Phillips & Phillips 1999), what the *Windrush* trajectory actually represents is 'the Irresistible Rise of Bi-Racial Britain'.

The *Windrush* trajectory demands a specific reinvention of 'black British' in narrow, racialized terms, one that excludes Asians and subsumes Africans.[5] Paul Gilroy has argued that this restrictive redefinition 'betoken[s] a general retreat into the dubious comfort of ethnic particularity' (1993, p.31), one which too easily reifies 'race' as a collective identification and belies the more complex fragmentations internal to this identity, most notably on class (Gilroy 2000b). The assertion of racially homogeneous identities, bounded by the rather disingenuous appeal to shared 'African' descent, becomes the refuge of the emergent black middle class, 'securing the unity of an emergent black *petit bourgeois* and . . . mystifying their intrinsically problematic relationship to those they are supposed to serve' (Gilroy 1993, p.31). At the same time, these reified boundaries belie the shared structural, geographical, even cultural spaces, however fraught, that cut across neatly bounded and labelled racial/ethnic packages.

This re-racialized black identity also facilitates a trans-Atlantic connection, which conflates African-Caribbean experience in Britain to African-American experience. Interestingly, African-Caribbeans in the United States (or the Caribbean itself) do not form part of this equation any more than Africans in Britain. The Black Atlantic then shrinks to a bi-polar marketplace, a trajectory that trades national and historical specificities as universalisms one way and black British academics the other.

On the other hand, if the claims of 'new ethnicities' or 'the politics of difference' were to disband the notion of unproblematized racial identities and substitute a more fluid and contested matrix of identity formations, the focus would not be on bounded cultures but on networks, border zones and boundary crossings, on ambiguity and transgression: what Mercer has called the more 'messy and ambivalent intermezzo worlds' (2000b, p. 235).

Theoretically at least, 'new ethnicities' aimed to refute bounded notions of homogeneous racial identities and to replace them with the identities formed in process and through inequalities of power. The claim was to make explicit the processes of domination, subordination and resistance which forged racialized identities and to make visible the fractured and unpredictable nature of their living through (Hall 1996). The central theoretical pillars of these new identities were diaspora, hybridity, the third space, becoming. In the re-imagination of non-essentialized black identities, this post-modernist, post-structuralist-inflected version of difference promised liberation from absolutist notions of cultural identity; most notably in relation to black/African-Caribbean identities. But as Kobena Mercer has argued, 'the subversive potential once invested in notions of hybridity has been subject to pre-millennial downsizing' (2000b, p.235). The co-optation of this once-potentially radical 'difference', the erasure of its implicit 'politics', has a number of implications for the interpretation of African-Caribbean communities in Britain.

Firstly, the commodification of difference as fashion iconography has led to increasing discomfort with the material realities of structural inequality and disadvantage, and the separation of structure and culture, leading to the valorization of the margin as radical chic. This 'downsized', castrated difference has been partly engineered through the work of culture brokers, who have assumed the burden of representation using this version of 'difference' to invalidate a class perspective and validate at the same time an integrative philosophy. If all identities are constructed and fragmented and contested then class, along with gender, sexuality, age, location and politics is in the mix, just another ready-to-wear part of multicultural, multiracial 'cool Britannia'; individualistic, inclusive, meritocratic, marketable, with just a hint of colour for emblematic danger. Same difference, safe difference.

Secondly, the valorization of 'difference' as an end in itself has led to the reinscription of a new binary: 'difference' versus 'culture' or 'community', perhaps even 'identity'. Rather than exploring the forms of continuity, ambiguity, imagination and transformation within seemingly rigid or exclusive forms of African-Caribbean identification (Hall 1990), the tendency has been to exclude these forms from the discussion, banished to the circle of the academic Inferno reserved for cultural or ethnic absolutists: fundamentalists, militants, nationalists and other intellectual tricksters. Hybridity itself becomes exclusionary and rigidified: thus Mercer cites Fisher, 'hybridity risks becoming an essentialist opposite to the new denigrated "cultural purity"' (2000b, p. 240).

This version of 'difference' actually works, then, through the exclusion and demonization of what are viewed as reactionary or essentialized identity construc-tions, a process of rendering uncomfortable or unacceptable identities invisible and consigning them to the unfashionable margin. 'Difference' is seen as primarily a positive process of creation, with negative formulations viewed as throwbacks to less enlightened times. Such theories have proved reluctant to take on gender relations, homophobia, violence and so on as part of this version of 'difference', placing them more as obstacles which stand in the way of the achievement of true 'difference', which in turn becomes an end-goal rather than a process – or a 'property' rather than a 'relation' (Hutnyk 2001). What remains is the acceptable face of 'difference', one which stresses inclusion, openness and, ironically, similarity: the disappearance into Britishness. In this it re-inscribes rather than challenges the reductive racial posturing of the *Windrush* trajectory, amounting more to the challenging of stereotypes, the assertion of complex identities and the appeal to a common humanity than an attack on structures and discourses which maintain inequality. As John Hutnyk has asserted:

> The self-approving liberalism that proclaims this as a radical cosmopolitan recognition worthy of progressive change, proceeds to ignore the historical consequences of those factors – race, class, gender, imperialism

– that create difference in the first place. This is not a progressive politics . . . it is . . . a mode of Fundamentalism (2001, p. 128)

It is perhaps unsurprising that the 'politics of difference' has tended to remain largely at the level of theory and to avoid its rather messier, incommensurable realities. African-Caribbean identities have been textualized rather than realized, reflecting a broader privileging of theory over the empirical in the academic fashion stakes. Take it from an ethnographer, removing lived experiences renders the application of theory a much tidier and more convincing narrative. What the politics of difference has failed to do – perhaps because it has never really tried – is to account for the problems and issues confronting many African-Caribbean communities: school exclusions, unemployment, drugs and violence, deaths in police custody, racial murders – either as victims or perpetrators.

If the triumph of 'difference' in the representation of African-Caribbean identities has been achieved through the drawing of internal exclusionary barriers and the silencing of internal 'Others' it can also be seen that its version of 'black Britain' is performed through the 'Othering' of exterior once-black-now-ethnic-minority communities, particularly Asians. Increasingly, the notion of 'black Britain' itself is constructed through the exclusion of Asian communities from its remit, a closure achieved through the projection of an alternative notion of 'cultural difference' founded on absolute and antipathetic value systems and beliefs (Modood *et al.* 1997).[6] Gilroy, for example, has commented on the way in which black British identity has engineered an inclusion contingent on the marginalization of Asian communities, particularly in the aftermath of *The Satanic Verses* affair:

> What do we say when the political and cultural gains of the emergent
> black Brits go hand in hand with a further marginalisation of 'Asians'
> in general and Muslims in particular? (1993, p. 94)

If the current academic scene is anything to go by, apparently nothing. This silence is facilitated and legitimated through the convenient abandonment of 'black' as a common category, which means that Asian communities no longer have anything to do with African-Caribbean communities, or African-Caribbean academics, and can be abandoned on the discursive margins to fend for themselves. At the same time, African-Caribbean experience remains the primary defining position for all non-white groups; the benchmark for 'race relations': Notting Hill Carnival, Stephen Lawrence, Big Brother.[7] African-Caribbeans are then made both to stand apart from unacceptable/unassimilable 'Others' in the construction of multiracial Britain and to represent and subsume them within the same discourse – the epitome of 'black' success.

(In)visible Asians

Of course, it could be argued, probably legitimately, that the secession from 'black' was largely precipitated from within 'the Asian community' itself.[8] Historical and common-sense orthodoxy tells us that 'black' obscured too many cultural differences and opposed agendas to remain useful, that it rendered invisible both the contribution of Asian communities and their supposed success vis à vis their African-Caribbean counterparts, that it reduced black experience to a list of disadvantages and oppressions. Tariq Modood thus argues that 'black' erased cultural differences and economic successes; that it ignored the specificities of emergent forms of 'cultural racism', especially in relation to Islam and Islamophobia; and that it privileged an African-Caribbean agenda masquerading as an inclusive political movement (1992a). More than this, Asians have simply never been seen, or have ever seen themselves, as 'black'.[9] For Modood, the major problem with 'black' is, ultimately, a question of culture – broadly, that Asians have a separate cultural tradition which imbues them with a strong value system: family, hard work, education, and provides them with a basis for economic success, whereas African-Caribbeans, implicitly lacking the same values and traditions, retreat to 'black' as a compensatory negative political and cultural identity founded on narratives of racial disadvantage: culture versus colour, 'mode of being' versus 'mode of oppression' (1992a, p.55).[10]

The Satanic Verses affair of 1989 probably sounded the death knell for 'black' in its peculiarly British formation. Certainly, images of Muslim men on the streets of Northern towns burning books were not easily compatible with the liberal image of peaceable Asian communities or anti-racist bids for inclusion in the economic, social and cultural life of a reimagined nation. Nor did they fit with notions of radical civil unrest and revolutionary potential, if anyone still believed in that by 1989, a script of national disavowal rehearsed through the events of the spring and summer of 2001 across the towns of northern England. Although there were different interpretations of the Rushdie affair (Samad 1992; Housee & Sharma 1999), the version that emerged triumphant played directly into dominant popular perceptions of Asian communities – the-everything-you-ever-knew-about-Asians-but-were-afraid-to-say narrative. This version signals an easy retreat into the axioms of the 'race relations' paradigm; Asians are different, they are different because of their culture, it is this culture which structures their interactions with wider British society (Parekh 2000, pp. 30–31). Hardly surprising then, if Bhikhu Parekh, should in 1997 still be talking about 'immigrants' and 'integration' (1997, Foreword).

This story turns crucially on a resurrected notion of cultural difference, one which employs the old-style anthropological paradigm of culture as tradition, ritual, belief rather than the construction of meaning; one with clearly defined collective features and institutions rather than individual creativity; and complete with handy corporeal tribal markers for the disoriented tourist. And, of course, with clearly defined, impenetrable boundaries, impossible to escape, undesirable to access. Interestingly, the inscription of cultural absolutes shares much in common with conservative and new racist perspectives on family, community, belonging and nationhood, on values and tradition (Gilroy 2000b) though without the repatriation clause, obviously.[11]

This neo-culturalist version of difference can be contrasted revealingly with the cultural-studies version of 'difference' discussed above. Thus, while African-Caribbean communities are defined as outward looking, moving into mainstream culture, re-defining notions of Britishness, Asians, in contrast, are seen as inward looking, static, culture-bound and exclusive, outside mainstream national culture and, increasingly, incompatible with it.[12] Whereas African-Caribbean cultures are defined as forward looking, individualistic, late- or post-modern, Asian cultures are placed as anachronistic, collective, pre-modern. African-Caribbean identities have been wrenched free of any ties of community, but Asian identities remain mired in questions of authenticity. It is interesting to reflect that while African-Caribbean cultures are primarily defined through youth, Asian cultures are envisaged through age: what Koushik Banerjea might typify as 'men with beards'.

Herded behind the cultural barricades, Asian communities remain largely invisible, in two senses. Firstly, Asian cultural identities are seen as distinct from wider national cultures and are therefore not represented within it, or are positioned as an alien threat to it. Secondly, Asians remain invisible in the sense that they are not presented in any complex way, appearing only as stereotypes or ideal types – and this is true of academic work as well as more generally.[13] Asian subjectivity seems almost to be a contradiction in terms. This is particularly striking given the amount of empirical ink spilt on Asian communities in Britain, an omission only paralleled by the almost total absence of theoretical work on those same communities.

The reculturation of Asian communities in the period after 'black' has seen an increasing proliferation of narrowly defined ethnic identities, premised on the privileging of national, regional and religious identifications, what Sivanandan has evocatively termed 'cultural enclaves and feuding nationalisms' (2000, p. 423). Feted as the celebration of cultural diversity (Modood 1992a), the inscription of absolute barriers between Asian groups has led instead to a focus on cultural antipathies and socio-economic differentiation, a division increasingly conflated with religion (Modood et al. 1997). This has seen the emergence of Islam into the spotlight as the latest object of academic desire, with Muslim communities fast becoming the newest occupants of the 'problem/victim' analytical space (Alexander 2000a). Overdetermined cultural difference has been used as a marker and explanation for internal economic differentiation, facilitating a dichotomy between Muslims and non-Muslims, or what Modood terms 'believers' and 'achievers' (Modood 1992a). Some cultures, that is, Muslim cultures, then become not a resource but an obstacle; most particularly an obstacle to integration and the success that is thereby guaranteed (Modood et al. 1997, p. 147). Parekh's assertion that (implicitly Muslim) communities need to yield up elements of their 'culture' to fulfil the 'moral covenant' and ease British acceptance is a logical consequence of this position: 'some of their values and practices might be unacceptable and then they need to be changed, by consensus when possible and by law if necessary' (1997, p. x).[14]

Thinking back to Benson's earlier formulation, it can be seen that Asians now not only have culture but that culture is itself the problem – at least, if you are Muslim. While the reimagination of black Britain turns upon the exclusion of Asian communities, then, the claims of Asian communities to British citizenship – if not cultural belonging – itself turns on the exclusion of Muslims. Muslims thus become the ultimate 'Other', transfixed through the racialization of religious identity to stand at the margins: undesired, irredeemable, alien.

It is particularly striking that the proponents of post-modern difference have largely acquiesced in this culturalist niche marketing, silently excluding Asians from the attribution of agency, stumbling over the stubbornly un-hybrid assertion of religious identity and supposed gendered antipathies (Anthias & Yuval-Davis 1992; Parekh 2000, p. 28). The experience of Asian communities then has remained un(der)theorized, trapped in culturalist bubbles to be discovered, translated and represented by empirical (and too often empiricist) explorers or neo-Orientalist 'cultural commissars' (Hutnyk 2001, p. 128). The exception to this dominant 'zoological perspective' (Goulbourne 1991) is the emerging work of younger Asian cultural theorists, such as the *TranslAsia* group, who have broken new ground – though significantly more in cultural studies than in sociology – in rendering South Asian experience opaque and complex (Sharma, Hutnyk and Sharma 1996; Kaur & Hutnyk 1999).

Shirin Housee and Sanjay Sharma, in a perceptive revisiting of the role of 'black' in anti-racist activism, have argued strongly for the need to place 'Asian' as a discursively produced construct, rather than a 'privileged experiential authenticity outside political processes or history' (1999, p. 117). Works such as *DisOrienting Rhythms* (1996) and *Travel Worlds* (1999) are crucial in challenging, often scathingly, the desire to 'know' and hence control Asian communities, and have insisted on the networks and dialogues that comprise this experience. Importantly, this work recognizes the tapestry of cultural exchange within and between communities, not merely across an Asian/white divide but with African-Caribbean, North American and Subcontinental cultural forms[15] (Banerjea & Banerjea 1996). The authors strongly critique both the uncritical celebration of theoretical difference and the reification of cultural difference, arguing for the structured and unequal nature of the dialogue between minorities and the academic establishment, and the erasure of complex realities for easy solutions on both sides of the debate over difference (Sharma, Hutnyk & Sharma 1996). In choosing the theoretical and textual over the empirical, however, the work potentially faces the same denial of lived experience which has erased African-Caribbean research.[16] The retreat into the supposedly morally pure ground of theory effectively leaves the sociological and anthropological field(work), unreconstructed and untouched, to the culture-seekers.

Beyond black: consequences and considerations

These two versions of difference should not be seen as autonomous and innocent theoretical exercises; indeed, they are intimately linked in opposition and bound up with issues of power, not only in the versions of power employed within them but in relation to the academy itself, that is, who does the defining. Like much else in the picture outlined above, this is no longer a black/white issue – being an academic of colour (or culture) is no longer an emblem of innocence, nor a guarantee of 'Truth'. The partition of 'black' has precipitated more than a terminological divide, it has led to the imposition of distinct and opposed versions of culture, which have formed the parameters of a new theoretical common sense in the study of race and ethnicity in post-millennial Britain. The contours of this partition have been traced above. What I now want to do is to consider some of the implications of this argument for research.

The first consequence is the way in which a recognition of shared structural positioning has been replaced with an implicit discourse of antipathy within and between Britain's once-black communities. African-Caribbeans and Asians have been positioned as the objects of opposed and irreconcilable versions of cultural difference – the one moving towards inclusion in and similarity with a reimagined

Britishness, the other excluded, willingly or unwillingly, from this process, perhaps even the price of this inclusion. Increasingly, this can be typified as the 'difference-as-colour' versus the 'difference-as-culture' position.[17] At the same time, and ironically, the fragmentation of 'black' as a political and discursive category has signalled a retreat to naturalized and essentialized marginal identities (cf Banerjea and St Louis, this volume) which privilege notions of racial or ethnic authenticity and belonging over historical and social processes (Housee & Sharma 1999).

Secondly, this theoretical bi-lateral declaration of independence has led to the disavowal of structure; that is, the discussion of racism and inequality has largely disappeared from the agenda of research or debate. On the one hand, 'cultural difference' becomes a ready-to-serve explanation for socio-economic disadvantage and discrimination; while on the other, the 'new ethnicities' narrative has been stripped of its core concerns with power and resistance and focused on the fetishization of marginality as a privileged site of knowledge and action in and of itself (Sharma, Hutnyk & Sharma 1996). One of the consequences of the abandonment of 'black' as an inclusive category is the removal and eventual erasure of a focus on structural positioning in favour of a commodified culturalism, which privileges oppression (if it appears at all) as a feature of identity, or a marketing ploy, rather than a practice to be challenged. Studies of racism, even in the wake of the Lawrence inquiry, seem to have become rare and unfashionable, perhaps even seeming uncomfortably anachronistic; not at all the stuff of *Newsnight*, *Start the Week* or other media hotspots which have now become the objects of academic aspiration.

Thirdly and relatedly, the fragmentation of 'black' has led to the redefinition of links between race/ethnicity and socio-economic disadvantage. Ironically, given that one of the primary arguments against 'black' was the association of the term solely with discrimination and the denial of divergent socio-economic positioning between African-Caribbean and Asian groups, the rise of ethnic differentiation has led to a renewed scramble for the category of 'most disadvantaged' in an increasingly shifting hierarchy of oppression, but one which still lays the emphasis on an uncritical privileging of racial/ethnic identity (Modood 1992a; Modood et al. 1997; Small 1994). This has obscured not only the emergence of internal class differentiation, through which black and Asian academics play a crucial role in 'speaking for' the folk,[18] but the continuance of shared geographical, social, cultural and economic locations between diverse once-black groups. The insistence on clearly bounded, internally homogeneous 'margins' has also overlooked the ways in which discourses about supposedly distinct racialized groups are used to validate or critique other groups (Gilroy 1993; Prashad 2000; Song 2001), or are mapped across boundaries; for example, on issues of violence and masculinity (Alexander 2000a,b).

Fourthly, there remains an academic division of labour, in which the majority of empirical work is centred on Asian communities and theoretical work focuses on African-Caribbean cultural production. This carries with it a bi-polar hierarchy in which empirical work becomes the only thought-work considered worthy of funding and with an emphasis on utilitarianism, whereas theoretical work becomes the only thoughtwork able to get publishing contracts and travel the Atlantic. At the same time, empirical work is considered second-tier at best, and collusion with the enemy at worst, by the theoretical purists, and theory is cast as high/over-blown and out of touch with reality by field-workers.

Perhaps what we need, is a third space, but one that is more than notional. This is one which holds on to the recognition of diversity within Britain's black communities but does not lose sight of the commonalities of experience, socio-economic, spatial, cultural, even emotional, which exist; one which recognizes internal differentiation, especially around class, and the questions that this raises for the intellectual process; one which brings together theory and praxis in a way that goes beyond empirical lip service and theoretical abstraction, and that truly allows for ambiguity and dangerous, unfashionable resistance, or capitulation. More than this, it is critical to take seriously the intersection of culture and structure which underlies the 'new ethnicities' paradigm, which does not allow for the easy reification of either culture or marginality. It is insufficient to continue to apply different versions of cultural identity to African-Caribbean and Asian communities; either to deny continuity, solidarity and history to the one, or agency and complex subjectivity to the other.

If 'difference' is to be a useful concept, it must be applicable to all communities and to all individuals; it is clearly inadequate to represent some as outside relations of power or as incapable of intervention in their own destiny. At the same time, 'difference' must be able to account for elements that run apparently counter to it, to be able to make space for articulations of 'sameness' and of specificity, of community and of its once more negative manifestations and performances. It must be able to narrate 'being' as well as 'becoming' as part of the same ambivalent process, exclusion as the inevitable corollary of inclusion, and recognize the inequalities of agency without erasing its presence or celebrating it as a shortcut to intellectual or spiritual enlightenment. And it must be able to ground this analysis, without dilution and without compromise, in the complex empirical realities of twenty-first-century Britain.

In short, I think we need to take difference seriously, to refuse to accept either the naturalization of cultural identity or the celebratory marginality of the 'politics of difference', which from seemingly opposed perspectives serve equally to obscure the complex relations of power that construct difference and keep Britain's black communities trapped within it.

Notes

1   Cf Tony Sewell's recent comments on black male underachievement in schools in *The Observer* newspaper (Adebayo, 22/8/2000).
2   The exception would be the spotlight on the work of cultural workers such as Salman Rushdie and Hanif Kureishi, though it is interesting that these are often positioned against, and opposed to, the notion of a more static, pre-modern notion of Asian (especially Islamic) cultural identity.
3   It is interesting that even the Parekh report on *The Future of Multi-Ethnic Britain* takes the *Windrush* as the central icon in post-war migration (2000, p. 104)
4   The exception would be the crisis over the arrival of East African Asians in 1967/8 which receives a passing mention in *Windrush* (Phillips & Phillips 1999). Significantly, *The Satanic Verses* affair, Gulf War, Bradford riots, Satpal Ram etc. receive no mention at all. It is also revealing that the recent events of Oldham, Leeds, Bradford etc (spring/summer 2001) have been viewed by some (for

example, by Lee Jasper) simply as the repetition of an earlier, distinct African-Caribbean struggle; a stance which denies the ongoing struggles of Asian communities since the 1950s and any autonomous existence for those communities outside a predetermined black/white paradigm.

5 A clear example of this dual process of exclusion and assimilation can be found in Owusu's *Black British Culture and Society* reader (2000). It is interesting to contrast this with the approach adopted by Mirza's earlier *Black British Feminism* (1997), which still employs an inclusive use of 'black'.

6 Belief is particularly significant at this moment where 'difference' is increasingly defined through religious identification, particularly Christian versus Muslim.

7 Housee and Sharma thus argue that 'in the legitimate and important theoretical move to de-essentialize Black, it is not only reconstructed as the cardinal anti-racist signifier, but has become an over-determined site – overburdened as a vehicle for racial emancipation on all fronts (1999, p. 111).

8 There has been some dispute among Asian academics between those keen to consign the concept to the scrapheap of negligent and outdated sociological concepts (Modood 1992a,b), and those keen to retain a recognition of structural solidarity (Brah 2000; Sharma, Hutnyk & Sharma 1996; Sivanandan 2000).

9 Cf Housee & Sharma's (1999) and Avtar Brah's critique of Modood's position (2000). Also see Rattansi's overview of these debates (2000).

10 A revealing comparison may be made with the ambivalent situation of Asian Americans as an ethnically bound 'model minority' vis à vis African-American communities; cf Song 2001 for a discussion of this issue.

11 Rattansi (2000) has also argued that these culturalist views of Asian communities have also been portrayed as congruent with mainstream political values in the fight for the 'ethnic vote' by all parties – a portrait which excludes and silences alternative accounts of Asian identity, as regards gender, sexuality, class, etc.

12 The Parekh Report (2000) thus writes of 'Asian' communities, 'Maintaining cultural and religious traditions is critical to their sense of identity . . . Traditions of origins are strongest in familial, personal and religious contexts, where there is a strong sense of extended kinship' (2000, p. 30). This is revealingly contrasted with the description of African-Caribbean communities as diluted by numerous cross-cultural influences conscious of their subordinate, racialised place in global power systems . . . familiarised . . . with many aspects of British life and institutions' (2000, p. 29)

13 There are exceptions in work done on Asian women, cf. Brah 1996; also work by John Eade on Bangladeshi youth in Tower Hamlets (1997).

14 I am grateful to Shamser Sinha for drawing my attention to Parekh's notion of the moral covenant, which centres on the negotiation of cultural plurality within a framework of shared nationhood (unpublished PhD, 2000).

15 Vijay Prashad's book *The Karma of Brown Folk* (2000) looks at these interactions and intersections in an American context.

16 Although as Housee and Sharma's (1999) article makes clear, there are inescapable implications of this position for political work; unfortunately, however, the authors do not expand this more grounded dimension.

17 This new dichotomy renders invisible other minority groups, such as the Chinese, Vietnamese, African, Indo-Caribbean, Turkish communities. It becomes increasingly fraught with the debates on immigration, refugees and asylum seekers.

18   It is significant that 'class' is one of the forms of internal differentiation that has not been given serious consideration to date. Rather, interest has been focused on gender and sexuality, most usually as a form of claiming the position of double/triple marginality.

References

Adebayo, Diran 2000 'Caught in the rap trap', *The Observer*, 22/8

Alexander, Claire 1996 *The Art of Being Black: the Creation of Black British Youth Identities*, Oxford: Oxford University Press

—— 2000a *The Asian Gang: Ethnicity, Identity, Masculinity*, Oxford: Berg

—— 2000b '(Dis)entangling the Asian gang: ethnicity, identity, masculinity', in Barnor Hesse (ed. *Un/Settled Multiculturalisms*, London: Zed Press

Anthias, Floya and Yuval-Davis, Nira 1992 *Racialised Boundaries: Race, Nation, Gender, Colour and Class an the Anti-racist Struggle*, London: Routledge

Anwar, Muhammad 1994 *Young Muslims in Britain*, Leicester: Islamic Foundation

—— 1998 *Between Cultures*, London: Routledge

Back, Les 1996 *New Ethnicities and Urban Culture*, London: UCL Press

Banerjea, Koushik and Banerjea, Partha 1996 'Psyche and soul: a view from the "South"', in Ashwani Sharma, John Hutnyk and Sanjay Sharma (eds), *DisOrienting Rhythms*, London: Zed Press

Baumann, Gerd 1996 *Contested Cultures: Discourses of Identity in Multi-ethnic London*, Cambridge: Cambridge University Press

Benson, Susan 1996 'Asians have culture, West Indians have problems', in Terence Ranger, Yunas Samad and Ossie Stuart (eds), *Culture, Identity & Politics*, Aldershot: Avebury

Brah, Avtar 1996 *Cartographies of Diaspora*, London: Routledge

—— 2000 Difference, diversity, differentiation', in John Solomos and Les Back (eds), *Theories of Race and Racism*, London: Routledge

CCCS Collective 1982 *The Empire Strikes Back*, London: Hutchinson

Eade, John 1997 'Identity, nation and religion: educated young Bangladeshis in London's East End', in John Eade (ed.), *Living in the Global City: Globalisation as a Local Process*, London: Routledge

Gilroy, Paul 1993 *Small Acts*, London: Serpent's Tail

—— 2000a 'The sugar you stir . . .', in Paul Gilroy, Lawrence Grossberg and Angela McRobbie (eds), *Without Guarantees: In Honour of Stuart Hall*, London: Verso

—— 2000b 'The dialectics of diaspora identification', in John Solomos and Les Back, (eds), *Theories of Race and Racism*, London: Routledge

Goulbourne, Harry 1991 *Ethnicity and Nationalism in Post-imperial Britain*, Cambridge: Cambridge University Press

Hall, Stuart 1990 'Cultural identity & diaspora', in Jonathan Rutherford (ed.), *Identity: Community, Culture, Difference*, London: Lawrence & Wishart

—— 1996 'Who needs identity?', in Stuart Hall & Paul DuGay (eds), *Questions of Cultural Identity*, London: Sage

—— 2000a 'Old and new identities, old and new ethnicities', in John Solomos and Les Back (eds), *Theories of Race and Racism*, London: Routledge

—— 2000b 'Frontlines and backyards', in Kwesi Owusu (ed.), *Black British Culture and Society*, London: Routledge

Housee, Shirin and Sharma, Sanjay 1999 "Too black too strong"?: Anti-racism and the making of South Asian political identities in Britain', in Tim Jordan & A. Lent (eds), *Storming the Millennium*, London: Lawrence & Wishart

Hutnyk, John 2001 'The right to difference is a fundamental human right', in P. Wade (ed.), *Left Curve*, No. 25, pp 112–37

Kaur, Raminder and Hutnyk, John (eds) 1999 *Travel Worlds: Journeys in Contemporary Cultural Politics*, London: Zed

Mercer, Kobena 2000a 'Identity and diversity in postmodern politics', in John Solomos and Les Back (eds), *Theories of Race and Racism*, London: Routledge

—— 2000b 'A sociography of diaspora', in Paul Gilroy, Lawrence Grossberg and Angela McRobbie (eds), *Without Guarantees: In Honour of Stuart Hall*, London: Routledge

Mirza, Heidi (ed.) 1997 *Black British Feminism*, London: Routledge

Modood, Tariq 1992a *Not Easy Being British*, Stoke on Trent: Trentham

—— 1992b 'British Asian Muslims and the Rushdie affair', in James Donald and Ali Rattansi (eds), *'Race', Culture & Difference*, London: Sage

Modood, Tariq *et al.* 1997 *Ethnic Minorities in Britain: Diversity and Disadvantage*, London: Policy Studies Institute

Owusu, Kwesi (ed.) 2000 *Black British Culture and Society*, London: Routledge

Parekh, Bhikhu 1997 'Foreword', in Tariq Modood *et al.*, *Ethnic Minorities in Britain: Diversity and Disadvantage*, London: Policy Studies Institute

Parekh, Bhikhu *et al.* 2000 *The Future of Multi-Ethnic Britain*, London: Profile Books

Phillips, Mike and Phillips, Trevor 1999 *Windrush: The Irresistible Rise of Multi-Racial Britain*, London: Harper Collins

Prashad, Vijay 2000 *The Karma of Brown Folk*, Minneapolis: University of Minnesota Press

Rttansi, Ali 1992 'Changing the subject? Racism, culture and education', in James Donald and Ali Rattansi (eds), *'Race', Culture and Difference*, London: Sage

—— 2000 'On being and not being brown/black British', *Interventions*, Vol. 2, No. 1, pp. 118–34

Samad, Yunas 1992 'Book burning and race relations: the political mobilisation of Bradford Muslims', *New Community*, vol. 18, no.4 pp. 507–19

Sharma, Ash, Hutnyk, John and Sharma, Sanjay (eds) 1996 *Dis-Orienting Rhythms: The Politics of the New Asian Dance Music*, London: Zed

Shaw, Alison 1988 *A Pakistani Community in Oxford*, Oxford: Basil Blackwell

Sivanandan, A. 1981/2 'From resistance to rebellion: Asian and Afro-Caribbean struggles in Britain', *Race and Class*, Vol. 23, Nos 2–3, pp. 111–51

—— 2000 'A radical black political culture', in Kwesi Owusu (ed.), *Black British Culture and Society*, London: Routledge

Song, Miri 2001 'Comparing minorities' ethnic options: do Asian Americans possess "more" ethnic options than African Americans?', Ethnicities, Vol. 1, No. 1

Small, Stephen 1994 *Racialised Barriers: the Black Experience in the United States and England in the 1980s*, London: Routledge

Werbner, Pnina 1999 *The Migration Process: Capital, Gifts and Offerings among British Pakistanis*, Oxford: Berg

West, Cornel 1993, 'The new cultural politics of difference', in S. During (ed.), *The Cultural Studies Reader*, London: Routledge

Chapter 15

David Theo Goldberg

RACIAL KNOWLEDGE

[. . .]

WHAT I AM CALLING 'racial knowledge' is defined by a dual movement. It is dependent upon – it appropriates as its own mode of expression, its premises, and the limits of its determinations – those of established scientific fields of the day, especially anthropology, natural history, and biology. This scientific cloak of racial knowledge, its formal character and seeming universality, imparts authority and legitimation to it. Its authority is identical with, it parasitically maps onto the formal authority of the scientific discipline it mirrors. At the same time, racial knowledge – racial science, to risk excess – is able to do this because it has been historically integral to the emergence of these authoritative scientific fields. Race has been a basic categorical object, in some cases a founding focus of scientific analysis in these various domains. This phenomenon has no doubt been facilitated by the definitive importance of difference in modernity's development of knowledge. As Foucault remarks:

> [A]ll knowledge, of whatever kind, proceeded to the ordering of its material by the establishment of differences and defined those differences by the establishment of an order; this was true for mathematics, true also for *taxonomies* . . . and for the sciences of nature; and it was equally true for all those approximative, imperfect, and largely spontaneous kinds of knowledge which are brought into play in the construction of the least fragment of discourse or in the daily process of exchange; and it was true finally for philosophical thought.[1]

Racial knowledge consists *ex hypothesi* in the making of difference; it is in a sense and paradoxically the assumption and paradigmatic establishment of difference. An epistemology so basically driven by difference will 'naturally' find racialized thinking comfortable; it will uncritically (come to) assume racial knowledge as given.

Power is exercised epistemologically in the dual practices of naming and evaluating. In naming or refusing to name things in the order of thought, existence is recognized or refused, significance assigned or ignored, beings elevated or rendered invisible. Once defined, order has to be maintained, serviced, extended, operationalized. Naming the racial Other, for all intents and purposes, *is* the Other. There is, as Said makes clear in the case of the Oriental, no Other behind or beyond the invention of knowledge in the Other's name. These practices of naming and knowledge construction deny all autonomy to those so named and imagined, extending power, control, authority, and domination over them. To extend Said's analysis of the 'Oriental' to the case of race in general, social science of the Other establishes the limits of knowledge about the Other, for the Other is just what racialized social science knows. It knows what is best for the Other – existentially, politically, economically, culturally: In governing the Other, racialized social science will save them from themselves, from their own Nature. It will furnish the grounds of the Other's modification and modernization, establishing what will launch the Other from the long dark night of its prehistory into civilized time. The wiser, the more knowledgeable the governors are about subject races – at home or abroad, colonially or postcolonially – the less will their administrative rule or government require raw force. 'Good racial government' thus requires information about racial nature: about character and culture, history and traditions, that is, about the limits of the Other's possibilities. Information, thus, has two senses: detailed facts about racial nature; and the forming of racial character. Information is accordingly furnished both by academic research and through practical expertise, through reading and observation, in schools and universities, in courts and prisons.

Production of social knowledge about the racialized Other, then, establishes a library or archive of information, a set of guiding ideas and principles about Otherness: a mind, characteristic behavior or habits, and predictions of likely responses. The Other, as object of study, may be employed but only as informant, as representative translator of culture. The set of representations thus constructed and cataloged in turn confines those so defined within the constraints of the representational limits, restricting the possibilities available to those rendered racially other as it delimits their natures. The spaces of the Other – the colonies, plantations, reservations, puppet governments and client states, the villages and townships, or the prisons, ganglands, ghettoes, and crowded inner cities – become the laboratory in which these epistemological constructs may be tested. Even the literature, art, languages, and general cultural expression are appropriated as proper objects of 'scientific' evaluation. They are judged not as works among works of art in general, but the works or languages or expressions of the Other, representative of the cultural condition and mentality, of the state of Otherness – artifacts not art, primitive formulations not rationally ordered linguistic systems, savage or barbaric or uncivilized expressions not high culture. Learned societies linked to the colonial condition, even disciplines emerged for the sole purpose of studying various racial Others, or the racial Other as such, *its* metaphysical being. These societies have served to inform the colonial or urban administration on whose account they have flourished, but they have also been defined and confined by the relation: what they could experience or represent, who and under what conditions objects could be approached, engaged, studied. Knowledge, accordingly, is socially managed, regulated by the general concerns of social authority, and self-imposed by the specific interests and concerns of the disciplinary specialist.[2]

So the central role of scientific authority in constituting Otherness cements such constitution into an objective given, a natural law. The characterizations accompanying, promoting, or instrumental to such constitutional creation of Others become reified, objectified as unalterable, basic parts of people's natures. In this way, the various divisions of racialized personhood become set as naturally given, as universal and unavoidable. This epistemological manufacture of Otherness mirrors the abstraction typical if not inherent in philosophy's constitution of its discursive object, namely, pure concepts indicative of universal, objective truths. Here, in the philosophical setting and interrelations of personhood (of mind and body), of civil society, and of the State, it is not that the Other is necessarily denied or abnegated (though this has often been so). Rather, in the abstraction of ideas about persons, society, and politics, the philosophical abstraction becomes objectified, once objectified reified as natural, and so extended universally. Part, indeed, an idealized part, is substituted for the whole, and the specificity of the Other, or Otherness itself is silently denied. Those thus rendered Other are sacrificed to the idealization, excluded from the being of personhood, from social benefits, and from political (self-)representation.[3] Erased in the name of a universality that has no place for them, the subjects of real political economy are denied and silenced, ontologically and epistemologically and morally evicted. The universal claims of Western knowledge, then, colonial or postcolonial, turn necessarily upon the deafening suppression of its various racialized Others into silence.

This process of silencing furnishes the solution to what Bauman identifies as the 'technological challenge' faced by social knowledge in the face of the erratic, and so unpredictable behavior of an Other unruled, or insufficiently ruled, by Reason. Admitting the Other's subjectivity is at once to give up epistemological and political control; it is to admit scientific and administrative inefficiency. To retain control, the scientist as much as the administrator, the theoretical expert as much as the advisor and consultant has to control the variables, to manage the environment. The outcomes must be predictable, the more strictly so the better. Calculation is methodologically central, the more formalized the more acceptable. As Foucault remarks, 'Recourse to mathematics, in one form or another, has always been the simplest way of providing positive knowledge about man with a scientific style, form, and justification.' Racialized knowledge in the nineteenth and twentieth centuries has been no exception: witness phrenology, the measurement and weighing of skulls, IQ testing, and crime statistics.[4]

Implicit in these remarks is a hint of the relation between formally produced racialized knowledge, especially at the hands of social science, and the State. Etienne Balibar insists that the relationship to the Other at the heart of modern racism is necessarily mediated by State intervention.[5] One of the basic modes this intervention assumes is concern over production of racialized knowledge. State conceptual mediation is as old as the category of *race* itself. But state mediation basically reinvents itself with each of the major conceptual developments in racialized thinking: with polygenism and the colonial encounter, with social Darwinism and eugenics, with IQ testing, and, as we saw, with race relations analysis. We should pursue the conceptual relations between racialized social science and the State a little further.

Race, social science, and the State

Social science is important to the modern State both *functionally* and *ideologically*. In the former sense, social science furnishes the State and its functionaries with information, and it is often employed in formulating and assessing State policies to satisfy social needs. Ideologically, the State often invokes expedient analyses and the results of social science, whether by collaboration or appropriation, to legitimize State pursuits and to rationalize established relations of power and domination. I do not mean to suggest that the functional and ideological exhaust State support of social science, still less that these forms exhaust social science itself. The State may support a research program because of its scientific value; and much social science may have little formally to do with the State as such, though work that studiously avoids *the social* barely deserves the name. More important, the State – or some particular state – may be the object of a *critical* social science concerned with uncovering and attacking modes of repression. So State Functional and State Ideological Social Science could both be objects of critical analysis.

What I am calling State Functional Social Science can be conducted *in virtue of* or *in service of* State ideology. Consider, for example, two related claims: 'People [in South Africa] . . . do define themselves, in the first instance, as members of a population group'; and 'The research . . . showed that population group/race/ nationality are first-order interpretations, categorizations or characteristics in terms of which others are perceived'.[6] These assumptions are so deeply entrenched in South African state ideology as to be unquestioned, and they are unquestioningly endorsed by the research that reproduces them. The claims hold, if at all, only *in virtue of* accepting the premises that ground the ideology; and in turn they give foundation to the conclusion that possible 'solutions' to the South African dilemma must be limited to producing 'constructive intergroup relations'.[7]

Consider, by contrast, the claim that white settlers arrived at the Cape of Good Hope at the close of the seventeenth century coincidentally with African tribes migrating from the north. Asserted by amateur colonial historians Theal and Cory early in the twentieth century, common in most school history texts, and until quite recently propounded by serious Afrikaner scholars, this claim was made *in service of* state ideology.[8] (Perhaps it should be said that the claim *functions* as ideology.) It was designed to substantiate the idea that whites originally laid equal claim to the land with blacks and historically acquired control over (at least) 87 percent of South African territory by way of a 'just', and so justified war. The deeper insinuation here, of course, is one of white superiority.

It seems obvious that State Ideological Social Science – the development and use of (a) social theory to rationalize, legitimize, or conceal repressive or unjust modes of social relation and expression – has functional value. That is, ideologically State Social Science need not merely define but may serve given state interests. It remains an open question, however, whether State Functional Social Science –

social science prompted by State defined purposes and structures – signifies ideologically. One is tempted to say that the ideology expressed by a State committed technocratically to functional social science is a form of *instrumental* pragmatism. Here, knowledge is treated as strictly instrumental to predefined State purposes, never as sustaining critique. Untheorized pragmatisms either generate or (more usually) cover up underlying ideological rationalizations of events, relations, and structures.

The relevance of these distinctions to an understanding of racialized social science should become apparent as I proceed. Yet their application is seldom quite so straightforward. For example, during the 1980s, many South Africans were fond of citing data showing that the majority of that country's black population did not support the call to disinvest. It is difficult to establish, without knowing considerably more and in the context of political hegemony, whether the data and, more significantly, the studies that produced them were functional or ideological; whether the studies were performed in virtue or in service of (function as) state ideology, or simply from the desire to know; and whether the *use* of the data thus collected was purely pragmatic, or in virtue, or in service of state ideology.

The distinction between data and their use is one the positivist might appeal to in objecting that State Ideological Social Science is not social science at all; and I suspect that one who pursued this line of criticism would conclude likewise for functional social science in the way I have defined it. But this form of positivistic critique misses the deeper point that needs highlighting, namely, that social science – the study and analysis of human beings past, present, and future in their social relations – is affected in all kinds of ways by the *Weltanschauung* in terms of which it is conducted, that it is often conducted by and for the State, that it may be formative in constructing the 'imagined community' of racialized State- or nationhood, and that once collected the data has to be interpreted before conclusions about social policy or action can be drawn. In short, there is nothing remotely resembling pure social data whose meaning and truth are incontestably self-evident.

Racialized knowledge production, and social science in particular, has been integral to State designs in both functional and ideological terms. It has often been noted that anthropology was handmaiden to colonialism. In furnishing information about those societies under the colonizing gun, anthropology both serviced the perceived needs of colonizing states and rationalized colonization as morally necessary for the sake of the colonized. Nevertheless, as Foucault reminds us, it should not be concluded that anthropology is nothing but a colonial discipline.[9] This was, understandably, the general sense of many suffering at the hands of anthropologizing colonialisms. This conclusion might be implied from the fact that with independence, especially in Africa, anthropology departments were replaced largely by sociology faculties at local universities. It should be remembered, though, that while Western governments may have withdrawn from former colonial territories, Western social scientists clearly did not. With the growing move to independence in those states marked as racially Other, political scientists were substituted for anthropologists in representing the functional and ideological interests of the West. Capitalism required new markets, and capital investment presupposed political stability. Western models of state formation were offered as necessary preconditions for the takeoff state[10] of modernizing economic development: Rational political organization – for example, the Westminster model for former British colonies – would rationalize efficient use of economic resources. Indigenous political organization reflected prehistory, objects for anthropological study not modernization. Once the battle for ongoing political allegiance had been more or less won by the lure of capital, economists almost automatically replaced political scientists as the prevailing postcolonial experts of choice. If imperialist direct rule was replaced under colonialism by indirect rule (a prototype of the sort of independence to follow), the outmoding of indirect rule by independence was accompanied by the institution of rule by other means – by economic control. The influence of economists, of direct representatives of Western capital, and of local technicians trained in the West furnished the skills necessary to rationalize control, in both senses of the term.[11] More or less radical social science, while undertaking to alter the thrust of epistemological colonization, has nevertheless done little to transform the terms of racialized knowledge production.

The terms used by social scientists to represent the racialized Other in the nineteenth and twentieth centuries reflected popular representations in dominant Western culture at the times in question. This truncated and all too partial reading of the history of social science in colonial and postcolonial control shows that the terms of popular representations of racialized Others were in many cases set by prevailing modes dominant in social science at the time. What follows is a critical reading of three conceptual schemata hegemonic in the production of contemporary racialized knowledge that now define and order popular conceptions of people racially conceived: the Primitive, the Third World, and the Underclass. These terms and the conceptual schemes they mark are the most prominent and general in silently ordering formal and popular knowledge of the Other in and through the study of cultural, political, and economic relations. [. . .]

The primitive

The word 'primitive' was first used in the late fifteenth century to refer to origins. In that sense, it assumed the connotations that were thought to accompany the image of an early, ancient, or first state, age, or period: old-fashioned, or rough, or rude. (It later acquired more neutral technical meanings in relation to the original words in a language, or members of the early Church.) The Enlightenment interest in human origins was, as we've seen, largely defined in physical terms. Original peoples or races were thought to have little or no social organization or cultural achievements worthy of mention, and the meaning of 'primitive' at the time seems to reflect this. It was in Darwin's wake that scholarly interest in the 'original' social and cultural condition of society really flourished, though even at this time the concept of *the Primitive* was not necessarily racialized. Many of the major theorists of 'primitive society' in the late nineteenth century initially approached the object of study as a set of legal issues, the standard for which was an analysis of Roman law. Included in the conception, accordingly, were Greek and Roman societies, those societies taken to be the primitive or early forerunners of modern Europe. The influence of this scholarly bent is reflected in the fact that art history initially included in the extension of the term 'primitive art' only pre-Renaissance Italian and Flemish painters. By the end of the century, the term had been broadened to include all ancient art; and by 1920, art's historical connotation had assumed the racialized reference it had long had beyond the boundaries of that discipline, referring strictly to art of non-Western cultures: Africa, Oceania, and South America.[12]

The idea of a *primitive society* invented, as Adam Kuper points out, by nineteenth-century legal anthropologists referred to some primeval origin to which society could be archaeologically traced. The idea reified the 'existence' of its referent through the crafting of a set of specialized instruments, ultimately those of applied mathematics, to get objectively at the 'real' nature of primitive society. Like *race*, then, the concept of *the Primitive* proved theoretically adaptable, appropriating novel theoretical developments as its own by being appropriable as a concept central and so seemingly necessary to theoretical advance. Almost as vacuous in connotation as *race*, *the Primitive* transformed in meaning as *race* did.[13] The Primitive assumed synonymy with the racial Other, a technical nomenclature for a popular category. Popular and scientific discourse merged, mutually influencing the terms of discursive formalization and expression. Indeed, the set of meanings that attaches to contemporary usage of 'the Primitive' and 'primitive societies', and by extension to 'Primitivism' is a legacy of this past century of scholarly and popular coproduction. Its transformative capacity makes it particularly suited as a basic trope, a primary element of racist expression.

Formally, primitive societies were theorized in binary differentiation from a civilized order: nomadic rather than settled; sexually promiscuous, polygamous, and communal in family and property relations rather than monogamous, nuclear, and committed to private property; illogical in mentality and practicing magic rather than rational and scientific. In popular terms, nonwhite primitives have come to be conceived as childlike, intuitive, and spontaneous; they require the iron fist of 'European' governance and paternalistic guidance to control inherent physical violence and sexual drives.[14] If, Platonistically, there is conceived to be a primitive lurking deep in the soul of the civilized, it is ruled by Reason, contained and controlled by civility and the institutions of civil society. For the Civilized have a history, but the Primitive have none: their histories are frozen.[15]

It is a remarkable conceit, this, to think of 'a people' having no history, no past, no movement from one time to another, frozen stiff like a wax figure in Madame Tussaud's or the Museum of Man. Remarkable in its arrogance, in its abnegation of those seemingly so unlike themselves that *they* can assume away humanity, banish it to the shadows of their assumptions about what human beings are or are not; remarkable in its lack of self-conscious skepticism about their own limits and excesses, their own warts and odors and blemishes, of what they can or cannot do or know, of their own productive capacities and incapacities, developments and destructions. Remarkable, too, in its denial of the invented relationships between Self and Other in modernity and now postmodernity that have been necessary in making possible the standard of living achieved by the 'civilized', 'developed', 'progressive', 'historical' beings. If the Primitive has no history at all, it is only because the theoretical standard-bearers of Civilization have managed first to construct a Primitive Subject and then to obliterate *his* history.

I do not mean to deny the importance of the anthropological critique of the primitivist discourse throughout much of this century. Two related points need stressing about the counterdiscourses. First, if Kuper is correct, although primitivist ideas no longer dominate anthropological theory, they continue to stamp initiation into the discipline and to be circulated at the fringes. Indeed, they continue to structure popular ideas about the racial and distant Other, as in the Blair brothers' popular 'Adventure' public television series, or National Geographic features, or coffee table books.[16] Second, this popular discourse of the Primitive has partially been sustained by the fact that the anthropological critique of the discourse is *internal*, so much so that it reproduces (even if it transforms) key concepts: primitive society, the primitive or savage mind, totemism, and animism. Contemporary sophisticates often know all too fashionably the critical references but are largely ignorant of their content. This partial, superficial knowing promotes reproduction of the categories under critique rather than internalizing the point of the critique itself.

There is an important sense in which this latter criticism also applies to scholarly production about the Primitive that borrows from, but is strictly beyond, anthropological confines. Two examples, quite different in various ways, will illustrate the point. The first is Marianna Torgovnick's widely cited book, *Gone Primitive*, to which I have already referred in passing. The second is the controversial Museum of Modern Art exhibition on 'Primitivism', and its accompanying two-volume catalog. While Torgovnick discusses the MOMA exhibition in considerable detail, I will analyze each in turn.

Torgovnick is concerned with the way modernists and postmodernists construct notions of the Primitive and import them into contemporary culture. She studies the various ways in which the discourse of primitivism signifies, both in racialized terms and in ways that have little if anything to do with racialized conceptions. In spite of her self-conscious resolve to distance herself from the discourse, it silently takes hold of her. On one hand, Torgovnick insists that in constructing a notion of the Primitive 'we become primitive'. One would think she would accordingly take more seriously Kuper's warning that there never was anything like a 'primitive society', that there is no coherent way of specifying what it is, that the history of the discourse is 'a history of an illusion'.[17] On the other hand, Torgovnick repeatedly, if tentatively, reaffirms the existence of primitive cultures that differ from 'our' modern or postmodern ones.[18] A critique of primitivist discourse that so readily reiterates the discursive terms at issue tends to reproduce the terms it is committed to resisting.

In an interesting and revealing discussion of the Tarzan phenomenon as primitivizing texts, Torgovnick offers a good example of the penetration of social scientific categories of racial Otherness into, and their distribution by, popular culture. Edgar Rice Burroughs, Tarzan's American author, conducted nonprofessional research on plant and animal life in Africa, and he was no doubt familiar with popular anthropological knowledge in the first half of the twentieth century. So, as Torgovnick points out, the reticence and ultimate denial of miscegenation that Burroughs constructs of Tarzan's sexual relations with female apes is reflective of and reinforces prevailing dispositions in the United States toward interracial intercourse. But it is one deeply reflective, at the same time, both of the polygenic

presuppositions lingering from nineteenth-century anthropology in popular literature and of eugenic dispositions socially influential in the United States well into
the 1920s.[19]

Torgovnick's understated commitment to the categories of primitivist discourse
is reflected in her appreciation of Burroughs having Tarzan join the Waziri of West
Africa in 'their dance and fashioning within their societal norms'. There is an unstated
assumption throughout that the reader is one with the postmodernist 'we', that
the Primitive is in no position to read such a text. The 'we' here, of which Tarzan
represents a recent predecessor, is identical with the anthropological 'we'. Indeed,
Tarzan may be read as the figure of an anthropologist. He enters the 'primitive'
world of Africa 'to learn what hierarchies exist in the human world and by suppressing
his doubts about their inevitability and basis'.[20] This is the anthropological drive,
and the implication of this 'realist' ethnography – seemingly neutral in its objectivity
but masking the imperialist imperative – is the affirmation of 'Western hierarchies',
of superiority and subjection.[21]

Thus, Gone Primitive becomes an example of the production of social knowledge reproducing certain sorts of established presuppositions about relations
between racialized natures. Torgovnick approves of what she takes to be the central
thematic of the Tarzan series: leaving nature as it is, being true to nature, living
in 'harmony with nature, without troubling relations of hierarchy and otherness'.[22]
It is as though this utopian naturalism escapes racist expression, which may yet be
advanced through the assumption of natural difference. It also leaves resistance to
racisms unproblematically coming to terms with nature, with what Torgovnick
leaves (and one is left to assume she takes) as natural difference, with the differences
of racialized natures – analogized in keeping with a long history of racist expression
in terms of apes! 'Going primitive' in Torgovnick's reading, then, is ultimately to
'go home' to a space of comfort and balance, to a space that is supposed to save
us from 'our estrangement from ourselves and our culture'.[23] While this domesticated
construal at least centralizes the inventedness of the Primitive, it uncritically
recreates the notion of the West's power over its creation, its appropriation as its
own, as 'home' precisely, a place of comfort, a 'return to origins'. If this is a
place to which it belongs, to which it has privileged access – or which belongs to
it – the Western self must surely be justified in its appropriation. What is missing
from the text is an account of the expense of the appropriation, the real life and
death expense, for those so constructed as primitive. [. . .]

The Third World

[. . .] The theory of three worlds was first proposed in 1952 by a French
demographer, Alfred Sauvy, writing in the newspaper L'Observateur. Sauvy
provocatively suggested that the notion of the 'Third World' was a product of
developing superpower antagonisms expressing themselves in terms of the cold
war. The notion came to reflect superpower anxiety about escalating postcolonial
conflict, the fear of expanding rival spheres of interest over vast territories, numbers
of people, and resources. It also expressed alarm among the newly decolonized
or decolonizing at revitalized control by the iron fist of superpower domination.

In this sense, as Pletsch argues, the concept of a *Third World* is nothing more than the by-product of aggression between the First and Second worlds.

This threefold division has been accompanied by, indeed, it has been defined in terms of sets of accompanying characterizations.[24] For social scientists and political theorists who have been seminal in constructing the model, the First World is strictly modern, scientifically and technologically ordered, ruled by utilitarian decision procedures. Governed by the laws of economic nature, of rational self-interest, it is unconstrained and self-regulating, the embodiment of the liberal, autonomous Kantian state. Of all societies, it is (as Pletsch says) the most natural, that which all others should seek to emulate, for it is guided by the invisible hand of universal Reason. The First World is thus efficient, democratic, and free.

The Second World, the space of (once) communist domination, is conceived as modernized and technologically developed, and so partially rational. But it is stricken unnaturally by ideology and by a socialist elite who must rely upon repression to maintain its privileges. This ideological veil and repressive reliance prevents the Second World from being completely efficient, and unless it emulates the First World, it is destined sooner or later to stagnate. (The recent economic and political devolution of the Second World is being taken in many ways as triumphant vindication of the naturalism of the First, and so as confirmation of the model.)

The Third World is also defined in economic and political terms. The accompanying geographical, environmental, and psychological characterizations are more or less expressly linked to racialized premises. Pletsch suggests that, but possibly for 'left' and 'right', the three-world division is 'the most primitive' scheme of political classification in social science. The rootedness of racialized discourse in modernity and the centrality of 'black' and 'white' within this discourse suggests that these racial designations are classificatory 'primitives' as basic perhaps as 'left' and 'right'.[25] It is in virtue of this racializing of the Third World that the First and Second worlds also silently assume racial character. The Third World is located baking beneath the tropical sun in contrast to the moderate climate of the Northern Hemisphere so conducive to intellectual productivity. It is the world of tradition and irrationality, underdeveloped and overpopulated, disordered and chaotic. It is also non-European and nonwhite.

There has been considerable debate about how the world should be divided in three. Different configurations will result when one employs only economic or only political criteria, or some mix. The divisions will differ again from one interpretation of economic criteria to another, from level of production or development or technology, say, to capacity of the rich countries to exploit the poor. The climatic–geographic consideration, historically associated with race, has led a country like Greenland, for example, to be considered part of the First World, while others like Korea or Singapore or Taiwan, Kuwait or Saudi Arabia, at least until recently, to 'belong' to the Third World, and still others like some Southern European countries to hover politically, and economically, and ideologically between the two. States with populations considered racially polarized, like Israel or South Africa, are ambiguous: Under one interpretation of the criteria they turn out to 'belong' to the First World; under the other, to *be* Third. I am not interested here, at least not primarily, in pursuing the theoretical politics of representing the three worlds. Rather, my concern is to indicate how in its conception and articulation this tripartite division is racialized; how it perpetuates, conceptually and actually, racialized relations – relations of domination, subjugation, and exclusion.

From the outset, the concept of *the Third World* captured the popular, political, and scientific imaginations. Journalists took to the term like vultures to a slain carcass. It came to dominate the way social science conceived of the world, of the basic differences between states, of what Pletsch calls the division of labor within the social sciences. The three-world scheme ordered the focal object of each discipline: Mainstream economics, sociology, and political science respectively concentrated on wealth, status, and power, especially in capitalist societies. Communist studies and international relations focused on the Second World. Area studies, development economics, and anthropology analyzed the 'underdeveloped' and 'traditional societies' of the Third World.[26] The study of Western civilization, the classics or the Great Books is regarded as foundational, as the base and structure for knowledge, value, morality, and good citizenship. By contrast, area studies, and in particular specialization in geographical and cultural fields concerning Otherness are standardly taken to have little if any intrinsic value. They are, if anything, deemed only instrumentally valuable. They are not pursued as knowledge *of* the field for its own sake, for the value inherent in it. At best, they are thought to furnish knowledge *about* the Other, the better to deal with *him*. This amounts to 'knowing *how*', not 'knowing *that*', to use a well-known epistemological distinction. The instrumental knowledge promoted concerns how to civilize, how to approach and relate to the Other.

More significantly, perhaps, the terms 'First World' and 'Second World' are rarely used. States so conceived are usually called capitalist or (formerly) communist, the West or the East, and their populations are termed European, (North) American and, generically, Westerners or East Europeans. 'The West' is similarly a sliding sign. Initially designating countries west of the iron curtain, its scope came to include those countries and their inhabitants that are capitalist in their mode of production, politically free with democratic institutions, culturally modernized, and largely white. Thus, the designation usually includes Australasia, which is almost as far east as one can go without being west, but excludes Japan (surely a First World state if there are any) and does so implicitly on racialized grounds, as in the title of a recent book by a British official with the European Community, *Japan Versus the West*. Indeed, 'the West' has included South Africa insofar as that country has been considered white or non-African. (Under *apartheid*, Japanese have been considered, for obvious reasons, 'honorary whites'.) The grandson of H. F. Verwoerd, for example, expressed a common sentiment among whites in South Africa when he once explained to me that he had 'gone over to Africa' (he meant Zambia). This is reiterated in a plaque at the Afrikaans Language Monument near Cape Town (which ironically is located on a hill across from the prison, in the valley below, from which Nelson Mandela was finally released): 'Afrikaans', the plaque reads, 'is the language that links western Europe and Africa; . . . it forms a bridge between the enlightened West and magical Africa.' Implicit in these claims is a deep-seated presupposition that South Africa is a European country (in racial, cultural, political, and economic commitments), not an African one. Within a historical context of political economy, power, and dominant culture, this characterization strikes me as highly suggestive.[27]

By contrast, 'Third World' is the generic term of choice in referring not only to those states that are taken to be underdeveloped but to populations considered traditional in their productive and cultural ways. Sometimes, 'the Third World' carries no racialized connotation: Argentina, for example, is often regarded as a Third World country (though not one that immediately comes to mind when using the term generically), and its population is not usually considered to be racially Other. Yet here, too, racial characterization can take over: Argentinean players in the 1990 World Cup were repeatedly described by British football commentators, in a reinvocation of themes of the Falkland campaign, as 'naturally violent', displaying the sort of behaviour to be expected of 'the Latin temperament'. Equally, the 'exotic' players of the 'Cinderella team' from the Cameroon – some players sported dreadlocks and wore 'traditional' jewelry – were characterized as 'exciting', but 'wild' and 'undisciplined'.[28]

The racial connotations carried by the ascription, 'the Third World', are captured most clearly in their usage by those in the United States and Europe who warn that blacks, the *Gastarbeiter* immigrants, and asylum seekers are turning their respective societies economically and culturally into Third World countries. In the political and cultural theater of the United States, Kirk Varnedoe is not that far from David Duke or Patrick Buchanan, or indeed from George Bush, in claiming that 'Third World nations have intensified their concern for the integrity of their own tribal arts'. As a range of conservative political figures portray an undifferentiated blackness or Otherness for political effect and reduce it to an unspecified Third World, so Varnedoe reifies an undifferentiated Third World and reduces it to the level of the Primitive. In a recent *New York Sunday Times* article on the declining fortunes of Detroit, Ze'ev Chafets draws a similar analogy between what he describes as the tragic decline of that city under black rule and the inevitable decline of independent African nations.[29] In a similar vein, the racialized situation of guest workers in Europe, not that different from Mexican migrants in California, is increasingly obviated against the reconstructed measuring stick of a European identity. Their strictly economic status as guest workers transforms into a supranational, superracial one against the backdrop of a European identity. Europe, after all, was central to the initial manufacture of racialized identities and racist exclusions. It is an irony too great to be bypassed that the unification of a European 'we', racially exclusionary in reinvented fashion, occurs exactly half a millennium after voyages of discovery that prompted the initial manufacture of racial Otherness. Whereas European racism might initially be described as exclusion at a distance, it is now what Balibar terms 'internal exclusion', and it takes place at the world level.[30] Migrant labour, then, is nothing else than racialized exploitation, an off-the-books form of what Worsley calls 'cost-free aid from the Third World to the First'.[31] The analogy with South Africa is accordingly worth pursuing [. . .]. Insofar as South Africa is considered a black country, it is 'naturally' designated Third World. In a recent visit to South Africa, I found whites widely bemoaning their observation that 'the new South Africa' is fast becoming 'a Third World country'. It follows that the notorious migrant labor system *apartheid* merely formalized must be a form of relatively free service to those identified as (ex-)European. [. . .]

The underclass

The notion of *the Underclass* has been present in social science literature for some considerable time. Myrdal used the term in passing in *The American Dilemma* and returns to it more firmly nearly twenty years later. Myrdal's use was strictly economic, designating the persistently unemployed and underemployed, those marginalized or completely excluded from the postindustrial economy.[32] With structural transformations in the capitalist economy that began to be obviated towards the close of the 1970s, the connotation of the term in social science shifted from degrees of unemployment to deep-seated, chronic poverty. This shift signaled a series of conceptual chains forged as much by the popular media as by social scientists. The Underclass population came to be characterized in behavioral terms, as a set of pathological social attitudes, actions, and activities. The outward, visible sign of these pathologies was race. Thus, the notion was relinked to the nineteenth-century conceptions of the 'undeserving poor', the 'rabble', and the 'lumpenprole-tariat'.[33] Accordingly, 'the Underclass' has come to signify not just the unemployed but the permanently unemployed and unemployable. It has come to include, particularly in the popular but also in the academic and political imaginations, those poor considered unmotivated to work – especially, women on welfare, vicious street criminals, drug pushers and addicts, hustlers and urban gangs, winos and the mentally deranged homeless. If these conditions are permanent, then they are necessary, and necessarily unchangeable, and so it would seem there is no responsibility for doing anything about them save improving the criminal justice response.

The conditions of the Underclass are accordingly reduced to individual pathologies and the poverty of culture that generates the social disease of deviance. '"Underclass" describes a state of mind and a way of life. It is at least as much a cultural as an economic condition.'[34] The claim that the Underclass consists of pathological individuals is 'established' by way of comparison with the 'deserving poor', those adult, law-abiding, two-parent families that, despite steady male employment, are unable to make ends meet.[35] The supposed fact that the underclass condition is produced by the poverty of culture is 'explained' in terms of the absence of moral virtues disabling individuals from 'deferring gratification, planning ahead, and making sacrifices for future benefit'.[36] So the social conditions of the undeserving poor can be blamed upon their own character.

The interpenetrating lists of individual pathologies and cultural poverty that have been taken by social scientists and journalists alike to make up the Underclass condition carry patently racialized connotations. Though technically and historically the Underclass is purported to be 'interracially' constituted (poverty is supposed to know no color), it is obvious that blacks are for the most part being thus chronically identified. If there is a single identifying criterion of Underclass membership, it is *idleness*. And as J. M. Coetzee makes clear in relation to the history of white South African writing, idleness has long expressed a central idea of racialized representation.[37] In group terms, blacks in the United States, Britain, and now South Africa are often aggregated into Underclass characterization by the term's conceptual extension: by police, on the street, in the media, at school. And they are so referenced whether they technically meet the sliding criteria or not.

Inner city culture conjures up the very real political economy of racialized space that the concept of the *Underclass* is assumed to be theorizing. The individual pathologies and wanting culture of the Underclass are seen to be expressed against the blighted backdrop of the urban ghetto. Causal responsibility for the set of Underclass conditions nevertheless is largely traced not to urban location – this is thought to be a mere manifestation, a symptom – but to the pathological population, to its culture. It is this causal inversion that William Julius Wilson undertakes to rectify in his important work on the Underclass.

Wilson has been careful to evade the poverty of culture thesis. He conceptualizes the Underclass as the set of individuals lacking training and skills, those experiencing long-term unemployment, and those not part of the labor force. Wilson seeks to explain the social position of the Underclass primarily in terms of the 'mismatch' hypothesis.[38] Inner city residents in the past two decades have been caught by structural changes in the U.S. economy that have left them without the technological skills necessary for the financial service jobs their spatial position would otherwise give them access to. This dislocation has two main effects: The 'concentration effect' results in a large number of single parent families, the unemployed, and criminals ghettoized into a relatively small and intense urban area with diminishing social services. The 'isolation effect' leaves these people cut off from the ameliorating influence of a middle class, black and white, who have fled for the suburbs.

Though Wilson dismisses the poverty of culture position, he has not found the case for individual pathologies quite so objectionable. Included in his underclass membership are street criminals, welfare mothers, and other social deviants. His notion of *the Underclass* is thus identified against a paradigm of a healthy body politic from which the Underclass population by definition diverges.[39] Although Wilson stresses that the Underclass includes many nonblacks, he is equally clear that his work focuses on the much larger black segment of the Underclass. These considerations prompt two implications for Wilson's analysis. The first is that he racializes the concept almost in spite of himself. The weight of Wilson's scientific stature behind the use of the concept authorizes even its more dubious, racially obvious policy and popular usages, no matter Wilson's own guarded qualifications. The second implication is at the explanatory level. Wilson predicates his structural economic analysis of the state of the Underclass on the idea of isolated, albeit spatially concentrated individuals. It is this methodological assumption that leaves Wilson holding on to the descriptive schemata of individual pathology. And it is in part this assumption that leads him to downplay the place of racism in his explanatory account of the black Underclass, as well as to de-emphasize race-specific programs as viable solutions.

Wilson finds it important, particularly in his more recent work, to recognize the effects on the black Underclass of racism, past and present. Nevertheless, his overriding emphasis throughout has been to stress the relatively greater weight of class considerations in the explanation of Underclass conditions. Class *structure* is specified in terms of individuals' 'attachment to the labor force'; in terms, that is, of *individual* job opportunities or access to job network and information systems.[40] Contrast this, for example, with Marx's notion of 'the proletariat', which is conceived as the *group* whose members own nothing but their labor power. This individualist methodological presupposition – perhaps it is even ontological – forces Wilson to underplay the influence of group effects. Similarly, Wilson thinks nonracialized programs aimed universally at alleviating poverty have far better political prospects in the racially tense political arena of the United States than race-based programs, which he takes to be racially polarizing. However, it is well-known that universally cast legislation and class- rather than race-specific antipoverty programs end up benefiting the white poor far more than the black.[41] One explanation for this is the ongoing perception among enforcers and administrators, linked to the prevailing image of the Underclass, that the former are deserving poor, the latter undeserving. Wilson has undertaken to integrate structural factors in the plight of the Underclass with individual and cultural ones. This is a commendable undertaking, but it is Wilson's peculiar mix that proves troubling. Thus, while he acknowledges racialized experiences and racism, they are almost completely untheorized in the explanatory schema and openly criticized in relation to policy considerations.

Wilson's analysis has been widely influential, even upon critics of his work. One of his deeper influences is related to this individualizing that is at the heart of his conceptual and explanatory account. In a set of interesting critical remarks on Wilson's work, Jennifer Hochschild praises Wilson's courage for insisting on the disturbing shift in the social values of the inner city black poor. As evidence of this shift, Hochschild quotes from unpublished work of the urban sociologist Elijah Anderson. Anderson notes the 'general sense of alienation, lack of opportunity, and demoralization of certain aspects of the black community'. Nevertheless, Anderson seems to be noting something more subtly complex than Hochschild is implying, namely, that the shift in values among the urban black poor is structurally related, a frustrated response to the perception of perpetuated, racially defined limits the black poor find themselves facing. The frustration has become especially acute in light of the failed promises the civil rights era seemed to hold out.[42] Anderson's structurally defined observation is at odds with Hochschild's ambivalent individualism, an individualism that becomes highlighted in Hochschild's analysis of possible courses of action. Here, she locates responsibility for responding to the plights and problems of the racialized poor primarily with those closest to the problems: the individuals directly in touch with those whose values are seen to need transforming. These include parents, schoolteachers, social workers, police, potential employers, and local politicians. True, Hochschild proceeds from here to structural considerations and state obligations, but the latter are secondary, an afterthought, though a recognizably necessary one. Hochschild individualizes the issues by locating the nexus of both the problem of poverty and of the starting point for transforming its complex of individual and structural considerations with the poverty of culture. She works out from this localized individual space of responsibility, expanding the universe of obligation outward from the 'problematic individual' ultimately to the political.[43] This presupposes that the problems lie foremost with deviant individual expression and only vaguely with policies, prejudice, economic structure and political self-interest, the failure of moral imagination and application, and the poverty of political discourse.

Experience might have taught us that where technologies of conceptualization create distance between what is needed and those with the responsibility and means to respond to the needs, little is likely to be done. The virtue of Wilson's work is its recognition of the complex interaction all the way up and down, so to speak, between individual responsibilities (local *and* distant) and transformed structures. *The Underclass*, I want to insist, is one conceptual technology that stands in the way of fully satisfying that recognition. Naming the Underclass makes the Underclass, nominates it into existence, and constitutes its members at once as Other.

Wilson's understanding of the force of race and the effects of racisms in the account of contemporary poverty in a deeply racialized social order like the United States rests upon his underestimating the perpetual disadvantages blacks continue to suffer, irrespective of their class position. Employment opportunities for whites are considerably greater than for blacks across the class spectrum. Geographically defined unemployment rates for blacks are often double that for whites. The rates of unemployment for both male and female blacks with one or more years of college are greater than those for whites who failed to complete high school. Unlike the experience of inadequately educated immigrants, many educated blacks have to settle for relatively poor jobs, while uneducated blacks have to live with no legitimate work at all. As Fainstein concludes in his subtle and convincing analysis of Wilson's 'mismatch' analysis, racism pervades the U.S. economy. It is

> built into the routine decisions of employers: the way they organize
> the division of labor, how they allocate men, women, blacks, and whites
> among jobs; what they decide to pay different kinds of workers, and
> the implicit criteria they utilize in hiring and promotion. Combined
> with virulent racism in housing markets, which keeps blacks concentrated
> in residential ghettoes in central cities and increasingly in suburban
> jurisdictions, outright discrimination along with more subtle forms of
> channeling in labor markets goes a long way toward explaining black
> economic disadvantage.[44]

Managing inflation through unemployment, for example, is a tax on the poor and, in the context of deeply racialized employment differentiation, upon blacks in particular.[45] This further disadvantages the truly disadvantaged, and it benefits those relatively well-off in ways analogous to the largely free aid Third World migrant labor finds itself 'forced' into furnishing the First World.

So, in general, the notion of *the Underclass* explicitly erases the exclusionary experiences of racisms from social science analysis while silently enthroning the demeaning impact of race-based insinuations and considerations. It distinguishes the especially impoverished from the ordinary poor while aggregating together those whose conditions of experience in various ways – in terms of race, gender, and class – may be quite different. It thus promotes a single policy solution for perhaps very different difficulties and social problems people find themselves facing.[46]

In a society whose advantages and opportunities are racially ordered, a concept like *the Underclass* will almost inevitably assume racial connotation. No matter the protestations of social scientists of Wilson's standing, race will likely be tied to pathological considerations of an *under*class. As others have noted, in analyses where there is an underclass, there too implicitly must be supposed to be an overclass. However, we find both in social science and popular accounts no mention of this.

The justification Wilson offers for using the concept turns on its identification of the structurally marginal position of some people in the labor force and the linking of this economic marginality to spatial location. He rightly criticizes Hochschild's substitute, 'the estranged poor', for failing to reflect the relationship between people's experience in the labor market and their neighborhood environment.[47] If Wilson's notion of *the Underclass* passes for the most part silently over the racial characterization of this relationship, Hochschild's term seems to erase it altogether. I would like to suggest *the racially marginalized* as an alternative. It explicitly captures the class dimension of economic marginality; it references the ghetto as the spatial location of the racially marginalized (Wilson admits that the white poor seldom live in ghetto areas); it differentiates those who are racialized but nonmarginal from those who deeply experience the material effects of exclusion, namely, the racial poor; and in foregrounding the processes of marginalization, it refuses moralistic judgments as first causes of the marginal condition. Accordingly, it directs analysis properly away from individualized character traits, or their lack, to what Hughes identifies as the 'isolated deprivation of the (impacted) ghetto'. The concept of *the racially marginalized* thus clearly captures the intersection of race and class that multiplies the depth of structural dislocation.[48] It also bridges the imaginary conceptual divide between those ghettoized in the racialized locations of urban sites, the 'urban jungles' throughout 'the West' and those marginalized in 'the Third World', between those situated as the 'Underclass' and those whose (supposed lack of) history is reduced to 'the Primitive'.[49]

There is a further dimension to the power of social science in effecting the 'objects' of its studies, one that is especially pertinent in the case of the racially marginalized. Debates in social science concerning important policy-related questions take place over a specified time span – a decade, say. During this time, the exchange becomes more precise – in the conceptual apparatus used, in hypothesis specification, testing, data accumulation, and analysis. Wilson's 'mismatch' hypothesis is a case in point. In the meantime, *en passant*, policy decisions are implemented on the basis of one or another of the contesting positions in the unresolved debate, a debate that may never see satisfactory resolution. The policies are necessarily partial (in both senses), just as the debate is incomplete. Researchers proceed to new issues, driven by perceived social needs, or their own interests, or available funding. Monies for research on the black super poor, or for that matter on black racial attitudes[50] have been notoriously difficult to come by, especially after the Moynihan and Kerner reports were issued in the late 1960s. Of course, there are real lives that are affected by the policies. So all too often the resolution of the issues under debate, insofar as there is resolution at all, is embodied in the lives of those trapped between the threads of tattered policies.

Blauner and Wellman emphasize the political and economic power major research universities represent to poor black populations whose neighborhoods are often adjacent to and controlled by the university trustees. University researchers are seen by communities to stand in positions of control, power, and exploitation, with little or no benefits accruing to the 'objects' of the research.[51] I have argued that racialized power is primarily conceived through conceptual orders like the Primitive, the Third World, and the Underclass. These are constitutive metaphors of racialized experience, the power of which consists in their ability to order and order anew racialized exclusions. In terms of social science, power is here expressed, managed, and extended in and through representing racial Others – to themselves and to the world.

As with 'black', it may be possible for those objectified by these categories to appropriate them, assuming the categories in assertive self-ascription. This appropriation is what I earlier called 'standing inside the terms', making them one's own, giving new meaning to and thereby redirecting them as forms of political engagement and critique. Of the three notions, 'the Third World' has come closest to this, perhaps because it is less deeply positioned in the history and rhetoric of racialized discourse than the other two. Nevertheless, it has to take extraordinary effort on the part of all, or nearly all, so characterized to redirect the original connotations the three terms carry. For a term like 'primitive' this would prove exceptionally difficult. Where it is still used, its referential scope proves to be partial and vague, temporally vacant and spatially diffuse. Those so referenced are rarely in a position of power, politically and technologically, to take on the category as a form of self-reference, even should they choose to. In the case of 'the Underclass', the lack of representational power seems equally obvious. Indeed, it might be added that to the extent that people so referenced assume some semblance of representational authority, they cease under the imposed criteria to be 'underclass' or 'primitive'.

As we have seen, it is not necessary that members of any group get racialized, though some groups – blacks and American Indians especially – are more likely than others to be. Nor once racialized does it necessarily follow that all members will be treated in racial terms or that any one member be so treated all or even much of the time. Once a group is racialized, and especially where the racial creation of the group runs deep into the history of its formation, however, the more likely will it be that the group and its members are made to carry its racialized nature with them.

Thus, not only is it the case, as Bauman observes, that the great effort exerted by the social sciences in studying race and racism has done little to alter the self-conception of the social sciences,[52] it is perhaps more emphatically the case that the social sciences have done much to create, authorize, legitimate, and extend both the figures of racial Otherness and the exclusions of the various racisms. The ways in which the production of social knowledge in the name of science continues more or less silently, more or less explicitly, to do so will be obviated by analyzing two contemporary texts produced in and representative of differing though not unrelated racialized contexts. The first reads race strictly as Africa; the second undertakes to normalize racial comprehension in/of South Africa by reinventing it in terms of 'Western' social science.

A dying racism?

Terence Ranger has long been concerned with representing Africa to and in the West. Where earlier social scientists engaged in what Mudimbe properly calls inventing Africa,[53] Ranger is committed to reinventing it. In the text I want to focus on here, his definitive statement on 'race relations', Ranger re-presents the civilizing mission of liberal good works in terms of charity beginning not at but from the home. Like earlier social science about the Other, then, it could be said that Ranger pursues Torgovnick's primitivizing search for (a) home in modernity's space-time of 'transcendental homelessness'. And as before, the invention of this idealized home can only be sustained by the destructive denial of the Other's actual home.

The auspicious occasion of Ranger's remarks is his inaugural lecture in 1987 as (Cecil John) Rhodes Professor of Race Relations at Oxford University. Ranger might thus be permitted some largesse, but the form the lecture assumes is the metaphor of a reimagined imperialism. In the address, 'Rhodes, Oxford, and the Study of Race Relations', Ranger engages in a range of metaphorical transmutations: metaphorical in the literary construction of his lecture; metaphorical in standing for the epistemological reproduction of the rule over Africa (which by implication cannot epistemologically rule itself, for it requires Oxford once again to know it, to be represented to itself); and metaphorical again for the place of racialized representation in Britain, in the terms of Ranger's, of Rhodes's Oxford.

Ranger's lecture transposes the Rhodes Chair of Race Relations into a Central African Kingdom; the Oxford pro-vice-chancellor, the highest-ranking university representative present, into a tribal elder; Ranger himself into an ascending king, a ruler over the domain of African Studies, not just at Oxford but universally; thus, Race Relations (itself a severe circumscription of a domain and a reification of its terms of representation as givens) into a certain sort of African Studies; race into what *others* are; and finally, Cecil John Rhodes, of all people, into a 'tutelary deity', a 'patron divinity' of Africa, of Race Relations as African Studies.[54]

The rhetorical medium of Ranger's transmutations is the description of the figure of Rhodes as deity of African Studies. Ranger admits the Janus-faced nature of the figure: At once appealing and fraternal, paternalistic and condescending to local Africans, Rhodes approached African leaders as equals and as servants. Expressing a desire to live as peaceful neighbor or landlord, Rhodes was consumed with the drive for and expression of personal, political, and economic power. This figure of contradictory power Ranger contrasts with an antidotive figure, a 'companion deity' with whom Ranger more easily identifies, a figure representing 'abnegation and powerlessness'. This is the figure of Arthur Shearly Cripps – British, white, a missionary (though 'radical'), and above all 'a quintessential Oxford man'. Yet, concludes Ranger with just a hint of melancholy, Cripps's humanism – his 'pastoralism and medievalism', traveling on foot in his missionary Africa 'like *his* African *flock*' – is inadequate to salvage Africa for Oxford; it is unable 'to conceptualize Africa'.[55]

The moral of Ranger's narrative for Oxford – the University, that is – is neither to save nor ruthlessly to modernize (Rhodes's) Africa. 'Oxford must settle for a relationship of equality (if it is not in itself absurd to speak of equality between a university and a continent).'[56] It is self-evidently absurd to speak in this way. But Ranger, recall, is speaking not anymore of a university but of the Oxfordian Kingdom, not of Africa but of African Studies, not of Africans but of Race Relations, over all of which he is assuming titular control. In moving to the concluding moments of his inauguration, to the assumption of his throne, Ranger reveals the state-to-be of the study of race relations at Oxford: an African Studies Centre not in the mold of any white divinity of the past – a Rhodes or Cripps or Smuts –

but with the view to the need for understanding Africa 'as much as Africa needs to understand us'.[57]

It is unclear in whose name the 'us' is being spoken here – Oxford, Britain, Europe, or the West. Postmodern irony and self-consciousness are not beyond the assertion of postcolonial power. What is clear is that Ranger refers by 'race' only to Africans, to the traditional Other; and clearer yet what his intentions are in representing Africa: to bring Africans to Oxford so as to be able 'to render [them] accurately – to speak of, sometimes even *for* Africans in Oxford'.[58] The power of representation remains fit for the king. In his construction of race and ethnicity in the name of Rhodes, not a word about race in contemporary Britain, about the 'empire striking back' or the 'lack of black in the Union Jack'; no mention of the vast study of race relations and the critical debate about racial construction and exclusion. Not a word, that is, about the state of British race analysis impossible to ignore beyond the shadows of Oxford's ivied bastions. No reference to race in the city of Oxford, of the testy relation between racialized town dwellers and the wearers of the university gown. Nothing about the fact that there are more African students attending Oxford than there are black British students, nor about the almost total lack of black faculty representation.

Ranger is at one with Oxford's past, the appropriate wearer of Rhodes's crown: Race is Africa! The World Bank would do no better than to respond to Ranger's explicit appeal, to buy its knowledge of Africa – of an undifferentiated Africa if the language of this document is anything to go by, and despite all its qualifications – to fund his Centre. Ranger's Kingdom is a market, a place to trade, to bring Africans once more to sell – this time their intellectual energy and their knowledge[59] (though sometimes, too, the Other must understand, knowledge will have to be given them, they will have to be re-presented). Once more, African labor, this time intellectual, becomes foreign aid for the glorification of the great white man's rule. [. . .]

Notes

1   Foucault (1970), p. 346.
2   I have adapted loosely and liberally from Said's stimulating analysis of Orientalism. Said (1979a), pp. 31–49. Cf. Wolf (1981), p. 388; Mudimbe (1988), pp. 1–43; and on art, Nettleton and Hammond-Tooke, eds. (1989).
3   This expresses philosophically what anthropological ethnography has long practiced: 'given the dominant rhetoric of anthropological discourse, the Other's ethnographic presence goes together with his theoretical absence. In ethnography, as we know it, the Other is displayed, and therefore contained, as an object of representation; the Other's voice, demands, teachings are usually absent from our theorizing.' Fabian (1990), p. 771.
4   Foucault (1970), p. 351; more generally, see Bauman (1989), pp. 179–80. And on the epistemological politics of the social sciences in historical context, see Mafeje (1976).
5   Balibar (1991), p. 15.
6   Human Sciences Research Council (HSRC of South Africa) (1985), p. 6. This may seem an extreme case. But substituting various other states for South Africa

in the quotations – the United States, Israel, Britain, to name only the more obvious – will hardly change their significance. In the case of the United States, there may be more self-consciousness and skepticism about the designations, a greater personal and institutional wrestling with the identifications than may have once been the case in South Africa, though even in this respect the latter may now be in the process of emulating the former. I have learned, not without cost and whether one intends it or not, that claims about South Africa, however generally stated, are dated: This is written in June 1991.

7   HSRC (1985), p. 157. It should be pointed out that leading South African ideologues are no longer committed to this claim, which is not the same as saying that they are no longer committed to some more or less formal racialized dispensation. I will be analyzing this document in greater detail later in the chapter.

8   A booklet published by the South African state in 1969, *Progress through Separate Development*, makes just this claim. However, the South African Museum, a state-sponsored national institution, for example, now acknowledges the arrival of blacks in South Africa two thousand years ago.

9   For evidence of the collaboration between anthropological study and colonial administration: 'It has been said that modern anthropology is destined to be of great assistance to colonial governments in providing the knowledge of the social structure of native groups upon which a sound and harmonious Native Administration, as envisaged in indirect Rule, should be built. Let me say that I for one firmly believe in the possibility of such cooperation between anthropologists and administrators.' S. F. Nadel, *A Black Byzantium* (1942), quoted in Frank (1979), p. 206. Cf. Foucault (1988), p. 162. Anthropologists have become much more self-conscious about the processes of what Johannes Fabian calls 'othering'. They no longer assume 'the givenness of the Other as the object of their discipline'. Fabian (1990), p. 755. In the first draft, I used 'peoples' in referring to the colonized. Alena Goldberg reminded me most forcefully that this, too, was to invoke, perhaps euphemistically, a category of the sort I am engaged in critiquing.

10 Theorization of 'development' in terms of stages can be traced to the Enlightenment. The four-stage theory of human development proposed by the Russian Semyon Efimovich Desnitsky, a student of Adam Smith's, is typical: The earliest mode of human development consists of 'peoples' living by hunting-gathering. The second stage consists of 'peoples' engaged in the pastoral lives of shepherds. The third stage is agricultural. And the fourth consists of 'peoples' living by commerce. ('Peoples' is the term used by Desnitsky in the eighteenth century.) See Meek (1976), p. 5. W. W. Rostow's five-stage theory of economic development has been the major influence in mainstream developmental economics in the past three decades.

11 See Mafeje (1976); and Mudimbe (1988), p. 44. The contemporary experience of South Africa in relation to the World Bank and the IMF is revealing. With the lifting of sanctions, the South African government is voluntarily subjecting itself to the 'advice' of these funding bodies without expecting further loans in the short term. Thus, they are using the economic expertise now being exported in the name of the G7 to rationalize greater privatization of nationalized industries, reduction in the tax rates, and introduction of an increasingly regressive tax structure in the form of a comprehensive value added tax, reduced government social service expenditures, and diminished welfare commitments.

12   Cf. Kuper (1988), pp. 1–4; Torgovnick (1990), pp. 18–19; Rubin (1984), p. 2.

13   Kuper thinks that *transformations* in the significations of theoretical concepts have played a major role in science, at least as significant as the role advocated by Kuhn's 'paradigms'. Kuper (1988), pp. 10–14.

14   On the formal qualities of the Primitive, see Kuper (1988), p. 5; on the popular conception, see Torgovnick (1990), pp. 8, 99, 192. Torgovnick points out that the concept was also used to rationalize control of 'lower classes, minorities, and women . . . the primitives at home' (p. 192). This rationalization was sustained by the economy of conceptual identification in the late nineteenth century between racial Others, mainly blacks and Jews, women, and the working class. Torgovnick also points out that primitive society became the 'testing ground' for early twentieth-century psychoanalytic hypotheses about human sexuality (p. 7). She is only partially correct in ascribing this to the anthropological constitution of the Other and its corollary assumption that the Primitive was the Other in us, the precivilized form through which, in the form of our ancestry, we passed. The rush of sex theorists into the field of anthropological study also had to do with prevailing Victorianism in sexual matters, the veil of taboos prohibiting frank, open, unbiased study of sex in civilized society. If Victorianism proved to be the push, the lure of the Savage was the invitation behind the veil of taboos, the pull of an object pristine and pure, unself-conscious, and so perhaps a view into the unconscious.

15   Levi-Strauss, perhaps a little gingerly, refers to these (non)histories as 'cold'. Wolf (1981), p. 385.

16   Kuper (1988), pp. 13–14. Compare Leni Riefenstahl's popular photographic collection of African bodies with Lawrence and Lorne Blair's *Ring of Fire*, an account of their journeys through Indonesia. For more on the latter, see Torgovnick (1990), pp. 177–82.

17   Torgovnick (1990), p. 38; Kuper (1988), pp. 7–9.

18   Three brief quotes should suffice: '[The Asmat of New Guinea] is a good example of how rare an untouched example of a primitive culture really is'. 'The tropes and categories through which we view primitive societies establish relations of power between them and us.' And '[these are] some of our greatest thinking and thinkers about the primitive'. Torgovnick (1990), p. 280 n. 3, pp. 11 and 190.

19   Torgovnick (1990), ch. 2. Torgovnick (p. 186) badly misrepresents the history of racial theorizing in claiming that post-Darwinist views on race were a return to the monogenist conception that predated polygenism, and that monogenism 'became the antiracist position' while polygenism 'became the assumption of the racist position'. That Gould, in another context, calls this a common misreading of the debate does not mitigate her mistake. Gould (1991), p. 13.

20   Torgovnick (1990), pp. 69–70. My emphases.

21   On realism as the dominant mode of ethnographical writing, see Fabian (1990).

22   Torgovnick (1990), p. 71. Similarly, she approves largely of the 1980s film *Greystoke: The Story of Tarzan*, failing to question why this film at that time.

23   Ibid., p. 185.

24   My characterization of the three worlds has been informed by Pletsch (1981), pp. 569–74; and Worsley (1984), ch. 1, and p. 308. See also Tipps (1973), esp. pp. 204, 208.

25   Pletsch (1981), p. 565.

26   Ibid., p. 581.
27   Gorra suggests that the characterization can be generalized in the colonial context to Africa as (being) Europe's, as belonging to Europe. Gorra (1991), p. 87. This spatial appropriation of Africa is accompanied, as Patricia Williams so forcefully argues, by an eviction of the cultural legacy of Africa from the denial of black contributors to the canon of 'Western civilization'. P. J. Williams (1991), pp. 113–14.
28   As I was composing this, an article appeared in *The New York Sunday Times*, June 23, 1991, on the expressed commitment of the Congress Party in India (newly returned to power after Rajiv Ghandi's assassination) to a 'free market' economy. The article referred to the encouragement of this newfound capitalism as expressed by 'a senior *Western* diplomat'. Whose interests, one wonders, does this diplomat represent? The cementing of 'the West' in the aftermath of the Gulf War seems at once and paradoxically impenetrable and transparent. By contrast, adding a 'Fourth World' to distinguish between different sorts of non-Western states simply reiterates the restrictions of the three-world system.
29   See Ridgeway (1990), p. 21; Varnedoe (1984a), p. 679. Chafets (1990), pp. 20–6.
30   Balibar (1991a), p. 14; cf. Balibar (1990), pp. 283–94. Two points attest to this growing phenomenon: In Germany, those initially deemed *Gastarbeiter* were later referred to as 'foreign workers' and now just as 'the foreigners'. There is no immigration law, only *Auslandergesetz*, or 'foreigner's law', dating back to 1965 and evocative of 1938 Nazi legislation, which it appears to emulate. Non-alien residents of European Community countries have the right of entry, employment, and self-employment. Rathzel (1990), pp. 32 ff.
31   Worsley (1984), pp. 238, 236.
32   Myrdal (1962).
33   Gans (1990), p. 271; Jencks (1988), p. 23; Innis and Feagin (1989), p. 14.
34   Magnet (1989), p. 130.
35   Jencks (1988), p. 23; Reed (1988). An article in the *Chronicle of Higher Education* in 1988 described the 'social pathologies' as including 'teenage pregnancies, out of wedlock births, single parent families, poor educational achievement, chronic unemployment, welfare dependency, drug abuse, and crime'. Coughlin (1988).
36   This is Boxill's critical characterization of the 'poverty of culture' thesis. Boxill (1991), p. 588.
37   For an explicit expression of the Underclass in terms of idleness, see Jencks (1988), p. 24. Cf. Coetzee (1989), pp. 12–35. Another indication of the racialized character of the Underclass is revealed in its popular use to characterize animal pecking orders. Gans reports finding a new story referring to 'underclass Mexican iguanas'. Gans (1990), p. 272.
38   Wilson (1987), p. 126. In a more recent paper, Wilson seeks to develop a 'broader theoretical . . . framework that integrates social structural and cultural arguments'. Wilson (1991b), p. 1.
39   Reed (1988), p. 168.
40   Wilson (1991a), p. 600.
41   Where they help blacks in any measure at all, these programs tend to assist the black middle class more than the black poor, for the former are in a better position to take advantage of them because of better knowledge, greater institutional access, and more available resources.

42   Hochschild (1991), p. 564. Contrast E. Anderson (1990), pp. 72, 112–13.

43   Hochschild (1991), pp. 575 ff.

44   Fainstein (1986), p. 440. See also pp. 418, 439. Duster notes that when inner
     city businesses relocate to areas where employment of black youth is less likely,
     the proportion of blacks in the community may be one of the decisive
     considerations. Duster (1988), p. 3. Jencks also addresses this point. Jencks
     (1988). Even in respect to welfare treatment, whites on welfare fare better than
     those who are not white. See Torres (1988), p. 1058.

45   Hochschild (1991), p. 563.

46   On this latter point, see Gans (1990), p. 274.

47   Wilson (1991a), pp. 600–602. Cf. Hochschild (1991), p. 561. In his presidential
     address to the American Sociological Association, Wilson pertinently substitutes
     for his use of 'the Underclass' the term 'the ghetto poor'. And he does this
     commendably 'to focus our attention less on controversy and more on research
     and theoretical issues'. He nevertheless emphasizes that he 'hop[es] that I would
     not lose any of the theoretical meaning that this concept [the Underclass] has had
     in my writing'. Wilson (1991b), p. 11.

48   Hughes (1989), pp. 191–2.

49   Defending the Bush administration's new 'violence initiative' to 'identify early
     in their lives people who may be prone to violent or antisocial behaviour', the
     senior health official in the Health Department, Dr. Frederick Goodwin, argued
     that 'male monkeys, especially in the wild . . . roughly half of them survive to
     adulthood. The other half die by violence. That is the natural way of it for males,
     to knock each other off . . . the same hyperaggressive monkeys who kill each
     other are also hypersexual, so they copulate more. . . . Maybe it isn't just
     the careless use of the word when people call certain areas of certain cities
     jungles, that we may have gone back to what might be more natural, without
     all of the social controls that we have imposed on ourselves as a civilization
     over thousands of years in our own evolution.' The New York Times, February
     28, 1992, p. A:7. Torgovnick also insists on using the term the 'urban jungle'
     in her analysis of contemporary primitivism discussed above. Theodore Lowi
     rightly asks why we now need concepts like 'culture of poverty' and 'underclass'
     in relation to black ghettos but not formerly in relation to Jewish or
     Irish ones. Lowi (1988), p. 855. On 'the West', see Young (1990), Derrida
     (1992).

50   Surveys of racial attitudes of whites in the United States date at least to
     the 1950s. The first major social science survey of the racial attitudes of
     blacks nationwide in over twenty years only recently appeared. Sigelman and
     Welch (1991). The same is largely true in South Africa. Blauner and Wellman
     discuss some of the political issues involved in conducting attitude research
     among the black poor. Blauner and Wellman (1973), pp. 310–30. The title of
     Ladner's well-known volume, The Death of White Sociology, strikes one with the
     hindsight of nearly two decades and in spite of some dramatic changes, as overly
     optimistic.

51   Blauner and Wellman (1973), p. 315.

52   Bauman (1989), p. 85.

53   See, for example, the book Becoming More Civilized by self-described liberal social
     psychologist Leonard Doob. Published in 1960, Doob's study is concerned with
     the psychological effects of Africans as they 'become more civilized'. 'Civilization

is intended as a description of the differences between the values of people who 'unwittingly live next to one another in the bush and those who wittingly live on top of one another in modern apartment houses'. Though Doob does not intend the term to designate or justify inferiority or superiority, the comparison of the irrational necessity of bush life with the free choice of modernity reproduces a presumption long considered to be well-established. See Doob (1960), pp. ix–x.

54   Ranger (1989), pp. 1–3.
55   Ibid., pp. 1–13, 18. My emphasis. Religious animism is converted into referential animalism – again!
56   Ibid., p. 19.
57   Ibid., p. 21.
58   Ibid., p. 22. My emphasis.
59.   Ibid., p. 24.

References

Anderson, E. (1990) *Streetwise: Race, Class, and Change in an Urban Community* (Chicago: University of Chicago Press).

Balibar, E. (1991) '*Es Gibt Keinen Staat in Europa*: Racism and Politics in Europe Today', *New Left Review* 187 (May-June): 5–19.

Balibar, E. (1990) 'Paradoxes of Universality'. In D. T. Goldberg, ed., *Anatomy of Racism* (Minneapolis: University of Minnesota Press).

Bauman, Z. (1989) *Modernity and the Holocaust* (Oxford: Polity Press).

Blauner, R. and Wellman, D. (1973) 'Toward the Decolonization of Social Research'. In J. Ladner, ed., *The Death of White Sociology* (New York: Random House).

Boxill, B. (1991) 'Wilson on the Truly Disadvantaged', *Ethics* 101 (April): 579–92.

Chafets, Z. (1990) 'The Tragedy of Detroit', *New York Sunday Times Magazine* (July 29): 20–6, 38, 42, 50–1.

Coetzee, J. M. (1989) *White Writing* (New Haven: Yale University Press).

Coughlin, E. K. (1988) 'Worsening Plight of the Underclass Catches Attention', *The Chronicle of Higher Education* (March): A5.

Derrida, J. (1992) *The Other Heading* (Bloomington: Indiana University Press).

Doob, L. (1960) *Becoming More Civilized* (New Haven: Yale University Press).

Duster, T. (1988) 'Social Implications of the "New" Black Underclass', *The Black Scholar* (May/June): 2–9.

Fabian, J. (1990) 'Presence and Representation: The Other and Anthropological Writing', *Critical Inquiry* 16 (Summer): 753–72.

Fainstein, N. (1986) 'The Underclass/Mismatch Hypothesis as an Explanation for Black Economic Deprivation', *Politics and Society* 15, 4: 403–51.

Foucault, M. (1988) 'The Political Technologies of Individuals'. In L. H. Martin, H. Gutman, and P. Hutton, eds., *Technologies of the Self*, (Minneapolis: University of Minnesota Press).

Foucault, M. (1970) *The Order of Things* (New York: Random House).

Frank, A. G. (1979) 'Anthropology = Ideology, Applied Anthropology = Politics'. In G. Huizer and B. Mannheim, eds., *The Politics of Anthropology* (The Hague: Mouton).

Gans, H. (1990) 'Reconstructing the Underclass: The Term's Dangers as a Planning Concept', *APA Journal* 271 (Summer): 271–77.

Gorra, M. (1991) 'Tact and Tarzan', *Transition* 52: 80–91.

Gould, S. J. (1991) 'The Birth of the Two-Sex World', *New York Review of Books* XXXVIII, 11 (June 13): 11–13.

Hochschild, J. (1991) 'The Politics of the Estranged Poor', *Ethics* 101 (April): 560–78.

Hughes, M. A. (1989) 'Misspeaking Truth to Power: A Geographical Perspective on the "Underclass" Fallacy', *Economic Geography* 65, 3 (July): 187–207.

Human Sciences Research Council (HSRC) (1985) *The South African Society: Realities and Future Prospects* (New York: Greenwood Press).

Innis, L. and Feagin, J. (1989) 'The Black "Underclass" Ideology in Race Relations Analysis', *Social Justice* 16, 4 (Winter): 13–34.

Jencks, C. (1988) 'Deadly Neighborhoods', *The New Republic* (June 13): 23–32.

Kuper, A. (1988) *The Invention of Primitive Society* (London: Routledge).

Lowi, T. (1988) 'The Theory of the Underclass: A Review of Wilson's *The Truly Disadvantaged*', *Policy Studies Review* 7, 4 (Summer): 852–8.

Mafeje, A. (1976) 'The Problem of Anthropology in Historical Perspective: An Inquiry into the Growth of the Social Sciences', *Canadian Journal of African Studies* X, 2: 307–33.

Magnet, M. (1989) 'America's Underclass: What to Do?', *Fortune* 115 (May 11): 130.

Meek, R. L. (1976) *Social Science and the Noble Savage* (Cambridge: Cambridge University Press).

Mudimbe, V. (1988) *The Invention of Africa* (Bloomington, IN: Indiana University Press).

Myrdal, G. (1962) *The Challenge to Affluence* (New York: Vintage Books).

Nettleton, A. and Hammond-Tooke, D., eds (1989) *African Art in Southern Africa: From Tradition to Township* (Johannesburg: Ad. Donker).

Pletsch, C. (1981) 'The Three Worlds, or the Division of Labor in the Social Sciences, circa 1950–75', *Comparative Studies in Society and History* 23, 4 (October): 565–90.

Ranger, T. (1989) *Rhodes, Oxford, and the Study of Race Relations* (Oxford: Clarendon Press).

Rathzel, N. (1990) 'Germany: One Race, One Nation?', *Race and Class* 32, 3: 31–48.

Reed, A. (1988) 'The Liberal Technocrat', *The New Republic* (Feb. 6): 167–70.

Ridgeway, J. (1990) 'Here He Comes, Mr. America', *The Village Voice* (October 9): 21.

Rubin, W., ed. (1984) *"Primitivism" in 20th Century Art: Affinity of the Tribal and the Modern* Vols I and II (New York: Museum of Modern Art).

Said, E. W. (1979a), 'Knowing the Oriental'. In E. W. Said, *Orientalism* (New York: Vintage Books).

Sigelman, L. and Welch, S. (1991) *Black Americans' Views of Racial Inequality: The Dream Deferred* (Cambridge: Cambridge University Press).

Tipps, D. (1973) 'Modernization Theory and the Comparative Study of Societies: A Critical Perspective', *Comparative Studies in Society and History* 15, 2: 119–226.

Torgovnick, M. (1990) *Gone Primitive: Savage Intellects, Modern Lives* (Chicago: University of Chicago Press).

Torres, G. (1988) 'Local Knowledge, Local Color: Critical Legal Studies and the Law of Race Relations', *San Diego Law Review* 25 (December): 1043–107.

Varnedoe, K. (1984a) 'Contemporary Explorations'. In W. Rubin, ed., *"Primitivism" in 20th Century Art: Affinity of the Tribal and the Modern* Vol. II (New York: Museum of Modern Art).

Williams, P. J. (1991) *The Alchemy of Race and Rights: Diary of a Law Professor* (Cambridge: Harvard University Press).

Wilson, W. J. (1991a) 'The Truly Disadvantaged Revisited: A Response to Hochschild and Boxill', *Ethics* 101 (April): 593–609.

Wilson, W. J. (1991b) 'Studying Inner City Social Dislocations: The Challenge of Public Agenda Research', *American Sociological Review* 56 (February): 1–14.

Wilson, W. J. (1987) *The Truly Disadvantaged: The Inner City, the Underclass, and Public Policy* (Chicago: Chicago University Press).

Wolf, E. (1981) *Europe and the People Without History* (Berkeley: University of California Press).

Worsley, P. (1984) *The Three Worlds* (London: Weidenfeld and Nicolson).

Young, R. (1990) *White Mythologies: Writing History and the West* (London: Routledge).

Guide to Further Reading

Key texts

Cornell, S. and Hartmann, D. (2007) *Ethnicity and Race: Making Identities in a Changing World*, Second edition, Thousand Oaks: Pine Forge Press (a general account of the changing role of race and ethnicity in the modern world).

Goldberg, D. T. (1993) *Racist Culture*, Oxford: Blackwell (a critical account of race and racism, that seeks to link theoretical analysis with an exploration of racist practices in specific contexts).

Knowles, C. (2003) *Race and Social Analysis*, London: Sage (a critical analysis of debates about race in the social sciences that focuses on the social construction of racial identities).

Miles, R. (1993) *Racism after 'Race Relations'*, London: Routledge (a collection of essays that provide an overview of some debates about the nature of racism and race relations).

Wieviorka, M. (1995) *The Arena of Racism*, London: Sage (an analysis of racism that draws on classical and contemporary European and American theories).

Background reading

Anthias, F. and Yuval-Davis, N. (1992) *Racialized Boundaries*, London: Routledge (an analysis of the construction of racial boundaries that emphasises links to gender, class and ethnicity).

Baker Jr, H. A., Diawara, M. and Lindeborg, R. H. (eds) (1996) *Black British Cultural Studies: A Reader*, Chicago: University of Chicago Press (a collection of essays about contemporary black British cultural studies, including papers by Hall, Gilroy and Carby).

Donald, J. and Rattansi, A. (eds) (1992) *'Race', Culture and Difference*, London: Sage (a collection of papers focusing on contemporary theories about race and cultural difference).

Eze, E. C. (ed.) (1997) *Race and the Enlightenment: A Reader*, Cambridge, MA: Blackwell (a collection of classical philosophical texts on race).

Gilroy, P. (1993) *The Black Atlantic: Modernity and Double Consciousness*, London: Verso (an influential reconstruction of the black diasporic experience from slavery to the present).

Goldberg, D. T. (2002) *The Racial State*, Oxford: Blackwell (a detailed theoretical analysis of the formation of racial states in different social and political contexts).

Guillaumin, C. (1995) *Racism, Sexism, Power and Ideology*, London: Routledge (a collection of essays that analyse the development of racism and sexism).

Malik, K. (1996) *The Meaning of Race: Race, History and Culture in Western Society*, London: Macmillan (an analysis of the relationship between ideas about race and post-enlightenment Western thought).

Marx, A. W. (1997) *Making Race and Nation: A Comparison of the United States, South Africa, and Brazil*, Cambridge: Cambridge University Press (a comparative analysis of the making of ideas about race and nation from the perspective of historical sociology).

Mills, C. W. (1997) *The Racial Contract*, Ithaca: Cornell University Press (an attempt to analyse ideas about race within contemporary philosophical terms).

—— (2003) *From Class to Race: Essays in White Marxism and Black Radicalism* Lanham: Rowman and Littlefield (a collection of essays that focus of the shifting meanings of race and class in the United States).

Mostern, K. (1996) 'Three Theories of Race of W. E. B. Du Bois', *Cultural Critique* 34, 27–63 (an exploration of different ideas about race in the work of Du Bois).

Outlaw Jr, L. T. (1996) *On Race and Philosophy*, New York: Routledge (a study of the relationship between race, philosophy and modernity).

Park, R. (1950) *Race and Culture*, New York: Free Press (a classic collection of papers by Robert Park that trace the development of his thinking on race relations from the early part of the twentieth century).

Reed Jr, A. L. (1997) *W. E. B. Du Bois and American Political Thought: Fabianism and the Color Line*, New York: Oxford University Press (an exploration of Du Bois's thinking on race, that suggests links to more contemporary debates).

Rex, J. (1983) *Race Relations in Sociological Theory*, Second edition, London: Routledge and Kegan Paul (a classic attempt to outline a theoretical basis for the study of race relations).

Stanfield II, J. H. (1985) *Philanthropy and Jim Crow in American Social Science*, Westport: Greenwood Press (a study of the development of early research on race relations in America during the Jim Crow period).

Key Questions

- How does Robert Park's concept of the 'race relations cycle' explain the development of race and ethnic relations in cities?
- John Rex's work seeks to outline a model for a 'distinct field of race relations studies'. What are the key elements of his model and how successful is it?
- Robert Miles argues that race constitutes a notion that that may be a common term of reference within everyday discourse but is not useful analytically. Why does he argue this and what are the consequences of his analysis?
- Stuart Hall argues that in contemporary societies we are seeing the development of new ethnicities that cannot be grounded in a set of fixed trans-cultural or transcendental racial categories. How does this argument help us to understand the changing patterns of race and ethnic relations in today's world?
- What does Claire Alexander mean when she says that 'we need to take difference seriously'? Discuss this argument in relation to specific examples.
- David Goldberg argues that racial identities have become increasingly ambivalent and ambiguous, and that they need to be contextualised in terms of time and space. How would you utilise this argument to analyse the changing forms of racial identity in contemporary societies?

PART THREE

Racism and anti-semitism

INTRODUCTION

O NE OF THE REGRETTABLE FEATURES of much contemporary
theorising about race and racism has been the tendency to leave the question
of anti-semitism to one side, treating it almost as a separate issue. This is despite
the ways in which one of the most consistent themes that runs through racist
thinking and the values articulated by racist and fascist movements throughout
this century has been anti-semitism. The extracts we have been able to include in
this part are, of course, merely examples of a much wider body of work that has
been produced over the years (see *Guide to Further Reading*). But in including
these extracts we hope that we have at least given an indication of the kinds of
questions that we need to think about in exploring the relationship between racism
and anti-semitism.

The first extract from George Mosse sets out to provide a brief overview of
the ways in which myths and counter-myths about 'the Jew' emerged and evolved.
Drawing on a variety of historical sources Mosse attempts to situate what he sees
as the main elements of myths about Jews and the way these myths evolved and
changed over time. In addition he is concerned to show how the evolving racial
mythologies about Jews helped to construct them as a kind of 'race apart'. To
take the particular example of the image of the 'wandering Jew', Mosse attempts
to show that such myths helped to construct Jews as the 'eternal foreigner' who
would be unable to become a part of the 'people'. Interestingly enough Mosse's
argument also shows that at least some Jews were influenced by racial thought
and to some extent sought to develop 'counter-myths' about race and Jewish identity
in order to question anti-semitism.

The next extract by Theodor Adorno and Max Horkheimer was originally written in 1944. Both Adorno and Horkheimer were leading members of the Frankfurt School of critical theory and they were in exile in the United States at the time. Given their experience as exiles from Nazi Germany it is perhaps not surprising that they saw the main arguments of their work on anti-semitism as an attempt to understand 'the actual reversion of enlightened civilisation to barbarism'. More specifically, however, Adorno and Horkheimer's analysis is preoccupied by the need to make sense of how anti-semitism in Nazi Germany led to the policy of 'extermination', the idea that 'Jews must be wiped from the face of the earth'. This is of course a question on which much has been written, both in the period immediately after the Second World War and in more recent times. But this extract helps to pose the need for an explanation of the relationship between anti-semitism and the Holocaust.

Perhaps the most influential recent attempt to provide a theoretical framework for the analysis of anti-semitism is to be found in the work of the sociologist Zygmunt Bauman. Bauman is particularly concerned with the question of the reasons why the Holocaust could happen in the context of modernity. The broad outline of his argument links up with some of the analytical arguments to be found in the work of Adorno and Horkheimer as well as the historical accounts of Mosse. A recurrent theme in his analysis is the way he attempts to show that the extermination and genocide of the Jews by the Nazi racial state was not the product of irrationality, but very much an integral part of the 'rational world of modern civilisation'. From this basic premise he attempts to show how it was precisely the development of technology, large impersonal state bureaucracies and modern science that provided the necessary conditions for the institutionalisation of a policy of extermination against Jews.

The next two extracts focus on the question of the role of images and stereotypes in the construction of 'the Jew'. The first extract is from Sander Gilman, one of the most prolific and controversial figures in this field, and is concerned particularly with the changing terms of debate about the body in discourses about Jews. Using recent debates in America about the construction of Jews as white Gilman sets out to show the tenuous and historically contingent nature of this ascription of 'whiteness'. Writing in his usual powerful narrative style Gilman uses the imagery of 'the Jewish nose' as a way of exploring the changing representations of the skin colour of Jews from the nineteenth century onwards. His account links up with the broader discussion of whiteness that has become such an important theme in debates about race and racism in recent years (see contributions by Ruth Frankenberg in Part Five and by David Roediger in Part Six).

Gilman's analysis also links up with the concerns of the final extract in this part, by Matthew Jacobson. This extract is symptomatic of a renewed interest by historians and others about the meanings attached to whiteness in America, particularly in relation to immigrant groups such as the Irish, Jews and Italians, among others. Drawing on research about the construction of Jewishness in American culture from the nineteenth century onwards, Jacobson's account is specifically concerned with the ways in which Jews have been constructed as both white and Other. He also argues forcefully that images based on 'racial Jewishness' were not simply the product of anti-semitism, since Jewish writers and commentators were also constructing their own versions of what 'Jewishness' meant. In this sense Jacobson's analysis can be taken as a case study of the importance of historical and cultural processes in shaping the meanings that are attached to racial categories.

Chapter 16

George L. Mosse

THE JEWS: MYTH AND COUNTER-MYTH

THE MYSTERY OF RACE TRANSFORMED the Jew into an evil principle. This was nothing new for the Jew; after all, anti-Christ had been a familiar figure during the Middle Ages. But in the last decades of the nineteenth century and the first half of the twentieth, the traditional legends which had swirled about the Jews in the past were revived as foils for racial mysticism and as instruments of political mobilization. Accusations of ritual murder, the curse of Ahasverus the wandering Jew, and fantasies about the universal Jewish world conspiracy had never vanished from the European consciousness even during the Enlightenment. Now they were to be revitalized and given renewed force.

The accusation of ritual murder – the so-called blood libel – had medieval roots in the legend that Jews murdered Christian children and drank their blood during the feast of Passover. As part of their religious ceremonial, the Jews allegedly performed a "ritual murder," typical of the perverse nature of their religion and the evil it represented. Moreover, this Jewish use of blood blasphemed the sacrifice of Christ on the Cross, for Easter and Passover coincided. The blood libel provided the basis for an accusation of atavism, because in contrast to civilized people, Jews supposedly practiced human sacrifice. The so-called Jewish conspiracy against the Gentile world was also built into this myth from the beginning, for no Jew, so it was thought, would inform on any other Jew, while talkative Gentiles were bribed with gold to remain silent about this ritual of human sacrifice.

The myth of the use and misuse of the sacred substance of blood served to separate out the Jews from the Christians. Blood libel had always surfaced in periods of stress. At the end of the nineteenth century, the times seemed out of joint and ritual murder accusations once more swept through eastern Europe. Between 1890 and 1914, there were no less than twelve trials of Jews for ritual murder; the last murder charge was leveled as late as 1930, in the Rutho-Carpathian Mountains by the prosecutor of the Czechoslovak government.[1]

The blood libel remained alive chiefly in the underdeveloped countries of eastern Europe and the Russian Empire. Within the Russian Empire the government shrewdly exploited the belief in order to provoke pogroms, and every lost Christian child was a menace to the local Jewish community, one of whose members might be accused of murder. Western and central Europe had also made use of this legend, but in these regions the accusations receded in time, especially among urban segments of the population where secularism had made large inroads. In rural regions the myth continued, encouraged in particular by the Catholic Church, which had trouble ending its long association with the accusation of ritual murder. Local priests still proclaimed its truth at times during the nineteenth and even into the twentieth century, and medieval saints like Simon of Trent, who were worshipped into our own day, kept the legend of martyred children supposedly brutally murdered by the Jews before the eyes of the pious.[2]

[. . .] If the blood libel encouraged Christians to look upon the Jew as harbinger of evil, the legend of the wandering Jew exemplified the curse laid upon that race by Christ himself. The figure of Ahasverus appears in legend as a Jew who sped Christ along to his crucifixion and refused him comfort or shelter. As a result, Ahasverus is doomed to a life of wandering, without a home, despised as rootless and disinherited. The wandering Jew, who can neither live nor die, also heralds terror and desolation.[3] This medieval tale of the "wicked Jew" (as Ahasverus was often called) did not fade in the nineteenth century but instead became symbolic of the cursed fate of the Jewish people. The restless age and the restless Jew both became symbols of a desolate modernity.

Ahasverus in legend is also associated with conspiracies against the righteous. In France, he symbolized the conspiracy of Jews and Masons against the nation. However, at times the wandering Jew could become a hero and the conspiracy be laid on other shoulders. Eugène Sue's The Wandering Jew (Le Juif Errant, 1844–45), the most famous Ahasverus story of the century, turns him into a hero who foils a Jesuit conspiracy. Then again, during the First World War the English satirized Emperor William II as Ahasverus who had driven Christ from his door and was now wandering through Europe in the vain search of peace.[4] Nevertheless, for the most part the ancient legend retained its original form, and remained symbolic of the curse which the Jewish people brought upon themselves and all they touched. These legends, whether the blood libel or that of the wandering Jew, offered explanation and coherence in a world of industrialization, instability, and bewildering social change, just as they had earlier been used as explanation for famines, sickness, and all manner of natural catastrophes.

The legend of the wandering Jew re-enforced the view of the Jew as the eternal foreigner, who would never learn to speak the national language properly or strike roots in the soil. This myth, in turn, was linked to the supposed oriental origin of the Jew as described in the Bible. The Jew was assumed to be fixed for all time as a desert nomad wandering through the Sinai. The Viennese Orientalist Adolf Wahrmund popularized this image in his Law of the Nomads and Contemporary Jewish Domination (Das Gesetz des Nomadenthums und die heutige Judenherrschaft, 1887). The Jews had been nomads in the past, and were still nomads today, claimed Wahrmund. This explained their shiftlessness in commerce, and their rootless, cosmopolitan way of thought, as opposed to the rooted Aryan peasantry. Wahrmund carried on the tradition of proving Aryan peasant origins through linguistics. Both as nomads and Asians, the Jews were indeed Ahasverus, not because of the curse of Christ, but because they were still a desert people.[5] Thus, an anti-Jewish image rooted in religion was secularized and given new credence by means of a pseudo-scientific environmentalism.

Such legends catered to the love of the romantic and the unusual. The nine-teenth century, which popularized Frankenstein and human vampires, was fascinated by horror stories that had a real people as their foil. The novel *Biarritz*, written in 1868 by Hermann Goedsche (under the pen name Sir John Redcliffe), was not only typical of this love of the unusual, but also significant as one of the chief sources of the notorious forged *Protocols of the Elders of Zion*.

The setting of *Biarritz* is the Jewish cemetery of Prague. Significantly, other more famous writers, such as Wilhelm Raabe, used the identical setting to tell stories of Jewish mysteries and secret deeds. The Jewish cemetery in Prague was a romantic site; moreover, it was accessible, for Prague, although part of the Austrian Empire, was considered a German city. It was easy to travel there and to see for oneself the sights of the ghetto, while the other ghettos of eastern Europe were in regions with "obscure" languages and difficult to reach. The tourist from Germany or Austria, for example, would feel at home staying in the large German section of Prague and visiting the picturesque sights. The clash of different cultures, which was exemplified by the ghettos still existing in eastern Europe, could be symbolized through the Jewish cemetery in Prague with its mysterious graves and caftaned figures – at least as seen by the tourist from the West. Goedsche summed up this symbolism when he wrote that Prague was the only German city where Jews still lived in isolation.[6]

In this way, Goedsche set the scene for a meeting of the thirteen Jewish elders in the cemetery. He named them the "cabalistic Sanhedrin," referring to the many legends associated with the Jewish Cabalah and thus giving a wider historical dimension to the assembly at the cemetery. For Goedsche, the mystery of the Cabalah consisted in "the power of gold."[7] Thus through the Cabalah he cemented the traditional association of the Jews with base materialism. One of the elders is Ahasverus, the wandering Jew; his presence among the thirteen clearly shows how Goedsche exploited old anti-Semitic traditions.[8]

The elders meet as the representatives of the chosen people, who show "the tenacity of a snake, the cunning of a fox, the look of a falcon, the memory of a dog, the diligence of an ant, and the sociability of a beaver."[9] The association of Jews with animal imagery should not surprise us; it was noted earlier when discussing the rise of the stereotype in the eighteenth century. The blacks suffered an identical fate when they were constantly compared to monkeys. Likening the so-called inferior races to animals put them low on the chain of being and, by analogy, robbed them of their humanity.

In the eerie setting of the cemetery, the elders conspire to take over the world. They plot to concentrate all capital into their hands; to secure possession of all land, railroads, mines, houses; to occupy government posts; to seize the press and direct all public opinion. This bizarre plan was later to be borrowed from *Biarritz* and, as a "Rabbi's speech," circulated all over the Russian and Austrian Empires.

The myth of the sinister Jewish conspiracy was not confined to eastern Europe. Only a year after *Biarritz* appeared, Gougenot de Mousseaux in a polemic against the Jews of France depicted them as devotees of a secret mystery-religion presided over by the devil himself.[10] Thus, the rapidly growing belief in occult forces during the last decades of the nineteenth century intersected with a revitalized medieval demonology. Indeed, Mousseaux declared that the devil was the King of the Jews, and his version of the Jewish plot would become part of the more famous *Protocols*, just as *Biarritz* also fed into this forgery.

The Protocols of the Elders of Zion became both the climax and the synthesis of these conspiracy theories. They were forged in France in the midst of the Dreyfus Affair, with the assistance of the Russian secret police, probably between 1894 and 1899. The French right wanted a document in order to link Dreyfus to the supposed conspiracy of his race, and the Russian secret police needed it to justify czarist anti-Jewish policy. This time the "learned elders of Zion," again meeting in the Jewish cemetery of Prague, reflected every aspect of the modern world which the reactionaries in France and Russia, but also in the rest of Europe, feared so much.

The weapons that the elders were to use to achieve world domination ranged from the use of the French Revolution's slogan, "Liberty, Equality, Fraternity," to the spreading of liberalism and socialism. The people of the world would be deprived of all faith in God and their strength undermined by encouraging public criticism of authority. At the same time, a financial crisis would be provoked and gold in the hands of the Jews would be manipulated in order to drive up prices. Eventually, "there should be in all states in the world, besides ourselves, only the masses of the proletariat, a few millionaires devoted to our interests and our own police and soldiers."[11] Blind obedience would then be demanded to the King of Jews, the ruler of the universe. In short, the conspiracy myth fed into the uncertainties and fears of the nineteenth century, bridging the gap between ancient anti-Semitic legend and the modern Jews in a world of dramatic change.

What if the Gentiles discovered this plot and began to attack the Jews? In this case the elders would use a truly horrible weapon, for soon all the national capitals of the world would be undermined by a network of underground railways. If there should be danger to the Jews, these tunnels would be used to blow up the cities and kill their inhabitants. Such a nightmare bears traces of the fear of a new technology, but also of the stories of horror and fantasy so popular at the time. Furthermore, the elders would destroy the Gentiles by inoculating them with diseases.

Opposition to inoculation was to become a part of racist thought. In 1935 the *Weltkampf*, a Nazi anti-Jewish journal, stated that inoculation had been invented by the Jews in order to subvert the Aryan blood, citing the *Protocols* as its evidence.[12] Racism is basic to the nightmare of the *Protocols*, for the Jews were considered an evil race, coherent and well organized. The mystery of race had found one of its most popular supposed proofs in the conspiracy of the elders of Zion.

Conspiracy theories might have been less popular and effective had it not been for certain past and present Jewish organizations which to some Gentiles seemed to serve a sinister purpose. In Russia it was charged that the Jewish communal organizations, which had been dissolved by Czar Nicholas I in 1844, were still alive and active as a secret Jewish government linked to foreign interests.[13] An element of spurious reality was lent to these conspiracy charges with the founding of the "Alliance Israélite Universelle" in 1860 by French Jews. The Alliance was intended to aid Jews in nations where they were deprived of civic rights, and to support schools for North African Jews. These worthy purposes were, of course, ignored and the Alliance seen as the exposed tip of an iceberg of conspiracy.

Aside from the reality of the Alliance, anti-Semites and racists pointed to the Masons as another existing secret conspiracy directed by Jews – the *Protocols* had linked Jewish and Masonic conspiracies. The fight against Masons in turn called the Catholic Church into action. The Anti-Masonic World Congress of 1897 was supported by Pope Leo XIII, and was placed under the protection of the Virgin Mary. During the Congress, the Jews were specifically linked to the anti-Catholic Masonic conspiracy, and the Union Antimaçonnique which was founded at that time received support from Drumont and other French racists.[14] An anti-Masonic movement also existed in Germany, and eventually, under the Nazis, an anti-Masonic museum was established, but this particular myth was strongest in Catholic France.

Powerful though the groups might have been that at times supported such theories and pointed to the Alliance or Masons as proof, they were still a minority (except, perhaps, among the Catholic clergy). Such myths and legends about the Jews were used in order to mobilize those who wanted to protect both traditional Christianity and traditional society. But much of the future importance of these anti-Jewish myths consisted in their association with a secular nationalism which lacked the traditional Christian inhibitions against embracing racism. Certainly, as we shall see, the line between Christian anti-Semitism and racism was thin; but the national mystique could without question accept these myths as inherent in the Jewish race. There was no need for secular nationalism to confront the problem of how Jews could be changed into Christians through baptism if their race was inherently evil, nor was it necessary as a part of the drama of Christian salvation to disentangle the Jews of the Old Testament from their inferior racial status. All racists did better to ignore Christianity whenever possible.

In this regard, a journalist like Wilhelm Marr in Germany was typical. His *Jewry's Victory over Teutonism* (*Der Sieg des Judentums über das Germanentum*, 1879) rejected the Christian accusations against the Jews as unworthy of the enlightened, but then repeated all the myths about rootless and conspiratorial Jews. For Marr the Jews were stronger than the Germans, for they were winning the racial battle for survival. He suggested a counteroffensive, spearheaded by anti-Semitic Russia.

The one-time member of the German diet, Hermann Ahlwardt, became more famous than Marr with the publication of his *The Desperate Struggle Between Aryan and Jew* (*Der Verzweiflungskampf der arischen Völker mit dem Judentum*, 1890). Two years later, this primary school principal wrote a book in a similar vein entitled *New Revelations: Jewish Rifles* (*Neue Enthüllungen Judenflinten*, 1892), in which he once more sounded the alarm against the Jewish threat. Here, he contended that the Jewish armament firm of Löwe was selling defective rifles to the German army as part of a universal world Jewish conspiracy to destroy the Reich. And for all the absurdity of the allegation, the government initiated an inquiry into the charges.[15]

As yet, the attempts to act as if the Jewish conspiracy were true remained on the fringes of European thought and, apart from Russia, unsuccessful in immediate terms. They were forerunners of the concerted war against the Jews which began only after the trauma of the First World War, in 1918, and of men like Hitler who not only believed in the *Protocols* but eventually had the means to act as if they were true. The anti-Masonic and anti-Jewish lodge founded by Jules Guérin in Paris during the 1890's was seen as ludicrous.[16] And the first international congress of the tiny rival anti-Semitic groups (mainly from Germany, Austria, and Hungary) meeting in Dresden in 1882 seemed scarcely more important, though it conceived itself as a rallying point against the Jewish world conspiracy. Its purpose was to consolidate the anti-Jewish struggle, but the congress could not overcome tensions between Christian anti-Semites like Adolf Stoecker and the racists, who were prone to violence and who denied that a baptized Jew differed from the rest of his race. The second meeting of this congress in 1883 bore the title "Alliance Antijuive Universelle" and clearly pointed to the Alliance Israélite as symbolic of the enemy.[17]

The legends about the Jews, as part of racial mysticism, penetrated beyond the relatively small groups who were obsessed with the Jewish conspiracy and had little time for other concerns. More important, however, such legends became a mechanism through which rightist movements sought to change society. The imaginary threat posed by the Jews could be used to rally people behind such interest groups as agriculture unions and conservative parties in their battle with liberals and Socialists. But Catholic and Protestant movements could also appeal to traditional legends about the Jews in order to fight atheism more effectively. Above all, those who wanted to reinvigorate the national mystique by emphasizing equality among the people used the Jews as a foil. Here, typically enough, an agitator like Wilhelm Marr, who was a democrat believing in universal suffrage and freedom of thought, accused the Jews of being liberals – a people without roots, who sought to substitute the slavery of finance capital for that of oppression by kings.[18] Such National Socialists, as they were called long before Adolf Hitler usurped the term, will occupy us later. Moreover, racism was firmly allied to nationalism through the mystery of race and even to science through Darwinism. Within these frameworks, the legends about the Jews which we have mentioned were kept alive, now as part of the race war that seemed imminent.

Even "The Universal Races Congress" of 1911, held in London and intended to reflect humanistic and Christian values, assumed that "pure" races could be said to exist, though such opponents of racism as John Dewey, Annie Besant, and the American black leader W. E. B. DuBois attended.[19] This Congress was one more sign of the abiding and deep interest in race.

Were the Jews themselves exempt from the influence of racial thought which seemed so widely spread throughout European society? Did the Jews themselves counter the myth of the Jew as an evil principle with a myth of the Jew as a pure and noble race? Many, indeed most Jews who were highly assimilated in central or western Europe regarded themselves as full members of the nations in which they lived – not as separate people but rather as one of the tribes, like the Saxons, Bavarians, or Alsatians, which made up the larger nation. The First World War enhanced such tendencies, and after 1918 Jewish veterans associated in many

European nations provided the principal support for such attempted national integration. However, those Jews who regarded themselves as a separate people must be our special concern. Did Jewish nationalism follow European nationalism in making an alliance with racism?

The racial ideas of Gobineau had been introduced to the readers of the Zionist *Die Welt* in 1902, not merely to sing the praises of racial purity, but mainly to counter the accusation that Jews were degenerate people. Gobineau had admired the Jews precisely because they had not given in to modern degeneracy, and now his theories could be used to best advantage in order to prove that "Jewry has maintained its . . . toughness, thanks to the purity of its blood." Miscegenation must be avoided at all costs. The Jewish and Aryan races could not interpenetrate, they could only live side by side in mutual understanding.[20] The influences of racism were clearly accepted here, even if the concept of the blood was not defined in terms of "blood and soil," but rather as the vehicle of the drives and peculiarities of the soul. Yet, this annexation of Gobineau (and of Houston Stewart Chamberlain, as we shall see later) proved the exception rather than the rule among Jews. If some Jews were attracted to racism, it was the science of race which seemed to have more appeal to them.

Jews, for example, contributed to the German *Journal for Racial and Social Biology*. But like most of the contributors to that journal, a belief in the reality of race did not mean that any one race was necessarily superior to another. For example, Elias Auerbach, one of the pioneers of Zionist settlement in Palestine, wrote in 1907 that while the Jewish race had been a mixture in the dim past, it was now pure because it had kept itself separate through centuries. He concluded his article with a quote from Gobineau to the effect that a Volk will never die while it can maintain its purity and uniqueness of composition.[21] Yet Auerbach advocated a binational Jewish–Arab Palestine, and opposed any domination of one people by another. It was possible to believe in pure races and still not be a racist; indeed, this was a trait shared by most Jews who believed in a Jewish race, and by many Gentiles as well.

Auerbach did not stand alone in his belief in race. The German writer J. M. Judt in *Jews as Race* (*Die Juden als Rasse*, 1903) was more specific, for he wrote that, as a race, Jews share common physical and physiognomic traits.[22] Even earlier, in 1881, Richard Andree, a German who was not a Jew but the founder of the discipline of ethnography and demography as applied to the Jews, had asserted that they represented a definite racial type kept intact through thousands of years. But for Andree, Jews and Aryans had a common root: both were Caucasians. Both were also the bearers of modern culture, in contrast to blacks who had remained in their primitive state.[23] Andree, like Judt, attempted to base his arguments on anthropology as well as physiognomy.

But it was the Austrian physician, anthropologist, and Zionist Ignaz Zollschan (1877–1948) who became the most famous theoretician of the Jews as a race. His major work, *The Racial Problem with Special Attention to the Theoretical Foundation of the Jewish Race* (*Das Rassenproblem unter Besonderer Berücksichtigung der Theoretischen Grundlagen der Jüdischen Rassenfrage*, 1910), held that race is transmitted by the human cell and thus not subject to outside influence. In this large work Zollschan praised Houston Stewart Chamberlain's racial ideals, such as the nobility that racial purity confers on a group and the necessity of developing the race to ever greater heights of heroism. Zollschan thought that Chamberlain was right about race, but wrong about the Jews. He felt that the evolution of culture could not be due to one race alone (such as the Aryans), but must be created by a series of pure races, including the Jews. The undesirable, materialistic aspect of the contemporary Jewish race would vanish when it found nationhood and escaped the ghetto.[24] Zollschan's ideal, as he restated it in 1914, was for a nation of pure blood, untainted by diseases of excess or immorality, with a highly developed sense of family, and deep-rooted, virtuous habits.[25] The linkage of racial mysticism and middle-class morality could hardly be demonstrated with greater clarity.

Zollschan broke with Zionism after the First World War, believing quite erroneously that the postwar world would see the decline of anti-Semitism and the end of ideas of national sovereignty.[26] At the same time, he also began to reject his earlier belief in races – a process which culminated in his *Racism Against Civilization* (published in London in 1942). By this time, the lengthening shadow of the Nazis in Europe made it difficult for any Jew to uphold ideas of race, even if he had done so earlier.

However, before the Nazis, and especially before the First World War, the debate among Jews as to whether or not Jews were a race had been a lively one, especially in the German *Journal of Jewish Demography and Statistics*. The guiding spirit behind this journal was the social Darwinist Arthur Ruppin. Ruppin was in charge of Jewish settlement in Palestine from 1908 until his death in 1942. Like Auerbach he believed, however ambivalently, in the existence of races. Yet during his many decades in Palestine he was a committed binationalist. At first Ruppin thought race to be an instinct which could not be changed, though typically enough his *Darwinism and Social Science* (*Darwinismus und Sozialwissenschaft*, 1903) advocated eugenics, and not a doctrine of racial superiority. Beauty and strength depended on factors of inheritance, not on environment, and in this connection Ruppin did talk about racial types. When he contemplated *The Jewish Fate and Future* (*Jüdisches Schicksal und die Zukunft*) in 1940, however, he condemned the confusion of "people" with "race," and referred to Virchow's findings among the German schoolchildren which denied the existence of pure races.

Jewish acceptance of the notion of race was ambivalent at best; being the foil of racism did not necessarily mean imitating the enemy. What about those orthodox religious Jews who believed in the reality of the concept of the chosen people? For the majority of such Jews, chosenness meant giving a living example of how life should be lived, and did not entail any claims to domination. Moreover, all peoples could be considered righteous, even Gentiles, provided they observed the seven Noahic laws instead of the 613 commandments binding on pious Jews. Thus belief in monotheism, and obedience to commandments against stealing, murder, false judgment, and adultery, as well as abstinence from eating live limbs of animals, would qualify anyone as chosen. No racism was inherent in this orthodoxy.

To be sure, the Hasidic rabbinical dynasties believed that qualities of leadership were at times transmitted by the blood; but this was not held to consistently, and in any case was no more racist than traditional notions of royal descent. But for all the denial of racism in theory, the borderline to racism was at times as furtively crossed by such orthodox Jews as by believing Christians, who were also supposed to reject it. The true believer in the nineteenth and twentieth centuries always retained some secular elements of superiority and domination within his belief.[27]

Again, Zionism was not in fact racist in its orientation, in spite of the occasional ideas of Zollschan or even Auerbach, both of whom were not really important in the movement. Yet, Theodor Herzl himself once wrote that whether Jews remained in their host nations or emigrated, the race must first be improved wherever it was found. It was necessary to make it work-loving, warrior-like, and virtuous.[28] Herzl often reflected his Viennese environment, whether in his vague and general use of the word "race" or in his condemnation of "kikes" who refused to follow his lead. Nevertheless, he stated that "No nation has uniformity of race."[29]

Much more typical were those influential young Zionists who at the beginning of this century believed in a national mystique without at the same time believing in race. Whenever the Zionist movement attempted to be scientific, they proclaimed in 1913, it got mired in skull measurement and all sorts of "racial nonsense."[30] Judaism, instead, was an inner cultural unity, the revelation of belief in the substance of Jewish nationality. World history, as the young Zionist Robert Weltsch put it in 1913, is not made by zoologists but by ideas. He compared Jewish nationality to Bergson's *élan vital*. The mystery of the Volk was accepted, but the racism which was often part of these mysteries in Gentile society was rejected.[31]

Even during the 1930's, when Max Brod asserted that race was basic to Jewish separateness, he meant this as an exhortation to eugenics; but for Brod, as for Martin Buber, the Jewish Volk became only a stepping stone to human unity and equality reflecting the oneness of God. Jewish nationalism did not embrace racism at a time when other nationalisms in Europe were becoming ever more racist themselves.

Those who did not believe in the existence of any Jewish race – and they were the overwhelming majority among the Jews – referred to the Jewish physician Maurice Fishberg's influential *Racial Characteristics of Jews* (*Die Rassenmerkmale der Juden*, 1913). Fishberg, a famed doctor and anthropologist living in New York, held that Jews have no such characteristics, and attacked Elias Auerbach for believing in a Jewish race. As proof for his contention, Fishberg cited the existence of those blond Jews who could be found all over Europe, tall Jews with long heads, Greek noses, and blue eyes. This "Aryan type among Jews," as he called it, must be the result of miscegenation with the Nordic and the Slavic races.[32] But another, even more influential and non-Jewish voice was raised to contend that Jews were no race or even a separate people. Felix von Luschan, an Austrian professor at the University of Berlin, had already replied to Auerbach that there was no Jewish race, but only a Jewish religious community, and that Zionism seemed opposed to all culture by forcing Jews back into the Orient where barbarism ruled. This highly respected Gentile anthropologist asserted that Jews, like everyone else, were a racial mixture. Indeed, for von Luschan there was only one race, *Homo sapiens*. No inferior races existed, only people with different cultures from our own; and the characteristics which divided men had their origin in climatic, social, and other environmental factors. Men like Chamberlain, he wrote, were not scientists but poets.[33]

Many Zionists who used words like "blood" or "race" actually agreed with von Luschan. Despite the scientific predilections of the nineteenth century, the use of terms like "blood," "race," "people," and "nation" was often imprecise and interchangeable. Blood and race were sometimes shorthand for the transmission of spiritual factors and had nothing to do with appearance or racial purity. The "new man" of whom both racists and Zionists dreamed was opposed to rationalism, but for the Zionists he represented a "humanitarian nationalism" that was both voluntaristic and pluralistic.[34]

Ideas about the mystery of race remained strongest in central Europe, though the legends about Jews found a home in France as well as in the more primitive Balkan regions. Rootless and conspiratorial, the Jew became a myth. As revealed by Ahasverus or by the *Protocols of the Elders of Zion*, he was the adversary, all the more effective in that medieval myths were applied to modern times. The fears and superstitions of a bygone age had sunk deeply into the European consciousness, and could be used to mobilize people against the frustrations of the present. Still, European civilization was, after all, a Christian civilization, in spite of the increasing inroads of secularism. If racism had presented itself as a science and as a national belief, what was to be the attitude of the Christian churches toward race?

Notes and references

1   *The Jews of Czechoslovakia*, The Society for the History of Czechoslovak Jews (Philadelphia – New York, 1968), 152.

2   See, for example, Jeannine Verdes-Leroux, *Scandale Financier et Antisémitique: Le Krach de l'Union Générale* (Paris, 1969), 223.

3   George K. Anderson, *The Legend of the Wandering Jew* (Providence, 1965), 21, 22.

4   *Raemaeker's Cartoons* (n.d., n.p.), Part 3, p. 69.

5   Josef Müller, *Die Entwicklung des Rassenantisemitismus in den Letzten Jahrzehnten des 19. Jahrhunderts* (Berlin, 1940), 25, 67; Müller analyzes the *Antisemitische Correspondenz* from, roughly, 1887 until 1892.

6   Quoted in Herman Bernstein, *The History of a Lie* (New York, 1921), 23.

7   *Ibid.*, 32.

8   *Ibid.*

9   *Ibid.*, 33.

10   Norman Cohn, *Warrant for Genocide* (New York, 1966), 43. I have followed this classic work in my discussion of the *Protocols*.

11   *Protocols of the Learned Elders of Zion* (Union, N.J., n.d.), 25. This is a modern version of the English edition of 1922.

12   *Ibid.*, 33; *Arbeiterzeitung* (Vienna), December 3, 1933 (Wiener Library Clipping Collection, Tel Aviv).

13   H. Lutostanski, *The Talmud and the Jew* (n.p., 1876), *passim*.

14   *Actes du Premier Congrès Antimaçonnique Internationale*, September 24 to 30, 1894, at Trente (Fournay, 1897), 119, 124.

15   Paul W. Massing, *Rehearsal for Destruction* (New York, 1967), 94.

16   The Paris police called it "anti-Jewish confetti," Archives de la Préfecture de Police, Paris, B. a/1341.

17   *Schmeitzner's Internationale Monatsschrift*, II (January 1883), *passim*; *ibid.*, II (May 1883), *passim*. Schmeitzner was the secretary of the congress.

18   Mosche Zimmermann, "Gabriel Riesser und Wilhelm Marr im Meinungsstreit," *Zeitschrift des Vereins für Hamburgische Geschichte*, vol. 61 (1975), 59–84.

19   Michael D. Biddiss, "The Universal Races Congress of 1911," *Race*, XIII (July 1971), 43.

20   Max Jungmann, "Ist das Jüdische Volk degeneriert?", *Die Welt*, 6. Jahrg., Nr. 24 (June 13, 1902).

21   Elias Auerbach, "Die Jüdische Rassenfrage," *Archiv für Rassenund Gesellschafts Biologie*, IV (1907), 333.

22   J. M. Judt, *Die Juden als Rasse: Eine Analyse aus dem Gebiet der Anthropologie* (Berlin, 1903), 213. This was published by the Jewish publishing house, Jüdischer Verlag.

23   Richard Andree, *Zur Volkskunde der Juden* (Bielefeld and Leipzig, 1881), 3, 10, 25.

24   Ignaz Zollschan, *Das Rassenproblem unter Besonderer Berücksichtigung der Theoretischen Grundlagen der Jüdischen Rassenfrage* (Vienna and Leipzig, 1910), 8, 235, 260ff., 427.

25   Ignaz Zollschan, *The Jewish Question* (New York, 1914), 14.

26   Adolf Böhm, *Die Zionistische Bewegung*, II (Tel Aviv, 1937), 84.

27   No study of this problem exists. I am grateful to Miss Deborah Herschmann and Mr. Warren Green for the information upon which this discussion of orthodox Jewry is based. See also the reliance on Noahic law as a code of morals for non-Jews in Germany in Sidney M. Bolkosky, *The Distorted Image: German Jewish Perceptions of Germans and Germany, 1918–1935* (New York, 1975), 80.

28   Theodor Herzl quoted in *Die Welt*, XVIII (July 3, 1914).

29   Amos Elon, *Herzl* (New York, 1975), 171, 251.

30   Moses Calvary in *Die Welt*, XVII (November 7, 1913), 540.

31   Robert Weltsch in *Die Welt*, XVII (March 21, 1913), 366.

32   Maurice Fishberg, *Die Rassenmerkmale der Juden* (Munich, 1913), 49, 51; see also Maurice Fishberg, "Zur Frage der Herkunft des blonden Elementes in Judentum," *Zeitschrift für Demographie und Statistik der Juden* (1907).

33   Felix von Luschan, *Völker, Rassen, Sprachen* (Berlin, 1922), 25, 169.

34   Gustav Krojanker, *Zum Problem des Neuen Deutschen Nationalismus* (Berlin, 1932), 17, 19.

Chapter 17

Theodor W. Adorno and
Max Horkheimer

ELEMENTS OF ANTI-SEMITISM
The limits of Enlightenment

[. . .]

FOR SOME PEOPLE TODAY anti-Semitism involves the destiny of mankind; for others it is a mere pretext. The Fascists do not view the Jews as a minority but as an opposing race, the embodiment of the negative principle. They must be exterminated to secure happiness for the world. At the other extreme we have the theory that the Jews have no national or racial characteristics and simply form a group through their religious opinions and tradition. It is claimed that only the Jews of Eastern Europe have Jewish characteristics, and then only if they have not been fully assimilated. Neither doctrine is wholly true or wholly false.

The first is true to the extent that Fascism has made it true. The Jews today are the group which calls down upon itself, both in theory and in practice, the will to destroy born of a false social order. They are branded as absolute evil by those who are absolutely evil, and are now in fact the chosen race. Whereas there is no longer any need for economic domination, the Jews are marked out as the absolute object of domination pure and simple. No one tells the workers, who are the ultimate target, straight to their face – for very good reasons; and the Negroes are to be kept where they belong: but the Jews must be wiped from the face of the earth, and the call to destroy them like vermin finds an echo in the heart of every budding fascist throughout the world. The portrait of the Jews that the nationalists offer to the world is in fact their own self-portrait. They long for total possession and unlimited power, at any price. They transfer their guilt for this to the Jews, whom as masters they despise and crucify, repeating *ad infinitum* a sacrifice which they cannot believe to be effective.

The other, liberal, theory is true as an idea. It contains the image of a society in which irrational anger no longer exists and seeks for outlets. But since the liberal theory assumes that unity among men is already in principle established, it serves as an apologia for existing circumstances. The attempt to avert the extreme threat by a minorities policy and a democratic strategy is ambiguous, like the defensive stance of the last liberal citizens. Their impotence attracts the enemy of impotence. The existence and way of life of the Jews throw into question the generality with which they do not conform. The inflexible adherence to their own order of life has brought the Jews into an uncertain relationship with the dominant order. They expected to be protected without themselves being in command. Their relationship with the ruling nations was one of greed and fear. But the arrivistes who crossed the gulf separating them from the dominant mode of life lost that cold, stoic character which society still makes a necessity. The dialectical link between enlightenment and domination, and the dual relationship of progress to cruelty and liberation which the Jews sensed in the great philosophers of the Enlightenment and the democratic, national movements are reflected in the very essence of those assimilated. The enlightened self-control with which the assimilated Jews managed to forget the painful memories of domination by others (a second circumcision, so to speak) led them straight from their own, long-suffering community into the modern bourgeoisie, which was moving inexorably toward reversion to cold repression and reorganization as a pure "race." But race is not a naturally special characteristic, as the folk mystics would have it. It is a reduction to the natural, to sheer force, to that stubborn particularity which in the status quo constitutes the generality. Today race has become the self-assertion of the bourgeois individual integrated within a barbaric collective. The harmony of society which the liberal Jews believed in turned against them in the form of the harmony of a national community. They thought that anti-Semitism would distort that order which in reality cannot exist without distorting men. The persecution of the Jews, like any other form of persecution, is inseparable from that system of order. However successfully it may at times be concealed, force is the essential nature of this order – and we are witnessing its naked truth today.

[. . .] Modern society, in which primitive religious feelings and new forms of religion as well as the heritage of revolution are sold on the open market, in which the Fascist leaders bargain over the land and life of nations behind locked doors while the habituated public sit by their radio sets and work out the cost; a society in which the word which it unmasks is thereby legitimized as a component part of a political racket: this society, in which politics is not only a business but business the whole of politics, is gripped by a holy anger over the retarded commercial attitudes of the Jews and classifies them as materialists, and hucksters who must give way to the new race of men who have elevated business into an absolute.

Bourgeois anti-Semitism has a specific economic reason: the concealment of domination in production. In earlier ages the rulers were directly repressive and not only left all the work to the lower classes but declared work to be a disgrace, as it always was under domination; and in a mercantile age, the industrial boss is an absolute monarch. Production attracts its own courtiers. The new rulers simply took off the bright garb of the nobility and donned civilian clothing. They declared that work was not degrading, so as to control the others more rationally. They claimed to be creative workers, but in reality they were still the grasping overlords of former times. The manufacturer took risks and acted like a banker or commercial wizard. He calculated, arranged, bought and sold. On the market he competed for the profit corresponding to his own capital. He seized all he could, not only on the market but at the very source: as a representative of his class he made sure that his workers did not sell him short with their labor. The workers had to supply the maximum amount of goods. Like Shylock, the bosses demand their pound of flesh. They owned the machines and materials, and therefore compelled others to produce for them. They called themselves producers, but secretly everyone knew the truth. The productive work of the capitalist, whether he justifies his profit by means of gross returns as under liberalism, or by his director's salary as today, is an ideology cloaking the real nature of the labor contract and the grasping character of the economic system.

And so people shout: Stop thief! – but point at the Jews. They are the scapegoats not only for individual maneuvers and machinations but in a broader sense, inasmuch as the economic injustice of the whole class is attributed to them. The manufacturer keeps an eye on his debtors, the workers, in the factory and makes sure that they have performed well before he pays them their money. They realize the true position when they stop to think what they can buy with this money. The smallest magnate can dispose of a quantity of services and goods which were available to no ruler in the past; but the workers receive a bare minimum. It is not enough actually to experience how few goods they can buy on the market; the salesmen continue to advertise the merits of things which they cannot afford. The relationship between wage and prices shows what is kept from the workers. With their wages they accept the principle of settlement of all their demands. The merchant presents them with the bill which they have signed away to the manufacturer. The merchant is the bailiff of the whole system and takes the hatred of others upon himself. The responsibility of the circulation sector for exploitation is a socially necessary pretence.

The Jews were not the sole owners of the circulation sector. But they had been active in it for so long that they mirrored in their own ways the hatred they had always borne. Unlike their Aryan colleagues, they were still largely denied access to the origins of surplus value. It was a long time before, with difficulty, they were allowed to own the means of production. Admittedly, in the history of Europe and even under the German emperors, baptized Jews were allowed high positions in industry and in the administration. But they had to justify themselves with twice the usual devotion, diligence, and stubborn self-denial. They were only allowed to retain their positions if by their behavior they tacitly accepted or confirmed the verdict pronounced on other Jews: that was the purpose of baptism. No matter how many great achievements the Jews were responsible for, they could not be absorbed into the European nations; they were not allowed to put down roots and so they were dismissed as rootless. At best the Jews were protected and dependent on emperors, princes or the absolute state. But the rulers themselves all had an economic advantage over the remainder of the population. To the extent that they could use the Jews as intermediaries, they protected them against the masses who had to pay the price of progress. The Jews were the colonizers for progress. From the time when, in their capacity as merchants, they helped to spread Roman civilization throughout Gentile Europe, they were the representatives – in harmony with their patriarchal religion – of municipal, bourgeois and, finally, industrial conditions. They carried capitalist ways of life to various countries and drew upon themselves the hatred of all who had to suffer under capitalism. For the sake of the economic progress which is now proving their downfall, the Jews were always a thorn in the side of the craftsmen and peasants who were declassed by capitalism. They are now experiencing to their own cost the exclusive, particularist character of capitalism. Those who always wanted to be first have been left far behind. Even the Jewish president of an American entertainment trust lives hopelessly on the defensive in his cocoon of cash. The kaftan was a relic of ancient middle-class costume. Today it indicates that its wearer has been cast onto the periphery of a society which, though completely enlightened, still wishes to lay the ghosts of its distant past. Those who proclaimed individualism, abstract justice, and the notion of the person are now degraded to the condition of a species. Those who are never allowed to enjoy freely the civil rights which should allow them human dignity are referred to, without distinction, as "the Jew." Even in the nineteenth century the Jews remained dependent on an alliance with the central power. General justice protected by the state was the pledge of their security, and the law of exception a specter held out before them. The Jews remained objects, at the mercy of others, even when they insisted on their rights. Commerce was not their vocation but their fate. The Jews constituted the trauma of the knights of industry who had to pretend to be creative, while the claptrap of anti-Semitism announced a fact for which they secretly despised themselves; their anti-Semitism is self-hatred, the bad conscience of the parasite.

[. . .] The howling voice of Fascist orators and camp commandants shows the other side of the same social condition. The yell is as cold as business. They both expropriate the sounds of natural complaint and make them elements of their technique. Their bellow has the same significance for the pogrom as the noise generator in the German flying bomb: the terrible cry which announces terror is simply turned on. The cry of pain of the victim who first called violence by its name, the mere word to designate the victim (Frenchman, Negro, or Jew), generates despair in the persecuted who must react violently. The victims are the false counterparts of the dread mimesis. They reproduce the insatiability of the power which they fear. Everything must be used and all must obey. The mere existence of the other is a provocation. Every "other" person who "doesn't know his place" must be forced back within his proper confines – those of unrestricted terror. Anyone who seeks refuge must be prevented from finding it; those who express ideas which all long for, peace, a home, freedom – the nomads and players – have always been refused a homeland. Whatever a man fears, that he suffers. Even the last resting place is emptied of peace. The destruction of cemeteries is not a mere excess of anti-Semitism – it is anti-Semitism in its essence. The outlawed naturally arouse the desire to outlaw others. Violence is even inflamed by the marks which violence has left on them. Anything which just wants to vegetate must be rooted out. In the chaotic net regulated escape reactions of the lower animals, in the convolutions of the sudden swarm, and the convulsive gestures of the martyred, we see the mimetic impulse which can never be completely destroyed. In the death struggle of the creature, at the opposite pole from freedom, freedom still shines out irresistibly as the thwarted destiny of matter. It is opposed by the idiosyncracy which claims anti-Semitism as its motive.

The mental energy harnessed by political anti-Semitism is this rationalized idosyncracy. All the pretexts over which the Führer and his followers reach agreement, imply surrender to the mimetic attraction without any open infringement of the reality principle – honorably, so to speak. They cannot stand the Jews, yet imitate them.

There is no anti-Semite who does not basically want to imitate his mental image of a Jew, which is composed of mimetic cyphers: the argumentative movement of a hand, the musical voice painting a vivid picture of things and feelings irrespective of the real content of what is said, and the nose – the physiognomic *principium individuationis*, symbol of the specific character of an individual, described between the lines of his countenance. The multifarious nuances of the sense of smell embody the archetypal longing for the lower forms of existence, for direct unification with circumambient nature, with the earth and mud. Of all the senses, that of smell – which is attracted without objectifying – bears clearest witness to the urge to lose oneself in and become the "other." As perception and the perceived – both are united – smell is more expressive than the other senses. When we see we remain what we are; but when we smell we are taken over by otherness. Hence the sense of smell is considered a disgrace in civilization, the sign of lower social strata, lesser races and base animals. The civilized individual may only indulge in such pleasure if the prohibition is suspended by rationalization in the service of real or apparent practical ends. The prohibited impulse may be tolerated if there is no doubt that the final aim is its elimination – this is the case with jokes or fun, the miserable parody of fulfillment. As a despised and despising characteristic, the mimetic function is enjoyed craftily. Anyone who seeks out "bad" smells, in order to destroy them, may imitate sniffing to his heart's content, taking unrationalized pleasure in the experience. The civilized man "disinfects" the forbidden impulse by his unconditional identification with the authority which has prohibited it; in this way the action is made acceptable. If he goes beyond the permitted bounds, laughter ensues. This is the schema of the anti-Semitic reaction. Anti-Semites gather together to celebrate the moment when authority permits what is usually forbidden, and become a collective only in that common purpose. There rantings are organized laughter. The more terrible their accusations and threats and the greater their anger, the more compelling their scorn. Anger, scorn, and embittered imitation are actually the same thing. The purpose of the Fascist formula, the ritual discipline, the uniforms, and the whole apparatus, which is at first sight irrational, is to allow mimetic behavior. The carefully thought out symbols (which are proper to every counterrevolutionary movement), the skulls and disguises, the barbaric drum beats, the monotonous repetition of words and gestures, are simply the organized imitation of magic practices, the mimesis of mimesis. The leader with his contorted face and the charisma of approaching hysteria take command. The leader acts as a representative; he portrays what is forbidden to everyone else in actual life. Hitler can gesticulate like a clown, Mussolini strike false notes like a provincial tenor, Goebbels talk endlessly like a Jewish agent whom he wants murdered, and Coughlin preach love like the savior whose crucifixion he portrays – all for the sake of still more bloodshed. Fascism is also totalitarian in that it seeks to make the rebellion of suppressed nature against domination directly useful to domination.

This machinery needs the Jews. Their artificially heightened prominence acts on the legitimate son of the gentile civilization like a magnetic field. The gentile sees equality, humanity, in his difference from the Jew, but this induces a feeling of antagonism and alien being. And so impulses which are normally taboo and conflict with the requirements of the prevailing form of labor are transformed into conforming idiosyncracies. The economic position of the Jews, the last defrauded frauds of liberalistic ideology, affords them no secure protection. Since they are so eminently fitted to generate these mental induction currents, they serve such functions involuntarily. They share the fate of the rebellious nature as which Fascism uses them: they are employed blindly yet perspicaciously. It matters little whether the Jews as individuals really do still have those mimetic features which awaken the dread malady, or whether such features are suppressed. Once the wielders of economic power have overcome their fear of the Fascist administrators, the Jews automatically stand out as the disturbing factor in the harmony of the national society. They are abandoned by domination when its progressive alienation from nature makes it revert to mere nature. The Jews as a whole are accused of participating in forbidden magic and bloody ritual. Disguised as accusation, the subconscious desire of the aboriginal inhabitants to return to the mimetic practice of sacrifice finds conscious fulfillment. When all the horror of prehistory which has been overlaid with civilization is rehabilitated as rational interest by projection onto the Jews, there is no restriction. The horror can be carried out in practice, and its practical implementation goes beyond the evil content of the projection. The fantasies of Jewish crimes, infanticide and sadistic excess, poisoning of the nation, and international conspiracy, accurately define the anti-Semitic dream, but remain far behind its actualization. Once things have reached this stage, the mere word "Jew" appears as the bloody grimace reflected in the swastika flag with its combination of death's head and shattered cross. The mere fact that a person is called a Jew is an invitation forcibly to make him over into a physical semblance of that image of death and distortion. [. . .]

Chapter 18

Zygmunt Bauman

MODERNITY, RACISM, EXTERMINATION

[. . .]

THERE IS AN APPARENT PARADOX in the history of racism, and Nazi racism in particular.

In the by far most spectacular and the best known case in this history, racism was instrumental in the mobilization of anti-modernist sentiments and anxieties, and was apparently effective primarily because of this connection. Adolf Stöcker, Dietrich Eckart, Alfred Rosenberg, Gregor Strasser, Joseph Goebbels, and virtually any other prophet, theorist and ideologue of National Socialism used the phantom of the Jewish race as a lynch-pin binding the fears of the past and prospective victims of modernization, which they articulated, and the ideal *volkisch* society of the future which they proposed to create in order to forestall further advances of modernity. In their appeals to the deep-seated horror of the social upheaval that modernity augured, they identified modernity as the rule of economic and monetary values, and charged Jewish racial characteristics with responsibility for such a relentless assault on the *volkisch* mode of life and standards of human worth. Elimination of the Jews was hence presented as a synonym of the rejection of modern order. This fact suggests an essentially pre-modern character of racism; its natural affinity, so to speak, with anti-modern emotions and its selective fitness as a vehicle for such emotions.

On the other hand, however, as a conception of the world, and even more importantly as an effective instrument of political practice, racism is unthinkable without the advancement of modern science, modern technology and modern forms of state power. As such, racism is strictly a modern product. Modernity made racism possible. It also created a demand for racism; an era that declared achievement to be the only measure of human worth needed a theory of ascription to redeem boundary-drawing and boundary-guarding concerns under new conditions which made boundary-crossing easier than ever before. Racism, in short, is a thoroughly modern weapon used in the conduct of pre-modern, or at least not exclusively modern, struggles.

From heterophobia to racism

Most commonly (though wrongly), racism is understood as a variety of inter-group resentment or prejudice. Sometimes racism is set apart from other sentiments or beliefs of the wider class by its emotional intensity; at other times, it is set apart by reference to hereditary, biological and extra-cultural attributes which, unlike the non-racist variants of group animosity, it normally contains. In some cases writers about racism point out the scientific pretensions that other, non-racist yet similarly negative stereotypes of foreign groups, do not usually possess. Whatever the feature chosen, however, the habit of analysing and interpreting racism in the framework of a larger category of prejudice is seldom breached.

As racism gains in saliency among contemporary forms of intergroup resentment, and alone among them manifests a pronounced affinity with the scientific spirit of the age, a reverse interpretive tendency becomes ever more prominent; a tendency to extend the notion of racism so as to embrace all varieties of resentment. All kinds of group prejudice are then interpreted as so many expressions of innate, natural racist predispositions. One can probably afford not to be too excited by such an exchange of places and view it, philosophically, as just a question of the definitions, which can, after all, be chosen or rejected at will. On a closer scrutiny, however, complacency appears ill-advised. Indeed, if all inter-group dislike and animosity are forms of racism, and if the tendency to keep strangers at a distance and resent their proximity has been amply documented by historical and ethnological research as a well-nigh universal and perpetual attribute of human groupings, then there is nothing essentially and radically novel about the racism that has acquired such a prominence in our time; just a rehearsal of the old scenario, though admittedly staged with somewhat updated dialogues. In particular, the intimate link of racism with other aspects of modern life is either denied outright or left out of focus.

In his recent impressively erudite study of prejudice,[1] Pierre-André Taguieff writes synonimically of racism and heterophobia (resentment of the different). Both appear, he avers, 'on three levels', or in three forms distinguished by the rising level of sophistication. The 'primary racism' is in his view universal. It is a natural reaction to the presence of an unknown stranger, to any form of human life that is foreign and puzzling. Invariably, the first response to strangeness is antipathy, which more often than not leads to aggressiveness. Universality goes hand-in-hand with spontaneity. The primary racism needs no inspiring or fomenting; nor does it need a theory to legitimize the elemental hatred – though it can be, on occasion, deliberately beefed up and deployed as an instrument of political mobilization.[2] At such a time it can be lifted to another level of complexity and turn into a 'secondary' or (rationalized) racism. This transformation happens when a theory is supplied (and internalized) that provides logical foundations for resentment. The repelling Other is represented as ill-willed or 'objectively' harmful – in either case threatening to the well-being of the resenting group. For instance, the resented category can be depicted as conspiring with the forces of evil in the form construed by the resenting group's religion, or it can be portrayed as an unscrupulous economic rival; the choice of the semantic field in which 'harmfulness' of the resented Other is theorized is presumably dictated by the current focus of social relevance, conflicts and divisions. Xenophobia, or more particularly ethnocentrism (both coming into their own in the age of rampant nationalism, when one of the most closely defended lines of division is argued in terms of shared history, tradition and culture), is a most common contemporary case of 'secondary racism'. Finally, the 'tertiary', or mystifactory, racism, which presupposes the two 'lower' levels, is distinguished by the deployment of a quasi-biological argument.

In the form in which it has been constructed and interpreted by Taguieff, the tri-partite classification seems logically flawed; if the secondary racism is already characterized by the theorizing of primary resentment, there seems to be no good reason for setting aside just one of the many possible ideologies that can (and are) used for this purpose as a distinctive feature of a 'higher-level' racism. The third-level racism looks much like a unit in the second-level set. Perhaps Taguieff could defend his classification against this charge were he, instead of separating biological theories because of the supposedly 'mystifactory' nature (one can argue without end about the degree of mystification in all the rest of the second-level racist theories), pointing to the tendency of biological argument to emphasize the irreversibility and incurability of the damaging 'otherness' of the Other. One could indeed point out that – in our age of artificiality of the social order, of the putative omnipotence of education and, more generally, of social engineering – biology in general, and heredity in particular, stand in public consciousness for the area still off-limits for cultural manipulation; something we do not know yet how to tinker with and to mould and reshape according to our will. Taguieff, however, insists that the modern biological–scientific form of racism does not appear 'different in nature, operation and function, from traditional discourses of disqualifying exclusion',[3] and focuses instead on the degree of 'deliric paranoia' or extreme 'speculativess' as on distinctive features of the 'tertiary racism'.

I suggest, on the contrary, that *it is precisely the nature, function and the mode of operation of racism that sharply differ from heterophobia* – that diffuse (and sentimental rather than practical) unease, discomfort, or anxiety that people normally experience whenever they are confronted with such 'human ingredients' of their situation as they do not fully understand, cannot communicate with easily and cannot expect to behave in a routine, familiar way. Heterophobia seems to be a focused manifestation of a still wider phenomenon of anxiety aroused by the feeling that one has no control over the situation, and that thus one can neither influence its development, nor foresee the consequences of one's action. Heterophobia may appear as either a realistic or an irrealistic objectification of such anxiety – but it is likely that the anxiety in question always seeks an object on which to anchor, and that consequently heterophobia is a fairly common phenomenon at all times and more common still in an age of modernity, when occasions for the 'no control' experience become more frequent, and their interpretation in terms of the obtrusive interference by an alien human group becomes more plausible.

I suggest as well that, so described, *heterophobia ought to be analytically distinguished from contestant enmity*, a more specific antagonism generated by the human practices of identity-seeking and boundary-drawing. In the latter case, sentiments of antipathy and resentment seem more like emotional appendages to the activity of separation; separation itself demands an activity, an effort, a sustained action. The alien of the first case, however, is not merely a too-close-for-comfort, yet clearly separate category of people easy to spot and keep at a required distance, but a collection of people whose 'collectiveness' is not obvious or generally recognized; its collectiveness may be even contested and is often concealed or denied by the members of the alien category. The alien in this case threatens to penetrate the native group and fuse with it – if preventive measures are not set out and vigilantly observed. The alien, therefore, threatens the unity and the identity of the alien group, not so much by confounding its control over a territory or its freedom to act in the familiar way, but by blurring the boundary of the territory itself and effacing the difference between the familiar (right) and the alien (wrong) way of life. This is the 'enemy in our midst' case – one that triggers a vehement boundary-drawing bustle, which in its turn generates a thick fall-out of antagonism and hatred to those found or suspected guilty of double loyalty and sitting astride the barricade.

Racism differs from both heterophobia and contestant enmity. The difference lies neither in the intensity of sentiments nor in the type of argument used to rationalize it. *Racism stands apart by a practice of which it is a part and which it rationalizes: a practice that combines strategies of architecture and gardening with that of medicine – in the service of the construction of an artificial social order, through cutting out the elements of the present reality that neither fit the visualized perfect reality, nor can be changed so that they do.* In a world that boasts the unprecedented ability to improve human conditions by reorganizing human affairs on a rational basis, racism manifests the conviction that a certain category of human beings cannot be incorporated into the rational order, whatever the effort. In a world notable for the continuous rolling back of the limits to scientific, technological and cultural manipulation, racism proclaims that certain blemishes of a certain category of people cannot be removed or rectified – that they remain beyond the boundaries of reforming practices, and will do so for ever. In a world proclaiming the formidable capacity of training and cultural conversion, racism sets apart a certain category of people that cannot be reached (and thus cannot be effectively cultivated) by argument or any other training tools, and hence must remain perpetually alien. To summarize: in the modern world distinguished by its ambition to self-control and self-administration racism declares a certain category of people endemically and hopelessly resistant to control and immune to all efforts at amelioration. To use the medical metaphor; one can train and shape 'healthy' parts of the body, but not cancerous growth. The latter can be 'improved' only by being destroyed.

The consequence is that *racism is inevitably associated with the strategy of estrangement.* If conditions allow, racism demands that the offending category ought to be removed beyond the territory occupied by the group it offends. If such conditions are absent, racism requires that the offending category is physically exterminated. Expulsion and destruction are two mutually exchangeable methods of estrangement.

Of the Jews, Alfred Rosenberg wrote: 'Zunz calls Judaism the whim of [the Jewish] soul. Now the Jew cannot break loose from this "whim" even if he is baptized ten times over, and the necessary result of this influence will always be the same: lifelessness, anti-Christianity and materialism.'[4] What is true about religious influence applies to all the other cultural interventions. Jews are beyond repair. Only a physical distance, or a break of communication, or fencing them off, or annihilation, may render them harmless.

Racism as a form of social engineering

Racism comes into its own only in the context of a design of the perfect society and intention to implement the design through planned and consistent effort. In the case of the Holocaust, the design was the thousand-year *Reich* – the kingdom of the liberated German Spirit. It was that kingdom which had no room for anything but the German Spirit. It had no room for the Jews, as the Jews could not be spiritually converted and embrace the *Geist* of the German *Volk*. This spiritual inability was articulated as the attribute of heredity or blood – substances which at that time at least embodied the other side of culture, the territory that culture could not dream of cultivating, a wilderness that would be never turned into the object of gardening. (The prospects of genetic engineering were not as yet seriously entertained.)

The Nazi revolution was an exercise in social engineering on a grandiose scale. 'Racial stock' was the key link in the chain of engineering measures. In the collection of official plaidoyers of Nazi policy, published in English on Ribbentrop's initiative for the purposes of international propaganda and for this reason expressed in a carefully tempered and cautious language, Dr Arthur Gütt, the Head of the National Hygiene Department in the Ministry of Interior, described as the major task of the Nazi rule 'an active policy consistently aiming at the preservation of racial health', and explained the strategy such policy had necessarily to involve: 'If we facilitate the propagation of healthy stock by systematic selection and by elimination of the unhealthy elements, we shall be able to improve the physical standards not, perhaps, of the present generation, but of those who will succeed us.' Gütt had no doubt that the selection-cum-elimination such a policy envisaged 'go along the lines universally adopted in conformity with the researches of Koch, Lister, Pasteur, and other celebrated scientists'[5] and thus constituted a logical extension – indeed, a culmination – of the advancement of modern science.

Dr Walter Gross, the Head of the Bureau for Enlightenment on Population Policy and Racial Welfare, spelled out the practicalities of the racial policy: reversing the current trend of 'declining birth-rate among the fitter inhabitants and unrestrained propagation among the hereditary unfit, the mentally deficient, imbeciles and hereditary criminals, etc.'[6] As he writes for an international audience unlikely to applaud the determination of the Nazis, unencumbered as they were by things so irrational as public opinion or political pluralism, to see the accomplishment of modern science and technology to their logical end, Gross does not venture beyond the necessity to sterilize the hereditary unfit.

The reality of racial policy was, however, much more gruesome. Contrary to Gütt's suggestion, the Nazi leaders saw no reason to restrict their concerns to 'those who will succeed us'. As the resources allowed, they set about to improve the *present* generation. The royal road to this goal led through the forceful removal of *unwertes Leben*. Every vehicle would do to secure progress along this road. Depending on circumstances, references were made to 'elimination', 'ridding', 'evacuation', or 'reduction' (read 'extermination'). Following Hitler's command of 1 September 1939, centres had been created in Brandenburg, Hadamar, Sonnenstein and Eichberg, which hid under a double lie: they called themselves, in hushed conversations between the initiated, 'euthanasia institutes', while for the wider consumption they used still more deceitful and misleading names of a Charitable Foundation for 'Institutional Care' or the 'the Transport of the Sick' – or even the bland 'T4' code (from 4 Tiergartenstrasse, Berlin, where the co-ordinating office of the whole killing operation was located).[7] When the command had to be rescinded on 28 August 1941 as the result of an outcry raised by a number of prominent luminaries of the Church, the principle of 'actively managing the population trends' was in no way abandoned. Its focus, together with the gassing technologies that the euthanasia campaign had helped to develop, was merely shifted to a different target: the Jews. And to different places, like Sobibór or Chelmno.

Unwertes Leben remained the target all along. For the Nazi designers of the perfect society, the project they pursued and were determined to implement through social engineering split human life into worthy and unworthy; the first to be lovingly cultivated and given *Lebensraum*, the other to be 'distanced', or – if the distancing proved unfeasible – exterminated. Those simply alien were not the objects of strictly racial policy: to them, old and tested strategies traditionally associated with contestant enmity could be applied: the aliens ought to be kept beyond closely guarded borders. Those bodily and mentally handicapped made a more difficult case and called for a new, original policy: they could not be evicted or fenced off as they did not rightfully belong to any of the 'other races', but they were unworthy to enter the thousand-year *Reich* either. The Jews offered an essentially similar case. They were not a race like the others; they were an anti-race, a race to undermine and poison all other races, to sap not just the identity of any race in particular, but the racial order itself. (Remember the Jews as the 'non-national nation', the incurable enemy of the nation-based order as such.) With approval and relish, Rosenberg quoted Weiniger's self-deprecatory verdict on the Jews as 'an invisible cohesive web of slime fungus (plasmodium), existing since time immemorial and spread over the entire earth'.[8] Thus the separation of the Jews could only be a half-measure, a station on the road to the ultimate goal. The matter could not possibly end with the cleansing of Germany of the Jews. Even residing far from the German borders, the Jews would continue to erode and disintegrate the natural logic of the universe. Having ordered his troops to fight for the supremacy of the *German* race, Hitler believed that the war he kindled was waged in the name of *all races*, a service rendered to racially organized humankind.

In this conception of social engineering as a scientifically founded work aimed at the institution of a new, and better, order (a work which necessarily entails the containment, or preferably elimination, of any disruptive factors), racism was indeed resonant with the world-view and practice of modernity. And this, at least, in two vital respects.

First, with the Enlightenment came the enthronement of the new deity, that of Nature, together with the legitimation of science as its only orthodox cult, and of scientists as its prophets and priests. Everything, in principle, had been opened to objective inquiry; everything could, in principle, be known – reliably and truly.

Truth, goodness and beauty, that which is and that which ought to be, had all become legitimate objects of systematic, precise observation. In turn, they could legitimize themselves only through objective knowledge which would result from such observation. In George L. Mosse's summary of his most convincingly documented history of racism, 'it is impossible to separate the inquiries of the Enlightenment philosophies into nature from their examination of morality and human character . . . [From] the outset . . . natural science and the moral and aesthetic ideals of the ancient joined hands.' In the form in which it was moulded by the Enlightenment, scientific activity was marked by an 'attempt to determine man's exact place in nature through observation, measurements, and comparisons between groups of men and animals' and 'belief in the unity of body and mind'. The latter 'was supposed to express itself in a tangible, physical way, which could be measured and observed'.[9] Phrenology (the art of reading the character from the measurements of the skull) and physiognomy (the art of reading the character from facial features) captured most fully the confidence, strategy and ambition of the new scientific age. Human temperament, character, intelligence, aesthetic talents, even political inclinations, were seen as determined by Nature; in what way exactly, one could find out through diligent observation and comparison of the visible, material 'substratum' of even the most elusive or concealed spiritual attributes. Material sources of sensual impressions were so many clues to Nature's secrets; signs to be read, records written down in a code which science must crack.

What was left to racism was merely to postulate a systematic, and genetically reproduced distribution of such material attributes of human organism as bore responsibility for characterological, moral, aesthetic or political traits. Even this job, however, had already been done for them by respectable and justly respected pioneers of science, seldom if ever listed among the luminaries of racism. Observing *sine ira et studio* the reality as they found it, they could hardly miss the tangible, material, indubitably 'objective' superiority that the West enjoyed over the rest of the inhabited world. Thus the father of scientific taxonomy, Linnaeus, recorded the division between the residents of Europe and inhabitants of Africa with the same scrupulous precision as that which he applied while describing the difference between crustacea and fishes. He could not, and he did not, describe the white race otherwise than 'as inventive, full of ingenuity, orderly, and governed by laws . . . By contrast the Negroes were endowed with all the negative qualities which made them a counterfoil for the superior race: they were regarded as lazy, devious, and unable to govern themselves.'[10] The father of 'scientific racism', Gobineau, did not have to exercise much inventiveness to describe the black race as of little intelligence, yet of overdeveloped sensuality and hence a crude, terrifying power (just as the mob on the loose), and the white race as in love with freedom, honour and everything spiritual.[11]

In 1938, Walter Frank described the persecution of Jews as the saga of 'German scholarship in a struggle against World Jewry'. From the very first day of the Nazi rule, scientific institutes, run by distinguished university professors of biology, history and political science, had been set up to investigate 'the Jewish question' according to the 'international standards of advanced science'. Reichinstitut für Geschichte des neuen Deutschlands, Institut zum Studium der Judenfrage, Institut zur Erforschung des jüdischen Einflusses auf das deutsche kirchliche Leben, and the notorious Rosenberg's Institut zur Enforschung der Judenfrage were just a few of the many scientific centres that tackled theoretical and practical issues of 'Jewish policy' as an application of scholarly methodology, and never were they short of qualified staff with academically certified credentials. According to a typical rationale of their activity, the

> whole cultural life for decades has been more or less under the influence of biological thinking, as it was begun particularly around the middle of the last century, by the teachings of Darwin, Mendel and Galton and afterwards has been advanced by the studies of Plötz, Schallmayer, Correns, de Vries, Tschermak, Baur, Rüdin, Fischer, Lenz and others . . . It was recognized that the natural laws discovered for plants and animals ought also be valid for man.[12]

Second – from the Enlightenment on, the modern world was distinguished by its activist, engineering attitude toward nature and toward itself. Science was not to be conducted for its own sake; it was seen as, first and foremost, an instrument of awesome power allowing its holder to improve on reality, to re-shape it according to human plans and designs, and to assist it in its drive to self-perfection. Gardening and medicine supplied the archetypes of constructive stance, while normality, health, or sanitation offered the archmetaphors for human tasks and strategies in the management of human affairs. Human existence and cohabitation became objects of planning and administration; like garden vegetation or a living organism they could not be left to their own devices, lest should they be infested by weeds or overwhelmed by cancerous tissues. Gardening and medicine are functionally distinct forms of the same activity of *separating and setting apart useful elements destined to live and thrive, from harmful and morbid ones, which ought to be exterminated*. [. . .]

From repellence to extermination

'Christian theology never advocated extermination of the Jews', writes George L. Mosse, 'but rather their exclusion from society as living witnesses to deicide. The pogroms were secondary to isolating Jews in ghettos.'[13] 'A crime', Hannah Arendt asserts, 'is met with punishment; a vice can only be exterminated.'[14]

Only in its modern, 'scientific', racist form, the age-long repellence of the Jews has been articulated as an exercise in sanitation; only with the modern re-incarnation of Jew-hatred have the Jews been charged with an ineradicable vice, with an immanent flaw which cannot be separated from its carriers. Before that, the Jews were sinners; like all sinners, they were bound to suffer for their sins, in an earthly or other-worldly purgatory – to repent and, possibly, to earn redemption. Their suffering was to be seen so that the consequences of sin and the need for repentance are seen. No such benefit can possibly be derived from watching vice, even if complete with its punishment. (If in doubt, consult Mary Whitehouse.) Cancer, vermin or weed cannot repent. They have not sinned, they just lived according to their nature. There is nothing to punish them for. By the nature of their evil, they have to be exterminated. Alone with himself, in his diary,

Joseph Goebbels spelled this out with the same clarity we previously noted in the abstract historiosophy of Rosenberg: 'There is no hope of leading the Jews back into the fold of civilized humanity by exceptional punishments. They will forever remain Jews, just as we are forever members of the Aryan race.'[15] Unlike the 'philosopher' Rosenberg, Goebbels was, however, a minister in a government wielding an awesome and unchallenged power; a government, moreover, which – thanks to the achievements of modern civilization – could conceive of the possibility of life without cancer, vermin or weeds, and had at its disposal material resources to make such a possibility into a reality.

It is difficult, perhaps impossible, to arrive at the idea of extermination of a whole people without race imagery; that is, without a vision of endemic and fatal defect which is in principle incurable and, in addition, is capable of self-propagation unless checked. It is also difficult, and probably impossible, to arrive at such an idea without the entrenched practice of medicine (both of medicine proper, aimed at the individual human body, and of its numerous allegorical applications), with its model of health and normality, strategy of separation and technique of surgery. It is particularly difficult, and well-nigh impossible, to conceive of such an idea separately from the engineering approach to society, the belief in artificiality of social order, institution of expertise and the practice of scientific management of human setting and interaction. For these reasons, *the exterminatory version of anti-Semitism ought to be seen as a thoroughly modern phenomenon*; that is, something which could occur only in an advanced state of modernity.

These were not, however, the only links between exterminatory designs and the developments rightly associated with modern civilization. Racism, even when coupled with the technological predisposition of the modern mind, would hardly suffice to accomplish the feat of the Holocaust. To do that, it would have had to be capable of securing the passage from theory to practice – and this would probably mean energizing, by sheer mobilizing power of ideas, enough human agents to cope with the scale of the task, and sustaining their dedication to the job for as long as the task would require. By ideological training, propaganda or brainwashing, racism would have to imbue masses of non-Jews with the hatred and repugnance of Jews so intense as to trigger a violent action against the Jews whenever and wherever they are met.

According to the widely shared opinion of the historians, this did not happen. In spite of the enormous resources devoted by the Nazi regime to racist propaganda, the concentrated effort of Nazi education, and the real threat of terror against resistance to racist practices, the popular acceptance of the racist programme (and particularly of its ultimate logical consequences) stopped well short of the level an emotion-led extermination would require. As if further proof was needed, this fact demonstrates once again *the absence of continuity or natural progression between heterophobia or contestant enmity and racism*. Those Nazi leaders who hoped to capitalize on the diffuse resentment of the Jews to obtain popular support for the racist policy of extermination were soon forced to realize their mistake.

Yet even if (an unlikely case, indeed) the racist creed was more successful, and volunteers for lynching and throat-cutting were many times more numerous, mob violence should strike us as a remarkably inefficient, blatantly pre-modern form of social engineering or of the thoroughly modern project of racial hygiene.

Indeed, as Sabini and Silver have convincingly put it, the most successful – widespread and materially effective – episode of mass anti-Jewish violence in Germany, the infamous *Kristallnacht*, was

> a pogrom, an instrument of terror . . . typical of the long-standing tradition of European anti-Semitism not the new Nazi order, not the systematic extermination of European Jewry. Mob violence is a primitive, ineffective technique of extermination. It is an effective method of territorizing a population, keeping people in their place, perhaps even of forcing some to abandon their religious or political convictions, but these were never Hitler's aims with regard to the Jews: he meant to destroy them.[16]

There was not enough 'mob' to be violent; the sight of murder and destruction put off as many as it inspired, while the overwhelming majority preferred to close their eyes and plug their ears, but first of all to gag their mouths. Mass destruction was accompanied not by the uproar of emotions, but the dead silence of unconcern. It was not public rejoicing, but public indifference which 'became a reinforcing strand in the noose inexorably tightening around hundreds of thousands of necks.'[17] *Racism is a policy first, ideology second. Like all politics, it needs organization, managers and experts.* Like all policies, it requires for its implementation a division of labour and an effective isolation of the task from the disorganizing effect of improvization and spontaneity. It demands that the specialists are left undisturbed and free to proceed with their task.

Not that indifference itself was indifferent; it surely was not, as far as the success of the Final Solution was concerned. It was the paralysis of that public which failed to turn into a mob, a paralysis achieved by the fascination and fear emanating from the display of power, which permitted the deadly logic of problem-solving to take its course unhampered. In Lawrence Stoke's words, 'The failure when the regime first set insecurely in power to protest its inhumane measures made prevention of their logical culmination all but impossible, however unwanted and disapproved this undoubtedly was.'[18] The spread and the depth of heterophobia was apparently sufficient for the German public not to protest against violence, even if the majority did not like it and remained immune to racist indoctrination. Of the latter fact the Nazis found numerous occasions to convince themselves. In her impeccably balanced account of German attitudes Sarah Gordon quotes an official Nazi report which vividly expressed Nazi disappointment with public responses to the *Kristallnacht*:

> One knows that anti-Semitism in Germany today is essentially confined to the party and its organizations, and that there is a certain group in the population who have not the slightest understanding for anti-Semitism and in whom every possibility of empathy is lacking.
>
> In the days after *Kristallnacht* these people ran immediately to Jewish businesses . . .
>
> This is to a great extent because we are, to be sure, an anti-Semitic people, an anti-Semitic state, but nevertheless in all manifestations of

life in the state and people anti-Semitism is as good as unexpressed . . .
There are still groups of *Spiessern* among the German people who talk
about the poor Jews and who have no understanding for the anti-Semitic
attitudes of the German people and who interceded for Jews at every
opportunity. It should not be that only the leadership and party are
anti-Semitic.[19]

Dislike of violence – particularly of such violence as could be seen and was
meant to be seen – coincided, however, with a much more sympathetic attitude
towards administrative measures taken against Jews. A great number of Germans
welcomed an energetic and vociferously advertised action aimed at the segregation,
separation, and disempowering of the Jews – those traditional expressions and
instruments of heterophobia or contestant enmity. In addition, many Germans
welcomed the measures portrayed as the punishment of the Jew (as long as one
could pretend that the punished was indeed the conceptual Jew) as an imaginary
(yet plausible) solution to quite real (if subconscious) anxieties and fears of
displacement and insecurity. Whatever the reasons of their satisfaction, they seemed
to be radically different from those implied by the Streicher-style exhortations to
violence as an all-too-realistic way of repaying imaginary economic or sexual crimes.
From the point of view of those who designed and commanded the mass murder
of the Jews, Jews were to die not because they were resented (or at least not
primarily for this reason); *they were seen as deserving death (and resented for that reason)*
because they stood between this one imperfect and tension-ridden reality and the hoped-for
world of tranquil happiness. [. . .] the disappearance of the Jews was instrumental in
bringing about the world of perfection. The absence of Jews was precisely the
difference between that world and the imperfect world here and now.

Examining neutral and critical sources in addition to official reports, Gordon
has documented a widespread and growing approval of 'ordinary Germans' for the
exclusion of Jews from positions of power, wealth and influence.[20] The gradual
disappearance of Jews from public life was either applauded or studiously overlooked.
Unwillingness of the public to partake personally of the persecution of the Jews
was, in short, combined with the readiness to go along with, or at least not to
interfere with, the action of the State. 'If most Germans were not fanatical or
"paranoid" anti-Semites, they were "mild", "latent", or passive anti-Semites, for
whom the Jews had become a "depersonalized", abstract, and alien entity beyond
human empathy and the "Jewish Question" a legitimate subject of state policy
deserving solution.'[21]

These considerations demonstrate once more the paramount importance of
the other, operational rather than ideological, link between the exterminatory form
of antisemitism and modernity. The *idea* of extermination, discontinuous with the
traditional heterophobia and dependent for that reason on the two implacably
modern phenomena of racist theory and the medical-therapeutic syndrome, provided
the first link. But the modern idea needed also suitably modern means of
implementation. It found such means in modern bureaucracy.

The only adequate solution to problems posited by the racist world-view is a
total and uncompromising isolation of the pathogenic and infectious race – the
source of disease and contamination – through its complete spatial separation or

physical destruction. By its nature, this is a daunting task, unthinkable unless in conjunction with the availability of huge resources, means of their mobilization and planned distribution, skills of splitting the overall task into a great number of partial and specialized functions and skills to co-ordinate their performance. In short, the task is inconceivable without modern bureaucracy. To be effective, modern exterminatory antisemitism had to be married to modern bureaucracy. And in Germany it was. In his famous Wandsee briefing, Heydrich spoke of the 'approval' or 'authorization' of the RSHA Jewish policy by the *Führer*.[22] Faced with the *problems* arising from the idea and the purpose this idea determined (Hitler himself preferred to speak of 'prophecy' rather than of a purpose or a task), the bureaucratic organization called *Reichsicherheithauptamt* set about designing proper practical *solutions*. It went about it the way all bureaucracies do: counting costs and measuring them against available resources, and then trying to determine the optimal combination. Heydrich underlined the need to accumulate practical experience, stressed the graduality of the process, and the provisional character of each step, confined by as-yet-limited practical know-how; RSHA was actively to seek the best solution. The *Führer* expressed his romantic vision of the world cleansed of the terminally diseased race. The rest was the matter of a not at all romantic, coolly rational bureaucratic process.

The murderous compound was made of a typically modern ambition of social design and engineering, mixed with the typically modern concentration of power, resources and managerial skills. In Gordon's terse and unforgettable phrase, 'when the millions of Jewish and other victims pondered their own imminent deaths and wondered "why must I die, since I have done nothing to deserve it?" probably the simplest answer would have been that power was totally concentrated in one man, and that man happened to hate their "race".'[23] The man's hatred and the concentrated power did not have to meet. (Indeed, no satisfactory theory has been offered to date which proves that antisemitism is functionally indispensable for a totalitarian regime; or, *vice versa*, that the presence of antisemitism in its modern, racialist, form, inevitably results in such a regime. Klaus von Beyme has found in his recent study that, for instance, Spanish falangists took particular pride in the absence of a single antisemitic remark in all the writings of Antonio Primo de Rivera, while even such a 'classical' Fascist as Franco's brother-in-law Serrano Suñer declared racism in general as a heresy for a good Catholic. French neo-Fascist Maurice Bardech stated that the persecution of the Jews was Hitler's greatest error and remained *hors du contrat fasciste*.[24]) But they did. And they may meet again.

Looking ahead

The story of modern antisemitism – in both its heterophobic and in its modern, racist, forms – is unfinished, as is the history of modernity in general and the modern state in particular. Modernization processes seem to move in our days away from Europe. Though some sort of boundary-defining device seemed to be necessary in the passage modern, 'garden-type' culture, as well as during the most traumatic dislocations in societies undergoing the modernizing change, the selection of Jews for the role of such a device was in all probability dictated by the particular vicissitudes of European history. The connection between Judeophobia and European modernity was historical – and, one may say, historically unique. On the other hand, we know only too well that cultural stimuli travel relatively freely, if also unaccompanied by structural conditions closely related to them in their place of origin. Stereotype of the Jew as an order-disturbing force, as an incongruous cluster of oppositions that saps all identities and threatens all efforts at self-determination, has been long ago sedimented in the highly authoritative European culture and is available for export and import transaction, like everything else in that culture which is widely recognized as superior and trustworthy. This stereotype, like so many other culturally framed concepts and items before, can be adopted as a vehicle in the solution of local problems even if historical experience of which it was born has been locally missing; even if (or perhaps particularly if) societies which adopt it have had no previous first-hand knowledge of the Jews.

It has been recently noted that antisemitism survived the populations it had been ostensibly targeted against. In countries where the Jews have all but disappeared, antisemitism (as sentiment, of course, married now to practices related primarily to other targets than the Jews) continues unabated. Even more remarkable is the dissociation between the acceptance of anti-Jewish sentiments and any other national, religious or racial prejudices, with which it was thought to be closely correlated. Neither are the antisemitic feelings related today to group or individual idiosyncracies, and particularly to anxiety-generating unresolved problems, acute uncertainty etc. Bernd Martin, who explored the Austrian case of 'antisemitism without Jews' has coined the term *cultural sedimentation* to account for a relatively new phenomenon: certain (usually morbid or otherwise unprepossessing or shameful) human features or behavioural patterns have come to be defined in popular consciousness as Jewish. In the absence of practical tests of such conjunction, the negative cultural definition and the antipathy to the features to which it refers feed and reinforce each other.[25]

To many other cases of contemporary antisemitism, however, the explanation in terms of 'cultural sedimentation' does not fit. In our global village, news travels fast and wide, and culture has long become a game without frontiers. *Rather than a product of cultural sedimentation, contemporary antisemitism seems to be subject to the processes of cultural diffusion*, today much more intense than at any time in the past. Like other objects of such diffusion, antisemitism, while retaining affinity with its original form, is on the way transformed – sharpened or enriched – to adapt to the problems and needs of its new home. Of such problems and needs there is no shortage in the times of 'uneven development' of modernity with its attendant tensions and traumas. Judeophobic stereotype offers a ready-made intelligibility to the otherwise puzzling and frightening dislocations and previously unexperienced forms of suffering. For instance, in Japan it has become in recent years increasingly popular as a universal key to the understanding of unanticipated obstacles in the path of economic expansion; the activity of world Jewry is proposed as the explanation of events so diverse as the over-valuation of the yen and the alleged threat of fall-out in the case of another Czernobyl-style nuclear mishap followed by another Soviet cover-up.[26]

One variety of antisemitic stereotype that travels easily is described in length by Norman Cohn as the image of the Jews as an international conspiracy set on ruining all local powers, decomposing all local cultures and traditions, and uniting the world under Jewish domination. This is, to be sure, the most vituperative and potentially lethal form of antisemitism; it was under the auspices of this stereotype that extermination of the Jews was attempted by the Nazis. It seems that in the contemporary world the multi-faceted imagery of Jewry, once drawing inspiration from multiple dimensions of 'Jewish incongruity', tends to be tapered down to just one fairly straightforward attribute: that *of a supra-national elite, of invisible power behind all visible powers, of a hidden manager of allegedly spontaneous and uncontrollable, but usually unfortunate and baffling turns of fate.*

The now dominant form of antisemitism is a product of theory, not of elementary experience; it is supported by the process of teaching and learning, not by intellectually unprocessed responses to the context of daily interaction. At the beginning of this century by far the most widespread variant of antisemitism in the affluent countries of Western Europe was one aimed at impoverished and strikingly alien masses of Jewish immigrants; it arose from the unmediated experience of the native lower classes, which were alone in touch with the strange and bizarre foreigners and which responded to their disconcerting and destabilizing presence with mistrust and suspicion. Their feelings were seldom shared by the elites, who had no direct experience of interaction with Yiddish-speaking newcomers and for whom the immigrants were not essentially distinct from the rest of the unruly, culturally depressed and potentially dangerous lower classes. As long as it remained unprocessed by a theory which only middle-class or upper-class intellectuals could offer, the elemental heterophobia of the masses stayed (to paraphrase the famous adage of Lenin) at the level of 'trade-union consciousness'; it could hardly be lifted from there as long as reference was made only to the low-level experience of intercourse with the Jewish poor. It could be generalized into a platform for mass unrest simply by adding up individual anxieties and presenting private troubles as shared problems (as it has been in the case of Mosley's British Movement, aimed above all against London's East End, or the present-day British National Front, aimed at the likes of Leicester and Notting Hill, and the French, targeted at Marseilles). It could advance as far as the demand to 'send the aliens back where they came from'. Yet there was no road leading from such heterophobia or even boundary-drawing anxiety of the masses, in a way a 'private affair' of the lower classes, to sophisticated antisemitic theories of universal ambitions, like this of a deadly race or the 'world conspiracy'. To capture popular imagination, such theories must refer to facts normally inaccessible and unknown to the masses and certainly not located within the realm of their daily and unmediated experience.

Our previous analysis has brought us, however, to the conclusion that the true role of the sophisticated, theoretical forms of antisemitism lay not so much in its capacity to foment the antagonist practices of the masses, as in its unique link with the social-engineering designs and ambitions of the modern state (or, more precisely, the extreme and radical variants of such ambitions). On the evidence of the present trends towards withdrawal of the Western state from direct management of many areas of previously controlled social life, and towards a pluralism-generating, market-led structure of social life, it seems unlikely that a racist form of antisemitism may be again used by a Western state as an instrument of a large-scale social-engineering project. For a *foreseeable* future, to be more precise; the post-modern, consumer-oriented and market-centred condition of most Western societies seems to be founded on a brittle basis of an exceptional economic superiority, which for the time being secures an inordinately large share of world resources but which is not bound to last forever. One can assume that situations calling for a direct take-over of social management by the state may well happen in some not too distant future – and then the well-entrenched and well-tested racist perspective may again come handy. In the meantime, the non-racist, less dramatic versions of Judeophobia may be on numerous less radical occasions deployed as means of political propaganda and mobilization.

With the Jews moving today massively towards the upper-middle classes, and hence out of reach of the direct experience of the masses, group antagonisms arising from freshly fomented concerns with boundary-drawing and boundary-maintenance tend to focus today in most Western countries on immigrant workers. There are political forces eager to capitalize on such concerns. They often use a language developed by modern racism to argue in favour of segregation and physical separation: a slogan successfully used by the Nazis on their road to power as a means of gaining the support of the combative enmity of the masses for their own racist intentions. In all countries that attracted in the time of post-war economic reconstruction large numbers of immigrant workers, the popular press and the populistically-inclined politicians supply innumerable examples of the new uses to which racist language is currently put. Gérard Fuchs, as well as Pierre Jouve and Ali Magoudi,[27] have recently published large collections and convincing analyses of these uses. One can read of *Le Figaro* magazine of 26 October 1985 dedicated to the question 'Will we still be French in thirty years?' or of prime minister Jacques Chirac speaking in one breath of his government's determination to fight with great firmness for the strengthening of personal security and of the identity of the French national community. The British reader, to be sure, has no need to look to French authors in the search for quasi-racist, segregationist language in the service of the mobilization of popular heterophobia and boundary fears.

However abominable they are, and however spacious is the reservoir of potential violence they contain, heterophobia and boundary-contest anxieties do not result – directly or indirectly – in genocide. *Confusing heterophobia with racism and the Holocaust-like organized crime is misleading and also potentially harmful, as it diverts scrutiny from the genuine causes of the disaster, which are rooted in some aspects of modern mentality and modern social organization*, rather than in timeless reactions to the strangers or even in less universal, yet fairly ubiquitous identity conflicts. In the initiation and perpetuation of the Holocaust, traditional heterophobia played but an auxiliary role. The truly indispensable factors lay elsewhere, and bore at the utmost a merely historical relation to more familiar forms of group resentment. The *possibility* of the Holocaust was rooted in certain universal features of modern civilization: its *implementation* on the other hand, was connected with a specific and not at all universal relationship between state and society. [. . .]

Notes and references

1   Cf. Pierre-André Taguieffe, *La force du préjugé: essai sur le racism et ses doubles* (Parish: La Decouverte, 1988).

2   Taguieff, *La force du préjugé*, pp. 69–70. Albert Memmi, *Le racisme* (Paris: Gallimard, 1982) maintains that 'racism, not anti-racism, is truly universal' (p. 157), and explains the mystery of its alleged universality by reference to another mystery: the instinctive fear invariably inspired by all difference. One does not understand the *different*, which by the same token turns into the *unknown* and the unknown is a source of terror. In Memmi's view, the horror of the unknown 'stems from the history of our species, in the course of which the unknown was the source of danger' (p. 208). It is suggested therefore that the putative universality of racism is a product of species learning. Having thus acquired a pre-cultural foundation, it is essentially immune to the impact of individual training.

3   Taguieff, *La force du préjugé*, p. 91.

4   Alfred Rosenberg, *Selected Writings* (London: Jonathan Cape, 1970), p. 196.

5   Arthur Gütt, 'Population Policy', in *Germany Speaks* (London: Thornton Butterworth, 1938), pp. 35–52.

6   Walter Gross, 'National Socialist Racial Thought', in *Germany Speaks*, p. 68.

7   Cf. Gerald Fleming, *Hitler and the Final Solution* (Oxford: Oxford University Press, 1986), pp. 23–5.

8   Alfred Rosenberg (ed.), Dietrich Eckart: Ein Vermächtnis (Munich, Frz. Eher, 1928). Quoted after George L. Mosse, *Nazi Culture: A Documentary History* (New York: Schocken Books, 1981), p. 77.

9   George. L. Mosse, *Toward a Final Solution: A History of European Racism* (London, J. M. Dent & Son, 1978), p. 2.

10   Mosse, *Toward the Final Solution*, p. 20.

11   Cf. Mosse, *Toward the Final Solution*, p. 53.

12   Max Wienreich, *Hitler's Professors: The Part of Scholarship in Germany's Crimes against the Jewish People* (New York: Yiddish Scientific Institute, 1946), pp. 56, 33.

13   Mosse, *Toward the Final Solution*, p. 134.

14   Hannah Arendt, *Origins of Totalitarianism* (London: Allen & Unwin, 1962), p. 87.

15   Diary of Joseph Goebbels, in *Survivors, Victims, and Perpetrators: Essays on the Nazi Holocaust*, ed. Joel E. Dinsdale (Washington: Hemisphere Publishing Company, 1980), p. 311.

16   John R. Sabini & Maury Silver, 'Destroying the Innocent with a Clear Conscience: A Sociopsychology of the Holocaust', in *Survivors, Victims, and the Perpetrators*, p. 329.

17   Richard Grünberger, *A Social History of the Third Reich* (London: Weidenfeld & Nicholson, 1971), p. 460.

18   Lawrence Stokes, 'The German People and the Destruction of the European Jewry', *Central European History*, no. 2 (1973), pp. 167–91.

19   Quoted after Sarah Gordon, *Hitler, Germans, and the 'Jewish Question'* (Princeton: Princeton University Press, 1984), pp. 159–60.

20   Cf. Gordon, *Hitler, Germans, and the 'Jewish Question'*, p. 171.

21   Christopher R. Browning, *Fateful Months* (New York: Holmes & Meier, 1985), p. 106.

22   *Le dossier Eichmann et la solution finale de la question juive* (Paris: Centre de documentation juive contemporaine, 1960), pp. 52–3.

23   Gordon, *Hitler, Germans, and the 'Jewish Question'*, p. 316.

24   Klaus von Beyme, *Right-Wing Extremism in Western Europe* (London: Frank Cass, 1988), p. 5. In a recent study Michael Balfour surveyed conditions and motives which prompted various strata of German Weimar society to offer enthusiastic,

mild or lukewarm support to the Nazi thrust for power, or at least refrain from active resistance. Many reasons are listed, general as well as specific to a given section of the population. The direct appeal of Nazi antisemitism figures prominently, however, in only one case (of the educated part of the *obere Mittelstand*, who felt threatened by the 'disproportionate competition' of the Jews), and even in this case merely as one of many factors found attractive, or at least worth trying, in the Nazi programme of the social revolution. Cf. *Withstanding Hitler in Germany 1933–45* (London: Routledge, 1988), pp. 10–28.

25 Cf. Bernd Martin, 'Antisemitism before and after Holocaust', in *Jews, Antisemitism and Culture in Vienna*, ed. Ivor Oxaal (London: Michael Pollak and Gerhard Botz, 1987).

26 *Jewish Chronicle*, 15 July 1988, p. 2.

27 Cf. Gérard Fuchs, *Ils resteront: le défi de l'immigration* (Paris: Syros, 1987); Pierre Jouve & Ali Magoudi, *Les dits et les non-dits de Jean-Marie Le Pen: enquéte et psychanalyse* (Paris: La Decouverte, 1988).

Chapter 19

Sander L. Gilman

ARE JEWS WHITE?
Or, The History of the Nose Job

[. . .]

THE PERSONAL COLUMNS IN the *Washingtonian*, the local city magazine in Washington, D.C., are filled with announcements of individuals "in search of" mates ("in search of" is the rubric under which these advertisements are grouped). These advertisements are peppered with various codes so well known that they are never really explained: "DWM [Divorced White Male] just recently arrived from Boston seeks a non-smoking, financially secure 40+ who loves to laugh" . . . or "SJF [Jewish Single Female], Kathleen Turner type, with a zest for life in search of S/DJM . . . for a passionate relationship." Recently, I was struck by a notice which began "DW(J)F [Divorced White (Jewish) Female] – young, 41, Ph.D., professional, no kids . . . seeks S/D/WWM, exceptional mind, heart & soul . . ."[1] What fascinated me were the brackets: advertisements for "Jews" or for "African Americans" or for "Whites" made it clear that individuals were interested in choosing their sexual partners from certain designated groups within American society. But the brackets implied that here was a woman who was both "White" and "Jewish." Given the racial politics of post-civil rights America, where do the Jews fit in? It made me ask the question, which the woman who placed the personals advertisement clearly was addressing: are Jews white? and what does "white" mean in this context? Or, to present this question in a slightly less polemical manner, how has the question of racial identity shaped Jewish identity in the Diaspora? I am not addressing what the religious, ethnic, or cultural definition of the Jew is – either from within or without Judaism or the Jewish community – but how the category of race present within Western, scientific, and popular culture, has shaped Jewish self-perception.

My question is not merely an "academic" one – rather I am interested in how the representation of the Jewish body is shaped and, in turn, shapes the sense of Jewish identity. My point of departure is the view of Mary Douglas:

> The human body is always treated as an image of society and . . . there
> can be no natural way of considering the body that does not involve
> at the same time a social dimension. Interest in its apertures depends
> on the preoccupation with social exits and entrances, escape routes and
> invasions. If there is no concern to preserve social boundaries, I would
> not expect to find concern with bodily boundaries.[2]

Where and how a society defines the body reflects how those in society define themselves. This is especially true in terms of the "scientific" or pseudo-scientific categories such as race which have had such an extraordinary importance in shaping how we all understand ourselves and each other. From the conclusion of the nineteenth century, the idea of "race" has been given a positive as well as a negative quality. We belong to a race and our biology defines us, is as true a statement for many groups, as is the opposite: you belong to a race and your biology limits you. Race is a constructed category of social organization as much as it is a reflection of some aspects of biological reality. Racial identity has been a powerful force in shaping how we, at the close of the twentieth century, understand ourselves – often in spite of ourselves. Beginning in the eighteenth century and continuing to the present, there has been an important cultural response to the idea of race, one which has stressed the uniqueness of the individual over the uniformity of the group. As Theodosius Dobzhansky noted in 1967: "Every person has a genotype and a life history different from any other person, be that person a member of his family, clan, race, or mankind. Beyond the universal rights of all human beings (which may be a typological notion!), a person ought to be evaluated on his own merits."[3] Dobzhansky and many scientists of the 1960s dismissed "race" as a category of scientific evaluation, arguing that whenever it had been included over the course of history, horrible abuses had resulted.[4] At the same time, within Western, specifically American culture of the 1960s, there was also a transvaluation of the concept of "race." "Black" was "beautiful," and "roots" were to be celebrated, not denied. The view was that seeing oneself as being a part of a "race" was a strengthening factor. We at the close of the twentieth century have, however, not suddenly become callous to the negative potential of the concept of "race." Given its abuse in the Shoah[5] as well as in neo-colonial policies throughout the world,[6] it is clear that a great deal of sensitivity must be used in employing the very idea of "race." In reversing the idea of "race," we have not eliminated its negative implications, we have only masked them. For it is also clear that the meanings associated with "race" impacts on those included within these constructed categories. It forms them and shapes them. And this can be a seemingly positive or a clearly negative response. There is no question that there are "real," i.e., shared genetic distinctions within and between groups. But the rhetoric of what this shared distinction comes to mean for the general culture and for the "group" so defined becomes central to any understanding of the implications of race.

Where I would like to begin is with that advertisement in the *Washingtonian* and with the question which the bracketed (J) posed: are Jews white? To begin to answer that question we must trace the debate about the skin color of the Jews, for skin colour remains one of the most salient markers for the construction of race in the West over time. The general consensus of the ethnological literature of the late nineteenth century was that the Jews were "black" or, at least, "swarthy." This view had a long history in European science. As early as 1691 François-Maximilien Misson, whose ideas influenced Bufon's *Natural History*, argued against the notion that Jews were black:

> 'Tis also a vulgar error that the Jews are all black; for this is only true of the Portuguese Jews, who marrying always among one another, beget Children like themselves, and consequently the Swarthiness of their Complexion is entail'd upon their whole Race, even in the Northern Regions. But the Jews who are originally of Germany, those, for example, I have seen at Prague, are not blacker than the rest of their Countrymen.[7]

But this was a minority position. For the eighteenth- and nineteenth-century scientist the "blackness" of the Jew was not only a mark of racial inferiority, but also an indicator of the diseased nature of the Jew. The "liberal" Bavarian writer Johan Pezzl, who travelled to Vienna in the 1780s, described the typical Viennese Jew of his time:

> There are about five hundred Jews in Vienna. Their sole and eternal occupation is to counterfeit, salvage, trade in coins, and cheat Christians, Turks, heathens, indeed themselves. . . . This is only the beggarly filth from Canaan which can only be exceeded in filth, uncleanliness, stench, disgust, poverty, dishonesty, pushiness and other things by the trash of the twelve tribes from Galicia. Excluding the Indian fakirs, there is no category of supposed human beings which comes closer to the Orang-Utan than does a Polish Jew. . . . Covered from foot to head in filth, dirt and rags, covered in a type of black sack . . . their necks exposed, the color of a Black, their faces covered up to the eyes with a beard, which would have given the High Priest in the Temple chills, the hair turned and knotted as if they all suffered from the "plica polonica."[8]

The image of the Viennese Jew is that of the Eastern Jew, suffering from the diseases of the East, such as the *Judenkratze*, the fabled skin and hair disease also attributed to the Poles under the designation of the "plica polonica."[9] The Jews' disease is written on the skin. It is the appearance, the skin color, the external manifestation of the Jew which marks the Jew as different. There is no question for a non-Jewish visitor to Vienna upon first seeing the Jew that the Jew suffers from Jewishness. The internal, moral state of the Jew, the Jew's very psychology, is reflected in the diseased exterior of the Jew. As mentioned earlier, "plica polonica" is a real dermatologic syndrome. It results from living in filth and poverty. But it was also associated with the unhygienic nature of the Jew and, by the mid-nineteenth century, with the Jew's special relationship to the most frightening disease of the period, syphilis.[10] For the non-Jew seeing the Jew it mirrored popular assumptions about the Jew's inherent, essential nature. Pezzl's contemporary, Joseph Rohrer, stressed the "disgusting skin diseases" of the Jew as a sign of the group's general infirmity.[11] And the essential Jew for Pezzl is the Galician Jew, the Jew from the Eastern reaches of the Hapsburg Empire.[12] (This late eighteenth-century view of the meaning of the Jew's skin color was not only held by non-Jews. The Enlightenment Jewish physician Elcan Isaac Wolf saw this "black yellow" skin color as a pathognomonic sign of the diseased Jew.[13]) Following the humoral theory of the times, James Cowles Pritchard (1808) commented on the Jews' "choleric and melancholic temperaments, so that they have in general a shade of complexion somewhat darker than that of the English people . . ."[14] Nineteenth-century anthropology as early as the work of Claudius Buchana commented on the "inferiority" of the "black" Jews of India.[15] By the mid-century, being black, being Jewish, being diseased, and being "ugly" come to be inexorably linked. All races, according to the ethnology of the day, were described in terms of aesthetics, as either "ugly" or "beautiful."[16] African blacks, especially the Hottentot, as I have shown elsewhere, became the epitome of the "ugly" race.[17] And being ugly, as I have also argued, was not merely a matter of aesthetics but was a clear sign of pathology, of disease. Being black was not beautiful. Indeed, the blackness of the African, like the blackness of the Jew, was believed to mark a pathological change in the skin, the result of congenital syphilis. (And, as we shall see, syphilis was given the responsibility for the form of the nose.) One bore the signs of one's diseased status on one's anatomy, and by extension, in one's psyche. And all of these signs pointed to the Jews being a member of the "ugly" races of mankind, rather than the "beautiful" races. In being denied any association with the beautiful and the erotic, the Jew's body was denigrated.[18]

Within the racial science of the nineteenth century, being "black" came to signify that the Jews had crossed racial boundaries. The boundaries of race were one of the most powerful social and political divisions evolved in the science of the period. That the Jews, rather than being considered the purest race, are because of their endogenous marriages, an impure race, and therefore, a potentially diseased one. That this impurity is written on their physiognomy. According to Houston Stewart Chamberlain, the Jews are a "mongrel" (rather than a healthy "mixed") race, who interbred with Africans during the period of the Alexandrian exile.[19] They are "a mongrel race which always retains this mongrel character." Jews had "hybridized" with blacks in Alexandrian exile. They are, in an ironic review of Chamberlain's work by Nathan Birnbaum, the Viennese-Jewish activist who coined the word "Zionist," a "bastard" race, the origin of which was caused by their incestuousness, their sexual selectivity.[20]

Jews bear the sign of the black, "the African character of the Jew, his muzzle-shaped mouth and face removing him from certain other races . . .," as Robert Knox noted at mid century.[21] The physiognomy of the Jew which is like that of the black ". . . the contour is convex; the eyes long and fine, the outer angles running towards the temples; the brow and nose apt to form a single convex line; the nose comparatively narrow at the base, the eyes consequently approaching each other; lips very full, mouth projecting, chin small, and the whole physiognomy, when swarthy, as it often is, has an African look."[22] It is, therefore, not only the color of the skin which enables the scientist to see the Jew as black, but also the associated anatomical signs, such as the shape of the nose. The Jews were quite literally seen as black. Adam Gurowski, a Polish noble, "took every light-colored mulatto for a Jew" when he first arrived in the United States in the 1850s.[23]

[. . .] Jews look different, they have a different appearance, and this appearance has pathognomonic significance. Skin color marked the Jew as both different and diseased. For the Jewish scientist, such as Sigmund Freud, these "minor differences in people who are otherwise alike . . . form the basis of feelings of strangeness and hostility between them." [24] This is what Freud clinically labeled as the "narcissism of minor differences." But are these differences "minor" either from the perspective of those labeling or those labeled? In reducing this sense of the basis of difference between "people who are otherwise alike," Freud was not only drawing on the Enlightenment claim of the universality of human rights, but also on the Christian underpinnings of these claims. For this "narcissism" fights "successfully against feelings of fellowship and overpower[s] the commandment that all men should love one another." It is the Christian claim to universal brotherly love that Freud was employing in arguing that the differences between himself, his body, and the body of the Aryan, are trivial. Freud comprehended the special place that the Jew played in the demonic universe of the Aryan psyche. But he marginalized this role as to the question of the Jew's function "as an agent of economic discharge . . . in the world of the Aryan ideal" rather than as one of the central aspects in the science of his time. [25] What Freud was masking was that Jews are not merely the fantasy capitalists of the paranoid delusions of the anti-Semites, they also mirror within their own sense of selves the image of their own difference.

By the close of the nineteenth century, the "reality" of the physical difference of the Jew as a central marker of race had come more and more into question. Antithetical theories, such as those of Friedrich Ratzel, began to argue that skin color was a reflex of geography, and could and did shift when a people moved from one part of the globe to another. Building on earlier work by the President of Princeton University at the close of the eighteenth century, Samuel Stanhope Smith (1787), the Jews came to be seen as the adaptive people par excellence. "In Britain and Germany they are fair, brown in France and in Turkey, swarthy in Portugal and Spain, olive in Syria and Chaldea, tawny or copper-coloured in Arabia and Egypt." [26] William Lawrence commented in 1823 that "their colour is everywhere modified by the situation they occupy." [27] The questionability of skin color as the marker of Jewish difference joined with other qualities which made the Jew visible.

By the latter half of the nineteenth century, Western European Jews had become indistinguishable from other Western Europeans in matters of language, dress, occupation, location of their dwellings and the cut of their hair. Indeed, if Rudolf Virchow's extensive study of over 10,000 German schoolchildren published in 1886 was accurate, they were also indistinguishable in terms of skin, hair, and eye color from the greater masses of those who lived in Germany. [28] Virchow's statistics sought to show that wherever a greater percentage of the overall population had lighter skin or bluer eyes or blonder hair there was a greater percentage of Jews also had lighter skin or bluer eyes or blonder hair. But although Virchow attempted to provide a rationale for the sense of Jewish acculturation, he still assumed that Jews were a separate and distinct racial category. George Mosse has commented, "the separateness of Jewish schoolchildren, approved by Virchow, says something about the course of Jewish emancipation in Germany. However, rationalized, the survey must have made Jewish schoolchildren conscious of their minority status and their supposedly different origins."[29] Nonetheless, even though they were labeled as different, Jews came to parallel the scale of types found elsewhere in European society.

A parallel shift in the perception of the Jewish body can be found during the twentieth century in the United States. It is not merely that second- and third-generation descendants of Eastern European Jewish immigrants do not "look" like their grandparents; but they "look" American. The writer and director Philip Dunne commented on the process of physical acculturation of Jews in Southern California during the twentieth century:

> You could even see the physical change in the family in the second generation – not resembling the first generation at all. Of course, this is true all across the country, but it is particularly noticeable in people who come out of very poor families. . . . One dear friend and colleague of mine was a product of a Lower East Side slum. He was desperately poor. And he grew up a rickety, tiny man who had obviously suffered as a child. At school, he told me, the goyim would scream at him. Growing up in California, his two sons were tall, tanned, and blond. Both excelled academically and in athletics. One became a military officer, the other a physicist. They were California kids. Not only American but Californian.[30]

But the more Jews in Germany and Austria at the fin de siècle looked like their non-Jewish contemporaries, the more they sensed themselves as different and were so considered. As the Anglo-Jewish social scientist Joseph Jacobs noted, "it is some quality which stamps their features as distinctly Jewish. This is confirmed by the interesting fact that Jews who mix much with the outer world seem to lose their Jewish quality. This was the case with Karl Marx . . ."[31] And yet, as we know, it was precisely those Jews who were the most assimilated, who were passing, who feared that their visibility as Jews could come to the fore. It was they who most feared being seen as bearing that disease, Jewishness, which Heinrich Heine, said the Jews brought from Egypt.

In the 1920s, Jacob Wassermann chronicled the ambivalence of the German Jews towards their own bodies, their own difference. Wassermann articulates this difference within the terms of the biology of race. He writes that: "I have known many Jews who have languished with longing for the fair-haired and blue-eyed individual. They knelt before him, burned incense before him, believed his every word; every blink of his eye was heroic; and when he spoke of his native soil, when he beat his Aryan breast, they broke into a hysterical shriek of triumph."[32] Their response, Wassermann argues, is to feel disgust for their own body, which even when it is identical in *all* respects to the body of the Aryan remains different: "I was once greatly diverted by a young Viennese Jew, elegant, full of suppressed ambition, rather melancholy, something of an artist, and something of a charlatan. Providence itself had given him fair hair and blue eyes; but lo, he had no confidence in his fair hair and blue eyes: in his heart of hearts he felt that they were spurious."[33] The Jew's experience of his or her own body was so deeply impacted by anti-Semitic rhetoric that even when that body met the expectations for perfection in the community in which the Jew lived, the Jew experienced his or her body as flawed, diseased.[34] If only one could change those aspects of the body which marked one as Jewish!

But nothing, not acculturation, not baptism, could wipe away the taint of race. No matter how they changed, they still remained diseased Jews. And this was marked on their physiognomy. Moses Hess, the German–Jewish revolutionary and political theorist commented, in his *Rome and Jerusalem* (1862) that "even baptism will not redeem the German Jew from the nightmare of German Jew-hatred. The Germans hate less the religion of the Jews than their race, less their peculiar beliefs than their peculiar noses. . . . Jewish noses cannot be reformed, nor black, curly, Jewish hair be turned through baptism or combing into smooth hair. The Jewish race is a primal one, which had reproduced itself in its integrity despite climactic influences. . . . The Jewish type is indestructible:"[35] The theme of the Jew's immutability was directly tied to arguments about the permanence of the negative features of the Jewish race.

On one count, Hess seemed to be wrong – the external appearance of the Jew did seem to be shifting. His skin seemed to be getting whiter, at least in his own estimation, though it could never get white enough. Jews, at least in Western Europe, no longer suffered from the disgusting skin diseases of poverty which had once marked their skin. But on another count, Hess was right. The Jew's nose could not be "reformed." Interrelated with the meaning of skin was the meaning of the Jew's physiognomy, especially the Jew's nose. And it was also associated with the Jew's nature. George Jabet, writing as Eden Warwick, in his *Notes on Noses* (1848) characterized the "Jewish, or Hawknose," as "very convex, and preserves its convexity like a bow, throughout the whole length from the eyes to the tip. It is thin and sharp." Shape also carried here a specific meaning: "It indicates considerable Shrewdness in worldly matters; a deep insight into character, and facility of turning that insight to profitable account."[36] Physicians, drawing on such analogies, speculated that the difference of the Jew's language, the very mirror of his psyche, was the result of the form of the his nose. Thus Bernhard Blechmann's rationale for the *Mauscheln* of the Jews, their inability to speak with other than a Jewish intonation, is that the "muscles, which are used for speaking and laughing are used inherently different from those of Christians and that this use can be traced . . . to the great difference in their nose and chin."[37] The nose becomes one of the central loci of difference in seeing the Jew. [. . .]

Notes and references

1   *Washingtonian* 26, 4 (January 1991), p. 196.
2   Mary Douglas, *Natural Symbols* (New York: Pantheon Books, 1970), p. 70.
3   Theodosius Dobzhansky, "On Types, Genotypes, and the Genetic Diversity in Populations," in J.N. Spuhler, ed., *Genetic Diversity and Human Behavior* (Chicago: Aldine, 1967), p. 12.
4   See for example, Peter A. Bochnik, *Die mächtigen Diener: Die Medizin und die Entwicklung von Frauenfeindlichkeit und Antisemitismus in der europäischen Geschichte* (Reinbek bei Hamburg: Rowohlt, 1985).

5   Robert Jay Lifton, *The Nazi Doctors: Medical Killing and the Psychology of Genocide* (New York: Basic Books, 1986).

6   See Oliver Ransford, *"Bid the Sickness Cease": Disease in the History of Black Africa* (London: John Murray, 1983).

7   François-Maximilien Misson, *A New Voyage to Italy*, 2 vols. (London: R. Bonwicke, 1714), 2: 139.

8   Johan Pezzl, *Skizze von Wien: Ein Kultur- und Sittenbild aus der josephinischen Zeit*, ed. Gustav Gugitz and Anton Scholssar (Graz: Leykam-Verlag, 1923), pp. 107–8.

9   On the meaning of this disease in the medical literature of the period see the following dissertations on the topic: Michael Scheiba, *Dissertatio inauguralis medica, sistens quaedam plicae pathologica: Germ. Juden-Zopff, Polon. Koltun: quam . . . in Academia Albertina pro gradu doctoris . . . subjiciet defensurus Michael Scheiba . . .* (Regiomonti: Litteris Reusnerianis, 1739) and Hieronymus Ludolf, *Dissertatio inauguralis medica de plica, vom Juden-Zopff . . .* (Erfordiae: Typis Groschianis, 1724)

10   Harry Friedenwald, *The Jews and Medicine: Essays.* 2 vols. (Baltimore: The Johns Hopkins University Press, 1944), 2: 531.

11   Joseph Rohrer, *Versuch über die jüdischen Bewohner der östereichischen Monarchie* (Vienna: n.p., 1804), p. 26. The debate about the special tendency of the Jews for skin disease, especially "plica polonica," goes on well into the twentieth century. See Richard Weinberg, "Zur Pathologie der Juden," *Zeitschrift für Demographie und Statistik der Juden* 1 (1905): 10–11.

12   Wolfgang Häusler, *Das galizische Judentum in der Habsburgermonarchie im Lichte der zeitgenössischen Publizistik und Reiseliteratur von 1772–1848* (Vienna: Verlag für Geschichte und Politik, 1979). On the status of the debates about the pathology of the Jews in the East after 1919 see *Voprosy biologii i patologii evreev* (Leningrad: State Publishing House, 1926).

13   Elcan Isaac Wolf, *Von den Krankheiten der Juden* (Mannheim: C.F. Schwan, 1777), p. 12.

14   James Cowles Pritchard, *Researches into the Physical History of Man* (Chicago: The University of Chicago Press, 1973), p. 186.

15   Claudius Buchanan, *Christian Researches in Asia, with Notices of the Translation of the Scriptures into the Oriental Languages* Boston: Samuel T. Armstrong, 1811), p. 169. On the background to these questions see George W. Stocking, Jr., *Victorian Anthropology* (New York: The Free Press, 1987).

16   Léon Poliakov, *The Aryan Myth: A History of Racist and Nationalist Ideas in Europe*, trans. Edmund Howard (New York: Basic Books, 1974), pp. 155–82.

17   Sander L. Gilman, *On Blackness without Blacks: Essays on the Image of the Black in Germany*, Yale Afro-American Studies (Boston: G. K. Hall, 1982).

18   See Cheryl Herr, *"The Erotics of Irishness,"* *Critical Inquiry* 17 (1990): 1–34.

19   Houston Stewart Chamberlain, *Foundations of the Nineteenth Century*, trans. John Lees, 2 vols. (London: John Lane/The Bodley Head, 1913), 1: 389.

20   Nathan Birnbaum, "Uber Houston Stewart Chamberlain," in his *Ausgewählte Schriften zur jüdischen Frage* (Czernowitz: Verlag der Buchhandlung Dr. Birnbaum & Dr. Kohut, 1910), 2: 201.

21   Robert Knox, *The Races of Men: A Fragment* (Philadelphia: Lea and Blanchard, 1850), p. 134.

22   Knox, *Races of Men*, p. 133.

23   Adam G. De Gurowski, *America and Europe* (New York: D. Appleton, 1857), p. 177.

24   Sigmund Freud, *Standard Edition of the Complete Psychological Works of Sigmund Freud*, ed. and trans, J. Strachey, A. Freud, A. Strachey, and A. Tyson, 24 vols. (London: Hogarth, 1955–74), 11: 199; 18: 101; 21: 114.

25   ibid. 21: 120.

26   Samuel Stanhope Smith, *An Essay on the Causes of the Variety of Complexion and Figure in the Human Species* (Cambridge: MASS: The Belknap Press, 1965), p. 42.

27   William Lawrence, *Lectures on Physiology, Zoology, and the Natural History of Man* (London: James Smith, 1823), p. 468.

28   Rudolf Virchow, "Gesamtbericht über die Farbe der Haut, der Haare und der Augen der Schulkinder in Deutschland," *Archiv für Anthropologie* 16 (1886): 275–475.

29   George L. Mosse, *Toward the Final Solution: A History of European Racism* (New York: Howard Fertig, 1975), pp. 90–91.

30   Cited from an interview by Neal Gabler, *An Empire of Their Own: How the Jews Invented Hollywood* (New York: Crown, 1988), pp. 242–42.

31   "Types," *The Jewish Encyclopedia*. 12 vols (New York: Funk and Wagnalls, 1906), 12: 295.

32   Wassermann, *My Life*, p. 156

33   Wassermann, *My Life*, p. 156.

34   On the cultural background for this concept see Jacob Katz, *Out of the Ghetto: The Social Background of Jewish Emancipation 1770–1870* (Cambridge, MASS: Harvard University Press, 1973) and Rainer Erb and Werner Bergmann, *Die Nachtseite der Judenemanzipation: Der Widerstand gegen die Integration der Juden in Deutschland 1780–1860* (Berlin: Metropol. 1989).

35   Moses Hess, *Rom und Jerusalem*. 2nd ed. (Leipzig: M. W. Kaufmann, 1899), Brief IV. Cited in the translation from Paul Lawrence Rose, *Revolutionary Antisemitism in Germany from Kant to Wagner* (Princeton: Princeton University Press, 1990), p. 323.

36   Eden Warwick, *Notes on Noses* (1848: London: Richard Bentley, 1864), p. 11. On the general question of the representation of the physiognomy of the Jew in mid-nineteenth-century culture see Mary Cowling, *The Artist as Anthropologist: The Representation of Type and Character in Victorian Art* (Cambridge: Cambridge University Press, 1989), pp. 118–19, 332–33.

37   Bernhard Blechmann, *Ein Beitrag zur Anthropologie der Juden* (Dorpat: Wilhelm Just, 1882), p. 11.

Chapter 20

Matthew F. Jacobson

LOOKING JEWISH, SEEING JEWS

WHEN JOHANN BLUMENBACH sat down to delineate *The Natural Varieties of Man* in 1775, he lighted upon the "racial face" of the Jews as the most powerful example of "the unadulterated countenance of nations." The principle of stable racial types was illustrated "above all [by] the nation of the Jews, who, under every climate, remain the same as far as the fundamental configuration of face goes, remarkable for a racial character almost universal, which can be distinguished at the first glance even by those little skilled in physiognomy."[1]

The racial character of Jewishness in the New World ebbed and flowed over time. The saga of Jewishness-as-difference in North America properly begins as early as 1654, when Peter Stuyvesant wrote to the Amsterdam Chamber of the Dutch West India Company that Christian settlers in New Amsterdam had "deemed it useful to require [Jews] in a friendly way to depart." Stuyvesant went on to pray "that the deceitful race – such hateful enemies and blasphemers of the name of Christ – be not allowed further to infect and trouble this new colony."[2] In the early republic Jewishness was most often taken up as a matter not of racial difference marked by physicality, but of religious difference marked by a stubborn and benighted failure to see Truth. Jews were "un-Christian," as in the laws limiting the right of office-holding in Maryland; they were "infidels" in more heated rhetoric. Then, like other non-Anglo-Saxon immigrants who entered under the terms of the 1790 naturalization law, Jews were increasingly seen as a racial group (in their case as Orientals, Semites, or Hebrews) in the mid to late nineteenth century – particularly as the demographics of immigration tilted away from German and other West European Jews, and toward the Yiddish-speaking Jews of Eastern Europe. Finally, again like other non-Anglo-Saxon immigrants, Jews gradually became Caucasians over the course of the twentieth century.

Thus anti-Semitism and the racial odyssey of Jews in the United States are neither wholly divisible from nor wholly dependent upon the history of whiteness and its vicissitudes in American political culture. When Henry James writes, "There were thousands of little chairs and almost as many little Jews; and there was music in the open rotunda, over which Jews wagged their big noses," it is useful to know that he is drawing upon a long European tradition of anti-Jewish imagery buttressed by arrangements of institutional power and political custom. It is also useful to know, however, that James's sensibilities could be as easily unsettled by a gang of Italian "ditchers" or a variety of other immigrant arrivals. After a visit to "the terrible little Ellis Island" in 1906, James ventured that the sight would bring "a new chill in [the] heart" of any long-standing American, as if he had "seen a ghost in his supposedly safe old house." American natives, he wrote, had been reduced to a state of "*unsettled possession*" of their own country; and it was not the Jew alone, but the "inconceivable alien" in general, who had him so worried.[3]

Yet as with Irish immigrants, who came ashore already carrying the cultural and political baggage of Saxon oppression, the Jews' version of becoming Caucasian cannot be understood apart from their particular history of special sorrows in the ghettos of Eastern Europe, apart from the deep history of anti-Semitism in Western culture, apart from anti-Semitic stereotypes that date back well before the European arrival on North American shores, or apart, finally and most obviously, from the historic cataclysm of the Holocaust.

[. . .] Like Irishness, Italianness, Greekness, and other probationary whitenesses, visible Jewishness in American culture between the mid-nineteenth and mid-twentieth centuries represented a complex process of social value *become* perception: social and political meanings attached to Jewishness generate a kind of physiognomical surveillance that renders Jewishness itself discernible as a particular pattern of physical traits (skin color, nose shape, hair color and texture, and the like – what Blumenbach called "the fundamental configuration of face." The visible markers may then be interpreted as outer signs of an essential, immutable, inner moral–intellectual character; and that character, in its turn – attested to by physical "difference" – is summoned up to explain the social value attached to Jewishness in the first place. The circuit is ineluctable. Race is social value become perception; Jewishness seen is social value naturalized and so enforced.

This is not to say that people all "really" look alike; rather, it is to argue that those physical differences which register in the consciousness as "*difference*" are keyed to particular social and historical circumstances. (We might all agree that Daniel Patrick Moynihan "looks Irish," for instance; but unlike our predecessors, we at the turn of the twenty-first century are not likely to note his Irishness first thing.) Thus a writer defending the "better" Jews (what a later generation would tellingly call "white Jews") in the North American Review in 1891 could collapse the distinction between behavior and physicality, arguing that "among cultured Jews the racial features are generally less strongly defined." (When Jews are of the "better" type, that is, the observing eye need not scout their Jewishness.)[4] That same year, meanwhile, in The Witch of Prague, the novelist Marion Crawford could thoroughly fuse physicality and inner character in his portrait of Jewish evil. In the Jewish quarter one encountered

> throngs of gowned men, crooked, bearded, filthy, vulture-eyed . . .
> hook-nosed and loose-lipped, grasping fat purses, in lean fingers, shaking

greasy curls that straggled out under caps of greasy fur, glancing to the
left and right with quick, gleaming looks that pierced the gloom like
fitful flashes of lightening . . . a writhing mass of humanity, intoxicated
by the smell of gold, mad for its possession, half hysteric with fear of
losing it, timid, yet dangerous, poisoned to the core by the sweet sting
of money, terrible in intelligence, vile in heart, contemptible in body,
irresistible in the unity of their greed – the Jews of Prague.[5]

Not, indeed, have conceptions of a racial Jewishness necessarily been confined
to negative depictions. The point is a critical one. [. . .] Yiddish writers like Abraham
Cahan and Morris Winchevsky were as quick as their non-Jewish contemporaries
to assign a distinctly racial integrity to Jewishness and Jews. Racial perceptions of
Jewishness are not simply a subject for the annals of anti-Semitism, in other words;
nor does racial ascription necessarily denote a negative assessment of a given group
in every case. Among the secularized Jews of the *haskala*, or Jewish enlightenment,
responses to "the Jewish Question" (such as Zionism, or bundist Yiddish socialism)
rested solidly upon *racial* notions of a unified Jewish "peoplehood." In the sciences,
too, it was not only the virulent Madison Grants and the Lothrop Stoddards, but
Jewish scientists like Maurice Fishberg and Joseph Jacobs, who advanced the
scholarly idea of Jewish racial purity.[6] (Nor, for that matter, were Jewish versions
of Jewish racial difference in every instance *positive*, either: as the *American Hebrew*
remarked in response to the immigrant waves from further east in Europe [1894],
the acculturated German Jew "is closer to the christian sentiment around him than
to the Judaism of these miserable darkened Hebrews.")[7]

Thus the history of racial Jewishness is not merely the history of anti-Semitism;
it encompasses the ways in which both Jews and non-Jews have construed Jewishness
– and the ways in which they have *seen* it – over time. It encompasses not only
arguments, like Madison Grant's, that "the mixture of a European and a Jew is a
Jew," or the view of Jews as "mud people" – the progenitors of all nonwhites –
which circulates in far right theology in the 1990s.[8] It also comprises the race pride
of a Morris Winchevsky or a Leon Kobrin, and the social forces under whose
influence such conceptions of peoplehood have largely given way. By 1950 Ludwig
Lewisohn could assert that "no sane man regards Jewish characteristics as 'racial.'"[9]
And yet as late as the 1970s Raphael Patai would still be trying to dispel "the myth
of the Jewish race"; and later still Philip Roth would be wincing at the "nasty
superstitions" attached to racial Jewishness.

A few remarks on the strategy of the present inquiry are in order. The definition
of "Jewishness" under investigation here is quite narrow. Surely religion and culture
can figure prominently in the ascription of Jewishness by Jews or non-Jews, anti-
Semites or philo-Semites. This discussion does not seek to exhaust Jewishness in
all of its dimensions or in its full range of possibilities; rather, it investigates strictly
ethnoracial conceptions and perceptions of Jewishness (answers to the question, is
Jewishness a parcel of biological, heritable traits?). Such conceptions, and the
inevitable debates over them, have been central to some Jews themselves as they
pondered their common destiny irrespective of religious devotion, and to non-
Jews wrestling with questions of immigration, inter-group relations, and the smooth
functioning of the polity. I begin by sketching the emergence of a visible, physical

– biological – Jewishness in common American understanding during the period preceding the mid-twentieth century. This history loosely parallels the chronology laid out for whiteness in general [. . .], although in the case of Jews World War II will present a sharper turning point than 1924 in the final transformation toward Caucasian whiteness. The investigation ends, then, with a close reading of Arthur Miller's *Focus* (1945), a sustained inquiry into the properties of Jewishness rendered at precisely that post-Nazi moment – like *Gentleman's Agreement* – when "racial" Jewishness was still alive, yet a newly intolerable, conception.

"Are Jews white?" asks Sander Gilman. The question gets at the fundamental instability of Jewishness as racial difference, but so does its wording fundamentally misstate the contours of whiteness in American political culture.[10] From 1790 onward Jews were indeed "white" by the most significant measures of that appellation: they could enter the country and become naturalized citizens. Given the shades of meaning attaching to various racial classifications, given the nuances involved as whiteness slips off toward Semitic or Hebrew and back again toward Caucasian, the question is not *are* they white, nor even how white are they, but how have they been both white and Other? What have been the historical terms of their probationary whiteness? [. . .]

The idea of a unique Jewish physicality or Jewish "blood" was not new to nineteenth-century America. As James Shapiro has recently argued, theology heavily influenced early modern conceptions of both racial and national difference in Europe, and so the alien Jew figures prominently in European discussion as early as the sixteenth century. In 1590 Andrew Willet argued that "Jews have never been grafted onto the stock of other people." In 1604 the Spaniard Prudencio de Sandoval combined a proto-racialist argument of hereditary Jewish evil with a kind of racialism-by-association with the other Other, the Negro: "Who can deny that in the descendants of the Jews there persists and endures the evil inclination of their ancient ingratitude and lack of understanding, just as in Negroes [there persists] the inseparability of their blackness?" Such ideas evidently crossed the Atlantic early on in the settlement of the New World, assuming even more directly racialist overtones in Increase Mather's comments on the "blood" of nations and the purity of the Jews in 1669:

> The providence of God hath suffered other nations to have their blood mixed very much, as you know it is with our own nation: there is a mixture of British, Roman, Saxon, Danish, [and] Norman blood. But as for the body of the Jewish nation, it is far otherwise. Let an English family live in Spain for five or six hundred years successively, and they will become Spaniards. But though a Jewish family live in Spain a thousand years, they do not degenerate into Spaniards (for the most part).[11]

Until the second half of the nineteenth century, however, it was generally not their "blood" but their religion that marked the Jews as a people apart. The Jew was the perpetual "Historical Outsider," in Frederic Jaher's phrase, whose perceived difference derived above all from "Christian hostility." The Jew's difference was primarily cast in terms of the "infidel" or the "blasphemer" (one Jacob Lambrozo was indicted in Maryland for denouncing Jesus as a "necromancer," for example), and discussion was occasionally infused with a dose of long-standing European rumor (such as the twelfth-century "blood libel" that Jews needed Christian blood for certain holiday fêtes) or stereotypes of Jews as well-poisoners and usurers. Although the popular view of Jews was "amply negative" in the colonies, by Jaher's account, it was far better there than in Europe; and their status was characterized by a general state of toleration disrupted only by occasional anti-Semitic outbursts, as when the New York Assembly disfranchised them in 1737, or when Savannah freeholders resisted the expansion of a Jewish cemetery in 1770.[12]

These religiously grounded ideas about the Jewish alien could occasionally take on a racialist cast in the new nation, just as they had in early modern Europe. In a rabid denunciation of the Jacobin propensities of the Democratic Society in 1795, for instance, one Federalist publisher asserted that the democrats would be "easily known by their physiognomy"; they seem to be "of the tribe of Shylock: they have that leering underlook and malicious grin."[13] But generally Jews remained "free [though unchristian] white persons" in the early republic, and the overt depictions of the Jew as a racial Other rose sharply only in the second half of the nineteenth century, particularly in the decades after what John Higham has called "a mild flurry of ideological anti-Semitism" during the Civil War. Now it was not only that Jews could be known in their greed (or their Jacobinism or their infidelism or their treachery) by their physiognomy, but that their physiognomy itself was significant – denoting, as it did, their essential unassimilability to the republic. Only now did the "Israelitish nose" stand for something in and of itself – not greed, or usury, or infidelism, or well-poisoning, but simply "difference." Only now was the dark Jew equated with "mongrelization," that catch-all term for "unfitness" in American political culture.[14] Thus a century after Johann Blumenbach introduced as scientific fact the remarkable stability of the Jews when it came to "the fundamental configuration of face," the New York *Sun* offered this vernacular explanation of "why the Jews are kept apart" (1893):

> Other races of men lose their identity by migration and by inter-marrying with different peoples, with the result that their peculiar characteristics and physiognomies are lost in the mess. The Jewish face and character remain the same as they were in the days of PHARAOH. Everybody can distinguish the Jewish features in the most ancient carvings and representations, for they are the same as those seen at this day. Usually a Jew is recognizable as such by sight. In whatever country he is, his race is always conspicuous . . . After a few generations other immigrants to this country lose their race identity and become Americans only. Generally the Jews retain theirs undiminished, so that it is observable by all men.[15]

Others, as we have seen, strongly contested the blithe assertion that "other im-migrants to this country lose their race identity," but the *Sun* was nonetheless expressing a point of impressive consensus on the unassimilability of the Jews.

This intensifying perception of a distinctly racial Jewishness coincided with two entangling developments between the 1850s and the early twentieth century:

the rise of the racial sciences, and the rise of what John Higham has called "discriminatory" (as opposed to "ideological") anti-Semitism.[16] Popular accounts of the racial Otherness of Jews, that is, at once framed, and were framed by, a scientific discourse of race on the one hand, and a set of social practices (including hiring and admissions patterns, and the barring of Jews from certain Saratoga resorts) on the other. This coincidence of scientific racialism, discriminatory practice, and the popular expression of racial Jewishness attests to the centrality of race as an organizer of American social life. It also attests to the similarity between the Jewish odyssey from white to Hebrew and, say, the Irish odyssey from white to Celt. Despite its capacity to absorb and adapt unique, long-standing anti-Semitic notions of Jewish greed and the like, the racial ideology encompassing Jewishness in the United States in the latter half of the nineteenth century did set Jews on a social trajectory similar to that traveled by many other probationary "white persons." The full texture of anti-Semitism in this country thus combined strains of an international phenomenon of Jew-hatred with the mutability of American whiteness.[17]

The rise of races and phenotypes in scientific discourse, as described earlier, was a creature of the age of European expansionism and exploration. Non-European races were "discovered" and became "known" through the technologies of conquest; then scientific accounts of these races, in their turn, justified and explained colonial domination and slavery. But Jews received a fair amount of attention even in this context, in part because of the mutual accommodations of scientific and religious understandings of genesis (or Genesis) and "difference," and in part because, as somewhat anomalous Europeans, Jews put stress upon the ideas of consanguinity and race which undergirded emergent European nationalisms. Just as the alien Jew raised questions as to who could or could not be truly "English" in Shakespeare's England, so romantic nationalisms of the nineteenth century had to come to terms with the anomalous Jew in an effort to theorize and police the "imagined community" of the nation. As one scholar puts it, science itself was "often either motivated by or soon annexed to political causes."[18] Just as the plunder of exploration and slavery formed the context within which Africans became "known" to Western science, so Jewish emancipation, debates over citizenship, and the emergence of modern nationalism formed the context within which science comprehended "the Jewish race." Were "Jewish traits" properly attributed to social isolation, environment, or immutable character? Could Jews be compatriots of non-Jews? Could they be redeemed as Europeans?

Thus from the outset scientific writings on Jews in Europe tended to focus upon questions of assimilation, most often emphasizing the race's stubborn immutability – which is to say, its unassimilability. As Gobineau wrote in his essay *Sur l'Inégalité des Races Humaines*, the "Jewish type" has remained much the same over the centuries; "the modifications it has undergone . . . have never been enough, in any country or latitude, to change the general character of the race. The warlike Rechabites of the Arabian desert, the peaceful Portuguese, French, German and Polish Jews – they all look alike . . . The Semitic face looks exactly the same as it appears on the Egyptian paintings of three or four thousand years ago."[19] The Jews may be incorporated, but they will forever be Jews. In *Races of Man* (1950), Robert Knox similarly noted Jews' essential physicality, leaving little doubt as to the further question of racial merit:

Brow marked with furrows or prominent points of bone, or with both; high cheek-bones; a sloping and disproportioned chin; and elongated, projecting mouth, which at the angles threatens every moment to reach the temples; a large, massive, club-shaped, hooked nose, three or four times larger than suits the face – these are features which stamp the African character of the Jew, his muzzle-shaped mouth and face removing him from certain other races . . . Thus it is that the Jewish face never can [be], and never is, perfectly beautiful.[20]

The presumed immutability of the Jews became a staple of American science by mid-century as well, even though slavery and the question of Negro citizenship still dominated racial discussion. In *Types of Mankind* (1855) Josiah Nott remarked that the "well-marked Israelitish features are never beheld out of that race"; "The complexion may be bleached or tanned . . . but the Jewish features stand unalterably through all climates." In *Natural History of the Human Races* (1869) John Jeffries, too, argued that "the Jews have preserved their family type unimpaired; and though they number over five million souls, each individual retains the full impress of his primitive typical ancestors".[21] And of course we have already seen where these "observations" on Jewish racial integrity tended in the age of eugenics.

In this connection the British scholar Joseph Jacobs deserves special attention. A Jew himself, Jacobs was, as he announced in the preface to *Studies in Jewish Statistics* (1891), "inclined to support the long-standing belief in the substantial purity of the Jewish race."[22] For Jacobs, according to the historian John Efron, Jewish race science represented "a new form of Jewish self-defense" and his own work a new genre of political resistance, "the scientific apologia." But if aimed toward the redemption, rather than the renunciation, of racial Jewishness, Jacobs's work rests upon the same logic of "difference" as the most virulent of his anti-Semitic contemporaries. Indeed, it is in Jacobs's work perhaps above all that we glimpse the depth of "difference" associated with Jewish racial identity in this period. "Even more in Jewesses than in Jews," he wrote, "we can see that cast of face in which the racial so dominates the individual that whereas of other countenances we say, 'That is a kind, a sad, a cruel, or a tender face,' of this our first thought is, 'That is a Jewish face.' . . . Even the negroes of Surinam, when they see a European and a Jew approaching, do not say, 'Here are two whites,' but, 'Here is a white and a Jew.'"[23]

Just as earlier scientific approaches to the righteousness of slavery (the work of Josiah Nott and John Van Evrie, for instance) had seized upon the degeneracy of the "mulatto" as proof of the unbridgeable divide separating black from white, so Jacobs went into great detail on the "infertility of mixed marriages" between Jews and non-Jews, on the basis of statistics kept in Prussia and Bavaria between 1875 and 1881. The variance in fecundity, according to Jacobs, was an average of 4.41 children for Jewish–Jewish marriages to 1.65 for Jewish–Gentile marriages in Prussia; and 4.7 to 1.1 in Bavaria. He also charted various physical characteristics of Jews and non-Jews in different regions, including the color of eyes, hair, and skin. (Only 65.4 percent of Austrian Jews had "white" skin, he found, as compared with more than 80 percent of the Gentiles.)[24]

Like conceptions of Anglo-Saxon, Celtic, or Teutonic racial character, scientific observations on the Hebrew passed from the rarified discourse of ethnological journals into the American vernacular and the American visual lexicon of race as well. Racial depiction did not necessarily entail a negative judgment; racially accented declarations of *philo*-Semitism were common enough. William Cullen Bryant lamented that Edwin Booth's rendering of Shylock, for instance, failed to do justice to "the grandeurs of the Jewish race." He later sang of "the wonderful working of the soul of the Hebrew."[25] James Russell Lowell, in an ambivalent twist, couched highly sympathetic remarks on Jewishness in a language of physicality and character, but also drew upon the common, anti-Semitic imagery of his day. "All share in government of the world was denied for centuries to perhaps the ablest, certainly the most tenacious, race that ever lived in it," he wrote compassionately in "Democracy" (1884), " . . . a race in which ability seems as natural and hereditary as the curve of their noses . . . We drove them into a corner, but they had their revenge . . . They made their corner the counter and banking house of the world, and thence they rule it and us with the ignoble scepter of finance."[26] Lowell's respect for "perhaps the ablest" race is the basis for an indictment of Christian political conduct, and particularly its lamentable exclusions. Even if blame lies at the doorstep of Christians, however, the Jewish "revenge" Lowell envisions taps the popular currents of nineteenth-century anti-Semitism.

[. . .] In *The Ambivalent Image*, her study of Jews in American cultural imagery, Louise Mayo has amassed an invaluable compendium of racial figures of Jewishness across time. Although Mayo's project did not entail theorizing the relationship between racial Jewishness and the American social order, her work supports the trajectory of Anglo-Saxondom and its Others sketched out above. Racial depictions of Jews would become most urgent, of course, as immigration figures climbed in the decades following Russia's May Laws of 1881. Nonetheless, as Mayo has so nicely laid bare in her cultural excavations, Hebrews appeared as a counterpoint to Anglo-Saxons in American cultural representation long before actual Hebrews began to disembark in huge numbers at Castle Garden and Ellis Island toward the end of the century. This seems part of the reflex toward an Anglo-supremacist exclusivity beginning in the 1840s. Thus in the cosmos of American popular literature, for instance, George Lippard could remark in *Quaker City* (1844), "Jew was written on his face as though he had fallen asleep for three thousand years at the building of the Temple"; in Peter Hamilton Meyers's *The Miser's Heir* (1854) a certain character's "features . . . proclaim him a Jew"; and in J. Richter Jones's *Quaker Soldier* (1866), a Jew is characterized by the "hereditary habits of his race."[27] By the early twentieth century a Jewish group could organize a grassroots boycott of certain New York theaters, protesting their "scurrilous and debasing impersonations of the Hebrew type." Judge Hugo Pam, the leader of the boycott, argued that the theater was fostering "race prejudice" because so many theater goers "get their impressions of the race from the stage Jew." (Significantly, this group took its cue from Irish activists, who, Pam said, had succeeded in eliminating "stage lampoons of the Celtic race" from popular theater.)[28]

Racial depictions of Jewishness circulated not only in cultural productions themselves, but also in cultural commentary, as when *Harper's Weekly* reported that the audience of the Yiddish theater was "remarkably strange in appearance to an

Anglo-Saxon," or when *Bookman* reviewed Abraham Cahan's *Yekl* as a penetrating look at the Yidish immigrant's "racial weakness." William Dean Howells, too, discussed Cahan's novella in racial terms, identifying Cahan as a "Hebrew" and his ghetto sketches as "so foreign to our race and civilization."[29]

Wherever "difference" was cast as race, certainly, the weight of the culture in general tended most often toward negative depiction. Nativist discussion of immigration restriction in the 1890s and the eugenics movement of the earlier twentieth century, of course, states Jewish difference most boldly. Sounding the familiar chord of race and republicanism, Henry Cabot Lodge warned that Jews "lack the nobler abilities which enable a people to rule and administer and to display that social efficiency in war, peace, and government without which all else is vain." The *Illustrated American* was blunter still, crying in 1894 that "the inroad of the hungry Semitic barbarian is a positive calamity." In a piece on immigration and anarchism, the *New York Times*, too, lamented the arrival of "unwashed, ignorant, unkempt, childish semi-savages," and remarked upon the "hatchet-faced, sallow, rat-eyed young men of the Russian Jewish colony." In response to Franz Boas's innovative argument that in fact no biological chasm did separate new immigrants from America's "old stock," Lothrop Stoddard dismissed his views as "the desperate attempt of a Jew to pass himself off as 'white.'"[30]

Franz Boas's argument notwithstanding, increasingly in the years after the Russian May Laws and the pogroms of 1881, Jews, too, embraced race as a basis for unity. This was particularly true among some Zionists and freethinkers for whom religion had ceased meaningfully to explain their ties to the "folk." The "Jewish Question" as it was posed during the period of pogroms in the East and the Dreyfus Affair in the West generated new secular and political notions of Jewish peoplehood in response. It was in this period, for instance, that Joseph Jacobs began his forays into Jewish race science in Europe. And, as John Efron has amply documented, the *racial* individuality of the Jews as a people was of particular interest within the budding Zionist movement. Aron Sandler's *Anthropologie und Zionismus* (1904), for instance, mobilized the scientific language of a distinct racial genius in order to press the necessity of a Jewish territory where that genius could properly take root and develop.[31]

Indeed, a much longer tradition entwined Jewish nationalism with Jewish racialism. The proto-Zionist Moses Hess, in *Rome and Jerusalem* (1862), had flatly announced that "Jewish noses cannot be reformed, nor black, curly, Jewish hair be turned through baptism or combing into smooth hair. The Jewish race is a primal one, which had reproduced itself in its integrity despite climatic influences . . . The Jewish type is indestructible."[32] The American proto-Zionist Emma Lazarus, too, wrote in *Epistle to the Hebrews* (1887) that Judaism was emphatically *both* a race and a religion. She rhapsodized over the Jews' "fusion of Oriental genius with Occidental enterprise and energy," "the fire of our Oriental blood," and "the deeper lights and shadows of [Jews'] Oriental temperament." She lamented that Jews in America tended to be condemned "as a race" for failings of a single individual. At once demonstrating her own commitment to racialism, yet marking the extent to which race was a contested concept, she lamented the Jews' lack of unanimity on their own racial status: "A race whose members are recognized at a glance, whatever be their color, complexion, costume or language, yet who dispute the cardinal fact as to whether they are a race, cannot easily be brought into unanimity upon more doubtful propositions," she sighed.[33]

In the 1890s and early 1900s immigrant writers in the United States like Abraham Cahan, Leon Kobrin, Abraham Liessen [Abraham Wald], and Bernard Gorin also lighted upon race both as a way of understanding their own secular Jewishness and as a way of couching their (socialist) appeals to the Yiddish masses. And even as late as the 1920s and 1930s a literature of Jewish assimilation toyed with race in its exploration of Jewish destiny in the New World.[34] What of today and of America?" asked Ludwig Lewisohn. "Were the Jews Germans? Are they Americans? . . . I am not talking about citizenship and passports or external loyalties. What are the inner facts?"[35]

The Island Within (1928), an immigrant saga tracing several generations of a German–Jewish family from Germany in the mid-nineteenth century to the United States in the early twentieth, is Lewisohn's exploration of precisely these "inner facts." "How was it," the novel's young hero, Arthur, wants to know, "that, before they went to school, always and always, as far back as the awakening of consciousness, the children knew that they were Jews? . . . There was in the house no visible symbol of religion and of race." What does Jewishness consist in? What is its basis, especially in the crucible of a transnational history in which questions of national belonging are so vexed?

Arthur vows to understand. Along the way in this ethnoracial *Bildungsroman*, he takes up anthropology and studies the "variableness of racial types" (but later discovers, to his distaste, that his professor rather undemocratically believes in "fixed qualitative racial differences," and so he searches elsewhere). A neighbor, Mrs. Goldman, provides a simple formula: "Jews always have been Jews and they always will be." The tautology actually foreshadows Arthur's own resolution at the end of the novel.[36]

Throughout the quest, race is central both to Arthur's crisis and to its resolution; for him it becomes a measure of his own alienation. He first registers the degree of his assimilation when he discovers that his own father "looks Jewish" to him: "His father's profile under the hat, pale and unwontedly sorrowful, looked immemorially Jewish . . . Arthur realized instantly that this perception of his was itself an un-Jewish one and showed how he had grown up to view his very parents slightly from without and how, indeed, in all thoughts and discussions, he treated the Jews as objects of his discourse." Some two hundred pages later, after a good deal of soul-searching and after many tortured conversations on the subject of Jewishness, Arthur discovers and reclaims his own "island within" – his own immutable, unshakable Jewishness. "You didn't know you were going to resurrect the Jew in you?" asks his Gentile wife, Elizabeth. He responds, "You're quite right . . . But really I didn't even have to resurrect the Jew. I just put away a pretense." Thus eternal Jewishness (what a generation of Yiddish speakers had called *dos pintele yid*, "the quintessence of the Jew"), if racially ambiguous, does have distinctly racial connotations. "It's kind of an argument, isn't it, against mixed marriages?" asks Elizabeth. "I'm afraid it is."[37]

In *I Am a Woman – and a Jew* (1926), Leah Morton [Elizabeth Stern], too, recounted her marriage to a non-Jew, her foray into the world of social work, her secularization, and her eventual re-embrace of Jewishness (if not exactly of

Judaism), all in the terms of her relationship to the "race." The authenticity of this narrative has recently been questioned; but it is nonetheless significant that this public embrace of her Jewish identity – however real or imagined – is cast in the thoroughly racial terms of the period's public discourse of Jewishness as difference.[38] Of New York's Bohemia, she wrote, "They were frankly Jewish. They had Jewish names, Jewish faces and the psychology of the Jew." Upon her first taste of public life in the settlement house movement, Leah came to realize that "here, in this office, I was not a girl representing a race. I was not a Jewish maiden responsible to a race, as at home." This fairly conveys Morton's own version of that Jewish immutability so stressed by writers from Knox and Gobineau to Jacobs and Cahan. "Was there a Jewish 'race'?" she asks. "Scientists were taking sides, saying, yes, or no, as they decided. What did it matter to us who were Jews? There was a Jewish people, something that belonged to us," in Moreton's estimation, finally comes through when she discovers and embraces "all that we, who are Jews, 'part Jews' or 'all Jews' share." This is Morton's version of the "island within": "We Jews are alike. We have the same insensities, the sensitiveness, poetry, bitterness, sorrow, the same humor, the same memories. The memories are not those we can bring forth from our minds: they are centuries old and are written in our features, in the cells of our brain."[39]

This, then, was the vision of difference that the blackface of an Al Jolson or an Eddie Cantor sought to efface. *The Jazz Singer* marks the beginning of the drift by which American Jews became racial Caucasians and illustrates Frantz Fanon's contention that, when it comes to race-hatred or race-acceptance, "one has only not to be a nigger."[40] As with all racial transformations, the next leg of the Jews' odyssey – the cultural trek from Hebrew to Caucasian – would be a gradual affair, glacial rather than catastrophic. A new paradigm was in ascendance in the 1920s and after; perhaps nothing demonstrates so well the power of that paradigm in redefining Jews as the odd, archaic ring that so much of the material in the foregoing pages now has. Whether it is Leah Morton writing proudly of the features and the brain cells of the eternal Jew, or Lothrop Stoddard commenting upon the slim prospects of Franz Boas's passing himself off as "white," these commentators from the mid-nineteenth century to the early twentieth were clearly speaking from a racial consciousness not our own. [. . .]

Jews did not disappear from racial view overnight in the mid-1920s, nor had racial Jewishness vanished completely even by the 1940s. An *Atlantic Monthly* piece entitled "The Jewish Problem in America" (1941) could still assert that the Jew had become European "only in residence; by nature he did not become an Occidental; he could not possibly have done so." Comparing Jews to another problematic "Oriental" group, Armenians, this writer went on to wonder "whether [differences] can be faded out by association, *miscegenation*, or other means of composition."[41] When Nazi policy began to make news in the 1930s and early 1940s, too, headlines in journals like the *Baltimore Sun* and the *Detroit Free Press* revealed the extent to which Americans and Germans shared a common lexicon of racial Jewishness: American papers unself-consciously reported upon the Nazis' "steps to solve [the] race problem," "laws restricting [the] rights of Hebrews," and the "persecution of members of the Jewish race." Hearst papers remarked upon the "extermination of an ancient and cultured race," while the Allentown (Pennsylvania) *Chronicle and News* commented upon Jews' inability to assimilate with "any other race."[42]

World War II and the revelations of the horrors of Nazi Germany were in fact part of what catapulted American Hebrews into the community of Caucasians in the mid-twentieth century.[. . .] The feverish and self-conscious revision of "the Jewish race" was at the very heart of the scientific project to rethink the "race concept" in general – the racial devastation in Germany, that is, was largely responsible for the mid-century ascendance of "ethnicity."

Changes wrought in the U.S. social order by the war itself and by the early Cold War, too, helped to speed the alchemy by which Hebrews became Caucasian. From A. Phillip Randolph's threatened march on Washington, to African–Americans' campaign for Double Victory, to the major parties' civil rights planks in 1944 and the rise of the Dixiecrats in 1948, the steady but certain ascendance of Jim Crow as *the* pressing political issue of the day brought the ineluctable logic of the South's white–black binary into play with new force in national life. Postwar prosperity and postindustrial shifts in the economy, too, tended to disperse Jews geographically, either to outlying suburbs or toward sunbelt cities like Los Angeles and Miami – in either case, to places where whiteness itself eclipsed Jewishness in racial salience. As scholars like Deborah Dash Moore and Karen Brodkin Sacks have written, Jews became simply "white or Anglo" in the regional racial schemes of the sunbelt; and racially tilted policies like the GI Bill of Rights and the Federal Housing Authority's "whites only" approach to suburban housing loans re-created Jews in their new regime of racial homogenization. Nikhil Singh has rightly called the postwar suburban boom a case of "state sponsored apartheid;" its hardening of race along exclusive and unforgiving lines of color held tremendous portent for Jews and other white races.[43] And finally, ironically, if racialism had historically been an important component of Zionism, the establishment of a Jewish state ultimately had the opposite effect of whitening the Jews in cultural representations of all sorts: America's client state in the Middle East became, of ideological necessity and by the imperatives of American nationalism, a *white* client state. This revision was popularized not only in mainstream journalism, but in Technicolor extravaganzas on Middle Eastern history like *The Ten Commandments* and *Exodus*.[44] [. . .]

Notes and references

1   Johann Fredrich Blumenbach, *On the Natural Varieties of Mankind* [1775, 1795] (New York: Bergman, 1969), p. 234.

2   In Morris U. Schapps,. ed., *A Documentary History of Jews in the United States*, 1654–1875 (New York: Schoken, 1950, 1971), pp. 1–2.

3   Henry James, "Glasses," *Atlantic Monthly*, Feb. 1896, p. 145; William Boelhower, *Through a Glass Darkly: Ethnic Semiosis in American Literature* (New York: Oxford, 1987), pp. 17–40, 21; Henry James, *The American Scene* [1906] (n.l.: Library of America, 1993), pp. 425–427. See also Karen Brodkin Sacks, "How Did Jews Become White Folks?" in Steven Gregory and Roger Sanjek, eds, *Race* (New Brunswick: Rutgers University Press, 1994), pp. 79–85.

4   *North American Review*, 152 (1891), p. 128. On "white Jews" see Louis Binstock, "Fire-Words," *Common Ground*, Winter 1947, pp. 83–84, and Laura Z. Hobson, *Gentleman's Agreement* (New York: Simon and Schuster, 1947), pp. 154–155.

5   F. Marion Crawford, *The Witch of Prague* (1891) (London: Sphere Books, 1974), p. 186.

6   Matthew Frye Jacobson, *Special Sorrows: The Diasporic Imagination of Irish, Polish, and Jewish Immigrants in the United States* (Cambridge: Harvard University Press, 1995), pp. 102–105, and " 'The Quintessence of the Jew': Polemics of Nationalism and Peoplehood in Turn-of-the-Century Yiddish Fiction," in Werner Sollors and Marc Schell, eds, *Multilingual America* (New York: New York University Press, forthcoming); John Efron, *Defenders of the Race: Jewish Doctors and Race Science in Fin-de-Siècle Europe* (New Haven: Yale University Press, 1994).

7   Hasia Diner, *In the Almost Promsied Land: American Jews and Blacks, 1915–1935* [1977] (Baltimore: Johns Hopkins University Press, 1995), pp. 8–9.

8   Madison Grant, *The Passing of the Great Race: or, The Racial Basis of European History* (New York: Scribners, 1916), pp. 15–16: James William Gibson, *Warrior Dreams: Violence and Manhood in Post-Vietnam America* (New York: Hill and Wang, 1994), p. 72.

9   Ludwig Lewisohn, *The American Jew: Character and Destiny* (New York: Farrar, Straus and Co., 1950), p. 23.

10   Sander Gillman, *The Jew's Body* (New York: Routledge, 1991), chapter 7; Sacks, "How Did Jews Become White Folks?"

11   James Shapiro, *Shakespeare and the Jews* (New York: Columbia University Press, 1996), pp. 36, 168, 169, 170; see pp. 167–193 on early modern English conceptions of nationality and the Jewish alien.

12   Frederic Cople Jaber, *A Scapegoat in the New Wilderness: The Origins and Rise of Anti-Semitism in America* (Cambridge: Harvard University Press, 1994), pp. 17, 82, 87–88, 106, 112. For Jaher's view of the Christian roots of the Jew as "Historical Outsider," see pp. 17–81 passim.

13   Jaher, *Scapegoat*, p. 133.

14   Ibid., pp. 222, 232; on the worsening image, see pp. 170–241; on the proto-racialism of older stereotypes, see pp. 192–194. John Higham, *Send These to Me: Immigrants in Urban America* [1975] (Baltimore: Johns Hopkins University Press, 1984), p. 123. Jeffrey Melnick notes an interesting swing in American discourse between the Jew as "mongrel" and the Jew as racially "pure" – both are bad. *A Right to Sing the Blues* (Cambridge: Harvard University Press, forthcoming).

15   *New York Sun*, April 24, 1893, p. 6.

16   Higham, *Send These to Me*, pp. 117–152. On Jews and the racial sciences see Robert Singerman, "The Jew as Racial Alien: The Genetic Component of American Anti-Semitism," in David Gerber, ed., *Anti-Semitism in American History* (Urbana: University of Illinois Press, 1987), pp. 103–128, and below.

17   John Higham, "Ideological Anti-Semitism in the Gilded Age," and "The Rise of Social Discrimination," in *Send These to Me*, pp. 95–116, 117–152. On "status panic" and American anti-Semitism, see p. 141.

18   Efron, *Defenders*, p. 63.

19   Michael Bediss, ed., Arthur Comte de Gobineau, *Selected Political Writings* (New York: Harper and Row, 1970), p. 102: William Stanton, *The Leopard's Spots: Scientific Attitudes towards Race in America, 1815–59* (Chicago: University of Chicago Press, 1960), pp. 147–148: George Stocking, ed., *Bones, Bodies, Behavior: Essays*

on Biological Anthropology (Madison: University of Winconsin Press, 1988); Thomas Gossett, *Race: The History of an Idea in America* (New York: Schocken, 1963).

20 Quoted in Efron, *Defenders*, p. 51.

21 Josiah Nott, *Types of Mankind* (Philadelphia: Lippincott, 1855), pp. 117, 118; John P. Jeffries, *Natural History of the Human Races* (New York: Edward O. Jenkins, 1869), p. 123.

22 Joseph Jacobs, *Studies in Jewish Statistics, Social, Vital, and Anthropometric* (London: D. Nutt, 1891), p. xxx.

23 Ibid., p. xxviii; Efron, *Defenders*, pp. 58–90, 59.

24 Jacobs, *Jewish Statistics*, pp. v, xiv; Efron, *Defenders*, pp. 79–80; Maurice Fishberg, *The Jews: A Study of Race and Environment* (n.l.: Walter Scott, 1911); Sander Gilman, *The Case of Sigmund Freud: Medicine and Identity at the Fin de Siècle* (Baltimore: Johns Hopkins University Press, 1993), pp. 11–68; Sander Gilman, *Freud, Race, and Gender* (Princeton: Princeton University Press, 1993), pp. 12–48.

25 Quoted in Louise Mayo, *The Ambivalent Image: Nineteenth-Century America's Perception of the Jew* (Rutherford: Fairleigh Dickinson University Press, 1988), p. 77.

26 James Russell Lowell, "Democracy" [1884], in *Essays, Poems, and Letters* (New York: Odyssey Press, 1948), p. 153.

27 Mayo, *Ambivalent Image*, pp. 44, 53, 54.

28 New York *Times*, April 25, 1913, p. 3.

29 Mayo, *Ambivalent Image*, pp. 75–76, 154; Howells quoted in Bernard Richards, "Abraham Cahan Cast in a New Role," in Cahan, *Yekl, the Imported Bridegroom, and Other Stories* (New York: Dover, 1970), p. vii.

30 Mayo, *Ambivalent Image*, pp. 58, 156, 172; Stoddard quoted in Michael Rogin, *Blackface, White Noise: Jewish Immigrants in the Hollywood Melting Pot* (Berkeley: University of California Press, 1996), p. 89. The Dillingham Commission was uncharacteristically sanguine regarding Jews' prospects for assimilation in 1911, asserting that "the Jews of to-day are more truly European than Asiatic or Semitic." Nonetheless, the report did note that "Israelites" were "preserving their own individuality to a marked degree." *Reports of the Immigration Commission: Dictionary of Races and peoples* (Washington D.C.: Government Printing Office, 1911), pp. 73, 74.

31 Efron, *Defenders*, pp. 123–174.

32 Quoted in Gilman, *The Jew's Body*, p. 179.

33 Emma Lazarus, *An Epistle to the Hebrews* [1887] (New York: Jewish Historical Society, 1987), pp. 9, 20, 21, 78, 80.

34 Jacobson, *Special Sorrows*, pp. 97–111; Melnick, *A Right to Sing the Blues*.

35 Ludwig Lewisohn, *The Island Within* (New York: Modern Library, 1928), p. 43.

36 Ibid., pp. 103–104, 146, 154–155, 168.

37 Ibid., pp. 148, 346.

38 Laura Browder, "*I Am a Woman – And a Jew*: Ethnic Imposter Autobiography and the Creation of Immigrant Identity," paper delivered at the ASA annual conference, Kansas City, November 1, 1996.

39 Leah Morton [Elizabeth Stern], *I Am a Woman – And A Jew* [1926] (New York: Markus Wiener, 1986), pp. 347, 62, 193, 360. The text also contains racialized references to Irish and Polish immigrants and to Nordic natives, pp. 175, 245, 299.

40   Frantz Fanon, *Black Skin, White Masks* [1952] (New York: Grove Wiedenfeld, 1967), p. 115.

41   Albert Nock, "The Jewish Problem in America" *Atlantic Monthly*, July 1941, p. 69 (emphasis added). In rebuttal, see Marie Syrkin, "How Not to Solve the 'Jewish Problem,'" *Common Ground*, Autumn 1941, p. 77.

42   Deborah Lipstadt, *Beyond Belief: The American Press and the Coming of the Holocaust, 1933–1945* (New York: Free Press, 1986), pp. 59–60, 88, 93, 157. See also Elazar Barkan, *The Retreat of Scientific Racism: Changing Concepts of Race in Britain and the United States between the World Wars* (Cambridge: Cambridge University Press, 1992), chapter 6; Stefan Kuhl, *The Nazi Connection: Eugenics, American Racism, and German National Socialism* (New York: Oxford, 1994).

43   Deborah Dash Moore, *To The Golden Cities: Pursuing the American Jewish Dream in Miami and L.A.* (New York: Free Press, 1994), p. 55; Sacks, "How Did Jews Become White Folks?" pp. 86–98; Rogin, *Blackface, White Noise*, p. 265; Nikhil Pal Singh, "'Race' and Nation in the American Century: A Genealogy of Color and Democracy" (Ph.D. diss., Yale University, 1995), Douglass Massey and Nancy Denton, *American Apartheid: Segregation and the Making of the Underclass* (Cambridge: Harvard University Press, 1993), pp. 51–54.

44   Moore, *Golden Cities*, pp. 227–261; Alan Nadel, *Containment Culture: American Narratives, Postmodernism, and the Atomic Age* (Durham: Duke University press, 1995), pp. 90–116. On the racial dynamics of American involvement in the Middle East, see also Soheir A. Morsy, "Beyond the Honorary 'White' Classification of Egyptians: Societal Identity in Historical Context," in Gregory and Senjak, *Race*, pp. 175–198.

Guide to Further Reading

Key texts

Arendt, H. (1973) *The Origins of Totalitarianism*, New edition, San Diego: Harcourt Brace (influential analysis of the historical basis of the origins of anti-semitism and its impact on Nazi thought).

Bauman, Z. (1989) *Modernity and the Holocaust*, Oxford: Blackwell (a sociological analysis of social and historical conditions that made the Holocaust possible).

Gilman, S. L. and Katz, S. T. (eds) (1991) *Anti-Semitism in Times of Crisis*, New York: New York University Press (a valuable collection of papers on the experience of anti-semitism in specific historical settings).

Gross, J. T. (2006) *Fear: Anti-Semitism in Poland after Auschwitz*, Princeton: Princeton University Press (an insightful analysis of the continuing significance of anti-semitism in Poland after the Second World War).

Perry, M. and Schweitzer, F. M. (eds) (2008) *Antisemitic Myths: A Historical and Contemporary Anthology*, Bloomington: Indiana University Press (using original documents as a key point of reference this anthology explores key myths in the shaping of historical and contemporary forms of anti-semitism).

Background reading

Adorno, T. W. and Horkheimer, M. (1986) *Dialectic of Enlightenment*, London: Verso (contains an insightful analysis of the origins of anti-semitism and its role under Nazism).

Berman, P. (1994) *Blacks and Jews: Alliances and Arguments*, New York: Delta (a collection of papers that discuss anti-semitism among African-Americans as well as a discussion of broader aspects of Black and Jewish relations in America).

Biale, D., Galchinsky, M. and Heschel, S. (eds) (1998) *Insider/Outsider: American Jews and Multiculturalism*, Berkeley: University of California Press (a collection that focuses on the changing cultural and identity politics of American Jews).

Burleigh, M. and Wippermann, W. (1991) *The Racial State: Germany 1933–1945*, Cambridge: Cambridge University Press (a masterful overview of the institutions and mechanisms of extermination developed by the Nazi racial state).

Cheyette, B. (1993) *Constructions of 'the Jew' in English Literature and Society: Racial Representations, 1875–1945*, Cambridge: Cambridge University Press (an account of ideas about Jews, focusing on images in English literature from the late nineteenth to the early twentieth century).

Cheyette, B. (ed.) (1996) *Between 'Race' and Culture: Representations of 'the Jew' in English and American Literature*, Stanford: Stanford University Press (a collection of papers that brings together recent English and American research on literary representations of 'the Jew').

Cheyette, B. and Marcus, L. (eds) (1998) *Modernity, Culture and 'The Jew'*, Cambridge: Polity Press (an important collection of papers that explore representations of Jewishness from the angle of literary theory and cultural studies).

Cohn, N. (1970) *Warrant for Genocide: The Myth of the Jewish World-Conspiracy and the Protocols of the Elders of Zion,* Harmondsworth: Penguin (a classic account of the role of conspiracy theories in anti-semitic discourses).

Finkelstein, N. G. (2003) *The Holocaust Industry: Reflections on the Exploitation of Jewish Suffering,* London: Verso (a critical exploration of what the author sees as the exploitation of the Holocaust for ideological purposes).

Gay, P. (1978) *Freud, Jews and Germans: Masters and Victims in Modernist Culture,* Oxford: Oxford University Press (an insightful account of the changing images of Jews in German culture).

Geras, N. (1998) *The Contract of Mutual Indifference: Political Philosophy after the Holocaust,* London: Verso (an attempt to situate the relevance of the Holocaust in terms of contemporary intellectual and political developments).

Gilman, S. L. (1986) *Jewish Self-Hatred: Anti-Semitism and the Hidden Language of the Jews,* Baltimore: The Johns Hopkins University Press (an exploration of the notion of 'self-hatred' among Jews from a historical and contemporary perspective).

—— (1991) *The Jew's Body,* New York: Routledge (an innovative account of the role of images about the body in discourses about Jews).

—— (1996) *Smart Jews: The Construction of the Image of Jewish Superior Intelligence,* Lincoln: University of Nebraska Press (an exploration of ideas about Jews and intelligence in scientific thought and popular culture).

Goldberg, D. T. and Krausz, M. (eds) (1993) *Jewish Identity,* Philadelphia: Temple University Press (an exploration of the changing patterns of contemporary Jewish identity).

Goldhagen, D. J. (1996) *Hitler's Willing Executioners: Ordinary Germans and the Holocaust,* London: Little, Brown and Company (a controversial history of the role of anti-semitism in German society in shaping the Holocaust).

Hitler, A. (1992) *Mein Kampf,* London: Pimlico (contains a version of Hitler's thoughts about Jews, race and related issues).

Hutton, C. M. (2005) *Race and the Third Reich,* Cambridge: Polity (a detailed account of the study of race under the Nazi regime, which includes a discussion of links between Nazi ideas and other traditions).

Kushner, T. (1994) *The Holocaust and the Liberal Imagination,* Oxford: Blackwell (an exploration of political and social responses to the Holocaust from the 1930s onwards).

Mayer, A. J. (1990) *Why Did the Heavens Not Darken: The 'Final Solution' in History,* London: Verso (an analysis of the conditions that led to the final solution).

Mosse, G. L. (1971) *Germans and Jews,* London: Orbach and Chambers (contains an insightful account of the development of the changing images of Jews in German society).

Poliakov, L. (1974) *The History of Anti-Semitism,* 4 Volumes, London: Routledge and Kegan Paul (an exhaustive historical analysis of anti-semitism in different historical settings).

Pulzer, P. (1988) *The Rise of Political Anti-Semitism in Germany and Austria,* London: Peter Halban (an exploration of the politicisation of anti-semitic thought and its impact on political culture).

Rose, P. L. (1990) *German Question/Jewish Question: Revolutionary Antisemitism in Germany from Kant to Wagner,* Princeton: Princeton University Press (an account of the links between anti-semitic thought and the development of German nationalism).

Sartre, J.-P. (1976) *Anti-Semite and Jew*, New York: Schocken Books (a classic attempt to construct a philosophical understanding of anti-semitism).

Taguieff, P.-A. (2004) *Rising from the Muck: The New Anti-Semitism in Europe*, Chicago: Ivan R. Dee (an analysis of new currents of anti-semitism in France and other societies, focusing particularly on the emergence of new discourses and perspectives).

Todorov, T. (1999) *Facing the Extreme: Moral Life in the Concentration Camps*, London: Weidenfeld and Nicolson (a critical examination of the moral significance of the Holocaust, including reflections on accounts by perpetrators and survivors, as well as wider philosophical issues).

Key Questions

- Theodor Adorno and Max Horkheimer argue that 'the fascists do not view the Jews as a minority but an opposing race'. What does this argument tell us about the nature of Nazi anti-semitism?
- Critically review George Mosse's analysis of the relationship between anti-semitism and racism.
- Zygmunt Bauman has argued 'modern civilisation was not the Holocaust's sufficient condition; it was, however, most certainly its necessary condition'. Review the implications of this argument for the analysis of the Holocaust.
- Analyse Sander Gilman's account of the role of changing images of 'the Jew' in racial discourses.
- 'The history of racial Jewishness is not merely the history of anti-semitism' (Mathew Jacobson). What do you understand by this argument?
- Should the analysis of anti-semitism be seen as separate from the question of racism?
- Some commentators have talked of the existence of 'anti-semitism without Jews'. Discuss the implications of this argument.

PART FOUR

Colonialism, race and the other

INTRODUCTION

T HE ROLE OF COLONIALISM and its associated institutions in shaping
contemporary ideas about race and racism has been an underlying concern in
some of the more historical literature in this field. For example, the connection
between scientific racism and imperialism and colonialism has been explored is
some detail by a number of scholars. But in recent years the growth of interest
in postcolonial theory, particularly in the fields of literary theory and cultural
studies, has brought about a new interest in the role that race played in structuring
social relationships in colonial societies. The various extracts in this part are all
in one way or another concerned with various aspects of this question. The first
extract is from the work of Frantz Fanon, which has exerted an influence on
theoretical debates about race and colonialism for over four decades now. Indeed
'The Fact of Blackness' is one of the most referenced texts in this area and has
been interpreted in a variety of ways. An underlying theme in Fanon's work is that
colonialism represented a relationship of domination and subordination, the
oppression of one racialised group by another and the production of racialised
meanings about both the 'coloniser' and the 'colonised'. Fanon is particularly
concerned with the ways in which colonial institutions and the ideologies associated
with them constructed ideas about race through representations of 'blackness', the
'negro', the 'native' and other notions. Perhaps more importantly he is also
concerned with the ways in which the colonised 'Others' saw themselves and their
position within colonial societies and the struggle against colonialism.

A number of the other extracts in this part engage in one way or another with
Fanon's work, although they often have a more specific focus on particular
expressions of colonial discourse. The next two extracts, by Lola Young and Ann

McClintock, are a case in point. Both are concerned with cultural mechanisms for the expression of colonial ideas and values. Young's concern is with the question of representations of race, gender and sexuality in the cinema, and she bases much of her argument on a detailed analysis of particular films. But from a broad conceptual angle she is also concerned with questions that were at the heart of Fanon's account of the colonial situation. What is particularly interesting about Young's account, however, is that she seeks to use the analysis of 'imperial culture' as represented in films as a way of framing the changing ideas about race as well as gender and sexuality.

The extract from Anne McClintock's work explores some of the same territory as Young, though her focus in this extract is on the narratives of Henry Rider Haggard, a British colonial administrator and writer. McClintock's focus on a nuanced textual analysis of Haggard's writings reflects the influence of literary theory in this field and the attempt to utilise an analysis of texts to uncover the workings of colonial and postcolonial discourses. Whatever the merits of the shift towards textual analysis that has become evident in recent years, part of the strength of McClintock's account is precisely the result of the attention to the representations of race, gender and sexuality that underpin the work of writers such as Haggard. Taking Haggard's classic *King Solomon's Mines* as her main point of reference she attempts to show how key themes in his work linked up to wider fears about race and degeneration in both Britain and the colonies.

The next extract, from Chandra Talpade Mohanty, is closely linked to arguments that have been going on within feminist scholarship for the past two decades, and it should thus be read in conjunction with the extracts in Part Five as well as the other extracts in this part. Mohanty's critical account of Western feminist discourses focuses particularly on what she sees as the lacunae of feminist theorising in relation to questions about race and colonialism. At a broader level she suggests that there is a need to broaden the boundaries of feminist scholarship in order to allow for a fuller understanding of the important differences that exist in the ways women in the West are positioned as compared to women in other parts of the globe. Underlying Mohanty's argument is a concern to explore the continuities and discontinuities between the experiences of different groups of women, and to highlight the relevance of class in shaping other patterns of inequality.

The contributions of both Young and McClintock have already touched upon the issue of the question of sexuality in the colonial situation. The extract by Ann Stoler takes this argument a step further by exploring in some detail the interrelationship between 'sexual affronts' and 'racial frontiers' in colonial South East Asia. Stoler's analysis is particularly focused on the interweaving of sexual desire for the 'Other' with the fear of 'race mixing' and its consequences that characterised colonial situations. Drawing on her research in relation to the Dutch East Indies she highlights the ways in which both sexual and racial boundaries were used to construct images of both 'Europeans' and the colonial 'Others'. But she also insists on the need to look closely at the ways in which the colonial administrations needed to set up complex institutional mechanisms to police these boundaries.

The final voice in this part is that of Homi Bhabha, whose work has done much to popularise the study of race within the emerging field of postcolonial studies. Bhabha's work is deeply influenced, somewhat idiosyncratically, by the work of both Fanon and by the conceptual framework of Michel Foucault. His work has become an important influence on the development of postcolonial theory. In this particular extract Bhabha focuses on the relationship between race, time and modernity. Starting his account with a discussion of Fanon's work he moves on to discuss the ways in which questions of race and identity have been reconfigured by wider processes of social and cultural change which are dislocating the central structures and processes of modern societies and undermining the frameworks which gave individuals stable anchorage in the social world. This in turn links up with a recurrent theme in this reader as a whole, namely the question of how modern societies deal with 'difference'.

Chapter 21

Frantz Fanon

THE FACT OF BLACKNESS

Translated by Charles Lam Markmann

"**D**IRTY NIGGER!**"** Or simply, "Look, a Negro!"
    I came into the world imbued with the will to find a meaning in things, my spirit filled with the desire to attain to the source of the world, and then I found that I was an object in the midst of other objects.

Sealed into that crushing objecthood, I turned beseechingly to others. Their attention was a liberation, running over my body suddenly abraded into nonbeing, endowing me once more with an agility that I had thought lost, and by taking me out of the world, restoring me to it. But just as I reached the other side, I stumbled, and the movements, the attitudes, the glances of the other fixed me there, in the sense in which a chemical solution is fixed by a dye. I was indignant; I demanded an explanation. Nothing happened. I burst apart. Now the fragments have been put together again by another self.

As long as the black man is among his own, he will have no occasion, except in minor internal conflicts, to experience his being through others. There is of course the moment of "being for others," of which Hegel speaks, but every ontology is made unattainable in a colonized and civilized society. It would seem that this fact has not been given sufficient attention by those who have discussed the question. In the *Weltanschauung* of a colonized people there is an impurity, a flaw that outlaws any ontological explanation. Someone may object that this is the case with every individual, but such an objection merely conceals a basic problem. Ontology – once it is finally admitted as leaving existence by the wayside – does not permit us to understand the being of the black man. For not only must the black man be black; he must be black in relation to the white man. Some critics will take it on themselves to remind us that this proposition has a converse. I say that this is false. The black man has no ontological resistance in the eyes of the white man. Overnight the Negro has been given two frames of reference within which he has had to place himself. His metaphysics, or, less pretentiously, his customs and the sources on which they were based, were wiped out because they were in conflict with a civilization that he did not know and that imposed itself on him.

The black man among his own in the twentieth century does not know at what moment his inferiority comes into being through the other. Of course I have talked about the black problem with friends, or, more rarely, with American Negroes. Together we protested, we asserted the equality of all men in the world. In the Antilles there was also that little gulf that exists among the almost-white, the mulatto, and the nigger. But I was satisfied with an intellectual understanding of these differences. It was not really dramatic. And then . . .

And then the occasion arose when I had to meet the white man's eyes. An unfamiliar weight burdened me. The real world challenged my claims. In the white world the man of color encounters difficulties in the development of his bodily schema. Consciousness of the body is solely a negating activity. It is a third-person consciousness. The body is surrounded by an atmosphere of certain uncertainty. I know that if I want to smoke, I shall have to reach out my right arm and take the pack of cigarettes lying at the other end of the table. The matches, however, are in the drawer on the left, and I shall have to lean back slightly. And all these movements are made not out of habit but out of implicit knowledge. A slow composition of my *self* as a body in the middle of a spatial and temporal world – such seems to be the schema. It does not impose itself on me; it is, rather, a definitive structuring of the self and of the world – definitive because it creates a real dialectic between my body and the world.

For several years certain laboratories have been trying to produce a serum for "denegrification"; with all the earnestness in the world, laboratories have sterilized their test tubes, checked their scales, and embarked on researches that might make it possible for the miserable Negro to whiten himself and thus to throw off the burden of that corporeal malediction. Below the corporeal scheme I had sketched a historico-racial schema. The elements that I used had been provided for me not by "residual sensations and perceptions primarily of a tactile, vestibular, kinesthetic, and visual character,"[1] but by the other, the white man, who had woven me out of a thousand details, anecdotes, stories. I thought that what I had in hand was to construct a physiological self, to balance space, to localize sensations, and here I was called on for more.

"Look, a Negro!" It was an external stimulus that flicked over me as I passed by. I made a tight smile.

"Look, a Negro!" It was true. It amused me.

"Look, a Negro!" The circle was drawing a bit tighter. I made no secret of my amusement.

"Mama, see the Negro! I'm frightened!" Frightened! Frightened!" Now they were beginning to be afraid of me. I made up my mind to laugh myself to tears, but laughter had become impossible.

I could no longer laugh, because I already knew that there were legends, stories, history, and above all *historicity*, which I had learned about from Jaspers. Then, assailed at various points, the corporeal schema crumbled, its place taken by a racial epidermal schema. In the train it was no longer a question of being aware of my body in the third person but in a triple person. In the train I was given not one but two, three places. I had already stopped being amused. It was not that I was finding febrile coordinates in the world. I existed triply: I occupied space. I moved toward the other . . . and the evanescent other, hostile but not opaque, transparent, not there, disappeared. Nausea. . . .

I was responsible at the same time for my body, for my race, for my ancestors. I discovered my blackness, my ethnic characteristics; and I was battered down by tom-toms, cannibalism, intellectual deficiency, fetishism, racial defects, slave-ships, and above all else, above all: "Sho' good eatin'."

On that day, completely dislocated, unable to be abroad with the other, the white man, who unmercifully imprisoned me, I took myself far off from my own presence, far indeed, and made myself an object. What else could it be for me but an amputation, an excision, a hemorrhage that spattered my whole body with black blood? But I did not want this revision, this thematization. All I wanted was to be a man among other men. I wanted to come lithe and young into a world that was ours and to help to build it together.

But I rejected all immunization of the emotions. I wanted to be a man, nothing but a man. Some identified me with ancestors of mine who had been enslaved or lynched: I decided to accept this. It was on the universal level of the intellect that I understood this inner kinship – I was the grandson of slaves in exactly the same way in which President Lebrun was the grandson of tax-paying, hard-working peasants. In the main, the panic soon vanished.

In America, Negroes are segregated. In South America, Negroes are whipped in the streets, and Negro strikers are cut down by machine-guns. In West Africa, the Negro is an animal. And there beside me, my neighbor in the university, who was born in Algeria, told me: "As long as the Arab is treated like a man, no solution is possible."

"Understand, my dear boy, color prejudice is something I find utterly foreign. . . . But of course, come in, sir, there is no color prejudice among us. . . . Quite, the Negro is a man like ourselves. . . . It is not because he is black that he is less intelligent than we are. . . . I had a Senegalese buddy in the army who was really clever. . . ."

Where am I to be classified? Or if you prefer, tucked away?

"A Martinican, a native of 'our' old colonies."

Where shall I hide?

"Look at the nigger! . . . Mama, a Negro! . . . Hell, he's getting mad. . . . Take no notice, sir, he does not know that you are as civilized as we. . . ."

My body was given back to me sprawled out, distorted, recolored, clad in mourning in that white winter day. The Negro is an animal, the Negro is bad, the Negro is mean, the Negro is ugly; look, a nigger, it's cold, the nigger is shivering, the nigger is shivering because he is cold, the little boy is trembling because he is afraid of the nigger, the nigger is shivering with cold, that cold that goes through your bones, the handsome little boy is trembling because he thinks that the nigger is quivering with rage, the little white boy throws himself into his mother's arms: Mama, the nigger's going to eat me up.

All round me the white man, above the sky tears at its navel, the earth rasps under my feet, and there is a white song, a white song. All this whiteness that burns me. . . .

I sit down at the fire and I become aware of my uniform. I had not seen it. It is indeed ugly. I stop there, for who can tell me what beauty is?

Where shall I find shelter from now on? I felt an easily identifiable flood mounting out of the countless facets of my being. I was about to be angry. The fire was long since out, and once more the nigger was trembling.

"Look how handsome that Negro is! . . ."

"Kiss the handsome Negro's ass, madame!"

Shame flooded her face. At last I was set free from my rumination. At the same time I accomplished two things: I identified my enemies and I made a scene. A grand slam. Now one would be able to laugh.

The field of battle having been marked out, I entered the lists.

What? While I was forgetting, forgiving, and wanting only to love, my message was flung back in my fact like a slap. The white world, the only honorable one, barred me from all participation. A man was expected to behave like a man. I was expected to behave like a black man – or at least like a nigger. I shouted a greeting to the world and the world slashed away my joy. I was told to stay within bounds, to go back where I belonged.

They would see, then! I had warned them, anyway. Slavery? It was no longer even mentioned, that unpleasant memory. My supposed inferiority? A hoax that it was better to laugh at. I forgot it all, but only on condition that the world not protect itself against me any longer. I had incisors to test. I was sure they were strong. And besides . . .

What! When it was I who had every reason to hate, to despise, I was rejected? When I should have been begged, implored, I was denied the slightest recognition? I resolved, since it was impossible for me to get away from an *inborn complex* to assert myself as a BLACK MAN. Since the other hesitated to recognize me, there remained only one solution: to make myself known.

In *Anti-Semite and Jew* (p. 95), Sartre says: "They [the Jews] have allowed themselves to be poisoned by the stereotype that others have of them, and they live in fear that their acts will correspond to this stereotype. . . . We may say that their conduct is perpetually overdetermined from the inside."

All the same, the Jew can be unknown in his Jewishness. He is not wholly what he is. One hopes, one waits. His actions, his behavior are the final determinant. He is a white man, and, apart from some rather debatable characteristics, he can sometimes go unnoticed. He belongs to the race of those who since the beginning of time have never known cannibalism. What an idea, to eat one's father! Simple enough, one has only not to be a nigger. Granted, the Jews are harassed – what am I thinking of? They are hunted down, exterminated, cremated. But these are little family quarrels. The Jew is disliked from the moment he is tracked down. But in my case everything takes on a *new* guise. I am given no chance. I am overdetermined from without. I am the slave not of the "idea" that others have of me but of my own appearance.

I move slowly in the world, accustomed now to seek no longer for upheaval. I progress by crawling. And already I am being dissected under white eyes, the only real eyes. I am *fixed*. Having adjusted their microtomes, they objectively cut away slices of my reality. I am laid bare. I feel, I see in those white faces that it is not a new man who has come in, but a new kind of man, a new genus. Why it's a Negro!

I slip into corners, and my long antennae pick up the catch-phrases strewn over the surface of things – nigger underwear smells of nigger – nigger teeth are white – nigger feet are big – the nigger's barrel chest – I slip into corners, I remain silent, I strive for anonymity, for invisibility. Look, I will accept the lot, as long as no one notices me!

"Oh, I want you to meet my black friend. . . . Aimé Césaire, a black man and a university graduate. . . . Marian Anderson, the finest of Negro singers. . . . Dr. Cobb, who invented white blood, is a Negro. . . . Here, say hello to my friend from Martinique (be careful, he's extremely sensitive). . . ."

Shame, Shame and self-contempt. Nausea. When people like me, they tell me it is in spite of my color. When they dislike me, they point out that it is not because of my color. Either way, I am locked into the infernal circle.

I turn away from these inspectors of the Ark before the Flood and I attach myself to my brothers, Negroes like myself. To my horror, they too reject me. They are almost white. And besides they are about to marry white women. They will have children faintly tinged with brown. Who knows, perhaps little by little. . . .

I had been dreaming.

"I want you to understand, sir, I am one of the best friends the Negro has in Lyon."

The evidence was there, unalterable. My blackness was there, dark and un-arguable. And it tormented me, pursued me, disturbed me, angered me.

Negroes are savages, brutes, illiterates. But in my own case I knew that these statements were false. There was a myth of the Negro that had to be destroyed at all costs. The time had long since passed when a Negro priest was an occasion for wonder. We had physicians, professors, statesmen. Yes, but something out of the ordinary still clung to such cases. "We have a Senegalese history teacher. He is quite bright. . . . Our doctor is colored. He is very gentle."

It was always the Negro teacher, the Negro doctor; brittle as I was becoming, I shivered at the slightest pretext. I knew, for instance, that if the physician made a mistake it would be the end of him and of all those who came after him. What could one expect, after all, from a Negro physician? As long as everything went well, he was praised to the skies, but look out, no nonsense, under any conditions! The black physician can never be sure how close he is to disgrace. I tell you, I was walled in: No exception was made for my refined manners, or my knowledge of literature, or my understanding of the quantum theory.

I requested, I demanded explanations. Gently, in the tone that one uses with a child, they introduced me to the existence of a certain view that was held by certain people, but, I was always told, "We must hope that it will very soon disappear." What was it? Color prejudice.

> It [colour prejudice] is nothing more than the unreasoning hatred of one race for another, the contempt of the stronger and richer peoples for those whom they consider inferior to themselves, and the bitter resentment of those who are kept in subjection and are so frequently insulted. As colour is the most obvious outward manifestation of race

it has been made the criterion by which men are judged, irrespective of their social or educational attainments. The light-skinned races have come to despise all those of a darker colour, and the dark-skinned peoples will no longer accept without protest the inferior position to which they have been relegated.[2]

I had read it rightly. It was hate; I was hated, despised, detested, not by the neighbor across the street or my cousin on my mother's side, but by an entire race. I was up against something unreasoned. The psychoanalysts say that nothing is more traumatizing for the young child than his encounters with what is rational. I would personally say that for a man whose only weapon is reason there is nothing more neurotic than contact with unreason.

I felt knife blades open within me. I resolved to defend myself. As a good tactician, I intended to rationalize the world and to show the white man that he was mistaken.

In the Jew, Jean-Paul Sartre says, there is

a sort of impassioned imperialism of reason: for he wishes not only to convince others that he is right; his goal is to persuade them that there is an absolute and unconditioned value to rationalism. He feels himself to be a missionary of the universal; against the universality of the Catholic religion, from which he is excluded, he asserts the "catholicity" of the rational, an instrument by which to attain to the truth and establish a spiritual bond among men.[3]

And, the author adds, though there may be Jews who have made intuition the basic category of their philosophy, their intuition

has no resemblance to the Pascalian subtlety of spirit, and it is this latter – based on a thousand imperceptible perceptions – which to the Jew seems his worst enemy. As for Bergson, his philosophy offers the curious appearance of an anti-intellectualist doctrine constructed entirely by the most rational and most critical of intelligences. It is through argument that he establishes the existence of pure duration, of philosophic intuition; and that very intuition which discovers duration or life, is itself universal, since anyone may practice it, and it leads towards the universal, since its objects can be named and conceived.[4]

With enthusiasm I set to cataloguing and probing my surroundings. As times changed, one had seen the Catholic religion at first justify and then condemn slavery and prejudices. But by referring everything to the idea of the dignity of man, one had ripped prejudice to shreds. After much reluctance, the scientists had conceded that the Negro was a human being; *in vivo* and *in vitro* the Negro had been proved analogous to the white man: the same morphology, the same histology. Reason was confident of victory on every level. I put all the parts back together. But I had to change my tune.

That victory played cat and mouse; it made a fool of me. As the other put it, when I was present, it was not; when it was there, I was no longer. In the abstract there was agreement: The Negro is a human being. That is to say, amended the less firmly convinced, that like us he has his heart on the left side. But on certain points the white man remained intractable. Under no conditions did he wish any intimacy between the races, for it is a truism that "crossings between widely different races can lower the physical and mental level. . . . Until we have a more definite knowledge of the effect of race-crossings we shall certainly do best to avoid crossings between widely different races."[5]

For my own part, I would certainly know how to react. And in one sense, if I were asked for a definition of myself, I would say that I am one who waits; I investigate my surroundings, I interpret everything in terms of what I discover, I become sensitive.

In the first chapter of the history that the others have compiled for me, the foundation of cannibalism has been made eminently plain in order that I may not lose sight of it. My chromosomes were supposed to have a few thicker or thinner genes representing cannibalism. In addition to the *sex-linked*, the scholars had now discovered the *racial-linked*.[6] What a shameful science!

But I understand this "psychological mechanism." For it is a matter of common knowledge that the mechanism is only psychological. Two centuries ago I was lost to humanity, I was a slave forever. And then came men who said that it all had gone on far too long. My tenaciousness did the rest; I was saved from the civilizing deluge. I have gone forward.

Too late. Everything is anticipated, thought out, demonstrated, made the most of. My trembling hands take hold of nothing; the vein has been mined out. Too late! But once again I want to understand.

Since the time when someone first mourned the fact that he had arrived too late and everything had been said, a nostalgia for the past has seemed to persist. Is this that lost original paradise of which Otto Rank speaks? How many such men, apparently rooted to the womb of the world, have devoted their lives to studying the Delphic oracles or exhausted themselves in attempts to plot the wanderings of Ulysses! The pan-spiritualists seek to prove the existence of a soul in animals by using this argument: A dog lies down on the grave of his master and starves to death there. We had to wait for Janet to demonstrate that the aforesaid dog, in contrast to man, simply lacked the capacity to liquidate the past. We speak of the glory of Greece, Artaud says; but, he adds, if modern man can no longer understand the *Choephoroi* of Aeschylus, it is Aeschylus who is to blame. It is tradition to which the anti-Semites turn in order to ground the validity of their "point of view." It is tradition, it is that long historical past, it is that blood relation between Pascal and Descartes, that is invoked when the Jew is told, "There is no possibility of your finding a place in society." Not long ago, one of those good Frenchmen said in a train where I was sitting: "Just let the real French virtues keep going and the race is safe. Now more than ever, national union must be made a reality. Let's have an end of internal strife! Let's face up to the foreigners (here he turned toward my corner) no matter who they are."

It must be said in his defense that he stank of cheap wine; if he had been capable of it, he would have told me that my emancipated-slave blood could not possibly be stirred by the name of Villon or Taine.

An outrage!

The Jew and I: Since I was not satisfied to be racialized, by a lucky turn of fate I was humanized. I joined the Jew, my brother in misery.

An outrage!

At first thought it may seem strange that the anti-Semite's outlook should be related to that of the Negro-phobe. It was my philosophy professor, a native of the Antilles, who recalled the fact to me one day: "Whenever you hear anyone abuse the Jews, pay attention, because he is talking about you." And I found that he was universally right – by which I meant that I was answerable in my body and in my heart for what was done to my brother. Later I realized that he meant, quite simply, an anti-Semite is inevitably anti-Negro.

[. . .] From time to time one would like to stop. To state reality is a wearing task. But, when one has taken it into one's head to try to express existence, one runs the risk of finding only the nonexistent. What is certain is that, at the very moment when I was trying to grasp my own being, Sartre, who remained The Other, gave me a name and thus shattered my last illusion. While I was saying to him:

> "My negritude is neither a tower nor a cathedral,
> it thrusts into the red flesh of the sun,
> it thrusts into the burning flesh of the sky,
> it hollows through the dense dismay of its own pillar of patience . . ."

while I was shouting that, in the paroxysm of my being and my fury, he was reminding me that my blackness was only a minor term. In all truth, in all truth I tell you, my shoulders slipped out of the framework of the world, my feet could no longer feel the touch of the ground. Without a Negro past, without a Negro future, it was impossible for me to live my Negrohood. Not yet white, no longer wholly black, I was damned. Jean-Paul Sartre had forgotten that the Negro suffers in his body quite differently from the white man.[7] Between the white man and me the connection was irrevocably one of transcendence.[8]

But the constancy of my love had been forgotten. I defined myself as an absolute intensity of beginning. So I took up my negritude, and with tears in my eyes I put its machinery together again. What had been broken to pieces was rebuilt, reconstructed by the intuitive lianas of my hands.

My cry grew more violent: I am a Negro, I am a Negro, I am a Negro. . . .

And there was my poor brother – living out his neurosis to the extreme and finding himself paralyzed:

THE NEGRO: I can't, ma'am.
LIZZIE: Why not?
THE NEGRO: I can't shoot white folks.
LIZZIE: Really! That would bother them, wouldn't it?
THE NEGRO: They're white folks, ma'am.
LIZZIE: So what? Maybe they got a right to bleed you like a pig just because they're white?
THE NEGRO: But they're white folks.

A feeling of inferiority? No, a feeling of nonexistence. Sin is Negro as virtue is white. All those white men in a group, guns in their hands, cannot be wrong. I am guilty. I do not know of what, but I know that I am no good.

> THE NEGRO: That's how it goes, ma'am. That's how it always goes with white folks.
>
> LIZZIE: You too? You feel guilty?
>
> THE NEGRO: Yes, ma'am.[9]

It is Bigger Thomas – he is afraid, he is terribly afraid. He is afraid, but of what is he afraid? Of himself. No one knows yet who he is, but he knows that fear will fill the world when the world finds out. And when the world knows, the world always expects something of the Negro. He is afraid lest the world know, he is afraid of the fear that the world would feel if the world knew. Like that old woman on her knees who begged me to tie her to her bed:

"I just know, Doctor: Any minute that thing will take hold of me."

"What thing?"

"The wanting to kill myself. Tie me down, I'm afraid."

In the end, Bigger Thomas acts. To put an end to his tension, he acts, he responds to the world's anticipation.[10]

So it is with the character in *If He Hollers Let Him Go*[11] – who does precisely what he did not want to do. That big blonde who was always in his way, weak, sensual, offered, open, fearing (desiring) rape, became his mistress in the end.

The Negro is a toy in the white man's hands; so, in order to shatter the hellish cycle, he explodes. I cannot go to a film without seeing myself. I wait for me. In the interval, just before the film starts, I wait for me. The people in the theater are watching me, examining me, waiting for me. A Negro groom is going to appear. My heart makes my head swim.

The crippled veteran of the Pacific war says to my brother, "Resign yourself to your color the way I got used to my stump; we're both victims."[12]

Nevertheless with all my strength I refuse to accept that amputation. I feel in myself a soul as immense as the world, truly a soul as deep as the deepest of rivers, my chest has the power to expand without limit. I am a master and I am advised to adopt the humility of the cripple. Yesterday, awakening to the world, I saw the sky turn upon itself utterly and wholly. I wanted to rise, but the disemboweled silence fell back upon me, its wings paralyzed. Without responsibility, straddling Nothingness and Infinity, I began to weep.

Notes

1 Jean Lhermitte, *L'Image de notre corps* (Paris, Nouvelle Revue critique, 1939), p. 17.
2 Sir Alan Burns, *Colour Prejudice* (London, Allen and Unwin, 1948), p. 16.
3 *Anti-Semite and Jew* (New York, Grove Press, 1960), pp. 112–13.
4 Ibid., p. 115.

5   Jon Alfred Mjoen, "Harmonic and Disharmonic Race-crossings," The Second International Congress of Eugenics (1921), *Eugenics in Race and State*, vol. II, p. 60, quoted in Sir Alan Burns, *op. cit.*, p. 120.

6   In English in the original. (Translator's note.)

7   Though Sartre's speculations on the existence of The Other may be correct (to the extent, we must remember, to which *Being and Nothingness* describes an alienated consciousness), their application to a black consciousness proves fallacious. That is because the white man is not only The Other but also the master, whether real or imaginary.

8   In the sense in which the word is used by Jean Wahl in *Existence humaine et transcendance*) (Neuchâtel, La Baconnière, 1944).

9   Jean-Paul Sartre, *The Respectful Prostitute*, in *Three Plays* (New York, Knopf, 1949), pp. 189, 191. Originally, *La Putain respectueuse* (Paris, Gallimard, 1947). See also *Home of the Brave,* a film by Mark Robson.

10 Richard Wright, *Native Son* (New York, Harper, 1940).

11 By Chester Himes (Garden City, Doubleday, 1945).

12 *Home of the Brave*.

Chapter 22

Lola Young

IMPERIAL CULTURE
The primitive, the savage and white civilization[1]

[. . .]

IN THIS CHAPTER I WILL examine how racialized discourses manifested themselves in texts, in terms of ideologies of superiority and inferiority
and where they connected with beliefs about femininity and masculinity, and sexuality. Critical analyses of orientalist, colonialist and primitivist discourses will be
considered in terms of their applicability to imperialist texts. I will analyse specific
representations of Otherness in some literary instances of the late nineteenth century,
suggesting how these images were subsequently consolidated and constituted in
the cinema.

This chapter marks the beginning of the analysis of specific films which are of
interest because of the ways in which they engage with racial and sexual issues. I am
not concerned here with films that have an aggressive imperialist vision since in many
respects these tend to be less interesting in terms of tensions and contradictions
within the text. The British archetype of this kind of jingoistic, compulsively
xenophobic film is probably *Sanders of the River* (1935). Films such as *The Song of
Freedom* (1936) and *Men of Two Worlds* (1946) are more engrossing as they slide
between an aggressive objectification of black African subjects, marking them as an
ignorant, 'primitive' undifferentiated mass, and an acknowledgement that specific
individuals can be redeemed by being properly schooled in the moral and cultural
values of western Europe. Another point of interest is that both *The Song of Freedom*
and *Men of Two Worlds* show the black protagonists living and working in England at
some stage and it is possible to see their interaction with white English people in
terms of class as well as 'race'. In *Sanders of the River* (1935), *Rhodes of Africa* (1936)
and other similar dramas, all the 'natives' are safely contained in Africa and the
virtues of colonialism unequivocally extolled. Another reason for including *The Song
of Freedom* and for devoting a chapter to imperialism and British cinema is that doing

so provides a context for the discussions in later chapters about the kinds of representations against which black film-makers in particular have reacted. [. . .]

Analysing colonial discourse

There have been a number of critiques of the discourses of Orientalism, primitivism and colonialism which have been helpful in identifying the role of ideology and discourse in the constitution of the colonized Other. A persistent critic of the way in which 'knowledge' and western European supremacist ideologies have constructed the Other and informed European culture, has been Edward Said (Said, 1985 and 1993). Although specifically referring to the way in which the notion of the Orient is a product of the western European imperial imagination, Said's theses in *Orientalism* can be usefully extended to a discussion of the way in which other cultures have been figured, although it is also necessary to bear in mind the specificities of the particular examples being discussed (Said, 1985). Said analyses Orientalism as an attempt to contain and control the Otherness of the Orient.

Said refers to a discourse of Orientalism, a set of terms, ideas and ways of constructing and thinking about the subject. Orientalism may be seen as preparing the way for colonialism discursively, ideologically and rhetorically. Both Orientalism and colonialism denied subject peoples' human agency and resistance and constructed explanatory models to account for the alterity of those subjects.

Similarly, much literary production during the late nineteenth century is replete with examples of 'knowledge' about the character of Africans based on white supremacist attitudes towards 'race'. In particular the notion of atavism – the belief that the 'primitive' people of Africa constituted an earlier stage of human development – often recurs: all the references to primeval swamps, to primitive rituals, the colonial subjects' perceived deficiency of language, intellect and culture attest to this belief. The texts are saturated with metaphors of 'darkness' infused with the presupposition of the positive associations of whiteness, light and so on, and negative attributes of blackness, dirtiness, ignorance, evil and so on.[2] The cultural (Christian) mission was, then, to introduce 'civilization' to the 'primitive' Other. Similar tropes are evident in the films of the 1930s such as *Sanders of the River* (1935), *The Song of Freedom* (1936), *King Solomon's Mines* (1937), *The Drum* (1938) and *The Four Feathers* (1939), and indeed, later in *Men of Two Worlds* (1947) and *Simba* (1955).

Marianna Torgovnick uses the idea of primitivism to identify and explicate a primitivist discourse in which the judgements of white Europeans about the intelligence, rationality and sexual practices of those deemed Other, are not acknowledged to be ideologically formed but are taken as categorical statements about the 'primitive' world (Torgovnick, 1990: 8).[3] Such convictions are abundant in the literature and cinema of imperialism. The necessity for Europeans of defining the primitive, Torgovnick argues, may be considered as an attempt to define the qualities and boundaries of white identity; an exploration of the self without problematizing the normalization of whiteness and its equation with civilization.

In specific instances, such as in the case of women, and in the case of the masses – frequently characterized as a teeming, primeval horde – some white people are attributed the qualities of 'primitiveness' thus becoming an internal Other. There are a number of instances when white women are positioned in ways analogous to the way in which black people – and working class people – are positioned albeit with variations in the woman's relative hierarchical status, and depending on her class and the degree of her heterosexual attraction. Torgovnick acknowledges this when she observes:

> gender issues always inhabit Western versions of the primitive. Sooner or later those familiar tropes for primitives become the tropes conventionally used for women. Global politics, the dance of colonizer and colonized, becomes sexual politics, the dance of male and female.
>
> (Torgovnick, 1990: 17)

Torgovnick's analysis conceptualizes these two issues – of primitivist discourse and patriarchal discourse – as parallel, linear developments and this does not allow for an analysis of the intersections and discontinuities. I argue that these discourses sometimes converge, and sometimes overlap in the cinematic examples which follow. Furthermore, in Torgovnick's examples there is little sense of the historical role of scientific and historiographical discourses in providing the 'objective proof' for the development of ideas about the relative statuses of black/white and male/female which I argue is crucial to an understanding of the potency and persistence of ideologies of racial and gender difference, and sexuality.[4]

As has been discussed [. . .], both Homi Bhabha and Edward Said in their accounts of colonialist and Orientalist discourses see the construction of stereotypes as crucial to the imperialist hegemonic project. Elaborating on Said's critique of the European 'archive' of knowledge, Bhabha asserts that colonial discourse is:

> a form of knowledge and identification that vacillates between what is always 'in place', already known, and something that must be anxiously repeated . . . as if the essential duplicity of the Asiatic or the bestial sexual licence of the African that needs no proof, can never really, in discourse, be proved.
>
> (Bhabha, 1983: 18)

The necessity for vacillation is occasioned because the discourse attempts to fix and stabilise that which is not static. The desire for scientism, exemplified in the valorization of systematic categorization based on empiricism, inevitably produces some instances which refuse to be contained by the conceptual boundaries established. In these cases either the lines of demarcation have to be re-ordered or the exceptions denied, and this is why stereotypes are protean rather than stable.

Although a good deal of what is expressed with regard to racial differences is contradictory there is 'a rigorous subconscious logic' which:

> defines the relations between the covert and overt policies and between the material and discursive practices of colonialism. The ideological functions of colonialist fiction . . . must be understood . . . in terms of the exigencies of domestic – that is, European and colonialist –

politics and culture; and the function of racial difference, of the fixation
on and fetishization of native savagery and evil, must be mapped in
terms of these exigencies and ideological imperatives.

> (JanMohamed, 1985: 62–63)

For this fetishization and demonization to cohere and 'make sense', there had to
be in place a systematic oppositional differentiation in *all* spheres, made between
colonizer and colonized: that such a dichotomous relationship existed was not often
challenged by the middle of the nineteenth century, even amongst those who had
opposed slavery. Once such notions enter the popular domain and hence discourse
and ideology, then they are, to all intents and purposes 'reality', since

> The work of ideology is to present the position of the subject as fixed
> and unchangeable, an element in a given system of differences which
> is human nature and the world of human experience, and to show
> possible action as an endless repetition of "normal", familiar action.
>
> (Belsey 1980: 90)

The conventional practices of colonial/imperial cinematic realist representations
attributed fixed, inferior characteristics to black people, basing such characterizations
on an archive of 'knowledge' about the African character, and, arguably, the
cumulative effect of such images was to limit informed public debate and to justify
policies regarding colonial rule. It is important to remember that the beginnings
of cinema coincided with the peak of colonial expansion towards the end of the
nineteenth and the first decades of the twentieth centuries. Imperialist growth and
policies had to be sustained and the emergent mass medium of the cinema offered
the opportunity to promote and consolidate colonial policy overseas. It should also
be noted, as Ella Shohat points out, that:

> Western cinema not only inherited and disseminated colonial discourse,
> but also created a system of domination through monopolistic control
> of film distribution and exhibition in much of Asia, Africa, and Latin
> America.
>
> (Shohat 1991:45)

Masculine, feminine

During the peak period of colonial expansion, a number of fictional works emerged
that were fantasized depictions of Africa and its people which served as an exotic
background against which white men could act out and test the prescribed masculine
qualities such as courage, tenacity and self-control. These narratives are characterized
by their vision of a robust, bourgeois, homosocial masculinity.

Newspapers, popular entertainment, postcards and comics in the first decade
of the twentieth century constantly reinforced the idea of war as glamorous,
character-building and fascinating: an activity which occurred in far-off exotic places,
away from what was seen as the stifling confinement of domesticity. These images
and fantasies were inextricably linked to conceptualizations of masculinity, and the

idea of what constitutes masculinity was a key site for confrontations springing from racial conflict, since in racially stratified societies, the notion of masculinity is not only determined by its being in opposition to femininity but by its racial specificity.

Ideas about masculinity, as is the case with other socially constructed categories, are in a continual state of flux and specific to historical time and place, although this is not always recognized to be the case. Particular ideas about what constitutes 'manliness' in terms of physical and athletic prowess became dominant in the late nineteenth century through public concern about British men's physical weakness at a time of expanding imperial conquests and the demand for the defence of existing colonies (Bristow, 1991; Roper and Tosh, 1991: 19).

There was also a crisis of masculinity which arose because of the success of the bourgeois vision of domestic life. Crucial to this lifestyle was the man's duty to provide moral and religious support, and the adoption of an ideology of hard work and thrift. In the bourgeois household, the home was the domain of the economically dependent wife whilst the rough world of industrial capitalism and work was the province of the male. The home was thus associated with the feminine since that was where the woman could exercise what power she did have. The bourgeois feminine world was that of domesticity, physical weakness, emotional displays, and masculinity was the antithesis of these characteristics.

White women – both middle and working class – and black people are again both implicated here as both were characterized as being dependent on others, and as being defined only through their oppositional relationship to white middle class men.[5] Although during the nineteenth century black and working class women were expected to carry out arduous physical labour, white middle class women were assigned a position of physical delicacy and fragility and were placed on a pedestal of sexual unattainability. The idealization of white female sexual purity and the valorization of 'masculine' attributes such as courage, autonomous action and independence served to privilege the celebration of essentialized characteristics of masculinity and femininity. Whilst it is the case that white middle class women were used and abused, they also colluded in shoring up the structures of supremacy and domination, supporting both class and racial stratification [. . .]

The desire to look on and control the female body had limited acceptability in regard to white women: with the institutionalization of black people's inferior status, no such inhibitions existed in regard to the bodies of African women. [. . .] During the late eighteenth and nineteenth centuries the black female body was subjected to rigorous scientific examination and her naked body placed on public display, the vast majority of such investigatory work being carried out, of course, by white male doctors and scientists. However, even into the twentieth century, the story was different when it came to white women who wished to exercise their privileged racial status through the right to look as is made clear in the following passage from a popular magazine, *Titbits,* 21 July, 1917:

> Some years ago we used to have large bodies of natives sent from Africa
> on military service or in some travelling show, and it was a revelation
> of horror and disgust to behold the manner in which English women
> would flock to see these men, whilst to watch them fawning upon these

black creatures and fondling them and embracing them, as I have seen
dozens of times, was a scandal and a disgrace to English womanhood.
How then is it possible to maintain as the one stern creed in the policy
of the Empire the eternal supremacy of white over black?

(quoted in Henriques, 1974:141)

Here the links between bestiality and sexuality, the gendering of the criteria by
which sexual impropriety is judged, femininity, and the putative effects of
transgressive sexual relations on the imperial project and white supremacy are
decisively articulated. [. . .]

Black femininity

[. . .] An analysis of representations of black femininity in the genre of colonial
and imperial literary adventures and their cinematic successors needs to take account
of the African women's metaphoric status which has arisen from the intersection
of these discourses on gender, 'race' and sexuality.[6] The literary texts are of note,
not just because of the recurring metaphors and themes, but because several important
films of the 1930s such as *King Solomon's Mines* (1937), *The Four Feathers* (1939)
and *Sanders of the River* (1935) were based on these novels.

In imperial literature regarding the terrain, there is much talk of 'penetration',
'conquering the interior' and so on. Africa is characterized as feminine with all
the contradictory connotations of passivity, uncontrollability, desire and danger
and indicating the extent to which colonial metaphors are gendered. An indicator
of the elision of African landscapes and the (forbidden) desire for (black) femity
is embedded in Freud's use of the term, 'dark continent'.

The seduction and conquest of the African woman became a metaphor
for the conquest of Africa itself. A powerful erotic symbolism linked
a woman's femininity so strongly to the attraction of the land that they
became one single idea, and to both were attributed the same irresistible,
deadly charm.

(Nicholas Monti, quoted in Doane, 1991: 213)

The feminization of the landscape points to a fascination with, and desire for,
African women which cannot be made explicit or elaborated due to its transgressive
nature: thus the desire may only be articulated through displacement. A prime
example of this figurative displacement occurs in H. Rider Haggard's novel *King
Solomon's Mines* (1885). From the perspective of the imperial 'I/eye' of his hero,
Alan Quatermain, Haggard gives a detailed description of the African landscape
which likens the mountainous panorama to a woman's breasts:

. . . I attempt to describe that extraordinary grandeur and beauty of
that sight, language seems to fail me. I am impotent even at its memory.
Before us rose two enormous mountains . . . These mountains . . . are
shaped after the fashion of a woman's breasts, and at times the mists

and shadows beneath them take the form of a recumbent woman veiled
mysteriously in sleep. Their bases swell gently from the plain, looking
at that distance perfectly round and smooth; and on top of each is a
vast hillock covered with snow, exactly corresponding to the nipple on
the female breast.

(Haggard, 1979: 56–57)

Significantly, Quatermain, white hero and narrator of the novel, on recalling the
beauty of the sight of that landscape admits to being cast back into the pre-symbolic
realm without language, rendered speechless and impotent 'even at its memory'
(Bristow, 1991: 127). The loss of the accoutrements of civilization and culture is
figured through sexual impotence: these fears are the continual fears of the oppressor.
Those African 'breasts' recall the dependency of infant on mother and as a
consequence, the anger experienced at being separated from her, the primary love-
object, and it is the enforced recognition of difference which produces 'impotence'.

That the sight of these 'breasts', the female's visible signifiers of sexual difference
and maternity. should generate such powerlessness and be effected through Africa
is indicative of the anxieties being displaced onto the land and onto black women.
If white men's fear of white women is based on the 'uncontrollable' sexual arousal
instigated by them, then since African women have been frequently described as
hypersexual and are phenotypically marked as inherently and immutably different,
the anxieties instigated by sexual difference are exacerbated. In the case of both
females and males, the contention that blacks are oversexed is historically linked
to and 'proven' by alleged anatomical excesses in one form or another. Whether
or not there was or is any empirical evidence to support or deny such beliefs is
irrelevant: it is the fact that such notions were, and still are, considered meaningful,
are still perpetuated either directly or indirectly, and are still the subject of many
ribald jokes, that is the significant issue.

At the same time as functioning as a contrast through which the white European
male could conceive of himself as fearless, active, independent, in control, virile
and so on, the African woman also represented a double negation of that heroic
self, being not-male, not-white. Freud's epistemology, as Shohat argues: 'assumes
the (white) male as the bearer of knowledge, who can penetrate woman and text,
while she, as a remote region, will let herself be explored until truth is uncovered'
(Shohat, 1991: 58). The question is, the truth about whom? Through the sexualization
of the feminized African landscape, lying passively on its (her) back displaying
naked splendour and availability (for penetration and conquest), the white male
unconscious can indulge itself in fantasizing about his assault on, his merging with
the forbidden object of fascination and desire. But there is fear embedded in that
desire, hence the necessity for denial.

Although black women were seen as 'not-male', neither were they seen as
women in the same sense that white women were. Since slavery, African females
had been seen as at once women – inasmuch as they were sexualized, reproductive
and subordinate – and not-women, that is not pure, not feminine, not fragile but
strong and sexually knowing and available. Thus an implicit contrast was established
between white (middle class) and black women and this generated the complex
set of relations under colonialism [. . .]

This in itself posed a number of problems for white men in their actual and fictional imperial adventures. Given the firmly established ideas about the inferiority of black people, it was unacceptable for white men on their travels across Africa to admit openly to engaging in interracial sexual activity. Referring to Edgar Wallace's eponymous hero, from the novel, *Sanders of the River,* Jeffrey Richards notes:

> Not surprisingly he [Sanders] is unshakeably opposed to miscegenation. When a succession of young officers become enamoured of the beautiful M'Lino he sends them home declaring: 'Monkey tricks of that sort are good enough for the Belgian Congo and for Togoland but they aren't good enough for this little strip of wilderness.'
>
> (Richards, 1973: 31)

Again, there is the linking of simian imagery with black people and sexual activity, and the often repeated assertion that the colonialism practised by other European powers was immoral and brutal as opposed to Britain's 'benign', paternalistic version.[7]

The European, as JanMohamed argues, has a choice when confronted with what she or he imagines as an unfathomable, alien Otherness. Hypothetically, she or he:

> has the option of responding to the Other in terms of identity or difference. If he assumes that he and the Other are essentially identical, then he would tend to ignore the significant divergences and to judge the Other according to his own cultural values. If, on the other hand, he assumes the Other is irremediably different, then he would have little incentive to adopt the viewpoint of that alterity: he would again turn to the security of his own perspective. Genuine and thorough comprehension of Otherness is possible only if the self can somehow negate or at least severely bracket the values, assumptions, and ideology of his culture.
>
> (JanMohamed, 1985: 64–65)

First though, white people have to recognize the 'values, assumptions and ideology' and to acknowledge the extent to which Otherness is a construction arising from those assumptions and beliefs. JanMohamed's argument is here locked into its own binarism, as he posits two alternatives and imputes a stability and cohesion in colonial and primitivist discourses which is illusory as has been argued by Homi Bhabha. Neither is it clear just what constitutes a significant difference or how singular a cultural perspective might be. Nonetheless, such an analysis recognizes the contradictions inherent in the colonialists' hazardous psychic positioning. Violation of the Other, whether literally, metaphorically, or representationally, must of necessity also be an act of cultural masochism since the Other is necessarily a part of the self constructed in and through difference.

> This establishment of the other *as* other is promoted by the initial drive to establish self-identity by identifying *with* the other. Negating others, *denigrating* them, becomes in part, thus, also self-negation and self-effacement.
>
> (Goldberg, 1993: 60)

This assertion regarding self-effacement should not be understood as a relinquishing of power, rather it comes as a result of possessing and naturalizing relations of power.

As the embodiment of an 'archive' of fantasies, 'primitives', 'orientals' and colonized black people have been expected to behave in particular ways and obliged to occupy particular positions in films. The power to define the Other – a power derived from economic and political dominance – is clearly demonstrated in the construction of the colonial subject represented in the literature and cinema of Empire: African men were at once feared and admired, being the objects of feelings of repulsion and veneration. White masculine cultural superiority is signified through the comparisons of weaponry (the 'savage' with the spear versus the gentleman with the revolver being a contest of phallic symbols), intelligence and courage. In these texts white masculinity is constantly revered, femininity excluded and derided and racism is naturalized.

The ambivalence that was structured into the consciousness of so many fictional adventurer heroes in Africa during that period finds expression in the recognition of the Africans' 'beauty' and the incongruity of their 'evil'. Rarely are Africans portrayed as individuated human beings. The primitive, homogeneous mass is emblematic of the Manichean confrontation between Self and Other; a scene often re-enacted in the cinema and literature of Empire.[8]

The testing of white masculinity was explicitly represented through combat with the savage Other: more covertly (though there are exceptions to which I will refer later) white masculinity was concerned with establishing white male virility within a heterosexual context, and the feminine metaphors used to describe Africa, including the controlling trope of the 'dark continent' itself indicate the repression of the feminine. Part of the explanation for the repression of the sexual element lies with the fact that:

> the whole genre bears the distinct imprint of the public school. The virtues and characteristics of the Imperial archetype are the virtues and characteristics bred into him by his public school. The male camaraderie and the subordinate role of women reflects the all-male environment of the public schools.
>
> (Richards, 1973: 220)

It would seem that the flight from the feminine and the domestic must be absolute: and with white women absent, homosexuality unspeakable and interracial hetero-sexual relations unthinkable, what is the white male hero to do in terms of sexual expression but circumscribe the field of sexual activity and sublimate sexual thoughts?

The cinema of empire

During the late 1920s, Britain's Colonial Office decided to exploit the propaganda qualities of film as it set out to explore how best to capitalize on cinema's potential for disseminating imperial ideology. By the 1920s North American cinema was already dominant. There was concern that some of the images of white people could be interpreted as deriding European or British culture and that steps should be taken to counter this. For example, the films of Charlie Chaplin were immensely popular but much of his work involved the humiliation of respectable male figures, men of authority and propriety such as clergymen and policemen, and eventually such texts were censored for screenings in the colonies (Smyth 1983: 129–143). In the USA during the 1920s the Hays Office codes ensured sexual propriety by establishing a code of conduct for film-makers which severely limited, in particular, the sexual content of films. The North American Production Code of the Motion Picture Producers and Directors of America, Inc. (1930–1934) made its policy on the representation of interracial sex explicit: 'Miscegenation (sex relation between the white and black races) is forbidden' (quoted in Shohat, 1991: 66). Also subject to censorship were any representations of white women behaving seductively (Smyth, 1983). In Kenya and Rhodesia (now Zimbabwe) where there were substantial white populations, viewing was racially segregated and censorship practised until at least the late 1940s according to whether the black population or white people were the intended audience.[9]

Although there were significant numbers of black people in Britain during the early part of the twentieth century, in the 1930s Otherness was almost always located 'out there' geographically, in adventure films such as *King Solomon's Mines* (1937), *The Drum* (1938) and *The Four Feathers* (1939). Africa was still conceptualized as belonging to prehistory, its peoples supposedly uncivilized.

In colonialist adventure films and literature, it is often the case that Africa's primeval existence is figured through the lush vegetative landscape, and edenic vistas. The strange animals and the strange people are seen as one entity, one powerful evocation of an exoticism impossible to find within the confines of Europe. However, although the primitive and the exotic were depicted as being in a location far removed from Britain, the texts in the imperial adventure genre served to confirm white European notions of cultural superiority and are thus, essentially parochial and introspective, telling us about how whiteness imagined itself rather than about these Other cultures.

An illustration of this 'speaking of self' in the guise of discussing the Other occurred when European men encountered tribal kinship structures based on polyandry and polygyny: they viewed these familial practices as expressions of an allegedly excessive black sexuality which was to be both tamed and exploited.

That such polygamous practices exemplified a supposed black male sexual potency which was both feared and envied is still evidenced in *Sanders of the River* (1935), where 'Sandy the strong, Sandy the wise' (Leslie Banks) dissuades ten young 'African' women who all wish to marry Bosambo (Paul Robeson in a revealing animal print loincloth) by proclaiming that Bosambo is already married to five older women, stronger than any of them. In fact Bosambo is not married to anyone but Sanders' role at this point is to actively control the potential reproduction of his favourite 'native' – an ex-convict – by introducing him to the concept of a monogamous heterosexual relationship. [. . .]

Different worlds

It would be misleading to suggest that Britain's hegemonic colonial practices met with or maintained uniform success or to assume that all black African opposition was located in Africa. Although the black population of Britain was still relatively small during the 1930s, there were a number of politically active people who saw the issue of black equality in this country as inextricable from questions of colonial policy. This activity led to the establishment of a number of organizations opposed to colonialism and racism. Pan-African sentiment grew whilst white people's participation in these political struggles was increasingly felt to be unacceptable: building on the connections between people of the African diaspora was considered to be the most effective way of organizing campaigns against oppression. Barbara Bush has noted that:

> In their efforts to improve race relations white liberals worked from a middle-class perspective, and thus to them "racial equality" usually implied equality for cultured, Europeanized blacks such as Paul Robeson and Harold Moody.
>
> (Bush, 1981: 47)[10]

Paul Robeson is a complex figure in terms of what he signified for both black and white audiences, and he did what he could to challenge supremacist ideologies in the film industry and wider society. He had the advantages of being both articulate and clever, and conforming to the conventional role of black male as performer and sporting personality, and – in the British context – of being from the USA.[11] African–American actors have often been preferred over British-based black people in a number of British films, a practice which still goes on today and which signals a degree of exoticism attributed to the black Other from 'elsewhere' which accrues in a limited way to the black Other within.[12]

Paul Robeson starred in *The Song of Freedom* (1936) with Elizabeth Welch, another African–American singer who lived in Britain. The film's opening sequence, beginning as it does with a mass of running, clamouring, African 'natives' – whose threatening, uncivilized demeanour is diminished by the angle of the shot which sees them running away from the camera – immediately draws the audience into the perspective of the explorer seeking to discover the Otherness of Africa. The legend, 'AFRICA' appears as the scene dissolves into a classic mountain/sea/landscape shot of a tropical island. Again, a caption appears in order to anchor the meaning of the visuals: 'The island of Casanga, off the west coast – in the year 1700 AD. The island had not yet attracted the attention of the slave traders on the mainland' we are told but 'its people suffered as fierce an oppression under their hereditary Queen Zinga – tyrant, despot, mistress of cruelty.' This last phrase may be indicative of a disaffection with female heads of state and matrilinearity and is significant if only because so few of the films set in Africa feature autonomous women. However to claim Queen Zinga as a powerful woman is to ignore the derisory treatment her character is given and the sadistic overtones of her 'mistress of cruelty' label.

Queen Zinga is played as a woman with a face fixed in a grimace, matted hair and an oiled body indicating a perpetual sweatiness. Zinga – wearing animal pelts, shells and beads – is flanked by further representations of primitiveness: tribal iconography consisting of archetypal primitive 'African' statues and two men whose bodies merge with the statues. In the face of the violent irrational matriarch, the men are reduced to ciphers. Zinga's men are passive male bodies, echoing the stance of the statues through both their physical positions and the way that they hold their shields. The interplay here between sexual and racial difference is marked. There is an appeal to white patriarchy: note that women who rule are insane megalomaniacs and to wield power is unnatural for them. Power strips women of their femininity – Zinga's gender is initially ambiguous – and men under matriarchy lack dignity, losing their ability to act autonomously.

This early sequence introduces us to a mad, cruel primitive African woman who is the opposite of most cinematic images of white femininity. In relation to her physical appearance and demeanour, the white male audience is interpellated as superior through their rationality, their intellect and the physical attraction of 'their' women. The primitivization of Zinga does not invite white women to identify with her or to be identified with her.

The process of cinematic identification of viewing subjects with characters and situations in the film is, however, a complex one and it should be acknowledged that identity may be characterized as fragmented with only an illusory coherence (Ellis, 1988: 43). It is not possible to assert that black people always or exclusively identify with black characters, although one can posit that black audiences viewing this type of film may experience a range of feelings which might vary according to context.

Fanon felt that, through representation:

> The Negro is a toy in the white man's hands . . . I cannot go to a film without seeing myself. I wait for me. In the interval, just before the film starts, I wait for me. The people in the theater are watching me, examining me, waiting for me.
>
> (Fanon, 1986: 140)

He then painfully reconstructs the sense of embarrassment and internalized self hatred which may entrap the black viewer of such texts: a viewer fixed by the gaze of the film-maker and white members of the audience. Fanon is explicit about the different effects that films such as *Tarzan* may have on black people, depending on the viewing context:

> In the Antilles, the young Negro identifies himself *de facto* with Tarzan against the Negroes. This is much more difficult for him in a European theater, for the rest of the audience, which is white, automatically identifies him with the savages on the screen.
>
> (Fanon, 1986: 152–153)

Paul Robeson is close to the 'noble savage' archetype in *The Song of Freedom*. His popularity as a singer is extensively brought into play in the film. His ability to sing is naturalized, reiterating the notion that all black people are able to sing spontaneously, without training: this 'natural' ability is then used as a crucial marker for his racially defined and differentiated subjectivity. John Zinga/Paul Robeson is both a 'natural' singer and a natural worker – he is, in this narrative, after all, of royal descent and thus not so feckless and unreliable as the average black male.

Perhaps this royal lineage is intended to account for his resilience, as, in spite of being conceived during the Middle Passage, into slavery – which according to the film was not an unpleasant experience – Zinga manages to make his way to England.

Zinga's naturalness is contrasted with the white upper class people who disembark from the ship in the docks where he is employed: they are remote from the world of physical labour which is going on around them. One of these passengers is an opera director, Gabriel Donozetti; his status as a foreign Other, albeit 'white' is established through his feminization: that is to say that arm and hand movements associated with 'feminine' gestures are deployed to signify both his exoticism and his distance from the experience of manual labour. Donozetti is a purveyor of opera, the exemplary cultural form of the privileged classes.

Part of what is interesting about this film is the fact that John Zinga's class allegiance is to the dockers with whom he works. The narrative posits a somewhat utopian vision of racial harmony in England where racism is clearly not an issue but where divisions based on social class are immutable and natural. 'Race' does, however, intrude on this cosy scenario on an unconscious level. For example, Zinga's nobility and royal lineage serve to make him only on a par with white workers, rather than according him the privileges of upper middle class English society. His entrée into the upper echelons of English society is made possible by his voice rather than by his birth and is strictly limited.

African–American film historian Donald Bogle describes John and Ruth Zinga as living 'a rather arch domestic life . . . who together are almost too wholesome and bourgeois to be true' (Bogle, 1988: 197). In her gingham dress the character of Ruth certainly looks as though she is designed to fit in with the minimum of visual disruption but their social status is rather that of the respectable, socially aspirant working class rather than the middle class.

John Zinga yearns to travel to Africa, even though he has no idea of his ancestry and it is posited that such a yearning is inbred. Richard Dyer suggests that this aspect of Robeson's characterization which surfaces in his other films too, may be an unconscious expression of the problematic relationship between African–Americans and Africa.[13] I think it has as much to do with white people's (sometimes unconscious) desire to see Africans returned to their 'natural' habitat; that is, Africa. The fact of black people being out of place here is emphasized by their isolation and the focus on their discomfiture in white English society.

Bogle's short commentary on *The Song of Freedom* is not able to be developed due to the encyclopedic nature of his book: it is beyond the scope of his work to attempt to account for some of the more interesting and contradictory aspects of the text. For example in the first domestic scene we see, John Zinga looks longingly at a poster depicting an 'African' landscape. This poster is in a pivotal location above the fireplace and the association here between home–hearth–heart is made clear as it becomes the focus of the audience's gaze, of Ruth's gaze and, of course, of Zinga's gaze. The caption on the poster encourages the reader to 'Go where there's sunshine! Christmas and New Year tours to South Africa': standing in front of this image is the ubiquitous archetypal African statue. The juxtaposition of these divergent representations of Africanness potentially establish a tension between the Zingas' English working-class lifestyle and what are held to be their cultural and racial origins. Ruth mildly castigates John for his desire to be in Africa by interrupting his fantasies with 'you're happy here: the people are kind' to which John responds with 'oh they're grand people . . . somewhere down there are *our* people Ruth and I've got a feeling they're grand people too. The people we belong to. Funny . . . that [white] fellow didn't want to go . . . natural – he's leaving his people to go out among strangers: he'll be out of place – lonely maybe. However hard I try, I always feel the same here.' Thus John Zinga makes explicit the 'unnaturalness' of black people in England whilst pointing to the reluctance of the white traveller as confirmation of the notion that people should remain with 'their own people'. It does not appear to matter how friendly or decent the host society is, these attempts at crossing the racial divide are bound to fail. Why Zinga should aspire to travel to South Africa is not established. It seems that the poster might be appropriate in a white working class home where South Africa would represent an opportunity to improve their social standing, and perhaps it is there in order to indicate the extent of Zinga's assimilation. It may perhaps also indicate that South Africa was considered an appropriate political system under which black people should work: clearly delineated statuses for black and white, systematic and inflexible ordering and categorization and supporting legislation were already in place by the 1930s. [. . .]

People from different worlds

Men of Two Worlds does not have the presence of a star persona such as Paul Robeson but ten years after *The Song of Freedom*, it is still foregrounding similar issues and themes. Interestingly, the title *Men of Two Worlds* resonates with more recent descriptions of young black people in Britain as being 'trapped between two cultures' [. . .]

This time the black male protagonist is named Kisenga – which sounds similar to Casanga, the island in *The Song of Freedom* – and he is a concert pianist rather than an opera singer but still firmly located within the realms of high rather than the emergent popular culture. Kisenga's music is a hybrid of traditional 'African' and classical European music, signifying that Kisenga is Europeanized but retains, as he puts it, 'the thousand years of Africa in his blood.' He decides to go to Africa to help 'his' people plagued by the tsetse fly which causes sleeping sickness.

Again the ignorance and primitivism of the 'African native' is embodied in the figure of the manipulative witch doctor who will not allow his fellow villagers to take the medicine prescribed by Doctor Munroe (Phyllis Calvert), the white female doctor. As is the case in *The Song of Freedom,* the principal evil of the witch doctor's rule is seen as his rejection of European values and his abhorrence of white people's presence in Africa.

A rationale for refusing to move away from the infestation is not attributed to this 'primitive' tribal community: they merely act, they do not think. This re-inforces white European assumptions about rational motivation being absent amongst 'primitive' people. In contrast to the childlike Africans, the archetypal figure of the District Commissioner, Randall (Eric Portman), is the voice of Europe masculine reason, trying to get the Litu – Kisenga's people – to move to a place which is not infested with tsetse flies. When the community, influenced by the 'witch doctor' reject European medicine it is seen as evidence of their irrationality and they thus forfeit any claim to be thought of as autonomous human beings. This is a similar justification for domination to that proposed during the eighteenth and nineteenth centuries.

Another point to note is how, just as in the earlier imperial literature described above, 'natives' are depicted as a primeval, undifferentiated horde. This colonialist tendency is identified by Albert Memmi as a strategy of depersonalization named by him as 'the mark of the plural.' Memmi, talking in general terms, notes: 'The colonized is never characterized in an individual manner; he is only to drown in an anonymous collectivity ("They are this." "They are all the same.")' (Memmi, 1990: 151). In *Sanders of the River* (1935), *The Song of Freedom* (1936), *Men of Two Worlds* (1947) and *Simba* (1955), only the quiescent or Europeanized Africans are allowed the privilege of individual subjectivity and the limits of this autonomy are strictly defined.

Men of Two Worlds has the characteristics of a film which was a tired attempt to revitalize and sustain the myth of benevolent British paternal colonial rule when it was already clear that the British Empire had little life left in it. However, there is a point of interest to which I would draw attention: Phyllis Calvert's performance as the doctor. Her disgust at the sight and proximity of the black people in the film is almost palpable. Her whole body seems to be infused with a nervous tension that manifests itself in the way she speaks, moves and relates to the other actors. She refuses to engage in eye contact with Kisenga and on occasion acts as though he does not exist, talking and looking through or past him. She barely acknowledges his presence and ensures that their bodies are never close enough to make contact even when they pass each other in narrow spaces. The extent to which Calvert's demeanour is intended to be a trait of her character is not clear. It could be that this hypertense performance is attributable to the repression of sexuality which informs the film and the taboos regarding interracial relationships between black men and white women which were even more marked then than they are today.

Made in 1955 *Simba*, represents yet another reworking of these themes of the black African male who is educated and has taken on in some clearly signalled sense western European culture. Here though, British fear regarding the increasingly vociferous demands for autonomy, and colonial subjects' rebellion against the experience of subordination is manifested in what Dyer calls 'the rigid binarism, with white standing for modernity, reason, order, stability, and black standing for backwardness, irrationality, chaos and violence' (Dyer, 1988: 49). The role of the bad Other is displaced from the witch doctor and intensified in relation to the Mau-Mau in *Simba*. This text is a late entry into the colonial adventure canon, coming as it did towards the end of British colonial rule in Africa. It does not engage with the black presence in England and may be seen as representing the terror of the imminent end of Empire and the assumption of white supremacy.

Conclusion

It was necessary to conceptualize and depict the colonial Other as an infantile, sexually licentious savage in order to justify continued economic exploitation, surveillance and the ruthless wielding of power. Bhabha sees the attribution of such qualities as perverse contradictions:

> The black is both savage (cannibal) and yet the most obedient and dignified of servants (the bearer of food); he is the embodiment of rampant sexuality and yet innocent as a child; he is mystical, primitive, simple-minded and yet the most worldly and accomplished liar, and manipulator of social forces. In each case what is being dramatised is a separation – *between* races, cultures, histories, within *histories* – a separation between *before* and *after* that repeats obsessively the mythical moment of disjunction.
>
> (Bhabha, 1983: 34)

Attributing cannibalism to savage Others serves at once as justification for taming those savages, as a confirmation of white European supremacy and as a screen onto which to project guilty repression of the knowledge that it is the white oppressor who behaves in a cannibalistic manner. The act of cannibalism also functions as a useful metaphor for colonial exploitation [. . .] There is also in evidence in these anxious repetitions of colonial tropes, the fear of being re-absorbed into the dark, articulated as a fear of the dark or being swallowed, or ingested by the Other. In order to exercise 'mastery' over that 'darkness', to pre-empt the retaliation that they guiltily fear will be enacted against them, acts of violation are perpetrated, such as rapine penetration, and genocide.

The notion of British colonialism as a global civilizing mission is explicit in *Sanders of the River* (1935), *The Song of Freedom* (1936), and *Men of Two Worlds* (1946), and reflects the narcissism embedded in colonial and neo-colonial fantasies. The central character of the white male is represented as whole, unified and coherent, a perception constantly in danger of disruption through the mirror-image of the black Other. Embedded in the psyche is the 'knowledge' that difference – specifically racial and sexual difference – subverts and disrupts the notion of cohesion and order and this anxiety needs to be constantly mollified. These films served as comforting narratives for a nation which, used to assuming spiritual, cultural and political superiority, was traumatised by the Indian 'mutiny' and the subsequent fear of further destabilizing uprisings and acts of resistance. Through cinema – and literature – the old self-assurance could be re-asserted with the likes of 'Sandy the strong, Sandy the wise' able to rule over devoted black subjects, in spite of being vastly outnumbered.

Five years before *Simba* was made, Basil Dearden's *Pool of London* was released. This film indicates a significant break with the colonial adventure genre since no direct link is made between the black male character and Africa. Although he works on a ship which necessitates him spending long periods away from London, his presence is not specifically marked as unnatural or out of place. However, attempts to date a white woman are thwarted in order to avoid any controversy.

Significant numbers of black settlers from Africa, South Asia and the Caribbean came to Britain after the Second World War and it is to these groups that film-makers who wished to explore racial difference turned in the latter part of the 1950s. Exoticism and Otherness no longer had to be sought 'out there' – indeed, could not now be with the imminent demise of this phase of colonialism – since the Other was actually 'here'. This marks the moment where the *numbers* of black people became imbued with more significance than they had been before. Although represented as living in Britain, in *The Song of Freedom* (1936), *The Proud Valley* (1939) and *Men of Two Worlds* (1946), black people posed little threat because one way or another they did not settle in or reproduce in Britain. The numbers of black people involved outside of well-established communities in Cardiff, Bristol and Liverpool were perceived as insignificant. The narratives dealt with such problems as did arise by removing the source – in these three examples the African men – through death or repatriation. Vast numbers of Africans in Africa were not so problematic since one efficient District Commissioner could control them all with the assistance of a compliant 'native' chief.

The term 'racial problem' – previously associated with the racial traumas of South Africa and the USA – took on a whole new dimension in the 1950s when black people started to settle across Britain and themes relating to sexuality which had previously been studiously avoided became issues demanding attention.

Notes

1   Raymond Williams notes the ambiguities and uncertainties which have accrued to the term 'imperialism'. In the late nineteenth century, imperialism was usually defined as 'primarily a political system in which colonies are governed from an imperial centre' (Williams, 1988: 159). However, imperialism also has a set of meanings where the emphasis is on the economic rather than the political, thus the term connotes 'an economic system of external investment and the penetration and control of markets and sources of raw materials' (ibid.: 159–160). In the context of this book, the emphasis is on the former meaning, rather than the latter.

There are several variations on this genre of film and literature: of particular note is the representation of the Indian sub-continent and its peoples. This is, however, outside the scope of this book.

2   However, these texts should not be thought of as ideologically homogeneous tracts as there is often evidence of contradictory feelings about the Empire and the demands it made, particularly on young men: see Joseph Conrad's *Heart of Darkness* (1989) for example which is, broadly speaking, anti-imperialist but suffused with imperial rhetoric. In his concluding chapter, Joseph Bristow (1991) discusses some of the ambivalences in writing of the late nineteenth century. For debates conducted amongst Victorians, see Christine Bolt (1971); for an informative account of Conrad's stance on imperialism as evidenced in his writings, see Benita Parry (1983); for an introduction to, and references for the role of the Pan-African movement in the 1920s and 1930, see Peter Fryer (1984), and Walter Rodney (1988); a leading Pan-Africanist who came to Britain whose work is relevant here is George Padmore, (1936).

3   Torgovnick's use of 'we' and 'they' is problematic since it serves to reinforce the Euro-American dominant cultural status in determining who is 'us' and who is 'them'. Torgovnick attempts to justify it thus:

> The 'we' as I use it in this section basically denotes the 'we' that imagines a primitive 'them', a cultural 'we' . . . I use the we strategically, to prevent

myself and my reader from backing away, too easily, from the systems of us/them thinking that structure all discourse about the civilized and the primitive . . . But at times . . . that 'we' is intended to produce a sense of discomfort or misfit. The 'we' is necessary to expose a shared illusion: the illusion of a representative primitive 'them' as opposed to a monolithic unified, powerful 'us'.

(Torgovnick, 1990: 6)

Unfortunately, the effect of using that 'we' is to consolidate white European dominance as the extent to which her desire to make 'us' feel uncomfortable will be experienced as helpful by those who have always felt excluded from the academic 'we' is questionable.

4   For a cogent analysis of the metaphoric status of this comparison between black people and women, see Nancy Leys Stepan (1990: 38–57).

5   For more on the formation and consolidation of ideas about masculinity and dependency in the Victorian era, see Catherine Hall (1992).

6   A substantial body of critical work which engages with gender and racial relations, the realm of the psyche and the material aspects of British colonialist and imperialist cinema has not been established, However, much productive analytical work has been carried out on nineteenth century literature. For more detailed analysis in this subject area, see Brian Street (1975); Benita Parry (1983); Patrick Brantlinger (1988); Joseph Bristow (1991). For work on cultural forms other than literature, see John Mackenzie (1984), and for an exploration of the links between white English public school life, masculinity and the literature and films of Empire, see Jeffrey Richards (1973).

7   Both the association of animal imagery with black women and the inferior model of colonization offered by the Belgians are evident in Joseph Conrad's *Heart of Darkness* (1989: 80).

8   These ideas about the massed 'native' Other were also the mainstay of the Western genre of North American cinema where the confrontation would be between Native American and Euro-American.

9   For examples of some of the films affected by censorship in Kenya and Northern Rhodesia in the 1940s, see Rosaleen Smyth (1983: 346, note 28).

10 Harold Moody was founder of the League of Coloured People in 1931.

11 For an examination of Paul Robeson's cross-over appeal, see Richard Dyer (1986).

12 For example, in the casting of African–American Denzil Washington as a former black soldier from London in *For Queen and Country* (1988) and similarly, Forrest Whittaker in *The Crying Game* (1992).

13 See Dyer (1986). Interestingly, in a biography of Robeson, it is claimed that he felt that *The Song of Freedom* was the 'first true one he has done about that continent [Africa]' (Foner, 1978: 31).

References

Belsey, C. (1980) *Critical Practice,* London: Methuen.

Bhabha, H. K. (1983) 'The Other Question . . .' in *Screen,* volume 24, number 6, November/December: 18–36.

Bogle, D. (1988) *Blacks in American Films and Television: An Illustrated Encyclopedia,* New York: Simon and Schuster Inc.

Bolt, C. (1971) *Victorian Attitudes to Race*, London: Routledge and Kegan Paul.

Brantlinger, P. (1988) *Rule of Darkness: British Literature and Imperialism*, Ithaca: Cornell University.

Bristow, J. (1991) *Empire Boys: Adventures in a Man's World*, London: HarperCollins Academic.

Bush, B. (1981) 'Blacks in Britain: the 1930s' in *History Today*, September.

Conrad, J. (1989) *Heart of Darkness*, London: Penguin, (originally published in 1902).

Doane, M. A. (1991) *Femmes Fatales: Feminism, Film Theory, Psychoanalysis*, New York: Routledge.

Dyer, R. (1988) 'White' in *Screen: The Last 'Special Issue' on Race?'* volume 29, number 4, Autumn: 44–65.

Ellis, J. (1988) *Visible Fictions: Cinema, Television, Video*, London: Routledge.

Fanon, F. (1986) *Black Skin, White Masks*, (translated by Charles Lam Markmann), London: Pluto Press, (originally published in 1952).

Foner, P. S. (1978) *Paul Robeson Speaks: Writings, Speeches, Interviews: 1918–1974*, London: Quartet.

Fryer, P. (1984) *Staying Power: The History of Black People in Britain*, London: Pluto Press.

Goldberg, D. T. (1993) *Racist Culture: Philosophy and the Politics of Meaning*, Cambridge, Massachusetts and Oxford, UK: Blackwell.

Haggard, H. R. (1979) *King Solomon's Mines*, London: Octopus Books, (originally published in 1885).

Hall, C. (1992) *White, Male and Middle Class: Explorations in Feminism and History*, Cambridge: Polity Press.

Henriques, F. (1974) *Children of Caliban: Miscegenation*, London: Secker and Warburg.

JanMohamed, A. R. (1985) 'The Economy of Manichean Allegory: The Function of Racial Difference in Colonialist Literature' in *Critical Enquiry*, number 12, Autumn: 59–87.

MacKenzie, J. (1984) *Propaganda and Empire: The Manipulation of Public Opinion, 1880–1960*. Manchester: Manchester University Press.

Memmi, A. (1990) *The Colonizer and the Colonized*, (translated by Howard Greenfield), London: Earthscan Publications, (originally published in 1957).

Padmore, George (1936) *Africa: How Britain Rules Africa*, London: Wishart Books.

Parry, B. (1983) *Conrad and Imperialism: Ideological Boundaries and Visionary Frontiers*, London: Macmillan.

Richards, J. (1973) *Visions of Yesterday*, London: Routledge and Kegan Paul Ltd.

Rodney, W. (1988) *How Europe Underdeveloped Africa*, London: Bogle L'Ouverture Publications.

Roper, M. and Tosh, J. (eds) (1991) *Manful Assertions: Masculinities in Britain Since 1800*, London: Routledge.

Said, E. W. (1985) *Orientalism*, Harmondsworth: Penguin.

Said, E. W. (1993) *Culture and Imperialism*, London: Chatto and Windus.

Shohat, E. (1991) 'Gender and the Culture of Empire: Toward a Feminist Ethnography of the Cinema' in *Quarterly Review of Film and Video*, volume 13: 45–84.

Smyth, R. (1983) 'Movies and Mandarins: the Official Film and British Colonial Africa' in J. Curran, and V. Porter (eds) *British Cinema History*, London: Weidenfeld and Nicholson: 129–43.

Stepan, N.L. (1990) 'Race and Gender: the Role of Analogy in Science' in D. T. Goldberg (ed.) *Anatomy of Racism*, Minneapolis: University of Minnesota Press.

Torgovnick, M. (1990) *Gone Primitive: Savage Intellects, Modern Lives*, Chicago and London: University of Chicago Press.

Williams, R. (1988) *Keywords: A Vocabulary of Culture and Society*, London: Fontana.

Chapter 23

Anne McClintock

THE WHITE FAMILY OF MAN
Colonial discourse and the reinvention of patriarchy

UNTIL THE 1860S SOUTH AFRICA was, from the imperial point of view, a far-flung outpost of scant allure. In 1867, however, an Afrikaner child chanced upon the first South African diamond. The discovery of the diamond fields at once drew "this most stagnant of colonial regions" into the eddies of modern imperial capitalism and "a land that had seen boat-load after boat-load of emigrants for New Zealand and Australia pass it unheeding by now saw men tumbling on to its wharves and hurrying up country to the mines."[1]

Among these new arrivals was Henry Rider Haggard, an obscure youth of nineteen, who, after a few years of unremarkable service in the colonial administration, returned to Britain to become the most spectacularly successful novelist of his time.[2] In 1885, a few months after the carving up of Africa among the "lords of humankind" at Berlin, Haggard published *King Solomon's Mines*, instantly and easily outselling all his contemporaries.[3] *She* appeared soon after, in 1887, to a riotous fanfare of applause. Almost overnight, this obscure youth had become an author of unparalleled commercial success and renown.[4]

King Solomon's Mines was intimately concerned with events in South Africa following the discovery of diamonds and then gold: specifically, the reordering of women's sexuality and work in the African homestead and the diversion of black male labor into the mines. The story illuminates not only relations between the imperial metropolis and the colonies but also the refashioning of gender relations in South Africa, as a nascent capitalism penetrated the region and disrupted already contested power relations within the homesteads. Despite recent recognition that some of the crucial conflicts in the nineteenth century took place over the African homestead economy, for the most part the story of women's work and women's resistance has been shunted to the sidings of history. Because women were the chief farmers, they were the primary producers of life, labor and food in the precolonial era. Their work was thus the single most valuable resource in the country, apart from the land itself. Yet we know very little about how pre-colonial societies were able to subordinate women's work and as little about the changes wrought on these societies by colonial conquest and the penetration of merchant and mining capital.

Haggard's *King Solomon's Mines* offers an unusual glimpse into some of the fundamental dynamics of that contest. The novel was in large part an attempt to negotiate contradictions in the colonial effort to discipline female sexuality and labor, both in the European metropolis and in the colonies. The conflicts between male and female generative power and between domesticity and imperialism, were not only the obsessive themes of Haggard's work but also a dominant preoccupation of his time. Much of the fascination of Haggard's writing for male Victorians was that he played out his phantasms of patriarchal power in the arena of empire, and thus evoked the unbidden relation between male middle- and upper-middle-class power in the metropolis and control of black female labor in the colonies. In this way, *King Solomon's Mines* becomes more than a Victorian curiosity; instead it brings to light some of the fundamental contradictions of the imperial project as well as African attempts to resist it. [. . .]

The regeneration of the family of man: an imperial narrative

Although Haggard was mediocre and disinherited in Britain, once he stepped onto South African soil, he rose immediately into the most exclusive white elite of the country. His appointment to the colonial administration was nothing more glamorous than housekeeper to the largely male family of white bureaucrats in Pietermaritsburg, Natal. But as general factotum to Sir Henry Bulwer, tasked with handling the "champagne and sherry policy" of Natal's brass-band and cavalry administration, his prestige and self-esteem were enormously enhanced.[5] Standing discreetly at the elbow of the paramount white authority in Natal, he was a far cry from the hapless dolt at Scoones. Indeed, a local newspaper announced the new arrival in Cape Town of a "Mr. Waggart."

Haggard's regenerative arrival in South Africa is illuminating in this respect, for the turnabout in his career rehearses a critical moment in late male Victorian culture: the transition, that Said identifies, from filiation to affiliation. Haggard's redemption in the colonial service vividly rehearses this transition from failed filiation within the feudal family manor – essentially a failure of class reproduction – to affiliation with the colonial bureaucracy. Through affiliation with the colonial administration, he was quite explicitly compensated for his loss of place in the landed, patriarchal family and was, moreover, provided with a surrogate father in the form of Theophilus Shepstone, Natal's Administrator of Native Affairs. Haggard was in this respect representative of a specific moment in imperial culture, in which the nearly anachronistic authority of the vanishing feudal family, invested in its sanctioned rituals of rank and subordination, was displaced onto the colonies and reinvented within the new order of the colonial administration.

This displacement gives rise to a paradox. One witnesses in the colonies a strange shadow-effect of the state of the family in Britain. George Orwell once acidly described the British ruling class as "a family with the wrong members in control." Drawing on the by now well-established figure of organic degeneration, he had a vision of Britain ruled over by a decrepit family of "irresponsible uncles and bedridden aunts."[6] Yet, as Williams notes, what Orwell regretted was not so much the existence of a ruling family but rather its decay of ability. The image of the family as the model of social order has so powerful a hold over Orwell's imagination that he could not yet dispense with it in favor of a notion such as class, and he could express his unease only in terms of biological decay. At the same time, for Orwell, a family ruled by irresponsible uncles and bedridden aunts was a pathological family, for the father was nowhere to be seen. It did not seem noteworthy, either to Orwell or to Williams, that the image also admits no mother.

Here an important relation makes itself felt. Orwell saw the social group from which he came, the great service families, "pushed down in importance by the growth of the centralized bureaucracy and by the monopoly trading companies."[7] The failure of the idea of filiation within the great landed and service families stemmed in part from the growth of the imperial bureaucracy, which not only usurped the social function of the service families, displacing administrative power beyond the network of the family but also seriously undermined the image of the patriarchal paterfamilias as ultimate originary power. Yet if the growth of the bureaucracy unseated the patriarch as the image of centralized and individual male power, one witnesses in the colonies the reinvention of the tradition of fatherhood, displaced onto the colonial bureaucracy as a surrogate, restored authority. In other words, the figure of the paterfamilias was most vigorously embraced in the colonies at just that moment when it was withering in the European metropolis. The colony became the last opportunity for restoring the political authority of fatherhood, and it is therefore not surprising that one finds its most intense expressions in the colonial administration, the very place that threatened it. Nor is it surprising that the reinvention of the patriarch in the colonies took on a pathological form.

Patriarchal regeneration: *King Solomon's Mines*

Allan Quartermain – gentleman, hunter, trader, fighter and miner (named, not accidentally, after a father surrogate who had befriended Haggard as a youth) – began to write "the strangest story" that he knows for prophylactic reasons, as an act of biological hygiene. A confounded lion having mauled his leg, he is laid up in Durban in some pain and is unable to get about. Writing the book will relieve some of the frustration of his impotence – it will return him to health and manhood. Further, he will send it to his son, who is studying to be a doctor at a London hospital and is therefore obliged to spend a good deal of his time cutting up dead bodies. Quartermain intends his imperial adventure to breathe "a little life into things" for his boy, Harry, who will as a result be better fitted to pursue the technology of sanitation, the task of national hygiene, the restoration of the race. The book will thus be a threefold narrative of imperial recuperation, embracing three realms and moving from one to the other in a certain privileged order: from the physical body of the white patriarch restored in the colonies to the familial bond with the son/doctor in Britain to the national body politic. At the same time, the narrative reveals that the attempted regeneration of late Victorian Britain depended on the reordering of labor in the colonies; in this case, the attempted reconstruction of the Zulu nation through control of female reproductive and labor power.

The task of paterfamilial restoration that motivates the narration of the journey to King Solomon's Mines finds its analog in the motivation for the fictional journey itself. Quartermain, Captain Good and Sir Henry Curtis set out for King Solomon's Mines primarily to find Sir Henry's younger brother, Neville. Left without a profession or a penny when his father died intestate, Neville quarreled with Sir Henry and set off for South Africa in search of a fortune – a small mimicry of the flight of many of the distressed gentry to the colonies. At the end of the novel Neville is found in the wilderness, clad in ragged skins, his beard grown wild, his leg crushed in an accident – a living incarnation of the degeneration and wounded manhood thought to imperil the white race when abandoned too long in the racial "wilderness." Thus at both the level of the telling of the story and of the story told, the narrative is initiated through a double crisis of male succession and is completed with the regeneration of ruptured family bonds, promising therewith the continuity, however tenuous, of the landed patriarch.

Yet as it happens, Haggard's family romance of fathers, sons and brothers regenerating each other through the imperial adventure is premised on the reordering of another family: the succession of the Kukuana royal family. This reordering requires the death of the "witch-mother" Gagool. Only with her death is female control over generation aborted and the "legitimate" king restored, presided over by the regenerated white "fathers," who will carry away the diamonds to restore the landed gentry in Britain.

[. . .] In *King Solomon's Mines* we find two theories of human racial development. Both are intimately dependent on each other and both are elaborated within the metaphor of the family. On one hand, the narrative presents the historical decline from white ("Egyptian") fatherhood to a primordial black degeneracy incarnated in the black mother. On the other hand, the narrative presents the story of the familial progress of humanity from degenerate native "child" to adult white father. Haggard shared the popular notion that civilization as embodied by colonials was hazardous to the African, who, "by intellect and by nature . . . is some five centuries behind. . . . Civilization, it would seem, when applied to black races, produces effects diametrically opposite to those we are accustomed to in white nations: it debases before it can elevate." Most crucially, the dynamic principle that animates the hierarchy of racial and gender degeneration, transforming a static depiction of debasement into a narrative of historical progress, is the principle of imperial conquest.

Feminizing the "Empty Lands"

The journey to King Solomon's mines is a genesis of racial and sexual order. The journey to origins, as Pierre Macherey points out is "not a way of showing the absolute or beginning but a way of determining the genesis of order, of succession."[8] Donna Haraway has observed that the colonial safari was a kind of traveling minisociety, an icon of the whole enterprise of imperialism fully expressive of its racial and sexual division of labor.[9] It is therefore fitting that Quartermain's party consists of three white gentlemen; a Zulu "gentleman" ("*kesbla*" [sic] or "ringed man"), who nevertheless lags in development some five hundred years behind the whites; three Zulu "boys," still in a state of native "childhood" in relation to the whites; and the racially degenerate "Hottentot," Ventvogel. Thus we set out with the Family of Man in place, fully expressive of fixed divisions of class and race, with the female entirely repressed – a fitting racial hierarchy with which to reinvent the genesis of the species.

True to the trope of anachronistic space, the journey into the interior is, like almost all colonial journeys, figured as a journey forward in space but backward in time. As the men progress, they enter the dangerous zones of racial degeneration. Entering the fever lands and the place of the tsetse fly, the men leave their sick animals and proceed on foot. On the edge of the burning desert that stretches between them and Solomon's blue mountains, they cross into the borderlands of pathology. Stepping into the desert, they step into the zone of prehistory. Their journey across the untenanted plain traces an evolutionary regression from adult virility into a primordial landscape of sun and thirst inhospitable to all except insect life. True to the narrative of recapitulation that underlies the journey, the men slowly slough off their manhood. The sun sucks their blood from them; they stagger like infants unable to walk and escape death only by digging a womb-hole in the earth in which they bury themselves.

Notably, Ventvogel here enters his proper racial element. "Being a Hottentot," and therefore untouched by the sun, his "wild-bred" instincts awaken and he sniffs the air "like an old Impala ram." Uttering guttural exclamations, he runs about and smells out the "pan bad water" (39). Again in keeping with the narrative of recapitulation, adult racial degeneration to the primitive state of the "Hottentot" is accompanied by sexual degeneration to the "female" condition, and both states are attended by linguistic degeneration to an infantile state of preverbal impotence. As we know from the map, the "pan bad water" represents the corrupted female head. At this point, just over the perilous threshold of race, the place of prehistory merges with the place of the female. The landscape becomes suddenly feminized – the sky blushes like a girl, the moon waxes wan and at the very moment that Ventvogel smells the bad water, the men lay eyes for the first time on Sheba's Breasts.

Here, the prescribed narrative of racial, sexual and linguistic degeneracy confirms itself. At the sight of the mountains "shaped exactly like a woman's breasts," their snowy peaks "exactly corresponding to the nipple on the female breast," Quartermain plunges into the condition of reduced manhood and linguistic degeneration characteristic of the "Hottentot" female state. He "cannot describe" what he saw: "Language seems to fail me. . . . To describe the grandeur of the whole view is beyond my powers" (38, 39). This crisis of representation is a ritualistic moment in the colonial narrative whereby the colonized land rises up in all its unrepresentability, threatening to unman the intruder: "I am impotent even before its memory." Yet this is a subterfuge, a pretense of the same order as writing "cannibals" on the colonial map, for Quartermain contains the eruptive power of the black female by inscribing her into the narrative of racial degeneracy.

As the men leave the plains of prehistory and scale Sheba's Breasts, Ventvogel's racial debility begins to tell. "Like most Hottentots" he cannot take the cold and freezes to death in the cave on Sheba's nipple, proving himself unfit to accompany the other men on their journey to the restoration of the paternal origin. At the same time, his death discloses a prior historical failing. In the cave where Ventvogel dies, they find, in fetal position, the frozen skeletal remains of the Portuguese trader, Jose da Silvestre. These remains are a memento of the racial and class unfitness of the first wave of colonial intruders in these parts and thereby a historical affirmation of the superior evolutionary fitness of the English gentry over the Portuguese trader. To inscribe this liminal moment of succession into history, Quartermain takes up da Silvestre's "rude pen," the "cleft-bone" signifying mastery and possession: "It is before me as I write – sometimes I sign my name with it" (45).

Standing aloft on Sheba's Breasts, the men re-enter history. Monarchs of all they survey, their proprietary act of seeing inscribes itself on the land.[10] Leaving Ventvogel and the tongueless zone of prehistory, they re-enter language. Nevertheless, this moment is not a moment of origin but rather the beginning of a historical return and regression, for the journey has already been made. As Macherey has observed, the colonial journey "cannot be an exploration in the strict sense of the word but only discovery, retrieval of a knowledge already complete."[11] The landscape before them is not originary – it cannot find its principle of order within itself. "The landscape lay before us like a map," written over with European history. The mountain peaks are "Alplike", Solomon's Road looks at first like "a sort of Roman road," then like Saint Gothard's in Switzerland. The landscape is not, properly speaking, African, because it is already the subject of conquest. One of the tunnels through which the men pass is carved in ancient statuary, one "exceedingly beautiful" representing a whole battle-scene with a convoy of captives being marched off in the distance. Thus, "the journey . . . is disclosed as having ineluctably happened before. . . . To explore is to follow, that is to say, to cover once again, under new conditions, a road already actually travelled. . . . The conquest is only possible because it has already been accomplished."[12]

Macherey's observations are important because if the narrative of origins is, more properly speaking, the genesis of an order and a hierarchy and if the order the white men intend to impose is that of colonization and the primary stages of the primitive stages of the primitive accumulation of capital, then their conquest finds its legitimacy only by virtue of the fact that the conquest had already taken place at a previous moment in history. King Solomon, whom Haggard regarded as white, had already proved his titular right to the treasure of the mines, had already carved his road over the land. All that had to be accomplished to succeed to the treasure was a demonstration of *family* resemblance. A poetics of blood inheritance had to be written whereby the white gentlemen could succeed as rightful heirs to the riches. [. . .]

Inventing traditions: white fathers and black kings

Natal, where Haggard found himself in 1875, was one of the most unpromising of British colonies. Lacking any vital raw materials for export and lying hundreds of miles from the markets of Cape Town, it was poor, isolated and vulnerable. During the early years of the nineteenth century, the area had seen much turbulence and distress as local chiefdoms rivaled each other for land and power under the pressure of narrowing environmental resources. Between 1816 and 1828, the Zulu leader Shaka had fashioned from the upheavals a formidable military kingdom that drew into its orbit many smaller clans, destroying or scattering the rest in a great chain effect of disruption (the *mfecane*). The small bands of fierce Boer nomads, pushed into this cleared buffer zone in the 1830s. The British, however, had been granted land on the coast by Shaka and bristled at the prospect of Port Natal falling into the hostile hands of the Voortrekkers. They hastily summoned troops from the Cape and snatched Natal from the Boers in 1843. Nevertheless, the British were reluctant to lose the Boers themselves, for they needed denser settlement to counter the potentially overwhelming presence of the Zulus in Zululand which hemmed them in to the north (the principle source, with Zimbabwe, of Haggard's Kukuanaland). The British offered the Boers huge farms over the heads of the indigenous Africans, but many Boers preferred to trek inland once more, becoming absentee owners or selling their land to speculators. Huge areas of land in Natal were left fallow and untended, yet closed to settlement. This was the paradox that plagued Natal's white farmers: a shortage of land in a vast country of thousands of acres and a shortage of labor in a land with a population of thousands of Africans.

After the discovery of diamonds in 1867 and gold in 1884 the paradox deepened as black labor left for the mineral fields and better wages of the interior. Haggard, in 1882, in his first published writing, *Cetywayo and His White Neighbours*, called this paradox "the unsolved riddle of the future, the Native Question."[13] It is this riddle that *King Solomon's Mines* attempts to resolve, revealing in the process that the problems of land and labor are rooted in the fundamental question of who was to control the women's labor – an issue fought out at a number of levels: between black women and men within the Zulu homestead, among black men and between white colonists and black men.

Many elements of the Zulu family drama are present in *King Solomon's Mines*. In 1856 a crisis had broken out over the rightful heir of the Zulu king, Mpande, a struggle that prefigured the crisis of male succession reenacted in the novel. As in Haggard's tale, the blood rivalry between Mpande's sons, Cetshwayo and Mbulazi, climaxed in a battle in 1856: an eyewitness account of the actual battle provided Haggard with many of the details he used for the battle scene in the novel. Haggard's depiction of the degenerate usurper king, Twala, is resonant of racist images of Cetshwayo as a gorilla-like monster in the popular illustrated papers. In both the novel and its historical counterpart, moreover, white men interfere in the crisis of male inheritance and arrogate to themselves the powers of white *patria potestas*. This gives them the authority to inaugurate what they believe will be a subservient black monarch, on terms favorable to the colonial state.

In the historical case, Cetshwayo emerged as victor and Shepstone visited the Zulu court to confer official blessings on him in 1861. However, instead of the adulatory welcome he confidently expected, Shepstone, like Haggard's heroes, only narrowly avoided death. Nevertheless, the parties were reconciled and in September 1873 Shepstone proceeded to enact a pompous ceremony of monarchical recognition that he alone took seriously. Cetshwayo was proclaimed king with a great deal of pomp and ritual invented by Shepstone for the occasion. Shepstone saw himself grandly "standing in the place of Cetshwayo's father and so representing the nation" and enunciated four articles that he regarded as necessary for putting an end to "the continual slaughter that darkens the history of Natal." These articles are strikingly similar to the articles of control Haggard's heroes would demand in *King Solomon's Mines*.

Shepstone clearly felt he had been instituted as nominal founding father of the Zulu nation, and he and Haggard made a good deal of rhetorical fuss of his new status as father of the Zulus. The coronation was not simply Shepstone's whimsy, however, but was a symptomatic replica of the invented traditions of monarchical inauguration that colonials were enacting all over British Africa. In what Terence Ranger has called "the invented tradition of the 'Imperial Monarchy' " the colonists – lacking, as they did, a single body of legitimating ritual – offered Africans a fantastic mummery of tinsel and velvet royalty that bore scant resemblance to the political reality of the British monarchy.[14] In Britain the monarch had shrunk to a ceremonial figurehead. The centers of political power lay elsewhere, on the desks of industrial magnates, in the corridors of parliament, in the shipyards and mills. In the African colonies, however, the figure of the king rose to its feet and walked abroad again. The anachronistic ideology of the imperial monarchy became a widespread administrative cult, full of invention and pretense, of which Shepstone's coronation of Cetshwayo (like Haggard's coronation of Umbopa) were symptomatic.

Ranger calls "the 'theology' of an omniscient, omnipotent and omnipresent monarchy . . . almost the sole ingredient of imperial ideology as it was represented to the Africans."[15] He thereby neglects, however, what was arguably the most authoritative and influential of all invented rituals in the colonies: the patriarch, or landed paterfamilias. Most significant in political impact, moreover, was the newly invented hierarchy between the white "father" and the black king.

In colonial documents, for example, Shepstone is referred to with ritualistic insistence as the "father-figure" of Natal. Sir Henry Bulwer called him "one of the Colonies' earliest fathers – the very Nestor of the Colony."[16] Shepstone was generally referred to by black people (no doubt obliging his fantasy) as "Somtsewu," which, as Jeff Guy says, "notwithstanding much speculation on its meaning along the lines of 'mighty hunter' . . . is a word of Sesotho origin meaning 'Father of Whiteness'."[17] Haggard, like Shepstone himself, understood the name to carry the entirely unfounded implication that the Zulus regarded Shepstone as the originary potentate of the black people themselves: Shepstone is "par excellence their great white chief and 'father'." In a message to Lobengula, chief of the Ndebele, Shepstone announced portentously: "The Lieutenant Governor of Natal is looked upon as the Father of all."[18]

Shepstone took the title of father and everything that sprang from it in terms of political authority very seriously indeed, not only as a title but as a political and administrative practice that had serious consequences for the history of South Africa. One example from many can suffice. In the 1850s he and Bishop Colenso of Natal, before their famous squabble, hatched a megalomaniacal plot to solve the "native question" by founding a Black Kingdom (like Kukuanaland) south of Natal, over which they would rule autocratically as founding patriarchs – each embodying, respectively, the absolute powers of "Father of the Church" and "Father of the state." In a letter to members of the Church of England, Colenso claimed he was called "Sokuleleka" ("Father of Raising Up") and "Sobantu" ("Father of the People"). Not to be outdone, Shepstone would be "Father of Whiteness." Both men thus arrogated to themselves, as Haggard's heroes do, all powers of male generation and succession. Their roles would be nothing less than the generators of civilization and the regenerators of the ancient Family of Man.

Shepstone manipulated the invented traditions of fathers and kings, mimicking allegiance to certain customs of Zulu chieftainship, while retaining for himself the superior status of father – the same solution to conflicting patriarchies that Haggard's tale rehearses. Thus Shepstone drew on an ideology of divine fatherhood, as preordained and natural, the founding source of all authority. The black king, on the other hand, was his symbolic reproduction, mortal, invested with authority only by virtue of his mimicry of the originary power of the father.

For these reasons, I suggest, the reinvention of fathers and kings in South Africa can be seen as a central attempt to mediate a number of contradictions: between the imperial bureaucracy and the declining landed gentry in Britain; between the colonial ruling patriarchy and the indigenous patriarchies of precapitalist polities; and last but most significantly, between women and men of all races. Here we come across the final and most important dynamic underlying both Haggard's tale and the emergent economy of the colonial state.

The invention of idleness

Shepstone's policy was based on an intimate sense of the precarious balance of power in Natal and Zululand. He knew that the frail colony could ill afford to antagonize the Zulus and that it lacked the military muscle and the finances to forcibly drive black men off their lands and into wage labor. As the missionary Henry Callaway asked ruefully, "How are 8,000 widely scattered whites to compel 200,000 coloureds to labor, against their will?"[19] Out of this riddle rose the exceptionally vituperative discourse on the degenerate "idleness" of the blacks. Of all the stigmata of degeneration invented by the settlers to mark themselves from the Africans, the most tirelessly invoked was idleness: the same stigma of racial unworth that Haggard saw as marking the Kukuana's degeneration and loss of title to the diamonds.

It is scarcely possible to read any travel account, settler memoir or ethnographic document without coming across a chorus of complaints about the sloth, idleness, indolence or torpor of the natives, who, the colonists claimed, preferred scheming and fighting, lazing and wanton lasciviousness to industry. Typical is Captain Ludlow's remark on visiting the Umvoti Mission Station: "The father of the family leant on his hoe in his mielie garden, lazily smoking his pipe. . . . It is amusing to watch one of them pretending to work."[20] Haggard saw the racial hatred of whites rooted in this stubborn abstraction of African labor: "The average white man . . . detests the Kaffir and looks on him as a lazy good-for-nothing, who ought to work for him and will not work for him."[21]

The idea of idleness was neither descriptively accurate of the laboring black farmers nor new. The settlers brought with them to South Africa the remnants of a three-hundred-year-old British discourse that associated poverty with sloth.

Beginning in the sixteenth century in Britain, an intricate discourse on idleness had emerged, not only to draw distinctions between laboring classes but also to sanction and enforce social discipline, to legitimize land plunder and to alter habits of labor. After 1575, the unemployed or unruly poor, for example, were no longer banished beyond the city walls but were dragooned into "houses of correction" where they were treated as a resource to meet the needs of the growing manufactures. Walling up discontent and fettering the desperate during the crises of unemployment, the houses of confinement, often attached to manufactures and providing them with labor, also taught new habits and forms of industry. It appears that many of the inmates of the houses of correction were women, suggesting that the houses were threshold institutions, mediating the gradual transfer of productive labor from the family to the factory.

The discourse on idleness is, more properly speaking, a discourse on work – used to distinguish between desirable and undesirable labor. Pressure to work was, more accurately, pressure to alter traditional habits of work. During the land revolution and the war on the cottages of the eighteenth century, Official Board of Agriculture reports of the time praised the land enclosures for robbing the lower orders of economic independence, thereby forcing laborers to work every day of the year. At the same time, the discourse on idleness is also a register of labor resistance, a resistance then lambasted as torpor and sloth.

Colonists borrowed and patched from British discourses and couched their complaints in the same images of degeneracy, massing animal menace and irrationality familiar to European descriptions of the dangerous urban underclasses. The missionary Aldin Grout wrote to James Kitchenham: "They see our tools and our work but seldom ask a question about these or express a wish to do the other." Lady Barker opined: "It is a new and revolutionary idea to a Kaffir that he should do any work at all." James Bryce agreed: "The male Kaffir is a lazy fellow who likes talking and sleeping better than continuous physical exertion and the difficulty of inducing him to work is the chief difficulty that European mine-owners in South Africa complain of."

But the African pastoralists differed markedly from the uprooted and immiserated British proletariat with which the settlers were familiar. The Africans still enjoyed a measure of self-sufficiency and were, on the whole, better farmers than the white interlopers.[22] As Slater notes, "many whites in fact came to depend upon African agricultural produce for their very subsistence."[23] Settler fortunes were constantly imperiled by the self-sufficiency of the black farmers. Complaints about black sloth were as often complaints about different habits of labor. If black people entered into wage relations for whites, it was often reluctantly or briefly, to earn money, buy guns or cattle, then to return home. Thus the discourse on idleness was not a monolithic discourse imposed on a hapless people. Rather it was a realm of contestation, marked with the stubborn refusal of Africans to alter their customs of work as well as by conflicts within the white communities.

Most importantly, I suggest, the assault on African work habits was at its root an assault on polygyny and the women farmers: the fundamental dynamic underlying both *King Solomon's Mines* and the native policy of Natal. The question, bitterly contested for decades, was who was to benefit from women's labor.

Marriage maidens and mines

One need not look far to see that the root of the problem of black labor lay in women's role in production. When Froude visited Natal, he noted grimly: "The government won't make the Kaffirs work." Then at once he came upon the cause of the problem. Male "indolence," he saw, was rooted regrettably but inevitably in the "detestable systems of polygamy and female slavery."

> My host talks much and rather bitterly on the Nigger question. If the Kafir would work, he would treble his profits. . . . It is an intricate problem. Here in Natal are nearly 400,000 natives. . . . They are allowed as much land as they want for their locations. They are polygamists and treat their women as slaves, while they themselves are idle or worse.[24]

Missionaries and colonists voiced their repugnance for polygyny in moral tones, placing it firmly within the discourse of racial degeneration. The practice of polygyny was seen to mark African men, as Haggard had marked King Twala, as wallowing in the depths of sexual abandon: the "African sin." Yet colonial documents readily reveal that the assault on polygyny was an assault on African habits of labor that withheld from the resentful farmers the work of black men and women. The excess labor that a black man controlled through his wives was seen as a direct and deadly threat to the profits of the settlers. As Governor Pine complained: "How can an Englishman with one pair of hands compete with a native with five to twenty slave wives?"[25] Likewise, Haggard's knowledge of women's productive power animates his fear of Gagool in *King Solomon's Mines*.

Black women in Natal become the ground over which white men fought black men for control of their land and labor. As Guy has shown, precapitalist societies in southern Africa depended on the control of *labor power*, rather than the control of *products*. The fundamental unit of Zulu society was the homestead (*umuzi, imizi*), in which a single male (*ummumzana*) held authority over his wife or wives, their children, livestock, gardens and grazing lands. Each homestead was more or less independent, with women growing food on land held in trust for the chief of the clan. Each wife worked her own fields, living with her children in a separate house that took its name from her. A strict gendered division of labor prevailed, as women did most of the agricultural and domestic work – hoeing, planting, gathering and tending the crops, building and tending the houses, making implements and clothes, taking care of the daily cooking and the houses, as well as the bearing and raising of the children. The men broke the ground in the first stages, made some of the implements and tended the cattle. In short, the homestead was based on the systematic exploitation of women's labor and the transformation of that labor into male social and political power.

The symbolic means for transforming woman's work into male power was the *ukulobolo,* or marriage exchange. A new homestead was formed when a man was given permission to leave the royal barracks, or his father's homestead and marry a wife from a different clan. The marriage was formalized by the transfer of *lobolo* from the new husband to the wife's father, usually in the form of cattle. Colonialists berated this system as base and commercial: but it was, rather, a ceremonial exchange that guaranteed the transfer of a woman's labor and sexuality. If she did not produce children or the work expected, the cattle could be reduced in number, or returned and the marriage dissolved. At the same time, the cattle could be retained if the new husband was seen to ill-treat his wife. Nevertheless, the society was not egalitarian and most of the homesteads had only one or two wives. Power in the form of cattle and wives was gathered in the upper reaches of the chiefly lineages, and chiefs distributed power back down the social hierarchy by controlling the distribution of cattle and wives to their sons and loyal supporters. *Labolo* was thus a symbolic, rather than a commercial, exchange whereby women's labor power was embodied in movable herds of cattle and exchanged among men across time and space.

At the same time, it is of the greatest significance that women's work freed men to fight in the Zulu army. The relation between women's labour and the Zulu fighting force is crucial. Women in the family homesteads provided a surplus of food for themselves and for the men in the barracks. The unequal distribution of women allowed male power to be hierarchically ranked within an arena of male competition for the basic resource of labor power. Thus whoever controlled the regulation of marriage controlled the power base of the economy. The dominant class was men over the marriageable age, the subordinate class women and children. Guy calls this "a fundamental cleavage so deep it can usefully be called one of class," but the fundamental division was gender, for a male child could leave the subordinate class at a certain age when he entered into marriage with a woman, that is, into a gendered division of labor in which he exploited his wife's labor power.

In *Cetywayo*, Haggard devoted a good deal of space to polygyny, which he recognized as lying at the heart of Zulu power. In a metaphor that nicely expressed the relation between matrimonial and military power, he advised: "Deprive them of their troops of servants in the shape of wives and thus force them to betake themselves to honest labor like the rest of mankind."[26] Tampering with the circulation of women was thus tantamount to severing the jugular vein of male Zulu power.

Indeed, this approach was precisely Shepstone's policy. In the face of the bitter ire of the farmer-settlers, Shepstone doggedly pursued a policy of segregation, administration and compromise. In the reserves, wretchedly apportioned as they were, blacks were allowed to retain access to land under "customary law" (as were the Kukuanas in Haggard's tale). The communal household was to be retained, since black resistance to changes in polygyny proved too tenacious. But the family would be gradually modified by diverting the profits of female labor out of the homestead into the colonial treasury in the form of hut and marriage taxes.

Knowing that an outright ban on polygyny was impractical, both Shepstone and Haggard favored a hut tax. The hut tax was, in fact, a tax on wives and thus the surest means of driving African men into wage labor. By legislating control of the rates of the hut taxes over the years, the Shepstone administration tried to take control of the traffic in women's work out of black men's hands, while driving these men into work on the white farms and mines. This put an administrative fetter on polygyny even as it turned the women's labor power into a sizable source of revenue for the dwindling treasury. The tax on women's labor would in fact become the principle source of revenue for the state. Significantly, what this fact reveals is that there was no objection to exploiting marriage and women's work as a commercial transaction as long as white men and not black men benefited from it. At the same time, to administer this gradual process of cultural attrition, ductile chiefs would be appointed to supervise and implement the process.

However, in 1876 the situation abruptly changed. The discovery of diamonds marked a new imperial initiative in southern Africa as Lord Carnarvon, British Secretary of State for the Colonies, hatched a scheme to confederate South Africa. Shepstone was given the responsibility of annexing the Transvaal and it was Haggard himself who raised the British flag over a reluctant Boer republic in 1876. The annexation shattered the uneasy balance between the Boers, Natal and the Zulus and set in train a series of events that led inexorably to the invasion of Zululand. Both Shepstone and Haggard deplored the invasion on the practical grounds that it was untimely and doomed to disaster. They remained convinced that the surest way to control the labor and land of South Africa was by segregation, indirect rule through selected chiefs, and the regulated diversion of labor from the reserves into the state economy.

Indeed, Haggard's fanatical tale is faithful to Shepstone's political blueprint for Zululand – Kukuanaland would remain territorially separate but in effect a "black colony" of Natal, while a compliant black leader who accepted the racial patrimony of the whites would be installed. True to Shepstone's segregationist policy, white men would not be allowed to settle there. At the same time, true to Haggard's own class loyalties – though not to the outcome of history – the booty from the mines would be placed in the hands of the landed gentry, not in the hands of the mining capitalists. Finally, the labor of black women is hidden from history, rendered as invisible as Gagool crushed beneath the rock.

In this way, *King Solomon's Mines* figures the reinvention of white imperial patriarchy through a legitimizing racial and gender politics. It asserts a white patriarch in control of a subservient black king, who grants white racial superiority and entitlement to the diamonds. It reorganizes production and reproduction within the black family by usurping the chief's control of the lives and labor of women. At the same time, it violently negates the African women's sexual and labor power.

Indeed, the Victorian obsession with treasure troves and treasure maps is a vivid example of commodity fetishism – the disavowal of the origins of money in labor. Finding treasure implies that gold and diamonds are there simply to be discovered, thereby denying the work of digging them out of the earth and thus the contested right to ownership. In the treasure fetish, money is seen to breed itself – just as in Haggard's tale the men give birth to themselves in the mine-womb.

Thus the narrative of phallic regeneracy is assured by the control of women in the arena of empire. The plundering of the land and the minerals is given legitimacy through the erasure of the mother and the reinvention of white patriarchy within the organic embrace of the regenerated Family of Man. It is only fitting, therefore that Haggard was himself enabled (by the fantastically approving British reception of his tale of phallic and racial regeneration) to buy the landed estate from which he had been disinherited.

Notes and references

1 C. W. De Kiewet, *A History of South Africa: Social and Economic* (London: Oxford University Press, 1941), p. 119.

2 Haggard was in South Africa from 1875 to 1881. In 1876 he personally raised the British flag over a disgruntled Transvaal.

3 Henry Rider Haggard, *King Solomon's Mines* (London: Signet, 1965). All further references to this edition are cited in the text by page number.

4 *King Solomon's Mines* was reprinted four times in the first three months, sold 31,000 copies in the first year and has never been out of print since its publication. *She*, too, was an instant bestseller and has been translated into over twenty languages and made into numerous films and plays as well as an opera. It too has not been out of print in Britain in the last century. Ella Shohat discusses film versions of both novels in "Gender and the Culture of Empire: Toward a Feminist Ethnography of the Cinema," *Quarterly Review of Film and Video*, 13, 1–3 (Spring 1991): 45–84.

5 Henry Rider Haggard, *Days of My Life* (London: Longmans Green and Co., 1926), p. 36.

6 George Orwell, in S. Orwell and I. Angus eds, *The Collected Essays, Journalism and Letters of George Orwell*, vol. 11 (London: Secker and Warburg, 1968), p. 67.

7 Raymond Williams, *George Orwell: A Collection of Critical Essays* (Engelwood Cliffs: Prentice Hall, 1975), p. 20.

8 Pierre Macherey, *A Theory of Literary Production* (London: Routledge & Kegan Paul, 1978), p. 265.

9 Donna Haraway, *Private Visions: Gender, Race and Nature in the World of Modern Science* (London: Routledge, 1989), p. 52.

10 See Mary Louise Pratt's fine analysis of this trope in *Imperial Eyes: Travel Writing and Transculturation* (New York: Routledge, 1992).

11 Macherey, *A Theory of Literary Production*, p. 183.

12 Macherey, *A Theory of Literary Production*, p. 183.

13 Haggard, *Cetywayo and His White Neighbours* (London: Trubner and Co., 1882), p. 281. See also Jeff Guy, *The Destruction of the Zulu Kingdom* (Johannesburg: Ravan Press, 1982); and H. Slater, "The Changing Pattern of Economic Relations in Rural Natal, 1838–1914," in Shula Marks and A. Atmore, eds, *Economy and Society in Pre-Industrial South Africa* (London: Longmans, 1980).

14 Terence Ranger, "The Invention of Tradition in Colonial Africa," in Eric Hobsbawm and Terence Ranger, eds., *The Invention of Tradition* (Cambridge: Cambridge University Press, 1983). See also David Cannadine, "The Context, Performance and Meaning of Ritual: The British Monarchy and the 'Invention of Tradition,' 1820–1977," in Hobsbawm and Ranger. For an excellent exploration of the invention of Zulu tradition, see Shula Marks, *The Ambiguities of Dependence: Class, Nationalism and the State in Twentieth Century Natal* (Johannesburg: Ravan Press, 1986).

15 Ranger, *The Invention of Tradition*, p. 212.

16 Quoted by Ruth E. Gordon, *Shepstone: The Role of the Family in the History of South Africa, 1820–1890* (Cape Town: Balkema, 1968), p. 309.

17 Guy, *The Destruction of the Zulu Kingdom*, p. 51 (n).

18 Haggard, *Days of My Life*, p. 9.

19   Henry Callaway, *A Memoir*, ed. M. S. Benham (London: 1896), p. 88.
20   W. R. Ludlow, *Zululand and Cetywayo* (London: Simpkin, Marshal, 1882), p. 18.
21   Haggard, *Cetywayo*, p. 57.
22   Patrick Harries, "Plantations, Passes and Proletarians: Labor and the Colonial State in Nineteenth Century Natal," *Journal of Southern African Studies* 13, 2, 375.
23   H. Slater, *The Changing Patterns*, p. 156.
24   Froude, *Short Studies*, p. 370–71.
25   Quoted in H. J. Simons. *African Women: Their Legal Status in South Africa* (Evanston: Northwestern University Press, 1968), p. 21.
26   Haggard, *Cetywayo*, p. 52.

Chapter 24

Chandra Talpade Mohanty

UNDER WESTERN EYES
Feminist scholarship and colonial discourses[1]

ANY DISCUSSION OF THE INTELLECTUAL and political construction of "third world feminisms" must address itself to two simultaneous projects: the internal critique of hegemonic "Western" feminisms, and the formulation of autonomous, geographically, historically, and culturally grounded feminist concerns and strategies. The first project is one of deconstructing and dismantling; the second, one of building and constructing. While these projects appear to be contradictory, the one working negatively and the other positively, unless these two tasks are addressed simultaneously "third world" feminisms run the risk of marginalization or ghettoization from both mainstream (right and left) and Western feminist discourses.

It is to the first project that I address myself. What I wish to analyze is specifically the production of the "third world woman" as a singular monolithic subject in some recent (Western) feminist texts. The definition of colonization I wish to invoke here is a predominantly *discursive* one, focusing on a certain mode of appropriation and codification of "scholarship" and "knowledge" about women in the third world by particular analytic categories employed in specific writings on the subject which take as their referent feminist interests as they have been articulated in the U.S. and Western Europe. If one of the tasks of formulating and understanding the locus of "third world feminisms" is delineating the way in which it resists and *works against* what I am referring to as "Western feminist discourse," an analysis of the discursive construction of "third world women" in Western feminism is an important first step.

Clearly Western feminist discourse and political practice is neither singular nor homogeneous in its goals, interests, or analyses. However, it is possible to trace a coherence of *effects* resulting from the implicit assumption of "the West" (in all its complexities and contradictions) as the primary referent in theory and praxis. My reference to "Western feminism" is by no means intended to imply that it is a monolith. Rather, I am attempting to draw attention to the similar effects of various textual strategies used by writers which codify Others as non-Western and hence themselves as (implicitly) Western. It is in this sense that I use the term *Western feminist*. Similar arguments can be made in terms of middle-class urban African or Asian scholars producing scholarship on or about their rural or working-class sisters which assumes their own middle-class cultures as the norm, and codifies working-class histories and cultures as Other. Thus, while this essay focuses specifically on what I refer to as "Western feminist" discourse on women in the third world, the critiques I offer also pertain to third world scholars writing about their own cultures, which employ identical analytic strategies.

It ought to be of some political significance, at least, that the term *colonization* has come to denote a variety of phenomena in recent feminist and left writings in general. From its analytic value as a category of exploitative economic exchange in both traditional and contemporary Marxisms (cf. particularly contemporary theorists such as Baran 1962, Amin 1977, and, Gunder-Frank 1967) to its use by feminist women of color in the U.S. to describe the appropriation of their experiences and struggles by hegemonic white women's movements (cf. especially Moraga and Anzaldúa 1983, Smith 1983, Joseph and Lewis 1981, and Moraga 1984), colonization has been used to characterize everything from the most evident economic and political hierarchies to the production of a particular cultural discourse about what is called the "third world."[2] However sophisticated or problematical its use as an explanatory construct, colonization almost invariably implies a relation of structural domination, and a suppression – often violent – of the heterogeneity of the subject(s) in question.

My concern about such writings derives from my own implication and invest-ment in contemporary debates in feminist theory, and the urgent political necessity (especially in the age of Reagan/Bush) of forming strategic coalitions across class, race, and national boundaries. The analytic principles discussed below serve to distort Western feminist political practices, and limit the possibility of coalitions among (usually white) Western feminists and working-class feminists and feminists of color around the world. These limitations are evident in the construction of the (implicitly consensual) priority of issues around which apparently *all* women are expected to organize. The necessary and integral connection between feminist scholarship and feminist political practice and organizing determines the significance and status of Western feminist writings on women. In the third world, for feminist scholarship, like most other kinds of scholarship, is not the mere production of knowledge about a certain subject. It is a directly political and discursive *practice* in that it is purposeful and ideological. It is best seen as a mode of intervention into particular hegemonic discourses (for example, traditional anthropology, sociology, literary criticism, etc.); it is a political praxis which counters and resists the totalizing imperative of age-old "legitimate" and "scientific" bodies of knowledge. Thus, feminist scholarly practices (whether reading, writing, critical, or textual) are inscribed in relations of power – relations which they counter, resist, or even perhaps implicitly support. There can, of course, be no apolitical scholarship.

The relationship between "Woman" – a cultural and ideological composite Other constructed through diverse representational discourses (scientific, literary, juridical, linguistic, cinematic, etc.) – and "women" – real, material subjects of their collective histories – is one of the central questions the practice of feminist scholarship seeks to address. This connection between women as historical subjects and the re-presentation of Woman produced by hegemonic discourses is not a relation of direct identity, or a relation of correspondence or simple implication.[3] It is an arbitrary relation set up by particular cultures. I would like to suggest that the feminist writings I analyze here discursively colonize the material and historical heterogeneities of the lives of women in the third world, thereby producing/re-presenting a composite, singular "third world woman" – an image which appears arbitrarily constructed, but nevertheless carries with it the authorizing signature of Western humanist discourse [4]

I argue that assumptions of privilege and ethnocentric universality, on the one hand, and inadequate self-consciousness about the effect of Western scholarship on the "third world" in the context of a world system dominated by the West, on the other, characterize a sizable extent of Western feminist work on women in the third world. An analysis of "sexual difference" in the form of a cross-culturally singular, monolithic notion of patriarchy or male dominance leads to the construction of a similarly reductive and homogeneous notion of what I call the "third world difference" – that stable, ahistorical something that apparently oppresses most if not all the women in these countries. And it is in the production of this "third world difference" that Western feminisms appropriate and "colonize" the constitutive complexities which characterize the lives of women in these countries. It is in this process of discursive homogenization and systematization of the oppression of women in the third world that power is exercised in much of recent Western feminist discourse, and this power needs to be defined and named.

[. . .] My critique is directed at three basic analytic principles which are present in (Western) feminist discourse on women in the third world. Since I focus primarily on the Zed Press Women in the Third World series, my comments on Western feminist discourse are circumscribed by my analysis of the texts in this series.[5] This is a way of focusing my critique. However, even though I am dealing with feminists who identify themselves as culturally or geographically from the "West," as mentioned earlier, what I say about these presuppositions or implicit principles holds for anyone who uses these methods, whether third world women in the West, or third world women in the third world writing on these issues and publishing in the West. Thus, I am not making a culturalist argument about ethnocentrism; rather, I am trying to uncover how ethnocentric universalism is produced in certain analyses. As a matter of fact, my argument holds for any discourse that sets up its own authorial subjects as the implicit referent, i.e., the yardstick by which to encode and represent cultural Others. It is in this move that power is exercised in discourse.

The first analytic presupposition I focus on is involved in the strategic location of the category "women" vis-à-vis the context of analysis. The assumption of women as an already constituted, coherent group with identical interests and desires, regardless of class, ethnic or racial location, or contradictions, implies a notion of gender or sexual difference or even patriarchy which can be applied universally and cross-culturally. (The context of analysis can be anything from kinship structures and the organization of labor to media representations.) The second analytical presupposition is evident on the methodological level, in the uncritical way "proof" of universality and cross-cultural validity are provided. The third is a more specifically political presupposition underlying the methodologies and the analytic strategies, i.e., the model of power and struggle they imply and suggest. I argue that as a result of the two modes – or rather, frames – of analysis described above, a homogeneous notion of the oppression of women as a group is assumed, which, in turn, produces the image of an "average third world woman." This average third world woman leads an essentially truncated life based on her feminine gender (read: sexually constrained) and her being "third world" (read: ignorant, poor, uneducated, tradition-bound, domestic, family-oriented, victimized, etc.). This, I suggest, is in contrast to the (implicit) self-representation of Western women as educated, as modern, as having control over their own bodies and sexualities, and the freedom to make their own decisions [. . .]

"Women" as a category of analysis, or: we are all sisters in struggle

By women as a category of analysis, I am referring to the crucial assumption that all of us of the same gender, across classes and cultures, are somehow socially constituted as a homogeneous group identified prior to the process of analysis. This is an assumption which characterizes much feminist discourse. The homogeneity of women as a group is produced not on the basis of biological essentials but rather on the basis of secondary sociological and anthropological universals. Thus, for instance, in any given piece of feminist analysis, women are characterized as a singular group on the basis of a shared oppression. What binds women together is a sociological notion of the "sameness" of their oppression. It is at this point that an elision takes place between "women" as a discursively constructed group and "women" as material subjects of their own history[6] Thus, the discursively consensual homogeneity of "women" as a group is mistaken for the historically specific material reality of groups of women. This results in an assumption of women as an always already constituted group, one which has been labeled "powerless," "exploited," "sexually harassed," etc., by feminist scientific, economic, legal, and sociological discourses. (Notice that this is quite similar to sexist discourse labeling women weak, emotional, having math anxiety, etc.) This focus is not on uncovering the material and ideological specificities that constitute a particular group of women as "powerless" in a particular context. It is, rather, on finding a variety of cases of "powerless" groups of women to prove the general point that women as a group are powerless.

   In this section I focus on five specific ways in which "women" as a category of analysis is used in Western feminist discourse on women in the third world. Each of these examples illustrates the construction of "third world women" as a homogeneous "powerless" group often located as implicit *victims* of particular socioeconomic systems. I have chosen to deal with a variety of writers – from Fran Hosken, who writes primarily about female genital mutilation, to writers from the Women in International Development school, who write about the effect of development policies on third world women for both Western and third world audiences. The similarity of assumptions about "third world women" in all these texts forms the basis of my discussion. This is not to equate all the texts that I analyze, nor is it to equalize their strengths and weaknesses. The authors I deal with write with varying degrees of care and complexity; however, the *effect* of their representation of third world women is a coherent one. In these texts women are defined as victims of male violence (Fran Hosken); victims of the colonial process (Maria Cutrufelli); victims of the Arab familial system (Juliette Minces); victims of the economic development process (Beverley Lindsay and the [liberal] WID School); and finally, victims of *the* Islamic code (Patricia Jeffery). This mode of defining women primarily in terms of their *object status* (the way in which they are affected or not affected by certain institutions and systems) is what characterizes this particular form of the use of "women" as a category of analysis. In the context of Western women writing/studying women in the third world, such objectification (however benevolently motivated) needs to be both named and challenged. As Valerie Amos and Pratibha Parmar argue quite eloquently, "Feminist theories which examine our cultural practices as 'feudal residues' or label us 'traditional,' also portray us as politically immature women who need to be versed and schooled in the ethos of Western feminism. They need to be continually challenged . . ." (1984, 7).

Women as victims of male violence

Fran Hosken, in writing about the relationship between human rights and female genital mutilation in Africa and the Middle East, bases her whole discussion/ condemnation of genital mutilation on one privileged premise: that the goal of this practice is "to mutilate the sexual pleasure and satisfaction of woman" (1981, 11). This, in turn, leads her to claim the woman's sexuality is controlled, as is her reproductive potential. According to Hosken, "male sexual politics" in Africa and around the world "share the same political goal: to assure female dependence and subservience by any and all means" (14). Physical violence against women (rape, sexual assault, excision, infibulation, etc.) is thus carried out "with an astonishing consensus among men in the world" (14). Here, women are defined consistently as the *victims* of male control – the "sexually oppressed."[7] Although it is true that the potential of male violence against women circumscribes and elucidates their social position to a certain extent, defining women as archetypal victims freezes them into "objects-who-defend-themselves," men into "subjects-who-perpetrate violence," and (every) society into powerless (read: women) and powerful (read: men) groups of people. Male violence must be theorized and interpreted within specific societies, in order both to understand it better and to effectively organize to change it.[8] Sisterhood cannot be assumed on the basis of gender; it must be forged in concrete historical and political practice and analysis.

Women as universal dependents

Beverly Lindsay's conclusion to the book *Comparative Perspectives of Third World Women: The Impact of Race, Sex and Class* (1983, 298, 306) states: "dependency relationships, based upon race, sex and class, are being perpetuated through social, educational, and economic institutions. These are the linkages among Third World Women." Here, as in other places, Lindsay implies that third world women constitute an identifiable group purely on the basis of shared dependencies. If shared dependencies were all that was needed to bind us together as a group, third world women would always be seen as an apolitical group with no subject status. Instead, if anything, it is the *common context* of political struggle against class, race, gender, and imperialist hierarchies that may constitute third world women as a strategic group at this historical juncture. Lindsay also states that linguistic and cultural differences exist between Vietnamese and black American women, but "both groups are victims of race, sex, and class." Again black and Vietnamese women are characterized by their victim status.

Similarly, examine statements such as "My analysis will start by stating that all African women are politically and economically dependent" (Cutrufelli 1983, 13), "Nevertheless, either overtly or covertly, prostitution is still the main if not the only source of work for African women" (Cutrufelli 1983, 33). *All* African women are dependent. Prostitution is the only work option for African women as a *group*. Both statements are illustrative of generalizations sprinkled liberally through a recent Zed Press publication, *Women of Africa: Roots of Oppression,* by Maria Rosa Cutrufelli, who is described on the cover as an Italian writer, sociologist, Marxist, and feminist. In the 1980s, is it possible to imagine writing a book entitled *Women of Europe: Roots of Oppression?* I am not objecting to the use of universal groupings for descriptive purposes. Women from the continent of Africa can be descriptively characterized as "women of Africa." It is when "women of Africa" becomes a homogeneous sociological grouping characterized by common dependencies or powerlessness (or even strengths) that problems arise — we say too little and too much at the same time.

This is because descriptive gender differences are transformed into the division between men and women. Women are constituted as a group via dependency relationships vis-à-vis men, who are implicitly held responsible for these relationships. When "women of Africa" as a group (versus "men of Africa" as a group?) are seen as a group precisely because they are generally dependent and oppressed, the analysis of specific historical differences becomes impossible, because reality is always apparently structured by divisions — two mutually exclusive and jointly exhaustive groups, the victims and the oppressors. Here the sociological is substituted for the biological, in order, however, to create the same — a unity of women. Thus, it is not the descriptive potential of gender difference but the privileged positioning and explanatory potential of gender difference as the *origin* of oppression that I question. In using "women of Africa" (as an already constituted group of oppressed peoples) as a category of analysis, Cutrufelli denies any historical specificity to the location of women as subordinate, powerful, marginal, central, or otherwise, vis-à-vis particular social and power networks. Women are taken as a unified "powerless" group prior to the analysis in question Thus, it is then merely a matter of specifying the context *after the fact*. "Women" are now placed in the context of the family, or in the workplace, or within religious networks, almost as if these systems existed outside the relations of women with other women, and women with men.

The problem with this analytic strategy, let me repeat, is that it assumes men and women are already constituted as sexual–political subjects prior to their entry into the arena of social relations. Only if we subscribe to this assumption is it possible to undertake analysis which looks at the "effects" kinship structures, colonialism, organization of labor, etc., on women, who are defined in advance as a group. The crucial point that is forgotten is that women are produced through these very relations as well as being implicated in forming these relations. As Michelle Rosaldo argues, "woman's place in human social life is not in any direct sense a product of the things she does (or even less, a function of what, biologically, she is) but the meaning her activities acquire through concrete social interactions" (1980, 400). That women mother in a variety of societies is not as significant as the value attached to mothering in these societies. The distinction between the act of mothering and the status attached to it is a very important one – one that needs to be stated and analyzed contextually.

Married women as victims of the colonial process

In Lévi-Strauss's theory of kinship structure as a system of the exchange of women, what is significant is that exchange itself is not constitutive of the subordination of women; women are not subordinate because of the *fact* of exchange, but because of the *modes* of exchange instituted, and the values attached to these modes. However, in discussing the marriage ritual of the Bemba, a Zambian matrilocal, matrilineal people, Cutrufelli in *Women of Africa* focuses on the fact of the marital exchange of women before and after Western colonization, rather than the value attached to this exchange in this particular context. This leads to her definition of Bemba women as a coherent group affected in a particular way by colonization. Here again, Bemba women are constituted rather unilaterally as victims of the effects of Western colonization.

Cutrufelli cites the marriage ritual of the Bemba as a multistage event "whereby a young man becomes incorporated into his wife's family group as he takes up residence with them and gives his services in return for food and maintenance" (43). This ritual extends over many years, and the sexual relationship varies according to the degree of the girl's physical maturity. It is only after she undergoes an initiation ceremony at puberty that intercourse is sanctioned, and the man acquires legal rights over her. This initiation ceremony is the more important act of the consecration of women's reproductive power, so that the abduction of an uninitiated girl is of no consequence, while heavy penalty is levied for the seduction of an initiated girl. Cutrufelli asserts that the effect of European colonization has changed the whole marriage system. Now the young man is entitled to take his wife away from her people in return for money. The implication is that Bemba women have now lost the protection of tribal laws. However, while it is possible to see how the structure of the traditional marriage contract (versus the postcolonial marriage contract) offered women a certain amount of control over their marital relations, only an analysis of the political significance of the actual practice which privileges an initiated girl over an uninitiated one, indicating a shift in female power relations as a result of this ceremony, can provide an accurate account of whether Bemba women were indeed protected by tribal laws *at all times*.

However, it is not possible to talk about Bemba women as a homogeneous group within the traditional marriage structure. Bemba women *before* the initiation are constituted within a different set of social relations compared to Bemba women *after* the initiation. To treat them as a unified group characterized by the fact of their "exchange" between male kin is to deny the sociohistorical and cultural specificities of their existence, and the differential *value* attached to their exchange before and after their Initiation. It is to treat the initiation ceremony as a ritual with no political implications or effects. It is also to assume that in merely describing the *structure* of the marriage contract, the situation of women is exposed. Women as a group are positioned within a given structure, but there is no attempt made to trace the effect of the marriage practice in constituting women within an obviously changing network of power relations. Thus, women are assumed to be sexual–political subjects prior to entry into kinship structures.

Women and familial systems

Elizabeth Cowie (1978), in another context, points out the implications of this sort of analysis when she emphasizes the specifically political nature of kinship structures which must be analyzed as ideological practices which designate men and women as father, husband, wife, mother, sister, etc. Thus, Cowie suggests, women as women are not *located* within the family. Rather, it is *in* the family, as an effect of kinship structures, that women as women are *constructed,* defined within and by the group. Thus, for instance, when Juliette Minces (1980) cites *the* patriarchal family as the basis for "an almost identical vision of women" that Arab and Muslim societies have, she falls into this very trap (see especially p. 23). Not only is it problematical to speak of a vision of women shared by Arab and Muslim societies (i.e., over twenty different countries) without addressing the particular historical, material, and ideological power structures that construct such images, but to speak of the patriarchal family or the tribal kinship structure as the origin of the socioeconomic status of women is to again assume that women are sexual–political subjects prior to their entry into the family. So while on the one hand women attain value or status within the family, the assumption of a singular patriarchal kinship system (common to all Arab and Muslim societies) is what apparently structures women as an oppressed group in these societies! This singular, coherent kinship system presumably influences another separate and given entity, "women." Thus, all women, regardless of class and cultural differences, are affected by this system. Not only are *all* Arab and Muslim women seen to constitute a homogeneous oppressed group, but there is no discussion of the specific *practices* within the family which constitute women as mothers, wives, sisters, etc. Arabs and Muslims, it appears, don't change at all. Their patriarchal family is carried over from the times of the prophet Mohammed. They exist, as it were, outside history.

Women and religious ideologies

A further example of the use of "women" as a category of analysis is found in cross-cultural analyses which subscribe to a certain economic reductionism in describing the relationship between the economy and factors such as politics and ideology. Here, in reducing the level of comparison to the economic relations between "developed and developing" countries, any specificity to the question of women is denied. Mina Modares (1981), in a careful analysis of women and Shi'ism in Iran, focuses on this very problem when she criticizes feminist writings which treat Islam as an ideology separate from and outside social relations and practices, rather than a discourse which includes rules for economic, social, and power relations within society. Patricia Jeffery's (1979) otherwise informative work on Pirzada women in purdah considers Islamic ideology a partial explanation for the status of women in that it provides a justification for the purdah. Here, Islamic ideology is reduced to a set of ideas whose internalization by Pirzada women contributes to the stability of the system. However, the primary explanation for purdah is located in the control that Pirzada men have over economic resources, and the personal security purdah gives to Pirzada women.

By taking a specific version of Islam as *the* Islam, Jeffery attributes a singularity and coherence to it. Modares notes " 'Islamic Theology' then becomes imposed on a separate and given entity called 'women.' A further unification is reached: Women (meaning *all women*), regardless of their differing positions within societies, come to be affected or not affected by Islam. These conceptions provide the right ingredients for an unproblematic possibility of a cross-cultural study of women" (63). [. . .]

Women and the development process

The best examples of universalization on the basis of economic reductionism can be found in the liberal "Women in Development" literature. Proponents of this school seek to examine the effect of development on third world women, sometimes from self-designated feminist perspectives. At the very least, there is an evident interest in and commitment to improving the lives of women in "developing" countries. Scholars such as Irene Tinker and Michelle Bo Bramsen (1972), Ester Boserup (1970), and Perdita Huston (1979) have all written about the effect of development policies on women in the third world.[9] All three women assume "development" is synonymous with "economic development" or "economic progress." As in the case of Minces's patriarchal family, Hosken's male sexual control, and Cutrufelli's Western colonization, development here becomes the all-time equalizer. Women are affected positively or negatively by economic development policies, and this is the basis for cross-cultural comparison.

For instance, Perdita Huston (1979) states that the purpose of her study is to describe the effect of the development process on the "family unit and its individual members" in Egypt, Kenya, Sudan, Tunisia, Sri Lanka, and Mexico. She states that the "problems" and "needs" expressed by rural and urban women in these countries all center around education and training, work and wages, access to health and other services, political participation, and legal rights. Huston relates all these "needs" to the lack of sensitive development policies which exclude women as a group or category. For her, the solution is simple: implement improved development policies which emphasize training for women fieldworkers, use women trainees, and women rural development officers, encourage women's cooperatives, etc. Here again, women are assumed to be a coherent group or category prior to their entry into "the development process." Huston assumes that all third world women have similar problems and needs. Thus, they must have similar interests and goals. However, the interests of urban, middle-class, educated Egyptian housewives, to take only one instance, could surely not be seen as being the same as those of their uneducated, poor maids. Development policies do not affect both groups of women in the same way. Practices which characterize women's status and roles vary according to class. Women are constituted as women through the complex interaction between class, culture, religion, and other ideological institutions and frameworks. They are not "women" – a coherent group – solely on the basis of a particular economic system or policy. Such reductive cross-cultural comparisons result in the colonization of the specifics of daily existence and the complexities of political interests which women of different social classes and cultures represent and mobilize.

Thus, it is revealing that for Perdita Huston, women in the third world countries she writes about have "needs" and "problems," but few if any have "choices" or the freedom to act. This is an interesting representation of women in the third world, one which is significant in suggesting a latent self-presentation of Western women which bears looking at. She writes, "What surprised and moved me most as I listened to women in such very different cultural settings was the striking commonality – whether they were educated or illiterate, urban or rural – of their most basic values: the importance they assign to family, dignity, and service to others" (1979, 115). Would Huston consider such values unusual for women in the West?

What is problematical about this kind of use of "women" as a group, as a stable category of analysis, is that it assumes an ahistorical, universal unity between women based on a generalized notion of their subordination. Instead of analytically *demonstrating* the production of women as socioeconomic political groups within particular local contexts, this analytical move limits the definition of the female subject to gender identity, completely bypassing social class and ethnic identities. What characterizes women as a group is their gender (sociologically, not necessarily biologically, defined) over and above everything else, indicating a monolithic notion of sexual difference. Because women are thus constituted as a coherent group, sexual difference becomes coterminous with female subordination, and power is automatically defined, in binary terms: people who have it (read: men), and people who do not (read: women). Men exploit, women are exploited. Such simplistic formulations are historically reductive; they are also ineffectual in designing strategies to combat oppressions. All they do is reinforce binary divisions between men and women.

What would an analysis which did not do this look like? Maria Mies's work illustrates the strength of Western feminist work on women in the third world which does not fall into the traps discussed above. Mies's study of the lace makers of Narsapur, India (1982), attempts to carefully analyze a substantial household industry in which "housewives" produce lace doilies for consumption in the world market. Through a detailed analysis of the structure of the lace industry, production and reproduction relations, the sexual division of labor, profits and exploitation, and the overall consequences of defining women as "non-working housewives" and their work as "leisure-time activity," Mies demonstrates the levels of exploitation in this industry and the impact of this production system on the work and living conditions of the women involved in it. In addition, she is able to analyze the "ideology of the housewife," the notion of a woman sitting in the house, as providing the necessary subjective and sociocultural element for the creation and maintenance of a production system that contributes to the increasing pauperization of women, and keeps them totally atomized and disorganized as workers. Mies's analysis shows the effect of a certain historically and culturally specific mode of patriarchal organization, an organization constructed on the basis of the definition of the lace makers as "non-working housewives" at familial, local, regional, statewide, and international levels. The intricacies and the effects of particular power networks not only are emphasized, but they form the basis of Mies's analysis of how this particular group of women is situated at the center of a hegemonic, exploitative world market. [. . .]

Methodological universalisms, or: women's oppression is a global phenomenon

Western feminist writings on women in the third world subscribe to a variety of methodologies to demonstrate the universal cross-cultural operation of male dominance and female exploitation. I summarize and critique three such methods below, moving from the simplest to the most complex.

First, proof of universalism is provided through the use of an arithmetic method. The argument goes like this: the greater the number of women who wear the veil, the more universal is the sexual segregation and control of women (Deardon 1975, 4–5). Similarly, a large number of different, fragmented examples from a variety of countries also apparently add up to a universal fact. For instance, Muslim women in Saudi Arabia, Iran, Pakistan, India, and Egypt all wear some sort of a veil. Hence, this indicates that the sexual control of women is a universal fact in those countries in which the women are veiled (Deardon 1975, 7, 10). Fran Hosken writes, "Rape, forced prostitution, polygamy, genital mutilation, pornography, the beating of girls and women, purdah (segregation of women) are all violations of basic human rights" (1981, 15). By equating purdah with rape, domestic violence, and forced prostitution, Hosken asserts its "sexual control" function as the primary explanation for purdah, whatever the context. Institutions of purdah are thus denied any cultural and historical specificity, and contradictions and potentially subversive aspects are totally ruled out.

In both these examples, the problem is not in asserting that the practice of wearing a veil is widespread. This assertion can be made on the basis of numbers. It is a descriptive generalization. However, it is the analytic leap from the practice of veiling to an assertion of its general significance in controlling women that must be questioned. While there may be a physical similarity in the veils worn by women in Saudi Arabia and Iran, the specific meaning attached to this practice varies according to the cultural and ideological context. In addition, the symbolic space occupied by the practice of purdah may be similar in certain contexts, but this does not automatically indicate that the practices themselves have identical significance in the social realm. For example, as is well known, Iranian middle-class women veiled themselves during the 1979 revolution to indicate solidarity with their veiled working-class sisters, while in contemporary Iran, mandatory Islamic laws dictate that all Iranian women wear veils. While in both these instances, similar reasons might be offered for the veil (opposition to the Shah and Western cultural colonization in the first case, and the true Islamicization of Iran in the second), the concrete *meanings* attached to Iranian women wearing the veil are clearly different in both historical contexts. In the first case, wearing the veil is both an oppositional and a revolutionary gesture on the part of Iranian middle-class women; in the second case, it is a coercive, institutional mandate (see Tabari 1980 for detailed discussion). It is on the basis of such context-specific differentiated analysis that effective political strategies can be generated. To assume that the mere practice of veiling women in a number of Muslim countries indicates the universal oppression of women through sexual segregation not only is analytically reductive, but also proves quite useless when it comes to the elaboration of oppositional political strategy.

Second, concepts such as reproduction, the sexual division of labor, the family, marriage, household, patriarchy, etc., are often used without their specification in local cultural and historical contexts. Feminists use these concepts in providing explanations for women's subordination, apparently assuming their universal applicability. For instance, how is it possible to refer to "the" sexual division of labor when the *content* of this division changes radically from one environment to the next, and from one historical juncture to another? At its most abstract level, it is the fact of the differential assignation of tasks according to sex that is significant; however, this is quite different from the *meaning* or *value* that the content of this sexual division of labor assumes in different contexts. In most cases the assigning of tasks on the basis of sex has an ideological origin. There is no question that a claim such as "women are concentrated in service-oriented occupations in a large number of countries around the world" is descriptively valid. Descriptively, then, perhaps the existence of a similar sexual division of labor (where women work in service occupations such as nursing, social work, etc., and men in other kinds of occupations) in a variety of different countries can be asserted. However, the concept of the "sexual division of labor" is more than just a descriptive category. It indicates the differential *value* placed on "men's work" versus "women's work."

Often the mere existence of a sexual division of labor is taken to be proof of the oppression of women in various societies. This results from a confusion between and collapsing together of the descriptive and explanatory potential of the concept of the sexual division of labor. Superficially similar situations may have radically different, historically specific explanations, and cannot be treated as identical. For instance, the rise of female-headed households in middle-class America might be construed as a sign of great independence and feminist progress, whereby women are considered to have *chosen* to be single parents, there are increasing numbers of lesbian mothers, etc. However, the recent increase in female-headed households in Latin America,[10] where women might be seen to have more decision-making power, is concentrated among the poorest strata, where life choices are the most constrained economically. A similar argument can be made for the rise of female-headed families among black and Chicana women in the U.S. The positive correlation between this and the level of poverty among women of color and white working-class women in the U.S. has now even acquired a name: the feminization of poverty. Thus, while it is possible to state that there is a rise in female-headed households in the U.S. and in Latin America, this rise cannot be discussed as a universal indicator of women's independence, nor can it be discussed as a universal indicator of women's impoverishment. The *meaning* of and *explanation* for the rise obviously vary according to the sociohistorical context.

[. . .] To summarize: I have discussed three methodological moves identifiable in feminist (and other academic) cross-cultural work which seeks to uncover a universality in women's subordinate position in society. The next and final section pulls together the previous sections, attempting to outline the political effects of the analytical strategies in the context of Western feminist writing on women in the third world. These arguments are not against generalization as much as they are for careful, historically specific generalizations responsive to complex realities. Nor do these arguments deny the necessity of forming strategic political identities and affinities. Thus, while Indian women of different religions, castes, and classes might forge a political unity on the basis of organizing against police brutality toward women (see Kishwar and Vanita 1984), an *analysis* of police brutality must be contextual. Strategic coalitions which construct oppositional political identities for themselves are based on generalization and provisional unities, but the analysis of these group identities cannot be based on universalistic, ahistorical categories.

This last section returns to an earlier point about the inherently political nature of feminist scholarship, and attempts to clarify my point about the possibility of detecting a colonialist move in the case of a hegemonic first–third world connection in scholarship. The nine texts in the Zed Press Women in the Third World series that I have discussed[11] focused on the following common areas in examining women's "status" within various societies: religion, family/kinship structures, the legal system, the sexual division of labor, education, and finally, political resistance. A large number of Western feminist writings on women in the third world focus on these themes. Of course the Zed texts have varying emphases. For instance, two of the studies, *Women in Palestine* (Bendt and Downing 1982) and *Indian Women in Struggle* (Omvedt 1980), focus explicitly on female militance and political involvement, while *Women in Arab Society* (Minces 1980) deals with Arab women's legal, religious, and familial status. In addition, each text evidences a variety of methodologies and degrees of care in making generalizations. Interestingly enough, however, almost all the texts assume "women" as a category of analysis in the manner designated above.

Clearly this is an analytical strategy which is neither limited to these Zed Press publications nor symptomatic of Zed Press publications in general. However, each of the particular texts in question assumes "women" have a coherent group identity within the different cultures discussed, prior to their entry into social relations. Thus, Omvedt can talk about "Indian women" while referring to a particular group of women in the State of Maharashtra, Cutrufelli about "women of Africa," and Minces about "Arab women" as if these groups of women have some sort of obvious cultural coherence, distinct from men in these societies. The "status" or "position" of women is assumed to be self-evident, because women as an already constituted group are *placed* within religious, economic, familial, and legal structures. However, this focus whereby women are seen as a coherent group across contexts, regardless of class or ethnicity, structures the world in ultimately binary, dichotomous terms, where women are always seen in opposition to men, patriarchy is always necessarily male dominance, and the religious, legal, economic, and familial systems are implicitly assumed to be constructed by men. Thus, both men and women are always apparently constituted whole populations, and relations of dominance and exploitation are also posited in terms of whole people – wholes coming into exploitative relations. It is only when men and women are seen as different categories or groups possessing different *already constituted* categories of experience, cognition, and interests as *groups* that such a simplistic dichotomy is possible.

What does this imply about the structure and functioning of power relations? The setting up of the commonality of third world women's struggles across classes and cultures against a general notion of oppression (primarily the group in power – i.e., men) necessitates the assumption of what Michel Foucault (1980, 135–45) calls the "juridico-discursive" model of power, the principal features of which are "a negative relation" (limit and lack), an "insistence on the rule" (which forms a binary system), a "cycle of prohibition," the "logic of censorship," and a "uniformity" of the apparatus functioning at different levels. Feminist discourse on the third world which assumes a homogeneous category – or group – called women necessarily operates through the setting up of originary power divisions. Power relations are structured in terms of a unilateral and undifferentiated source of power and a cumulative reaction to power. Opposition is a generalized phenomenon created as a response to power – which, in turn, is possessed by certain groups of people.

The major problem with such a definition of power is that it locks all evolutionary struggles into binary structures – possessing power versus being powerless. Women are powerless, unified groups. If the struggle for a just society is seen in terms of the move from powerless to powerful for women as a *group*, and this is the implication in feminist discourse which structures sexual difference in terms of the division between the sexes, then the new society would be structurally identical to the existing organization of power relations, constituting itself as a simple *inversion* of what exists. If relations of domination and exploitation are defined in terms of binary divisions – groups which dominate and groups which are dominated – surely the implication is that the accession to power of women as a group is sufficient to dismantle the existing organization of relations? But women as a group are not in some sense essentially superior or infallible. The crux of the problem lies in that initial assumption of women as a homogeneous group or category ("the oppressed"), a familiar assumption in Western radical and liberal feminisms.[12]

What happens when this assumption of "women as an oppressed group" is situated in the context of Western feminist writing about third world women? It is here that I locate the colonialist move. By contrasting the representation of women in the third world with what I referred to earlier as Western feminisms' self-presentation in the same context, we see how Western feminists alone become the true "subjects" of this counterhistory. Third world women, on the other hand, never rise above the debilitating generality of their "object" status.

While radical and liberal feminist assumptions of women as a sex class might elucidate (however inadequately) the autonomy of particular women's struggles in the West, the application of the notion of women as a homogeneous category to women in the third world colonizes and appropriates the pluralities of the simultaneous location of different groups of women in social class and ethnic frameworks; in doing so it ultimately robs them of their historical and political *agency*. Similarly, many Zed Press authors who ground themselves in the basic analytic strategies of traditional Marxism also implicitly create a "unity" of women by substituting "women's activity" for "labor" as the primary theoretical determinant of women's situation. Here again, women are constituted as a coherent group not on the basis of "natural" qualities or needs but on the basis of the sociological "unity" of their role in domestic production and wage labor (see Haraway 1985, esp. p. 76). In other words, Western feminist discourse, by assuming women as a coherent, already constituted group which is placed in kinship, legal, and other structures, defines third world women as subjects *outside* social relations, instead of looking at the way women are constituted *through* these very structures.

Legal, economic, religious and familial structures are treated as phenomena to be judged by Western standards. It is here that ethnocentric universality comes into play. When these structures are defined as "underdeveloped" or "developing" and women are placed within them, an implicit image of the "average third world woman" is produced. This is the transformation of the (implicitly Western) "oppressed woman" into the "oppressed third world woman." While the category of "oppressed woman" is generated through an exclusive focus on gender difference "the oppressed third world woman" category has an additional attribute – the "third world difference!" The "third world difference" includes a paternalistic attitude toward women in the third world.[13] Since discussions of the various themes I identified earlier (kinship, education, religion, etc.) are conducted in the context of the relative "underdevelopment" of the third world (which is nothing less than unjustifiably confusing development with the separate path taken by the West in its development, as well as ignoring the directionality of the first–third world power relationship), third world women as a group or category are automatically and necessarily defined as religious (read "not progressive"), family-oriented (read "traditional"), legal minors (read "they-are-still-not-conscious-of-their-rights"), illiterate (read "ignorant"), domestic (read "backward"), and sometimes revolutionary (read "their-country-is-in-a-state-of-war; they-must-fight!") This is how the "third world difference" is produced.

When the category of "sexually oppressed women" is located within particular systems in the third world which are defined on a scale which is normed through Eurocentric assumptions, not only are third world women defined in a particular way prior to their entry into social relations, but since no connections are made between first and third world power shifts, the assumption is reinforced that the third world just has not evolved to the extent that the West has. This mode of feminist analysis, by homogenizing and systematizing the experiences of different groups of women in these countries, erases all marginal and resistant modes and experiences.[14] It is significant that none of the texts I reviewed in the Zed Press focuses on lesbian politics or the politics of ethnic and religious marginal organizations in third world women's groups. Resistance can thus be defined only as cumulatively reactive, not as something inherent in the operation of power. If power, as Michel Foucault has argued recently, can really be understood only in the context of resistance,[15] this misconceptualization is both analytically and strategically problematical. It limits theoretical analysis as well as reinforces Western cultural imperialism. For in the context of a first/third world balance of power, feminist analyses which perpetrate and sustain the hegemony of the idea of the superiority of the West produce a corresponding set of universal images of the "third world woman," images such as the veiled woman, the powerful mother, the chaste virgin, the obedient wife, etc. These images exist in universal, ahistorical splendor, setting in motion a colonialist discourse which exercises a very specific power in defining, coding, and maintaining existing first/third world connections.

To conclude, then, let me suggest some disconcerting similarities between the typically authorizing signature of such Western feminist writings on women in the third world, and the authorizing signature of the project of humanism in general – humanism as a Western ideological and political project which involves the necessary recuperation of the "East" and "Woman" as Others. Many contemporary thinkers, including Foucault (1978, 1980), Derrida (1974), Kristeva (1980), Deleuze and Guattari (1977), and Said (1978), have written at length about the underlying anthropomorphism and ethnocentrism which constitute a hegemonic humanistic problematic that repeatedly confirms and legitimates (Western) Man's centrality. Feminist theorists such as Luce Irigaray,(1981), Sarah Kofman (see Berg 1982), and Helene Cixous (1981) have also written about the recuperation and absence of woman/women within Western humanism. The focus of the work of all these thinkers can be stated simply as an uncovering of the political *interests* that underlie the binary logic of humanistic discourse and ideology whereby, as a valuable recent essay puts it, "the first (majority) term (Identity, Universality, Culture, Disinterested-ness, Truth, Sanity, Justice, etc.), which is, in fact, secondary and derivitive (a construction), is privileged over and colonizes the second (minority) term (difference, temporality, anarchy, error, interestedness, insanity, deviance, etc.), which is in fact, primary and originative" (Spanos 1984). In other words, it is only insofar as "Woman/Women" and "the East" are defined as *Others*, or as peripheral, that (Western) Man/Humanism can represent him/itself as the center. It is not the center that determines the periphery, but the periphery that, in its boundedness determines the center. Just as feminists such as Cristeva and Cixous deconstruct the latent anthropomorphism in Western discourse, I have suggested a parallel strategy in this essay in uncovering a latent ethnocentrism in particular feminist writings on women in the third world.[16]

As discussed earlier, a comparison between Western feminist self-presentation and Western feminist re-presentation of women in the third world yields significant results. Universal images of "the third world woman" (the veiled woman, chaste virgin, etc.), images constructed from adding the "third world difference" to "sexual difference," are predicated upon (and hence obviously bring into sharper focus) assumptions about Western women as secular, liberated, and having control over their own lives. This is not to suggest that Western women *are* secular, liberated, and in control of their own lives. I am referring to a *discursive* self-presentation, not necessarily to material reality. If this were a material reality, there would be no need for political movements in the West. Similarly, only from the vantage point of the West is it possible to define the "third world" as underdeveloped and economically dependent. Without the overdetermined discourse that creates the *third* world, there would be no (singular and privileged) first world. Without the "third world woman," the particular self-presentation of Western women mentioned above would be problematical. I am suggesting, then, that the one enables and sustains the other. This is not to say that the signature of Western feminist writings on the third world has the same authority as the project of Western humanism. However, in the context of the hegemony of the Western scholarly establishment in the production and dissemination of texts, and in the context of the legitimating imperative of humanistic and scientific discourse, the definition of "the third world woman" as a monolith might well tie into the larger economic and ideological praxis of "disinterested" scientific inquiry and pluralism which are the surface manifestations of a latent economic and cultural colonization of the "non-Western" world. It is time to move beyond the Marx who found it possible to say: They cannot represent themselves; they must be represented.

Notes

This essay would not have been possible without S. P. Mohanty's challenging and careful reading. I would also like to thank Biddy Martin for our numerous discussions about feminist theory and politics. They both helped me think through some of the arguments herein.

1   This is an updated and modified version of an essay published in *Boundary 2* 12, no. 3/13, no. 1 (Spring/Fall 1984), and reprinted in *Feminist Review*, no. 30 (Autumn 1988).

2   Terms such as *third* and *first world* are very problematical both in suggesting oversimplified similarities between and among countries labeled thus, and in implicitly reinforcing existing economic, cultural, and ideological hierarchies which are conjured up in using such terminology. I use the term "*third world*" with full awareness of its problems, only because this is the terminology available to us at the moment. The use of quotation marks is meant to suggest a continuous questioning of the designation. Even when I do not use quotation marks, I mean to use the term critically.

3   I am indebted to Teresa de Lauretis for this particular formulation of the project of feminist theorizing. See especially her introduction in de Lauretis, *Alice Doesn't: Feminism, Semiotics, Cinema* (Bloomington: Indiana University Press, 1984) see also Sylvia Wynter, "The Politics of Domination," unpublished manuscript.

4   This argument is similar to Homi Bhabha's definition of colonial discourse as strategically creating a space for a subject people through the production of knowledges and the exercise of power. The full quote reads: "[colonial discourse is] an apparatus of power . . . an apparatus that turns on the recognition and disavowal of racial/cultural/historical differences. Its predominant strategic function is the creation of a space for a subject people through the production of knowledges in terms of which surveillance is exercised and a complex form of pleasure/unpleasure is incited. It (i.e. colonial discourse) seeks authorization for its strategies by the production of knowledges by coloniser and colonised which are stereotypical but antithetically evaluated" (1983, 23).

5   The Zed Press Women in the Third World series is unique in its conception. I choose to focus on it because it is the only contemporary series I have found

which assumes that "women in the third world" are a legitimate and separate subject of study and research. Since 1985, when this essay was first written, numerous new titles have appeared in the Women in the Third World series. Thus, I suspect that Zed has come to occupy a rather privileged position in the dissemination and construction of discourses by and about third world women. A number of the books in this series are excellent, especially those which deal directly with women's resistance struggles. In addition, Zed Press consistently publishes progressive feminist, antiracist, and antiimperialist texts. However, a number of the texts written by feminist sociologists, anthropologists, and journalists are symptomatic of the kind of Western feminist work on women in the third world that concerns me. Thus, an analysis of a few of these particular works in this series can serve as a representative point of entry into the discourse I am attempting to locate and define. My focus on these texts is therefore an attempt at an internal critique: I simply expect and demand more from this series. Needless to say, progressive publishing houses also carry their own authorizing signatures.

6 Elsewhere I have discussed this particular point in detail in a critique of Robin Morgan's construction of "women's herstory" in her introduction to *Sisterhood Is Global: The International Women's Movement Anthology* (New York: Anchor Press/Doubleday, 1984). See my "Feminist Encounters: Locating the Politics of Experience," *Copyright* 1, "Fin de Siècle 2000," 30–44, especially 35–37.

7 Another example of this kind of analysis is Mary Daly's (1978) *Gyn/Ecology*. Daly's assumption in this text, that women as a group are sexually victimized, leads to her very problematic comparison between the attitudes toward women witches and healers in the West, Chinese footbinding, and the genital mutilation of women in Africa. According to Daly, women in Europe, China, and Africa constitute a homogeneous group as victims of male power. Not only does this label (sexual victims) eradicate the specific historical and material realities and contradictions which lead to and perpetuate practices such as witch hunting and genital mutilation, but it also obliterates the differences, complexities, and heterogeneities of the lives of, for example, women of different classes, religions, and nations in Africa. As Audre Lorde (1983) pointed out, women in Africa share a long tradition of healers and goddesses that perhaps binds them together more appropriately than their victim status. However, both Daly and Lorde fall prey to universalistic assumptions about "African women" (both negative and positive). What matters is the complex, historical range of power differences, commonalities, and resistances that exist among women in Africa which construct African women as "subjects" of their own politics.

8 See Eldhom, Harris, and Young (1977) for a good discussion of the necessity to theorize male violence within specific societal frameworks, rather than assume it as a universal fact.

9 These views can also be found in differing degrees in collections such as Wellesley Editorial Committee, ed., *Women and National Development: The Complexities of Change* (Chicago: University of Chicago Press, 1977), and *Signs*, Special Issue, "Development and the Sexual Division of Labor," 7, no. 2 (Winter 1981). For an excellent introduction of WID issues, see ISIS, *Women in Development: A Resource Guide for Organization and Action* (Philadelphia: New Society Publishers, 1984). For a politically focused discussion of feminism and development and the stakes for poor third world women, see Gita Sen and Caren Grown, *Development Crises*

and Alternative Visions: Third World Women's Perspectives (New York: Monthly Review Press, 1987).

10   Olivia Harris, "Latin American Women – An Overview," in Harris, ed *Latin American Women* (London: Minority Rights Group Report no. 57, 1983), 4–7. Other MRG Reports include Ann Deardon (1975) and Rounaq Jahan (1980).

11   List of Zed Press publications: Patricia Jeffery, *Frogs in a Well: Indian Women in Purdah* (1979); Latin American and Caribbean Women's Collective, *Slaves of Slaves: The Challenge of Latin American Women* (1980); Gail Omvedt, *We Shall Smash This Prison: Indian Women in Struggle* (1980); Juliette Minces, *The House of Obedience: Women in Arab Society* (1980); Bobby Siu, *Women of China: Imperialism and Women's Resistance, 1900–1949* (1981); Ingela Bendt and James Downing, *We Shall Return: Women in Palestine* (1982); Maria Rosa Cutrufelli, *Women of Africa: Roots of Oppression* (1983); Maria Mies, *The Lace Makers of Narsapur: Indian Housewives Produce for the World Market* (1982); Miranda Davis, ed., *Third World/Second Sex: Women's Struggles and National Liberation* (1983).

12   For succinct discussions of Western radical and liberal feminisms, see Hester Eisenstein. *Contemporary Feminist Thought* (Boston: G. K. Hall & Co., 1983), and Zillah Eisenstein, *The Radical Future of Liberal Feminism* (New York: Longman, 1981).

13   Amos and Parmar (1984) describe the cultural stereotypes present in Euro-American feminist thought: "The image is of the passive Asian woman subject to oppressive practices within the Asian family with an emphasis on wanting to 'help' Asian women liberate themselves from their role. Or there is the strong, dominant Afro-Caribbean woman, who despite her 'strength' is exploited by the 'sexism' which is seen as being a strong feature in relationships between Afro-Caribbean men and women" (9). These images illustrate the extent to which *paternalism* is an essential element of feminist thinking which incorporates the above stereotypes, a paternalism which can lead to the definition of priorities for women of color by Euro-American feminists.

14   I discuss the question of theorizing experience in my "Feminist Encounters" (1987) and in an essay coauthored with Biddy Martin, "Feminist Politics: What's Home Got to Do with It?" in Teresa de Lauretis, ed., *Feminist Studies/Critical Studies* (Bloomington: Indiana University Press, 1986), 191–212.

15   This is one of M. Foucault's (1978, 1980) central points in his reconceptualization of the strategies and workings of power networks.

16   For an argument which demands a *new* conception of humanism in work on third world women, see Marnia Lazreg (1988). While Lazreg's position might appear to be diametrically opposed to mine, I see it as a provocative and potentially positive extension of some of the implications that follow from my arguments. In criticizing the feminist rejection of humanism in the name of "essential Man," Lazreg points to what she calls an "essentialism of difference" within these very feminist projects. She asks: "To what extent can Western feminism dispense with an ethics of responsibility then writing about different women? The point is neither to subsume other women under one's own experience nor to uphold a separate truth for them. Rather, it is to allow them to *be* while recognizing that what they are is just as meaningful, valid, and comprehensible as what we are. . . . Indeed, when feminists essentially deny other women the humanity they claim for themselves, they dispense with any ethical constraint. They engage in the act of splitting the social universe into us and them, subject and objects" (99–100).

This essay by Lazreg and an essay by S. P. Mohanty (1989) entitled "Us and Them: On the Philosophical Bases of Political Criticism" suggest positive directions for self-conscious cross-cultural analyses, analyses which move beyond the deconstructive to a fundamentally productive mode in designating overlapping areas for cross-cultural comparison. The latter essay calls not for a "humanism" but for a reconsideration of the question of the "human" in a posthumanist context. It argues that (1) there is no necessary "incompatibility between the deconstruction of Western humanism" and such "a positive elaboration" of the human, and moreover that (2) such an elaboration is essential if contemporary political–critical discourse is to avoid the incoherences and weaknesses of a relativist position.

References

Amin, Samir. 1977. *Imperialism and Unequal Development*. New York: Monthly Review Press.

Amos, Valerie, and Pratibha Parmar. 1984 "Challenging Imperial Feminism." *Feminist Review* 17:3–19.

Baran, Paul A. 1962. *The Political Economy of Growth*. New York: Monthly Review Press.

Berg, Elizabeth. 1982, "The Third Woman." *Diacritics* (Summer):11–20.

Bhabha, Homi. 1983. "The Other Question – The Stereotype and Colonial Discourse." *Screen* 24. no. 6:23.

Boserup, Ester. 1970. *Women's Role in Economic Development*. New York: St. Martin's Press; London: Allen and Unwin.

Cixous, Helene. 1981. "The Laugh of the Medusa." In Marks and De Courtivron (1981).

Cowie, Elizabeth. 1978. "Woman as Sign." *m/f* 1:49–63.

Cutrufelli, Maria Rosa. 1983. *Women of Africa: Roots of Oppression*. London: Zed Press.

Daly, Mary. 1978. *Gyn/Ecology: The Metaethics of Radical Feminism*. Boston: Beacon Press.

Deardon, Ann, ed. 1975. *Arab Women*. London: Minority Rights Group Report no. 27.

de Lauretis, Teresa. 1984. *Alice Doesn't: Feminism, Semiotics, Cinema*. Bloomington: Indiana University Press.

—— 1986. *Feminist Studies/Critical Studies*. Bloomington: Indiana University Press.

Deleuze. Giles, and Felix Guattari. 1977. *Anti-Oedipus: Capitalism and Schizophrenia*. New York: Viking.

Derrida, Jacques. 1974. *Of Grammatology*. Baltimore. Johns Hopkins University Press.

Eisenstein, Hester. 1983. *Contemporary Feminist Thought*. Boston: G. K. Hall and Co.

Eisenstein, Zillab. 1981. *The Radical Future of Liberal Feminism*. New York: Longman.

Eidhom, Felicity, Olivia Harris, and Kate Young. 1977. "Conceptualising Women." *Critique of Anthropology "Women's Issue"*, no. 3.

Foucault, Michel. 1978. *History of Sexuality: Volume One*. New York: Random House.

—— 1980. *Power/Knowledge*. New York: Pantheon.

Gunder-Frank, Audre. 1967. *Capitalism and Underdevelopment in Latin America*. New York: Monthly Review Press.

Haraway, Donna. 1985. "A Manifesto for Cyborgs: Science, Technology and Socialist Feminism in the 1980s." *Socialist Review* 80 (March/April):65–108.

Harris, Olivia. 1983a. "Latin American Women – An Overview." In Harris (1983b).

——— 1983b. *Latin American Women.* London: Minority Rights Group Report no. 57.

Hosken Fran. 1981. "Female Genital Mutilation and Human Rights." *Feminist Issues* 1, no. 3.

Huston, Perdita. 1979. *Third World Women Speak Out.* New York: Praeger.

Irigaray, Luce. 1981. "'This Sex Which Is Not One" and "When the Goods Get Together." In Marks and De Courtivron (1981).

Jahan. Rounaq, ed. 1980. *Women in Asia.* London: Minority Rights Group Report no. 45.

Jeffery, Patricia. 1979. *Frogs in a Well: Indian Women in Purdah.* London: Zed Press.

Joseph, Gloria, and Jill Lewis. 1981. *Common Differences: Conflicts in Black and White Feminist Perspectives.* Boston: Beacon Press.

Kishwar, Madhu, and Ruth Vanita. 1984. *In Search of Answers: Indian Women's Voices from Manushi.* London: Zed Press.

Kristeva, Julia. 1980. *Desire in Language.* New York: Columbia University Press.

Lazreg, Marnia. 1988. "Feminism and Difference: The Perils of Writing as a Woman on Women in Algeria." *Feminist Issues* 14, no. 1 (Spring):81–107.

Lindsay, Beverley, ed. 1983. *Comparative Perspectives of Third World Women: The Impact of Race, Sex and Class.* New York: Praeger.

Lorde, Audre. 1983. "An Open Letter to Mary Daly." In Moraga and Anzaldua (1983), 94–97.

Mies Maria. 1982. *The Lace Makers of Narsapur: Indian Housewives Produce for the World Market.* London: Zed Press.

Minces Juliette. 1980. *The House of Obedience: Women in Arab Society.* London: Zed Press.

Modares, Mina. 1981. "Women and Shi'ism in Iran." *m/f* 5 and 6:61–82.

Mohanty, Chandra Talpade. 1987. "Feminist Encounters: Locating the Politics of Experience." *Copyright* 1, "Fin de Siecle 2000," 30–44.

Mohanty, Chandra Talpade, and Biddy Martin. 1986. "Feminist Politics: What's Home Got to Do with It?" In de Lauretis (1986).

Mohanty, S. P. 1989. "Us and Them: On the Philosophical Bases of Political Criticism." *Yale Journal of Criticism* 2 (March):1–31.

Moraga, Cherríe. 1984. *Loving in the War Years.* Boston: South End Press.

Moraga, Cherríe, and Gloria Anzaldúa, eds. 1983. *This Bridge Called My Back: Writings by Radical Women of Color.* New York: Kitchen Table Press.

Morgan, Robin, ed. 1984. *Sisterhood Is Global: The International Women's Movement Anthology.* New York: Anchor Press/Doubleday; Harmondsworth: Penguin.

Rosaldo, M. A. 1980. "The Use and Abuse of Anthropology: Reflections on Feminism and Cross-Cultural Understanding." *Signs* 53:389–417.

Said, Edward. 1978. *Orientalism.* New York: Random House.

Sen, Gita, and Caren Grown. 1987. *Development Crises and Alternative Visions: Third World Women's Perspectives.* New York: Monthly Review Press.

Smith, Barbara, ed. 1983. *Home Girls: A Black Feminist Anthology.* New York: Kitchen Table Press.

Spanos, William V. 1984. "Boundary 2 and the Polity of Interest: Humanism, the 'Center Elsewhere' and Power." *Boundary* 2 12, no. 3/13, no. 1 (Spring/Fall).

Tabari, Azar. 1980. "The Enigma of the Veiled Iranian Women." *Feminist Review* 5:19–32.

Tinker, Irene, and Michelle Bo Bramsen, eds. 1972. *Women and World Development.* Washington, D.C.: Overseas Development Council.

Chapter 25

Ann L. Stoler

SEXUAL AFFRONTS AND
RACIAL FRONTIERS
European identities and the cultural politics
of exclusion in colonial Southeast Asia

T HIS ESSAY IS CONCERNED WITH the construction of colonial categories and national identities and with those people who ambiguously straddled, crossed, and threatened these imperial divides. It begins with a story about *métissage* (interracial unions) and the sorts of progeny to which it gave rise (referred to as *métis,* mixed bloods) in French Indochina at the turn of the century. It is a story with multiple versions about people whose cultural sensibilities, physical being, and political sentiments called into question the distinctions of difference which maintained the neat boundaries of colonial rule. Its plot and resolution defy the treatment of European nationalist impulses and colonial racist policies as discrete projects, since here it was in the conflation of racial category, sexual morality, cultural competence and national identity that the case was contested and politically charged. In a broader sense, it allows me to address one of the tensions of empire which this essay only begins to sketch: the relationship between the discourses of inclusion, humanitarianism, and equality which informed liberal policy at the turn of the century in colonial Southeast Asia and the exclusionary, discriminatory practices which were reactive to, coexistent with, and perhaps inherent in liberalism itself.[1]

Nowhere is this relationship between inclusionary impulses and exclusionary practices more evident than in how métissage was legally handled, culturally inscribed, and politically treated in the contrasting colonial cultures of French Indochina and the Netherlands Indies. French Indochina was a colony of commerce occupied by the military in the 1860s and settled by *colons* in the 1870s with a métis population which numbered no more than several hundred by the turn of the century.[2] The Netherlands Indies by contrast, had been settled since the early 1600s with those of mixed descent or born in the Indies numbering in the tens of thousands in 1900. They made up nearly three-quarters of those legally designated as European. Their *Indische* mestizo culture shaped the contours of colonial society for its first two hundred years.[3] Although conventional historiography defines sharp contrasts between French, British, and Dutch colonial racial policy and the particular national metropolitan agendas from which they derived, what is more striking is that similar discourses were mapped onto such vastly different social and political landscapes.[4]

In both the Indies and Indochina, with their distinct demographics and internal rhythms, métissage was a focal point of political, legal, and social debate. Conceived as a dangerous source of subversion, it was seen as a threat to white prestige, an embodiment of European degeneration and moral decay.[5] This is not to suggest that the so-called mixed-blood problem was of the same intensity in both places nor resolved in precisely the same ways. However, the issues which resonated in these different colonies reveal a patterned set of transgressions that have not been sufficiently explored. I would suggest that both situations were so charged, in part because such mixing called into question the very criteria by which Europeanness could be identified, citizenship should be accorded, and nationality assigned. Métissage represented not the dangers of foreign enemies at national borders, but the more pressing affront for European nation-states, what the German philosopher, Fichte, so aptly defined as the, essence of the nation, its "interior frontiers."[6]

The concept of an interior frontier is compelling precisely because of its contradictory connotations. As Etienne Balibar has noted, a frontier locates both a site of enclosure and contact, of observed passage and exchange. When coupled with the word interior, frontier carries the sense of internal distinctions within a territory (or empire); at the level of the individual, frontier marks the moral predicates by which a subject retains his or her national identity despite location outside the national frontier and despite heterogeneity within the nation-state. As Fichte deployed it, an interior frontier entails two dilemmas: the purity of the community is prone to penetration on its interior and exterior borders, and the essence of the community is an intangible "moral attitude," "a multiplicity of invisible ties."[7]

Viewing late nineteenth-century representations of a national essence in these terms, we can trace how métissage emerges as a powerful trope for internal contamination and challenge conceived morally, politically, and sexually.[8] The changing density and intensity of métissage's discursive field outlines the fault lines of colonial authority: In linking domestic arrangements to the public order, family to the state, sex to subversion, and psychological essence to racial type, métissage might be read as a metonym for the biopolitics of the empire at large.

In both Indochina and the Netherlands Indies, the rejection of métis as a distinct legal category only intensified how the politics of cultural difference were played out in other domains.[9] In both colonies, the *métis-indo* problem produced a discourse in which facile theories of racial hierarchy were rejected, while confirming the practical predicates of European superiority at the same time. The early Vietnamese and Indonesian nationalist movements created new sources of colonial vulnerability, and some of the debates over the nature and definition of Dutch and French national identity must be seen in that light. The resurgence of European nationalist rhetoric may partly have been a response to nationalist resistance in the colonies, but it cannot be accounted for in these terms alone.[10] For French Indochina, discourses about the dangers of métissage were sustained in periods of quiescence and cannot be viewed as rhetorics of reaction *tout court*. This is not to suggest that there was no correspondence between them.[11] But anticolonial challenges in Indo-china, contrary to the discourse which characterized the métis as a potential subversive vanguard, were never predominantly led nor peopled by them. And in the Indies, where persons of mixed descent made up a potentially powerful constituency, the bids they made for economic, social, and political reform were more often made in contradistinction to the demands of the native population, not in alliance with them.

Although the content of the métis problem was partially in response to popular threats to colonial rule, the particular form that the securing of European privilege took was not shaped in the colonies alone. The focus on moral unity, cultural genealogy, and language joined the imagining of European colonial communities and metropolitan national entities in fundamental ways. Both visions embraced a moral rearmament, centering on the domestic domain and the family as sites in which state authority could be secured or irreparably undermined.[12]

[. . .] I explore that question here by working off of a seemingly disparate set of texts and contexts: a criminal court proceeding in Haiphong in 1898; the Hanoi campaign against child abandonment in the early 1900s; the protracted debate on mixed marriage legislation in the Indies between 1887 and 1898; and finally, the confused and failed efforts of the Indo-European movement itself in the Indies to articulate its opposition to "pure-blood" Dutch by calling upon race, place, and cultural genealogy to make its demands.

In each of these texts, class, gender, and cultural markers deny and designate exclusionary practices at the same time. We cannot determine which of these categories is privileged at any given moment by sorting out the fixed primacy of race over gender or gender over class. On the contrary, I trace an unstable and uneven set of discourses in which different institutional authorities claimed primacy for one over another in relationship to how other authorities attempted to designate how political boundaries were to be protected and assigned. For mid-Victorian England, Mary Poovey argues that discourses about gender identity were gradually displaced in the 1850s by the issue of national identity.[13] However, the contestations over métissage suggest nothing linear about these developments. Rather, class distinctions, gender prescriptions, cultural knowledge, and racial membership were simultaneously invoked and strategically filled with different meanings for varied projects.

Patriarchal principles were not always applied to shore up government priorities. Colonial authorities with competing agendas agreed on two premises: Children had to be taught both their place and race, and the family was the crucial site in which future subjects and loyal citizens were to be made. These concerns framed the fact that the domestic life of individuals was increasingly subject to public scrutiny by a wide range of private and government organizations that charged themselves with the task of policing the moral borderlands of the European community and the psychological sensibilities of its marginal, as well as supposedly full-fledged, members.

At the heart of this tension between inclusionary rhetorics and exclusionary practices was a search for essences that joined formulations of national and racial identity – what Benedict Anderson has contrasted as the contrary dreams of "historical destinies" and "eternal contaminations."[14] Racism is commonly understood as a visual ideology in which somatic features are thought to provide the crucial criteria of membership. But racism is not really a visual ideology at all; physiological attributes only signal the non-visual and more salient distinctions of exclusion on which racism rests. Racism is not to biology as nationalism is to culture. Cultural attributions in both provide the observable conduits, the indices of psychological propensities and moral susceptibilities seen to shape which individuals are suitable for inclusion in the national community and whether those of ambiguous racial membership are to be classified as subjects or citizens within it. If we are to trace the epidemiologies of racist and nationalist thinking, then it is the cultural logics that underwrite the relationship between fixed, visual representations and invisible protean essences to which we must attend. This convergence between national and racial thinking achieves particular clarity when we turn to the legal and social debates in the colonies that linked observable cultural styles of parenting and domestic arrangement to the hidden psychological requirements for access to French and Dutch citizenship in this period.

Cultural competence, national identity, and métissage

In 1898 in the French Indochinese city of Haiphong, the nineteen-year-old son of a French minor naval employee, Sieur Icard, was charged with assaulting without provocation a German naval mechanic, striking his temple with a whip, and attempting to crush his eye. The boy was sentenced by the tribunal court to six months in prison.[15] Spurred by the father's efforts to make an appeal for an attenuated prison term, some higher officials subsequently questioned whether the penalty was unduly severe. Clemency was not accorded by the Governor-General, and the boy, referred to by the court as "Nguyen van Thinh *dit* Lucien" (called Lucien) was sentenced to bear out his full term. The case might have been less easily dismissed if it were not for the fact that the son was métis, the child of a man who was a French citizen and a woman who was a colonial subject, his concubine and Vietnamese.

The granting of a pardon rested on two assessments: whether the boy's cultural identity and his display of French cultural competence supported his claim to French citizenship rights. Because the Governor-General's letters listed the boy as Nguyen van Thinh dit Lucien, they thereby invoked not only the double naming of the son, privileging first Nguyen van Thinh over Lucien, but suggested the dubious nature of his cultural affinities, giving the impression that his real name was Nguyen van Thinh, although he answered to the name Lucien. The father, Sieur Icard, attempted to affirm the Frenchness of his son by referring to him as Lucien and eliminated reference to Nguyen. But the angry president of Haiphong's tribunal court used only the boy's Vietnamese name, dropping Lucien altogether and put the very kinship between the father and son in question by naming Icard as the "alleged" father.

Icard's plea for pardon, which invoked his own patriotic sentiments as well as those of his son, was carefully conceived. Icard protested that the court had wrongly treated the boy as a *"vulgaire annamite"* (a common Annamite) and not as the legally recognized son of a French citizen. Icard held that his son had been provoked and only then struck the German in retaliation. But more important, Lucien had been raised in a French patriotic milieu, in a household in which Germans were held in "contempt and disdain." He pointed out that their home was full of drawings of the 1870 (Franco-Prussian) War and that like any impressionable [French] boy of his age, Lucien and his imagination were excited by these images.

The tribunal's refusal to accept the appeal confronted and countered Icard's claims. At issue was whether Nguyen van Thinh dit Lucien could really be considered culturally and politically French and whether he was inculcated with the patriotic feelings and nationalist sentiments which might have prompted such a loyal response. The tribunal argued that Icard was away sailing too much of the time to impart such a love of *patrie* to his son and that Icard's "hate of Germans must have been of very recent origin since he had spent so much time sailing with foreigners."[16] The non-French inclinations of the boy were firmly established with the court's observation that Lucien was illiterate and knew but a few French words. Icard's argument was thus further undermined since Icard himself "spoke no annamite" and therefore shared no common language with his offspring.

Although these counter-arguments may have been sufficient to convince the Governor-General not to grant leniency, another unclarified but damning reason was invoked to deny the son's case and the father's appeal: namely, the "immoral relations which could have existed between the detainee and the one who declared himself his father.[17] Or as put by Villeminot, the city attorney in Haiphong charged with further investigating Icard's appeal, the boy deserved no leniency because "his morality was always detestable" and the police reports permitted one "to entertain the most serious suspicions concerning the nature of the relations which Nguyen van Thinh maintained with his alleged father."[18]

Whether these were coded allegations of homosexuality or referred to a possibly illegal recognition of the boy by Icard (pretending to be his father) is unclear. Icard's case came up at a time when acts of "fraudulent recognition" of native children were said to be swelling the French citizenry with a bastard population of native poor.[19] Perversion and immorality and patriotism and nationalist sentiments were clearly considered mutually exclusive categories. As in nineteenth-century Germany, adherence to middle-class European sexual morality was one implicit requisite for full-fledged citizenship in the European nation-state.[20]

But with all these allusions to suspect and duplicitous behavior perhaps what was more unsettling in this case was another unspeakable element in this story: Namely, that Icard felt such a powerful sentiment between himself and his son and that he not only recognized his Eurasian son but went so far as to plead the case of a boy who had virtually none of the exterior qualities (skin tone, language, or cultural literacy), and therefore could have none of the interior attributes of being French at all. What the court seemed to have condemned was a relationship in which Icard could have shown such dedication and love for a child who was illiterate, ignorant of the French language, and who spent most of his time in a cultural milieu that was much less French than Vietnamese. Under such circumstances, Icard's concern for Lucien was inappropriate and improper; his fatherly efforts to excuse his son's misdeeds were neither lauded by the lower courts nor the Governor-General. On the contrary, paternal love and responsibility were not to be disseminated arbitrarily as Icard had obviously done by recognizing his progeny but allowing him to grow up Indochinese. In denying the father's plea, the court passed sentence both on Icard and his son: Both were guilty of transgressing the boundaries of race, culture, sex, and patrie. If Icard (whose misspellings and profession belied his lower-class origins) was not able to bring his son up in a proper French milieu, then he should have abandoned him all together.

What was perhaps most duplicitous in the relationship was that the boy could both be Nguyen van Thinh in cultural sensibilities and Lucien to his father, or, from a slightly different perspective, that Lucien's physical and cultural non-French affinities did not stand in the way of the father's love. Like the relationship with the boy's mother, which was easily attributed to carnal lust, Icard's choice to stand up for his son was reduced to a motive of base desires, sexual or otherwise. Neither father nor son had demonstrated a proper commitment to and identification with those invisible moral bonds by which racist pedigrees and colonial divides were marked and maintained.

Cultural neglect, native mothers, and the racial politics of abandonment

The story invokes the multiple tensions of colonial cultures in Southeast Asia and would be of interest for that alone. But it is all the more startling because it so boldly contradicts the dominant formulation of the "métis question" at the turn of the century as a problem of "abandonment," of children culturally on the loose, sexually abused, economically impoverished, morally neglected, and politically dangerous. European feminists took up the protection of abandoned mixed-blood children as their cause, condemning the irresponsibility and double standards of European men, but so too did colonial officials who argued that these concubinary relations were producing a new underclass of European paupers, of rootless children who could not be counted among the proper European citizenry, whose sartorial trappings merely masked their cultural incompetence, who did not know what it meant to be Dutch or French. The consequences of mixed unions were thus collapsed into a singular moral trajectory, which, without state intervention, would lead to a future generation of Eurasian paupers and prostitutes, an affront to European prestige and a contribution to national decay.

If we look more closely at what was identified as abandonment, the cultural and historical peculiarities of this definition become more apparent. In his comprehensive history of child abandonment in western Europe, John Boswell commonly uses "abandonment" to refer to "the *voluntary* relinquishing of control over children by their natural parents or guardians" and to children who were exposed at the doors of churches or in other public spaces and less frequently for those intentionally exposed to death.[21] Boswell argues that ancient and contemporary commentators have conflated abandonment with infanticide far more than the evidence suggests. Nevertheless, perceptions and policies on abandonment were integrally tied to issues of child mortality. Jacques Donzelot argues that in nineteenth-century France abandonment often led to high rates of child mortality and that the intensified policing of families was morally justified for those reasons among others.[22] This does not suggest that abandonment always led to death nor that this was always its intent. The point is that in the colonial context, in contrast, discussions of abandonment rarely raise a similar concern for infanticide or even obliquely address this eventuality.

The abandonment of métis children invoked, in the colonial context, not a biological but a social death – a severing from European society, a banishment of "innocents" from the European cultural milieu in which they could potentially thrive and where some reformers contended they rightfully belonged.[23] Those officials who wrote about métis children argued that exposure in the colonial context was to the native milieu, not the natural elements, and to the immoral influence of native women whose debased characters inclined them to succumb to such illicit unions in the first place. Moreover, abandonment, as we shall see, was not necessarily voluntary, nor did both parents, despite the implication in Boswell's definition, participate in it. The statutes of the Society for the Protection and Education of Young French Métis of Cochinchine and Cambodia defined the issue of abandonment in the following way:

> Left to themselves, having no other guide than their instincts and their passions, these unfortunates will always give free rein to their bad inclinations; the boys will increase the ranks of vagabonds, the girls those of prostitution.
>
> Left to their mothers and lost in the milieu of Annamites, they will not become less depraved. It must not be forgotten that in most cases, the indigenous woman who consents to live with a European is a veritable prostitute and that she will never reform. When, after several years of free union with Frenchmen, the latter disappear or abandon her, she fatally returns to the vice from which she came and she nearly always sets an example of debauchery, sloth, and immorality for her children. She takes care of them with the sole purpose of later profiting from their labor and especially from their vices.
>
> For her métis son, she seeks out a scholarship in a school with the certainty that when her child obtains a minor administrative post, she will profit from it. But, in many cases, the child, ill-advised and ill-directed, does not work and when he leaves school, abandons himself to idleness and then to vagabondage; he procures his means of existence by extortion and theft.
>
> Abandoned métisse girls are no better off; from the cradle, their mothers adorn them with bracelets and necklaces and maintain in them a love of luxury innate in the Annamites. Arriving at the age of puberty, deprived of any skills which would help them survive, and pushed into a life by their mothers that they have a natural tendency to imitate, they will take to prostitution in its diverse forms to procure the means necessary to keep themselves in luxury.[24]

Here, abandonment has specific race, cultural, and gender coordinates. Most frequently, it referred to the abandonment of métis children by European fathers and their abandonment of the children's native mothers with whom these men lived outside of marriage. The gaze of the colonial state was not directed at children abandoned by native men but only at the progeny of mixed unions. Most significantly, the child, considered abandoned whether he or she remained in the care of the mother, was most frequently classified that way precisely because the child was left to a native mother and to the cultural surroundings in which she lived. But the term abandonment was also used freely in another context to condemn those socially déclassé European men who chose to reside with their mixed-blood children in the supposedly immoral and degraded native milieu. In designating cultural rather than physical neglect, abandonment connoted at least two things: that a proper French father would never allow his offspring prolonged contact nor identification with such a milieu and that the native mother of lower class origins would only choose to keep her own children for mercenary purposes.

If abandonment of métis offspring by European men was considered morally reprehensible, the depraved motives of colonized women who refused to give up their children to the superior environment of state institutions were considered worse. Thus the president of The Hanoi Society for the Protection of Métis Youths in 1904 noted that "numerous mothers refuse to confer their children to us . . . under the *pretext* of not wanting to be apart from them, despite the fact that they may periodically visit them at school." [25] But if maternal love obscured more mercenary quests to exploit their young for profits and pleasure, as was often claimed, why did so many women not only refuse to hand over their children but reject any form of financial assistance for them? Cases of such refusal were not uncommon. In 1903 the Haiphong court admonished a métisse mother who was herself "raised with all the exterior signs of a European education" for withdrawing her daughter from a government school "for motives which could not be but base given the mother's character." [26] Resistance also came from the children themselves: in 1904, the seventeen-year-old métisse daughter of an Annamite woman cohabited with the French employer of her mother's Annamite lover, declaring that she *volontairement* accepted and preferred her own situation over what the Society for the Protection of Métis Youths could offer. [27] Numerous reports are cited of métisse girls forced into prostitution by *concubin*, that is, by native men who were the subsequent lovers of the girls' native mothers. These cases expressed another sexual and cultural transgression that metropolitan social reformers and colonial authorities both feared: namely, a "traffic in *filles françaises*" for the Chinese and Annamite market, not for Europeans. [28]

The portrait of abandonment and charitable rescue is seriously flawed, for it misses the fact that the channeling of abandoned métis children into special state institutions was part of a larger (but failed) imperial vision. These children were to be molded into very special colonial citizens; in one scenario, they were to be the bulwark of a future white settler population, acclimatized to the tropics but loyal to the state. [29] As proposed by the French Feminist caucus at the National Colonial Exposition of 1931, métisse young women could:

> marry with Frenchmen, would accept living in the bush where young women from the metropole would be hesitant to follow their husbands, . . . [and would form] the foundation of a bourgeoisie, attached at one and the same time to their native land and to the France of Europe. [30]

This perspective on mixed marriages was more optimistic than some, but echoes the commonly held view that if métisse girls were rescued in time, they could be effectively educated to become *bonnes menagères* (good housekeepers) of a settled Indochina, wives or domestics in the service of France. Similar proposals, as we shall see, were entertained in the Indies in the same period and there too met with little success. However, in both contexts, the vision of fortifying the colonial project with a mixed-blood yeomanry was informed by a fundamental concern: What could be done with this mixed population, whose ambiguous positioning and identifications could make them either dangerous adversaries or effective partisans of the colonial state?

Fraudulent recognitions and other dangers of métissage

The question of what to do with the métis population prompted a number of different responses, but each hinged on whether métis should be classified as a distinct legal category subject to special education or so thoroughly assimilated into French culture that they would pose no threat. In French Indochina, the model treatment of métis in the Netherlands Indies was invoked at every turn. In 1901, Joseph Chailley-Bert, director of the *Union Colonial Française,* was sent on a government mission to Java to report on the status of métis in the Indies and on the efficacy of Dutch policy towards them. Chailley-Bert came away from Batavia immensely impressed and convinced that segregation was not the answer. He was overwhelmed by the sheer numbers of persons of mixed descent who occupied high station in the Indies, with wealth and cultivation rivaling those of many "full-blooded" Europeans. He argued that the Dutch policy not to segregate those of mixed descent nor distinguish between illegitimate and legitimate children was the only humane and politically safe course to pursue. He urged the government to adopt several Dutch practices: that abandoned métis youth be assigned European status until proof of filiation was made, that private organizations in each legal grouping (i.e., European and native) be charged with poor relief rather than the government; and that European standing not be confined to those with the proper "dosage of blood" alone. In the Indies he noted that such a ruling would be impossible because the entire society was in large part métis and such a distinction would allow a distance between the aryan without mix and the asiatic hybrids."[31]

Monsieur A. July, writing from Hanoi in 1905, similarly applauded "the remarkably successful results" of the Indies government policy rejecting the legal designation of métis as a caste apart. He argued that France's abolition of slavery and call for universal suffrage had made a tabula rasa of racial prejudice; however, he was less sanguine that France's political system could permit a similar scale of naturalization as that practiced by the Dutch, since not all young métis could be recognized as *citoyen français* for reasons he thought better not to discuss. Firmin Jacques Montagne, a head conductor in the Department of Roads and Bridges also urged that French Indochina follow the Indies path, where the Dutch had not only "safeguarded their prestige, but also profited from a force that if badly directed, could turn against Dutch domination."[32] Based on the account of a friend who administered a plantation on Java he urged that métis boys in Indochina, as in the Indies, should be educated in special institutions to prepare them to be soldiers and later for modest employment in commerce or on the estates.

These appeals to Dutch wisdom are so curious because they reflected neither the treatment of the poor Indo-European population in the Indies, nor what administrative quandaries were actually facing Dutch officials there. In the very year of Chailley-Bert's visit to Batavia, the Indies government began a massive investigation of the recent proliferation of European pauperism and its causes. Between 1901 and 1903 several thousands of pages of government reports outlined the precarious economic conditions and political dangers of a population legally classified as European but riddled with impoverished widows, beggars, vagrants, and abandoned children who were mostly Indo-Europeans.[33] The pauperism commission identified an "alarming increase" of poor Europeans born in the Indies or of mixed parentage, who could neither compete for civil service positions with the influx of "full-blooded" Dutch educated in Europe nor with the growing number of better-educated Indonesians now qualified for the same jobs.[34]

The Dutch did investigate Indo-European adult life and labor, but the focus of the commissions' concern was on children and their upbringing in the parental home (*opvoeding in de ouderlijkewoning*).[35] Among the more than 70,000 legally classified Europeans in the Indies in 1900, nearly 70 percent knew little Dutch or none at all. Perhaps the more disturbing finding was that many of them were living on the borderlands of respectable bourgeois European society in styles that indicated not a failed version of European culture but an outright rejection of it.[36]

The causes of the situation were found in the continued prevalence of concubinage, not only among subaltern European military barred from legal marriage but also among civil servants and European estate supervisors for whom marriage to European women was either formally prohibited or made an economically untenable option. Although government and private company policies significantly relaxed the restrictions imposed on the entry of women from Europe after the turn of the century, non-conjugal mixed unions, along with the gendered and racist assumptions on which they were based, were not about to disappear by government fiat. In Indochina, French officials had to issue repeated warnings against concubinage from 1893 to 1911 (just when the societies for protection of métis youth were most active), suggesting the formation of another generation that threatened not to know where they belonged.[37] The pauperism commission condemned the general moral environment of the Indies, targeting concubinage as the source of a transient "rough and dangerous pauper element" that lived off the native population when they could, disgracing European prestige and creating a financial burden for the state.[38]

But Indo-European pauperism in the Indies could not be accounted for by concubinage alone. The pauperism commission's enquiry revealed a highly stratified educational system in which European youths educated in the Indies were categorically barred from high-level administrative posts and in which middling Indo-Europeans were offered only a rudimentary training in Dutch, a basic requisite for any white collar job.[39] European public (free) schools in the Indies, like those in Indochina, were largely schools for the poor (*armenscholen*) attended by and really only designed for a lower-class of indigent and mixed-blood Europeans.[40]

A concrete set of reforms did form a response, to some extent, to concubinage and educational inequities, but European pauperism was located in a more unsettling problem: It was seen to have deeper and more tenacious roots in the surreptitious penetration of inlanders into the legal category of European.[41] Because the European legal standing exempted men both from labor service and from the harsher penal code applied to those of native status, officials argued that an underclass of European soldiers and civilians was allegedly engaged in a profitable racket of falsely recognizing native children who were not their own for an attractive fee. Thus, the state commission argued, European impoverishment was far more limited than the statistics indicated: The European civil registers were inflated by lowlife mercenaries and, as in Indochina, by *des sans-travail* (the unemployed), who might register as many as thirty to forty children who did not have proper rights to Dutch or French citizenship at all.[42]

The issue of fraudulent recognition, like concubinage, hinged on the fear that children were being raised in cultural fashions that blurred the distinctions between ruler and ruled and on the fear that uneducated native young men were acquiring access to Dutch and French nationality by channels, such as false filiation, that circumvented state control. Such practices were allegedly contingent on a nefarious class of European men who were willing to facilitate the efforts of native mothers who sought such arrangements. Whether there were as many fraudulent recognitions of métis children in Indochina, or *kunstmatig gefabriceerde Europeanen* (artificially fabricated Europeans) in the Indies as authorities claimed is really not the point. The repeated reference to fictitious, fraudulent, and fabricated Europeans expressed an underlying preoccupation of colonial authorities, shared by many in the European community at large, that illicit incursions into the Dutch and French citizenry extended beyond those cases labelled fraudulent recognition by name. We should remember that Nguyen van Thinh dit Lucien's condemnation was never explicitly argued on the basis of his suspect parentage, but on the more general contention that his behavior had to be understood as that of an *indigene* in disguise, not as a citizen of France. Annamite women who had lived in concubinage were accused of clothing their métisse daughters in European attire, while ensuring them that their souls and sentiments remained deeply native.[43]

Colonial officials wrestled with the belief that the Europeanness of métis children could never be assured, despite a rhetoric affirming that education and upbringing were transformative processes. Authorities spoke of abandoned métisse daughters as *les filles françaises* when arguing for their redemption, but when supporting segregated education, these same authorities recast these youths as physically marked and morally marred with "the faults and mediocre qualities of their [native] mothers" as "the fruits of a regrettable weakness."[44] Thus, abandoned métis children not only represented the sexual excesses and indiscretions of European men but the dangers of a subaltern class, degenerate *(verwilderen)* and lacking paternal discipline *(gemis aan vaderlijke tucht),* a world in which mothers took charge.[45] To what extent the concern over neglected métis children was not only about the negative influence of the native milieu but about the threat of single-mother families as in Europe and America in the same period is difficult to discern.[46] The absence of patriarchal authority in households of widows and native women who had exited from concubinary domestic arrangements was clearly seen as a threat to the proper moral upbringing of children and sanctioned the intervention of the state. Métis children undermined the inherent principles upon which national identity thrived – those *liens invisibles* (invisible bonds) that all men shared and that so clearly and comfortably marked off *pur-sang* French and Dutch from those of the generic colonized.

The option of making métis a legal category was actively debated in international colonial fora through the 1930s but was rejected on explicitly political grounds. French jurists persuasively argued that such a legal segregation would infest the colonies with a destructive virus, with a "class of *déraciné, déclassé*," "our most dangerous enemies," "insurgents, irreconcilable enemies of our domination."[47] The legal rejection of difference in no way diminished the concern about them. On the contrary, it produced an intensified discourse in which racial thinking remained the bedrock on which cultural markers of difference were honed and more carefully defined.

This was nowhere clearer than in the legal discussion about whether and by what criteria children of unknown parents should be assigned French or native nationality.[48] Under a 1928 *décret,* all persons born in Indochina (that is, on French soil) of unknown parents of which one was presumed to be French could obtain recognition *of "la qualité de français."*[49] Presumed Frenchness rested on two sorts of certainty: the evaluation of the child's "physical features or race" by a "medico-legal expert" and a "moral certainty" derived from the fact that the child "has a French name, lived in a European milieu and was considered by all as being of French descent."[50] Thus, French citizenship was not open to all métis but restricted by a "scientific" and moral judgment that the child was decidedly non-indigene.[51] As we have seen in the case of Nguyen van Thinh dit Lucien, however, the name Lucien, the acknowledged paternity by Icard, and the patriotic ambience of the household were only sufficient for the child to be legally classified as French, not for him to be treated as French by a court of law. Inclusionary laws left ample room for an implementation based on exclusionary principles and practices.

The moral outrage and crusade against abandonment attended to another underlying dilemma for those who ruled. Métis youth not only had to be protected from the "demoralisation of the special milieu" in which they were raised but, as important, educated in a way that would not produce unreasonable expectations nor encourage them to harbor desires for privilege above their station simply because French or Dutch blood flowed in their veins. The aim of the Hanoi society for the protection of métis youth was "to inculcate them with our sense of honor and integrity, while only suggesting to them modest tastes and humble aspirations."[52] Similarly, in the Indies, Indo-European pauperism was commonly attributed to the "false sense of pride" of Indos who refused to do manual labor or take on menial jobs, who did not know that "real Dutchmen" in the Netherlands worked with their hands. The assault was double-edged. It blamed those impoverished for their condition but also suggested more subtly that if they were really Dutch in spirit and drive, such problems of pauperism would not have arisen. [. . .]

Jus sol, jus sanguinis, and nationality

> In the civilized world, no one may be without a relationship to the
> state.[53]

J. A. Nederburgh, one of the principal architects of Indies colonial law in 1898,
engaged the question of national identity and membership more directly than many
of his contemporaries. He argued that in destroying racial purity, colonialism had
made obsolete the criteria of *jus soli* (place of birth) and *jus sanguinis* (blood descent)
for determining nationality. Colonial *vermenging* (mixing or blending), he contended,
had produced a new category of "wavering classes," large groups of people whose
place of birth and mixed genealogies called into question the earlier criteria by
which rights to metropolitan citizenship and designations of colonial subject had
once been assigned. Taking the nation to be those who shared "morals, culture,
and perceptions, feelings that unite us without one being able to say what they
are," Nederburgh concluded that one could not differentiate who had these
sensibilities by knowing birthplace and kinship alone. He pointed to those of "pure
European blood" who

> for years remained almost entirely in native surroundings [*omgeving*] and
> became so entirely nativized [*verlandschen*] that they no longer felt at
> ease among their own kind [*rasgenooten*] and found it difficult to defend
> themselves against *Indische* morals and points of view.[54]

He concluded that surroundings had an "overwhelming influence," with "the power
to almost entirely neutralise the effects of descent and blood."[55] Although
Nederburgh's claim may seem to suggest a firm dismissal of racial supremacy, we
should note that he was among the most staunchly conservative legalists of his time,
a firm defender of the superiority of Western logic and law.[56] By Nederburgh's cultural
account, Europeans, especially children "who because of their age are most susceptible
and often the most exposed" to native influence in school and native servants at home,
who remained too long in the Indies "could only remain *echte-Europeesch* (truly
European) in thought and deed with much exertion."[57] While Nederburgh insisted
that he was not "against *Indische* influence per se," he recommended that the state
allocate funds to bring up European children in Holland.[58] Some eight years later,
at the height of the Ethical Policy, another prominent member of the colonial elite
made a similar but more radical recommendation to close all schools of higher
education in Batavia and to replace them with state-subsidized education in Holland
to improve the quality of the colored *(kleuringen)* in the civil servant ranks.[59] Both
proposals derived from the same assumption: that it was "impossible for persons
raised and educated in the Indies to be bearers [*dragers*] of Western culture and
civilization."[60]

Attention to upbringing, surroundings, and milieu did not disengage personal
potential from the physiological fixities of race. Distinctions made on the basis of
opvoeding (upbringing) merely recoded race in the quotidian circumstances that
enabled acquisition of certain cultural competencies and not others. The focus on
milieu naturalized cultural difference, sexual essence, and moral fiber of Europeanness

in new kinds of ways. I have discussed elsewhere how the shift in the colonies to white endogamy and away from concubinage at the turn of the century, an intensified surveillance of native servants, and a sharper delineation of the social space in which European children could be brought up and where and with whom they might play marked out not only the cultural borders of the European community but indicated how much political security was seen to reside in the choices of residence, language, and cultural style that individuals made. Personal prescriptions for inclusion as citizens of the Dutch state were as stringent and intimate as those that defined the exclusion of its subjects.[61] The wide gap between prescription and practice suggests why the prescriptions were so insistently reiterated, updated, and reapplied. Among those classified as European, there was little agreement on these prescriptions, which were contested, if not openly defied.

In 1884, legal access to European equivalent status in the Indies required a "complete suitability [geschiktheid] for European society," defined as a belief in Christianity, fluency in spoken and written Dutch, and training in European morals and ideas.[62] In the absence of an upbringing in Europe, district authorities were charged with evaluating whether the concerned party was "brought up in European surroundings as a European."[63] But European equivalence was not granted simply on the display of a competence and comfort in European norms. It required that the candidate "no longer feel at home" (niet meer thuis voelt) in native society and has already "distanced" himself from his native being (Inlander-zijn). In short the candidate could neither identify nor retain inappropriate senses of belonging or longings for the milieu from which she or he came.[64] The mental states of potential citizens were at issue, not their material assets alone. Who were to be the arbitrators? Suitability to which European society and to which Europeans? The questions are disingenuous because the coding is clear: cultural competence, family form, and a middle-class morality became the salient new criteria for marking subjects, nationals, citizens, and different kinds of citizens in the nation-state. As European legal status and its equivalent became accessible to an ever broader population, the cultural criteria of privilege were more carefully defined. European women who subscribed to the social prescription of white endogamy were made the custodians of a new morality – not, as we shall see, those "fictive" European women who rejected those norms.

Colonial practice contradicted the moral designations for European national and racial identity in blatant ways: which European morality was to be iconized? That embraced by those European men who cohabited with native women, became nativized, and supported their offspring? Or the morality of European men who retained their cultural trappings as they lived with native women who bore métis children, then departed for Europe unencumbered when their contracts were done? Or was it the morality of colonial officials who barred the filing of paternity suits against European men by native women or the morality of those who argued for it on the grounds that it would hinder fraudulent acknowledgments and easy recognitions by lower-class European men? What can we make of the ruling on European equivalence for non-native residents that stipulated that candidates must be from regions or states that subscribed to a monogamous family law?[65] How did this speak to the thousands of Indisch Dutch men for whom concubinage was the most frequently chosen option? And finally, if national identity was, as often stated, "an indescribable set of invisible bonds," what did it mean when a European woman upon marriage to a native man was legally reclassified to follow his nationality? As we shall see, these invisible bonds, in which women only had a conjugal share by proxy to their husbands, were those enjoyed by some but not all men. The paradox is that native women married to European men were charged with the upbringing of children, with the formative making of Dutch citizens, and with culturally encoding the markers of race. Colonial cultures created problematic contexts in which patriarchal principles and criteria for citizenship seemed to be at fundamental odds. At a time when European feminists were turning to motherhood as a claim to citizenship, this notion of "mothers of citizens" meant something different in colonial politics, where definitions of proper motherhood served to clarify the blurred boundaries of nation and race.[66]

The mixed-marriage law of 1898

The mixed-marriage law of 1898 and the legal arguments which surrounded it are of special interest on several counts. Nowhere in the Dutch colonial record is the relationship between gender prescription, class membership, and racial category so contentiously debated and so clearly defined; nowhere is the danger of certain kinds of mixing so directly linked to national image while references to race are denied.[67] This is a liberal discourse ostensibly about the protection of native (men's) rights and later viewed as the paragon of ethical intent to equalize and synchronize colonial and metropolitan law. But, as Willem Wertheim noted nearly forty years ago, it did far more to buttress racial distinctions than to break them down.[68]

Legal attention to mixed marriages was not new in the Indies but had never been formalized as it was to be now.[69] Mixed marriages had been regulated by government decree and church decretals soon after the East Indies Company established a settlement in Batavia in the early seventeenth century. The decree of 1617 forbidding marriages between Christian and non-Christian remained intact for over 200 years. With the new Civil Code of 1848, the religious criteria were replaced with the ruling that marriage partners of European and native standing would both be subject to European law.

The legislation on mixed marriages prior to 1898 was designed to address one kind of union but not others. The 1848 ruling allowed European men already living in concubinage with non-Christian native women to legalize those unions and the children borne from them. Although the civil law of 1848 was derived from the Napoleonic civil code, a dominant principle of it had been curiously ignored: that upon marriage a woman's legal status was made that of her husband. As Dutch jurists were to argue a half-century later because mixed marriages had then been overwhelmingly between European men and native women, the latter's legal incorporation could be easily assumed. This, however, was no longer the case in the 1880s when Indies colonial officials noted two troubling phenomena: First, more women classified as European were choosing to marry non-European men; and second, concubinage continued to remain the domestic arrangement of choice over legal marriage.[70] Legal specialists argued that concubinage was a primary cause of Indo-European impoverishment and had to be discouraged. However, the mixed-marriage rulings as they stood, were so complicated and costly that people continued to choose cohabitation over legal marriage. Perhaps more disturbing still, some European, Indo-European, and native women opted to retain their own legal standing (thereby protecting their own material assets and those they could bestow on their children), thus rejecting marriage altogether.[71]

Colonial lawyers were thus faced with a conundrum: How could they implement a ruling that would facilitate certain kinds of mixed marriages (over concubinage) and condemn others. Two basic premises were accepted on all sides: that the family was the bulwark of state authority and that the unity of the family could only be assured by its unity in law.[72] Thus, legitimate children could not be subject to one law and their father to another, nor could women hold native status while their husbands retained that of a European.[73] Given this agreement there were two possible solutions: either the "superior European standing" of either spouse would determine the legal status (and nationality) of the other; or, alternatively, the patriarchal principle – that is, a woman follows the legal status of her husband (regardless of his origin) – would be applied. Principles of cultural and male supremacy seem to be opposed. Let us look at why they were not.

Those who argued that a European woman should retain her European standing in a mixed marriage did so on the grounds, among others, that European prestige would be seriously compromised. The liberal lawyer, J. H. Abendanon, cogently argued that European women would be placed in a "highly unfavorable and insecure position"; by being subject to adat, she risked becoming no more than a concubine if her native husband took a second wife, as polygamy under Islamic law was not justification for divorce. Others pointed out that she would be subject to the penal code applied to those of native status. Should she commit a crime, she would be treated to "humiliating physical and psychological punishment," for which her "physical constitution" was unsuited. Her relegation to native status would thus cause an "outrageous scandal" in the European community at large.[74]

The argument above rested on one central but contested assumption: that all women classified as European deserved the protection and privilege of European law. However, those who made the countercase that the patriarchal principle be applied regardless of origin, argued that the quality of women with European standing was not the same. Although the state commission noted that mixed marriages between European women and native men were relatively few, it underlined their marked and "steady increase among certain classes of the inhabitants".[75] Such mixed marriages, all but unthinkable in 1848 but now on the rise among Indo-European and even full-blooded European women with native men, were attributed to the increasing impoverishment and declining welfare of these women on the one hand and of the "intellectual and social development" among certain classes of native men on the other.[76] The latter issue, however, was rarely addressed because the gender hierarchy of the argument was contingent on assuming that women who made such conjugal choices were neither well-bred nor deserving of European standing.

One lawyer, Taco Henny, argued that the category, European, was a legal fiction not indicative of those who actually participated in the cultural and moral life of the European community and that the majority of women who made such choices were "outwardly and inwardly indistinguishable from natives." Because these women tended to be of lower-class origin or mixed racial descent, he held that they were already native in culture and inclination and needed no protection from that cultural milieu in which they rightly belonged. Similarly, their subjection to the native penal code was no reason for scandal because it was appropriate to their actual station. They were already so far removed from Dutch society proper that it would cause no alarm.

If Taco Henny's argument was not convincing enough, Pastor van Santen made the case in even bolder terms:

> The European woman who wants to enter into such a marriage has already sunk so deep socially and morally that it does not result in ruin, either in her own eyes or those of society. It merely serves to consolidate her situation.[77]

Such arguments rested on an interior distinction between echte Dutch women and those in whom "very little European blood actually flowed in their veins" within the category of those classified as European. Pastor van Santen's claim that this latter group had already fallen from cultural and racial grace had its "proof" in yet another observation: "that if she was still European in thought and feeling, she would never take a step that was so clearly humiliating and debasing in the eyes of actual (werkelijk) European women."[78] This reasoning (which won in the end) marshaled the patriarchal tenets of the civil code to exclude women of a certain class and cultural milieu from Dutch citizenship rights without directly invoking race in the legal argument.

But this gendered principle did more work still and could be justified on wider grounds. First, such legislation defined a "true" European woman in accepted cultural terms: first, by her spousal choice, and, second, by her maternal sentiments. She was to demonstrate that she put her children's interests first by guarding their European standing, which would be lost to her future progeny if she married a non-European under the new law. As such, it strongly dissuaded "true" European women from choosing to marry native men. This was its implicit and, according to some advocates, its explicit intent. In addition, it spoke on the behalf of well-to-do native men, arguing that they would otherwise lose their access to agricultural land and other privileges passed from fathers to sons under adat law.[79] Finally, the new legislation claimed to discourage concubinage, as native men could thus retain their customary rights and would not be tempted to live with Indo-European and "full-blooded" European women outside of marriage. But perhaps most important, this appeal to patriarchy prevented the infiltration of increasing numbers of native men into the Dutch citizenry, particularly those of the middling classes, who were considered to have little to lose and much to gain by acquiring a Dutch nationality. Those who supported "uplifting" native men to European status through marriage would in effect encourage marriages of convenience at the expense of both European women who were drawn to such unions and those who prided themselves on the cultural distinctions that defined them as European."[80] Here again, as in the fraudulent recognitions of métis children, at issue was the undesirability of an increase in "the number of persons who would only be European in name."[81]

In the end, the mixed-marriage ruling and the debates surrounding it were more an index than a cause of profound changes in thinking about sexual practice, national identity, and colonial morality. Mixed marriages increased between native women and European men between 1900 and 1920. This was evident in the declining number of acknowledgments of children born out of wedlock and in an increased number of single European men who now married their *huishoudster* (housekeeper or sexual companion or both).[82] Condemnation of concubinage came simultaneously from several sources. The Pauperism Commission had provided new evidence that concubinage was producing an underclass of Indos that had to be curbed. By treating prostitution and the huishoudster system in the colonies as similar phenomena, the *Nederlandschen Vrouwenbond* (Dutch Women's Association) conflated the distinct options such arrangements afforded women and rallied against both.[83] The *Sarekat Islam*, one of the strongest native nationalist organizations, also campaigned against concubinage on religious grounds that may have discouraged some native women from such unions.[84] Still, in 1920 half the métis children of a European father and native mother were born outside of marriage. After 1925 the number of mixed marriages fell off again as the number of Dutch-born women coming to the Indies increased fourfold.

Hailed as exemplary liberal legislation, the mixed-marriage ruling was applied selectively on the basis of class, gender, and race. By reinvoking the Napoleonic civil code, European men were assured that their "invisible bonds" of nationality remained intact regardless of their legal partner. European women, on the other hand, were summarily (but temporarily) disenfranchised from their national community on the basis of conjugal choice alone.[85] Those mixed marriages which derived from earlier cohabitations between European men and native women were not the unions most in question, and jurists of different persuasions stated as much throughout the debate. These marriages were considered unproblematic on the assumption that a native woman would be grateful for, and proud of, her elevated European status and content with legal dependence on a European man. Were native women easily granted European legal standing and Dutch citizenship because there was no danger that they could or would fully exercise their rights? The point is never discussed because racial and gender privileges were in line.

But what about the next generation of métis? Although the new ruling effectively blocked the naturalization of native adult men through marriage, it granted a new generation of métis children a European standing by affixing their nationality to their father's. Would this generation be so assuredly cut from their mother's roots as well? The persistent vigilance with which concern for omgeving, upbringing, class, and education were discussed in the 1920s and 1930s suggests that there were resounding doubts. The Netherlands Indies Eugenics Society designed studies to test whether children of Europeans born in the Indies might display different "racial markers" than their parents.[86] Eugenicist logic consolidated discussions about national identity and cultural difference in a discourse of "fitness" that specified the interior frontiers of the nation, reaffirming yet again that upbringing and parenting were critical in deciding who would be marked as a fictive compatriot or true citizen.

Although the race criterion was finally removed from the Indies constitution in 1918 under native nationalist pressure, debates over the psychological, physical, and moral make-up of Indo-Europeans intensified in the 1920s and 1930s more than they had before. A 1936 doctoral dissertation at the University of Amsterdam could still "explain the lack of energy" of Indo-Europeans by the influence of a sapping and warm, dank climate; by the bad influence of the "energy-less Javanese race" on Indo-Europeans; and by the fact that "halfbloods" were not descended from the "average European" and the "average Javanese."[87] In the 1920s, the European-born Dutch population was visibly closing its ranks, creating new cultural boundaries while shoring up its old ones. Racial hate *(rassenhaat)* and representation were watchwords of the times. A renewed disdain for Indos permeated a discourse that heightened in the Depression as the nationalist movement grew stronger and as unemployed "full-blooded" Europeans found "roaming around" in native villages blurred with the ranks of the Indo poor. How the colonial state distinguished these two groups from one another and from "natives" on issues of unemployment insurance and poor relief underscored how crucial these interior frontiers were to the strategies of the emerging welfare state.[88]

Indo-Europeans and the quest for a fatherland

The slippage between race and culture, as well the intensified discussions of racial membership and national identity, were not invoked by the echte-Europeesche population alone. We have seen that the moral geography of the colonies had a metonymic quality: Despite the huge numbers of Europeans of mixed parentage and substantial economic means, the term Indo was usually reserved for that segment who were *verindische* (indianized) and poor. Less clear are the cultural, political, and racial criteria by which those of mixed descent identified themselves. The contradictory and changing criteria used by the various segments of the Indo-European movement at the turn of the century highlight how contentious and politically contingent these deliberations were.

It is not accidental that the term Indo-European is difficult to define. In the Indies it applied to those of *mengbloeden* (mixed blood) of European and native origin, to Europeans born in the Indies of Dutch nationality and not of native origin, and to those pur-sang Europeans born elsewhere who referred to the Indies as a "second fatherland."[89] The semantics of mixing thus related to blood, place, and belonging to different degrees and at different times. *Soeria Soemirat,* one of the earliest publications of the Indo-European constituency in the late 1890s, included among its members all Indies-born Europeans and took as its central goal the uplifting of the (Indo)-European poor. The *Indisch Bond* formed in 1898, was led by an Indies-born European constituency that spoke for the Indo poor but whose numbers were rarely represented in their ranks. At the heart of both organizations was the push for an *Indisch vaderland,* contesting both the popular terms of Indonesian nationalism and the exclusionary practices of the Dutch-born *(totok)* society.[90]

The Indo-European movement never developed as a nationalist movement. As "socially thin" as Benedict Anderson suggests its creole counterpart was in the Americas, it could neither enlist a popular constituency nor dissociate from its strong identification with the European-born Dutch elite. The Indisch movement often made its bids for political and economic power by invoking Eurasian racial superiority to inlanders while concurrently denying racial criteria for judging their status vis-à-vis European-born Dutch. The subsequent effort in 1912 to form an *Indische Partij* with the motto "Indies for the Indiers") was stridently antigovernment, with a platform that addressed native as well as poor Indo welfare. Despite an inclusionary rhetoric, its native and poor Indo constituency were categorically marginalized and could find no common political ground.[91] By 1919, when native nationalist mobilization was gaining strength, the need for a specifically *Indo-Bond* took on new urgency and meaning. As its founder argued, it would be a "*class-verbond* (class-based association) to support the interests of the larger Indo-group."[92] This organization, eventually called the Indo-Europeesch Verbond (IEV), with more than 10,000 members in 1924, continued to plead the cause of the Indo poor while remaining unequivocally loyal to the Dutch colonial state. This truncated version of a much more complicated story, nevertheless, illustrates the unsettling point that the poor Indo constituency never achieved a political voice. However large their numbers, they were silently rejected from the early Indonesian nationalist movement and could only make their demands based on claims to a cultural and racial alliance with those Dutch who ruled.[93] [. . .]

Rootlessness and cultural racism

With rootedness at the center stage of nationalist discourse, the notion of rootlessness captured a range of dangers about métissage.[94] Abandoned métis youths were generically viewed as vagrants in Indochina, as child delinquents in the Indies, as de facto stateless subversives without a patrie.[95] In times of economic crisis "free-roaming European bastards" were rounded up for charity and goodwill in efforts to avert a racial disgrace. Liberal colonial projects spent decades creating a barrage of institutions to incorporate, inculcate, and insulate abandoned métis youths. But the image of rootlessness was not only applied to those who were abandoned.

In 1938, government officials in Hanoi conducted a colony-wide enquiry to monitor the physical and political movements of métis. The Resident of Tonkin recommended a comprehensive state-sponsored social rehabilitation program to give métis youths the means to function as real *citoyens* on the argument that with "French blood prevailing in their veins," they already "manifested an instinctive attachment to France."[96] But many French in Indochina must have been more equivocal about their instinctive patriotic attachments. The fear that métis might revert to their natural inclinations persisted, as did a continuing discourse on their susceptibility to the native milieu, where they might relapse to the immoral and subversive states of their mothers.

Fears of métissage were not confined to colonial locales. We need only read the 1942 treatise, *Les Métis*, of René Martial who combined his appointment on the faculty of medicine in Paris with eugenic research on the *anthro-biologie des races*. For him, métis were categorically persons of physical and mental deformity. He saw métis descent as a frequent cause both of birth defects in individuals and of the contaminated body politic of France. As he put it,

> Instability, the dominant characteristic of métis, . . . is contagious, it
> stands in opposition to the spirit of order and method, it generates
> indeterminable and futile discussion and paralyzes action. It is this state
> of mind that makes democracies fail that live with this chimera of racial
> equality, one of the most dangerous errors of our times, defended with
> piety by pseudo-French who have found in it a convenient means to
> insinuate themselves everywhere.[97]

That Martial's spirit continues to thrive in contemporary France in the rhetoric of
Le Pen is not coincidental. The discourses on métissage in the early twentieth
century and in LePen's rhetoric on immigrant foreigners today are both about
external boundaries and interior frontiers. Both discourses are permeated with
images of purity, contamination, infiltration, and national decay. For both Martial
and LePen, cultural identities refer to human natures and psychological propensities
inimical to the identity of the French nation and a drain on the welfare state.[98]

On cultural hybridity and domestic subversions

These historically disparate discourses are striking in how similarly they encode
métissage as a political danger predicated on the psychological liminality, mental
instability, and economic vulnerability of culturally hybrid minorities.[99] But could
we not re-present these discourses by turning them on their heads, by unpacking
what the weakness of métissage was supposed to entail? Recast, these discourses
may be more about the fear of empowerment, not about marginality at all; about
groups that straddled and disrupted cleanly marked social divides and whose diverse
membership exposed the arbitrary logic by which the categories of control were
made.[100] These discourses are not unlike those about Indische women that, in
disparaging their impoverished and hybrid Dutch and non-European tastes, eclipsed
the more compelling reality that they could "sometimes pass between ethnic
communities, cross lines drawn by color and caste and enter slots for which they
had no birthright, depending on their alliance with men."[101] The final clause is
critical because through these varied sexual contracts citizenship rights were accorded
and métis identities were contested and remade.[102] The management of sexuality,
parenting, and morality were at the heart of the late imperial project. Cohabitation,
prostitution, and legally recognized mixed marriages slotted women, men, and
their progeny differently on the social and moral landscape of colonial society.
These sexual contracts were buttressed by pedagogic, medical, and legal evaluations
that shaped the boundaries of European membership and the interior frontiers of
the colonial state.

Métissage was first a name and then made a thing. It was so heavily politicized
because it threatened both to destabilize national identity and the Manichean
categories of ruler and ruled. The cultural density of class, gender, and national
issues that it invoked converged in a grid of transgressions which tapped into
metropolitan and colonial politics at the same time. The sexual affront that it
represented challenged middle-class family order and racial frontiers, norms of
childrearing and conjugal patriarchy, and made it increasingly difficult to distinguish

between true nationals and their sullied, pseudo-compatriots. The issue of fraudulent recognition could be viewed in a similar light. Poor white men and native women who arranged legal recognition of their own children or those of others, defied the authority of the state by using the legal system to grant Dutch and French citizenship to a younger generation.[103]

The turn of the century represents one major break point in the nature of colonial morality and in national projects. In both the Indies and Indochina, a new humanitarian liberal concern for mass education and representation was coupled with newly recast social prescriptions for maintaining separatist and exclusionary cultural conventions regarding how, where, and with whom European colonials should live. Virtually all of these differentiating practices were worked through a psychologizing and naturalizing impulse that embedded gender inequalities, sexual privilege, class priorities, and racial superiority in a tangled political field. Colonial liberalism in its nationalist cast opened the possibilities of representation for some while it set out moral prescriptions and affixed psychological attributes which partially closed those possibilities down.

But the exclusionary strategies of the colonial state were not meted out to a passive population, nor is it clear that many of those who inhabited the borderlands of European colonial communities sought inclusion within them. At the core of the métis problem were cultural contestations of gender and class that made these "laboratories of modernity" unwieldy sites of engineering.[104] The experiments were reworked by their subjects, not least of all by women who refused to give "up" their children to charitable institutions for European training and by others who chose cohabitation (not concubinage) over marriage. Women and men who lived culturally hybrid lifestyles intercepted nationalist and racist visions. Without romanticizing their impoverishment, we might consider the possibility that their choices expressed a domestic subversion, a rejection of the terms of the civilizing mission. For those who did not adhere to European bourgeois prescripts, cultural hybridity may have affirmed their own new measures of civility.

Notes

1   Uday Mehta outlines some features of this relationship in "Liberal Strategies of Exclusion," *Politics and Society*, 18:(4) (1990), 427–54. He cogently argues for the more radical claim that the theoretical underpinnings of liberalism are exclusionary and cannot be explained as "an episodic compromise with the practical constraints of implementation" (p. 429).

2   Cochinchine's European population only increased from 594 in 1864 to 3,000 by 1900 (Charles Meyer, *De Français en Indochine, 1860–1910*. 70 (Paris: Hachette, 1985]). By 1914 only 149 planters qualified as electors in the Chamber of Agriculture of Tonkin and Annam; on Java alone there were several thousand (John Laffey. "Racism in Tonkin before 1914," *French Colonial Studies*, no. 1 [1977], 65–81). In 1900 approximately 91,000 persons were classified as European in the Indies. As late as 1931 there were just under 10,500 French civilians in Indochina, when the Indies census counted 244,000 Europeans for the same year (see A. van Marle, "De groep der Europeanen in Nederlands-Indie, iets over ontstaan en groei," *Indonesie*, 5:5 (1952), 490; and Gilles de Gante, *La population*

française au Tonkin entre 1931 et 1938, 23 [Mémoire de Maitrise, Université de Provence], 1981.

3   See Jean Taylor's subtle gendered analysis of the mestizo features of colonial culture in the Netherlands Indies *(The Social World of Batavia* [Madison: University of Winconsin Press, 1983]). The term *Indisch* is difficult to translate. According to Taylor, it is a cultural marker of a person who "partook of Mestizo culture in marriage, practice, habit and loyalty" (p. xx). It is most often used in contrast to the life style and values of the Dutch *totok* population comprised of Hollanders born and bred in Europe who refused such cultural accommodations and retained a distinct distance from inlander (native) customs and social practice. Thus, for example, the European *blivjers* (those who stayed in the Indies) were commonly referred to as Indisch as opposed to *vertrekkers* (those Europeans who treated their residence in the Indies as a temporary assignment away from their native metropolitan homes).

4   See Martin Lewis, "One Hundred Million Frenchmen: The 'Assimilation' Theory in French Colonial Policy," *Comparative Studies in Society and History.* 3:4 (1961), 129–51. While the social positioning of Eurasians in India is often contrasted to that in the Indies, there are striking similarities in their changing and contradictory legal and social status in the late nineteenth century. See Mark Naidis, "British Attitudes toward the Anglo-Indians," *South Atlantic Quarterly,* LXII:3 (Summer 1963), 407–22; and Noel Gist and Roy Wright, *Marginality and Identity: Anglo-Indians as a Racially-Mixed Minority in India,* especially 7–20 (Leiden, 1973).

5   For an extended discussion of the politics of degeneracy and the eugenics of empire, see my "Carnal Knowledge and Imperial Power: The Politics of Race and Sexual Morality in Colonial Asia" in *Gender at the Crossroads: Feminist Anthropology in the Post-Modern Era,* 51–101, Micaela di Leonardo, ed. (University of California Press, 1991).

6   In the following section I draw on Etienne Balibar's discussion of this concept in "Fichte et la Frontière Intérieure: A Propos des *Discours a la nation allemande,* "*Les Cahiers de Fontenay, 58/59* (June 1990).

7   Fichte quoted in Balibar, "Fichte et la Frontière Intérieure," 4.

8   See my "Carnal Knowledge and Imperial Power" on métissage and contamination. Also see Andre-Pierre Taguieff's *La Force du Préjugé* (1987), in which he discusses "la hantisse due métissage" and argues that the métis problem is not a question of mixed-blood but a question of the indeterminate "social identity" which métissage implies (p. 345).

9   This is not to suggest that the French and Dutch rejection of métis as a legal category owed the same trajectory or occurred in the same way. As I later show, the legal status of métis children with unknown parents was still a subject of French juridical debate in the 1930s in a discourse in which race and upbringing were offered as two alternative criteria for judging whether a métis child should be granted the rights of a *citoyen.* See Jacques Mazet, *La condition juridique des métis dans les possession françaises* (Paris: Domat-Montchresiten, 1932).

10 Paul Rich, *Race and Empire in British Politics* (Cambridge: Cambridge University Press, 1986), argues that the anti-black riots in Liverpool and Cardiff in 1919 represented "the extension of rising colonial nationalism into the heart of the British metropolis itself at a time when nationalist ferment was being expressed in many parts of the empire" (p. 122).

11 The profusion of French juridical tracts in the 1930s debating whether métis should be made a separate legal category (distinct from European and *indigène)* and what were the political effects of doing so were forged in the tense environment in which Vietnamese nationalists were making their opposition most strongly felt. See David Marr's two important studies of the Vietnamese nationalist movements, *Vietnamese Anticolonialism, 1885–1925* (Berkeley: California Press, 1971) and *Vietnamese Tradition on Trial. 1920–1945* (Berkeley: California Press, 1981). It is noteworthy that Marr makes no reference to the métis problem (generally or as it related to citizenship, immigration and education) in either text.

12 This is not to suggest, however, that the battles for legal reform regarding, for example, paternity suits, illegitimate children, and family law waged by jurists, feminists, and religious organizations in the Netherlands and the Indies at the turn of the century were animated by the same political projects or fears; on the contrary, in the colonies, the social menace of illegitimate children, as we shall see, was not only about future criminals and prostitutes but also about mixed-blood criminals and prostitutes, about European paternity, and native mothers – and thus about the moral landscape of race and the protection of European men by the Dutch colonial state. For contrasting discourses on paternity suits in the Indies and Holland, compare Selma Sevenhuijsen's comprehensive study of this political debate *(De Orde van het Vaderschap: Politieke debatten over ongehuwd moederschap, afstamming en huwelijk in Nederland 1870–1900* [Amsterdam: Stichting Beheer IISG. 1987]) to R. Kleyn's "Onderzock nar het vaderschap" *(Het Recht in Nederlandsch-Indie,* 67 [1896], 130–50).

13 See Mary Poovey's *Uneven Developments: The Ideological Work of Gender in Mid-Victorian England* (Chicago: Chicago University Press, 1988).

14 Benedict Anderson, *Imagined Communities,* 136 (London: Verso, 1983).

15 Archives d'Outre-Mer, Protectorat de l'Annam et du Tonkin, no. 1506, 17 December 1898.

16 See Archives d'Outre Mer, December 1898, No. 39127, Report from Monsieur E. Issaud, Procureur-Général to the Résident Superieure in Tonkon at Hanoi.

17 Relations immorales qui ont pu exister entre le détenue et celui qui s'est declaré son père" (Archives d'Outre Mer [hereafter, AOM], Fonds Amiraux, No. 1792, 12 December 1898).

18 AOM, Aix-en-Provence, No. 1792, 12 December 1898. Report of M. Villemont, Procureur in Haiphong, to the Procureur-Général, Head of the Judicial Service in Hanoi.

19 According to the procureur-général, Raoul Abor, these fraudulent acknowledgments were threatening to submerge the French element by a deluge of naturalized natives (see Raoul Abor, *Des Reconnaisances Frauduleuses d'Enfants Naturels en Indochine,* 25 [Hanoi: Imprimerie Tonkinoise, 1917]).

20 George Mosse, *Nationalism and Sexuality* (Madison: University of Wisconsin Press, 1985).

21 John Boswell's *The Kindness of Strangers: The Abandonment of Children in Western Europe from Late Antiquity to the* Renaissance (New York: Pantheon, 1988). According to Boswell, this relinquishment might occur by "leaving them somewhere, selling them, or legally consigning authority to some other person or institution" (p. 24). As we shall see, abandonment in colonial practice did not fit this definition at all.

22   See Jacques Donzelot's *The Policing of* Families, 29.

23   I do not use this term in the sense employed by Orlando Patterson with regard to slavery but to suggest the definitive exile from European society which abandonment implied.

24   AOM, Amiraux 7701, 1899, Statute of the "Société de protection et d'éducation des Jeunes Métis Français de la Cohcinchine et du Cambodge."

25   AOM, No. 164, 11 May 1904 (my emphasis).

26   AOM, 13 November 1903.

27   Letter from the Administrative Resident in Bac-giang to the Résident Superieure in Hanoi.

28   AOM, Letter (No. 151) to the Governor-General in Hanoi from Monsieur Paris, the President of the Société de Protection et d'Education des Jeunes Métis Française abandonnés, 29 February 1904. This concern over the entrapment of European young women in the colonies coincides with the concurrent campaigns against the white slave trade in Europe (see Frank Mort, *Dangerous Sexualities: Medico-Moral Politics in England Since 1830*, 126–7 [London: Routledge and Kegan Paul, 1987]).

29   For such recommendations, see A. Brou, "Le métis franco annamite," *Revue Indochinois* (July 1907), 897–908; Douchet, *Métis et congaies d'Indochine* (Hanoi, 1928); Jacques Mazet, *La conditions juridique des métis* (Paris: Domat-Montchrestien 1932); Philippe Gossard, *Études sur le métissage principalement en A.O.F.* (Paris: Les Presses Modernes, 1934).

30   Etats-Generaux du Feminisme, *Exposition Coloniale Internationale de Paris 1931, rapport général présenté par le Gouverneur Général Olivier*, 139 (Paris: Imprimerie Nationale, 1931).

31   AOM, Amiraux 7701, *Report on Métis in the Dutch East Indies* (1901).

32   "Courte notice sur les métis d'Extreme Orient et en particulier sur ceux de l'Indochine," Firmin Jacques Montagne, AOM, Amiraux 1669 (1903), 1896–1909.

33   The fact that the issue of poor whites loomed large on a diverse number of colonial landscapes at this time, in part, may derive from the fact that white poverty itself was coming to be perceived in metropole and colony in new ways. In Calcutta nearly one-fourth of the Anglo-Indian community in the late nineteenth century was on poor relief (N. Gist and R. Wright, *Marginality and Identity: Anglo-Indians as a Racially Mixed Minority in India,* 16 [Leiden: Brill, 1973]). Colin Bundy argues for South Africa that white poverty was redefined "as a social problem to be tackled by state action rather than as a phenomenon of individual failure to be assuaged by charity" (p. 104). In the Indies, this reassignment of poor relief from civic to state responsibility was hotly contested and never really made.

34   *Rapport der Pauperisme-Commissie* (Batavia: Landsdrukkerij, 1902); *Uitkomsten der Pauperisme-Enquete: Algemeen Verslag* (Batavia: Landsdrukkerij, 1902); *Het Pauperisme onder de Europeanen in Nederlandsch-Indie,* Parts 3, 5 (Batavia: Landsdrukkerij, 1901); *Uitkomsten der Pauperisme-Enquete: Gewestelijke Verslagen* (Batavia: Landsdrukkerij, 1901); *De Staatsarmenzorg voor Europeanen in Nederlandsch-Indie* (Batavia: Landsdrukkerij, 1901).

35   See Petrus Blumberger's *De Indo-Europeesche Beweging in Nederlandsch-Indie*, 26 Harlem: Tjeenk Willink, 1939).

36   See J. M. Coetzee, *White Writing: On the Culture of Letters in South Africa* (New Haven: Yale University Press, 1988), in which he argues that the British railed

against Boer idleness precisely because they refused the possibility that an alternative, native milieu may have been preferred by some European men and have held a real attraction.

37 AOM, Archives Centrales de l'Indochine, nos. 9147, 9273, 7770, 4680.

38 *Encyclopedie van Nederlandsch-Indie* (1919), 367.

39 In 1900, an educational survey carried out in Dutch elementary schools in the Indies among 1,500 students found that only 29 per cent of those with European legal standing knew some Dutch and more than 40 per cent did not know any (Paul van der Veur, "Cultural Aspects of the Eurasian Community in Indonesian Colonial Society," *Indonesia*, no. 6 (1968), 45.

40 See Dr. I. J. Brugmans, *Geschiedenis van het onderwijs in Nederlandsch-Indie* (Batavia: Walters, 1938).

41 See J. F. Kohlbrugge, "Prostitutie in Nederlandsch-Indie," *Indisch Genootschap*. 19 February 1901, 26–28.

42 See n.a., "Ons Pauperisme," *Mededeelingen der Vereeniging "Soeria Soemirat,"* no. 2 (1892), 8. One proof of the falsity of the claim was that these fathers often conferred upon these children "repulsive and obscene" names frequently enough that a government ruling stipulated that no family name could be given that "could humiliate the child" (G. H. Koster, "Aangenomen Kinderen en Staatsblad Europeanen," *De Amsterdammer,* 15 July 1922).

43 Letter from the Administrative Resident in Bac-giang to the Resident Superieure, Hanoi, AOM, No. 164, 11 May 1904.

44 See Jacques Mazet, *La Condition Juridique de Métis* (Paris: Domat-Montchrestien, 1932) and Douchet *Métis et congaies d'Indochine.*

45 Kohlbrugge, "Prostitutie in Nederlandsch-Indie," 23.

46 See Linda Gordon's discussion of this issue for early twentieth-century America in *Heroes of Their Own Lives: The Politics and History of Family Violence* (New York: Vintage, 1988).

47 See Mazet, *La Condition Juridique de Métis,* 37, 42.

48 Questions about the legal status of métis and the political consequences of that decision were not confined to the French alone. The International Colonial Institute in Brussels created by Joseph Chailley-Bert in 1893 engaged this question in at least three of its international meetings in 1911, 1920, and 1924. See *Comptes Rendus de l'institut Colonial International* (Bruxelles: Bibliotheque Coloniale Internationale, 1911, 1920, 1924).

49 Mazet, *La Condition Jurdique de Métis,* 114.

50 Ibid., 80.

51 Ibid., 90.

52 Statue of the "Societé de protection des enfants métis," 18 May 1904, Article 37.

53 "In de beschaafd wereld, niemand zonder staatsverband mag zijn" (K. H. Beyen, *Het Nederlanderschap in verband met het international recht* [Utrecht, 1890]), quoted in J.A. Nederburgh, *Wet en Adat,* 83 [Batavia: Kolff and Co., 1898]). The word *staatsverband* literally means "relationship to the state." Nederburgh distinguishes it from nationality and defines it as "the tie that exists between the state and each of its members, the membership of the state" (p. 91). Dutch scholars of colonial history say the term is rarely used but connotes citizenship.

54 Ibid., 87–88.

55 Ibid., 87.

56   See Willem Wertheim's incisive review of Prof. R. D. Kollewijn's *Intergentiel Recht, Indonesie,* 19 (1956), 169–73. Nederburgh's name comes up in this critique of Kottewijn, whose liberal rhetoric and opposition to such conservatives as Nederburgh belied the fact that he praised the virtues of the Indies mixed-marriage legislation of 1898, despite the racist principles that underwrote It.

57   Nederburgh, *Wet en Adat,* 88.

58   Ibid., 90.

59   Kooreman 1906.

60   Ibid.

61   See my "Rethinking Colonial Categories: European Communities and the Boundaries of Rule," *Comparative Studies in Society and History,* 31:1 (1989), 134–61; and "Carnal Knowledge and Imperial Power."

62   W. E. van Maszenbroek, *De Historische Ontwikkeling van de Staatrechtelijke Indeeling der Bevolking van Nederlandsch-Indie* 70 (Wageningen: Veenam, 1934).

63   See W. F. Prins, "De Bevolkingsgroepen in het Nederlandsch-Indische Recht," *Kolonlal Studien,* 17 (1933), 652–88. especially 677.

64   Ibid., 677; Van Marle, "De groep der Europeanen in Nederlands," *Indonesie,* 5:2 (1951), 110.

65   See William Mastenbroek, *De Historische Ontwikkeling van de Staatsrechtelijke Indeeling der Bevolking van Nederlandsch-Indie,* 87.

66   See Karen Offen's "Depopulation, Nationalism and Feminism in Fin-de-Siècle France," *American Historical Review,* 89:3 (1984), 648–76.

67   The following discussion is based on several documents that I will abbreviate in referring to in the section below as follows: *Verslag van het Verhandelde in de Bijeenkomsten der Nederlandsch-Indische Juristen-Vereeninging* on 25, 27, and 29 June 1887 in Batavia [hereafter, JV]; "Voldoet de wetgeving betreffende huwelijken tusschen personen behoorende tot de beide staatkundige categorien der Nederlandsch Indische bevolking (die der Europeanen en met hen, en die der Inlanders en met hen gelijkgestelden) aan de maatschappelijke behoefte? Zoo neen, welke wijzigingen zijn noodig? (1887) [hereafter, VW]; J. A. Nederburgh, *Gemengde Huwelijken, Staatsblad 1898, No. 158: Officiele Bescheiden met Eenige Aanteekeningen* [hereafter, GH].

68   Werhein, *Intergentiel Recht.*

69   The term mixed marriages (*gemengde huwelijken*) had two distinct but overlapping meanings in the Indies at the turn of the century. Common usage defined it as referring to contracts between a man and a woman of different racial origin; the state defined it as "a marriage between persons who were subject to different laws in the Netherlands Indies" with no reference to race. The distinction is significant for at least two reasons: (1) because the designations of legal standing as inlander versus European cut across the racial spectrum, with generations of mixed bloods falling on different sides of this divide and (2) because adat (customary) and Dutch law followed different rulings with respect to the marriage contract, divorce, inheritance, and child custody.

70   Although the hierarchies of gender and race of Indies colonial society in part account for the fact that in 1895 more than half of the European men in the Indies still lived with native women outside of marriage, this may only tell one part of the story. The juridical debates on legal reform of mixed marriages suggest that there were women who chose cohabitation over legal marriage. At the very least, this suggests that concubinage may not have been an appropriate

term for some of these arrangements, nor does it necessarily reflect what options
women may have perceived in these arrangements.

71   W. F. Prins, "De bevolkingsgroepen in het Nederlandsch-Indische recht," *Koloniale
Studien*, 17, 665. That some women chose cohabitation over legal mixed marriages
is rarely addressed in the colonial or secondary literature on the assumption that
all forms of cohabitation could be subsumed by the term concubinage, signaling
the moral degradation of a "kept woman" that the latter term implies. References
in these legal debates to the fact that some women chose not to marry suggests
that this issue needs further investigation.

72   Nederburgh, *GH*, 17.

73   As the chairman of the commission poignantly illustrated, a woman with native
legal standing could be arrested for wearing European attire at the very moment
she emerged from the building in which she had just married a European. Nor
could a European man and his wife of native standing take the short boat trip
from Soerabaya to Madura without prior permission of the authorities since sea
passage for natives was forbidden by law (*JV*, 29–30).

74   Nederburgh, *GH*, 20.

75   Ibid., 13.

76   Ibid., 13.

77   *JV*, 39.

78   *Idem*.

79   Ibid., 51.

80   Ibid., 40. The arguments presented over the mixed-marriage ruling are much
more numerous and elaborate than this short account suggests. There were
indeed those such as Abendanon (the lawyer friend of Kartini), whose proposals
raised yet a whole different set of options than those offered in these accounts.
He argued that both man and woman should be given European status, except
in those cases in which a native man preferred to retain his rights under adat
law. Abendanon also singlehandedly countered the claim that any European woman
who chose to marry a native man was already debased, arguing that there were
many Dutch girls in the Netherlands for whom this was not the case. But these
arguments were incidental to the main thrust of the debate and had little sway
in the final analysis.

81   Nederburgh, *GM*, 64.

82   See A. van Marle's "De Groep der Europeanen in Nederlands-Indie, iets over
ontstaan en groei," *Indonesie*. 5:3 (1952), 322, 328. Van Marle suggests that the
much larger number of illiterate women of European standing in central Java
and the Moluccas compared to the rest of the Indies indicates that the number
of mixed marriages in these regions was particularly high (p. 330). But this was
not the case everywhere. In East Java, European men acknowledged more of
their métis children but continued to cohabit with the native mothers of their
children outside of marriage (p. 495).

83   Mevrouw Douaire Klerck, *Eenige Beschouwingen over Oost-Indische Toestanden*, 3–19
(Amsterdam: Versluys, 1898).

84   S. J. Ratu-Langie, *Sarekat Islam*, 21 (Baarn: Hollandia Drukkerij, 1913).

85   A woman who had contracted a mixed marriage could, upon divorce or death
of her husband, declare her desire to reinstate her original nationality as long as
she did so within a certain time. However, a native woman who married a

European man and subsequently married and divorced a man of non-European status could not recoup her European status.

86   Ernest Rodenwalt, "Eugenetische Problemen in Nederlandsch-Indie," *Ons Nages-lacht*, 1–8 (1928).

87   Johan Winsemius, *Nieuw-Guinee als kolonisatie-gebied voor Europeanen en van Indo-Europeanen*, 227 (Ph.D. Disser., Faculty of Medicine, University of Amsterdam, 1936).

88   Jacques van Doorn emphasizes the dualistic policy on poverty in the 1930s in "Armoede en Dualistisch Beleid" (unpublished); I would refer to it as a three-tiered policy, not a dualistic one.

89   J. Th. Petrus Blumberger, *De Indo-Europeesche Beweging in Nederlandsch-Indie*, 5 Haarlem: Tjeenk Willink, 1939).

90   See Paul van der Veur's "The Eurasians of Indonesia: A Problem and Challenge in Colonial History. "*Journal of Southeast Asian History*. 9:2 (September 1966), 191–207, and his "Cultural Aspects of the Eurasian Community in Indonesian Colonial Society," *Indonesia*, 6 (October 1968), 38–53.

91   On the various currents of Eurasian political activity, see Paul W. van der Veur's "The Eurasians of Indonesia: A Problem and Challenge in Colonial History," On the importance of Indo individuals in the early Malay press and nationalist movement, see Takashi Shiraishi's *An Age in Motion: Popular Radicalism in Java, 1912–1926*, especially 37, 58–59 (Ithaca: Cornell University Press. 1990). Neither account addresses the class differences within Eurasian groups and where their distinct allegiances lay.

92   Blumberger, *De Indo-Europeesche Beweging*, 50.

93   According to the historian, Rudolph Mrazek, the early silent rejection of the Indo-European community from the Indonesian nationalist project turned explicit under Soekarno in the mid-1920s, when Indo-Europeans were categorically barred from membership in nationalist political organizations. Mrazek suggests that this silence among Dutch-educated nationalist leaders on the Indo question should be understood as a response from their own cultural formation and identification as cultural hybrids themselves (personal communication).

94   This issue of rootlessness is most subtly analyzed in contemporary contexts. Liisa Malkki explores the meanings attached to displacement and uprootedness in the national order of things "National Geographic: The Rooting of Peoples and the Territorialization of National Identity among Scholars and Refugees," *Cultural Anthropology* (1992). André-Pierre Taguieff examines LePen's nationalist rhetoric on the dangers of the rootlessness of immigrant workers in France. See Pierre-André Taguieff's excellent analysis of LePen's rhetoric in "The Doctrine of the National Front in France (1972–1989)," in *New Political Science*, no. 16/17, 29–70.

95   See A. Braconier, "Het Pauperisme onder de in Ned. Oost-Indie levende Europeanen," *Nederlandsch-Indie*, no. 1 (1917), 291–300, at 293.

96   Enquete sur Métissage, AOM, Amiraux 53.50.6.

97   René Martial, *Les Métis*, 58 (Paris: Flammarion. 1942).

98   See Taguieff, "The Doctrine of the National Front".

99   On the recent British discourse on Britishness and the cultural threat of Islam to that identity, see Talal Asad's rich analysis in "Multiculturalism and British Identity in the Wake of the Rushdie Affair," *Politics and Society*, 18:4 (December 1990), 455–80.

100 Hazel Carby ("Lynching, Empire and Sexuality," *Critical Enquiry,* 12:1 (1985), 262–77) argues that Afro-American women intellectuals at the turn of the century focused on the métis figure because it both enabled an exploration and expressed the relations between the races, because it demythologized concepts of pure blood and pure race while debunking any proposition of degeneracy through amalgamation. Such black women writers as Pauline Hopkins embraced the mulatto to counter the official script that miscegenation was not the inmost desire of the nonwhite peoples but the result of white rape (p. 274). In both the Indies and the United States at the same time, the figure of the Indo-mulatto looms large in both dominant and subaltern literary production, serving to convey strategic social dilemmas and political messages. It is not surprising, then, that the portrayal of the Indo in fiction was widely discussed in the Indies and metropolitan press by many more than those who were interested in literary style alone.

101 Taylor, *The Social World of Batavia*, 155.

102 Carole Pateman argues that the sexual contract is fundamental to the functioning of European civil society, in that the principle of patriarchal right defines the social contract between men, and the individual and citizen as male *(The Sexual Contract* [Stanford: Stanford University Press, 1988]).

103 I thank Luise White for pressing me to think out this point.

104 Gwendolyn Wright, "Tradition in the Service of Modernity: Architecture and Urbanism in Colonial Policy, 1900–1930," *Journal of Modern History*, 59 (June 1987), 291–316, at 297.

Chapter 26

Homi K. Bhabha

'RACE' TIME AND THE REVISION OF MODERNITY

'Dirty nigger!' Or simply, Look, a Negro!'

Frantz Fanon, *The Fact of Blackness*

I

WHENEVER THESE WORDS ARE SAID in anger or in hate, whether of the Jew in that *estaminet* in Antwerp, or of the Palestinian on the West Bank, or the Zairian student eking out a wretched existence selling fake fetishes on the Left Bank; whether they are said of the body of woman or the man of colour; whether they are quasi-officially spoken in South Africa or officially prohibited in London or New York, but inscribed nevertheless in the severe staging of the statistics of educational performance and crime, visa violations, immigration irregularities; whenever 'Dirty nigger!' or, 'Look, a Negro!' is not said at all, but you can see it in a gaze, or hear it in the solecism of a still silence; whenever and wherever I am when I hear a racist, or catch his look, I am reminded of Fanon's evocatory essay 'The Fact of Blackness' and its unforgettable opening lines.[1]

I want to start by returning to that essay, to explore only one scene in its remarkable staging, Fanon's phenomenological performance of what it means to be *not only a nigger* but a member of the marginalized, the displaced, the diasporic. To be amongst those whose very presence is both 'overlooked' – in the double sense of social surveillance and psychic disavowal – and, at the same time, over-determined – psychically projected made stereotypical and symptomatic. Despite its very specific location a Martinican subjected to the racist gaze on a street corner in Lyons – I claim a generality for Fanon's argument because he talks not simply of the historicity of the black man, as much as he writes in 'The Fact of Blackness' about the temporality of modernity within which the figure of the 'human' comes to be *authorized*. It is Fanon's temporality of emergence – his sense of the *belatedness of the black man* – that does not simply make the question of ontology inappropriate for black. identity, but somehow *impossible* for the very understanding of humanity in the world of modernity:

> You come too late, much too late, there will always be a world – a white world between you and us. (My emphasis)

It is the opposition to the ontology of that white world – to its assumed hierarchical forms of rationality and universality – that Fanon turns in a performance that is iterative and interrogative – a repetition that is initiatory, instating a differential history that will not return to the power of the Same. Between *you and us* Fanon opens up an enunciative space that does not simply contradict the metaphysical ideas of progress or racism or rationality; he distantiates them by 'repeating' these ideas, makes them uncanny by displacing them in a number of culturally contradictory and discursively estranged locations.

What Fanon shows up is the liminality of those Ideas – their ethnocentric margin – by revealing the *historicity* of its most universal symbol – Man. From the perspective of a postcolonial 'belatedness', Fanon disturbs the *punctum* of man as the signifying, subjectifying category of Western culture, as a unifying reference of ethical value. Fanon performs the desire of the colonized to identify with the humanistic, enlightenment ideal of Man: 'all I wanted was to be a man among other men. I wanted to come lithe and young into a world that was ours and build it together.' Then, in a catachrestic reversal he shows how, despite the pedagogies of human history, the performative discourse of the liberal West, its quotidian conversation and comments, reveal the cultural supremacy and racial typology upon which the universalism of Man is founded. 'But of course, come in, sir, there is no colour prejudice among us. . . . Quite, the Negro is a man like ourselves. . . . It is not because he is black that he is less intelligent than we are.'

Fanon uses the fact of blackness, of belatedness, to destroy the binary structure of power and identity: the imperative that 'the Black man must be Black; he must be Black in relation to the white man.' Elsewhere he has written: 'The Black man is not. [caesura] Any more than the white man' (my interpolation). Fanon's discourse of the 'human' emerges from that temporal break or caesura effected in the contuinist, progressivist myth of Man. He too speaks from the signifying time-lag of cultural difference that I have been attempting to develop as a structure for the representation of subaltern and postcolonial agency. Fanon writes from that temporal caesura, the time-lag of cultural difference, in a space between the symbolization of the social and the 'sign' of its representation of subjects and agencies. Fanon destroys two time schemes in which the historicity of the human is thought. He rejects the 'belatedness' of the black man because it is only the opposite of the framing of the white man as universal, normative – *the white sky all around me:* the black man refuses to occupy the past of which the white man is the future. But Fanon also refuses the Hegelian-Marxist dialectical schema whereby the black man is part of a transcendental sublation: a minor term in a dialectic that will emerge into a more equitable universality. Fanon, I believe, suggests another time, another space.

It is a space of being that is wrought from the interruptive, interrogative, tragic experience of blackness, of discrimination, of despair. It is the apprehension of the social and psychic question of 'origin' – and its erasure – in a negative side that 'draws its worth from an almost substantive absoluteness . . . [which has to be] ignorant of the essences and determinations of its being . . . an absolute density . . . an abolition of the ego by desire'. What may seem primordial or timeless is, I believe, a moment of a kind of 'projective past' whose history and signification I shall attempt to explore here. It is a mode of 'negativity' that makes the enunciatory present of modernity disjunctive. It opens up a time-lag at the point at which we speak of humanity through its differentiations – gender, race, class – that mark an excessive marginality of modernity. It is the enigma of this form of temporality which emerges from what Du Bois also called the 'swift and low of human doing',[2] to face Progress with some unanswerable questions, and suggest some answers of its own.

In destroying the 'ontology of man' Fanon suggests that 'there is not merely one Negro, there are *Negroes*'. This is emphatically not a post-modern celebration of pluralistic identities. As my argument will make clear, for me the project of modernity is itself rendered so contradictory and unresolved through the insertion of the 'time-lag' in which colonial and postcolonial moments emerge as sign and history, that I am sceptical of those transitions to postmodernity in Western academic writings which theorize the experience of this 'new historicity' through the appropriation of a 'Third World' metaphor; 'the First World . . . in a peculiar dialectical reversal, begins to touch some features of third-world experience. . . . The United States is . . . the biggest third-world country because of unemployment, nonproduction, etc.'[3]

Fanon's sense of social contingency and indeterminacy, made from the perspective of a postcolonial time-lag, is not a celebration of fragmentation, *bricolage*, pastiche or the 'simulacrum'. It is a vision of social contraction and cultural difference – as the disjunctive space of modernity – that is best seen in a fragment of a poem he cites towards the end of 'The Fact of Blackness':

> As the contradiction among the features
> creates the harmony of the face
> we proclaim the oneness of the suffering
> and the revolt.

II

The discourse of race that I am trying to develop displays the *problem of the ambivalent temporality of modernity* that is often overlooked in the more 'spatial', traditions of some aspects of postmodern theory.[4] Under the rubric 'the discourse of modernity', I do not intend to reduce a complex and diverse historical moment, with varied national genealogies and different institutional practices, into a singular shibboleth – be it the 'idea' of Reason, Historicism, Progress – for the critical convenience of postmodern literary theory. My interest in the question of modernity resides in the influential discussion generated by the work of Habermas, Foucault,

Lyotard and Lefort, amongst many others, that has generated a critical discourse around historical modernity as an epistemological structure.[5] To put it succinctly, the question of ethical and cultural judgement, central to the processes of subject formation and the objectification of social knowledge, is challenged at its 'cognitivist' core. Habermas characterizes it as a form of Occidental self-understanding that enacts a cognitive reductionism in the relation of the human being to the social world:

> Ontologically the world is reduced to a world of entities *as a whole* (as the totality of objects . . .); epistemologically, our relationship to that world is reduced to the capacity of know[ing] . . . states of affairs . . . in a purposive-rational fashion; semantically it is reduced to fact-stating discourse in which assertoric sentences are used.[6] (My emphasis)

Although this may be a stark presentation of the problem, it highlights the fact that the challenge to such a 'cognitivist' consciousness displaces the problem of truth or meaning from the disciplinary confines of epistemology – the problem of the referential as 'objectivity' reflected in that celebrated Rortyesque trope, the mirror of nature. What results could be figuratively described as a preoccupation not simply with the reflection in the glass – the idea or concept in itself – but with the frameworks of meaning as they are revealed in what Derrida has called the 'supplementary necessity of a parergon'. That is the performative, living description of the *writing* of a concept or theory, 'a relation to the history of its writing and the writing of its history also'.[7]

If we take even the most cursory view of influential postmodern perspectives, we find that there is an increasing *narrativization* of the question of social ethics and subject formation. Whether it is in the conversational procedures and 'final vocabularies' of liberal ironists like Richard Rorty, or the 'moral fictions' of Alisdair Macintyre that are the sustaining myths 'after virtue'; whether it is the *petits récits* and *phrases* that remain from the fall-out of the grand narratives of modernity in Lyotard; or the projective but ideal speech community that is rescued *within* modernity by Habermas in his concept of communicative reason that is expressed in its pragmatic logic or argument and a 'decentred' understanding of the world: what we encounter in all these accounts are proposals for what is considered to be the essential gesture of Western modernity, an 'ethics of self-construction' – or, as Mladan Dolar cogently describes it:

> What makes this attitude typical of modernity is the constant reconstruction and the reinvention of the self. . . . The subject and the present it belongs to have no objective status, they have to be perpetually (re)constructed.[8]

I want to ask whether this synchronous constancy of reconstruction and reinvention of the subject does not assume a cultural temporality that may not be universalist in its epistemological moment of judgement, but may, indeed, be ethnocentric in its construction of cultural 'difference'. It is certainly true, as Robert Young argues, that the inscription of alterity within the self can allow for a new relation to ethics';[9] but does that *necessarily* entail the more general case argued by Dolar, that 'the persisting split [of the subject] is the condition of freedom'?

If so, how do we specify the historical conditions and theoretical configurations of 'splitting' in political situations of 'unfreedom' – in the colonial and postcolonial margins of modernity? I am persuaded that it is the catachrestic postcolonial agency of 'seizing the value-coding' – as Gayatri Spivak has argued – that opens up an interruptive time-lag in the 'progressive' myth of modernity, and enables the diasporic and the postcolonial to be represented. But this makes it all the more crucial to specify the discursive and historical temporality that interrupts the enunciative 'present' in which the self-inventions of modernity take place. And it is this 'taking place' of modernity, this insistent and incipient *spatial* metaphor in which the social relations of modernity are conceived, that introduces a temporality of the 'synchronous' in the structure of the 'splitting' of modernity. It is this 'synchronous and spatial' representation of cultural difference that must be reworked as a framework for cultural otherness *within* the general dialectic of doubling that postmodernism proposes. Otherwise we are likely to find ourselves beached amidst Jameson's 'cognitive mappings' of the Third World, which might work for the Bonaventura Hotel in Los Angeles, but will leave you somewhat eyeless in Gaza.[10] Or if, like Terry Eagleton, your taste is more 'other worldly' than Third World, you will find yourself somewhat dismissive of the 'real' history of the 'other' – women, foreigners, homosexuals, the natives of Ireland – on the basis of 'certain styles, values, life-experiences which can be appealed to now as a form of political critique' because 'the fundamental political question is that of demanding an equal right with others of what one might become, not of assuming some fully-fashioned identity which is merely repressed.'[11]

It is to establish a *sign* of *the present,* of modernity, that is not that 'now' of transparent immediacy, and to found a form of social individuation where communality is *not predicated on a transcendent becoming,* that I want to pose my questions of a contra-modernity: what is modernity in those colonial conditions where its imposition is itself the denial of historical freedom, civic autonomy and the 'ethical' choice of refashioning?

III

I am posing these questions from within the problematic of modernity because of a shift within contemporary critical traditions of postcolonial writing. There is no longer an influential separatist emphasis on simply elaborating an anti-imperialist or black nationalist tradition 'in itself'. There is an attempt to interrupt the Western discourses of modernity through these displacing, interrogative subaltern or postslavery narratives and the critical–theoretical perspectives they engender. For example, Houston Baker's reading of the modernity of the Harlem Renaissance strategically elaborates a 'deformation of mastery', a vernacularism, based on the enunciation of the subject as 'never a simple coming into being, but a release from being possessed'.[12] The revision of Western modernism, he suggests, requires both the linguistic investiture of the subject and a practice of diasporic performance that is metaphorical. The 'public culture' project that Carol Breckenridge and Arjun

Appadurai have initiated focuses on the transnational dissemination of cultural modernity. What becomes properly urgent for them is that the 'simultaneous' global locations of such a modernity should not lose sense of the conflictual, contradictory locations of those cultural practices and products that follow the 'unequal development' of the tracks of international or multinational capital. Any transnational cultural study must 'translate', each time locally and specifically, what decentres and subverts this transnational globality, so that it does not become enthralled by the new global technologies of ideological transmission and cultural consumption.[13] Paul Gilroy proposes a form of populist modernism to comprehend both the aesthetic and political transformation of European philosophy and letters by black writers, but also to make sense of the secular and spiritual *popular* forms – music and dance – that have handled the anxieties and dilemmas involved in a response to the *flux of modern life*'.[14]

The power of the postcolonial translation of modernity rests in its *permative, deformative* structure that does not simply revalue the contents of a cultural tradition, or transpose values 'cross-culturally'. The cultural inheritance of slavery or colonialism is brought *before* modernity *not* to resolve its historic differences into a new totality, nor to forego its traditions. It is to introduce another locus of inscription and intervention, another hybrid, 'inappropriate' enunciative site, through that temporal split – or time-lag – that I have opened up [. . .] for the signification of postcolonial agency. Differences in culture and power are constituted through the social conditions of enunciation: the temporal caesura, *which is also the historically tranformative moment*, when a lagged space opens up *in*-between the *inter*subjective 'reality of signs . . . deprived of subjectivity' and the historical development of the subject in the order of social symbols.[15] This transvaluation of the symbolic structure of the cultural sign is absolutely necessary so that in the renaming of modernity there may ensue that process of the active agency of translation – the moment of 'making a name for oneself' that emerges through 'the undecidabiity . . . [at work] in a struggle for the proper name within a scene of genealogical indebtedness'.[16] Without such a reinscription of the sign itself – without a transformation of the site of *enunciation* – there is the danger that the mimetic contents of a discourse will conceal the fact that the hegemonic structures of power are maintained in a position of authority through a *shift in vocabulary* in the position of authority. There is for instance a kinship between the normative paradigms of colonial anthropology and the contemporary discourse of aid and development agencies. The 'transfer of technology' has not resulted in the transfer of power or the displacement of a neo-colonial tradition of political control through philanthropy – a celebrated missionary position.

What is the struggle of translation in the name of modernity? How do we catachrestically seize the genealogy of modernity and open it to the postcolonial translation? The 'value' of modernity is not located, a priori, in the passive fact of an epochal event or idea – of progress, civility, the law – but has to be negotiated *within* the 'enunciative' present of the discourse. The brilliance of Claude Lefort's account of the genesis of ideology in modern societies is to suggest that the representation of the rule, or the discourse of generality that symbolizes authority, is ambivalent because it is split off from its effective operation.[17] The *new or the contemporary* appear through the splitting of modernity as event and enunciation, the epochal and the everyday. Modernity as a *sign* of the present emerges in that process of splitting, that *lag,* that gives the practice of everyday life its consistency as *being contemporary*. It is because the present has the value of a 'sign', that modernity is iterative; a continual questioning of the conditions of existence; making problematic its own discourse not simply 'as ideas' but as the position and status of the locus of social utterance.

IV

'It is not enough . . . to follow the teleological thread that makes progress possible; one must isolate, within the history [of modernity], an event that will have the value of a sign.'[18] In his reading of Kant's *Was ist Aufklärung?* Foucault suggests that the sign of modernity is a form of decipherment whose value must be sought in *petits récits*, imperceptible events, in signs apparently *without* meaning and value – empty and excentric – in events that are outside the 'great events' of history.

The sign of history does not consist in an essence of the event itself, nor exclusively in the *immediate consciousness* of its agents and actors, but in its form as a *spectacle*; spectacle that signifies *because of* the distanciation and displacement between the event and those who are its spectators. The indeterminacy of modernity, where the struggle of translation takes place, is not simply around the ideas of progress or truth. Modernity, I suggest, is about the historical construction of a specific position of historical enunciation and address. It privileges those who 'bear witness', those who are 'subjected', or in the Fanonian sense with which I began, historically displaced. It gives them a representative position through the spatial distance, or the *time-lag* between the Great Event and its circulation as a historical sign of the 'people'; or an 'epoch' that constitutes the memory and the moral of the event *as a narrative*, a disposition to cultural communality, a form of social and psychic identification. The discursive address of modernity – its structure of authority – decentres the Great Event, and speaks from that moment of 'imperceptibility', the supplementary space 'outside' or uncannily beside (*abseits*).

Through Kant, Foucault traces 'the ontology of the present' to the exemplary event of the French Revolution and it is there that he stages his sign of modernity. But it is the spatial dimension of distance – *the perspectival distance from which the spectacle is seen* – that installs a cultural homogeneity into the sign of modernity. Foucault introduces a Eurocentric perspective at the point at which modernity installs a 'moral disposition in mankind'. The Eurocentricity of Foucault's theory of cultural difference is revealed in his insistent spatializing of the time of modernity. Avoiding the problems of the sovereign subject and linear causality, he nonetheless falls prey to the notion of the 'cultural' as a social formation whose discursive doubleness – the transcendental and empirical dialectic – is contained in a temporal frame that makes differences repetitively 'contemporaneous', regimes of sense-as-synchronous. It is a kind of cultural 'contradictoriness' that always presupposes a correlative spacing. Foucault's *spatial distancing* seals the sign of modernity in 1789 into a 'correlative', overlapping temporality. Progress brings together the three moments of the sign as:

a *signum rememorativum*, for it reveals that disposition [of progress] which has been present from the beginning; it is a *signum demonstrativum* because it demonstrates the present efficacity of this disposition; and it is also *signum prognosticum* for, although the Revolution may have certain questionable results, one cannot forget the disposition [of modernity] that is revealed through it.[19]

What if the effects of 'certain questionable results' of the Revolution create a disjunction, between the *signum demonstrativum* and the *signum prognosticum?* What if in the geopolitical space of the colony genealogically (in Foucault's sense) related to the Western metropolis, the symbol of the Revolution is partially visible as an unforgettable, tantalizing promise – a *pedagogy* of the values of modernity – while the 'present efficacy' of the sign of everyday life – its *political performativity*– repeats the archaic aristocratic racism of the *ancien régime*?

The ethnocentric limitations of Foucault's spatial sign of modernity become immediately apparent if we take our stand, in the immediate postrevolutionary period, in San Domingo with the Black Jacobins, rather than Paris. What if the 'distance' that constitutes the meaning of the Revolution as sign, the *signifying lag* between event and enunciation, stretches not across the Place de la Bastille or the rue des Blancs-Monteaux, but spans the temporal difference of the colonial space? What if we heard the 'moral disposition of mankind' uttered by Toussaint L'Ouverture for whom, as C. L. R. James so vividly recalls, the signs of modernity, 'liberty, equality, fraternity . . . what the French Revolution signified, was perpetually on his lips, in his correspondence, in his private conversations.'[20] What do we make of the figure of Toussaint – James invokes Phèdre, Ahab, Hamlet – at the moment when he grasps the tragic lesson that the moral, *modern* disposition of mankind, enshrined in the sign of the Revolution, only fuels the archaic racial factor in the society of slavery? What do we learn from that split consciousness, that 'colonial' disjunction of modern times and colonial and slave histories, where the reinvention of the self and the remaking of the social are strictly out of joint?

These are the issues of the catachrestic, postcolonial translation of modernity. They force us to introduce the question of subaltern agency, into the question of modernity: what is this 'now' of modernity? Who defines this present from which we speak? This leads to a more challenging question: *what is the desire of this repeated demand to modernize? Why does it insist, so compulsively, on its contemporaneous reality, its spatial dimension, its spectatorial distance?* What happens to the sign of modernity in those repressive places like San Domingo where progress is only heard (of) and not 'seen', is that it reveals the problem of the disjunctive moment of its utterance: the space which enables a postcolonial contra-modernity to emerge. For the discourse of modernity is *signified* from the time-lag, or temporal caesura, that emerges in the tension between the epochal 'event' of modernity as the symbol of the continuity of progress, and the interruptive temporality of the sign of the present, the contingency of modern times that Habermas has aptly described as its 'forward gropings and shocking encounters'.[21]

In this 'time' of repetition there circulates a contingent tension within modernity: a tension between the *pedagogy* of the symbols of progress, historicism, modernization, homogeneous empty time, the narcissism of organic culture, the onanistic search for the origins of race, and what I shall call the 'sign of the present': the performativity of discursive practice, the *récits* of the everyday, the repetition of the empirical, the ethics of self-enactment, the iterative signs that mark the non-synchronic *passages* of time in the archives of the 'new'. This is the space in which the question of modernity *emerges as a form of interrogation*: what do I belong to in this present? In what terms do I identify with the 'we', the intersubjective realm of society? This process cannot be represented in the binary relation of archaism/modernity, inside/outside, past/present, because these questions block off the forward drive or teleology of modernity. They suggest that what is read as the 'futurity' of the modern, its ineluctable progress, its cultural hierarchies, may be an 'excess' a disturbing alterity, a process of the marginalization of the symbols of modernity.

Time-lag is not a circulation of nullity, the endless slippage of the signifier or the theoretical anarchy of aporia. It is a concept that does not collude with current fashions for claiming the heterogeneity of ever-increasing 'causes', multiplicities of subject positions, endless supplies of subversive 'specificities', 'localities', 'territories'. The problem of the articulation of cultural difference is not the problem of free-wheeling pragmatist pluralism or the 'diversity' of the many; it is the problem of the not-one, the minus in the origin and repetition of cultural signs in a doubling that will not be sublated into a similitude. What is *in* modernity *more* than modernity is this signifying 'cut' or temporal break: it cuts into the plenitudinous notion of Culture splendidly reflected in the mirror of human nature; equally it halts the endless signification of difference. The process I have described as the sign of the present – *within modernity* – erases and interrogates those ethnocentric forms of cultural modernity that 'contemporize' cultural difference: it opposes both cultural pluralism with its spurious egalitarianism – different cultures in the same time ('The Magicians of the Earth', Pompidou Centre, Paris, 1989) – or cultural relativism – different cultural temporalities in the same 'universal' space 'The Primitivism Show', MOMA, New York, 1984).

V

This caesura in the narrative of modernity reveals something of what de Certeau has famously described as the non-place from which all historiographical operation starts, the lag which all histories must encounter in order to make a beginning.[22] For the emergence of modernity – as an ideology of *beginning, modernity as the new* – the template of this 'non-place' becomes the colonial space. It signifies this in a double way. The colonial space is the *terra incognita* or the *terra nulla*, the empty or wasted land whose history has to be begun, whose archives must be filled out; whose future progress must be secured in modernity. But the colonial space also stands for the *despotic* time of the Orient that becomes a great problem for the definition of modernity and its inscription of the history of the colonized from the perspective of the West. Despotic time, as Althusser has brilliantly described it, is 'space without places, time without duration'.[23] In that double-figure which haunted the moment of the enlightenment in its relation to the *otherness* of the Other, you can see the historical formation of the time-lag of modernity. And lest it be said that this disjunctive present of modernity is merely my theoretical abstraction, let me also remind you that a similar, signifying caesura occurs within the invention of progress in the 'long imperialist nineteenth century'. At the mid-point of the century questions concerning the 'origin of races' provided modernity with an ontology of its present and a justification of cultural hierarchy within the West and in the East. In the structure of the discourse, however, there was a recurrent ambivalence between the developmental, organic notion of cultural and racial 'indigenism' as the justification of supremacy, and the notion of evolution as abrupt cultural transition, discontinuous progress, the periodic eruption of invading tribes from somewhere mysterious in Asia, as the guarantee of progress.[24]

The 'subalterns and ex-slaves', who now seize the spectacular event of modernity do so in a catachrestic gesture of reinscribing modernity's 'caesura' and using it to transform the locus of thought and writing in their postcolonial critique. Listen to the ironic naming, the interrogative repetitions, of the critical terms themselves: black 'vernacularism' repeats the minor term used to designate the language of the native and the housebound slave to make demotic the grander narratives of progress. Black 'expressivism' reverses the stereotypical affectivity and sensuality of the stereotype to suggest that 'rationalities are produced *endlessly*' in populist modernism.[25] New ethnicity' is used by Stuart Hall in the black British context to create a discourse of cultural difference that marks ethnicity as the struggle against ethnicist 'fixing' and in favour of a wider minority discourse that represents sexuality and class. Cornel West's genealogical materialist view of race and Afro-American oppression is, he writes, 'both continuous and discontinuous with the Marxist tradition; and shares an equally contingent relation to Nietzsche and Foucault.'[26] More recently, he has constructed a prophetic pragmatic tradition from William James, Niebuhr and Du Bois suggesting that 'it is possible to be a prophetic pragmatist and belong to different political movements, e.g. feminist, Black, chicano, socialist, left-liberal ones.'[27] The Indian historian Gyan Prakash, in an essay on postorientalist histories of the Third World, claims that:

> it is difficult to overlook the fact that . . . third world voices . . . speak within and to discourses familiar to the 'West'. . . . The Third World, far from being confined to its assigned space, has penetrated the inner sanctum of the 'First World', in the process of being 'Third Worlded' – arousing, inciting, and affiliating with the subordinated others in the First World . . . to connect with minority voices.[28]

The intervention of postcolonial or black critique is aimed at transforming the conditions of enunciation at the level of the sign – where the intersubjective realm is constituted – not simply setting up new symbols of identity, new 'positive' images' that fuel an unreflective 'identity politics'. The challenge to modernity comes in redefining the signifying relation to a disjunctive 'present': staging the past as *symbol*, myth, memory, history, the ancestral – but a past whose iterative *value as sign* reinscribes the 'lessons of the past' into the very textuality of the present that determines both the identification with, and the interrogation of, modernity: what Is the 'we' that defines the prerogative of my present? The possibility of inciting cultural translations across minority discourses arises because of the disjunctive present of modernity. It ensures that what *seems* the 'same' within cultures is negotiated in the time-lag of the 'sign' which constitutes the inter-subjective, social realm. Because that lag is indeed the very structure of difference and splitting within the discourse of modernity, turning it into a performative process, then each repetition of the sign of modernity is different, specific to its historical and cultural conditions of enunciation.

    This process is most clearly apparent in the work of those 'postmodern' writers who, in pushing the paradoxes of modernity to its limits, reveal the margins of the West.[29] From the postcolonial perspective we can only assume a disjunctive and displaced relation to these works; we cannot accept them until we subject them to a *lagging*: both in the temporal sense of postcolonial agency with which you are now (over)familiar, and in the obscurer sense in which, in the early days of settler colonization, to be lagged was to be transported to the colonies for penal servitude!

    In Foucault's Introduction to the *History of Sexuality*, racism emerges in the nineteenth century in the form of an historical retroversion that Foucault finally disavows. In the 'modern' shift of power from the juridical politics of death to the biopolitics of life, race produces a historical temporality of interference, overlapping, and the displacement of sexuality. It is, for Foucault, the great historical irony of modernity that the Hitlerite annihilation of the Jews was carried out in the name of the archaic, premodern signs of race and sanguinity – the oneiric exaltation of blood, death, skin – rather than through the politics of sexuality. What is profoundly revealing is Foucault's complicity with the logic of the 'contemporaneous' within Western modernity. Characterizing the 'symbolics of blood' as being retroverse, Foucault disavows the time-lag of race as the sign of cultural difference and its mode of repetition.

    The *temporal* disjunction that the 'modern' question of race would introduce into the discourse of disciplinary and pastoral power is disallowed because of Foucault's spatial critique: 'we must conceptualize the deployment of sexuality on the basis of the techniques of power that are *contemporary* with it' (my emphasis).[30] However subversive 'blood' and race may be they are in the last analysis merely an 'historical retroversion'. Elsewhere Foucault directly links the 'flamboyant rationality' of Social Darwinism to Nazi Ideology, entirely ignoring colonial societies which were the proving grounds for Social Darwinist administrative discourses all through the nineteenth and early twentieth centuries.[31]

    If Foucault normalizes the time-lagged, 'retroverse' sign of race, Benedict Anderson places the 'modern' dreams of racism 'outside history' altogether. For Foucault race and blood interfere with modern sexuality. For Anderson racism has its origins in antique ideologies of class that belong to the aristocratic 'pre-history' of the modern nation. Race represents an archaic ahistorical moment outside the 'modernity' of the imagined community: 'nationalism thinks in historical destinies, while racism dreams of eternal contaminations . . . outside history.'[32] Foucault's spatial notion of the conceptual contemporaneity of power-as-sexuality limits him from seeing the double and overdetermined structure of race and sexuality that has a long history in the *peuplement* (politics of settlement) of colonial societies; for Anderson the 'modern' anomaly of racism finds its historical modularity, and its fantasmatic scenario, in the colonial space which is a belated and hybrid attempt to 'weld together dynastic legitimacy and national community. . . to shore up domestic aristocratic bastions'.[33]

The racism of colonial empires is then part of an archaic acting out, a dream-text of a form of historical retroversion that 'appeared to confirm on a global, modern stage antique conceptions of power and privilege'.[34] What could have been a way of understanding the limits of Western imperialist ideas of progress within the genealogy of a 'colonial metropolis' – a hybridizing of the Western nation – is quickly disavowed in the language of the *opéra bouffe* as a grimly amusing *tableau vivant* of 'the [colonial] bourgeois gentilhomme speaking poetry against a backcloth of spacious mansions and gardens filled with mimosa and bougainvillea'.[35] It is in that 'weld' of the colonial site as, contradictorily, both 'dynastic and national', that the modernity of Western national society is confronted by its colonial double. Such a moment of temporal disjunction, which would be crucial for understanding the colonial history of contemporary metropolitan racism in the West, is placed 'outside history'. It is obscured by Anderson's espousal of 'a simultaneity across homogeneous empty time' as the modal narrative of the imagined community. It is this kind of evasion, I think, that makes Partha Chatterjee, the Indian 'subaltern' scholar, suggest, from a different perspective, that Anderson 'seals up his theme with a sociological determinism . . . without noticing the twists and turns, the suppressed possibilities, the contradictions still unresolved'.[36]

These accounts of the modernity of power and national community become strangely symptomatic at the point at which they create a rhetoric of 'retroversion' for the emergence of racism. In placing the representations of race 'outside' modernity, in the space of historical retroversion, Foucault reinforces his 'correlative spacing' by relegating the social fantasy of racism to an archaic daydream, Anderson further universalizes his homogeneous empty time of the 'modern' social imaginary. Hidden in the disavowing narrative of historical retroversion and its archaism, is a notion of the time-lag that displaces Foucault's spatial analytic of modernity and Anderson's homogeneous temporality of the modern nation. In order to extract the one from the other we have to see how they form a double boundary: rather like the more general intervention and seizure of the history of modernity that has been attempted by postcolonial critics.

Retroversion and archaic doubling, attributed to the ideological 'contents' of racism, do not remain at the ideational or pedagogical level of the discourse. Their inscription of a structure of retroaction returns to disrupt the enunciative function of this discourse and produce a different 'value' of the sign and time of race and modernity. At the level of content the archaism and fantasy of racism is represented as 'ahistorical', outside the progressive myth of modernity. This is an attempt, I would argue, to universalize the spatial fantasy of modern cultural communities as living their history 'contemporaneously', in a 'homogeneous empty time' of the People-as-One that finally deprives minorities of those marginal, liminal spaces from which they can intervene in the unifying and totalizing *myths* of the national culture.

However, each time such a homogeneity of cultural identification is established there is a marked disturbance of temporality in the *writing of modernity*. For Foucault it is the awareness that retroversion of race or sanguinity haunts and doubles the contemporary analytic of power and sexuality and may be subversive of it: we may need to think the disciplinary powers of race as sexuality in a hybrid cultural formation that will not be contained within Foucault's logic of the contemporary. Anderson goes further in acknowledging that colonial racism introduces an awkward weld, a strange historical 'suture' in the narrative of the nation's *modernity*. The archaism of colonial racism, as a form of cultural signification (rather than simply an ideological content), reactivates nothing less than the 'primal scene' of the modern Western nation: that is, the problematic historical transition between dynastic, lineage societies and horizontal, homogeneous secular communities. What Anderson designates as racism's 'timelessness', its location 'outside history' is in fact that form of time-lag, a mode of repetition and reinscription, that *performs* the ambivalent historical temporality of modern national cultures – the *aporetic coexistence*, within the cultural history of the *modern* imagined community, of both the dynastic, hierarchical, prefigurative 'medieval' traditions (the past), and the secular, homogeneous, synchronous cross-time of modernity (the present). Anderson resists a reading of the modern nation that suggests – in an iterative time-lag – that the hybridity of the colonial space may provide a pertinent problematic within which to write the history of the 'postmodern' national formations of the West.

To take this perspective would mean that we see 'racism' not simply as a hangover from archaic conceptions of the aristocracy, but as part of the historical traditions of civic and liberal humanism that create ideological matrices of national aspiration, together with their concepts of 'a people' and its imagined community. Such a privileging of ambivalence in the social imaginaries of nation*ness*, and its forms of collective affiliation, would enable us to understand the coeval, often *incommensurable* tension between the influence of traditional 'ethnicist' identifications that coexist with contemporary secular, modernizing aspirations. The enunciative 'present' of modernity, that I am proposing, would provide a political space to articulate and negotiate such culturally hybrid social identities. Questions of cultural difference would not be dismissed – with a barely concealed racism – as atavistic tribal instincts that afflict Irish Catholics in Belfast or 'Muslim fundamentalists' in Bradford. It is precisely such unresolved, transitional moments within the disjunctive present of modernity that are then projected into a time of historical retroversion or an inassimilable place outside history.

The *history* of modernity's antique dreams is to be found in the *writing out* of the colonial and postcolonial moment. In resisting these attempts to normalize the time-lagged colonial moment, we may provide a *genealogy* for postmodernity that is at least as important as the 'aporetic' history of the Sublime or the nightmare of rationality in Auschwitz. For colonial and postcolonial texts do not merely tell the modern history of 'unequal development' or evoke memories of underdevelopment. I have tried to suggest that they provide modernity with a modular moment of *enunciation:* the locus and locution of cultures caught in the transitional and disjunctive temporalities of modernity. What is in modernity *more* than modernity is the disjunctive 'postcolonial' time and space that makes its presence felt *at the level of enunciation*. It figures, in an influential contemporary fictional instance, as the contingent margin between Toni Morrison's indeterminate moment of the 'not-there' – a 'black' space that she distinguishes from the Western sense of synchronous tradition – which then turns into the 'first stroke' of slave rememory, the *time* of communality and the narrative of a history of slavery. This translation of the meaning of time into the discourse of space; this catachrestic seizure of the signifying 'caesura' of modernity's presence and *present;* this insistence that power must be thought in the hybridity of race and sexuality; that nation must be reconceived liminally as the dynastic-in-the-democratic, race-difference doubling and splitting the teleology of class-consciousness: it is through these iterative interrogations and *historical initiations* that the cultural location of modernity shifts to the post-colonial site. [. . .]

Notes

1   All citations from Fanon In the following pages come from 'The Fact of Blackness', in *Black Skin, White* Masks, Foreword by H. Bhabha (London: Pluto, 1986). pp. 109–40.

2   W. B. Du Bois, *The Souls of Black Folk* (New York: Signet Classics, 1982), p. 275.

3   'A conversation with Fredric Jameson', in A. Ross (ed.) *Universal Abandon: The Politics of Postmodernism* (Edinburgh: Edinburgh University Press, 1988), p. 17.

4   See my reading of Renan in *The Location of Culture*, Chapter 8, 'DissemiNation'.

5   Each of these writers has addressed the problem of modernity in a number of works so that selection becomes invidious. However, some of the most directly relevant are the following: J. Habermas, *The Philosophical Discourse of Modernity* (Cambridge: Polity Press, 1990), esp. chs 11 and 12; M. Foucault, *The History of Sexuality. Volume One: An Introduction* (London: Allen Lane, 1979); see also his 'The art of telling the truth', in L. D. Kritzman (ed.), *Politics, Philosophy and Culture* (New York Routledge, 1990); J.-F. Lyotard, *The Differend* (Minneapolis: University of Minnesota Press, 1988); C. Lefort, *The Political Forms of Modern Society*, J. B. Thompson (ed.) (Cambridge: Polity Press), especially Part II, 'History, ideology and the social imaginary'.

6   Habermas, *The Philosophical Discourse of Modernity*, p 311.

7   J. Derrida, *The Post Card: From Socrates to Freud and Beyond*, A. Bass (trans.) (Chicago: Chicago University Press, 1987), pp 303–4.

8   M. Dolar, *The Legacy of the Enlightenment: Foucault and Lacan*, unpublished manuscript.

9   R. J. C. Young, *White Mythologies: Writing, History and the West* (London: Routledge, 1990), pp. 16-17. Young argues a convincing case against the Eurocentrism of historicism through his exposition of a number of 'totalizing' historical doctrines, particular in the Marxist tradition, while demonstrating at the same time that the spatializing anti-historicismn of Foucault remains equally Eurocentric.

10   Cf. Young, *White Mythologies*, pp. 116–17.

11   T. Eagleton, *The Ideology of the Aesthetic* (Oxford: Blackwell, 1990), p. 414.

12   H. A. Baker, Jr, *Modernism and the Harlem Renaissance* (Chicago: Chicago University Press, 1987), p. 56.

13   C. Breckenridge and A. Appadurai, *The Situation of Public Culture*, unpublished manuscript. For the general elaboration of this thesis see various issues of *Public Culture: Bulletin of the Project for Transnational Cultural Studies* (University of Pennsylvania).

14   P. Gilroy, 'One nation under a groove', in D. T. Goldberg (ed.) *Anatomy of Racism* (Minneapolis: University of Minnesota Press, 1990), p. 280.

15   Although I introduce the term 'time-lag' more specifically in *The Location of Culture*, Chapters 8 and 9, it is a structure of the 'splitting' of colonial discourse that I have been elaborating and illustrating – without giving it a name – from my very earliest essays.

16   J. Derrida, 'Des Tours de Babel', in *Difference in Translation*, J. F. Graham (ed.) (Ithaca: Cornell University Press, 1985), p. 174.

17   Lefort, *The Political Forms of Modern Society*, p. 212.

18   Foucault, 'The art of telling the truth', p. 90.

19   Ibid., p. 93.

20   C. L. R. James, *The Black Jacobins* (London: Allison and Busby, 1980), pp. 290–1.

21   J. Habermas, 'Modernity: an incomplete project', in H. Foster (ed.) *Postmodern Culture* (London: Pluto, 1985).

22   M. de Certeau, 'The historiographical operation', in his *The Writing of History*, T. Conley (trans.) (New York: Columbia University Press, 1988), p. 91.

23   L. Althusser, *Montesquieu, Rousseau, Marx* (London: Verso, 1972), p. 78.

24   P. J. Bowler, *The Invention of Progress* (Oxford: Blackwell, 1990), ch. 4.

25   Gilroy, 'One nation under a groove', p. 278.

26   C. West, 'Race and social theory: towards a genealogical materialist analysis', in M. Davis, M. Marable, F. Pfeil and M. Sprinker (eds) *Towards a Rainbow Socialism* (London: Verso, 1987), pp. 86 ff.

27   C. West, *The American Evasion of Philosophy* (London: Macmillan, 1990), pp. 232–3.

28   G. Prakash, 'Post-orientalist third-world histories', *Comparative Studies in Society and History*, vol. 32, no. 2 (April 1990), p. 403.

29   Robert Young, in *White Mythologies*, also suggests, in keeping with my argument that the colonial and postcolonial moment is the liminal point, or the limit-text, of the holistic demands of historicism.

30   Foucault, *The History of Sexuality*, p. 150.

31   M. Foucault, *Foucault Live*, J. Johnstone and S. Lotringer (trans.) (New York: Semiotext(e), 1989), p. 269.

32   B. Anderson, *Imagined Communities* (London: Verso, 1983), p. 136.

33   Ibid., p. 137.

34   Ibid.

35   Ibid.

36   P. Chatterjee, *Nationalist Thought and the Colonial World* (London: Zed, 1986), pp. 21–2.

Guide to Further Reading

Key texts

Alexander, M. J. and Mohanty, C. T. (eds) (1997) *Feminist Genealogies, Colonial Legacies, Democratic Futures*, New York: Routledge (an important collection of papers that explore questions about race and gender in colonial and postcolonial situations).

Bhabha, H. (1994) *The Location of Culture*, London: Routledge (an influential collection of papers that explore various facets of Bhabha's theoretical model).

Mbembe, A. (2001) *On the Postcolony*, Berkeley: University of California Press (a critique of postcolonial theories drawing on a critical analysis of power and subjectivity in Africa).

Stoler, A. L. (1995) *Race and the Education of Desire: Foucault's History of Sexuality and the Colonial Order of Things*, Durham, NC: Duke University Press (an attempt to link Foucault's analysis of sexuality to an analysis of colonialism).

Stoler, A. L. (2002) *Carnal Knowledge and Imperial Power: Race and the Intimate in Colonial Rule*, Berkeley: University of California Press (a detailed analysis of the role of race and intimacy in colonial situations).

Stoler, A. L. (ed.) (2006) *Haunted by Empire: Geographies of Intimacy in North American History*, Durham and London: Duke University Press (an attempt to bring a postcolonial perspective to bear on North American histories).

Background reading

Adas, M. (1989) *Machines as the Measure of Men: Science, Technology and Ideologies of Western Dominance*, Ithaca: Cornell University Press (an analysis of changing ideas about race and civilisation through the nineteenth and early twentieth centuries).

Appiah, K. A. (1992) *In My Father's House: Africa in the Philosophy of Culture*, London: Methuen (an exploration of questions about race and identity in Africa).

Brantlinger, P. (1988) *Rule of Darkness: British Literature and Imperialism 1830–1914*, Ithaca: Cornell University Press (explores the interrelationship between literature and imperialism).

Calhoun, C., Cooper, F. and Moore, K. W. (eds) (2006) *Lessons of Empire: Imperial Histories and American Power*, New York: New Press (a collection of papers that focuses on the role of colonialism and power in the history of the United States).

Cesaire, A. (1972) *Discourse on Colonialism*, New York: Monthly Review Press (a classical exploration of the cultural and social impact of colonialism).

Coombes, A. (1994) *Reinventing Africa: Museums, Material Culture and Popular Imagination in Late Victorian and Edwardian England*, London: Yale University Press (an exploration of representations of Africa and Africans in museums and popular culture).

Cooper, F. and Stoler, A. L. (eds) 1997) *Tensions of Empire: Colonial Cultures in a Bourgeois World*, Berkeley: University of California Press (an analysis of the refashioning of modernity as a consequence of the colonial encounters).

Diawara, M. (1998) *In Search of Africa*, Cambridge, MA: Harvard University Press (a biographical narrative of the author's return to his native Guinea and exploration of everyday features of the postcolonial situation in West Africa).

Dirks, N. B. (ed.) 1992) *Colonialism and Culture*, Ann Arbor: University of Michigan Press (a collection of historical papers on the cultural impact of colonialism).

Eze, E. C. (ed.) (1997) *Postcolonial African Philosophy: A Critical Reader*, Cambridge, MA: Blackwell (a collection of papers on current debates about postcolonial African philosophy).

Frantz Fanon (1986) *Black Skin, White Masks*, London: Pluto (a classic account of the psychological impact of colonialism).

Füredi, F. (1998) *The Silent War: Imperialism and the Changing Perception of Race*, London: Pluto Press (an analysis of the role of imperialism in shaping ideas about race).

Gordon, L. R. (1997) *Her Majesty's Other Children: Sketches of Racism from a Neocolonial Age*, Lanham, MD: Rowman and Littlefield (a collection of essays that explore historical and contemporary features of racism).

Greenblatt, S. (1991) *Marvelous Possessions: The Wonder of the New World*, Chicago: University of Chicago Press (an account of the impact of the discovery of the New World on images of other cultures).

Hobsbawm, E. (1987) *The Age of Empire 1875–1914*, London: Weidenfeld and Nicolson (an influential history of the high-point of European imperial expansion).

Hulme, P. (1986) *Colonial Encounters: Europe and the Native Caribbean*, London: Methuen (an analysis of the emergence of colonialism in the Caribbean).

Kiernan, V. G. (1969) *The Lords of Humankind: Black Man, Yellow Man, and White Man in the Age of Empire*, Harmondsworth: Penguin (a classic account of the articulation of changing ideas about race in the context of colonialism).

Lewis, R. (1996) *Gendering Orientalism: Race, Femininity and Representation*, London: Routledge (an analysis of the intersections between race and gender in orientalist discourses).

Low, G. C.-L. (1996) *White Skins, Black Masks: Representation and Colonialism*, London: Routledge (a study of literary representations of colonialism, focusing on Haggard and Kipling).

Lowe, L. (1991) *Critical Terrains: French and British Orientalisms*, Ithaca: Cornell University Press (a comparative analysis of the changing images of race and the other to be found in French and British orientalisms).

Mani, L. (1998) *Contentious Traditions: The Debate on Sati in Colonial India*, Berkeley: University of California Press (a detailed analysis of how colonial discourses constructed ideas of tradition in India).

Mannoni, O. (1964) *Prospero and Caliban: The Psychology of Colonization*, New York: Frederick A. Praeger (a classic account of the psychological impact of colonialism, based on a study of Madagascar).

Mudimbe, V. Y. (1994) *The Idea of Africa*, Bloomington: Indiana University Press (an account of ideas about Africa from ancient times to the present).

Nandy, A. (1988) *The Intimate Enemy: Loss and Recovery of Self Under Colonialism*, Second edition, Delhi: Oxford University Press (a discussion of the impact of colonialism on ideas about self and other).

Padgen, A. (1995) *Lords of All the World: Ideologies of Empire in Spain, Britain and France c.1500–c.1800*, New Haven and London: Yale University Press (a comparative account of early ideologies of empire).

Parry, B. (1998) *Delusions and Discoveries: India in the British Imagination, 1880–1930*, New edition, London: Verso (an exploration of evolving British ideas about Indian culture and society).

Parsons, N. (1998) *King Khama, Emperor Joe and the Great White Queen: Victorian Britain Through African Eyes*, Chicago: University of Chicago Press (an innovative look at Victorian society through the eyes of Africans).

Pieterse, J. N. and Parekh, B. (ed.) (1995) *The Decolonization of Imagination: Culture, Knowledge and Power*, London: Zed Books (an exploration of discourses of colonial domination and decolonisation).

Pratt, M. L. (1992) *Imperial Eyes: Travel Writing and Transculturation*, London: Routledge (a study that focuses on travel writings and how they constructed images of other people in the nineteenth and early twentieth century).

Ross, R. (ed.) (1982) *Racism and Colonialism*, The Hague: Martinus Nijhoff (an important collection of papers that explore the relationship between racism and colonialism).

Said, E. (1978) *Orientalism*, Harmondsworth: Penguin (the foundational statement of the orientalist thesis).

Scott, D. (1999) *Refashioning Futures: Criticism after Postcoloniality*, Princeton: an Princeton University Press (a critical account of postcolonial theories and their application to specific contexts).

UNESCO (1977) *Race and Class in Post-Colonial Society*, Paris: UNESCO (a collection of papers that is focused on the relationship between class and race, particularly in the Caribbean and Latin America).

Yegengolu, M. (1998) *Colonial Fantasies: Towards a Feminist Reading of Orientalism*, Cambridge: Cambridge University Press (a feminist reading of the debates about orientalism).

Young, R. J. C. (1995) *Colonial Desire: Hybridity in Theory, Culture and Race*, London: Routledge (an influential analysis of changing ideas about race and hybridity from the nineteenth century onwards).

Key Questions

- How can Frantz Fanon's essay on 'The Fact of Blackness' be used to analyse the development of racism in colonial societies?
- In what ways were racial ideas and institutions an integral element of the colonial situation?
- What are the implications of Chandra Talpade Mohanty's critical analysis of western feminist discourses for an analysis of racism?
- Explore the implications of Ann Stoler's argument that colonialism involved the construction of both racial and sexual boundaries?
- Examine Homi Bhabha's argument that postcolonial writing involves a critical dialogue within and beyond the limits of modernity?
- Discuss the ways in which Ann McClintock's essay on 'The White Family of Man' illustrates the interface between race, gender and sexuality in structuring colonialism.

PART FIVE

Feminism, difference and identity

INTRODUCTION

A N IMPORTANT FEATURE OF DEBATES on race and racism over the past two decades has been the development of what some writers have defined as a gendered perspective on race and racism. We have discussed the broad contours of this transformation in the Introduction and a number of the papers in earlier parts of the Reader, particularly in Part Four, have touched upon the growing emphasis on linking the analysis of racism to questions of gender and sexuality. In this part we have included a group of extracts that explore this dimension is depth, focusing specifically on those writers whose work has been influential in shaping the contours of academic and public debates about this issue.

The first extract is from the writings of Hazel Carby, whose work on feminism and race has done much to influence debate on both sides of the Atlantic about this issue. Carby's influential text was written in the early 1980s and was part of a critical engagement by black and minority feminists with what they saw as some of the limitations of white feminist discourses. At the time most feminist publications were practically all white and their content dealt almost exclusively with white women in the United States or in Europe. One consequence of this situation was that for many feminist theorists writing at this time all men were equivalent oppressors and all family structures were bastions of patriarchy. As Carby argues, however, for many black feminists this was perceived to be a position that took little account of the specific aspects of the experience of black communities and of the history of slavery or racial discrimination. A recurrent refrain in Carby's contribution, which led to intense debate at the time, was on the need for white feminists to show a critical awareness of the role that racism played in shaping the everyday lives of both black and white women and to explore the need to include the experiences of minority women within the conceptual frameworks that they were using. Although it is clear that the tenor of the public debates within feminism and in academia about these issues has moved in the period since Carby's contribution was first published, we have included it here in order to highlight the terms within which debates about this issue were framed as late as the 1980s.

In the two decades since the original publication of hooks and Carby's interventions there has been a rapid expansion of scholarship in this field, and there is an identifiable sub-field of black feminist theorising that has come to the fore in recent years. One of the key contributors to this work is the American sociologist Patricia Hill Collins, and the extract from her work that we include here is symptomatic of the concerns to be found in her work and that of others. A particular feature of Collins's argument is the need to explore the intersections between gender, race and class in structuring the position of African American women. Another recurrent theme in her work is the need to situate the position of African American women in relation to family structures, churches, and other community organisations in order to gain a fuller understanding of the way they are positioned within specific communities and localities. She also emphasises the need to understand that the conditions of the black women's oppression are specific and complex, and that it is therefore important to seek particularised methodologies that might reveal the ways in which that oppression is experienced.

Collins account of black feminism is followed by Kimberly Springer's analysis of the new waves of black feminist theorising, focusing on trends and developments in the United States. Springer's account touches on key facets of the different ways in which she sees new voices emerging to address the relevance of feminist theorising to the position of black communities and women of colour. A recurring theme in her account is the need to think about the ways in which black feminist activism is not a singular process but a process that is likely to take new direction in the early decades of the twenty-first century.

Another influential contributor to theorising in this field is Patricia Williams, whose book *The Alchemy of Race and Rights* attracted much attention when it was published in the early 1990s. Written in a style that is both personal and analytical at the same time, Williams's book eschews much of the jargon of academic feminist writing in this field and adopts a discursive essay form. At its broadest level Williams's work explores the changing experiences of black American women and how their everyday lives continue to be shaped by race, class, gender and other social relations. The extract we have included here gives a flavour of the way Williams seeks to explore the changing boundaries of race and gender in contemporary America, and provide a fascinating insight into the ways in which these issues are talked about among the academic milieu of which she is a part.

The following extract, from Avtar Brah, takes up the issue of how to theorise ideas about difference and diversity in relation to questions of race and gender. Drawing on debates that have become a recurrent theme among black and white feminists in both Britain and America, Brah seeks to show that there is a need for theorising on race and gender to open up new ways to understand the complex variety of subject positions that are occupied by different groups of women in contemporary societies. Her argument links up with the debates about 'new ethnicities' that have been initiated by Stuart Hall among others. But it also seeks to go beyond what she sees as the limitations of current debates in feminist circles about race and gender.

The next extract, from Ruth Frankenberg, reflects another important trend in this field, namely the attempt to use insights derived from the study of the social construction of whiteness to explore the position of white women in American society. Frankenberg's account of this question is framed by her in-depth life history interviews with white women and by her attempt to provide a broader framework as to how issues of race and gender are talked about by these women. There has been an explosion of theorising about 'whiteness' in recent years (see Part Six), but what is particularly important about Frankenberg's analysis is the way she seeks to situate her work within a life history approach in order to uncover what she sees as the complexities of the relationship between racial and gender relations in the contemporary environment.

Following on from Frankenberg's engagement with the issue of whiteness and gender, the final extract in this part is from Sarita Srivastava, and it is focused on the intersections between anti-racist politics and women's organisations and social movements. Drawing equally on current theoretical debates and empirical research on social movements Srivastava's analysis seeks to question the simplistic reduction of antiracism to political goodness and therapy. In doing so she provides a nuanced and critical perspective on the articulation of feminism with antiracist social and political discourses.

Chapter 27

Hazel V. Carby

WHITE WOMAN LISTEN!
Black feminism and the boundaries
of sisterhood

I'm leaving evidence. And you got to leave evidence too. And your
children got to leave evidence. . . . They burned all the documents.
. . . We got to burn out what they put in our minds, like you burn
out a wound. Except we got to keep what we need to bear witness.
That scar that's left to bear witness. We got to keep it as visible as
our blood.[1]

THE BLACK WOMEN'S CRITIQUE of *his*tory has not only involved
us in coming to terms with 'absences'; we have also been outraged by the
ways in which it has made us visible, when it has chosen to see us. *His*tory has
constructed our sexuality and our femininity as deviating from those qualities with
which white women, as the prize objects of the Western world, have been
endowed. We have also been defined in less than human terms.[2] Our continuing
struggle with *his*tory began with its 'discovery' of us. However, this chapter will
be concerned with herstory rather than *his*tory. We wish to address questions to
the feminist theories which have been developed during the last decade; a decade
in which black women have been fighting, in the streets, in the schools, through
the courts, inside and outside the wage relation. The significance of these struggles
ought to inform the writing of the herstory of women in Britain. It is fundamental
to the development of a feminist theory and practice that is meaningful for black
women. We cannot hope to reconstitute ourselves in all our absences, or to rectify
the ill-conceived presences that invade herstory from *his*tory, but we do wish to
bear witness to our own herstories. The connections between these and the
herstories of white women will be made and remade in struggle. Black women
have come from Africa, Asia and the Caribbean and we cannot do justice to all
their herstories in a single chapter. Neither can we represent the voices of all black
women in Britain, our herstories are too numerous and too varied. What we will

do is to offer ways in which the 'triple' oppression of gender, race and class can be understood, in their specificity, and also as they determine the lives of black women.

Much contemporary debate has posed the question of the relation between race and gender, in terms which attempt to parallel race and gender divisions. It can be argued that as processes, racism and sexism are similar. Ideologically for example, they both construct common sense through reference to 'natural' and 'biological' differences. It has also been argued that the categories of race and gender are both socially constructed and that, therefore, they have little internal coherence as concepts. Furthermore, it is possible to parallel racialized and gendered divisions in the sense that the possibilities of amelioration through legislation appear to be equally ineffectual in both cases. Michèle Barrett, however, has pointed out that it is not possible to argue for parallels because as soon as historical analysis is made, it becomes obvious that the institutions which have to be analysed are different, as are the forms of analysis needed.[3] We would agree that the construction of such parallels is fruitless and often proves to be little more than a mere academic exercise; but there are other reasons for our dismissal of these kinds of debate. The experience of black women does not enter the parameters of parallelism. The fact that black women are subject to the *simultaneous* oppression of patriarchy, class and 'race' is the prime reason for not employing parallels that render their position and experience not only marginal but also invisible.

In arguing that most contemporary feminist theory does not begin to adequately account for the experience of black women we also have to acknowledge that it is not a simple question of their absence, consequently the task is not one of rendering their visibility. On the contrary we will have to argue that the process of accounting for their historical and contemporary position does, in itself, challenge the use of some of the central categories and assumptions of recent main-stream feminist thought. We can point to no single source for our oppression. When white feminists emphasize patriarchy alone, we want to redefine the term and make it a more complex concept. Racism ensures that black men do not have the same relations to patriarchal/capitalist hierarchies as white men.

[. . .] It is only in the writings by black feminists that we can find attempts to theorize the interconnection of class gender and race as it occurs in our lives and it has only been in the autonomous organizations of black women that we have been able to express and act upon the experiences consequent upon these determinants. Many black women had been alienated by the non-recognition of their lives, experiences and herstories in the WLM. Black feminists have been, and are still, demanding that the existence of racism must be acknowledged as a structuring feature of our relationships with white women. Both white feminist theory and practice have to recognize that white women stand in a power relation as oppressors of black women. This compromises any feminist theory and practice founded on the notion of simple equality.

Three concepts which are central to feminist theory become problematic in their application to black women's lives: 'the family', 'patriarchy' and 'reproduction'. When used they are placed in a context of the herstory of white (frequently middle-class) women and become contradictory when applied to the lives and experiences of black women.

[. . .] The use of the concept of 'dependency', is also a problem for black feminists. It has been argued that this concept provides the link between the 'material organisation of the household, and the ideology of femininity'. How then can we account for situations in which black women may be heads of households, or where, because of an economic system which structures high black male unemployment, they are not financially dependent upon a black man? This condition exists in both colonial and metropolitan situations. Ideologies of black female domesticity and motherhood have been constructed, through their employment (or chattel position) as domestics and surrogate mothers to white families rather than in relation to their own families. West Indian women still migrate to the United States and Canada as domestics and in Britain are seen to be suitable as office cleaners, National Health Service domestics, etc. In colonial situations Asian women have frequently been forced into prostitution to sexually service the white male invaders, whether in the form of armies of occupation or employees and guests of multinational corporations. How then, in view of all this, can it be argued that black male dominance exists in the same forms as white male dominance? Systems of slavery, colonialism, imperialism, have systematically denied positions in the white male hierarchy to black men and have used specific forms of terror to oppress them.

Black family structures have been seen as pathological by the state and are in the process of being constructed as pathological within white feminist theory. Here, ironically, the Western nuclear family structure and related ideologies of 'romantic love' formed under capitalism, are seen as more 'progressive' than black family structures.

[. . .] Too often concepts of historical progress are invoked by the left and feminists alike, to create a sliding scale of 'civilized liberties'. When barbarous sexual practices are to be described the 'Third World' is placed on display and compared to the 'First World' which is seen as more 'enlightened' or 'progressive'. The metropolitan centres of the West define the questions to be asked of other social systems and, at the same time, provide the measure against which all 'foreign' practices are gauged. In a peculiar combination of Marxism and feminism, capitalism becomes the vehicle for reforms which allow for progress towards the emancipation of women. The 'Third World', on the other hand, is viewed as retaining pre-capitalist forms expressed at the cultural level by traditions which are more oppressive to women.

[. . .] It can be seen from this brief discussion of the use of the concept 'the family' that the terms 'patriarchy' and 'reproduction' also become more complex in their application. It bears repetition that black men have not held the same patriarchal positions of power that the white males have established. Michèle Barrett argues that the term patriarchy has lost all analytic or explanatory power and has been reduced to a synonym for male dominance. She tries therefore to limit its use to a specific type of male dominance that could be located historically.

> I would not . . . want to argue that the concept of patriarchy should
> be jettisoned. I would favour retaining it for use in contexts where
> male domination is expressed through the power of the father over
> women and over younger men. . . . Hence I would argue for a more

precise and specific use of the concept of patriarchy, rather than one which expands it to cover all expressions of male domination and thereby attempts to construe a descriptive term as a systemic explanatory theory.[4]

Barrett is not thinking of capitalist social organization. But if we try to apply this more 'classic' and limited definition of patriarchy to the slave systems of the Americas and the Caribbean, we find that even this refined use of the concept cannot adequately account for the fact that both slaves and manumitted males did not have this type of patriarchal power. Alternatively, if we take patriarchy and apply it to various colonial situations it is equally unsatisfactory because it is unable to explain why black males have not enjoyed the benefits of white patriarchy. There are very obvious power structures in both colonial and slave social formations and they are predominantly patriarchal. However, the historically specific forms of racism force us to modify or alter the application of the term 'patriarchy' to black men. Black women have been dominated 'patriarchally' in different ways by men of different 'colours'.

In questioning the application of the concepts of 'the family' and 'patriarchy' we also need to problematize the use of the concept of 'reproduction'. In using this concept in relation to the domestic labour of black women we find that in spite of its apparent simplicity it must be dismantled. What does the concept of reproduction mean in a situation where black women have done domestic labour outside of their own homes in the servicing of white families? In this example they lie outside of the industrial wage relation but in a situation where they are providing for the reproduction of black labour in their own domestic sphere, simultaneously ensuring the reproduction of white labour power in the 'white' household. The concept, in fact, is unable to explain exactly what the relations are that need to be revealed. What needs to be understood is, first, precisely *how* the black woman's role in a rural, industrial or domestic labour force affects the construction of ideologies of black female sexuality which are different from, and often constructed in opposition to, white female sexuality; and second, how this role relates to the black woman's struggle for control over her own sexuality.

If we examine the recent herstory of women in post-war Britain we can see the ways in which the inclusion of black women creates problems for hasty generalization. In pointing to the contradiction between 'home-making as a career' and the campaign to recruit women into the labour force during post-war reconstruction, Elizabeth Wilson fails to perceive migration of black women to Britain as the solution to these contradictory needs. The Economic Survey for 1947 is cited as an example of the ways in which women were seen to form 'the only large reserve of labour left', yet, as we know, there was a rather large pool of labour in the colonies that had been mobilized previously to fight in World War II. The industries that the survey listed as in dire need of labour included those that were filled by both male and female black workers, though Elizabeth Wilson does not differentiate them.

> The survey gave a list of the industries and services where labour was most urgently required. The boot and shoe industry, clothing, textiles,

> iron and steel, all require female workers, as did hospitals, domestic
> service, transport, and the women's land army. There was also a shortage
> of shorthand typists, and a dire shortage of nurses and midwives.[5]

This tells us nothing about why black women were recruited more heavily into
some of these areas than others; perhaps we are given a clue when the author goes
on to point out that women were welcomed into the labour force in a 'circumscribed
way'.

> as temporary workers at a period of crisis, as part-time workers, and
> as not disturbing the traditional division of labour in industry along sex
> lines – the Survey reflected the view which was still dominant, that
> married women would not naturally wish to work.[6]

Not all black women were subject to this process: Afro-Caribbean women, for
example, were encouraged and chose to come to Britain precisely to work.
Ideologically they were seen as 'naturally' suitable for the lowest paid, most menial
jobs. Elizabeth Wilson goes on to explain that 'work and marriage were still
understood as alternatives . . . two kinds of women . . . a wife and a mother or
a single career woman'. Yet black women bridged this division. They were viewed
simultaneously as workers and as wives and mothers. Elizabeth Wilson stresses
that the post-war debate over the entry of women into the labour force occurred
within the parameters of the question of possible effects on family life. She argues
that 'wives and mothers were granted entry into paid work only so long as this
did not harm the family'. Yet women from Britain's reserve army of labour in the
colonies were recruited into the labour force far beyond any such considerations.
Rather than a concern to protect or preserve the black family in Britain, the state
reproduced common-sense notions of its inherent pathology: black women were
seen to fail as mothers precisely because of their position as workers.

One important struggle, rooted in these different ideological mechanisms,
which determine racially differentiated representations of gender, has been the
black woman's battle to gain control over her own sexuality in the face of racist
experimentation with the contraceptive Depo-Provera and enforced sterilizations.[7]

It is not just our herstory before we came to Britain that has been ignored by
white feminists, our experiences and struggles here have also been ignored. These
struggles and experiences, because they have been structured by racism, have been
different to those of white women. Black feminists decry the non-recognition of
the specificities of black women's sexuality and femininity, both in the ways these
are constructed and also as they are addressed through practices which oppress
black women in a gender-specific but nonetheless racist way.

This non-recognition is typified by a very interesting article on women in Third
World manufacturing by Diane Elson and Ruth Pearson. In analysing the employment
of Third World women in world market factories they quote from an investment
brochure designed to attract foreign firms:

> The manual dexterity of the oriental female is famous the world over.
> Her hands are small and she works fast with extreme care. Who,

therefore, could be better qualified by *nature and inheritance* to contribute to the efficiency of a bench-assembly production line than the oriental girl?[8] (original emphasis)

The authors, however, analyse only the naturalization of gender and ignore the specificity signalled by the inclusion of the adjective 'oriental', as if it didn't matter. The fact that the sexuality of the 'oriental' woman is being differentiated, is not commented upon and remains implicit rather than explicit as in the following remarks.

It is in the context of the subordination of women as a gender that we must analyse the supposed docility, subservience and consequent suitability for tedious, monotonous work of young women in the Third World.[9]

In concentrating an analysis upon gender only, Elson and Pearson do not see the relation between the situation they are examining in the periphery and the women who have migrated to the metropole. This last description is part of the common-sense racism that we have described as being applied to Asian women in Britain to channel them into 'tedious, monotonous work'. Elson and Pearson discuss this ascription of docility and passivity and compare it to Frantz Fanon's analysis of colonized people, without putting together the ways in which the women who are their objects of study have been oppressed not by gender subordination alone but also by colonization. The 'oriental' sexuality referred to in the advertising brochure is one of many constructions of exotic sexual dexterity promised to Western male tourists to South East Asia. This ideology of 'Eastern promise' links the material practice of the move from the bench – making microchips – to the bed, in which multinational corporate executives are serviced by prostitutes. This transition is described by Elson and Pearson but not understood as a process which illustrates an example of racially demarcated patriarchal power.

If a woman loses her job in a world market factory after she has re-shaped her life on the basis of a wage income, the only way she may have of surviving is by selling her body. There are reports from South Korea, for instance, that many former electronics workers have no alternative but to become prostitutes. . . . A growing market for such services is provided by the way in which the tourist industry has developed, especially in South East Asia.[10]

The photographs accompanying the article are of anonymous black women. This anonymity and the tendency to generalize into meaninglessness, the oppression of an amorphous category called 'Third World women', are symptomatic of the ways in which the specificity of our experiences and oppression are subsumed under inapplicable concepts and theories. Black feminists in the US have complained of the ignorance, in the white women's movement, of black women's lives.

The force that allows white feminist authors to make no reference to racial identity in their books about 'women' that are in actuality about white women, is the same one that would compel any author writing exclusively on black women to refer explicitly to their racial identity. That force is racism. . . . It is the dominant race that can make it seem that their experience is representative.[11]

In Britain too it is as if we don't exist.

There is a growing body of black feminist criticism of white feminist theory and practice, for its incipient racism and lack of relevance to black women's lives.[12] The dialogues that have been attempted[13] have concentrated more upon visible, empirical differences that affect black and white women's lives than upon developing a feminist theoretical approach that would enable a feminist understanding of the basis of these differences. The accusation that racism in the women's movement acted so as to exclude the participation of black women, has led to an explosion of debate in the USA.

> from a black female perspective, if white women are denying the existence of black women, writing 'feminist' scholarship as if black women are not a part of the collective group American women, or discriminating against black women, then it matters less that North America was colonised by white patriarchal *men* who institutionalised a racially imperialist social order, than that white women who purport to be feminists support and actively perpetuate anti-black racism.[14]

What little reaction there has been in Britain has been more akin to lighting a damp squib, than an explosion. US black feminist criticism has no more been listened to than indigenous black feminist criticism. Yet, bell hooks's powerful critique has considerable relevance to British feminists. White women in the British WLM are extraordinarily reluctant to see themselves in the situations of being oppressors, as they feel that this will be at the expense of concentrating upon being oppressed. Consequently the involvement of British women in imperialism and colonialism is repressed and the benefits that they – as whites – gained from the oppression of black people ignored. Forms of imperialism are simply identified as aspects of an all embracing patriarchy rather than as sets of social relations in which white women hold positions of power by virtue of their 'race'.

> Had feminists chosen to make explicit comparisons between . . . the status of black women and white women, it would have been more than obvious that the two groups do not share an identical oppression. It would have been obvious that similarities between the status of women under patriarchy and that of any slave or colonized person do not necessarily exist in a society that is both racially and sexually imperialistic. In such a society, the woman who is seen as inferior because of her sex can also be seen as superior because of her race, even in relationship to men of another race.[15]

The benefits of a white skin did not just apply to a handful of cotton, tea or sugar plantation mistresses; all women in Britain benefited – in varying degrees – from the economic exploitation of the colonies. The pro-imperialist attitudes of many nineteenth- and early-twentieth-century feminists and suffragists have yet to be acknowledged for their racist implications. However, apart from this herstorical work, the exploration of contemporary racism within the white feminist movement in Britain has yet to begin.

Feminist theory in Britain is almost wholly Eurocentric and, when it is not ignoring the experience of black women 'at home', it is trundling 'Third World women' onto the stage only to perform as victims of 'barbarous', 'primitive' practices in 'barbarous', 'primitive' societies.

It should be noted that much feminist work suffers from the assumption that it is only through the development of a Western-style industrial capitalism and the resultant entry of women into waged labour that the potential for the liberation of women can increase. For example, foot-binding, clitoridectomy, female 'circumcision' and other forms of mutilation of the female body have been described as 'feudal residues', existing in economically 'backward' or 'underdeveloped' nations (i.e. not the industrialized West). Arranged marriages, polygamy and these forms of mutilation are linked in reductionist ways to a lack of technological development. [. . .]

Constructing alternatives

It should be an imperative for feminist herstory and theory to avoid reproducing the structural inequalities that exist between the 'metropoles' and the 'peripheries', and within the 'metropoles' between black and white women, in the form of inappropriate polarizations between the 'First' and 'Third World', developed/underdeveloped or advanced/backward. We have already argued that the generalizations made about women's lives across societies in the African and Asian continents, would be thought intolerable if applied to the lives of white women in Europe or North America. These are some of the reasons why concepts which allow for specificity, whilst at the same time providing cross-cultural reference points – not based in assumptions of inferiority – are urgently needed in feminist work. The work of Gayle Rubin and her use of discrete 'sex/gender systems' appears to provide such a potential, particularly in the possibility of applying the concept within as well as between societies. With regard to the problems with the concept of patriarchy discussed above, she has made the following assessment:

> The term 'patriarchy' was introduced to distinguish the forces maintaining sexism from other social forces, such as capitalism. But the use of 'patriarchy' obscures other distinctions.[16]

In arguing for an alternative formulation Gayle Rubin stresses the importance of maintaining, a distinction between the human capacity and necessity to create a sexual world, and the empirically oppressive ways in which sexual worlds have been organized. Patriarchy subsumes both meanings into the same term. Sex/gender system, on the other hand, is a neutral term which refers to the domain and indicates that oppression is not inevitable in that domain, but is the product of the specific social relations which organize it.[17]

This concept of sex/gender systems offers the opportunity to be historically and culturally specific but also points to the position of relative autonomy of the sexual realm. It enables the subordination of women to be seen as a 'product of the relationships by which sex and gender are organized and produced'.[18] Thus, in order to account for the development of specific forms of sex/gender systems, reference must be made not only to the mode of production but also to the complex totality of specific social formations within which each system develops. Gayle Rubin argues that kinship relations are visible, empirical forms of sex/gender systems. Kinship relations here is not limited to biological relatives but is rather a 'system of categories and statuses which often contradict actual genetic relationships'.

What are commonly referred to as 'arranged marriages' can, then, be viewed as the way in which a particular sex/gender system organizes the 'exchange of women'. Similarly, transformations of sex/gender systems brought about by colonial oppression, and the changes in kinship patterns which result from migration, must be assessed on their own terms, not just in comparative relation to other sex/gender systems. In this way patterns of subordination of women can be understood historically, rather than being dismissed as the inevitable product of pathological family structures.

[. . .] We need to counteract the tendency to reduce sex oppression to a mere 'reflex of 'economic forces'[19] whilst at the same time recognizing that:

> sexual systems cannot, in the final analysis, be understood in complete isolation. A full-bodied analysis of women in a single society, or through out history, must take everything into account: the evolution of commodity forms in women, systems of land tenure, political arrangements, subsistence technology, etc.[20]

We can begin to see how these elements come together to affect the lives of black women under colonial oppression in ways that transform the sex/gender systems which they live but that are also shaped by the sex/gender system of the colonizers. If we examine changes in land distribution we can see how capitalist notions of the private ownership of land (a primarily economic division) and ideas of male dominance (from the sex/gender system) work together against the colonized.

> Another problem affecting women's agricultural work is that as land ownership shifts from the collective 'land-use rights' of traditional village life, in which women shared in the distribution of land, to the European concept of private ownership, it is usually only the men who

have the necessary cash to pay for it (by virtue of their cash-cropping income). In addition, some men traditionally 'owned' the land, while women 'owned' the crops as in the Cameroons in West Africa. As land becomes increasingly scarce, men begin to rent and sell 'their' land, leaving women with no recourse but to pay for land or stop their agricultural work.[21]

It is impossible to argue that colonialism left pre-capitalist or feudal forms of organization untouched. If we look at the West Indies we can see that patterns of migration, for both men and women, have followed the dictates of capital.

When men migrated from the islands for work in plantations or building the Panama canal, women migrated from rural to urban areas. Both have migrated to labour in the 'core' capitalist nations. Domestic, marginal or temporary service work has sometimes been viewed as a great 'opportunity' for West Indian women to transform their lives. But as Shirley-Ann Hussein has shown,

> Take the case of the domestic workers. A development institution should be involved in more than placing these women in domestic jobs as this makes no dent in the society. It merely rearranges the same order. Domestic labour will have to be done away with in any serious attempt at social and economic reorganisation.[22]

If, however, imperialism and colonialism have ensured the existence of a world market it still remains necessary to explain how it is in the interests of capitalism to maintain social relations of production that are non-capitalist – that is, forms that could not be described as feudal because that means pre-capitalist, but which are also not organized around the wage relation. If we return to the example of changes in ownership of land and in agricultural production, outlined above, it can be argued that:

> the agricultural division of labor in the periphery – with male semi-proletarians and female agriculturalists – contributes to the maintenance of a low value of labor power for peripheral capital accumulation through the production of subsistence foodstuffs by the noncapitalist mode of production for the reproduction and maintenance of the labor force.[23]

In other words the work that the women do is a force which helps to keep wages low. To relegate 'women of colour' in the periphery to the position of being the victims of feudal relations is to aid in the masking of colonial relations of oppression. These relations of imperialism should not be denied. Truly feminist herstory should be able to acknowledge that:

> Women's economic participation in the periphery of the world capitalist system, just as within center economies, has been conditioned by the requirements of capital accumulation . . . (but) the economic participation of women in the Third World differs significantly from women's economic participation within the center of the world capitalist system.[24]

Black women have been at the forefront of rebellions against land seizures and struggle over the rights of access to land in Africa, Latin America and the Caribbean. Adequate herstories of their roles in many of these uprisings remain to be written. The role of West Indian women in the rebellions preceding and during the disturbances in Jamaica in 1938, for example, though known to be significant has still not been thoroughly described. White feminist herstorians are therefore mistaken when they portray black women as passive recipients of colonial oppression. As Gail Omvedt has shown in her book *We Will Smash This Prison*,[25] women in India have a long and complex herstory of fighting oppression both in and out of the wage relation. It is clear that many women coming from India to Britain have a shared herstory of struggle, whether in rural areas as agricultural labourers or in urban districts as municipal employees. The organized struggles of Asian women in Britain need to be viewed in the light of this herstory. Their industrial battles, and struggles against immigration policy and practice, articulate the triple oppression of race, gender and class that have been present since the dawn of imperialist domination.

In concentrating solely upon the isolated position of white women in the Western nuclear family structure, feminist theory has necessarily neglected the very strong female support networks that exist in many black sex/gender systems. These have often been transformed by the march of technological 'progress' intended to relieve black women from aspects of their labour.

> Throughout Africa, the digging of village wells has saved women enormous amounts of time which they formerly spent trekking long distances to obtain water. But it has often simultaneously destroyed their only chance to get together and share information and experiences. Technological advances such as household appliances do not free women from domestic drudgery in any society.[26]

Leghorn and Parker, in *Women's Worth*, attempt to create new categories to describe, in general terms, the diversity of male power across societies. Whilst they warn against the rigid application of these categories – few countries fit exactly the category applied to them – the work does represent an attempt to move away from Euro-American racist assumptions of superiority whether political, cultural or economic. The three classifications that they introduce are 'minimal', 'token' and 'negotiating power' societies. Interestingly, from the black women's point of view, the most salient factor in the categorization of a country has

> usually been that of women's networks, because it is the existence, building or dissolution of these networks that determines women's status and potential for change in all areas of their lives.[27]

These categories cut through the usual divisions of First/Third World, advanced/ dependent, industrial/non-industrial in an attempt to find a mechanism that would 'free' thinking from these definitions. Space will not allow for a critical assessment of all three categories but it can be said that their application of 'negotiating power' does recognize as important the 'traditional' women's organizations to be found in West Africa, and described [. . .] in relation to the Igbo. Leghorn and Parker are careful to stress that 'negotiating power' is limited to the possibilities of negotiating, it is not an absolute category of power that is held *over* men by women. The two examples of societies given in their book, where women hold this negotiating position are the Ewe, in West Africa, and the Iroquois. Both of course, are also examples where contact with the whites has been for the worse. Many of the Ewe female institutions disintegrated under colonialism whilst the institutions that afforded Iroquois women power were destroyed by European intrusion. In contrast to feminist work that focuses upon the lack of technology and household mechanical aids in the lives of these women, Leghorn and Parker concentrate upon the aspects of labour that bring women together. Of the Ewe they note:

> Women often work together in their own fields, or as family members preparing meals together, village women meeting at the stream to do the wash, or family, friends and neighbours, walking five to fifteen miles a day to market together, sitting near each other in the market, and setting the day's prices together. They share childcare, news, and looking after each other's market stalls. In addition to making the time more pleasant, this shared work enables women to share information and in fact serves as an integral and vital part of the village communications system. Consequently, they have a tremendous sense of solidarity when it comes to working in their collective interest.[28]

It is important not to romanticize the existence of such female support networks but they do provide a startling contrast to the isolated position of women in the Euro-American nuclear family structure.

In Britain, strong female support networks continue in both West Indian and Asian sex/gender systems, though these are ignored by sociological studies of migrant black women. This is not to say that these systems remain unchanged with migration. New circumstances require adaptation and new survival strategies have to be found.

> Even childcare in a metropolitan area is a big problem. If you live in a village in an extended family, you know that if your child's outside somewhere, someone will be looking out for her. If your child is out on the street and your neighbour down the road sees your child in some mess, that woman is going to take responsibility of dealing with that child. But in Brooklyn or in London, you're stuck in that apartment. You're there with that kid, you can't expect that child to be out on the street and be taken care of. You know the day care situation is lousy, you're not in that extended family, so you have a big problem on your hands. So when they talk about the reduction of house-work, we know by now that that's a lie.[29]

However, the transformations that occur are not merely adaptive, neither is the black family destroyed in the process of change. Female networks mean that black women are key figures in the development of survival strategies, both in the past, through periods of slavery and colonialism, and now, facing a racist and authoritarian state.

> There is considerable evidence that women – and families – do not . . .
> simply accept the isolation, loss of status, and cultural devaluation
> involved in the migration. Networks are re-formed, if need be with
> non-kin or on the basis of an extended definition of kinship, by strong,
> active, and resourceful women. . . . Cultures of resistance are not simple
> adaptive mechanisms; they embody important alternative ways of organ-
> izing production and reproduction and value systems critical of the
> oppressor. Recognition of the special position of families in these cultures
> and social structures can lead to new forms of struggle, new goals.[30]

In arguing that feminism must take account of the lives, herstories and experiences of black women we are not advocating that teams of white feminists should descend upon Brixton, Southall, Bristol or Liverpool to take black women as objects of study in modes of resistance. We don't need that kind of intrusion on top of all the other information-gathering forces that the state has mobilized in the interest of 'race relations'. White women have been used against black women in this way before and feminists must learn from history. After the Igbo riots [. . .], two women anthropologists were sent by the British to 'study the causes of the riot and to uncover the organisational base that permitted such spontaneity and solidarity among the women'.[31] The WLM, however, does need to listen to the work of black feminists and to take account of autonomous organizations like OWAAD (Organisation of Women of Asian and African Descent) who are helping to articulate the ways in which we are oppressed as black women.

In addition to this it is very important that white women in the women's movement examine the ways in which racism excludes many black women and prevents them from unconditionally aligning themselves with white women. Instead of taking black women as the objects of their research, white feminist researchers should try to uncover the gender-specific mechanisms of racism amongst white women. This more than any other factor disrupts the recognition of common interests of sisterhood.

In *Finding a Voice* by Amrit Wilson, Asian women describe many instances of racial oppression at work from white women. Asian women

> are paid low salaries and everything is worse for them, they have to
> face the insults of supervisors. These supervisors are all English women.
> The trouble is that in Britain our women are expected to behave like
> servants and we are not used to behaving like servants and we can't.
> But if we behave normally . . . the supervisors start shouting and
> harassing us. . . . They complain about us Indians to the manager.[32]

Black women do not want to be grafted onto 'feminism' in a tokenistic manner as colourful diversions to 'real' problems. Feminism has to be transformed if it is to address us. Neither do we wish our words to be misused in generalities as if what each one of us utters represents the total experience of all black women. Audre Lourde's address to Mary Daly is perhaps the best conclusion.

I ask that you be aware of how this serves the destructive forces of racism and separation between women – the assumption that the herstory and myth of white women is the legitimate and sole herstory and myth of all women to call for power and background, and that non-white women and our herstories are note-worthy only as decorations, or examples of female victimisation. I ask that you be aware of the effect that this dismissal has upon the community of black women, and how it devalues your own words. . . . When patriarchy dismisses us, it encourages our murders. When radical lesbian feminist theory dismisses us, it encourages its own demise. This dismissal stands as a real block to communication between us. This block makes it far easier to turn away from you completely than attempt to understand the thinking behind your choices. Should the next step be war between us, or separation? Assimilation within a sole Western-European herstory is not acceptable.[33]

In other words, of white feminists we must ask, what exactly do you mean when you say 'WE'??

Notes and references

1 Gayle Jones, *Corregidora* (Random House 1975), pp. 14, 72.
2 Winthrop Jordan, *White Over Black* (Penguin 1969), pp. 238, 495, 500.
3 My thanks to Michèle Barrett who, in a talk given at the Social Science Research Council's Research Unit on Ethnic Relations, helped to clarify many of these attempted parallels.
4 Michèle Barrett, *Women's Oppression Today* (Verso 1980).
5 Elizabeth Wilson, *Only Halfway to Paradise: Women in Postwar Britain 1945–1968* (Tavistock 1980), pp. 43–4.
6 ibid.
7 OWAAD, *Forward*, no. 2 (1979).
8 Diane Elson and Ruth Pearson, 'Nimble fingers make cheap workers: an analysis of women's employment in Third World export manufacturing', *Feminist Review*, no. 7 (Spring 1981), p. 93.
9 ibid., p. 95.
10 ibid.
11 bell hooks, *Ain't I a Woman* (South End Press 1981), p. 138.
12 Much of this critical work has been written in America but is applicable to the WLM in Britain. Apart from the books cited in this chapter, interested readers should look out for essays and articles by Gloria Joseph, Audre Lorde, Barbara Smith and Gloria Watkins that represent a range of black feminist thought. In Britain, the very existence of the feminist Organisation of Women of Asian and African Descent (OWAAD) is a concrete expression of black feminists critical distance from 'white' feminism. See also: Valerie Amos and Pratibha Parmar, 'Resistances and responses: black girls in Britain', in A. McRobbie and T. McCabe (eds), *Feminism For Girls: An Adventure Story* (Routledge and Kegan Paul 1982), who criticize the WLM for its irrelevance to the lives of black girls in Britain.

13   See: Gloria Joseph and Jill Lewis, *Common Differences: Conflicts in Black and White Feminist Perspectives* (Anchor 1981), for an attempt at a dialogue that shows just how difficult it is to maintain.

14   bell hooks, *Ain't I a Woman* (South End Press 1981), pp. 123–4.

15   ibid., p. 141

16   Gayle Rubin, 'The traffic in women: notes on the political economy of sex', in R. Reiter (ed.) *Toward an Anthropology of Women* (Monthly Review Press 1975), p. 167.

17   ibid., p. 168.

18   ibid., p. 177.

19   Gayle Rubin, 'The traffic in women: notes on the political economy of sex', in R. Reiter (ed.) *Toward an Anthropology of Women* (Monthly Review Press 1975), p. 203.

20   ibid., p. 209.

21   Lisa Leghorn and Katherine Parker, *Women's Worth, Sexual Economics and the World of Women* (Routledge and Kegan Paul 1981), p. 45.

22   Shirley-Ann Hussein, 'Four views on women in the struggle', in *Caribbean Women in the Struggle*, p. 29; quoted in Leghorn and Parker, p. 52.

23   Carmen Diane Deere, 'Rural women's subsistence production', in Robin Cohen *et al.* (eds), *Peasants and Proletarians: The Struggles of Third World Women Workers* (Monthly Review 1979), p. 143.

24   ibid., p. 133.

25   Gail Omvedt, *We Will Smash this Prison* (Zed Press 1980).

26   Lisa Leghorn and Katherine Parker, *Women's Worth, Sexual Economics and the World of Women* (Routledge and Kegan Paul 1981), p. 55.

27   ibid., p. 60.

28   ibid., p. 88.

29   Margaret Prescod-Roberts and Norma Steele, *Black Women: Bringing it all Back Home* (Falling Wall Press 1980), p. 28.

30   Mina Davis Caufield, 'Cultures of resistance', in *Socialist Revolution,* 20, vol. 4, no. 2, October 1974, pp. 81, 84.

31   Leis, 'Women in groups', quoted in Mina Davis Caufield, ibid.

32   Amrit Wilson, *Finding a Voice: Asian Women in Britain* (Virago 1978), p. 122.

33   Audre Lorde, 'An open letter of Mary Daly', in Moraga and Anzaldúa (eds), *This Bridge Called My Back: Writings by Radical Women of Color* (Persephone Press 1981), p. 96.

Chapter 28

Patricia Hill Collins

BLACK FEMINIST THOUGHT

WIDELY USED YET RARELY DEFINED, Black feminist thought encompasses diverse and contradictory meanings. Two interrelated tensions highlight issues in defining Black feminist thought. The first concerns the thorny question of who can be a Black feminist. One current response, explicit in Patricia Bell Scott's (1982b) "Selected Bibliography on Black Feminism," classifies all African-American women, regardless of the content of our ideas, as Black feminists. From this perspective, living as Black women provides experiences to stimulate a Black feminist consciousness. Yet indiscriminately labeling all Black women in this way simultaneously conflates the terms *woman* and *feminist* and identifies being of African descent – a questionable biological category – as being the sole determinant of a Black feminist consciousness. As Cheryl Clarke points out, "I criticized Scott. Some of the women she cited as 'black feminist' were clearly not feminist at the time they wrote their books and still are not to this day" (1983, 94).

The term *Black feminist* has also been used to apply to selected African-Americans – primarily women – who possess some version of a feminist consciousness. Beverly Guy-Sheftall (1986) contends that both men and women can be "Black feminists" and names Frederick Douglass and William E. B. DuBois as prominent examples of Black male feminists. Guy-Sheftall also identifies some distinguishing features of Black feminist ideas: namely, that Black women's experiences with both racial and gender oppression result in needs and problems distinct from white women and Black men, and that Black women must struggle for equality both as women and as African-Americans. Guy-Sheftall's definition is helpful in that its use of ideological criteria fosters a definition of Black feminist thought that encompasses both experiences and ideas. In other words, she suggests that experiences gained from living as African-American women stimulate a Black feminist sensibility. But her definition is simultaneously troublesome because it makes the biological category of Blackness the prerequisite for possessing such thought. Furthermore, it does not explain why these particular ideological criteria and not others are the distinguishing ones.

The term Black feminist has also been used to describe selected African–American women who possess some version of a feminist consciousness (Beale 1970; hooks 1981; Barbara Smith 1983; White 1984). This usage of the term yields the most restrictive notion of who can be a Black feminist. The ground-breaking Combahee River Collective (1982) document, "A Black Feminist Statement," implicity relies on this definition. The Collective claims that "as Black women we find any type of biological determinism a particularly dangerous and reactionary basis upon which to build a politic" (p.17). But in spite of this statement, by implying that only African-American women can be Black feminists, they require a biological prerequisite for race and gender consciousness. The Collective also offers its own ideological criteria for identifying Black feminist ideas. In contrast to Beverly Guy-Sheftall, the Collective places a stronger emphasis on capitalism as a source of Black women's oppression and on political activism as a distinguishing feature of Black feminism.

Biologically deterministic criteria for the term *black* and the accompanying assumption that being of African descent somehow produces a certain consciousness or perspective are inherent in these definitions. By presenting race as being fixed and immutable – something rooted in nature – these approaches mask the historical construction of racial categories, the shifting meaning of race, and the crucial role of politics and ideology in shaping conceptions of race (Gould 1981: Omi and Winant 1986). In contrast, much greater variation is afforded the term feminist. Feminists are seen as ranging from biologically determined – as is the case in radical feminist thought, which argues that only women can be feminist – to notions of feminists as individuals who have undergone some type of political transformation theoretically achievable by anyone.

Though the term Black feminist could also be used to describe any individual who embraces Black feminist ideas, the separation of biology from ideology required for this usage is rarely seen in the works of Black women intellectuals. Sometimes the contradictions among these competing definitions can be so great that Black women writers use all simultaneously. Consider the following passage from Deborah McDowell's essay "New Directions for Black Feminist Criticism":

> I use the term here simply to refer to Black female critics who analyze the works of Black female writers from a feminist political perspective. But the term can also apply to any criticism written by a Black woman regardless of her subject or perspective – a book written by a male from a feminist or political perspective, a book written by a Black woman or about Black women authors in general, or any writings by women.
>
> (1985, 191)

While McDowell implies that elite white men could be "black feminists," she is clearly unwilling to state so categorically. From McDowell's perspective, whites and Black men who embrace a specific political perspective, and Black women regardless of political perspective, could all potentially be deemed Black feminist critics.

The ambiguity surrounding current perspectives on who can be a Black feminist is directly tied to a second definitional tension in Black feminist thought: the question of what constitutes Black feminism. The range of assumptions concerning the relationship between ideas and their advocates as illustrated in the works of Patricia Bell Scott, Beverly Guy-Sheftall, the Combahee River Collective, and Deborah McDowell leads to problems in defining Black feminist theory itself. Once a person is labeled a "Black feminist," then ideas forwarded by that individual often become defined as Black feminist thought. This practice accounts for neither changes in the thinking of an individual nor differences among Black feminist theorists.

A definition of Black feminist thought is needed that avoids the materialist position that being Black and/or female generates certain experiences that automatically determine variants of a Black and/or feminist consciousness. Claims that Black feminist thought is the exclusive province of African-American women, regardless of the experiences and worldview of such women, typify this position. But a definition of Black feminist thought must also avoid the idealist position that ideas can be evaluated in isolation from the groups that create them. Definitions claiming that anyone can produce and develop Black feminist thought risk obscuring the special angle of vision that Black women bring to the knowledge production process.

The dimensions of a black women's standpoint

Developing adequate definitions of Black feminist thought involves facing this complex nexus of relationships among biological classification, the social construction of race and gender as categories of analysis, the material conditions accompanying these changing social constructions, and Black women's consciousness about these themes. One way of addressing the definitional tensions in Black feminist thought is to specify the relationship between a Black women's standpoint – those experiences and ideas shared by African-American women that provide a unique angle of vision on self, community, and society – and theories that interpret these experiences.[1] I suggest that Black feminist thought consists of specialized knowledge created by African-American women which clarifies a standpoint of and for Black women. In other words, Black feminist thought encompasses theoretical interpretations of Black women's reality by those who live it.

This definition does not mean that all African-American women generate such thought or that other groups do not play a critical role in its production. Before exploring the contours and implications of this working definition, understanding five key dimension of a Black women's standpoint is essential.

The core themes of a black women's standpoint

All African-American women share the common experience of being Black women in a society that denigrates women of African descent. This commonality of experience suggests that certain characteristic themes will be prominent in a Black women's standpoint. For example, one core theme is a legacy of struggle. Katie Cannon observes, "throughout the history of the United States, the interrelationship of white supremacy and male superiority, has characterized the Black woman's reality as a situation of struggle – a struggle to survive in two contradictory worlds simultaneously, one white, privileged, and oppressive, the other black, exploited, and oppressed" (1985, 30). Black women's vulnerability to assaults in the workplace, on the street, and at home has stimulated Black women's independence and self-reliance.

In spite of differences created by historical era, age, social class, sexual orientation, or ethnicity, the legacy of struggle against racism and sexism is a common thread binding African-American women. Anna Julia Cooper, a nineteenth-century Black woman intellectual, describes Black women's vulnerability to sexual violence:

> I would beg . . . to add my plea for the *Colored Girls* of the South – that large, bright, promising fatally beautiful class . . . so full of promise and possibilities, yet so sure of destruction; often without a father to whom they dare apply the loving term, often without a stronger brother to espouse their cause and defend their honor with his life's blood; in the midst of pitfalls and snares, waylaid by the lower classes of white men, with no shelter, no protection.
>
> (Cooper 1892, 240)

Yet during this period Black women struggled and built a powerful club movement and numerous community organizations (Giddings 1984, 1988; Gilkes 1985).

Age offers little protection from this legacy of struggle. Far too many young Black girls inhabit hazardous and hostile environments. In 1975 I received an essay entitled "My World" from Sandra, a sixth-grade student who was a resident of one of the most dangerous public housing projects in Boston. Sandra wrote, "My world is full of people getting rape. People shooting one another. Kids and grownups fighting over girlsfriends. And people without jobs who can't afford to get a education so they can get a job . . . winos on the streets raping and killing little girls." Her words poignantly express a growing Black feminist sensibility that she may be victimized by racism and poverty. They also reveal her awareness that she is vulnerable to rape as a gender-specific form of sexual violence. In spite of her feelings about her community, Sandra not only walked the streets daily but managed safely to deliver three younger siblings to school. In doing so she participated in a Black women's legacy of struggle.

This legacy of struggle constitutes one of several core themes of a Black women's standpoint. Efforts to reclaim the Black feminist intellectual tradition are revealing Black women's longstanding attention to a series of core themes first recorded by Maria W. Stewart (Richardson 1987). Stewart's treatment of the interlocking nature of race, gender, and class oppression, her call for replacing denigrated images of Black womanhood with self-defined images, her belief in Black women's activism as mothers, teachers, and Black community leaders, and her sensitivity to sexual politics are all core themes advanced by a variety of Black feminist intellectuals.

Variation of responses to core themes

The existence of core themes does not mean that African-American women respond to these themes in the same way. Diversity among Black women produces different concrete experiences that in turn shape various reactions to the core themes. For example, when faced with stereotypical controlling images of Black women, some women – such as Sojourner Truth – demand, "ain't I a woman?" By deconstructing the conceptual apparatus of the dominant group, they invoke a Black women's legacy of struggle. In contrast, other women internalize the controlling images and come to believe that they are the stereotypes (Brown-Collins and Sussewell 1986).

A variety of factors explain the diversity of responses. For example although all African-American women encounter racism, social class differences among African-American women influence how racism is experienced. A young manager who graduated with honors from the University of Maryland describes the specific form racism can take for middle-class Blacks. Before flying to Cleveland to explain a marketing plan for her company, her manager made her go over it three or four times in front of him so that she would not forget *her* marketing plan. Then he explained how to check luggage at an airport and how to reclaim it. "I just sat at lunch listening to this man talking to me like I was a monkey who could remember but couldn't think," the Black female manager recalled. When she had had enough, she responded, "I asked him if he wanted to tie my money up in a handkerchief and put a note on me saying that I was an employee of this company. In case I got lost I would be picked up by Traveler's Aid, and Traveler's Aid would send me back" (Davis and Watson 1985, 86). Most middle-class Black women do not encounter such blatant incidents, but many working-class Blacks do. For both groups the racist belief that African-Americans are less intelligent than whites remains strong.

Sexual orientation provides another key factor. Black lesbians have identified homophobia in general and the issues they face living as Black lesbians in homophobic communities as being a major influence on their angle of vision on everyday events (Shockley 1974; Lorde 1982, 1984; Clarke et al. 1983; Barbara Smith 1983). Beverly Smith describes how being a lesbian affected her perceptions of the wedding of one of her closest friends: "God, I wish I had one friend here. Someone who knew me and would understand how I, feel. I am masquerading as a nice, straight, middle-class Black 'girl'" (1983, 172). While the majority of those attending the wedding saw only a festive event, Beverly Smith felt that her friend was being sent into a form of bondage.

Other factors such as ethnicity, region of the country, urbanization, and age combine to produce a web of experiences shaping diversity among African-American women. As a result, it is more accurate to discuss a Black *women's* standpoint than a Black *woman's* standpoint.

The interdependence of experience and consciousness

Black women's work and family experiences and grounding in traditional African-American culture suggest that African-American women as a group experience a world different from that of those who are not Black and female. Moreover, these concrete experiences can stimulate a distinctive Black feminist consciousness concerning that material reality.[2] Being Black and female may expose African-American women to certain common experiences, which in turn may predispose us to a distinctive group consciousness, but it in no way guarantees that such a consciousness will develop among all women or that it will be articulated as such by the group.

Many African-American women have grasped this connection between what one does and how one thinks. Hannah Nelson, an elderly Black domestic worker, discusses how work shapes the perspectives of African-American and white women: "Since I have to work, I don't really have to worry about most of the things that most of the white women I have worked for are worrying about. And if these women did their own work, they would think just like I do – about this, anyway" (Gwaltney 1980, 4). Ruth Shays, a Black inner-city resident, points out how variations in men's and women's experiences lead to differences in perspective. "The mind of the man and the mind of the woman is the same" she notes "'but this business of living makes women use their minds in ways that men don' even have to think about" (Gwaltney 1980, 33).

This connection between experience and consciousness that shapes the everyday lives of all African-American women pervades the works of Black women activists and scholars. In her autobiography, Ida B. Wells describes how the lynching of her friends had such an impact on her worldview that she subsequently devoted much of her life to the antilynching cause (Duster 1970). Sociologist Joyce Ladner's (1972) *Tomorrow's Tomorrow,* a ground-breaking study of Black female adolescence, emerged from her discomfort with the disparity between the teachings of mainstream scholarship and her experiences as a young Black woman in the South. Similarly, the transformed consciousness experienced by Janie, the light-skinned heroine of Zora Neale Hurston's (1937) classic *Their Eyes Were Watching God,* from obedient granddaughter and wife to a self-defined African-American woman, can be directly traced to her experiences with each of her three husbands. In one scene Janie's second husband, angry because she served him a dinner of scorched rice, underdone fish, and soggy bread, hits her. That incident stimulates Janie to stand "where he left her for unmeasured time" and think. Her thinking leads to the recognition that "her image of Jody tumbled down and shattered . . . she had an inside and an outside now and suddenly she knew how not to mix them" (p. 63).

Consciousness and the struggle for a self-defined standpoint

African-American women as a group may have experiences that provide us with a unique angle of vision. But expressing a collective, self-defined Black feminist consciousness is problematic precisely because dominant groups have a vested interest in suppressing such thought.[3] As Hannah Nelson notes, "I have grown to womanhood in a world where the saner you are, the madder you are made to appear" (Gwaltney 1980, 7). Ms. Nelson realizes that those who control the schools, media, and other cultural institutions of society prevail in establishing their viewpoint as superior to others.

An oppressed group's experiences may put its members in a position to see things differently, but their lack of control over the ideological apparatuses of society makes expressing a self-defined standpoint more difficult. Elderly domestic worker Rosa Wakefield assesses how the standpoints of the powerful and those who serve them diverge:

> If you eats these dinners and don't cook 'em, if you wears these clothes and don't buy or iron them, then you might start thinking that the good fairy or some spirit did all that. . . . Black folks don't have no time to be thinking like that. . . . But when you don't have anything else to do, you can think like that. It's bad for your mind, though.
>
> (Gwaltney 1980, 88)

Ms. Wakefield has a self-defined perspective growing from her experiences that enables her to reject the standpoint of more powerful groups. And yet ideas like hers are typically suppressed by dominant groups. Groups unequal in power are correspondingly unequal in their ability to make their standpoint known to themselves and others.

Individual African-American women have long displayed varying types of consciousness regarding our shared angle of vision. By aggregating and articulating these individual expressions of consciousness, a collective, focused group consciousness becomes possible. Black women's ability to forge these individual, unarticulated, yet potentially powerful expressions of everyday consciousness into an articulated, self-defined, collective standpoint is key to Black women's survival. As Audre Lorde points out, "it is axiomatic that if we do not define ourselves for ourselves, we will be defined by others – for their use and to our detriment" (1984, 45).

One fundamental feature of this struggle for a self-defined standpoint involves tapping sources of everyday, unarticulated consciousness that have traditionally been denigrated in white, male-controlled institutions. For Black women, the struggle involves embracing a consciousness that is simultaneously Afrocentric and feminist. What does this mean?

Research in African-American Studies suggests that an Afrocentric worldview exists which is distinct from and in many ways opposed to a Eurocentric worldview (Okanlawon 1972; Asante 1987; Myers 1988). Standard scholarly social constructions of blackness and race define these concepts as being either reflections of quantifiable, biological differences among humans or residual categories that emerged in response to institutionalized racism (Lyman 1972; Bash 1979; Gould 1981; Omi and Winant 1986). In contrast, even though it often relies on biological notions of the "race," Afrocentric scholarship suggests that "blackness" and Afrocentricity reflect long-standing belief systems among African peoples (Diop 1974; Richards 1980; Asante 1987). While Black people were forced to adapt these Afrocentric belief systems in the face of different institutional arrangements of white domination, the continuation of an Afrocentric worldview has been fundamental to African-Americans' resistance to racial oppression (Smitherman 1977; Webber 1978; Sobel 1979; Thompson 1983). In other words, being Black encompasses *both* experiencing white domination *and* individual and group valuation of an independent, long-standing Afrocentric consciousness.

African-American women draw on this Afrocentric worldview to cope with racial oppression. But far too often Black women's Afrocentric consciousness remains unarticulated and not fully developed into a self-defined standpoint. In societies that denigrate African ideas and peoples, the process of valuing an Afrocentric worldview is the result of self-conscious struggle.

Similar concerns can be raised about the issue of what constitutes feminist ideas (Eisenstein 1983; Jaggar 1983). Being a biological female does not mean that one's ideas are automatically feminist. Self-conscious struggle is needed in order to reject patriarchal perceptions of women and to value women's ideas and actions. The fact that more women than men identify themselves as feminists reflects women's greater experience with the negative consequences of gender oppression. Becoming a feminist is routinely described by women (and men) as a process of transformation, of struggling to develop new interpretations of familiar realities.

The struggles of women from different racial/ethnic groups and those of women and men within African-American communities to articulate self-defined standpoints represent similar yet distinct processes. While race and gender are both socially constructed categories, constructions of gender rest on clearer biological criteria than do constructions of race. Classifying African-Americans into specious racial categories is considerably more difficult than noting the clear biological differences distinguishing females from males (Patterson 1982). But though united by biological sex, women do not form the same type of group as do African-Americans, Jews, native Americans, Vietnamese, or other groups with distinct histories, geographic origins, cultures, and social institutions. The absence of an identifiable tradition uniting women does not mean that women are characterized more by differences than by similarities. Women do share common experiences, but the experiences are not generally the same type as those affecting racial and ethnic groups (King 1988). Thus while expressions of race and gender are both socially constructed, they are not constructed in the same way. The struggle for an Afrocentric feminist consciousness requires embracing both an Afrocentric worldview and a feminist sensibility and using both to forge a self-defined standpoint.[4] [. . .]

Who can be a Black feminist? The centrality of Black women intellectuals to the production of Black feminist thought

I aim to develop a definition of Black feminist thought that relies exclusively neither on a materialist analysis – one whereby all African-American women by virtue of biology become automatically registered as "authentic Black feminists" – nor on an idealist analysis whereby the background, worldview, and interests of the thinker are deemed irrelevant in assessing his or her ideas. Resolving the tension between these two extremes involves reassessing the centrality Black women intellectuals assume in producing Black feminist thought. It also requires examining the importance of coalitions with Black men, white women, people of color, and other groups with distinctive standpoints. Such coalitions are essential in order to foster other groups' contributions as critics, teachers, advocates, and disseminators of a self-defined Afrocentric feminist standpoint.

Black women's concrete experiences as members of specific race, class, and gender groups as well as our concrete historical situations necessarily play significant roles in our perspectives on the world. No standpoint is neutral because no individual or group exists unembedded in the world. Knowledge is gained not by solitary individuals but by Black women as socially constituted members of a group (Narayan 1989). These factors all frame the definitional tensions in Black feminist thought.

Black women intellectuals are central to Black feminist thought for several reasons. First, our experiences as African-American women provide us with a unique standpoint on Black womanhood unavailable to other groups. It is more likely for Black women as members of an oppressed group to have critical insights into the condition of our own oppression than it is for those who live outside those structures. One of the characters in Frances Ellen Watkins Harper's 1892 novel, *Iola Leroy*, expresses this belief in the special vision of those who have experienced oppression:

> Miss Leroy, out of the race must come its own thinkers and writers. Authors belonging to the white race have written good books, for which I am deeply grateful, but it seems to be almost impossible for a white man to put himself completely in our place. No man can feel the iron which enters another man's soul.
>
> (Carby 1987, 62)

Only African-American women occupy this center and can "feel the iron" that enters Black women's souls, because we are the only group that has experienced race, gender, and class oppression as Black women experience them. The importance of Black women's leadership in producing Black feminist thought does not mean that others cannot participate. It does mean that the primary responsibility for defining one's own reality lies with the people who live that reality, who actually have those experiences.

Second, Black women intellectuals provide unique leadership for Black women's empowerment and resistance. In discussing Black women's involvement in the feminist movement, Sheila Radford-Hill points out the connections among self-definition, empowerment, and taking actions in one's own behalf:

> Black women now realize that part of the problem within the movement was our insistence that white women do for/with us what we must do for/with ourselves: namely, frame our own social action around our own agenda for change. . . . Critical to this discussion is the right to organize on one's own behalf. . . . Criticism by black feminists must reaffirm this principle.
>
> (1986, 162)

Black feminist thought cannot challenge race, gender, and class oppression without empowering African-American women. "Oppressed people resist by identifying themselves as subjects, by defining their reality, shaping their new identity, naming their history, telling their story," notes bell hooks (1989, 43). Because self-definition is key to individual and group empowerment, using an epistemology that cedes the power of self-definition to other groups, no matter how well-meaning, in essence perpetuates Black women's subordination. As Black feminist sociologist Deborah K. King succinctly states, "Black feminism asserts self-determination as essential" (1988, 72).

Stressing the importance of Black women's centrality to Black feminist thought does not mean that all African-American women exert this leadership. While being an African-American woman generally provides the experiential base for an

Afrocentric feminist consciousness, these same conditions suppress its articulation. It is not acquired as a finished product but must continually develop in relation to changing conditions.

Bonnie Johnson emphasizes the importance of self-definition. In her critique of Patricia Bell Scott's bibliography on Black feminism, she challenges both Scott's categorization of all works by Black women as being Black feminist and Scott's identification of a wide range of African-American women as Black feminists: "Whether I think they're feminists is irrelevant. *They* would not call themselves feminist" (Clarke et al. 1983, 94). As Patrice L. Dickerson contends, "a person comes into being and knows herself by her achievements, and through her efforts to become and know herself, she achieves" (personal correspondence 1988). Here is the heart of the matter. An Afrocentric feminist consciousness constantly emerges and is part of a self-conscious struggle to merge thought and action.

Third, Black women intellectuals are central in the production of Black feminist thought because we alone can create the group autonomy that must precede effective coalitions with other groups. This autonomy is quite distinct from separatist positions whereby Black women withdraw from other groups and engage in exclusionary politics. In her introduction to *Home Girls, A Black Feminist Anthology,* Barbara Smith describes this difference: "Autonomy and separatism are fundamentally different. Whereas autonomy comes from a position of strength, separatism comes from a position of fear. When we're truly autonomous we can deal with other kinds of people, a multiplicity of issues, and with difference, because we have formed a solid base of strength" (1983, xi). Black women intellectuals who articulate an autonomous, self-defined standpoint are in a position to examine the usefulness of coalitions with other groups, both scholarly and activist, in order to develop new models for social change. However, autonomy to develop a self-defined, independent analysis does not mean that Black feminist thought has relevance only for African-American women or that we must confine ourselves to analyzing our own experiences. As Sonia Sanchez points out, "I've always known that if you write from a black experience, you're writing from a universal experience as well . . . I know you don't have to whitewash yourself to be universal" (in Tate 1983, 142).

While Black feminist thought may originate with Black feminist intellectuals, it cannot flourish isolated from the experiences and ideas of other groups. The dilemma is that Black women intellectuals must place our own experiences and consciousness at the center of any serious efforts to develop Black feminist thought yet not have that thought become separatist and exclusionary. bell hooks offers a solution to this problem by suggesting that we shift from statements such as "I am a feminist" to those such as "I advocate feminism." Such an approach could "serve as a way women who are concerned about feminism as well as other political movements could express their support while avoiding linguistic structures that give primacy to one particular group" (1984, 30).

By advocating, refining, and disseminating Black feminist thought, other groups – such as Black men, white women, white men, and other people of color – further its development. Black women can produce an attenuated version of Black feminist thought separated from other groups. Other groups cannot produce Black feminist thought without African-American women. Such groups can, however, develop self-defined knowledge reflecting their own standpoints. But the full actualization of Black feminist thought requires a collaborative enterprise with Black women at the center of a community based on coalitions among autonomous groups [. . .]

What constitutes black feminism? The recurring humanist vision

A wide range of African-American women intellectuals have advanced the view that Black women's struggles are part of a wider struggle for human dignity and empowerment. In an 1893 speech to women, Anna Julia Cooper cogently expressed this alternative worldview:

> We take our stand on the solidarity of humanity, the oneness of life, and the unnaturalness and injustice of all special favoritisms, whether of sex, race, country, or condition. . . . The colored woman feels that woman's cause is one and universal; and that . . . not till race, color, sex, and condition are seen as accidents, and not the substance of life; not till the universal title of humanity to life, liberty, and the pursuit of happiness is conceded to be inalienable to all; not till then is woman's lesson taught and woman's cause won – not the white woman's nor the black woman's, not the red woman's but the cause of every man and of every woman who has writhed silently under a mighty wrong.
>
> Loewenberg and Bogin 1976, 330–31)

Like Cooper, many African-American women intellectuals embrace this perspective regardless of particular political solutions we propose, our fields of study, or our historical periods. Whether we advocate working through separate Black women's organizations, becoming part of women's organizations, working within existing political structures, or supporting Black community institutions, African-American women intellectuals repeatedly identify political actions such as these as a *means* for human empowerment rather than ends in and of themselves. Thus the primary guiding principle of Black feminism is a recurring humanist vision (Steady 1981, 1987).[5]

Alice Walker's preference for the term *womanist*, a term she describes as "womanist is to feminist as purple is to lavender," addresses this notion of the solidarity of humanity. To Walker, one is "womanist" when one is "committed to the survival and wholeness of entire people, male and female." A womanist is "not a separatist, except periodically for health" and is "traditionally universalist, as is 'Mama, why are we brown, pink, and yellow, and our cousins are white, beige, and black?' Ans.: 'Well, you know the colored race is just like a flower garden, with every color flower represented'" (1983, xi). By redefining all people as "people of color," Walker universalizes what are typically seen as individual struggles while simultaneously allowing space for autonomous movements of self-determination.

In assessing the sexism of the Black nationalist movement of the 1960s, Black feminist lawyer Pauli Murray identifies the dangers inherent in separatism as opposed to autonomy, and also echoes Cooper's concern with the solidarity of humanity:

> The lesson of history that all human rights are indivisible and that the
> failure to adhere to this principle jeopardizes the rights of all is particularly
> applicable here. A built-in hazard of an aggressive ethnocentric movement
> which disregards the interests of other disadvantaged groups is that it
> will become parochial and ultimately self-defeating in the face of hostile
> reactions, dwindling allies, and mounting frustrations. . . . Only a broad
> movement for human rights can prevent the Black Revolution from
> becoming isolated and can insure ultimate success.
>
> (Murray 1970, 102)

Without a commitment to human solidarity, suggests Murray, any political movement
– whether nationalist, feminist or antielitist – may be doomed to ultimate failure.

bell hook's analysis of feminism adds another critical dimension that must be
considered: namely, the necessity of self-conscious struggle against a more generalized
ideology of domination:

> To me feminism is not simply a struggle to end male chauvinism or a
> movement to ensure that women will have equal rights with men; it
> is a commitment to eradicating the ideology of domination that permeates
> Western culture on various levels – sex, race, and class, to name a
> few – and a commitment to reorganizing U.S. society so that the self-
> development of people can take precedence over imperialism, economic
> expansion, and material desires.
>
> (hooks 1981, 194)

Former assemblywoman Shirley Chisholm also points to the need for self-conscious
struggle against the stereotypes buttressing ideologies of domination. In "working
toward our own freedom, we can help others work free from the traps of their
stereotypes" she notes. "In the end, antiblack, antifemale, and all forms of
discrimination are equivalent to the same thing – antihumanism. . . . We must
reject not only the stereotypes that others have of us but also those we have of
ourselves and others" (1970, 181).

This humanist vision is also reflected in the growing prominence of international
issues and global concerns in the works of contemporary African-American women
intellectuals (Lindsay 1980; Steady 1981, 1987). Economists Margaret Simms and
Julianne Malveaux's 1986 edited volume, *Slipping through the Cracks: The Status of
Black Women,* contains articles on Black women in Tanzania, Jamaica, and South
Africa. Angela Davis devotes an entire section of her 1989 book, *Women, Culture,
and Politics,* to international affairs and includes essays on Winnie Mandela and on
women in Egypt. June Jordan's 1985 volume, *On Call,* includes essays on South
Africa, Nicaragua, and the Bahamas. Alice Walker writes compellingly of the types
of links these and other Black women intellectuals see between African-American
women's issues and those of other groups: "To me, Central America is one large
plantation; and I see the people's struggle to be free as a slave revolt" (1988, 177).

The words and actions of Black women intellectuals from different historical
times and addressing markedly different audiences resonate with a strikingly similar
theme of the oneness of all human life. Perhaps the most succinct version of the

humanist vision in Black feminist thought is offered by Fannie Lou Hamer, the daughter of sharecroppers, and a Mississippi civil rights activist. While sitting on her porch, Ms. Hamer observed "Ain' no such thing as I can hate anybody and hope to see God's face" (Jordan 1981, xi).

Taken together, the ideas of Anna Julia Cooper, Pauli Murray, bell hooks, Alice Walker, Fannie Lou Hamer, and other Black women intellectuals too numerous to mention suggest a powerful answer to the question "What is Black feminism?" Inherent in their words and deeds is a definition of Black feminism as a process of self-conscious struggle that empowers women and men to actualize a humanist vision of community.

Notes

1 For discussions of the concept of standpoint, see Hartsock (1983a, 1983b), Jaggar (1983), and Smith (1987). Even though I use standpoint epistemologies as an organizing concept in this volume, they remain controversial. For a helpful critique of standpoint epistemologies, see Harding (1986). Haraway's (1988) reformulation of standpoint epistemologies approximates my use here.

2 Scott (1985) defines consciousness as the symbols, norms, and ideological forms people create to give meaning to their acts. For de Lauretis (1986), consciousness is a process, a "particular configuration of subjectivity . . . produced at the intersection of meaning with experience . . . Consciousness is grounded in personal history, and self and identity are understood within particular cultural contexts. Consciousness. . . is never fixed, never attained once and for all, because discursive boundaries change with historical conditions" (p. 8).

3 The presence of a Black women's culture of resistance (Terborg-Penn 1986; Dodson and Gilkes 1987) that is both Afrocentric and feminist challenges two prevailing interpretations of the consciousness of oppressed groups. One approach claims that subordinate groups identify with the powerful and have no valid independent interpretation of their own oppression. The second assumes the oppressed are less human than their rulers, and are therefore less capable of interpreting their own experiences (Rollins 1985; Scott 1985). Both approaches see any independent consciousness expressed by oppressed groups as being either not of their own making or inferior to that of the dominant group. More important, both explanations suggest that the alleged lack of political activism on the part of oppressed groups stems from their flawed consciousness of their own subordination.

4 Even though I will continue to use the term *Afrocentric feminist thought* interchangeably with the phrase *Black feminist thought*, I think they are conceptually distinct.

5 My use of the term *humanist* grows from an Afrocentric historical context distinct from that criticized by Western feminists. I use the term to tap an Afrocentric humanism as cited by West (1977–78), Asante (1987) and Turner (1984) and as part of the Black theological tradition (Mitchell and Lewter 1986; Cannon 1988). See Harris (1981) for a discussion of the humanist tradition in the works of three Black women writers. See Richards (1990) for a discussion of African–American spirituality, a key dimension of Afrocentric humanism. Novelist Margaret

Walker offers one of the clearest discussions of Black humanism. Walker claims:. "I think it is more important now to emphasize humanism in a technological age than ever before, because it is only in terms of humanism that society can redeem itself. I believe that mankind is only one race – the human race. There are many strands in the family of man – many races. The world has yet to learn to appreciate the deep reservoirs of humanism in all races, and particularly in the Black race" (Rowell 1975, 12).

References

Asante, Molefi Kete. 1987. *The Afrocentric Idea*. Philadelphia: Temple University Press.

Bash, Harry H. 1979. *Sociology, Race and Ethnicity*. New York: Gordon and Breach.

Beale, Frances. 1970 "Double Jeopardy: To Be Black and Female." In *The Black Woman: An Anthology*, edited by Toni Cade (Bambara), 90–100, New York: Signet.

Brown-Collins, Alice, and Deborah Ridley Sussewell. 1986. "The Afro-American Women's Emerging Selves" *Journal of Black Psychology* 13(1): 1–11.

Cannon, Katie G. 1985. "The Emergence of a Black Feminist Consciousness." In *Feminist Interpretations of the Bible*, edited by Letty M. Russell, 30–40, Philadelphia: Westminster Press.

——. 1988. *Black Womanist Ethics*. Atlanta: Scholars Press.

Carby, Hazel. 1987. *Reconstructing Womanhood: The Emergence of the Afro-American Woman Novelist*. New York: Oxford.

Chisholm, Shirley. 1970. *Unbought and Unbossed*. New York: Avon.

Clarke, Cheryl. 1983. "The Failure to Transform: Homophobia in the Black Community." In *Home Girls: A Black Feminist Anthology*, edited by Barbara Smith, 197–208. New York: Kitchen Table Press.

——, Jewell L. Gomez, Evelyn Hammonds, Bonnie Johnson, and Linda Powell. 1983. "Conversations and Questions: Black Woman on Black Women Writers." *Conditions: Nine* 3 (3): 88–137.

The Combahee River Collective. 1982. "A Black Feminist Statement." In *But Some of Us Are Brave*, edited by Gloria T. Hull, Patricia Bell Scott, and Barbara Smith, 13–22, Old Westbury, NY: Feminist Press.

Cooper, Anna Julia. 1892. *A Voice from the South: By a Black Woman of the South*. Xenia, OH: Aldine Printing House.

Davis, Angela Y. 1981. *Women, Race and Class*. New York: Random House.

——. 1989. *Women, Culture and Politics*. New York: Random House.

Davis, George and Glegg Watson. 1985. *Black Life in Corporate America*. New York: Anchor.

de Lauretis, Teresa. 1986. "Feminist Studies/Critical Studies: Issues, Terms and Contexts." In *Feminist Studies/Critical Studies*, edited by Teresa de Lauretis, 1–19. Bloomington: Indiana University Press.

Diop, Cheikh. 1974. *The African Origin of Civilization: Myth or Reality*. New York: L. Hill.

Dodson, Jualyne E., and Cheryl Townsend Gilkes. 1987. "Something Within: Social Change and Collective Endurance in the Sacred World of Black Christian Women." In *Women and Religion in America, Volume 3: 1900–1968*, edited by Rosemary Reuther and R. Keller, 80–130. New York: Harper and Row.

Duster, Alfreda M., ed. 1970. *Crusade for Justice: The Autobiography of Ida B. Wells.* Chicago: University of Chicago Press.

Eisenstein, Hester. 1983. *Contemporary Feminist Thought.* Boston: G. K. Hall.

Giddings, Paula. 1984. *When and Where I Enter . . . The Impact of Black Women on Race and Sex in America.* New York: William Morrow.

——. 1988. *In Search of Sisterhood: Delta Sigma Theta and the Challenge of the Black Sorority Movement.* New York: William Morrow.

Gilkes, Cheryl Townsend. 1985. " 'Together and in Harness': Women's Traditions in the Sanctified Church." *Signs* 10(4): 678–99.

Gould, Stephen Jay. 1981. *The Mismeasure of Man.* New York: W. W. Norton.

Guy-Sheftall, Beverly. 1986. "Remembering Sojourner Truth: On Black Feminism." *Catalyst* (Fall): 54–57.

Gwaltney, John Langston. 1980. *Drylongso, A Self-Portrait of Black America.* New York: Vintage.

Haraway, Donna. 1988. "Situated Knowledges: The Science Question in Feminism and the Privilege of Partial Perspective." *Feminist Studies* 14(3): 575–99.

Harding, Sandra. 1986. *The Science Question in Feminism*, Ithaca, NY: Cornell University Press.

Harris, Trudier. 1981. "Three Black Women Writers and Humanism: A Folk Perspective." In *Black American Literature and Humanism*, edited by R. Baxter Miller, 50–74. Lexington: University of Kentucky Press.

Hartsock, Nancy M. 1983a. "The Feminist Standpoint: Developing the Ground for a Specifically Feminist Historical Materialism." In *Discovering Reality*, edited by Sandra Harding and Merrill B. Hintikka, 283–310. Boston: D. Reidel.

——. 1983b. *Money, Sex and Power.* Boston: Northeastern University Press.

hooks, bell. 1981. *Ain't I a Woman: Black Women and Feminism.* Boston: South End Press.

——. 1984. *From Margin to Center.* Boston: South End Press.

——. 1989. *Talking Back: Thinking Feminist, Thinking Black.* Boston: South End Press.

Hurston, Zora Neale. [1937] 1969. *Their Eyes Were Watching God.* Greenwich, CT: Fawcett.

Jaggar, Alison M. 1983. *Feminist Politics and Human Nature.* Totawa, NJ: Rowman & Allanheld.

Jordan, June. 1981. *Civil Wars.* Boston: Beacon.

——. 1985. *On Call.* Boston: South End Press.

King, Deborah K. 1988. "Multiple Jeopardy, Multiple Consciousness: The Context of a Black Feminist Ideology." *Signs* 14(1): 42–72.

Ladner, Joyce. 1972. *Tomorrow's Tomorrow.* Garden City, NY: Doubleday.

Lindsay, Beverly, ed. 1980. *Comparative Perspectives of Third World Women: The Impact of Race, Sex and Class.* New York: Praeger.

Loewenberg, Bert J., and Ruth Bogin, eds. 1976. *Black Women in Nineteenth-Century American Life.* University Park: Pennsylvania State University Press.

Lorde, Audre. 1982. *Zami, A New Spelling of My Name.* Trumansberg, NY: The Crossing Press.

——. 1984. *Sister Outsider.* Trumansberg, NY: The Crossing Press.

Lyman, Stanford M. 1972. *The Black American in Sociological Thought: A Failure of Perspective.* New York: Capricorn.

McDowell, Deborah E. 1985. "New Directions for Black Feminist Criticism." In *The New Feminist Criticism*, edited by Elaine Showalter, 186–99, New York: Pantheon.

Mitchell, Henry H., and Nicholas Cooper Lewter. 1986. *Soul Theology: The Heart of American Black Culture*. San Francisco: Harper & Row.

Murray, Pauli. 1970. "The Liberation of Black Women." In *Voices of the New Feminism*, edited by Mary Lou Thompson, 87–102. Boston: Beacon.

Myers, Linda James. 1988. *Understanding an Afrocentric World View: Introduction to an Optimal Psychology*. Dubuque, IA: Kendall/Hunt.

Narayan, Uma. 1989. "The Project of Feminist Epistemology: Perspectives from a Nonwestern Feminist." In *Gender/Body/Knowledge: Feminist Reconstructions of Being and Knowing*, edited by Alison M. Jaggar and Susan R. Bordo, 256–69, New Brunswick, NJ: Rutgers University Press.

Okanlawon, Alexander. 1972. "Africanism – A Synthesis of the African World-View." *Black World* 21(9): 40–44, 92–97.

Omi, Michael, and Howard Winant, 1986. *Racial Formation in the United States: From the 1960s to the 1980s*. New York: Routledge & Kegan Paul.

Patterson, Orlando. 1982. *Slavery and Social Death*. Cambridge, MA: Harvard University Press.

Radford-Hill, Sheila. 1986. "Considering Feminism as a Model for Social Change." In *Feminist Studies/Critical Studies*, edited by Teresa de Lauretis, 157–72. Bloomington: Indiana University Press.

Richards, Dona. 1980. "European Mythology: The Ideology of 'Progress.'" In *Contemporary Black Thought*, edited by Molefi Kete Asante and Abdulai Sa. Vandi, 59–79. Beverly Hills, CA: Sage.

——. 1990. "The Implications of African-American Spirituality." In *African Culture: The Rhythms of Unity*, edited by Molefi Kete Asante and Kariamu Welsh Asante, 207–31, Trenton, NJ: Africa World Press.

Richardson, Marilyn, ed. 1987. *Maria W. Stewart, America's First Black Woman Political Writer*. Bloomington: Indiana University Press.

Ritchie, Beth. 1985. "Battered Black Women: A Challenge for the Black Community." *Black Scholar* 16: 40–44.

Rollins, Judith. 1985. *Between Women, Domestics and Their Employers*. Philadelphia: Temple University Press.

Rowell, Charles H. 1975. "An Interview with Margaret Walker." *Black World* 25(2): 4–17.

Scott, James C. 1985. *Weapons of the Weak: Everyday Forms of Peasant Resistance*. New Haven, CT: Yale University Press.

Scott, Patricia Bell. 1982a. "Debunking Sapphire: Toward a Non-Racist and Non-Sexist Social Science." in *But Some of Us Are Brave*, edited by Gloria T. Hull, Patricia Bell Scott, and Barbara Smith, 85–92. Old Westbury, NY: Feminist Press.

——. 1982b. "Selected Bibliography on Black Feminism." In *But Some of Us Are Brave*, edited by Gloria T. Hull, Patricia Bell Scott, and Barbara Smith, 23–36. Old Westbury, NY: Feminist Press.

Shockley, Ann Allen. 1974. *Loving Her*. Hallahassee, FL: Naiad Press.

Simms, Margaret C. and Julianne Malveaux, eds. 1986. *Slipping through the Cracks: The Status of Black Women*. New Brunswick, NJ: Transaction.

Smith, Barbara. 1983. "Introduction." In *Home Girls: A Black Feminist Anthology*, edited by Barbara Smith, xix–lvi. New York: Kitchen Table Press.

Smith, Beverly. 1983. "The Wedding." In *Home Girls: A Black Feminist Anthology*, edited by Barbara Smith, 171–76. New York: Kitchen Table Press.

Smith, Dorothy. 1987. *The Everyday World as Problematic*. Boston: Northeastern University Press.

Smitherman, Geneva. 1977. *Talkin and Testifyin: The Language of Black America*. Boston: Houghton Mifflin.

Sobel, Mechal. 1979. *Trabelin' On: The Slave Journey to an Afro-Baptist Faith*. Princeton: Princeton University Press.

Steady, Filomina Chioma. 1981. "The Black Woman Cross-Culturally: An Overview." In *The Black Woman Cross-Culturally*, edited by Filomina Chioma Steady, 7–42. Cambridge, MA: Schenkman.

——. 1987. "African Feminism: A Worldwide Perspective." In *Women in Africa and the African Diaspora*, edited by Rosalyn Terborg-Penn, Sharon Harley, and Andrea Benton Rushing, 3–24. Washington, DC: Howard University Press.

Tate, Claudia, ed. 1983. *Black Women Writers at Work*. New York: Continuum Publishing.

Terborg-Penn, Rosalyn. 1986. "Black Women in Resistance: A Cross-Cultural Perspective." In *In Resistance: Studies in African, Caribbean and Afro-American History*, edited by Gary Y. Okhiro, 188–209. Amherst: University of Massachusetts Press.

Thompson, Robert Farris. 1983. *Flash of the Spirit: African and Afro-American Art and Philosophy*. New York: Vintage.

Walker, Alice. 1983. *In Search of Our Mothers' Gardens*. New York: Harcourt Brace Jovanovich.

——. 1988. *Living by the Word*. New York: Harcourt Brace Jovanovich.

Webber, Thomas L. 1978. *Deep Like the Rivers*. New York: W. W. Norton.

West, Cornel. 1977–78. "Philosophy and the Afro-American Experience." *Philosophical Forum* 9(2–3): 117–48.

White, E. Frances. 1984. "Listening to the Voices of Black Feminism." *Radical America* 18(2–3): 7–25.

Chapter 29

Kimberly Springer

THIRD WAVE BLACK FEMINISM?

BLACK FEMINISTS IN THE 1970s expended disproportionate
amounts of energy attempting to legitimize themselves in the eyes of Black
communities – so much so that often their organizing suffered (Springer 2001).[1]
It is compelling to note similarities between 1970s Black feminists and those
writing in the 1990s. Writings in the 1990s continue to refute the idea that working
against gender oppression is somehow counter to antiracist efforts. Both attempt
to strike a balance between adequately theorizing race and gender oppression as
they intersect in the United States. Black feminists writing then and now struggle
with advocating a love for Black men while passionately hating Black sexism.

And while older Black feminists are wrestling with past dilemmas and strive
to impart knowledge about the struggle for racial and gender justice, younger
Black women are also joining the dialogue through their activism, music, and
writing. This article evokes three central questions about *contemporary* young Black
women's views on gender and race: Is there a third wave Black feminist politic?
What issues are contemporary young Black feminists prioritizing? How do these
young women contextualize their experiences and their politics?

The article begins with a discussion of the term *third wave* and how this
model excludes feminists of color. Looking closely at this term is key to positioning
young Black women along the continuum of feminist history in the United States,
as well as intervening in the exclusion of these voices from contemporary feminist
theorizing and organizing. I examine three texts: Lisa Jones's collection of essays
Bulletproof Diva: Tales of Race, Sex, and Hair (1994), Joan Morgan's essays *When
Chickenheads Come Home to Roost: My Life as a Hip-Hop Feminist* (1999; hereafter
known as *Chickenheads*), and Veronica Chambers's memoir *Mama's Girl* (1996).
These texts stand out as they speak explicitly from or about young Black feminist
perspectives in the 1990s. Jones's and Morgan's essays effectively meld the third
wave penchant for personal narrative with second wave theoretical underpinnings,
creating a case for interrogating the politics of style and the style of politics.

Chambers's book is the outlier of the three, as it is the only memoir. Though she was only twenty-five years old when she wrote it, and the production of memoirs has spiraled exponentially in the past ten years, it is important to examine Chambers's book because it is one of the few written by a young African-American woman. Her narrative's inflections of the complex interweaving of gender, class, and race reaffirm the value of memoir for relaying and contextualizing experiences that some might think are unimportant. These three texts have much to contribute to women's studies, African-American studies, and other fields concerned with examining the daily functioning of interlocking systems of oppression. Moreover, as texts that examine popular culture, they convey valuable, transferable messages for activists working around gender, race, and class in U.S. Black communities.[2]

Three themes emerged from my reading of these texts. The first is young Black women's relationship to our personal and political histories. This history includes our relationships to past social movements, our biological mothers, and our political foremothers. The next theme is a familiar one that spans the history of Black women's writing: relationship to self. Morgan, Chambers, and Jones all tackle the myth of the "strong-blackwoman" and what it means for how we relate to our mothers, other Black women, and ourselves. Finally, the authors I analyze write about Black women's relationships to Black men: biological brothers, brothers in the political sense, and fathers.

There are still young Black women continuing feminist analyses of Black life, but they are not necessarily claiming the label of *third wave*. Their reasons, however, are different than those of women who fear feminism as an ideology. These women share their life stories in the public forum as a way of asserting a contemporary Black female identity that is mindful of historical context and community imperatives. The recuperation of the self in a racist and sexist society is a political enterprise and a Black feminist one that deprioritizes generational differences in the interest of historical, activist continuity.

I conclude with a proposal for ways that we can use these writings to move Black feminist theorizing and action out of the classroom and the more cerebral realms of reading and contemplation. How might we, as activists and teachers, pair the readings I discuss in this article with popular culture representations in conversations with schools, community groups, and other public arenas in the Black community that so desperately need what Johnnetta Cole and Beverly Guy-Sheftall (in press) call "gender talk"?

Black feminism: Drowned out by the wave

Feminist activists and women's movement historians use the "wave" model to describe the women's movement in the United States. This model obscures the historical role of race in feminist organizing. If we consider the first wave as that moment of organizing encompassing woman suffrage and the second wave as the women's liberation/women's rights activism of the late 1960s, we effectively disregard the race-based movements before them that served as precursors, or windows of political opportunity, for gender activism.

In relationship to the first wave, the oration, organizing, writing, and agitation skills that white women gleaned from their work in the abolitionist movement, as well as the cues taken from Black women involved in antislavery, antilynching, and suffrage work, were instrumental to the evolution of the first wave. Consider these three examples. In Boston, Maria Stewart, a free Black from Connecticut, gave a public lecture to a racially mixed audience of men and women; she was the first woman of any race to do so. In the 1850s, Mary Shadd Cary, the first Black woman newspaper editor in North America, published the *Provincial Freeman*, which was an abolitionist paper with the motto "Self-Reliance is the True Road to Independence." Anna Julia Cooper, author of *A Voice from the South by a Black Woman of the South* (1988), wrote the first book-length feminist treatise on the condition of African Americans. A pivotal text of Black feminist thought, Cooper argues for women's leadership in the Black community, as well as the need for Black women to work separately from white feminists because of racism experienced personally, political betrayals, and the strategic need for separatism.

Inserting these women into the public record of feminist activism challenges the notion that "race women" were not also concerned about gender. African-American women, if inserted into this wave model, make the wave, shall we say, a much bigger swell. Remaining mindful of the links between the struggles for freedom from racism and sexism is critical as future social justice coalition work depends on accurate – for better or worse – historical memory.

More disruptive of the wave model is the work of scholars such as Angela Davis and Deborah Gray White on enslaved African women's forms of resistance to gendered violence. As Davis observes in her pioneering article "Reflections on the Black Woman's Role in the Community of Slaves" ([1971] 1995), and as White notes in *Ar'n't I a Woman: Female Slaves in the Plantation South* (1985), enslaved women actively resisted rape, forced pregnancy, and separation from their children on plantations. Through natural abortion methods and fighting back against nonconsensual sexual relations when they could, they enacted an early form of feminist resistance to distinctly gendered oppression aimed at women. Harriet Jacobs's (1987) emancipation narrative, for example, is one of the few historical documents written from a Black woman's perspective demonstrating early feminist resistance to slavery and sexual abuse. None of this is meant to discount the gendered atrocities that Black men faced in the slave economy (e.g., castration and other attempts at demasculinization), but it is meant to highlight the ways in which, early on, Black women enacted feminist politics that acknowledged the ways that they were oppressed as Blacks and women. This resistance to *gendered* violence predates that of the abolition movement, but it also happened while the movement emerged. Thus, we can make the case that the idea of a first wave beginning with suffrage excludes the fact that Black women resisted gendered oppression during the antebellum period.[3]

In sum, as we learn more about women of color's feminist activism, the wave analogy becomes untenable. What might, for example, the inclusion of American Indian women's gendered resistance do to even my time line? Reexamining the wave model of the women's movement can only benefit the movement as we continue to expand the category of "women" and make sure that, as bell hooks asserts, "feminism is for everybody" (hooks 2000).

Another way that this critique of waves dismisses race is the evolution of the term third wave itself. My initial reading of writings labeled as third wave, such as the Barbara Findlen anthology *Listen Up! Voices from the Next Feminist Generation* (1995) and Rebecca Walker's volume *To Be Real: Telling the Truth and Changing the Face of Feminism* (1995), triggered memories of women of color using the term *third wave* in the late 1980s. Barbara Smith, founder of Kitchen Table, Women of Color Press and editor of, among other works, *Home Girls: A Black Feminist Anthology* (1983), confirms that Kitchen Table set out to publish a book on racism called *The Third Wave*. In this conceptualization of third wave that emerged in the late 1980s, the book was to describe an antiracist, women-of-color-led feminism for the coming decade. Smith notes quite logically that it is only common sense, based on the first wave and second wave analogies, for those seeking to define a new direction of feminism to call it the "third wave" (Orr 1997; Smith 2001).

The term *third wave feminism* as we now know it signals a new generation of feminists. It came to public consciousness, or at least leftist consciousness, in the form of Rebecca Walker's founding of the Third Wave Foundation in 1992, which initially conducted a Freedom Summer-styled voter registration campaign that same year.[4] This generation of third wave feminism credits previous generations for women-centered social and political advances. This acknowledgment, however, took the form of seeming ungratefulness and historical amnesia in Walker's anthology, *To Be Real* (Steinem 1995; Walker 1995). Some contributors voiced a sense of feeling stifled by the previous generation's organizing style and seemed to reduce the third wave's argument to a gripe about feminism as lifestyle dogma. Yet, more recent writings about third wave feminism – particularly Jennifer Baumgardner and Amy Richards's recent book *Manifesta: Young Women, Feminism, and the Future* (2000) – attempt to define third wave politics and mend the generational rift that arose between some older and younger white feminists. Moreover, *Manifesta* at least gives lip service to the role of women of color, lesbians, and, to a lesser degree, poor women in the third wave women's movement.[5]

The wave model perpetuates the exclusion of women of color from women's movement history and feminist theorizing. Still, as it is so deeply embedded in how we examine the history and future of the women's movement, it remains useful for internal critique. As it is used historically and today, it is too static. To serve a wide range of women's needs, it is imperative that the wave model includes women of color's resistance to gender violence.

What to do with our mothers' gardens

If we proceed with this idea of third wave feminism in its most obvious form, that of denoting generations of feminism, what is the relationship between Black feminists of differing generations? Does a generational rift exist between them? One aspect of the generational tensions between feminists in general is the frustration that older feminists feel at watching younger women reinvent the wheels of social change. Michele Wallace, in retrospect, recognized the irritation of her mother and other women of her mother's generation. In her essay "To Hell and Back," Wallace writes of the late 1960s: "My thesis had been that I and my generation were reinventing youth, danger, sex, love, blackness, and fun. But there had always been just beneath the surface a persistent countermelody, . . . what I might also call my mother's line, a deep suspicion that I was reinventing nothing, but rather making a fool of myself in precisely the manner that untold generations of young women before me had done" (1997, 11). Other than this autobiographical insight by Wallace, few sources speak of conflicts or distinctions between Black feminists of different generations.

In interviews with Black feminists who participated in 1970s feminist activism, some voiced a mix of disappointment and understanding at young Black women's seeming lack of interest in feminism.[6] Their understanding came from intimate knowledge of the struggle, name-calling, and painful awakening around claiming feminism as a political stance. Simultaneously, older Black feminists also seemed disappointed that young Black women could appear to turn their backs on the foundations of Black feminist activism, which made possible, at the very least, a few societal gains for the next generation.

The few articles about Black feminism that have made it into the mainstream press either lament the lack of formal Black feminist organizations or pick up where *Essence* left off in the 1970s – questioning the need for feminism in Black women's lives.[7] As an example of the questioning of the existence of Black feminism on the organizational level, the most recent, high-profile article is Kristal Brent Zook's (1995) essay "A Manifesto of Sorts for a Black Feminist Movement," which appeared in the *New York Times Magazine*. She calls Black women to task for their failure to organize on the behalf of Black women and for serving instead as auxiliaries to male-centered causes like the Million Man March or the "Endangered Black Male" crusades of figures such as O. J. Simpson, Tupac Shakur, and Mike Tyson. Zook also voices frustration with an older generation that continues to define leadership as male-centered and rooted in traditions such as NAACP conventions and benefit fashion shows.[8]

Jones, Morgan, and Chambers all address the question of generation – along with the benefits and drawbacks of being born after the 1960s and 1970s social movements that drastically altered the sociopolitical landscape of racial and sexual polities. They give credit to the Civil Rights, women's, and Black nationalist movements for the place of privilege that those movements put some of us in, in terms of opportunities. Yet, they also recognize the complacency that such awe-inspiring heroes encouraged in Generation X.[9] Chambers recalls being a fifth grader and watching documentaries about Black history:

> It seemed that all the big black battles were over by the time I was born. . . . Watching footage of the bus boycotts, the sit-ins, and the marches . . . I would wonder if I would have been brave. My brother and I used to say, "No way were we sitting on the back of the bus!" but the look my mother would give us told me that we had no idea what we would or wouldn't have done. Deep down inside, I wondered. As bad as those times were, I wished sometimes that there was some sort of protest or something that I could get involved with. (Chambers 1996, 52)

Chambers lived with both parents until her father left the family when she was ten years old. At the time of Chambers's reminiscence, her parents had always provided the basics for her and her brother, and the fact that they had always lived in a house with a yard is a significant marker of the class security that she felt as a child. Chambers's parents instituted a "Black History Day" in their home before Black History Month came into existence, so their daughter had an early sense of the sacrifices they made, particularly her mother, but felt none of those barriers herself. Chambers's memories of contemplating what she would have done during the height of the Civil Rights movement is the luxury of a generation that benefited from that particular struggle.

Is contemplation of the past a luxury of middle-class ascendancy? Or do past struggles at least provide the room to dream about middle- or upper-class status? Morgan views successful social movements, in terms of the sometimes temporary gains of the Civil Rights movement, as having a lulling effect on Generation X. The introduction to Morgan's book is entitled "Dress Up." In it, she recalls envying her mother's generation of women, not because their lives were easy but because of the simultaneous emergence of the women's movement and dissemination of ideas about independence and self-fulfillment at that time. Women of her mother's generation also had the cultural explosion of Black women's literature to affirm their existence and the circumstances of "being black, female and surviving" (Morgan 1999, 19). Morgan was ten years old when Ntozake Shange's choreopoem *for colored girls who have considered suicide when the rainbow was not enuf* premiered in New York. When her mother refused to take her, a young Joan tried every trick in her arsenal – from whining, to singing "the Five Stairsteps' 'O-o-h child things are going to get easier' over and over again – attitudinal and loud – until I was two seconds shy of an ass whooping" (Morgan 1999, 19). But when she was older Morgan understood that "the play held crucial parts of her [mother] – parts she needed to share with her husband and not her ten-year-old daughter" (Morgan 1999, 20).

In this retelling we see a nod to the previous generation of women who, whether they identified as feminist or not, made possible Morgan's self-described position as a hip-hop feminist. When she attends the twentieth anniversary run of *for colored girls* in Manhattan, Morgan hopes that it will reveal "the secrets of black womanhood" that she thought her mother withheld when she saw the play (Morgan 1999, 21). This was not the case. She says, "As a child of the post-Civil Rights, post-feminist, post-soul hip-hop generation my struggle songs consisted of the same notes but they were infused with distinctly different rhythms" (1999, 21–22). In realizing that she was waiting for someone to write a *for colored girls* for her generation, Morgan calls to task her own complacency, as well as that of her generation. She cautions that "relying on older heads to redefine the struggle to encompass our generation's issues is not only lazy but dangerous. Consider our foremothers' contributions a bad-ass bolt of cloth. We've got to fashion the gear to our own liking" (22). Linking generational style and politics, Morgan calls upon the hip-hop generation to create a language and culture that signifies more than a lifestyle but also a political stance worthy of definition.

By describing herself as "a child of the *post*-Civil Rights, *post*-feminist, *post*-soul hip-hop generation," Morgan is not implying that, as a society, we are somehow finished with the struggle for civil or women's rights. The popular press's use of the term *postfeminist* signifies a uniquely liberated, sexy, young woman who believes that feminism is dead or all the battles have been won. Morgan uses the prefix post to signal the end of a particular era of tactics and action. She in no way indicates that the goals or hopes of those movements were fulfilled or are no longer relevant to current generations. She does openly recognize that "we are the daughters of feminist privilege" (Morgan 1999, 59). The "we" means college-educated, middle-class Black girls who believe that there is nothing we cannot achieve because we are women, though sexism and racism might fight us every step of the way. Morgan attempts to craft a collective identity for a new generation of thinkers and organizers. This is a unifying move meant to reach out to women like Chambers who long for significant struggles like those of past eras, as well as to those who feel as though the movements of the 1960s were failures because of conservative backlash, without taking into account our own lack of political vigilance.

Jones issues a similar call to action for the post-Civil Rights, postfeminist generation. Though the subtitle of her book only mentions race, sex, and hair, she is also class-conscious, either explicitly or implicitly, in the forty-four essays that make up her book. About the differences between generations, Jones parallels Morgan in her observations of the cultural production of the 1970s:

> The renaissance of fiction by black women in the seventies, we caught that too. Those books made us feel less invisible, though their stories were far from our own lives as big-city girls; girls who took ballet and were carted off to Planned Parenthood in high school so as not to risk that baby that Mom, not Mama, warned would have "ruined our lives." College was expected. The southern ghosts of popular black women's fiction, the hardships and abuse worn like purple hearts, the clipped wings were not ours. We had burdens of our own. Glass ceilings at the office and in the art world, media and beauty industries that saw us as substandard, the color and hair wars that continued to sap our energy. We wanted to hear about these. (1994, 133–34)

As young white feminists are seeking to step outside of what they consider rigid lifestyle instructions of their feminist foremothers (e.g., stylistic and political), young Black women are attempting to stretch beyond the awe-inspiring legendary work of women like Fannie Lou Hamer, Coretta Scott King, Ruby Doris Smith Robinson, Barbara Smith, bell hooks, and Angela Davis. Their work cannot be matched. When Jones poses the question, "Do you know who speaks through you?" (1994, 26), she poses a rhetorical question that recognizes the significance of history in giving current struggles meaning.

Morgan and Jones exhort the post-Civil Rights, postfeminist, hip-hop generation to pay homage to past struggles but not to rest on our ivory tower degrees. Both recognize the class implications of being exposed to Black feminists' texts as assigned reading in college. Morgan, while recognizing historical reasons for Black women's lack of engagement with feminism – for example, racism in the women's movement, feminism's alleged irrelevancy to Black lives – believes that what it comes down to is that Black women are "misguidedly over-protective, hopelessly male-identified, and all too often self-sacrificing" (Morgan 1999, 55). She interprets homecoming parades for Tyson on his release from prison after serving a sentence for sexual assault and blind support for conservative Supreme Court Justice nominee Clarence Thomas as knee-jerk reactions to centuries of racist violence. However, jumping to the defense of Black men – even when Black women are the victims of male violence – does nothing for current and future generations struggling against gender bias within the Black community. Critiquing popular culture and writing openly from a Black feminist perspective in periodicals, such as the hip-hop magazine *Vibe* and the *Village Voice*, Morgan and Jones most likely reach a mix of middle-class Blacks and white readerships. Still, in their writings they reference a continuum of Black and women's struggle, overlaying historical context onto contemporary manifestations of racism and sexism, that can be useful for articulating a vision for attacking battering, rape, and gender violence in the Black community.

Strongblackwomen/Bulletproof Divas

"Some writers write to tell the world things, others of us write to find something out," Jones commented to a reporter for the *Boston Herald* (Young 1994, 20). Morgan writes that we, Black women, need to take an honest look at ourselves and then tell the truth about it (Morgan 1999, 23). Jones, Morgan, and Chambers want to tell the truth about, in part, the myths that circumscribe the lives of Black women. Yet, similar to some Black Panther Party women's critique of feminism, Morgan raises the culpability of Black women in keeping these myths alive (The Movement 1969). All three women dissect external messages from white society about beauty and how these messages wreak havoc with Black women's self-esteem. These authors also pry apart the layers of self-hatred that work to smother Black women within the Black community. The solutions they offer all involve, to some degree, letting go of the past and opening up to a future as fallible human beings and not women of mythical proportions.

Morgan situates the standard of the strongblackwoman in the history of slavery and the ways that Black women were expected to persevere under any circumstances. Referencing Wallace's explanation of the myths of the superwoman, the mammy, the jezebel, and the sapphire, Morgan contends that these myths have metamorphosed into the contemporary figures of among others, the "Ghetto Bitch . . . Hoochie Mama . . . Skeezer . . . Too independent . . . Don't need no man . . . [and] Waiting to Exhale" women (Morgan 1999, 100). She believes that the older myths justifying slaveowners' brutality against Black women metamorphosed into contemporary conservative welfare myths. We have internalized new myths and have been indiscriminate in crafting our identities from them.[10] At one point in her life, Morgan begins to feel like she is suffocating under the burden of trying always to appear in control and strong. A friend diagnoses her as succumbing to "strongblackwoman" syndrome. The motto of the strongblackwoman? "No matter how bad shit gets, handle it alone, quietly, and with dignity" (Morgan 1999, 72).

Morgan writes "strongblackwoman" as one word and abbreviates it to SBW, signifying the transformation of a stereotype into an accepted and recognizable identity trait for Black women. This linguistic move solidifies the idea of "strong," "black," and "woman" as nonseparable parts of a seemingly cohesive identity. In this title, there is no room for being just one of the three identities at any given time. There is the expectation in the Black community that Black women will be all three, *at all times*. This is not a new concept. Nineteenth- and early twentieth-century crusaders trumpeted the strongblackwoman as a model for "lifting as we climb," but Wallace and contributors to Toni Cade Bambara's *The Black Woman* (1970) deconstructed this model in the 1970s. Morgan wants to take apart the strongblackwoman image for what it is: a way for Black women to deny emotional, psychic, and even physical pain, all the while appearing to keep it together – just like our mothers appeared to do.

Once when she was about thirteen years old, Chambers told her mother that she was depressed. Her mother gave her a scolding about being ungrateful for all that she had, and she let Veronica know that depression was a "white girls" domain. Black women were strong and did not get depressed, and, her mother added, Veronica would not be able to count on the world to make her happy (Chambers 1996, 72).

As much as Chambers's mother warns against the realities of a racist and sexist world, she can never fully explain *why* these realities exist. This is not a personal failure, but the inability of adult, Black Americans to explain a number of social realities to their children. The worsening of poverty in Black communities, the continued degradation of women, the rescinding of civil rights gained in the 1960s, and the lack of a clear course of action from Black leaders (or the lack of Black leaders, period) are equally incomprehensible to children, as well as to adults living in a so-called democracy.

After a series of struggles and achievements – including abuse at the hands of her father and stepmother, putting herself through Simon's Rock College (entering at the age of sixteen), recognition as one of *Glamour* magazine's Top Ten College Women of 1990, and several successful magazine internships – Chambers burns out. She goes through a period of not eating and not sleeping, though she is exhausted. She keeps this information from her mother because she believes "depression was absolutely not allowed." She likens Black women to magicians, "masters of emotional sleight of hand. The closer you get, the less you can see. It was true of my mother. It is also true of me" (Chambers 1996, 73).

Veronica lived with an aunt at the time of her depression, and it is she who reports to Veronica's mother that something is amiss with her daughter. When Veronica does open up to her mother about her exhaustion and depression, she learns that her mother always assumed that everything was fine. Her mother was so busy worrying about her brother, who was not doing well in school and would later deal drugs and end up in jail, that she was just happy not to have to worry about Veronica. This conversation, Chambers's "coming out" to her mother as *not* always strong, begins her process of letting go of the strongblackwoman image. She is aided in this process by a group of college sistah-friends with whom she can relax and speak freely, peppering her language with affectionate "chile, pleases," "girlfriends," "sis's," and "flygirls" (Chambers 1996, 145). Through them and a better relationship with her mother, Chambers is able to recapture a feeling that she had not had since her childhood days of playing double Dutch in Brooklyn, New York. Of those days she says, "There is a space between the two ropes where nothing is better than being a black girl. The helix encircles you and protects you and there you are strong. I wish she'd [Chambers's mother] let me show her. I could teach her how it feels" (Chambers 1996, 7).

The solutions that Morgan, Jones, and Chambers offer to fighting strongblack-woman syndrome are not unlike those that Black feminists in the 1970s offered. In addition to fighting the racist and sexist implications of this myth, Morgan and Jones call for redefinition. Morgan calls it her "Memo of Retirement." In it she addresses white people, people in her life who are overdependent on her to comfort them, and men who expect her to support them unequivocally without having needs of her own. She resolves, "The fake 'Fine' and compulsory smile? Gone. Deaded. Don't look for it . . . Some days I really am an evil black woman" (Morgan 1999, 85). Ultimately, when Morgan has her bout with depression, she leaves New York and moves to San Francisco for the winter. There she allows herself to fall apart with people who are not afraid of her fragility and do not expect her to be a strongblackwoman.

Many women, particularly women of color, do not have the resources to take a winter sabbatical. Yet, the more accessible aspect of Morgan's cure for depression is "claiming the right to imperfections and vulnerabilities" (Morgan 1999, 110). Across classes, Black women are taught to hide their imperfections for fear of being a discredit to the race or vilified as welfare queens. Perhaps more challenging than finding the monetary resources to take a mental health break is finding those people, female or male, with whom a Black woman can be less than strong.

Jones, though more casual in her approach, calls for redefinition of self as key to recuperating an image of Black women that is not detrimental to our individual and collective well-being. She advocates the creation of the "Bulletproof Diva," defining not only what she is but also what she is *not*. I quote extensively from Jones to demonstrate the range of experience that she allows for in this redefinition:

> Consider this a narrative in which we invent our own heroine, the Bulletproof Diva. A woman whose sense of dignity and self cannot be denied; who, though she may live in a war zone like Brownsville, goes out everyday greased, pressed, and dressed, with hair faded and braided and freeze-dried and spit-curled and wrapped and locked and cut to a sexy baldie (so she is all eyes and lips) and piled ten inches high and colored siren red, cobalt blue, and flaming yellow. She is fine and she knows it. She has to know it because who else will. . . . A Bulletproof Diva is not, I repeat, *not* that tired stereotype, the emasculating black bitch too hard for love or piety. It's safe to assume that a Bulletproof Diva is whoever you make her – corporate girl, teen mom, or the combination – as long as she has the lip and nerve, *and as long as she uses that lip and nerve to raise up herself and the world.* (Jones 1994, 3; emphasis mine)

Morgan's "Memo of Retirement" and Jones's definition of the Bulletproof Diva do not advocate dropping out of politics or individualism. Rather they remind us of the road that Black women have traveled to get to this point in our collective history. They open up the possibility of self-preservation and community activism as intersecting, reinforcing objectives on the road to Black liberation.

Another aspect of Black women's relationships is how Black women relate to one another. Young Black women writers both highlight the support they feel from other Black women and bear witness to the misguided power that Black women, sharing similar experiences around racism and sexism, exert over one another to wound in unfathomable ways. Competition, vying for status, and degraded self-worth can be Black women's worst interpersonal enemies. Morgan, Chambers, and Jones heed Audre Lorde's call in her essay "Eye to Eye" (1984) for Black women to face how we treat one another and what that says about how we feel about ourselves.

Chambers recalls encounters with other Black girls that, while not unusual, emphasize the ways that African-American women try to hold one another back, from calling Chambers a "sellout" to accusing her of "talking white" because she takes her education seriously. Morgan, in her chapter entitled "Chickenhead Envy," cogently calls out the behavior of said Chickenheads (Morgan 1999, 185–86).[11] To her credit, she is also self-reflective, exploring what so-called Chickenheads reflect back to Black women who are independent and ambitious. Morgan is initiating much-needed dialogue about Black women's culpability in our own oppression and how we oppress one another, especially in the areas of class, color, and sexual orientation. Morgan and Chambers, in fact, disrupt the notion that there is a unified Black sisterhood. While that may be the ideal, these authors point out how Black sisterhood is sometimes far from the reality of our relationships.

For all the emphasis on truth telling and exploring the totality of Black women's lives, the writers explored here are noticeably silent on issues of heterosexism, homophobia in the Black community, and Black women's sexuality in general. Jones and Morgan cogently delve into the history of stereotyping Black women as hyper-sexual and animalistic, yet there is no discussion of what a positive Black female sexuality would look like. Instead, Black women's (hetero)sexuality is alluded to in their musing on "fine brothers" and dating mores. Black women's sexuality is something to be repressed, except on a surface level of relationships with Black men.

Chambers's only mention of her own sexuality, for example, discusses her fear of an unwanted pregnancy derailing her educational and career goals. This deprioritizing of teen sexuality sheds light on her mother's understated reaction to Veronica's first menstrual cycle. Rather than celebrating her step into young womanhood, her mother makes sure Veronica knows how not to get pregnant. In her later potentially sexual encounters with young men, Chambers can only call on the experiences of friends raised by single mothers, as she was, and friends who were single mothers. Of flirting and potential intimate involvements, Chambers says, "No guy ever said a word to me that didn't sound like a lie. The answer [to sex] was always no" (Chambers 1996, 70–71). While access to her sexuality is by no means dependent on engaging in sexual relations with anyone, blanket denials of her sexual self vis-à-vis young men also deny Chambers access to her own sexual agency. Even an avocation of abstinence would be an exertion of sexual agency.

Given the abundance of writing by African-American lesbians and their influence on Black feminist theory, the lack of attention to heterosexism is a step backward in moving a Black feminist agenda forward. In her chapter on "The F-Word," Morgan declares her allegiance to feminism because she feels feminism claimed her. The most she says about lesbians or heterosexism is a toned-down rebuttal to a man who said she must just need the right man, "as if I'd consider being mistaken for a lesbian an insult instead of an inaccuracy" (Morgan 1999, 42). Yet, in the context of these three texts, examining heterosexuality as a construct is ignored. Instead, within the texts it is a given that they are "straight girls."

The absence of frank discussions about sexuality is an odd repression that barely even acknowledges the authors' own sexuality, much less the variability of human sexuality. This is a noticeable elision given their attentive focus on the complexity of Black women's identities. This omission, or tentative dance, around Black women's sexuality leaves one to conclude that sexual stereotypes have been so debilitating that refuting them only results in the negation of a fuller spectrum for Black female sexual expression. When Black women, for example Alice Walker, Michele Wallace, and Rebecca Walker, frankly discuss their own and Black women's sexuality – be they heterosexual, lesbian, bisexual, or transgender – they run a constant threat of censure inside and outside the Black community through the deployment of degrading, historically rooted stereotypes of licentious Black female sexuality.

In "Toward a Genealogy of Black Female Sexuality," Evelyn Hammonds makes critical note of Black feminist theorizing on Black women's sexuality. In particular, she observes that "historically, Black women have reacted to the repressive force of the hegemonic discourse on race and sex and this image [Black women as empty space] with silence, secrecy, and a partially self-chosen invisibility" (Hammonds 1997, 171). Hammonds later calls not only for intervention that disrupts negative stereotypes about Black women's sexuality but also for critical engagement between Black heterosexual women and Black lesbians to develop a fuller Black feminist praxis around sexuality.

In light of the historical, strategic use of silence around Black women's sexuality by nineteenth-century reformers and the contemporary maligning of Black women such as Anita Hill and Lani Guinier, it is not surprising that Morgan, Jones, and Chambers skirt the issue of Black women's sexuality. The challenge that comes from analyzing their work is, as Hammonds (1997) suggests, the disruption of stereotypes but also the frank discussion of Black women's relationship to their sexual lives through consciousness-raising at all age levels.

The brothas

The recurring point of contention that Black women have with feminism is its impact on Black male/female relationships. Many times, Black feminists in the 1970s spent so much time reaffirming their commitment to Black men and the Black community that their gender critiques and actions to end sexism fell by the wayside. Thus it is incumbent on young Black feminist writers to tread a line between – to apply the Combahee River Collective Statement to the present – struggling with Black men *against* racism but also struggling with Black men about sexism (Combahee River Collective 1986, 12). Chambers, Jones, and Morgan do this to varying degrees by writing about Black men as fathers, as mothers' sons, as biological brothers, as spiritual/artistic brothers, as potential lovers, and as lifetime partners. In their personal and political examination of their lives, these writers show that the love Black women feel for Black men is sometimes diluted by the mutual disrespect and mistrust engendered by slavery and kept alive through women's and men's sustained patriarchal notions about gender.

Black fathers make brief appearances in these texts. Both Morgan's and Chambers's fathers left their families when they were young, and Jones's parents (writers Hettie Jones and Amiri Baraka, then LeRoi Jones) divorced. The emphasis that the Black community and media have placed on Black men's role in raising their sons has resulted, Morgan contends, in "precious little attention [being paid to] the significant role Black men play in shaping their daughters' ideas about themselves and love" (Morgan 1999, 123). More than a dismissal of the role of fathers, the pain these women experience around the father-daughter relationship slips in and out of their narratives. This pain is unresolved and, therefore, unspoken and untheorized. Morgan, in her chapter entitled "babymother," does attempt to address men's rights to choose, or not to choose, fatherhood as a reproductive rights issue with which feminists must deal if we desire equality. However, the reader is left to wonder how much of Morgan's anxiety about men's reproductive rights is linked to the emotional and political fallout of her own father's absence. Such a revelation would do much of the professed work of feminist theory by connecting theory and personal experience.

The physical or emotional absence of fathers in a number of Black homes allows both Chambers and Morgan to confront Black women about the significant differences in the ways that they rear girl children and boy children. Chambers knew from an early age that her mother and her mother's closest friends, also immigrants from Panama, prized their boy children while girls were an afterthought. " 'And Veronica,' they would say eventually. 'She's fine. All A's as usual,' " her mother would say in a sad voice that Veronica interpreted as a display of her mother's overriding concern for her brother, Malcolm (Chambers 1996, 46–47). Malcolm began exhibiting behavioral problems after their father left. Chambers is consistently aware of sexist ideologies and their impact on girls. However, when lamenting her brother's drug problem and incarceration, Chambers appears resistant to considering his problems to result from sexist and racist ideologies as well. The endangered Black male dialogue of the late 1980s and 1990s was problematic, but a broader political analysis of Black men's vulnerability and subsequent understanding of her brother's life under white supremacy are buried under Chambers's sibling rivalry.

Morgan offers a fuller analysis of the disparities in how Black women love their sons and raise their daughters, perhaps because her examination focuses more on the connections between sons and the lovers/partners/ husbands they become. This is the closest that any of these authors comes to lobbing a generational grenade and assigning culpability for perpetuating the strongblackwoman and endangered blackmale roles, which are compatible only in that they encourage an enabler/ dependent relationship. Morgan wonders how older women can teach their daughters to be independent and ambitious and then comment that they are too strong willed to be acceptable to any man. Morgan also notes that these are the same women who loved their sons but did not teach young men about mutuality in relationships.

The doppelganger to this portrayal of Black mothers is, according to Morgan, those women who maintain "all men are dogs" (Morgan 1999, 137). This might be a defensive stance to pass on to daughters, but what message does this impart to their sons about self-worth? And what behavior do mothers condone or abet if they think men are meant to have many girlfriends, to be "playas"? Women who believe their sons can *do* no wrong and those who believe their sons can only *be* wrong, and therefore need constant protection, pass along a fatalistic stance that ignores all the Black men who are, Morgan notes, "taking care of their kids, working and contributing to their communities" (1999, 131).

The writers examined here clearly are conflicted about how Black women and Black men relate to one another. Jones recalls the Black men who responded to her feminist performance group's work as artistic and intellectual compatriots. Yet in her chapter "Open Letter to a Brother," she ponders the ways that sexual liberation enabled Black men to reinforce negative myths about themselves, resulting in what she calls "the Dog Syndrome." Offering much-needed critiques of Black masculinity, Jones seeks to delve deeper into how Black men's lack of access to political and economic power became so entrenched in obtaining sexual power. The Dog Syndrome is in fact, according to Jones, "black male impotence masquerading as power" (1994, 217).

Jones's and Morgan's essays, read with Chambers's more personal backdrop, begin to offer a direction for open discussion in the Black community about Black masculinity and femininity, Black men and Black women. If generational politics come into play in Black feminist thought for these women, it is in putting contemporary tensions into historical perspective. Rather than blaming the past for the distrust that plagues Black women and men, younger Black feminists are, read in conjunction, asking Black men to forgo atonement for the past and take responsibility for male privilege in the present. Being a Black man in U.S. society is much more complex than adopting a pose and maintaining it. Yet, critically, these Black feminists, Morgan in particular, are offering complementary suggestions for Black women to check their behavior and expectations of men and relationships. How do we participate in our own oppression and that of future generations? What is our stake in maintaining gender relations that can only lead to continued trauma?

[. . .]

Young Black feminists are not uniform in political thought, so it would be dishonest to assert that Black women still feel the need to apologize for engaging feminist politics. Yet, in linking with the work of feminist foremothers, contemporary, young Black feminist writers continue to explain feminism's relevance to Black communities. Far from reinventing the feminist wheel, young Black feminists are building on the legacy left by nineteenth-century abolitionists, antilynching crusaders, club women, Civil Rights organizers, Black Nationalist revolutionaries, and 1970s Black feminists. They are not inserting themselves into the third wave paradigm as much as they are continuing the work of a history of Black race women concerned with gender issues. These three writers in particular also have in common with their ancestors the gift of literacy and the privilege of education.

Sheila Radford-Hill's *Further to Fly: Black Women and the Politics of Empowerment* advocates an "authentic feminism." This is not another brand of feminism but a call for Black feminism not to "fall in love with the sound of its own voice" and return to an applied feminism (Radford-Hill 2000, xxi). Young Black feminist writers might, in fact, need to fall in love with the sounds of their own voices. In a discriminatory society that continues to marginalize the theorizing of women of color, who but ourselves will honor our words as we continue the legacy of struggle to end racism, sexism, heterosexism, ablism, and classism? The key to that honoring, as Chambers, Morgan, and Jones note in their writing and as the hip-hop generation insists, is to keep it real.

Notes

1   I capitalize "Black" to denote the 1970s political history of Black empowerment from which Black feminist theorizing and activism emerged.

2   My omission of sexuality and sexual orientation is strategic because, as I explain later in this essay, these authors' discussions of sexuality are distinctly abbreviated and circumscribed.

3   I first heard this critique of the wave model posed by Guy-Sheftall in a graduate course on Black women's history.

4   Today, the Third Wave Foundation focuses on inspiring and cultivating feminist activism among women ages fifteen to thirty, who are considered within the demographic of the third wave. Defining the waves of feminism according to generation also raises the question of where women who are older than thirty, but were children during the height of second wave activism, fall in this generational schemata.

5   Disability as an issue for women is wholly absent from this text, as well as the texts by young Black feminists examined here.

6   For another research project on the history of Black feminist organizations, I conducted twenty-two oral history interviews with Black feminists active during the 1970s about their organizations (Springer in press). The last question I posed to them was on their thoughts about Black feminist activism today. This question was not specifically about young Black women, but some of my interviewees did wonder cynically, "What Black feminism?" as if young women had not picked up the torch. Others who I interviewed spoke positively in terms of continuing their activism and working with young Black women who they encountered daily to nurture a Black feminist politic.

7   As Cheryl Hicks (2001) notes, *Essence* is interesting in this regard as it was founded and continues to be published by African-American men, though several African-American women have served as editor-in-chief.

8   Barbara Ransby criticizes Zook, claiming that Zook "distorted and obscured more about black feminism than she revealed" (2000, n. 1). Though she does not elucidate this claim, I believe that Ransby is referring to the lack of attention that Zook pays to grassroots, decentralized Black feminist organizing in the interest of raising compelling questions about the invisibility of a national Black feminist activism (2000).

9   Generation X consists of people born between 1961 and 1981. Unlike the wave model, this bracketing of generations adapts to the age of the members of the generation. That is, baby boomers, regardless of how old they are, remain baby boomers. Those born between 1961 and 1981, though getting older, remain within that particular social designation of Generation X.

10 Radford-Hill makes a similar observation. In her book *Further to Fly: Black Women and the Politics of Empowerment*, she claims that Black women have been experiencing a crisis in identity since 1965, roughly coinciding with the publication of the

Moynihan Report, which demonized Black women as the root cause of Black "pathology" (2000, xx).

11 A "chickenhead" is a woman who is a materialist, dresses in barely there outfits ("skankwear"), and, according to Morgan, is adept at stroking the male ego (185). She is also calculating, cunning, and savvy when it comes to getting what she wants – all acceptable traits for men in white, capitalist patriarchy but wholly unacceptable for Black women.

References

Bambara, Toni Cade, ed. 1970. *The Black Woman: An Anthology*. New York: New American Library.

Baumgardner, Jennifer, and Amy Richards. 2000. "Thou Shalt Not Become Thy Mother." In their *Manifesta: Young Women, Feminism and the Future*, 219–34. New York: Farrar, Straus, & Giroux.

Chambers, Veronica. 1996. *Mama's Girl*. New York: Riverhead.

Cole, Johnnetta, and Beverly Guy-Sheftall. In press. *Gender Talk*. New York: Ballantine.

Combahee River Collective. 1986. *The Combahee River Collective Statement: Black Feminist Organizing in the Seventies and Eighties*. New York: Kitchen Table, Women of Color Press.

Cooper, Anna Julia. 1988. *A Voice from the South by a Black Woman of the South*. New York: Oxford University Press.

Davis, Angela. (1971) 1995. "Reflections on the Black Woman's Role in the Community of Slaves" In *Words of Fire: An Anthology of African-American Feminist Thought*, ed. Beverly Guy-Sheftall, 200–218. New York: New Press.

Farley, Christopher John. 1998. "Neo-Soul on a Roll." *Time*, July 6.

Findlen, Barbara, ed. 1995. *Listen Up! Voices from the Next Feminist Generation*. Seattle: Seal.

Hammonds, Evelyn. 1997. "Toward a Genealogy of Black Female Sexuality: The Problematic of Silence." In *Feminist Genealogies, Colonial Legacies, Democratic Futures*, ed. M. Jacqui Alexander and Chandra Talpade Mohanty, 170–81. New York: Routledge.

Hicks, Cheryl. 2001. Conversation with author, May 2.

hooks, bell. 2000, *Feminism Is for Everybody: Passionate Politics*. Boston: South End.

Jacobs, Harriet. 1987. *Incidents in the Life of a Slave Girl: Written by Herself*. Ed. Jean Fagin Yellin. Cambridge, Mass.: Harvard University Press.

Jones, Lisa. 1994. *Bulletproof Diva: Tales of Race, Sex, and Hair*. New York: Doubleday.

Lorde, Audre. 1984. "Eye to Eye: Black Women, Hatred and Anger." In her *Sister Outsider*, 145–75. Trumansburg, N.Y.: Crossing.

Morgan, Joan. 1999. *When Chickenheads Come Home to Roost: My Life as a Hip-Hop Feminist*. New York: Simon & Schuster.

Movement, The. 1969. *Black Panther Sisters Talk about Women's Liberation*. Pamphlet. N.p.: New England Free Press.

Orr, Catherine. 1997. "Charting the Currents of the Third Wave." *Hypatia* 12(3): 29–45.

Radford-Hill, Sheila. 2000. *Further to Fly: Black Women and the Politics of Empowerment*. Minneapolis: University of Minnesota Press.

Ransby, Barbara. 2000. "Black Feminism at Twenty-One: Reflections on the Evolution of a National Community." *Signs: Journal of Women in Culture and Society* 25(4):1215–21.

Smith, Barbara. 2001. Conversation with author, April 14.

Smith, Barbara, ed. 1983. *Home Girls: A Black Feminist Anthology*. New York: Kitchen Table, Women of Color Press.

Springer, Kimberly. 2001. "Practicing Politics in the Cracks: The Interstitial Politics of Black Feminist Organizations." *Meridians* 1(2):155–91.

———. In press. *Living for the Revolution: Black Feminist Organizations, 1968–1980*. Chapel Hill, NC.: Duke University Press.

Steinem, Gloria. 1995. "Foreword," In Walker 1995, xiii–xxviii.

Walker, Rebecca. 1995. *To Be Real: Telling the Truth and Changing the Face of Feminism*. New York: Anchor.

Wallace, Michele. 1997. *To Hell and Back: On the Road with Black Feminism*. Pamphlet. Brooklyn, N.Y.: Olympia X.

White, Deborah. 1985. *Ar'n't I a Woman: Female Slaves in the Plantation South*. New York: Norton.

Young, Bob. 1994. "Books Columnist Writes to 'Find Something Out." *Boston Herald*, April 23, 20.

Zook, Kristal Brent. 1995. "A Manifesto of Sorts for a Black Feminist Movement." *New York Times Magazine*, November 12, 86–89.

Chapter 30

Patricia J. Williams

RACE AND RIGHTS

A T A FACULTY MEETING ONCE, I raised several issues: racism among my students, my difficulty in dealing with it by myself, and my need for the support of colleagues. I was told by a white professor that "we" should be able to "break the anxiety by just laughing about it." Another nodded in agreement and added that "the key is not to take this sort of thing too seriously."

Sometime after that, the *New York Times* ran a story about the arrest of one hundred parole violators who had been lured to a brunch with promises of free tickets to a Washington Redskins–Cincinnati Bengals football game: "The suspects reported to the Washington Convention Center after receiving a letter saying they had won the tickets from a cable television company, which had been set up as part of the police operation."[1] That evening, the televised news accounts of this story were infinitely more graphic. They showed one hundred black men entering a hall dressed for a party, some in tuxedos, some with fresh shiny perms, some with flowers in their lapels, some clearly hungry and there for the promised food, some dressed in the outfits of anticipatory football spectators, in raccoon coats and duckbill hats that said "Redskins." One hundred black men rolling up the escalators to the convention hall were greeted by smiling white (undercover) masters of ceremony, popping flashbulbs, lots of cameras, and pretty white women in skimpy costumes. Everyone smiled and laughed, like children at a birthday party. Everyone looked as though they were about the business of having a good time together. We saw the one hundred black men being rounded up by a swarm of white men, white women (also undercover agents) dressed as cheerleaders bouncing up and down on the side, a policeman dressed as a chicken with an automatic hidden in the lining, a SWAT team dressed in guerrilla-warfare green bursting in with weapons drawn.

My faculty colleagues have urged me not to give the voices of racism "so much power." Laughter is the way to disempower the forces of evil, I am told. But is it the racism I am disempowering if I laugh? Wouldn't this betray the deadly seriousness of it all? Laughing purposefully at what is hurtful seems somehow related to a first lesson in the skill of staged humiliation. Racism will thus be reduced to fantasy, a slapstick vaunting of good over evil – except that it is real. The cultural image of favored step-siblings laughing and pointing at such stupidity, at the sheer disingenuousness of bad children falling for the promise that they will get gifts, of even daring to imagine that they will get wonderful gifts too . . . if I laugh, don't I risk becoming that or, worse, a caricature of that image, that glossy marketing of despair?

Those who compose the fringe of society have always been the acceptable scapegoats, the butt of jokes, and the favored whipping boys. It resembles the pattern within psychotic families where one child is set up as "sick" and absorbs the whole family's destructiveness. The child may indeed be sick in unsociably visible and dramatically destructive ways, but the family is unhealthy in its conspiracy not to see in themselves the emanation of such sickness. The child becomes the public mirror of quietly enacted personality slaughter. Resistance to seeing the full reality is played out in the heaving of blame and, most cowardly of all, in disempowering others and ourselves by making fun of serious issues. The alternative (and infinitely more difficult) course is to face the interconnectedness, the enmeshed pattern of public dismissiveness and private humiliation, of private crimes and publicly righteous wrongs, of individual disappointments and national tragedies.

In sum, I see the problem at hand not as one of *my* giving racism too much power, but of how we may all give more power to the voices that racism suppresses.

I am attending a conference called The Sounds of Silence. The topic of the day is the social construction of race and gender and oppression. People hurl heavy names at one another: Hegel, Foucault, Adorno. The discussion is interesting, but the undercurrent is dialectical war; there are lots of authority-bullets whizzing through the air.

I think: my raciality is socially constructed, and I experience it as such. I feel my blackself as an eddy of conflicted meanings – and meaninglessness – in which my self can get lost, in which agency and consent are tumbled in constant motion. This sense of motion, the constant windy sound of manipulation whistling in my ears, is a reminder of society's constant construction of my blackness.

Somewhere at the center, my heart gets lost. I transfigure the undesirability of my racial ambiguity into the necessity of deference, the accommodation of condescension. It is very painful when I permit myself to see all this. I shield myself from it wherever possible. Indeed, at the conference it feels too dangerous to say any of this aloud, so I continue to muse to myself, pretending to doze. I am awakened suddenly to a still and deadly serious room: someone has asked me to comment on the rape of black women and the death of our children.

Caught with my guard down, I finesse the question with statistics and for-gotten words. What actually comes to my mind, however, is a tragically powerful embodiment of my ambiguous, tenuous, social positioning: the case of Tawana Brawley, a fifteen-year-old black girl from Wappinger Falls, New York. In late November 1987, after a four-day disappearance, she was found in a vacant lot, clothed only in a shirt and a plastic garbage bag into which she had apparently crawled; she was in a dazed state, not responding to noise, cold, or ammonia;

there was urine-soaked cotton stuffed in her nose and ears; her hair had been chopped off; there were cigarette burns over a third of her body; "KKK" and "Nigger" had been inscribed on her torso; her body was smeared with dog feces.[2] This much is certain, "certain" because there were objective third persons to testify as to her condition in that foundling state (and independent "objective" testimony is apparently what is required before experience gets to be labeled truth) although even this much certainty was persistently recast as nothing-at-all in the subsequent months. By September the *New York Times* was reporting that "her ears and nose were *protected* by cotton wads"; that it was not her *own* hair that was cut, but hair extensions "woven into her own short hair" that had either been torn or cut out; that only her clothes and not her body had been burned; that, from the moment she was found, "*seemingly* dazed and degraded, [she] assumed the mantle of victim"; and that her dazed condition was "ephemeral" because, in the emergency room, after resisting efforts to pull open her eyes, "Dr. Pena concluded that Tawana was not unconscious and was aware of what was going on around her . . . In a moment of quiet drama, Dr. Pena confronted Miss Brawley: 'I know you can hear me so open your eyes,' she commanded. Tawana opened her eyes and was able to move them in all directions by following Pena's finger."[3]

This much is certainly worth the conviction that Tawana Brawley has been the victim of some unspeakable crime. No matter how she got there. No matter who did it to her – and even if she did it to herself. Her condition was clearly the expression of some crime against her, some tremendous violence, some great violation that challenges comprehension. And it is this much that I grieve about. The rest of the story is lost, or irrelevant in the worst of all possible ways.

But there is a second version of the story. On July 14, 1988, New York State Attorney General Robert Adams stated that "there may not have been any crime committed here."[4] A local television call-in poll showed that the vast majority of New Yorkers – the vast majority of any potential jury pool, in other words – agreed with him. Most people felt either that if she were raped it was "consensual" (as cruel an oxymoron that ever was) or that she "did it to herself" (as if self-mutilation and attempted suicide are free-enterprise, private matters of no social consequence with reference to which the concern of others is an invasion of privacy). It was a surprise to no one, therefore, when a New York grand jury concluded that Tawana Brawley had made the whole thing up.[5]

When Tawana Brawley was finally able to tell her story – she remained curled in fetal position for several days after she was found – she indicated that she had been kidnapped and raped by six white men:

> Nodding or shaking her head to questions . . . Miss Brawley gave contradictory answers. She indicated that she had been subjected to acts of oral sex, and after first indicating she had not been raped, she suggested she had been assaulted by three white men . . . Asked who assaulted her, she grabbed the silver badge on his uniform but did not respond when he asked if the badge she saw was like this. He then gave her his notebook and she wrote "white cop." Asked where, she wrote "woods." He then asked her if she had been raped, and she wrote: "a lot" and

drew an arrow to "white cop" . . . This response was the closest Miss
Brawley ever came to asserting to authorities that she had been raped;
her family and advisers, however, asserted many times that she was
raped, sodomized and subjected to other abuse.[6]

The white men she implicated included the district attorney of Wappinger Falls,
a highway patrolman, and a local police officer. This accusation was not only the
first but also the last public statement Tawana Brawley ever made. (One may well
question why she, a minor and a rape victim, was ever put in the position of
making public statements at all. One might also inquire why the Child Protective
Services Agency, which is supposed to intervene in such cases, did not.[7])

What replaced Tawana's story was a thunderous amount of media brouhaha,
public offerings of a thousand and one other stories, fables, legends, and myths.
A sampling of these enticing distractions includes:

- Tawana's mother, Glenda Brawley, who fled to the sanctuary of a church to
  avoid arrest for failing to testify before a grand jury and to protest the failure
  of the same grand jury to subpoena the men named by her daughter.

- Tawana's stepfather, from whom she had allegedly run away on prior occasions;
  by whom she had allegedly been beaten many times before – once even in
  a police station, in the presence of officers before they had a chance to
  intervene; and who served seven years for manslaughter in the death of his
  first wife, whom he stabbed fourteen times and, while awaiting trial for that
  much, then shot and killed.

- Tawana's boyfriend, who was serving time on drug charges in an upstate
  facility and whom she had gone to visit shortly before her disappearance.

- Tawana's lawyers, civil-rights activists Alton Maddox and C. Vernon Mason,
  who advised their client not to cooperate with investigating authorities until
  an independent prosecutor was appointed to handle the case.

- Tawana's spiritual counselor, the Reverend Al Sharpton, described variously
  as a "minister without a congregation" ("Mr. Sharpton, who is still a member
  of the Washington Temple Church of God in Christ, does not serve as the
  pastor of any church. 'My total time is civil rights,' he said. 'It's kind of
  hard to do both.'"[8]) and as an informer for the FBI ("The Rev. Al Sharpton,
  a Brooklyn minister who has organized civil disobedience demonstrations and
  has frequently criticized the city's predominantly white political leadership,
  assisted law-enforcement officials in at least one recent criminal investigation
  of black community groups, Government sources said. He also allowed
  investigators to wiretap a telephone in his home, the sources said."[9]). Al
  Sharpton, a man who had a "long and well-publicized history of involvement
  in the wiretapping of civil rights leaders, yet *mirabile dictu* a sudden but
  "trusted adviser" to the Brawley family. Al Sharpton, tumbling off the stage
  in a bout of fisticuffs with Roy Innis on the Morton Downey television show,
  brought to you Live! from the Apollo Theater.[10] Al Sharpton, railing against
  the court order holding Glenda Brawley in contempt, saying to the television
  cameras, "Their arms are too short to box with God."

It was Al Sharpton who proceeded to weave the story where Tawana left off. It was he who proceeded, on the Phil Donahue show, to implicate the Irish Republican Army, a man with a missing finger, and the Mafia. And it was he who spirited Tawana Brawley off into hiding, shortly after the police officer she had implicated in her rape committed suicide.

More hiding. As if it were a reenactment of her kidnap, a re-reenactment of her disappearing into the middle of her own case. It was like watching the Pied Piper of Harlem, this slowly replayed television spectacle of her being led off by the hand, put in a car, and driven to "a secret location"; a dance into thin air that could be accounted for by nothing less than sheer enchantment. I had a terrible premonition, as I watched, that Tawana Brawley would never be heard from again.

She has not been heard from again. From time to time there are missives from her advisers to the world: Tawana is adjusting well to her new school; Tawana wants to be a model; Tawana approves of the actions of her advisers; and, most poignantly, Tawana is "depressed," so her advisers are throwing her a party.

But the stories in the newspapers are no longer about Tawana anyway. They are all about black manhood and white justice; a contest of wills between her attorneys, the black community, and the New York state prosecutor's office. Since Tawana's statement implicated a prosecutor, one issue was the propriety of her case's being handled through the usual channels, rather than setting up a special unit to handle this and other allegations of racial violence. But even this issue was not able to hold center stage with all the thunder and smoke of raucous male outcry, curdling warrior accusations, the flash of political swords and shields – typified by Governor Cuomo's gratuitous offer to talk to Tawana personally; by Al Sharpton's particularly gratuitous statement that Tawana might show up at her mother's contempt hearing because "most children want to be in court to say good-bye to their mothers before they go to jail"[11]; by Phil Donahue's interview with Glenda Brawley, which he began with "No one wants to jump on your bones and suggest that you are not an honorable person but . . ."; by the enlistment of the support of Louis Farrakhan and a good deal of antisemitic insinuation; by the mishandling and loss of key evidence by investigating authorities; by the commissioning of a so-called Black Army to encircle Glenda Brawley on the courthouse steps; by the refusal of the New York attorney general's office to take seriously the request for an independent prosecutor; and by the testimony of an associate of Sharpton's, a former police officer named Perry McKinnon, that Mason, Maddox, and Sharpton did not believe Tawana's story. (On television I hear this story reported in at least three different forms: [McKinnon says Tawana lied; McKinnon says Sharpton lied about believing Tawana's story; McKinnon says that Mason and Maddox made up the whole thing in order to advance their own political careers. Like a contest, or a lottery with some drunken, solomonic gameshow host at the helm, the truth gets sorted out by a call-in poll. Channel 7, the local ABC affiliate, puts the issue to its viewers: Do you believe Sharpton? Or do you believe McKinnon? I forgot to listen to the eleven o'clock news, when the winner and the weather were to have been announced.)

To me, the most ironic thing about this whole bad business – as well as the thread of wisdom that runs at the heart of the decision not to have Tawana Brawley testify – is that were she to have come out of hiding and pursued trial in the conventional manner, she would no doubt have undergone exactly what she did undergo, in the courts and in the media. Without her, the script unfolded at a particularly abstract and fantastical level, but the story would be the same: wild black girl who loves to lie, who is no innocent (in New York television newscasters inadvertently, but repeatedly, referred to her as the "defendant") and whose wiles are the downfall of innocent, jaded, desperate white men; this whore-lette, the symbolic consort of rapacious, saber-rattling, buffoonish black men asserting their manhood, whether her jailbird boyfriend, her smooth-headed FBI drugbuster informant of a spiritual adviser; or her grandstanding, unethically boisterous so-called lawyers who have yet to establish "a *single* cognizable legal claim."[12]

Tawana's terrible story has every black woman's worst fears and experiences wrapped into it. Few will believe a black woman who has been raped by a white man. In one of the more appallingly straightforward statements to this effect, Pete Hamill, while excoriating the "racist hustlers" Sharpton, Mason, and Maddox for talking "about 'whites' as if they were a monolith" asked: "After Tawana Brawley, who will believe the next black woman who says she was raped by white men? Or the one after her?"[13] A slightly more highbrow version of the same sentiment was put forth in a *New York Times* editorial: "How can anyone know the depths of cynicism and distrust engendered by an escapade like this? Ask the next black person who is truly victimized – and meets skepticism and disbelief. Ask the next skeptic, white or black."[14]

If anyone believes that some white man even wanted her, no one will believe that she is not a whore. (White women are prostitutes; black women are whores. White women sell themselves, in implied Dickensian fashion, because they are jaded and desperate; black women *whore* as a way of being, as an innateness of sootiness and contamination, as a sticky-sweet inherency of black womanhood persistently imaged as overripe fruit – so they whore, according to this fantasy-script, as easily as they will cut your throat or slit open said deep sweet fruit, spitting out afterwards a predictable stream of blood and seeds and casual curses.) Black women whore because it is sensual and lazy and vengeful. How can such a one be raped? Or so the story goes.

It is no easier when a black woman is raped by a black man (many of the newspapers have spun eager nets of suspicion around Tawana's stepfather[15] or a boyfriend). Black-on-black rape is not merely the violation of one woman by one man; it is a sociological event, a circus of stereotypification.[16] It is a contest between the universalized black man and the lusty black female. The intimacy of rape becomes a public display, full of passion, pain and gutsy blues.

Tawana Brawley herself remains absent from all this. She is a shape, a hollow, an emptiness at the center. Joy Kogawa's "white sound":

> There is a silence that cannot speak.
> There is a silence that will not speak.
> Beneath the grass the speaking dreams and beneath the dreams is a
> sensate sea. The speech that frees comes forth from that amniotic deep.
> To attend its voice, I can hear it say, is to embrace its absence. I fail
> the task. The word is stone.[17]

There is no respect or wonder for her silence. The world that created her oppression now literally countenances it, filling the void of her suffering with sacrilegious noise, clashing color, serial tableaux of lurid possibility. Truth, like a fad, takes on life of its own, independent of action and limited only by the imagination of self-proclaimed visionaries; untruth becomes truth through belief, and disbelief untruths the truth. The world turns upside-down; the quiet, terrible, nearly invisible story of her suffering may never emerge from the clamor that overtook the quest for "what happened" and polarized it into the bizarre and undecideable litigation of "something happened" versus "nothing happened."

In the face of all this, there is some part of me that wanted this child to stay in hiding, some part of me that understands the instinct to bury her rather than expound. Exposure is the equivalent of metarape, as hiding with Al Sharpton is the equivalent of metakidnap. It feels as if there are no other options than hiding or exposing. There is danger everywhere for her, no shelter, no protection. There is no medicine circle for her, no healing society, no stable place to testify and be heard, in the unburdening of one heart.

There are three enduring pictures I have of Tawana Brawley. The first is drawn from the images that both signaled and sensationalized the public controversy: the "television cameras invading the Brawley home to zoom in for a close-up of Tawana lying on a couch, looking brutalized, disoriented, almost comatose." And the pictures that were either leaked or "escaped" from the attorney general's office, the "police-evidence photographs showing Tawana Brawley as she looked when she was first brought by ambulance to a hospital following her rape: unconscious, dirty, half-naked, a 'censorship band' on the pictures covering only the nipples on her otherwise exposed breasts."[18] Her body so open and public; her eyes closed, her face shuttered, her head turned always away from the cameras.

The second image I carry of her is the widely circulated picture of her standing just behind Al Sharpton as he spoke for her. It is an image retained from innumerable photographs, taken from every angle and published over and over again, for months, everywhere: Al Sharpton with his mouth open, the perpetually open mouth. Tawana standing in his shadow clothed in silence, obedient and attentive, patient, wide-eyed, and unremittingly passive.

The third image is one described by a student of mine. At the height of the controversy, Tawana attended a comedy show at the Apollo Theater in Harlem. One of the comedians called attention to her presence in the audience and, in a parody of the federal antisex and antidrug campaigns, advised her to "just say no next time." As the audience roared with merriment and the spotlight played on her, Tawana threw back her head and laughed along with the crowd. She opened her mouth and laughed, in false witness of this cruel joke. It is the only image I have of Tawana with her mouth open – caught in a position of compromise, of satisfying the pleasure and expectations of others, trapped in the pornography of living out other people's fantasy.

I also take away three images of the men in whose shadow Tawana always stood. The first, and just plain weirdest, is that of Al Sharpton boxing with Roy Innis on the ultraconservative and ultrapsychotic Morton Downey show:

> Conservative black leader Roy Innis toppled Tawana Brawley adviser
> Al Sharpton while taping a TV program on black leadership, and the
> two civil rights gadflies vowed yesterday to settle their dispute in a
> boxing ring . . . "He tried to 'Bogart' me in the middle of my statement,"
> said Innis . . . "I said no dice . . . We stood up and the body language
> was not good. So I acted to protect myself. I pushed him and he went
> down" . . . As the rotund preacher tumbled backward, Downey and
> several bodyguards jumped between the pair. Neither man was hurt
> . . . Sharpton said he hoped boxing promoter Don King would help
> organize a Sharpton–Innis charity boxing match . . . but said he would
> promote it himself if necessary . . . "The best part is that we will be
> giving a very positive lesson" to young black people in this city about
> conflicting resolution – but not on the street with guns and knives,"
> Innis said. "It will be an honest, clean and honorable contest."[19]

The second image I have is of heavyweight champion Mike Tyson, whose own
tumultuous home life was momentarily overshadowed when, with a great deal of
public ceremony, he presented Tawana with a gold Rolex watch and ringside
tickets for his next match. Yet there was an odd intersection in the Brawley and
Tyson stories: in the contemporaneous coverage of the marital spats between Tyson
and his wife, actress Robin Givens – and in the face of uncontested allegations
that Tyson used his lethal million-dollar fists to beat her up – it was somehow
Givens and her mother, like Tawana and hers, who became everyone's favorite
despised object in supermarket-checkout conversation.[20] Tyson's image as a big
harmless puppy whose uncontrolled paws were only a feature of his exuberant
lovability found ultimate and ironic expression, as cultured in the media, with his
visit and gifts to the Brawley family.

The last image is one I saw in the newspaper shortly after the grand-jury report
had been published, of Louis Farrakhan, unkindly captured with his mouth wide
open. The story says that Tawana Brawley has surfaced from her long silence and

> expressed a desire to become a Muslim and will receive a new Muslim
> name . . . Mr. Farrakhan [leader of the Nation of Islam] . . . told an
> audience of 10,000 on Sunday that he . . . rejected the grand jury's
> findings, and he vowed vengeance on those who, he said, had attacked
> the girl. "You raped my daughter and I will kill you and dismember
> your body and feed it to the fowl of the air."[21]

The photo also shows Tawana, standing just behind Farrakhan. She is wrapped and
turbanned in white, the image of chastity, of rigid propriety, of womanhood's
submission to rule and ritual in a world where obedience is an unendingly
complicated affair. There is a prayerful expression on her face. Her eyes are
unreadable, and her mouth is closed.

Notes and references

1   "Police, Marshals and Chicken Lure Fugitives into Custody," *New York Times*, December 16, 1985, p. B17.

2   E. Diamond, "The Brawley Fiasco," *New York Magazine*, July 18, 1988, p. 22.

3   "Evidence Points to Deceit by Brawley," *New York Times*, September 27, 1988, p. A1, italics added.

4   M. Cottman, "Abrams' Brawley Update: There Might Be No Crime," *New York Newsday*, July 15, 1988, p. 5.

5   Robert McFadden, "Brawley Made Up Story of Assault, Grand Jury Finds," *New York Times*, October 7, 1988, p. 1.

6   *New York Times,* September 27, 1988, p. A1.

7   "What first signalled to me that a Black girl was about to become a public victim was hearing the *name* of an alleged rape victim – Tawana Brawley – given on a local radio news show. Since when does the press give the name of any rape victim, much less one who is underage? Obviously when the victim is Black, and thus not worthy of the same respect and protection that would be given a white child." Audrey Edwards, "The Rape of Tawana Brawley," *Essence*, November 1988, p. 80.

     As NAACP attorney Conrad Lynn observed, "State law provides that if a child appears to have been sexually molested, then the Child Protective Services Agency is supposed to take jurisdiction and custody of that child. Now, Tawana Brawley was 15 at the time of the incident. If that had been done, as I proposed early on, the agency would have given her psychiatric attention and preserved evidence, if there were evidence . . . But there was a state decision that the agency shouldn't be involved." Editorial, "What happened to Tawana Brawley's Case – and to Attitudes about Race and Justice," *New York Times*, October 9, 1988, p. E8.

8   E. R. Shipp, "A Flamboyant Leader of Protests," *New York Times*, January 21, 1988, p. B6.

9   M. A. Farber, "Protest Figure Reported To Be a U.S. Informant," *New York Times*, January 21, 1988, p. B1. "Mr. Sharpton said that he – not investigators – had put a recording device on his phone, but only to serve as a 'hot line' for people turning in crack dealers" (p. B6).

10   "Roy Innis Pushes Al Sharpton: Fracas at 'Downey Show' Taping: Boxing Match Planned," *Washington Post*, August 11, 1988, p. D4.

11   A. Bollinger, "Tawana's Mom to Get 'Black Army' Escort," *New York Post*, June 3,1988, p. 7

12   Howard Kurtz, "New York Moves Against Brawley Lawyers," *Washington Post,* October 7, 1988, p. A1.

13   Pete Hamill, "Black Media Should Tell the Truth" *New York Post*, September 29, 1988, p. 5.

14   "The Victims of the Brawley Case," *New York Times*, September 28, 1988, p. A22.

15   "One witness said Mr. King 'would watch her exercise' and talked to the girl 'in a real sexual way,' sometimes describing her as a 'fine fox' " *New York Times*, September 27, 1988, p. A16.

16   "Then it was off to the airport cafeteria for a strategy session and some cheeseburgers with advisers Alton Maddox, C. Vernon Mason and the Rev. Al Sharpton. 'The fat one, he ate the most,' said Carmen, the cashier. 'He and the

skinny one [an aide] bought about $50 or $60 of cheeseburgers, orange juice, chocolate cake, pasta salad and pie,' she added." J. Nolan, "Traveling Circus Has 'Em Rollin' in Aisles," *New York Post*, September 29, 1988, p. 4.

17   Joy Kogawa, *Obasan* (Boston: David Godine, 1981), p. 1.

18   Edwards, "The Rape of Tawana Brawley," p. 80.

19   *Washington Post*, August 11, 1988, p. D4.

20   Under the caption "Robin Givens: Waiter, A Tonic with Slime for the Lady," even *Ms* magazine wrote: "We sympathized with the fights. We understood the divorce. But this crazy libel suit we don't get. Was it his personality and his pecs, or did you just want the bucks all along?" E. Combs and M. Suh, "Women Who Made Us Cringe," *Ms*, January–February 1989, p. 96.

21   "Brawley to Get Muslim Name," *New York Times*, October 11, 1988, p. B3.

Chapter 31

Avtar Brah

DIFFERENCE, DIVERSITY, DIFFERENTIATION
Processes of racialisation and gender

DIFFERENCE, DIVERSITY, PLURALISM, HYBRIDITY – these are some of the most debated and contested terms of our time. Questions of difference are at the heart of many discussions within contemporary feminisms. In the field of education in Britain, questions of identity and community continue to dominate debates surrounding multiculturalism and anti-racism. In this chapter, I consider how these themes might help us to understand the racialisation of gender. However often the concept is exposed as vacuous, 'race' still acts as an apparently ineradicable marker of social difference. What makes it possible for the category to act in this way? What is the nature of social and cultural differences and what gives them their force? How does 'racial' difference then connect to difference and antagonisms organised around other markers, like 'gender' or 'class'? Such questions are important because they can help to explain people's tenacious investment in notions of identity, community and tradition.

One recurrent problem in this area is essentialism: that is, a notion of ultimate essence that transcends historical and cultural boundaries. Here I argue against an essentialist concept of difference while simultaneously problematising the issue of 'essentialism'. At what point, and in what ways, for example, does the specificity of a particular social experience become an expression of essentialism? In reviewing feminist debates, I suggest that black and white feminism should not be seen as essentially fixed oppositional categories but rather as historically contingent fields of contestation within discursive and material practices in a post-colonial society. In similar vein, I shall be arguing that analysis of the interconnections between racism, class, gender and sexuality must take account of the positionality of different racisms with respect to one another. Overall, I underline the importance of a macro-analysis that studies the inter-relationships between various forms of social differentiation empirically and historically, but without necessarily deriving them all from a single determining instance. In other words, I shall also be trying to avoid the danger of 'reductionism'.

The article is divided into three parts. In the first, I address the various notions of 'difference' that have emerged in recent discussions of how extensively the term 'black' can be used to define the experience of African-Caribbean and south Asian groups in post-war Britain. The second section is concerned with the ways in which issues of 'difference' have been framed with respect to racism within feminist theory and practice. My primary focus here is on the ongoing debate in Britain. I conclude with a brief examination of some conceptual categories used in the theorisation of 'difference' and suggest that greater clarity in how we conceptualise 'difference' may aid in developing sharper political strategies for social justice.

What's in a name? What's in a colour?

Over the past few years the usage of the term 'black' to refer to people of African-Caribbean and south Asian descent in Britain has been the subject of considerable controversy. It is relevant to address some of these arguments as they often centre around notions of difference.

The African-Caribbean and south Asian people who migrated to Britain in the post-war period found themselves occupying a broadly similar structural position within British society, as workers performing predominantly unskilled or semi-skilled jobs on the lowest rungs of the economy. Although the ideologies which racialised them were not identical in content there were similarities in their encounters with racism in arenas such as the workplace, the education system, the housing market and the health services. Their 'non-whiteness' was a common referent within the racism confronting them. These groups were then commonly described in popular, political and academic discourses as 'coloured people'. This was not a simple descriptive term. It had been the colonial code for a relationship of domination and subordination between the coloniser and colonised. Now the code was reworked and reconstituted in and through a variety of political, cultural and economic processes in post-war Britain.

The term 'black' was adopted by the emerging coalitions amongst African-Caribbean and south Asian organisations and activists in the late 1960s and 1970s. They were influenced by the way that the Black Power movement in the USA, which had turned the concept of Black on its head, divested it of its pejorative connotations in racialised discourses, and transformed it into a confident expression of an assertive group identity. The Black Power movement urged black Americans to construe the black community not as a matter of geography but rather in terms of the global African diaspora. Eschewing 'chromatism' – the basis of differentiation amongst blacks according to lighter or darker tone of skin – 'black' became a political colour to be worn with pride against colour-based racisms. The African-Caribbean and south Asian activists in Britain borrowed the term from the Black Power movement to foster a rejection of chromatism amongst those defined as 'coloured people' in Britain.

The politics of solidarity between African-Caribbean and south Asian activists of the period were also influenced by the history of anti-colonial struggles in Africa, Asia and the Caribbean. The fusion of these two influences in the formation of a project concerned to address the social condition of post-colonial subjects in the heart of the British metropolis meant that the concept of black has been associated with rather distinctive and somewhat different meanings in Britain as compared with the USA.

Recently British usage of the term 'black' has been criticised by commentators like Hazareesingh (1986) and Modood (1988). They argue that the 'black' in Black Power ideology referred specifically to the historical experience of people of sub-Saharan African descent, and was designed to create a positive political and cultural identity amongst black Americans. When used in relation to south Asians the concept is *de facto* emptied of those specific cultural meanings associated with phrases such as 'black music'. The concept can incorporate south Asians in a political sense only, and they therefore conclude that it denies Asian cultural identity. Clearly there is some force in this argument. It is certainly the case, as we have already noted, that the Black Power movement's mobilisation of the term 'black' was an attempt at reclaiming an African heritage that had been denied to black Americans by racism. But, as a historically specific political project located in the socio-political and economic dynamics in the USA, the Black Power ideology did not simply reclaim a pre-given ancestral past. In that very process, it also constructed a particular version of this heritage. Given that cultural processes are dynamic, and the process of claiming is itself mediated, the term 'black' does not have to be construed in essentialist terms. It can have different political and cultural meanings in different contexts. Its specific meaning in post-war Britain cannot be taken to have denied cultural differences between African, Caribbean and south Asian people when cultural difference was not the organising principle within this discourse or political practice. The concrete political struggles in which the new meaning was grounded acknowledged cultural differences but sought to accomplish political unity against racism. In any case, the issue of cultural difference cannot be posed purely in terms of differences between south Asian and African–Caribbean cultures. There are, for example, many differences between African and Caribbean cultures (which also include cultures of people of south Asian descent). Cultures in the diasporas always have their own specificity. In other words, even when the use of the 'black' is restricted to sub-Saharan Africa and its diasporas, it can be said, within the parameters of the terms set by the critics, to deny the cultural specificities of these diverse groups.

A second criticism of the ways in which 'black' has been employed in Britain has been that the concept is meaningless since many south Asians do not define themselves as black, and many African-Caribbeans do not recognise them as such. This assertion hinges partly on the criterion of numbers, but without providing supporting numerical evidence. In my own research I have found that south Asians will frequently describe themselves as 'kale' (black) when discussing issues of racism. But since the whole social being of south Asian and African-Caribbean peoples is not constituted only by the experience of racism, they have many other identifications based on, for example, religion, language and political affiliation. Moreover, as many demonstrations and campaigns show, the concept of black was mobilised as part of a set of constitutive ideas and principles to promote collective action. As a social movement, black activism has aimed to generate solidarity; it has not necessarily assumed that all members of the diverse black communities inevitably identify with the concept in its British usage.

Another area of contention has centred on the distribution of resources by the state to different categories of consumers. It is argued that the term 'black' serves to conceal the cultural needs of groups other than those of African-Caribbean origin. This particular critique is often steeped in 'ethnicism'. Ethnicism, I would suggest, defines the experience of racialised groups primarily in 'culturalist' terms: that is it posits 'ethnic difference' as the primary modality around which social life is constituted and experienced. Cultural needs are defined largely as independent of other social experiences centred around class, gender, racism or sexuality. This means that a group identified as culturally different is assumed to be internally homogeneous, when this is patently not the case. The 'housing needs' of a working-class Asian living in overcrowded conditions on a housing estate, for instance, cannot be the same as those of a middle-class Asian living in a semi-detached house in suburbia. In other words, ethnicist discourses seek to impose stereotypic notions of 'common cultural need' upon heterogeneous groups with diverse social aspirations and interests. They often fail to address the relationship between 'difference' and the social relations of power in which it may be inscribed. It is clearly important that the state should be sensitive to the plurality of needs amongst its citizens. But we need to be attentive to the ways in which 'needs' are socially constructed and represented in various discourses.

[. . .] The main point I wish to stress through this foray into the debate surrounding the use of 'black' in Britain is to highlight how difference is constructed within these competing discourses. That is, the usage of 'black', 'Indian' or 'Asian' is determined not so much by the nature of its referent, but by its semiotic function within different discourses. These various meanings signal differing political strategies and outcomes. They mobilise different sets of cultural or political identities, and set limits to where the boundaries of a 'community' are established. This debate has to an extent been echoed within feminism. And it is against this general background that I turn to issues of 'difference' within feminism.

Is sisterhood global?

In 1985 I attended the International Women's Conference in Nairobi. It was a gathering of over 10,000 women from over 150 countries. There we were all gathered together as women to address questions of our universal subordination as a 'second sex', yet the most striking aspect of this conference was the heterogeneity of our social condition. The issues raised by the different groups of women present at the conference, especially those from the Third World, served to underline the fact that issues affecting women cannot be analysed in isolation from the national and international context of inequality (Brah 1988; Mohanty 1988).

Our gender is constituted and represented differently according to our differential location within the global relations of power. Our insertion into these global relations of power is realised through a myriad of economic, political and ideological processes. Within these structures of social relations we do not exist simply as women but as differentiated categories such as working-class women, peasant women, migrant women. Each description references a specificity of social condition. And real lives are forged out of a complex articulation of these dimensions. As is currently being increasingly recognised in feminist theory and practice, woman is not a unitary category. Yet, this does not mean that the noun 'woman' is meaningless. It too has its own specificity constituted within and through historically specific configurations of gender relations. But in different womanhoods the noun is only meaningful – indeed only exists – with reference to a fusion of adjectives which symbolise particular historical trajectories, material circumstances and cultural experiences. Difference in this sense is a difference of social condition. At this level of analysis the focus is on the social construction of different categories of women within the broader structural and ideological processes within societies. No claims are made that an individual category is internally homogeneous. Working-class women, for instance, comprise very diverse groups of people both within and between societies. Class position signals certain commonalities of location within the social structure, but class articulates with other axes of differentiation such as racism, heterosexism or caste in delineating the precise social position of specific categories of women.

The primary objective of feminism has been to change the social relations of power embedded within gender. Since gender inequalities pervade all spheres of life, feminist strategies have involved a challenge to women's subordinated position within both state institutions and civil society. The driving force behind feminist theory and practice in the post-war period has been its commitment to eradicate inequalities arising from a notion of sexual difference inherent in biologically deterministic theories which explain women's position in society as a result of innate differences. Despite evidence that sex differences in cognitive behaviour among infants are slight, and the psychological similarity between men and women is very high, research to establish innate differences continues unabated (Segal 1990; Rose, Kamin and Lewontin 1984). Feminists do not, of course, ignore women's biology, but they challenge ideologies which construct and represent women's subordination as resulting from their biological capacities.

The ways in which questions of biology are addressed and taken account of vary within different feminisms. Radical feminist accounts, for example, tend to identify women's biologically-based subordination as the fundamental basis of gender inequality. The relations of power between men and women are seen as the primary dynamic of women's oppression almost to the exclusion of other determinants such as class and racism. Radical feminist perspectives often represent women's procreative abilities as an indicator of certain psychological qualities which are uniquely and universally female. These qualities are assumed to have been undermined through patriarchal domination and thus have to be rediscovered and reclaimed. They may often celebrate sexual difference in the form of presumed unique female attributes and qualities. It has been argued that whilst repudiating biological determinism embedded within patriarchal discourses, some versions of radical feminism in turn construct a trans-historical notion of essential femaleness in need of rescuing and recapturing beyond patriarchal relations (Weedon 1987; Segal 1987; Spellman 1988).

Socialist feminism, on the other hand, has been based on the assumption that human nature is not essential but is socially produced. The meaning of what it is to be a woman – biologically, socially, culturally and psychically – is considered to be historically variable. Socialist feminism has mounted a powerful critique of those materialist perspectives which prioritise class, neglect the social consequences of the sexual division of labour, privilege heterosexuality and pay scant attentions to the social mechanisms which prevent women from attaining economic, political and social equality. This strand of feminism distances itself from the radical feminist emphasis on power relations between the sexes as the almost exclusive determinant of women's subordination.

On the whole, and especially until very recently, western feminist perspectives of whatever kind have paid little attention to the processes of racialisation of gender, class or sexuality. Processes of racialisation are, of course, historically specific, and different groups have been racialised differently under varying circumstances, and on the basis of different signifiers of 'difference'. Each racism has a particular history. It arose from a particular set of economic, political and cultural circumstances, has been reproduced through specific mechanisms, and has found different expression in different societies. Anti-black racism, anti-Irish racism, anti-Jewish racism, anti-Arab racism, different varieties of orientalisms: all have distinctive features.

The specific histories of these various racisms place them in particular relationship to each other. For example, there are several similarities in the social experience of the Irish and black groups in Britain. Both sets of people have a history of being colonised by Britain, their migration patterns to Britain share common features, both groups occupy a predominantly working-class position within the British class structure, and they both have been subjected to racism. But anti-black and anti-Irish racism situate these groups differently within British society. As white Europeans, the great majority of Irish people are placed in a dominant position *vis-à-vis* black people in and through the discourses of anti-black racism, even when the two groups may share a similar class location. In other words, we assume different subject positions within various racisms. Analysis of the interconnections between racism, class, gender and sexuality must take account of the positionality of different racisms with respect to one another.

A second example may illustrate the above point further. African-Caribbean and south Asian communities have developed differing responses to racism because their experiences of racism, though similar in many ways, have not been identical (Brah and Deem 1986). State policies have impacted differently on these communities. African-Caribbean communities have mobilised far more around their collective experience of the criminal justice system, particularly the police and the courts, whereas Asian groups have been much more actively involved in defending communities against violent racial attacks, racial harassment on housing estates, and in organising campaigns against deportations and other issues arising from the effects of immigration laws. The stereotypic representations of African-Caribbean and south Asian communities have also been substantially different. The gendered discourses of the 'nigger' and the 'Paki' in post-war Britain represent distinctive ideologies, yet they are two strands of a common racism structured around colour/phenotype/culture as signifiers of superiority and inferiority in post-colonial Britain. This means that African-Caribbean, south Asian and white groups are relationally positioned within these structures of representation. By their behaviour and actions they may reinforce these structures or alternatively they may assume a political practice which challenges these different strands of anti-black racism.

There is a tendency in Britain to see racism as 'something to do with the presence of black people'. But it is important to stress that both black and white people experience their gender, class and sexuality through 'race'. Racialisation of white subjectivity is often not manifestly apparent to white groups because 'white' is a signifier of dominance, but this renders the racialisation process no less significant. We need to analyse the processes which construct us as 'white female', 'black female', 'white male', 'black male' etc. We need to examine how and why the meanings of these words change from plain descriptions to hierarchically organised categories under given economic, political and social circumstances.

Black feminism, white feminism

During the 1970s there was a lack of much serious and sustained engagement with issues of gendered exploitation of post-colonial labour in the British metropolis, racism within state policies and cultural practices, the racialisation of black and white subjectivity in the specific context of a period following the loss of empire, and the particularities of black women's oppression within feminist theory and practice. This played an important part in the formation of black feminist organisations as distinct from the 'white' Women's Liberation Movement. These organisations emerged against the background of a deepening economic and political crisis and an increasing entrenchment of racism. The 1970s was a period when the Powellism of the 1960s came to suffuse the social fabric, and was gradually consolidated and transmuted into Thatcherism in the 1980s. The black communities were involved in a wide variety of political activity throughout the decade. There were major industrial strikes of which several were led by women. The Black Trade Union Solidarity Movement was formed to deal with racism in employment and trade unions. There were massive campaigns against immigration control, fascist violence, racist attacks on person and property, modes of policing that resulted in the harassment of black people, and against the criminalisation of black communities. There were many self-help projects concerned with educational, welfare and cultural activities. Black women were involved in all these activities, but the formation of autonomous black women's groups in the late 1970s injected a new dimension into the political scene.

The specific priorities of local black women's organisations, a number of which combined to form a national body – the Organisation of Women of Asian and African Descent (OWAAD), varied to an extent according to the exigencies of the local context. But the overall aim was to challenge the specific forms of oppression faced by the different categories of black women. The commitment to forging unity between African, Caribbean and Asian women demanded sustained attempts to analyse, understand and work with commonalities as well as heterogeneity of experience. It called for an interrogation of the role of colonialism and imperialism and that of contemporary economic, political and ideological processes in sustaining particular social divisions within these groups. It required black women to be sensitive to one another's cultural specificities while constructing common political strategies to confront sexism, racism and class inequality. This was no easy task, and it is a testimony to the political commitment and vision of the women involved that this project thrived for many years, and some of the local groups have survived the divisive impact of ethnicism and remain active today (Bryan, Dadzie and Scafe 1985; Brixton Black Women's Group 1984).

The demise of OWAAD as a national organisation in the early 1980s was precipitated by a number of factors. Many such divisive tendencies have been paralleled in the women's movement as a whole. The organisations affiliated to OWAAD shared its broad aims but there were political differences amongst women on various issues. There was general agreement that racism was crucial in structuring our oppression in Britain, but we differed in our analysis of racism and its links with class and other modes of inequality. For some women racism was an autonomous structure of oppression and had to be tackled as such; for others it was inextricably connected with class and other axes of social division. There were also differences in perspectives between feminists and non-feminists in OWAAD. For the latter, an emphasis on sexism was a diversion from the struggle against racism. The devaluation of black cultures by the onslaughts of racism meant that for some women the priority was to 'reclaim' these cultural sites and to situate themselves 'as women' within them. Whilst this was an important project there was, at times, more than a hint of idealising a lost past. Other women argued that, whilst the empowering aspects of culture did need to be affirmed and validated, it was equally important to examine how culture is also a terrain on which women's oppression is produced and reproduced. The problem of male violence against women and children, the unequal sexual division of labour in the household, questions of dowry and forced marriages, clitoridectomy, heterosexism and the suppression of lesbian sexualities: all these were issues demanding immediate attention. Although most women in OWAAD did recognise the importance of these issues, there were nonetheless major differences about priorities and political strategies to deal with them.

Alongside these tendencies there was an emerging emphasis within the women's movement as a whole on identity politics. Instead of embarking on the complex but necessary task of sifting out the specificities of particular oppressions, identifying their similarities or connections with other oppressions, and building a politics of solidarity, some women were beginning to differentiate these specificities into hierarchies of oppression. The mere act of naming oneself as a member of an oppressed group was assumed to vest one with moral authority. Multiple oppressions came to be regarded not in terms of their patterns of articulation/interconnections – but rather as separate elements that could be added in a linear fashion, so that the more oppressions a woman could list the greater her claims to occupy a higher moral ground. Assertions about authenticity of personal experience could be presented as if they were an unproblematic guide to an understanding of processes of subordination and domination. Declarations concerning self-righteous political correctness sometimes came to substitute for careful political analysis (Adams 1989; Ardill and O'Sullivan 1986).

Despite the fragmentation of the women's movement, black women in Britain have continued to raise critical questions about feminist theory and practice. As a result of our location within diasporas formed by the history of slavery, colonialism and imperialism black feminists have consistently argued against parochialism and stressed the need for a feminism sensitive to the international social relations of power (Carby 1982; Parmar 1982; Feminist Review 1984; Brah and Minhas 1985; Brah 1987; Phoenix 1987; Grewal, Kay, Landor, Lewis and Parmar 1988; Mama 1989; Lewis 1990). Hazel Carby's article 'White Woman Listen!', for instance, presents a critique of such key feminist concepts as 'patriarchy', 'the family' and 'reproduction'. She criticises feminist perspectives which use notions of 'feudal residues' and 'traditionalism' to create sliding scales of 'civilised liberties', with the 'Third World' seen at one end of the scale and the supposedly progressive 'First World' at the other. She provides several illustrations of how a certain type of western feminism can serve to reproduce rather than challenge the categories through which 'the west' constructs and represents itself as superior to its 'others'.

These critiques have generated some critical self-reflection on the part of white feminist writers. Barrett and McIntosh (1985), for example, have attempted to reassess their earlier work. They acknowledge the limitations of the concept of patriarchy as unambiguous and invariable male dominance undifferentiated by class or racism, but wish to retain the notion of 'patriarchal' as signifying how 'particular social relations combine a public dimension of power, exploitation or status with a dimension of personal servility' (p.39). Having made this point, they fail to explore in any systematic way how and why the concept of the 'patriarchal' helps us to engage with the interconnections between gender, class and racism. The mere substitution of the concept of patriarchy by patriarchal relations will not by itself deal with the charges of ahistoricism, universalism or essentialism that have been levelled at the former (although, as Walby (1990) argues, it is possible to provide historicised accounts of patriarchy). As a response to recent reconceptualisations of patriarchy, Joan Acker suggests that it might be more appropriate to shift 'the theoretical object from patriarchy to gender, which we can define briefly as structural, relational, and symbolic differentiations between women and men' (Acker 1989: 238). She remains cautious about this shift, however, as 'gender', according to her, lacks the critical political sharpness of 'patriarchy' and could much more easily be co-opted and neutralised within 'mainstream' theory.

Patriarchal relations are a specific form of gender relations in which women inhabit a subordinated position. In theory, at least it should be possible to envisage a social context in which gender relations are not associated with inequality between the sexes *qua* women and men. I would argue in favour of retaining the concept of 'patriarchal' without necessarily subscribing to the concept of 'patriarchy' – whether historicised or not – because I hold serious reservations about the analytic or political utility of maintaining system boundaries between 'patriarchy' and the particular socio-economic and political formation (e.g. capitalism or state socialism) with which it articulates. The issue is not whether patriarchal relations predate capitalism or state socialism, for they patently do, but how they are manifested within these systems in the context of a history of colonialism and imperialism in different parts of the globe. Structures of class, racism, gender and sexuality cannot be treated as 'independent variables' because the oppression of each is inscribed within the other – is constituted by and is constituted of the other.

Acknowledging the black feminist critique, Barrett and McIntosh stress the need to analyse the ideological construction of white femininity through racism. This in my view is essential since there is still a tendency to address questions of inequality through a focus on the victims of inequality. Discussions around feminism and racism often centre around the oppression of black women rather than exploring how both black and white women's gender is constructed through class and racism. This means that white women's 'privileged position' within racialised discourses (even when they may share a class position with black women) fails to be adequately theorised, and processes of domination remain invisible. The representation of white women as 'the moral guardians of a superior race', for instance, serves to homogenise white women's sexuality at the same time as it fractures it across class in that the white working-class woman, although also presented as 'carrier of the race', is simultaneously constructed as prone to 'degeneracy' because of her class background. Here we see how class contradictions may be worked through and 'resolved' ideologically within the racialised structuration of gender.

Barrett and McIntosh's article generated considerable debate (Ramazanoglu, Kazi, Lees and Safia-Mirza in *Feminist Review*, 22, 1986; Bhavnani and Coulson 1986). Whilst acknowledging the importance of the reassessment of a part of their work by two prominent white feminists, the critics argued that their methods of re-examination failed to provide the possibility of radical transformation of previous analysis, thus leaving the ways in which 'race' features within social reproduction largely untheorised. Although Barrett and McIntosh note that socialists are divided as to whether the social divisions associated with ethnicity and racism should be seen as absolutely autonomous of social class, as reducible to social class, or as having historical origins but articulating now with the divisions of class in capitalist society (p.38), they do not signal their own analytical preference on these issues. This is a surprising silence in an article whose aim is to advance our understanding of conceptual and theoretical concerns in the field.

I would argue that racism is neither reducible to social class or gender nor wholly autonomous. Racisms have variable historical origins but they articulate with patriarchal class structures in specific ways under given historical conditions. Racisms have independent effectivity but to suggest this is not the same as saying, as Caroline Ramazanoglu (1989) does, that racism is an 'independent form of domination'. The search for grand theories specifying the interconnections between racism, gender and class has been less than productive. They are best construed as historically contingent and context-specific relationships. Hence, we can focus on a given context and differentiate between the demarcation of a category as an object of social discourse, as an analytical category, and as a subject of political mobilisation without making assumptions about their permanence or stability across time and space. This means that 'white' feminism or 'black' feminism in Britain are not essentialist categories but rather they are fields of contestation inscribed within discursive and material processes and practices in a post-colonial terrain. They represent struggles over political frameworks for analysis; the meanings of theoretical concepts; the relationship between theory, practice and subjective experiences; and over political priorities and modes of mobilisations, but they should not, in my view, be understood as locating 'white' and 'black' women as 'essentially' fixed oppositional categories.

More recent contributions to the debate make the point that irrespective of the intentions of the authors, anti-racist feminist discourses of the late 1970s and 1980s did not always facilitate political mobilisation. Knowles and Mercer (1990), for example, take the position that Carby's and Bourne's emphasis on the inscription of racism and gender inequality within processes of capitalism, colonialism and patriarchal social systems produced functionalist arguments – that sexism and racism were inherent within these systems and served the needs of these systems to perpetuate themselves. They believe that this approach demanded nothing short of an all-embracing struggle against these 'isms' that thereby undermined more localised, small-scale political responses. Their own method of dealing with this is to suggest that racism and sexism be 'viewed as a series of effects which do not have a single cause'. I would accept the arguments that the level of abstraction at which categories such as 'capitalism' or 'patriarchal relations' are delineated does not provide straightforward guidelines for concrete strategy and action, and also that racism and sexism are not monocausal phenomena. Nonetheless, I am not sure how treating racism and sexism as a 'series of effects' provides any clearer guidelines for political response. The same 'effect' may be interpreted from a variety of political positions, and lead to quite different strategies for action. Taking up a specific political position means that one is making certain assumptions about the nature of the various processes that underline a social phenomenon of which a particular event may be an effect. A focus only on 'effects' may render invisible the workings of such ideological and material processes, thereby hindering our understanding of the complex basis of inequalities. Although crucial in mobilising specific constituencies the single-issue struggles as ends in themselves may delimit wider-ranging challenges to social inequalities. The language of 'effects' in any case assumes the existence of some causes. The main issue is not whether we should jettison macro-level analysis of gender or racism in relation to capitalism, colonialism or state socialism in favour of empirically grounded analysis of the concrete manifestations of racism in a given local situation, but how each is overdetermined by, and also helps to determine, the others.

I share Knowles and Mercer's reservations about analytical and political perspectives in which social inequality comes to be personified in the bodies of the dominant social groups – white people, men, or heterosexual individuals in relation to racism, sexism or heterosexism – but we cannot ignore the social relations of power that inscribe such differentiations. Members of dominant groups do occupy privileged positions within political and material practices that attend these social divisions, although the precise interplay of this power in specific institutions or in interpersonal relations cannot be stipulated in advance, may be contradictory and can be challenged. [. . .]

Difference, what difference?

It is evident that the concept of difference is associated with different meanings in different discourses. But how are we to understand 'difference'? A detailed discussion of this topic is beyond the scope of this chapter but I would like to suggest four ways in which difference may be conceptualised and addressed.

Difference as experience

Experience has been a key concept within feminism. Women's movements have aimed to give a collective voice to women's personal experiences of social and psychic forces that constitute the 'female' into the 'woman'. The everyday of the social relations of gender – ranging from housework and child care, low-paid employment and economic dependency to sexual violence and women's exclusion from key centres of political and cultural power – have all been given a new significance through feminism as they have been brought out of the realm of the 'taken for granted' to be interrogated and challenged. The personal with its profoundly concrete yet elusive qualities, and its manifold contradictions, acquired new meanings in the slogan 'the personal is political' as consciousness-raising groups provided the forums for exploring individual experiences, personal feelings and women's own understandings of their daily lives.

The limitations of the consciousness-raising method (empowering though it was for some women) as a strategy for systematically challenging the structures of gender inequality have been widely acknowledged. Nonetheless there was at least an implicit recognition in this mode of working that experience did not transparently reflect reality, but instead it was a constellation of mediated relationships, a site of contradictions to be addressed collectively. This insight is quite often missing from current discussions about differences between women where difference and experience are used primarily as a 'commonsensical term' (Barrett 1987). Hence, the need to re-emphasise a notion of experience not as unmediated guide to 'truth' but as a practice of making sense, both symbolically and narratively; as struggle over material conditions and over meaning.

Difference as social relation

The emphasis here is on social relations at the level of the social structure. A group usually mobilises the concept of difference in this sense of a social relation when addressing the structural, political and historical basis of the commonality of its experience. Experience is understood here primarily in terms of collective histories.

In practice, the everyday of lived experience and experience as a social relation do not exist in mutually exclusive spaces. For example, if we speak of 'north African women in France', we are, on the one hand, referring to the social relations of gendered post-coloniality in France. On the other hand, we are also making a statement about the everyday experience of this post-coloniality on the part of such women, although we cannot specify, in advance, the particularity of individual women's lives or how they interpret and define this experience. In both instances, the question of how difference is defined remains paramount. Are perceptions of difference in a given context a basis of affirming diversity or a mechanism for exclusionary and discriminatory practices? Do discourses of difference legitimise progressive or oppressive state policies and practices? How are different categories of women represented within such discourses? How do the women themselves construct or represent the specificity of their experience? Under what circumstances does 'difference' become the basis of asserting a collective identity?

Difference as subjectivity

Issues of difference have been central to theoretical debates around subjectivity. A key question facing us is: how are racialised subjects formed? But the question of racialisation of subjectivity has not yet received much attention within feminist theory, which has been preoccupied primarily with the status of 'sexual difference' in the formation of subjectivity. Feminists have turned to psychoanalysis (notably its post-structuralist and object-relations variants) and to forms of deconstructionist thought to understand the processes of identity formation.

With the growing awareness that women's innermost emotions, feelings, desires and fantasies with their multiple contradictions could not be understood purely in terms of the imperatives of the social institutions and the forces of male domination, feminists have approached psychoanalysis for a more complex account of the trials and tribulations of psychic life. Dissatisfied with the social conditioning approaches to women's psychology, some feminists have looked to Lacan's rereading of Freud for a non-reductive understanding of subjectivity. Post-structuralist accounts have proved attractive to feminism, for they seek to problematise 'sexual difference': sexual difference is something to be explained rather than assumed. Subjectivity is seen as neither unified nor fixed – rather it is something that is constantly in progress. Compelling arguments have been made in favour of the importance of psychoanalysis for feminism against those critics who assume that the notion of a fragmented sexual identity constantly in process is at odds with the feminist project of constructing oppositional consciousness through collective action (cf. Rose 1986; Penley 1989; Minsky 1990).

These arguments are convincing, but certain issues still need to be addressed. The enormous contribution of individuals such as Fanon notwithstanding, much work is yet to be undertaken on the subject of how the racialised 'other' is constituted in the psychic domain. How is post-colonial gendered and racialised subjectivity to be analysed? Does the privileging of 'sexual difference' and early childhood in psychoanalysis limit its explanatory value in helping understand psychic dimensions of social phenomena such as racism? How do the 'symbolic order' and the social order articulate in the formation of the subject? In other words, how is the link between social and psychic reality to be theorised? There is also the issue of how certain psychoanalytical discourses are themselves implicated in the inscription of racism (Dalal 1988).

Difference as identity

Our struggles over meaning are also our struggles over different modes of being: different identities (Minh-ha 1989). Identity is never a fixed core. On the other hand, changing identities do assume specific, concrete patterns, as in a kaleidoscope, against particular sets of historical and social circumstances. Our cultural identities are simultaneously our cultures in process but they acquire specific meanings in a given context. Social phenomena such as racism seek to fix and naturalise 'difference' and create impervious boundaries between groups. The modalities of difference inscribed within the particularities of our personal and collective historical, cultural and political experience – our ethnicities – can interrogate and challenge the strangulating imagination of racism, but the task is a complex one, for ethnicities are liable to be appropriated by racism as signifiers of permanent boundaries. Hence, the 'Englishness' of a particular class can come to represent itself via racism as 'Britishness' against those ethnicities that it subordinates – such as those of the

Irish, Scottish, Welsh, black British, or the ethnicities of the formerly colonised world. But, as I noted earlier, 'white'/European ethnicities are subordinated differently from non-white, non-European ethnicities.

It should be possible through political practice to retrieve ethnicity from racialised nationalist discourses so that it can be manifested as a non-essentialist horizontality rather than hierarchically organised difference. As Stuart Hall says:

> The fact that this grounding of ethnicity in difference was deployed, in the discourse of racism, as a means of disavowing the realities of racism and repression does not mean that we can permit the term to be permanently colonised. That appropriation will have to be contested, the term disarticulated from its position in the discourse of 'multi-culturalism' and transcoded, just as we previously had to recuperate the term 'black', from its place in a system of negative equivalences
>
> Hall 1988: 27

But the project is always beset with difficulties. Since ethnicities are always gendered they construct sexual difference in specific ways. The appropriation of a particular ethnicity cannot be assumed necessarily to involve challenging gender inequalities unless this is undertaken as a conscious objective. Indeed, the reverse may be the case. Similarly, depending upon the context, ethnicities may legitimise class or caste divisions by proclaiming and stressing only the unity of an otherwise heterogeneous group.

So how can we claim ethnicities that do not reinforce inequalities? The project is complex but broadly will entail a variety of concrete practices at the economic, political and cultural level designed to undermine the relations of power that underlie these inequalities. There will be the need to remain vigilant of the circumstances under which affirmation of a particular collective experience becomes an essentialist assertion of difference. This problem may arise not only in relation to dominant ethnicities but also dominated ethnicities. In their struggle against the hegemonic, universalising imperatives of the former, the latter may also take recourse to constructing essentialist differences. This can be especially problematic for women if the cultural values that the groups in question excavate, recast, and reconstruct are those that underscore women's subordination.

Although I have argued against essentialism, it is not easy to deal with this problem. In their need to create new political identities, dominated groups will often appeal to bonds of common cultural experience in order to mobilise their constituency. In so doing they may assert a seemingly essentialist difference. Spivak (1987) and Fuss (1989) have argued in favour of such a 'strategic essentialism'. They believe that the 'risk' of essentialism may be worth taking if framed from the vantage point of a dominated subject position. This will remain problematic if a challenge to one form of oppression leads to the reinforcement of another. It may be over-ambitious, but it is imperative that we do not compartmentalise oppressions, but instead formulate strategies for challenging all oppressions on the basis of an understanding of how they interconnect and articulate.

References

Acker, J. (1989) 'The Problem with Patriarchy', *Sociology*, 23, 2: 325–40

Adams, M. L. (1989) 'Identity Politics', *Feminist Review* 31: 22–34

Ardill, S. and O'Sullivan, S. (1986) 'Upsetting an Applecart: Difference, Desire and Lesbian Sadomasochism', *Feminist Review*, 23: 31–57

Barrett, M. (1987) 'The Concept of Difference', *Feminist Review*, 26: 29–43

Barrett, M. and McIntosh, M. (1985) 'Ethnocentrism and Socialist-Feminist Theory', *Feminist Review*, 20: 23–49

Bhavnani, K. K. and Coulson, M. (1986) 'Transforming Socialist Feminism: The Challenge of Racism,' *Feminist Review*, 23: 81–92

Brah, A. (1987) 'Women of South Asian Origin in Britain: Issues and Concerns', *South Asia Research* 7, 1: 39–55

——— (1988) 'A Journey to Nairobi', in S. Grewal et al. (eds) *Charting the Journey*, London, Sheba

Brah, A. and Deem, R. (1986) 'Towards Anti-Sexist and Anti-Racist Schooling', *Critical Social Policy*, 16: 65–79

Brah, A. and Minhas, R. (1985) 'Structural Racism or Cultural Difference: Schooling for Asian Girls', in G. Weiner (ed), *Just A Bunch of Girls*, Milton Keynes, Open University Press

Bryan, B., Dadzie, S. and Scafe, S. (1985) *Heart of the Race*, London, Virago Press

Carby, H. (1982) 'White Woman Listen! Black Feminism and Boundaries of Sisterhood', in CCCS, *The Empire Strikes Back*, London, Hutchinson

Dalal, F. (1988) 'The Racism of Jung', *Race and Class*, 29, 3: 1–23

Feminist Review (1984) 'Many Voices, One Chant: Black Feminist Perspectives', *Feminist Review*, 17, Special Issue

——— (1986) 'Feedback: Feminism and Racism', *Feminist Review*, 22: 82–105

Fuss, D. (1989) *Essentially Speaking*, London, Routledge

Grewal, S., Kay, J., Landor, L., Lewis, G. and Parmar, P. (1988) *Charting The Journey*, London, Sheba

Hall, S. (1988) 'New Ethnicities', in *ICA Documents: Black Film British Cinema*, London, ICA

Hazareesingh, S. (1986) 'Racism and Cultural Identity: An Indian Perspective', *Dragons Teeth*, Issue 24

Knowles, C. and Mercer, S. (1990) 'Feminism and Anti-Racism', in A. X. Cambridge and S. Feuchtwang (eds), *Anti-racist Strategies*, Aldershot, Avebury

Lewis, G. (1990) 'Audre Lorde: Vignettes and Mental Conversations', *Feminist Review*, 34: 100–15

Mama, A. (1989) 'Violence against Black Women: Gender, Race, and State Responses', *Feminist Review*, 32: 30–48

Minh-ha, T. (1989) *Women, Native, Other: Writing Post Coloniality and Feminism*, Bloomington, Indiana University Press

Minsky, R. (1990) '"The Trouble is It's Ahistorical": The Problem of the Unconscious in Modern Feminist Theory', *Feminist Review*, 36: 4–15

Modood, T. (1988) '"Black" Racial Equality and Asian Identity', *New Community*, 14, 3: 397–404

Mohanty, C. T. (1988) 'Under Western Eyes: Feminist Scholarship and Colonial Discourses', *Feminist Review*, 30: 61–89

Parmar, P. (1982) 'Gender, Race and Class: Asian Women in Resistance' , in CCCS, *The Empire Strikes Back*, London, Hutchinson

Penley, C. (1989) *The Future of an Illusion: Film, Feminism and Psychoanalysis*, London, Routledge

Phoenix, A. (1987) 'Theories of Gender and Black Families', in Weiner, G. and Arnot, M. (eds) *Gender Under Scrutiny*, London: Hutchinson

Ramazanoglu, C. (1989) *Feminism and the Contradictions of Oppression*, London, Routledge

Rose, J. (1986) *Sexuality in the Field of Vision*, London, Verso

Rose, S., Kamin, J. and Lewontin, R. C. (1984) *Not In Our Genes*, Harmondsworth, Pelican

Segal, L. (1987) *Is The Future Female?* London, Virago Press

—— (1990) *Slow Motion: Changing Masculinities, Changing Men*, London, Virago Press

Spellman, E. V. (1988) *Inessential Woman: Problems of Exclusion in Feminist Thought*, London, Women's Press

Spivak, G. (1987) *In Other Worlds: Essays in Cultural Politics*, London, Methuen

Walby, S. (1990) *Theorizing Patriarchy*, Oxford, Basil Blackwell

Weedon, C. (1987) *Feminist Practice and Poststructuralist Theory*, Oxford, Basil Blackwell

Chapter 32

Ruth Frankenberg

WHITE WOMEN, RACE MATTERS
The social construction of whiteness

MY ARGUMENT IN THIS BOOK is that race shapes white women's lives. In the same way that both men's and women's lives are shaped by their gender, and that both heterosexual and lesbian women's experiences in the world are marked by their sexuality, white people *and* people of color live racially structured lives. In other words, any system of differentiation shapes those on whom it bestows privilege as well as those it oppresses. White people are "raced," just as men are "gendered." And in a social context where white people have too often viewed themselves as nonracial or racially neutral, it is crucial to look at the "racialness" of white experience. Through life history interviews, the book examines white women's places in the racial structure of the United States at the end of the twentieth century and views white women's lives as sites both for the reproduction of racism and for challenges to it.

If race shapes white women's lives, the cumulative name that I have given to that shape is "whiteness." Whiteness, I will argue in the pages that follow, has a set of linked dimensions. First, whiteness is a location of structural advantage, of race privilege. Second, it is a "standpoint," a place from which white people look at ourselves, at others, and at society.[1] Third, "whiteness" refers to a set of cultural practices that are usually unmarked and unnamed. This book seeks to begin exploring, mapping, and examining the terrain of whiteness.

There are two analytic dimensions to the book. In beginning to research the significance of race in white women's lives, I expected to learn about, and document, the daily experience of racial structuring and the ways race privilege might be crosscut by other axes of difference and inequality: class, culture, ethnicity, gender, and sexuality. From there, I hoped to comprehend how that daily experience shapes white women's perceptions of the significance of race in the social structure as a whole. As my work proceeded, however, a second dimension of analysis became equally significant, for it became clear that, as much as white women are located in – and speak from – physical environments shaped by race, we are also located in, and perceive our environments by means of, a set of discourses on race, culture, and society whose history spans this century and, beyond it, the broader sweep of Western expansion and colonialism.[2]

The material and discursive dimensions of whiteness are always, in practice, interconnected. Discursive repertoires may reinforce, contradict, conceal, explain, or "explain away" the materiality or the history of a given situation. Their interconnection, rather than material life alone, is in fact what generates "experience"; and, given this, the "experience" of living as a white woman in the United States is continually being transformed. Analytically, chapters of the book at times foreground that which is clearly concrete, tangible, and material about white women's experience of race – childhood, interracial relationships, political activism. At other times my focus is on issues of discourse – the meaning and apparent emptiness of "white" as a cultural identity; the political contexts, strengths, and limitations of different ways of "thinking through race"; the persistence of a discourse against interracial relationships.

Points of origin

This book emerged out of the 1980s, the decade in which white feminist women like myself could no longer fail to notice the critique of white feminist racism by feminist/radical women of color (a critique that had, in fact, marked the entire "second wave" of feminism).[3] More specifically, the research project had as its inception my own passage through that decade, and my own despair over the confused mess that white feminist women's response to charges of racism had collectively become by 1983–84. At worst – and it appeared from where I was standing that "worst" was much of the time – it seemed as though we white feminists had a limited repertoire of responses when we were charged with racism: confusion over accusations of racism; guilt over racism; anger over repeated criticism; dismissal; stasis. Feminist/radical women of color would also, it seemed, go through phases: anger over racism; efforts to communicate with white women about racism, despite it; frustration; and the temptation (acted upon temporarily or permanently) to withdraw from multiracial work.

Sites of productive multiracial feminist dialogue and activity existed, but they were few and far between.[4] Too often, I witnessed situations in which, as predominantly white feminist workplaces, classrooms, or organizations tried to move to more multiracial formats or agendas, the desire to work together rapidly deteriorated into painful, ugly processes in which racial tension and conflict actually seemed to get worse rather than better as the months went by. There were, it appeared, multiple ways in which the racism of the wider culture was simply being replayed in feminist locations.

Increasingly, this generated for me a sense of contradiction, a need to know more. As a white feminist, I knew that I had not previously known I was "being racist" and that I had never set out to "be racist." I also knew that these desires and intentions had had little effect on outcomes. I, as a coauthor, in however modest a way, of feminist agendas and discourse, was at best failing to challenge racism and, at worst, aiding and abetting it. How had feminism, a movement that, to my knowledge, intended to support and benefit all women, turned out not to be doing so?

In the early 1980s, I found myself straddling two sides of a "race line." On the one hand, I spent time sitting with white feminist university friends (roughly my age, roughly my class), at times in discussion groups and at other times more informally, as we struggled to make sense of the "racism question." The issue was anything but trivial to us. For one thing, it was startling in its implication that we were about to lose our newly found grip on the reins of liberation. (My friends and I were mostly socialist feminists. I, for one, liked the idea that, as women – apparently racially undefined – we had a distinctively radical purview of society, premised in part upon our status as structurally oppressed in relation to men – again apparently racially undefined. We were, however, analytically honest enough to realize that analyses such as that proposed by the Combahee River Collective, pointing to the structural subordination of women of color, and the potentially radical standpoint arising out of that position, changed all that!)[5] Because we were basically well-meaning individuals, the idea of being part of the problem of racism (something I had associated with extremists or institutions but not with myself) was genuinely shocking to us. And the issue was also terrifying, in the sense that we constantly felt that at any second we might err again with respect to racism, that we didn't know the rules and therefore didn't know how to prevent that happening. There was, perhaps, a way racism was disembodied in our discussions, sometimes an issue of standpoint, sometimes one of etiquette, and definitely an issue that provoked the intense frustration that came of not being able to "get it," or to "get it right."

Meanwhile, I was also spending a great deal of time with a friendship/support network of working-class women of color and white women, some of whom I had also first met through the university. These women were mainly parents (I was not), as well as older, poorer, and positioned very differently than I in the relations of racism in the United States. As I sat with them and traveled their daily pathways – thanks to an unexpectedly profound connection to one woman in particular – an inventory of meanings of racism, of racist behaviors began, de facto, to accumulate in my consciousness. In part, the inventory felt necessary to my ability to cope in those gatherings without offending anyone, but in part my friend made it her business to educate me. I learned by proximity what it means to navigate through a largely hostile terrain, to deal with institutions that do not operate by one's own logic nor in one's interests, and to need those institutions to function in one's favor if one is to survive, let alone to achieve. I realized for almost the first time in my life the gulf of experience and meaning between individuals differentially positioned in relation to systems of domination, and the profundity of cultural difference. (I say *almost* the first time because the culture shock of moving to the United States from Britain at the age of twenty-one had opened my eyes to the latter.)

Uniting the divergent experiences of being both a part of that network and a graduate student was, and remains, beyond my capability. In any case, doing so, and especially conveying the experiences of women of color, in general or in particular, is not my goal in any direct way.[6] More relevant here is the multi-faceted impact of both affiliations, and their disjunction, on my own understanding of racism and on the genesis of this project. When my white sisters and I struggled to comprehend a situation we did not understand and had not meant to create, critical questions for me were: How did this happen? How did we get into this mess? What do "they" mean when they tell us white feminism is racist? Translated into research, the same questions looked something like this:

- (How) does racism shape white women's lives?
- What are the social processes through which white women are created as social actors primed to reproduce racism within the feminist movement?
- (How) can white women's lives become sites of resistance to the reproduction of racism?

Socialist feminism had also given me an analytical commitment to three axioms: first, that in "societies structured in dominance"[7] we, as feminists, must always remember that we act from within the social relations and subject positions we seek to change; second, that experience constructs identity; and, third, that there is a direct relationship between "experience" and "worldview" or "standpoint" such that any system of domination can be seen most clearly from the subject positions of those oppressed by it. As the project developed, applying those axioms to positions of privilege or domination, or to subjects simultaneously privileged and oppressed, required me to complicate the second and third of these axioms. The first remained not only intact but even more challenging than it had appeared at the outset.

From the network predominantly made up of women of color, of which I was in some way a part, I carried into the research three realizations: first, that there is frequently a gulf of experience of racism between white people and people of color; second, that white women might have a range of awareness in relation to racism, with greater awareness based on, among other things, their long-term connectedness to communities of color (I did not, I should perhaps clarify, include myself in the latter category at that time); third, that there *is* a cultural/racial specificity to white people, at times more obvious to people who are not white than to white individuals.

What's in a name?

When I began work on this book, I described it as one that would examine the relationship between white women and racism. In the years between then and now, I have added another conceptualization of it, one that perhaps overlaps, without displacing, my earlier description. For I now also describe this book as a study of the social construction of whiteness.

Calling the project a study of white women and racism marked out the set of concerns that motivated me to begin it, namely, emphasizing that racism was and is something that shapes white women's lives, rather than something that people of color have to live and deal with in a way that bears no relationship or relevance to the lives of white people. For when white people – and I was especially concerned about white feminists, since the project had its origins in the feminist movement – look at racism, we tend to view it as an issue that people of color face and have to struggle with, but not as an issue that generally involves or implicates us. Viewing racism in this way has serious consequences for how white women look at racism, and for how antiracist work might be framed. With this view, white women can see antiracist work as an act of compassion for an "other," an optional, extra project, but not one intimately and organically linked to our own lives. Racism can, in short, be conceived as something external to us rather than as a system that shapes our daily experiences and sense of self.

The "and" in "white women and racism" implies, but does not really define, a link between the two terms. The need to speak of whiteness further specifies what is at stake in speaking of racism in relation to white people. To speak of "the social construction of whiteness" asserts that there are locations, discourses, and material relations to which the term "whiteness" applies. I argue in this book that whiteness refers to a set of locations that are historically, socially, politically, and culturally produced and, moreover, are intrinsically linked to unfolding relations of domination. Naming "whiteness" displaces it from the unmarked, unnamed status that is itself an effect of its dominance. Among the effects on white people both of race privilege and of the dominance of whiteness are their seeming normativity, their structured invisibility. This normativity is, however, unevenly effective. I will explore and seek to explain the invisibility and modes of visibility of racism, race difference, and whiteness. To look at the social construction of whiteness, then, is to look head-on at a site of dominance. (And it may be more difficult for white people to say "Whiteness has nothing to do with me – I'm not white" than to say "Race has nothing to do with me – I'm not racist.") To speak of whiteness is, I think, to assign *everyone* a place in the relations of racism. It is to emphasize that dealing with racism is not merely an option for white people – that, rather, racism shapes white people's lives and identities in a way that is inseparable from other facets of daily life.

To name whiteness also broadens the focus of my study, first because it makes room for the linkage of white subjects to histories not encompassed by, but connected to, that of racism: histories of colonialism and imperialism, and, secondarily, histories of assimilationism in the United States. Second, it allows me to view certain practices and subject positions as racialized (that is, structured by relations of race, usually alongside other structuring principles) rather than necessarily racist – although whiteness is for the most part racialized in the context of racism. Third, by examining and naming the terrain of whiteness, it may, I think, be possible to generate or work toward antiracist forms of whiteness, or at least toward antiracist strategies for reworking the terrain of whiteness.

Several distinct but, I believe, compatible theoretical and methodological orientations have been distilled into my approach. First, I share in a feminist commitment to drawing on women's daily lives as a resource for analyzing society. Second, I also share what is, in a sense, the converse of that commitment (and also an approach adopted by feminists): the belief that women's daily life experiences can only be adequately understood by "mapping" them onto broader social processes. Third, then, in order to better comprehend the social processes involved in the construction of whiteness, I have drawn on both theoretical and substantive analyses of race, racism, and colonialism in the United States and beyond.

Feminism: personal, political, theoretical

My decision, in 1984, to begin to explore whiteness through white women's life histories drew on a strong current of feminist thought that has used accounts of women's experience as ground for the construction and critique of theory and strategy. Since the consciousness-raising groups of the late 1960s, feminists have transformed accounts of personal experience into politicized and theorized terrain.[8] Through this process, the private, the daily, and the apparently trivial in women's activities came to be understood as shared rather than individual experiences, and as socially and politically constructed. The personal, in short, became political.

In addition to anchoring theories of gender and of society in general, women's accounts of personal experience have served as leverage points from which to criticize canons, whether of social theory or of political movements' agendas for change. During the "second wave" of feminism, from the late 1960s to the present, this kind of critique has challenged at least two canons that are especially relevant here. First, white feminists and feminist/radical women of color have critized the lack of attention to gender domination – and effective male-centredness – of left and anti-racist movements. Second, feminist/radical women of color have challenged feminisms dominated by white-centered accounts of female experience. As women activists of a range of racial identities criticized theory based on male standpoints, it became clear that such standpoints obscured or ignored female subordination. And again, as women of color challenged white feminist accounts of "women's place" in society, the partiality of those accounts became visible.

Theorizing "from experience" rested on several key epistemological claims that, over time, became staples of feminist "common sense." The first of these was a critique of "objectivity" or "distance" as the best stances from which to generate knowledge. For, feminists argued, there is a link between where one stands in society and what one perceives. In addition, this epistemological stance made another, stronger claim: that the oppressed can see with the greatest clarity not only their own position but also that of the oppressor/privileged, and indeed the shape of social systems as a whole.[9]

To theorize "from experience" is thus to propose that there is no firm separation to be drawn between woman as member of society and woman as thinker, theorist, or activist. And therefore, as became clear in the context of a critique of white feminist racism, there are multiple problems in attempting (by default) to use white women's lives as a resource for analyzing gender domination in its entirety. Through the 1980s and into the present, work predominantly by women of color has been transforming feminist analysis, drawing attention to the white-centredness, and more generally the false universalizing claims, of much feminist discourse.[10] Ethnocentrism based on the racial specificity of white women's lives, it was pointed out, limits feminist analysis and strategy in relation to issues such as the family[11] and reproductive rights.[12] In the realm of theory, women of color were the first to advance frameworks for understanding the intersection in women's lives of gender, sexuality, race, and class[13] as well as visions and concepts of multiracial coalition work.[14]

The issue here was not only that white women's daily experiences *differed* from those of our sisters of color. If that had been the case, simply adding more accounts by women from a variety of racial locations would have resolved the problem. Instead, it became clear that white feminist women accounting for our experience were missing its "racialness" and that we were not seeing what was going on around us: in other words, we lacked an awareness of how our positions in society were constructed in relation to those of women – and men – of color.

One of my concerns, as I looked at white women's lives through a specifically racial lens, was, as a result, trying to comprehend those lacunae in perception. I needed to understand not only how race is lived, but also how it is seen – or more often, in my immediate political and social networks, *not* seen. In 1983 (before beginning the interviews for this book) I argued that the extent to which white women were "missing" or "not getting" the significance of race in either our or anyone else's experience had everything to do with standpoint: because we were race privileged, I argued, we were not in a structural position to see the effects of racism on our lives, nor the significance of race in the shaping of U.S. society.[15]

But by themselves, the material, daily relations of race cannot adequately explain whether, when, and in what terms white women perceive race as structuring either their own or anyone else's experience. The "dailiness" of racial separation and the inescapability of whiteness as a position of relative privilege cannot explain the *content* of white women's descriptions of others and of themselves – the ways, for example, masculinity and femininity are divided in racial and cultural terms. Similarly, they cannot explain why some white women learn or contest explicitly racist attitudes from childhood onward, while for others racial inequality is, in the words of one of the women I interviewed, "a reality enjoyed, but not acknowledged, a privilege lived in, but unknown."

Through the second half of the 1980s, several ongoing areas of feminist work were critical as I interviewed white women and analyzed their narratives. First, feminist scholars, mainly women of color, engaged in the painstaking work of refracting gender through the lenses of race and culture: examining, for example, how constructions of womanhood have always been racially and culturally marked and, in a racist society, even racially exclusive.[16] This work of rigorous specification exposes the universalism of the second wave of feminism as largely false – and calls, I suggest, for the reciprocal specification of *white* womanhood.[17] Second, feminists of all racial groups (but, as noted earlier, in a process initiated by women of color) made richer and more complex our theorizations of subjectivity and of society in general. Thus, for example, theorists described the "simultaneity" of the impact of race, class, and gender in shaping the lives of women of color[18] (and, I would add, white women too) and emphasized that subjectivity is "[displaced] across a multiplicity of discourses"[19] rather than produced out of the single axis of gender domination or the twin poles of capitalism and patriarchy. Third, more complex views of the subject produced correspondingly complex epistemologies, understood as emerging out of multifaceted political locations.[20]

While feminist women of color have worked to specify their histories and the contemporary shape of their lives in gendered and racial terms, however, a corresponding particularism has too often been lacking on the part of white feminist women. Thus, as white feminists participate alongside women of color in developing new theoretical articulations of "difference" and the "multiplicity" of women's experiences, there is, I fear, a danger that while increasingly theorists of color speak from concrete conceptualizations of what that multiplicity means to them, for white women visions of "difference" and "multiplicity" may remain abstract.

There are critical exceptions here. In a productive approach to questions about white women and racism, some white feminists began in the late 1970s and 1980s to examine through autobiography the ways race privilege and racism have shaped their own lives.[21] Thus, as these women and others like them continue to articulate feminist practice, they do so with a more multifaceted understanding of the social forces that made them who they are.

My study, and the exploration of white women's life histories upon which this book is based, share these women's commitment to careful and detailed analysis of how racism enters and shapes white women's lives, and to making more visible how our lives are embedded in a range of histories, political struggles, and social forces. My assumption here is one I've held since I first came to politics in the 1970s: that knowledge about a situation is a critical tool in dismantling it.

[. . .] The majority of the women I interviewed for this study did not consider themselves particularly interested in the racial order, or especially implicated in racism. All of them, however, said a great deal that was relevant to both. Successive chapters of this book have traveled the terrain of whiteness as material, cultural, and subjective location, exploring childhood, interracial relationships, discursive repertoires on race, and constructions of culture and identity. This process has, I hope, rendered more explicit and complex the meaning – or better, meanings – of whiteness in the contemporary United States. I have attempted to mark out the historical and contemporary conditions, material and discursive, that define and limit it. Through reading white women's life histories, I have examined the ways in which region, class, generation, and ethnicity further subdivide the terrain of lived experiences of whiteness. I have also indicated in preliminary ways how gender and sexuality may intersect with whiteness. In addition to marking out the limits and the "givenness" of whiteness, I have argued that the women I interviewed actively negotiated it. I have explored in detail the forms and content of that negotiation process.

Whiteness changes over time and space and is in no way a transhistorical essence. Rather, as I have argued, it is a complexly constructed product of local, regional, national, and global relations, past and present. Thus, the range of possible ways of living whiteness, for an individual white woman in a particular time and place, is delimited by the relations of racism *at that moment and in that place*. And if whiteness varies spatially and temporally, it is also a relational category, one that is coconstructed with a range of other racial and cultural categories, with class and with gender. This coconstruction is, however, fundamentally asymmetrical, for the term "whiteness" signals the production and reproduction of dominance rather than subordination, normativity rather than marginality, and privilege rather than disadvantage.[22]

In this text, the coconstruction of gender and whiteness were most visible in the arena of interracial sexuality and relationships. There, I argued, first, that the discourse against interracial relationships entails specifically racialized constructions of white femininity in relation to racialized masculinities. Second, I suggested that white women and men were placed, respectively, as victim and rescuer in the discourse against interracial sexuality, vis-à-vis the supposed sexual threat posed by men of color toward white women. Third, and in a sense exceeding the terms of the discourse against interracial sexuality, I suggested that white heterosexual women's choices of primary partners at times involved negotiations over preferred modes of living out femininity and living with men. Fourth, I argued that both heterosexual and lesbian white women's strategies for coping with the burdens that racism placed on interracial couples seemed at times to be distinctively "female" ones.

To speak about the intersections of femininity or femaleness and whiteness in the context of sexuality and partnerships is, however, only the beginning of the story. A range of further questions, most of which are beyond the scope of this study, present themselves. One set of questions concerns childhood. Here one might ask, for example, whether white boys and white girls use their environments in different ways. Were this so, boys might have different contexts from girls in which to interact with boys and girls, or men and women, of color. In relation to the fearful response of many white girls to peers of color, one can also ask whether white boys and white girls are socialized differently with regard to racial Others and hence whether white boys might be more hostile than fearful in interracial situations. (In fact, this difference, if it did exist, would be partly explicable in the context of the discourse on interracial sexuality just discussed.) Here I am, of course, speculating, for questions of this kind would have to be addressed in the context of a study that included both women and men.

How does the interweaving of material and discursive limitation, "local" variation, ascription, agency, and self-consciousness translate into individual trajectories through and within whiteness? On one level, it is impractical to unravel these strands, since they are lived, second by second, as interwoven. However, it is also possible analytically – if artificially – to separate these strands and place them on a continuum of fixity and mutability. And it is also, I suggest, necessary to do so, for such an exercise might expose more clearly the points of pressure, of potential challenge to racial domination.

[. . .] White women also inhabited as given a universe of discourses on race, on whiteness, on racial Others, and on racism, each of which could be identified temporally and spatially in terms of their emergence, but that coexisted in the present in uneven and complex ways. The key discursive repertoires in question here were, first, modes of naming culture and difference associated with west European colonial expansion; second, elements of "essentialist" racism again linked to European colonialism but also critical as rationale for Anglo settler colonialism and segregationism in what is now the USA; third, "assimilationist" or later "color- and power-evasive" strategies for thinking through race first articulated in the early decades of this century; and, fourth, what I have called "race-cognizant" repertoires that emerged in the latter half of the twentieth century and were linked both to U.S. liberation movements and to broader global struggles for decolonization. For the most part, I have argued, a color- and power-evasive repertoire was dominant, at least as a public language of race, in the times and places at which these interviews took place. Nonetheless, elements of the other repertoires were also in play.

This discursive environment was given, then, according to a complex logic and temporality. For I have argued that these white women lived, negotiated, appropriated, and rejected, at some times more consciously and intentionally than at others, the entire array of discursive repertoires. It was possible to identify individual trajectories of change with respect to discursive repertoires, which themselves mapped onto much broader social processes, both national and regional. Individual women at times self-consciously deployed one discursive repertoire against another (color evasiveness against essentialist racism, race cognizance against color evasiveness), and at other times appeared simultaneously caught within and critical of specific elements of one or another. In these ways, discourse was "given" and yet more fluid than the material relations of race. In ways that defied dualistic analysis, the women were apparently both self-conscious about the discursive history of race and not conscious of it; apparently both capable and not capable of changing their discursive repertoires.

In arguing that race shapes white women's lives, then, I am making a claim with two linked dimensions. First, white women's lives are marked by their diverse locations in the materiality of the racial order. But, second, white women's senses of self, other, identity, and worldview are also racialized, for they emerged here as repositories of the key elements of the history of the idea of race, in the United States and beyond. The white subject and the white imaginary thus by no means confine themselves to the present in their construction, but rather draw, consciously and unconsciously, on moments in the racial order long past in material terms.

[. . .] Attention to the construction of white "experience" is important, both to transforming the meaning of whiteness and to transforming the relations of race in general. This is crucial in a social context in which the racial order is normalized and rationalized rather than upheld by coercion alone. Analyzing the connections between white daily lives and discursive orders may help make visible the processes by which the stability of whiteness – as location of privilege, as culturally normative space, and as standpoint – is secured and reproduced. In this context, reconceptualizing histories and refiguring racialized landscapes are political acts in themselves.

Analyzing the construction of whiteness is important as a means of reconceptualizing the grounds on which white activists participate in antiracist work. In that regard, this book may help generate a checklist of existing conceptualizations of both whiteness and racism and the potential strengths and weaknesses of each. I have, for example, criticized the "power-evasive" view that reduces racism to individual, intentional acts. Not only does that view distract white people's attention from the results of individual actions, it also evades a much broader range of historical and contemporary processes through which the racial order is maintained. Again, I have criticized conceptions of white complicity with racism that deploy as metaphor colonialism or neocolonialism but do not trace in practical terms the real and varying relationships of white people to either project. Operating as, in a sense, secularized metaphors for "sin" and "evil," such conceptions are in fact simultaneously reductive and excessive, and actually have the potential to disempower and short-circuit white antiracism. By contrast, I have argued here that white complicity with racism should be understood – and challenged – in the complex, multifaceted terms in which it operates.

Examining the coconstruction of whiteness and other racial identities is useful because it may help lead white activists (and also, for that matter, activists of color) away from the incorporation of "old" discursive elements into "new" strategies. I have, for example, argued that we need to displace the colonial construction of whiteness as an "empty" cultural space, in part by refiguring it as constructed and dominant rather than as norm. Without reconceptualizing culture, we run the risk of reifying and dehistoricizing *all* cultural practices, valorizing or romanticizing some while discounting others as not cultural at all. But a dualistic framework is retained, for example, in new curricular programs that include attention to nondominant cultures but do not simultaneously reconceptualize or reexamine the status, content, and formation of whiteness. Similarly, references to women of color, but not white women, as "racial-ethnic women," implicitly suggest that race does *not* shape white identities or experience.

Beyond a point, however, the reinterpretation of white women's experience and the historicizing of whiteness are simply retellings of the same tale. Analysis of the place of whiteness in the racial order can and should be, rather than an end in itself, only one part of a much broader process of social change leveled both at the material relations of race and at discursive repertoires. It is not, in any case, realistic or meaningful to reconceptualize whiteness outside of racial domination when, in practical terms, whiteness still confers race privilege. It would be similarly naive to imagine that political will alone might bring about the kinds of shifts necessary to challenge those discourses that most effectively stabilize the racial order.

Ultimately, the process of altering present and future meanings of whiteness is inextricably connected to that of altering the meanings of other, coconstructed racial and cultural identities. That process is in turn linked to the effort to transform the racial order in both material and discursive terms and to alter, perhaps, more than anything, the distribution of power. Clearly, that project is not individual but collective. Nor does it rest with white activists alone, so much as with collective actions by people from a range of locations in the racial order.

Notes

1   Following Nancy Hartsock, "The Feminist Standpoint: Developing the Ground for a Specifically Feminist Historical Materialism," in *Discovering Reality*, ed. Sandra Harding and Merrill B. Hintikka (Dordrecht: D. Riedel, 1983), 283–310, the word "standpoint" has two linked meanings. The first is the perspective that arises out of a class's or gender's received and unanalyzed engagement with its material environment, perceived through the worldview of the dominant group. The second is the self-conscious perspective on self and society that arises out of a class (or gender) grouping's critical apprehension of itself and its location in relation to the system it inhabits. With respect to gender, Hartsock styles the former "women's standpoint" and the latter "feminist standpoint." No such distinction is currently available for my purposes. In referring here to whiteness as a standpoint, I intend, loosely, an analogy with Hartsock's "women's standpoint." The most appropriate analogy for Hartsock's "feminist standpoint" would be "white antiracist standpoint." At points in this book, I and some interviewees articulate elements of a white antiracist standpoint. Finally, it should be emphasized that the analogy is by no means perfect, since both "feminist" and "proletarian"

standpoints refer to the self-conscious engagements of oppressed groups with their own positioning, whereas, of course, a "white antiracist standpoint" refers to self-conscious and self-critical engagement with a *dominant* position in the racial order.

2   "Discourses" may be understood in this book as historically constituted bodies of ideas providing conceptual frameworks for individuals, made material in the design and creation of institutions and shaping daily practices, interpersonal interactions, and social relations. "Western" is capitalized here to draw attention to its status as a discursive rather than a geographical construct. In the geographical sense, "west" is of course a relative term (tied to "east," "north," and "south," as well as to a particular point in space from which a given calculation emanates). But "west," *in* the West, tends to be understood to refer to the capitalist European countries, North America, Australia, New Zealand, and, on occasion, Japan(!). Discursively, too, "West" and "Western" are relational terms, constructed out of opposition to non-Western Others or "Orientals." Westernness implies a particular, dominative relationship to power, colonial expansion, a belonging to center rather than margin in a global capitalist system, and a privileged relationship to institutions – be they academic or oriented to mass communication – for the production of knowledge. Not all people in the (pseudogeographical) West/west are, within the terms of a discourse on West-non-West, Westerners. This is because the cultural content of Westernness draws on Christian, rationalist, north and west European customs and patterns of thought and because, discursively, Westernness is racially exclusive and tends to mean only Caucasian. Thus, for example, Ward Churchill, in describing the stages of European colonization of Native Americans, remarks that, "In the beginning, troops arrive to butcher the indigenous population. Later, the 'savages' are seen as worthy of being 'educated' and 'civilized' to white, *Western* standards, dealing a devastating blow to the cultures possessed by the survivors of the slaughter." Ward Churchill, *Fantasies of the Master Race: Literature, Cinema and the Colonization of American Indians*, ed. Annette Jaimes (Monroe, Maine: Common Courage Press, 1992), 264 (emphasis mine).

3   I use "second wave" to refer to feminism from the late 1960s to the present. "Third wave" has at times been used to characterize, optimistically, the emergence of distinctively multiracial feminisms through the 1980s.

4   Examples of the published record of Black–white feminist dialogue in particular are Tia Cross, Frieda Klein, Barbara Smith, and Beverley Smith, "Face-to-Face, Day-to-Day: Racism CR [Consciousness Raising]," *Heresies* 3: 3, 66–67; Elly Bulkin, Minnie Bruce Pratt, and Barbara Smith, *Yours in Struggle: Three Feminist Perspectives on Anti-Semitism and Racism* (Brooklyn, N.Y.: Long Haul Press, 1984; Ithaca, N.Y.: Firebrand, 1988); Gloria I. Joseph and Jill Lewis, *Common Differences: Conflicts in Black and White Feminist Perspectives* (Garden City, N.Y.: Anchor, 1981). See also Chandra Talpade Mohanty, Ann Russo, and Lourdes Torres, eds., *Third World Women and the Politics of Feminism* (Bloomington: Indiana University Press, 1991), ix, for reference to the conference Common Differences: Third World Women and Feminist Perspectives, University of Illinois, Urbana-Champaign, April 1983.

5   Combahee River Collective, "A Black Feminist Statement," in *Capitalist Patriarchy and the Case for Socialist Feminism*, ed. Zillah R. Eisenstein (New York: Monthly Review Press, 1979), 362–72. The statement argues for the need to analyze

U.S. society in terms of four interlocking axes of oppression based on race, class, gender, and sexuality. It also articulates an identity politics that linked the positioning of Black women who are targets of all four systems of domination with a unique purview and political agency.

6   In fact, bell hooks and Chela Sandoval, two women I met at that time at the University of California, Santa Cruz, have written precisely about the political and strategic implications for women of color of their positioning within webs of power and systems of domination. Both of these women have been critical to my thinking about racism, and Sandoval's work has been crucial to my thinking about power and political strategy. bell hooks, *Ain't I a Woman? Black Women and Feminism* (Boston: South End Press, 1981); *Feminist Theory: From Margin to Center* (Boston: South End Press, 1984); *Talking Back: Thinking Feminist, Thinking Black* (Boston: South End Press, 1989). Chela Sandoval, "The Struggle Within: Women respond to Racism – Report on the National Women's Studies Conference, Storrs Connecticut" (Oakland, California: Occasional Paper, Center for Third World Organizing, 1982) (revised version of this paper is published in *Making Face, Making Soul, Haciendo Caras: Creative and Critical Perspectives by Women of Color*, ed. Gloria Anzaldúa, [San Francisco: Aunt Lute, 1990], 55–71); "U.S. Third World Feminism: The Theory and Method of Oppositional Consciousness in the Postmodern World," *Genders* 10 (Spring 1991): 1–24.

7   I owe this term to Stuart Hall, "Race, Articulation, and Societies Structured in Dominance," in *UNESCO: Sociological Theories, Race and Colonialism* (Paris: UNESCO Press, 1980), 305–45.

8   For accounts of the uses and effectiveness of consciousness raising in the second wave of feminism, see Anna Coote and Beatrix Campbell, *Sweet Freedom: The Struggle for Women's Liberation* (London: Picador, 1982); Alice Echols, *Daring to Be Bad: Radical Feminism in America, 1967–75* (Minneapolis: University of Minnesota Press, 1989); Katie King, "The Situation of Lesbianism as Magical Sign: Contests for Meaning in the U.S. Women's Movement, 1968–72," *Communications* 9 (1986): 65–91.

9   From a white feminist perspective, the clearest articulation of this position is Hartsock, "The Feminist Standpoint." Articulations of a similar epistemological stance by U.S. women of color include Combahee River Collective," A Black Feminist Statement"; Aida Hurtado, "Relating to Privilege: Seduction and Rejection in the Subordination of White Women and Women of Color," *Signs* 14, no. 4 (1989): 833–55; and Patricia Hill Collins, "The Social Construction of Black Feminist Thought," *Signs* 14, no. 4 (1989): 745–73.

10 A key text here is Cherríe Moraga and Gloria Anzaldúa, eds., *This Bridge Called My Back: Writings by Radical Women of Color* (Watertown, Mass.: Persephone, 1981; New York: Kitchen Table Women of Color Press, 1983).

11 Among others, see Hazel Carby, "White Woman Listen! Black Feminism and the Boundaries of Sisterhood," Center for Contemporary Cultural Studies, *The Empire Strikes Back: Race and Racism in '70s Britain* (London: Hutchinson, 1981), 212–35; Kum Kum Bhavnani and Margaret Coulson, "Transforming Socialist Feminism: The Challenge of Racism," *Feminist Review* 23 (Summer 1986): 81–92.

12 See, for example, Angela Y. Davis, *Women, Race and Class* (New York: Random House, 1981), 202–21.

13 The founding text here is, I believe, the Combahee River Collective's "A Black Feminist Statement."

14   For example, Bernice Johnson Reagon, "Coalition Politics: Turning the Century," in *Home Girls: A Black Feminist Anthology*, ed. Barbara Smith (New York: Kitchen Table Women of Color Press, 1983), 356–69; Cherríe Moraga and Gloria Anzaldúa's concept of "El Mundo Zurdo/The Left Handed World," *This Bridge Called My Back*, 195–96.

15   Ruth Frankenberg, "Different Perspectives: Interweaving Theory and Practice in Women's Work," qualifying essay, Board of Studies in the History of Consciousness, University of California, Santa Cruz, 1983.

16   Among such developments, Chicana scholars have examined how the figure of La Malinche constructs Chicana femininity (for example, Norma Alarcon, "Chicana's Feminist Literature: A Revision Through Malintzin/or Malintzin: Putting Flesh Back on the Object," Moraga and Anzaldúa. *This Bridge Called My Back*, 182–90. Similarly, Hortense Spillers builds on the work of African–American historians to show how, given the material conditions of Black women's lives, they were "excluded" from racially dominant notions of femininity, "Mama's Baby, Papa's Maybe: An American Grammar book," *Diacritics*, Summer 1987: 65–81. Rayna Green, in "The Pocahontas Perplex: The Image of Indian Women in American Culture," in *Unequal Sisters*, ed. Ellen Carol DuBois and Vicki L. Ruiz (New York: Routledge, 1990), 15–21, analyzes the ideological construction of the figure of Native American women within a colonial matrix.

17   Such work has been undertaken by, for example, Gloria I. Joseph and Jill Lewis, *Common Differences*, who examine the differences in perspective, experience, and sense of self between white and Black women; Vron Ware, *Beyond the Pale: White Women, Racism and History* (London: Verso, 1992), who articulates in particular the place of white womanhood in the discursive economies of racism and imperialism; and Teresa L. Amott and Julie A. Matthaei, *Race, Gender, and Work: A Multicultural History of Women in the United States* (Boston: South End Press, 1991), who by juxtaposing and contrasting the histories of U.S. women across racial and ethnic lines enable greater attention to the specification of gender by race and class.

18   Patricia Zavella, "The Problematic Relationship of Feminism and Chicana Studies," *Women's Studies* 17 (1988): 123–34.

19   Norma Alarcon, "The Theoretical Subjects of *This Bridge Called My Back* and Anglo-American Feminism," in *Haciendo Caras*, ed. Anzaldúa, 356–69.

20   Chandra Talpade Mohanty, "Feminist Encounters: Locating the Politics of Experience," *Copyright* 1, no. 1 (1984); Donna J. Haraway, "Situated Knowledges: The Science Question and the Privilege of Partial Perspective," in Donna J. Haraway, *Simians, Cyborgs and Women: The Reinvention of Nature* (New York: Routledge, 1991), 183–202.

21   Foremost in this regard were Elly Bulkin ("Hard Ground: Jewish Identity, Racism and Anti-Semitism") and Minnie Bruce Pratt ("Identity: Skin, Blood, Heart") in Bulkin, Pratt, and Smith, *Yours in Struggle*, 89–228 and 9–64; Mab Segrest, *My Mama's Dead Squirrel: Lesbian Essays on Southern Culture* (Ithaca, N.Y.: Firebrand, 1985); Adrienne Rich, "Disloyal to Civilization: Feminism, Racism, Gynephobia," in Adrienne Rich, *On Lies, Secrets and Silence: Selected Prose, 1966–1978* (New York: Norton, 1979), 275–310; and Adrienne Rich, "Notes Toward a Politics of Location," in Adrienne Rich, *Blood, Bread and Poetry: Selected Prose, 1979–1985* (New York: Norton, 1986), 210–31.

22   As I have repeatedly emphasized, this does not mean that all white individuals have absolute privilege, any more than all male individuals have absolute privilege. Rather, it means that individuals whose ascribed characteristics include whiteness (or maleness) will find the benefits of that ascription accruing to them.

Chapter 33

Sarita Srivastava

"YOU'RE CALLING ME A RACIST?"
The moral and emotional regulation of antiracism and feminism

[. . .]

RAGE, TEARS, AND CONFUSION often follow even the most tentative discussions of racism and explorations of antiracism. Feminist scholars in particular have observed that antiracist challenges in feminist organizatons and classrooms can elicit emotional responses from white feminists (Anzaldúa 1990; Friedman 1995; Fellows and Razack 1998). Ruth Frankenberg's well-known research on whiteness, for example, stemmed from her own "despair" over white feminists' "limited repertoire" of emotional responses to charges of racism (1993, 2). It becomes clear that while emotional aspects of solidarity have always been vital to building progressive communities of feminists and other activists, they are also the unsteady foundations on which antiracist change falters. However, there have been few sustained observations of how and why these emotional responses have been able to block, defuse, and distract from change in feminist, pedagogical, and social movement sites. I should emphasize that my aim is not to critique or dismiss the range of excellent antiracist work that has been undertaken by both white and nonwhite activists, and most notably by feminists, but rather to explore the subtle and not-so-subtle resistance to this work as well as the pitfalls of well-meaning efforts. While some might suggest that resistance to antiracism is a minor or temporary blot in the history of social movements rather than an ongoing phenomenon, we must acknowledge that there is ample evidence to the contrary (hooks 1983; Moraga and Anzaldda 1983; Dua and Robertson 1999) [. . .]

Writers such as Mariana Valverde (1991), Ann Laura Stoler (1995), and Richard Dyer (1997) provide an important beginning to my analysis, showing that colonial and contemporary representations of virtue, honesty, and benevolence have been a historical foundation of whiteness, bourgeois respectability, and femininity. My contribution is to show further that the history of Western feminist movements adds another layer of moral imperative to these historical constructions of racial innocence. Many authors have already elaborated on the state as a regulator of gendered and racialized systems of morality and social control (Corrigan 1981; Little 1999). However, we must recognize that social movement organizations have also been important in promoting values that support state moral regulation and nation building (Valverde and Weir 1988, 32; Valverde 1991, 17). At the same time, social movement organizations are also active in creating their own social spaces, or "heterotopia" (Foucault 1986; Hetherington 1997), with local codes of morality that may counter state aims. So social movements may be both implicated in state multiculturalism policy and influenced by alternative discourses of equity and antiracism. My own study attends to these unique characteristics of contemporary social movement organizations – as well as to their historical particularity in the past two decades of feminist organizing. I argue that within social movements such as feminism, and in nations such as Canada, we can discern distinct moral accounts of self that disallow open discussions of what it might mean to be antiracist.

In undertaking this analysis, it is important to acknowledge the ongoing historical shifts in the moral narratives shared by many white feminists. Over the past two decades, as Western feminist practice has gradually integrated antiracist thought, it seems that ideas about what makes a good feminist have also shifted. My analysis finds, however, that as some white feminists move toward new ideals of antiracist feminism, they often move toward deeper self-examination rather than toward organizational change. These findings suggest that some of the deadlocks of antiracist efforts are linked to these preoccupations with morality and self.

Method and methodology

The analysis here is based on semistructured interviews with feminists involved in antiracism, on the published reflections of feminists, and on observations of organizational efforts. I conducted twenty-one confidential interviews with fifteen feminists involved in antiracist efforts in eighteen women's organizations based in Toronto, Canada, including drop-in centers, shelters, feminist advocacy groups, and feminist publications and publishers. Two-thirds of those interviewed identified themselves as women of color; one-third identified themselves as white. All those interviewed had been involved in antiracist efforts within at least one community or social movement organization. Some of the women were interviewed more than once, as several had been involved in antiracist efforts in more than one organization. I also draw on observations of twelve antiracist workshops or workshop series as well as on numerous organizational meetings in a variety of sites, including feminist, environmental, social justice, and popular educational organizations and an aboriginal youth conference. In five of these workshop series I was either participant or facilitator. While my interest is in the practice of antiracism within organizations, I do not focus on the structure, goals, or work of these organizations. While detailed interview accounts of personal reflections and debates among activists are central to this study, I do not attempt to do a detailed analysis of or make proposals about interpersonal communication and individual motivation. Rather, I use these accounts by and about individual activists to understand better how discourses and practices of antiracism in organizations are shaped by broader historical relations of gender, race, and nation.[1]

I begin by tracing historical representations of white, innocent femininity and feminism and then show how these are conjoined with the moral conventions of the contemporary feminist community. I then turn to the observations and reminiscences of nonwhite and white antiracist feminists to illustrate these links in the context of antiracist debates.

Morality, whiteness, and women

A number of scholars have investigated the making of the white subject and its place in constructions of culture, nation, and empire. These studies provide the foundation for interpreting the racial and moral politics of antiracist debate between white and nonwhite feminists today.[2]

That representations of morality are racialized is well demonstrated. David Goldberg has argued that moral reason itself has been racialized by "constituting racial others outside the scope of morality" (1993, 39). Dyer (1997) demonstrates this racialization of morality in his close study of visual representations of white people in Western culture, showing that the moral symbolism of the color white is in turn reflected in the repetitive association of white skin with virtue. Tracing visual and literary representations from Renaissance painting to Hollywood film, Dyer argues that the equation of whiteness with goodness underlies all representations of white and nonwhite people. He concludes, "To be white is to be at once of the white race and 'honourable' and 'square-dealing'" (65).

Representations of morality have also been historically gendered. Dyer, for example, traces the historic tendency of visual depictions of white women to draw on images of the glowingly angelic. But the image of the good, caring woman has been further shaped by imperialism (Enloe 1989; Valverde 1991; Ware 1992). Stoler's work in particular shows that nineteenth-century imperialist discourses cast white women as the "custodians" of bourgeois morality (1995, 130). The protection of white women from the supposed immoral passions of men of color in the colonies, for example, was justified by gendered and racialized representations of virtue. The White Women's Protection Ordinance of Papua New Guinea is but one piece of colonial legislation that cemented these constructions (Stoler 1995) Furthermore, in their roles as missionaries and teachers, European women in colonial settings often styled themselves as the overseers of black souls and "guardian of white morals" (Ware 1992, 120).

However, not only feminine but also feminist moral identity has been historically focused on benevolence and innocence. Research has shown that these historical representations of the benevolent Anglo-Saxon bourgeois woman as a standard of moral and racial purity have also played an enduring part in first-wave feminist discourse (Valverde 1992), not only in colonial settings but also in U.S. and Canadian movements. Nineteenth-century and early twentieth-century maternal feminism, for example, reproduced images of women as keepers of morality in the family and the nation (Valverde 1992). Valverde (1992) shows how discourses of whiteness, light, and purity in the turn-of-the-century Canadian maternal feminist movement produced an image of vote-deserving women as the cultural, moral, and biological "mothers of the race," a position clearly inhabitable only by some white women.

Vron Ware (1992) and Paula Giddirigs (1984) have made similar observations about the suffragist movements in Britain and in the United States.

The turn-of-the-century moral reform movement in North America, closely linked to first-wave feminism, echoed these constructions of femininity and gendered morality. By rescuing or studying immigrant, "feeble-minded," or poor women, middle-class Anglo-Saxon Protestant women thereby emphasized their own supposed benevolence, superiority, and innocence (Valverde 1991, 62). Similarly, the ideals of women's liberation that U.S. women brought to their work as missionaries in India in the late nineteenth and early twentieth centuries were bolstered by their belief that their superior domestic, cultural, and religious position must be adopted by supposedly "down-trodden" Indian women (Flemming 1992, 192). In other words, the role of moral leader, reformer, and expert allowed some white women to attain respectability and status (Valverde 1991; Fellows and Razack 1998).

Contemporary feminism: Threads of heterotopia, history, and nation

How, then, are these histories expressed in contemporary sites? While discussions of racism continue to be shaped by imperialist histories, these preoccupations with innocence and morality have a more contemporary and more complex expression. Specific to Western second-wave feminist organizations are the ways that these historical and gendered representations of racial innocence and superiority come together with two other threads: feminist ideals of justice and egalitarian community and national discourses of tolerance, benevolence, and nonracism.

[. . .]

However, even as they produce distinct ethical practices and moral communities, second-wave feminist efforts are also overlaid with the contemporary national discourses of tolerance, multiculturalism, or nonracism common to Western nations such as Canada, the Netherlands, New Zealand, and the United States. Here, I use the term *nonracist* to refer to a liberal discourse of equality that denies the systemic nature of racism and its presence in our everyday language and practices.[3] In Canada, the "national story" of benevolence and generosity toward outsiders is particularly powerful (Ng 1992; Razack 2000). In Carol Schick's study of Canadian student teachers' reflections on racism, Canada was described as a "lovable," "not evil" place where everyone receives equitable treatment (1998, 310). Not surprisingly, Schick found that the teachers' claims to their own innocence concerning racism drew on this national discourse of tolerance and benevolence. Similarly, in the Netherlands, writes Philomena Essed (1991), the reluctance of citizens to acknowledge racist acts is tied to the national self-image of tolerance and nondiscrimination. In Frankenberg's interviews with white women in the United States, a similar "color-evasive" and "power-evasive" repertoire was predominant (1993, 14). In New Zealand, Margaret Wetherell and Jonathan Potter (1992) outline similar discursive strategies of denial that New Zealanders use to avoid being seen as prejudiced. As many have argued, these kinds of liberal and "color-blind" representations have been central not only to the denial but also to the perpetuation of racism and exclusion (see, e.g., Razack 2000).[4]

These discourses have been influential in feminist politics as well, although here nonracism has been joined by antiracism, a political philosophy and practice committed to challenging racism as systemic in institutions and everyday life. As a historically humanist project, feminism, like liberal democratic nations, has often been imagined as inherently egalitarian and inherently nonracist. In other words, nonracist feminist discourse expresses concerns about racism not as an active political project but as an impediment to an otherwise inherent egalitarianism. Within feminist organizations, however, this broader liberal discourse is joined with a feminist vision of radical democracy and revolution. Ware argues that this implicit progressive egalitarianism was a tenet of British feminism in the 1980s, one that stood in the way of antiracist activism: "To begin with, there was almost an assumption among many women that as feminism was a progressive, even revolutionary force, it contained within it an automatic anti-racism position" (Ware 1992, 18). Lynda Hurst's *Toronto Star* article about racial conflict among feminists in Canada suggests rhetorically, "Surely feminism, a movement based on equality, has always been implicitly anti-racist?" (1992, D1). Feminism, in this representation, is a place of just practices, egalitarian relations, revolutionary goals, and good individuals.

These three threads – imperial representations of innocence, imagined egalitarian communities, and national discourses of tolerance – can become intertwined in contemporary women's feminist, service, and professional work. A number of writers have made links between the historical foundations of gendered and racialized morality and contemporary discussions of racism or oppression in feminist forums (Enloe 1989; Ware 1992; Fellows and Razack 1998). As Mary Louise Fellows and Sherene Razack suggest, in contemporary feminist debates women whose dominance is contested often respond with an "emotional attachment to innocence" (1998, 343). Fellows and Razack argue that this attachment to innocence can be linked to colonial representations of white, innocent femininity. In other words, just as first-wave feminism was shaped by the backdrop of imperialism and nation building, contemporary feminist communities have been similarly shaped by representations of morality rooted in racist and imperial histories. Other scholars have convincingly demonstrated that these nineteenth-century representations continue to structure many contemporary white women's motivations in feminist psychotherapy (Roger 1998) and international development (Heron 1999). Barbara Heron shows that the desire of white Canadian women to do development work in Africa is inextricable from the "enduring legacy of . . . middle-class women's moral role" (1999, 86). The women she interviewed, for example, typically said that their motivation to work in Africa was to "make myself better by doing something for someone somewhere" (1999, 102). However, in the context of the feminist movement or "progressive" communities, historical representations of white innocence are also joined by the newly theorized ideals of social justice and of the political integrity of an egalitarian community. Images of benevolence and nonracism remain meaningful, but they are also tied to profound moral visions of social justice and commitments to activism. For example, Heron quotes the white development workers she interviewed as wanting to "do something to improve the state of the world" (1999, 107). Heron argues that although these statements can be read as an expression of "white bourgeois subjects seeking to situate themselves in a global context," they may also be read as "a determined resistance to both racism and injustice" (107).

Links among these three threads may also be visible in the ways that national ideals of liberal democracy, freedom, and equality have been significant in some feminist and popular discourse on sexism and racism and in some feminist and antiracist appeals to the state. We might suggest, for example, that representations of women in Afghanistan and Iraq as oppressed have not only been important in justifying "liberation" by the U.S. military but have also reinforced implicit images of women of color as needing liberation from men of color and of third-world women as more oppressed than first-world women, assumptions that have been prominent in some feminist commentary on female genital surgery, the veil, and violence against women (see, e.g., Uma Narayan's 1997 essay contrasting the ways in which violence against women in the United States and in India are framed).

These links among discourses of nation, femininity, and feminism are clearly demonstrated in some of the responses to antiracist challenges within feminist organizations. With these challenges, the assertion of the good, white woman easily becomes a spectacle within and outside feminist organizations. A well-known Toronto example is the antiracist challenge raised by women of color working at Nellie's Hostel, a shelter for battered women. At a turbulent Nellie's board meeting in 1990, staff member Joan Johnson read aloud a letter outlining concerns of racism. However, the chair of the board, prominent Canadian philanthropist June Callwood, was quick to remind Johnson of what she owed to white women at Nellie's – years earlier, Johnson had been sheltered at Nellie's Hostel while seeking legal immigration status. "Are you the same Joan Johnson all these women helped?" the chair demanded. Johnson understood the meaning of Caliwood's reproach. She replied, "You want me on my knees forever" (interview transcripts, May 1996; Dewar 1993, 37). Any discussion of racism in the organization was stopped short by a reminder of the good women who had helped a needy woman of color years before. In this exchange, Callwood questions the gratitude of a woman who would raise the specter of racism against her rescuers. However, the woman's response – "You want me on my knees forever" – is an explicit political challenge to the historical representation of the benevolent, white, middle-class helper of the "less fortunate," to what has been called the "Lady Bountiful" image (Harper 1995). Furthermore, the vociferous public and organizational defense of Callwood, recipient of the Order of Canada, centered around familiar images not only of the good woman and philanthropist but also of the good nation.[5] However, Callwood's defenders were not only other prominent Canadians but also some other feminists, showing how the projection of innocence is crucial both to national self-image and to the white feminist political project. In other words, the defense of Callwood demonstrates a morality founded on representations of innocent femininity, the tolerant nation, and an egalitarian and nonracist feminism.

Moral identity

A liberal nonracist discourse projects innocence not only onto the tolerant and benevolent nation but also onto the individual, by defining racism as acts done by bad or ignorant individuals and ameliorated by education. Because the heterotopias, or imagined moral communities, of social movement organizations are concerned not only with the production of ethical practices and values but also with the production of ethical selves, this notion of nonracism can have particular strength and unique manifestations. As Hetherington (1997) notes, the making of the good place is about creating a space for the perfection not only of society but also of the individual within it. Ethical practices, or the ways that we monitor and make ethical selves, are, in other words, of particular interest in understanding social movements and organizations that hope to change conduct and codes of morality.[6] In freemasonry, Hetherington suggests, the ethical practices of trust, tolerance, and fraternity transformed ethical selves and collective identities "from isolated stranger to trustworthy brother" (97). The phrase "the personal is political," for example, gives us the sense that we might create a more just world through the practice of ethical self-regulation. This used to be referred to in activist circles as "politically correct," or behavior that "adheres to a movement's morality and hastens its goals" (Dimen 1984, 139).[7]

Sherryl Kleinman uses the term *moral identity* to refer to "an identity that people invest with moral significance; our belief in ourselves as good people depends on whether we think our actions and reactions are consistent with that identity" (1996, 5). In social movements – or those social spaces that are organized around alternative social justice – distinct organizational rituals, discourses, and shared values can produce specific moral identities. These may be labeled variously as "activist," "feminist," "progressive," and so on, depending on the local social movement context; all moral identities, as Margaret Walker says, are "produced by and in these histories of specific relationship" (1997, 69).

However, not all measure up to these moral identities or participate equally in the moral community. Benedict Anderson (1992) reminds us that the making of nation or community requires not only imagining sameness and communion but also forgetting difference and oppression. The ideas of community are conjured, Anderson says, because "regardless of the actual inequality and exploitation that may prevail in each, the nation is always conceived as a deep, horizontal comradeship" (1992, 7). The forgetting of difference has similarly been a central problem for social movements. It has been possible to imagine solidarity and sisterhood among all women only because relations of power and anger among women have been "forgotten." Imagining the good feminist requires similar omissions. We need to ask new questions about the ethical subject of feminism: Who is "good," or seen as good? Does *good feminist* mean good, white feminist? Does *good feminist* imply a nonracism that glides over inequitable relations of race?

My interview with Yasmin, a young Muslim woman active in making an antiracist challenge at a feminist agency, demonstrates that feminist moral identity has indeed been shaped by race and class relations and that not everyone therefore measures up to the community's moral scrutiny. Yasmin described "my fear of being seen as not feminist"; she was continually aware that she was constantly judged by coworkers on whether her lifestyle was "alternative" enough (interview transcripts). She highlights the omissions in the imagining of the just, "alternative" identity and world, suggesting that these are premised on racialized and classed conceptions of justice and gender: "Everything they embodied was this alternative way of being. 'I'm not going to drink tap water,' 'I'm going to send my child to an alternative school.' And it went on and on. . . . So in some ways, it prevented certain people from feeling comfortable here too" (interview transcripts, April 1996). Yasmin is neither invited to imagine nor desires to imagine the moral community and alternative identity that her coworkers imagine.

Similarly, the implicit nonracism that has been present in some feminist communities or discussions absents the antiracist concerns of Yasmin and other women of color and shapes talk and behavior on these concerns. Here nonracist may be used to refer both to those who do "not see" racial inequality as well as to those who acknowledge racism as a concern "out there" but deny that they, their organizations, movements, or nations are implicated in racist practices or discourses. My interviews and my review of feminist media suggest that many white feminists see nonracism or antiracism as integral not only to their identity as tolerant Canadians but also, and primarily, to their identity as feminists, as people working toward a more just world. As Frankenberg observes about her own growing awareness of antiracist feminism, "Because we were basically well-meaning individuals, the idea of being part of the problem of racism was genuinely shocking to us" (1993, 3). The incident at Nellie's Hostel, for example, reinforces the notion that if one is generous and committed to social change, the taint of racism is unthinkable.

The struggle by some white feminists and feminist organizations to maintain an ethical nonracist feminist identity can then become an impediment to meaningful antiracist analysis and change. Kleinman's (1996) study of moral identity confirms that the struggle to maintain an "alternative" identity can ironically hamper social change. In the alternative health organization Kleinman studied, the members' sense of self-worth was dependent on their belief that they were "doing something different" (5), that they were truly alternative. However, Kleinman says, their deep investment in this alternative moral identity "kept them from seeing how their behaviours contradicted their ideals" when they perpetuated inequalities inside their organization (1996, 11). Kleinman argues that "we become so invested in our beliefs as radicals or 'good people' that we cannot see the reactionary or hurtful consequences of our behaviours" (11). In other words, an alternative moral identity can both foster and impede social change.

"You're calling me a racist?": Emotion and morality

The political context of alternative moral identities also explains why being seen as nonracist or antiracist is more likely to be a highly emotional concern for feminists and other activists or community workers and more likely to be crucial to their moral identity or sense of self. This political and ethical climate means that there is a great deal at stake – not only one's sense of goodness and sense of self but also one's political identity, one's career as activist or worker in a feminist organization. The effort to maintain an ethical, innocent, and nonracist face often produces an emotional resistance to antiracism, typified in my interviews by the incredulous or tearful phrase, "You're calling me a racist?" An understanding of the individual and psychic aspects of moral regulation gives us new insight into the emotional resistance to antiracism in feminist communities. We need to acknowledge that experiments in creating a new social order, a social movement, create not only spaces of new ethics but also new emotions. Historical analyses of the ethical and emotional climate of fraternity have some parallels to that of sisterhood: "Fraternity had a very strong emotional content, uniting something like the sentiments of kinship, friendship and love. . . . Hence – as in freemasonry – it also had a very strong ethical content" (Hobsbawm 1975, 472).

Similarly, new social movements produce moral climates that become emotional spaces for the production of ethical selves. In Kleinman's (1996) study, members of an alternative health organization used emotional rituals to reinforce their alternative moral community and identity. Rituals of emotional expression and personal experience have also been important in building feminist moral identity, particularly in organizations that draw on consciousness-raising and feminist therapy models. The U.S. National Lesbian Conference in 1991 had several "vibes watchers" – women whose job it was to monitor the emotional climate and advise the participants when to take a deep breath, take a moment of silence, or scream (Taylor 1995). Staff at a feminist health clinic studied by Sandra Morgen (1995) had regular "feelings meetings" to air out the emotional "fallout" of their work and to deal with interpersonal conflicts: a typical comment might be, for example, "I'm getting hurt by your personal style" (245). There is a clear link between ethical and emotional practices in shaping the imagined feminist community.

So what happens when nonracist feminist discourses and identities are challenged? It is these discourses and rituals of emotion that have helped to maintain and defend the nonracist heterotopia and moral identities of the feminist movement. When this imagined nonracism is challenged by antiracist feminists, the denials and defense often are not only couched in personal ethical terms but also can be highly emotional. My interviews show that antiracist efforts are often met with emotional resistance by white women – with anger, even tears. According to my interviews about antiracist discussions, white participants may speak in an emotional manner about their commitment, hope, solidarity, complicity, guilt, lack of complicity, failure to understand, disbelief, hurt, and anger that they have been accused; tears are the most commonly described reaction. The problem, as the antiracist activists interviewed point out, is not that emotional expression is inherently negative; the problem is that discussions about personnel, decision making, or programming become derailed by emotional protestations that one is not a racist and by efforts to take care of colleagues upset by antiracist challenges. In other words, it is the effects and the racialized power relations of this emotional expression that are problematic rather than emotion itself.

One of the most common angry and indignant reactions described in my interviews was "How can you call me racist?" (interview transcripts, December 1996). Lynn describes the emotional aftermath after one particularly acrimonious board meeting: "And [one of the board members] was bawling her eyes out and saying that she wasn't going to apologize for anything that she had done" (interview transcripts, May 1996). Vijaya, one of the activists I interviewed, echoed a common sentiment that white women's tears flow more openly in these discussions: "White women cry all the fucking time, and women of color never cry" (interview transcripts, December 1996). Rayna's description notes that anger, indignation – "You're calling me a racist?" – and tears are typical responses of whites to organizational discussions of racism: "The indignant response, anger, the rage that turns into tears, the foot stomping, temper tantrums, which are very typical responses. Every single organization that I have been in, every single one. So I realized that it wasn't about me . . . after a while [laughter]" (interview transcripts, April 1996).

If one's identity as feminist, as woman, as Canadian, as liberal rests on being tolerant and just, then antiracist challenges profoundly unsettle that foundation. Here, as elsewhere, some whites may direct anger and defensiveness at those who have disturbed that imagined identity. For example, the defensive reactions that accompanied antiracist change in a local feminist community organization are described by Samantha, a white manager whom I interviewed: "Oh, lots of defensiveness, definitely – 'That's not racism,' or 'I can't believe you think that.' Or, 'She didn't mean that.' Or, 'I'm not racist.' You certainly heard that a lot" (interview transcripts, December 1996). In my interviews this is a strikingly common description. Catherine, a white executive director of a women's agency, describes the kinds of reactions she sees as she begins to broach antiracism as an organizational issue: "I'm not prejudiced,' 'I've never discriminated against anybody in my life" (interview transcripts, December 1996).

Other white feminists respond with fear and terror that their moral accounts of self will be challenged. Minnie Bruce Pratt speaks of the "clutch of fear around my heart," the "terror" she feels on being "found out" as a white person who has "wronged others" and is about to be "punished" (1984, 17). Frankenberg's story of confronting antiracist feminism echoes these feelings: "And the issue was also terrifying, in the sense that we constantly felt that at any second we might err again with respect to racism, that we didn't know the rules" (1993, 3). She and her white feminist friends were terrified, she says, of "not being able to 'get it right' " (4).

Empathy

According to interview accounts, some white women openly demonstrate their remorse and empathy when they come face to face with the everyday meaning of racism for women of color. Samantha, a white woman involved in antiracist change in her organization, reflected on her own tearful reaction, saying, "One horrible incident makes me want to cry, when I hear about it" (interview transcripts, December 1996). We can see that, like anger, expressions of empathy and care help to construct and maintain a self-image of the good feminist. In feminist moral philosophy, displaying empathy and care for the other is generally characterized as a desirable expression of the caring and political connection among women, as well as of egalitarian relations. In fact, feminist philosophers have argued for the importance of empathy in working across difference, as it is seen as central to moral judgment about oppression (Bartky 1997; Meyers 1997).

Ironically, this is precisely why the expression of empathy and sympathy can become problematic in organizational settings: empathic expressions often revolve around an individual's moral self-image rather than organizational change. In the context of feminist psychotherapy Kerstin Roger (1998) argues that empathy reinforces the notion of the universally kind, helping white woman. For example, Nina tells the story of her organization, one in turmoil over accusations of racism. One of the white board members showed up at the women of color caucus meeting to voice her support but instead spoke about herself and cried. Nina recalls: "She came to the women of color caucus, and then she just talked about herself. . . . And she started crying, she was bawling her eyes out in fact, and saying, 'It's terrible, I don't know how you guys stand it" (interview transcripts, December 1996). This white board member clearly sought out a space to publicly display her revulsion of racism, even as the same self-preoccupation left her unwilling to actually do anything to support antiracist change. Her public display of revulsion – "I don't know how you guys stand it" – was also a necessary display of her inherent antiracism, inherent goodness.

Himani Bannerji, in her recollections of antiracist feminist discussions, writes that "claims about sharing 'experience,' having empathy" are meant to show that white feminists are "doing good" to feminists of color (1992, 10). Thus it is empathy "rather than questions, criticisms and politics" that emanates from these women: "Why" she asks, "do they . . . only talk about racism as understanding us, doing good to 'us'?" (11).

Contrary to the arguments of many feminist philosophers, these displays of empathy are clearly not helpful but offensive. Here we see that empathy about racism implies that the problem belongs to women of color and requires only the sympathetic feelings of white women – it emphasizes, in other words, the unequal relations of power. In the context of feminist discussions of racism, displays of empathetic feelings also reinforce the "goodness" in being a feminist – they show that one is highly sensitive to injustice.

Innocence and sin

As I have suggested, the defensive, angry, tearful, and empathic responses to antiracist challenges may be traced in part to the struggle to maintain a good, innocent, and egalitarian moral identity. When it comes to discussing racism, the moral terrain of the feminist movement can take on a dramatic tenor: the nonracist must be not just good but also innocent and pure. That desire for innocence underlies many conflicts about social difference in feminist forums. Fellows and Razack (1998) describe several feminist roundtables in which they were participants and show how the presumption of innocence – this "deeply felt belief that each of us, as women, is not implicated in the subordination" of others – underlies the deep fracture that opens when feminists talk about race (364). These contemporary relations between white and nonwhite feminists have been shaped by an imperial history of respectability and benevolence on the part of white women – an image of benevolence that becomes difficult to maintain when women of color begin to highlight racism or to criticize efforts to make the movement more inclusive (Grewal 1996; Fellows and Razack 1998).

My interviews with Ginny, a woman of color active in antiracist struggles, echo Fellows and Razack's analysis. Reflecting on some of the common reactions to antiracism that she has experienced in women's organizations, Ginny notes that the resistance comes from a deep incredulity that women feel about being implicated in any oppressive practice: "I think a lot of time the white women that are in power, they don't actually think of themselves as having power, they think of themselves as victims, as women, so that when they're told that they've done something to hurt somebody, they just can't believe it. 'Me? But I'm the one who's been a victim all my life. I went through . . .' de da de da de . . ." (interview transcripts, April 1996). [. . .]

Strategic innocence

In turn, protestations of innocence and expressions of empathy appear to be used as a way of tempering white women's feelings of desolation and of protecting them from anger and criticism by women of color. For example, Yasmin describes a typical reaction by some white women who were challenged for not having contributed to an antiracist workshop exercise. That, Yasmin says, "just led to tears on the part of the white women . . . and blah, blah . . . things like, 'I've tried really hard to see where I've come from, and who I've oppressed as a white woman" (interview transcripts, May 1996). One can hear these women's anxiety that their endeavors to be good antiracist feminists should be recognized; they remain anxious to present themselves as good feminists with good intentions.

There can be no clearer illustration of "innocence" as protection and strategic response than in the racial tensions documented by Métis writer Maria Campbell and white actor Linda Griffiths in the writing of their award-winning feminist play Jessica, based on Campbell's Métis ancestry and performed by Griffiths.[8] In reflecting on their difficult collaboration, Campbell explains that it was Griffiths's innocent facade, her smile, her "Virgin face" that both infuriated Campbell and compelled her to give Griffiths what she wanted – the painful details of her experience and history as a Métis woman (Griffiths and Campbell 1999, 70). As Griffiths admits, "It was the only way I could protect myself, with innocence, niceness. I just couldn't figure out why anyone would want to get mad at someone who was trying so hard. . . . My only protection was my innocence, my little white hand on your arm – 'Maria, why are you angry? Why don't you like me?' – hating myself for the smile on my face" (Griffiths and Campbell 1999, 71). Griffiths's "innocence" protects her against Campbell's anger – anger at Griffiths's privilege and presumption. Like the women in Yasmin's organization who proclaimed, "I've tried really hard to see where I've come from as a white woman," Griffiths deliberately uses her innocent face to portray herself as "someone who was trying so hard" – a strategy she uses to not only shield herself but also to obtain the information she needs.

Trauma

Recent theorizations of the trauma people experience on learning about racism and violence are helpful in explaining resistance to antiracist change. Deborah Britzman (1998) argues that the trauma of learning "difficult knowledge" (117) – knowledge of ethnic hatred and social violence – leads to a crisis of the self. This crisis of the self, Britzman shows, also leads to a profound resistance to learning. She uses the term passion for ignorance for the refusal to learn from these traumatic moments, a passion we have certainly seen in accounts of some white feminists' angry and tearful diversions. Shoshana Felman's (1992) psychoanalytic take on the trauma her students experience on hearing Holocaust stories is similarly helpful in understanding the intensity and limits of white feminists' emotional responses. Her descriptions of her students' panic, anxiety, anger, and tremendous "need to talk" (49) echo the reactions of white women on confronting the details of racism in women's lives and confronting their own complicity. The pedagogy of confronting antiracism has clear parallels to Felman's classroom; the trauma of facing questions of morality, complicity, or oppression is surely common to both pedagogical encounters. As I have suggested earlier, the refusals of some feminists to confront concerns about racism may also stem from a refusal to face certain questions of morality and complicity. These theorizations of trauma are relevant to understanding the responses of people when they confront the difficult knowledge that their self-image or moral identity as just activists, good feminists, alternative folks, and tolerant Canadians may be suspect; as we have seen, they may display a similar passion for ignorance and emotional and verbal expression.

The resulting emotional reactions are echoed in Don Laub's (1992) analysis of trauma. He outlines the kinds of defensive emotions that people use to fend off the upheaval – the pedagogical opportunity – of confronting the difficult knowledge of genocide: "a sense of total paralysis . . . a sense of outrage and anger unwittingly directed at the victim . . . a flood of awe and fear; we endow the survivor with a kind of sanctity, both to pay our tribute to him and to keep him at a distance, to avoid the intimacy entailed in knowing . . . hyperemotionality which superficially looks like compassion and caring. The testifier is simply flooded, drowned and lost in the listener's defensive affectivity" (Laub 1992, 72). As we have seen, the resistance to learning about racism is suffused with similar refusals. Recall Nina's fellow board member who comes to the women of color caucus to "bawl her eyes out" and "just talk about herself" and the pain she feels. We might suggest that she has experienced the trauma both of learning about racism from the perspective of women of color and of having her moral identity challenged. She is feeling, as Felman and Laub predict, a tremendous need to talk, a hyperemotionality that helps her deal with that upheaval. Here Judith Butler's (1997) use of Sigmund Freud's concept of melancholia or mourning also aptly describes this coworker's tearful focus on herself. Melancholia or mourning is defined as the sorrow at the loss of a person or ideal – here, the loss of the ideal of a just, nonracist feminist community and identity. One of the expressions of this loss is the "shameless voicing of self-beratement in front of others" (181), a form of narcissism in which "I revile myself and rehabilitate the other . . . . I refuse to speak to or of the other, but I speak voluminously about myself" (183).

It is important to extend these theorizations of trauma by reiterating that these preoccupations are also shaped by the unique history of feminist contexts, including imagined feminist heterotopia, feminist practices of emotional disclosure, and even colonial histories of white femininity. As Butler (1997) argues in her attempt to break down the categories of "inner" psychic life versus "exterior" social life, these psychic dramas are structured by social relations. For example, in feminist organizations, forms of social power emerge that regulate which losses can and cannot be grieved and who is allowed to grieve for which losses. In other words, the crisis of self that Britzman, Felman, and Laub discuss is colored by the unique heterotopic, emotional, and historic undertones of feminist organizations. In discussions of racial privilege in feminist organizations, white women's expressions of grief or loss are sometimes facilitated and are even respectable. Many feminist contexts have provided the political climate that allowed Nina's coworker to openly display her empathy and to receive care and understanding for her emotionality.

Shifts in moral identity, steps toward antiracism

At the same time, this social context of feminism, nonracism, and antiracism has been continually shifting in ways that continue to shape emotional and organizational responses to antiracist challenges. Neither moral community nor identity maintains a static and homogeneous nonracist frame. As Walker points out, "Communities of people who hold each other morally accountable reconfigure over time [their] shared understandings" (1997, 71). Over the past two decades an antiracist ethical discourse has evolved after years of challenges and writing by women of color, who argued for an integrative antiracist perspective (Dua 1999). There have been accompanying shifts in the imagined moral community and in what makes a good feminist.

For example, a new ethical practice that grew out of early shifts was the prefacing of commentary with a statement of social location: "I am a white, middle-class heterosexual urban woman."[9] Within social movements such as feminism, antiracism has similarly often been interpreted as personalized ethical practice requiring the self-examination, declaration, and regulation of an individual's racist beliefs. For example, as I have demonstrated elsewhere (Srivastava 1996), many antiracist workshops use knowledge of the individual and self-knowledge to teach whites about and to challenge racism. In this model, antiracist practice is seen in part as providing a key to the self. We might call this a personalized antiracist ethic.

As Foucault has suggested, the historical development of techniques such as confession and psychotherapy means that modern ethical practices have become focused primarily on self-examination, "self-decipherment," and "salvation," with the goal being "transformations" of the self (Foucault 1985, 29). In other words, techniques of self-examination have become important in determining "how the individual is supposed to constitute himself as a moral subject" (Foucault 1983, 238). These ethical practices of self-decipherment also describe the route of some white feminists moving toward antiracism.

This route has been influenced by the evocative accounts of many white feminists who in the 1980s began writing self-reflective accounts of their racial histories and antiracist journeys. Two of the best known of these is Pratt's 1984 essay "Identity: Skin/Blood/Heart" and Mab Segrest's 1985 *My Mama's Dead Squirrel*. Pratt, for example, argues that to regain the self-respect lost in becoming aware of racial privilege, "we need to find new ways to be *in* the world, those very actions a way of creating a positive self" (1984, 42). More broadly, the powerful discourse that "the personal is political" has also been influential in encouraging feminists to make these links between their personal lives and political change. In Frankenberg's 1993 study, the "race-cognizant" (159) white feminists focused on their personal identity, practices, and behaviors when asked about race. For many of them, the idea of "practising your antiracism" (168) – in other words, "the personal is political" – had become an ethical yardstick. This focus on self-examination and personal "process" is apparent when one of these white feminists talks about confronting the racism expressed by her old friends but remarks, "I think it's someone's own process to go through" (Frankenberg 1993, 166).

Unfortunately, as my interviews show, some women may become mired in self-examination and stuck in deliberations on morality and salvation. Not surprisingly, this ethical self-transformation is still framed by the poles of good versus evil, newly interpreted as the fraudulent nonracist versus the authentic antiracist. A number of the white feminists I interviewed, newly involved in antiracism, clearly struggle with their own place on this moral and political trajectory. Having started with a nonracist image of feminism and self, as they move toward a more systemic understanding of racism they find they also need to shift their understandings of moral community and self. Look again at Catherine's full description of some of the other white women in her organization: "There's people who say, 'I'm feeling attacked. Why am I being attacked? I'm not racist, I'm not prejudiced. . . . I've never discriminated against anybody in my life.' *So you're at that stage*" (interview transcripts, December 1996).

Catherine's reference to "that stage" highlights the variability of responses to antiracism over time. It also signals the extended and predictable stages many white feminists move through as they learn about antiracism. As a closer examination of both interview transcripts and feminist literature will show, we may characterize the stages in this discourse of moral progression as follows: first, being color-blind, being unaware of color and race; second, becoming aware that racism is a problem and being committed to your own nonracism; third, becoming aware of your own racism and feeling terrible about it; and finally, being able to accept and live with the fact that you might be racist rather than fearing it.

Segrest (1985) uses much the same language of moral progression to speak about the disorienting process of finding a new basis for her identity as a white, Southern woman. She also describes the process as having four stages – beginning with total unawareness of privilege and moving, finally, toward connection with other women:

> First, I am so racist, class-privileged, Christian that I don't even realize it, but assume that I am naturally wonderful. . . . Then I begin to see the false status that I get from my race and class and Christian privilege. And as soon as I do, I begin to see lies everywhere, and everywhere my own responsibility, my own complicity. . . . As I begin to feel what slavery did to Black people, I look up and see – God, we killed the Indians too. Then I hit the third stage of intense self-hatred. . . . I think the reason why white women avoid their racism . . . and can act so weird around women of color is because deep down we are afraid that this third level is all that there is. . . . That we will end up stuck in despair. . . . But I believe that underneath there is another level, a self that longs for wholeness and connection. (Segrest 1985, 171)

Contained within these stages of moral progression are both the nonracist ethic and personalized antiracist ethic.

Yet the movement between these stages is neither smooth nor linear. These are unsettled and discontinuous states, for both individuals and organizations. Britzman's discussion of the pedagogy of "difficult knowlsedge" as an inconstant process is helpful: "The psychic time of learning [is] one in which the confronted self vacillates, sometimes violently, sometimes passively, sometimes imperceptibly and sometimes shockingly, between resistance as symptom and the working through of resistance" (1998, 119). It is important to remember that for feminist activists, this learning is going on within a social movement and organizational context. As feminist activists learn about racial privilege, the context of a changing feminist moral order adds another unsettled layer. Since the mid-1980s the broader climate of feminist politics has shifted away from nonracism, and the imagined moral community is increasingly fragmented. Thus for those in the process of shifting their ethical self-image, the nonracist selfimage no longer makes sense to them, but the antiracist ethic is still hazy within the larger feminist community. As the political and moral climate of an organization and a movement shifts, individuals also move slowly and erratically between these apparent poles. Not surprisingly, women hover between two unattainable poles, between two cloudy and unreachable spaces of purity – nonracist and antiracist.

If we follow Samantha, a white senior manager working on antiracist change, we can see that the movement from nonracist to antiracist ethical *self-image* is both ambivalent and highly personalized. Looking more closely at her reflections, we can trace not only her evolving emotional responses but also the shift in how she thinks about herself in relation to women of color and racism: "I can't imagine what it is like. I can hear people's stories that tell me a bit of what it's like. But I'm not dealing with it. Because one horrible incident makes me want to cry, when I hear about it. But, then think about it, if you had a life like that, each incident is just the accumulation of that experience – I can't even begin to imagine what it's like to be in that place" (interview transcripts, December 1996).

As Samantha struggles toward understanding the daily experience of racism, she falls into the expected tearful empathetic response common in this initial nonracist stage of ethical practice. Empathy is often the first step in dealing with difficult knowledge of others, suggests Britzman: "Initially the learner attaches to the experience of the other by way of wondering what she or he would have done had such an event occurred in her or his own life" (1998, 118). However, like the antiracist activists I have interviewed, Britzman notes that "this experiment in empathy" can not only provoke resistance but also "impedes an understanding of the differences between the learner's knowledge and the knowledge of the other" (118). Interestingly, even as Samantha expresses her empathy, she also appears to acknowledge the disjuncture of knowledges that Britzman highlights, recognizing the difference between hearing or crying about racism and experiencing racism day to day.

However, Samantha's journey is still expressed as a personal moral progression. Even when Samantha discusses her organization, she describes progress on antiracism in terms of the individuals' ethical shifts: "I think that we got to the place where . . . we were working on discussions, and 'let's just talk about racism, what does it look like here,' getting to the point where we could sit at a table anywhere in the agency and say racism and people wouldn't run. . . . I think that is a really big step. And it is hard to acknowledge. And it's critical" (interview transcripts, December 1996). On the one hand, we can see how, within the four-step model of moral progression, getting individuals to talk openly about racism is indeed "a big step." In contrast, however, feminists of color to whom I spoke generally identify this stage – "let's just talk about racism" – as stagnation, even a frustrating full stop.

Samantha's own movement through these four stages, and her shift from seeing *racist* as anathema to seeing *racist* as part of her feminist identity, highlights not only her ambivalence but also the inadequacy of this framework for antiracism: "Throughout the agency . . . I think there was real fear of being called 'racist.' . . . It is hard for me to reflect back on where I was then, but I am sure that's where I was too. I was more afraid of being called 'racist' than anything else. And now, if someone were to say that, I would say, 'you're probably right' " (interview transcripts, December 1996). The four-stage moral progression traps Samantha between two unsatisfactory stages: if she were to say with complete ease "I am racist" to her colleagues or to the woman of color interviewing her, she risks criticisms that she is complacent or glib about racism. If she were to outright deny being racist, she knows she would be stuck in an unacceptable ethical position. Samantha's discomfort suggests that problematic narratives of purity and impurity remain from nonracist discourse.

Instead of innocent versus racist, however, the poles of purity versus impurity in commentaries such as Samantha's are more likely to signify knowledge versus ignorance, the antiracist feminist versus other unenlightened feminists. Samantha indicates that she has reached a more advanced understanding of racism than her colleagues. Similarly, when Catherine, another white senior manager, explains how routine practice can perpetuate racism, she says, "And even I – 'even I' – after a lot of years of experience, I can find myself doing things a certain way, just because they've always been done that way" (interview transcripts, December 1996). With her phrase "even I," Catherine, like Samantha, gestures to her higher level of awareness in comparison to other women in her organization. Both Samantha's and Catherine's commentary shows that a personalized antiracist ethical discourse contains a new yardstick for measuring other feminists: it is the self-made antiracist white feminist who is good, other white feminists who are not good enough. Catherine even catches herself perpetuating this dichotomy; repeating "even I" in an ironic aside, she mocks herself and her tendency to present herself as morally superior. Yet her slip shows that this dichotomy, between thinking of herself as "pure" and others as racist, ironically underlies her transition toward antiracism.

This discourse of moral progression and self-examination is further supported by feminist discourses of emotional self-care and therapy. In explaining why it is important to examine oneself in antiracist discussion, Samantha highlights the emotional benefits: "It's like doing any of your own work – it's really scary to look at the ghosts in your own closet. But if you know that by looking at them you're going to feel better, then you are more likely to look at them than just trying to keep the door shut" (interview transcripts, December 1996). In other words, we attempt to extirpate our racist beliefs because we will know ourselves better and "feel better" – therapeutic sentiments that are further shaped by a desire for ethical self-transformation. By remaining focused on the self rather than on organizational practice, these individualized discourses of therapy and moral progression make a broader antiracist analysis difficult.

Salvation

Despite the ambiguity of her position, Samantha's commentary shows that the focus on self-examination of one's personal antiracist practice leads ultimately to a "once was lost, now am found" narrative. As in "Amazing Grace," the slave trader's song from which this phrase is drawn, Samantha's redemption comes from a turning point of personal salvation.

In this muddy arena of moral uncertainty, antiracist caucuses, task forces, experts, facilitators, and antiracist policy can take on particular moral significance and moral authority. If one is failing in the task of self-contemplation, one may look to another person or policy to provide an easier route to salvation. Samantha reflects on the deference staff and board members have toward the new antiracist task force in her organization: "Like if someone says, 'the [anti-racist] task force says this,' people go, 'Ohhh.' . . . I think partly it's that we don't really know all the answers. So, if someone thinks they know the answers, *that's great*" (interview transcripts, December 1996).

In Yasmin's organization, women's desire for moral guidance and salvation is even more strikingly expressed in their awe of a well-known black antiracist consultant from the United States whom her coworkers want to hire:

> She's seen as an expert, and . . . people take her word as the goddess's word. . . . There was this awe surrounding her. There would be this hesitation, by all three women, to even phone her. There was this reverence about her – "What are we going to say to her?" . . . I just really thought that was bizarre, that people were all tongue-tied at the thought of her. . . . Phone her up, she's charging us $1,000 a day, you can damn well think of something to say!
>
> It was like suddenly, she was this catalyst of change, just as Martin Luther King was. You could make that parallel: this great woman was going to make change for us. And I think that was the problem, that there was this dependence on her already, before they even phoned her.
>
> *Author*: She was going to make things right.
>
> Right. (Interview transcripts, May 1996)

Both goddess and godsend, the antiracist consultant appears to inspire the emotional and religious reverence of a spiritual leader, of a great civil rights leader. Without a clear moral guide to antiracist behavior, people look for guidance, even a savior. Yasmin's description of lost sheep looking for moral guidance suggests a moral community in transition, uncertain of its new parameters, ethical practices, and language, and preferring to follow rather than to act. People then pin impossible expectations for solving the problem on a brief visit by an antiracist facilitator and expert. Yasmin's language also recalls Laub's (1992) description of the self-protective awe, fear, and sanctity with which people endow the recounter of genocide. Laub suggests this response allows people to put distance between themselves and difficult knowledge. In Yasmin's organization, by constructing a sacred image of moral superiority, those struggling with a new understanding of racism can distance themselves from their own responsibility for ethical decisions and organizational action.

Conclusions and alternatives

Like the heterotopia of which Hetherington (1997) writes, feminism as a modern humanist project has produced a new ethical subject and social order. However, antiracist feminist challenges have highlighted the interlocking relations of race and gender that are implicated in the construction of this moral community. As we have seen in the rocky history of antiracism in the feminist movement, a crisis arises when people realize that the imagined utopic community, or the "transparent community of beautiful souls," is neither possible nor universally desired.[10]

One reaction to this crisis has been to reassert and refine feminism's moral boundaries. Wendy Brown's discussion of social movements facing the loss of universal visions is apt: "It is when the telos of the good vanishes but the yearning for it remains that morality appears to dissolve into moralism in politics" (2001, 28). We can see that this attempt to recuperate the vision of the just, nonracist feminist continues within organizations today. In tracing the narratives of white feminists in various stages of refusal, it becomes clear that not only imperial histories of innocent white femininity but also historical constructions of a just feminist community underlie some feminists' emotional protestations of innocence.

Of course, not all white feminists coming face-to-face with antiracist challenges react to the difficult knowledge of racial privilege with emotional refusals. Those active in antiracist work also struggle to find their own place in it. Yet in their desire to leave the nonracist ethic behind, they may still become trapped in attempts to construct a personalized antiracist ethic that implicitly relies on a discourse of moral progression, one that requires either self-examination, utterances of purification, or salvation by others. As the political and moral climate of their movement shifts toward antiracism, these individuals, and often the organizations they run, can become stalled as they vacillate between these apparent moral poles.

Yet why not be introspective about racialized ideas and practices and thereby become a "better person"? Frankenberg believes that this approach, expressed only in her interviews with white feminists, is important (1993, 159). According to Samantha, this approach did allow her organization to draft an antiracist policy and create an antiracist committee.

However, personal accounts of ethical practices that are framed around poles of purity and impurity in turn shape and limit the kinds of antiracist organizational debates and actions that are possible. Samantha recognizes that the "big step" her organization took when members acknowledged their own racism was also a resting place where organizational structure was not addressed. Says Samantha: "So, we got to that place. But what happened was that nothing happened because we weren't working on the structural stuff" (interview transcripts, December 1996). In other words, practices of self-examination and self-improvement may shift the moral and ethical climate or facilitate antiracist initiatives but lead to limited organizational change. A liberalist discourse that frames racism as done by ignorant or bad people and extirpated by confession dictates an individual solution. In social movements, these broader discourses are interpreted within moral communities that tie the personal to the political, rionracism to political goodness, and therapy and emotional expression to social change.

Is there a way to shift the centrality of this moral preoccupation? Does racism inevitably raise questions of individual morality and personal ethics? Tracing the construction and conflicts of imagined moral communities within feminist polities opens the possibility that we may move beyond the seesaw of purity versus corruption that appears currently to structure responses to antiracist critique. These preoccupations may seem unavoidable in social movements directed by a moral code to not oppress others – to act, in fact, to challenge oppression. Yet certainly many white feminists do not frame antiracism as a question of innocence versus sin, and some openly criticize this approach. Frankenberg (1993) found that this is particularly true of older feminists involved in early antiracist struggles, from the 1940s on. Frankenberg shows that the historical context of race blindness, which necessitated white women's soul-searching in the first place, has not shaped older activists' responses. One of the younger white feminist activists whom Frankenberg interviewed perhaps provides an example of how a moral framework may move outside the poles of complicity versus noncomplicity. This woman reflects that it is important to finally admit, "Well, yeah, our hearts are in the right place, but it's still not coming together" and to discuss why (1993, 175). It seems that she too sees this as a moral obligation, yet her response to her feelings of guilt differs from earlier examples. She is more interested in why antiracist change is not happening and less interested in her own moral acceptability.

Many workshop and consciousness-raising approaches have taught us to "know better," "feel better," and be better people. Yet in addition to knowing more and feeling better, we might want to think better and do better. A comprehensive discussion of alternative strategies is beyond the scope of this article, but we must continue to investigate an alternative to these moral preoccupations – a third way that starts with the goal of systemic antiracist change yet still acknowledges the individual preoccupations that may impede that work. Could we not imagine discussions of racism as collective political and social analyses rather than as individual preoccupations with morality? For example, in one feminist collective, two women of color, fed up with the personalized focus of the antiracist workshops and facilitator, intervened by gathering data on the racialized division of labor among collective members and demonstrated that women of color carried a far greater burden of administrative and behind-the-scenes work.

Beginning with this kind of focus on political analysis and action rather than with nostalgic moral visions of a united community or attempts at ethical self-transformation might better avoid the pitfalls we have seen here. Bartky (1997) suggests that antiracist feminist change aims at a transformation of self. I would argue, rather, that an antiracist feminism might aim at an unbalancing of historical links between racism and the poles of innocence versus evil, knowledge versus ignorance.

Notes

1   Rosemary Pringle's study of secretaries and bosses, *Secretaries Talk* (1989), and Frankenberg's study of whiteness, *White Women, Race Matters* (1993), use similar approaches to integrating interview material into sociological analysis.
2   See Goldberg 1993; Stoler 1995; Dyer 1997; Frankenberg 1997.

3   This term was suggested to me by Roxana Ng, Ontario Institute for Studies in Education, University of Toronto. Donna Baines (1998) has used Ng's term in her study of progressive social workers she interviewed.

4   Frankenberg uses the more accurate terms *color-evasive* and *power-evasive* in preference to *color blindness* because the former refers to the strategies people use to avoid acknowledging racism rather than to their supposed inability to see racism.

5   Extensive newspaper coverage included a full-page spread in the national newspaper *Globe and Mail* (Rose 1992); a *Globe and Mail* editorial, "A Question of the Pot Calling the Kettle White" (Thorsell 1992); "If Callwood Is a Racist Then So Are We All" (Berton 1992); and "Unsaid Words on Racism" (Paris 1992). Magazine coverage included the now-infamous "Wrongful Dismissal" (Dewar 1993); a cover story in *Quota*, a lesbian monthly, "Checking In: June Callwood Talks about Her Feelings, Her Faults, and the Failing of Feminist Groups Struggling with Issues of Racism" (Douglas 1993); and Adele Freedman's (1993) "White Woman's Burden" in *Saturday Night*.

6   Valverde's (1999) study of Alcoholics Anonymous, for example, shows that the organization's primary practices can be described as ethical techniques – practices aimed at changing the self, one's own desires and habits – as opposed to medical or psychological techniques.

7   In the past decade, this meaning of *politically correct* has been caricatured and remade by many conservative writers. For a discussion of this "anti-PC" discourse, see Richer and Weir 1995.

8   *Jessica* had successful runs across Canada in the mid-1980s and won a number of awards, including the 1986 Dora Mayor Moore Award for Outstanding New Play.

9   For further discussion of the history of this practice, see Mary Louise Adams, who argues that 'together we ascribed a moral significance to our individual litanies of oppression" (1989, 22).

10   Valverde, e-mail communication, March 2002.

References

Adams, Mary Louise. 1989. "There's No Place Like Home: On the Place of Identity in Feminist Politics." *Feminist Review* 31 (Spring): 23–33.

Anderson, Benedict. 1992. *Imagined Communities: Reflections on the Origin and Spread of Nationalism*. New York: Verso.

Anzaldúa, Gloria, ed. 1990. *Making Face, Making Soul/Haciendo Caras: Creative and Critical Perspectives by Feminists of Color*. San Francisco: Aunt Lute Books.

Baines, Donna. 1998. "Everyday Practices of Race, Class and Gender." PhD dissertation, University of Toronto.

Bannerji, Himani. 1992. "Racism, Sexism, Knowledge and the Academy: Re:Turning the Gaze." *Resources for Feminist Research* 20(3/4):5–11.

Bartky, Sandra Lee. 1997. "Sympathy and Solidarity: On a Tightrope with Scheler." In *Feminists Rethink the Self*, ed. Diana Tietjens Meyers, 177–96. Boulder, CO: Westview.

Berton, Pierre. 1992. "If Callwood Is a Racist Then So Are We All." *Toronto Star*, May 23, H3.

Britzman, Deborah P. 1998. *Lost Subjects, Contested Objects: Toward a Psychoanalytic Inquiry of Learning*. Albany: State University of New York Press.

Broadside Collective. 1986. "No to Racism!" *Broadside Collective* 7(5):3.

Brown, Wendy. 2001. "Moralism as Anti-politics." In her *Politics Out of History*, 18–44. Princeton, NJ: Princeton University Press.

Butler, Judith. 1997. *The Psychic Life of Power: Theories in Subjection*. Stanford, CA: Stanford University Press.

Carroll, William, and Robert Ratner. 1996. "Master Frames and Counter-hegemony: Political Sensibilities in Contemporary Social Movements." *Canadian Review of Sociology and Anthropology* 33(4):407–35.

Corrigan, Philip. 1981. "On Moral Regulation: Some Preliminary Remarks." *Sociological Review* 29(2):313–38.

Dewar, Elaine. 1993. "Wrongful Dismissal." *Toronto Life*, March, 32–45.

Dimen, Muriel. 1984. "Politically Correct? Politically Incorrect?" In *Pleasure and Danger: Exploring Female Sexuality*, ed. Carol S. Vance, 138–48. Boston: Routledge & Kegan Paul.

Douglas, Catherine. 1993. "Checking In: June Callwood Talks about Her Feelings, Her Faults, and the Failing of Feminist Groups Struggling with Issues of Racism." *Quota*, April, 6.

Dua, Enakshi. 1999. "Introduction." In Dua and Robertson 1999, 7–31.

Dua, Enakshi, and Angela Robertson, eds. 1999. *Scratching the Surface: Canadian Anti-racist Feminist Thought*. Toronto: Women's Press.

Dyer, Richard. 1997. *White*. New York: Routledge.

Enloe, Cynthia. 1989. *Bananas, Beaches and Bases: Making Feminist Sense of International Politics*. London: Pandora.

Essed, Philomena. 1991. *Understanding Everyday Racism: An Interdisciplinary Theory*. London: Sage.

Fellows, Mary Louise, and Sherene Razack. 1994. "Seeking Relations: Law and Feminism Roundtables." *Signs: Journal of Women in Culture and Society* 19(4): 1048–83.

———.1998. "The Race to Innocence: Confronting Hierarchical Relations among Women." *Journal of Gender, Race and Justice* 1(2):335–52.

Felman, Shoshana. 1992. "Education and Crisis, or the Vicissitudes of Teaching." In *Testimony: Crises of Witnessing in Literature, Psychoanalysis, and History*, ed. Shoshana Felman and Don Laub, 1–56. New York: Routledge.

Flemming, Leslie. 1992. "A New Humanity: American Missionaries' Ideals for Women in North India, 1870–1930." In *Western Women and Imperialism: Complicity and Resistance*, ed. Nupur Chaudhuri and Margaret Strobel, 191–206. Bloomington: Indiana University Press.

Foucault, Michel. 1983. "On the Genealogy of Ethics." In *Michel Foucault: Beyond Structuralism and Hermeneutics*, ed. Henry Dreyfus and Paul Rabinow, 229–52. Chicago: University of Chicago Press.

———.1985. *The History of Sexuality*. Vol. 2, The Use of Pleasure. New York: Pantheon.

———.1986. "Of Other Spaces." *Diacritics* 16(1):22–27.

Frankenberg, Ruth. 1993. *White Women, Race Matters: The Social Construction of Whiteness*. Minneapolis: University of Minnesota Press.

———, ed. 1997. *Displacing Whiteness: Essays in Social and Cultural Criticism*. Durham, NC: Duke University Press.

Freedman, Adele. 1993. "White Woman's Burden." *Saturday Night*, April, 40–44, 74–84.

Friedman, Susan. 1995. "Beyond White and Other: Relationality and Narratives of Race in Feminist Discourse." *Signs* 21(1);1–49.

Giddings, Paula. 1984. *When and Where I Enter: The Impact of Black Women on Race and Sex in America*. New York: Morrow.

Goldberg, David Theo. 1993. *Racist Culture: Philosophy and the Politics of Meaning*. Cambridge: Blackwell.

Grewal, Inderpal. 1996. *Home and Harem: Nation, Gender, Empire, and the Cultures of Travel*. Durham, NC: Duke University Press.

Griffiths, Linda, and Maria Campbell. 1999. *The Book of Jessica: A Theatrical Transformation*. Toronto: Playwrights Union of Canada.

Harper, Helen. 1995. "Danger at the Borders: The Response of High School Girls to Feminist Writing Practices." PhD dissertation, University of Toronto.

Heron, Barbara. 1999. "Desire for Development: The Education of White Women as Development Workers." PhD dissertation, University of Toronto.

Hetherington, Kevin. 1997. *The Badlands of Modernity: Heterotopia and Social Ordering*. New York: Routledge.

Hobsbawm, Eric. 1975. *The Age of Capital, 1848–1875*. London: Weidenfeld & Nicolson.

hooks, bell. 1983. *Ain't I a Woman: Black Women and Feminism*. Boston: South End.

Hurst, Lynda. 1992. "Feminism's Fault Lines." *Toronto Star*, November 28, D1, D4.

Kleinman, Sherryl. 1996. *Opposing Ambitions: Gender and Identity in an Alternative Organization*. Chicago: University of Chicago Press.

Laub, Don. 1992. "An Event without a Witness: Truth, Testimony and Survival." In *Testimony: Crises of Witnessing in Literature, Psychoanalysis, and History*, ed. Shoshana Felman and Don Laub, 75–92. New York: Routledge.

Little, Margaret Hillyard. 1999. "'A Fit and Proper Person': The Moral Regulation of Single Mothers in Ontario, 1920–1940." In *Gendered Pasts: Historical Essays in Femininity and Masculinity in Canada*, ed. Kathryn McPherson, Cecilia Morgan, and Nancy M. Forestell, 123–38. Don Mills, Ontario: Oxford University Press.

Meyers, Diana Tietjens. 1997. "Emotion and Heterodox Moral Perception: An Essay in Moral Social Psychology." In *Feminists Rethink the Self*, ed. Diana Tietjens Meyers, 197–218. Boulder, CO: Westview.

Moraga, Cherríe, and Gloria Anzaldúa, eds. 1983. *This Bridge Called My Back: Writings by Radical Women of Color*. New York: Kitchen Table.

Morgan, Robin, ed. 1984. *Sisterhood Is Powerful: The International Women's Movement Anthology*. New York: Anchor.

Morgen, Sandra. 1995. "'It was the best of times, it was the worst of times': Emotional Discourse in the Work Cultures of Feminist Health Clinics." In *Feminist Organizations: Harvest of the New Women's Movement*, ed. Myra Marx Ferree and Patricia Yancey Martin, 234–47. Philadelphia: Temple University Press.

Narayan, Uma. 1997. "Cross-Cultural Connections, Border-Crossings, and 'Death by Culture': Thinking about Dowry-Murders in India and Domestic-Violence Murders in the United States." In her *Dislocating Cultures: Identities, Traditions, and Third World Feminism*, 81–118. New York: Routledge.

Ng, Roxana. 1992. "Multiculturalism as Ideology: A Textual Accomplishment." Paper presented at the ninety-first annual meeting of the American Anthropological Association, San Francisco, December.

Paris, Erna. 1992. "Unsaid Words on Racism." *Globe and Mail*, July 21, A14.

Pratt, Minnie Bruce. 1984. "Identity: Skin/Blood/Heart." In *Yours in Struggle: Three Feminist Perspectives on Anti-Semitism and Racism*, ed. Minnie Bruce Pratt, Elly Bulkin, and Barbara Smith, 11–63. New York: Longhaul.

Pringle, Rosemary. 1989. *Secretaries Talk*. London: Verso.

Razack, Sherene. 2000. "Your Place or Mine? Transnational Feminist Collaboration." In *Anti-Racist Feminism: Critical Race and Gender Studies,* ed. Agnes Calliste and George J. Sefa Dei, 39–53. Halifax: Fernwood.

Richer, Stephen, and Lorna Weir, eds. 1995. *Beyond Political Correctness: Toward the Inclusive University*. Toronto: University of Toronto Press.

Roach, Kiké, and Judy Rebick. 1996. *Politically Speaking*. Vancouver: Douglas & McIntyre.

Roger, Kerstin. 1998. "Fairy Fictions: White Women as Professional Helpers." PhD dissertation, University of Toronto.

Rooney, Ellen. 1989. "Commentary: What's to Be Done?" In *Coming to Terms: Feminism, Theory, and Politics*, ed. Elizabeth Weed, 230–39. New York: Routledge.

Rose, Barbara Wade. 1992. "Trouble at Nellie's: Accusations of Racism at the Toronto Hostel for Abused Women Lead to the Resignation of Its Biggest Name, June Callwood." *Globe and Mail*, May 9, Dl.

Schick, Carol. 1998. "By Virtue of Being White: Racialized Identity Formation and the Implications for Anti-racist Pedagogy." PhD dissertation, University of Toronto.

Segrest, Mab. 1985. *My Mama's Dead Squirrel: Lesbian Essays on Southern Culture*. Ithaca, NY: Firebrand.

Srivastava, Santa. 1996. "Song and Dance? The Performance of Antiracist Workshops." *Canadian Review of Sociology and Anthropology* 33(3):292–315.

———. Forthcoming. "Tears, Fears and Careers: Anti-racism, Emotion and Social Movement Organizations." *Canadian Journal of Sociology*.

Stoler, Ann Laura. 1995. *Race and the Education of Desire: Foucault's "History of Sexuality" and the Colonial Order of Things*. Durham, NC: Duke University Press.

Taylor, Verta. 1995. "Watching for Vibes: Bringing Emotions into the Study of Feminist Organizations." In *Feminist Organizations: Harvest of the New Women's Movement*, ed. Myra Marx Ferree and Patricia Yancey Martin, 223–33. Philadelphia: Temple University Press.

Thorsell, William. 1992. "A Question of the Pot Calling the Kettle White." *Globe and Mail*, May 23, D6.

Valverde, Mariana. 1991. *The Age of Light, Soap and Water: Moral Reform in English Canada, 1885–1935*, Toronto: McClelland & Stewart.

———. 1992. "When the Mother of the Race Is Free': Race, Reproduction, and Sexuality in First-Wave Feminism." In *Gender Conflicts: New Essays in Women's History*, ed. France Iacovetta and Mariana Valverde, 3–26. Toronto: University of Toronto Press.

———. 1999. "One Day at a Time' and Other Slogans for Everyday Life: The Ethical Practices of Alcoholics Anonymous." *Sociology* 33(2):393–410.

Valverde, Mariana, and Lorna Weir. 1988. "The Struggles of the Immoral: Preliminary Remarks on Moral Regulation." *Resources for Feminist Research* 17(3): 31–34.

Walker, Margaret Urban. 1997. "Picking Up Pieces: Lives, Stories, and Integrity." In *Feminists Rethink the Self*, ed. Diana Tictjens Meyers, 62–84. Boulder, CO: Westview.

Ware, Vron. 1992. *Beyond the Pale: White Women, Racism and History*. London: Verso.

Wetherell, Margaret, and Jonathan Potter. 1992. *Mapping the Language of Racism: Discourse and the Legitimation of Exploitation*. Hemel Hempstead: Harvester Wheatsheaf.

Guide to Further Reading

Key texts

Alcoff, L. M. (2006) *Visible Identities: Race, Gender and the Self*, New York: Oxford University Press (an account of the formation of identities based on race and gender and the role they play in mobilising identity politics).

Alexander, C. and Knowles, C. (eds) (2005) *Making Race Matter: Bodies, Space & Identity*, Basingstoke: Palgrave Macmillan (a collection of papers exploring the mechanisms through which racial bodies are made and re-made).

Collins, P. H. (1990) *Black Feminist Thought*, London: Unwin Hyman (a critical analysis of the emergence of black feminism and its contribution to the understanding of the position of black women).

Mirza, H. S. (ed.) (1997) *Black British Feminism: A Reader*, London: Routledge (a collection of some important contributions to the development of black British feminism).

Nagel, J. (2003) *Race, Ethnicity, and Sexuality: Intimate Intersections, Forbidden Frontiers*, New York: Oxford University Press (a formative text that explores the intersections of race, ethnicity and sexuality).

Williams, P. J. (1991) *The Alchemy of Race and Rights*, Cambridge, MA: Harvard University Press (an exploration of everyday experiences of race and gender in American society).

Background reading

Bhattacharyya, G. (1998) *Tales of Dark-Skinned Women: Race, Gender and Global Culture*, London: UCL Press (a series of stories that explores the encounter between black women and the West).

Brody, J. D. (1998) *Impossible Purities: Blackness, Femininity, and Victorian Culture*, Durham, NC: Duke University Press (a historical reconstruction of images of femininity and blackness in the Victorian imagination).

Bryan, B., Dadzie, S. and Scafe, S. (1985) *The Heart of the Race: Black Women's Lives in Britain*, London: Virago (an early attempt to explore the experiences of black women in contemporary Britain).

Carby, H. V. (1998) *Race Men*, Cambridge, Mass.: Harvard University Press (an innovative account of the articulation of ideas about black masculinity in American culture, with a focus on Du Bois and other important figures in black American history).

Christian, B. (1985) *Black Feminist Criticism: Perspectives on Black Women Writers*, New York: Pergamon Press (an important collection of papers on key black women writers).

Davis, A. Y. (1982) *Women, Race & Class*, London: The Women's Press (an influential early attempt to link the analysis of race with questions about class and gender).

Frankenberg, R. (1993) *White Women, Race Matters: The Social Construction of Whiteness*, London: Routledge (an investigation of the meanings of race and whiteness among a sample of white women in America).

Gates Jr, H. L. (ed.) (1990) *Reading Black, Reading Feminist: A Critical Anthology*, New York: Meridian (a collection of recent critical perspectives on black women's writing in America).

hooks, b. (1990) *Yearning: Race, Gender and Cultural Politics*, Boston: South End Press (an influential analysis of the new cultural politics of race and gender in America).

Ifekwunigwe, J. O. (1999) *Scattered Belongings: Cultural Paradoxes of 'Race', Nation and Gender*, London: Routledge (mixes biography and academic analysis to map the borders between race and gender in the contemporary environment).

James, J. (ed.) (1998) *The Angela Y. Davis Reader*, Oxford: Blackwell (a collection of Davis's writings on race, class and gender).

James, S. and Busia, A. (eds) (1993) *Theorizing Black Feminisms*, London: Routledge (a collection of papers on various aspects of contemporary black feminism).

Jarrett-Macauley, D. (ed.) (1996) *Reconstructing Womanhood, Reconstructing Feminism: Writings on Black Women*, London: Routledge (a collection of papers on debates within black British feminism).

Mama, A. (1995) *Beyond the Masks: Race, Gender and Subjectivity*, London: Routledge (an account of psychological discourses about race and Africans).

Mohanty, C. T., Russo, A. and Torres, L. (eds) (1991) *Third World Women and the Politics of Feminism*, Bloomington: Indiana University Press (an influential collection of papers that explore feminism from a third world perspective).

Mullings, L. (1997) *On Our Own Terms: Race, Class and Gender in the Lives of African American Women*, New York: Routledge (an analysis of the changing experiences of African American women).

Nelson, D. D. (1998) *National Manhood: Capitalist Manhood and the Imagined Fraternity of White Men*, Durham, NC: Duke University Press (a historical analysis of ideas about nation, race and gender in America).

Parker, A., Russo, M., Sommer, D. and Yaeger, P. (eds) (1992) *Nationalisms and Sexualities*, New York: Routledge (a collection of papers that explore the relationship between nationalism and sexuality in a variety of contexts).

Spivak, G. C. (1988) *In Other Worlds: Essays in Cultural Politics*, London: Routledge (a collection of influential essays, including Spivak's critical analysis of Western feminism).

—— (1993) *Outside in the Teaching Machine*, New York: Routledge (a collection of essays, including questions of multiculturalism, postcolonialism and feminism).

Sudbury, J. (1998) *'Other Kinds of Dreams': Black Women's Organisations and the Politics of Transformation*, London: Routledge (an account of forms of self-organisation among black women in Britain).

Ware, V. (1992) *Beyond the Pale: White Women, Racism and History*, London: Verso (a historical treatment of the role of white women in relation to colonialism and racism).

Key Questions

- How has the analysis of race and racism been influenced by debates about gender, sexuality and masculinity?
- Is Hazel Carby right to argue that in contemporary debates 'terms like women, gender, and sexuality have a decorative function only'? How can this situation be changed?
- Discuss Patricia Hill Collins's analysis of the intersections of race, class and gender in structuring the position of women in African-American communities.
- Critically evaluate Springer's argument that we have seen the emergence of third wave black feminism.
- In what ways can Patricia Williams's work be seen as giving 'more power to the voices that racism suppresses'?
- Avtar Brah argues that it is important that 'we do not compartmentalize oppressions'. Analyse her argument and how it may help to move us beyond compartmentalisation.
- What does Ruth Frankenberg mean when she says that 'race shapes white women's lives'.
- Critically review Sarita Srivastava's argument that antiracist feminism is preoccupied with self-examination, morality and self.

PART SIX

Changing boundaries and spaces

INTRODUCTION

T HE FOCUS OF THE MATERIAL INCLUDED in the preceding parts
has been largely, though not exclusively, on the elaboration of key theoretical
and conceptual debates about race and racism. Within the limitations of one volume
we have attempted to be as open as we could be to the inclusion of extracts from
the major authors who have helped to shape in one way or another the course
of academic debate in this field over the years, though we are aware that there
is also much that cannot be fitted into the specific parameters of this Reader. In
doing so we have also sought to give a flavour of the passion and political feeling
that questions about race and racism are bound to give rise to in one way or
another. Much of the most intense debate in this field has been focused on how
to conceptualise the boundaries of race and racism, particularly in an environment
that is rapidly changing. This is the dimension that we turn to in this part, where
we shift focus somewhat by bringing together a series of extracts that raise questions
that are likely to be the subject of extensive debate and scholarship in the years
to come.

The first extract is from Paul Gilroy, who is one of the most original
contemporary theorists in this field. Gilroy takes up a question that has been the
focus of much of his influential oeuvre, namely the changing patterns of identity
formation within the African diaspora in a context of social change and transformation that characterises the everyday realities within which diasporic
communities live and interact with other social groups. This is an issue that has
been at the heart of much of the more recent theorising in this field both in the
United States and in Europe and raises important questions about the complex
forms that diasporic identification often takes among particular communities and

groups within them. The arguments developed by Gilroy also link up with some of the key contributions to be found in Parts Four and Five and it may be useful to explore some of these linkages in thinking through the implications of his analysis for future research.

A related set of questions is taken up by Kobena Mercer, who provides an insightful account of the changing patterns of identity politics within the context of increasing social and cultural diversity. Linking his analysis to broader debates about postmodernism, Mercer is particularly concerned with analysing the contradictions within identity politics, and he seeks to situate the preoccupation with both identity and diversity in the new social and cultural politics that have emerged in contemporary societies.

In the past two decades we have seen a rapid growth in studies of whiteness. Some aspects of this field have been covered in Part Five in relation to the work of Ruth Frankenberg. In this part we have included a masterful overview of aspects of critical white studies by one of its main exponents David R. Roediger. His account is deeply imbued with a historical perspective, particularly through the lens of labour history, and it helps to highlight the importance to any rounded analysis of race and racism of a critical understanding of the formations of whiteness. In particular he suggests that there is a need to see whiteness as a problem that needs to be researched both from a historical and sociological perspective.

The extracts from Kimberlé Crenshaw and Stephen Steinberg shift the focus from theory to the level of political institutions and ideas. From rather different angles they take up questions at the heart of the changing politics of race in the United States of America and the impact of state policies aimed at ameliorating the effects of racism. Both authors focus on the diverse initiatives and programmes that were brought into existence by the racial conflicts of the 1950s and 1960s in the United States. Crenshaw's analysis, which is part of what is called 'critical race theory' in the United States, seeks to challenge conceptions of anti-discrimination policies that do not take fully into account the complex linkages between race, class and gender in structuring the everyday experiences of African Americans in the period since the 1960s. Crenshaw's contribution is followed by Stephen Steinberg, who is one of the most astute and vocal critics of what he sees as a 'retreat from racial justice' in the period since the 1980s. Steinberg's analysis focuses on the ways in which the political and social discourses of both the Conservative Right and of Liberals can be seen as representing a retreat from the promise of reform and action to tackle the root causes of racial inequality in the United States that was much in evidence in the aftermath of the Civil Rights Movement. Both of these extracts highlight important conceptual issues as to the way we can attempt to understand the impact of political institutions on questions of racial inequality and exclusion.

The question of contemporary racial trends is explored further in the extracts from Jennifer L. Hochschild and Eduardo Bonilla-Silva. Hochschild's discussion is focused on recent scholarly and public debates about the future of race and ethnicity in the United States. She provides a masterful overview of how the position of African Americans has changed over the past century, arguing nevertheless that whatever future scenarios may develop, 'African Americans will remain a distinct although not always subordinated social grouping'. It is interesting to note here that her account resonates with some of the more historical extracts that we included in Part One of the Reader. Bonilla-Silva's account covers some of the same ground as Hochschild, although it is more focused on the emergence of a 'tri-racial' pattern of racial stratification in the post-Civil Rights period. His contribution highlights the complex role of race, class and racism in shaping the position of 'blacks', 'Latinos' and 'Asians' in the contemporary morphology of the United States. In a detailed analysis of emerging empirical data he argues forcefully that scholars in this field will have to critically question how far the categories we use are meaningful in the ever-changing landscape of the present.

The extract by Anthony Appiah is a nuanced exploration of the dilemmas faced in thinking about the boundaries of racial identification, and was written as part of a dialogue between himself and the political theorist Amy Gutmann. But in many ways it can be seen as neatly capturing dilemmas that are at the heart of contemporary debates about the changing boundaries of racial identity. What is particularly interesting about Appiah's account is the way he does not lose sight of the need to situate the new patterns of identity formation that characterise contemporary societies against the background of historical trends and processes. In this he reminds us that we need to know as much about where racial ideas come from as we do about where they are going at the present time.

The final concluding extract, from Howard Winant provides a useful endpoint for the Reader as a whole. Winant's starting point is that we need to develop an account of globalised race and racism that is capable both of understanding the present and of looking forward to the trends and developments that are likely to shape the first part of the twenty-first century. He is particularly concerned to move beyond a frame of reference on the nation state and to look into the transnational processes that are likely to come to the fore in the coming decades. Along with the other contributions in this part of the Reader, his account is indicative of the changing boundaries of both scholarly and public debate on race and racism. It is also suggestive of the need for more dialogue across disciplines and scholarly traditions.

Chapter 34

Paul Gilroy

THE DIALECTICS OF DIASPORA
IDENTIFICATION

[. . .]

THE SUBJECT OF THIS PAPER is culture and resistance and I want to begin by asking you to consider how resistance itself is to be understood. I think that our recent political history, as people in but not necessarily of the modern, Western world, a history which involved processes of political organization that are explicitly transcultural and international in nature, demands that we consider this question very carefully. What is being resisted and by what means? Slavery? Capitalism? Coerced industrialization? Racial terror? Or ethnocentrism and European solipsism? How are the discontinuous, plural histories of diaspora resistance to be *thought*, to be theorized by those who have experienced the consequences of racial domination?

In this paper, I want to look specifically at the positions of the nation-state, and the idea of nationality in accounts of black resistance and black culture, particularly music. Towards the end, I will also use a brief discussion of black music to ask implicit questions about the tendencies towards ethnocentrism and ethnic absolutism of black cultural theory. The problem of weighing the claims of national identity against other contrasting varieties of subjectivity and identification has a special place in the intellectual history of blacks in the West. W. E. B. Du Bois's concept of 'double consciousness'[1] is only the best-known resolution of a familiar problem which points towards the core dynamic of racial oppression as well as the fundamental antinomy of diaspora blacks. How has this doubleness, what Richard Wright calls the 'dreadful objectivity'[2] which flows from being both inside and outside the West, affected the conduct of political movements against racial oppression and towards black autonomy? Can the inescapable pluralities involved in the movements of black peoples, in Africa and in exile, ever be synchronized? How would these struggles be periodized in relation to modernity: the fatal intermediation of capitalism, industrialization and a new conception of political democracy? Does even posing these questions in this way signify nothing except the reluctant intellectual affiliation of diaspora blacks to an approach which attempts a premature totalization of our infinite struggles, an approach which has deep roots within the ambiguous intellectual traditions of the European enlightenment?

In my view, the problematic intellectual heritage of Euro-American modernity still determines the manner in which nationality is understood within black political discourse. In particular, it conditions the continuing aspiration to acquire a supposedly authentic, natural and stable identity. This identity is the premise of a thinking 'racial' self that is both socialized and unified by its connection with other kindred souls encountered usually, though not always, within the fortified frontiers of those discrete ethnic cultures which also happen to coincide with the contours of a sovereign nation-state that guarantees their continuity. Consider for a moment the looseness with which the term 'black nationalism' is used both by its advocates and by sceptics. Why is a more refined political language for dealing with these crucial issues of identity, kinship and affiliation such a long time coming?

This area of difficulty has recently become associated with a second, namely the over-integrated conceptions of culture which mean that black political struggles are construed as somehow automatically *expressive* of the national or ethnic differences with which they are articulated. This over-integrated sense of cultural and ethnic particularity is very popular today and blacks do not monopolize it. It masks the arbitrariness of its own political choices in the morally charged language of ethnic absolutism and this poses significant dangers because it overlooks the development of political ideology and ignores the restless, recombinant qualities of our affirmative political cultures. The critical political project forged in the journey from slave ship to citizenship is in danger of being wrecked by the seemingly insoluble conflict between two distinct but currently symbiotic perspectives which can be loosely identified as the essentialist and the pluralist standpoints.

The antagonistic relationship between these outlooks is especially intense in discussions of black art and cultural criticism. The essentialist view comes in gender-specific forms, but has often been characterized by an archaic pan-Africanism that, in Britain at least, is now politically inert. In the newer garb of Africentricity it has still proved unable to specify precisely where the highly prized but doggedly evasive essence of black artistic sensibility is currently located. This perspective sees the black artist as a potential leader. It is often allied to a realist approach to aesthetics which minimizes the substantive political and philosophical issues involved in the processes of artistic representation. Its absolutist conception of ethnic cultures can be identified by the way in which it registers uncomprehending disappointment with the actual cultural choices and patterns of the mass of black people in this country. It looks for an artistic practice that can disabuse them of the illusions into which they have been seduced by their condition of exile. The community is felt to be on the wrong road and it is the artist's job to give them a new direction, first by recovering and then by donating the racial awareness that the masses seem to lack.

This perspective currently confronts a pluralistic position which affirms blackness as an open signifier and seeks to celebrate complex representations of a black particularity that is *internally* divided: by class, sexuality, gender, age and political consciousness. There is no unitary idea of black community here and the authoritarian tendencies of those who would 'police' black cultural expression in the name of their own particular history or priorities are rightly repudiated. Essentialism is replaced by a libertarian alternative: the saturnalia which attends 'the dissolution of the essential black subject'. Here, the polyphonic qualities of black cultural expression form the main aesthetic consideration and there is often an uneasy but exhilarating fusion of 'modernist' and populist techniques and styles. From this perspective, the cultural achievements of popular black cultural forms like music are a constant source of inspiration and are prized for their implicit warning against the pitfalls of artistic conceit. The difficulty with this second tendency is that, in leaving racial essentialism behind by viewing 'race' itself as a social and cultural construction, it has been insufficiently alive to the lingering power of specifically 'racial' forms of power and subordination. Each outlook attempts to compensate for the obvious weaknesses in the other camp but so far there has been little open and explicit debate between them.

This conflict, initially formulated in debates over black aesthetics and cultural production, is valuable as a preliminary guide to some of the dilemmas faced by cultural and intellectual *historians* of the African diaspora. The problems it raises become acute, particularly for those who seek to comprehend cultural developments and political resistances which have had scant regard for either modern borders or pre-modern frontiers. At its worst, the lazy, casual invocation of cultural insiderism which characterizes the essentialist view is nothing more than a melancholy symptom of the growing cleavages *within* the black communities. There, uneasy spokespeople of the black middle classes – some of them professional cultural commentators, artists, writers, painters and film-makers as well as career politicians – have fabricated a volkish political outlook as an expression of their own contradictory position. Although the 'neo' is never satisfactorily explained, this is often presented as a neo-nationalism. It incorporates meditation on the special needs and desires of the relatively privileged castes within black communities, but its most consistent trademark is the persistent mystification of that group's increasingly problematic relationships with the black poor who, after all, supply them with a dubious entitlement to speak on behalf of black people in general.

The idea of blacks as a 'national' or proto-national group with its own hermetically enclosed culture plays a key role in this mystification and, though seldom overtly named, the misplaced idea of a 'national interest' gets invoked here as a means to silence dissent and censor political debate.

These problems take on a specific aspect in Britain, which still lacks anything that can credibly be called a black bourgeoisie. However, they are not confined to this country and they cannot be overlooked. The idea of nationality and the assumptions of cultural absolutism come together in various other ways.[3] For example, the archaeology of black critical knowledges in which we are engaged, currently involves the construction of canons which seems to be proceeding on an exclusively *national* basis – Afro-American, Anglophone Caribbean and so on. (This is not just my oblique answer to the pressure to produce an equivalent inventory of black English or British cultural forms and expressions.) If it seems indelicate to ask whom the formation of such canons might serve, then the related question of where the impulse to formalize and codify elements of our cultural heritage in this particular pattern comes from may be a better one with which to commence.

The historiography of canon formation raises interesting issues for the intellectual historian in and of itself. But if the way that these issues occur around the question of the canon appears too obscure, similar problems are also evident in recent debates over hip-hop culture, the powerful expressive medium of America's urban black poor. Rap is a hybrid form rooted in the syncretic social relations of the South Bronx where Jamaican sound-system culture, transplanted during the 1970s, put down new roots and in conjunction with specific technological innovations, set in train a process that was to transform black America's sense of itself and a large portion of the popular music industry as well. How does a form which flaunts and glories in its own malleability as well as its transnational character become interpreted as an expression of some authentic Afro-American essence? Why is rap discussed as if it sprang intact from the entrails of the blues?[4] What is it about Afro-America's writing elite which means that they need to claim this diasporic cultural form in such an assertively nationalist way?[5] Hip-hop culture has recently provided the raw material for a bitter contest between black vernacular expression and repressive censorship of artistic work. This has thrown some black commentators into a quandary which they resolve by invoking the rhetoric of cultural insiderism and drawing the distinctive cloak of ethnicity even more tightly around their shoulders. It is striking, for example, that apologists for the woman-hating antics of the 2 Live Crew have been so far unconcerned that the vernacular tradition they desire to affirm has its own record of reflection on the specific ethical obligations and political responsibilities which constitute the unique burden of the black artist. This may have generational, even authoritarian, implications because the 'racial' community is always a source of constraint as well as a source of support and protection for its artists and intellectuals but, leaving the question of misogyny aside for a moment, to collude in the belief that black vernacular is *nothing* more than a playfully parodic cavalcade of Rabelaisian subversion decisively weakens the positions of the artist, the critical commentator[6] and the community as a whole. What is more significant is surely the failure of either academic or journalistic commentary on black popular music in America to develop a reflexive political aesthetics capable of distinguishing the 2 Live Crew and their ilk from their equally 'authentic' but possibly more compelling and certainly more constructive peers.[7] I am not suggesting that the self-conscious racial pedagogy of artists like KRS1, The Poor Righteous Teachers, Lakim Shabazz or The X Clan can be straightforwardly counterposed against the carefully calculated affirmative nihilism of Ice Cube, Above The Law and Compton's Most Wanted. The different styles and political perspectives expressed within the music are linked both by the bonds of a stylized but aggressively masculinist discourse and by formal borrowings from the linguistic innovations to Jamaica's distinct traditions of 'kinetic orality'.[8] The debt to Caribbean forms is more openly acknowledged in the ludic Afrocentrisms of The Jungle Brothers, De La Soul and A Tribe Called Quest, which may represent a third alternative – in its respectful and egalitarian representation of women and in its ambivalent relationship to America. This stimulating and innovative work operates a rather different conception of black authenticity which effectively contrasts the local (black nationalism) with the global (black internationalism) and Americanism with Ethiopianism. It is important to emphasize that all three strands within hip-hop contribute to a folk-cultural constellation where neither the political compass of weary leftism nor the shiny navigational instruments of premature black post-modernism[9] in aesthetics offer very much that is useful.

An additional, and possibly more profound, area of political difficulty comes into view where the voguish language of absolute cultural difference I have described provides an embarrassing link between the practice of blacks who comprehend racial politics through it and the activities of their foresworn opponents – the racist New Right – who approach the complex dynamics of race, nationality and ethnicity through a similar set of precise, culturalist equations. [. . .]

[. . .] I want to make all these abstract and difficult points more concrete and accessible by turning to some of the lessons to be learned from considering the musical traditions of blacks in the West. The history and significance of these musics are consistently overlooked by black writers for two reasons: first, because they escape the frameworks of national or ethnocentric analysis, and second, because talking seriously about the politics and aesthetics of black vernacular cultures demands a confrontation with the order of 'intra-racial' differences. These may be to do with class, gender, sexuality or other factors, but they provide severe embarrassment to the rhetoric of racial and cultural homogeneity. As these internal divisions have grown, the price of that embarrassment has been an aching silence.

To break that silence, I want to examine the role of black musical expression in reproducing what Zygmunt Bauman has called a distinctive 'counter culture of modernity'. The shifting relationship of music-making to other modes of black cultural expression requires a much more sustained treatment that I can give it here. However, I want to use a brief consideration of black musical development to move our critical thoughts beyond an understanding of cultural processes which, as I have already suggested, is currently torn between seeing them as either the expression of an essential, unchanging, sovereign racial self or as the effluent from a constituted subjectivity that emerges contingently from the endless play of racial signification conceived solely in terms of the inappropriate model which *textuality* provides. The vitality and complexity of this musical culture offers a means to get beyond the related oppositions between essentialists and pluralists on the one hand and between tradition, modernity and post-modernity on the other.

Black music's obstinate and consistent commitment to the idea of a better future is a puzzle to which our enforced separation from literacy and the compensatory refinement of musical art supplies less than half an answer. The power of music in developing our struggles by communicating information, organizing consciousness and testing out, deploying or amplifying the forms of subjectivity which are required by political agency – individual and collective, defensive and transformational – demands attention to both the formal attributes of this tradition of expression and its distinctive *moral* basis. The formal qualities of this music are becoming better known,[10] so I shall concentrate here on the moral aspects and in particular on the disjunction between the ethical value of the music and its ethnic significance.

In the simplest possible terms, by posing the world as it is against the world as the racially subordinated would like it to be, this musical culture supplies a great deal of the courage required to go on living in the present. It is both produced by and expressive of that 'transvaluation of all values' precipitated by the history of racial terror in the new world. It contains a theodicy but moves beyond theodicy because the profane dimensions of that racial terror made theodicy impossible.[11]

I have considered its distinctive critique of capitalist social relations elsewhere.[12] Here, because I want to suggest that its critical edge includes but also surpasses anti-capitalism, I want to draw out some of its inner philosophical dynamics and place emphasis on the connection between its normative character and its utopian aspirations. These are interrelated and even inseparable from each other and from the critique of racial capitalism.[13] Comprehending them requires us to link together analysis of the lyrical content and the forms of musical expression as well as the often hidden social relations in which these deeply encoded oppositional practices are created and consumed. The issue of normative content focuses attention on what might be called the politics of fulfilment:[14] the notion that a future society will be able to realize the social and political promise that present society has left unaccomplished. Reflecting the primary semantic position of the Bible, this is primarily a discursive mode of communication. Though by no means literal, it relates mainly to what is said, shouted, screamed or sung. The issue of utopia is more complex not least because it strives continually to move beyond the grasp of the merely linguistic, textual or discursive. It references what, following Seyla Benhabib's suggestive lead, I propose to call the politics of transfiguration. This emphasizes the emergence of qualitatively new desires, social relations and modes of association within the racial community of interpretation and resistance *and* between that group and its erstwhile oppressors. It points specifically to the formation of a community of needs and solidarity which is magically made audible in the music itself and palpable in the social relations of its cultural consumption and reproduction.

The politics of fulfilment practiced by the descendants of slaves demands that bourgeois civil society lives up to the promises of its own rhetoric and offers a means whereby demands for justice, rational organization of the productive processes, etc., can be expressed. It is immanent within modernity and is no less a valuable element of modernity's counter-discourse for being so consistently ignored. Created under the nose of the overseer, the utopian desires which fuel the politics of transfiguration must be invoked by other deliberately opaque means. This politics exists on a lower frequency where it is played, danced and acted, as well as sung about, because words, even words stretched by melisma and supplemented or mutated by the screams which still index the conspicuous power of the slave sublime, will never be enough to communicate its unsayable claims to truth. The wilfully damaged signs which betray the utopian politics of transfiguration therefore partially transcend modernity. This is not a counter-discourse but a counter-culture that defiantly constructs its own critical, intellectual and moral genealogy anew in a partially hidden public sphere of its own. The politics of transfiguration therefore reveals the internal problems in the concept of modernity. The bounds of politics are extended precisely because this tradition of expression refuses to accept that the political is a readily separable domain. Its basic desire is to conjure up and enact the new modes of friendship, happiness and solidarity that are consequent on the overcoming of the racial oppression on which modernity and the duality of rational Western progress as excessive barbarity relied. Thus the vernacular arts of the children of slaves give rise to a verdict on the role of art which is strikingly in harmony with Adorno's reflections on the dynamics of European artistic expression in the wake of Auschwitz:

> Art's Utopia, the counterfactual yet-to-come, is draped in black. It goes
> on being a recollection of the possible with a critical edge against the
> real; it is a kind of imaginary restitution of that catastrophe, which is
> world history; it is a freedom which did not pass under the spell of
> necessity and which may well not come to pass ever at all.[15]

These sibling dimensions of black sensibility, the politics of fulfilment and the politics of transfiguration, are not coextensive. There are significant tensions between them but they are closely associated in the vernacular cultures of the diaspora. They can also be used to reflect the doubleness with which I began and which is often argued to be our constitutive experience in the modern world: in the West but not of it. The politics of fulfilment is content to play occidental rationality at its own game. It necessitates a hermeneutic orientation which can assimilate the semiotic, verbal and textual. The politics of transfiguration strives in pursuit of the sublime, struggling to repeat the unrepeatable, to present the unpresentable. Its rather different hermeneutic focus pushes towards the mimetic, dramatic and performative.

It seems especially significant that the cultural traditions which these musics allow us to map out, do not seek to exclude problems of inequality or to make racial justice an exclusively abstract matter. Their grounded ethics offers, among other things, a continuous commentary on the systematic and pervasive relations of domination that supply its conditions of existence. Their grounded aesthetics is never separated off into an autonomous realm where familiar political rules cannot be applied and where, as Salman Rushdie puts it, 'the little room of literature' can continue to enjoy its special privileges as a heroic resource for the well-heeled adversaries of liberal capitalism.[16]

I am proposing then, that we re-read and rethink this tradition of cultural expression not simply as a succession of literary tropes and genres, but as a philosophical discourse which refuses the modern, occidental separation of ethics and aesthetics, culture and politics. The traditional teaching of ethics and politics – practical philosophy – came to an end some time ago, even if its death agonies were prolonged. This tradition had maintained the idea that a good life for the individual and the problem of the best social and political order for the collectivity could be discerned by rational means. Although it is seldom acknowledged even now, this tradition lost its exclusive claim to rationality, in part, through the way that slavery became internal to Western civilization and through the obvious complicity which both plantation slavery and colonial regimes revealed between rationality and the practice of racial terror.

Not perceiving its residual condition, blacks in the West eavesdropped on and then took over a fundamental question from that tradition. Their progress from the status of slaves to the status of citizens led them to enquire into what the best possible forms of social and political existence might be. The memory of slavery, actively preserved as a living, intellectual resource in their expressive political culture, helped them to generate a new set of answers to this enquiry. They had to fight – often through the invocation of spirituality – to hold on to the unity of ethics and politics sundered from each other by modernity's insistence that the true, the good and the beautiful had distinct origins and belong to different domains of knowledge. First, slavery itself and then their memory of it induced many of them to query the foundational moves of modern philosophy and social thought whether they came from the natural-rights theorists who sought to distinguish between the spheres of morality and legality, the idealists who wanted to emancipate politics from morals so that it could become a sphere of strategic action, or the political economists of the bourgeoisie who first formulated the separation of economic activity from both ethics and politics. The brutal excess of the slave plantation supplied a set of moral and political responses to each of these attempts.

The history of black music enables us to trace something of the means through which the unity of ethics and politics has been reproduced as a form of folk knowledge. This sub-culture often appears to be the intuitive expression of some racial essence but is in fact an elementary historical acquisition produced from the viscera of an alternative tradition of cultural and political expression which considers the world critically from the point of view of its emancipatory transformation. In the future, it will become a place which is capable of satisfying the (redefined) needs of human beings that will emerge once the violence – epistemic and concrete – of racial typology is at an end. Reason is thus reunited with the happiness and freedom of individuals and the reign of justice within the collectivity.

I have already implied that there is a degree of convergence here with other projects towards a critical theory of society, particularly Marxism. However, where lived crisis and systemic crisis come together, Marxism allocates priority to the latter while the memory of slavery insists on the priority of the former. Their convergence is also undercut by the simple fact that in the critical tradition of blacks in the West, social self-creation through labour is not the core of emancipatory hopes. For the descendants of slaves, work signifies only servitude, misery and subordination. Artistic expression, expanded beyond recognition from the grudging gifts offered by the masters as a token substitute for freedom from bondage, therefore becomes the means towards both individual self-fashioning and communal liberation. Poiesis and poetics begin to coexist in novel forms – autobiographical writing, special and uniquely creative ways of manipulating spoken language and, above all, the music.

Antiphony (call and response) is the principal formal feature of these musical traditions. It reaches out beyond music into other modes of cultural expression, supplying, along with improvisation, montage and dramaturgy, the hermeneutic keys to the full medley of black artistic practices from kinesics to rhetoric. The intense and often bitter dialogues, which make the black arts movement move, offer a small reminder that there is a 'democratic' moment enshrined in the practice of antiphony which anticipates new, non-dominating social relationships. Lines between self and other are blurred and special forms of pleasure are created as a result. Ellison's famous observation on the inner dynamics of jazz uses visual art as its central analogy and can be extended beyond the specific context it was written to illuminate:

> There is in this a cruel contradiction implicit in the art form itself. For true jazz is an art of individual assertion within and against the group. Each true jazz moment . . . springs from a contest in which the artist challenges all the rest; each solo flight, or improvisation, represents

(like the canvasses of a painter) a definition of his identity: as individual, as member of the collectivity and as a link in the chain of tradition. Thus because jazz finds its very life in improvisation upon traditional materials, the jazz man must lose his identity even as he finds it. . .[17]

By way of a conclusion, I want to illustrate these arguments further by very briefly bringing forward two concrete historical instances in which the musical traditions of the black Atlantic world acquired a special political valency. These examples are simultaneously both national, in that they had a direct impact on British politics, and diasporic, in that they tell us something fundamental about the limit of that national perspective. They are not, of course, the only examples I could have chosen. They have been selected somewhat at random, although the fact that they span a century will, I hope, be taken as preliminary evidence for the existence of fractal[18] patterns of cultural and political affiliation which will need further elaboration and detailed critical consideration. Both, in rather different ways, reflect the special position of Britain within the black Atlantic world, standing at the apex of the semi-triangular structure which saw commodities and people shipped to and fro across the ocean.

The first relates to the visits by the Fisk University Jubilee Singers[19] to England, Ireland, Wales and Scotland in the early 1870s under the philanthropic patronage of the Earl of Shaftesbury. The Fisk Singers have a profound historical importance because they were the first group to perform spirituals on a public platform, offering this form of black music as mass entertainment.[20] Their success is especially significant amidst the changed cultural and ideological circumstances that attended the 're-making' of the English working class in the era of imperialism.[21] In explicit opposition to minstrelsy, which was becoming an established element in popular culture by this time,[22] the Fisk Singers constructed an aura of seriousness and projected the memory of slavery outwards as the means to make their musical performances intelligible and pleasurable. The choir had taken to the road seven years after the founding of their Alma Mater to raise funds. They produced books to supplement the income from their concert performances and these volumes ran to over 60,000 copies sold between 1877 and the end of the century. Interestingly, these publications included a general historical account of Fisk and its struggles, some unusual autobiographical statements from the members of the ensemble and the music and lyrics of between 104 and 139 songs from their extensive repertoire. In my opinion, this unusual combination of communicative modes and genres is especially important for anyone seeking to locate the origins of the polyphonic montage technique developed by Du Bois in *The Souls of Black Folk*.

The Fisk Singers' text describes Queen Victoria listening to 'John Brown's body' 'with manifest pleasure', the Prince of Wales requesting 'No More Auction Block for Me' and the choir being waited upon by Mr and Mrs Gladstone after their servants had been dismissed.[23] These images are important, although the choir's performances to enormous working-class audiences in British cities may be more significant for contemporary anti-racism struggling to escape the strictures of its own apparent novelty. It is clear that for their liberal patrons, the music and song of the Fisk Singers offered an opportunity to feel closer to God while the memory of slavery, recovered by their performances, entrenched the feelings of moral rectitude which flowed from the commitment to political reform for which the imagery of elevation from slavery was emblematic long after emancipation. The Fisk Singers' music can be shown to have articulated what Du Bois calls 'the articulate message of the slave to the world' into British culture and society at several distinct and class-specific points. The spirituals enforced the patrician moral concerns of Shaftesbury and Gladstone but also introduced a specific moral sensibility into the lives of the lower orders who, it would appear, began to create Jubilee choirs of their own.[24]

My second example of diasporic cultural innovation is contemporary, although it relates to the song 'I'm So Proud', originally written and performed by the Chicagoan vocal trio The Impressions at the peak of their artistic and commercial success in the mid-1960s. The Impressions' 1960s hits like 'Gypsy Woman', 'Grow Closer Together', 'Minstrel and Queen' and 'People Get Ready' were extremely popular among blacks in Britain and in the Caribbean. In Jamaica, the male vocal trio format popularized by the band inaugurated a distinct genre within the vernacular musical form which would eventually be marketed internationally as reggae.[25] The Wailers were only one of many groups that patterned themselves on The Impressions and strove to match the singing of the Americans for harmonic texture, emotional dynamics and black metaphysical grace. A new version of The Impressions' hit 'I'm So Proud' has recently topped the reggae charts in Britain. Re-titled 'Proud of Mandela', it was performed by the toaster Macka B and the Lovers' Rock singer Kofi who had produced her own version of the tune itself, patterned on another soft soul version issued by the American singer Deniece Williams in 1983.

I want to make no special claims for the formal, musical merits of this particular record, but I think that it is exemplary in that it brings Africa, America, Europe and the Caribbean seamlessly together. It was produced in Britain by the children of Caribbean and African settlers from raw materials supplied by black Chicago but filtered through Kingstonian sensibility in order to pay tribute to a black hero whose global significance lies beyond his partial South African citizenship and the impossible national identity which goes with it. The very least that this music and its history can offer us today is an analogy for comprehending the lines of affiliation and association which take the idea of the diaspora beyond its symbolic status as the fragmentary opposite of an imputed racial essence. Foregrounding the role of music allows us to see England, or perhaps London, as an important junction point on the web of black Atlantic political culture: a place where, by virtue of local factors like the informality of racial segregation, the configuration of class relations and the contingency of linguistic convergences of global phenomena such as anti-colonial and emancipationist political formations are still being sustained, reproduced and amplified.

Notes and references

I have taken the title of this essay directly from lyrics written and performed by Rakim (W. Griffin). In his recordings with his sometimes partner Eric B, Rakim has persistently returned to the problem of diasporic identification and the connected issue of the relationship between local and global components of blackness. His 'I Know You got

Soul' (1987) was received as a classic recording in London's soul underground, and since then he has produced what I regard as the most complex and exciting poetry to emerge from the hip-hop movement. The dread recording which directly inspired the production of this essay is called 'The Ghetto' and is included on the MCA (1990) album 'Let the Rhythm Hit 'Em'. I wish to thank my children for tolerating the repeated playing of this cut at bone-breaking volume, Vron Ware for her insight and bell hooks for the transatlantic dialogue which has helped me to frame this piece of work.

1   W. E. B. Du Bois, *The Souls of Black Folk* (1903) reprinted Bantam, New York, 1989. See also the discussion of this in ch. 4 of my book *The Black Atlantic*.

2   This phrase is taken from Wright's novel *The Outsider*, Harper and Row, New York, 1965. In his book of essays, *White Man Listen!*, Anchor Books, New York, 1964, he employs the phrase 'dual existence' to map the same terrain.

3   Etienne Balibar and Immanuel Wallerstein, *Race, Nation, Class*, Verso, London, 1991.

4   Nelson George, *The Death of Rhythm and Blues*, Omnibus, London, 1988.

5   I should emphasize that it is the assimilation of these cultural forms to an unthinking notion of nationality which is the object of my critique here. Of course, certain cultural forms become articulated with sets of social and political forces over long periods of time. These forms may be played with and lived with as though they were 'natural' emblems of racial and ethnic particularity. This may even be an essential defensive attribute of the interpretive communities involved. However, the notion of nationality cannot be borrowed as a ready-made means to make sense of the special dynamics of this process.

6   Henry Louis Gates jnr, 'Rap Music: Don't knock it if you're not onto its "lies"', *Herald Tribune*, 20 June 1990.

7   I am prepared to defer to black Americans who argue that it is probably necessary to be both defenders and critics of the 2 Live Crew. However, watching the MTV video of their hit single, 'Banned in the USA', I found it difficult to accept the way in which the powerful visual legacy of the black movement of the 1950s and 1960s had been appropriated and made over so that it became readily and unproblematically continuous with the group's own brand of American patriotism.

8   Cornel West, 'Black Culture and Postmodernism' in B. Kruger and P. Mariani (eds), *Re-Making History*, Dia Foundation, Bay Press, Seattle, 1989.

9   Trey Ellis's famous piece on the new black aesthetic in a recent issue of *Callaloo* exemplifies the perils of this casual, 'anything goes' post-modernism for the black arts movement. It was striking how, for example, profound questions of class antagonism within the black communities were conjured out of sight. Apart from his conflation of forms which are not merely different but actively oppose one another, Ellis does not seriously consider the notion that the NBA might have a very particular and highly class-specific articulation within a small and isolated segment of the black middle class which struggles with its own dependency on the cultural lifeblood of the black poor.

10   Anthony Jackson's dazzling exposition of James Jamerson's bass style is, in my view, indicative of the type of detailed critical work which needs to be done on the form and dynamics of black musical creativity. His remarks on Jamerson's use of harmonic and rhythmic ambiguity and selective employment of dissonance were especially helpful. To say that the book from which it is taken has been

geared to the needs of the performing musician rather than the cultural historian is to indict the current state of cultural history rather than the work of Jackson and his collaborator, Dr Licks. See 'An Appreciation of the Style' in Dr Licks (ed.) *Standing in the Shadows of Motown*, Hal Leonard, Detroit, 1989.

11 I am thinking here both of Wright's tantalizing discussion of 'The Dozens' in the essay on the 'Literary Tradition of the Negro in the United States' in *White Man Listen!* and also of Levinas's remarks on useless suffering in another context: 'useless and unjustifiable suffering [is] exposed and displayed . . . without any shadow of consoling theodicy' (see 'Useless Suffering' in R. Bernasconi and D. Wood (eds), *The Provocation of Levinas*, Routledge, London, 1988). Jon Michael Spencer's thoughtful but fervently Christian discussion of what he calls the Theodicy of the Blues is also relevant here. See *The Theology of American Popular Music*, a special issue of *Black Sacred Music*, vol. 3, no. 2, Fall 1989 (Duke University Press). I do not have space to develop my critique of Spencer here.

12 *There Ain't No Black in the Union Jack: The Cultural Politics of Race and Nation*, Hutchinson, London, 1987, ch. 5.

13 Cedric Robinson, *Black Marxism*, Zed Press, London, 1982.

14 This concept and its pairing with the politics of transfiguration have been adapted from Seyla Benhabib's inspiring book *Critique, Norm and Utopia*, Columbia University Press, New York, 1987.

15 *Aesthetic Theory*, Routledge, London, p. 196.

16 Salman Rushdie, *Is Nothing Sacred?* The Herbert Read Memorial Lecture 1990, Granta, Cambridge.

17 Ralph Ellison, *Shadow and Act*, Random House, New York, 1964, p. 234. There are in Ellison's remarks the components of a definitive response to the position of Adorno in 'Uber Jazz'; see also Susan Buck Morss, *The Origin of Negative Dialectics*, Free Press, New York pp. 108–10.

18 I am thinking of fractal geometry as an analogy here because it allows for the possibility that a line of infinite length can enclose a finite area. The opposition between totality and infinity is thus recast in a striking image of the scope for agency in restricted conditions.

19 The radical historian Peter Linebaugh has recently discussed the etymology of the word 'jubilee' and some of the political discourses that surround it: 'Jubilating', *Midnight Notes*, Fall 1990. Reviews of the singers' performances in England can be found in *East Anglian Daily Times*, 21 November 1874 and the *Surrey Advertiser*, 5 December 1874.

20 John M. MacKenzie (ed.), *Imperialism and Popular Culture*, Manchester University Press, 1986.

21 Gareth Stedman Jones, 'Working-class Culture and Working-class Politics in London 1870–1900: Notes on the remaking of a working class' in *Languages of Class*, Cambridge University Press, Cambridge, 1983.

22 An 'Eva Gets Well' version of *Uncle Tom's Cabin* was doing excellent business on the London stage in 1878. See also Robert C. Toll, *Blacking Up: The Minstrel Show in Nineteenth Century America*, Oxford University Press, Oxford, 1974; Barry Anthony, 'Early Nigger Minstrel Acts in Britain', *Music Hall*, vol. 12, April 1980; and Josephine Wright, 'Orpheus Myron McAdoo', *Black Perspective in Music*, vol. 4, no. 3, Fall 1976.

23 These events are described in Gladstone's diaries for 14 and 29 July 1873. Apart from the singers' own text, there is a lengthy discussion of these events in the

New York *Independent*, 21 August 1873. See also Ella Sheppard Moore, 'Historical Sketch of The Jubilee Singers', *Fisk University News*, October 1911, p. 42.

24   In his essay on the Fisk Singers in Britain, Doug Seroff cites the example of the East London Jubilee Singers of Hackney Juvenile Mission, a 'ragged school' formed after an inspirational visit by the Fisk Singers to Hackney in June 1873. John Newman, the manager of the Mission, 'felt that such singing from the soul should not be forgotten, and speedily set to work to teach the children of the Mission the songs the Jubilee singers had sung'; see R. Lotz and I. Pegg (eds), *Under the Imperial Carpet: Essays in Black History 1780–1950*, Rabbit Press, Crawley, 1986. Listening recently to my 7-year-old son's primary school singing 'Oh Freedom' in furtherance of the multicultural and anti-racist educational policies of the Borough of Islington was confirmation that slave songs are still being sung in inner London schools in the 1990s.

25   The phenomenon of Jamaican male vocal trios is discussed by Randall Grass, 'Iron Sharpen Iron: The great Jamaican harmony trios' in P. Simon (ed.), *Reggae International*, Thames & Hudson, London, 1983. Key exponents of this particular art would be The Heptones, The Paragons, The Gaylads, The Meditations, The Itals, Carlton and The Shoes, Justice Hines and The Dominoes, Toots and The Maytals, Yabby Yu and The Prophets, The Gladiators, The Melodians, The Ethiopians, The Cables, The Tamlins, The Congoes, The Mighty Diamonds, The Abyssinians, Black Uhuru, Israel Vibration and, of course, The Wailers, whose Neville O'Reilly/Bunny Livingstone/Bunny Wailer does the best Curtis Mayfield impersonation of the lot.

Chapter 35

Kobena Mercer

IDENTITY AND DIVERSITY IN POSTMODERN POLITICS

JUST NOW EVERYBODY WANTS to talk about identity. As a keyword in contemporary politics it has taken on so many different connotations that sometimes it is obvious that people are not even talking about the same thing. One thing at least is clear – identity only becomes an issue when it is in crisis, when something assumed to be fixed, coherent and stable is displaced by the experience of doubt and uncertainty. From this angle, the eagerness to talk about identity is symptomatic of the postmodern predicament of contemporary politics.

The salient ambiguity of the word itself draws attention to the breakup of the traditional vocabulary of Left, Right and Center. Our conventional maps are no longer adequate to the territory, as the political landscape has been radically restructured over the last decade by the hegemony of the New Right. Hence, in no uncertain terms, the 'identity crisis' of the Left. After ten years of Thatcherism, the attitudes, assumptions and institutions of the British Left have been systematically demoralized, disorganized and disaggregated. Neoliberal hegemony has helped to transform the political terrain to the point where the figurative meaning of the Left/Right dichotomy has been totally reversed. This was always a metaphor for the opposition between progressive and reactionary forces, derived in fact from the seating arrangements of the General Assemblies after the French Revolution. But today the word 'revolution' sounds vaguely embarrassing when it comes out of the mouths of people on the Left: it only sounds as if it means what it says when uttered in the mouths of the radicalized Right. In the modern period, the Left anticipated the future with optimism, confident that socialism would irreversibly change the world. Today such epic beliefs seem to be disappearing into the grand museum, as it is the postmodern Right that wants to 'revolutionize' the entire society and remake our future in its own millennial image of neoliberal market freedom.

The identity crisis of the Left is underlined not only by the defeat experienced by trade unions and other organizations that make up the labor movement, but

above all by the inability of the Labour Party to articulate an effective 'opposition.'
Even so, the problem goes beyond the official theater of parliamentary democracy.
The classical Marxist view of the industrial working classes as the privileged agent
of revolutionary historical change has been undermined and discredited from below
by the emergence of numerous social movements – feminisms, black struggles,
national liberation, antinuclear and ecology movements – that have also reshaped
and redefined the sphere of politics. The ambiguity of 'identity' serves in this
regard as a way of acknowledging the presence of new social actors and new
political subjects – women, black people, lesbian and gay communities, youth –
whose aspirations do not neatly fit into the traditional Left/Right dichotomy.
However I am not sure that 'identity' is what these movements share in common:
on the contrary, within and between the various new movements that have arisen
in postwar, Western, capitalist democracies, what is asserted is an emphasis on
'difference.' In a sense, the 'newness' of these struggles consists precisely in the
fact that such differences cannot be coded or programmed into the same old formula
of Left, Right and Center. The proliferation of differences is highly ambivalent,
as it relativizes the Big Picture and weakens the totalizing universalist truth claims
of ideologies like Marxism, thus demanding acknowledgment of the *plural* sources
of oppression, unhappiness and antagonism in contemporary capitalist societies.

On the other hand, the downside of such diversification and fragmentation is
the awareness that there is no necessary relationship between the new social
movements and the traditional labor movement, or to put it another way, it cannot
be taken for granted that there is common cause in the project of creating a socialist
society. This question arises with a double sense of urgency, not only because it
has become difficult to imagine what a socialist society looks like as something
'totally' different from any other type of society, but because the new social subjects
have no necessary belonging on either side of the distinction between progressive
and reactionary politics, which is to say they could go either way.

Difference and division

I want to examine the unwieldy relationship between the Left and the new social
movements because they both share problems made symptomatic in terms of
'identity,' and yet there is no vocabulary in which to conduct a mutual dialogue
on the possibility of alliances or coalitions around a common project, which is the
starting point for any potentially hegemonic project. This dilemma was forcefully
brought to light in the experiments in municipal socialism led by the Greater
London Council (GLC) and other metropolitan local authorities in Britain in the
early to mid-1980s. Such initiatives mobilized popular enthusiasm for socialist
politics, but now that the whole experience is a fast-fading memory, what is mostly
remembered is the mess created by the microantagonisms that erupted precisely
in the relationship between the traditional Left and the political movements
articulated around race, gender, ethnicity and sexuality.

The scenario of fragmentation that emerged was further dramatized by the
conflictual differences within and between the new social movements themselves.
The tabloid discourse of 'Loony Leftism' picked up on this state of affairs and

created a reactive populist parody to which the Labour leadership readily capitulated. In the aftermath of a local campaign for 'Positive Images' of lesbians and gays in Haringey schools in 1987, the Labour Party disassociated itself from the GLC's somewhat ragged rainbow coalition with the dismissive and divisive remark that 'the lesbian and gay issue is costing us dear among the pensioners.' The so-called 'London factor' was held to be responsible for yet another electoral defeat, but in the search for something to blame, Labour not only rationalized its unwillingness to construct new alliances, but helped pave the way for the hateful, authoritarian logic of Clause 28. Why could Labour not articulate pensioners *and* lesbians and gays within the same discourse? Was it not conceivable that pensioners and lesbians and gay men might even have a common interest in constructing an alternative to the unremitting 'new reality' of Thatcherite Britain?

What was important and exciting about the GLC in that briefly optimistic moment around 1983 was precisely the attempt to find forms of democratic representation and participation that would be responsive to the diversity of social identities active in the contemporary polity. Looking back, was it any wonder the experiment failed given that *this was the first time it had ever been contemplated*? The question of alliances between the labor movement, the Left and the various new social movements arose in the 1970s in trade union strikes, single-issue protest campaigns, localized community action and cultural mobilizations such as Rock Against Racism. While these experiences helped to create a fragile network of association either in the workplace or in civil society, the GLC experiment attempted to remobilize alliances around a socialist program *within* the institutional spaces of the local state. The shift was important because of the symbolic and material resources invested in local government as an apparatus of the state, but by the same token it proved impossible to translate the connections between the various elements once they were 'inside' the bureaucratic machinery of 'representative democracy.'

The Labour Left administration of the 1981 to 1986 GLC was the first of its kind to take the demands of the new movements seriously and to go beyond the tokenistic management of noisy 'minorities.' Conversely, this was the first time many community-based activists had operated within the framework of officialdom, whereas their previous extraparliamentary 'autonomy' made them skeptical of having anything to do with it. What happened when the two came face to face was that expectations about equal participation and representation were converted into sectional demands and competing claims about the legitimation of different needs. The possibility of coalition building was preempted by the competitive dynamic of who would have priority access to resources.

The worst aspects of the new social movements emerged in a rhetoric of 'identity politics' based on an essentialist notion of a fixed hierarchy of racial, sexual or gendered oppressions. By playing off each other to establish who was more authentically oppressed than whom, the residual separatist tendencies of the autonomous movements played into the normative calculation of 'disadvantage' inscribed in welfare statism. For their part, the generation of New Left activists who became the managers of state bureaucracy could only take over, rather than transform, the traditional top-down conception of meeting needs. Hence official rhetoric acknowledged diversity in a discourse of 'race, class and gender,' which became the policy repertoire in which each element was juggled about and administered according to expediency, patronage and good old Labourite pragmatism. The rationing of meager resources became a means of regulating and controlling 'difference' because, as the various actors perceived it, one group's loss was another group's gain. In this zero-sum game the only tangible consequence of diversity was dividedness.

[. . .] Like 'identity,' difference, diversity and fragmentation are keywords in the postmodern vocabulary, where they are saturated with groovy connotations. But it should be clear that there is nothing particularly groovy about the postmodern condition at all. As a best-seller ideology in artistic and intellectual circles, the postmodern paradigm has already been and gone, but as a pervasive sensibility in everyday life its smelly ideological effect lingers on. Postmodernism means many different things to many different people, but the key motifs of displacement, decentering and disenchantment have a specific resonance and relevance for the Left and new social movements after the demoralizing decade of Thatcherism.

In philosophical terms, postmodernism has been discussed as a weakening, fading or relativization of the absolutist or universalist values of the Western Enlightenment. The master narratives are collapsing, which is to say we no longer have the confidence to invest belief in the foundational myths of inevitable human rationality or social progress. Certain intellectuals, however (like Baudrillard), are apt to exaggerate the effect in a rather stupefied apocalyptic manner simply because they can no longer adopt the universalist postures they once did. Just like the organized Left, a whole generation of postwar intellectuals have been thrown into identity crisis as philosophies of Marxism and Modernism have begun to lose their adversarial aura. The loss of faith in the idea of a cultural avant-garde parallels the crisis of credulity in now-discredited notions of political vanguardism or 'scientific socialism.' But the narcissistic pathos expressed within the prevailing postmodern ideology obscures the more generalized effect of decentering acknowledged in common sense. Everybody intuitively knows that everyday life is so complex that no singular belief system or Big Story can hope to explain it all. We don't need another hero. But we do need to make sense of the experiences that characterize postmodern structures of feeling.

In sociological terms, this means a recognition of the fragmentation of traditional sources of authority and identity, the displacement of collective sources of membership and belonging, such as 'class' and 'community,' that help to construct political loyalties, affinities and identifications. One does not need to invoke the outmoded base/superstructure metaphor to acknowledge the impact of deterritorialized and decentralized forms of production in late-modern capitalism. While certain structures associated with the highly centralized logic of mass production and mass consumption give way to more flexible transnational arrangements that undermine the boundaries of the sovereign nation-state, other boundaries become more rigid, such as those that exclude the late-modern underclass from participation in free-market choices – 'you can have anything you want, but you better not take it from me.'[1] The New Right is not at the origin of these changes, but its brutalizing reassertion of competitive individualism and archaic 'Little Englandism' has hegemonized the commonsense terms in which the British are invited to make sense of and live through the vertiginous experience of displacement and decentering that these processes entail. It is here that we arrive at the political terms of postmodernism, in the sense that Thatcherism represents a new type of hegemony which has totally displaced the mythical 'Center' of the postwar social democratic consensus.

Identity is a key motif of post-consensus politics because the postwar vocabulary of Left, Right and Center, in which individual and collective subjects identified their loyalties and commitments, has been shot to pieces. The decentering of the social-democratic consensus, which was historically constructed around the axioms of welfare-state capitalism, was partly the result of its own internal economic and political contradictions. But, as Stuart Hall's analyses (1988) of Thatcherism have shown, it was the neoliberal agenda of 'free market and strong state' (Gamble, 1988), crystallized in the mid-1970s, that took the lead in answering the task of constructing a new form of popular consent by creating a new form of governmentality – 'authoritarian populism.'[2] If one identifies 1968 as the turning point in the deepening crisis of social-democratic consensus, it can be said that it was the New Right, not the New Left or the new social movements, that won out historically. It is precisely for this reason that we need to undertake an archaeology of the recent past, in which the problematic relationship between the Left and the new social movements developed.

Children of the revolution

> And my brother's back at home, with his Beatles and his Stones, We never got it off on that revolution stuff, What a drag, Too many snags.
> *All the Young Dudes*[3]

One way of clarifying what is at stake in the postmodern is to point out that the grammatical prefix 'post' simply means that the noun it predicates is 'past.' The ubiquitous prefix thus suggests a generalized mood or sensibility which problematizes perceptions of the past in relation to the contemporary horizon from which we imagine the future. Jacques Donzelot has characterized this as a new 'apprehension of time'[4] resulting from the exhaustion of the rationalist myth of progress: new future or no future, adapt or die, that is how it feels, especially on the Left and among the oppositional movements that once thought that time was on our side. In this sense, as a shift in popular memory that results in a changed disposition towards the past, one recognizes that the cultural forms of postmodernism – the pervasive *mode retro*, nostalgia and recycling aesthetic, or the prevalence of pastiche and parody – are implicated in a logic that problematizes the recent past by creating ironic distance between 'then' and 'now.' The sixties and seventies are effectively historicized in much the same way as historians treat 'the twenties' or 'the forties.' What happened the day before yesterday now looks like it happened a long time ago, and sometimes it looks as if it never happened at all. While ex-leftist intellectuals are eager to repudiate and renounce the radical political fantasies of '1968,' a more generalized process of erasure and effacement is at work, selectively wiping out certain traces of the recent past sedimented in common sense by the progressive gains of the 1960s.

Taking this analysis a step further, Lawrence Grossberg (1988) has suggested a reading of this postmodern sensibility as a crucial resource for the hegemony of the New Right. Neoconservatism dominates our ability to imagine the future by performing on the postmodern 'frontier effect' in popular memory. Although Grossberg's analysis is addressed to the experience of Reaganism in the United States, it pertains to the British experience, because he argues that the sense of disillusionment with the radical aspirations of the sixties is central to the mobilization of popular support for the neoliberal programme of restructuring state and civil society in the present:

> If the state hegemonic project of the New Right entails deconstructing the postwar social democratic consensus, its cultural hegemonic project entails disarticulating the central relationship between the national identity, a specific set of generational histories, and the equation of the national-popular with postwar youth culture.
>
> (Grossberg, 1988: 52)

One has only to recall those images of Harold Wilson and the Beatles (fresh from Buckingham Palace with their OBEs) to appreciate the resonance of the equation between postwar modernization in Western capitalist democracies and the cultural presence of a new social subject, the teenager. In this equation 'youth' came to embody the promise of modernity within the ethos of social democracy. Grossberg argues that the repudiation of capitalist modernization within the youth counter-cultures of the late 1960s marked the cutoff point or threshold of dissensus against the Center. The neoconservative onslaught against 'the sixties' has since become a crucial component in winning consent for neoliberal democracy, or, as Conservative minister Francis Pym once put it, 'I think public expectations are too high. We have an end to the language of the Sixties. Today we have got to rid ourselves of these outlooks and look at economic and social matters in a new light.'[5]

During its period of opposition in the 1970s, Thatcherism mobilized a frontier effect which polarized the political field into two antagonistic positions. Labourism was identified with the interventionist state, while the Tories positioned themselves 'out there' with the people, against the state, to recruit support for a market-led definition of freedom detached from the welfarist conception of equality.[6] Since 1979 the Tories have never stopped using the state to pursue monetarist economic policies, but as an ideology that has now achieved considerable 'leadership' in official institutions and popular common sense, Thatcherism seeks to maintain its sources of support by playing on the binary polarity in which the Left is identified with the past and the Right monopolizes the imaginary horizon of the future. There can be no return to the bad old days of dissensus, which is to say that in popular consciousness the possibility of a future for socialism is rendered 'unthinkable' because the prevailing image of the Left is fixed in 'the winter of discontent' of 1979, a vestige of the past which occasionally flickers up in television documentaries.

The 'active forgetting' of the recent past is further underlined by Thatcherite identity politics, in which 'Little Englandism,' the peculiarly English combination of racism, nationalism and populism, becomes the predominant framework of the imagined community in which the 'collective will' is constructed – 'it's great to be Great again,' as the 1987 Tory election slogan put it. The Falklands War and Royal Weddings, Victorian values and Raj nostalgia movies are all recycled in the Great British heritage industry, and not just for the benefit of Japanese or American tourists either. Workers in Sunderland or Derbyshire know that their futures might well depend on decisions taken in Tokyo or Chicago, but the British do not like to think of themselves as a Third World nation run on a service economy. So the nation is enjoined to travel back to the future in a rewriting of history which leapfrogs over the recent past in order to retrieve an entirely fictional image of systemic 'national-popular' unity based on the retrieval and recycling of the wretched age of Empire.

Dick Hebdige (1987) has called this 'digging for Britain,' in that historicity and popular conceptions of the past have become a key site in which the changed circumstances of the present are apprehended and defined. One only has to consider the retrieval of historical *counter*memory in black pop culture (where the 'cut 'n' mix' aesthetic informs the narration of stories precisely hidden from history in dominant discourses of the past) to recognize the sources of popular resistance to the postmodern frontier effect, something underlined in a recent comment by the pop group Tears for Fears:

> The Tories are renowned for evoking memories of the Victorian era 'cos it falls in line with their paternalistic morality. What I wanted to do was bring back memories of that era when Britain was 'great' – the era of Harold Wilson, The Beatles, the red London bus, Twiggy and the mini. . . . There was a time when it was okay to be idealistic or, dare I say it, spiritual. And I wanted to jog everybody's memory.[7]

A few years ago Judith Williamson rightly criticized a simple-minded left-wing populism which merely imitated and capitulated to neoconservative definitions of popularity, and indeed one might also note a tendency towards culturalism or 'cultural substitutionism,' among Left intelligensia for whom 'postmodernism' just means going to the shops.[8] In one sense this is symptomatic of the Left's deeply demoralizing experience of being actively disarticulated as a result of the postmodern frontier effect. The withdrawal and retreat into culturalism further underlines another ironic twist of the Thatcher decade, as cultural studies has been appropriated into a knowledge-producing apparatus that services the reproduction of hyper-consumption in the culture industry.

These indicative signs of the times underscore the identity crisis of the Left, but the *contradictoriness* of the postmodern requires a *relational* emphasis, because what is experienced as the loss of identity and authority in some quarters is also an empowering experience which affirms the identities and experiences of others *for precisely the same reasons*. The 1980s have seen a significant renewal and revitalization of black politics. Whether this has occurred despite Thatcherism or because of it, issues of race and ethnicity have been irrevocably inscribed on the national political agenda, a process which represents a considerable advance on the previous decades. Indeed, if I think about the intensity of all those discussions about 'the definition of black' which occurred in the post-1981 scenario after the 'inner-city' riots, the experience of decentering has been highly empowering, as it has also articulated an experience of demarginalization, in which new forms of collective subjectivity and imagined community have been mobilized by various political and cultural activities.

What was so important about the demand for 'black representation' that could be heard in Britain in the early 1980s was an extension of radical democracy in which a marginalized and subordinate group affirmed and asserted their political rights to representation. The shift from 'ethnic minority' to 'black' registered in the language of political discourse, demonstrated a process in which the objects of racist ideology reconstituted themselves as subjects of social, cultural and political change, actively making history, albeit under circumstances not of their own choosing. A minority is literally a minor, not simply the abject and dependent childlike figure necessary for the legitimation of paternalistic ideologies of assimilation and integration, but a social subject that is *in-fans*, without a voice, debarred and disenfranchised from access to political representation in a liberal or social democracy.

The rearticulation of black as a political rather than racial category among Asian, Caribbean and African peoples, originating from a variety of ethnic backgrounds and sharing common experiences of British racism, thus created a new form of symbolic unity out of the signifiers of racial difference. For over four centuries the sign /black/ had nothing but negative connotations, as it signified racialized identities within Manichaean dualism, an absolute division between 'the West' and 'the rest' in which the identity of the black subject was negated as Other, ugly and ultimately unhuman. The decentering of 'Man,' the centered subject of Western liberal humanism, is nothing if not a good thing, as it has radically demonstrated the coercive force and power implicated in the worldly construction of the Western rational *cogito* – the subject of logocentrism and all the other 'centrisms' that construct its representations of reality. Western 'Man' consisted of a subject whose identity and subjectivity depended on the negation, exclusion and denial of Others. Women, children, slaves, criminals, madmen and savages were all alike in as much as their otherness affirmed 'his' identity as the universal norm represented in the category 'human.' Indeed, if the period after the modern is when the Others of modernity talk back, what is revealed is the fictional character of Western universality, as the subject who arrogated the power to speak on behalf of humanity was nothing but a minority himself – the hegemonic, white, male, bourgeois subject whose sovereign, centered identity depended on the 'othering' of subordinate class, racial, gendered and sexual subjects who were thereby excluded from the category 'human' and marginalized from democratic rights to political subjectivity. [. . .]

1968: What did you do in the war?

Chantal Mouffe (1988) has brought such critical tasks into focus by calling for the 'institutionalization of a true pluralism' on the Left which recognizes and respects the diversified character of political struggles which have radicalized democracy in postwar capitalist societies. By grounding her analysis of 'new democratic struggles' in terms of a view which emphasizes the processes that enable or prevent the extension of the subversive logic of democratic 'equality,' Mouffe argues that:

> The progressive character of a struggle does not depend on its place
> of origin . . . but rather on its link with other struggles. The longer
> the chain of equivalences set up between the defence of the rights of
> one group and those of other groups, the deeper will be the
> democratization process and the more difficult it will be to neutralize
> certain struggles or make them serve the ends of the Right. The concept
> of solidarity can be used to form such a chain of democratic equivalences.
>
> (Mouffe, 1988: 100)

Laclau's metaphorical concept of frontier effects (1977) refers precisely to the
formation of imaginary unities and political solidarities, crystallized out of numerous
microalliances or systems of equivalence that polarize the political field into
democratic antagonism. The 'us and them' logic of authoritarian populism, and
the paranoid policing of the 'enemy within' articulated by Thatcherite ideology
represent one such frontier effect that has hegemonized popular consciousness in
the present. But to understand the effectiveness of this right-wing closure (which
largely explains why the Left is so defeated and demoralized) we have to grasp
the reversals by which the New Right disarticulated and rearticulated the
emancipatory identifications which the new social movements opened up against
the 'Center' by inaugurating the democratic revolutions of the 1960s.

As Mouffe notes, forms of oppression and inequality based on racism and
patriarchy predate industrial capitalism, but the contradictory development of
democracy within the universalized commodification of social relations in the
postwar period was one of the key conditions by which the demand for equality
was radicalized in the politics of feminism and black struggles. Just like women,
the colonized participated equally in the war effort against facism, and in this
respect were interpellated as 'equal' in one set of discourses, while the terms of
social democratic consensus repositioned them – in the labor process, in the political
process, in social relations – once more as 'unequal.' Mouffe argues that this
contradictory interpellation created the conditions for new forms of democratic
antagonism, not because people 'naturally' aspire towards freedom, equality and
solidarity, but because such values were placed at the center of social and political
life by social democracy, which nevertheless denied access to such values to its
subordinate subjects and marginalized citizenry. It is from this perspective that 'we
can see the widening of social conflict as the extension of the democratic revolution
into more and more spheres of social life' (1988: 100). It seems to me that a
historical reading of this concrete conjuncture would reveal the *privileged metaphor
of 'race'* within the radicalization of the postmodern democratic imaginary.

At one level this is acknowledged globally in the geopolitical metaphor of
First, Second and Third Worlds. In the context of the Cold War, whose 'Iron
Curtain' polarized two rival superpowers, the assertion of US hegemony in a new
phase of multinational capitalism required the presence of the underdeveloped
world to stabilize and reproduce the logic of modernization necessary to the existence
of the overdeveloped world. But politically speaking, the Third World was brought
into existence by the anticolonial struggles of the colonized, by the historical presence
of subjects who were formerly objects of imperialism. In such movements as Pan-
Africanism or Gandhi's non-violent mobilization on the Indian subcontinent, localized

regional, ethnic and 'tribal' identities were hegemonized by revolutionary nationalisms. Western forms of nationhood were appropriated and articulated with
'syncretic' traditionalism and indigenous 'folklore' to encode the demand of new
collective historical subjects for democratic self-determination, liberation and
independence. In Kwame Nkrumah's speculations about the existence of an 'African
personality,' and in Frantz Fanon's diagnosis of the political unconscious of
colonialism (and the psychic reality of its 'superiority/inferiority' complex as
constitutive of white/black subjectivities), what we see is not the description of
preexisting, already formed identities, but intellectual reflection on the transformative
practices, made possible by new democratic antagonisms, that were bringing new
forms of postcolonial subjectivity into being.[9] Aside from the chain of equivalence
constructed within anticolonial movements for national liberation, we also see an
extension of the same process within the metropolitan First World in terms of the
radicalized demand for autonomy.

   The Afro-American civil rights movement in the United States during the
1950s and early 1960s acted as the catalyst in which the radical democratic chain
of equivalence reconstituted political subjects across the metaphorical boundary of
racial difference itself. On the one hand, this unfolded internally as a radicalization
of subaltern racial identity inscribed in the transition from 'Negro' to 'Black.' The
reformist character of Martin Luther King's leadership, through which the demand
for equal citizenship rights was articulated, was transformed in the Northern urban
setting by nationalist ideologies, such as those advocated by Malcolm X, to extend
beyond legal and social rights into an existential affirmation of a negated subjectivity
(exactly that which was designated under erasure as simply 'X'). This resulted in
the mid-1960s in the highly volatile and indeterminate metaphor of 'Black Power.'
As Manning Marable (1984) has pointed out, this rallying cry was articulated into
right-wing positions (and even President Nixon became an advocate, as he endorsed
it as a form of black capitalism), as well as the left-wing positions associated with
the Black Panther Party and its charismatic leadership which, for a brief moment
around the late 1960s, became a counter-hegemonic subject capable of leading and
directing a range of positions into the chain of radical democratic equivalence.

   One of the factors behind this process lay in the transracial identifications by
which the codified symbols and imaginary metaphors of 'black liberation' were
taken up, translated and rearticulated among postwar generations of white youth.
Among student activists, within the bohemian 'underground,' within second-wave
feminism, and in the nascent gay and lesbian liberation movement, the signs and
signifiers of radical blackness were appropriated into a chain of equivalences that
empowered subordinate identities within *white* society. Of course, this most often
took a cultural rather than conventionally political form of solidarity. The mass
diffusion of black expressive culture through the pop and rock music industry
played a key role in the dissemination of such imaginary modes of alternative
identification, culminating in the 1969 Woodstock Festival, where the predominantly
white, middle-class youth who gathered there thought they constituted a nation
within the nation, a new imagined community. In psychedelic Britain this was the
imaginary space in which representations of an 'alternative society' were constructed.
Here we see the vicissitudes of ambivalence, inversion and othering in the political
identifications made possible by the cultural forms of antagonism which articulated

the extension of the radical democratic chain of equivalences. At its liminal point, whiteness was emptied out in a direct imitation of empowered black subjectivity, such as when the activist John Sinclair formed the short-lived White Panther Party in the United States in 1968.[10]

Some of the contradictions inherent in the unfolding of this system of equivalences became apparent both at the frontier with the 'law and order' state (which effectively wiped out and repressed the guerrilla strategies of the far Left), and within the counterculture itself, where the masculinist character of its antiauthoritarianism was contested by women and gay men. But it was precisely in this respect that the radicalization of sexual politics from 1970 onwards derived significant momentum from imaginary equivalences with black struggles, as 'black pride' and 'brotherhood' acted as metonymic leverage for the affirmation of 'gay pride' and the assertion that 'sisterhood is strength.' Finally, although it should be pointed out that such radicalization also affected the increasing militancy of the labor movement in the early 1970s (as shown in the miners' strike of 1973), in the context of the polyvocal anticonsensus populism of the period it was ultimately the New Right, and not the New Left nor the new social movements, that got hold of what the Situationists used to call 'the reversible connecting factor' (Debord, 1981).

The metaphor of 'race' was privileged in the sense that it was also crucial to the emergence of a neoconservative populism which, in Britain, was forcefully articulated in 1968 by the dramatic interventions of Enoch Powell. Volosinov noted that 'the social multi-accentuality of the sign . . . has two faces, like Janus,' and that 'this inner dialectic quality of the sign comes out into the open only in times of social crises or revolutionary changes,' because 'in ordinary circumstances . . . the ideological sign in an established dominant ideology . . . always tries to stabilize the dialectical flux' (Volosinov, 1973: 23–24). In his political speeches on race and nation, culminating in the 'Enemies Within' speech in 1970, Powell encoded the dialectical flux of the crisis of authority into a populist chain of equivalences in which issues of race and immigration opened up a broader ideological attack against the Centre, radically destabilizing the values of social democracy. As an advocate of free-market capitalism, and a staunch defender of the primacy of the nation-state in politics, Enoch Powell prefigured and helped pave the way for the logic of authoritarian populism we now know as Thatcherism.[11] But what also needs acknowledging is the fact that the three lines of force which divided the field of political antagonism between the new social movements, the New Left and the New Right were all implicated in the *same* struggle over the 'communifying' logic of democratic equivalences, set in motion by the decentering of the consensual Center. What is at issue in our understanding of the moment of 1968 is how these three nuclei of political identification competed for the collective will of society. Contrary to the impression given by academic deconstructionists, the moment of indeterminacy, undecidability and ambivalence is never a neutral or purely textual affair – it is when politics is experienced at its most intense.

As someone who was eight years old in 1968, I have no direct experience, memory or investment on which to draw, as more recent dates like 1977 or 1981 punctuate more formative experiences in the political consciousness of my generation. Yet precisely as a textual construction in popular memory, '1968' has an affective resonance that I feel needs to be defended and conserved against the 'active forgetting' which the contemporary postmodern frontier effect encourages. What is demanded by the shift in popular memory is not a history that aims to 'articulate the past the way it really was,' but a mode of storytelling which, in Walter Benjamin's (1973) phrase, aims to 'seize hold of a memory as it flashes up at a moment of danger.' In lieu of a concrete historical account of the postmodern crisis of social democracy (which should be backdated to the period between 1956 and 1968), my sketch of radical democratic equivalences is really only an inventory arising out of my own formation growing up in the aftermath of the post-'68 conjuncture. Nevertheless, by asking 'whatever happened to the empowering identifications of the sixties?' we might arrive at a clearer understanding of why the 1980s have been so awful.

Between the fragments: citizenship in a decentred society

> We no longer regard ourselves as the successive incarnations of the absolute spirit – Science, Class, Party – but as the poor men and women who think and act in a present which is always transient and limited; but that same limitation is the condition of our strength – we can be ourselves and regard ourselves as constructors of the world only insofar as the gods have died. There is no longer a logos.
>
> (Ernesto Laclau, 1988: 21)

> Our diversity is a strength: let's value it.
>
> (Mobil Corporation advertising logo)[12]

Ten years ago such narrative strategies informed the counterhistory undertaken by the influential socialist-feminist text, *Beyond the Fragments* (Rowbotham, Wainwright, Segal, 1979). Taking stock of the uneven development of a dialogue between the male-dominated Left and the 1970s women's liberation movement, it emphasized the important differences between the organizational form of political parties and the participatory politics of social movements such as feminism. Sheila Rowbotham's nuanced account of the political culture of sectarianism on the British Left – dominated by macho dogmatism and the authoritative stance of Leninist vanguard leadership – drew attention to the 'emotionally terrorizing morality' (*ibid.*: 126) of having to be 'politically correct' in order to lay claim to the identity of being a 'true' socialist. Considering the transformative impact of various feminisms over the past two decades, it seems to me that the contrasting decline of the organized Left can be accounted for by just such unpleasant behaviors concerning the policing of one's 'correct' credentials. Such attitudes also contribute to the widespread apathy and boredom inspired by conventional Left/Right politics today. In the wake of heroic models of modernist commitment, the withdrawal of affective involvement from formal politics, like the decline of the public sphere itself, underlines postmodern indifference and the privatization of political passions (the so-called 'crisis of caring') as much as it underpins the rise of 'conviction politics' and all sorts of fundamentalism which speak in the name of the silent majorities.

So where is the passion that was once invested in the Left? Such passion certainly exists, as has been seen in the system of equivalences unfolding in the ex-Communist world as a result of glasnost and perestroika. Gramsci argued for a symbolic view of politics and power, as his conception of the party as a 'modern prince' was based on the argument that all forms of living practice necessarily produce *myth*, which is

> expressed neither in the form of a cold utopia nor as learned theorizing, but rather by a creation of concrete phantasy which acts on a dispersed and shattered people to arouse and organize its collective will.
>
> (Gramsci, 1971: 126)

The New Right has certainly heeded such Gramscian advice: since 1968 the 'concrete phantasy' that has aroused and organized the collective will of the British people has been hegemonized and directed by the bifurcated neoconservative vision of shrinking freedom and deepening inequalities. The myth of a socialist society, on the other hand, for so long institutionalized in the image of the 'caring' welfare state, is tattered, torn and untenable. Moreover, the prospects for reconstruction look bleak, as the organized Left – what is left of it – has shown no sign of being able to grasp the imaginary and symbolic dimensions of hegemonic strategy. Even when sections of the British Left have mobilized an alternative populism against the Tories, as occurred in the GLC experience (borrowing 'rainbow coalition' imagery from Jesse Jackson's Democratic campaigns in the US), the 'thinkability' of new alliances has been undermined from within by the conservative traditionalism of the Left, as well as by the essentialist tendencies of 'identity politics' on the part of the new movements.

Since the 1950s, the new social movements have autonomously constructed diverse political myths and fantasies which have not only empowered people in their everyday lives, but which have thereby enriched and expanded the horizon of popular politics. But in the plurality of particularisms, what can also be seen at the outer limits of the new diversified and decentred public sphere is the paradoxical replication of an authoritarian desire for a center. The Left's sectarian or doctrinaire anxiety over the 'correct' interpretation of the master thinkers Marx, Lenin and Trotsky is reproduced at a subjective level in the new movements by the ethical imperative of 'authenticity,' expressed in the righteous rhetoric of being 'ideologically right-on.' The moral masochism that informs the attitude policing and credibility inspection routines so characteristic of the separatist tendencies of some of the autonomous movements reproduces the monological and puritanical conception of agency found in Marxist economism and class essentialism. The search for an authentic, essential 'self' in adversarial ideologies such as black cultural nationalism or lesbian–feminist separatism, to cite just two examples, often replays the vanguardist notion that there can be only *one* privileged agent of social and historical change. However tactically necessary in the 'war-of-maneuver' against white/male supremacist ideologies, the consequences of such separatism is self-defeating, as it mimics the authoritarian power to which it is initially opposed by simply inverting the binarism of discourses that legitimate domination. In any case, such fixed beliefs in immutable identity within the new antagonisms of race, gender, ethnicity and sexuality have been called into question by the pluralization effect that occurs in the encounter between the different movements – something that has become more progressively pronounced in the 1980s. The emergence of black women as a distinct 'class' or group in politics, for example, has relativized radical feminist notions of 'global sisterhood' by raising issues of racial and ethnic oppression that cut across experiences of power and powerlessness among women. By the same logic, black feminist positions disrupt complacent notions of a homogeneous and self-identical 'black community' by highlighting gender antagonisms and the divisive consequences of masculinist rhetoric in black political strategies (see Barbara Smith, 1983; Amos, Lewis, Mama and Parmar, 1984; hooks, 1989).

Essentialist notions of identity and subjectivity surface in the vortex of this bewildering experience of difference because of the absence of a common idea of what diversity really means for the multitude of subjects who are deeply unhappy with, and antagonistic towards, New Right hegemony. One appreciates the awfulness of this condition (which marks out the historic failure of the Left) by recognizing that the only available ideology which has taken diversity seriously is the social-democratic discourse on 'multiculturalism,' which enjoys little credibility among both racists and antiracists, Left and Right alike. But insofar as the British Left evacuates and abandons the terrain, it is colonized by the Right, and monocultural essentialism is mobilized in the defence of 'our way of life' to deny the very existence of diversity and difference.

Beyond the Fragments was influential (and informed the GLC's project of participatory democracy) because it recognized the diverse sources of antagonism in capitalist society: as Hilary Wainwright said, 'it is precisely the connections between these sources of oppression, both through the state and through the organization of production and culture, that makes a piecemeal solution impossible' (1979, *op. cit.*: 4). But in the scenario of further fragmentation and detotalization that has characterized the 1980s, who really has the confidence to assume that there is such a transcendental realm of the 'beyond'? Should we not begin again by relativizing the perspective to examine the contradictions that characterize the complex relations 'between'? This would mean deepening and extending the analysis of the interdependency of culture and politics in the process by which men and women 'acquire consciousnessness through social relations.' It would also entail a more detailed understanding of the salient differences and similarities between political parties and social movements. Alain Touraine has remarked that 'the labour movement, whose power is frequently invoked to underscore the weakness of the new social movements, is not really a wholly social movement' (1988: 131), because it has confined itself to class contradictions at the expense of other social antagonisms that do not arise directly out of the conflict of capital and labor. However, to understand the combined and uneven development of potentially counter-hegemonic forces, it is the very dichotomy between the state and civil society that also needs to be reformulated.

First, because it obscures the double-edged situation whereby the incorporation and neutralization of the industrial labor movement (in corporatism, bureaucracy and other forms of state mediation) is paralleled by the cultural appropriation and commodification of the new movements in the marketplace, where many radical slogans (such as 'the personal is political') have been hijacked, objectified and sold back to us an ever-widening range of 'life-style' options for those who can afford to pay. Yet, just as the welfare state did deliver limited gains by extending citizenship rights from the legal and political to the social arena, the new movements have had significant impact on personal relations and lived experience precisely through the diffusion of their ideologies in the commodified forms of the cultural marketplace.

Second, the concrete problems of political representation that came to light in the GLC experiment demonstrated that the distinction between state formation and the public sphere is not an impassable or absolute boundary, but nevertheless a boundary through which it is difficult simply to translate correspondences from one to the other. Paul Gilroy's (1987: 114–152) reading of the 'success' of the Rock Against Racism campaign in civil society in the 1970s, and the 'failure' of top-down bureaucratic methods of municipal antiracism in the 1980s, highlights the degree of incommensurability between the two. But because the analysis remains within the state/civil society dichotomy it describes, it does not identify the pragmatic points of entry from which to conduct or prefigure counter-hegemonic strategy 'in and against' the state. Given the legacy of statism within the British labor movement, one cannot evade the task of conceptualizing the necessary transformation of the state and its role in socialist strategy.

The official discourse of antiracism failed precisely because it imposed a one-dimensional view of racial antagonism in practices such as 'racism awareness training,' which simply reinforced existing relations of minority representation. Problems of tokenism – in which the one black person on the committee or in the organization is positioned, or rather burdened, with the role of a 'representative' who 'speaks for' the entire community – were left intact. Black subjects historically marginalized from political representation by exclusionary practices reproduced within the Left were legitimately angry. But the encoding of such anger often took the displaced form of 'guilt-tripping' in which potential allies were paralyzed by the sins of their past. While activists recognized the untenable innocence of conciliatory liberal pluralism, but without a common set of terms in which to openly share criticism and disagreements, alliance-building was inhibited by the fear of being seen to be 'incorrect' or not 'ideologically right-on.' Rather than learn from the educative value of active mistakes and errors, action was inhibited by a dogmatic discourse of antiracism which merely disguised the guilt, anger and resentment that gave urgency to issues of race and racism. In my view solidarity does not mean that everyone thinks in the same way; it begins when people have the confidence to disagree over issues of fundamental importance precisely because they 'care' about constructing common ground. It is around such passions encountered in the pluralized and diversified forms of contemporary democracy that the issue of alliances needs to be rethought, through an expanded and thoroughly modernized conception of citizenship.

The concept of citizenship is crucial because it operates in the hinge that articulates civil society and the state in an open-ended or indeterminate relationship. In the modern period, somewhere between 1880 and 1920, the industrial labor movement contested the narrow range of citizenship rights of 'the people' within liberal democracy. The gradual enfranchisement of excluded and marginalized subjects, as the result of class struggles in relation to the state, constituted the form of government defined after 1945 as social democracy. In the postindustrial word, however, the democratic image of 'the people' has been radically pluralized and hybridised by the proliferation of new antagonisms, and by the presence of a diversity of social subjects whose needs and interests can no longer be programmed around the limited citizenship rights inscribed in the welfare state. Yet neoliberal democracy – the freedom and inequality pursued by the New Right – threatens to erode and reduce even such minimal rights by prioritizing the market over society as the ultimate site upon which basic needs and rights are guaranteed only by individual initiative. As Margaret Thatcher told us, 'there is no such thing as society, only individual men and women and families.'

The prospects for a radical renewal of the 'myth' of a socialist society cannot lie in the revival or recycling of Labourite welfare statism, although the defence of minimal civil rights to employment, housing, health care, education and freedom of association has never been more necessary than it is now. Is it possible to envisage a minimalist state capable of guaranteeing such basic rights of citizenship against the structured inequalities produced by free-market forces? John Keane and others have argued that only a new constitutional settlement around an expanded conception of democratic citizenship can make socialism thinkable again.[13] Some sections of the Left in Britain, like *Marxism Today* magazine, would have us believe that the process of rethinking is already underway. But I have yet to hear the chorus of a genuinely plural discourse of the Left which actually acknowledges the sheer difficulty of living with difference.

The postimperial decline of British manufacturing was once explained as a consequence of the uniquely British resistance to postwar modernization. Politically, the British Left still resists and retreats from the democratic task that confronts it, namely to thoroughly modernize its conception of what a socialist society could and should be. To date there has been very little sustained analysis of what went wrong in the GLC,[14] and such 'active forgetting,' of course, serves the purpose of the Tories quite nicely. If, however, as Stuart Hall has remarked, the noise produced in its attempt to find new forms of democratic representation and participation 'is the positive sound of a real, as opposed to phoney and pacified democracy at work . . . a positive recognition of the necessary tension between civil society and the state' (1988: 235), then instead of withdrawing into quiet conformity, the Left has to recognize that it is being called upon to actively enjoy and encourage such noise if it is to arouse and organize a popular counter-hegemonic conception of radical democracy in a plural society. If this is what 'socialist pluralism in a real democracy will be like,' we cannot go back to the future, so bring the noise.

Notes

1   'Welcome to the Jungle,' from Guns 'N Roses, *Appetite for Destruction*, Geffen Records, 1988.

2   See, also, Claus Offe, *Contradictions of the Welfare State* (London: Hutchinson, 1984).

3   Written by David Bowie (1972), performed by Mott the Hoople, *Mott the Hoople Greatest Hits*, CBS Records, 1976.

4   Jacques Donzelot, 'The Apprehension of Time,' in Don Barry and Stephen Mueke, eds., *The Apprehension of Time* (Sydney: Local Consumption Publications, 1988).

5   Cited in Jon Savage, 'Do You Know How to Pony? The Messianic Intensity of the Sixties,' (1982) reprinted in Angela McRobbie, ed., *Zoot Suits and Second-Hand Dresses: An Anthology of Fashion and Music* (London: Macmillan, 1989), 121.

6   Stuart Hall, 'Popular Democratic vs. Authoritarian Populism: Two Ways of Taking Democracy Seriously,' (1980) in Hall (1988); the concept of frontier effects is originally developed in Ernesto Laclau (1977).

7   *Melody Maker* (August 19, 1989), 41.

8   Judith Williamson, 'The Problem with Being Popular,' *New Socialist* (September 1986).

9   See Kwame Nkrumah, *I Speak of Freedom: An African Ideology* (London: Heineman, 1961); and Frantz Fanon, 1970 [1952] and 1967 [1961].

10   The White Panther manifesto, the 'Woodstock Nation,' and other documents from the countercultures in Britain, Europe and the United States are collected in Peter Stansill and David Zane Mairowitz, eds., *BAMN (By Any Means Necessary): Outlaw Manifestoes and other Ephemera, 1965–1970* (Harmondsworth: Penguin 1971). On the 'alternative society' in Britain, see David Widgery, *The Left in Britain, 1956–1968* (Harmondsworth: Penguin, 1976). On feminist and gay equivalences, see Robin Morgan, 'Goodbye to All That,' in *BAMN*; and Aubrey Walter, ed., *Come Together: The Years of Gay Liberation, 1970–1973* (London: Gay Mens Press, 1980).

11   Key speeches of the 1960s are gathered in Enoch Powell, *Freedom and Reality* (Farnham: Elliot Right Way Books, 1969); see also, John Elliot, ed., *Powell and the 1970 Election* (Farnham, Elliot Right Way Books, 1970); and for a Marxist account, see Tom Nairn, *The Break-Up of Britain: Crisis and Neo-Nationalism*, (London: New Left Books, 1981), especially chapter six, 'English Nationalism: The Case of Enoch Powell.'

12   Advertisement in *Black Enterprise* magazine (January–February 1989).

13   See John Keane, ed., *Democracy and Civil Society* (London: Verso, 1988).

14   An important exception is Franco Bianchini, 'GLC RIP: Cultural Policies in London, 1981–1986,' *New Formations*, 1 (Spring 1987).

References

Amos, Valerie, Gail Lewis, Amina Mama, Pratibha Parmar, eds. (1984) 'Many Voices, One Chant,' *Feminist Review*, 17.

Benjamin, Walter (1973 [1940]) 'Theses, on the Philosophy of History,' *Illuminations*, London: Fontana.

Debord, Guy (1981 [1959]) 'Detournment as Negation and Prelude,' in Knabb, ed. *Situationist International Anthology*, Berkeley: Bureau of Public Secrets.

Gamble, Andrew (1988) *The Free Economy and the Strong State: The Politics of Thatcherism*, London: Macmillan.

Gilroy, Paul (1987) *There Ain't No Black in the Union Jack: The Cultural Politics of Race and Nation*, London: Hutchinson.

Gramsci, Antonio (1971 [1930]) *Selections from the Prison Notebooks*, London: Lawrence & Wishart.

Grossberg, Lawrence (1988) *It's a Sin: Essays on Postmodernism, Politics and Culture*, Sydney: Power Institute.

Hall, Stuart (1988) *The Hard Road to Renewal: Thatcherism and the Crisis of the Left*, London: Verso.

Hebdige, Dick (1987) 'Digging for Britain: an Excavation in Seven Parts,' in *The British Edge*, Boston: Institute of Contemporary Arts.

hooks, bell (1989) *Talking Back: Thinking Feminist, Thinking Black*, London: Sheba Feminist Publishers.

Laclau, Ernesto (1977) *Politics and Ideology in Marxist Theory*, London: New Left Books.

——(1990[1988]) 'Building a New Left' [interview] *Strategies*, 1, reprinted in *New Reflections on the Revolution of Our Time*.

——and Chantal Mouffe (1985) *Hegemony and Socialist Strategy: Towards a Radical Democratic Politics*, London: Verso.

Marable, Manning (1984) *Race, Reform and Rebellion: The Second Reconstruction of Black America, 1945–1982*, London: Macmillan.

Mouffe, Chantal (1988) 'Hegemony and New Political Subjects: Towards a New Concept of Democracy,' in Cary Nelson and Lawrence Grossberg, eds. *Marxism and the Interpretation of Culture*, London: Macmillan.

Rowbotham, Sheila, Hilary Wainwright, Lynne Segal (1979) *Beyond the Fragments: Feminism and the Making of Socialism*, London: Merlin.

Smith, Barbara, ed. (1983) *Home Girls: A Black Feminist Anthology*, New York: Kitchen Table/Women of Color Press.

Touraine, Alain (1988) *The Return of the Actor: Social Theory in Post-Industrial Society*, Minneapolis: University of Minnesota Press.

Volosinov, V. N. (1973 [1929]) *Marxism and the Philosophy of Language*, Cambridge: Harvard University Press.

Chapter 36

David R. Roediger

ALL ABOUT EVE, CRITICAL WHITE STUDIES, AND GETTING OVER WHITENESS

Is race over?

THE COVER OF A RHAPSODIC 1993 special issue of *Time* showed us "The New Face of America." Within, the newsmagazine proclaimed the United States to be "the first universal nation," one that supposedly was not "a military superpower but . . . a multicultural superpower." Moving cheerfully between the domestic and the global, an article declared Miami to be the new "Capital of Latin America." Commodity flows were cited as an index of tasty cultural changes: "Americans use 68% more spices today than a decade ago. The consumption of red pepper rose 105%, basil 190%." Chrysler's CEO, Robert J. Eaton, best summed up the issue's expansive mood in a lavish advertising spread:

> At the Chrysler Corporation, our commitment to cultural diversity ranges from programs for minority-owned dealerships to the brand-new jeep factory we built in ethnically diverse downtown Detroit. And our knowhow is spreading to countries from which the immigrants came. We're building and selling Jeep vehicles in China, minivans in Austria and trucks in Mexico. We're proud to be associated with this probing look [by *Time*] at a multicultural America. We hope you enjoy it.[1]

Remarkably, *Time* sustained such euphoria amid many passages confessing to doubts, troubling facts, and even gloom. In the U.S.-led "global village," readers learned, there were more telephones in Tokyo than in the whole of Africa. The "exemplary" Asian American immigrants had succeeded, but at tremendous cost. The host population that benefited from the wonders of "our new hybrid forms" told *Time's* pollsters that it strongly supported curbs on legal immigration (60 percent to 35 percent). By a smaller majority, those polled also backed the unconstitutional initiatives being floated in 1993 to prevent the children of noncitizens from acquiring citizenship. One article in this issue of *Time* held that, "with a relatively static force of only 5600 agents [patrolling immigration], the U.S. has effectively lost control of its territorial integrity." Richard Brookhiser's "Three Cheers for the WASPs" fretted that liberty- and wealth-producing White Anglo-Saxon Protestants' values were being elbowed aside as the "repressed" habits of an "ice person." In one of many bows to an older language of race – one key article called intermarriage "crossbreeding" – that the issue claimed to be transcending, Brookhiser lamented that the WASP's "psychic genes" were no longer dominant and revered. The balance sheet on recent immigration was a close one for *Time*: "Though different and perhaps more problematic than those who have come before, the latest immigrants are helping to form a new society."[2]

The ability to keep smiling amid contradictory crosscurrents hinged on the image that looked out at readers from the magazine's cover. She was "Eve", the result of sending the computerized photographs of fourteen models (of "various ethnic and racial backgrounds") through the Morph 2.0 computer software program. With the aid of a multicultural crew of technicians, the program pictured serially the offspring likely to eventuate from various couples. The writers had trouble deciding how seriously we ought to take Eve and the morphing process. The exercise mapped "key facial features" with "pinpoint" accuracy. At the same time, it was portrayed as merely a playful "way to dramatize the impact of interethnic marriage which has increased dramatically in the U.S. during the latest wave of immigration," making for a society "intermarried with children." State-of-the-art technology made "no claim to scientific accuracy," but the magazine presented the results "in the spirit of fun and experiment." The crowning morph ("as in metamorphosis, a striking change in structure or appearance," a writer added) was a miracle and a cover story. The managing editor recalled, "Little did we know what we had wrought. As onlookers watched the image of our new Eve begin to appear on the computer screen, several staff members promptly fell in love. Said one: 'It really breaks my heart that she doesn't exist.' We sympathize with our lovelorn colleagues, but even technology has its limits. This is a love that must forever remain unrequited."[3]

But then again, maybe not. After all, *Time's* cover proclaimed Eve who was described there as a mixture of "races," (with a caffè latte skin tone) to be the nation's "new face." The beauty of that face helped to explain why the modern Eve had magazine staffers lining up to join Adam in the ranks of apple pickers. But the Eden that she represented mattered at least as much in accounting for her appeal. In connecting her face to the nation's future, Time implied that she is what the United States will look like at that twenty-first-century point when, as they put it, "the descendants of white Europeans, the arbiters of our national culture for most of its existence, are likely to slip into minority status." Not only did Eve reassure us that all will be well when that happens, but also she already existed in cyberspace to mock allegedly outmoded emphases on the ugliness and exploitation of race relations in the United States. The collection of morphed photos carried the headline "Rebirth of a Nation." As Michael Rogin's prescient analysis of the cover gently puts it, the title was perhaps chosen "without . . . full consciousness of its meaning." Unlike the racist film classic *The Birth of a Nation*, in which race mixing is cast as Black-on-white rape, the rebirth-in-progress was (con)sensual, even as it was chastely mediated by technology. Although associations with a fall from grace persist, Eve was decidedly presented as good news. Toni Morrison's reminder that race has often been brutally figured on a Black-white axis stuck out like a sore thumb in the special issue. Her telling warnings that immigrants have historically had to "buy into the notion of American blacks as the real aliens" in order to assimilate fully seemed a dour refusal to join the fun of Eve's cyber-wonderland. Morrison was left describing the United States as "Star spangled. Race strangled" at the very moment when the computer could show us the end to all that. An article gratuitously attacking the "politics of separation" on college campuses underlined *Time's* point that it is time to get over racial (and feminist and gay) politics.[4]

The less slickly marketed recent analysis of demographic trends by the historian and sociologist Orlando Patterson ends with conclusions that precisely mirror those of Time. Writing in *The New Republic* under the headline "Race Over," Patterson allows that W. E. B. Du Bois may have been "half-right" in arguing that the "color line" was the problem of the century just past. But, he adds, those who project that problem into the new century are "altogether wrong." Because "migratory, sociological, and biotechnological developments" are undermining race, the outlook for the future is clear to Patterson: "By the middle of the twenty-first century, America will have problems aplenty. But no racial problem whatsoever." Patterson breezily develops four regional patterns. The "California system," destined to prevail on the U.S. and Canadian Pacific Rim, features "cultural and somatic mixing" generating a population that is mostly "Eurasian – but with a growing Latin element." On the West Coast, the "endless stream of unskilled Mexican workers" will drive away "lower-class Caucasians, middle-class racial purists and most African Americans." In the "Caribbean-American system," the Caribbean nations will be integrated into the United States, via economic collapse in the West Indies. Florida will become the "metropolitan center" of this system, which will also produce "transnational and post-national" Afro-Latin communities in northeastern cities. The rest of the Northeast and the urban Midwest will continue to rust, and a declining public sector, the end of affirmative action, and competition from West Indian immigrants will devastate African American and U.S.-born Latino communities. But the Black and Latino poor will be joined in cities and inner suburbs by "European American lower classes." Gated communities will house the middle class. "Social resentment and a common, lumpen-proletarian, hip-hop culture" will produce unity even amid "murderous racial gang fights." The victims of deindustrialization will be "lower-class, alienated and out of control." But they "will be hybrid nonetheless." In discussing the Southeast, Patterson suddenly declines to make a case for metamorphosis. The "Atlanta system" (as Patterson calls it, oddly choosing a southern city whose Third World immigrant population is skyrocketing) will feature continuing segregation. "The old Confederacy," we are told, "will remain a place where everyone knows who is white and who is black and need reckon no in-between." Somehow this prediction still leaves Patterson's "Race Over" prognostications intact, however. Over the next century, "the Southern model will become an increasingly odd and decreasingly relevant anachronism." In any case, science is likely to create new methods of changing hair texture and skin color, enabling African Americans to "enhance their individuality" by "opt[ing] for varying degrees of hybridity" through biotechnology. By 2050, "the social virus of race will have gone the way of smallpox."[5]

Time and Patterson are scarcely alone in arguing that the movement of immigrants, the demographics of intermarriage, and the global consumption of commodities associated with exotic others signal that "race" is over, or at least doomed. The influential website/social movement known as Interracial Voice touts the "intermarried with children" pattern as the key to change. Since, in the view of "Interracial Voice," "political leaders 'of color' and . . . black 'leaders' specifically" prop up the old racial order, the "mixed race contingent" is destined to usher in the "ideal future of racelessness."[6] The journalist Neil Bernstein extols "blond cheerleaders" who claim Cherokee ancestry and the "children of mixed marriages [who] insist that they are whatever race they say they are" as frontline troops "facing the complicated reality of what the 21st century will be."[7] Writing in the New York Times Magazine, the critic Stanley Crouch almost precisely anticipates Patterson's basic point, under the title "Race Is Over." Crouch concludes, "One hundred years from today Americans are likely to look back on the ethnic difficulties of our time as quizzically as we look at earlier periods of our history." Although his essay comments on Americans as a "culturally miscegenated people," it is lavishly illustrated with pictures like those in Time, serving as "previews" of the future flesh-and-blood individuals who are "Pakistani-African-American," "Russian-Polish Jewish/Puerto Rican," and "Dutch/Jamaican/Irish/African-American/Russian Jewish." The caption of the 20 pictures is "WHAT WILL WE LOOK LIKE?"[8]

The case against the "race is over" thesis

It is not possible to assent to the Time/Patterson/Crouch vision of an automatic transition to a raceless nation. The many objections to such a view turn on two difficulties. The first of these is an inattention to change over time, and the second is an absence of discussions of power and privilege. In its conviction that everything is new regarding race, the "race is over" school tends to cut off the present and future from any serious relationship to the past. If, as Alexander Saxton argues, "white racism is essentially a theory of history," Eve announces that we are excused from paying serious attention to either racism or history. Time's special issue does offer a short, rosy, and inaccurate history of immigration, but that history is written in such a distorted way as to leave no scars and set no limits. For example, the glories of U.S. multiculturalism arise, according to Time, from the nation's "traditional open door polity" toward immigrants. In fact, of course, the historical Open Door Policy of the United States insisted on free movement of American goods in Asia, while Asian migrants were excluded from the United States on openly racial grounds. If everything is new – Time writes, "During the past two decades America has produced the greatest variety of hybrid households in the history of the world' – then doing serious history can itself become a symptom of a mordant commitment to raking over old coals instead of stepping into the nonracial and multicultural sunshine. Significant in this regard is the tendency of the "postrace-ists" to keep using the hoary language of biological race as though it carries no meaning, now or in the future, to speak of crossbreeding and refer to the children of intermarriage as hybrids. Indeed, so sure are some advocates of hybridity that mixing and morphing can dissolve race that they put "race" inside wary quotation marks that (rightly) signal its scientifically spurious status but abandon all wariness when "multiracial" is invoked as a category.[9] Inattention to history leaves discussions of the transcendence of race fully saddled with the very preoccupation with biological explanations that it declares to be liquidated.

Taking history seriously also calls into question the proposition that demographic trends can easily be extrapolated into the future to predict racial change. Not only do trends shift, but the very categories that define race can also change dramatically. The idea that "crossbreeding" will disarm racism is at least 140 years old. Demographics simply are not always decisive. Southern states in the nineteenth century with large – sometimes majority – Black populations and very substantial mixing of the races were *slaveholding* states. In the recent past, California celebrated its move toward becoming a white-minority state by passing a raft of anti-Black and anti-immigrant initiatives, becoming, as George Lipsitz puts it, "the Mississippi of the 1990s." That the 1996 anti-affirmative action initiative's triumph occurred in a state in which the population was less than 53 percent white but the registered voters were over 80 percent white reminds us that politics matters at least as much as head counts.[10]

At the start of the twentieth century [. . .] predictions in which the changed racial character of the United States was plotted and graphed looked very much as they did in the 1990s. Reactions a century ago ranged from a sense of alarm at the threat of "degeneration," of Anglo-Saxon "race suicide," and of "mongreliza-tion," to optimistic rhetoric regarding the creation of a new and invigorated "American race." If immigration continued and mixed marriages spread, the "pure white," "Nordic" domination of the United States was doomed. Immigration from southern and eastern Europe did continue massively for a time, but then it was decimated via political action restricting its flow. Mixed marriages grew dramatically, joining (for example) racially suspect newcomers from Poland, Greece, and Italy with each other and with older groups. But the prediction of racial change never quite became fact. Somewhere along the line, the "new immigrants" from southern and eastern Europe became fully accepted as white. It may be that, as *Time* puts it, "Native American-black-white-Hungarian-French-Catholic-Jewish-American" young people will lead the United States to an "unhyphenated whole." But the "Polish-Irish-Italian-Jewish-Greek-Croatian" offspring of the twentieth century also seemed to hold out that hope. In very many cases they ended unhyphenated, all right, but as whites. We simply do not know what racial categories will be in 2060. As Ruben Rumbaut's and Mary Waters's provocative works show, we do not know how the diverse children imagined in *Time* will be seen or will see themselves in terms of identity. Although white supremacy can certainly exist without a white majority, the question of whether such a majority might yet be cobbled together through the twenty-first century remains. These questions, to which we shall return at the conclusion of this volume, are political ones, and even Morph 2.0 cannot answer them.[11]

The important recent work of the population specialists Sharon M. Lee, Barry Edmonston, and Jeffrey Passel underlines this point. Their projections for the year

2100 show a U.S. population 34 percent mixed race, up from about 8 percent today. (Less than a third of the latter percentage actually chose the new "multiracial" category on the 2000 census.) The Asian American/multiple-origin population, in these estimates, will rise to 42 million in the next century, rivaling in size the 56 million U.S. residents whose ancestry is "purely" Asian. Among Latinos, the 184 million persons of Latino/multiple-origin ancestry will vastly outnumber the 77 million whose ancestry is Latino on both sides. Among African Americans, lower rates of intermarriage will result in 66 million persons with African American ancestry on both sides and 39 million persons of African American/multiple-origin descent. Among "whites," the "pure" population is projected also to outnumber the white/multiple-origin one by 165 million to 90 million. Even though all of the "purities" are laughable historically, and although the new century will surely surprise us in many ways, the study's broader implications are vital. As the authors emphasize, the answer to whether there might be 77 million, or fewer, or three times that many, Latinos in 2100 will be decided historically and politically, not just demographically. Particularly important will be the actions and consciousness of those whom Cherrie Moraga calls "21st century mestizos" – those "born of two parents of color of different races and/or ethnicities." At issue too is whether the projected relative "purity" of Black-white racial categories will make that divide more rather than less salient or leave the 66 million residents with African American ancestry on both sides in a particularly exposed racial position.[12]

Eve leaves studiously vague the possibility that the "new face" of the United States might stay white. She is, the editor tells us, 35 percent southern European and 15 percent Anglo-Saxon but also 17.5 percent Middle Eastern and 7.5 percent Hispanic. Thus, in the curious racelessness that Time proposes, Eve remains white even as the text chatters about the nonwhite-majority nation of the future. Chicana students in my classes sometimes see Eve's picture as that of a chicana; Puerto Rican students see her as Puerto Rican; Italian Americans likewise take her as their own. When a new Betty Crocker was introduced as the "mythic spokesperson" for baking products in 1996, the General Mills Corporation's icon morphed into a figure that looks very much like Eve. Her creators announced the marketing value of the figure's ambiguity clearly: "Women of different backgrounds will see someone different: Native American, African-American, Hispanic, Caucasian."[13]

More subtle are the ways in which Eve's seductiveness blurs the line between present and future. Eve appealingly appears – but in cyberspace, not in time. She belongs in some sense to the present, insofar as she is already used to mock antiracist initiatives as anachronistic and wrong. However, Eve exists in 2050, or maybe 2060 or 2100. Those who conjure her up thus ask us to practice (or abandon) the politics of racial justice in the shadow of someone who does not exist. This problem is exacerbated by the fact that white residents of the United States believe that whites are a minority in the United States. In a 1996 poll, white respondents estimated whites in the United States population at 49.9 percent. The accurate figure was 74 percent. They thought that the United States was 23.8 percent African American, twice the enumerated Black population. At 10.8 percent, Asian Americans existed in the white psyche in 3½ times their numbers in the census. Hispanics were imagined to constitute 14.7 percent of the population; they represent 9.5 percent. Such misperceptions clearly fueled the anti-immigrant initiatives of the 1990s. Lovable as Eve seemed to the editors, *Time's* special issue remained equivocal at best on favoring relatively open immigration, and its collapsing of present and future in Eve made nativist folklore credible.[14]

The evasions of questions of power and privilege in the "race is over" literature also obscure the extent to which the fiction of race still structures life chances in the United States. If whiteness continues to confer substantial material advantages, and if large groups of Black and Latino people exist in grinding poverty, then the wholesale abandonment of older categories of racial categorization and identificatior seems unlikely. Evidence that such advantages are ending is unimpressive. The *Wall Street Journal's* dissection of trends from 1992 through 1998 featured a chart with two telling headlines regarding race and wealth. The first was "A Wide Divide in Family Income." Figures under it showed "Nonwhite or Hispanic Income" rising somewhat more rapidly than that of "White non-Hispanics" (10.4 percent to 74 percent). These were the good years. From 1970 to 1993, by contrast, the median income of white households rose 3.4 percent; for Black households, the figure was 0.8 percent. Later (1990s) gains still left Black and Latino family incomes at less than 63 percent of white family incomes. More revealing, as Melvin Oliver and Thomas Shapiro have eloquently argued, are patterns of wealth. The *Journal's* second heading ran "And a Wider Divide in Family Wealth." The boom of the Clinton years left the net worth of "Nonwhite or Hispanic" families at 17.28 percent of the net worth of "White non-Hispanic" families. The rise was infinitesimal, up from 17.13 percent.[15]

Given the prevalence of what the sociologists Douglas Massey and Nancy Denton call "American Apartheid," such gaping disparities in resources are concentrated in communities. As the legal scholar John Powell has shown, of the 8 million U.S. residents living in "areas of concentrated poverty" (defined as census tracts where 40 percent of the population have incomes below the official poverty line) in 1990, half were African American and a quarter were Hispanic. Clinton-era "welfare reform" enforces what Alejandra Marchevsky and Jeanne Theohatis call the "racialization of entitlement," using ostensibly *individualistic* criteria to limit eligibility for benefits of racial groups isolated from jobs. In future economic downturns, the reforms will further devastate whole communities. In those areas of concentrated misery known as prisons, the growth in numbers of Black and Hispanic inmates has been astronomical. The years 1985 to 1995 saw a 204 percent increase in Black women's incarceration and a 143 percent increase for Black men. About two-thirds of all prisoners are Black or Hispanic. Given a sixfold increase in the prison population between 1972 and 1997, and with the total number of U.S. inmates reaching 2 million, such disparities massively affect communities. Black males born in 1991 are estimated to have a 29 percent chance of being imprisoned at some point in their lives. For Hispanics the figure is 16 percent and for whites just 4 percent. If the imprisoned were counted as unemployed, joblessness in African American and Latino communities would still be at Great Depression levels amid record job creation.[16]

That white poverty is consistently underestimated by the media and by the U.S. residents who are polled makes some sense in terms of such material realities. Poverty among whites appears as situational, not structural, and as unattached to alleged racial traits. Moreover, whereas the poorest 20 percent of the Black population made almost 60 percent of the income of the poorest fifth of the white population in 1967, by 1992 that figure had fallen to 50 percent. The longstanding idea that "whiteness is property," which *ought* to pay off even if it is not doing so at the moment, survives with distressing ease amid such trends, even as income inequalities *within* the Black, white, and Hispanic population have grown tremendously.[17]

The idea that laws, social practices, and the personal opinions of whites in the United States are now "colorblind," and the corollary that antiracism is therefore irrational, counterproductive, or even itself racist, also undergird much of the "race is over" argument. As powell notes, conservatives have increasingly become the leading advocates of "colorblindness." They argue "that since we have learned that race is an illusion, rather than a scientific fact, we should drop racial categories altogether . . . [and that] only those who are either racist or badly misinformed would insist that we continue to utilize these pernicious categories." As Neil Gotanda's riveting work shows, the legal ideology of colorblindness has often also entailed blindness to "white racial domination" where constitutional law is concerned.[18]

The broader notion that whites are generally colorblind animates recent studies arguing for an abandonment of affirmative action and other partly race-based reforms. From the work of Paul Sniderman through that of Stephan and Abigail Thernstrom, to that of Joel Rogers and Ruy Teixeira, advocates of such a position consistently reach sanguine conclusions based on opinion polls in which whites report their own increasing enlightenment on racial matters. We learn, for example, that in 1997 only 1 percent of whites told pollsters that they would or might move if a Black person moved in next door. The changes in polling data are "large and all are in the same direction: more tolerance, less racism."[19]

These attitudinal shifts, which underpin "race is over" arguments, are suspect for three reasons. One is that racist practices may function despite reported shifts in attitude, and segregation in housing is perhaps the most dramatic example. Second, studies sometimes presume that white respondents are the experts on changing racial attitudes ani practices. Polls among people of color may tell a different story. In a recent poll conducted in the Chicago area, for example, 61 percent of white respondents thought that there was "fairly little," "almost none," or no hiring discrimination against Blacks. Only 19 percent of Black respondents agreed; and 43 percent reported believing that there was a "great deal" of discrimination.[20] Finally, although racism may no longer be exhibited openly in political discourse, it is not so decisively defeated in the culture. Huge numbers of whites, for example, tell pollsters that Blacks are relatively lazy. When Charles Murray wrote a proposal for the racist tract he coauthored, *The Bell Curve*, he reportedly promised that it would cause many whites to "feel better about things they already think but do not know how to say." The huge sales of the book combine with polling data to suggest that he was not entirely wrong.[21] In justifying its own interest in *The Bell Curve, The New Republic* offered the striking editorial opinion that "the notion that there might be resilient ethnic difference in intelligence is not, we believe, an inherently racist notion."[22]

Specific invocations of the idea that Eve has made race passé often leave unexamined the question of what then is to become of white privilege and instead specifically argue for an end of African Americas racial identity. The Interracial Voice website, for example, currently features the leading spokesperson of the anti-affirmative action movement, Ward Connerly, predicting that "by 2070, perhaps sooner, 'black, 'brown,' and 'white' will be historical concepts. Café-au-lait will be reality." The good news is that "in California today, there are more children born to 'interracial' couples than are born to two black parents." The better news for the colorblind right is that the "California trend" will soon sweep the nation. Its fondest hope is that " 'African Americans' [will] readily and proudly acknowledge the diversity of their backgrounds [and] then the concept of 'race' will disintegrate." Similarly, mainstream journals of opinion give very respectful attention to the idea that because race is happily over, African Americans should give up their identities. In May 1997, for example, both *Harper*'s and *Atlantic Monthly* featured long pleas for an "end of blackness." Meanwhile, the idea that whiteness should disappear is treated as defining the outer limits of academic zaniness.[23] This disparity between the professed goal of nonracialism and the concentration of contemporary fire on the racial politics of activists of color detracts from even so sophisticated a work as Paul Gilroy's recent *Against Race: Imagining Political Culture Beyond the Color Line*. (Even so, we will miss a greal opportunity if debate about Gilroy's book is focused simply on its unfortunate title and not on the possibilities and limits of its insistently antifascist politics.)[24]

A final way in which the "race is over" stance ignores existing inequalities is more subtle. In declaring race to be utterly malleable, proponents of this idea often then turn to gender and sexuality as the "real" differences on which the future is to be founded. *Time*, as Michael Rogin observes, rejected one image produced by Morph 2.0. Because it showed a "distinctly feminine face – sitting atop a muscular neck and hairy chest," the article proclaimed, "Back to the mouse on that one." The insistence on Eve as a love object and on "intermarriage" and "breeding" as the antidotes to racial division defines a future sexual and gender universe as static as the racial frontier is dynamic. Variations on this theme play themselves out more broadly in the abandonment of attempts to build coalitions that address racism and sexism together and in the striking coexistence of usually masculine challenges to the color line with homophobic rants in hip-hop.[25]

The presence of race and the possibility of nonwhiteness

Obviously, some of the recent penchant for projecting an assured non-racial future derived from a specific media demand for end-of-decade/century/millennium prognostications. Even so, it seems likely that such predictions will have enduring ideological force growing out of real, though highly complicated, changes in demographics, mass culture, and markets. Sheer exhaustion in the wake of 30 years of grappling, with difficult racial questions without effective government commitments to justice and without compelling visions of liberation articulated by a mass movement also make the idea of a raceless new beginning very attractive.

We organize and write, like it or not, in the face of Eve's appeal, and the appeal of Eve's face frankly causes serious problems for antiracists. The charges made against us have decisively shifted. For a long time, such charges were clear:

too visionary, too impatient, too little aware of the weight of history and tradition. Now the accusation becomes that we are atavistic – so eager to dwell on the bleak past that we miss the glorious future. With astonishing speed, the idea that race is too fixed a category to allow for the "fixing" of racial injustice has given way to a recipe for inaction that features the fluidity of race: If it ain't fixed, don't bother to fix it. From such an aphorism, it is but a short leap to seeing antiracists as the *cause* of continued race-thinking in an imagined nation whose culture is supposed to be hybrid, whose laws are supposed to be colorblind, whose white citizens are supposed to have gotten over racism, and whose very population is soon supposed to make race irrelevant. If Dr. Martin Luther King, Jr., felt compelled to explain the question "Why we can't wait," we are put in the position of explaining "Why we can't celebrate."[26] In answering, we risk seeming joyless, dated, and parochial. We also run the more serious risk of so defensively insisting on the continuing relevance of race as to miss tremendous changes and the opportunities for resistance that they open. We miss the occasion to decide what we *do* want to celebrate.

At its best, the love of Eve's image expresses a deep desire for the United States to stop being a white nation. We cannot but share that desire. Nor can we ignore the fact that in the last century, the props have been kicked out from under much old-style racism. If white supremacy seemed a century ago to rest on scientific racism, on Jim Crow segregation, on disenfranchisement, and on color bars against the entry and the naturalization of nonwhite immigrants, it survives with none of these barbarisms intact. The arguments being made here thus imply not that struggles for racial justice must continue on the same terrain, but only that they must continue. Indeed, taking advantage of new terrain is one critical task in carrying on such struggles before us.

The title and the structure of this book are intended to convey both the changed situation in which we write and the loads we carry. *Colored White* derives from a line delivered by the great African American comedian Redd Foxx. Playing a junk dealer and crime victim in an episode of his 1970s television series, *Sanford and Son*, Foxx answered an inevitable question regarding his attackers: "Yeh, they was colored – white!" A quarter-century later we are in a much better position to hope that Foxx's barbed point – that whites too carry and act on racial identities – would be broadly intelligible. The much-publicized spate of works in "whiteness studies" (better called critical studies of whiteness) have inched the "white problem" onto mainstream intellectual agendas. These studies have drawn on the works of previously marginalized people of color who had long reflected, and continue to reflect, on why some people think it is important to be white.[27] "Colored white" also carries the connotation that race is, to use Frantz Fanon's term, "epidermal." It is produced in social relations over time and is not biological and fixed. The triumph of such ideas regarding race, although it has been achieved by starts and fits and continues to encounter resistance, is one grand achievement of twentieth-century science and of the century's freedom movements. At the same time, however, that very triumph sets the stage for the conservative and neoliberal arguments rehearsed above, which miss the tragic gravity of Fanon's remarks on the epidermalization of race and indeed seek to forget race by confusing its biological inconsequence and superficiality with the deep inequalities it structures.[28] [. . .]

The last decade has seen a dramatic increase in the attention paid to scholarship that casts whiteness as a problem and insists that both the origins and the persistence of white identity demand explanation. Publications that address intellectual and cultural trends have lavished attention on studies of whiteness in the United States. A special issue of *Voice Literary Supplement*, a review essay in *Lingua Franca*, and even an article in the popular music magazine *Spin* all proclaimed the arrival of this putatively new area of inquiry. Special, massive issues of *Transition*, *Hungry Mind Review*, and *Minnesota Review* quickly appeared. Cleverly titled collections proliferated: *Displacing Whiteness*, *Off White*, *White Reign*, *Whiteness: A Critical Reader*, *Outside the Whale*, *Critical White Studies*, and more.[29] Although it has been predominantly a U.S. phenomenon, the study of whiteness has also gathered momentum in Britain and its empire, in Japan, in South Africa, in Australia, and elsewhere, often acknowledging inspiration from, and pointing to problems with, U.S.-centered studies.[30] Most strikingly, the April 1997 "Making and Unmaking of Whiteness" conference at Berkeley drew extensive national and international press coverage.[31]

Such attention has come complete with its share of problems. The new scholarship has been seen as portraying whiteness as just another identity at the table of multiculturalism, thus redirecting scholarly attention to whites in a way that minimizes consideration of power and privilege. As Angie Chabram-Dernersesian's excellent "Whiteness in Chicana/o Discourses" puts it, emphasizing what whites say and feel about their racial identities risks "tak[ing] the jagged edges off the kind of social practices and material effects" associated with racism. The way in which President William Jefferson Clinton briefly enlisted the uncompromisingly radical work of the historian of whiteness Noel Ignatiev in the service of smoothing out "jagged edges" illustrates both the visibility of the new scholarship and the process that Chabram-Dernersesian describes. In 1998 Clinton gave his jocular, admiring, and fractured version of Ignatiev's *How the Irish Became White*. The president told audiences, "I got . . . this book the other day from a friend of mine who's got a terrific sense of humor who talked about how unfortunate it was that a lot of my [Irish American] forebears turned reactionary, because when we first came here we were treated just like the recently freed slaves."[32]

The clearest barometer of the ease with which the study of whiteness has gotten attention, and of its difficulty in getting a serious hearing, is the insistence of some popularizers that such study is brand new and is a white thing. In 1997, for example, a *New York Times Magazine* reporter interviewed me for her "whiteness studies" story. She led off by remarking that her research was winding down and enumerated those scholars with whom she had spoken. My objection that she had spoken only with white writers was twice waved away. She first held that this was a new field being pioneered by white writers like myself and then shifted to the safer claim that the "news" was that whites were now studying whiteness. Even so, I hoped that our talk had convinced her that such views missed the point of the study of whiteness, that she was overlooking its intellectual leaders, and that she would add interviews and change her emphasis. When the celebrated Minneapolis photographer Ken Pickett later was hired by the *Times* to take my picture for the story, my illusions vanished. Somewhat puzzled, Pickett told me that the magazine wanted oddly adjusted exposures for my picture and those of others who were quoted in the article. When I asked what fooling with the exposure in such a way would do, Pickett replied, "It will make you look whiter." The article itself mocked the study of whiteness as trendy, self-absorbed, and white.[33] Historically and now, however such study has been anything but those things.

If the defining intellectual thrust in the critical study of whiteness is to make white identity into a problem worth historicizing and investigating, it stands to reason that those groups for whom white behavior and attitudes have been most problematic would have inquired most searchingly into the dynamics of whiteness. Indeed, studying whiteness as a problem is perfectly consistent with an African American tradition, extending from Frederick Douglass forward, of insisting that talk of a "Negro problem" missed the point and that the "white problem" instead deserved emphasis. Similarly, the question of white values and the problem of the expansion of the white nationalism of the United States have focused the reflections of Native American thinkers. If slave folklore represents one point of departure for the critical study of whiteness, then the Chicana/o tales collected by Américo Paredes in *Uncle Remus con Chile* define another such point. When W. E. B. Du Bois claimed "singularly clairvoyant" knowledge of the "souls of white folk," his grounding for that claim lay not in any mystique of racial essentialism. Rather, as he, James Baldwin, bell hooks, and others understood, such knowledge was situated in particular "points of vantage."[34] However ignored, intellectuals of color have made searching inquiries into whiteness for a long time. In the writings of Robert Lee, Neil Foley, Cheryl Harris, john powell, Cherrie Moraga, Tomás Almaguer, Gloria Anzaldúa, and bell hooks, such intellectuals have likewise produced the recent texts that have most boldly extended such inquiries.[35] As universities have become less white places, such work has gained influence.

Characterizing the study of whiteness as a project of white scholars thus represents both a continued insistence on placing whites at the center of everything and a continuing refusal to take seriously the insights into whiteness that people of color offer. The enduring and scandalous inability of historians to come to grips with Du Bois as an expert on the past of the *white* South is one index of this failure. More direct evidence comes from the nearly simultaneous denunciation by both *Time* and *Newsweek* of the fiction of the great American Indian expert on race Leslie Marmon Silko, as somehow "antiwhite," despite her nuanced portrayals of race and her sympathetic development of the view that whites are but a symptom of "witchery" and not the source of evils.[36]

In briefly surveying the content of critical studies of whiteness, it is well to begin with a series of questions posed long ago but still much in need of answers. As World War II ended, the great novelist Chester Himes had a character in *If He Hollers Let Him Go* begin "wondering when white folks started getting white – or rather, when they started losing it." Twenty years ago, in the essay "The Little Man at Chehaw Station," Ralph Ellison puzzled, "What, by the way, is one to make of a white youngster who, with a transistor radio, screaming a Stevie Wonder tune, glued to his ear, shouts racial epithets at black youngsters trying to swim at a public beach?" The oldest of the questions is the most difficult. In a February 1860 contribution to *Anglo-Africa Magazine*, the Brooklyn schoolteacher William J. Wilson, writing as "Ethiop," framed his subject with a title question: "What Shall We Do with the White People?"[37]

If the critical study of whiteness cannot fully answer the profound questions raised by Ethiop, Himes, and Ellison, at least it offers promising ways to address them. Its first and most critical contribution lies in "marking" whiteness as a particular – even peculiar, – identity, rather than as the presumed norm. This insight crosses disciplinary lines dramatically. For example, Toni Morrison's work of literary criticism, *Playing in the Dark*, lays bare the tendency to assume that *American*, absent another adjective, means white American. Richard Dyer's essay on cinema, "White," argues that its title describes the normative color of the silver screen. Allan Bérubé joins Baldwin, Siobhan B. Somerville, and others in challenging durable, troubled, and often not consciously noticed connections of whiteness with both "vanilla" heterosexual and queer sexualities. The fact that people of color often regard white identity as crying out for explanation undergirds such important writings as Mia Bay's The White Image in the Black Mind and Keith Basso's *Portraits of "The Whiteman": Linguistic Play and Cultural Symbols among the Western Apache*. [38]

In "marking" whiteness, the historical approach suggested by Himes's question has moved debate forward decisively. Critical studies of whiteness have begun to describe not the origins of generalized white identity but the ways in which specific strata of the population came to think that they are white. In particular, the adoption of white identity by groups themselves subordinated, exploited, and even racialized as "not quite white" has proved fascinating to historians. In his 1935 classic *Black Reconstruction*, for example, W. E. B. Du Bois initiated specific historical discussion of the "white worker" and of why the adjective so often received stronger accent than the noun in the identity of this group. His emphasis on *both* the "income-bearing value" of whiteness and the "public and psychological wages" offered to those categorized as white informs much recent writing on the white worker, including Dana Frank's superb "White Working-Class Women and the Race Question." In Robert Lee's *Orientals*, this body of work is dramatically extended in a deeply gendered account of how the post–Civil War white working class coalesced around the idea of a "family wage" earned by a male breadwinner, in opposition to images of the Chinese immigrant as "a racial Other unfit for white work or white wives." The appearance of scholarship that closely roots white workers in specific locales, labor processes, and political economies marks a further advance. [39]

The painful, uneven ways in which immigrants from European groups were historically seen as racially different and even as less-than-fully-white have long occupied the attention of writers of color. For their deft balancing of "choice" and "coercion" in the process through which immigrants whitened, for their sure sense of racial learning among immigrants as a great drama and tragedy, and for their seminal influence on recent writings on whiteness and immigration, James Baldwin's The Price of the Ticket and his "On Being 'White' . . . and Other Lies" deserve specific mention. Outstanding among the recent historical works following the trail Baldwin blazed are those by Robert Orsi, Karen Brodkin, Michael Rogin, and Noel Ignatiev. More impressionistic accounts by the art critic Maurice Berger and the theologian Thandeka perhaps approach Baldwin's boldness even more fully, as does Camille Cosby's article on how her son's murderer, an eastern European immigrant, might have learned to hate Blacks in the United States. Such accounts remind us that whiteness has functioned both as a category, into which immigrants were or were not put, and as a consciousness, which immigrants embraced and rejected in specific circumstances.[40]

The racial identity of white women has engaged the urgent attention of African American thinkers from the slave narratives, through the antilynching agitation of Ida B. Wells, to the recent, provocative, and highly compressed reflections of the philosopher Lewis Gordon. Cheryl Harris's "Finding Sojourner's Truth" offers the closest study of the ways in which gender oppression made the situation of white women like that of African American women (and men), as well as the clearest account of differences that all but ensured that white women would both accept and contest their oppression as women while accepting a white identity. The leading book-length study that takes white womanhood in the United States as a problem for investigation remains Ruth Frankenberg's sensitive ethnography *White Women, Race Matters*, which charts the various ways in which white and female identities interact in daily lives. Vron Ware's *Beyond the Pale* and Louise Newman's *White Women's Rights* cross oceans to put white womanhood and feminism in a context of colonialism as well as of slavery.[41]

Perhaps the central overarching theme in scholarship on whiteness is the argument that white identity is decisively shaped by the exercise of power and the expectation of advantages in acquiring property. This insistence that white identity derived from the experience of dominating, rather than from biology or culture, has long found expression in African American thought. Both Amiri Baraka and Malcolm X, for example, insisted that whiteness is not a color but rather an ideology that developed out of desires to rule and the exigencies of ruling. The leading U.S. historians of whiteness, Theodore Allen and Alexander Saxton, consistently view white identity in terms of class and domination. Equally forceful in connecting whiteness with the exercise of power is Ian Haney Lopez's *White by Law*, the first full treatment of the protracted use of U.S. state power, via naturalization law, to determine who was and who was not white.[42]

The pervasiveness of terror and of the witness of terror – from slave patrols to lynchings to contemporary mass incarceration – in the construction of white identities is another old, and newly rediscovered, theme. When such contemporary writers as Paul Gilroy and bell hooks emphasize that whiteness has been and is still often experienced as terror by people of color, they can easily reach back to the autobiographies of slaves for examples. But those autobiographies also showed how watching and committing acts of racial violence incorporated children, women, and the poor unequally but surely into the white population and kept them there. Gloria Anzaldúa's "We Call Them Greasers" makes poetry out of the impact of such terror. Her poem is narrated by a white man who uses fraud, rustling of livestock, courts, fire, the English language, rape, and murder to gain land from Mexican American victims, some of whom had "black eyes like an Indian." The verses imagine a point at which even "his boys" are so repelled that they refuse to look the father/narrator in the eyes. At that critical juncture, the father requires his sons to lynch the last victim. The story echoes a number of African American works, all written from a "white" viewpoint, on the effects that witnessing terror had on whites. As Ralph Ellison, himself the author of an arresting short story recounting a lynching from the point of view of a white youth, once put it, whiteness worked as "a form of manifest destiny which designated Negroes as its territory and its challenge."[43] In the recent past, Lewis Gordon, Robyn Wiegman, Nell Irvin Painter, and Trudier Harris have likewise described the connections between violence and the development of white collective identities.[44]

The most arresting effort to connect whiteness with power lies in Cheryl Harris's long and remarkable *Harvard Law Review* essay "Whiteness as Property," [. . .] Harris moves away from older arguments that simply detail the privileges a white skin confers in obtaining property in the United States to contend that whiteness historically became, and remains, *itself* a form of property. Developing in counterpoint to the dispossession of American Indian property, the owning of slave property, and later, the systematic property advantages channeled toward whites by segregation and other state policies, whiteness itself possesses value and has at times been seen by courts to do so. Harris, like the Chicana writers Linda Lopez McAlister and Linda M. Pierce, features family histories of passing as a member of the white race as openings onto the connections between whiteness and property. George Lipsitz's and Martha Mahoney's accounts of the role of federal housing policies in fostering what Lipsitz calls a "possessive investment in whiteness" merit reading as complements to Harris's article.[45] Ironically, such work is especially important in analyzing the behavior and thought of the millions of whites who acquire no property and the many more who acquire no productive property. Along with valuable emerging scholarship on "propertyless" whiteness, Harris's point that poor whites *do* possess the property of whiteness helps to recast debate on the tragedy of why those who derive so little material benefit from white supremacy often firmly cling to white identity, the only property they hold. [46] Harris's work, like nearly all of the best critical studies of whiteness old and new, implicitly warns us against claims that any significant drama in U.S. history is "really about race" or that any single dynamic is isolated from the social processes within which it unfolds. As we turn, then, to a brief description of the sections of this book, let us first note that the essays seek to place race in dialectical relationship to factors such as class, ethnicity, gender, age, and sexuality in the belief that doing so enhances our understanding of the pervasive presence of race in the United States.

Notes

1   All citations here and in nn. 2, 3, and 4 below are in *Time* 142 (Fall 1993), a special issue not in weekly sequence. On the "universal nation" and "open door," see Editors, "America's Immigrant Challenge," 3, quoting Ben J. Wattenberg; Pico Tye "The Global Village Finally Arrives," 87, quoting Federico Mayor Zaragoza on "superpower"; Cathy Booth, "The Capital of Latin America: Miami," 82; Robert Eaton in Chrysler advertisement at 23. On "special issues" of popular magazines, nativism, and gender, see Lauren Berlant, *The Queen of America Goes to Washington City: Essays on Sex and Citizenship* (Durham: Duke University Press, 1997), 596.

2   Tyer, "Global Village," 87; James Walsh, "The Perils of Success," 55; Bruce W. Nelan, "Not Quite So Welcome Anymore," 10–13; Michael Walsh, "The Shadow of the Law," 17; Richard Brookhiser, "Three Cheers for the WASPs," 78–79; Editors, "America's Immigrant Challenge," 6. On efforts to end "birthright

citizenship" in the United States in the 1990s, see Dorothy E. Roberts, "Who May Give Birth to Citizens: Reproduction, Eugenics, and Immigration," in Juan F. Perea's important collection *Immigrants Out! The New Nativism and the Anti-Immigrant Impulse in the United States* (New York: New York University Press, 1997), 208 and 205–19 passim.

3   "Rebirth of a Nation, Computer-Style," 66; James Gaines, "From the Managing Editor," a; Jill Smolowe, "Intermarried . . . With Children," 64–65.

4   Front cover, Editors, "America's Immigrant Challenge," 5; "Rebirth of the Nation," 66. On *The Birth of a Nation*, see Michael Rogin, "The Sword Became a Flashing Vision': D. W. Griffith's *The Birth of a Nation*," in Robert Lang, ed., *The Birth of a Nation* (New Brunswick, NJ: Rutgers University Press, 1994), 250–93; Toni Morrison, "On the Backs of Blacks," William A. Henry III, "The Politics of Separation," 73–74. For Michael Rogin, see his *Blackface, White Noise: Jewish Immigrants in the Hollywood Melting Pot* (Berkeley: University of California Press, 1996), 7–8 and 76–79.

5   Orlando Patterson, "Race Over," *New Republic* 222 (January 10, 2000), 6.

6   See the Interracial Voice website for September–October 1996 at http://www.coml-intvoice/.

7   Neil Bernstein, "Goin' Gangsta, Choosin' Cholita," as reprinted in *Utne Reader* (March–April 1995), 87–90, from West, a supplement to the *San Jose Mercury News*.

8   Molly O'Neill, "Hip-Hop at the Mall," *New York Times Magazine* (January 9, 1994), 43; Stanley Crouch, "Race Is Over: Black, White, Red, Yellow – Same Difference," *New York Times Magazine* (September 29, 1996), 170–71.

9   Alexander Saxron, The Rise and Fall of the White Republic: Class Politics and Mass Culture in Nineteenth-Century America (London and New York Verso, 1990), 390; Smolowe, "Intermarried . . . With Children," 64–65 and the Interracial Voice website; Steven Masami Ropp, "Do Multiracial Subjects Really Challenge Race? Mixed-Race Asians in the United States and the Caribbean," *Amerasia Journal* 2.3 (1997), 1–16. On the peculiar mixture of race-transcendent claims with crudely essentialist notions of race, see also Josephine Lee's insightful "Disappointing Othellos: Cross-Racial Casting and the Baggage of Race" (Asian American Studies Workshop Series, University of Illinois, Urbana-Champaign, April, 2001).

10   See Lydia Chávez, *The Color Bind: California's Battle to End Affirmative Action* (Berkeley: University of California Press, 1998), asp. 36–37; George Lipsitz, *The Possessive Investment in Whiteness* (Philadelphia: Temple University Press, 1998), 211–34; George Fredrickson, *The Black Image in the White Mind: The Debate on Afro-American Character and Destiny, 1817–1914* (Middletown, CT: Wesleyan University Press, 1987, originally 1971), 120–22.

11   [. . .] Smolowe, "Intermarried . . . With Children," 65; Stanley Lieberson, "Unhyphenated Whites in the United States," *Ethnic and Racial Studies* 8 (January 1985), 159–80 explores the most extreme case of this identification with whiteness to the exclusion of "any clearcut identification with, and/or knowledge of, a specific European origin" (159); Stanley Lieberson and Mary C. Waters, "The Ethnic Response of Whites: What Causes Their Instability, Simplification, and Inconsistency?" *Social Forces* 72 (December 1993), 421–50; see also Mary C. Waters, *Ethnic Options: Choosing Identities in America* (Berkeley: University of California Press, 1990); Ruben Rumbaut, "The Crucible Within: Ethnic Identity,

Self-Esteem and Segmented Assimilation," *International Migration Review* 18 (1994), 748–94.

12   Barry Edmonston, Sharon M. Lee, and Jeffrey Passel, "Recent Trends in Intermarriage and Immigration and Their Effects on the Future Racial Composition of the U.S. Population," paper presented at the "Multiraciality: How Will the New Census Data Be Used?" conference at Bard College (September 2000) and available on webcast at http://www.levy.org; Cherrie Moraga, *The Last Generation: Prose and Poetry* (Boston: South End Press, 1993), 128. See also Joel Perlmann, "Reflecting the Changing Face of America," *Levy Institute Public Policy Brief*, Number 3 5 (1997); Mia Tuan, *Forever Foreigners or Honorary Whites: The Asian Ethnic Experience Today* (New Brunswick, NJ, and London: Rutgers University Press, 1998), 152–67, and Clarence Page, 'Piecing It all Together," *Chicago Tribune* (March 14, 2001).

13   Gaines, "From the Managing Editor," 2; Lee Svitak Dean, "Recipe for a New Betty Crocker," *Minneapolis Star-Tribune* (March 20, 1996), 1.

14   Priscilla Labovitz, "Immigration – Just the Facts," *New York Times* (March 25, 1996); Nelan, "Not Quite So Welcome," 10–12; Editors, "America's Immigrant Challenge," 3–9; Walsh, "Shadow of the Law," 17.

15   Yochi J. Dreazen, "U.S. Racial Wealth Gap Remains Huge," *Wall Street Journal* (March 14, 2000), A–2 and A–22; Unsigned (Doug Henwood, editor), "Race and Money," *Left Business Observer* 69 (September, 1995), 4–5. Melvin Oliver and Thomas Shapiro, *Black Wealth/White Wealth: A New Perspective on Racial Inequality* (New York: Routledge, David Savran, "The Sadomasochist in the Closet: White Masculinity and the Culture of Victimization," *differences: A Journal of Feminist Cultural Studies* 8 (1996), 137. More broadly, see Mary C. Waters and Karl Eschbach, "Immigration and Racial Inequality in the United States," *Annual Review of Sociology* 21 (1995) 419–46.

16   Douglas A. Massey and Nancy A. Denton, *American Apartheid: Segregation and the Making of the Underclass* (Cambridge, MA: Harvard University Press., 1993); john powell, "Sprawl, Fragmentation and the Persistence of Racial Inequality: Limiting Civil Rights by Fragmenting Space," forthcoming; Alejandra Marchevsky and Jeanne Theoharis, "Welfare Reform, Globalization, and the Racialization of Entitlement," *American Studies* 41 (Summer–Fall 2000), 235–65. Marc Mauei; *Race to Incarcerate* (New York: New Press, 1999), esp. 20, 118–20, 125, and 168–69; Joy James, ed., States of *Confinement: Policing, Detention and Prisons* (New York: St. Martin's Press, 2000). The category "Hispanic" is used in official statistics on concentrated poverty and on prison populations.

17   Unsigned, "Race and Money," 4–5-

18   john a. powell, "The Colorblind Multiracial Dilemma: Racial Categories Reconsidered," *University of San Francisco Law Review* 31 (Summer 1997), 790; Neil Gotanda, "A Critique of 'Our Constitution Is Color-Blind," *Stanford Law Review* 44 (November 1991), 2.

19   Stephan Thernstrom and Abigail Thernstrom, *America in Black and White: One Nation Indivisible* (New York: Simon and Schuster, 1997); Paul Sniderman, *The Scar of Race* (Cambridge, MA: Harvard University Press, 1993); Paul Sniderman and Edward G. Carmines, *Reaching Beyond Race* (Cambridge, MA: Harvard University Press, 1997); Roy Teixeira and Joel Rogers, *America's Forgotten Majority: Why the White Working Class Still Matters* (New York: Basic Books, 2000), 40 (emphases original).

20   Don Hayner and Mary A. Johnson, "In the Workplace: Most Whites See No Hiring Bias, But 82% of Blacks Disagree," *Chicago Sun-Times* (January 12., 1993), 16.

21   Alexander Star, "Dumbskulls," *The New Republic* 4163 (October 3', 1994), 11; Richard J. Herrnstein and Charles Murray, *The Bell Curve: Intelligence and Class Structure in American Life* (New York: The Free Press, 1995). Among several devastating critiques of *The Bell Curve*, see Joe Kincheloe, Shirley R. Steinberg, and Aaron D. Greeson, eds., *Measured Lies:* The Bell Curve *Examined* (New York: St. Martin's Press, 1996). On the continuing stereotyping of Blacks, especially as lazy, see Martin Gilens, *Why Americans Hate Welfare: Race, Media and the Politics of Antipoverty Policy* (Chicago: University of Chicago Press, 1999), 68–72 and passim, and Joe R. Feagin, *Racist America: Roots, Current Realities, and Future Reparations* (New York and London: Routledge, 2000), 110–11 and 116–17.

22   Editors, "The Issue," *The New Republic* 4163 (October 31, 1994), 9.

23   Ward Connerly, "*Loving* America," Interracial Voice website at http://www. web.com/~intvoice/. On Connerly, see Lydia Chávez, *The Color Bind*, esp. 24–34, 63–65, and 73–76; Randall Kennedy, "My Race Problem – And Ours," *Atlantic Monthly* 279 (May 1997), 55–66; Jim Sleeper, "Toward an End of Blackness," *Harper's* 294 (May 1997), 35–44. Cf. Margaret Talbot, "Getting Credit for Being White," *New York Times Magazine* 42 (November 30, 1997), 6.

24   Paul Gilroy, *Against Race: Imagining Political Culture Beyond the Color Line* (Cambridge, MA: Harvard University Press, 2000). For an acute commentary on Walter Bents Michaels's attempts to move beyond race, see Avery Gordon and Christopher Newfield, "White Philosophy," *Critical Inquiry* 20 (Summer 1994), 737–57. Cf. David Hollinger, *Postethnic America: Beyond Multiculturalism* (New York: Basic Books, 1995), esp. 84–86.

25   Rogin, *Blackface, White Noise*, 8; "Rebirth of a Nation," 66–67.

26   Martin Luther King, *Why We Can't Wait* (New York: Harper & Row, 1964).

27   Foxx as quoted in Christopher Porterfield, "The New TV Season: Toppling Old Taboos," *Time* 100 (September 25, 1972), 49.

28   Frantz Fanon, *Black Skins, White Masks*, trans. Charles Lam Markmann (London: Pluto Press, 1986, originally 1952), 110–11; Elazar Barkan, *The Retreat of Scientific Racism: Changing Concepts of Race in Britain and the United States Between the World Wars* (Cambridge, England: Cambridge University Press, 1992); Micaela di Leonardo, *Exotics at Home: Anthropologists, Others, American Modernity* (Chicago: University of Chicago, 1998), esp. 299–204; James B. McKee, *Sociology and the Race Problem* (Urbana and Chicago: University of Illinois Press, 1993), esp. 55–102; Lee Baker, *From Savage to Negro: Anthropology and the Construction of Race, 1896–1954* (Berkeley: University of California Press,1998).

29   Carl Swanson, "The White-Boy Shuffle," *Spin* 13 (October 1997), 54; Peter Erickson, "Seeing White," *Transition* 67 (1996), 166–85; David W. Stowe, "Uncolored People: The Rise of Whiteness Studies," *Lingua Franca* (September/ October 1996), 68–77; Judith Levine, "The Heart of Whiteness," *Voice Literary Supplement* (September 1994), 11-16; the *Minnesota Review* special issue is Number 47 (Spring 1997); Frankenberg, ed., *Displacing Whiteness*; Michelle Fine, Lois Weis, Linda C. Powell, and L. Mung Wong, eds., *Off White: Readings on Race, Power and Society* (New York and London: Routledge, 1997); Vron Ware and Les Back, eds., *Outside the Whale: Essays on Whiteness, Politics and Culture* (forthcoming from University of Chicago Press); Chris J. Cuomo and Kim Q. Hall, eds.,

Whiteness: Critical Philosophical Reflections (Lanham, MD: Rowman and Littlefield, 1999); Mike Hill, ed., Whiteness: *A Critical Reader* (New York: New York University Press, 1997); Richard Delgado and Jean Stefanic, eds., *Critical White Studies: Looking Beyond the Mirror* (Philadelphia: Temple University Press, 1997); Joe L. Kincheloe, Shirley R. Steinberg, Nelson M. Rodriguez, and Ronald E. Chennault, eds., *White Reign: Deploying Whiteness in America* (New York: St. Martin's Press, 1998).

30   Richard Dyer, *White* (London and New York: Routledge, 1997); Vron Ware, *Beyond the Pale: White Women, Racism and History* (London and New York: Verso, 1992); Ware and Back, *Outside the Whale*, forthcoming; Jeremy Krikler, "Lessons from America," *Journal of Southern African Studies* 20 (December 1994), 663–69; Alastair Bonnett, *White Identities: Historical and International Perspectives* (Harlow, England: Prentice-Hall, 2000); Bronwen Walter, *Outsiders Inside: Whiteness, Place and Irish Women* (New York and London: Routledge, 2000); Ghasson Hage, *White Nation: Fantasies of White Supremacy* (New York: Routledge, 2000); Gillian Cowlishow, *Rednecks, Eggheads and Blackfellas: A Study of Racial Power and Intimacy in Australia* (Ann Arbor: University of Michigan Press, 1999); note also the focus on whiteness in recent conferences in Japan (Kyoto American Studies Seminar, 2000), Canada (University of Toronto, 2000), and South Africa (History Workshop, 2001).

31   Quentin Hardy, "School of Thought: The Unbearable Whiteness of Being," *Wall Street Journal* (April 24, 1997); "Nationline," *USA Today* (April 7, 1997); Peter S. Goodman, "Conference Seeks to Clear Up What It Means to Be White," *Washington Post* (April 12, 1997).

32   Angie Chabram-Dernersesian, "On the Social Construction of Whiteness Within Selected Chicana/o Discourses," in Frankenberg, ed., *Displacing Whiteness*, 110; Clinton's remarks are from a reception in Portland, Oregon, *Weekly Compilation of Presidential Documents, William J. Clinton* 341 (June 1998), 1114–19.

33   Margaret Talbot, "Getting Credit for Being White,"*New York Times Magazine* (November 30, 1997) 116–18, which includes the photos.

34   Waldo E. Martin, Jr., *The Mind of Frederick Douglass* (Chapel Hill and London: University of North Carolina Press, 1984), 112; Editors of *Ebony, The WHITE Problem in America* (Chicago: Johnson Publications, 1966). See also the introduction to my edited volume, *Black on White: Black Writers on What It Means to Be White* (New York: Schocken, 1998); Crispin Sartwell, *Act Like You Know: African American Autobiography and White Identity* (Chicago: University of Chicago Press, 1998); Betsy Lucal, "Seeing Ourselves Through Others' Eyes: An Examination of African American Perspectives on Whiteness" (unpublished paper presented at the Eastern Sociological Society in Philadelphia in 1998); Jane Davis, *The White Image in the Black Mind: A Study in African American Literature* (Westport, CT: Greenwood, 2000) Américo Paredes, *Uncle Remus con Chile* (Houston: Arte Publico Press, 1993) Du Bois, as reprinted in Julius Lester, ed., The Seventh Son: *The Thought and Writings of W. E. B. Du Bois*, 2 vols. (New York: Random House, 1971), 1:485

35   Moraga, *The Last Generation*, 98–131; Gloria Anzaldúa, *Borderlands/La Frontera: The New Mestiza* (San Francisco: Spinsters/Aunt Lute 1987), esp. 7–8, 101–3, and 134–35; Robert G. Lee, *Orientals: Asian Americans in Popular Culture* (Philadelphia: Temple University Press, 1999); Neil Foley, *The White Scourge: Mexicans, Blacks, and Poor Whites in Texas Cotton Culture* (Berkeley: University of

California Press, 1997); john a. powell. "Whites Will Be Whites: The Failure to Interrogate Racial Privilege," *University of San Francisco Law Review* 34 (Spring 2000), 419–64; Toni Morrison, *Playing in the Dark: Whiteness and the Literary Imagination* (Cambridge, MA Harvard University Press, 1990); Tómas Almaguer, *Racial Fault Lines: The Historical Origins of White Supremacy in California* (Berkeley: University of California Press, 1994), esp. 45–74.

36   Carl Abbott, "Tracing the Trends in U.S. Regional History" (American Historical Association) *Perspectives* 28 (February 1990), 8 (on Du Bois); on Silko, see Sharon Patricia Holland's important *Raising the Dead: Readings o) Death and (Black) Subjectivity* (Durham and London: Duke University Press, 2000), 68 and 70–102, passim, and Leslie Marmon Silko, *Ceremony* (New York: Viking, 1977), 132–38.

37   Ralph Ellison, "The Little Man at Chehaw Station," in *Going to the Territory* (New York: Random House, 1987); Chester Himes, *If He Hollers Let Him Go* (New York: Doubleday, 1945), 42; Ethiop [William J. Wilson], "What Shall We Do with the White People?" *Anglo-African Magazine* 2 (February 1860), 41.

38   Morrison, *Playing in the Dark*, 47–50; Richard Dyer, "White," *Screen* 29 (1988), 141–63; Allan Bérubé, "How Gay Stays White" (paper delivered at "The Making and Unmaking of Whiteness" Conference, Berkeley, April 1997); Tracy D. Morgan, "Pages of Whiteness: Race, Physique Magazines and the Emergence of Public Gay Culture" in Brett Beemyn and Mickey Eliason, eds., *Queer Studies* (New York: New York University Press, 1997), passim; James Baldwin, "Here Be Dragons," in *The Price of the Ticket: Collected Nonfiction, 1948–1985* (New York: St. Martin's Press, 1985), esp. 682–83; John Howard, *Men Like That: A Southern Queer History* (Chicago and London: University of Chicago Press, 1999), 155 and 211; Siobhan Somerville, *Queering the Color Line: Race and the Invention of Homosexuality in American Culture* (Durham and London: Duke University Press, 2000), esp. 138–40; Mia Bay, *The White Image in the Black Mind* (Oxford and New York: Oxford University Press, 2000); Keith H. Basso, *Portraits of "The Whiteman": Linguistic Play and Cultural Symbols Among the Western Apache* (Cambridge, England, and New York: Cambridge University Press, 1978).

39   W. E. B. Du Bois, *Dusk of Dawn: An Essay toward an Autobiography of a Race-Concept* (New York: Harcourt, Brace, 1940), 129; Du Bois, *Black Reconstruction in America, 1860–1880* (New York: Atheneum, 1992, originally 1935), 17–31 and 700–1; David R. Roediger, *The Wages of Whiteness: Race and the Making of the American Working Class* (New York and London: Verso, 1991); Eric Lott, *Love and Theft: Blackface Minstrelsy and the American Working Class* (New York and Oxford: Oxford University Press, 1993); Dana Frank, "White Working-Class Women and the Race Question," *International Labor and Working Class History* 54 (Fall 1998), 80–102; Lee, *Orientals*, 82; Bruce Nelson, *Divided We Stand: American Workers and the Struggle for Black Equality* (Princeton: Princeton University Press, 2001).

40   Piri Thomas, Down These Mean Streets (New York: New American Library, 1967), 33–47; James Baldwin, *The Price of the Ticket* and "On Being 'White' . . . and Other Lies," *Essence* (April 1984), 90–9 2; Noel Ignatiev *How the Irish Became White* (New York and London: Routledge, 1995); Karen Brodkin, *How Jews Became White Folks and What That Says About Race in America* (New Brunswick, NJ: Rutgers University Press, 1998); Rogin, *Blackface, White Noise*; Matthew Jacobson, *Whiteness of a Different Color: European Immigrants and the Alchemy of Race* (Cambridge, MA: Harvard University Press, 1998); Robert Orsi, "The Religious Boundaries of an Inbetween People: Street *Feste* and the Problem of the Dark-Skinned 'Other' in Italian Harlem,"

American Quarterly 44 (September 1992), 313–47; Maurice Berger, *White Lies: Race and the Myths of Whiteness* (New York: Farrar, Straus & Giroux, 1999), esp. 5–8; Thandeka, *Learning to Be White: Money, Race and God in America* (New York: Continuum, 1999), 61–70; Camille O. Cosby, "America Taught My Son's Killer to Hate Blacks," USA Today (July 8, 1998),15–A.

41   Lewis Gordon, *Bad Faith and Antiblack Racism* (Atlantic Highlands, NJ: Humanities Press, 1995); Cheryl Harris, "Finding Sojourner's Truth," *Cardozo Law Review* 18 (November 1998), 309–410; Ruth Frankenberg, *White Women, Race Matters: The Social Construction of Race* (Minneapolis: University of Minnesota Press, 1994); Vron Ware, *Beyond the Pale: White Women, Racism and History* (London: Verso, 1992); Louise Newman, *White Women's Rights: The Racial Origins of Feminism in the United States* (New York: Oxford University Press, 1999); Aida Hurtado, "The Trickster's Play: Whiteness in the Subordination and Liberation Process," in Rodolfo D. Torres, Louis F. Mirón, and Jonathan Xavier Inda, eds., *Race, Identity and Citizenship: A Reader* (Maiden, MA: Blackwell, 1999), 229–36; Linda Martin Alcoff, "What Should White People Do?" *Hypatia* 13 (Summer 1998), 11–12.

42   Theodore W. Allen, *The Invention of the White Race*, 2 vols. (New York and London: Verso, 1994 and 1997); Saxton, *Rise and Fall of the White Republic*; Ian Haney Lopez, *White by Law: The Legal Construction of Race* (New York and London: New York University Press, 1996).

43   Paul Gilroy, *The Black Atlantic: Modernity and Double Consciousness* (Cambridge, MA: Harvard University Press, 1993), 174–75; bell books, *Black Looks: Race and Representation* (Boston: South End Press, 1992.), 172; Ralph Ellison, "A Party Down at the Square," in John E. Callahan, ed., *Flying Home and Other Stories* (New York: Random House, 1996), 3–11 Anzaldúa, *Borderlands/La Frontera*, 134–3; Roediger, ed., *Black on White*, 318–49.

44   Gordon, *Bad Faith and Antiblack Racism*; Trudier Harris, *Exorcising Blackness: Historical and Literary Lynching and Burning Rituals* (Bloomington: Indiana University Press, 1984); Robyn Wiegman, *American Anatomies: Theorizing Race and Gender* (Durham and London: Duke University Press, 1995); Grace Elizabeth Hale, *Making Whiteness: The Culture of Segregation in the South, 1890–1940* (New York: Pantheon, 1998); Nell Irvin Painter, "Soul Murder and Slavery: Toward a Fully Loaded Cost Accounting," in Linda K. Kerber, Alice Kessler Harris, and Kathryn Kish Sklas eds., *U.S. History as Women's History: New Feminist Essays* (Chapel Hill and London: University of North Carolina Press, 1995), 115–46.

45   Cheryl Harris, "Whiteness as Property," 1710–91; Linda Lopez McAlister; "My Grandmother's Passing," and Linda M. Pierce, "Pinay White Woman," both in Chris J. Cuomo and Kim Q. Hall, eds., *Whiteness*, 15–27 and 45–52; George Lipsitz, *The Possessive Investment in Whiteness: How White People Profit from Identity Politics* (Philadelphia: Temple University Press, 1998), 1–23; Martha R. Mahoney, "Segregation, Whiteness, and Transformation," *University of Pennsylvania Law Review* 143 (1995); 1659–840.

46   Matt Wray and Annalee Newitz, *White Trash: Race and Class in America* (New York and London: Routledge, 1997). The most telling discussion of "poor whites" remains Ralph Ellison, "An Extravagance of Laughter," in *Going to the Territory*, 145–97. "Propertyless" whiteness is from Mike Hill's "Can Whiteness Speak?" in *White Trash*, 160. See also John Hartigan's provocative *Racial Situations: Class Predicaments of Whiteness in Detroit* (Princeton: Princeton University Press, 1999).

Chapter 37

Kimberlé Williams Crenshaw

RACE, REFORM, AND RETRENCHMENT
Transformation and legitimation in antidiscrimination law

[. . .]

IN 1984, PRESIDENT RONALD REAGAN signed a bill that created the Martin Luther King, Jr. Federal Holiday Commission.[1] The commission was charged with the responsibility of issuing guidelines for states and localities to follow in preparing their observances of King's birthday. The commission's task would not be easy. Although King's birthday had come to symbolize the massive social movement that grew out of African-Americans' efforts to end the long history of racial oppression in America,[2] the first official observance of the holiday would take place in the face of at least two disturbing obstacles: first, a constant, if not increasing, socioeconomic disparity between the races,[3] and second, a hostile administration devoted to changing the path of civil rights reforms which many believe responsible for most of the movement's progress.[4]

The commission, though, was presented with a more essential difficulty: a focus on the continuing disparities between blacks and whites might call not for celebration but for strident criticism of America's failure to make good on its promise of racial equality. Yet such criticism would overlook the progress that has been made, progress that the holiday itself represents. The commission apparently resolved this dilemma by calling for a celebration of progress toward racial equality while urging continued commitment to this ideal. This effort to reconcile the celebration of an ideal with conditions that bespeak its continuing denial was given the ironic, but altogether appropriate title "Living the Dream."[5] The "Living the Dream" directive aptly illustrates Derrick Bell's observation that "[m]ost Americans, black and white, view the civil rights crusade as a long, slow, but always upward pull that must, given the basic precepts of the country and the commitment of its people to equality and liberty, eventually end in the full enjoyment by blacks of all rights and privileges of citizenship enjoyed by whites."[6]

[. . .] Throughout American history, the subordination of blacks was rationalized by a series of stereotypes and beliefs that made their conditions appear logical and natural. Historically, white supremacy has been premised upon various political, scientific, and religious theories, each of which relies on racial characterizations and stereotypes about blacks which have coalesced into an extensive legitimating ideology. Today, it is probably not controversial to say that these stereotypes were developed primarily to rationalize the oppression of blacks. What is overlooked, however, is the extent to which these stereotypes serve a hegemonic function by perpetuating a mythology about both blacks and whites even today, reinforcing an illusion of a white community that cuts across ethnic, gender, and class lines.

[. . .] Racism does not support the dominant order simply because all whites want to maintain their privilege at the expense of blacks, or because blacks sometimes serve as convenient political scapegoats; rather, the very existence of a clearly subordinated Other group is contrasted with the norm in a way that reinforces identification with the dominant group. Racism helps to create an illusion of unity through the oppositional force of a symbolic "other."[7] The establishment of an Other creates a bond, a burgeoning common identity of all nonstigmatized parties – whose identity and interests are defined in opposition to the other.

According to the philosophy of Jacques Derrida, a structure of polarized categories is characteristic of Western thought:

> Western thought . . . has always been structured in terms of dichotomies or polarities: good vs. evil, being vs. nothingness, presence vs. absence, truth vs. error, identity vs. difference, mind vs. matter, man vs. woman, soul vs. body, life vs. death, nature vs. culture, speech vs. writing. These polar opposite do not, however, stand as independent and equal entities. The second term in each pair is considered the negative, corrupt, undesirable version of the first, a fall away from it. . . . In other words, the two terms are not simply opposed in their meanings, but are arranged in a hierarchical order which gives the first term priority. . . .[8]

Racist ideology replicates this pattern of arranging oppositional categories in a hierarchical order; historically, whites have represented the dominant element in the antinomy, while blacks came to be seen as separate and subordinate. This hierarchy is reflected in the list on p. 551; note how each traditional negative image of blacks correlates with a counterimage of whites (see Table).

The oppositional dynamic exemplified in this list was created and maintained through an elaborate and systematic process. Laws and customs helped to create "races" out of a broad range of human traits. In the process of creating races, the categories came to be filled with meaning: whites were characterized one way and associated with normatively positive characteristics, whereas blacks were characterized another way and became associated with the subordinate, even aberrational characteristics. The operation of this dynamic, along with the important political role of racial oppositionalism, can be illustrated through a few brief historical references.

Edmund Morgan provides vivid illustration of how slaveholders from the seventeenth century onward created and politicized racial categories in order to maintain the support of nonslaveholding whites. Morgan recounts how the planters "lump[ed] Indians, mulattoes, and Negroes in a single slave class," and how these categories became "an essential, if unacknowledged, ingredient of the republican ideology that enabled Virginians to lead the nation."[9] Having accepted a common interest with slaveholders in keeping blacks subordinated, even those whites who had material reasons to object to the dominance of the slaveholding class could challenge the regime only so far. The power of race-consciousness convinced whites to support a system that was opposed to their own economic interests. As George Fredrickson put it, "racial privilege could and did serve as a compensation for class disadvantage."[10]

Domination through race-consciousness continued throughout the post-Reconstruction period. Historian C. Vann Woodward has argued that the ruling plantocracy was able to undermine the progressive accomplishments of the Populist movement by stirring up antiblack sentiment among poor whites farmers; racism was articulated as the "broader ground for a new democracy."[11] As racism formed the new base for a broader notion of democracy, class differences were mediated through reference to a racial community of equality.[12] A tragic example of the success of such race-conscious political manipulation is the career of Tom Watson, the leader of the progressive Populist movement of the 1890s. Watson, in his attempts to educate the masses of poor farmers about the destructive role of race-based politics, repeatedly told black and white audiences: "You are made to hate each other because upon that hatred is rested the keystone of the arch of financial despotism which enslaves you both. You are deceived and blinded that you may not see how this race antagonism perpetuates a monetary system which beggars you both."[13] Yet by 1906, Watson had joined the movement to disenfranchise blacks; according to Woodward, Watson had "persuaded himself that only after the Negro was eliminated from politics could Populist principles gain a hearing. In other words, the white men would have to unite before they could divide."[14]

White race-consciousness also played a role in the nascent labor movement in the North. Labor historian Herbert Hill has demonstrated that unions of virtually all trades excluded black workers from their ranks and often entirely barred black employment in certain fields. Immigrant labor unions were particularly adamant about

Historical oppositional dualities

WHITE IMAGES	BLACK IMAGES
industrious	lazy
intelligent	unintelligent
moral	immoral
knowledgeable	ignorant
enabling culture	disabling culture
law-abiding	criminal
responsible	shiftless
virtuous/pious	lascivious

keeping out black workers; indeed, it was precisely in order to assimilate into the American mainstream that immigrant laborers adopted these exclusionary policies.[15]

The political and ideological role that race-consciousness continues to play is suggested by racial polarization in contemporary presidential politics. Several political commentators have suggested that many whites supported Ronald Reagan in the belief that he would correct a perceived policy imbalance that unjustly benefited blacks, and some argue further that Reagan made a direct racist appeal to white voters. . . . Reagan received nearly 70 percent of the white vote, whereas 90 percent of black voters cast their ballots for Mondale. Similarly, the vast majority of blacks – 82 percent – disapproved of Reagan's performance, whereas only 32 percent of whites did.

Even the Democratic party, which has traditionally relied on blacks as its most loyal constituency, has responded to this apparent racial polarization by seeking to distance itself from black interests. Although some have argued that the racial polarization demonstrated in the 1984 election does not represent a trend of white defections from the Democratic party, it is significant that, whatever the cause of the party's inability to attract white votes, Democratic leaders have expressed a willingness to moderate the party's stand on key racial issues in an effort to recapture the white vote.[16]

[. . .] Prior to the civil rights reforms, blacks were formally subordinated by the state. Blacks experienced being the "other" in two aspects of oppression, which I shall designate as symbolic and material.[17] Symbolic subordination refers to the formal denial of social and political equality to all blacks, regardless of their accomplishments. Segregation and other forms of social exclusion – separate restrooms, drinking fountains, entrances, parks, cemeteries, and dining facilities – reinforced a racist ideology that blacks were simply inferior to whites and were therefore not included in the vision of America as a community of equals.

Material subordination, on the other hand, refers to the ways that discrimination and exclusion economically subordinated blacks to whites and subordinated the life chances of blacks to those of whites on almost every level. This subordination occurs when blacks are paid less for the same work, when segregation limits access to decent housing, and where poverty, anxiety, poor health care, and crime create a life expectancy for blacks that is five to six years shorter than for whites.

Symbolic subordination often created material disadvantage by reinforcing race-consciousness in everything from employment to education. In fact, symbolic and material subordination were generally not thought of separately: separate facilities were usually inferior facilities, and limited job categorization almost invariably brought lower pay and harder work. Despite the pervasiveness of racism, however, there existed even before the civil rights movement a class of blacks who were educationally, economically, and professionally equal – if not superior – to many whites; yet even these blacks suffered social and political exclusion as well.

It is also significant that not all separation resulted in inferior institutions. School segregation – although often presented as the epitome of symbolic and material subordination – did not always bring about inferior education. It is not separation per se that made segregation subordinating; rather, this result is more properly attributable to the fact that it was enforced and supported by state power, and accompanied by the explicit belief in African-American inferiority.[18]

The response to the civil rights movement was the removal of most formal barriers and symbolic manifestations of subordination. Thus, "whites only" notices and other obvious indicators of the social policy of racial subordination disappeared – at least in the public sphere. The disappearance of these symbols of subordination reflected the acceptance of the rhetoric of formal equality, signaling the demise of white supremacy rhetoric as expressing America's normative vision. In other words, it could no longer be said that blacks were not included as equals in the American political vision.

Removal of these public manifestations of subordination was a significant gain for all blacks, although some benefited more than others. The eradication of formal barriers meant more to those whose oppression was primarily symbolic than to those who suffered lasting material disadvantage. Yet despite these disparate results, it would be absurd to suggest that no benefits came from these formal reforms, especially in regard to racial policies, such as segregation, that were partly material but largely symbolic. Thus, to say that the reforms were "merely symbolic" is to say a great deal: these legal reforms and the formal extension of "citizenship" were large achievements precisely because much of what characterized black oppression was symbolic and formal.

Yet the attainment of formal equality is not the end of the story. Racial hierarchy cannot be cured by the move to facial race-neutrality in the laws that structure the economic, political, and social lives of black people. White race-consciousness, in a new but nonetheless virulent form, plays an important, perhaps crucial, role in the new regime that has legitimated the deteriorating day-to-day material conditions of the majority of blacks.

The end of Jim Crow has been accompanied by the demise of an explicit ideology of white supremacy. The white norm, however, has not disappeared; it has only been submerged in popular consciousness. It continues in an unspoken form as a statement of the positive social norm, legitimating the continuing domination of those who do not meet it. Nor have the negative stereotypes associated with blacks been eradicated. The rationalizations once used to legitimate black subordination based on a belief in racial inferiority have now been reemployed to legitimate the domination of blacks through reference to an assumed cultural inferiority.

Thomas Sowell, for example, suggests that underclass blacks are economically depressed because they have not adopted the values of hard work and discipline. He further implies that blacks have not pursued the need to attain skills and marketable education, and have not learned to make the sacrifices necessary for success. Instead, he charges, blacks view demands for special treatment as a means for achieving what other groups have achieved through hard work and the abandonment of racial politics.

Sowell applies the same stereotypes to the mass of blacks that white supremacists had applied in the past, but bases these modern stereotypes on notions of "culture" rather than genetics. Sowell characterizes underclass blacks as victims of self-imposed ignorance, lack of direction, and poor work attitudes: culture, not race, now accounts for this Otherness. Except for vestigial pockets of historical racism, any possible connection between past racial subordination and the present situation has been severed by the formal repudiation of the old race-conscious policies. The same dualities that historically have been used to legitimate racial subordination in the name of genetic inferiority have now been adopted by Sowell as a means for explaining the subordinated status of blacks today in terms of cultural inferiority.[19]

Moreover, Sowell's explanation of blacks' subordinated status also illustrates the treatment of the now-unspoken white stereotypes as the positive social norm. His assertion that the absence of certain attributes accounts for the continued subordination of blacks implies that it is the presence of these attributes that explains the continued advantage of whites. The only difference between this argument and the older oppositional dynamic is this: whereas the latter explained black subordination through reference to the ideology of white supremacy, the former explains black subordination through reference to an unspoken social norm. That norm – although no longer explicitly white supremacist – nevertheless, remains a white norm.

White race-consciousness, which includes the modern belief in cultural inferiority, furthers black subordination by justifying all the forms of unofficial racial discrimination, injury, and neglect that flourish in a society only formally dedicated to equality. Indeed, in ways more subtle, white race-consciousness reinforces and is reinforced by the myth of equal opportunity which explains and justifies broader class hierarchies.

Race-consciousness also reinforces whites' sense that American society truly is meritocratic, and thus it helps to prevent them from questioning the basic legitimacy of the free market. Believing both that blacks are inferior and that the economy impartially rewards the superior over the inferior, whites see that most blacks are indeed worse off than whites are, which reinforces their sense that the market is operating "fairly and impartially"; those who logically should be on the bottom are on the bottom. This strengthening of whites' belief in the system in turn reinforces their beliefs that blacks are indeed inferior. After all, equal opportunity is the rule, and the market is an impartial judge; if blacks are on the bottom, it must reflect their relative inferiority. Racist ideology thus operates in conjunction with the class components of legal ideology to reinforce the status quo, both in terms of class and race.

To bring a fundamental challenge to the way things are, whites would have to question not just their own subordinate status but also both the economic and the racial myths that justify the status quo. Racism, combined with equal opportunity mythology, provides a rationalization for racial oppression, making it difficult for whites to see the black situation as illegitimate or unnecessary. If whites believe that blacks, because they are unambitious or inferior, get what they deserve, it becomes that much harder to convince whites that something is wrong with the entire system. Similarly, a challenge to the legitimacy of continued racial inequality would force whites to confront myths about equality of opportunity which justify for them whatever measure of economic success they may have attained.

[. . .] Rights discourse provided the ideological mechanisms through which the conflicts of federalism, the power of the presidency, and the legitimacy of the courts could be orchestrated against Jim Crow. Movement leaders used these tactics to force open a conflict between whites, which eventually benefited black people. Casting racial issues in the moral and legal rights rhetoric of the prevailing ideology helped to create the political controversy without which the state's coercive function would not have been enlisted to aid blacks.

Merely critiquing the ideology from without or making demands in language outside the rights discourse would have accomplished little. Rather, blacks gained by using a powerful combination of direct action, mass protest, and individual acts of resistance, along with appeals, both to public opinion and to the court, that were couched in the language of the prevailing legal consciousness. The result was a series of ideological and political crises in which civil rights activists and lawyers induced the federal government to aid blacks and triggered efforts to legitimate and reinforce the authority of the law in ways that benefited blacks. Merely insisting that blacks be integrated or speaking in the language of "needs" would have endangered the lives of those who were already taking risks – and with no reasonable chance of success. President Eisenhower, for example, would not have sent federal troops to Little Rock simply at the behest of protesters demanding that black schoolchildren receive an equal education. Instead, the successful manipulation of legal rhetoric led to a crisis of federal power that ultimately benefited blacks.

Some critics of legal reform movements seem to overlook the fact that state power has made a significant difference – sometimes between life and death – in the efforts of black people to transform their world. Attempts to harness the power of the state through the appropriate rhetorical and legal incantations should be appreciated as intensely powerful and calculated political acts. In the context of white supremacy, engaging in rights discourse should be seen as an act of self-defense. This was particularly true once the movement had mobilized people to challenge the system of oppression, because the state could not assume a position of neutrality regarding black people; either the coercive mechanism of the state had to be used to support white supremacy, or it had to be used to dismantle it. We know now, with hindsight, that it did both.[20]

Blacks did use rights rhetoric to mobilize state power to their benefit against symbolic oppression through formal inequality and, to some extent, against material deprivation in the form of private, informal exclusion of the middle class from jobs and housing. Yet today the same legal reforms play a role in providing an ideological framework that makes the present conditions facing underclass blacks appear fair and reasonable. However, the eradication of barriers has created a new dilemma for those victims of racial oppression who are not in a position to benefit from the move to formal equality. The race neutrality of the legal system creates the illusion that racism is no longer the primary factor responsible for the condition of the black underclass; instead, as we have seen, class disparities appear to be the consequence of individual and group merit within a supposed system of equal opportunity. Moreover, the fact that some blacks are economically successful gives credence both to the assertion that opportunities exist and to the backlash attitude that blacks have "gotten too far." Psychologically, for blacks who have not made it, the lack of an explanation for their underclass status may result in self-blame and other self-destructive attitudes.

Another consequence of the formal reforms may be the loss of collectivity among blacks. The removal of formal barriers created new opportunities for some blacks which were not shared by various other classes of African-Americans; as blacks moved into different spheres, the experience of being black in America became fragmented and multifaceted, and the different contexts presented opportunities to experience racism in different ways. The social, economic, and even residential distance between the various classes may complicate efforts to unite behind issues as a racial group. Although "whites only" signs may have been crude and debilitating, they at least presented a readily discernible target around which to organize. Now, the targets are obscure and diffuse, and this difference may create doubt among some blacks as to whether there is enough similarity between their own life experiences and those of other blacks to warrant collective political action.

Formal equality significantly transformed the black experience in America. With society's embrace of formal equality came the eradication of symbolic domination and the suppression of white supremacy as the norm of society. Future generations of black Americans would no longer be explicitly regarded as America's second-class citizens. Yet the transformation of the oppositional dynamic – achieved through the suppression of racial norms and stereotypes, and the recasting of racial inferiority into assumptions of cultural inferiority – creates several difficulties for the civil rights constituency. The removal of formal barriers, although symbolically significant to all and materially significant to some, will do little to alter the hierarchical relationship between blacks and whites until the way in which white race-consciousness perpetuates norms that legitimate black subordination is revealed. This is not to say that white norms alone account for the conditions of the black underclass; it is, instead, an acknowledgement that until the distinct racial nature of class ideology is itself revealed and debunked, nothing can be done about the underlying structural problems that account for the disparities. The narrow focus of racial exclusion – that is, the belief that racial exclusion is illegitimate only where the "whites only" signs are explicit – coupled with strong assumptions about equal opportunity, makes it difficult to move the discussion of racism beyond the societal self-satisfaction engendered by the appearance of neutral norms and formal inclusion.

[. . .] For blacks, the task at hand is to devise ways to wage ideological and political struggle while minimizing the costs of engaging in an inherently legitimating discourse. A clearer understanding of the space we occupy in the American political consciousness is a necessary prerequisite to the development of pragmatic strategies for political and economic survival. In this regard, the most serious challenge for blacks is to minimize the political and cultural cost of engaging in an inevitably co-optive process in order to secure material benefits. Because our present predicament gives us few options, we must create conditions for the maintenance of a distinct political thought that is informed by the actual conditions of black people. Unlike the civil rights vision, this new approach should not be defined and thereby limited by the possibilities of dominant political discourse; rather, it should maintain a distinctly progressive outlook that focuses on the needs of the African-American community.

Notes and references

1   Act of Aug. 27, 1984, Pub. L. No. 98–399, 98 Stat. 1473. President Reagan's signing is reported in 20 *Weekly Comp. Pres. Doc.* 1192 (Sept. 3, 1984).

2   I shall use "African-American" and "black" interchangeably. . . . The naming of Americans of African descent has had political overtones throughout history. See W. E. B. Du Bois, 2 *The Seventh Son*, 12–13 (1971) (arguing that the "N" in Negro was always capitalized until, in defense of slavery, the use of the lower case "N" became the custom in "recognition" of Blacks' status as property; that the usage was defended as a "description of the color of a people"; and that the capitalization of other ethnic and national origin designations made the failure to capitalize "Negro" an insult). "African-American" is now preferred by some because it is both culturally more specific and historically more expansive than the traditional terms that narrowly categorize us as America's Other. . . .

3   Continuing disparities exist between African-Americans and whites in virtually every measurable category. In 1986, the African-American poverty rate stood at 31 percent, compared with 11 percent for whites; see Williams, "Urban League Says Blacks Suffered Loss over Decade," *New York Times*, Jan. 15, 1988, A10:1. "[B]lack median income is 57 percent that of whites, a decline of about four percentage points since the early 1970's"; Bernstein, "20 Years After the Kerner Report: Three Societies, All Separate," *New York Times*, Feb. 29, 1988, B8:2. Between 1981 and 1985, black unemployment averaged 17 percent, compared to 7.3 percent for whites; see National Urban League, *The State of Black America 1986*, 15 (1986). In 1986, approximately 44 percent of all black children lived in poverty; see Lauter and May, "A Saga of Triumph, a Return to Poverty: Black Middle Class Has Grown but Poor Multiply," *Los Angeles Times*, April 2, 1988, 1. 16:1. Blacks comprise 60 percent of the urban underclass in the United States; *id.* at 16:3.

The African-American socioeconomic position in American society has actually declined in the last two decades. Average annual family income for African-Americans dropped 9 percent from the seventies to the eighties, see Williams, *supra*, A10:1. Since 1969, the proportion of black men between 25 and 55 earning less than $5000 a year rose from 8 to 20 percent, see Lauter and May, *supra*. African-American enrollment in universities and colleges is also on the decline; see Williams, *supra*, A10:2.

The decline in the African-American socioeconomic position has been paralleled by an increase in overt racial hostility. See generally U.S. Commission on Civil Rights, *Intimidation and Violence: Racial and Religious Bigotry in America* (1983). In addition to well-publicized incidents of racial violence like the Howard Beach attack . . . and the lynching of Michael Donald, . . . racial unrest has risen dramatically on university campuses; see Wilkerson, "Campus Blacks Feel Racism's Nuances," *New York Times*, April 17, 1988, 1.1:3.

For a comprehensive analysis of the conditions afflicting the black urban underclass, see W. Wilson, *The Truly Disadvantaged: The Inner City, the Underclass, and Public Policy* (1987).

4   The principal civil rights reforms are the Civil Rights Act of 1964, Pub. L. No. 88–352,. 78 Stat. 243 (codified as amended at 42 U.S.C. ss 2000(e)–2000(h)(6) (1982)); the Voting Rights Act of 1965, Pub. L. No. 89–110, 79 Stat. 437 (codified as amended at 42 U.S.C. ss 1971–1974 (1982)); U.S/CONST. amends. XIII–XV; 42 U.S.C. ss 1981, 1983, 1985 (1982); Exec. Order No. 11,246, 3 C.F.R. 339 (1964–1965 comp.); and the Equal Employment Opportunity Commission regulations, 29 C.F.R. ss 1600–1691 (1987).

See ACLU, *In Contempt of Congress and the Courts – The Reagan Civil Rights Record* (1984); Chambers, "Racial Justice in the 1980's," 8 *Campbell L. Rev.*, 29, 31–34 (1985); Devins, "Closing the Classroom Door to Civil Rights," 11 *Hum. Rts.*, 26 (1984); Selig, "The Reagan Justice Department and Civil Rights: What Went Wrong," 1985 *U. Ill. L. Rev.*, 785; Wolvovitz and Lobel, "The Enforcement of Civil Rights Statutes: The Reagan Administration's Record," 9 *Black L.J.*, 252 (1986); see also Hernandez, Weiss, and Smith, "How Different Is the World of 1984 from the World of 1964?," 37 *Rutgers L. Rev.*, 755, 757–60 (1985).

Some scholars have been critical of the overall development of civil rights law over the past decade, positing that we have reached the end of the "Second Reconstruction"; see generally D. Bell, *And We Are Not Saved* (1987); Bell, "The Supreme Court, 1984 Term – Foreword: The Civil Rights Chronicles," 99 *Harv. L. Rev.*, 4 (1985).

5   Martin Luther King, Jr., Federal Holiday Commission, *Living the Dream* (1986).
6   D. Bell, *Race, Racism and American Law* (2nd ed. 1981).
7   The notion of blacks as a subordinated Other in Western culture has been a major theme in scholarship exploring the cultural and sociological structure of racism. See Trost, "Western Metaphysical Dualism as an Element in Racism," in J. Hodge, D. Struckmann, and L. Trost, eds., *Cultural Bases of Racism and Group Oppression* 49 (1975) (arguing that black and white are seen as paired antinomies, and that there is a hierarchy within the antimonies, with Caucasians and Western culture constituting the preferred or higher antinomy). Frantz Fanon has summarized the attitude of the West toward blackness as a projection of Western anxiety concerning the Other in terms of skin color: "In Europe, the black man is the symbol of Evil. . . . The torturer is the black man, Satan is black, one talks of shadow, when one is dirty one is black – whether one is thinking of physical dirtiness or moral dirtiness. It would be astonishing, if the trouble were taken to bring them all together, to see the vast number of expressions that make the black man the equivalent of sin. In Europe, whether concretely or symbolically, the black man stands for the bad side of the character. As long as one cannot understand this fact one is doomed to talk in circles about the 'black problem.' Blackness, darkness, shadow, shades, night, the labyrinths of the earth, abysmal depths, blacken someone's reputation; and on the other side, the bright look of innocence, the white dove of peace, magical, heavenly light"; F. Fanon, *Black Skins, White Masks*, 188–89 (1967); see S. Gilman, *Difference and Pathology: Stereotypes of Sexuality, Race, and Sadness*, 30 (1985) (arguing that the notion that "blacks are the antithesis of the mirage of whiteness, the ideal of European aesthetic values, strikes the reader as an extension of some 'real,' perceived difference to which the qualities of 'good' and 'bad' have been erroneously applied. But the very concept of color is a quality of Otherness, not of reality."); Isaacs, "Blackness and Whiteness," *Encounter*, 8 (Aug. 1963); see also W. Jordan, *White Over Black: American Attitudes Toward the Negro, 1650–1712* (1968) (discussing how sixteenth- and seventeenth-century English writers used the concept that blacks were the Europeans' polar opposites in order to establish an elaborate hierarchy to classify other colored people in the world). Others who have used the concept of Otherness as a framework for examining black/white relations include C. Degler, *Neither Black Nor White: Slavery and Race Relations in Brazil and The United States* (1971), and Copeland, "The Negro as a Contrast

Conception," in E. Thompson, ed., *Race Relations and the Race Problem: A Definition and An Analysis*, 152–79 (1939).

8   J. Derrida, *Dissemination*, viii, trans. B. Johnson (1981) (emphasis is original).

9   E. Morgan, *American Slavery – American Freedom*, 386 (1975).

10   G. Fredrickson, *White Supremacy: A Comparative Study in American and South African History*, (1981).

11   C. Vann Woodward, *The Strange Career of Jim Crow*, 76 (1958).

12   One might argue that the fact that many poor whites were simultaneously disenfranchised cuts against the idea that racist ideology was the glue that organized and held whites together across class lines. In reality, the ability to exclude lower-class whites was achieved politically, via racist rhetoric.

13   *Id.* at 44–45.

14   *Id.* at 73–74.

15   "The historical record reveals that the embrace of white supremacy as ideology and as practice was a strategy for assimilation by European working class immigrants, the white ethnics who were to constitute a major part of the membership and leadership of organized labor in the United States"; . . . Hill, "Race and Ethnicity in Organized Labor: The Historical Sources of Restrictions to Affirmative Action," *J. Intergroup Rel.*, 6 (winter 1984). Even today, unions that are supposed to represent the "consciousness of the working class" often still fail to represent the interests of the black American worker. For an account of the racist history of the AFL-CIO, see Hill, "The AFL-CIO and the Black Worker: Twenty-Five Years After the Merger," *J. Intergroup Rel.*, 5 (Sept. 1982).

16   This effort to minimize black influence reflects what Derrick Bell, Jr., has called the principle of "involuntary sacrifice"; see D. Bell, *Race, Racism, and American Law*, U 1.8, at 29–30. . . . Bell asserts that throughout American history, Black interests have been sacrificed when necessary to reestablish the bonds of the white community, "so that identifiably different groups of whites may settle a dispute and establish or reestablish their relationship"; *id.* at 30.

17   These two manifestations of racial subordination are not mutually exclusive. In fact, it only makes sense to separate various aspects of racial oppression in this post-civil rights era in order to understand how the movement changed some social norms and reinforced others. Most blacks probably did not experience or perceive their oppression as reflecting two separate structures.

18   Socially, many blacks lived in a society comparable in many ways to that of the white elites. Hardly strangers to debutante balls, country clubs, and vacations abroad, these blacks lived lives of which many whites only dreamed. Nevertheless, despite their material wealth, upper-middle-class blacks were still members of a subordinated group. Where rights and privileges were distributed on the basis of race, even a distinguished African-American had to take a back seat to each white – no matter how poor, ignorant, or uneducated the white might be.

19   Sowell exemplifies what may be the worst development of the civil rights movement – that some blacks who have benefited the most from the formal gestures of equality now identify with those who attempt to affirm the legitimacy of oppressing other blacks. Clearly, this legitimation and desertion by some blacks has been politically damaging and may undermine future efforts to organize.

20   Consider, for example, the possible police responses to students who violated local ordinances by sitting in at segregated lunch counters and demanding service. Government officials could have ordered the students arrested, thereby upholding

the segregation policy, or they could have ignored them, which would have incidentally supported the students' efforts. Both tactics were followed throughout the course of the movement. Because officials sometimes had a degree of choice in the matter, and courts had the ultimate power to review the legitimacy of the laws and the officials' actions, black protesters' use of rights rhetoric can be seen as an effort to defend themselves against arrest or conviction for violating the norms of white supremacy.

Chapter 38

Stephen Steinberg

AMERICA AGAIN AT
THE CROSSROADS

W HEN THIS NATION'S FOUNDING FATHERS betrayed the noble principles enshrined in the Declaration of Independence and the Constitution, and surrendered to temptation and greed by sanctioning the slave trade, they placed the nation on a calamitous path of racial division and conflict that continues down to the present. Yet the thirteen decades since the abolition of slavery are littered with lost opportunities – golden moments when the nation could have severed this historical chain, but either failed to do so or did not go far enough in eradicating the legacy of slavery.

The first lost opportunity, of course, was the failure of Reconstruction. The Thirteenth, Fourteenth, and Fifteenth Amendments to the Constitution elevated blacks to full citizenship, and ushered in a period of biracial democracy in which blacks voted, held office, and, despite a general pattern of social segregation, enjoyed a modicum of civil equality.[1] However, these gains were tenuous and short-lived. As W.E.B. Du Bois wrote in his 1935 study *Black Reconstruction in America*: "The slave went free; stood a brief moment in the sun; then moved back again toward slavery."[2]

Had the promise of Reconstruction been kept, then this would have obviated the need for a civil rights revolution a century later. Nor can blame for the failure of Reconstruction be placed wholly on the South. As Neil McMillen writes in his history of Jim Crow in Mississippi: "Without the ready acquiescence of northern white sentiment, the national Republican party, and the three branches of the federal government, blacks could not have been driven from politics in any state."[3] Indeed, Northern acquiescence to black disfranchisement persisted until 1965, when Congress, under unrelenting pressure from the black protest movement, passed the Voting Rights Act. During the preceding century, however, even anti-lynching legislation was beyond the pale of political possibility.

The failure of Reconstruction goes beyond the subversion of the Reconstruction amendments. After two centuries of slavery, the bestowal of political rights on blacks scarcely began to address the needs of an expropriated people. Genuine reconstruction would have included a massive redistribution of land, as envisioned by a few "radical" Republicans. Not only would this have placed freedmen on a path toward self-sufficiency, but it also would have secured their newly won political rights as well. As Thaddeus Stevens commented when he submitted his proposal for a land redistribution to Congress in 1865: "How can republican institutions, free schools, free churches, free social intercourse exist in a mingled community of nabobs and serfs?"[4]

Indeed, "forty acres and a mule" epitomized the dream of blacks at the end of the Civil War. This was a dream unfulfilled, however. The legislation establishing the Freedmen's Bureau in March 1865 had provided for the distribution of land confiscated from Confederate soldiers and their supporters, but within months President Johnson ordered that the land be returned to its former owners. Most blacks ended up working as sharecroppers or tenant farmers, a system that amounted to a form of debt servitude that restricted the freedoms of workers and kept them tied to the land. As Myrdal lamented in *An American Dilemma*: "The story of the Negro in agriculture would have been a rather different one if the Negro farmer had greater opportunity to establish himself as an independent owner."[5]

The subjugation of the South's black population was so complete that we can only imagine how the course of race history might have been altered if white America had delivered on the promise of "forty acres and a mule." One historical example provides a glimpse into the future that never was: the so-called "exoduster movement." This involved a migration of tens of thousands of Southern blacks to Kansas in the spring of 1879. Kansas was only one of a number of emigration schemes that were explored by blacks desperate to escape the tightening noose of racial oppression. Emissaries had gone as far away as Haiti, Canada, and even Liberia. Kansas emerged as an option because it was in need of settlers, and the abolitionist Republicans who ruled the state accepted blacks on a parity with whites.[6] Word of "cheap land in Kansas" spread like wildfire throughout the South, with the help of blacks working on steamboats and railroads.

As the migration gained momentum, it assumed messianic overtones. Migrants, who were called "exodusters," saw themselves as fleeing Egypt for the Promised Land. The leader of the movement, "Pap" Singleton, was dubbed the Father of the Exodus and the Moses of the Colored People. In some respects the story parallels the one told by Leon Uris in *Exodus*. The land available for black settlement had been passed over during the westward migration because of the dearth of water. Lacking trees and shelter, settlers were forced to live in dugouts gouged out of the arid soil. Many gave up in frustration and resumed their northward migration. However, several "colonies" were established that eventually developed into flourishing agricultural communities, replete with churches, newspapers, hotels, businesses, and all of the other accouterments and amenities of a Midwestern town.

Like the rest of rural America, the black towns were hard hit by the Depression and the Dust Bowl, and most of the residents dispersed to cities in the North and West. However, one community, Nicodemus, still exists, a living symbol of "what might have been" if blacks had been masters of their own destiny.

I stumbled upon Nicodemus in 1975 while doing research on the impact of European immigration on African Americans. The research began with the naive question: why did so few blacks migrate to the Northern cities that offered opportunity to millions of immigrants at the turn of the century? The social science literature was of little help. In *An American Dilemma*, for example, Gunnar Myrdal puzzled about why so few blacks migrated to the North and West, conceding that this was "a mystery."[7] Historians, for their part, are so riveted on chronicling "what happened" that they tend to ignore non-events – in this case, the *non-migration* of blacks to the North during this period.[8] Nor in 1975 were there any major studies of the exoduster movement.[9] I found one nugget of information in the Kansas volume of the Federal Writer's Project that described Nicodemus as the "last survivor of Kansas' three colonies settled by the exodusters." I decided to go see for myself.[10]

On my first field trip to Nicodemus I interviewed two women: Hattie Burney and Ola Scruggs Wilson, both octagenarians who had been schoolteachers to generations of Nicodemus's youth. They were repositories of memory, and filled my notebook with stories about life on the prairie where they battled droughts, dust storms, rattlesnakes, and fierce winters; gave birth to children with the help of midwives; and, despite the many privations, cultivated a singular grace and sophistication. Mrs. Burney's eyes filled with tears as she recalled what breakfast was like, with her eight siblings encircling the breakfast table, and the overpowering sense of gratitude that they felt for their father who, despite hardships, had provided them with their daily bread. She also loaned me a manuscript that her father had written late in his life. It was a history of Nicodemus that traced its origins and development, and celebrated its triumph over adversity.

Mrs. Wilson, who prided herself as Nicodemus's historian, rebuffed some of my questions, accusing me of "stealing her thunder." Like all historians, she jealously guarded her sources. But she did tell me about the racism in the surrounding communities, and how Nicodemus was crippled when the decision was made to run the railroad through the neighboring town of Bogue. She also described her mother's joy upon learning of her freedom. I was struck by the ease with which Mrs. Wilson invoked the word "master." For me this word had a cold abstract meaning. But here was a woman, only a generation removed from slavery, for whom the word was replete with deep personal significance. And here I was, conversing with someone whose *mother* had been a slave. It was a chilling reminder of how proximate slavery is to the present.

I returned to Nicodemus a year later for the annual Homecoming. Originally it was called "Emancipation Day," but the event was later redefined as a homecoming. Between four and five hundred descendants return every August for a week of festivities. The community boasts of a judge in Denver, an assistant attorney general in Colorado, and a big-league football player, but aside from these success stories, most of Nicodemus's progeny seem to have "made it" in various walks of life. They returned to Nicodemus in late-model cars, with a sense of pride, both of their shared origins and of their second lives in the diaspora. To be sure, Nicodemus is a historical anomaly, but it signifies "what might have been" – if more blacks had been able to escape the yoke of Southern oppression, if they had been free to own land and develop their own communities, if Reconstruction had not wound up a broken promise.

A second lost opportunity spans the period between 1880 and 1924, the years of the last great wave of European immigration. With the notable exception of Eastern European Jews, these immigrants – like blacks – generally came from peasant origins and had high rates of illiteracy. They were a surplus rural population drawn to America primarily by the prospect of jobs in its burgeoning industries. Between 1880 and 1920 some 24 million immigrants arrived. At the beginning of this period – 1880 – the entire African-American population totaled only 6.6 million, 90 percent of whom lived in the South. Despite the "Great Migration" during the First World War, 85 percent of blacks still lived in the South in 1920. The chief reason so few migrated North should have been obvious. A color line, maintained by employers and workers alike, barred blacks from virtually the entire industrial sector. This simple truth may have eluded Myrdal, but it is clearly enunciated in a 1944 book by an obscure black scholar, John G. Van Deusen, who wrote:

> Regardless of qualifications, most Northern Negroes at this time found themselves forced into domestic and personal service or restricted to odd jobs at unskilled labor. History does not show many peoples who have migrated because of persecution alone. The Negro is not dissimilar to others, and where no economic base was assured, he preferred to endure those ills he had rather than fly to others he knew not of.[11]

In the categorical exclusion of blacks from the industrial work force, the nation missed a unique opportunity to incorporate blacks into the mainstream of the economy at a time when there was rapid growth and a dire shortage of labor. Needless to say, Europe's "wretched refuse" were hardly embraced as racial kin. They, too, were regarded as pariahs, feared and despised for their ethnic peculiarities, and ruthlessly exploited. Nativists of various stripes were determined to make Americans of them. But this is precisely the point: as whites they could be naturalized and assimilated into the body politic. In the final analysis immigration policy and employment practices were predicated on the racist assumption that even the most reprobate Europeans were preferable to African-Americans.

A third lost opportunity came with the Second World War, when powerful forces for racial change were set into motion. On the level of ideology, the war against fascism served as a backlight on America's own racist and fascist tendencies. The contradiction of drafting blacks into a Jim Crow army to fight for American democracy could no longer be patched over, and A. Philip Randolph launched a "double-V campaign," standing for victory abroad *and* at home. Expectations ran high among blacks and whites alike that blacks would be rewarded for their patriotism. With characteristic optimism, Myrdal wrote: "There is bound to be a redefinition of the Negro's status in America as a result of this War."[12]

No less important were the economic and demographic changes wrought by the war. Rapid growth, combined with the mobilization of the armed forces, generated a need for black labor. A million and a half black workers were part of the war-production work force alone, and the income of black workers increased twice as fast as that of whites. The opening up of the Northern labor markets to blacks stimulated the migration of Southern blacks. Between 1940 and 1950 net migration reached an all-time high of 1.6 million.

The ancillary effects of these changes were far-reaching. Blacks developed large and cohesive communities in major Northern cities. Membership in the NAACP mushroomed to 85,000.[13] Northern residence translated into greater political leverage, evident in the fact that black voters provided the margin of victory in the election of Truman in 1948. For the first time blacks consolidated the economic and institutional base from which they could mount resistance to white oppression.[14]

The momentum was quickly blunted, however. The Fair Employment Practices Commission that Roosevelt established during the war in order to forestall Randolph's march on Washington was a feeble organization with a skeletal staff and no enforcement powers. Even so, it was embroiled in controversy from the outset, and after a Southern filibuster in 1946 the agency was dismantled. Here was an early portent that the federal government would not be a champion of black rights during the postwar period. Black soldiers returning home had to accept the bitter fact that victory had been secured on one front only. For African-Americans the return to normalcy – the hallmark of the 1950s – meant a return to second-class citizenship.

The fourth lost opportunity has been the [. . .] failure to follow through on the momentous changes wrung out of white society by the civil rights movement. The passage of civil rights legislation in 1964 and 1965 was a monumental achievement. In securing civil rights for African-Americans, they signified the end to official racism. Of paramount importance, the state of terror, so graphically documented in *An American Dilemma*, was brought to an end. Segregation in public accommodations, long the trademark of the Southern way of life, virtually disappeared. Eventually blacks derived benefits from the franchise, at least in municipalities with a black population majority.[15] After much foot-dragging and circumvention, school desegregation was implemented throughout the South, even more successfully than in the North. By the standard of what preceded it, the post-civil rights era amounted to a great social metamorphosis.

On the other hand, to paraphrase James Baldwin, the crimes of the past cannot be used to gloss over the inequities of the present. The appropriate benchmark for assessing progress is not how much worse things were as we move closer to slavery, but rather, how much blacks continue to lag behind whites in terms of major social indicators. When these comparisons are made, a far less sanguine picture emerges – one of persistent and even widening gaps between blacks and whites in incomes and living standards.[16]

In their totality these four lost opportunities represent the greatest failure of American democracy: to come to terms with the legacy of slavery. Moreover, this failure occurred during the most expansive and prosperous period in its history, the century after slavery when the United States emerged as an industrial monolith, providing opportunity to tens of millions of immigrants, and boasting the highest standard of living in the world. Here, then, is the present conundrum: If the United States failed to come to terms with the legacy of slavery in an era of empire, what can we hope for in an era of decline?

That is to say, if the nation failed to incorporate African-Americans into the economic mainstream during a century marked by overall growth and prosperity, what can we hope for at a time when real wages are declining and the nation's overall level of prosperity and standard of living are undergoing a secular decline? If white America turned a deaf ear to black demands in the halcyon days of "the affluent society," how will it respond in a time of national hand-wringing over "the end of the American dream" and "the fall of the middle class?"[17] What will the nation have to offer African-Americans who were never included in the American dream and who never made it to the middle class?

The answers are becoming painfully obvious. In the first place, the number of blacks below the official poverty line (currently $14,763 for an urban family of four) has steadily *increased* over the past two decades – from 7.5 million in 1970 to 8.6 million in 1980, to 9.8 million in 1990, to 10.9 million in 1993. Today blacks, who are 12 percent of the population, account for 29 percent of the poor, the same proportion as in 1960.[18] Even these figures underestimate the extent to which poverty is concentrated among blacks. Nearly half of all black children under age eighteen are being raised in families below the poverty line, as compared to 16 percent of whites.[19] Poverty among blacks is also far more likely to be long-term. One study devised a measure of "persistent poverty," which applied to households that were below the official poverty level in at least eight of the ten years under examination. It found that persistent poverty was more than seven times as prevalent among urban blacks as among the rest of the urban population.[20] Another recent study found that blacks account for 58 percent of the "severely distressed" in ninety-five major cities.[21]

[. . .] The nation's failure, even at propitious moments in its history, to come to terms with its legacy of slavery has always had regressive implications for race and politics alike. As Eric Foner wrote at the conclusion of *Reconstruction*:

> If racism contributed to the undoing of Reconstruction, by the same token Reconstruction's demise and the emergence of blacks as a disenfranchised class of dependent laborers greatly facilitated racism's further spread, until by the twentieth century it had become more deeply embedded in the nation's culture and politics than at any time since the beginning of the antislavery crusade and perhaps in our entire history. The removal of a significant portion of the nation's laboring population from public life shifted the center of gravity of American politics to the right, complicating the tasks of reformers for generations to come.[22]

In much the same way, the failure of the Second Reconstruction, as the civil rights revolution has been called, to remedy the deep-seated inequalities between blacks and whites has engendered both racism and reaction, each feeding on the other.

This is the context for the recent recrudescence of scientific racism, in the form of Richard Herrnstein and Charles Murray's *The Bell Curve*.[23] This retrograde book represents the apogee of the backlash, the culmination of forces of retreat that have been building for three decades, fueled not only by the agents of racism and reaction, but also by the white liberals and black conservatives who have made the fatal mistake of shifting the focus of blame away from societal institutions onto the individuals and groups who have been cast to the fringes of the social order. As Adolph

Reed has written: "We can trace Murray's legitimacy directly to the spinelessness, opportunism and racial bad faith of the liberals in the social-policy establishment. . . . Many of those objecting to Herrnstein and Murray's racism embrace positions that are almost indistinguishable, except for the resort to biology."[24]

One would think from the extraordinary attention that has been showered on *The Bell Curve* that the book offered something new to the debate over inequality. Notwithstanding all the cybernetics that the authors bring to bear – a daunting array of statistics and graphs – the book's major tenets are only a rarefied version of arguments that began with the development of IQ testing early in this century: that there is a unitary thing called intelligence, that it exists independently of environmental influences and can be accurately measured by conventional IQ tests, that the source of intelligence is in the gene and is therefore a matter of biological inheritance, and that some groups – notably African-Americans – have lower average intelligence and this genetic deficit explains why they occupy the lowest strata of society. Far from new, this timeworn model had long ago been relinquished to the trashbin of history, and perhaps would have remained there if not for the persistence and largess of the Pioneer Fund, an ultrarightist foundation that was founded by eugenicists in the 1930s and has subsidized much of the research that forms the basis for *The Bell Curve*.[25]

The question that needs to be addressed, therefore, is: Why now? What accounts for the book's publication by a major publishing house, and its extraordinary reception in the mass media? *The New York Times Magazine* christened the publication with a cover story under the title "Daring Research or 'Social Science Pornography'?" *Newsweek* and *Time* followed with feature stories. *The New Republic* printed a lengthy excerpt, along with an apologia from the editors explaining why such a reversion to scientific racism should appear on the pages of an ostensibly liberal journal.[26] Thanks to this media blitz, augmented with appearances by Charles Murray on numerous television programs, *The Bell Curve* rapidly climbed to second place on the *New York Times* Best Seller List. Against this background, it behooves us to ask: What is it about this book and the times that make them "right" for each other?

Biological determinism originally fell into disrepute not only because its knowledge-claims were debunked by the emerging social sciences, but also because the prevailing system of social relations was no longer conducive to maintaining a theory that defined social status as immutable and fixed. Notions of biological inferiority had been perfectly tailored to a caste-like society where, in the words of one anthropologist, "everyone is sentenced for life to a social cell shared by others of like birth, separated from and ranked relative to all other social cells."[27] In the twentieth century, however, the forces of industrialization, urbanization, and modernity transformed traditional society, and threw into question the ideological justifications of the old order, including the pseudo-scientific theories that consigned whole groups – racial minorities, women, and the poor – to permanent inferiority. Especially as these groups were elevated in status, it became increasingly difficult to maintain the postulates of biological determinism. To state the obvious, if this nation had followed through on the promise of the civil rights revolution, and enacted the changes that would have established a basic parity between blacks and whites in socioeconomic status and living standards, we would not today be debating whether black subordination is a product of genes.

Clearly, it is the existence of a "permanent underclass" that is sustaining the recrudescence of scientific racism. *The Bell Curve* comes on stream at a time when the American class system has become more static, when poverty is on the increase, when the gap between the haves and have-nots is growing wider, and when many of the middle rungs on the ladder of success have been eliminated, making it more difficult than ever to escape poverty.[28] For the black poor in particular, who must cope with the impediments of race as well as the disabilities of class, their situation is not far removed from one where "everyone is sentenced for life to a social cell shared by others of like birth." The significance of *The Bell Curve* is that it provides ideological justification for this rigidification of class lines. The book is driven by the same ideological agenda as Murray's previous work, *Losing Ground*, which argued that social programs to uplift the poor are futile and even counterproductive, in that they foster a welfare dependency that keeps their beneficiaries trapped in poverty. Thanks to his collaboration with Richard Herrnstein, Murray has added a biological twist to this argument. The underclass is destined by nature to remain on the tail end of the socioeconomic curve. Ameliorative social policy is destined to failure. We can only resign ourselves to the dictates of nature in the name of a perverse multiculturalism.

Yet it would be premature to conclude that *The Bell Curve* represents a decisive shift in the prevailing paradigm. For one thing, an avalanche of criticism was heaped on the book, even before it had been reviewed in scholarly journals. As Adolph Reed has noted, "Even illiberals like Pat Buchanan, John McLaughlin and Rush Limbaugh . . . are eloquently dissenting from Herrnstein and Murray's unsavory racial messages."[29] The same is true of a number of conservatives who participated in a symposium on *The Bell Curve* in *The National Review*.[30] The reason these conservatives do not want "to play the IQ card," as one put it, is not that they have seen the liberal light, but rather that they prefer the neoconservative model that traces inequality to aberrant values rather than defective genes. As far as they are concerned, Murray had it right the first time, and his fling into biology along with Herrnstein threatens to discredit the entire conservative paradigm. Besides, the idea that this is a nation where *everyone* can rise to the top – where people are judged by the content of their character – is the ideological linchpin of the American myth, irreconcilable with Herrnstein and Murray's conception of a Brave New World stratified by the content of one's germ plasm.

In the final analysis, *The Bell Curve* is flourishing on its notoriety, on its petulant flouting of ideas long considered taboo. In this sense the publication of the book, and the wide public discussion that has ensued, represents the triumph of the anti-PC campaign. Nevertheless, there is good reason to think that, like the earlier publications of William Shockley, Arthur Jensen, and Herrnstein himself, *The Bell Curve* is destined to collect layers of merciful dust on our bookshelves.

As Myrdal noted in *An American Dilemma*, periods of racial advance have typically been followed by periods of retreat, though "not as much ground was lost as had been won."[31] Race history, one might say, has observed the pattern of two steps forward and one step back. *The Bell Curve* represents that metaphoric step back. It leaves "America Again at the Crossroads" – the title that Myrdal chose for the concluding chapter of *An American Dilemma*. Indeed, this is the tragedy of history – that half a century later the nation finds itself again at the crossroads, still uncertain whether to take the road back to the benighted past, or to forge a new path leading to a historical reconciliation between the black and white citizens of this nation.

What will it take to move history forward again? Clearly, there is no return to the civil rights movement: it was the product of forces unique to that time, and it fulfilled its chief purpose, which was the passage of civil rights legislation that brought an end to Jim Crow. Indeed, this has been the quandary that has stymied the liberation movement ever since: how to develop a theory and praxis for attacking the institutionalized inequalities that constitute the enduring legacy of slavery. Given the recent ascendancy of the political right, based in large part on its cynical use of race and racism to launch an attack on the welfare state, it is difficult even to imagine a political scenario leading to the fulfillment of Martin Luther King's celebrated dream.

Yet the lesson of history is that the flame of liberation cannot be extinguished. Racial oppression has always originated at the top echelons of society, but the irrepressible forces for black liberation have always sprung from the bottom. Not from the political establishment – its leaders, the political parties, or the vaunted institutions of American democracy. Not from white liberals who have too often equivocated and temporized, offering little more than a kinder and gentler version of the racial status quo. Certainly not from some armchair theorist or policy maven who has lit on some hitherto elusive truth. Not even from the civil rights establishment that, despite valiant efforts, must settle for meager concessions extracted from white power structures.

To be sure, democratic institutions, liberals, scholars, and civil rights organizations may again serve as constructive agents for change, as they have in the past. However, the paramount truth is that this nation has never had the political will to address the legacy of slavery until forced by events to do so. As in the past, the catalyst for change will be "the mounting pressure" that emanates from those segments of black society that have little reason to acquiesce in the racial status quo. It has yet to be seen exactly what form resistance and protest will take. However, we can take comfort from Lerone Bennett's astute observation: "There has been . . . a Negro revolt in every decade of this century. Each revolt failed, only to emerge in the next decade on a higher level of development."[32]

Our nation has chosen to canonize the Martin Luther King who, in his celebrated "I Have a Dream" oration, projected a racial nirvana in some indefinite future. But let us also remember the King who in the same speech said: "The whirlwinds of revolt will continue to shake the foundations of our nation until the bright day of justice emerges."[33]

Notes and references

1   Eric Foner, *Reconstruction: America's Unfinished Revolution, 1863–1877* (New York: Harper & Row, 1988).

2   W. E. B. Du Bois, *Black Reconstruction* (New York: Harcourt, Brace, 1935), p. 30.

3   Neil R. McMillen, *Dark Journey: Black Mississippians in the Age of Jim Crow* (Urbana and Chicago: University of Illinois Press, 1989), p. 38.

4   Foner, *Reconstruction: America's Unfinished Revolution, 1863–1877*, p. 236.

5   Gunnar Myrdal, *An American Dilemma: The Negro Problem and Modern Democracy* (New York: Harper & Row, 1944), p. 237.

6   Nell Irvin Painter, *Exodusters* (New York: Knopf, 1977), p. 159.

7   Myrdal, *An American Dilemma*, pp. 189–90.

8   An exception is Peter Uhlenberg, "Noneconomic Determinants of Nonmigration: Sociological Considerations for Migration Theory," *Rural Sociology* 38 (Fall 1973): 296.

9   Nell Irvin Painter's excellent study, *Exodusters*, was published in 1977.

10   A second field trip involved oral histories and the production of a film under a grant from the Ethnic Heritage Studies Program of the Office of Education.

11   John G. Van Deusen, *The Black Man in White America* (Washington, D.C.: Associated Publishers, 1944), p. 30. See also Stephen Steinberg, *The Ethnic Myth* (Boston: Beacon Press, 1989), Chapter 7.

12   Myrdal, *An American Dilemma*, p. 997.

13   Ibid., p. 821.

14   Francis Fox Piven and Richard A. Cloward, *Poor People's Movements* (New York: Vintage Books, 1979), p. 205.

15   For an assessment of the impact of the civil rights movement on Southern blacks, see James Button, *Blacks and Social Change* (Princeton, N.J.: Princeton University Press, 1989).

16   For detailed analyses of income trends and related issues, see Gerald David Jaynes and Robin M. Williams, Jr., A *Common Destiny* (Washington, D.C.: National Academy Press, 1989), especially Chapter 6. See also Gerald David Jaynes, "The Labor Market Status of Black Americans: 1939–1985," *Journal of Economic Perspectives* (Fall 1990); 9–24; James P. Smith and Finis R. Welch, "Black Economic Progress After Myrdal," *Journal of Economic Literature* 27 (June 1989): 119–164; and Reynolds Farley, *Blacks and Whites: Narrowing the Gap?* (Cambridge, Mass.: Harvard University Press, 1984).

17   These themes are at the center of a number of recent works: Katherine S. Newman, *Falling from Grace: The Experience of Downward Mobility in the American Middle Class* (New York: Free Press, 1988); Michael W. Haga, *Is the American Dream Dying?* (Denver: Acclaim Publishing, 1994); Lillian B. Rubin, *Families in the Front Line* (New York: HarperCollins, 1994).

18   *Statistical Abstracts of the United States, 1994* (Washington, D.C.: Government Printing Office, 1994), p. 475; *Income, Poverty, and Valuation of Non-Cash Benefits*, Current Population Reports, series P-60, no. 188 (Washington, D.C.: Government Printing Office, 1993).

19   *Statistical Abstracts of the United States, 1994* (Washington, D.C.: Government Printing Office, 1994), p. 475.

20   The time period under examination was 1974–1983. Terry K. Adams, Greg J. Duncan, and Willard L. Rodgers, "The Persistence of Urban Poverty," in *Quiet Riots*, ed. Fred R. Harris and Roger W. Wilkins (New York: Pantheon, 1988), pp. 83–85. Another study reports that while 63 percent of whites who are in poverty are there for only one year, the figure for blacks is 48 percent. The percentage of those in poverty for seven years or more is 4 percent for whites, but 15 percent for blacks; Peter Gottschalk, Sara McLanahan, and Gary D. Sandefur, "The Dynamics and Intergenerational Transmission of Poverty and Welfare Participation," in *Confronting Poverty*, ed. Sheldon H. Danziger, Gary D.

Sandefur, and Daniel H. Weinberg (Cambridge, Mass.: Harvard University Press, 1994), p. 94.

21   "The severely distressed" is a composite measure consisting of five factors: low education; single parenthood; poor work history; public assistance recipiency; and poverty. John D. Kasarda, "The Severely Distressed in Economically Transforming Cities," in *Drugs, Crime, and Social Isolation*, ed. Adele V. Harrell and George E. Peterson (Washington, D.C.: The Urban Institute Press, 1992), pp. 49–54.

22   Eric Foner, *Reconstruction: America's Unfinished Revolution, 1863–1877*, p. 604.

23   Richard J. Herrnstein and Charles Murray, *The Bell Curve: Intelligence and Class Structure in American Life* (New York: Free Press, 1994).

24   Adolph Reed, Jr., "Looking Backward," *The Nation* (November 28, 1994): 661–62.

25   According to Charles Lane, Herrnstein and Murray cite thirteen scholars who were beneficiaries of grants over the last two decades totalling over $4 million. Seventeen researchers cited in the bibliography have contributed to *Mankind Quarterly*, a neo-fascist journal that espouses the genetic superiority of the white race; "The Tainted Sources of 'The Bell Curve,'" *New York Review of Books* (December 1, 1994), p. 15. The role of the Pioneer Fund in underwriting research on race and IQ was also the subject of a report on ABC news with Peter Jennings, November 22, 1994.

26   Jason DeParle, "Daring Research or 'Social Science Pornography'?" *New York Times Magazine* (October 9, 1994): p. 48; "IQ: Is It Destiny?" *Newsweek* (October 24, 1994); Richard Lacayo, "For Whom the Bell Curves: A New Book Raises a Ruckus by Linking Intelligence to Genetics and Race," *Time* (October 24, 1994). Charles Murray and Richard J. Herrnstein, "Race, Genes and I.Q. – An Apologia," *The New Republic* (October 31, 1994): 27–37; the issue included responses from an array of critics.

27   Gerald D. Berryman, "Race, Caste, and Other Invidious Distinctions in Social Stratification," reprinted in *Majority and Minority*, ed. Norman R. Yetman (Boston: Allyn & Bacon, 1991), p. 22.

28   For recent documentation of the increase in the absolute and relative rates of poverty, and the growing gap between those at the top and those at the bottom of the income distribution, see Sheldon H. Danziger and Daniel H. Weinberg, "The Historical Record: Trends in Family Income, Inequality, and Poverty," in *Confronting Poverty*, ed. Sheldon H. Danziger, Gary D. Sandefur, and Daniel H. Weinberg, pp. 18–50.

29   Reed, "Looking Backward," p. 661.

30   "*The Bell Curve*: A Symposium," *The National Review* (December 5, 1994): 32–61.

31   Myrdal, *An American Dilemma*, p. 997.

32   Lerone Bennett, "Tea and Sympathy: Liberals and Other White Hopes," in Bennett, *The Negro Mood and Other Essays* (Chicago: Johnson Publications, 1963), p. 22.

33   Martin Luther King, Jr., *I Have a Dream: Writing and Speeches that Changed the World*, ed. James Melvin Washington (New York: HarperCollins, 1992), p. 103.

Chapter 39

Jennifer L. Hochschild

LOOKING AHEAD: RACIAL TRENDS IN THE UNITED STATES

I N A P R I L O F 2 0 0 4 , the quarterly newsletter *Migration News* summarized the most recent data on race and ethnicity from the U.S. Census Bureau "In 2000, the racial/ethnic makeup of US residents was: White, 69 percent; Hispanic and Black, 13 percent each: and Asian and other, six percent. By 2050, these percentages are projected to be: 50, 24, 15, and 13." For anyone who has been studying racial trends in America these figures weren't surprising.[1] But the newsletter's conclusion certainly was: "It is possible that, by 2050, today's racial and ethnic categories will no longer be in use."

Migration News is a scholarly publication that "summarizes the most important immigration and integration developments."[2] It is produced by Migration Dialogue, a group at the University of California, Davis, that aspires to provide "timely, factual and nonpartisan information and analysis of international migration issues." *Migration News* cannot by any stretch of the imagination be described as fanciful or ideological – and yet in the middle of a summary of census data its authors produced the astonishing prognosis that "by 2050, today's racial and ethnic categories will no longer be in use." If *Migration News* is correct, residents of the United States will, within the lifetime of many readers of this issue of *Dædalus*, no longer talk of blacks, whites, Asians, Latinos, and Native Americans, but will instead speak of – what?

This essay explores possible answers to that tantalizing question. By looking backward at racial and ethnic constructions and practices in the United States over the past century, we will be better situated to project possible racial and ethnic constructions and practices over the next one. *Migration News* might well he right – although, as I will argue, that is a far cry from predicting that the old shameful racial hierarchies will disappear.

The idea of ethnicity did not exist in 1900; the term 'ethnic' was invented around World War I and came into widespread use in the 1930s. 'The term 'race' did much of the work that we now assign to 'ethnicity'; phrases such as 'the Irish race,' 'the Yankee race,' and 'the Hebrew race' were common and uncontested. But race meant a lot more than ethnicity. Edgar Allen Poe wrote of "the race of Usher," Charles Dickens, of "the race of Evrémonde." Biologists measured cranial capacities and developed intelligence testing in order to make what they perceived to be scientific determinations of the biological differences among races of humans. In 1939 Carleton Coon, a physical anthropologist at Harvard University, published *The Races of Europe*, a textbook that named eighteen races that were spread across the continent, including "Partially Mongoloid," "Brunn strain, Tronder etc., unreduced, only partly brachycephalized," "Pleistocene Mediterranean Survivor," "Neo-Danubian." and so on. Meanwhile, the Negro and Indian races were routinely distinguished from the white race.

A century later we retain the term 'race,' but only in the last of these usages, that is, distinguishing a few major groups from each other. A family is described by ancestry, lineage, or descent – not by race. The Irish are an ethnic group; to identify someone as a Yankee is to evoke a regional or cultural distinction; Jews are an amalgam of religion, ethnicity, and perhaps culture. Anthropologists no longer make racial distinctions among Europeans; in fact, current research in the field of cultural studies typically identifies all Europeans, from Swedes to Arabs, as a single race distinguished by its whiteness.

The biology of race has also changed dramatically. A century ago, biologists held that there were many races, that races could be distinguished from one another in objective and quantifiable ways, and that less measurable but nonetheless real differences in intelligence and emotional maturity were closely associated with measurable differences in skull size or proportion of white ancestry. Some still held that races had different origins or were even different subspecies. By the middle of the twentieth century, however, the number of commonly recognized races had shrunk to a few (in grade school, I learned about Caucasoids, Mongoloids, Negroids, and Indians). And by the end of the century, conventional wisdom, at least among scholars, held that a race was a purely social construction with no notable biological differences.

The wheel may be turning again, however. That well-known exemplar of postmodern deconstructionism, the U.S. census, is leading the way in proliferating racial identities: the census now recognizes 126 ethnoracial groups (or a mere 63 racial groups!) and, as Kenneth Prewitt points out, many more could come in quick succession. At the same time, some scientists and medical doctors are contesting the view that race is nothing but a social construction; as Neil Risch and his coauthors put it, "a 'race-neutral' or 'color-blind' approach to biomedical research is neither equitable nor advantageous, and would not lead to a reduction of disparities in disease risk or treatment efficacy between groups."[3] People of different races or ethnicities may react differently to particular medications, maybe especially susceptible to specific diseases, or may have bone marrow or kidneys compatible only with some co-ethnics. Most new biological research has been purified of the old eugenicist motivations; even the dean of Howard University Medical School has endorsed a major initiative to collect DNA samples from his hospital's (mostly black) patients for medical research on diseases to which African Americans are especially prone, such as high blood pressure, asthma, and prostate cancer. By 2050 the historical seesaw between biology and social constructivism may be superseded by genomic research that disaggregates individuals at levels far below any groupings by race, ethnicity, geography, or culture.

In parallel with the changing meanings of race, we have witnessed the rise and perhaps fall of the concept of ethnicity. That concept was invented partly in opposition to the idea of race, since it was taken to denote possibly malleable culture rather than biologically fixed characteristics. It was elaborated as a way to make distinctions within a given race, usually among whites; Michael Novak wrote in 1972 of "the rise of the unmeltable ethnics" within various European nationalities. Some analysts continue to insist that the two terms should be defined in opposition to each other. I, like other undergraduate lecturers, have taught my students that Latinos have a common ethnicity shared among multiple races, whereas Pacific Rim Asians are a single race with multiple ethnicities.

But scholars and activists are now working to confound the distinction that was developed over most of the past century, Ian Haney López, for example, wrote in 1997 that "conceptualizing Latinos/as in racial terms is warranted. . . . The general abandonment of racial language and its replacement with substitute vocabularies, in particular that of ethnicity, will obfuscate key aspects of Latino/a lives."[4] Four in ten of those who identified as Hispanic or Latino on the ethnicity question in the 2000 census rejected all the racial categories offered to them in the next question, in favor of "some other race," Whether that represents a principled refusal to distinguish race from ethnicity, or just respondents' confusion with the census form, as the Census Bureau interpreted it, remains to be seen. David Hollinger has pointed out one of the more resonant ironies of American racial politics: the same federal government that separates Hispanic ethnicity from race in the census treats Hispanics as legally equivalent to African Americans in antidiscrimination policies such as affirmative action, voting rights, and minority set-asides.

Residents of the United States began the twentieth century by not distinguishing a race from an ethnicity; they spent most of that century elaborating the differences between the two concepts; and they appear now to be collapsing the distinction. The number of recognized races shrank drastically and is now expanding again. When the century began, the concept of race was tightly connected with the biological sciences; that bond was almost snapped but now may be regaining strength. I am not making a simple cyclical argument: the proliferation of races through multiple self-definitions is very different from the mapmaking of a physical anthropologist, and the biology of eugenics is unconnected with the biology of the genome project. Nevertheless, the transformations of the past century show that *Migration News*'s casual suggestion that by 2050 today's racial and ethnic categories may no longer be in use is not as farfetched as it initially appears to be.

Definitions and usages of concepts such as race and ethnicity matter because they help us to understand the practice of racial and ethnic interaction. If immigrants are regarded as a race apart, biologically distinct from the rest of us, they will be treated very differently than if they are regarded as belonging to another ethnicity, similar in crucial ways to all the others. The structure of racial hierarchy will be different if races are conceived as discrete and insular (i.e., one can be black or white but not both) rather than if they are conceived as occurring along a continuum.

The degree to which such conceptions and practices have changed over the past century can give us hints as to how they are likely to change over the next one.

Consider immigrants first. Ever alert to its responsibility as the newspaper of record, *The New York Times* reminded readers in the1880s of "a powerful 'dangerous class,' who care nothing for our liberty or civilization, . . . who burrow at the roots of society, and only come forth in the darkness and in times of disturbance, to plunder and prey on the good things which surround them, but which they never reach." This is, the *Times* proceeded to warn, "the poorest and lowest laboring class . . . [who] drudge year after year in fruitless labor . . . [but] never rise above their position . . . They hate the rich . . . They are densely ignorant, and easily aroused by prejudice or passion." The members of this class "are mainly Irish Catholics."

Not only words were invoked to control the dangerous classes. Of the 1,713 lynchings in the decade after 1882, (the first year for which accurate records exist), half of the victims were white (largely Jewish or Catholic); in the succeeding decade, a quarter were. 'Hunkies,' Italians, and Russian Jews could live and socialize only in a 'foreign colony' in an undesirable part of town. Unless there was a substantial black population in the area, most new immigrants occupied the lowest-skilled and lowest-paying jobs in the lowest-status industries. When able to attain jobs that required more expertise, they were paid less than their northern European counterparts.

Eventually, however, the despised races became the celebrated white ethnics. The reasons included genuine assimilation, the desire to become white in order not to be black, the almost complete cessation of new European immigration after World War I, upward mobility in a growing labor force, and political incorporation through party machines. By the 1960s, Irish Catholic families enjoyed on average $2,500 more than the national average family income.[5] An Irish Catholic has been president of the nation, and during his presidential campaign John Kerry was coy about the fact that he is not Irish. Intermarriage rates among white ethnics are so high that demographers have largely given up trying to trace socioeconomic differences among nationalities. In short, the ethnic boundaries at the turn of the twentieth century that were sometimes etched in violence have mostly dissolved into shades of whiteness.

The transformation of the status of Asian immigrants has been even more phenomenal. In 1877, a U.S. Senate committee investigating Chinese immigration to California concluded that "the Chinese do not desire to become citizens of this country, and have no knowledge or appreciation for our institutions. . . . An indigestible mass in the community, distinct in language, pagan in religion, inferior in mental and moral qualities, and all peculiarities, is an undesirable element in a republic, but becomes especially so if political power is placed in its hands." Until the middle of the twentieth century, members of most Asian nationalities were prohibited from immigrating, becoming naturalized citizens, or owning certain types of property. Most Japanese Americans were interned in World War II, although few German Americans or Italian Americans were.

But now Asian Americans are perceived, often to their chagrin, as the 'model minority.' Elite private universities are rumored to use informal quotas to keep too many from beating out their non-Asian competitors. At the most prestigious state universities in California, where no such restrictions hold, Asian American students typically fill two-fifths of the student seats (in a state whose population is 12 percent Asian American). Almost half of adult Asian Americans have a college degree or more education, compared with three in ten Anglos, two in ten African Americans, and one in ten Latinos. A *Newsweek* cover story lauds the sex appeal of Asian men; analysts report that "Anglos living in close proximity to large Asian populations are more likely than racially and ethnically isolated Anglos to favor increased immigration."[6] As of 1990, a fifth of the children who had one Asian parent also had a parent of a different race; that proportion is surely much higher now. In the same year, 30 percent of Asians who married wed a non-Asian American, and that figure too is rising. While discrimination persists, virulently at times, and the label of 'foreigner' sometimes seems impossible to escape, it is not crazy to think that Asians may by 2050 have followed the path of Irish Catholics and Polish Jews into the status of 'just American.'

Conversely, another group of immigrants – Mexican Americans, or Latinos more generally – might become more sharply differentiated from other residents of the United States over the next few decades. Samuel Huntington argues that the "extent and nature of this immigration differ fundamentally from those of previous immigrations, and the assimilation successes of the past are unlikely to be duplicated with the contemporary flood of immigrants from Latin America. This reality poses a fundamental question: Will the United States remain a country with a single national language and a core Anglo-Protestant culture?"[7] In this view, Latinos will follow the opposite trajectory from that of the Irish and Asians: Latinos, once perceived as part of an ethnicity with an identifiable but permeable culture, are becoming a race with increasingly defined boundaries.

The research evidence is completely mixed on this point. U.S-born children of Mexican parents consistently receive more education than their parents, speak English better, earn more at higher-status jobs, move away from gateway cities more frequently, marry more non-Mexicans, and vote more. However, discrimination and subordination persist, and scholars such as Richard Alba and his coauthors find 'no convincing sign of convergence in the educational attainments of later-generation Mexican Americans and Anglos."[8] That is, after the second generation, assimilation may lose its momentum. Sociologists even point to the possibility of a reversal, such that children and grandchildren of poor immigrants may lose ground economically, disengage politically, and end up with poorer health, higher rates of crime, or greater family instability than their ancestors or counterparts in their native country.

Huntington articulates a deeper anxiety: that the sheer magnitude of immigration and the high birth rates among Latinos who share a language, religion, and background and who mostly live in a distinct section of the United States are creating "a de facto split between a predominantly Spanish-speaking United States and an English-speaking United States." In my view, this concern is unwarranted; the culture of the United States is certainly changing in response to massive immigration from Latin America, but the immigrants are changing just as much, if not more. From the perspective of African Americans, in fact, the danger maybe altogether too much assimilation rather than too little – creating once again a society in which immigrants get to become American by stepping over the only group that cannot, and does not want to, attain whiteness (or at least nonblackness).

Beyond the empirical complexities, I cannot forecast whether today's racial and ethnic categories will no longer be in use with regard to immigrants in zoo, because of a crucial but unpredictable feature of immigration: the level and composition of immigration is largely a matter of political choice. U.S. immigration has not been drastically curtailed after forty years of increase, as it was in 1924 after about fifty years of a proportionally similar increase. But will it be? On the one hand, there are few signs of an impending cutoff. So the long period of incorporation with few newcomers that the United States experienced from 1920 until 1965 is unlikely to be repeated in the near future.

On the other hand, the war against terrorism may yet dramatically affect immigration laws and the treatment of immigrants. So far only a small segment of the population has been significantly affected. But arguably precedents have been set that could have powerful and, in my view, terrible consequences for the United States's treatment of 'foreigners.' And with a few more terrorist attacks, residents of the United States could develop a powerful nativism tinged with religious and ethnic hostility and fueled by a genuine and warranted fear. The effect such developments would have on the racial and ethnic categories of 2050 is anyone's guess.

For most of the twentieth century, the boundary between black and white was as firmly fixed in law and self-definition as it was blurred in practice. This boundary did not always exist; in the 1600s, the Virginia legislature had to outlaw interracial marriages because too many white indentured servants were marrying black proto-slaves. Interracial sexual activity persisted, of course, and government policy in the centuries since then has shifted from counting mulattoes, quadroons, and octoroons to establishing "one drop of blood" laws in thirty states by 1940. In some states or legal jurisdictions, not only blacks but also South Asians, Chinese and Japanese Americans, and Mexican Americans were forbidden to marry European Americans. Opponents used rumors of interracial sex to try to discredit Abraham Lincoln, the Populist movement, labor unions, New Deal agencies, desegregation in the Army, and the civil rights movement. The Supreme Court refused to take on cases of interracial marriage in the 1950s for fear of evoking uncontrollable anger; Justice Harlan is reported to have said, with Thurgood Marshall's concurrence, that "one bombshell at a time is enough."

Most of that sentiment has disappeared, or at least gone underground. Multiracial identity is now a point of public pride and private assertion; a social movement built around multiracial identity has shown surprising strength. In 1958, only 4 percent of whites endorsed interracial marriage; the most recent Gallup poll shows that 70 percent now do. A recent cover of *Parade* magazine is adorned with smiling, adorable children under the headline of "The Changing Faces of America"; Mattel has introduced Kayla, whom it describes as "Barbie's racially ambiguous playmate"; *The New York Times* showcases "Generation E.A.: Ethnically Ambiguous"; *Newsweek* shows yet another set of adorable children in a story on "The New Face of Race." Whatever motives one attributes to the marketing of racial complexity, the fact that multiracialism now has commercial appeal shows how far it has moved from connotations of mongrelization and degeneration.

How much actual multiracialism there is in the United States is indeterminate. The answer depends on what one defines as a race (is a marriage between a Mexican

American and a European American interracial?), whether interethnic marriages are factored in (how about a marriage between a Korean and a Japanese?), how far back one goes in a person's ancestry to determine multiraciality, and what individuals know or acknowledge in their own family history. Nevertheless, it is probably safe to say that intermarriage is rising, along with the number of children who are, or who are recognized as being, multiracial. Up to 12 percent of youth can now readily be called multiracial, and plausibly by 2050 about 10 percent of whites and blacks and over so percent of Latinos, Asians, and American Indians will marry outside their group.

Since families are comprised of more than only parents and children, a single intermarriage can have a wide impact. As of 1990, "one in seven whites, one in three blacks, four in five Asians, and more than 19 in 20 American Indians are closely related to someone of a different racial group. Despite an intermarriage rate of about 1 percent, about 20 percent of Americans count someone from a different racial group among their kin."[9] And those calculations include neither marriages between or offspring of a Latino and a non-Latino, nor individuals with multiracial ancestry who consider themselves to be members of one racial group.

These changes in sentiment and behavior may grow even stronger over the next few decades, as Latinos' celebration of *mestizaje*, the mixing of races, as a cultural identity and social environment, rather than as a description of an individual's ancestry, spreads across the nation. Similarly, the census's invitation to identify with more than one race may spread, for simple bureaucratic and non-ideological reasons, to schools, state governments, corporations, hospitals, the criminal justice system, the military, and other far-reaching institutions. A frequently repeated offer to "check one or more" may encourage people to think of themselves as 'more than one.' If the trajectory of multiracialism persists, *Migration News*'s speculation that today's racial and ethnic categories will no longer be in use in a few decades seems even less farfetched.

We cannot evaluate the impact of the unstable meanings of race and ethnicity, the fluctuating status of various immigrant groups, and the evolving connotation of muitiracialism without considering African Americans. They are the perennial losers in the hierarchies of status, wealth, and power in the United States. The boundaries around blackness have been the most stringently monitored, first by oppressors and now perhaps by African Americans themselves; their relations with white Americans have been and continue to be the most fraught. If we knew how much the meaning of being black in the United States will change by 2050 – or more contentiously, whether racial oppression will be significantly underminedwe would know how seriously to take the speculation that our current racial and ethnic categories may become outmoded.

The standing of African Americans has changed dramatically over the past century: Republican President Roosevelt was widely criticized for once entertaining Booker T. Washington in the White House; Republican President Bush has entrusted two of the most important cabinet-level positions to African Americans. The highest paid corporate executive on Wall Street in 2003 was black; some African Americans hold high elective office or judgeships; some are esteemed socially and culturally. Overall, using criteria that encompass roughly half of the white population, about a third of American blacks can be described as middle class. Affluent African Americans can now pass their status on to their children, so a fully developed class structure has emerged in the black community.

Still, perhaps a third of African Americans remain at the bottom of the various hierarchies in the United States. Compared with all other groups, poor blacks are more deeply poor, for longer periods of their life and from earlier in childhood; they are more likely to live among other poor people. Black children who begin their education with roughly the same knowledge and skills as white children lose ground in the public school system. Blacks are more likely to be victimized by crime than any other group, and black men are much more likely to be incarcerated and subsequently disfranchised for life than are white men.

More generally, we cannot dismiss the possible persistence of what Orlando Patterson once called the "homeostatic principle of the entire system of racial domination," in which racial subordination is repressed in one location only to burst forth in another.[10] Regardless of their income, African Americans are overcharged for used cars, less likely to receive appropriate treatment for heart attacks, and less likely to receive excellent service from realtors and bankers. Blacks have drastically less wealth than whites with the same earnings. Whites seldom vote for black candidates when they have an alternative, and even less often move into substantially black neighborhoods, schools, and churches.

I am not sure what would count as persuasive evidence that the racial hierarchy in the United States is on a certain path to extinction. Certainly a strong black class structure that persists across generations would be essential (although it may merely substitute one hierarchy for another). A sense among African Americans that they can let down their guard – that embracing multiracialism is not just a way of inching closer to whiteness, that racism is only infrequently part of the explanation for a failure, that a commitment to racial solidarity need not take precedence over values such as feminism or patriotism or simple idiosyncrasy – would also be good evidence. And changed behavior by nonblacks, such as choosing a home or a child's school because of its quality rather than its racial composition, or repudiating implicit as well as explicit racial appeals by political candidates, or recognizing and disavowing the privileges that come with being the apparently raceless norm in U.S. society, would also be necessary.

Until we can he clear on what it will take to abolish racial hierarchy in the United States, and on how far we have moved toward that abolition, we cannot say whether by 2050 today's racial and ethnic categories will no longer be in use. If racial hierarchy persists, so will the categories of black and nonblack. Multiracialism and the history of American racial politics over the past few decades are on balance encouraging, but they are not dispositive.

I turn finally to discrimination by skin tone, which may be the deepest and most tenacious form of racism in the United States. The connection between lightness and virtue is at least as old as Shakespeare, whose Timon of Athens learned too late that enough gold "will make black white, foul fair, wrong right, base noble, old young, coward valiant."

Europeans have not always denigrated dark-skinned people in favor of light-skinned ones, as Werner Sollors shows in *An Anthology of Interracial Literature*, but by the mid-nineteenth century, few residents of the United States publicly contested the view that lighter was better. Skin-color hierarchy held a fortiori across what we now call races; northern European whites were dominant, southern Europeans and Latinos held intermediate positions, and blacks were subordinated to all. But skin-color hierarchy also obtained within racial and ethnic groups, as phrases like 'the black Irish' and 'the brown paper hag test' and the advertising jingle asserting that 'blonds have more fun' attest. The history of each racial or ethnic group includes its own variant of skincolor ranking. Spanish and Portuguese colonizers of Latin America elaborated rules for ranking according to a complex mixture of race, physical appearance, wealth, cultural heritage, and enslavement:

> Whites generally have a superior slatus. People of Indian racial background whose cultural practices are mainly of Portuguese or Spanish derivation . . . would be next on the social ladder. Mestizos, people of mixed indigenous and white background, would have a higher rating than those of largely Indian background. At the bottom of the social pyramid would be Afro-Americans, with mulattos occupying a higher social status than blacks.[11]

My research (conducted with Traci Burch and Vesla Weaver) suggests that skin-color ranking has had an equally powerful impact on African Americans. Compared with their darker-skinned counterparts, lighter-skinned black soldiers in the Civil War's Union Army were more likely to have been skilled workers than field hands before they entered the service. Sergeants and lieutenants were most likely to be light-skinned, and black soldiers with light skin were more likely than their darker-skinned counterparts to be promoted white in the Army. They were significantly taller (a measure of nutrition) and – most striking of all – the lightest members of the black regiments were significantly less likely to die in service.[12]

Asian societies are not immune from the bias of skin-color ranking. An ancient Japanese proverb holds that "white skin makes up for seven defects," and Indian newspapers and websites carry personal ads for women whose parents boast of their daughters' purity and light skin in order to attract a husband. European Americans hold light skin in the same regard, as elucidated by that noted sociologist F. Scott Fitzgerald in *This Side of Paradise*. During a conversation about the virtues of strenuous exercise, Fitzgerald's Byrne suddenly observes,

> "Personal appearance has a lot to do with it."
> "Coloring?" Amory asked eagerly.
> "Yes."
> "That's what Tom and I figured." Amory agreed. "We took the year-books for the last ten years and looked at the pictures of the senior council. . . . It does represent success here [at Princeton University] in a general way. Well, I suppose only about thirty-five per cent of every class here are blonds, are really light – yet *two-thirds* of every senior council are light . . .."
> "It's true," Byrne agreed. "The light-haired man *is* a higher type, generally speaking. I worked the thing out with the Presidents of the

United States once, and found that way over half of them were light-haired, yet think of the preponderant number of brunettes in the race."

They go on for several more paragraphs in the same vein, apropos of nothing in the book's plot.

Such examples range across several centuries because the importance of skin tone has changed relatively little, despite the growth of a black cultural aesthetic, the Latino celebration of *mestizaje*, and the Asian drive for panethnic unity. Surveys from the 1990s show that lighter-skinned African Americans and Hispanics continue to enjoy higher incomes and more education than their darker counterparts. They are more likely to own homes and to live among white neighbors, and less likely to be on welfare. Darker blacks and Latinos have higher rates of incarceration and unemployment; dark-skinned Mexican Americans speak less English and are less likely to be unionized if they are workers. Dark-skinned black men convicted of a crime receive longer sentences than lighter-skinned counterparts. Both blacks and whites attach more negative and fewer positive attributes to images of dark-skinned, compared with light-skinned, blacks.

Controls for class background reduce but do not eliminate these differences. That is, light-skinned people are more likely to come from a well-off family reflecting the historical advantages of light skin – *and* they are more likely to he treated well by police, employers, teachers, and other citizens. The magnitude of these effects is impressive. One study found complexion to be more closely connected than was parents' socioeconomic status to blacks' occupation and income; another found that "dark-skinned blacks suffer much the same disadvantage relative to light-skinned blacks that blacks, in general, suffer relative to whites."[13] Even if racial and ethnic categories change drastically by 2050, one cannot assume that skin-color hierarchy will do the same.

Qver the past century, the meaning of race and ethnicity has changed a lot, as have the status of most immigrants and the connotations of multiracialism. Skin-color hierarchy has changed little, and the subordination of African Americans has been challenged but not yet overthrown. Combining these dynamics in various ways and with varying degrees of emphasis permits us to envision at least six possible futures:

- The United States might persist in a structure of black exceptionalism, or an updated Jim Crow. In this scenario, skin tone and ethnicity would matter, but the main divide would continue to be between those identified as black and all others. That is, race as we now understand it would trump skin tone and ethnicity among blacks, even if skin tone or ethnicity complicates the meaning of race for all other residents of the United States. Biracial individuals would be treated as simply black or nonblack, and would mostly identify according to that binary, rather than become a liminal or new category.
- A similar possible scenario is white exceptionalism. Here too, skin tone and ethnicity would continue to matter, but the main divide would be between those identified as white and all others. Skin tone and ethnic identification would continue to matter little among European Americans, who would all

share to a greater or lesser degree in white privilege. Appearance and ethnic groupings might matter a great deal for sorting the rest of the population, but only within a shared subordinate status,

- Alternatively, the United States might move toward a South African model, That would combine the first two scenarios, producing a nation sorted into three groups: whites and 'honorary whites' (most Asians, some Latinos, and some biracials), coloreds (some Asians, most Latinos, some biracials, and a few African Americans), and blacks and almost-blacks (indigenous Latinos, many Native Americans, and some biracials, as well as African Americans). Levels of affluence, status, power, and vulnerability to discrimination would on average vary accordingly, with wider variations between rather than within the groups.[14]

- Perhaps the United States will sort along a more complex set of racial and ethnic dimensions, with new understandings of race and ethnicity. One possibility is sharper regional divides. Thus the Northwest would mingle Asians, Native Americans, and Anglos; the Southwest would mix Latinos, Native Americans, and Anglos; the Midwest would remain largely Anglo; the South would continue to hold mostly separate populations of blacks and Anglos, and so on. These regional divides could develop important political and cultural implications, even if not at the level of the antebellum North, South, and West as described by Anne Norton, among others.[15] Or the nation might divide along lines of nativity, so that the most salient characteristic is whether one is foreign- or native-born. Perhaps class lines or intensity of religious commitment or isolationism would cut across lines of race, ethnicity, and skin tone alike.

- The United States might be moving toward the eventual elimination of distinct racial and ethnic groups in favor of a skin-color hierarchy, *tout court*. Socioeconomic status, prestige, and political power would in that case depend on one's location on that continuum; identity, beliefs, and perceptions would eventually follow. Whether such a continuum would improve the United States's racial order by substituting fluidity for rigidity, or worsen it by disguising persistent racial stigma through a series of small gradations, remains to be seen.

- Finally, the United State might blur distinct racial and ethnic groups into a multiracial mélange. The logic of multiracialism differs from that of skin color since the former is not inherently hierarchical: black/white individuals have the same standing qua 'multiracials' as do Asian/Latino individuals. The crucial divide in this scenario would be between those who identify as monoracials and seek to protect cultural purity and those who identify as multiracials and celebrate cultural mixing. Skin tone, along with conventional distinctions of race and ethnicity, would recede in importance.

Prediction is a fool's game. The future will be partly controlled by political and policy choices not yet made, perhaps not yet even imagined. Furthermore, [. . .] the very categories that we employ to measure racial and ethnic change will themselves affect the direction and magnitude of that change. The census is not a neutral bean counter; Heisenberg's principle holds for the social as well as the physical world. Nevertheless, I will venture a guess: skin tone will continue to be associated with invidious distinctions; African Americans will remain a distinct although not always subordinated social grouping; and everything else in this arena – our understandings of race and ethnicity, our treatment of immigrants, our evaluation of people and cultures that cut across formerly distinct categories – is up for grabs.

Notes

1   This essay is part of a joint research project with Traci Burch and Vesla Weaver, both Ph.D. students at Harvard University. I thank them for their contributions to our shared enterprise. The views expressed in this essay are my own, and not necessarily shared by these coauthors of the larger project.

2   <http://migration.ucdavis.edu/>.

3   Neil Risch, Esteban Burchard, Elad Ziv, and Hua Tang, "Categorization of Humans in Biomedical Research: Genes, Race, and Disease," *Genome Biology* 3 (7) (1002): 1–12.

4   Ian Haney López, "Race, Ethnicity, Erasure: The Salience of Race to LatCrit Theory," *California Law Review* 85 (5) (1997):1143–11–11.

5   Andrew Greeley, "Ethnic Minorities in the United States: Demographic Perspectives." *International Journal of Group Tensions* 7 (3 and 4) (1977): 64–97. See table 5-C for data.

6   M. V. Hood III and Irwin Morris, "¿Amigo o Enemigo? Context, Attitudes, and Anglo Public Opinion Toward Immigration," *Social Science Quarterly* 78 (2) (1997): 309–323.

7   Samuel P. Huntington, "The Hispanic Challenge," *Foreign Policy* (March/April 2004): 30–45.

8   Richard Alba, Dalia Abdel-Hady, Tariqul Islam, and Karen Marotz, "Downward Assimilation and Mexican Americans: An Examination of Intergenerational Advance and Stagnation in Educational Attainment." University at Albany, SUNY, Albany, N.Y., 2004.

9   Joshua R. Goldstein, "Kinship Networks that Cross Racial Lines: The Exception or the Rule?" *Demography* 36 (3) (August 1999): 399–407.

10   Orlando Patterson, "Toward a Study of Black America.' *Dissent* (Fall 1989): 476–486.

11   Robert J. Cottrol, "The Long Lingering Shadow: Law, Liberalism, and Cultures of Racial Hierarchy and Identity in the Americas," *Tulane Law Review* 76 (November 2001): 11–79.

12   These data are drawn from Jacob Metzer and Robert A. Margo, *Union Army Recruits in Black Regiments in the United States, 1862–1865*, computer file, University of Michigan, Interuniversity Consortium for Political and Social Research, Ann Arbor, Mich., 1990.

13   Michael Hughes and Bradley R. Hertel, "The Significance of Color Remains: A Study of Life Chances, Mate Selection, and Ethnic Consciousness Among Black Americans." *Social Forces* 68 (4) (1990): 1105–1120; Verna Keith and Cedric Herring, "Skin Tone and Stratification in the Black Community," *American Journal of Sociology* 97 (3): 760–778.

14 For more on this scenario, see Eduardo Bonilla-Silva, "We Are All Americans!: The Latin Americanization of Race Relations in the United States," in Maria Krysan and Amanda Lewis, eds., *The Changing Terrain of Race and Ethnicity* (New York: Russell Sage Foundation, 2004): 149–183.

15 Anne Norton, *Alternative Americas : A Reading of Antebellum Political Culture* (Chicago, Ill: University of Chicago Press, 1986).

Chapter 40

Eduardo Bonilla-Silva

FROM BI-RACIAL TO TRI-RACIAL

[. . .]

FOR DEMOGRAPHIC (the relative large size of the black population) and historical reasons (the centrality of blacks to the national economic development from the seventeenth to the middle part of the twentieth century), the United States has had a bi-racial order (white versus the rest) fundamentally anchored on the black-white experience (Feagin 2000).[1] Albeit regions such as the Southwest, states such as California (Almaguer 1994), and sub-areas in some states (the case of 'tri-racial isolates', see Daniels 2002) have had more complex racial dynamics, the larger bi-racial system has always posed the outer limits. This has meant historically that those on the nonwhite side of the divide (blacks, Native Americans, Asians, and Latinos) have shared similar experiences of colonialism, oppression, exploitation, and racialization (Ammott and Matthai 1991). Hence, being nonwhite has meant having restricted access to the multiple 'wages of whiteness' (Roediger 1991) such as good housing, decent jobs, and a good education.

Nevertheless, the post-civil rights era has brought changes in how racial stratification seems to operate. For example, significant gaps in status have emerged between groups that previously shared a common denizen position in the racial order. Asian Americans in particular have almost matched the socio-economic standing of whites and, in some areas (e.g., educational attainment), have surpassed them (but see Note 4). For example, in selective colleges across the nation, Asian Americans are represented at three to ten times their national proportion (US News and World Report 2003). Another example of the changes is the high rate of interracial dating and marriage between Latinos and Whites and Asians and Whites (Qian and Lichter 2000; Moran 2001). These interracial unions, coupled with the collapse of formal segregation, have created the political space for 'multiracial activists' to force the Census Bureau in 2000 to allow respondents to pick all the races they felt apply to them (Parker and Song 2001; Daniels 2002).

Yet another instance of the changes in contemporary America is that few whites endorse segregationist views in surveys. This has been heralded by some as reality as 'the end of racism' (D'Souza 1995) or as 'the declining significance of race' (Wilson 1978). Lastly, blacks have been surpassed by Latinos as the largest minority group (by 2001, the Census noted that Hispanics were 13 per cent of the population and blacks 12 per cent).

I propose that all this reshuffling denotes that the bi-racial order typical of the United States, which was the exception in the world-racial system,[2] is evolving into a complex and loosely organized tri-racial stratification system similar to that of many Latin American and Caribbean nations (Degler 1986; Wade 1997). Specifically, I argue the emerging tri-racial system will be comprised of 'whites' at the top, an intermediary group of 'honorary whites' – similar to the coloureds in South Africa during formal apartheid (Fredrickson 1981), and a nonwhite group or the 'collective black' at the bottom. In Figure 1, I sketch what these three groups may look like.[3] I hypothesize that the white group will include 'traditional' whites, new 'white' immigrants and, in the near future, totally assimilated white Latinos (e.g., former

---

"Whites"

Whites New Whites (Russians, Albanians, etc.)
Assimilated white Latinos
Some multiracials
Assimilated (urban) Native Americans
A few Asian-origin people

"Honorary Whites"

Light-skinned Latinos
Japanese Americana
Korean Americans
Asian Indians
Chinese Americans
Middle Eastern Americans
Most multiracials
Filipino Americans

"Collective Black"

Vietnamese Americans
Hmong Americans
Laotian Americans
Dark-skinned Latinos
Blacks
New West Indian and African immigrants
Reservation-bound Native Americans

Figure 1 Preliminary map of tri-racial system in the USA

Secretary of Education Lauro Cabazos, the football coach of The University of Wisconsin Barry Alvarez, and actors such as Martin Sheen), lighter-skinned multi-racials (Rockquemore and Brunsma 2002), and other sub-groups; the intermediate racial group or honorary whites will comprise most light-skinned Latinos (e.g., most Cubans and segments of the Mexican and Puerto Rican communities), Japanese Americans, Korean Americans, Asian Indians, Chinese Americans, Filipinos, and most Middle Eastern Americans; and, finally, that the collective black group will include blacks, dark-skinned Latinos, Vietnamese, Cambodians and Laotians.

As a tri-racial system (or Latin- or Caribbean-like racial order), race conflict will be buffered by the intermediate group, much like class conflict is when the class structure includes a large middle class (Bottomore 1968). Furthermore, colour gradations, which have always been important matters of within-group differentiation, will become more salient factors of stratification. Lastly, Americans, like people in complex racial stratification orders, will begin making nationalists' appeals ('We are all Americans'), decry their racial past, and claim they are 'beyond race' (Martínez-Echazabal 1998). [. . .]

Why would a tri-racial system be emerging in the USA now?

Why would race relations in the United States be moving towards a tri-racial regime at this point in history? The reasons are multiple. First, the demography of the nation is changing. Racial minorities are up to 30 per cent of the population and, as population projections suggest, may become a numeric majority in the year 2050 (US Bureau of the Census 1996). And these projections may be slightly off downward as early releases from the 2000 Census suggest that the Latino population was about 12.5 per cent of the population, almost one percentage point higher than the highest projection and the proportion of the white population (77.1 per cent white or in combination) was slightly lower than originally expected (Grieco and Cassidy 2001).

The rapid darkening of America is creating a situation similar to that of many Latin American and Caribbean nations where the white elites realized their countries were becoming 'black' or 'Indian' and devised a number of strategies to whiten their population and maintain white power (Helg 1990). Although whitening the population through immigration or classifying many newcomers as white (Warren and Twine 1997; Gans 1999) is a possible solution to the new American demography, a more plausible accommodation to the new racial reality, and one that would still help maintain 'white supremacy' (Mills 1997), is to (1) create an intermediate racial group to buffer racial conflict, (2) allow some newcomers into the white racial strata, and (3) incorporate most immigrants into the collective black strata.

Second, as part of the tremendous reorganization that transpired in America in the post-civil rights era, a new kinder and gentler white supremacy emerged which Bonilla-Silva has labelled elsewhere as the 'new racism' (Smith 1995; Bonilla-Silva 2001). In post-civil rights America the maintenance of systemic white privilege is accomplished socially, economically, and politically through institutional, covert, and apparently nonracial practices. Whether in banks or universities, in stores or housing markets, 'smiling discrimination' tends to be the order of the day. This kinder and gentler form of white supremacy has produced an accompanying ideology: the ideology of colour-blind racism. This ideology denies the salience of race, scorns those who talk about race, and increasingly proclaims that 'We are all Americans' (for a detailed analysis of colour-blind racism, see Bonilla-Silva 2003).

Third, race relations have become globalized (Lusane 1997). The once almost all-white Western nations have now 'interiorized the other' (Miles 1993). The new world-systemic need for capital accumulation has led to the incorporation of 'dark' foreigners as 'guest workers' and even as permanent workers (Schoenbaum and Pond 1996). Thus, today European nations have racial minorities in their midst who are progressively becoming an underclass (Castles and Miller 1993; Cohen 1997), have developed an internal 'racial structure' (Bonilla-Silva 1997) to maintain white power, and have a curious racial ideology that combines ethnonationalism with a race-blind ideology similar to the colour-blind racism of the United States today (for more on this, see Bonilla-Silva 2000).

This new global racial reality will reinforce the trend towards tri-racialism in the United States as versions of colour-blind racism will become prevalent in most Western nations (Winant 2001). Furthermore, as many formerly almost-all white Western countries (e.g., Germany, France, England, etc.) become more and more racially diverse, tri-racial divisions may surface in these societies too.

Fourth, the convergence of the political and ideological actions of the Republican Party, conservative commentators and activists, and the so-called 'multi-racial' movement (Rockquemore and Brunsma 2002), has created the space for the radical transformation of the way we gather racial data in America. One possible outcome of the Census Bureau categorical back-and-forth on racial and ethnic classifications is either the dilution of racial data or the elimination of race as an official category (Nobles 2000).

Lastly, the attack on affirmative action, which is part of what Stephen Steinberg (1995) has labelled as the 'racial retreat', is the clarion call signalling the end of race-based social policy in the United States. Although it is still possible to save a watered-down version of this programme, at this point, this seems doubtful. Again, this trend reinforces my thesis because the elimination of race-based social policy is, among other things, predicated on the notion that race no longer affects minorities' status. Hence, as in many countries of the world, the United States may eliminate race by decree and maintain – or even increase – the level of racial inequality (for recent data on Brazil, see Lovell and Wood 1998).

A look at the data

A) Objective indicators of standing of the three racial strata

If the racial order in the United States is becoming tri-racial, significant gaps in socio-economic status between whites, honorary whites, and the collective black should be developing. The available data suggest this is the case. In terms of income, as Table 1 shows, Latino groups that are mostly white (Argentines, Chileans, Costa Ricans, and Cubans) have per capita incomes that are 40–100 per cent higher that those of Latino groups that are predominantly comprised of dark-skinned people

(Mexicans, Puerto Ricans, Dominicans). The exceptions in Table 1 (Bolivians and Panamanians) are examples of self-selected immigrants. For example, four of the largest ten concentrations of Bolivians are in the state of Virginia, a state with just 7.2 per cent Latinos.[4] Table 1 also reveals a similar pattern for Asians: a severe income gap is emerging among honorary white Asians (Japanese, Koreans, Filipinos, and Chinese) and those I classify as belonging to the collective black (Vietnamese, Cambodian, Hmong, and Laotians). (Data on educational standing and poverty rates analysed elsewhere (Bonilla-Silva and Glover forthcoming) exhibit the same pattern.)

Substantial group differences are also evident in the occupational status of the groups (based on data from 1990 PUMS not shown in table form). White Latinos, although far from whites, are between 50–100 per cent more likely to be represented in the 'Managerial and Professional' and 'Technical' categories than dark-skinned Latinos (for example, whereas 32 per cent of Costa Ricans are in such categories, only 17 per cent of Mexicans are). Along the same lines, elite Asians are even more likely to be well-represented in the higher prestige occupational categories than underclass Asians (for example, 45 per cent of Asian Indians are in 'Professional' and 'Technical' jobs, but only 5 per cent of Hmong, 9 per cent of Laotians, 10 per cent of Cambodians, and 23 per cent of Vietnamese.[5]

B) Subjective indicators of 'consciousness' of three racial strata

Social psychologists have amply demonstrated that it takes very little for groups to form, develop a common view, and adjudicate status positions to nominal characteristics (Tajfel 1970; Ridgeway 1991). Thus, it should not be surprising if

Table 1 Mean Per Capita Income* ($) of Different Ethnic Groups, 1990

Latinos	Mean income	Asian Americans	Mean income
Mexican Americans	6,470.05	Chinese	12,695.05
Puerto Ricans	7,250.20	Japanese	15,801.93
Cubans	11,727.21	Koreans	10,177.38
Guatemalans	7,103.94	Asian Indians	15,857.61
Salvadorans	6,745.21	Filipinos	12,313.99
Costa Ricans	10,615.79	Taiwanese	13,310.58
Panamanians	10,701.25	Hmong	1,191.89
Argentines	15,506.40	Vietnamese	7,930.65
Chileans	12,727.60	Cambodians	3,759.82
Bolivians	10,661.95	Laotians	4,520.04
Whites	12,159.18	Whites	12,159.18
Blacks	7,210.56	Blacks	7,210.56

Source: 1990 PUMS 5% sample.

* I use per capita income as family income distort the status of some groups (particularly Asians and Whites) as some groups have more people than others contributing toward the family income.

objective gaps in income, occupational status, and education between these various groups is contributing to group formation. That is, honorary whites may be classifying themselves as 'white' or believing they are better than the 'collective black'. If this is happening, this group should also be in the process of developing white-like racial attitudes befitting their new social position and differentiating (distancing) themselves from the 'collective black'. In line with my thesis, I also expect whites to be making distinctions between honorary whites and the collective black, specifically, exhibiting a more positive outlook towards the former than towards the latter. Finally, if a tri-racial order is emerging, I speculate the 'collective black' will begin to exhibit a diffused and contradictory racial consciousness as blacks and Indians tend to do throughout Latin America and the Caribbean (Hanchard 1994; Wade 1997). I examine data for the first corollary and will mention general findings on the latter two in the final section.

1) *Latinos' self-reports on race*: Historically, most Latinos have classified themselves as 'white', but the proportion who do so varies tremendously by group. Hence, as Table 2 shows, whereas 60 per cent or more of the members of the Latino groups I regard as honorary white classify themselves as white, 50 per cent or less of the members of the groups I regard as belonging to the collective black do so. As a case in point, whereas Mexicans, Puerto Ricans, and Central Americans are very likely to report 'Other' as their preferred 'racial' classification, most Costa Ricans, Cubans, Chileans, and Argentines choose the 'white' descriptor. This Census 1990 data mirrors the results of the 1988 Latino National Political Survey (de la Garza *et al.* 1992).

2) *'Racial' distinctions among Asians*: While Asians tend to vote panethnically on political issues (Espiritu 1992), distinctions between native-born and foreign-born (e.g., American-born Chinese and foreign-born Chinese) and between economically successful and unsuccessful Asians, are developing. In fact, according to various

Table 2 Racial self-classification by selected Hispanic-origin group 1990

	White	Black	Other	Native American	Asian
Dominicans	29.34	24.61	44.79	0.78	0.49
Salvadorans	38.96	0.89	59.19	0.33	0.63
Guatemalans	41.55	1.41	54.97	0.54	1.54
Hondurans	47.80	8.17	43.48	0.36	0.19
Puerto Ricans	46.42	4.90	47.46	0.25	0.98
Mexicans	50.63	0.72	47.37	0.79	0.49
Costa Ricans	59.38	6.51	32.99	0.54	0.58
Colombians	64.07	0.25	33.55	0.32	0.49
Bolivians	68.08	0.35	30.99	0.06	0.53
Venezuelans	73.45	3.42	22.16	0.49	0.49
Chileans	74.61	0.25	24.17	0.44	0.54
Cubans	84.76	3.13	11.75	0.08	0.29
Argentines	85.06	0.23	14.33	0.02	0.36

Source: 1990 PUMS 5% sample.

analysts, given the tremendous diversity of experiences among Asian Americans, 'all talk of Asian panethnicity should now be abandoned as useless speculation' (San Juan 2000, p. 10). Leland Saito (1998), in his *Race and Politics*, points out that many Asians have reacted to the 'Asian flack' they are experiencing with the rise in Asian immigration by fleeing the cities of immigration, disidentifying from new Asians, and invoking the image of the 'good immigrant'. In some communities, this has led to older, assimilated segments of a community to dissociate from recent migrants. For example, a Nisei returning to his community after years of overseas military service, told his dad the following about the city's new demography: 'Goddamn dad, where the hell did all these Chinese come from? Shit, this isn't even our town anymore (Ibid., p. 59)'.

To be clear, my point is not that Asian Americans have not engaged in coalition politics and, in various locations, engaged in concerted efforts to elect Asian American candidates (Saito 1998). My point is that the group labelled 'Asian Americans' is profoundly divided along many axes and to forecast that many of those already existing divisions will be racialized by whites (e.g., sexploitation of Asian women by lonely white men in the 'Oriental bride' market) (Kitano and Daniels 1995) as well as by Asian Americans themselves (e.g., intra-Asian preferences seem to follow a racialized hierarchy of desire) (see data on this in Tuan 1998 and Moran 2001).

3) *Latinos' and Asians' racial attitudes*: The incorporation of the majority of Latinos as 'colonial subjects' (Puerto Ricans), refugees from wars (Central Americans), or illegal migrant workers (Mexicans) has foreshadowed subsequent patterns of integration into the American racial order. Nevertheless, the incorporation of a minority of Latinos as 'political refugees' (Cubans, Chileans, and Argentines) or as 'neutral' immigrants trying to better their economic situation (Costa Rica, Colombia) has allowed them a more comfortable ride in America's racial boat (Pedraza 1985). Therefore, whereas the incorporation of most Latinos has meant becoming 'nonwhite', for a few it has meant becoming almost white.

The identification of most Latinos as 'racial others' has led them to be more likely to be pro-black than pro-white. For example, the proportion of Mexicans and Puerto Ricans who indicate feeling very warm towards blacks is much higher (about 12 percentage points for Mexicans and 14 percentage points for Puerto Ricans) than towards Asians (the readings in the 'thermometer' range from 0 to 100 and the higher the 'temperature', the more positive are the feelings towards the group in question). In contrast, the proportion of Cubans who feel very warm towards blacks is 10 to 14 percentage points *lower* than Mexicans and Puerto Ricans. Cubans are also more likely to feel very warm towards Asians than towards blacks. More fitting of my thesis, as Table 3 shows, is that although Latinos who identify as 'white' express similar empathy towards blacks and Asians, those who identify as 'black' express the most positive feelings towards blacks (about 20 degrees warmer towards blacks than towards Asians).

Various studies have documented that Asians tend to hold anti-black and anti-Latino attitudes. For instance, Bobo, Zubrinsky, Johnson, and Oliver (1995) found that Chinese residents of Los Angeles expressed negative racial attitudes toward blacks. One Chinese resident stated, 'Blacks in general seem to be overly lazy' and another asserted, 'Blacks have a definite attitude problem' (Bobo, Zubrinsky, Johnson, and

Table 3 Latinos' affect toward Blacks and Asians by Latino ethnicity and racial self-classification

	Blacks	*Asians*
Latino ethnicity		
Mexicans	60.07	52.88
Puerto Ricans	60.24	50.81
Cubans	56.36	56.99
Racial self-classification		
White	57.71	53.49
Black	69.62	48.83
Latino self-referent	61.01	53.10

Source: Forman, Martinez, and Bonilla-Silva "Latinos' Perceptions of Blacks and Asians: Testing the Immigrant Hypothesis" (Unpublished Manuscript).

Oliver 1995, p. 78; for a more thorough analysis, see Bobo and Johnson 2000). Studies on Korean shopkeepers in various locales have found that over 70 per cent of them hold anti-black attitudes (Min 1996; Weitzer 1997; Yoon 1997).

C) Social interaction among members of the three racial strata

If a tri-racial system is emerging, one would expect more social (e.g., friendship, associations as neighbours, etc.) and intimate (e.g., marriage) contact between whites and honorary whites than between whites and members of the collective black. A cursory analysis of the interracial marriage and segregation data suggests this seems to be the case.

1) *Interracial marriage*: Although most marriages in America are still intra-racial, the rates vary substantially by group. Whereas 93 per cent of whites and blacks marry within-group, 70 per cent of Latinos and Asians do so and only 33 per cent Native Americans marry Native Americans (Moran 2001, p. 103). More significantly, when one disentangles the generic terms 'Asians' and 'Latinos', the data fit even more closely my thesis. For example, among 'Latinos', Cubans, Mexicans, Central Americans, and South Americans have higher rates of outmarriage than Puerto Ricans and Dominicans (Gilbertson, Fitzpatrick, and Yang 1996). Although interpreting the Asian American outmarriage patterns is very complex (groups such as Filipinos and Vietnamese have higher than expected rates partly due to the Vietnam War and the military bases in the Philippines), it is worth pointing out that the highest rate belongs to Japanese Americans and Chinese Americans (Kitano and Daniels 1995) and the lowest to Southeast Asians.

Furthermore, racial assimilation through marriage ('whitening') is significantly more likely for the children of Asian-white and Latino-white unions than for those of black-white unions. Hence, whereas only 22 per cent of the children of black fathers and white mothers are classified as white, the children of similar unions among Asians are twice as likely to be classified as white (Waters 1999). For Latinos, the data fit my thesis even closer as Latinos of Cuban, Mexican, and South

American origin have high rates of exogamy compared to Puerto Ricans and Dominicans (Gilbertson, Fitzpatrick, and Yang 1996). I concur with Moran's (2001) speculation that this may reflect the fact that because Puerto Ricans and Dominicans are generally more dark-skinned, they have restricted chances for outmarriage to whites in a highly racialized marriage market.

2) *Residential segregation of Latinos and Asians*: An imperfect measure of interracial interaction is the level of neighbourhood 'integration'. Researchers have shown that Latinos are less segregated from and are more exposed to whites than blacks (Massey and Denton 1987). Yet, they have also documented that dark-skinned Latinos (Dominicans and Puerto Ricans) experience rates of residential segregation which are similar to blacks. Thus, not surprisingly, in cities with a significant (10 per cent or higher) Latino presence, such as San Antonio, Chicago, New York, Long Beach, the index of residential dissimilarity[6] in 2000 is 60, 62, 67 and 63 per cent respectively (Lewis Mumford Center 2001).

Asians are generally less segregated from whites than blacks and Latinos. However, they have experienced an increase in residential segregation in recent years (White, Biddlecom and Guo 1993; Frey and Farley 1996). Part of the increase may be the result of the arrival of newer immigrants from Southeast Asia (Vietnam, Cambodia, and Laos) over the last two decades (Frey and Farley 1996). The relatively large Asian population in the San Francisco area, which accounts for about 21 per cent of the area's total population, has a dissimilarity index of .501, near the Latino index of .500, but less than the index for blacks at .640 (Logan 2001). Most metropolitan areas in the United States, however, do not have as large a population of Asians, and thus may not have reached the racial 'tipping point' that brings on residential segregation.

Concluding remarks: Tri-racial order, racial politics, and the future of white supremacy in America

I have presented a broad thesis about the future of race relations in the United States.[7] I argued that a new racial matrix, similar to that existing in Latin American and Caribbean societies, is developing and will eventually replace the old bi-racial one. In the emerging Amerikkka, 'blacks', 'Latinos', and 'Asians' can be found in any of the three loose racial strata. Therefore, as many members of minority groups experience 'racial redistricting' (Gallagher 2003), doing research on these groups will be more complex. Analysts will have to come to terms with the fact that many of the racial and ethnic categories we have used in the past are losing empirical purchase (how useful is the Latino category to comprehend the dissimilar experiences of Argentineans and Puerto Ricans?) as well as of the reality that members within some of these groups have vastly different experiences (is the category Cuban sufficient to understand the life trajectories of black and white 'Cubans'?).[8]

However, at this early stage of the analysis, and given the limitations of the available data on 'Latinos' and 'Asians' (most of the data is not parcelled out by subgroups and there is limited information by skintone), it is hard to make a conclusive case for Latin Americanization. Nevertheless, almost all the objective, subjective, and social interaction indicators I reviewed point in the direction one would expect if a tri-racial system is emerging. 'Honorary whites', the crucial group in my thesis, do better than members of the 'collective black', and have developed a racial attitudinal profile that is closer to that of whites, and prefer to associate with whites (a preference pattern that is reciprocated) than with members of the 'collective black'.[9]

Before I proceed to discuss the larger implications of Latin Americanization, I must clarify a number of points to avoid confusion. First, the three groups I describe will be *loosely organized* and need not act collectively or be conscious of their groupness to share a common social location. Borrowing from Marx's discussions on class, some of these racial strata will be 'race *in* itself' rather than 'race *for* itself'. Second, I expect higher levels of collective action and consciousness among the poles of the racial order (i.e., among whites and the collective black much as in Latin America and the Caribbean). Third, the honorary white strata, which will be the most unstable group in this new order, is the product of the socio-political needs of whites to maintain white supremacy given local and international changes but, at the same time, actors in this group will develop their own agency.'[10] Regardless of the reasons for its existence, members of this strata will defend their status vis-à-vis those below and try to achieve racial mobility through whitening as intermediate racial groups have done in the Caribbean and Latin America (Nettleford 1973; Wade 1997; Alleyne 2002).

If my prediction is right, what may be the consequences for race relations in the United States? First, racial politics will change dramatically. The 'us' versus 'them' racial dynamic will lessen as 'honorary whites' grow in size and social importance. This group is likely to buffer racial conflict – or derail it – as intermediate groups do in many Latin American countries. Two incidents reported by Norman Matloft in an Op-Ed piece in the *San Francisco Chronicle* (1997) are examples of things to come:

> In the newsletter of the Oakland chapter of the Organization of Chinese Americans, editor Peter Eng opined: "Chinese-Americans will need to separate and distance ourselves from other ethnic immigrant groups" and suggested that Latino immigration was a burden to society.

> Elaine Kim, a Korean-American UC Berkeley professor, has written that a major Latino organization suggested to her [actually to Korean community activist Bong Huan Kim-NM] that Asians and Latinos work together against blacks in an Oakland redistricting proposal. And an Asian/Latino coalition is suing Oakland, claiming it awards too many city contracts to black-owned firms.

Second, the ideology of colour-blind racism (Bonilla-Silva 2001, 2003) will become even more salient among whites and honorary whites and will also impact members of the collective black. This ideology will help to glue the new social system and further buffer racial conflict.

Third, if the state decides to stop gathering racial statistics, the struggle to document the impact of race in a variety of social venues will become monumental. More significantly, because state actions always impact upon civil society, if the state decides to erase race from above, the *social* recognition of 'races' in the polity may become harder. Americans may develop a Latin American- or Caribbean-like 'disgust' for even mentioning anything that is race-related.

Fourth, the deep history of black-white divisions in the United States has been such that the centrality of the black identity will not dissipate. Research on the 'black elite', for instance, shows they exhibit racial attitudes in line with their racial rather than class group (Dawson 1994). That identity may be taken up by dark-skinned Latinos as it is being rapidly taken up by most West Indians (Kasinitz, Battle, and Miyares 2001) and some Latinos (Rodriguez 2000). For example, Al, a fifty-three-year-old Jamaican engineer interviewed by Milton Vickerman (1999), stated:

> I have nothing against Haitians; I have nothing against black Americans.
> . . . If you're a nigger, you're a nigger, regardless of whether your are
> from Timbuktu. . . . There isn't the unity that one would like to see
> . . . Blacks have to appreciate blacks, no matter where they are from.
> Just look at it the way I look at it: That you're the same.

However, even among blacks, I predict some important changes. Their racial consciousness will become more diffused. For example, blacks are already developing a more disarticulated and blunted oppositional consciousness than ever before in American history (see Chapter 7 in Bonilla-Silva 2003). Furthermore, the external pressure of 'multiracials' in white contexts (Rockquemore and Brusma 2002) and the internal pressure of 'ethnic' blacks may change the notion of 'blackness' and even the position of some 'blacks' in the system. Colourism may become an even more important factor as a way of making social distinctions among 'blacks' (Keith and Herring 1991).

Fifth, the new order will force a reshuffling of *all* racial identities. Certain 'racial' and 'ethnic' claims may dissipate (or, in some cases, decline in significance) as mobility will increasingly be seen as based on (1) whiteness or near-whiteness and (2) intermarriage with whites (this seems to be the case among many Japanese Americans, particularly those who have intermarried). For example, the bi-racial project can be seen as a rejection of blackness hoping to achieve entrance into or, at least, nearness to whiteness (Minkalani 2003). This dissipation of ethnicity will not be limited to 'honorary whites' as members of the 'collective black' strata strive to position themselves higher in the new racial totem pole based on degrees of proximity or closeness to whiteness. Will Vietnamese, Hmongs, Laoatians and other members of the Asian underclass coalesce with blacks and dark-skinned Latinos or will they try to distance themselves from them and struggle to emphasize their 'Americanness'?

Lastly, the new racial stratification system will be more effective in maintaining 'white supremacy' (Mills 1997). Whites will still be at the top of the social structure but will face fewer race-based challenges, and racial inequality will remain and may even widen as is the case throughout Latin America and the Caribbean (Nascimento and Nascimento 2001). And, to avoid confusion about my claim regarding 'honorary whites', let me clarify that their standing and status will be dependent upon whites' wishes and practices. 'Honorary' means they will remain secondary, will still face discrimination, and will not receive equal treatment in society. For example, although Arab Americans will be regarded as 'honorary whites', their treatment in the post-11 September era suggests their status as 'white' and 'American' is tenuous at best.[11] Likewise, albeit substantial segments of the Asian American community may become 'honorary white', they will also continue to suffer from discrimination and be regarded in many quarters as 'perpetual foreigners'.

Therein lie some weaknesses of the emerging tri-racial order and the possibilities for challenging it. Members of the 'collective black' must be the backbone of the movement challenging the new order, as they are the ones who will remain literally 'at the bottom of the well'. However, if they want to be successful, they must wage, in coalition with progressive Asian and Latino organizations, a concerted effort to politicize the segments I label 'honorary whites' and make them aware of the *honorary* character of their status. This is the way out of the impending new racial quandary. We need to short-circuit the belief in near-whiteness as the solution to status differences and create a coalition of all 'people of colour' and their white allies. If the the tri-racial, Latin American- or Caribbean-like model of race prevails and 'pigmentocracy' crystallizes, most Americans will scramble for the meagre wages that near-whiteness will provide to those willing to play the 'we are all American' game.

Notes

1   This does not mean that blacks and whites have been the *only* racial actors in the United States's history or that more complex race relations have not existed before in some areas of the country. It just means that the macro-level racial dynamics in the United States, unlike those in many other parts of the world, have been bifurcated and that the black-white foundation has served as the yardstick to treat all other groups since the creation of the United States in 1776 (see Chapter 7 in Feagin 2000).

2   For a discussion on the racialization of the world-system, see Etienne Balibar and Immanuel Wallerstein, *Race, Nation, and Class: Ambiguous Identities* (London: Verso, 1991).

3   Figure 1 is heuristic rather than definitive and, thus, the main purpose of this map is to sketch how these three racial strata might look. Therefore, a few of [the] racial or ethnic groups I place in these loosely structured groups may be out of place and not all the ethnic groups that comprise the United States are included.

4   An important matter to disentangle empirically in the future is if the immigrant groups we label 'honorary whites' come with the racial, class, or race/class capital before they achieve honorary white status, that is, are they allowed to fit this intermediate position because of their class or because of their racial or because of a combination of race and class status? The case of West Indians-who come to the Unites States with class advantages (e.g., educational and otherwise) and yet 'fade to black' in a few generations (that is, become 'black') suggest that the 'racial' status of the group has an independent effect in this process (Kasinitz, Battle, and Miyares 2001). Similarly, Filipinos come to the United States highly educated and acculturated yet, because they experience severe racial

discrimination, second- and third-generation Filipinos' self-identify as Filipino-American (Le Espiritu and Wolf 2001. For a similar finding on Vietnamese, see Zhou 2001).

5   It is important to point out that occupational representation in a category does not mean equality. Chan (1991) shows that many Asians are pushed into self-employment after suffering occupational sedimentation in professional jobs. See also Ronald Takaki, *A Different Mirror: A History of Multicultural America* (Boston: Little, Brown & Co., 1993).

6   The index of residential dissimilarity expresses the percentage of a minority population that would have to move to result in a perfectly even distribution of the population across census tracts. This index runs from 0 (no segregation) to 100 (total segregation) and it's symmetrical (not affected by population size).

7   I am not alone in making this kind of prediction. Arthur K. Spears (1999), Suzanne Oboler (2000), Gary Okihiro (1994), Man Matsueda (1996) have made similar claims recently.

8   This separation within the Cuban ethnic group may already be happening. See Mirta Ojito (2001) 'Best of Friends, Worlds Apart', in *How Race is Lived in America*, Correspondents of the *New York Times*, pp. 23–39 (New York: Henry Holt and Company).

9   I recognize there are alternative interpretations to these findings. One could claim that what is happening is that class is becoming more salient than race (but see Note 3), or that education and nativity are becoming better predictors of mobility. Unfortunately, no data set includes all these elements as well as the ones I suggest are becoming central to control for all these variables. In the mean time, the fact that indicators in three different areas line up in the expected direction gives me confidence that my thesis is likely.

10 For an excellent collection analysing, among other things, the instability of intermediate mulatto and *mestizo* groups in Latin America and, at the same time, their agency in articulating a stake in whiteness, see *Race & Nation in Modern Latin America*, edited by Nancy P. Appelbaum *et al.* (Chapel Hill and London: University of North Carolina Press, 2003).

11 However, I still contend that most Arab Americans will be part of this intermediate strata. First, although recent immigrants remain loyal to their ethnic communities, older, well-established Arab Americans put their emphasis 'not on their ethnicity but on their Americanism' (Suleiman 1994). Second, even though recent immigrants experience some economic hardships, the Census data indicate that Arab Americans have levels of education, income, and occupational standing similar to the majority community (Schopmeyer 2000). Lastly, although I acknowledge the vulnerability of Arab Americans in post-11 September America, there are two things to note. First, this has not led Arab Americans to develop a political programme of identification and cooperation with racial minorities. Second, we must not forget that other groups, such as Japanese Americans, suffered equal indignities in the past (in the 1940s, they were interned in concentration camps, and in the 1990s they were treated as traitors during the 50th anniversary of Pearl Harbor) and yet did not become a racial underclass or change their racial attitudes and political behaviour towards the racial groups at the bottom of America's racial barrel.

References

Almaguer, Tomas 1994 *Racial Fault Lines: The Historical Origins of White Supremacy in California*, Berkeley, Los Angeles, and London: The University of California Press

Alleyne, Mervyn C. 2002 *The Construction and Representation of Race and Ethnicity in the Caribbean and the World*, Mona and Kingston: University of the West Indies Press

Amott, Teresa and Matteai, Leslie 1991 *Race, Gender, and Work: A Multi-cultural History of Women in the United States*, Boston, MA: South End Press

Applebaum, Nancy P., MacPherson, Anne S. and Rosemblatt, Karin Alejandra (eds) 2003 *Race & Nation in Modern Latin America*, Chapel Hill and London: University of North Carolina Press

Balibar, Etienne and Wallerstein, Immanuel 1991 *Race, Nation, and Class: Ambiguous Identities*, London: Verso

Bobo, Lawrence and Johnson, Devon 2000 'Racial attitudes in a prismatic metropolis: mapping identity, stereotypes, competition, and views on affirmative action', in Lawrence Bobo, Melvin Oliver, James Johnson and Abel Valenzuela (eds), *Prismatic Metropolis*, New York: Russell Sage Foundation, pp. 81–166

Bobo, Lawrence, Zubrinsky, Camille, Johnson, James JR, and Oliver, Melvin 1995 'Work orientation, job discrimination, and ethnicity', *Research in the Sociology of Work*, vol. 5 pp 45–85

Bonilla-Silva, Eduardo and Glover, Karen S. forthcoming 'We are all Americans! The Latin Americanization of race relations in the USA', in Amanda E. Lewis and Maria Krysan (eds), *The Changing Terrain of Race and Ethnicity: Theory, Methods and Public Policy*, New York: Russell Sage Foundation

Bonilla-Silva, Eduardo 2003 *Racism Without Racists: Color Blind Racism and the Persistence of Racial Inequality*, Boulder, CO: Rowman and Littlefield

—— 2001 *White Supremacy and Racism in the Post-Civil Rights Era*, Boulder, CO: Lynne Rienner Publishers

—— 2000 'This is a white country': The racial ideology of the Western nations of the world-system', *Sociological Inquiry*, vol. 70, no. 3, pp. 188–214

—— 1997 'Rethinking racism: towards a structural interpretation', *American Sociological Review*, vol. 62, no 3 pp 465–80

Bottomore, Thomas B. 1968 *Classes in Modern Society*, New York: Vintage Books

Castles, Stephen and Miller, Mark 1993 *The Age of Migration: International Population Movements in the Modern World*, Hong Kong: Macmillan

Chan, Sucheng 1991 *Asian Americans: An Interpretive History*, Boston, MA: Twayne Publishers

Cohen, Robin 1997 *Global Diasporas: An Introduction*, Seattle, WA: University of Washington Press

Daniels, Reginald 2002 *More Than Black? Multiracial Identity and the New Racial Order*, Philadelphia, PA: Temple University Press

Dawson, Michael C. 1994 *Behind the Mule: Race and Class in African American Politics*, Princeton, NJ: Princeton University Press

Degler, Carl N. 1986 *Neither Black nor White: Slavery and Race Relations in Brazil and the United States*, Madison, WI: The University of Wisconsin Press

De la Garza, Rodolfo, O., Desipio, Louis, Garcia, Chris, Garcia, John and Falcon, Angelo (eds) 1993 *Latino Voices: Mexican, Puerto Rican, & Cuban Perspectives on American Politics*, Boulder, San Francisco, and Oxford: Westview Press

D'Souza, Dinesh 1995 *The End of Racism: Principles for a Multiracial Society*, New York: Free Press

Espiritu, Yen Le 1992 *Asian American Panethnicity: Bridging Institutions and Identities*, Philadelphia, PA: Temple University Press

Espiritu, Yen Le and Wolf, Diane 2001 'The paradox of assimilation: Children of Filipino immigrants in San Diego', in Ruben Rumbaut and Alejandro Portes (eds), *Ethnicities: Children of Immigrants in America*, Berkeley and New York: University of California Press and Russell Sage Foundation

Feagin, Joe R. 2000 *Racist America: Roots: Current Realities, and Future Reparations*, London and New York: Routledge

Fredrickson, George M. 1981 *White Supremacy*, Oxford, New York, Toronto, and Melbourne: Oxford University Press

Frey, William H. and Reynolds, Farley 1996 'Latino, Asian, and Black segregation in U.S. metropolitan areas: are multi-ethnic metros different?', *Demography*, vol. 33, no 1 pp. 35–50

Gallagher, Charles A. 2003 'Racial redistricting: expanding the boundaries of whiteness', in Heather Dalmage (ed.), *The Multiracial Movement: The Politics of Color*, New York: SUNY Press

Gans, Herbert J. 1999 *The Possibility of a New Racial Hierarchy in the Twenty-First Century United States*, Chicago, IL: The University of Chicago Press

Ilbertson, Greta A., Fitzpatrick, Joseph P. and Lijun, Yang 1996 'Hispanic outmarriage in New York City-new evidence from 1991', *International Immigration Review*, vol. 30

Grieco, Elizabeth M. and Cassidy, Rachel C. 2001 *Overview of Race and Hispanic Origin 2000*, Washington: U.S. Government Printing Office

Hanchard, Michael 1994 *Orpheus and Power: The Movimiento Negro of Rio de Janeiro and São Paulo, Brazil, 1945–1988*, Princeton, NJ: Princeton University Press

Helg, Aline 1990 'Race in Argentina and Cuba, 1880–1930: Theory, policies, and popular reaction', in Richard Graham (ed.), *The Idea of Race in Latin America, 1870–1940*, Austin: University of Texas Press, pp. 37–69

Kasinitz, Philip, Battle, Juan and Miyares, Ines 2001 'Fade to black? The children of West Indian immigrants in southern Florida', in Ruben G. Rumbaut and Alejandro Portes (eds), *Ethnicities: Children of Immigrants in America*, Berkeley, CA: University of California Press pp 267–300

Keith, Verna M. and Herring, Cedric 1991 'Skin tone and stratification in the Black community', *American Journal of Sociology*, vol. 97, no. 3, pp. 760–78

Kitano, Harry H. L. and Daniels, Rogers 1995 *Asian Americans: Emerging Minorities*, 2nd edn, Englewood Cliffs, NJ: Prentice Hall

Lewis Mumford Centre 2001 *Racial and Ethnic Population Totals, Dissimilarity Indices and Exposure for Metropolitan Areas, 1990–2000*

Logan, John R. 2001 *From Many Shores: Asians in Census 2000*, in Report by the Lewis Mumford Center for Comparative Urban and Regional Research, Albany: University of Albany

Lovell, Peggy A. and Wood, Charles H. 1998 'Skin color, racial identity, and life chances in Brazil', *Latin American Perspectives*, vol. 25, no. 3, pp. 90–109

Lusane, Clarence 1997 *Race in the Global Era: African Americans at the Millennium*, Boston, MA: South End Press

Martinez-Echazabel, Lourdes 1998 'Mestizaje and the discourse of national/cultural identity in Latin America, 1845–1959', *Latin American Perspectives*, vol. 25, no. 3, pp. 21–42

Massey, Douglas S. and Denton, Nancy A. 1987 'Trends in the residential segregation of Blacks, Hispanics, and Asians: 1970–1980', *American Sociological Review*, vol. 52, no. 6, pp. 802–825

Matloff, Norman 1997 'Asians, Blacks, and intolerance', *San Francisco Chronicle*, 20 May

Matsueda, Mari J. 1996 *Where is Your Body? And Other Essays on Race, Gender and the Law*, Boston, MA: Beacon Press

Miles, Robert 1993 *Racism After 'Race Relations'*, London: Routledge

Mills, Charles W. 1997 *The Racial Contract*, Ithaca and London: Cornell University Press

Min, Pyong Gap 1996 *Caught in the Middle: Korean Communities in New York and Los Angeles*, Berkeley, CA: University of California Press

Minkalani, Minkah 2003 'Rejecting Blackness and claiming Whiteness: antiblack Whiteness in the biracial project', in Ashley Doane and Eduardo Bonilla-Silva (eds), *White Out: The Continuing Significance of Racism*, New York and London: Routledge, pp. 81–94

Moran, Rachel 2001 *Interracial Intimacy: The Regulation of Race and Romance*, Chicago and London: The University of Chicago Press

Nascimento, Abdias and Nascimento, Elisa Larkin 2001 'Dance of deception: a reading of race relations in Brazil', in Charles Hamilton *et al.* (eds), *Beyond Racism*, Boulder and London: Lynne Rienner Publishers, pp. 105–56

Nettleford, Rex 1973 'National identity and attitudes toward race in Jamaica', in David Lowenthal and Lambros Comitas (eds), *Consequences of Class and Color: West Indian Perspectives*, New York: Doubleday, pp. 35–55

Nobles, Melissa 2000 *Shades of Citizenship: Race and the Census in Modern Politics*, Stanford, CA: Stanford University Press

Okihiro, Gary 1994 *Margins and Mainstreams: Asians in American History and Culture*, Seattle, WA: University of Washington Press

Oboler, Suzanne 2000 'It must be a fake!' racial ideologies, identities, and the question of rights in Hispanics/Latinos', in Jorge J. E. Gracia and Pablo De Greiff (eds), *The United States: Ethnicity, Race, and Rights*, New York: Routledge, pp. 125–44

Ojito, Mirta 2001 'Best of friends, worlds apart', in Correspondents of the *New York Times* (eds), *How Race is Lived in America*, New York: Henry Holt and Company, pp. 23–39

Parker, David and Song, Miri 2001 *Rethinking 'Mixed Race'*, London: Pluto Press

Pedrza, Silvia 1985 *Political and Economic Migrants in America: Cubans and Mexicans*, Austin, TX: University of Texas Press

Qian, Zhenchao and Lichter, Daniel T. 2000 'Measuring marital assimilation: intermarriage among natives and immigrants', *Social Science Research*, vol. 30, pp. 289–312

Ridgeway, Cecilia L. 1991 'The social construction of status value: Gender and other nominal characteristics', *Social Forces*, vol. 70, no 2 pp. 367–86

Rockquemore, Kerry Ann and Brunsma, David L. 2002 *Beyond Black: Biracial Identity in America*, Thousand Oaks, CA: Sage Publications

Rodriguez, Clara E. 2000 *Changing Race: Latinos, the Census; and the History of Ethnicity in the United States*, New York: New York University Press

Roediger, David 1991 *The Wages of Whiteness: Race and the Making of the American Working Class*, New York: Verso

Saito, Leland T. 1998 *Race and Politics: Asian Americans; Latinos, and Whites in a Los Angeles Suburb*, Urbana: University of Illinois Press

San Juan, E. JR. 2000 'The limits of ethnicity and the horizon of historical materialism', in Esther Mikyung Ghymn (ed.) *Asian American Studies: Identity, Images, Issues Past and Present*, New York Peter Lang, pp. 9–34

Schoenbaum, David and Pond, Elizabeth 1996 *The German Question and Other German Questions*, New York: St. Martin's Press

Schopmeyer, Kim 2000 'A demographic portrait of Arab detroit', in Nabeel Abraham and Andrew Shyrock (eds), *Arab Detroit: From Margin to Mainstream*, Detroit: Wayne State University Press, pp. 61–94

Smith, Robert C. 1995 *Racism in the Post-Civil Rights Era: Now You See It, Now You Don't*, Albany: State University of New York Press

Spears, Arthur K. 1999 *Race and Ideology: Language, Symbolism, and Popular Culture*, Detroit: Wayne State University Press

Steinberg, Stephen 1995 *Turning Back: The Retreat from Racial Justice in American Thought and Policy*, Boston, MA: Beacon Press

Suleiman, Michael W. 1994 'Arab Americans and the political process', in Ernest McCarus (ed.), *The Development of Arab-American Identity*, Ann Arbor, MI: The University of Michigan Press pp 37–60

Takai, Ronald 1993 *A Different Mirror: A History of Multicultural America*, Boston, MA: Little, Brown & Co

Tajfel, H. 1970 'Experiments in intergroup discrimination', *Scientific American*, vol. 223, pp. 96–102

Tuan, Mia 1998 *Forever Foreigners or Honorary Whites? The Asian Ethnic Experience Today*, New Brunswick: Rutgers University Press

US Bureau Of The Census 1996 *Population Projections of the United States by Age, Sex, Race, and Hispanic Origin: 1995 to 2050*, Washington, DC: US Government Printing Office

US News and World Report 2003 *America's Best Colleges*, Washington, DC: US News and World Report

Vickerman, Milton 1999 *Crosscurrents: West Indian Immigrants and Race*, New York: Oxford University Press

Wade, Peter 1997 *Race and Ethnicity in Latin America*, London: Pluto Press

Warren, Jonathan W. and Twine, France Winddance 1997 'White Americans, the new minority?: Non-Blacks and the ever-expanding boundaries of Whiteness', *Journal of Black Studies*, vol. 28, no. 2, pp. 200–18

Waters, Mary C. 1999 *Black Identities: West Indian Immigrant Dreams and American Reality*, Cambridge, MA: Harvard University Press

Weitzer, Ronald 1997 'Racial prejudice among Korean merchants in African American Neighborhoods' *Sociological Quarterly*, vol. 38, no. 4, pp. 587–606

White, Michael J., Biddlecom, Ann E. and Guo, Shenyand 1993 'Immigration, naturalization, and residential assimilation among Asian Americans in 1980', *Social Forces*, vol. 72, no 1 pp 93–117

Wilson, William J. 1978 *The Declining Significance of Race*, Chicago, IL: The University of Chicago Press

Winant, Howard 2001 *The World is a Ghetto: Race and Democracy Since World War II*, New York: Basic Books

Yoon, In-Jin 1997 *On My Own: Korean Businesses and Race Relations in America*, Chicago, IL: University of Chicago Press

Zhou, Min 2001 'Straddling different worlds: The acculturation of Vietnamese refugee children', in Ruben G. Rumbaut and Alejandro Portes (eds), *Ethnicities: Children of Immigrants in America*, Berkeley, CA: University of California Press, pp. 187–227

Chapter 41

K. Anthony Appiah

RACIAL IDENTITY AND RACIAL IDENTIFICATION

[. . .]

IF WE FOLLOW THE BADGE of color from "African" to "Negro" to "colored race" to "black" to "Afro-American" to "African-American" (and this ignores such fascinating detours as the route by way of "Afro-Saxon") we are thus tracing the history not only of a signifier, a label, but also a history of its effects. At any time in this history there was, within the American colonies and the United States that succeeded them, a massive consensus, both among those labeled black and among those labeled white, as to who, in their own communities, fell under which labels. (As immigration from China and other parts of the "Far East" occurred, an Oriental label came to have equal stability.) There was, no doubt, some "passing"; but the very concept of passing implies that, if the relevant fact about the ancestry of these individuals had become known, most people would have taken them to be traveling under the wrong badge.

The major North American exception was in southern Louisiana, where a different system in which an intermediary Creole group, neither white nor black, had social recognition; but *Plessy v. Fergusson* reflected the extent to which the Louisiana Purchase effectively brought even that state gradually into the American mainstream of racial classification. For in that case Homer Adolph Plessy – a Creole gentleman who could certainly have passed in most places for white – discovered in 1896, after a long process of appeal, that the Supreme Court of the United States proposed to treat him as a Negro and therefore recognize the State of Louisiana's right to keep him and his white fellow citizens "separate but equal."

The result is that there are at least three sociocultural objects in America – blacks, whites and Orientals – whose membership at any time is relatively, and increasingly, determinate. These objects are historical in this sense: to identify all the members of these American races over time, you cannot seek a single criterion that applies equally always; you can find the starting point for the race – the subcontinental source of the population of individuals that defines its initial membership – and then apply at each historical moment the criteria of inter-temporal continuity that apply at that moment to decide which individuals in the next generation count as belonging to the group. There is from the very beginning until the present, at the heart of the system, a simple rule that very few would dispute even today: where both parents are of a single race, the child is of the same race as the parents.

The criteria applicable at any time may leave vague boundaries. They certainly change, as the varying decisions about what proportion of African ancestry made one black or the current uncertainty as to how to assign the children of white-yellow "miscegenation" demonstrate. But they always definitely assign some people to the group and definitely rule out others; and for most of America's history the class of people about whom there was uncertainty (are the Florida Seminoles black or Indian?) was relatively small.[1]

Once the racial label is applied to people, ideas about what it refers to, ideas that may be much less consensual than the application of the label, come to have their social effects. But they have not only social effects but psychological ones as well; and they shape the ways people conceive of themselves and their projects. In particular, the labels can operate to shape what I want to call "identification": the process through which an individual intentionally shapes her projects – including her plans for her own life and her conception of the good – by reference to available labels, available identities.

Identification is central to what Ian Hacking has called "making up people."[2] Drawing on a number of examples, but centrally homosexuality and multiple personality syndrome, he defends what he calls a "dynamic nominalism," which argues that "numerous kinds of human beings and human acts come into being hand in hand with our invention of the categories labeling them."[3] I have just articulated a dynamic nominalism about a kind of person that is currently usually called "African-American."

Hacking reminds us of the philosophical truism, whose most influential formulation is in Elizabeth Anscombe's work on intention, that in intentional action people act "under descriptions"; that their actions are conceptually shaped. It follows, of course, that what people can do depends on what concepts they have available to them; and among the concepts that may shape one's action is the concept of a certain kind of person and the behavior appropriate to that kind.

Hacking offers as an example Sartre's brilliant evocation, in *Being and Nothingness*, of the Parisian *garçon de café*: "His movement is quick and forward, a little too precise, a little too rapid. He comes towards the patrons with a step a little too quick. He bends forward a little too eagerly, his eyes express an interest too solicitous for the order of the customer."[4] Hacking comments:

> Sartre's antihero chose to be a waiter. Evidently that was not a possible choice in other places, other times. There are servile people in most societies, and servants in many, but a waiter is something specific, and a *garçon de café* more specific. . . .
>
> As with almost every way in which it is possible to be a person, it is possible to be a *garçon de café* only at a certain time, in a certain

place, in a certain social setting. The feudal serf putting food on my lady's table can no more choose to be a *garçon de café* than he can choose to be lord of the manor. But the impossibility is evidently of a different kind.[5]

The idea of the *garçon de café* lacks, so far as I can see, the sort of theoretical commitments that are trailed by the idea of the black and the white, the homosexual and the heterosexual. So it makes no sense to ask of someone who has a job as a *garçon de café* whether that is what he really is. The point is not that we do not have expectations of the *garçon de café*: that is why it is a recognizable identity. It is rather that those expectations are about the performance of the role; they depend on our assumption of intentional conformity to those expectations. As I spent some time arguing earlier, we *can* ask whether someone is really of a black race, because the constitution of this identity is generally theoretically committed: we expect people of a certain race to behave a certain way not simply because they are conforming to the script for that identity, performing that role, but because they have certain antecedent properties that are consequences of the label's properly applying to them. It is because ascription of racial identities – the process of applying the label to people, including ourselves – is based on more than intentional identification that there can be a gap between what a person ascriptively is and the racial identity he performs: it is this gap that makes passing possible.

Race is, in this way, like all the major forms of identification that are central to contemporary identity politics: female and male; gay, lesbian, and straight; black, white, yellow, red, and brown; Jewish-, Japanese-, and Korean-American; even that most neglected of American identities, class. There is, in all of them, a set of theoretically committed criteria for ascription, not all of which are held by everybody, and which may not be consistent with one another even in the ascriptions of a single person; and there is then a process of identification in which the label shapes the intentional acts of (some of) those who fall under it.

It does not follow from the fact that identification shapes action, shapes life plans, that the identification itself must be thought of as voluntary. I don't recall ever choosing to identify as a male;[6] but being male has shaped many of my plans and actions. In fact, where my ascriptive identity is one on which almost all my fellow citizens agree, I am likely to have little sense of choice about whether the identity is mine; though I *can* choose how central my identification with it will be – choose, that is, how much I will organize my life around that identity. Thus if I am among those (like the unhappily labeled "straight-acting gay men," or most American Jews) who are able, if they choose, to escape ascription, I may choose not to take up a gay or Jewish identity; though this will require concealing facts about myself or my ancestry from others.

If, on the other hand, I fall into the class of those for whom the consensus on ascription is not clear – as among contemporary so-called biracials, or bisexuals, or those many white Americans of multiple identifiable ethnic heritages[7] – I may have a sense of identity options: but one way I may exercise them is by marking myself ethnically (as when someone chooses to wear an Irish pin) so that others will then be more likely to ascribe that identity to me.

Differences among differences

Collective identities differ, of course, in lots of ways; the body is central to race, gender, and sexuality but not so central to class and ethnicity. And, to repeat an important point, racial identification is simply harder to resist than ethnic identification. The reason is twofold. First, racial ascription is more socially salient: unless you are morphologically atypical for your racial group, strangers, friends, officials are always aware of it in public and private contexts, always notice it, almost never let it slip from view. Second – and again both in intimate settings and in public space – race is taken by so many more people to be the basis for treating people differentially. (In this respect, Jewish identity in America strikes me as being a long way along a line toward African-American identity: there are ways of speaking and acting and looking – and it matters very little whether they are "really" mostly cultural or mostly genetic – that are associated with being Jewish; and there are many people, white and black, Jewish and Gentile, for whom this identity is a central force in shaping their responses to others.)

This much about identification said, we can see that Du Bois's analytical problem was, in effect, that he believed that for racial labeling of this sort to have the obvious real effects that it did have – among them, crucially, his own identification with other black people and with Africa – there must be some real essence that held the race together. Our account of the history of the label reveals that this is a mistake: once we focus, as Du Bois almost saw, on the racial badge – the signifier rather than the signified, the word rather than the concept – we see both that the effects of the labeling are powerful and real and that false ideas, muddle and mistake and mischief, played a central role in determining both how the label was applied and to what purposes.

This, I believe, is why Du Bois so often found himself reduced, in his attempts to define race, to occult forces: if you look for a shared essence you won't get anything, so you'll come to believe you've missed it, because it is super-subtle, difficult to experience or identify: in short, mysterious. But if, as I say, you understand the sociohistorical process of construction of the race, you'll see that the label works despite the absence of an essence.

Perhaps, then, we can allow that what Du Bois was after was the idea of racial identity, which I shall roughly define as a label, R, associated with *ascriptions* by most people (where ascription involves descriptive criteria for applying the label); and *identifications* by those that fall under it (where identification implies a shaping role for the label in the intentional acts of the possessors, so that they sometimes act *as an R*), where there is a history of associating possessors of the label with an inherited racial essence (even if some who use the label no longer believe in racial essences).

In fact, we might argue that racial identities could persist even if nobody believed in racial essences, provided both ascription and identification continue.

There will be some who will object to my account that it does not give racism a central place in defining racial identity: it is obvious, I think, from the history I have explored, that racism has been central to the development of race theory. In that sense racism has been part of the story all along. But you might give an account of racial identity in which you counted nothing as a racial essence unless it implied a hierarchy among the races;[8] or unless the label played a role in racist practices. I have some sympathy with the former strategy; it would fit easily into my basic picture. To the latter strategy, however, I make the philosopher's objection that it confuses logical and causal priority: I have no doubt that racial theories grew up, in part, as rationalizations for mistreating blacks, Jews, Chinese, and various others. But I think it is useful to reserve the concept of racism, as opposed to ethnocentrism or simply inhumanity, for practices in which a race concept plays a central role. And I doubt you can explain racism without first explaining the race concept.

I *am* in sympathy, however, with an animating impulse behind such proposals, which is to make sure that here in America we do not have discussions of race in which racism disappears from view. As I pointed out, racial identification is hard to resist in part because racial ascription by others is so insistent; and its effects – especially, but by no means exclusively, the racist ones – are so hard to escape. It is obvious, I think, that the persistence of racism means that racial ascriptions have negative consequences for some and positive consequences for others – creating, in particular, the white-skin privilege that it is so easy for people who have it to forget; and it is clear, too, that for those who suffer from the negative consequences, racial identification is a predictable response, especially where the project it suggests is that the victims of racism should join together to resist it. I shall return later to some of the important moral consequences of present racism and the legacy of racisms of the past.

But before I do, I want to offer some grounds for preferring the account of racial identity I have proposed, which places racial essences at its heart, over some newer accounts that see racial identity as a species of cultural identity.

[. . .] In the United States, not only ethnic but also racial boundaries are culturally marked. In *White Women, Race Matters: The Social Construction of Whiteness*,[9] Ruth Frankenberg records the anxiety of many white women who do not see themselves as white "ethnics" and worry, therefore, that they have no culture.[10] This is somewhat puzzling in people who live, as every normal human being does, in rich structures of knowledge, experience, value and meaning; through tastes and practices: it is perplexing, in short, in people with normal human lives. But the reason these women do not recognize that they have a culture is because none of these things that actually make up their cultural lives are marked as white, as belonging specially to them: and the things that *are* marked as white (racism, white privilege) are things they want to repudiate. Many African-Americans, on the other hand, have cultural lives in which the ways they eat, the churches they go to, the music they listen to, and the ways they speak *are* marked as black: their identities are marked by cultural differences.

I have insisted that African-Americans do not have a single culture, in the sense of shared language, values, practices, and meanings. But many people who think of races as groups defined by shared cultures, conceive that sharing in a different way. They understand black people as sharing black culture *by definition*: jazz or hip-hop belongs to an African-American, whether she likes it or knows anything about it, because it is culturally marked as black. Jazz belongs to a black person who knows nothing about it more fully or naturally that it does to a white jazzman. [. . .]

Identities and norms

I have been exploring these questions about culture in order to show how unsatisfactory an account of the significance of race that mistakes identity for culture can be. But if this is the wrong route from identity to moral and political concerns, is there a better way?

We need to go back to the analysis of racial identities. While the theories on which ascription is based need not themselves be normative, these identities come with normative as well as descriptive expectations; about which, once more, there may be both inconsistency in the thinking of the individuals and fairly widespread disagreement among them. There is, for example, a very wide range of opinions among American Jews as to what their being Jewish commits them; and while most Gentiles probably don't think about the matter very much, people often make remarks that suggest they admire the way in which, as they believe, Jews have "stuck together," an admiration that seems to presuppose the moral idea that it is, if not morally obligatory, then at least morally desirable, for those who share identities to take responsibility for each other. (Similar comments have been made increasingly often about Korean-Americans.)

We need, in short, to be clear that the relation between identities and moral life are complex. In the liberal tradition, to which I adhere, we see public morality as engaging each of us as individuals with our individual "identities": and we have the notion, which comes (as Charles Taylor has rightly argued[11]) from the ethics of authenticity, that, other things being equal, people have the right to be acknowledged publicly as what they already really are. It is because someone is already authentically Jewish or gay that we deny them something in requiring them to hide this fact, to "pass," as we say, for something that they are not. Charles Taylor has suggested that we call the political issues raised by this fact the politics of recognition: a politics that asks us to acknowledge socially and politically the authentic identities of others.

As has often been pointed out, however, the way much discussion of recognition proceeds is strangely at odds with the individualist thrust of talk of authenticity and identity. If what matters about me is my individual and authentic self, why is so much contemporary talk of identity about large categories – race, gender, ethnicity, nationality, sexuality – that seem so far from individual? What is the relation between this collective language and the individualist thrust of the modern notion of the self? How has social life come to be so bound up with an idea of identity that has deep roots in romanticism with its celebration of the individual over and against society?[12]

The connection between individual identity, on the one hand, and race and other collective identities, on the other, seems to be something like this: each person's individual identity is seen as having two major dimensions. There is a collective dimension, the intersection of her collective identities; and there is what I will call a personal dimension, consisting of other socially or morally important features of the person – intelligence, charm, wit, cupidity – that are not themselves the basis of forms of collective identity.

The distinction between these two dimensions of identity is, so to speak, a sociological rather than a logical distinction. In each dimension we are talking about properties that are important for social life. But only the collective identities count as social categories, kinds of person. There is a logical category but no social category of the witty, or the clever, or the charming, or the greedy: people who share these properties do not constitute a social group, in the relevant sense. The concept of authenticity is central to the connection between these two dimensions; and there is a problem in many current understandings of that relationship, a misunderstanding one can find, for example, in Charles Taylor's recent (brilliant) essay *Multiculturalism and the Politics of Recognition*. [. . .]

Beyond identity

The large collective identities that call for recognition come with notions of how a proper person of that kind behaves: it is not that there is *one* way that blacks should behave, but that there are proper black modes of behavior. These notions provide loose norms or models, which play a role in shaping the life plans of those who make these collective identities central to their individual identities; of the identifications of those who fly under these banners.[13] Collective identities, in short, provide what we might call scripts: narratives that people can use in shaping their life plans and in telling their life stories. In our society (though not, perhaps, in the England of Addison and Steele) being witty does not in this way suggest the life script of "the wit." And that is why what I called the personal dimensions of identity work differently from the collective ones.

This is not just a point about modern Westerners: cross-culturally it matters to people that their lives have a certain narrative unity; they want to be able to tell a story of their lives that makes sense. The story – my story – should cohere in the way appropriate by the standards made available in my culture to a person of my identity. In telling that story, how I fit into the wider story of various collectivities is, for most of us, important. It is not just gender identities that give shape (through, for example, rites of passage into woman- or manhood) to one's life: ethnic and national identities too fit each individual story into a larger narrative. And some of the most "individualist" of individuals value such things. Hobbes spoke of the desire for glory as one of the dominating impulses of human beings, one that was bound to make trouble for social life. But glory can consist in fitting and being seen to fit into a collective history: and so, in the name of glory, one can end up doing the most social things of all.

How does this general idea apply to our current situation in the multicultural West? We live in societies in which certain individuals have not been treated with equal dignity because they were, for example, women, homosexuals, blacks, Catholics. Because, as Taylor so persuasively argues, our identities are dialogically shaped, people who have these characteristics find them central – often, negatively central – to their identities. Nowadays there is a widespread agreement that the insults to their dignity and the limitations of their autonomy imposed in the name of these collective identities are seriously wrong. One form of healing of the self that those who have these identities participate in is learning to see these collective identities not as sources of limitation and insult but as a valuable part of what they centrally are. Because the ethics of authenticity requires us to express what we centrally are in our lives, they move next to the demand that they be recognized in social life as women, homosexuals, blacks, Catholics. Because there was no good reason to treat people of these sorts badly, and because the culture continues to provide degrading images of them nevertheless, they demand that we do cultural work to resist the stereotypes, to challenge the insults, to lift the restrictions.

These old restrictions suggested life scripts for the bearers of these identities, but they were negative ones. In order to construct a life with dignity, it seems natural to take the collective identity and construct positive life scripts instead.

An African-American after the Black Power movement takes the old script of self-hatred, the script in which he or she is a nigger, and works, in community with others, to construct a series of positive black life scripts. In these life scripts, being a Negro is recoded as being black: and this requires, among other things, refusing to assimilate to white norms of speech and behavior. And if one is to be black in a society that is racist then one has constantly to deal with assaults on one's dignity. In this context, insisting on the right to live a dignified life will not be enough. It will not even be enough to require that one be treated with equal dignity despite being black: for that will require a concession that being black counts naturally or to some degree against one's dignity. And so one will end up asking to be respected *as a black*.

I hope I seem sympathetic to this story. I *am* sympathetic. I see how the story goes. It may even be historically, strategically necessary for the story to go this way.[14] But I think we need to go on to the next necessary step, which is to ask whether the identities constructed in this way are ones we can all be happy with in the longer run. What demanding respect for people *as blacks* or *as gays* requires is that there be some scripts that go with being an African-American or having same-sex desires. There will be proper ways of being black and gay: there will be expectations to be met; demands will be made. It is at this point that someone who takes autonomy seriously will want to ask whether we have not replaced one kind of tyranny with another. If I had to choose between Uncle Tom and Black Power, I would, of course, choose the latter. But I would like not to have to choose. I would like other options. The politics of recognition requires that one's skin color, one's sexual body, should be politically acknowledged in ways that make it hard for those who want to treat their skin and their sexual body as personal dimensions of the self. And "personal" doesn't mean "secret" but "not too tightly scripted," "not too constrained by the demands and expectations of others."

In short, so it seems to me, those who see potential for conflict between individual freedom and the politics of identity are right. [. . .]

Notes and references

1   See Kevin Mulroy, *Freedom on the Border: The Seminole Maroons in Florida, the Indian Territory, Coahuila, and Texas* (Lubbock, Tex.: Texas Tech University Press, 1993).

2   Ian Hacking, "Making Up People" reprinted from *Reconstructing Individualism: Autonomy, Individuality and the Self in Western Thought*, ed. Thomas Heller, Morton Sousa, and David Wellbery (Stanford: Stanford University Press, 1986), in *Forms of Desire: Sexual Orientation and the Social Constructionist Controversy*, ed. Edward

Stein (New York: Routledge, 1992), pp. 69–88 (page references are to this version).

3   Hacking, "Making Up People," p. 87.

4   Cited in ibid., p. 81.

5   Ibid., p. 82.

6   That I don't recall it doesn't *prove* that I didn't, of course.

7   See Mary C. Waters, *Ethnic Options: Choosing Identities in America* (Berkeley and Los Angeles: University of California Press, 1990).

8   This is the proposal of a paper on metaphysical racism by Berel Lang at the New School for Social Research seminar "Race and Philosophy" in October 1994, from which I learned much.

9   Ruth Frankenberg, *White Women, Race Matters: The Social Construction of Whiteness* (Minneapolis: University of Minnesota Press, 1993).

10   The discussion of this work is shaped by conversation with Larry Blum, Martha Minow, David Wilkins, and David Wong.

11   Charles Taylor, *Multiculturalism and "The Politics of Recognition."* With commentary by Amy Gutmann, ed., K. Anthony Appiah, Jürgen Habermas, Steven C. Rockefeller, Michael Walzer, and Susan Wolf (Princeton: Princeton University Press, 1994).

12   Taylor reminds us rightly of Trilling's profound contributions to our understanding of this history. I discuss Trilling's work in chap. 4 of *In My Father's House.*

13   I say "make" here not because I think there is always conscious attention to the shaping of life plans or a substantial experience of choice but because I want to stress the antiessentialist point that there are choices that can be made.

14   Compare what Sartre wrote in his "Orphée Noir," in *Anthologie de la Nouvelle Poésie Nègre et Malagache de Langue Française*, ed. L. S. Senghor, p. xiv. Sartre argued, in effect, that this move is a necessary step in a dialectical progression. In this passage he explicitly argues that what he calls an "antiracist racism" is a path to the "final unity . . . the abolition of differences of race."

Chapter 42

Howard Winant

RACE AND RACISM: TOWARDS A GLOBAL FUTURE

[. . .]

WHAT IS THE FUTURE OF THE RACE CONCEPT, of racially-based social structures, of racial identities? How should we understand the meaning of race and of racism in a post-civil rights, post-apartheid, post-colonial world?

For a long time – indeed most of modern history – such questions would not have seemed logical. Race was once thought to be a natural phenomenon, not a social one. It was considered eternal, not transient. While its meaning might have varied in practical terms (among nations and empires, say, or over time), the *concept* of race retained its character as an essence. The supposed naturality of race, its givenness, was barely ever questioned. Race was understood as an ineluctable and natural framework of difference among human beings.[1]

That was then; this is now.

Today the race concept is more problematic than ever before. Racially-based social structures – of inequality and exclusion, and of resistance and autonomy as well – persist, but their legitimacy is questioned far more strongly than it was in the past. And racial identities also seem to be less solid and ineffable than they did in previous ages. While racial identity remains a major component of individuality and group recognition, it partakes of a certain flexibility and fungibility that was formerly rare.

This essay is framed by the perception (but it is not only mine) of a developing worldwide crisis in the meaning and structure of race. The age of empire is over; apartheid and Jim Crow have been ended; and a significant consensus exists among scientists (natural and social), and humanists as well, that the concept of race lacks an objective basis. Yet the concept persists, as idea, as practice, as identity, and as social structure. Racism perseveres in these same ways.[2]

Enormous discrepancies and contradictions continue as well, notably between official racial rhetorics and the actual dilemmas of racial experience and social organization. To list just a few major examples:

- Increasing mobility, both geographic and socio-economic, among subaltern racialized groups, coexists with ongoing patterns of exclusion and superexploitation of these same groups.
- Postcolonial states and national societies display substantial continuities with the 'bad old days' of empire, in both political-economic and cultural forms of domination and subordination.
- Post-apartheid South Africa, the post-civil rights US, and postcolonial Europe, perhaps the most significant national! regional stages upon which the postwar racial drama was played, have not significantly altered the 'life-chances' of their racially-defined subaltern populations. Similar statements can be made for other nation-states and regions. Although more racially democratic than their despotic earlier incarnations, these countries have by and large incorporated and 'normalized' their racial conflicts over the postwar years. Yet in many respects the conditions of blacks, Muslims, indigenous peoples, and undocumented migrants/denizens have also worsened in these settings.
- The extensive deployment of non- or anti-racialist rhetorics and policies (multiculturalism, diversity, racial pluralism, equal opportunity, etc.) has not significantly altered long-prevalent patterns of racialized identity-formation and cultural representation.
- Increasingly visible and complex transnational racial ties (diasporas, 'panethnic' movements and cultural forms, etc.) conflict with and undermine frameworks of citizenship and rights grounded in the logic of the nation-state.
- The reassertion of imperial geopolitical patterns, whether tacit or explicit, with embedded racial dynamics intact, casts the United States, still the world's hegemonic power, in a particularly ambiguous racial role.

This is the present racial crisis. '[C]risis,' Gramsci wrote, 'consists precisely in the fact that the old is dying and the new cannot be born: in this interregnum, a great variety of morbid symptoms appear' (Gramsci 1971, 276). The enormous advances made since WWII in overcoming such entrenched systems of racial despotism as apartheid in South Africa and segregation in the US, and the tremendous accomplishment of dismantling the various colonial archipelagos (British, French, Dutch, Portuguese, etc.), coexist with a system of ongoing racial stratification and injustice that substantially if more ambiguously manages to reproduce most of the conditions that have supposedly been abolished. What this suggests, if nothing else, is that *the global racial situation remains volatile and undertheorized.*

Although the intellectual endeavour required to rethink global racial conditions obviously exceeds the capacities of any single scholar, the task of framing the key problems presented by the contemporary situation is not beyond our grasp. Indeed, we must not desist from trying to make sense of the current world racial situation and of our role within it. A new account of race and racism is possible, one that addresses the emergent racial conditions of the twenty-first century. We can catch a glimpse of the global racial future by trying to reinterpret the racial present.

The racial present

We confront a contradictory combination of progress and stasis in racial institutions. This is paralleled in social life and personal experience by a similar unstable combination: that of *resilience and confidence* on the one hand, and *disappointment and vulnerability* on the other. This situation is intelligible: it is the variegated outcome of a complex process of mobilization and reform. It is the result of a cultural and political-economic shift that has been counterposed, over the post-WWII period, to the centuries-long tradition of racial domination, discrimination, exclusion, and violence that shaped colonialism and empire, and through them the world sociopolitical system *tout court*.[3]

To sort out the innumerable variations of this worldwide set of dilemmas is more than the present article can accomplish. In lieu of that sort of inventory-taking,[4] I propose to devote my attention to a set of five themes in contemporary patterns of racial formation on a world scale. These five issues, I suggest, play a significant part in the making and unmaking of worldwide patterns of race and racism. By grasping the contradictory sociopolitical forces at work in these five thematic areas, we can begin to visualize emerging parameters of the race concept, and to retheorize racism as well, as twenty-first century phenomena.

Nonracialism v. Race Consciousness: The production of racial categories, the classification of people within them, and the quotidian experience of living within such classifications, are all complex processes that link macro-level societal dynamics – censuses, the spatial organization of housing, labour, transport, etc., and social stratification in general – with micro-level ones,[5] such as acculturation and socialization, the 'testing' of attitudes and beliefs and risk-taking in everyday life, shifting interpretations of difference and identity, 'styles', etc. In the post-WWII era, the postcolonial era, it has been possible to claim that race is less salient than before in determining 'life-chances'; this is the nonracialist or 'colourblind' argument. At the same time social organization continues to function along racial lines; 'race consciousness' operates in the allocation of resources, the dynamics of social control, and the organization of movements for equality and social justice. At both the micro- and macro-social levels, in both cultural and political-economic frameworks, race must be signified and organized.

On what ground – however shaky and uncertain – do nonracialism and race consciousness meet? US Supreme Court Justice Harry Blackmun famously said that 'In order to get beyond racism, we must first take account of race' (Blackmun 1978). The 1955 South Africa Freedom Charter (the key programmatic document of the African National Congress) condemned racialism, but the postapartheid ANC government must struggle every day with issues of state racial policy (African National Congress, 1979 [1955]). How can we both take account of race and get beyond it, as the present situation seems to demand?[6]

Racial Genomics: Racial science has advanced and retreated in historical 'waves'. Before the current DNA-based breakthroughs there was the approach of eugenics (Duster 2003 [1990]). Much as genomics does today, the worldwide eugenics movement also claimed that it was a dispassionate advance over the benightedness of the past. Though particularly dangerous in the hands of right-wing and fascist movements and governments, eugenics also had left-wing and feminist adherents.

Tainted by its adoption by Nazism, eugenics 'retreated' (Barkan 1992), but has resurfaced under neoconservative and new right sponsorship in recent decades (Herrnstein and Murray 1994).

Today's racial genomics is at pains to distinguish itself from the eugenics of the past. Indeed it has dual effects that would have been unimaginable in the heyday of eugenics: it renders racial identity more fungible and flexible, quite the opposite of what occurred in the era of Fisher, Pearson, or Stoddard. Yet at the same time racial genomics is pressed into service for 'profiling'; it is harnessed to old and repressive practices (Duster 2004). Thus it simultaneously reinforces the same stereotypes its advocates profess to debunk. Recognizing the sociohistorical context in which the race-concept developed and in which it has been explained, it seems, does not prevent the periodic recurrence of biologically-based accounts. To what extent is current scientific knowledge about race distinct from previous scientific knowledge?

The Nation and its Peoples. Citizens, Denizens, Migrants: In the past, the commonsense view of 'the nation' was inflected by race (and to some extent by gender as well). The US, for example, was perceived as 'a white man's country', a herrenvolk republic, as David Roediger (1991) called it. South Africa explicitly institutionalized the herrenvolk model, first piecemeal, and then systematically after 1948. All the European empires struggled to distinguish between metropolitans/citizens and colonials/natives, especially as mixed-race populations expanded, miscegenation became commonplace, and 'creoles', 'kaffirs', and 'wogs' established themselves in London, Paris, Lisbon, Amsterdam, and elsewhere (Stoler 2002). Recurrent nativism was directed against immigrants, while anti-black racism and contempt for indigenous peoples underwrote state racial policy in both colony and metropole. In the US, for example, Anglo-Saxonism and 'anglo-conformity' shaped the national culture in various ways, sometimes relaxing and sometimes tightening the boundaries of membership, but always reflecting restrictive norms. Blacks only became citizens in a practical sense in the 1960s; many Asians only achieved naturalization rights in the 1950s, and native peoples only received their citizenship in the 1920s.

Today new nativist rumblings can be heard in the US as the spectre of a 'majority-minority' society looms. ('Doesn't a declining pool of middle-class manufacturing and service jobs endanger the US economy itself? Where is effective demand supposed to come from? Who will finance baby boomers' social security outlays?') The new threat to the norm of whiteness comes, we are told, from the Latinization of certain areas (Huntington 2004); the west coast is being transformed into 'Mexifornia' (Hanson 2003); and border-oriented vigilantism (the 'Minutemen') receives grudging support from mainstream politicians. Yet California voters have also punished those who promoted anti-immigrant initiatives, and many corporations too oppose heightened restriction. How lawns will be mowed, dishes washed, vegetables picked, or laundry done in a highly restrictive immigration regime remains an unanswered question. Meanwhile, economists differ markedly on the costs and benefits for the American economy of immigration, both low- and high-skilled, both capitalbearing and capital-deficient.

In Europe as well, citizenship rights were only gradually extended (and even more gradually granted in practice) to immigrants, Jews, and nonwhites. In Germany *jus sanguinis* policies were continued from the formation of the nation, through the

Nuremberg Laws and Holocaust, and into the establishment of the EU, when they were finally relaxed (only in the 1990s!). French 'racial differentialism' (Taguieff 2001 [1988]) struggles in vain to reconcile the exclusion and despair of the banlieues with the Jacobin/Napoleonic legacies of assimilationism and secularism (Wieviorka 1995; Noiriel 1996; Silverstein 2004). The Front Nationale in France, the German Republikaner, the Austrian FPO, the Belgian Vlaams Blok, the Northern League in Italy, and many 'mainstream' parties as well habitually associate racially-designated immigrants with crime and unemployment. In many of the Pacific rim countries, Chinese communities are attacked by nationalists as 'middleman minorities' and as agents of globalization, of the neoimperialism of the IMF and its structural adjustment policies (Chus 2002).

These examples could be multiplied. Most 'developed' countries (and not a few LDCs as well) maintain unstable and contentious immigration, citizenship, and naturalization policies.

Race/Gender/Class: Race/gender/class 'intersectionality' (Crenshaw 1994; Collins 1998) is the name we now give to the complex of deep attachments and conflicts among anti-racist/anticolonial movements, women's movements, and labour-based/anti-poverty movements. In the US (Lerner, 1972; Davis 1981; Zinn and Dill, 1994; Hine, 2005), in Britain (Rowbotham 1992; Ware 1992; McClintock 1995), France (Guillaumin 1995), and elsewhere these linkages have connected struggles for racial justice, women's rights, and labour rights for nearly two centuries. Today these intersections cross the whole racial spectrum. In post-coloniality approaches, notably in the 'subaltern studies' school, feminism has come to play a central role (Spivak 1987), not only in relation to colonial and postcolonial South Asia, but in regard to Latin America (Beverley 1999; Franco 2001) and Africa (Urdang 1989; Seidman 1993; Amadiume 2000).

The explanatory framework for intersectionality studies, however, remains elusive. Unquestionably a general parallel exists between racial and gender-based oppressions and emancipatory claims. De Beauvoir explicitly modelled her pioneering account in feminist theory, *The Second Sex* (1989 [1953]) on working-class and anticolonial struggles for emancipation. The key parallels she stressed, along with many others, included: rule through chattelization, the assignment of political status based on corporeal characteristics, 'isolation effects' and alienation, and the internalization of domination. Numerous other common experiences link these axes of power and resistance. Yet racebased, gender-based, and labour-based movements have always teetered between convergence and divergence, both in the US and elsewhere. That's at the macro-social, institutional level.

At the micro-social or experiential level a similar uncertainty operates: involvement in 'multiple oppressions', for example, often forces women of colour to 'choose their battles'. They confront competing demands for solidarity, often across race-, class-, or gender-lines. White women, too, must often choose between gender, race, and class solidarity. Rather than lamenting these dilemmas, we should learn from them about pragmatism and the instability *in practice* of the race-concept. Theorizing intersectionality requires a hefty dose of pragmatism, a strong recognition that 'self-reflective action' shapes the production and transformation of both individual and collective identities.[7] This phenomenon – of situatedness and strategic reflection in practice – is not necessarily problematic for emancipatory purposes;

it may indeed be unavoidable, a prerequisite, for all efforts (men's as well as women's) to create an emancipatory political framework.

The Trajectory of Empire, Race, and Neoconservatism: Empire has been a racial matter since the rise of Europe and the founding of the 'modern world-system'. It involves subduing 'others', tutoring them in the 'higher values' of advanced 'civilization', and also squeezing their resources and/or labour out of them. Though often justified by free-market ideology, this process is basically coercive; indeed some political economic and economic history approaches reject the idea that the extraction of mass labour and the drive for natural resources at the periphery are fundamentally market-based processes at all. This dimension of imperial activity – "extra-economic coercion" (Laclau 1977; Mann 1988; Brenner 1993; Mamdani 1996; Polanyi 2001[1944];) – is regaining its centrality in the supposedly postcolonial, but perhaps re-imperializing,[8] twenty-first-century world.

The divestment of the old European empires took place in the decades after WWII, sometimes peacefully and sometimes as a result of bloody conflict. The transition to a postcolonial world was accompanied by a rhetoric of anti-racism, democracy, and self-determination that had roots not only in revolutionary movements but also in Wilsonian principles (Singh 1998).

The global dismantling of European empire was paralleled by a fierce battle within the US. The connections between civil rights and racial freedom movements, on the one hand, and anticolonial ones on the other, have been extensively studied. But the US, as the leading global power, also defended the European empires during the decades after WWII, notably in Southeast Asia but elsewhere as well. Only after the end of the Vietnam war did that practice come largely to a halt.

This was roughly the same moment that the civil rights movement was being incorporated and institutionalized, a process that was shaped by *neoconservatism*. That viewpoint took shape in the 1970s as a disillusioned domestic racial liberalism that deplored segregation and redistribution of resources along racial lines in approximately equal measure.

Originally formulated as a set of social scientific and policy-oriented principles, neoconservatism developed into a grass-roots racial ideology ('reverse discrimination' etc.). Later still it developed an imperial cast, avowing US empire for the first time since the turn of the twentieth century (Kaplan 2001; Kagan 2003; Ferguson 2004). In its advocacy of US intervention in Iraq, neoconservatism drew both on the civil rights legacy and on the older imperial presuppositions: of tutelage, uplift, religious messianism, etc. These 'others' have waited too long for liberation; the US has an obligation to help them understand the ways of democracy and freedom; we must, in short, promote our 'way of life' and 'enlighten' our subjects abroad. Empire tends to have a racial subtext.

In university classrooms in the US today many of our students (especially but not only white students) tell us that they 'don't notice race', and that they 'treat everyone as an individual'. Their rejection of racism is no doubt genuine in its adoption of 'colourblindness' or nonracialism; but it also tends to ratify the existing inequalities and injustices that descend from the 'bad old days' of segregation. These positions reflect the dominant racial ideology in the US – neoconservatism – a view that seems more concerned with 'reverse discrimination' than with unchanged black and Latino poverty rates, infant mortality, or heightening, not declining, racial stratification (Oliver and Shapiro 1995). Thus domestic neoconservatism both undermines an older, more familiar racial mindset and reinvokes it.

In respect to Iraq and the 'war on terror', US foreign policy operates in parallel fashion, once again reflecting the contradictions of neoconservatism. 'Welcome to Injun country', Robert Kaplan (2005) quotes US officers telling him in Iraq. Leading US foreign policy intellectuals have spilt a great deal of ink on the theme of 'getting used to the American empire'. An effort is made to distinguish the US approach to 'projecting power' from that of the British or French a century ago. Unlike our predecessors, we bring democracy and freedom. But is the US (and its allies the British) not committed to its 'great game' in the Middle East every bit as much as were the British a century ago (Meyer and Brysac 1999)?

In short – to lapse into Bourdieu-ese for just a moment neoconservatism today combines a *habitus* of domination over the racialized other with a *doxa* of incorporation and respect for those who are no longer formally recognized as other at all.[9] And from the standpoint of those others – who are in practice still racially identified – there is a combination of responses as well: as we have already noted, not only a new resilience, but also a continuing vulnerability. It is the height of perversity that the civil rights legacy has been harnessed to the cause of global domination and 'preemptive' war, but the fact remains that some of its key tropes have been preserved by the neocons who once represented its 'moderate' wing.[10]

Towards the racial future

These contradictions are indications of the uncertainties of the current moment in racial politics. The necessarily brief review presented here suggests that a new racial hegemony has by no means been secured. There are fundamental instabilities in the ideologies of colourblindness, racial 'differentialism', and 'nonracialism'. Racial biologism is prospering; is it still a 'backdoor to eugenics' (Duster 2003 [1990])? Race/gender/class 'intersectionality' denotes the instability in *practice* – both at 'micro-social' and at 'macro-social' levels – not only of race and racism, but also of other axes of oppression. The link between racism and empire was wrongly considered terminated; instead it has been reinvented, principally through US neoconservatism. In fact none of the 'posts-' – post-civil rights, post-apartheid, post-coloniality – is sufficiently 'post'; none denotes a full break with the conditions their very names contain; all necessitate uneasy and continuous adjustments, both on the level of policy and politics, and on that of personal experience and identity, to the ongoing operation of racial conflicts.

So what is the meaning of these racial contradictions for the future? What do they suggest about the development of a new racial justice agenda, both globally and locally? Although the intellectual endeavour required to rethink global racial conditions is rather daunting, the political and personal commitments we 'movement scholars' have undertaken do not permit us to desist from trying to make sense of the current world racial situation and of our role within it. Neither do they allow us to 'stop thinking about tomorrow', as the popular song would have it.

Simply reasserting the continuing significance of race, while not mistaken, nevertheless has serious limits. Such an approach is insufficiently pragmatist, as well as deficient in its democratic commitments. As we learn from racial formation theory and critical race theory, race is a flexible concept that is constantly being reshaped in practical political activity. That the civil rights movement and the racial nationalisms of the 1960s were absorbed and rearticulated in a new racial hegemony was not only a contradictory outcome, one that combined some real achievements with some painful defeats; it was also a valuable lesson about racial politics.

Question: what happened to the civil rights movement ideal of a colourblind society? Answer: it morphed under the pressure of neoconservative politics into an abstract concept of equality, becoming available to the respectable racial right. Ironic, isn't it – downright annoying in fact – that the rearticulation of 'colourblind' racial ideology served to shore up the inequality and structural racism of US society. This was after all the same phenomenon that movement advocacy of nonracialism had originally aimed at overturning!

Similar pitfalls awaited 'nationalist' concepts of racial emancipation. Originally developed under conditions of colonial (or quasi-colonial) rule as the effort to restore democracy and 'self-determination', nationalist movements have proved susceptible to autocracy and caudillismo of various types: plagued by corruption, religious authoritarianism, and sexism, dependent upon charismatic leaders, they are often incapable of fulfilling in practice the democratic and emancipatory ideals that originally inspired them (Gilroy 2000).

Such is post-civil rights, postcolonial, post-apartheid racial hegemony. But is that the end of the story? Is this the end of the trajectory of racial politics? After the emancipatory insights of a movement have been absorbed and reinterpreted, after its radicalism has been so to speak bleached away, then what happens? What happens to a dream deferred?

By way of answer – for space here is limited – it is worth noting how unstable and problematic the ideas of colourblindness, nonracialism, differentialism, and postcolonialism are proving to be. Of course there is a significant movement critique of these supposedly post-racial positions, one that insists on the fulfilment of the still-incomplete agenda of the earlier post-WWIJ decades; demonstrates the continuity and depth of US racial injustice (Bonilla-Silva 2003; Brown *et al.* 2003); and notes the links between globalization and racism (Macedo and Panayota 2005). But this critique, for all its merits, has not yet developed a theoretical account capable of resolving the various contradictions of twenty-first-century racial dynamics – nonracialism, intersectionality, etc. – that are the central subjects here.

Meanwhile, back at the plantation, twenty-first-century racial hegemony has not been secured. Once again ironically, its major challenges originate, not from the critiques just mentioned, and not from the anti-racist left or from civil rights advocates or racial nationalists based in the global South or global East. Rather they have emerged *from the ongoing instabilities and conflicts of racial rule itself.* Taking the US (the world's only 'superpower') as a central case: the post-civil rights US racial regime must frequently negate its own insistence on colourblindness. This regime apparently cannot dispense with its practice of 'racial profiling': not only for reasons of 'national security' but also in carceral, policing, and welfare state practices. It has made substantial investments in racial genomics, which is now a big scientific enterprise as well as a developing system for social control. Driven by paranoia about immigration, the US is reviving nativist practices on the Mexican border and in the Pacific.

Not only because it has failed to fulfil the promise of racial equality and justice, but also because it defaults, so to speak, to racial rule as a key component of hegemonic rule, the contemporary US regime *must violate its own racial norms*, themselves the products of post-WWII civil rights and anti-imperial political struggles.

What does the foregoing analysis suggest about twenty-first-century movement politics oriented towards fomenting racial justice and expanding democracy? Instead of insisting on the fulfilment of twentieth-century demands, movement activists and theorists have to pose new questions about the actually existing and deeply conflicted dynamics of racial politics and racial identity; in short, we have to think about racial formation processes as they are unfolding today and in the future. Here I briefly (and artificially) distinguish the experiential dimensions of racial politics (micro-level raciality, the personal or smallscale aspects of racial formation) from the social structural dimensions of racial politics (macro-level raciality, the institutional, governmental, and world-systemic aspects of racial formation).[11]

At the micro-social, experiential level, we all experience race in a contradictory fashion. We must recognize once again, a century after DuBois introduced it (1989 [1903]), the importance of 'double consciousness'. His exploration of that contradiction in *Souls* ('An American, a Negro: two warring souls in one dark body. . .') points more than ever to the situated and flexible character of raciality as a practical matter. It applies to everybody, not just blacks, albeit in varying ways. This duality or even multiplicity is what shapes our racial identities *really*, not some ideal of a nonracialist world or of an undifferentiated, racially-defined group solidarity. Life is more complicated than that.

We know *both* that in the US – and across the whole planet – race continues to matter, that it shapes identities and 'life-chances'; *and* that racially-based identity can be problematic, uncertain, or overridden by other forms of solidarity. Racial identity can be called into question by mixed-race status, by strong ties that cut across racial lines, or by multiple identities (for example, racial and class-based identities can conflict). In real life-experience we are often forced to 'choose our battles' or make distasteful tactical alliances; we are sometimes uncertain what the racial meaning of a given situation or utterance might be ('Was that a racist remark, or not?').

At the social structural level, the macro-social level, we must recognize again, a century after DuBois, that we still live in an unfolding racial history, in which racial dynamics are linked to the struggle for democracy, for a socially just distribution of resources, and for the overcoming, if not of capitalism itself, at least of the wretched, cruel, and despotic excesses of capitalism. *Racism is a variety of despotism.* When we contemplate race and racism as global or national social structures, we are immediately struck by the extent to which they still stratify national societies and the social world as a whole. Yet we cannot operate effectively, we cannot think effectively, if we deny the significance of the racial transformations of recent decades.

If it is true that both at the 'micro-social' and at the 'macro-social' levels racial experience is now more patently contradictory than it was in earlier historical moments, this should be considered more as an opportunity than as a dilemma: a chance to develop new forms of political practice, and new theoretical insights as well, in pursuit of racial justice and racial democracy. Although the scope of this argument obviously exceeds the space presently available, in my view we must embrace and build upon *pragmatist* sources to help us realize this opportunity to advance a new racial theory for the twenty-first century. Pragmatist racial theory comes to us through DuBois, whose concepts of 'double consciousness' and of the 'veil' laid the foundation for an understanding of race that is radically democratic. From the standpoint of the radical pragmatist account of 'double consciousness', we can begin to grasp the improvisational and self-reflective processes that racial awareness demands in the post-civil rights, postapartheid, postcolonial era. From a radical pragmatist position we can better understand the heightened flexibility required of the racially oppressed and their allies as they conduct their freedom struggles in that 'post-' era. To be sure the pragmatist tradition has tended to emphasize the micro-social dimensions of action,[12] which has been a limitation. Nor are pragmatist approaches uniformly liberatory; pragmatist principles are also invoked by such conservative thinkers as Richard Posner (2005). But as I have argued elsewhere (Winant 2004, 188–204), promising *radical* pragmatist approaches to race are available; they are concerned with linking the micro-social and macrosocial dimensions of race; and they are being applied to such issues as the racial state, race-based social movements, and the racial dynamics of globalization.[13]

Thus we are compelled to ask, what would a racial justice-oriented set of policies, what would a racial justice-oriented political programme, look like in the twenty-first century? Let us not dismiss that as a rhetorical question, but instead attempt to respond from a radical pragmatist viewpoint, one that takes its commitments seriously.

Clearly such a programme would require redistribution of wealth/income nationally and globally via democratically selected means. This might take various forms: a 'global Marshall Plan' has been suggested (Rademacher *et al* 2004), the 'Tobin tax' scheme continues to attract attention (Ul Haq, Kaul, and Grunberg 1996; Patomaki 2003), and various reparation initiatives have been proposed (Yamamoto 1999; Feagin 2000; Thompson 2002; Bittker 2003 [1973]).[14]

'Now hold on a moment!', I hear my readers cry. 'Is all that stuff race-based? You're talking about big global issues!'

Perfectly true, but as a few moments' reflection will confirm, most of the 'big global issues' (as well as the big national ones) have significant racial dimensions. That is a logical consequence of global development in our postcolonial, post-Cold War epoch, which takes clear North-South (and now West-East) forms.

Continuing to take race and racism seriously is particularly logical in the aftermath of the vast wave of racial conflict and racial reform that succeeded WWII. That set of conflicts linked 'southern' anticolonial and 'northern' anti-racism very clearly. Thus, as the racial state has incorporated the demands of anti-apartheid, anti-Jim Crow, and anticolonial movements – in suitably 'moderate' form of course – it has become a more difficult target for racial justice movements.

Put another way, while movement activity on behalf of racial justice and racial equality must continue to address its demands towards the nation-state, it must also shift attention, as movements have frequently done in the past, away from the framework of the national and towards both local and transnational spheres of mobilization.[15]

The racial future remains uncertain. The concept of race and the social practices we designate as racism and anti-racism are in transition, for we are passing through a period of crisis when 'the old has died but the new cannot be born'. Today these conditions demand that we clarify the circumstances under which contested concepts of race, racially-based social structures, and race-based identities continue to operate. Yes, the accomplishments of the postWWII movements for racial justice and the end of colonial rule were significant; yes, the reforms achieved and revolutions carried through changed the global racial system. But these accomplishments, for all their importance, also had the perverse effect of reinforcing some of the very institutions they sought to overcome, of inoculating them, so to speak, with tolerable doses of their own oppositions, and thus immunizing them against the more severe 'diseases' of radical change. Hegemony operates, Gramsci said, by incorporating resistance.

The analysis presented here recognizes the pervasive contradictions and uncertainties of the post-civil rights and postcolonial era. This is fully consistent with noticing the ongoing social injustices and 'human waste' that remain at the core of the race-concept, and of racism as well, in all their forms: attitudinal, practical, and structural.

In the racial future, I venture to predict, there will be a combination of greater flexibility in the understanding of racial identity on the one hand, and a deepening structural racism on the other. That is to say: the global racial crisis will intensify, not diminish. The trend towards heightening disparities in 'life-chances' by race, towards increasing racial stratification on a planetary scale, is in large part congruent with general global tendencies towards mounting inequality. People around the world, and ordinary Americans as well, cannot long escape these troubling contradictions. In different ways, DuBois's 'double consciousness' now divides us all. This is itself both a great achievement and an injunction: to look deeper into our disciplines, our social institutions, our political activity, and ourselves.

Notes

1   Race is *concept which signifies and symbolizes sociopolitical conflicts and interests in reference to different types of human bodies.* Although the concept of race appeals to biologically-based human characteristics (so-called phenotypes), selection of these particular human features for purposes of racial signification is always and necessarily a social and historical process. There is no biological basis for distinguishing human groups along the lines of 'race', and the sociohistorical categories employed to differentiate among these groups reveal themselves, upon serious examination, to be imprecise if not completely arbitrary.

2   Racism consists of one or more of the following: (1) Signifying practice that essentializes or naturalizes human identities based on racial categories or concepts; (2) Social action that produces unjust allocation of socially valued resources, based on such significations; (3) Social structure that reproduces such allocations.

3   For more on the global racial 'break' that took place during and after WWII, see Winant 2001.

4   For some examples of such inventories, see Gurr *et al.* 1993; Gurr and Harif 1994; Chaliand and Rageau 1995.

5   As I have written elsewhere, the micro-macro distinction is merely analytical as it applies to racial formation: see Winant 2004, 200–202.

6   See the discussion of DuBoisian 'double consciousness' below.

7   This argument, which receives greater attention below, applies as well to other axes of oppression and resistance, quite obviously. Here I confine myself mainly to discussion about race.

8   Forgive this neologism: I refer to the resurgent imperial character of North-South (and to some extent West-East) international relationships and organizations such as the IMF and the WTO.

9   See Winant 1994, 24–29.

10   'We should never indulge in the condescending voices that allege that some people are not interested in freedom or aren't ready for freedom's responsibility. That view was wrong in 1963 in Birmingham, and it's wrong in 2004 in Baghdad' (Condoleeza Rice, Commencement Speech, Vanderbilt University, May 13, 2004).

11   See note 3, above, in respect to the micro-macro distinction in 'levels' of racial formation.

12   I am thinking here of Mead's (1967 [1934]) concept of self, and of the performative dimensions of identity in Blumer's (1969) work and its legacy, as well as in the œuvre of Erving Goffman.

13   Radical pragmatist approaches to racial theory are finally receiving the serious attention they deserve. Much of the credit for this advance belongs to Cornel West, whose early work on this theme (1989) remains indispensable. See also West and Mendieta 2004. Herbert Blumer's later work on race is indispensable; see his classic article of 1958; see also Blumer and Duster 1980. Fraser's (1998) work on Alain Locke should also be noted.

14   Reparations and redistribution projects have much to recommend them, but also must be approached with caution. Race/class intersectionality comes into play here; in other words, who pays for them counts as much as who benefits by them. Unless they can be structured as transfers not only from the racially privileged to the racially subaltern, but also as transfers from capital to labor, they will have the effect (indended or unintended) of heightening class divisions even as they reduce racial ones. As a general rule, reparations should be funded by wealth taxes rather than by transfers from general funds. See Winant 2004, 126.

15   The US civil rights movement did this quite consciously, shifting its political leverage from the state level, where segregationism and 'state's rights' arguments held greater sway, toward the US nation-state, where such matters as Cold War imperatives, northern voting and labor patterns, and liberal cultural norms were in play. Today, with the federal state under the control of reactionary and anti-democratic groups, we see movement activity emphasizing local and state-based political venues.

References

African National Congress 1979 *The Freedom Charter*. Adopted at the Congress of the People, Kliptown, June 26, 1955. New York: United Nations Centre Against Apartheid.

Amadiume, IFI 2000 *Daughters of the Goddess, Daughters of Imperialism: African Women Struggle for Culture, Power and Democracy*, New York: Zed/St. Martin's Press

Barkan, Elazar 1992 *The Retreat of Scientific Racism: Changing Concepts of Race in Britain and the United States Between the World Wars*, Cambridge; New York: Cambridge University Press

Beauvoir, Simone de 1989 (1953)*The Second Sex*; translated by H.M. Parshley. New York Vintage Books.

Beverley, John 1999 *Subalternity and Representation: Arguments in Cultural Theory*, Durham: Duke University Press

Bittker, Boris 2003 (1973) *Reparations: The Case for Black Reparations*, Boston: Beacon

Blackmun, Harry 1978 *University of California Regents v. Bakke*, 438 U.S. 265, concurring in part.

Blumer, Herbert and Duster, Troy 1980 'Theories of Race and Social Action', in O'Callaghan Marion (ed.), *Sociological Theories Race and Colonialism*, Paris: UNESCO

Blumer, Herbert 1958 'Race Prejudice as a Sense of Group Position'. *Pacific Sociological Review*, Vol. 1, no. I (Spring)

—— 1969 *Symbolic Interactionism: Perspective and Method*, Englewood Cliffs, NJ: Prentice-Hall

Bonilla-Silva, Eduardo 2003 *Racism Without Racists: Color-Blind Racism and the Persistence of Racial Inequality in the United States*, Lanham, MD: Rowman and Littlefield

Brenner, Robert 1993 *Merchants and Revolution: Commercial Change, Political Conflict, and London's Overseas Traders 1550–1653*, Princeton: Princeton University Press

Brown, Michael K., *et al.* 2003 *Whitewashing Race: The Myth of a Color-Blind Society*, Berkeley: University of California Press

Chaliand, Gerard and Rageau, Jean-Pierre 1995 *The Penguin Atlas of Diasporas*; with maps by Catherine Petit; translated by A.M. Berrett. New York: Viking

Chua, Amy 2002 *World on Fire: How Exporting Free Market Democracy Breeds Ethnic Hatred and Global Instability*, New York: Doubleday

Collins, Patricia Hill 1998 *Fighting Words: Black Women and the Search for Justice*, Minneapolis: University of Minnesota Press

Crenshaw, Kimberlé Williams 1994 'Mapping the Margins: Intersectionality, Identity Politics, and Violence Against Women of Color', in Martha Albertson Fineman and Roxanne Mikitiuk (eds), *The Public Nature of Private Violence*, New York: Routledge

Davis, Angela Y. 1981 *Women, Race, and Class*, New York: Random House

DuBois, W.E.B. 1989 [1903] *The Souls of Black Folk*, New York: Penguin

Duster, Troy 2003 [1990] *Backdoor to Eugenics*, New York: Routledge

—— 2004 'Selective Arrests, an Ever-Expanding DNA Forensic Database, and the Specter of an Early-Twenty-First-Century Equivalent of Phrenology', in David Lazer (ed.), *DNA and the Criminal Justice System: The Technology of Justice*, Cambridge, MA: MIT Press

Feagin, Joe R. 2000 *Racist America: Roots, Current Realities, and Future Reparations*, New York Routledge

Ferguson, Niall 2004 *Colossus: The Price of America's Empire*, New York: Penguin

Franco, Jean 2001 'Bodies in Contention'. *NACLA Report on the Americas* Vol. 34, no. 5 (March).

Fraser, Nancy 1998 'Another Pragmatism: Alain Locke, Critical Race Theory, and the Politics of Culture', in Morris Dickstein (ed.), *The Revival of Pragmatism: New Essays an Social Thought, Law, and Culture*, Durham, NC: Duke University Press

Gilroy, Paul 2000 *Against Race: Imagining Political Culture beyond the Color Line*, Cambridge, MA: Harvard University Press

Gramsci, Antonio 1971 *Selections from the Prison Notebooks*. Edited by Quinton Hoare and Geoffrey Nowell-Smith, New York: International Publishers

Guillaumin, Colette 1995 *Racism, Sexism, Power, and Ideology*, New York: Routledge

Gurr, Ted Robert and Harff, Barbara, 1994 *Ethnic Conflict in World Politics*, Boulder: Westview Press

Gurr, Ted Robert, *et al.* 1993 *Minorities at Risk: A Global View of Ethnopolitical Conflicts*, Washington: United States Institute of Peace Press

Hanson, Victor Davis 2003 *Mexifornia: A State of Becoming*, San Francisco: Encounter Books

Herrnstein, Richard and Murray, Charles 1994 *The Bell Curve: Intelligence and Class Structure in American Life*, New York: Free Press

Hine, Darlene Clark (ed.) 2005 *Black Women in America* (3 volumes), 2nd ed. New York: Oxford University Press

Huntington, Samuel P. 2004 *Who Are We? The Challenges to America's Identity*, New York: Simon and Schuster

Kagan, Robert 2003 *Of Paradise and Power: America and Europe in the New World Order*, New York: Knopf

Kaplan, Robert D. 2005 *Imperial Grunts: The American Military on the Ground*, New York: Random House

—— 2001 *The Coming Anarchy: Shattering the Dreams of the Post Cold War*, New York: Vintage

Laclau, Ernesto 1977 *Politics and Ideology in Marxist Theory: Capitalism, Fascism, Populism*, London: Verso

Lerner, Gerda (ed.) 1972 *Black Women in White America: A Documentary History*. New York: Pantheon

Macedo, Donaldo, and Gounari, Panayota (eds.) 2005 *The Globalization of Racism*. Boulder, CO: Paradigm

Mamdani, Mahmood 1996 *Citizen and Subject: Contemporary Africa and the Legacy of Late Colonialism*, Princeton, NJ: Princeton University Press

Mann, Michael 1988 *States, War, and Capitalism: Studies in Political Sociology*, New York: Blackwell

McClintock, Anne 1995 *Imperial Leather: Race, Gender, and Sexuality in the Colonial Conquest*, New York: Routledge

Mead, George Herbert 1967 (1934) *Mind, Self and Society: From the Standpoint of a Social Behaviorist*, Chicago: University of Chicago Press

Meyer, Karl E. and Brysac, Shareen Blair 1999 *Tournament of Shadows: The Great Game and the Race for Empire in Central Asia*, New York: Counterpoint

Noiriel, Gerrard 1996 *The French Melting Pot: Immigration, Citizenship, and National Identity*, translated by Geoffroy de Laforcade. Minneapolis: University of Minnesota Press

Oliver, Melvin L. and Shapiro, Thomas M. 1995 *Black Wealth/White Wealth: A New Perspective on Racial Inequality*, New York: Routledge

Patomäki, Heikki 2003 *Democratising Globalization: The Leverage of the Tobin Tax*, London: Zed

Polanyi, Karl 2001 [1944] *The Great Transformation*, Boston: Beacon Press

Posner, Richard A. 2005 *The Problems of Jurisprudence*, 2nd ed, Cambridge, MA: Harvard University Press

Radermacher, Franz Josef, *et al.* 2004 *Global Marshall Plan: A Planetary Contract*, Hamburg: Global Marshall Plan Initiative

Roediger, David R. 1991 *The Wages of Whiteness: Race and the Making of the American Working Class*, New York: Verso

Rowbotham, Sheila 1992 *Women in Movement: Feminism and Social Action*, New York: Routledge

Seidman, Gay 1993 'No Freedom without the Women: Mobilization and Gender in South Africa 1970–1992'. *Signs* Vol. 18. No 2

Silverstein, Paul 2004 Algeria in France: Transpolitics Race and Notion, Bloomington: Indiana University Press

Singh, Nikhil Pal 1998 'Culture/Wars: Recoding Empire in an Age of Democracy'. *American Quarterly* Vol. 50, no. 3 (September)

Stoler, Ann Laura 2002 *Carnal Knowledge and Imperial Power: Race and the Intimate in Colonial Rule*, Berkeley: University of California Press

Taguieff, Pierre-André 2001 *The Force of Prejudice: On Racism and Its Doubles*; translated by Hassan Melehy. Minneapolis: University of Minnesota Press; original French edition 1988

Thompson, Jana 2002 *Taking Responsibility for the Past: Reparation and Historical Injustice*, Malden, MA: Polity

Ul Haq, Mahbub, Inge Kaul, and Grunberg, Isabelle (eds) 1996 *The Tobin Tax: Coping with Financial Volatility*. New York: Oxford University Press

Urdang, Stephanie 1989 *And Still they Dance: Women, Destabilization, and the Struggle for Change in Mozambique*, New York: Monthly Review Press

Ware, Vron 1992 *Beyond the Pale: White Women, Racism and History*, London: Verso

West, Cornel 1989 *The American Evasion of Philosophy: A Genealogy of Pragmatism*, Madison: University of Wisconsin Press

West, Cornel, with Mendieta, Eduardo 2004 'Empire, Pragmatism, and War: A Conversation with Cornel West'. *Logos* Vol. 3, no, 3 (Summer)

Wieviorka, Michel 1995 *The Arena of Racism*, translated by Chris Turner, Thousand Oaks, CA: Sage

Winant, Howard 2004 *The New Politics of Race: Globalism, Difference, Justice*, Minneapolis: University of Minnesota Press

—— 2001 *The World Is a Ghetto: Race and Democracy Since World War II*, New York: Basic

—— 1994 *Racial Conditions: Politics, Theory, Comparisons*, Minneapolis: University of Minnesota Press

Yamamoto, Eric 1999 *Interracial Justice: Conflict and Reconciliation in Post-Civil Rights America*, New York: New York University Press

Zinn, Maxine Baca, and Dill, Bonnie, Thornton, (eds) 1994 *Women of Color in US. Society*. Philadelphia: Temple University Press

Guide to Further Reading

Key texts

Brown, M. K. *et al.* (eds) (2003) *Whitewashing Race: The Myth of a Color-Blind Society*, Berkeley: University of California Press (an overview of the continuing significance of race in the United States).

Frankenberg, R. (ed.) (1997) *Displacing Whiteness: Essays in Social and Cultural Criticism*, Durham, NC: Duke University Press (a collection of papers on current debates about whiteness from a variety of historical and contemporary angles).

Gilroy, P. (2004) *Between Camps: Nations, Cultures and the Allure of Race*, London: Routledge (a systematic reworking of the core conceptual critique of 'raciology' by one of the leading scholars of race and racism).

Krysan, M and Lewis, A. E. (2004) *The Changing Terrain of Race and Ethnicity*, New York: Russell Sage Foundation (an exploration of the shifting boundaries of race and ethnicity, focusing on social and economic issues).

Pateman, C. and Mills, C. W. (2007) *Contract and Domination*, Cambridge: Polity (a collaborative text that explores the role of gender and race in shaping power relations).

Lacy, K. R. (2007) *Blue-Chip Black: Race, Class, and Status in the New Black Middle Class*, Berkeley: University of California Press (an account of the role of race and class in shaping the lives of the black middle class in the United States).

Background reading

Alexander, J. C. (2006) *The Civil Sphere*, Oxford: Oxford University Press (a formative analysis that includes detailed discussion of the position of both black and Jewish Americans in the post-civil rights period).

Allen, T. W. (1994) *The Invention of the White Race. Volume One: Racial Oppression and Social Control*, London: Verso (an analysis of the history of ideas about whiteness in America).

Appadurai, A. (1996) *Modernity at Large: Cultural Dimensions of Globalization*, Minneapolis: University of Minnesota Press (a collection of papers that explores the changing boundaries of globalisation and identity).

Appiah, K. A. and Gates Jr, H. L. (eds) (1995) *Identities*, Chicago: University of Chicago Press (a collection of papers on changing processes of identity formation in relation to race, ethnicity, gender and related issues).

Appiah, K. A. and Gutmann, A. (1996) *Color Conscious: The Political Morality of Race*, Princeton: Princeton University Press (a collection of essays in which the authors outline their understandings of race and multiculturalism in contemporary America).

Austin, A. (2006) *Achieving Blackness: Race, Black Nationalism, and Afrocentrism in the Twentieth Century*, New York: New York University Press (a critical analysis of a range of mobilisation of blackness in the US during the twentieth century).

Balibar, E. and Wallerstein, I. (1991) *Race, Nation, Class: Ambiguous Identities,* London: Verso (a collection of papers in which the authors present their views on the relationship between race, nation and class).

Cohen, R. (1997) *Global Diasporas: An Introduction,* London: UCL Press (a systematic analysis of various diasporas and of their role in shaping global processes).

Delgado, R. and Stefancic, J. (eds) (1997) *Critical White Studies: Looking Behind the Mirror,* Philadelphia: Temple University Press (a comprehensive collection of historical and contemporary texts on various aspects of the construction of whiteness).

Foner, N. and Fredrickson, G. M. (eds) (2004) *Not Just Black and White: Historical and Contemporary Perspectives on Immigration, Race, and Ethnicity in the United States,* New York: Russell Sage Foundation (a collection of papers that link historical analysis with a contemporary overview of racial and ethnic questions in the United States).

Gilroy, P. (2004) *After Empire: Melancholia or Convivial Culture?,* London: Routledge (a critical analysis of contemporary debates about race and culture in British society).

Goldberg, D. T. (ed.) (1994) *Multiculturalism: A Critical Reader,* Oxford: Blackwell (an important collection of papers that encompasses both the theory and the practice of multiculturalism).

Gordon, A. F. and Newfield, C. (eds) (1996) *Mapping Multiculturalism,* Minneapolis: University of Minnesota Press (an exploration of the different uses of the concept of multiculturalism, with a focus on intellectual debates and political trends).

Gutmann, A. (ed.) (1994) *Multiculturalism: Examining the Politics of Recognition,* Princeton: Princeton University Press (a collection of papers debating Charles Taylor's notion of the 'politics of recognition').

Hannerz, U. (1996) *Transnational Connections: Culture, People, Places,* London: Routledge (explores the development of forms of transnationalism based on people, culture and movement).

Kymlicka, W. (1995) *Multicultural Citizenship: A Liberal Theory of Minority Rights,* Oxford: Oxford University Press (a discussion of the rights and status of minority cultures in multicultural societies).

Lasch-Quinn, E. (2001) *Race Experts: How Racial Etiquette, Sensitivity Training, and New-age Therapy Hijacked the Civil Rights Revolution,* New York: W.W. Norton (a critical analysis of the move away from seeing race as an issue of equality and justice and seeing it through the lens of therapy).

Levitt, P. and Waters, M. C. (eds) (2002) *The Changing Face of Home: The Transnational Lives of the Second Generation,* New York: Russell Sage Foundation (a collection of original research on transnationalism in the lives of second generation migrants in the US).

Lipsitz, G. (1998) *The Possessive Investment in Whiteness: How White People Profit from Identity Politics,* Philadelphia: Temple University Press (explores the values and meanings of whiteness in shaping politics, culture and public policy in American society).

Mann, M (2003) *Incoherent Empire,* London: Verso (a trenchant critical account of the economic and ideological foundations of the American empire in the aftermath of 9-11).

Mercer, K. (ed.) (2008) *Exiles, Diasporas and Strangers*, Cambridge, MA: MIT Press (focusing on artists and intellectuals, this collection explores the formation of global networks of travelling cultures).

Rattansi, A. and Westwood, S. (eds) (1994) *Racism, Modernity and Identity: On the Western Front*, Cambridge: Polity Press (a collection of essays that provide an overview of recent debates about racism, modernity and postmodernism).

Roediger, D. R. (ed.) (1998) *Black on White: Black Writers on What It Means to be White*, New York: Schocken Books (a collection that focuses on how black writers have defined the meaning of whiteness).

Smelser, N. J., Wilson, W. J. and Mitchell, F. (eds) (2001) *America Becoming: Racial Trends and Their Consequences*, 2 Volumes, Washington, DC: National Academy Press (a challenging overview of racial and social dynamics of American society today, with important insights into future research agendas).

Sollors, W. (1997) *Neither Black Nor White Yet Both: Thematic Explorations in Interracial Literature*, New York: Oxford University Press (a detailed analysis of interracial themes in literature and the visual arts, from the perspective of what this literature tells us about the construction of race and of the categories 'black' and 'white').

Van Hear, N. (1998) *New Diasporas: The Mass Exodus, Dispersal and Regrouping of Migrant Communities*, London: UCL Press (an appraisal of the development of new forms of migration and dispersal in the current global environment).

West, C. (1993) *Race Matters*, Boston: Beacon Press (an influential essay on current dilemmas about race in America).

Williams, P. J. (1997) *Seeing a Color-Blind Future: The Paradox of Race*, New York: The Noonday Press (a series of lectures that reflect on current dilemmas about racism and anti-racism).

Key Questions

- Paul Gilroy has argued: 'The idea of a common, invariant racial identity capable of linking divergent black experiences across different spaces and times has been fatally undermined.' What are the implications of this argument for the analysis of racial and other forms of identity in contemporary societies?
- How does Kobena Mercer explain the emergence of new forms of identity politics in the contemporary social and cultural environment?
- In what ways does David Roediger's analysis of whiteness help us to understand racism as a historical and contemporary phenomenon?
- Kimberlé Crenshaw argues that there is a need to reconceptualise race 'as a coalition between men and women of colour'. What are the consequences of this approach for anti-racist politics?
- What processes can help us to understand what Stephen Steinberg has called the 'retreat from racial justice' in American society?
- In what ways does Jennifer Hochschild argue that our understandings of race, ethnicity and immigration in the USA are changing?
- Eduardo Bonilla-Silva argues that the United States is moving from a bi-racial to a tri-racial system of racial stratification. What evidence is there that this new 'racial system' has emerged?
- How does Anthony Appiah account for the changing patterns of racial identity in contemporary societies?
- Critically evaluate Howard Winant's argument that the racial future will involve a combination of greater flexibility of racial identity and a deepening of structural racism

Index